JUDAISM AND HELLENISM

MARTIN HENGEL

JUDAISM
AND
HELLENISM

*Studies in their Encounter in Palestine
during the Early Hellenistic Period*

VOLUME ONE
TEXT

VOLUME TWO
NOTES & BIBLIOGRAPHY

FORTRESS PRESS   PHILADELPHIA

Translated by John Bowden from the German
Judentum und Hellenismus,
Studien zu ihrer Begegnung unter besonderer Berücksichtigung Palästinas
bis zur Mitte des 2 Jh.s v.Chr.,
no. 10 in the series Wissenschaftliche Untersuchungen zum Neuen Testament,
ed. D. Dr Joachim Jeremias and D. Otto Michel,
published by J. C. B. Mohr (Paul Siebeck), Tübingen,
second revised and enlarged edition 1973.

First published in America in two volumes by Fortress Press 1974

First one-volume edition 1981

Library of Congress Cataloging in Publication Data

Hengel, Martin.
  Judaism and Hellenism.

  Translation of Judentum und Hellenismus.
  A revision of the author's Habilitationsschrift,
Tübingen, 1966.
    Bibliography: p.
    Includes indexes.
    1. Judaism—Relations—Greek. 2. Greece—Religion.
3. Hellenism. I. Title.
BM536.G7H4613 1981   296′.09′014   80–39574
ISBN 0–8006–1495–X (pbk.)

9001K80   Printed in the United States of America   1–1495

TO MY WIFE

CONTENTS

VOLUME ONE

VOLUME TWO

VOLUME ONE

VOLUME ONE

PREFACE

This work was presented as a thesis to the Faculty of Protestant Theology of the Eberhard-Karls-Universität in Tübingen in November 1966 and was abbreviated or expanded further in a number of places before publication.

It sets out to make a contribution to the better understanding of the development of Judaism in the period between the Testaments, which to a considerable degree coincides with the age of Hellenism, and at the same time to illuminate the social, religious and historical background from which primitive Christianity emerged.

My thanks are due first to the Faculty of Protestant Theology of the University of Tübingen which, by granting me a research fellowship from 1964 onwards, created the conditions for my return to theology after many years of other work; also to the Deutsche Forschungsgemeinschaft, which supported the publication of the work by a substantial subsidy.

I am grateful to my honoured teacher Professor Michel for the lively interest which he has always shown in the work and to him and Professor Jeremias for accepting it in the Wissenschaftliche Untersuchungen zum Neuen Testament.

I also owe thanks to Professors Galling, Gese, Betz and Stuhlmacher, and to Dr H. P. Rüger and Dr P. Welten for valuable suggestions and conversations. The University Library in Tübingen has gone to endless trouble in obtaining widely-scattered literature for me, and has helped the process of publication on by its knowledgable and friendly collaboration.

For help over proofs and the compilation of the indices I am above all grateful to Klaus W. Müller and W. Lorenz, to Fräulein G. Krugmann and Herr H, Kienle.

Tübingen, October 1968

PREFACE TO THE SECOND EDITION

The first edition went out of print more quickly than was expected. For the second edition, mistakes and misprints have been removed and about ninety titles of more recent literature, together with further references to ancient sources, have been worked into the notes where this was possible.

I am particularly grateful to my assistants Klaus W. Müller and Helmut Kienle for their vigilant care in this work.

Tübingen, January 1973

INTRODUCTION
Terms of Reference

One fundamental presupposition of historical work on the New Testament which seems to be taken for granted is the differentiation, in terms of tradition, between 'Judaism' on the one hand and 'Hellenism' on the other. Distinctions are made between 'Jewish apocalyptic' and 'Hellenistic mysticism', between the 'Jewish, rabbinic tradition' and 'Hellenistic, oriental gnosticism', between 'Palestinian' and 'Hellenistic' Judaism, between a 'Palestinian' and a 'Hellenistic' community. Investigations of particular concepts, above all, usually result in a separation of these two 'lines of tradition', which are often traced back into the Old Testament or to classical Greece. This unavoidable distinction does, of course, pass too lightly over the fact that by the time of Jesus, Palestine had already been under 'Hellenistic' rule and its resultant cultural influence for some 360 years. Thus, even in Jewish Palestine, in the New Testament period Hellenistic civilization had a long and eventful history behind it. If New Testament scholars are to apply these unavoidable differentiations properly, and not just schematically, they must take account of the result of this history. The 'prehistory of Christianity', which goes by the unhappy designation 'history of New Testament times', and is often passed over all too quickly, is one of the indispensable foundations of a true understanding of the New Testament.

The present work sets out to depict the 'encounter between Judaism and Hellenism' in the first half of these 360 years, that is, until about the middle of the second century, though in certain issues the temporal limit will be exceeded. Furthermore, developments in Palestine itself will be deliberately given a central place, and events in the Diaspora will only be introduced in part, as by that time Jerusalem and Palestinian Judaism already formed the centre of the Diaspora as it spread out to the east and west. It is hoped that the investigation will be extended to cover the second half of the period at a later stage.

The two basic terms, 'Judaism' and 'Hellenism', used as they are with such great confidence, themselves already point to the many difficulties in the task we have set ourselves. The Greek counterpart to 'Judaism', ᾿Ιουδαϊσμός, derives from the middle of the period with which we are to deal. It appears for the first time in the account of the persecution under Antiochus IV in II Maccabees or its source in Jason of Cyrene, and conveys what even the ancient world found to be an astonishing state of affairs: the word means both political and genetic association with the Jewish nation and exclusive belief in the one God of Israel, together with observance of the Torah given by him.[1] From this it follows that if our work is to do justice to its subject it cannot be limited to 'religious' questions, but must also include politics and social questions.

The meaning of the corresponding Greek Ἑλληνισμός is limited to the philologically unobjectionable dominance of 'common Greek' as opposed to dialects and barbarisms.[2] We find one of the very rare divergences from this usage once again in II Maccabees (4.13), where ἀκμή τις Ἑλληνισμοῦ, i.e. 'a climax of Hellenizing tendencies', is mentioned in connection with the Hellenistic reform in Jerusalem. One might conclude from this first contrast between the two terms that Palestinian 'Judaism' and 'Hellenism' represent forces that are opposed in principle; this supposition is, of course, countered by the fact that the Jew Jason presented his defence of Ἰουδαϊσμός in the highly rhetorical garb of solemn *Hellenistic* historiography, of which his work is one of the best preserved examples (see below, pp. 95ff.).

It was J. G. Droysen who first gave the term 'Hellenism' the significance it now bears, by transferring it to the epoch of Greek expansion in the Orient which begins with Alexander the Great.

In work for his doctorate in 1831, Droysen, beginning with the long-established philological interpretation of the term which, starting from the 'Hellenists' in Acts 6.1, designated New Testament *koinē* the *dialectus hellenistica*,[3] defended the dubious theory that Christianity was nearer to Greece than to Judaism, basing it on the penetration of the Greeks into the lands of the East.[4] A little later he applied the designation 'Hellenism' to the epoch characterized by the union of Greece and the Orient and to the culture of that epoch: 'East and West were ripe for fusion, and cross-fertilization and metamorphosis quickly took place on both sides; newly-awakened popular life led to constantly new and further developments in the state and in knowledge, in commerce and in art, in religion and morality. May we be allowed to give this new principle in world history the name Hellenistic? Greece, invading the life of the world of the East and fertilizing it, developed that *Hellenism, in which the paganism of Asia and Greece, indeed antiquity itself, was destined to culminate.*'[5] He regarded Hellenism as the 'modern period of antiquity',[6] which found its goal and climax in the rise of Christianity: 'That is the point towards which the development of the old, pagan world strives, from which its history must be understood.'[7] Hence he set theology alongside philology as being 'the disciplines most deeply involved in the history of Hellenism'.[8] Unfortunately the former has had far too small a share in the investigation of this period.

Droysen thus already saw quite clearly the essential criterion of that time and its culture. Something fundamentally new arose in 'Hellenism' – through the encounter of Greece with the Orient – which differed from the time of classical Greece, just as Judaism – and here we return to our theme – underwent a gradual but deep-rooted change in the Hellenistic period through its encounter and conflict with the social, political and spiritual forces of this epoch, on the basis of which it differs in essential points from its earlier forms in the Old Testament.

There have, of course, been disputes over the dating of the Hellenistic period and the content that is to be assigned to the concept of Hellenism. This is not least because the concept has been used in a number of ways and therefore became very indefinite and variable; its content has tended to change according to the perspective in which it has been considered.[9] Thus it has to be remembered that the Hellenistic period was in the making throughout the fourth century,[10] and that Greek cultural influence was visible in the East, above all in Phoenicia and Egypt, even before Alexander's expeditions.[11] For the moment, the lower limit of the Hellenistic epoch concerns us less; for Syria and Palestine it should not be set at Actium, as is the case for Greece, but at the end of the last 'Hellenistic' city territories in Commagene, the kingdom of Agrippa II and the Nabateans under the Flavians, viz. Trajan. It is incomparably more difficult to define the characteristic content of Hellenism. Is it primarily a matter of the political, economic and cultural permeation of the East by the conquerors from Greece and Macedonia, or is it the fusion of oriental conceptions and Greek form, for which Oswald Spengler coined the concept of 'pseudomorphosis'?[12] The former aspect is dominant in the period of early Hellenism down to the end of the third century BC: the victorious course of Alexander the Great finally shattered the particularist narrowness of the *polis* and created a common Greek cultural consciousness which was especially developed in the newly-conquered territories, where the Greeks were rapidly bound together into a unity (see pp. 65ff. below). However, oriental influence grew with the decline of the kingdoms of the Diadochi after the beginning of the second century BC, giving rise to that process of fusion which is described in the religious sphere by the catchword 'syncretism'.[13]

Hellenism, then, must be treated as a complex phenomenon which cannot be limited to purely political, socio-economic, cultural or religious aspects, but embraces them all. The starting-point and point of reference is the expansion of Greece which was in the making in the fourth century BC, reached its political and military climax with the expedition of Alexander, and was followed by economic and cultural penetration; the East answered this in the religious sphere by accepting it, rejecting it and developing countermovements.

The 'encounter between Judaism and Hellenism' can therefore be described only in a complex way. This account of it begins, in accordance with historical developments, in Chapter I with political, military and socio-economic

developments, with emphasis on the third century BC. In Chapter II it moves
on to the problem of the proliferation of Greek language, Graecized names,
Greek education and literature. Chapter III deals most extensively with
religious and theological questions, and the account closes in Chapter IV with
the early Greek descriptions of Judaism and the Jewish attempt at reform in
Jerusalem. A brief summary has been attached to each chapter; in connection
with these, attempts are made from time to time to outline briefly those
aspects which have a bearing on the New Testament.

The first two chapters aim at a degree of completeness in literary and
archaeological material; the political and cultural background in the empire
of the Ptolemies or the Seleucids and in non-Jewish Palestine is also regularly
included. The real difficulties lie in the all-important third part, which extends
from Koheleth to early Essenism. At this point attention must be drawn to the
methodological discussion at the beginning of the chapter (see pp. 107ff.
below). It is not primarily a matter of demonstrating supposedly 'Greek
influences' here and there, especially as it is often impossible to distinguish
between analogies and real influences. Rather, an attempt is made to depict the
inner contours of Jewish and Palestinian thought in the tension between
acceptance and rejection of the Hellenistic *Zeitgeist*.

No 'history of scholarship' can be offered here, as this treatment of the
theme in its complex multiplicity is a first attempt; it is only possible to enter
discussion with the flood of secondary literature in connection with particular
problems. However, reference should be made to a number of fundamental
works to which the author owes a great deal. Pride of place goes to the work of
Schürer, unequalled in its wealth of material, even if some details are now
outdated; unfortunately it only begins at 175 BC. F. M. Abel's history of
Palestine and Tcherikover's great work *Hellenistic Civilization and the Jews*[14]
deal predominantly with political history, though Tcherikover also pays special
attention to economic and social conditions; unfortunately, he neglects
religious questions. Mention should also be made of the numerous and
always stimulating investigations of E. Bickermann, in whom knowledge of
Hellenistic history and Judaism are combined in a happy and, for the present,
probably a unique way. His masterly monograph, *Der Gott der Makkabäer*,
1937 (= *GM*), determined the direction of Chapter IV of this book. The work
of Bousset and Gressmann is still fundamental to a study of the religious
development of Palestinian Judaism in the pre-Rabbinic period, and A.
Schlatter's *Geschichte Israels* also contains a wealth of valuable observations.[15]
As an introduction to the Hellenistic world the works of Rostovtzeff were
helpful for politics and economics, as was that of Nilsson for Greek religion.[16]

The greatest burden to the author was the astonishing amount of published
material in very scattered form which swelled the work to its present size.
However, this very 'atomizing' of individual pieces of scholarship was a
stimulus to bring a comprehensive synthesis to some sort of meaningful

conclusion. In the process, it has not always been possible to satisfy the conflicting demands of a concise account and that convincing form of argument which depends on detail to avoid the charge of being a 'terrible simplification'.

The theme takes the investigation into the 'inter-testamental' period. The questions raised keep the New Testament in view, although the New Testament period is only reached as a number of lines are drawn further; as a rule the work breaks off 150–180 years earlier. It has not proved possible to anchor it backwards to the Jewish history of the Persian period, desirable though that would have been, because of lack of space. It is, however, clear that in some ways there is a remarkable degree of continuity between the Persian rule and the Hellenistic era, so that later developments were prepared at an earlier stage; furthermore, the ancient East and Greek tradition were not complete opposites, but on some lines each pressed towards a union. It was the unsuccessful attempt at Hellenistic reform that brought about the real breach in Judea. The profound shock which the Jewish people experienced in the following decades created the presuppositions for the spiritual and religious constellation which was later determinative for the New Testament period.

Because of the uncertain position over source material and its fragmentary nature, one often has to work with hypotheses. Attempts are made to indicate their different degrees of probability. The questionability of this kind of approach constantly becomes evident in the problem of dates. Nevertheless, the aim remains, despite all the potential errors in individual detail, to provide something like an overall historical picture of the encounter between Judaism and Hellenism in Palestine in the period under review.

I

Early Hellenism as a Political and Economic Force

1. The Historical Framework: Palestine as a Bone of Contention between Ptolemies and Seleucids

After the defeat of Antigonus at Ipsus in 301 BC, despite the objections of Seleucus I, Coele Syria and Palestine fell to Ptolemy I Soter, who since the beginning of 304 had been king of Egypt. The Lagid had left the risk of the decisive battle to his allies, and did not take part in it; indeed, preoccupied with the siege of Sidon, he had quickly left the province again as a result of a rumour of the defeat of his friends, leaving garrisons behind. Going against an earlier agreement, the victors now assigned Coele Syria in its entirety to Seleucus, but Ptolemy forestalled the latter in occupying the land and presented him with a *fait accompli*. Seleucus was unwilling to proceed by force against his former comrade-in-arms, to whose support he owed his successful rise, but he never gave up his claim to the territory that was his by right of victory. The opposition between the Ptolemies and the Seleucids which resulted was to determine the history of the Hellenistic East for the next 150 years.[1]

Even after Ipsus, Demetrius Poliorcetes, the son of Antigonus, had retained control of the sea and the Phoenician coastal cities of Tyre and Sidon because of his fleet, and from time to time he was able to cause unrest in Palestine. In 296 he is said to have destroyed Samaria, but he was not able to sustain his effort; we find him back in Greece again that same year.[2] The coastal cities also fell to Egypt by 286 BC at the latest. In occupying Coele Syria and Palestine, Ptolemy I was reviving the old policy of the Pharaohs. First, this territory formed a vital military buffer for Egypt against any attack from the north, and secondly, the harbours of Phoenicia and the forests of Lebanon were the basis for the naval might of the Ptolemies. Moreover, Palestine was a focal point for the commercial and caravan routes from Mesopotamia, the Persian Gulf and Southern Arabia; from an economic point of view, too, it represented a valuable extension to Egypt. Finally, the Ptolemies, who were primarily dependent almost entirely on foreign mercenaries for their army, were able to enlist Idumean, Arabian and Jewish auxiliaries here.[3] It is therefore no coincidence that with the loss of this territory about 200 BC,

Egypt also relinquished its political predominance in the eastern Mediterranean. All this enables us to see why the Ptolemies felt it important to keep a firm hand on their province not only militarily, but also fiscally and administratively. Its official name was 'Syria and Phoenicia', but it is often mentioned simply as 'Syria' in the sources; where that is the case, both Palestine and Phoenicia are also meant.[4]

An intensive penetration of the territory began especially during the long rule of the vigorous Ptolemy II Philadelphus (282–246 BC); the correspondence of Zeno gives us numerous instances of this. Zeno was the steward of a large estate in the newly reclaimed Fayum, which Apollonius, the 'finance minister', had received as a present from the king. Zeno carried on an extensive correspondence on his master's behalf, covering almost all the eastern Mediterranean under Egyptian domination; he collected it together carefully in an archive of which about two thousand items are extant, forty of them relating to Syria and Palestine. Before Zeno was entrusted with the administration of the estate he undertook prolonged journeys for his master which, as in 259 BC, took him the length and breadth of Palestine.[5] The accounts in the Zeno papyri are supplemented by a papyrus from Vienna which contains two royal decrees, especially concerning 'Syria and Phoenicia'.[6] This fills at least part of the gap in our knowledge of conditions in Palestine in the third century BC, caused by the lack of source material. The process of Hellenization proper will have begun with the administrative and economic development of Palestine.[7]

Leaving aside the invasion of Antiochus III (219/217 BC), about a hundred years of Ptolemaic rule brought a period of relatively peaceful development to the disputed provinces.[8] The first three Syrian wars seem to have touched the country only in the north.[9] Despite individual military setbacks, on the whole they did not turn out badly for the Ptolemies, and in their successful phases of the first and third wars the Seleucids were only able to penetrate as far as Damascus.[10] Nevertheless, Dan. 11.5–9 shows that the conflicts between the 'king of the south' and the 'king of the north' were followed attentively even in Jerusalem.[11] Throughout the third century the boundary of the two kingdoms remained relatively constant, apart from minor alterations. It began at the stream of Eleutheros north of Tripolis and ran southeastwards in the direction of Baalbek and from there to Damascus, which was disputed. Transjordania including Batanea and Trachonitis also belonged to the Ptolemies' kingdom.[12]

As early as 221, the young Antiochus III had failed in an attempt to attack the border fortresses of the Biqaʿ,[13] and it was only at this fourth encounter in 219 BC that he was able to occupy a large part of Coele Syria. He overpowered the coastal cities of Tyre and Acco-Ptolemais through the treachery of the *stratēgos* Theodotus and went on to lay siege to Dor. Negotiations proposed by Ptolemy IV Philopator, who had not yet completed his military preparations, came to nothing. So the following year, 218, Antiochus advanced along the Phoenician coast to Galilee, capturing Philoteria, Scythopolis and the fortress of Atabyrion on the Tabor. He crossed the Jordan, occupied Pella, Kamoun (*qāmōn*, Judg. 10.5 ?) and (G)ephron in Transjordania, stormed the fortresses of Gadara, Abila and Rabbath Ammon, and sent a detachment of troops to Samaria. We hear nothing of the fate of Jerusalem; presumably it was also occupied by the troops of Antiochus in connection with the last-mentioned undertaking. Antiochus III directed the main thrust of his attack against Transjordania and outflanked Palestine to the east because he was counting on Arab support. They immediately took his side and provided powerful aid (see below, pp. 15, 17f.). His successes were further facilitated by the fact that a number of Ptolemy's military leaders came over to his side;[14] the mismanagement and nepotism under Philopator (222–205 BC) ushered in the downfall of the Ptolemaic kingdom. If some of Ptolemy's officers were in such a doubtful mood, one may assume, despite remarks of Polybius to the contrary,[15] that at the time a large part of the populace were on the side of the Seleucids. The exception was those cities and territories which had close economic ties with Egypt, e.g. Sidon, which Antiochus was unable to occupy, Gaza and, according to Polybius, Samaria: presumably Judea was included in the τοὺς κατὰ Σαμάρειαν τόπους.[16] The fact that nevertheless Antiochus took two years to occupy Coele Syria and Palestine shows the degree to which the Ptolemies had fortified their first line of defence.

Meanwhile Philopator, or rather his minister Sosibius, had concluded preparations for war. On 22 June, 217 BC, the armies met at Raphia on the southern border of Palestine. Despite initial successes, Antiochus was unexpectedly defeated. A vital part in the result was played by the native Egyptian troops trained along Macedonian lines; in this way the national consciousness of the Egyptians was strengthened over against the Greek ruling class and expressed itself a few years later in a chain of rebellions.[17] Antiochus had to vacate immediately the territory he had won over the two previous years; on the other hand the victorious Philopator and his sister Arsinoe stayed on for almost four months in the province that they had recovered, visiting its cities and sanctuaries to receive the homage of the populace and to demonstrate their reverence for the gods of the country.[18] Honorific inscriptions in Joppa on the coast and in Marisa on the border of Idumea and Judea bear witness to the visit of the two rulers;[19] presumably they will also have visited Jerusalem. It is quite possible that there was a conflict with the Jews, as is hinted at in III Macc. 1.10ff., over the king's leanings towards mysticism and his exaggerated reverence for Dionysus.[20] Ptolemy III Euergetes had already visited the temple in Jerusalem and had sacrifices offered – probably after the victorious end to the third Syrian war.[21]

Despite the victory, the collapse of the Ptolemaic kingdom was now inevitable. The exploited Egyptian populace revolted, and the maladministration at court took worse and worse forms. Antiochus III, on the other hand, had surprising victories in Asia Minor and in the East, and appeared as the restorer of the kingdom of Seleucus I.[22]

After the mysterious deaths of Philopator and his sister and wife Arsinoe in 205 BC, the incompetence of the guardians of the five-year-old Ptolemy V Epiphanes made the weakness of Egypt utterly clear.[23] In 201 (202?) BC Antiochus, in alliance with Philip V of Macedon, again crossed the frontier, and the country came over to him much more easily than eighteen years earlier. Only Gaza, the terminus of Arabian trade with Egypt and therefore particularly closely bound up with it, offered resistance for any length of time.[24] In the autumn Antiochus departed from Palestine, leaving garrisons behind. The Ptolemaic leader Scopas took advantage of this in the winter of 201/200 for a counter-thrust by which he was able to win back considerable areas of the lost territory. Meanwhile a strong pro-Seleucid party had established itself in Jerusalem. The obscure saying in Dan. 11.14 probably hints at its resistance and the punishment meted out by Scopas: 'In those times many shall rise against the king of the south; and the men of violence (*pārīṣīm*) among your own people shall lift themselves up in order to fulfil the vision; but they shall fail.' The partisan warfare in the capital of Judea is confirmed by the interpretation of the passage in Jerome, which is dependent on Porphyry:[25] '*Pugnantibus contra se Magno Antiocho et ducibus Ptolemaei in medio Judaea posita in contraria studia scindebatur, aliis Antiocho aliis Ptolemaeo faventibus.*' A fragment of Polybius preserved in Josephus also suggests that the Jews were suppressed by force; i.e., probably that this time the majority of them were pro-Seleucid.[26]

In 200 BC, however, Scopas was overwhelmingly defeated by Antiochus at Paneion, by the source of the Jordan; he fled to Sidon and there had to surrender to the Seleucids in exchange for free conduct.[27] Now Antiochus had a free hand finally to occupy the province, and in the two following years 199/198 he brought his campaign to a conclusion. On this expedition the king attached great importance to gaining the favour of the populace. This is shown by an extensive inscription from the neighbourhood of Beth-Shean/Scythopolis. It contains two memoranda from Ptolemy son of Traseas, *stratēgos* of Syria and Phoenicia, to the king or his son, and six royal letters to subordinate officials from the period between 201 and 195 BC. In them soldiers are expressly forbidden to billet themselves on the populace of Ptolemy's villages or to drive them from their homes. In this way the king was probably countering the acts of violence which had been perpetrated by his troops. All this was to be engraved on stone and to be set up in public places.[28] Once again we find the majority of Jews on the side of the Seleucids; they supported the Syrians by besieging the Egyptian garrison in the citadel and victualling the troops and elephants.[29] But Jews also seem to have fought on the Ptolemaic side, for according to Jerome/Porphyry the '*optimates Ptolemæi partium*' were evacuated to Egypt.[30]

Jerusalem and Judea had suffered severely under the fighting of previous years.[31] It was therefore a considerable help that Antiochus III, in a decree (πρόσταγμα)[32] which was also addressed to the *stratēgos* Ptolemy, promised the Jews not only his support in rebuilding the city and the temple, but also exemption from tribute for three years and the release of Jewish prisoners. The temple personnel and the gerousia were exempted from all taxes. Furthermore the Jews were granted internal 'autonomy', i.e. were given the possibility of living according to their own laws.

With these 'royal marks of favour' (φιλάνθρωπα βασιλικά) which were negotiated through a Jewish delegation in Antioch,[33] the 'great king' Antiochus was probably deliberately taking up precedents from the earlier Persian period;[34] they also corresponded to the more 'federative constitution' of the Seleucid kingdom.[35] Moreover, the king was concerned to bind the Jews, whose military capabilities he had learnt to value,[36] more firmly to the new Seleucid rule, especially as he had to keep in mind permanently a conflict with a new, dangerous enemy over against which he needed to keep his rear secured: after Rome's victory over Philip V of Macedon in 197 BC, a war seemed inevitable.[37] For this reason, in 196 Antiochus promised his daughter Cleopatra as wife to the young Ptolemy V Epiphanes and raised his hopes that he might receive Coele Syria back again as a dowry. The wedding eventually took place two-and-a-half years later in 194/193, but Antiochus never returned the territory he had conquered.[38]

Defeat by the Romans at Magnesia (end of 190 BC) and the harsh peace of Apamea (188) not only put an end to the high-flown plans of Antiochus III, but at the same time ushered in the collapse of the Seleucid empire.[39] Above all, the territory won back in the East was quickly lost again. Only a year later Antiochus was killed plundering a temple of Bel in Susiana.[40] His son Seleucus IV Philopator (187–175) differed from his father in being a passive ruler. In Egypt, where there was disappointment that Coele Syria had not been returned at the peace of Apamea, hopes for the reconquest of the province rose again; perhaps first hostilities already came about, and it was probably only the constant internal unrest and the sudden death of Ptolemy V Epiphanes in 180 BC that prevented an attack on Syria.[41] Even in Jerusalem, sympathy for Egypt seems to have grown again. War reparations had to be paid to Rome by Seleucid subjects to the tune of 12,000 talents, so that the populace in Judea will no longer have detected much of the original alleviations of tribute.[42] The attempt of Heliodorus to sequestrate money in the temple in Jerusalem is connected with this acute financial crisis. At the same time this incident, which led to the journey of the high priest Onias III to Antioch and to his deposition, reveals the internal party struggle in Jerusalem.[43] When after the murder of Seleucus IV in 175 BC his more ambitious brother Antiochus IV Epiphanes took over the throne, Seleucid politics again became more active (see below, pp. 277f.).

Cleopatra I, the sister of the two brothers, had no plans for an aggressive military policy against the Seleucids, but after her death in 177/176 this attitude altered, when the one-time Syrian slave Lenaeus and Eulaeus, who was probably also an oriental eunuch, took over the guardianship of Ptolemy VI Philometor, who was still a minor.[44] Their incredibly clumsy and provocative politics (II Macc.4.21) gave Antiochus a pretext for attacking Egypt at the end of 170 or the beginning of 169 BC, and he found progress surprisingly easy as far as Alexandria. He concluded a treaty in his own favour with the young Philometor and left garrisons; presumably he believed that in the civil war which was now to be expected Philometor would remain dependent on him. On his return at the end of 169 BC he visited Jerusalem and plundered the temple treasury, which certainly exacerbated feelings towards the Seleucid regime. However, Ptolemy VI Philometor broke the agreements which had been made with Antiochus IV under compulsion and reconciled himself with his kinsfolk and co-regents.[45] During the second invasion of 168 BC, in which Antiochus also sacked Cyprus, the Roman ambassador C. Popilius Laenas met Antiochus at the beginning of July in Eleusis, near Alexandria, and in a brusque fashion required him to surrender the fruits of his victory.[46] Presumably the humiliation of the king, coupled with a rumour of his death, strengthened the anti-Seleucid forces in Palestine and Phoenicia, which had formerly been a province of the Ptolemies. The deposed high priest Jason undertook a successful surprise attack on Jerusalem from Transjordania, Antiochus had to overpower the city by force of arms, and let it feel his hand in punishment. At that time, too, it is probable that the sphere of influence of the Tobiad Hyrcanus, who had presumably supported Jason, in Ammanitis, was destroyed.[47] Phoenician Aradus also temporarily defected, and was severely punished, as perhaps were other parts of Phoenicia, too.[48] The great period of the Hellenistic monarchies of the east was finally over.

This compressed survey of political events down to the outbreak of the Maccabean revolt shows how much the destiny of the country was shaped by its role as a disputed buffer-state between the two great powers; the situation had much in common with the political position of Israel and Judah between the eighth and the sixth century BC.

Such an exposed position had by no means only negative consequences. These only become clear in the fourth and fifth Syrian wars, when Palestine became a theatre of war. Of quite positive significance is the fact that both powers turned their attention towards the political, military and economic development of the country and sought to influence it at least for some of the time in a favourable direction. More suspicious was the fact that parties in Jerusalem, even if they had a social or a religious background, easily acquired a political slant because they were regularly called to decide for or against one of the two powers. Even the apocalyptists, who did not commit themselves to either of the two powers, saw Jewish history determined by this opposition, as Dan.11 shows. The relationship between Jerusalem and the Diaspora was also damaged: 'The fact that Jerusalem, the spiritual centre of the Diaspora, belonged to one of the rival powers cast suspicion on the loyalty of the Jews under the domination of the other.'[49] These tensions could lead to the founding of competing sanctuaries, as under the Tobiad Hyrcanus in Transjordania or under Onias IV in Leontopolis (see below pp.274f.).

On the other hand, we must not overlook the fact that despite the struggles between Ptolemies and Seleucids which kept flaring up again and again, Palestine was above all granted a period of peace for eighty years, a time of relatively peaceable development such as the country was not to see again over the next three hundred years. We might ask whether this period, in which the first encounter between Judaism and Hellenism took place under favourable circumstances, was not of decisive significance for its further development. At the end of our epoch, in the crisis which became manifest in Jerusalem after 175, we find Judaism in a form which has changed in many ways, a Judaism which has essential differences from the Judaism to be seen at the time of Nehemiah and Ezra. This transformation is bound up with the influence of Hellenistic civilization on Judaism and began as early as the third century BC, when the fronts between Greece and Judaism had not yet hardened.[50]

Not the least important reason why the attempt at a Hellenistic reform in Jerusalem after 175 BC came to nothing, despite this long period of preparation, is that the great Hellenistic powers had by then passed the zenith of their strength, that Rome increasingly restricted their freedom of movement, and that also in Egypt and Iran the oriental nationalist reaction had gone over to the counter-offensive under the leadership of indigenous priests.[51]

2. Graeco-Hellenistic War and the Jews

In the first period after the expedition of Alexander, the encounter of Judaism with Hellenistic civilization did not take place in those spheres which one usually associates with the term 'Hellenism': Greek literature, art, philosophy or a syncretistic religious context. Rather, the Greek spirit first revealed its superiority to the people of the East in an inexorable, highly secular way: in a perfected, superior technique of war[52] and – particularly in the Egyptian sphere of influence – in a no less perfect and inexorable state administration, whose aim was the optimal exploitation of its subject territories.

Greek mercenaries were not unknown to the inhabitants of Palestine centuries before the expedition of Alexander. According to newly-discovered ostraca, *'kittīm'* were stationed on the southern border in Arad even at the end of the Jewish monarchy, under Josiah; they probably came from Cyprus or even from the Aegean.[53] At about the same time the Saite dynasty in Egypt enlisted Greek mercenaries who were settled in the country, and Greeks also fought earlier, from the beginning of the seventh century BC, in Assyrian armies.[54] A brother of the Lesbian poet Alcaeus, named Antimenidas, served under the king of Babylon, presumably Nebuchadnezzar, and perhaps took part in the siege of Ashkelon in 604 BC.[55] Later, Greeks were highly valued by the satraps of the western Persian provinces, and after Marathon and Plataea their participation in a war was almost regarded as decisive. Thus the long-drawn-out war over the independence of Egypt in the fourth century BC was carried on principally with Greek mercenaries on both sides, who from time to time also went through Palestine. It can be shown that a Greek army led by the Athenian Iphicrates was in Akē (Acco) between 380 and 374, to prepare for an attack on Egypt. Excavations at 'Aṭliṭ, six miles north of Dor, suggest that at that time Greek mercenaries were already settled at individual places on the coastal plain. The rebellion of Sidon, fomented by Egypt, after 350 also took place with the aid of Greek troops, and the same thing is also true of the sacking of Egypt by Artaxerxes III Ochus which followed; it was largely just a war between Greek mercenaries. Judea, too, seems to have been affected by the battles following the revolt of Sidon.[56]

But all this was merely a prelude. Alexander's unprecedented chain of victories, the successful sieges of Tyre and Gaza, the rapid and harsh punishment of the Samaritan rebels,[57] all this demonstrated even to the populace of the hill country of Judah the tremendous superiority of the Graeco-Macedonian technique of war. Alexander's drastic measures against Samaria, which changed the city into a Macedonian colony (see note 69), led to the resettlement of Shechem and thus probably also to the building of the temple on Gerizim, an event which made the schism between Jews and Samaritans final.[58] Alexander is one of the few Hellenistic leaders with whom apocalyptic, Alexandrian Jewish and even Rabbinic literature were extensively preoccupied at a later date.[59]

The Macedonians came as conquerors, with all the arrogance of the victor at whose feet the world lies. Their first concern was to secure the fruits of this victory over against the subject peoples and – after Alexander's premature death – against the rivals from their own ranks. Army and fleet formed the foundation of the Diadochi kingdoms which now arose, or rather, were the completely personal power of the rulers; the military assembly, represented by the guard, was the only institution which retained an independent function, e.g. the right of acclamation and the control of the succession.[60] (This was a relic from early Macedonian times.) The technical progress of the Hellenistic period accordingly manifested itself above all in the construction of astonishing machines of war, of increasingly large warships and in types of fortification.[61] The superiority of the Graeco-Macedonian monarchies over the 'barbarians' lay above all in the technical perfection of the way in which they waged war, beginning with pre-military training in the gymnasium, and progressing through tactics and strategy to the techniques of laying siege.[62] The decline of individual kingdoms began with the breaking of the monopoly of absolute military superiority. The armies of the Hellenistic period were for the most part mercenary armies, whose core was made up of the traditional 'Macedonian' phalanx.[63] Those soldiers who did not belong to the relatively small standing army were settled in times of peace in widely dispersed military colonies (κληρουχίαι, κατοικίαι) (that is, if they did not wish to return to their homelands) and thus formed a kind of reserve army which secured the territory against rebellion and invasion.[64] The relatively high pay or the royal gift of land, coupled with tax concessions, furthered the development of a well-to-do class of professional soldiers.[65] Especially in the Seleucid multi-nation state, the non-Greek elements kept increasing with time, so that in spite of an original division of detachments according to nationality, the army favoured the progress of miscegenation.[66]

Palestine was to savour to the full the fearfulness of Hellenistic warfare in the twenty-two years between the death of Alexander and Ipsus: it was crossed or occupied seven or eight times by armies;[67] Jerusalem itself was stormed by force at least once, and Ptolemy I had a large number of Jews brought captive to Egypt.[68] Those were also the years when the first Macedonian military colonies were established in Palestine. Perdiccas was probably the founder of the new Samaria and of Gerasa, where he was later venerated as 'ktistēs'.[69] Pella, Dion and some other cities with names from Macedonia or Northern Greece perhaps go back to Antigonus, who in this way sought to protect Transjordania against the Arabs.[70] The Ptolemies constructed their military buffer by a chain of fortifications and numerous strongholds: first along the coast, then between Lebanon and the Antilebanon, south of Lake Gennesaret and in Transjordania.[71] A fine example of the Hellenistic art of fortification is extant in the round towers from the early Ptolemaic period in Samaria; another fortified position discovered in Samaria dates from the time of the transition from Ptolemaic to Seleucid rule about 200. Fortifications of towers and walls from the Ptolemaic era have also been excavated in Philoteria on Lake Gennesaret.[72] The citadel of Beth Zur discovered by Sellers, the newly-discovered fortified tower of Tell 'Arad and the fortified position at 'Engedi perhaps belong to a Ptolemaic or Seleucid chain of fortifications intended to protect southern Palestine against marauding Arabs.[73]

The five city-foundations or renamings of earlier places known to us from Ptolemaic times also presumably had a military character: Acco-Ptolemais on the coast, Philotheria at the southern end of Lake Gennesaret, Rabbath-Ammon-Philadelphia in Transjordania, Pella-Berenice in the Jordan valley and Arsinoe, which either lay in the Biqaʿ or is even perhaps to be identified with Damascus. Possibly there were even two different cities of this name.[74] Scythopolis (bēt-šeʾān) was perhaps founded as a military colony of Greek mercenaries from the Bosphorus or of Scythian bowmen. As A. H. M. Jones infers from a comparison with names of Egyptian cities ending in -polis, a foundation by the Ptolemies seems most probable.[75] At first the military colonies proper had little economic or cultural significance, as the Macedonian, Thracian and Northern Greek mercenaries who predominated there were still half barbarians.[76] However, mingling with the native Semitic populace was to their advantage. One example of this is given by the Rainer papyrus, which is addressed to 'the soldiers and other (Graeco-Macedonian) settlers in Syria and Phoenicia', and states that their native-born concubines are exempted from the general census of slaves. Such relatively frequent associations thus seem to have been legitimized in this way.[77] As well as military settlers there were also garrison troops in the numerous fortresses. Polybius mentions a considerable number in his account of the fourth Syrian war, among them principally Abila, Gadara and Rabbath-Ammon (5,70f.). The Zeno papyri mention a garrison in Tripolis on the Seleucid boundary and with it a whole series of senior officers, like fortress-commanders, hipparchs, etc.[78]

An inscription on the tomb of a Cretan officer of the garrison, his young son and his granddaughter has been preserved in Gaza; an Aetolian son-in-law is also mentioned in the same place as an officer of Ptolemy. The monument presumably comes from the time of Philopator. It shows how Greek families settled in Palestine and remained in the country as early as the third century BC. A series of decorated tombs of soldiers of the occupation has also been found in Sidon.[79] An inscription in the same city mentions a *politeuma* of Caunians from Caria, the home town of Zeno, which presumably arose out of a Carian detachment of the occupying troops.[80] True, there is no evidence of a Ptolemaic garrison in Jerusalem until after the recapture of the city by Scopas in 200 BC, but the existence of a citadel makes the constant presence of a small Ptolemaic detachment of troops probable.[81] In the Seleucid period the force consisted of Cypriots and men from Asia Minor, and was a standing arrangement.[82] Most significant, however, is the existence of a military colony in the Ammanitis east of the Jordan consisting of Graeco-Macedonian, 'Persian' and Jewish soldiers and horsemen under the command of a Jewish sheikh Tobias, whose ancestors were settled in this area as early as the time of Nehemiah, as representatives of the Persian state. Here the Ptolemies took note of local circumstances and exploited the age-old hostility of the local sheikh against the Arab nomads who constantly threatened the cultivated land. Presumably this military colony under Jewish command also served to defend the province against the Arabs.[83] Wherever such garrisons were situated, mutual influence and miscegenation were unavoidable.

Here we also come up against a sphere in which we may suppose the earliest closer contacts between Jews and Greeks to have taken place: *the Jewish mercenaries*. According to Josephus (Ps. Hecataeus), even Alexander the Great had enlisted Jewish mercenaries, and there is no real reason to doubt this.[84] He was followed by Ptolemy I and his later successors, taking up a tradition of Jewish military settlements in Egypt going back to Psammetichus and the

Persian period. Thus the Aramaic Cowley Papyrus 81, *c.* 310 BC, newly edited by J. Hamatta, mentions ten places between Migdāl on the north-eastern border of Egypt and Syene in the south where Jews were settled; even two priests are mentioned, one from Thmuis in the south, where the Jewish temple mentioned in Isa. 19.19 was perhaps located. Later, Josephus and some inscriptions speak of Jewish garrisons in Egypt, Libya and Cyrenaica; the latter in particular had to be secured by non-Greek mercenaries: it was a border region inhabited by a Greek population who were passionately concerned for freedom. In Teucheira we find a Jewish burial ground from the early period of the empire, very probably going back to a Ptolemaic military colony; the same may be true of the great community in Berenice, to which countless inscriptions bear witness.[85] In the time of Sulla (85 BC), the Jews formed one of the four classes of population in Cyrene, and in Boreion the Jewish community claimed that its 'temple' went back to the time of Solomon: probably there had been a Jewish border garrison here at the extreme south-western corner of Cyrenaica since early Ptolemaic times.[86] The Ptolemies also enlisted Samaritans, Idumeans and Arabs as well as Jews in their eastern province, but strangely enough no Syrians, as these were apparently little suited to war service.[87] The Jewish units of troops and their generals acquired great political significance particularly in the second century, after the foundation of the temple of Leontopolis by Onias IV, together with the military colony that went with it.[88] Statistics show clearly that whereas the number of Semitic mercenaries increased in the second century BC, that of Greek and Thracian mercenaries and mercenaries from Asia Minor declined.[89] The Seleucids, too, seem to have used Jewish mercenaries in their service from the beginning.[90] According to a note which is legendary in the form in which it has come down, but probably goes back to a historical event, in II Macc. 8.16–18, Jewish mercenaries played a decisive role in a battle of Antiochus I against the Galatians in 275 BC.[91] The strong Jewish Diaspora inland in Asia Minor presumably goes back to the settling of two thousand Jewish cleruchs of the Babylonian Diaspora in Phrygia by Antiochus III, before 200 BC.[92] Under the Hasmonean high priests Jonathan (I Macc. 10.36; 11.43ff.) and John Hyrcanus (*Antt.* 13, 249ff.), self-contained Jewish contingents provided war service for their Seleucid overlords; they will have been engaged in this form even in pre-Maccabean times.[93] Alongside slaves, Jewish soldiers in Hellenistic armies may therefore have made the greatest contribution to the rise of the Diaspora in the Greek-speaking world. The Jewish military settlers transplanted to Egypt adopted the Greek language and Greek customs relatively quickly, as they had no desire to be counted among the down-trodden, native-barbarian population and, moreover, lived in closest contact with Greek and Macedonian soldiers (see below, p. 63. There is no evidence of self-contained Jewish units in the third century BC). This assimilation went so far that Jews could adopt the designation 'Macedonians', because they or their forbears had served in Macedonian units.[94] We may well associate with the growing significance of Jewish troops and officers, especially in Egypt, the romance of Artapanus that Moses invented the weapons and war machines of the Egyptian army, served as supreme commander of a peasant force of 100,000 men and waged war successfully with them for ten years in Ethiopia.[95] One might almost assume that in pre-Maccabean Judea there was a custom similar to the Reislauf in mediaeval Switzerland, of taking up mercenary service in the Hellenistic kingdoms, especially as the small, hilly country could hardly provide enough food for its constantly increasing population. The account by Hecataeus of Abdera from the last years of the fourth century BC about the attention devoted to warfare even by Moses, and the military training of Jewish youth (ἐποιήσατο ὁ νομοθέτης τῶν τε πολεμικῶν ἔργων πολλὴν πρόνοιαν καὶ τοὺς νέους ἠνάγκαζεν ἀσκεῖν ἀνδρείαν),[96] may go back to experiences with Jewish mercenaries in Ptolemaic Egypt.

This development was not without its effect on the mother country. Not all the Jews serving in the Egyptian army will have stayed in Egypt for ever; presumably at least a part of them – as was also the case with Greek mercenaries[97] – will have returned home to Judea. Moreover, there was a close link between the mother country and Alexandria.[98] These contacts formed an ever-increasing, effective counterbalance to the tendency appearing from the time of Ezra and Nehemiah towards an external segregation of the Jewish cultic community.

Encounter with Hellenistic techniques of war did not fail to have an influence also on Jewish thought. In *apocalyptic circles* the picture of the fourth world kingdom of the Greeks received its fearful traits above all because of its military superiority:

> A fourth beast, fearful and terrifying and extraordinarily strong; and it had great iron teeth . . . ; it devoured and broke in pieces, and stamped the residue with its feet. It was different from all the beasts that were before it . . .[99]

In the same way, in the LXX of Jer. 27 (MT 50).16, the 'sword of the oppressor' (*ḥereb hayyōnā*) which annihilates Babylon becomes a μάχαιρα Ἑλληνική. In the face of this godless, uncanny power, memories recalled the early Israelite tradition of the Holy War:

> For I bend Judah as a bow and make Ephraim its arrow. I summon your sons, O Zion, against the sons of Jawan and wield you like a warrior's sword . . .
> . . . for Yahweh Sebaoth cares for his flock, the house of Judah, and makes them like his proud steed in battle. Out of them comes the cornerstone, out of them the tent peg, out of them the battle bow, out of them every ruler. And they trample heroes in battle like the mire of the streets and

fight, for Yahweh is with them, and the riders on horses shall be put to shame . . .[100]

Alexander's expedition and the struggles of the Diadochi probably gave new life to the forecasts of prophets and apocalyptists (see pp. 180ff. below). The careful attention paid in Judea to political and military controversies in the third century BC is clear from I Macc. 1.1–10 and above all the historical outline in Dan. 11, with the enumeration of the various Syrian wars. The connection between Hellenistic techniques of war and the tradition of war in ancient Israel becomes quite clear in the War Scroll of Qumran, the earliest version of which surely goes back to the Hellenistic period. Here the idealized conception of the holy war of the end-time was fused with experiences of contemporary tactics, so that a double picture arose, partly realistic and partly utopian.[101] There is probably an intrinsic connection between the war service of Jewish mercenaries in Hellenistic armies, these apocalyptic traditions of war and the military success of the Jews in the Maccabean revolt. It is quite possible that former mercenaries formed the nucleus of the Maccabean army and gave it its superiority over the auxiliary forces of its Syrian neighbours, who had become unaccustomed to war (see below, pp. 275f.).

3. Administration and Taxation in Palestine under Hellenistic Rule

a) The organization of the Ptolemaic administration and the levy of taxes

In contrast to the Seleucids, who followed the decentralized Persian administration in organizing their far-flung, multi-national state,[102] the geographical and economic structure of Egypt under the Ptolemies required a centrally directed, tightly organized system of administration.[103] The old institutions of the time of the Pharaohs had been thrown into disorder both by the ultimately unsuccessful war of independence against the Persians – after 343 BC Egypt was sacked by Artaxerxes III and remained in Persian hands, apart from a brief interlude from 338–336, until the invasion of Alexander in 332[104] – and by internal confusion.[105] Above all under their first two rulers, Ptolemy I Soter (323) 304–283 and Ptolemy II Philadelphus (285) 282–246 BC, the Ptolemies now created a new state organization following on the old institutions, in which the ideals and insights of the Greek theory of the state also played a certain part.[106] This achievement is to be rated all the more highly in that the Macedonians and Greeks did not bring with them any explicit experience in the administration of large kingdoms. Hecataeus of Abdera, historian – the first Greek who also wrote about the Jews –, utopian and a philosophico-political supporter of Ptolemy I, could proclaim to the Greek world that state administration in Egypt came nearest to the concept of the philosophers' state.[107] Thus under the first Ptolemies the oriental idea of the divinely sanctioned omnipotence of the king was put into effect, with Greek logic, down to the final consequence.[108]

The starting point here was the conception that the whole land was the personal possession *(οἶκος)* of the king.[109] The titles of the Ptolemaic administrative officials therefore often derive from the terminology used in large private estates in Greece. The king 'managed the State as a plain Macedonian or Greek would manage his own household'.[110] The first man in the state beside the king was the *dioikētēs*, under Philadelphus from 261 BC the Apollonius who has already been mentioned, and from whose sphere the Zeno correspondence derives. He bore responsibility for the entire possessions and income of the king, i.e. everything connected with the finances, the economy and the administration of the state. He seems to have had tremendous gifts as an organizer and attached supreme importance to acquiring as much information as possible about the many and varied riches of the great empire.[111] Egypt itself had of old been divided into nomes, and these in turn into toparchies. The smallest administrative unit was the village. The most important officials in any district were the military *stratēgos*, the *oikonomos* for administration of finance and commerce, and a series of further functionaries presumably of equal status; under them was a hierarchically ordered host of subordinate officials. The leading places were exclusively in the hands of Greeks, but there were also many non-Greeks in the lower ranks of the administration.[112] Ptolemy III Euergetes (246–222) tried to tighten up the complicated and inflated administration along military lines and put the district *stratēgos* at the head of each nome. The juxtaposition of military and civil-economic administration thus came to an end.[113] However, the dangerous overall development could not be brought to a halt by individual measures, as the bifurcated system of administration inevitably led in the end to a bureaucratic formalism. In itself, the bureaucracy built up in its many gradations on the office of the 'scribe' was of oriental origin, and was in practice unknown to the Greeks, with their background of the *polis*. However, with their own logic they completed it to perfection.[114] By far the largest part of the land was the direct possession of the king and was worked by free tenants, the royal peasants, under the strict supervision of royal officials. The royal land also provided those portions of land which were assigned to military settlers or given as gifts to high officials like Apollonius. However, both could be repossessed by the king at any time, as they were his property. The temple land, too, was under strict state control.[115] The high incomes obtained from farming out the royal land were supplemented by a number of taxes which, following the Greek pattern, were farmed out to private individuals. However, the amount of them was accurately estimated and strict supervision was given to their collection. A further source of income was the state monopoly on the most important merchandise.[116] The riches of the Ptolemies which followed from this policy of firm administration and financial control gave them political superiority in the eastern Mediterranean during the third century BC. The reverse side of this concentration of power in the hands of the king was a state capitalism without parallel in the ancient world, by which the lower strata of the people, especially the native Egyptians, were burdened beyond bearing.[117] It was not until the administrative reform by Diocletian almost five hundred years later that an 'equally uniform state administration' was once again created.[118]

We must now ask how far the Ptolemies attempted to introduce this system into their foreign possessions, and above all into Palestine. Here conditions were very different from those in Egypt; whereas there the uniform population of fellahin and the natural characteristics of the country simplified a centralized administration and indeed made it necessary, 'Syria and Phoenicia' were relatively ununiform, both ethnologically and geographically. The country was divided by high mountains and deep chasms; politically it was made up of a whole series of former Phoenician 'city-states' on the coast from Orthosia to Gaza, the 'temple state' of Jerusalem with the Jewish *'ethnos'*, and the *'ethnē'* of the Idumeans and Samaritans, groups of people of Canaanite and Syrian descent, various cities in the interior including the Macedonian military colonies, and finally the Arabian and Nabatean tribes east of the Jordan and in the south.[119] On the one hand the Ptolemies had to take into account the special circumstances in their disputed boundary province and adopt themselves to the circumstances obtaining at the time; on the other hand, it is understandable that a system of administration that was accustomed to keep such a tight rein in its home country at least attempted to force the well-tried bureaucratic administration of the motherland on the province immediately adjoining it.

Like the nomes of Egypt and the other foreign Ptolemaic provinces, 'Syria and Phoenicia' also had a military *stratēgos* and a financial specialist as chief officers – later the *stratēgos* alone.[120] Acco was presumably the chief administrative centre; we can assume this both from its geographical position and from its frequent mention in the Zeno papyri and in the accounts in Polybius. Its name was changed to Ptolemais by Philadelphus, probably towards 261 BC, i.e. shortly before Zeno's travels. From this year we find the first coins of Ptolemy II made in Ptolemais. It rapidly gained in importance, and in Ptolemaic times was well on the way towards outstripping its Phoenician sister-cities, which did not have such a large hinterland.[121] The province was divided up into smaller administrative units which perhaps went back to Persian times and whose names kept changing. In the earliest official document we have relating to Ptolemaic administration in 'Syria and Palestine', they are called *'hyparchies'*.[122] The names of these administrative units have probably been preserved in the place-names ending in -itis, like Ammanitis, Esbonitis, Gaulanitis, Galaaditis, etc, as in Egypt the *'nomoi'* were Graecized in similar fashion. A further group is formed by the places ending in -ia:

Iudaia, Idumaia, Samareia and Galilaia.[123] The Seleucids also kept this
division at a later date.[124] Although only the *'oikonomoi'* of the hyparchies
are mentioned in the document to which reference has been made, here too
we may assume a division between military and financial matters with a
'hyparch' on one side and an *'oikonomos'* on the other; there is evidence of this
in Ptolemaic possessions in Asia Minor and later in the Seleucid period.[125]
Thus perhaps the *'hyparch'* Keraias mentioned by Polybius (5, 70, 10) had
Galilee under his command. Sometime a royal *'grammateus'* is mentioned –
outside Palestine – as a third official.[126] As in Egypt, the village, under the
'kōmarchēs', was at the bottom of the chain of command.[127] Presumably
Idumea formed such a *'hyparchy'*, with the administrative centre at Marisa,
about twenty-five miles south-west of Jerusalem.[128]

> Here the Zeno correspondence gives us an insight into the Ptolemaic
> administration: on travelling through Marisa in 259 BC, Zeno had purchased
> three young slaves from two prominent Idumean brothers. When he
> returned to Egypt, they escaped and went back to their old masters. The
> latter demanded a further sum for their surrender. Zeno now sent his agent
> Strato to Marisa with five letters. Two of them were to senior officials –
> perhaps the *'hyparch'* and the local police officer –, the third letter went to
> their executive department with the description of the slaves, and the last
> two letters were sent to personal friends for them to influence three further
> officials – probably in the finance department – in Zeno's favour.[129]
> Strato was not to be burdened in Marisa with any compulsory 'special
> tasks', e.g. the collecting of tax, etc. Zeno also sought to use the same
> Strato to collect a debt from a certain Jeddūs – presumably a Jew and
> *'komarch'* of a village. A higher official (Alexand)ros delegated the matter
> to his subordinate Oryas. However, the latter was 'prevented by illness' –
> perhaps because he did not want to incur the hostility of Jeddūs – and only
> allowed Strato to be accompanied by his slave. Jeddūs drove the two of
> them from the village by force, and Oryas could only send to his superior
> the resigned report that we now have.[130]

The two episodes show a flourishing bureaucracy even on the borders of
Judea and Idumea, and at the same time the difficulties with which the
officials, who were presumably all Greek, had to struggle in their barbarian
surroundings. Idumeans and Jews were not so easy to regulate as the Egyptian
fellahin, and even the right hand of the all-powerful finance minister instilled
little respect into them.

It was of decisive significance that the Ptolemies also introduced the
originally Greek system of tax-farming and delegation of tolls into their
foreign possessions. According to the Rainer papyrus, the whole matter was
regulated in a νόμος τῆς μισθώσεως specifically relating to 'Syria and Phoenicia';
unfortunately this is no longer extant.[131] In addition, the papyrus refers to
a whole series of royal ordinances (προστάγματα), regulations (διαγράμματα)

and a special royal decree. All this must be taken as the expression of special legislative activity for the province. The Zeno papyri report – for the first time, as far as Palestine is concerned – the activity of the τελῶναι in the mercantile centres of Gaza and Tyre.[132] In the Rainer papyrus, which among other things contains a decree of Ptolemy II about the valuation of livestock and slaves, the 'village tax farmers', together with the '*komarchs*', are entrusted with the execution and supervision of the livestock valuation.[133] In the domain of Apollonius in Galilean Beth-anath there appears a κωμομισθωτής whose tasks include hiring out the state land – or in this case the domain land, which probably comes from a royal gift – to the peasants of a village and making an exact calculation of the quantities to be delivered.[134] As a 'blend of farmer and royal official', he was probably competent in a multiplicity of duties.[135] This context fits Josephus' report from the story of the Tobiads that the taxes of the 'cities of Syria and Phoenicia' were farmed out year by year in Alexandria, by free tender, to the magistrates or principal citizens of that area.[136] The supervision of the collection of taxes was strict: fraud by false declaration or even refusal to pay tax were punished by severe penalties; informers were generously rewarded; those who owed taxes were threatened with prison or even compulsory selling into slavery.[137] As in Egypt, it is probable that state revenue officials worked alongside the tax-farmers or in their service, so that each supervised the other.

One important factor was the *royal land* in the direct possession of the Ptolemies which was worked in the form of domains or through the royal peasants. It was held for 'Syria and Palestine' as for Egypt that the whole province was a territory 'won by the spear' *(δορύκτητος χώρα)* and thus theoretically belonged to the king.[138] Even if this claim was considerably qualified because of practical political considerations, a quite considerable part was nevertheless under the direct control of the king. The settling of military peasants, the establishment of military colonies and the equipping of newly-founded cities of Greek constitution with the necessary land, together with the rewarding of deserving officials, like the *dioikētēs* Apollonius in Galilee or the *stratēgos* Ptolemy in Scythopolis, were all done through assignments from the royal estates.[139] A. Alt has sought to demonstrate the existence of such royal estates in Galilee, the plain of Megiddo and the Jordan valley.[140] In addition, one might point to the cleruchs under the command of Tobias in Ammanitis, who had certainly been settled on royal ground; or even to the famous balsam plantations of Jericho and Engedi, which were old domains going back to the time of the monarchy or of the Persians.[141] Recent investigations east of Jaffa suggest that there were also royal domains on the coastal plain, and perhaps military settlers were established there.[142] In Roman times, at any rate, the number of imperial estates in Palestine was again very significant.[143]

On the whole, then, a picture emerges which is very similar to that in

Egypt. The Ptolemies introduced a system of taxation and leasing so thoroughly organized down to the last detail that even the Seleucids – who exploited the country still more after an initial remission of taxation – took it over; indeed, its basic features continued down to Roman times.[144] On the other hand, by giving the upper class of the country a share in the risk and the gain of collecting taxes and revenues, the Ptolemies gained a hold on the aristocracy, who played a key role in determining the mood of the country.[145] Moreover, their interest in preserving the yield of the land resulted in a certain concern towards the ordinary population; this is shown by the prohibition against enslaving free natives of 'Syria and Phoenicia'. Probably the Graeco-Macedonian military settlers tried to make the Semitic peasants who worked their lots of land into their slaves, a custom which probably had hung on from the wars of the Diadochi.[146] The freeing of Jewish slaves in Egypt by Ptolemy II is also connected with this policy.[147]

b) *The Ptolemaic administration and the Jewish temple state*

The question now is whether the practice of administration and taxation depicted above held without qualification for the whole province or whether there were exceptions for certain *'semi-autonomous' areas*.[148] These latter would comprise in the first place the cities with a Greek constitution.[149] Those cities which can be recognized by their names as being Macedonian and Ptolemaic foundations have already been mentioned;[150] in addition, there are all the important coastal cities and at least part of the 'cities in Coele Syria', later restored by Pompey and Gabinius, which had been made subject by the Hasmoneans.[151] In individual instances, however, it can often no longer be established whether the places had full city rights or only had a 'city-like' character, or whether the elevation to the status of city took place in Ptolemaic times or only in the Seleucid period.[152] The significant Phoenician coastal cities, like Sidon, Tyre, Acco-Ptolemais, Gaza, Ashkelon, Joppa and Dor were certainly cities in the proper sense at an early date. On the other hand, the military settlements were not yet free *poleis* in the full sense, though they had features resembling those of the *polis*, as for instance a certain city territory and their own magistrates. They could be elevated to the status of *polis* at any time by royal decree. There were no completely 'free' cities in the ancient Greek sense within the Ptolemaic empire.[153] Whatever the individual details, in Palestine – as opposed to the mother country of Egypt – we find a relatively large number of 'free' or 'semi-free' cities with a constitution following the pattern of Greek models. In these, administration and the collection of taxes were carried out by the city magistrates and local tax-farmers, but, as the instance of Marisa and the Aegean cities and those in Asia Minor belonging to the Ptolemies shows, there was strict supervision by Ptolemaic officials, who maintained a constant presence.[154] There is no reason to assume that the royal *'prostagmata'* did not hold here.[155]

The second group of 'semi-autonomous' areas were the *'ethnē'*. Strabo names four such peoples in Palestine, who 'dwell intermingled with the Syrians, Coele Syrians and Phoenicians': Jews, Idumeans, Gazeans and Azoteans.[156] The Zeno correspondence shows that there was a considerable bureaucratic administrative apparatus for Idumea. So the Ptolemaic administration will not have made any fundamental exception in its treatment of the *Jewish 'ethnos'*,[157] and will not have been particularly lenient towards them. Like the rest of the population of Syria-Palestine, the Jews who settled outside their main territory in Galilee (I Macc. 5.20ff.), Idumea and Transjordania will – if they did not have a special status as cleruchs (see above, pp. 15f.) – have been regarded as σώματα λαϊκὰ ἐλεύθερα (see above, p. 15, nn. 146, 325). Even Judea itself, whose geographical extent – leaving aside one uncertain note in Josephus – largely corresponded, in all probability, to the former Persian province of Jehud,[158] was neither 'politically independent within the Ptolemaic kingdom', nor did it take 'the first steps towards political independence' with the high priest as a 'petty monarch'.[159] In addition, Judea not only formed the heart of an *'ethnos'*, but could at the same time be regarded as a *'temple state'*. The very fact that 'Jerusalem' was called 'Hierosolyma', contrary to the real wording, indicates that it was interpreted on an analogy with the temple cities of Syria and Asia Minor, which termed themselves *'hierapolis'*.[160] However, whereas the Seleucids allowed their 'temple states' relative freedom down to the defeat of Magnesia,[161] the rich Egyptian sanctuaries were carefully controlled by the crown, particularly in respect of finance. An *'epistatēs'* appointed by the king was responsible to the king for the finances of a particular sanctuary; the temple land itself was controlled by the fiscal authority.[162] The *dioikētēs* Apollonius in particular seems to have tightened this control of the temples.[163] The result was that the Egyptian sanctuaries partly became a stronghold of resistance against the Greeks. Of course, in Jerusalem the *high priest* was nominally at the head of the Jewish *'ethnos'* and the temple, but it would have been against the principles of Ptolemaic rule – especially under Philadelphus – if he could have held sway there like an independent ruler, apart from paying a certain amount of tax. Palestine was no peripheral territory, but of great strategic significance, bordering, as it did, in the north immediately on the territory of the old enemy, the Seleucids, and in the south and east on the constantly unsettled tribes of the Arabian desert.[164] Probably a special Jewish temple official, authorized by the foreign régime, worked alongside the high priest, responsible for the finance of Judea and the temple; presumably he collaborated with the Ptolemaic officials, who would no more have been absent from Jerusalem than from Idumean Marisa. This division between the religious-political office of the high priest and the financial administrator, which apparently goes back to the pre-Ptolemaic period and perhaps under Alexander took the place of the Persian division[165] between governor and high priest,[166] would accord with a rule which can also be noted elsewhere in the Hellenistic administration (see above, pp.19f.). We find one piece of evidence for it which probably comes from the Seleucid period: II Macc.3.4ff. records a bitter dispute between the προστάτης τοῦ ἱεροῦ Simon and the high priest Onias III over the 'agoranomia', an office which in itself comes from the Greek *polis* and was bound up, among other things, with police regulations.[167] The independence of this official over against the high priest is clear, for the latter was not in a position to override Simon and have him removed from office. Rather, Simon – presumably as the one responsible for finance – went to the Seleucid *stratēgos* of Coele Syria with the charge that Onias was keeping money hidden in the temple without justification.

> The office of στρατηγὸς τοῦ ἱεροῦ (sᵉgān hakkohᵃnîm), the representative of the high priest, attested in Josephus, in Acts 4.1; 5.24, 26 and in the Mishnah, may possibly have grown out of the earlier one of προστάτης τοῦ ἱεροῦ. Three treasurers were subordinate to him.[168]

Not least, the power of the high priest depended on the strength of his personality. The tax farmer Joseph could rob the weak Onias II of a good part of his political power, whereas the energetic Simon II made a strong position for himself at the time of the conquest of Jerusalem by Antiochus III. His son Onias III, however, found himself on the defensive.

P. W. Lapp has investigated pottery stamps inscribed with *jhd* in old Hebrew letters (and the sign ⊘) and *yršlm* (with a five-pointed star). These are probably connected with the Ptolemaic tax system. According to him, the signs served to distinguish between the taxes for the king and those for the sanctuary.[169] The only question one might add is whether the great vessels marked in this way might not have contained tax contributions from royal domains in Judea in addition to the natural taxes.[170] The *mṣh* stamp has also been associated with Persian crown property in Judea.[171] In the light of circumstances in Egypt, a common collection of taxes for the crown and the sanctuary was by no means unusual. This automatically resulted in an effective control of the temple finances, which was necessary simply because the foreign ruler was at the same time patron of the sanctuary. Even in Jerusalem, according to ancient tradition, the royal exchequer was responsible for at least part of the costs incurred in the sanctuary.[172] Whether one can attribute a 'nationalistic' tendency to the *yršlm* stamp is, of course, questionable.[173]

Presumably during Ptolemaic rule, another important institution developed, limiting the authority of the high priest: the *gerousia*. The origins of this body go back into Persian times, where we find the nobility, the heads of large families or even the elders as an influential group. However, they did not form a strictly demarcated nucleus; as can be seen from the change in designations, their boundary was still indeterminate.[174] The principal priests, who are still mentioned alongside the high priest in the writings of the Jews of

Elephantine,[175] presumably also had a share in the constitution of the *gerousia*. We meet it as a regular authority for the first time in the decree of Antiochus III after his seizure of Jerusalem, where the *gerousia*, together with the priests, temple scribes and temple singers are granted exemption from tax in gratitude for their support of the king in his capture of the country: ἡ γερουσία καὶ οἱ ἱερεῖς καὶ οἱ γραμματεῖς τοῦ ἱεροῦ καὶ οἱ ἱεροψάλται. A little later Sirach seems to give indications of the existence of the *gerousia*.[176] We may regard it as representative of the principal priests, the rich lay nobility, the great landowners and heads of clans, and we may assume that the Tobiads played a decisive role in this assembly down to the outbreak of the Maccabean revolt.

> 'Scribes', too – like Ben Sira (see below, pp. 131ff.) – will have been represented in it in small numbers, as the *gerousia* surely also had juristic functions. This could be the historical root for the fiction of the 'men of the great synagogue' (*'Ab.* I, 1a), who are said to have passed on the Mishnah between the prophets and Simon the Just. In the edict of Antiochus III, however, the 'temple scribes' are cited as a special group alongside the *gerousia*, and there – presumably down till the end of the second temple – the scribal element formed a minority. The Pharisees only gained absolute dominance at the Synod of Jabneh.[177]

Just because the *gerousia* formed an aristocratic and not a democratically elected body, we may not assume that it was constituted as a regular institution even during Persian times; there were also a whole series of assemblies with an aristocratic constitution under the Greek system, too, chief among which was Sparta. Indeed, Sparta was particularly attractive to the Jewish Hellenists, so that at an early stage they constructed a primal relationship between Jews and Spartans.[178] The Hellenistic reform programme put forward by Jason and the foundation of the new *polis* Antiochia in Jerusalem seems to have been sanctioned by a majority in the *gerousia*, so the *gerousia* was presumably also to form the supreme authority in the city to be founded; open protests by members of the senate only came about after the replacement of Jason by Menelaus.[179] Of course the attempt to turn Jerusalem into a Greek *polis* was only a brief – albeit momentous – episode.[180] Even in the Maccabean period, the *gerousia* retained its great significance, though surely with other members. This is shown by the introduction of Jonathan's letter to the Spartans: Ἰωναθαν ἀρχιερεὺς καὶ ἡ γερουσία τοῦ ἔθνους καὶ οἱ ἱερεῖς καὶ ὁ λοιπὸς δῆμος τῶν Ἰουδαίων Σπαρτιάταις τοῖς ἀδελφοῖς χαίρειν.[181] Here we can see not only the political status of the Jews as an '*ethnos*', but also, as their supreme head bore the title ἀρχιερεύς, the political form of Judea as a 'temple state'. The fact that the *gerousia* is mentioned before the priests shows that it was the second ruling authority alongside the high priest. However, we may not conclude from this that it was a purely lay body; rather, the leading priestly temple authorities will also have been represented in it. Through the rest of Jewish history, despite all the changes of political circumstances, the *gerousia* (from the time of Herod under the name of the Sanhedrin)[182] remained an important organ of the Jewish state. Its final constitution and acquisition of political influence probably goes far back into Ptolemaic times, and influence from Greek models is quite possible.[183] The Ptolemies and the Seleucids after them thus had the possibility of playing off different constitutional organs against one another, following the motto '*divide et impera*'. This was one of the chief reasons for the partisan struggles which broke out in Jerusalem as early as the third century BC.

When the high priest Onias II, probably under Ptolemy III Euergetes (see below, pp. 268ff.), suddenly refused to pay the tax, he did not do so, as the author of the Tobiad romance relates, from old-aged stubbornness and avarice, but because of the general weariness in face of constant regimentation by the Ptolemaic administration. Perhaps, too, he hoped for a change of régime under the impact of the temporary success of Seleucus II Callinicus towards the end of the third Syrian war.[184] The king immediately threatened a confiscation of Jewish territory and the settlement of military colonists. This threat was repelled by the intervention of the *Tobiad Joseph*. He received the office of '*prostasia*', i.e. he was entrusted with the representation of the Jewish '*ethnos*' to the royal administration.[185] In addition, because of his high offer, he acquired the right *to levy general taxation* throughout 'Syria and Phoenicia'. He was able successfully to break the resistance of a number of cities, like Ashkelon and Scythopolis (see above, p. 26, n. 75), which by then had already been largely Hellenized, and held the office of 'general taxation officer' for twenty-two years.[186] The report of Josephus that Euergetes 'after his occupation of all Syria, instead of making thank-offerings for victory to the gods in Egypt, came to Jerusalem and there offered many sacrifices to God according to our customs', could be connected with the new regulation of affairs in Jerusalem.[187] Probably the administrative apparatus constructed by his father and his *dioikētēs* had become too complicated for Euergetes; he concentrated military and political responsibility in the hand of the *stratēgos* (see above, p. 21), partly did away with the office of '*oikonomos*', and sought to relieve the state bureaucracy and at the same time raise the revenue from taxation by transferring the entire tax collection of the province to the Tobiad Joseph.[188] Whether he was successful in so doing is questionable. Probably the deposition of the financial genius Apollonius had a negative effect. The king found himself in financial difficulty and had to take refuge in a debasement of the coinage.[189] The considerably increased financial burden could – at least partially – be the reason for the sharp drop in finds of coins of the third and fourth Ptolemies in Palestine (see below, pp. 43f.), as any additional levy of taxes must have diminished the amount of currency in circulation. For the Jews themselves, the rise of the Tobiad Joseph to his influential position was certainly by no means unfavourable, as Jerusalem, which until that time was still relatively insignificant and indeed old-fashioned, will have gained economic and political significance, and perhaps even have won internal independence. Moreover, Joseph was able to protect his people against excessive exploitation.[190]

Two documents from Seleucid times give us some information about the nature and the level of the *taxes* paid in Judea. The decree of Antiochus III in favour of the Jews freed the temple personnel and the *gerousia* from three royal personal taxes: the salt tax, which was connected with the state monopoly in salt, the garland tax, presumably a compulsory gift on royal feast days, and the poll tax.[191] At least the first two were already levied by the Ptolemies. In addition to a three-year exemption from taxes, Antiochus granted the whole people remission of a third of the tribute previously paid to the Ptolemies.[192] Possibly Seleucus IV, under the pressure of the annual war reparations to Rome and Pergamon, revoked these concessions again and demanded 300 talents;[193] on the accession of Antiochus IV, Jason probably increased this contribution to 360,[194] and by the sale of the office of high priest to Menelaus it was screwed up to almost a double contribution of 660 talents – a third of the annual payment to Rome, with which Antiochus was in arrears.[195] The incomes of the temple and the priests were probably also taxed again.[196] After the Jewish rebellion Judea was apparently treated as a royal territory, as punishment for its disobedience; in addition to the royal personal taxes, it was required to pay a quota mentioned in the letter of Demetrius I in I Macc. 10.29f. of harvest produce to the extent of a third of sown produce and a half of fruit from trees.[197] These excessive tax demands will have helped the Maccabean independence movement and are perhaps the real cause for the smouldering of revolt after the death of Judas Maccabaeus.[198] It is reasonable to suppose that the sum of 300 talents mentioned often in the sources was the tax demand of the Ptolemies, based on the economic capability of the country, to which the special taxes mentioned above and the excise were added.[199] The sum of 8,000 talents given by Josephus in *Antt.* 12,175 as the tax contribution for 'Syria and Phoenicia' may be somewhat exaggerated, but is not 'so far from the truth';[200] of course the doubling of the sum by the Tobiad Joseph is an exaggeration. Porphyry gives the income of Ptolemy II Philadelphus from Egypt alone as 14,800 talents of silver and 1,500,000 *artaboi* of grain, probably not including the export monopoly (see below, p. 37).[201] A comparison with figures from Persian times shows how the Greeks and Macedonians could make subject lands financially profitable and exploit them: under Darius I the tribute for Phoenicia, Palestine and Cyprus was 350 (Babylonian) talents. Even if we must assume an essential change in economic structure for the two to three hundred years down to Ptolemaic or Seleucid rule, above all a transition from a natural economy to a money economy and thus a change in the price of precious metals, the figures given indicate the considerable increase in the income from taxation in Judea. This increase was only possible as the result of more intensive cultivation and the consequent increase in the fertility of the country.[202] In later times, on the other hand, it hardly grew at all. Archelaus took in 400 (*Bell.* 2,97) or 600 (*Antt.* 17,320) talents from Judea and Samaria, and Herod I and Agrippa I about 1200 from a much larger area.[203] It had reached its extreme limit in the Hellenistic period.

c) *Contemporary Jewish views on the power of the state*

The remarkable thing is that Jewish judgments on the foreign state and its rulers in the early Hellenistic period are still overwhelmingly positive. For Artapanus, the ordering of the Egyptian state was so impressive that he derived it from Joseph and Moses. Joseph was the first *dioikētēs* of the whole country (διοικητὴς τῆς ὅλης γενέσθαι χώρας), who introduced the surveying and distribution of the country (cf. Gen. 47.20ff.), set apart the temple land and – like Philadelphus in the Fayum – made much unfertile land arable. Moses' contribution was, among other things, the division into 36 nomes, the irrigation system and the absolute monarchy.[204] Here the motive of the 'culture-bringer' certainly plays a part; but the alien culture was the model. The Letter of Aristeas draws a completely ideal picture of the first two Ptolemies – in some contrast to the report of Agatharchides on Ptolemy I and his attitude to the Jews.[205] Philadelphus above all appears as a pure philanthropist, corresponding completely to the demands of the model which he draws up in question and answer form with the seventy-two elders.[206] Like the king, his officials and counsellors are also depicted in an ideal light. The cordiality and graciousness of the two Ptolemies also occupy the centre of the Tobiad romance. Its aim is to show that Joseph and his son Hyrcanus succeeded in gaining to an unlimited degree the favour of the king, his spouse and his friends.[207]

One could raise the objection that these stories come from the milieu of the Jewish Diaspora in Egypt, where in the second century above all a close collaboration was developed between Ptolemeans and Jews, and more than a few offices, from *stratēgos* to tax farmer, were occupied by Jews.[208] But even the 'court histories' preserved in Palestinian Judaism, though transferred to the Babylonian and Persian court – show in similar fashion an overwhelmingly positive attitude towards the foreign monarchy. With God's help Daniel succeeds in winning the favour of the various kings and retaining it in spite of all temptations and trials. Not only does he become counsellor to Nebuchadnezzar, but with his friends he reaches the highest posts in the administration of the pagan land, whose wisdom he has learnt better than all its native inhabitants.[209] A positive picture of the heathen king is also drawn in the Prayer of Nabonidus, which is related to the Daniel narratives, and after his healing by a Jewish miracle-worker – like Nebuchadnezzar in Dan. 4 – he becomes a worshipper of the true God.[210] Without going further into the difficult literary problems of the book of Daniel, we may state that the narratives of Dan. 1–6 and others of this nature – though still in simpler form –

were current in Jewish Palestine in the third century BC and had perhaps already been collected by that time.[211] In spite of all their criticism, for example towards the self-glorification of the divine monarchy – in which there is probably already a hint of the opposition to the ruler cult of the Hellenistic monarchs – they contain an openness towards the foreign kings which was hardly possible after Antiochus IV and the gaining of national independence.[212] We find further court histories built on a similar pattern at the beginning of the book of Tobit, which is influenced by the story of Ahikar,[213] and in more elaborate form in the book of Esther.[214] Both probably come from the Hellenistic period before the Maccabean revolt, and hint at a new stage of development in Hebrew literature which probably is a kind of analogy to the rise of the Hellenistic romance and the aretalogy.[215] Finally, the story of the three page boys (III Ezra 3.1–5.6) also belongs in this context; here Zerubbabel gains great honour and respect through his wisdom before the Persian king and his officials. With its oriental, fairy-tale like features and its primitive, Semitic-type Greek, it does not match the Alexandrian-Jewish literature known to us, and probably goes back to an Aramaic source. The parallels to Daniel and Esther are not the result of literary dependence, but arise because each is the same kind of narrative. It can hardly be put in the post-Maccabean period because of its secular tendency.[216] Significantly, e.g. the command of the king to rebuild Jerusalem is described by analogy with founding a *polis*.[217]

All these 'court stories' have a common model in the story of Joseph or even the story of Ahikar, thus going back to an oriental, *pre-Hellenistic* basic motif.[218] On the other hand, the story of the Jew who rose to power and honour under the great foreign king attracted the interest of the Jewish listener and reader particularly in the early Hellenistic period, as is shown by the number of contemporary examples listed above. Had the foreign, pagan monarchy been rejected in principle, these stories, which are attached to a predominantly friendly attitude of the Persian king towards the Jews, would hardly have been handed on further, been collected or fixed in writing. It is striking that the motif of the rise to power and indeed the whole genre of 'court history' no longer appears in this way in the literature of Judaism after the second century; the hostile additions in the Greek translation of the book of Esther show that difficulties were found even with the traditional stories.[219] Later stories in Jewish literature, like the book of Judith from the Maccabean period or III and IV Maccabees, which come from the Diaspora of the first century AD, have an outspokenly hostile attitude to the pagan state, for all their Hellenistic form. Typical of this attitude is the maxim of Shemaiah, head of a Pharisaic school at the time of the last Hasmoneans and Herod: 'Hate the dignity of the ruler and do not seek acquaintance with authority' (*'Ab.* 1, 10b). In the later Rabbinic period, it was in principle suspicious for anyone to be 'close to the government',[220] and prayers were offered in the synagogue for the speedy downfall of the 'wicked government'.[221] Significantly, by far the

greater majority of Jewish synagogue inscriptions in Egypt consist of dedications to the two Ptolemies, while such dedications in synagogues of the Roman
period are infinitesimally small.[222] So we may probably take the fondness
for 'court stories' at the beginning of the Hellenistic era as an expression of
openness to the world on the part of certain sections of the Jewish people, who
were in opposition to that apocalyptic view of history which expected the
imminent downfall of the Gentile world of nations (see below, pp. 180ff.); it is
understandable that examples of this kind awakened the desire, particularly
among young Jews of the aristocracy, to seek their fortunes far from the
narrowness of their homeland in the service of the Hellenistic kings, whether
as soldiers or as officials. This did not necessarily mean apostasy from
the faith of the fathers. Nehemiah had been a high Persian official, and in the
Hellenistic period Ps. Hecataeus was concerned to show that the Jews in the
service of Alexander and Ptolemy I kept faithfully to their ancestral beliefs.[223]
True, we can point to some apostates who gave up their faith for their
career in the state,[224] but these remained the exception. In Koheleth, which
probably comes from the third century BC (see below, pp. 115ff.), we find a
whole series of sayings which are concerned with behaviour towards the king.
Even if this was a traditional theme of the wisdom tradition – the 'court story'
as a whole has its origin in wisdom – these sayings cannot have been spoken
theoretically into the void, but could have been directed towards young nobles
in Jerusalem who were toying with the thought of going into the service of the
Ptolemies. Perhaps Koheleth himself had gained some of his experience
there.[225] Even Ben Sira, who took up a critical attitude towards Seleucid rule[226]
and could warn against royal service (7.4f.), nevertheless saw the service of
princes as an appropriate activity for the wise – probably looking back to his
own past:

> He serves among great men
> and appears before rulers.
> He travels through the land of foreign nations
> and learns good and evil among men.[227]

If we look for the reasons for this predominantly positive attitude, the
answer can be given in the words of H. Gressmann: 'Dread of the Greeks led
to wonderment at their success and their power.'[228] However, this was true
only for the Jewish aristocracy – rejection may have been stronger in the lower
strata of the people; it found its expression in apocalyptic speculation as this is
reflected, say, in the vision of the terrifying beast in Dan. 7, which is quite
different from what has gone before (7.8, 20, 23). This is matched by the
general verdict on the monarchs of the Diadochi between Alexander the Great
and Antiochus IV in I Macc. 1.9: 'and they caused many evils on the earth.'
That this negative judgment was not limited to Palestine – just as the positive
appreciation was not limited to the Diaspora – is shown by the way in which

the translation of Isa.9.10f. in the Septuagint, which presumably came into being in Egypt in the second half of the second century BC, is brought up to date: καὶ ῥάξει ὁ θεὸς τοὺς ἐπανισταμένους ἐπ᾽ ὄρος Σιὼν ἐπ᾽ αὐτοὺς καὶ τοὺς ἐχθροὺς αὐτῶν διασκεδάσει, Συρίαν ἀφ᾽ ἡλίου ἀνατολῶν καὶ τοὺς Ἕλληνας (for pᵉlištim) ἀφ᾽ ἡλίου δυσμῶν τοὺς κατεσθίοντας τὸν Ἰσραὴλ ὅλῳ τῷ στόματι. Here the reference is evidently to the successes of the Parthians against the Seleucids and the annihilation of Macedonia by the Romans. The essential feature of all these negative testimonies is of course that they were written at the time of the Maccabean revolt or later, under its influence.[229]

4. Hellenistic Influence on Trade, Commerce and Social Structure in Palestine

a) Greek influences in the pre-Hellenistic period

As a coastland, Palestine had had trade connections since the second millennium not only with Egypt, Mesopotamia, northern Syria and Arabia, but also over the sea with Cyprus and the islands of the Aegean. With the Greek mercenaries, for whom there is evidence back to the seventh century BC, Greek merchants, Greek goods and, after the sixth century, Greek coins came to Palestine. The import statistics in Ezek.27.11–25a, which probably come from the beginning of the fifth century BC, know Tyrian trade with Tartessus, Ionia and Greece, Asia Minor and Rhodes. About 460 BC, after the victory at Eurymedon, Athenians settled, probably for about a decade, at Dor on the Palestinian coast, and the city paid tribute to the Attic sea alliance.[230] Both Isaeus[231] and his pupil Demosthenes[232] mention a colony of Greek merchants some decades later in Akē (Acco). It is quite possible that merchants and mercenaries from Greece settled in other harbours on the coast of Palestine.[233] Conversely, from the fourth century there is evidence of a Sidonian community in the Piraeus, and as early as about 370 Strato, king of Sidon – presumably the founder of Strato's Tower on the coast south of Dor – was honoured by the Athenians with the *proxenia*. According to a bilingual inscription of the fourth century from the mercantile centre of Delos, the '*hieronautai*' of Tyre made an offering to Apollo there.[234]

All this indicates that it was the *Phoenicians* who were the mediators of Greek culture for Palestine in the pre-Hellenistic period. They lived for a long time on Cyprus and in the Western Mediterranean in close economic and cultural contact with the Greeks, and were more and more influenced by them. Through them Greece, and primarily Athens, exported valuable pottery and other luxury goods, receiving in exchange above all grain.[235] An Attic pottery fragment from Dor still bears the name of its Phoenician owner, and another has Greek marks on it; perhaps Greeks had settled there even after the end of the brief 'Athenian' era.[236] The Greek export of pottery to the orient was as ancient as the 'export' of Greek mercenaries; it can be found as early as the end of the seventh century BC – above all in the form of Athenian black lacquered and red figured ceramic ware – in a great many burial places in Palestine, not only on the coastal plain, where culture was more strongly developed and which from 475 down to the expedition of Alexander was in the possession of Tyre and Sidon,[237] but also in the hinterland, including Judea:[238] 'finds of Greek pottery are rather the rule than the exception for sites in Palestine.'[239]

With Attic pottery came Attic money. It was needed above all to pay the Greek mercenaries who were in the service of the Persians or the Phoenicians. The oldest coin found in Palestine was minted by Pisistratus between 555 and 546 BC and was discovered in a suburb of Jerusalem; a coin coming from north Greece about 500 BC was found in excavations in ancient Shechem.[240] Silver coins minted in Attica, which formed an almost international currency, were much more widespread in Syria and Palestine than Persian darics, which hardly played any part there. When the stream of Attic drachmae ceased after 404 BC, they were imitated by the local Persian governors. Even the governor of the Persian province 'Jehud' had coins minted on the Attic pattern and with the inscription of the province; a few examples are still extant. So it is certainly no coincidence that one of the few Greek loanwords in the Old Testament is the word *dark^{e}mōnīm*, a Hebrew form of the Greek genitive plural δραχμῶν.[241] On this W. F. Albright remarks: 'Virtually all coins found in Palestine excavations from the Persian period are Attic drachmas or imitations of them.' This is confirmed by D. Schlumberger in a survey of hoards of coins from Persian times in Syria and Palestine: none of the hoards discovered down to 1950 contained Persian darics.[242] In contrast to the 'monnaie vivante' of the Greeks and the imitations of it, Persian coinage was a 'monnaie quasi immobile'.[243]

Through Phoenician mediation, interest grew in artistic objects in Greek style. At Tell el-Fareʿ, about eighteen miles south of Gaza, in tombs of the Persian period, have been discovered three bronze vessels, presumably of Greek origin, and an elegant suite of bed and chair with 'almost pure Attic forms';[244] in addition, silverware in a 'mixture of Persian and Syrian style' has been found.[245] Thus Palestine became the meeting point of most varied spheres of influence, something which was only possible because a kind of international trade existed even in the Persian period. The terra cottas and miniatures found in a whole series of places in Palestine, above all on the coastal plain and in the Shephelah, indicate Egyptian and Persian models on the one hand, but the growing influence of Greek form is unmistakable. They may derive in part from Greek imports, but more probably they are local imitations or a product of Phoenician manufacturers.[246] One such was discovered in Ḥarayeb near Sidon; it extends from the fourth century well into the Hellenistic period. Here there are unmistakable links with Tanagra, the stronghold of Greek terra cotta manufacture.[247] The influence of Ḥarayeb is in turn demonstrable in the coastal region of Palestine.[248] A collection of small bronzes from the fourth century which was found in Ashkelon and contains above all representations of Egyptian gods shows elements of Greek style as well as strong Egyptian features.[249] Thus in the Phoenician sphere of influence, in which at that time almost all Palestine could be included, one can talk of a 'mixed culture' in which Egyptian, Persian and to an increasing extent Greek influences encountered each other. A typical picture is presented by the burial ground of ʿAṭlīṭ, between Haifa and Dor, from the fifth and fourth centuries BC. C. N. Johns, who excavated it, described it in the following way: 'Their culture was complex, an eclectic combination of Greek, Egyptian and oriental objects such as Attic vases, Egyptian amulets and scarabs in a mixed style.'[250]

The economic and cultural mediation of the Phoenicians was effective during the Persian epoch and well into the Hellenistic period. This is shown, among other things, by the Sidonian colonies in Marisa and Shechem and presumably also by a Tyrian colony in Rabbath-Ammon-Philadelphia, which flourished during the third and second centuries BC; probably these were originally mercantile settlements.[251] According to Neh. 13.16, as early as the fifth century BC Phoenician merchants, who had settled in the country, were working in Jerusalem; they were active in dealings with 'fish and all kinds of wares', i.e. in trade with places on the coast.[252] Presumably economic undertakings which went beyond the narrow borders of Judea were in their hands. Down to the Christian era, the Palestinian Jews themselves lived predominantly from agriculture and rearing livestock.[253] This is true to a considerable degree even for the Jewish diaspora outside Alexandria. The two Jewish wholesalers ʾAbihai and Jonathan, whose extensive list of debtors from the period before 310 BC is to be found in P. Cowley 81, certainly form an exception.[254] In ancient Israel and post-exilic Judaism, the terms for 'merchant' and 'Canaanite' were identical,[255] and the circles of strict Jews regarded the Phoenician and Canaanite merchants who imported luxury, the temptation of alien cults and ritual impurity into the country, with the utmost mistrust. Prophetic prediction of the early Hellenistic period saw it as a sign of eschatological salvation that 'there shall no longer be a trader ($k^ena^{\,c}ani$) in the house of Yahweh Sebaoth on that day'.[256] G. Boström in particular has demonstrated from Jewish wisdom literature the deep-rooted aversion of the conservative Jews to 'foreign' merchants and their Jewish representatives.[257] This attitude was furthered by the fact that from an economic point of view Judea was a dead end; the great trade routes passed it by. The Phoenicians dominated sea trade, the coastal plain and connections to the north; the Arabs (Nabateans) in the south and east dominated the caravan trade with southern Arabia and the Persian Gulf.[258] Moreover the imported luxury goods, e.g. the valuable Greek pottery, were of interest only to the thin upper stratum; the simple peasant of the hill country of Judea led a frugal life and with his few needs in life was largely self-sufficient. Nevertheless, Attic pottery has been found even in Jerusalem and other places in Judea,[259] and in the capital itself some terra-cotta heads of an Egyptian or Hellenistic type.[260] In comparison with Samaria, however, Judea was economically backward, not least because of the hostility of active religious circles to alien influences. This does not quite match up with the vigorous intellectual life of the Palestinian Jews which is attested by their rich literature (see below, pp. 112ff.). Perhaps this ambiguous situation is the reason why the liberal minority of the Jewish aristocracy stubbornly maintained contact with their northern neighbours, although they had the majority of the people against them on this point.[261]

b) The economic and social situation under Ptolemaic rule

The Macedonian conquest brought a manifold intensification of previous Greek influences. The vision of a uniform Graeco-Macedonian world empire from India to the pillars of Hercules indeed occupied the political horizon for only a short space of time, and so the subject peoples of the East were hardly aware of it. However, the trend towards international trade which was already there in the Persian period increased further, despite the division of Alexander's kingdom into the rival kingdoms of the Diadochi. The Greek language became the *lingua franca*, and Greek standards, weights, coins, ways of reckoning and trade usage became the general norm. Even the constant wars could not hinder the development of commercial connections. It was only the intervention of Rome in the East which introduced the economic decline.[262]

The fact that for 100 years Palestine came under the kingdom of the Ptolemies was of decisive significance. Here from the beginning the tight administration was supplemented by a no less purposeful state commerce which, in the form that it took, was a novelty and had not been practised before in any oriental state.[263] Rivalry with the Seleucid empire, which was considerably larger both in extent and in population, required that Egypt mobilized all its resources to create an effective balance of power. This notion dominated the great line of Ptolemaic economic policy in the third century: according to a phrase of W. W. Tarn's, Egypt became 'a money making machine'.[264] The starting point was the conception already mentioned, that the whole kingdom was the personal estate of the king. This led not only to his power of disposal over the country and its natural resources, but also – at least in theory – to the same power over its inhabitants.[265] The Greeks, to whom conceptions of this kind were alien, in the light of their native '*poleis*', were won over to collaboration in this new form of state because they were assigned a vital role in the development of the Ptolemaic state economy and at the same time a share in its fruits. So the first Ptolemies and their Greek helpers developed Egypt in the first half of the third century BC on the basis of the oriental idea of kingship in such a way that it became the leading state in the

Hellenistic world. In so doing they bound two systems very closely together, 'the immemorial practice of Egypt and the methods of the Greek State and the Greek private household'.[266]

It remains uncertain how far this new order had already come into being under Ptolemy I Soter, who ruled Egypt from 323 BC and took the title of king in 305/4.[267] According to the Aramaic Papyrus Cowley 81, the later monopoly was still unknown in Egypt towards 310 BC.[268] The transfer of the capital from Memphis to the new 'Greek' Alexandria was a far-sighted move; it increasingly became an economic and cultural bridge between Greece and the oriental world[269] and thus also influenced deeply the development of Judaism in Egypt and Palestine. Sources begin to flow more fully under Ptolemy II Philadelphus, primarily the Zeno papyri. What happened earlier remains largely in the dark. The foundation of the Ptolemies' riches was agriculture, above all the cultivation of wheat, which had probably been introduced into Egypt in Persian times. Here a subtle system of farming out, planned cultivation, supervision and taxation led to a huge increase in royal income over previous levels.[270] The king and his *dioikētēs* were concerned not only with a more extensive exploitation of the land but also with a real increase in its fertility by the reclamation of marshland, better irrigation, the introduction of new plants, breeding stock and improved methods of cultivation. The estate of Philadelphia in the Fayum, handed over to Apollonius as a royal '*dōrea*', with Zeno as its administrator, was at the same time a kind of experimental agricultural institute.[271] A further source of income was the royal '*monopoly*' on vegetable oils, linen cloth, metal, salt, spices and other important goods and merchandise.[272] Where it was not carried on in royal '*ergastēria*', industrial manufacture, too, was supervised by the state and, if that were necessary for its purpose, was taken over directly; the same was true of transport. The carriers needed state concessions; the level of interest and the price of essential goods were prescribed.[273] Thus in practice the state controlled the whole of the Egyptian economy in such a way that private initiative on the part of the individual entrepreneur was not excluded, but made use of where possible through a refined system of leases and the mutual supervision of the state treasury.[274] A further support of Ptolemaic commerce was the strictly preserved *monopoly in coinage*, which took further Alexander's idea of a uniform imperial currency. In contrast to the other Hellenistic states, Ptolemy I changed over from the Attic standard, already spread widely by Alexander (see above, p. 33), to the Phoenician, and his son continued this independent policy. Foreign coins coming into the country were called in and reminted; the independent city and feudal coinages were suspended in at least Cyprus, Phoenicia and Palestine, and Ptolemy's own royal gold, silver and copper coins were circulated in sufficient quantities. Copper coinage represented an innovation; it made coins popular even among the lower strata of the populace and limited the extent of barter. This policy over coinage was supplemented by a royal bank with its branches scattered throughout the empire, which made possible a kind of Giro credit transfer and establishment of private bank accounts.[275] Uniform imperial coins were also minted in the province of 'Syria and Phoenicia'; coins have been found in Scythopolis with the stamp of Philadelphus from Joppa, Ptolemais, Tyre and Sidon.[276]

Commercial policy within Egypt was supplemented by intensive trade with the foreign *provinces* of the Ptolemaic empire which to a large extent provided what Egypt itself lacked.[277] In addition, a proper export trade was also developed. The possession of the harbours of Palestine gave the Ptolemies the termini of the old profitable trade with the Mineans in Arabia Felix and Gerrha on the Persian Gulf. The Zeno correspondence mentions Gaza as the most important mercantile centre in Palestine, in which incense, myrrh and other aromatic goods, spices and luxury goods were all traded.[278] A special official was entrusted with supervision, as working in aromatic goods was a royal monopoly.[279] The trade itself was in the hands of the Nabateans and people related to them; the Zeno correspondence mentions, for example, a 'Moabite' Malichus, perhaps an intermediary between a caravan from Gerrha and the *dioikētēs*.[280] The *Nabateans*, who were still depicted as wild nomads at the end of the fourth century by Hieronymus of Cardia, had successfully withstood an attempt to subjugate them by Antigonus and his son Demetrius Poliorcetes,[281] but had to submit to the first Ptolemies, as these had the Palestinian termini of the caravan routes firmly in their hands; Philadelphus not only sent a fleet against them, but also set up coastal stations on the Red Sea and thus isolated them.[282] However, when Antiochus III invaded Palestine for the first time, 'the inhabitants of Arabia' immediately went over to his side and fought alongside him at Raphia.[283] The Maccabees later had friendly relations with them, and were probably given their support in the fight for freedom against the Seleucids.[284] Despite their independence, close trade connections, especially with Egypt, brought them visibly under the influence of Alexandrian Hellenistic culture, so that towards the end of the first century BC Strabo could depict them as a settled, highly civilized people.[285]

Ptolemaic trade policy could also be used as pressure even against over-populated *Greece*: to a large degree the Greek cities were dependent on Ptolemaic grain exports.[286] Ambitious Greeks regarded Ptolemaic Egypt and its colonies as the promised land, in which a man could easily make his fortune. 'Ptolemy is the best paymaster for a free man,' remarked Theocritus,[287] and at about the same time (beginning of the third century BC) Herondas praised the advantages of the 'new world' in a mime:

> For all that is and will be, can be found in Egypt:
> Riches, stadiums, power, fine weather,
> Reputation, theatres, philosophers, gold, young men,

> The sanctuary of the kindred gods, the king,
> A just one, the museum, wine, every good thing,
> Whatever you want, and women . . .[288]

This praise of the riches of the Ptolemies is matched by the family tomb-stone of two officers of Cretan or Aetolian origin from Gaza, which praises the παλαίπλουτοι βασιλῆες Αἰγύπτου.[289] Plato may still have seen curiosity to learn as the characteristic of the Greeks and avarice as the characteristic of the Phoenicians and Egyptians (*Republic* 435e/436a), but in the Hellenistic period these characteristics were exchanged: 'The Greeks came to Egypt to grow rich.'[290] The first Ptolemies had a great need for Greek soldiers, officials, inventors, craftsmen and other specialists, so that they favoured immigration. The political freedoms of the *polis*, which had become increasingly more questionable after Alexander, even in the mother country, were replaced by the economic advantages of belonging to a superior class and the possibility of alliance with *politeumata* of fellow-countrymen, in which a Greek way of life could be followed even in barbarian surroundings.[291] On precisely this point, the Jews in the Greek-speaking Diaspora were their apt imitators; they too allied together in *politeumata*, where the synagogues took the place of the gymnasium (see pp. 65ff. below) as the centre of their communal life.[292]

Thus the foundations of Ptolemaic politics rested above all on economic considerations, which had precedence over pure power politics. Apart from the founder of the dynasty, the Lagids, in contrast to the majority of the Seleucid rulers, were no longer significant generals. Here they displayed a tendency which was transferred to the Greeks settled in Egypt: 'The *homo politicus*, still alive in Greece, yielded place to the *homo oeconomicus* and to the *homo technicus* in Egypt.'[293] This specialization in the commercial sector was expressed *inter alia* in the specialist literature of the '*Geōrgika*', '*Kēpurgika*', etc.,[294] which, based on earlier Greek models, flourished particularly in Alexandria. It is a particularly striking manifestation of the 'rationalist and technical character of Greek culture',[295] which in the case of the mass of Graeco-Macedonian immigrants was completely directed towards economic success. As the Zeno papyri show, in the Ptolemaic 'foundation years' they worked with feverish activity and required the native inhabitants to do the same. The climate of work on the estate in Philadelphia is characterized by Apollonius' demand to Zeno to carry out his commands as quickly as possible: νύκτα ἡμέραν . . . ποιούμενος. The consequence was that some workers and slaves simply absconded:[296] 'Strike after strike, complaints, requests, trials are the order of the day.'[297] Unlike the king and his officials, who had to take care to preserve the working capacity of the native population and for whom, therefore, the demand for '*philanthrōpia*' had to some extent a real background, the Greeks of the developing upper class – 'pressés de s'enrichir' – showed hardly any trace of a social conscience for the Egyptian and Semitic 'barbarians' under them.[298] In a petition to Zeno, one of his lesser employees, presumably a Palestinian, laments bitterly that the wages which he has been promised many times keep being withheld from him, for 'they had seen that I am a barbarian . . .' and 'that I do not know how to live like a Greek *(ὅτι οὐκ ἐπίσταμαι ἑλληνίζειν)*'.[299] However, the lament of the '*katochos*' Ptolemy from the Serapeion in Memphis, in the middle of the second century BC, shows how much the situation was to change in a hundred years. He complains that he has been attacked by Egyptians 'because I am a Hellene'.[300] National unrest in Egypt breaking out after the end of the third century is a consequence of the failure of Ptolemaic internal policy.[301] This change of situation, furthered by social distress, is similarly to be found, perhaps to a still greater degree, in Palestine and in the east of the Seleucid empire. It was one of the reasons for the Maccabean revolt.

This situation gave the ever-increasing Jewish Diaspora in Egypt the alternatives of either becoming part of the Egyptian fellahin or advancing into the favoured class of Greeks, or at least obtaining an equivalent status, by learning to *ἑλληνίζειν*.[302] The Septuagint, the synagogue inscriptions and the Alexandrian Jewish literature show that the majority of Jews in Egypt adopted the latter course, though without giving up their particularity; this was a significant decision that was to have world-wide, historical importance.

c) The economic development of Palestine under the Ptolemies

Among the external provinces of the Ptolemaic kingdom, 'Syria and Phoenicia' were of special significance not only strategically, but also commercially. The role of Palestinian harbours as turn-round points for the aromatic trade has already been mentioned, and the Phoenician cities and the forests of Lebanon were the foundations of Ptolemaic sea power. But even the hinterland attracted the Greek entrepreneural spirit with the aim of better commercial exploitation. *The great journey which Zeno made through the length and breadth of Palestine as representative of the '*dioikētēs*'* was connected with this task. A papyrus of 261/260 BC shows the *dioikētēs* as an importer of considerable amounts of grain from Palestine;[303] he also had an estate in Beth-Anath in Galilee,[304] presumably a royal gift, in which he concentrated on producing wine.

A London papyrus gives us some interesting details. It is a letter from a certain Glaucias, who had been sent on a tour of inspection, to the *dioikētēs*. He seems to have been satisfied with the work being done and speaks of eighty thousand vines, the building of a cistern and the erection of sufficient living accommodation for the workers. The quality of the wine was so excellent that it was indistinguishable from the wine of the Aegean (Chios), which was imported into Palestine in very great quantities. We see from this that similar progressive and systematic methods were used in work on the estate in Galilee to those being used on the experimental estate in Philadelphia in the Fayum. Probably Apollonius had vines from Chios planted, in order to be independent of wine imports.[305]

Zeno, however, was not only concerned with the inspection of this estate but spent about thirteen or fourteen months in all, from the end of 260 to at least March 258 BC, in Palestine and Phoenicia. Moreover, his recall came unexpectedly as a sudden summons by Apollonius: he was to take over the direction of Philadelphia. From about the same time we also have the Revenue Laws (end 259) and the Rainer papyrus on 'Syria and Palestine' (see pp. 20ff. above); so these were years with particular financial and economic activity, which also concerned Palestine. We can still follow some of Zeno's journeyings. His first began at the end of January 259 from Strato's Tower on the coast and continued by Jerusalem, Jericho and Abella (*'ābel haššiṭṭīm*, Num. 33.49), into Transjordania to the stronghold *(βιρτα or Σουραβιττοις)* of Tobias in the Ammanitis. He reached there on 29 Dystros (25 April) 259 and probably stayed several days. He continued the journey in a northerly direction, making a detour to the south of Damascus and, going by the estate of Apollonius in Beth-Anath in Galilee, he again reached the coast at Ptolemais at the end of May.[306] At the end of May or the beginning of June he sent goods from a Palestinian harbour to Pelusium.[307] Presumably he also made a detour into some Phoenician cities; we also find him in the south, in Gaza and the Idumean cities of Marisa and Adora, right on the border of Judea.[308] He sent an agent with a caravan into the Hauran; another, who had been stationed in Cyprus for some time as a *'grammateus'* and was presumably summoned to Phoenicia by Zeno, requested an advance payment from Tyre to Berytus.[309] Finally, shortly before his sudden departure to Gaza, Zeno is given a considerable amount of grain at the special request of Apollonius.[310]

On his great excursion into Transjordania and to Galilee, in which he also crossed Judea and visited Jerusalem – we have a receipt from Jerusalem[311] – Zeno travelled with an extensive staff, like his master Apollonius on his inspection tours in Egypt: including Zeno, seventy-eight people are mentioned by name in the lists that we have, of whom only twelve have Semitic names. The rest have Greek names. Among them are high officials, like a certain Apelles, τῶν παρὰ τοῦ βασιλέως, presumably with a special commission for the king, possibly also Callicrates, the admiral of Ptolemy II, Dionysodorus, inspector of the accounts office of the *dioikētēs*, and several officers, Greeks from Athens, Aspendus, Miletus and Colophon. Ariston, a brother of Zeno, also belonged to the group.[312]

Mere consideration of this illustrious escort will suggest that Zeno undertook this journey less as a private concern of his master[313] than as an official commission, so to speak as his representative. Its long duration was determined by the multiplicity of tasks laid on him: intensive study of local conditions, taking up trade relationships, supervising the financial officials already working there, new organization and further extension of the net of agents – a number of members of his staff remained behind in the province even after his return. He was also concerned with any measures which could serve an improved exploitation of the productive capacity of Palestine. Presumably Zeno will also have investigated the possibility of direct participation in the aromatic trade to the exclusion of the Nabateans; this could be the reason for the expeditions into Transjordania and the Hauran, the business relations with the Moabite Malichus and the Jewish sheikh Tobias, and the intervention of Apollonius in the Palestinian caravan trade.[314] The foundation of the military colony under the command of Tobias in the Ammanitis, mentioned earlier, and the elevation of Rabbath-Ammon to the status of the city of 'Philadelphia' may also be connected with Ptolemaic politics towards the Nabateans.[315] Later letters from Tobias to Apollonius and the king and the various reports from agents of Zeno's about happenings from all over Palestine show that the connections established by Zeno's journey remained alive.[316] Officials, representatives of Apollonius, but also unscrupulous speculators must have worked there in large numbers. The *slave trade* in particular seemed to be a profitable business, as in Egypt the enslavement of free workers was forbidden by royal law.[317] Even Zeno bought slaves in Palestine, though they caused him some trouble; Tobias later sent three more with a eunuch as tutor as a present to the *dioikētēs*.[318] A more suspicious matter was when one of his agents bought slaves in Palestine on his own account and ran into trouble with the customs in Tyre in his attempt to sell them abroad without an export licence.[319] We also hear of two Greeks who spent a time as guides in the service of Apollonius and later carried on an open trade in girls; they travelled far and wide into the Hauran, Ammonite and Nabatean territory, taking their slave girls with them, buying here and selling there; they sold four of their victims as 'priestesses', i.e. probably as temple prostitutes, to Joppa, and hired out another to a '*horophylax*' in 'Pēgai', who ran a guesthouse.[320] We hear several times that Palestinian slaves absconded from their transport to Egypt; perhaps they felt the difference between the status of slave in the more patriarchal ordering of the oriental household and the purely economic approach of the Greeks.[321] Ben Sira later occupies a peculiar middle place between the harsh Greek and the milder patriarchal treatment of slaves.[322] Among the Greek upper class in Egypt there was a considerable need for 'Syrian' slaves for the household; they could hardly compete with the cheap 'free' working forces in agriculture and the crafts. There were surely also Jews among these σώματα ἀπὸ Συρίας, who are mentioned several times in the Zeno correspondence. Two slaves girls ’Ιωανα(ι) and ’Ανας, presumably with the Jewish names Johanna and Hanna, worked in the household of Apollonius. Ps. Aristeas also confirms the large number of Jewish slaves who had come to Egypt through the campaigns of Ptolemy I.[323] In addition, however, there were also free Jewish workers there; the Zeno correspondence mentions two vintners, a shepherd, a dog-watcher and a brickmaker, who even observed the sabbath in his work for the *dioikētēs*. A number of 'Syrian villages' with partial Jewish populations were scattered through the country.[324] All this points to a constant immigration from Palestine. The Rainer papyrus with the decree on the declaration of slaves in 'Syria and Phoenicia' is to bring an end to the widespread enslavement of σώματα λαϊκὰ ἐλεύθερα, i.e. the semi-free population.[325] An inscription of the early third century BC from Oropos on the borders of Attica and Boeotia concerning the freeing of the Jew Moschus son of Moschion on the ground of an incubation dream shows that Jewish slaves were sold even to Greece at a relatively early period.[326] This is an illustration of the threat against Tyre, Sidon and the 'regions of Philistia' in Joel 3.4–8, which threatens vengeance on them because of their plundering of Jerusalem and then continues:

> 'You have sold the people of Judah and Jerusalem to the Greeks (*libᵉnē hayyewānīm*), removing them far from their own border. But now I will stir them up from the place to which you have sold them . . . And I will sell your sons and daughters into the hands of the sons of Judah, and they will sell them to the Sabeans, to a nation far off . . .' The slave trade with southern Arabia is confirmed by the hierodule inscription of Ma'in, which mentions 28 slave girls from 'Gaza' and only 8 from Egypt.

The dating of the Joel passage remains uncertain; perhaps it is connected with the conquest of Jerusalem by Ptolemy I or events during the wars of the Diadochi in 323–301 BC which are unknown to us. The threat hardly fits the peaceful period of Ptolemaic rule, and a date in the Maccabean period is probably too late.[327] For this era, II Macc. 8.11 also mentions the Phoenicians as intermediaries in the slave trade, and at the same time the reports of freeings of Jewish slaves in Greece grow more frequent: in 163/162 BC an unknown Jewish slave was freed in Delphi; in 158/157 there follow a Jewess Antigone with her daughters Theodora and Dorothea.[328] The well-known cynic Menippus came at the beginning of the third century as a slave from his home town Gadara in Transjordania to Sinope on the Black Sea.[329] Without doubt, the slave trade in Palestine had great economic significance.

Palestine was also, given good harvests, an exporter of grain, and had to come to the rescue when the Egyptian harvest turned out badly. 'Syrian wheat' was highly prized in Egypt, and even planted there by Apollonius because of its rapid ripening.[330] A further export article was olive oil, indispensable to the Greeks, as Egypt produced almost nothing but vegetable oil. The government allowed private export dealings in both grain and oil, but watched them carefully because of its monopoly.[331] The deliveries from Apollonius' vineyard in Galilee show that wine, too, was exported to Egypt.[332] In addition, the Zeno papyri include lists of goods with an abundance of further items.[333] All in all, Palestine was the predominantly exporting partner; Egyptian shipments were largely of manufactured wares like papyrus, glass, pottery and fine textiles. There were also luxury goods, to the degree that Palestine became capable of purchasing them. Here Alexandria entered into the Greek heritage.[334] But even here, domestic production developed.

Because of their geographical position, Phoenicia and Palestine had long been countries of *transit*, above all for traffic between Egypt, Arabia, Mesopotamia and the rest of the Mediterranean. Merchant shipping consisted for a large part in coastal shipping, and Pelusium was only two days' journey distant from Gaza. A long list of goods with excise levied in Pelusium, and imported from 'Syria', contains many items coming from Greece and Asia Minor.[335] Illuminating here is the report of a truly international trade in furnishings: cushions, coverings, mattresses and bed linen, with sales or purchases in Miletus, Caunus in Caria – Zeno's homeland – Halicarnassus, Gaza, Rabbath Ammon and Ptolemais Acco; the wife of the entrepreneur, who, himself an agent of Apollonius, was really meant to be buying wool in Miletus, arranged the business in the meantime in Alexandria.[336] This shows at the same time that even in the period before Alexander, Palestine had close trade connections with the Aegean, especially the great mercantile centres like Rhodes, and later Delos. We have a whole series of reports from this area not only of Phoenician but also of Palestinian merchants. The relatively early evidence of Jewish communities in Delos and Rhodes is also to be explained in this way.[337] By and large the Zeno correspondence, even as far as Palestine is concerned, gives the picture of a very active, almost hectic commercial life, originated by that host of Greek officials, agents and merchants who flooded the land in the truest sense of the word and 'penetrated into the last village of the country'.[338]

This extraordinary activity, which took place even in Palestine under Philadelphus, is further confirmed from various quarters. Probably in the same decade in which Zeno travelled through Palestine, the Sidonians founded a trade settlement in the Idumean administrative centre of Marisa, which lay at the crossroads of the routes from Gaza to Jerusalem, Ashkelon to Hebron and Petra to Joppa. Probably they wanted to intervene from here in the traffic in aromatic goods and spices. They formed a *politeuma* of their own in Marisa, rapidly reached a state of prosperity, associated with the Idumean aristocracy, and together with them led the life of grand feudal lords, as the tomb paintings in their great rock tombs show. Linked with this was the adoption of strong Hellenistic and Alexandrian cultural influences and the Greek language.[339] At about the same time the Tyrians possibly founded a settlement in Rabbath Ammon in Transjordania and introduced there the cult of their city god Heracles-Melkart and his mother Asteria-Ashtoreth. The city – which was also an important fortress – was still given the name Philadelphia under the second Ptolemy. It, too, had great significance as a staging post for the caravan trade with the Persian Gulf and southern Arabia.[340]

Finds of coins are a further indication of the commercial boom in Palestine at this time. A comparison of the coins found in various excavations in early Hellenistic sites and strata shows that the coins minted by Ptolemy II exceed those of his father by four- to fivefold, and pre-Ptolemaic, Attic, Phoenician,

Philisto-Arabian coins and coins of Alexander by eightfold. However, after the second Ptolemy, the number of coins of the later Ptolemies declines sharply again, perhaps because the stock minted by Philadelphus was adequate, but more likely because there was no longer such positive commercial activity, and the pressure of taxation was increased (see above, p. 27). Almost no Seleucid coins from the third century BC have been found – because of the Ptolemaic money monopoly; they appear only after the conquest of the country by Antiochus III. At this time they appear in large quantities, whereas the Ptolemaic coins quickly disappear. The coins of Antiochus III, however, amount to little more than a third of those of Philadelphus. The absolute climax is reached with Antiochus IV Epiphanes, who even exceeds the second Ptolemy with his mintings, presumably because of the expeditions in Palestine carried out by him and his generals. The particularly large number of coins of Epiphanes in the citadel of Beth Zur shows that the soldiers brought coins into the country. By and large, one might say that minted money was finally established in Palestine only through Ptolemy II, and largely superseded barter.[341]

The increase of foreign trade in the course of the third century BC is attested by the many stamped – and partly datable – jars from Rhodes and other parts of the Aegean which are to be found throughout Palestine west of the Jordan, including Judea, Samaria and Galilee. There have even been some individual finds in Transjordania. Probably the soldiers of the occupation, the Greek officials and merchants, and indeed the members of the local aristocracy, preferred the wine and the oil of the Aegean islands and the coast of Ionia, which was 'bottled' in Rhodes and Cos and exported throughout the world, to native produce. This makes Apollonius' efforts towards a Galilean wine of Ionian quality understandable.[342] From an early date the enjoyment of Gentile wine had become impossible for strict Jews because of its ritual impurity.[343]

The interest shown by Philadelphus and his *dioikētēs* in improvement and greater fertility in agriculture suggests that on the great crown estates in Palestine and, say, in the *'dōrea'* of Apollonius in Galilee, they will have introduced new plants, animals and methods of growing.[344] Individual proof is difficult because of lack of evidence, but there are some hints from which one may draw conclusions to this effect. Theophrastus, the pupil of Aristotle, reports at the end of the fourth century BC on two *'paradeisoi'*, i.e. plantations of the Persian kings, in 'a valley in Syria'; the context shows this to be the Jordan valley, in which precious balsam was grown.[345] The later parallel reports of Diodorus, Strabo, Pompeius Trogus and Josephus directly indicate Jericho and 'Engedi.[346] According to the account of Diodorus, which goes back to Hieronymus of Cardia, a contemporary of Theophrastus, the growth of the *balsam shrub* was a real monopoly (οὐδαμοῦ μὲν τῆς ἄλλης οἰκουμένης εὑρισκομένου), which brought great profit (ἐξ οὗ πρόσοδον ἁδρὰν λαμβάνουσιν). Pompeius Trogus attributes the riches of the Jews to this monopoly; Horace makes it an especially valuable product of Herod.[347] According to Strabo the Jews are said to have limited growth in order to obtain the highest possible price for their monopoly.[348] All this explains why Mark Antony left the balsam plantations – perhaps in fulfilment of an old promise – to Cleopatra VII, and Herod had to buy their produce back again for a high fee.[349] Nevertheless, the balsam monopoly does not seem to have been fully enforceable, as the sources also speak of balsam being grown at Zoar to the south of the Dead Sea, in Scythopolis, by Lake Gennesaret, and in one instance even of Egypt, not to mention Arabia Felix, the home of the balsam shrub.[350] Pliny adds a note, depending on Theophrastus, that in the time of Alexander the crops of the two '*paradeisoi*' had been relatively small, but that in Roman times the produce had increased considerably: for a period of five years he mentions the sum of seventy to eighty million sesterces.[351] It is further striking that in ancient writers the balsam of Judea or Jericho, with the Dead Sea and the asphalt gained from it, excites the greatest interest, which is not exceeded even by the accounts of the temple in Jerusalem. This can best be explained from the great significance of this monopoly.[352] If one considers that there is a gaping chasm in historical tradition between the fourth and the first centuries BC and that the historians of the early empire mostly draw on Hellenistic sources which are largely lost,[353] it seems likely that the significance of the balsam monopoly was not just discovered in the Roman period, but already goes back to the first Ptolemies who, following their policy elsewhere, exploited as profitably as possible the domains in Jericho and 'Engedi which they took over from the Persians. They may therefore already have extended the size of the plantations and transferred the growing of balsam to Galilee and Egypt. In 'Engedi, too, where there was an estate producing balsam in the late monarchy, which flourished under Persian rule in the fifth century and then fell victim to nomad incursions, coins from the Ptolemaic period have been found together with the foundations of a strong citadel which protected the royal estate against the Arabs. It is therefore probable that the growth of balsam and palms which flourished in Roman times through terraced plantations with artificial irrigation was already begun in the Ptolemaic period.[354] Song of Songs 5.13; 6.2; 8.14 already speaks of balsam plantations of Jericho in connection with various aromatic goods. After the Maccabean uprising, the royal estates passed over into the hands of Hasmonean priests and later the Herods. Pliny, Solin and the Talmudic tradition show that they were imperial estates in the Roman period.[355]

The Dead Sea, with the *asphalt* rising in it, which was fished out by local Arabs, also excited the interest of ancient historians and geographers. Here we have the eye-witness report of Hieronymus of Cardia, who led an unsuccessful operation against the Arabs by the Dead Sea in the time of Antigonus, towards the end of the fourth century BC, which was meant to bring the acquisition of asphalt into Greek hands. Perhaps the intention at the same time was to prevent the export of asphalt to Egypt, as at the beginning of the Ptolemaic period it became quite important for embalming. Here too, as R. J. Forbes points out, there can hardly be any doubt that Philadelphus took the acquisition of asphalt under his own control in the course of his repression of the Nabateans.[356]

A. Schlatter has pointed out that *papyrus*, too, was planted in Palestine in the Hellenistic period, according to Theophrastus by Lake Gennesaret and according to a report of Josephus presumably in the Jordan valley.[357] A series of archaeological discoveries confirms vigorous commercial activity in the coastal plain: in the middle of the third century new agricultural settlements arose near Jaffa on land which had not been built on before,[358] and twelve miles east of Jaffa a great fortress-like warehouse was discovered with an oil press, considerable dyeing equipment and workshops, presumably the centre of an estate.[359] A *dye-works* has been found in Tell Mor, the harbour of Ashdod, connected with obtaining purple dye from murex shells. In Dor, too, the Phoenicians are said to have obtained purple. A 'wholesale business' for wool-dying was found in Hellenistic Gezer.[360] Further dyeing installations from the second century BC have been found at Tell el Fūl north of Jerusalem and in Beth Zur, where there was also a centre of the wool industry.[361] The dye-works of the Hellenistic period are at the same time an indication of extensive sheep-tending and weaving.[362]

Artificial irrigation was probably also introduced into Palestine at that time. The first express evidence of it is provided by Koheleth (2.6) and Jesus Sirach (24.30f.). Diodorus speaks of irrigation canals in the date-palm plantations of Jericho, and at Damascus the Chrysorrhoas was almost completely led off into canals, to irrigate a large area.[363] On the western slope of the Judean hill-country at Adullam[364] there were, in the Hellenistic period, a large number of artificial terraces, pools and canals which probably also served to improve agriculture and irrigation. According to the evidence of the Qumran *hodayot* and the archaeological discoveries there, the Essene agricultural settlement of 'Ein Feshka was also equipped with artificial irrigation, and in Roman times there is evidence of constructions in Jericho, by Lake Gennesaret and elsewhere in Galilee. They are taken for granted by the Jewish Talmudic tradition.[365] With their help, in climatically favourable areas, e.g. in the Jordan valley, two harvests a year could be obtained. By its very name, Taricheae at the southern end of Lake Gennesaret points to a fishing industry in Galilee founded in the Hellenistic period – perhaps as a royal domain;[366] according to the evidence of Rabbinic literature, agriculture, trade and commerce were much more intensive than in Old Testament times.[367] Unfortunately the sources do not allow us to present a historical development, but e.g. the excavations at Beth Zur give an impression of the lively commercial life of a small garrison city of the early Hellenistic period, and the discoveries at Ḥirbet Qumran and ʿEin Feshka show very varied economic activity even among the Essenes.[368] There are also individual indications of *technical improvements* at that time: thus a better form of oil and wine presses,[369] the treadmill,[370] the irrigation wheel[371] and the plough all seem to have been innovations. The latter was already known in ancient Babylon, but is first mentioned for Palestine in Jub. 11.23 as an invention of Abraham. Even in Egypt one only comes across it after the Hellenistic period.[372] Finally, mention should be made of building technique, which also made great progress at that time. Traces of this are to be found in Palestine. It extends from Hippodamus' 'gridiron' pattern of a city strictly divided into quadrilateral blocks of dwellings – ultimately deriving from the East – through wall-building technique to simple house-building. In addition there were the splendid public buildings in Hellenistic cities. Unfortunately we only have scanty remains of what was certainly considerable building activity in the early Hellenistic period. Interestingly, the Greek loanwords of the Mishnah are particularly concerned with the building sector.[373]

By and large it may be assumed that in Palestine, as in Egypt, agricultural and commercial production was considerably increased, leading not only to a substantial increase in the revenue from taxes but also to an increase in the population itself.[374] In the hill-country of Judah, where artificial irrigation was difficult and it was not so easy to secure an increase in crops, superfluous population may well have been forced to emigrate to non-Jewish parts of Palestine and to Egypt, especially in years when the harvest was bad.

An economic recession set in from the second century, as it did throughout the eastern Mediterranean. The confusion of war, with the conquest of Palestine by Antiochus III, the high Seleucid war damages to Rome which meant a heavy burden of taxation, and finally the Maccabean war of liberation followed by the Hasmonean war of conquest, did not favour future developments. A whole series of settlements were given up, partly through destruction, partly through improverishment and the departure of the inhabitants, including places like Gezer, Beth Zur, Lachish, Shechem and possibly also Bethel, Dothan, Shiloh, etc.[375] The political and economic isolation of the new Jewish state, combined with constant civil war and wars of expansion at the end of the second century, inevitably led to this decline.

d) The effects on Palestinian Judaism

On his journey, Zeno also came into close contact with Jews. The Jewish sheikh Tobias, commander of the Ptolemaic military colony in the Ammanitis, and according to Josephus the brother-in-law of Onias II, deserves first place here.[376] Not only was his fortress beyond the Jordan one of the most important destinations of the great caravan of Zeno in its journey to Transjordania, but Tobias also lent generous support to Zeno by giving him asses, three horses and animal drivers;[377] moreover, this was not just done after

Zeno's visit to the Ammanitis, but before the beginning of his journey. Both sides were interested in treating each other advantageously. Presumably Zeno sought the support of influential Jews as a counterbalance to the Arabs, whose position of power was to be limited: the Jew Tobias is the only non-Greek in Palestine to appear so extensively in the sources. Jews are also mentioned elsewhere: the village elder Jeddūs lent money to Zeno and had difficulty in getting it back again,[378] and a certain Simon led a grain caravan from Galilee to Sidon. It remains uncertain whether he is the same person who, as the editors assume, sent Apollonius a jar filled with mackerel.[379] In addition, Jews also appear in quite subordinate positions as escorts to the great caravans; we find a ʿΟσαῖος (Hoshea) and an ᾿Αυναῖος (Hanan).[380] Finally, mention should be made of the Jewish slaves in Zeno's service (see p. 41 above). The social division which seems to be appearing here was no coincidence: the Ptolemies were interested in contacts with the Semitic upper class because they needed them – here circumstances were different from those in Egypt – to maintain their rule. If the Semites were prepared to adopt the Greek language and Greek ways of life – as can be seen, for example, in Marisa (see below, pp. 61f.), they had the possibility of obtaining equal rights to the Greeks. These circles were the real active proponents of the trend towards Helleniza-tion. The simple populace, the σώματα λαϊκὰ ἐλεύθερα, appeared primarily as an object of exploitation, and the only notice needed to be taken of them was to see that their economic productivity was not limited. This tendency was increased by the fact that, as a result of their native inheritance, the Greeks were only interested in city culture and despised the open country, the *chōra*. They had no time for a cultural mission to the country populace. This attitude could not be accepted without further ado by the leading strata of non-Jewish Palestine, above all where the influence of Phoenician city and commercial culture had long been dominant, as in the coastal plain. In Jewish areas, on the other hand, it inevitably kept on meeting resistance on strongly religious grounds. In Israel from pre-exilic times a deep-rooted social tradition had been effective as a result of the preaching of the prophets – in complete contrast to Greece. Certain forms of the term 'poor' acquired virtually a positive religious significance, and in the sense of 'unjustly oppressed' the term came near to the word 'righteous',[381] a development which would have been impossible with the Greeks, who originally recognized only responsibility to the family and the polis, and not to their poverty-stricken fellow-men.[382] This contrast, explored most thoroughly by Bolkestein, probably rests in the end on a deep-rooted difference between the social conceptions of the East and those of the Graeco-Roman world, where the much wider spread of slavery had led to a hardening of social contrasts.

Even in the *pre*-Hellenistic period the *social conditions* in Judea were less than ideal: this is shown by the eloquent lament of some of the populace to Nehemiah:

We have to pledge (read *'ōr^ebīm* for *rabbīm*) our sons and daughters to get grain, so that we may eat and stay alive. Others said, 'We have borrowed money for the king's tax upon (add *'al*) our fields and our vineyards. Yet our flesh is as the flesh of our brethren, (and) our children are as good as theirs; and we are forcing our sons and daughters to be slaves, and some of our daughters have already been enslaved; but it is not in our power to help it, for other men have our fields and our vineyards.'[383]

Although Nehemiah himself was creditor on many counts, he did not take the part of his peers, the 'nobles and officials' (5.7, 10), but supported those who were weak in society; in the assembly of the people he brought about a general remission of debts. The fact that in his reforms he relied less on the priesthood than on the Levites and secured for the latter a tithe of the harvest as their income,[384] also has a social background as well as a religious and political one, and it is significant that in the Hellenistic period the priesthood applied the claim for the tithe to itself.[385] With the coming of the Ptolemaic 'economic and social policy', the social conflict which Nehemiah in his time strove to obviate must have grown substantially more acute, especially as religious motives were at work here. The new masters relied on the support of the 'nobles and officials', the aristocratic estate-owners and the leaders of the priesthood, on whom Nehemiah had delivered such a sharp judgment one hundred and fifty years before. In these circles the dominant attitude was one of resistance to the reforms of Nehemiah and Ezra together with the growing legal rigorism and separatism that these produced. Although this group could not make headway against the majority of the people, they never gave up contact with avowed opponents of reform, the house of Sanballat in Samaria and the 'Ammonite' Tobiads.[386] That now, in contrast to Persian times, they gained influence, is shown by the kinship of Tobias with the high priest and the move of the Tobiad family to Jerusalem, attested by Josephus.[387] These circles sought the profitable contact with the 'foreigners', whether these were Phoenician merchants or Greeks, which was so strongly attacked in Proverbs and also in Ben Sira.[388] From here, too, there probably came those who were responsible for collecting tax: the leading priestly families appointed the officials of the temple treasury, like that Hezekiah who emigrated to Egypt in the time of Ptolemy I and whose 'incomparable business efficiency', eloquence and close contact with the Greeks (συνήθης ἡμῖν γενόμενος) are so praised by Ps.-Hecataeus.[389] The priests and lay nobility also had the possibility of leasing all kinds of duties; the Ptolemaic tax system was many-sided enough. In addition, good relations were maintained with the leading men in Alexandria, as is shown by the example of Tobias, his son Joseph, and perhaps also the Simon who is mentioned above.

On both economic-social and religious grounds, a development is beginning here which carried within itself the germ of conflicts. A relatively small, but rich and powerful upper class, which moreover had the confidence of their

Greek masters and their immediate neighbours, faced on the one hand the representatives of a theocracy faithful to the Law, which was predominantly recruited from the lower priesthood and the Levites and whose conservative, legalistic and cultic attitude is manifested above all in the work of the Chronicler and those who revised it, together with Ben Sira,[390] and on the other those groups in which the prophetic tradition lived on and apocalyptic was coming to birth.[391] Although these groups were not completely at one within themselves, both regarded the growth in the power of the aristocracy and the penetration of Greek customs into Jerusalem with the utmost distaste. On the other hand, their members had to face the temptation to rise into the class of the privileged by compromising with the new masters and their way of life. The predilection for the genre of 'court stories' indicates that this temptation was by no means small for gifted Jews. It will emerge that the ideal of 'theocracy' was not strong enough by itself to withstand the manifold temptations of Hellenistic civilization (see above, p.31, and below, pp.267ff.). This 'tendency to compromise' must have appeared at an early stage, as Hecataeus of Abdera at the beginning of the third century BC already testifies that during the Persian and Macedonian rule the Jews had 'changed many of the laws that had come down from their forefathers' (πολλὰ τῶν πατρίων τοῖς Ἰουδαίοις νομίμων ἐκινήθη) because of 'their mingling with aliens' (ἐκ τῆς τῶν ἀλλοφύλων ἐπιμιξίας).[392]

It is difficult to say how far the *simple people* shared in the fruits of the intensification of economic life under the first Ptolemies. Probably their lot, too, will have improved through the long period of peace. However, as the elaborate system of taxes and duties pressed hard on them and the social gulf between the thin upper stratum favourable towards Greek customs and the mass of people became more striking, if not in fact greater, than in the Persian period, we must assume that the rule of the new foreigners found little approval in their sight. The contrast, so typical in Israel, between the godless rich and the poor, unjustly oppressed faithful, as it appears in prophetic preaching and in the Psalms,[393] made it possible to interpret the social contrast in religious terms. It is therefore very probable that hints of religio-social contrasts have been preserved in certain late psalms,[394] in the latest parts of Proverbs,[395] in the latest parts of the prophets[396] and above all in Koheleth.[397] They entered an acute stage in the Maccabean revolt (see below, p.290). Koheleth gives us some illustrations of the social situation of his time, which is best put in the third century BC between 280 and 230 BC (see below, pp.115ff.). He gives us an impressive description of the boundless struggle for riches:

He who loves money will not be satisfied with money;
nor he who loves wealth, with gain;
this also is vanity.
When goods increase, they increase who eat them. (Koh. 5.9f.)

The other side of this boundless desire for money is the subjection of the poor:

> And I went round and saw all the oppressions
> that are practised under the sun.
> And behold, the tears of the oppressed,
> and they had no one to comfort them;
> On the side of their oppressors there was power,
> and there was no one to comfort them.[398]

These and the following verses could reflect the pressure of the hierarchically gradated Ptolemaic bureaucratic administration which went hand in hand with the upper class in exploiting the population:

> If you see the poor oppressed
> and justice and right violently taken away in the province
> (*bam^edīnā* = νόμος),
> do not be amazed at the matter;
> for the high official is watched by a higher,
> and there are yet higher ones over them.

The apodosis perhaps indicates the interest of the Ptolemies in agriculture:

> But in all, this is an advantage for the land:
> A king where there are cultivated fields.[399]

The type of the restless business man who is so fascinated by the hunt for money that he has no possibility of enjoying it is a typical manifestation of the early Hellenistic period; the best examples are the *dioikētēs* Apollonius and Zeno himself. The Tobiad Joseph could represent a Jewish counterpart (see above, pp. 27f.). We find the presentation of this time simultaneously in Koheleth, Ben Sira and the New Comedy.[400] It is significant that the aristocratic wisdom teacher Koheleth, who himself stands 'in the shadow of money' (7.12), observes and notes the misdemeanours, but does not really criticize them. For him the social question is not an independent problem, as it is for the later Ben Sira; it merely serves as illustrative material for the inexplicability of human fate, on which he reflects in a new, critical way – probably already under the influence of the Hellenistic atmosphere in which he wrote (see below, pp. 116ff.).

This *change in the 'social climate'* because of the rational and technical order of the Greeks is perhaps illustrated by a small translation variant in the LXX, coming from the middle of the second century, on Isa. 58.6: whereas the Masoretic text demands in vivid imagery 'Is not this the fast that I choose . . . to undo the thongs of the yoke and to let the oppressed go free and for you (translations sing.) to break every yoke', the LXX puts this significantly in concrete terms: '. . . undo the thongs *of compulsory treaties (βιαίων συναλλαγμάτων)*, release the broken ones by letting them go free *(ἐν ἀφέσει)*, and *shatter every unjust treaty (πᾶσαν συγγραφὴν ἄδικον*

ιάσπα).' We encounter this new attitude, for example, in the negotiations
of the protesting Galilean peasants in Beth-Anath: the agents of Apollonius
refer to the agreement with the '*kōmōmisthōtēs*' and demand full payment on
time *(εὐτακτεῖν)*, PSI 554, ll.12ff., 33f. Only then has an appeal to the
'generosity' *(τὰ φιλάνθρωπα)* of the exalted lord any prospect of success.

Significantly, the assessments of social questions to be found in Jewish
wisdom literature do not agree in the way that we find in prophetic preaching:
riches and the independence that they produce are recognized and valued,[401]
and in Proverbs and Ben Sira poverty can be condemned, as in Greece,
as something that a man brings on himself.[402] However, alongside this there
is still the same emphasis on the condemnation of the unjust and arrogant rich
and sympathy for the poor. This contrast between the appreciation and the
condemnation of riches can be pursued down through the Rabbinic tradition.[403]
On the other hand, Hasidic and apocalyptic circles more clearly applied
themselves to condemnation of the rich and religious appreciation of the poor,
and this finds its consummate expression in the communism of Qumran and
the designation of 'the poor' (*'bywnym*) which they apply to themselves (see
below, p. 246). This opposition of the faithful to the acceptance of economic
and cultural contacts with the non-Jewish environment is most clearly
expressed by Ben Sira[404] in his polemic against the hectic concern with
earning money and against the – usually – deceptive merchant (see below,
pp. 137ff.). After the conquest of Jerusalem by Antiochus III in 198 BC, the
orthodox members of the priesthood, presumably under Simon the Just,
succeeded in obtaining from the king a regulation which – allegedly on grounds
of purity and to protect the sanctity of the temple – inevitably put considerable
limitations on dealings of aliens in the city and its significance in transit
dealings. Significantly, the dispute between Simon's son Onias III and the
financial administrator of the temple, Simon, a supporter of the Tobiads (see
above, pp. 24f. and below, p. 272), which finally led to the deposition of Onias
III, broke out over a question which also concerned trading in the city, the
'*agoranomia*'.

This *restriction on trade with foreigners* through ritual prescriptions occurs
to a still greater extent after the Maccabean period. Thus the first pair of
teachers of the *Pirqe 'Aboth* (see below, p.81), Jose b. Jo'ezer and Jose b.
Johanan, are said to have declared as levitically unclean 'the lands of the
heathen' and the glass vessels (cf. Job 28.17) imported as luxuries from
Alexandria, Tyre and Sidon. This decree was probably promulgated by the
Hasidim of the Maccabean period (see below, pp. 175ff.), in order to prevent
the emigration encouraged by the disasters of war and to make the import of
foreign luxury goods more difficult. Simeon b. Setah (*c.* 100 BC) later
consistently extended this regulation to all metal implements. These could
not be 'cleansed' again, even by melting down (*Shab.* 14b; *j.Pes.* 27d, 54ff.
and *j.Ket.* 32c, 4ff.; cf. *Shab.* 16b). Even before him, Jehoshua b.Perahya

(*c*.130 BC) is said to have forbidden the importation of 'wheat from Alexandria', as in Egypt the impure water of the Nile was brought to the cornfields by irrigation wheels (*'ntly'* = ἀντλία), and according to Lev.11.38 this made it unclean. His rigoristic attitude was, however, rejected, presumably in order to keep down the price of food and to guarantee the provision of grain during famine (*T. Mac.*3.4, 1.675). Conversely, an old Mishnah prohibited the sale of cattle to Gentiles (*Pes.*4.3 and A.Z. 1.6; cf. A.Z. 7b). We find a parallel regulation in CD 12.8f., where the sale of all *pure* animals and birds of Gentiles is prohibited, 'so that they do not sacrifice them'. The sale of the produce of 'threshing floor' and 'winepress' (12.10), i.e. of all corn and wine, to Gentiles is also utterly forbidden. Here, too, we seem to have rigorist, originally Hasidic regulations. The tendency to prohibit all trading with non-Jews by ritual commands and prohibitions, which amounted to an economic boycott, comes up again in the time of the first revolt in AD 66, when the importation of foreign oil and other foodstuffs was prohibited on grounds of impurity. [405]

A further important factor was that, as the only 'city' of Judea, *Jerusalem* completely dominated the country. Whereas even Nehemiah had to move some of the country population into the city through a compulsory synoicism, Judea could now be regarded by outside observers as the territory of what seemed to be the *'polis'* of Jerusalem, although this was not in fact the constitutional position. [406] The city, which underwent an economic revival under the tax farmer Joseph, now also attracted the interest of ancient writers. Timochares, the biographer and presumably also the contemporary of Antiochus IV Epiphanes, gives as its circumference the figure of 40 stadia (4.8 miles), which is probably set too high. The same figure also appears in Ps. Aristeas 105f., and at the same time or a little later the topographer Xenophon, or an anonymous writer, speaks – probably more realistically – of 27 stadia. Even for Greek conceptions, Jerusalem itself was no longer a small city. [407] But even now, the sanctuary formed the absolute centre and remained so until the end of the second temple. Polybius speaks of the Jews 'who live round the sanctuary named Hierosolyma' (*Antt.*12, 136, cf. *Sib.*3, 213f.). As the example of the Tobiads shows, the nobility lived more and more in the city. Whereas the sheikh Tobias still lived for the most part in his fortress in the Ammanitis – significantly, Zeno visited him there and not in Jerusalem, – we find his son Joseph and Joseph's sons principally in the capital. The preliminaries to the Maccabean revolt, in which the Tobiads played a decisive role, consist principally in partisan struggles in Jerusalem itself (see below, pp.277ff.). Hellenistic cultural influence, too, was limited for the most part to the capital. Thus the old opposition between city and the people of the land (*'am hā-āreṣ*) reached a new climax; it was also to play a decisive role in the further history of Judea down to the destruction of the holy city in AD 70. [408]

In view of this, it is not improbable that the *'faithful'* with their apocalyptic tendencies were recruited – as Max Weber thought[409] – predominantly from the growing middle class of the city. But the conservative, small-farmer population settled on the land also considered with mistrust the arrogant priests and the rich lay aristocracy who took up Greek customs. Thus the guerrilla war which was successfully waged against the Jewish friends of Greece and their Seleucid protectors did not begin from some prominent families in Jerusalem but from the sons of Mattathias, who belonged to the lower priesthood and perhaps even only to the levitical *clerus minor* from Modein, a small country town in the north-west, on the periphery of the territory of Judea (see below, pp.289f.). The degree to which this fight for freedom was helped on by the social division is shown by Jub.23.19ff., which in its context clearly refers to the Maccabean revolt:

> And they shall strive one with another, the young with the old . . . the poor with the rich, the lowly with the great, and the beggar with the prince, on account of the law and the covenant . . . And they shall stand (with bows and) swords and war to turn them back in the way; but they shall not return until much blood has been shed on the earth, one by another.

The primarily economic trend of Hellenistic civilization and its limitation to the upper classes and the cities resulted in a relaxation of *life-style* which during the course of the third century probably found an entry even into Palestine and certain circles in Jerusalem. The eloquent warnings of the latest part of Proverbs in particular, against adultery with the 'strange woman',[410] the picture of enjoyment of life and the delight of feasting on the one hand and the warning against a luxurious way of life on the other suggest that the 'Graeculi' were not just a phenomenon in the Rome of the late republic, but were also to be found in Palestine. In addition to the later wisdom literature, like the last part of Proverbs, Koheleth and Ben Sira,[411] some scenes from the Tobiad romance speak a language which is clear enough:[412]

> Bread is made for contentment,
> and wine gladdens life,
> and money answers everything. (Koh.10.19)

A reaction against the predominance of city life is shown in the agricultural ideal which keeps on appearing in the wisdom literature.[413] The laxer, materialistic spirit of the New Comedy and the mime was true not only of the citizens of Athens or Cos at the time of a Menander or a Herondas, but also of the Greek emigrants who brought it, for example, to Phoenicia and Palestine, where it easily found enough imitators among the natives.

> (They) certainly were selfish, their conception of life was materialistic, their ideals somewhat distasteful, and their morality low. What they wanted was a quiet and easy life of pleasure, with the minimum of work and worry. They showed very little interest in the State or in religion. Their main endeavour

was to increase their material possessions and to bequeath them to their posterity. Love plays an important part in their lives, but it was not the basis of marriage; the latter was simply a business transaction.[414]

The emigrants were perhaps less 'bourgeois' and therefore showed more of a 'pioneer spirit', but they were certainly even less bound by social considerations and religious taboos than those who remained at home. That the seed sown by them also came up in Syria and Palestine is shown by the picture outlined by Posidonius, with a certain pointed exaggeration, of the life of the rich bourgeoisie in the Syrian cities towards the end of the second century BC:

> Because of the richness of the land the inhabitants of the cities are liberated from concern for the necessities of life; they hold many assemblies at which they constantly dine. They use the gymnasiums as baths and anoint themselves (there) with valuable oils and ointments. They live in the '*grammateia*' – which is what they call their common dining rooms – as though they were their private dwellings, and for the greater part of the day fill their body with wine and food to such an extent that they can still take a good deal home with them; the sound of the bright-toned lyre rings so in their ears that whole cities echo with its noise.[415]

A perspective on life can be seen here which is also reflected in the epigrams of the Palestine poets Meleager and Philodemus, and is also vigorously reflected in the tomb-paintings and graffiti of Marisa (see below pp. 62, 84ff.).

5. Summary: Hellenistic Civilization as a Secular Force in Palestine

Even the Jews met the civilization of early Hellenism, coming in the wake of Alexander and the kingdoms of the Diadochi which followed him, as a fully secular force. This was the experience of the whole of the East. Its dominant feature was the impact made by the apparently insuperable war technique of Greece and Macedon, with which the Jews, too, gradually became familiar through Jewish mercenaries. This made its mark on the conception of the Holy War in Jewish apocalyptic and made possible the later Maccabean revolt and the Jewish expansionist policy which followed. A further deep impression was left by the strict Ptolemaic system of administration and taxation, and here above all by the typically Greek institution of farming out dues of all kinds. This became a firm institution in Judea over the centuries which followed: the power of the state was henceforward embodied not least in the hated τελῶναι. The development of the 'constitution' of the Jewish temple state as we know it from New Testament times, with the delicate balance between high priest and Sanhedrin, also probably goes back to the Ptolemaic period.

Other impressive features were the economic activity, the talent for organization and the logical and technical system which the Greeks developed in

Palestine, in the service of the Ptolemaic state and in their own interest, to draw more profitably than before on the riches of the country. At the same time they intensified domestic and export trade in Palestine in conjunction with the Phoenicians; not only were the trade connections of the country strengthened towards Egypt and Arabia, but also the Aegean and western Asia Minor attracted the interest of Palestine more than before. The Jewish Diaspora also began to expand further, partly through Jewish mercenaries and emigrants and partly through slaves; it not only grew stronger in Egypt and Cyrenaica, but also took root in Greece and Asia Minor. The long period of peace in the third century furthered favourable economic development, which probably reached its climax under Ptolemy II Philadelphus 285 (282)–246.

In Palestine itself, virtually every inhabitant of the country came into close contact with the new masters, whether he was a soldier, official, merchant or landowner. The *Phoenicians,* who had dominated the whole of the coastal region of Palestine since Persian times and also had great influence in the interior as a result of their trading colonies, took quick and skilful action to adjust to the new situation. But even the inhabitants of Judea could not close their eyes to it indefinitely. The theocratic programme of separation from the non-Jewish environment was now put to a severe test. Were the leading groups to seize the economic and social possibilities which Hellenistic civilization offered to them, as it did to other members of the Phoenician-Palestinian aristocracy, or were they to continue to persist in the enchanted sleep of a temple state set beyond great events, which at the same time enjoyed the reputation of separatism? There were certainly young and ambitious people who struggled to break through the narrowness of their homeland and to make more room for the new spirit which was gradually making itself felt even in Jerusalem. A concrete example of this can be found in the surprising rise of the Tobiad Joseph at the time of Ptolemy III Euergetes (246–222), in becoming the chief tax-farmer of 'Syria and Phoenicia'. Connections with the growing Diaspora of the Greek-speaking world, especially Egypt, which could not close its eyes to Hellenistic civilization precisely because of its social status, will have lent powerful support to these tendencies. An essential factor here is that in the economic sphere Hellenism brought about no radical break, but intensified developments which had already begun to take shape in Palestine in the Persian period through the mediation of the Phoenicians.

Interest in Hellenistic civilization, however, *remained predominantly limited to the well-to-do aristocracy of Jerusalem.* Intensive economic exploitation and the social unconcernedness of the new masters and their imitators, who were concerned purely with economics, only served to exacerbate the situation of the lower strata of the population. It prepared the ground for apocalyptic speculation and the later revolts, which had increasingly strong social elements, right down to the time of the Bar Kochba rebellion. Even the milieu of the parables of Jesus, with its great landowners, tax farmers, administrators, moneylenders, day-labourers and customs officials, with speculation in grain, slavery for debt and the leasing of land, can only be understood on the basis of economic conditions brought about by Hellenism in Palestine.

Now Hellenistic civilization was by no means an exclusively or even predominantly military, civic and socio-economic phenomenon – these were simply the areas in which its effects first became visible; rather, it was the expression of a force which embraced almost every sphere of life. It was a force of confusing fullness, an expression of the power of the Greek spirit which penetrated and shaped everything, expressive and receptive. Consequently it also had effects on areas which so far have been kept in the background of our investigation, literature, philosophy and religion. To penetrate into these regions, however, the foreigner needed a bridge, and this was provided for him by the common language of the Hellenistic world, which bound it all together, the *koinē*.

II

Hellenism in Palestine as a Cultural Force and its Influence on the Jews

1. The Greek Language in Palestinian Judaism

a) The penetration of the Greek language into Palestine

The bond which held the Hellenistic world together despite the fragmentation which began with the death of Alexander and continued thereafter, was Attic *koinē*.[1] Its sphere of influence went far beyond that of Aramaic, the official language of the Persian kingdom. Greek merchants dealt in it, whether in Bactria on the border of India or in Massilia; laws were promulgated in it and treaties concluded in accordance with a uniform basic scheme;[2] it was the language of both diplomats and men of letters; and anyone who sought social respect or even the reputation of being an educated man had to have an impeccable command of it. The word ἑλληνίζειν primarily meant 'speak Greek correctly', and only secondarily 'adopt a Greek style of life'. Impeccable command of the Greek language was the most important qualification for taking over Greek culture.[3] The final establishment and dissemination of the *koinē* was probably the most valuable and the most permanent fruit of Alexander's expedition. The way in which it dominated public and economic life in Egypt as virtually the only written language is shown by the Zeno correspondence. Among its approximately two thousand items, very few are in Demotic, and there is not one single piece of writing in Aramaic, although Jews, Idumeans, Syrians and Arabs (= Nabateans) are mentioned often enough; we have hardly two or three Aramaic or Hebrew writings from Jews in Egypt between 300 BC and AD 300.[4] In *Palestine*, the triumphal progress of Greek makes an impressive showing in *inscriptions*. It is no coincidence that if we disregard later Nabatean inscriptions in Transjordania and the typically Jewish tomb, ossuary and synagogue inscriptions, which rest upon a certain national self-awareness, from the third century BC we find almost exclusively Greek inscriptions in Palestine. This is true, to mention only the demonstrably early evidence of the third and second century BC, of official texts in honour of Ptolemy IV Philopator in Marisa and Joppa or of the great warning inscription with letters of Antiochus III and Seleucus IV from Hephzibah in Scythopolis as it is of the religious inscriptions in Ptolemais, Scythopolis, Samaria and Marisa or of the tomb inscriptions in Gaza, Marisa and now also in Shechem. Indeed, even graffiti were often written in Greek.[5] To this extent the official language was dominant in the public life of the non-Jewish cities of Palestine. *Outside the sphere of Judaism* the principle could probably very soon be applied that anyone who could read and write also had a command of Greek. Aramaic became the language of the illiterate, who needed no written remembrances. Weak beginnings of a non-Jewish, Aramaic literature only started to develop in the Byzantine-Christian period, when the significance of Greek in comparison with local vernaculars receded into the background. Here the Hellenization of the non-Jewish parts of Palestine seems to have been even stronger than that of Phoenicia, where a whole series of Phoenician inscriptions exists from the Hellenistic period, and where even local coins were minted with two languages,[6] a sign that the national consciousness of the Phoenicians was still alive, despite the Hellenistic varnish.

The situation in *Judea* is illuminated by the letters of the Jew Tobias to Apollonius and the king himself, which were all written in excellent Greek and beautiful handwriting by his Greek secretary in 257 BC.[7] A Jewish soldier son of Ananias appears as 'guarantor' alongside some pure Greeks, as a witness in a purchase arrangement concluded in the '*birta*' of Tobias; he too will have known Greek. Since Tobias was the commander of a cleruchy with Greek troops, it is further probable that he himself spoke Greek; his son Joseph certainly received a thorough education in Greek, as is shown by his success in the court in Alexandria: the important office of general tax farmer for 'Syria and Palestine' would not have been entrusted to an uneducated barbarian.[8] It is said explicitly of the grandchildren of Tobias that their father Joseph sent them 'one after the other to the famous teachers of the time', though Greek education seems to have been really successful only with the youngest of them, Hyrcanus; he went on to be Joseph's representative at the celebration of the birth of the heir to the throne at the court in Alexandria.[9] The grandchildren of Tobias and their sons later formed the nucleus of that party of Hellenists in Jerusalem who wanted to turn the city into a Greek *polis*. The high priest and the financial administrator of the temple will also have had impeccable Greek-speaking and Greek-writing secretaries for their correspondence with Ptolemaic offices and the court. If one goes on to include members of the Ptolemaic garrison, officials and merchants, even the Jerusalem of the third century BC may be assumed to have had a considerable Greek-speaking minority.

Clearchus of Soli records the meeting of Aristotle with a Greek-educated Palestinian Jew from Judea in Asia Minor about 345 BC. Although this report is unhistorical, we may conclude from it that at the time of Clearchus, about the middle of the third century BC, there were Jews from Palestine to whom the description that 'he was a Greek not only in his language but also in his soul' could be applied with some degree of accuracy.[10] The same is true of the

Letter of Aristeas. According to that, the high priest chose for the translation of the Torah into Greek six men from each tribe who were distinguished by their '*paideia*' and 'not only had a mastery of Jewish literature, but had also acquired a thorough knowledge of Greek'.[11] This report of 72 Jews knowing Greek at the time of Philadelphus may be an exaggeration, but we can conclude that at the time of the composition of the letter in the second half of the second century BC a knowledge of Greek could be taken for granted among Palestinian Jews of the aristocracy.[12] Moreover, the books of Maccabees clearly show that not only the members of the Hellenistic party but also many supporters of Judas and his brothers had a command of Greek: this is the only way in which the embassies to Rome and Sparta and the tedious negotiations with the Syrian rulers are conceivable.[13] There was no stopping the penetration of the Greek language even in Jewish Palestine, and the young Jew who wanted to rise a stage above the mass of the simple people had to learn it. This process was strengthened by contacts with the Diaspora in Egypt, Asia Minor and the Aegean, above all after the temple in Jerusalem attracted more and more festival pilgrims from there. The significance of Jerusalem grew with the growth of the western Diaspora, though it continued to remain the centre of world Judaism, now predominantly Greek-speaking.[14] There was no break in this development even as a result of the Maccabean revolt, but it was furthered because after Jewish independence had been won, the Hasmoneans followed a quite deliberate policy of influencing the Diaspora, which was then continued by Herod. It could not fail to affect the Jews in Palestine.[15] From the second century BC onwards we can trace the beginnings of a Graeco-Jewish literature in Palestine (see below, pp. 88–102). Finally, one need only mention the many Greek inscriptions in Jerusalem, which only in part derive from those who had returned from the Diaspora: they do belong, though, for the most part to the later period between Herod and AD 70.[16] Probably the earliest Greek inscription from Jerusalem is a graffito from the magnificent tomb of Jason, decked with drawings of ships. The tomb comes from the time of Alexander Jannaeus, 103–76 BC, and the graffito is composed in the style of the Hellenistic epitaph with the motto 'Enjoy life'.[17]

Greek loanwords give a further indication of the penetration of Greek. It is true that they are extraordinarily rare in Old Testament literature: in addition to the '*drachmae*', already mentioned, we find '*appiryōn* in the Song of Songs, which is perhaps derived from the Greek φορεῖον, 'sedan chair', and the various musical instruments in Dan. 3.[18] A deliberate purism based on religious and nationalistic grounds may be the reason why neither Sirach nor the extra-biblical Qumran texts have any Greek loanwords; conversely, the Greek papyri of Egypt and the *koinē* in general have hardly any 'barbaric' foreign words.[19] On the other hand, even the Essenes, who had a very critical attitude towards the Greek world, could not get by without the Greek language, as is shown by the Greek papyrus fragments found in Qumran, which include fragments of the Septuagint.[20] It was required of the 'overseer of the camp', among other things, that he 'was familiar with all the languages of the families (living in the camp)', and this surely included Greek. A similar demand was made in the Talmud of members of the Sanhedrin, 'so that they were not compelled to use an interpreter'.[21] Unlike literary Hebrew, popular Aramaic or Hebrew constantly adopted new Greek loanwords, as is shown by the language of the Mishnaic and Talmudic literature. While it reflects the situation at a later period, its origins go back well before the Christian era.[22] The collection of the loanwords in the Mishna to be found in Schürer shows the areas in which Hellenistic influence first became visible: military matters, state administration and legislature, trade and commerce, clothing and household utensils, and not least in building.[23] The so-called copper scroll with its utopian list of treasures also contains a series of Greek loanwords.[24] When towards the end of the first century BC, Hillel in practice repealed the regulation of the remission of debts in the sabbath year (Deut. 15.1–11) by the possibility of a special reservation on the part of the creditor, this reservation was given a Greek name introduced into Palestinian legal language: $p^e r \bar{o} z^e b b \bar{o} l = \pi \rho o \sigma \beta o \lambda \dot{\eta}$,[25] a sign that even at that time legal language was shot through with Greek.

b) *The advance of Greek names*

One measure of the advance of the Greek language is the introduction of Greek names. The first traces of this go back to the time before Alexander. Just as prominent Phoenicians, e.g. Strato, king of Sidon, had a Greek form of name,[26] so too the last 'Persian' governor of Samaria, Sanballat, seems to have given his daughter the Greek name Nikaso. She married Manasseh, the son of the Jewish high priest.[27] After the Macedonian conquest, the Phoenicians in particular, being more open to Greek culture than hitherto, took over Greek names. We know Philocles son of Apollodorus (Rešephiatan), the last king of Sidon and admiral of Demetrius Poliorcetes and Ptolemy II Philadelphus.[28] After his death Sidon went over to a democratic constitution, and in PZenMich 3 we hear of an '*archōn*' Theodotus, who sends the *dioikētēs* Apollonius a present. In a bill which speaks among other things of Gaza, incense and myrrh, and is thus connected with the trade in aromatics, a Zenodorus appears whose father still had the good Semitic name Abbaeus ('*abbā*' or '*abba*'y).[29] The *double name* was an intermediate stage in the Graecizing of names: for dealings with Greeks and on journeys a man had a Greek name, while at home and among Semites he had a Semitic name. Graeco-Phoenician bilingual evidence of the third century connects Šamaʻbaʻal with Diopeithes, Benḥodeš with Noumenius, ʻAbdtanit with Artemidorus, ʻAbdšemeš with Heliodorus; an Ashkelonite ʻAbdʻaštart calls himself Aphrodisius, two Tyrian brothers on Malta, ʻAbdʼosir and ʼOsiršamar, are called Dionysius and Sarapion, like their father and grandfather.[30] Here the giving of names indicates the syncretistic *interpretatio graeca* of the native gods.

The contamination of Greek and Semitic divine names is striking in Panabelus, the name of a travelling companion of Zeno in Palestine, or a formation like Patrobala, from the tomb inscriptions of Marisa on the Judaeo-Idumean border: the ending Baal was so obvious that it was not always Hellenized.[31] In the *tomb inscriptions of Marisa* from the end of the third century BC we find a motley mixture of Phoenician, Idumaean and above all Greek names, with a clear trend towards Hellenization: the Phoenician Sesmaius gave his son the name Apollophanes; the latter was then '*archōn*' of the Sidonian *politeuma* in Marisa for thirty-three years, his son had the same name and a granddaughter was called Demetria. However, a sister of Apollophanes had the Idumean name Sabo, and a brother was called Ammo(n)ius in Egyptian-Hellenistic manner. Ammo(n)ius named a son Kosnatanus after the Idumean God Kos (see below, p.261, n.27); he called his sons Babas and Babatas in Jewish-Idumean fashion, and a daughter, once again, Sabo. Alongside the great family of Sesmaius we find the Phoenician Meerbaal, who called his son Demetrius, who in turn had a descendant Ortas, bearing a Macedonian name. The Phoenician Zenodorus had a son Antagoras; Kosbanus, presumably an Idumean, was father of Callicrates, who again named his son Kosbanus after his grandfather. Another Idumean, Zabbaeus, had two sons Apollodorus and Ammonius. In tomb IV, which, according to Peters and Thiersch, was not one of the tombs of the Sidonian colony, what is perhaps a Jewish name, Sarya, appears among predominantly Greek women's names like Irene, Berenice, Demetria, daughter of Philo, and Aristeia.[32] Two other names which are possibly Jewish appear among the inscriptions of the special tomb V published by F. M. Abel; apart from a certain Σαλαμ (ψ) (for Σαλαμψω) and Ναουμα (feminine form of Nahum), it probably contains the names of female slaves who come from the region between eastern Asia Minor and the Caspian sea.[33] On the whole, the tomb inscriptions, composed throughout in Greek, together with the names, point to a very high degree of Hellenization in Marisa for the period from the end of the third century to the conquest of the city about 110 BC by John Hyrcanus, a finding which is also confirmed by the tomb paintings and inscriptions elsewhere. Conditions in the capital of Idumea are certainly to be understood as a parallel phenomenon to the Hellenizing tendencies in Jerusalem at the beginning of the second century BC, as it was a bare twenty-five miles away. It is interesting that the Idumean ancestors of Herod presumably descended from the Hellenized aristocracy of this city.[34] Greek names like 'Melantheus' are also found in the similar, but simpler rock tombs in Samaritan Shechem, which come from the Hellenistic period. Perhaps they are connected with the Sidonian colony in Shechem. A pottery fragment from the same place from the time between 250 and 150 BC, engraved before the firing of the vessel, has a long inscription in which the name Simonide(s) is still legible; perhaps this is the Graecizing of the Hebrew Simeon.[35]

Little can be said about Jewish names in Palestine during the third century
BC, as we have very little Judeo-Palestinian material from this period. However, circumstances in Egypt are very illuminating: whereas the many Jews
mentioned in the Aramaic P. Cowley 81 towards 310 BC have almost exclusively
Hebrew names,[36] fifty to a hundred years later we find predominantly
Greek names among the Jews of the Egyptian Diaspora. In an agreement of
April 260 BC we come across the Jewish soldier Alexander, son of Andronicus;
a trial account from 226 BC reports on the dispute between the Jew Dositheus
and the Jewess Heraclea; a complaint of 210 BC and an agreement of 201 BC
mention nine Jews in all, all of whom have Greek or – in one case – Egyptian
names and patronyms.[37] Only about twenty-five per cent of the Jewish
military settlers mentioned in the papyri have Jewish names; in reality the
percentage is still lower, as Jewish bearers of Greek names can only be
recognized by the addition of 'Ioudaios', and that was by no means always
made. 'The common life in the camps and military settlements, as well as in
mixed military units, brought about a rapid adoption of Greek names and
customs.'[38] Typically Jewish names are rather more frequent in the second
century BC, presumably because the Jewish military settlers at that time
settled more in self-contained groups; perhaps the national sensibility aroused
by the Maccabean revolt also made itself felt in Egypt. A certain tendency
towards double names or altering an original Hebrew name can also be
demonstrated, whether this came about through translation, assonance, or
quite freely, without any visible connection with the old name.[39] Even
pagan theophorous names were not excluded, as in a will of 238/7 BC, which
mentions an Apoll(odorus? . . .) ὃς καὶ Συριστὶ ᾽Ιωναθᾶς [καλεῖται . . .][40]
The theophorous names of Daniel and his companions in Babylonia show
that people were not so sensitive on this point in the early Hellenistic
period.[41] Nevertheless, the overwhelming majority of people in the Egyptian
Diaspora – like the Jews in Palestine – remained true to the faith of their
fathers; this is clear from the fact that in a comparison of all Jewish names, the
theophorous names Dositheus – which was used almost exclusively by Jews –
and Theodotus stand at the head by a long way. This may be taken as a kind
of confession of the one God in pagan surroundings. The most striking
instance of this kind is the Jewish slave Antigone, freed in Delphi in 158/157
BC, with her daughters Theodora and Dorothea.[42] There is certainly an
intrinsic connection between the rapid Hellenizing of the Jews of Egypt
attested by the names and the translation of the Pentateuch into Greek, which
also took place in the same century. The first synagogue inscriptions from the
time of Ptolemy III Euergetes (246–222 BC) are naturally composed in
Greek.[43]

From the moment when the sources for Palestine Judaism become fuller,
with the books of Maccabees, we come across an abundance of Greek names.
It is clear that the tendency to adopt them did not begin with Antiochus IV,

but had been at work even earlier. The first to carry a name which, if not Greek, at least sounded Greek to Jewish ears, was – as far as we can see – Hyrcanus the Tobiad, son of the tax farmer Joseph.[44] Antigonus of Socho, who according to '*Ab.*1, 3 received the Torah 'from Simon the Just', high priest and father of Onias III and Jason, is one of the early figures with a Greek name to appear in Jerusalem about the end of the third century BC. This is all the more striking as he did not come from Jerusalem, but from a small country town some fifteen miles south-west of Jerusalem.[45] The fathers of the ambassadors sent by Jonathan and Simon to Sparta or Rome, Numenius son of Antiochus, Antipater son of Jason and Alexander son of Dorotheus, may similarly have been born before the turn of the century.[46] John, of the priestly family of Haqqōṣ, who negotiated with Antiochus III, presumably in Antioch, after 200 BC over the φιλάνθρωπα βασιλικά for the Jews, called his son Eupolemus. Under Judas, Eupolemus later led the first embassy to Rome, perhaps with Jason, mentioned above, and presumably distinguished himself as a Jewish history writer in the Greek language.[47] According to II Macc.14.19, the parliamentarians who sent Nicanor to Judas for peace negotiations included a Theodotus and a Mattathias; perhaps this too was a person with a double name. Two Maccabean cavalry officers in Transjordania, who probably belonged earlier to the cleruchy of the Tobiads in Transjordania (see below, pp.275f.), bore the names Dositheus and Sosipater.[48] This tendency did not cease even during the Hasmonean period. A certain Lysimachus son of Ptolemy – presumably here, as in the case of Antiochus, who has already been mentioned, the names were at the same time political confessions – translated the book of Esther into Greek in Jerusalem; a priest Dositheus and his son Ptolemy then brought the work to Egypt, probably in the year 78/77 BC.[49] Mention should finally be made of Jeshua-Jason, the leader of the Hellenist party, the brothers Menelaus and Lysimachus, and the later high priest Eliakim-Alcimus; their Greek names were by no means extraordinary, but rather corresponded to a general tendency of nomenclature in the Jewish aristocracy, no matter whether persons were pro-Hellenist or pro-Maccabean. Among the seventy-two Palestinian elders, the Letter of Aristeas lists men with Greek names like Theodosius (three times), Theodotus, Theophilus, Dositheus and Jason (twice). Even if it is a Jewish-Alexandrian fiction, it would hardly have given individual Palestinians Greek names if this had not happened at the time.[50] Even the Hasmoneans again bore Hebrew/Greek double names after the second and third generations, i.e. after John Hyrcanus, his brother-in-law Ptolemy son of Abub, and his sons Jehuda-Aristobulus, Antigonus and Alexander Jannaeus.[51] Finally, it is certainly no coincidence that in the Hellenistic-Roman period up to about AD 200 the name Simeon-Simon is used most frequently in Palestine. First, it matched the strong national consciousness, for the last of the Maccabean brothers had borne it;[52] secondly, however, it was easily assimilable, as it was almost identical with the Greek name Simon.[53] The ambiguity which becomes evident in the popularity of this name is typical of Jewish history throughout this whole period.

2. Greek Education and Culture and Palestinian Judaism

a) *Hellenism as a force in education*

The Hellenistic period was a period of education. Thus H. I. Marrou defined Hellenism, in contrast to the preceding 'civilization of the πόλις' and the later 'civilization of the city of God', i.e. the later Byzantine and medieval Christian empire, as 'a civilization of *paideia*'.[54] Some time before Alexander, Isocrates had already broken through the old prejudices of the Greeks towards the 'barbarians' which had existed above all since the Persian wars and were still defended by Aristotle, in a revolutionary formulation:[55]

> The designation 'Hellene' seems no longer to be a matter of descent but of disposition, and those who share in our education have more right to be called Hellenes than those who have a common descent with us.[56]

Even if Isocrates was also setting out to express the intellectual superiority of Athens here, we can see in his words the conception of a 'universal concept of culture' pertaining to every man,[57] which for him was identical with the Greek *paideia*. A century later, under Stoic influence and in a defence of Alexander, Eratosthenes made the further proposal that men should no longer be classed as Greeks or barbarians, but according to ἀρετή and κακία, 'for in the one the sense of right and community, of education (παιδεία) and eloquence prevails, and in the other the contrary'. Thus the Hellenistic epoch produced a new picture of man, and the key concept in it was *paideia*.[58] Varro and Cicero were not wrong in later translating *paideia* as *humanitas*.[59]

Alexander's victorious expedition gave new possibilities to the idea of 'Greeks by *paideia*'. The Graeco-Macedonian soldiers, officials and merchants planted their customary institutions of education, the Greek school and above all the gymnasium – 'il n'existe . . . pas d'institution plus typiquement grecque'[60] – in the newly-conquered areas of the East. Both institutions developed predominantly on a private and at best on a communal basis.[61] Direct evidence for the Seleucid sphere is relatively limited,[62] but for Ptolemaic Egypt the sources are considerably richer. Here we have the indirect evidence of school papyri for the *elementary school*, and the overwhelming mass of Greek literary papyri from the *chōra*, which point to a widespread intellectual interest among the Greek-educated population, show that this private institution, so difficult to reconstruct from the sources, did not lack success. The best-known school papyrus, a handbook of instruction, comes from the third century BC and is typical of a conservative form of instruction, quite uninfluenced by the Egyptian homeland. The gymnasia, which encountered strong public interest, appear more frequently, partly in applications made to state offices and also in inscriptions. Like the elementary schools, they were to be found not only in the cities but even in larger villages, i.e., everywhere that Greeks settled in self-contained groups. The sponsoring body was as a rule an association, but often they were based on private foundations.[63] School and gymnasium together gave the Greek minority support against the threat of assimilation to the 'barbarian' environment; they were 'the basis on which Greek culture was built up'.[64] Here generation upon generation of the foreign ruling class received its traditional Greek education and life-style, which bound together all Greeks far beyond the boundaries of the world-empires. For political reasons, in Egypt even in Roman times strict precautions were taken to exclude native Egyptians as far as possible from the gymnasium and to accept only the sons of Greek parents, whose fathers had themselves passed through the gymnasium.[65] Nevertheless, above all in the Ptolemaic period, from time to time individual Egyptians succeeded in rising into the preferential class of Hellenes. Non-Greek foreigners were in a better position: prominent Persians and Jews, above all from the ranks of the military settlers, could gain access to the leading upper class by way of Greek education and the gymnasium.[66] The remarkable and probably historically unique fusion of Jewish and Hellenistic culture in Alexandria from the third century BC is only understandable on the grounds of the unhindered access of Egyptian Jews to the treasures of Greek education. Here the gymnasium became an important point of transition.

Instruction in the 'Greek school' was presumably divided into three age groups: school age from about 7 to 14/15, followed by the period of the ephebate which lasted one or two years, which was the real time of training in the gymnasium, dominated above all by physical exercise and also a degree of military training. This was in turn followed by the stage of the 'young men', who continued their instruction in the gymnasium until about the age of twenty.[67] Former pupils continued contacts with their place of education by means of associations. The honorary director of the gymnasium, the gymnasiarch, was one of the most important city dignitaries, as a rule a rich citizen who could contribute to the support of the institution from his own means. At the same time, the gymnasium was also always one of the central places of public life.[68] Instead of examinations and reports in our sense, the constant competitions served as an effective stimulus; these were not just limited to sports, but also included literary skills.[69] Literary instruction, which at least in the earlier period took third place behind physical training and musical education, was concentrated on one language, the Greek mother-tongue, and on one – it might almost be called the canonical – book, the epic work of Homer, especially the *Iliad*; at a higher level of instruction the later classic writers of 'canonical' status were also taken up. For example, the school book from the third century BC, mentioned above, contains among other things an elegy on the consecration of a temple of Homer by Ptolemy IV Philopator, together with a fragment of the *Odyssey* and Euripides' *Phoenician Women*.[70] The very idea of constant competition, the 'agonistic ideal of life', basically goes back to Homer:

$$\alpha i \grave{\epsilon} \nu \ \grave{\alpha} \rho \iota \sigma \tau \epsilon \acute{\nu} \epsilon \iota \nu \ \kappa \alpha \grave{\iota} \ \acute{\nu} \pi \epsilon \acute{\iota} \rho o \chi o \nu \ \acute{\epsilon} \mu \mu \epsilon \nu \alpha \iota \ \acute{\alpha} \lambda \lambda \omega \nu.^{71}$$

Despite all locally conditioned differences, Greek education, which hardly changed from the beginning of the Hellenistic age, maintained down the centuries a 'remarkable unity and steadfastness'.[72] It preserved its conservative traits and educated the young 'Hellenes' in a very uniform way. If its original aim, the training of a responsible citizen of the *polis*, had been suppressed in the Hellenistic monarchies, it still shaped the self-awareness of members of the Greek ruling class: 'Its overall object was to fashion the ideal of Greek gentlemen'.[73] In this way – not least because of its slant towards sport and because its spiritual foundation was rooted in the chivalrous ideals of the Homeric world – it acquired an expressly aristocratic character: and after hesitation at some unusual manifestations, like the competition of naked youths in the palaestra, had been overcome, it could also exercise a stronger attraction over the youths of subject peoples than the educational ideal of the oriental scribe, which was predominantly directed towards religious attitudes and traditional 'wisdom'.[74] 'Whereas Greek education was designed to produce gentlemen amateurs, Eastern education was designed to perpetuate a guild of professional scribes.'[75]

It is commonly stressed that the Greeks could contribute nothing to the peoples of the East in the sphere of religion, but rather that they themselves were to an increasing extent the receivers. This view pays too little attention to the influence of the Greek school. Constant reading of Homer kept alive knowledge of Greek mythology, and favoured the *interpretatio graeca* of the Oriental world of the gods. Moreover, the gymnasium possessed its own guardian deities, Hermes, Heracles and the muses,[76] and the countless festivals and competitions of the Greeks had a thoroughly religious character.[77] Young people at school played an important role in the feasts to honour the gods of the city, and in the Hellenistic monarchies the ruler cult gained overwhelming significance in the gymnasia in particular; it was the culmination of the tendency to revere human heroes and benefactors as gods, which began at an early stage in the gymnasium.[78] Much as freedom of religious conviction was allowed in the Greek *polis*, people could be very intolerant with their own citizens in questions of the official cult. At least *the Jew exposed to Hellenism in the Diaspora* could come up against difficulties if he wanted to undergo education in the gymnasium or acquire citizenship of his native town.[79] In a petition from Ionian cities to Marcus Agrippa between 16 and

13 BC the citizens demanded that Jews should give up their claim to equal rights, for 'if the Jews really belonged to them, they would also reverence their gods': εἰ συγγενεῖς εἰσιν αὐτοῖς ᾿Ιουδαῖοι, σέβεσθαι τοὺς αὐτῶν θεούς.[80] Similarly, Apion asked the Jews who laid claim to citizenship of Alexandria: '*quomodo ergo . . . si sunt cives, eosdem deos quos Alexandrini non colunt ?*'[81] The legendary III Maccabees reports that the Jews who allowed themselves to be initiated into the mysteries of Dionysus were honoured for their action with the citizenship of Alexandria, and that some could not resist this allure. Even if the framework of this book is for the most part unhistorical, the temptation to apostasy for political advantage may point back to a particular historical situation.[82] On the whole, the Jews of the Diaspora remained constant in face of these claims and temptations, but the inscription of the second century BC from Iasus in Ionia, according to which a 'Nicetas son of Jason from Jerusalem' contributed 100 drachmas for a feast of Dionysus, shows that they had to be very generous – above all in the early period, before the promulgation of privileges for the Jews by Caesar and his successors.[83] As far as the education of their sons was concerned, the Jewish upper class in the Diaspora was ready on occasion to compromise with the polytheistic basic tendency of gymnasium instruction, as is shown by the way in which Jewish names keep appearing in the lists of ephebes of Greek cities, which usually end with a formula of dedication to Hermes and Heracles.[84] However, this is not to be taken without qualification as an evasion of Jewish belief; partly, it is also a sign that the Judaism of the Diaspora had won an inner self-assurance over against its polytheistic environment.[85] The Letter of Aristeas, about 140 BC, with its frequent stress on the educational ideal of the καλοκἀγαθία, so loved in the gymnasium, already shows that this had been accepted and acknowledged by the Jewish upper class in Alexandria.[86] Philo, too, took it for granted that well-to-do Jews would be educated at the gymnasium.[87] The account of Josephus suggests that Jews were admitted to gymnasium education in Seleucid Antioch: he says that they laid claim to the official distribution of oil by the gymnasiarch; however, they could have received the equivalent in money.[88] The view of S. Applebaum in his controversy with V. Tcherikover, that gymnasium education 'must have been purchased with the betrayal of Judaism',[89] is, however, probably too sweeping. In Sardes in the second to fourth century AD, the great synagogue appears 'seemingly as an integral part of the city gymnasium', and thus in practice formed a building-complex with it. Prominent Jews proudly called themselves 'Sardianos', i.e. citizen of Sardes, and some of them were city councillors. The place of the synagogue probably goes back to a gift of the city to the Jews in the first century BC (*Antt.* 14, 260f.).[90] When by his famous letter of AD 41 Claudius finally deprived the sons of the Jewish aristocracy of entry to the gymnasium in Alexandria, which they coveted, and hence of the right to Alexandrian (and Roman) citizenship, it was a bitter blow against the leaders of Alexandrian

Judaism and led the way to the rebellion and the annihilation of the Jewish Diaspora in Egypt in AD 115–117.[91]

The normal course of Greek education communicated an 'ésprit de corps' and a marked self-awareness in the face of the barbarian environment, but hardly a comprehensive knowledge of great literature or even philosophy; here pupils were at best informed about certain fashions that were dominant.[92] Whether a person wanted to go beyond the normal course of education – which was itself already something of a selection – and to continue his studies until he had acquired a real ἐγκύκλιος παιδεία[93] was left to his individual financial and intellectual capacity. There will in any case have been very few who devoted themselves to a more thorough study of rhetoric, philosophy or other special disciplines. The best basis for such a more thorough 'university study' was provided in the early Hellenistic period by *Alexandria*. It was of decisive significance for later Jewish and Christian intellectual history that the first Ptolemies succeeded in making this city – which was so easily accessible from Palestine – into the spiritual centre of the Hellenistic world, and in this area too in achieving an absolute superiority over the Seleucid rulers.[94] In this way Alexandria exercised tremendous attraction not only as the greatest mercantile metropolis, but also as the centre of science and the arts.[95] The intellectual élite of the Greek-speaking Jews of Egypt could not escape this influence. They developed their own learned tradition, which lasted over several centuries – probably a unique phenomenon in the history of the Graeco-Roman world. The first stimulus towards this surely came from the translation of the Torah made under Ptolemy II Philadelphus, probably primarily for liturgical usage (see below, p. 102); the first representative we can note was Demetrius, who wrote a chronological work on 'the kings of the Jews' in a learned Alexandrian style, under Ptolemy IV Philopator, 222–204 BC. In this he was following the tracks of Manetho and Berossus, who had treated Egyptian and Babylonian history in a similar way before him; the goal which all had in common was to demonstrate the considerable age of the national tradition.[96] He was followed in the second century by the historical romancers like Artapanus and Cleodemus Malchus, or by poets who dealt with historical themes like the older Philo, the Samaritan Theodotus, Ezekiel the tragedian and – with an apocalyptic slant – the author of the earliest Jewish Sibyllines.[97] With the exception of Demetrius, they all elaborated quite considerably the material of Jewish history which they treated, and did not disdain to use even the colours of Greek mythology or at least the archaic language of classical models. In addition there were more serious historians like Aristeas, Ps.-Hecataeus and Jason of Cyrene, and the first beginnings of philosophical writing in Aristobulus (see below, pp. 110ff.), the Letter of Pseudo-Aristeas and the Wisdom of Solomon, which was composed in the first century BC. As the numerous fragments, mostly spurious, of Orpheus, Homer, Hesiod, Heraclitus, Aeschylus, etc., show, writers had their own views on monotheistic belief in creation or the sacred number seven confirmed by classical authorities.[98] This writing, which is usually designated apologetic or missionary literature,[99] served only exceptionally, however – as with Aristobulus –, to defend Judaism to the outside world; rather, it met the particular needs of a Greek-speaking Jewish readership with an intellectual interest.[100] It was supplemented by an abundance of translations of a more popular kind from Palestinian literature. Even in the mother country, an express need for a wider selection of reading material will have made itself felt as early as the Persian and early Hellenistic period (see below pp. 110ff.). The Greek learned world, on the other hand, did not bother much either with the Septuagint – the creation account was, perhaps, an exception (see below, p. 261, n. 24) – or with Hellenistic Jewish writings. The special exception of the collector of curiosities, Alexander Polyhistor, only proves the rule. Only with Philo and Josephus do we meet an apologetic deliberately aimed at outsiders. It is likely that the influences of the *literati* and learned men inspired by the genius of Ptolemaic Alexandria were not limited to Egypt, but also extended to nearby Judea. There too, the Greek language had made an entry since the middle of the third century BC, and in addition the themes of Jewish-Alexandrian literature frequently reflect their close connection of the author with the mother country and the holy city. So from the beginning of the second century we can find the first signs of a native literature in the Greek language in Alexandria itself (see below, pp. 88ff.). It may be assumed that the connections between Jerusalem and Alexandria were also of a cultural kind, and we cannot exclude the possibility that individual gifted sons of the Jerusalem aristocracy, like young Syrians from the Hellenized Palestinian cities, at some time pursued rhetorical studies in Alexandria or other intellectual centres of the Hellenistic world.[101]

b) Greek education and culture in Palestine and its influence on Judaism

The earliest account of the establishment of a *gymnasium*[102] in Syria and Palestine – leaving aside the mention of a gymnasium in Antioch on the Orontes from the middle of the third century BC[103] – is the narrative in the two books of Maccabees about the foundation of a gymnasium and the ephebate associated with it in Jerusalem, in 175 BC.[104] From a later period, too, we have only quite isolated evidence about gymnasia, for example the report of Josephus that Herod had built gymnasia in Damascus, Ptolemais-Acco and Tripolis at his own expense – presumably developing older institutions,[105] a Graeco-Phoenician bilingual inscription from Aradus, which mentions the gymnasiarchs, Hermes and Heracles,[106] and an inscription which is difficult to decipher and date from Philadelphia, which probably reports the honouring of a gymnasiarch devoted to the cult of Heracles by the council and citizens of the place.[107] Finally, we have the archaeological discovery of the gymnasium of Petra built at the end of the period.[108]

Alongside these and other more or less chance accounts of gymnasia in the Seleucid kingdom, e.g. in Babylon, where Antiochus IV is named as *ktistēs*,[109] there is indirect evidence, above all the inscriptions which report victories of Phoenician competitors in games in the Greek mother country.

As early as 270 BC an inscription from Delos mentions the Sidonian Sillis and the Byblian Timocrates as victors in the boxing.[110] The 'sufet' (δικαστής) Diotimus is celebrated in Sidon, his home city, towards 200 BC, with a skilful Greek verse inscription, as victor in the Pan-Hellenic Nemean chariot race in Argos, to which in principle only 'Hellenes' were admitted. The poem therefore explicitly stresses the mythological affinity between Argives, Thebans and Phoenicians.[111] An undated but probably contemporaneous inscription praises another Diotimus son of Abdubastius, who was victor in the wrestling under the *agōnothesia* of Apollophanes son of Abdyzomunus in the competition in Sidon in honour of Delphian Apollo.[112] Phoenicians are mentioned relatively frequently in the inscriptions of honour of the Pan-Athenian games in Athens: in 191 BC (or 182/181) the Sidonian Poseidonius son of Polemarchus won in the double race; his countryman Lysanias son of Theodorus followed in 184 BC as victor in the chariot race, and at the same time a Hieron from Phoenician Laodicea was victor in the horse racing.[113] Tyrians, too, were successful, in 180 BC a Dioscorides in the boxing,[114] and in one case a citizen from Ptolemais, perhaps Phoenician Acco.[115] Phoenicians even distinguished themselves in musical festivals in Greece, like the Sidonian Strato son of Strato, as *kitharistēs* in the Museia in Thespiae in Boeotia.[116]

Although they were at home in their ancestral language and maintained the traditional religious and political institutions, these Phoenicians competed as 'Hellenes' in their own right; not only did they have a command of the Greek language, but they had also undergone a gymnasium education and observed the rules of the contests as well as the Greeks of the mother country. Thus there will have been gymnasia not only in the Phoenician cities, but also in the larger Palestinian cities, especially in those which derived from Macedonian-Greek military colonies. When Jason-Jeshua,[117] in addition to the office of high priest, also purchased permission to 'establish by his authority a gymnasium and a body of youth for it' in *Jerusalem* and 'to enrol the men of Jerusalem as citizens of Antioch',[118] he had these examples in mind. Indeed his Jewish compatriots in Egypt had long had the possibility, if they belonged to the upper social strata of the populace, of obtaining equal rights to the Greeks by Greek education and training in the gymnasium and, like, e.g., the royal *hypomnēmatographos* Dositheus son of Drimylus, of rising to the highest offices of the state.[119]

Even the Phoenicians on the coast were well advanced here in comparison with 'backward' Jerusalem; they could regard themselves as 'Hellenes' of a special kind whose culture was older than that of Greece and from whom had descended mythical figures of Greek primeval time like Europa, Andromeda – who was associated with the Palestinian port of Joppa[120] – and above all Cadmus, the founder of Thebes.[121] A line of descent was also constructed in the reverse direction: Agenor, the first king of Sidon and father of Cadmus and – according to some mythographers – of Andromeda, was said in turn to have been a son of Phoronis, king of Argos.[122] Zenodotus the Stoic, otherwise unknown, expressed this high reputation of Phoenicia in an epigram on Zeno of Citium, the founder of the Stoa:

If Phoenicia bore you, who will find it fault?
Cadmus, from whom Greece learnt writing, was also a Phoenician.

εἰ δὲ πάτρα Φοίνισσα, τίς ὁ φθόνος; ἦν καὶ ὁ Κάδμος
κεῖνος, ἀφ’οὖ γραπτὰν Ἑλλὰς ἔχει σελίδα.

Diog. Laert. 7,30 = *Anth. Gr.* 7, 117

The legend of the *affinity between Jews and Spartans*, which surely goes back well into pre-Maccabean times, shows that even the Jews were interested in supporting their claims to equal rights with such primeval associations with Greece. Speculations of this kind were helped on by the fact that there was a certain analogy between the Jews and the Spartans with their strict laws, their lawgivers Moses and Lycurgus, and the divine authorization on Sinai or through Delphian Apollo. Just as the Jews, even according to the first Greek account of Hecataeus of Abdera, led a μισόξενον βίον, so according to Herodotus the Lacedaemonians were regarded as ξενοῖσι ἀπρόσμεικτοι, and while Lycurgus, the Spartan 'lawgiver', was designated friend of Zeus (Ζηνὶ φίλος) by the oracle at Delphi, so according to Exod. 33.11, God talked with Moses 'as with a friend'.[123] It is certainly no coincidence that Jason, author of the Hellenistic reform in Jerusalem, ended his life in Sparta. The reform party in particular seems to have had a quite special interest in this affinity, so that the origin of the legend is presumably to be sought in their circles. Possibly it goes back to an elaboration of the note in Gen. 25.1–4 on the sons of Keturah.[124] Here, too, we again have parallels from Phoenicia and Asia Minor: Tyrian writing preserved as an inscription in Delphi claims that the people of Delphi are similarly kin (συγγενεῖς),[125] and a series of cities in south-west Asia Minor claimed – without historical basis – to be Lacedaemonian colonies. All these instances are fundamentally cases of 'entrance tickets into European culture'.[126]

With his apparently revolutionary step, Jason was by no means treading a solitary course; according to the parallel report in I Macc. 1.11ff., an influential group with a considerable following were behind him:

In those days men came forth from Israel who were lawless (παράνομοι) and misled many (ἀνέπεισαν πολλούς), saying: 'Let us go and make a covenant with the Gentiles round about (διαθώμεθα διαθήκην μετὰ τῶν ἐθνῶν τῶν κύκλῳ ἡμῶν), for since we separated from them many evils have come upon us.' This proposal pleased them, and some of the people declared themselves ready to go to the king. He authorized them to introduce the ordinances *(τὰ δικαιώματα)* of the Greeks. So they built a gymnasium in Jerusalem, according to Gentile custom, had the foreskin restored, and abandoned the holy covenant. They joined with the Gentiles and sold themselves to do evil.

This bold decision of Jason and the men behind him was not just an offence against 'Jewish popular custom', as I. Heinemann thought in his critical discussion of the theses of E. Bickermann,[127] but a decisive change of course in the development of the Jewish temple state, an attempt to do away with the result of five hundred years of Israelite and Jewish history. The aim of this step, in which the initiative clearly came from the aristocracy in Jerusalem sympathetic to the Greeks, with the Oniad Jason, son of Simon the Just, at their head, was complete and final bridge-building with Hellenistic culture and the incorporation of the Jewish upper strata into the privileged class of 'Hellenes', i.e. those with Greek education.[128] For this purpose, everything that separated the Jews from their more progressive neighbours and had earned them the charge of hostility to foreigners had to be pushed into the background (see below, p. 261). Despite this decisive reorientation, Jason must have found many enthusiastic supporters in his undertaking. At first we hear nothing about the unrest or the resistance of the pious: presumably most of the citizens of Jerusalem were on his side, a sign that this development had been on the way for some time. The best young men of the Jerusalem nobility *(τοὺς κρατίστους τῶν ἐφήβων)* followed him; the high priest, gymnasiarch and archon of 'the Antiochenes in Jerusalem' were at one,[129] 'under the *petasos*', the broad-brimmed hat which was part of the 'uniform' of the ephebes.[130] The gymnasium was built in the immediate vicinity of the temple 'under the acropolis',[131] and as soon as the gong gave the sign, the priests gladly left temple and sacrifice to take part in what was going on in the palaestra.[132] We do not know whether the Greek guardian deities of the gymnasium, Heracles and Hermes, and the '*ktistēs*' Antiochus IV, were honoured there; the dilemma in which the Jewish Hellenists found themselves at this point is illustrated by the following episode: the musical and gymnastic festival in Tyre, founded by Alexander the Great and celebrated every five years, provided an admirable opportunity to demonstrate the solidarity of the new 'Hellenes' and 'Antiochenes of Jerusalem' with the 'Hellenes' of the Phoenician cities, a solidarity which, in the view of Jason himself, included sacrifice to the guardian deity of the festival, the Tyrian Heracles-Melkart. The fact that the envoys *(θεωροί)*, against their original commission, then gave the money to equip ships, shows that they could not rid themselves of ancestral custom so easily.[133] But this was only a question of interpretation: according to the contemporary Jewish 'historian' Eupolemus – who was probably a Palestinian and a faithful follower of the Maccabees – Solomon had already given a golden pillar to king Suron for the temple of 'Zeus' in Tyre.[134] Another

Jewish 'history writer' of the time, Cleodemus-Malchus, reports that the sons of Abraham by Keturah hastened to aid Heracles in his battle against Antaeus and that Heracles eventually married a granddaughter of Abraham.[135] In this way the sons of Abraham were given a share in the Phoenician colonization of Africa. Hellenistic Jewish learning offered many possibilities of 'interpreting' pagan-Greek cults and their mythology in the right way (see below, pp. 263ff.).

We have no detailed knowledge about the *training given in the gymnasium* in Jerusalem. It will, however, hardly have been different from the form usual in other Palestinian and Phoenician cities. Obviously the ephebes competed naked in sports, an offence about which the book of Jubilees becomes excited even two generations later.[136] The vigorous rejection of oil for anointing the body by the Essenes is presumably to be understood as an aversion to the Greek custom and indirectly as polemic against the similar use of oil in the palaestra.[137] The fact that Jewish ephebes attempted to undo the effects of circumcision by epispasm shows how far the tendency to assimilation went. This may at the same time be an indication that non-Jews took part in the gymnastic games.[138] II Macc. 4.10 states that Jason conformed the young ephebes completely to the Greek style of life by means of gymnasium education: ἐπὶ τὸν Ἑλληνικὸν χαρακτῆρα τοὺς ὁμοφύλους μετέστησεν; thus the instruction will have embraced not only sports, but also music and literature, like the reading of Homer.[139] Tcherikover's view 'that Jason's reform did not affect traditional religious life' is certainly too optimistic. The programme of the reformers, which Tcherikover himself describes as 'the end of self-differentiation from the Gentiles, which had been the tradition of generations since Ezra's time',[140] also had very serious consequences for Jewish religion. In the ancient world, and still more in Judaism, religion was indissolubly bound up with the cultural and political side of life.

The new institutions, the gymnasium, the ephebate and the establishment of 'Antiochenes in Jerusalem', also had a by no means insubstantial political background: the aim was to *transform* the Jewish *ethnos*, or the temple state of Jerusalem, into a Greek *polis*, with a limited, Greek-educated citizenry. The broad mass of the people were left on one side and were demoted to the status of *perioikoi*,[141] a development which was not such a heavy blow as it might seem, as the people had very little political influence, because of the aristocratic constitution of the Jewish *ethnos* (see above, pp. 25ff.). Nevertheless, a series of popular assemblies are recorded from pre-Maccabean and post-Maccabean times.[142] In the long run the new political order in Jerusalem seemed a convenient way of breaking the influence of the conservative opponents of all innovations, who were certainly still numerous. The social gulf which already existed was also extended and deepened by the Greek education of the upper class, which now became obligatory.[143] So with the unity of state and religious order which was particularly marked in the Jewish theocracy, the revolutionary innovations of Jason and his followers inevitably shook the Jewish temple state to its very foundations.[144]

According to II Macc. 4.13, these events marked 'an extreme of Hellenization' *(ἀκμή τις 'Ελληνισμοῦ)* in Jerusalem. They were only conceivable on the basis of a lengthy period of preparation, in which Hellenistic influences in Jerusalem had long been at work, though we do not know much about them.[145] One indication is given by Ben Sira with his polemic against apostasy from the law, religious laxity, the arrogance of the rich and religious scepticism (see below, pp. 138–53). The predilection for Greek names in the Jewish upper class of Jerusalem from the end of the third century BC also points in this direction. A man like Jason could only introduce his reform in Jerusalem and lead ephebes as 'gymnasiarch' because he himself had also undergone a certain degree of Greek education. The same is true of his contemporaries, the three brothers Simon, Menelaus and Lysimachus of the priestly family of Bilga (see below, pp. 279f.), who without hesitation supported the rapid Hellenization of the city. The name Menelaus in particular could on the one hand point to the 'affinity' with the Spartans and at the same time indicate a certain knowledge of Homer.[146]

> That *Homer* was recognized as the canonical book of Greek education in Jewish Palestinian circles even later is shown by the criticism made by the Sadduccees, reported in Jad. 4.6 and coming from the first century AD: 'We object against you Pharisees that you say that the holy scriptures make the hands unclean whereas the books of Homer (ספרי המירם) do not make the hands unclean.' Here the term 'books of Homer' is probably already a stereotyped description of Greek literature in general, and we may see here a sign that it had found a way into the everyday language of Palestinian Jews a long time before. Perhaps it goes back to the era of acute Hellenization after 175 BC.[147] Even in the later Rabbinic period Homer was not unknown to the Jews of Palestine and was even read again in more exalted circles close to Graeco-Roman civilization.[148] At about the same time as Jason's attempted reform, the Jewish 'peripatetic' Aristobulus quoted a series of lines from Homer, wholly or partially forged, in his dissertation to Ptolemy VI Philometor, to stress the significance of the seventh day, and in so doing attempted to press the highest authority of Greek education into the service of Jewish apologetic aims.[149] A few decades later, towards 140 BC, presumably under the influence of the anti-Hellenistic wave swollen by the victorious Maccabean revolt, the Jewish Sibyl condemned Homer as a *ψευδογράφος* by interpolating an earlier Greek text, a verdict in which she was later followed by Josephus, with a reference to Plato.[150] Thus the problem of Homer could be considered by Jews in very different ways; the early Christian fathers then took this many-sided approach further.[151]

The penetration of Greek education into Jewish circles in Palestine began – in analogy with the expansion of the Greek language – as early as the third century BC: there was already a Greek secretary in the family of the Tobiads in

257 BC (see above, p. 59), and later Greek tutors were probably at work. The situation may have been the same in the house of the high priest; the pioneer of Hellenization was indeed the second son of Simon the Just, who is praised so strikingly by the conservative Ben Sira (Sir. 50.1–21), and who in the *Pirqe 'Aboth* is the first teacher mentioned by name at the head of the chain of tradition after the prophets and the men of the 'great synagogue' (see below, pp. 161f.). In these leading circles, there need not have been conflict between a conscious preservation of the national tradition of the Jewish people and an affirmative attitude towards Greek education. There were also cross-connections with Judaism in Alexandria, which was certainly already strongly Hellenized: for example, the brother of the Tobiad Joseph sought to marry his daughter to a prominent Jew in Alexandria.[152] All these points suggest that even from the Ptolemean period the sons of the Jewish aristocracy in Jerusalem had the possibility of learning Greek language and customs; in other words, a long time before the establishment of the gymnasium and the ephebate there was something like a Greek elementary school – of course on a private basis.

Even after the Maccabean revolt, the Greek school does not seem to have vanished completely from Jerusalem. About the middle of the second century BC, the Palestinian Eupolemus – presumably the leader of a Jewish embassy to Rome – wrote a history of the Jewish kings in Greek (see below, pp. 92ff.). A Rabbinic legend reports the civil war between Hyrcanus II and Aristobulus II in Judea in 65 BC a short time before the invasion of Scaurus:

> When the Hasmoneans were waging war against each other, Hyrcanus was outside and Aristobulus inside (Jerusalem). Every day the besieged put denarii in a basket and took it up for the Tamid sacrifice. There was an old man who had insight into Greek wisdom (שהיה מכיר בחכמה יוונית). He spoke to them in Greek wisdom (לעז להם בח″ יוונית). As long as (the besieged) concern themselves with the worship of God, they will not fall into your hands. On the following day (the besieged) again took up denarii in a basket, and instead they found a pig . . . At that hour it was said, Cursed be the man who rears a pig and cursed be those who instruct their sons in Greek wisdom.[153]

As the legend appears in a slightly different form in Josephus, it may have a historical nucleus. The attached curse on learning 'Greek wisdom' may come from a later time; the association between 'Greek wisdom', the cessation of sacrifice and the desecration of the temple points back to the events under Antiochus IV and is thus presumably an interpretation of old tradition. The passage also contains the reminiscence that under the later Hasmoneans the leading circles in Jerusalem again came more strongly under the influence of Hellenistic culture: the uncle of the two disputing brothers, Aristobulus I, bore the surname Φιλέλλην, their father Alexander Jannaeus adopted the title of king, had coins minted with additional Greek legends and used mercenaries from Asia Minor.[154] All this shows that Hellenistic education and style of life once again gained ground in Jerusalem even before Herod. Herod himself seems to have been to the Greek elementary school in Jerusalem, in which the sons of the Jewish aristocracy were probably instructed. At an advanced age he then pursued philosophical, rhetorical and historical studies under the direction of Nicolaus of Damascus; he also had his sons brought up completely in the Greek style. Josephus calls his great-grandson Agrippa II and his kinsmen ἀνδρῶν τῆς Ἑλληνικῆς παιδείας ἐπὶ πλεῖστον ἡκόντων (*Vita* 359).[155] We should also presuppose Greek instruction later in the circles of the Jewish aristocracy, for example in the influential family of Simon son of Boethus, who was appointed high priest by Herod and who came from Alexandria,[156] or even in the young Josephus; otherwise he would hardly have been entrusted with the difficult embassy to Rome while he was still a young man.[157] Even after the catastrophes of AD 70 and 135 the positive attitude towards Greek education continued in the family of Jewish patriarchs descended from Hillel. Even towards the end of the fourth century AD the sons of the patriarch are said to have studied with the rhetorician Libanius in Antioch.[158]

Behind these very different reports of the emergence of Greek education in Jewish Palestine, extending over a period of six hundred years, there is one basic necessity. If the circles ruling there at the time wanted to gain greater influence over the Greek-speaking Diaspora and the changing foreign governments, they not only had to master the Greek language (see above, pp. 58ff.), but also to become familiar with certain basic forms of Greek rhetorical education. But this was true only for a certain upper stratum. For by and large the events between 175 and 167 BC which began with the introduction of gymnasium education and ended with the 'abomination of desolation' marked a unique and deep turning-point in the history of Palestinian Judaism during the Graeco-Roman period. Only in that brief space of about eleven years under the rule of Antiochus IV was Judaism in the acute danger of submitting to Hellenistic culture as the result of the assimilation furthered by a powerful aristocratic minority. This deep crisis, which led to the attempt – which was undertaken primarily by Jewish forces themselves – decisively altered the religious and spiritual face of Palestinian Judaism. The ground was laid for that polemical and legalistic accentuation of Jewish piety which characterizes it in the New Testament period. And even where the Greek language was, in fact, largely used and with it forms of rhetoric (see below, pp. 95ff., 102), this often only happened in order to stress the absolute superiority of the Jewish tradition and to show the impossibility of Greek polytheism and the lax morality of the non-Jews with the means of the Hellenistic criticism of religion. Thus 'Greek education' was put to serve the Jewish cause. The fathers of the early church took over a large part of their polemic and apologetic arsenal from Hellenistic Judaism (see below, pp. 169f., 266).

However, the richest fruit of what was at first such a threatening encounter with 'Greek education' began to grow as Judaism formed its own 'system of education' which in practice embraced the totality of the people and was decisively to shape its spiritual development.

Excursus 1: The development of the Jewish school

From pre-exilic times, there were certainly scribal schools in the temple and probably elsewhere in the country[159] which served primarily to instruct suitable priests and Levites, who would in turn instruct the people in the law on the great feast days and who had to make legal judgments also on the basis of the law and the legal tradition.[160] In this way the status of the γραμματεῖς τοῦ ἱεροῦ, witnessed for the first time in the edict of Antiochus III, developed (*Antt.*12, 142, cf.11, 128). It should be noted here that particularly in the Hellenistic period the temple had become the stronghold of the old national language and tradition in both Babylonia and Egypt.[161] This may also have been true to some extent of Jerusalem, though we can also see the opposite tendency, that the rich priestly nobility was particularly open to foreign cultural influences. As far as they can be named, those who supported the reform in Jerusalem were almost exclusively priests (see below, pp. 279ff.).

Thus at the beginning of the Hellenistic period the 'scribal schools' had two completely opposite possibilities of development; on the one side they could accept the new cultural and intellectual influences and the assimilation to Hellenism which those produced; on the other, they could be conservative and preserve the old tradition. The majority of them surely took the second course, but this did not exclude the adoption of new forms and conceptions. On the contrary, they were the first to provide the possibility of offering effective opposition to the danger of excessive foreign influence. In this sense the term 'sōpēr', like 'ḥākām', is not the name of a party but a professional or educational designation. There will have been sōpᵉrim and ḥᵃkāmîm in the camp friendly to Greece, just as there will have been with the rigoristic ḥᵃsîdîm; the same is true later, down to AD 70, of the Sadducees and Pharisees. Only from that time on were 'scribes' and 'learned men' necessarily also Pharisees. Nevertheless, we cannot overlook the fact that the 'scribal' element had decisive significance in the formation of the anti-Hellenist opposition and later Pharisaism.

Aristocratic laymen, too, were probably admitted for education at this scribal school – the author of Koheleth could be taken as an example of this –, but at first we hardly hear anything of them. In II Chron.34.13 the 'scribal office' appears as a privilege of the Levites, and even for Ben Sira, Aaron and his descendants were 'masters of law and right' (Sir.45.17). The Jewish wisdom tradition was probably native to such priestly-levitical circles; they may therefore also have been responsible for the 'Israelitizing and Yahweh-izing' of what was at first a predominantly secular and eudaimonistic, common oriental wisdom tradition.[162] The great men of the Israelite past like Solomon and David were also later characterized as 'wise men' and 'scribes'.[163] The great period of these *sōp͏ᵉrîm* lay in the two hundred years between the only two bearers of the title known to us by name, Ezra about 398 and Ben Sira about 180 BC; this is a period of considerable obscurity. Whereas Koheleth, about the middle of the third century (see below, p. 129), still hid behind a pseudonym, even though it was only partially observed, Ben Sira was the first to venture to emerge clearly as a personality (50.27). Here is the beginning of a new development, for the stressing of the personality of the individual teacher derived from Greek custom and was probably a sign that the individualism of the Hellenistic period was also gaining significance among the Jewish people.[164] From now on, more such teacher personalities were to emerge under their own names. Moreover, in his writing there appear for the first time the exact phrases 'Jewish house of learning' (בית המדרש) and the 'seat' (ישיבה) of the teacher; we can hardly go wrong in supposing that the two phenomena are also connected with the development of the institute of the synagogue in Palestine. We have the first report from a synagogue in the Diaspora at a rather later period.[165] Finally, his portrait of the *sōp͏ēr* demonstrates how the position of the teacher is breaking away from its association with the temple, a connection which is still strongly stressed in the work of the Chronicler. Koheleth no longer had any real connection with the cult (see below, pp. 120ff.), but he was an outspoken outsider; in Ben Sira, on the other hand, the *sōp͏ēr* seems to have relatively independent significance, even if in 45.17 he still depicts Aaron as the lawgiver pure and simple.[166] For him 'instruction' is an important key term (*mūsār*, see p. 132). With this ideal of instruction, grounded in old oriental wisdom but adapted to the new time, he is in immediate controversy with the influences of Hellenism in Jerusalem which are breaking up traditional custom. It was probably this intellectual struggle which brought the office of the *sōp͏ēr* more and more out of the exclusiveness of the privileged scribe, associated with the temple, and made it accessible to wider circles of the laity. Priests and Levites, even those who were at least partly infected with Hellenistic ideas, were no longer up to the new tasks on their own. The motto attributed to the 'men of the great synagogue', 'Put up many schools', points to this development; it is at the same time the basis for one of the chief aims of later Pharisaism, the intensive *instruction of the whole people in the law*. Even if the 'great assembly' is a very questionable entity in the form in which it has been handed down to us, its leading ideal may be connected with efforts to intensify the national traditions of Israel in the time of Simon the Just: 'Like their leader the High Priest, the members of the Great Assembly realized that Hellenism as a cultural movement could be offset only by a strong educational effort among the masses.'[167] The new programme of education, which was later developed by the Pharisees and was probably handed down above all by the pre-Maccabean Hasidim (see below, pp. 175ff.), was essentially different from the exclusive, status-conscious attitude of the earlier scribal schools. Even Ben Sira, as a scribe conscious of tradition, wanted to exclude peasants and craftsmen from the study of wisdom,[168] but on the other hand he stressed that 'the true wise men are wise for their people'. Here we clearly have a certain contradiction, which we also meet elsewhere. The aristocratic priestly tradition did not break off with the rise of the new 'plebeian' form of school; Josephus still knows about the special teaching reserved for the priests. Among the Essenes, too, the exposition of the Torah was above all a matter for the priests, especially the Zadokites.[169] However, the new attitude gained the upper hand; it is clear in the – presumably Hasidic – wisdom psalm 11 QPsᵃ 154:

> For to proclaim the glory of Yahweh is wisdom given . . . כי להודעי
> כבוד יהוה נתנה חכמה, to proclaim to the foolish (לפותאים) his power, to
> declare to those who are lacking in understanding (לחסרי לבב) his greatness,
> to those who are far from its (wisdom's) gates, who are driven from its
> entrances.

The social and political situation from the time before the Maccabean revolt is probably indicated in these verses, partially expanded in the Syriac translation:

> Praise Yahweh, who delivers the humble (גואל עני) from the hand of
> strangers and the innocent from the hand of the godless.[170]

Anyone who belonged to the people of God – even the proselyte – was now invited to study wisdom, i.e. the law (see below, pp. 16off.); and provided that he had the application and the aptitude, he had the possibility of being a great teacher of the law. This attitude 'was foreign to early Israel and the ancient Orient in general, but was part and parcel of the liberal Hellenistic ideal'.[171] The motto of Jose b. Jo'ezer, a contemporary of Sirach, who according to Rabbinic tradition was not only a priest and martyr, but also the uncle of the later high priest Eliakim-Alcimus, shows a similar 'democratic' tendency: 'Let your house be a meeting place for the wise, cover yourself with the dust of their feet and drink their word thirstily.' Immediately before the account of the execution of the sixty Hasidim by Alcimus – who probably included Jose b. Jo'ezer – I Macc. 7.12 speaks of the conference of a συναγωγὴ γραμματέων with Alcimus and the Seleucid general Bacchides, which examined the legitimacy of the Aaronite descent of the new high priest. The scribal 'wise' men appear here for the first time as an independent group in Judea; they probably formed the élite of the Hasidim (see below, pp. 176ff.), who were concerned not with a continuation of the struggle for freedom, but with peace, which was the essential presupposition for a settled adoption of the interpretation of the law, the education of the people and a life in accordance with the law. A generation later we hear of Joshua b. Peraḥya: 'Take a teacher (*rab*) and make yourself a companion (*ḥābēr*).'[172] These pre-Pharisaic, Hasidic 'wise men' were probably also responsible for the introduction of eschatological, anthropologically dualist and cosmological conceptions of Hellenistic and oriental origin, alien to conservative Judaism, which considerably transformed the picture of Jewish piety.[173]

The chain of teachers in *Pirqe 'Aboth*, which emerges from anonymity with Simon the Just, the high priest before 200 BC, and is continued after Antigonus in five pairs down to Hillel and Shammai (end of the first century BC), is certainly a later construction, but it shows that there was more interest than there had been in the personality of the individual teacher, just as elsewhere traditions about them were preserved in anecdotes. The form of this chain of authoritative tradents, which is traced back through the past as far as Moses for the purpose of legitimation, has, as E. Bickermann stressed, its nearest parallel in the chains of tradition of the heads of Greek philosophical schools and Roman law schools. There, too, was a tendency to extend these chains backwards to an authoritative origin.[174] Rengstorf points out that the way in which earlier authorities, and particularly a man's own teacher or the head of his school, are quoted in the Rabbinate runs parallel to the 'form usual in the Stoa' (*TDNT* 4,441). Particularly famous teachers like Shemaiah and Abtalion are said to have demanded teaching fees about the middle of the first century BC, like the Greek teachers;[175] later, of course, as in the case of Socrates, teaching was required to be given without payment: '. . . and if you accept payment for the words of the Torah, you will be found to be one who destroys the whole world.'[176] In this perspective, the comparison between the Jewish sects and the Greek philosophical schools in Josephus is not completely unjustified.[177] Even the master-pupil relationship in the Rabbinate, bound up with the principle of tradition, has its model less in the Old Testament, where it was not known in this strict form, than in Greece. The διδάσκαλος corresponded to the *rab* and the *talmīd* to the μαθητής.[178] The dialectical form of instruction which could almost be termed 'Socratic', with its sequence of question and answer, *quaestiones* and *solutiones*, may have been influenced by the model of the Greek rhetorical schools.[179] The same is true of the exegetical methods developed by the rabbis after Shemaiah and Abtalion and their pupil Hillel; this applies both to halachic exegesis which, on the basis of the seven *middōt* of Hillel in the controversy with the Sadducees, anchored the prescriptive right of the oral Torah in the Torah, and to haggadic exegesis, which, like the Homer exegesis of the Alexandrian grammatists, was meant to abolish and explain contradictions and stumbling blocks in the text.[180]

One significant consequence of the idea, which began with the Hasidic and later Pharisaic scribes and wisdom teachers, of educating the whole people in the Torah was the gradual introduction of *elementary schools* (*bēt sēper*). Simeon b. Seṭaḥ already ordained 'that the young boys should go to school'.[181] This tradition, which goes back to the end of the second century BC, is supplemented by a tradition in the name of Rab, according to which the school system in Jewish Palestine had been introduced by stages. First children's teachers had been appointed in Jerusalem, and then R. Joshua b. Gamla had had teachers installed in all the provinces and cities. The usual identification of this teacher with the high priest Jesus son of Gamaliel *c.* AD 63–65 was already doubted on good grounds by Bacher and S. Krauss; instead, they conjectured that Joshua ben Peraḥya, already mentioned above, was responsible for it in the time of Hyrcanus I, about 130 BC. Simeon b. Seṭaḥ would then have put his ordinance into force once again.[182] Without a considerable number of Jewish elementary schools, the rise of the Rabbinate, the extension of the popular Pharisaic movement and even the establishment of the institution of the synagogue, which presupposes a basic stock of people knowledgeable in the law in particular places, would be inconceivable: 'The beginnings of a popular school had to arise as a preliminary to the liturgy of reading and preaching.'[183] In the addition to the Essene community rule which probably comes from the first century BC, instruction 'from youth onwards in the book of contemplation' (ספר ההגו) is required for the whole community of the people of Israel ('*ēdā*); after this, instruction in 'the laws of the covenant' (בחוקי הברית) is called for, according to age. Young adults are to be instructed in the commandments for ten years. The book of Jubilees also stresses the great value of education, transferring it to the past: 'Jacob learnt the scripture, but Esau did not.'[184] The Testament of Levi, which probably derives from the same circles, admonishes parents: 'Also teach your children letters *(γράμματα)*, so that they have understanding in their whole life by reading the law of God incessantly' (13.2, cf. Ps. Philo 22.5f.; Philo, *Leg. C.* 115). Even the mild Hillel could stress the demand for learning in a harshly formulated Aramaic rhyme: 'Anyone who does not learn deserves death' (*'Ab.* 1,13). Josephus took it for granted that Jewish children were instructed in the law, and derived this from Moses.[185] A Rabbinic account, albeit late and certainly exaggerated, can report:

> There were 480 synagogues in Jerusalem, and each possessed a school house and a teaching house; a school house for biblical instruction and a teaching house for instruction in the Mishnah, and Vespasian took steps against all of them.[186]

The Theodotus inscription also points to the connection between the synagogue and instruction in the law *(εἰς διδαχὴν ἐντολῶν)*.[187] According to the tradition of Rab, the school age was set at 6–7 years of age as in the Greek elementary schools; non-Jews and even Samaritans were prohibited as teachers on principle. Instead of Homer, the Hebrew Bible, and especially the Pentateuch, held pride of place in instruction. That instruction traditionally began with the book of Leviticus is perhaps an indication that the Jewish school derived from the scribal school of the temple.[188] The fact that the

Jewish school gave the people unique support as a bulwark against alien rule and alien civilization is attested by a Rabbinic anecdote of the Cynic philosopher Oenomaus of Gadara,[189] about the *goyim* who lamented that they could not cope with the Israelites:

> Go and observe their synagogues and schools; as long as you find children there who twitter with their voice – i.e. who recite the Torah aloud – you cannot succeed, for their (heavenly) Father has promised them.

3. Greek Literature and Philosophy in Palestine

a) The intellectual influence of Hellenism in non-Jewish Palestine and Phoenicia

By means of Greek education, Hellenism also gained ground in Palestine as an intellectual force. Tcherikover's judgment that 'of the cultural activity of the Greek cities of Palestine in the Hellenistic period we hear absolutely nothing'[190] is incorrect in this bald form. Of course one cannot make comparisons with Alexandria, Rhodes or Pergamon, but in a narrower framework we can see a vigorous intellectual life in a series of places, especially if we include the Phoenician cities, which exercised a considerable influence on the Palestinian hinterland in the period with which we are concerned. However, in contrast to Egypt, where the rich material of the literary papyri is at our disposal, the accounts are fortuitous and scattered, though they speak for themselves. Thus in Gaza and Sidon we find two lengthy Greek verse inscriptions of unexceptionable form from the period around 200 BC, the epitaph of two Ptolemaic officers and their families and the victory inscription of Diotimus.[191] Still more astonishing is a graffito from tomb I of Marisa with an erotic poem, a 'Locrian song' in genre, in which a *hetaira* exults over her lover to whom she has shown the door, keeping his coat – according to Canaanite custom – as a pledge.[192] A further example of this popular poetry in the Greek language from Hellenistic, pre-Christian times is provided by a spell against fever on a papyrus of the first century BC which is ascribed to a 'Syrian woman' from *Gadara* and is composed in faultless hexameters: . . . Σύρας Γαδαρρήνης [ἐπαοιδὴ] πρὸς πᾶν κατάκαυμ[α. A counterpart in prose is offered by the forty-nine cursing tablets composed predominantly in Greek from Marisa, though from a literary point of view they are at a very low level.[193] *Gadara* seems to have acquired literary significance at a very early stage. The epitaph of Apion of Gadara which was found near Hippo on the east bank of Lake Gennesaret calls the dead man's home town χρηστομούσια,[194] an honorific title which Gadara really deserved. Despite its out-of-the-way situation east of the Jordan (see above, p.8), it produced a whole series of significant poets and philosophers. Strabo confuses Gadara with Gazara (Gezer), which became Jewish in the Maccabean period, but he mentions four famous writers coming from the city: 'Philodemus the Epicurean, Meleager, Menippus the satirist (σπουδογέλοιος) and Theodorus the rhetor from our days', who all belong to the pre-Christian period.[195] *Menippus* belongs to the last decades of the fourth century BC; presumably in the turmoil of the wars of the Diadochi he was sold as a slave to Sinope in Pontus of Asia Minor.[196] We may conclude from this that he was not a new Greek settler but a Syrian; he is an example of the way in which Semites could assimilate to Greek ways even at that time. Later freed and having a moderate sum of money, he purchased for himself the citizenship of Thebes. According to Diogenes Laertius, who significantly calls him a 'Phoenician', he was the most famous pupil of the cynic Metrocles.[197] In that case his real period of activity falls into the first half of the third century BC. Whereas Bion of Borysthenes developed the cynic 'diatribe' at about the same time, Menippus created his philosophical polemic form of satire. Both diatribe and satire exercised a strong influence on later Hellenistic and Roman literature, and even Jewish and Christian preaching were not uninfluenced by them.[198] Among other things, Menippus' satirical work contained a journey into the underworld, 'letters of the gods', 'testaments' and very probably also a journey to heaven.[199] Schmid and Stählin point out that similar literary genres and themes also appear in Jewish, apocalyptic literature, though in quite a different context.[200] Another peculiarity is the mixture of prose and verse, in which F. Dornseiff and M. Hadas see a typically Semitic form of style.[201] We also find this form, alien to the Greek sense of style, in contemporary Jewish literature, above all – significantly – in apocalyptic, say in Daniel (chs. 2;7), and also in the War Scroll, where hymns and prose passages alternate. Hardly any of the work of Menippus is directly extant, but the Syrian Lucian of Samosata has an affinity to him and deliberately took up his work; above all, he used his conversations of dead men and gods and his journeys to Hades and heaven as a model.[202] We might ask whether the caustic wit so typical of the two does not make an appearance again in Rabbinic anecdotes.

Meleager of Gadara,[203] who, two hundred years later, in his old age, still referred to the example of his countryman, shows that this great son of the city was still remembered in Gadara, although he ended his life in Greece and probably hardly saw his homeland again. Meleager was born about 140 BC and received his higher education in Tyre, where the 'Phoenician school', so significant for the development of Greek lyric poetry, was under the direction of *Antipater* of Sidon (about 170–100 BC).[204] He was the real creator of the Greek anthology, to which he himself contributed 132 epigrams and Antipater 65; at the same time he was a master of Hellenistic love poetry, which had perfect control of every degree of feeling. At the same time, however, he mixed parody in with it, for 'they (the Syrians) prized spirit and wit above feeling, and it is surely no coincidence that, as with Heine, we find the destruction of illusion prefigured among them.'[205] From Tyre, he later went to Cos, but he never denied his Palestinian homeland:

Island Tyre was my nurse, and Gadara, which is Attic, but lies in Syria, gave birth to me. From Eucrates I sprang, Meleager, who first by the help of the Muses ran abreast of the Graces of Menippus. If I am a Syrian, what wonder? Stranger, we dwell in one country, the world; one Chaos gave birth to all mortals.[206]

Νᾶσος ἐμὰ θρέπτειρα Τύρος· πάτρα δέ με τεκνοῖ
'Ατθὶς ἐν 'Ασσυρίοις ναιομένα Γαδάροις·
'Ευκράτεω δ'ἔβλαστον ὁ σὺν Μούσαις Μελέαγρος
πρῶτα Μενιππείοις συντροχάσας Χάρισιν.
εἰ δὲ Σύρος, τί τὸ θαῦμα; μίαν, ξένε, πατρίδα κόσμον
ναίομεν, ἕν θνατοὺς πάντας ἔτικτε Χάος.

Meleager's reference, while still in Cos, to the intellectual heritage of Menippus and his homeland, subjugated by the Jews under Alexander Jannaeus towards 100 BC,[207] and the fact that he even calls it the 'Assyrian Attica', shows his Syrian national pride and at the same time indicates that the Palestinian country town east of the Jordan had developed a vigorous intellectual life since the time of the Ptolemies, though it probably exercised little influence on the surrounding neighbourhood.[208] He also stresses 'holy' Tyre several times.[209] Alongside this, however, there also emerges the Cynic-Stoic feeling of the citizen of the world:[210] 'Stranger, we dwell in one country, the world.' Love of the homeland and cosmopolitan breadth are also connected in another epitaph:

Heavenborn Tyre and Gadara's holy soil reared him to manhood, and beloved Cos of the Meropes tended his old age. If you are a Syrian, 'Salam!' If you are a Phoenician, 'Naidius!' If you are a Greek, 'Chaire!', and say the same yourself.[211]

ὃν θεόπαις ἤνδρωσε Τύρος Γαδάρων θ'ἱερὰ χθών·
Κῶς δ'ἐρατὴ Μερόπων πρέσβυν ἐγηροτρόφει.
ἀλλ 'εἰ μὲν Σύρος ἐσσί, 'Σαλάμ', εἰ δ'οὖν σύ γε Φοῖνιξ,
'Αὐδονίς', εἰ δ' "Ελλην, 'Χαῖρε', τὸ δ'αὐτὸ φράσον.

His pride in his Syrian homeland also emerges in his nationalist solution to the old dispute over Homer's native land:

Meleager of Gadara claimed in his work 'The Graces' that Homer was a Syrian by origin, as according to the custom of his homeland he has the Achaeans eating no fish, although the Hellespont overflows with them.[212]

Antipater of Sidon, who was probably his teacher, resolves the question in an epigram in a universal sense:

Different men call different places your cradle. But if I may utter openly the wise prophecies of Phoebus, great heaven is your country, and your mother was no mortal woman, but Calliope.[213]

Here we have at the same time an indication of the significance of Homer even in Phoenicia and Palestine.

If Antipater of Sidon was close to Stoicism – among other things he composed an epitaph in honour of Zeno of Citium[214] – and Meleager was close to the Cynics, the third great Gadarene *Philodemus* (*c.* 100–40/35 BC) was an Epicurean. He too contributed a considerable number of delicate epigrams to the anthology. However, the chief work of this man with his all-round education was in the sphere of philosophy. Later he worked in Rome, and, like so many other educated men from Syria, became a teacher of the young Roman aristocracy. Part of his philosophical work has been preserved to us through the papyrus finds at Herculaneum.[215] He was a pupil of the Epicurean philosopher Zeno of Sidon, born about 160 BC and feared for his acuteness.[216] According to his tombstone, the Sidonian Philocrates son of Philocrates, coming from about the same time, was 'devoted from his earliest youth upwards to the easily understandable teaching of Epicurus'. He ended his life as a trainer for gymnastic contests in Greece.[217] Marginal mention should be made of the Epicurean Philonides, coming from Syrian Laodicea on the Sea, who instructed the young Demetrius I, son of Seleucus IV, and according to his own testimony also converted Antiochus IV Epiphanes to Epicurean philosophy. He founded a school of philosophy in Antioch, but later returned to his home town.[218] According to Strabo, *Sidon* had an old philosophico-mathematical and astronomical school tradition, and Posidonius can even report that the theory of atoms was invented not by Democritus, but by a Sidonian, Mochus, long before the Trojan war.[219] This report certainly derives from the competition of various peoples and cities over the 'first discoverers',[220] and has hardly more historical value than the Jewish reports of Moses and Abraham as the first teachers of astrology and philosophy (see below, pp. 89ff.), but it does show that in the Hellenistic period individual Phoenician cities laid claim to be leaders in the intellectual sphere. The unorthodox Stoic *Boethus of Sidon*, a pupil of Diogenes of Babylon (*c.* 240–152 BC), came from a rather earlier period (*c.* 180 BC). He broke with Stoic monism and divided the world: the godhead, an ethereal substance, has its place in the firmament. This change has been attributed to Aristotelian influences, but we should consider whether these beginnings of a theistic correction of the Stoa were not sponsored by the Semitic conception of the supreme God of heaven.[221] *Ashkelon* was also already an intellectual centre alongside Gadara and the Phoenician cities in pre-Christian times: 'Many from there made a name for themselves: as philosophers, Antiochus the Swan, Sosus, Antibius and Eubius, famous Stoics; as grammaticians the distinguished Ptolemy son of Aristarchus and Dorotheus, as historians Apollonius and Artemidorus . . .'[222] The most significant among them was probably *Antiochus* (*c.* 130–68 BC), who is usually simply called 'the Ashkelonite' in the sources. Sosus, to whom he devoted a disputation, was, like Posidonius, a pupil of Panaitius (*c.* 185–109

BC), and therefore was probably older than Antiochus. Perhaps he introduced the latter to the Stoa,[223] as Antiochus was not originally a Stoic, but an adherent of the Sceptic academy. However, he broke with Scepticism because he could find in it no basis for human action, and became head of the new-formed Academy in Athens, where Cicero heard him. However, instead of going back to the spirit of Plato himself, following the inclinations of the time he made considerable borrowings from the Stoa, which, of course, he traced back to Plato by way of justification, and became a real eclectic. The old philosophical schools, the Academy and the Peripatos, were, according to him, originally at one in their teaching, but at a later stage Zeno, Chrysippus and Epicurus, against whom in places he writes vigorous polemic, later introduced falsifications.[224] It is worth remembering that the eclectic combination of Platonism[225] and Stoicism, associated with a deliberate ethical trend and an appeal to the earliest tradition, was a basic feature of Jewish and Alexandrian philosophy. The motto of Antiochus, *veteres sequi*, was a fundamental principle of the late Hellenistic period and also corresponded to the Jewish principle of tradition.[226] In general, philosophical eclecticism was more and more predominant in the different schools from the second century BC on.[227]

A whole series of other Syrian-Phoenician philosophers can be cited from this period. A teacher or studying companion of Strabo was the Aristotelian Boethus of Sidon (not to be confused with the earlier Stoic of the same name), and his brother Diodotus is also mentioned as a philosopher.[228] The Sceptic Heracleitus came from Tyre; like Antiochus of Ashkelon he was a pupil of Philo of Larissa, but in contrast to him he had no leaning towards dogmatism, but remained faithful to Scepticism.[229] We also hear of the Tyrian Stoic Antipater, who introduced the younger Cato to Stoic philosophy, and Apollonius, who wrote a first history of the Stoic school of philosophy.[230] Two otherwise unknown Stoics, Diogenes and Apollonius of Ptolemais, complete the picture.[231] In this way, all the philosophical schools were represented in Palestine and Phoenicia, but the preponderance of the *Stoa* is unmistakable, above all if we add its most significant representative, Posidonius from North-Syrian Apamea, who had a decisive influence on the intellectual and religious development of the late-Hellenistic and Roman period (see below, pp. 258ff., 300f.). It is certainly no coincidence that it was the Stoic school which exerted particular influence in this region and found most adherents. First, as J. Kaerst stressed, the Stoa was the dominant philosophy of Hellenism, and secondly, its founders Zeno of Citium in Cyprus and Chrysippus of Soloi in Cilicia were very probably themselves Semites assimilated to Greek ways.[232] In his great work, M. Pohlenz often refers to the influence of Semitic thought-forms on the teaching edifice of the Stoa.[233] J. Bidez stressed Semitic and Syrian influence on the Stoa even more strongly; he was perhaps too one-sided in seeing in it a predominantly oriental spiritual movement.[234]

In view of all this, Tcherikover's judgment that there was no intellectual life worth mentioning in the 'Greek' cities of Palestine during the pre-Christian Hellenistic period is too one-sidedly negative. Even if the great men like Menippus, Meleager, Philodemus, etc., for the most part emigrated to Greece and Rome, it is astonishing that such gifts flourished in Palestine and Phoenicia at all, and could be nourished there. There was also a poetical and philosophical school at least in Sidon and Tyre. All this was only possible on the basis of a continuing intellectual tradition which probably arose as early as the third century BC. This development was probably stimulated by the constant cultural influence of neighbouring Alexandria and the cultural centres of the Aegean, like Rhodes, Cos and even Athens. Alexandrian influence can also clearly be demonstrated in the artistic sphere, say in the tomb paintings in Marisa and in the monument of the Tobiad Hyrcanus in 'Araq el Emir in Transjordania.[235] Here we come up against the question how far even Palestinian Judaism was influenced by the intellectual might of Hellenism in the pre-Christian Hellenistic period. But first we have to deal with the problem of a Jewish-Palestinian literature in Greek.

b) *Jewish literature in Greek in Palestine*

It is very probable that the Greek-educated friends of Hellenistic culture in Jerusalem made attempts to produce their own literature in the Greek language, following the pattern of their fellow-Jews in Alexandria. However, we have as little of this material as of the writings of the Jewish freedom movement before AD 70; the losing side seldom has its say in history.[236] A certain exception is perhaps the 'Tobiad romance' transmitted by Josephus, which is perhaps based on remnants of a family chronicle of the Tobiads. However, the romance was not composed in Palestine, but in Egypt, some time after the events depicted in it, and so it can only be included among 'Palestinian' literature with qualification.[237]

aa) The anonymous Samaritan

We do, however, have preserved for us in Eusebius' *Praeparatio Evangelica*, among the Jewish fragments of the collective work of Alexander Polyhistor, extracts from the work of an anonymous historiographer wrongly named Eupolemus,[238] who according to the investigations of Freudenthal was a Samaritan.[239] This anonymous writer, who probably wrote in Palestine between the Seleucid conquest in 200 BC and the Maccabean revolt,[240] attempted to combine the biblical creation stories and above all the haggadically elaborated Abraham narratives of Genesis with Babylonian-Greek mythology, by using non-Jewish sources like Berossus, Hesiod and perhaps also Ctesias.[241] The intention is to confirm the truth of the Old Testament account – which the anonymous writer treats very freely – and to glorify the figure of Abraham.

The proper names suggest that the author used the Septuagint in his work, but we must also suppose that he had a knowledge of Hebrew.[242] In addition, an acquaintance with the Jewish-apocalyptic tradition can be demonstrated: Enoch, who is named Atlas by the Greeks, is the inventor of astrology, and transmitted to posterity 'all that he learnt from the angels of God'.[243] Even more astounding is his interpretation of the stories of Gen.6–11: Noah and Nimrod are combined in one person and identified with Bel and Kronos. This superhuman figure is the only one of the 'giants' to have been rescued from the great flood; he founded Babylon and built the famous tower.[244] Here the Samaritan, freely reshaping his biblical model and misreading the genealogy, combined the sagas of the fall of the angels (Gen.6.4 LXX), the flood, the foundation of Babylon by the 'giant' Nimrod (Gen.10.9 LXX) and the building of the tower of Babel. At the same time, he combined these accounts with the narrative of Berossus about the foundation of Babylon by the creator God Bel[245] and the myth of the revolt of the Titans in Hesiod. The third book of the Sibyllines, composed about 140 BC, and probably dependent on the work of the anonymous Samaritan, also combined these sagas, but gave more prominence to the *Theogony* of Hesiod.[246] From now on the combination of the struggle of the Titans and the building of the tower of Babel became a favourite theme: it appears in Alexander Polyhistor, Thallus, Eusebius, etc.[247] The essential feature in all these mythological speculations is that despite their gigantic nature, the ancestral deities of Babylon and Greece, Bel and Kronos, are mortal men. Their descendants are punished by God for their sins and scattered over the earth. Thus the *demythologizing euhemerism* of the Samaritan dissolves the polytheistic pantheon of Greeks and Babylonians. The sequence of descent from Bel to Kronos to Noah is also instructive. Bel II (Shem) and Ham appear as sons. The latter has only one son, Canaan, 'the father of the Phoenicians'. Only from the latter – in contrast to Gen. 10.6 – do 'Chum' and 'Metzraeim', the ancestors of Ethiopia and Egypt, descend, a sign of the predominance of the Phoenicians and probably also of the non-Egyptian origin of the work.[248] In a similar way we find the euhemeristic humanization of pagan deities once again in the chronographer Thallus in the first century AD, who was possibly a countryman of the anonymous Samaritan, and at least a Syrian.[249] Further parallels are the identification of 'Hamor' (Gen.34.2) with 'Hermes', whose son Sikimios founded Shechem, in the Samaritan Theodotus (second century BC) who wrote in Homeric hexameters, and the mention of Heracles and Astarte (Asteria) as parents of Melchizedek in Epiphanius, who also knew his association with Shechem. Here, too, Phoenician influence is visible.[250]

Against this background of demythologized pagan sagas of the gods which are fundamentally intended merely to confirm the truth of the biblical account, the personality of *Abraham* shines out all the more brightly. 'He surpassed all in nobility and wisdom and . . . was well-pleasing to God through his special piety.'[251] Born in the tenth generation after the flood, he still belongs to the race of the 'supermen',[252] and, following the Enoch tradition, he becomes the (re)discoverer of astrology and 'the Chaldean art'.[253] At God's command he emigrated to 'Phoenicia' and taught the Phoenicians the 'course of the sun and the moon and all other (wisdom), to please their king'. When the Armenians – a change from the king of Shinar in Gen. 14 – conquered Phoenicia[254] and took Abraham's nephew prisoner, Abraham defeated the victors, but generously gave back to the enemy without ransom the wives and children he had taken captive. Then he met with the priest-king Melchizedek in the 'city sanctuary of Hargarizin', the 'mountain of the most high'.[255] Only after these events did he go to Egypt – a transposition of the sequence in Genesis – because of a famine. The episode with Sarah and the Pharaoh is transmitted similarly to the way in which it appears in the Genesis Apocryphon and in the Palestinian haggada.[256] Furthermore, he instructed the priests of Heliopolis in many ways, above all in astrology. Once again it is expressly said that this was not invented by the Egyptians but by the Babylonians, though the real authorship goes back to Enoch.[257] Presumably the anonymous Samaritan knew the report of Herodotus which mentioned the priests of Heliopolis as the wisest in Egypt and the Egyptians as the wisest men ($\lambda o\gamma\iota\acute{\omega}\tau\alpha\tau o\iota$) in the world.[258]

An explicit *interest in the history of culture* is manifest in this narrative; it is expressed both in the sequence of the tribal ancestors and in the journeys of Abraham: first Babylonia, then Phoenicia and Canaan, and only at the end Egypt. Thus Abraham becomes the bringer of culture for the Western peoples and indirectly also for the Greeks, since as the youngest people they drew their wisdom from the Phoenicians and the Egyptians. Here we find this claim to the $\pi\rho\hat{\omega}\tau o\varsigma$ $\epsilon\acute{v}\rho\acute{\epsilon}\tau\eta\varsigma$, which we have already noted among the Phoenicians, made for a biblical person. Abraham and Enoch were quite simply the wisest men in humanity. At this point the anonymous writer could take up the Greek tradition of Herodotus, Plato and above all Hecataeus, according to which the Greeks were instructed by the wisdom of the Egyptians. Now that Abraham is made the teacher of the (Phoenicians and the) Egyptians, the biblical tradition is proved to be the oldest wisdom of mankind. On this point the anonymous Samaritan was followed by the Palestinian Eupolemus (see below, pp. 92ff.) and the Alexandrians Aristobulus and Artapanus, down to Josephus and the church fathers. So here we have the first evidence for the Jewish and Christian-apologetic view that the Greek philosophers really drew their wisdom from the patriarchs and Moses.[259]

The identification of Canaanites and Phoenicians is also surprising. It is grounded in the predominant cultural and economic role that the Phoenicians had in Palestine in Persian and early Hellenistic times. It will be remembered that during the period of persecution under Antiochus IV Epiphanes, the Samaritans described themselves in a letter to the king as 'Sidonians', presumably because there was a Phoenician trading colony in Shechem similar to those in Marisa and Philadelphia. The Septuagint also calls Canaan or the Canaanites Phoenicia or Phoenicians on several occasions.[260] A further important point is the fact that the fragments which we have, apart from one statement about the sanctuary on Gerizim, could just as well come from a Jew with a Hellenistic education, that the Septuagint was used, and that often contacts with Jewish haggadic and apocalyptic tradition can be demonstrated. Despite the competing sanctuaries and the border disputes reported by Josephus, it seems probable that contacts between the Jewish upper classes and the Samaritans were not broken off in the third century BC: even in Alexandria, the final break only seems to have taken place under Ptolemy VI Philometor (180–145) – presumably in connection with the Maccabean revolt, despite previous disputes.[261] The 'syncretism' of the anonymous writer, said by Freudenthal to be typically Samaritan, is not present in this way. In him we find no traits tending towards polytheism, and one could with much greater justification apply the term syncretistic to the fictional biography of Moses by the Egyptian Jew Artapanus; it probably comes from about the same time, and states that Moses introduced the cult of animals into Egyptian territory and is himself to be identified with Hermes-Thoth and Musaeus, allegedly the teacher of Orpheus.[262]

The fragments rather have a rational and universalist trait. The anonymous writer is concerned 'to build a bridge between Babylonian and Greek culture on the ground of the biblical tradition, which provides his material and determines its form'. Here he is one of the first Palestinians to present the biblical history in the form of Hellenistic history writing.[263] The pagan myths are historicized and humanized; Abraham appears as the universal bringer of culture; the 'father of many nations' (Gen. 17.5 LXX) becomes the 'teacher of many nations'. Further, as the result of a certain academic and national interest, his own history is tied up with that of the nations. The freeing of the Armenian women and children is to be taken as a humanitarian trait. The divine retribution, revelations by angels, indeed even the efficacy of manticism, of course retain their validity, yet for all its national pride the religious attitude is free of narrowness and fanaticism. Abraham openly teaches the Phoenicians and the pagan priest of Heliopolis astrology or astronomy (they were identical at that time), which were highly prized and associated with Enoch and Abraham, the Chaldean. So we find it not only in the Jewish Hellenistic tradition in Alexandria, but also in Qumran and in Palestinian apocalyptic; its high valuation is a typical achievement of the Hellenistic period.[264] On the whole we find here a quite different spirit from that, say, in the later book of Jubilees, where attempts are made to trace back the validity of the Mosaic law even into the patriarchal narratives, and where there is even polemic against knowledge of the heavens. We probably have to imagine that the views of the moderate friends of Greece in Jerusalem were along similar lines. People were proud of their national history and of the extreme age of their own tradition, but on the other hand they were tolerant and interested in an expansion of their own horizon of education, and thus interested in a certain knowledge of the Greek intellectual world. Nor were people disinclined for contacts with Greeks and with their Hellenistic neighbours in the Palestinian-Phoenician cities. Abraham must have been of particular interest for this circle because of what one might almost call the 'international' breadth of his personality. By speculations about his journeys[265] or even about his manifold descendants, like the sons of Keturah, so briefly treated in the Bible, lines of affinity for the Jews could be traced to the Ethiopians, the Spartans and the Sophacians in Cyrenaica, or even to friendship with the Pergamenes.[266]

bb) The Jewish historian Eupolemus

In the excerpts of Alexander Polyhistor, further fragments are preserved of a history writer Eupolemus which, according to the researches of Freudenthal,[267] go back to a Greek-educated Palestinian Jew. In view of the time at which the history work begins, after 158/57 BC,[268] this Jew could be identical with Eupolemus son of John from the priestly family of Haqqos, mentioned in I Macc. 8.17 as leader of the Jewish delegation to Rome.[269]

The very title, 'About the kings in Judea', indicates the 'patriotic' character of this work, which has serious linguistic and stylistic deficiencies, and for that reason alone can hardly have been composed in Alexandria.[270] Like the anonymous Samaritan, the author uses the Septuagint, but like Josephus and Paul he also knew the Hebrew text.[271] There survive, first, a brief fragment about Moses, who is called the 'first wise man' ($\pi\rho\hat{\omega}\tau o\nu$ $\sigma o\phi \acute{o}\nu$) and is said to have been the first to have communicated the knowledge of the alphabet, or of the sciences in general, to the Jews.[272] The Phoenicians would then have received this knowledge from the Jews and the Greeks from the Phoenicians. Here we have basically the same 'invention' theme as in the anonymous Samaritan, except that the same thing is transferred, as with Artapanus, to Moses, and the invention of alphabetic writing, of which the Phoenicians were so proud, is shifted to the Jewish lawgiver. Probably the alphabet here represents literature and science in general. Perhaps this is meant to say that the Mosaic law was the first written document.

The identification of Moses and Hermes-Thoth in *Artapanus* points back to the myth reported by Plato in the Phaedrus, that the Egyptian 'Tut', in addition to number, logic, geometry, astronomy, dice and board games also invented writing ($\tau \grave{a}$ $\gamma \rho \acute{a}\mu\mu a\tau a$), and showed it to the king of Egypt. Hecataeus, a worshipper of Plato and an admirer of Egypt, further enlarged and elaborated this report[273] by having the wisest Greeks come to Egypt in primal times 'so that they could have a share in the laws and education there'. In first place he mentions Orpheus, who is said to have brought the

Greeks the mysteries from Egypt (Diod. I, 96). Thus for Artapanus, Moses-Hermes was not only the founder of Egyptian wisdom and religion, but also, as teacher of Orpheus, founder of Greek wisdom and religion, too (see above, n.262).

Similar themes appear elsewhere in a less 'syncretistic' form in the Jewish Alexandrian tradition.[274] For this reason, *Eupolemus* put the exodus from Egypt at an earlier date than the usual biblical chronology, in 1736 BC. The antiquity of the Jewish tradition could not be set high enough over against Egypt, Phoenicia and the Greeks.[275] According to a further fragment, Jeremiah announced deportation by the Babylonians to the Jews as a punishment for their idolatry. The king of Babylon heard of this prediction – in this way his resolve is fully rationalized – and allied himself with king Astibares of Media, a feature which the author could have borrowed from Ctesias.[276] The two kings first subjected 'Samaria, Galilee, Scythopolis and the Jews living in the Galaditis'[277] and then plundered Jerusalem; only the ark with the tables of the law was saved by Jeremiah.[278] The largest fragment contains the narrative of the building of the temple by Solomon; the central place is occupied by a fictitious correspondence between the king and Pharaoh Uaphres of Egypt and king Suron of 'Tyre and Sidon', based on the exchange of messengers between Solomon and Hiram in II Chron.2.2-15 (the Pharaoh is probably taken from Jer.44.30).[279] This is in accordance with the manner of Hellenistic history writing, which loved to insert 'official' archives. The letters were left unaltered by Polyhistor, who made excerpts from them; they therefore have particular value as sources. While elsewhere Polyhistor smoothed over the unskilful style of the author, here his linguistic inadequacy is evident, and we have also some echoes of the expressions to be found in the papyri letters and Ps. Aristeas.[280] Above all, the political picture of Solomon's kingdom which Eupolemus paints is remarkable. His father David had already defeated the Syrians in the neighbourhood of the Euphrates and in the Commagene – i.e. in the heart of Seleucid territory, and the 'Assyrians and Phoenicians'[281] living in the 'Galadene' east of the Jordan; he exacted tribute from his nearer neighbours, like the Idumeans, Ammonites, Moabites, Itureans, Nabateans, Nabdeans and finally even Suron, the king of Tyre and Sidon. He even exploited the golden island of Uphre in the Erithrean sea by means of the Arabian harbour of Elana. But with Pharaoh Uaphres he maintained friendly relations and concluded a covenant.[282] Here is a clear expression of the political situation of the Maccabean struggle and the beginning of Jewish expansion in Palestine, which relied on a good relationship with Ptolemaic Egypt. So in the letters of Solomon to Suron, Galilee, Samareitis (!), Moabitis, Ammanitis and Arabia appear as subject provinces, which have to contribute grain and sacrificial beasts as provisions for the builders of the temple and for sacrifices.[283] The letters of Solomon to the two kings are composed in brief as to subject peoples; the answers, in which Solomon is addressed as 'great king' *(βασιλεὺς μέγας)*,[284] like Antiochus III, are full of subservience. On the whole Eupolemus follows the account of Chronicles and the books of Kings in his portrait of the building of the temple, but he allows himself complete freedom in his elaboration, above all when it is a matter of the enlarging and more splendid decoration of the sanctuary. Its size was a cube of sixty cubits instead of the twenty of the biblical account, and the two iron pillars were covered with gold to the thickness of a finger; as in the description in the Mishnah, the temple building itself had skilful arrangements for driving away birds.[285] The broad-mindedness of the author is finally expressed in the note, mentioned above, that Solomon sent Suron a golden pillar which he erected in the temple of Zeus *(ἐν τῷ ἱερῷ τοῦ Διός)* in Tyre. According to *Contra Apionem* 1,113 (cf. 118), this was the Zeus Olympius identified with *Baʿal Šāmēm*.[286] Perhaps in the background here is the conception of pre-Maccabean Hellenists that the 'greatest God' *(θεὸς μέγιστος)* to whom Solomon owed his status as king, the God who gave him the commission to build the temple and whom Suron defined in his answer as 'creator of heaven and earth', was in the last resort, as the one God, also identical with the Zeus of the Phoenicians and Greeks.[287] Various parallel narratives suggest that this account comes from a more extensive collection of traditions originating in Phoenicia, which were concerned with the relationship between Hiram and Solomon. The friends of Hellenism in Jerusalem were surely interested in traditions in which Jerusalem appeared as a partner of the Phoenician cities with equal, if not superior, status.[288] Although Eupolemus was a supporter of the Maccabees, he also seems to have been influenced on this side. On the whole, however, a strong nationalistic tendency predominates in his work, which heralds the vigorous expansionist policy of the Hasmoneans in the following decades. Furthermore, the temple and its cult stand in the foreground. This may partially have been conditioned by the material in the fragments that we still have, but on the whole one may concur with the judgment of Dalbert: 'One is given the impression that the piety of Eupolemus is expressly directed towards a right ordering of the cult.'[289] The law is mentioned only once in passing.[290] Perhaps one may say that Eupolemus is a link between the work of the Chronicler – his primary source – and the strongly nationalistic colours of the Sadduceeism of the Hasmonean period. The Hellenistic element introduces a certain interest in and openness towards the wider world; thus Eupolemus paves the way for the positive attitude of the later Hasmonean kings towards Hellenism.

The anonymous Samaritan and Eupolemus have a number of things in common. A. Schlatter would not, therefore, allow the division made by Freudenthal, but derived the two groups of fragments from a great history work of an otherwise unknown Alexandrian Jewish historian Eupolemus, on whom Artapanus, Philo and to an especial degree Josephus were said to be dependent. However, this is an unprovable hypothesis: the stress on Shechem and the temple on Gerizim in the anonymous writer, and the demotion of Samaria to a dependent province and the glorification of the temple of Solomon in Eupolemus rule it out.[291]

Common to both is their great freedom towards the biblical text, which they both expand or alter at will in an effort to make the biblical tradition correspond with non-Jewish history writing or to give it an even more splendid appearance. To this end they refer back to Greek history writers: here we have an indirect proof that these were read in Jewish or Samaritan circles in Palestine. In addition there are the relationships with the Alexandrian Jewish tradition and the Palestinian haggada; indeed even apocalyptic material like the Enoch tradition is taken up by the anonymous writer.[292] In both works the Egyptians, and still more the Phoenicians, appear as the people with whom Israel and its ancestors were associated through close cultural relationships. Here perhaps the conditions of the time of the Ptolemaic-Seleucid rule are transferred to the past. One special concern is the strengthening of the author's own self-awareness by the assertion that decisive 'first inventions' come, like astrology, from Abraham, or like writing, from Moses. In this way the Torah becomes the earliest of all books; in the end, indeed, 'all Hellenism is made dependent on Moses'.[293] Another feature which the two have in common is their tendency towards rationalization, though this did not exclude the appearances of angels and predictions in the prophets.

The most essential difference, apart from the two competing sanctuaries on Gerizim and in Jerusalem, is the universalist breadth of the Abraham narrative in the anonymous Samaritan and the Judean nationalistic narrowness of the fragments of Eupolemus, where even the international relationships of Solomon only serve to the greater glory of the Jewish king and the sanctuary built by him. Furthermore, it is by no means the same thing whether Abraham or Moses appears as the 'first wise man'.[294] In one case the universalist tendency predominates, and in the other the nationalist. Here the change of conditions brought about by the Maccabean revolt is evident.[295]

cc) Jason of Cyrene and Palestinian-Jewish history writing

The very name of Jason of Cyrene, the author of the history work summarized in II Maccabees, indicates that he was not a real Palestinian but either came from the Jewish Diaspora in Cyrenaica or at least spent a good part of his life there. His work, which is 'profoundly influenced by the spirit of solemn Hellenistic historiography',[296] also presupposes that its author has received a thorough training in rhetoric, which he is most likely to have been able to obtain in Alexandria.[297] If despite this we consider his work, it is because its contents refer completely to Judea, and in its not inconsiderable extent of five books – which a later epitomator then forcibly compressed into one – must have dealt in comparatively great detail with a relatively short but decisive space of Jewish history extending over about fifteen years (say, 176–160 BC), i.e. the preliminaries to the Maccabean revolt and the acts of Judas.[298] Even in the severely compressed form of II Maccabees,[299] the work still has such a fullness of historical detail[300] that we must suppose that the author had a lengthy stay in Palestine and knew Aramaic or Hebrew. The question of his sources and the time of his writing is disputed: whereas Niese, Schürer, Jacoby, Abel and Tcherikover see Jason as an eye-witness who composed his work soon after the death of Judas and used principally oral tradition,[301] others, like E. Meyer, Bickermann, Pfeiffer and Schunck, believe in a later use of written sources (though these are hard to define), on which there is no agreement.[302] Schunck, who investigated the source problem in the greatest detail, assumed that a history of Judas was a common source for the otherwise completely independent historical works of Jason and I Maccabees; in addition, with a lesser degree of probability, he posited a chronicle of the Seleucids.[303] Furthermore, Jason is said to have drawn on the diaries of the high priests Onias, Jason and Menelaus, which were preserved in the archives of the temple in Jerusalem, for the preliminaries to the rebellion.[304] Knowledge of the proceedings in II Macc. 11, whose authenticity is now almost universally acknowledged, was communicated by the archive in Jerusalem.[305] Schunck would not rule out even oral tradition. His source theory, which is based above all on the double chronology of the books of Maccabees (especially of I Macc.), with the different beginnings of the Seleucid era in Autumn 312 and on 1 Nisan of early 311 BC, has, however, been outdated by the Sachs-Wiseman publication of the cuneiform chronology of the Seleucids and needs to be examined again.[306] Surprisingly, it has proved that the historical reliability of the work of Jason, which B. Niese already stressed so strongly (perhaps too strongly), has been confirmed in one point where Jason had previously been taken to be wrong: the report of the death of Antiochus IV was published in Babylon as early as the ninth month of the year 142 in the Seleucid era, i.e. between 20.11 and 18.12.164 BC; this means that the king did not die in early 163, but a short time *before* the reconsecration of the temple on 25 Chislev = 14 December 164.[307] The reason why in other places II Maccabees reports the historical order of events in a false sequence which deviates from the relatively ordered chronology of I Macc. may be that the epitomator altered Jason's order in the interest of an increase in the inner tension of the work, so that the victory over Nicanor could be depicted with supernatural colouring. He probably also omitted the death of Judas Maccabaeus, the real hero of the work, in the interest of a 'happy ending'.[308] A decisive factor is that despite the outward Hellenistic garb of Jason's work, his theological views are stamped much more with the piety of the Palestinian Hasidim than with the Jewish Hellenism of Alexandria.[309] This is true, say, of the depiction of the rigorous observance of the sabbath commandment[310] and of the food laws by the pious Jews who fled into the wilderness;[311] of the doctrine of the resurrection of the dead, presented several times, and the intercession of the departed faithful;[312] the extensive angelology[313] and the tradition of the holy war.[314] It is impossible – as Hanhart assumes, following Seeligmann[315] – that all these points could come from a Palestinian revision of the work of Jason by the epitomator. As the epitomator shared the approach of Jason's work – otherwise he would hardly have worked over it – he naturally abbreviated the purely historical parts and retained the 'edifying' parts, in this way strengthening the tendency of the work. On the other hand, the doctrine of retribution stressed particularly by Hanhart is not typically Jewish, but is also to be found in Hellenistic 'solemn' historiography, like the writing of Timaeus of Tauromenium, in whose footsteps Jason walks.[316] A special concern of the work – like that of Eupolemus and the books of Chronicles – was the glorification of the temple: the sanctuary, threatened several times by the Gentiles, is continually protected by God in new and wonderful ways.[317] On the other hand, interest in the later Hasmonean dynasty fades right into the background: we hear neither of its ancestor Mattathias nor of the priesthood of Judas nor of the high-priestly office of his brothers Jonathan and Simon; rather, the only regular Zadokite high priest Onias III is presented as a holy figure.[318] People have wanted to regard Jason as a representative of the Pharisaic movement, but against this it has rightly been stressed that one decisive Pharisaic feature, reference to oral tradition, is missing from his work.[319] His views are nearer to the pre-Pharisaic, Hasidic movement which we find in Daniel and in the older parts of the Essene tradition. In contrast to the first book of Maccabees, which here marks a clear distinction, he makes Judas the leader of the Hasidim.[320]

Tcherikover calls attention to one feature which is essential for the question of dating: in connection with the reform attempt of the high priest Jason, II Macc. 4.11 mentions a John as a successful negotiator with Antiochus III and adds, by way of explanation: 'the father of Eupolemus, who took part in the delegation to the Romans for a treaty of friendship and armaments'. As elsewhere the name of a person is defined more closely by his father's name, the mention of the son only makes sense if he was still known to the readers. Indeed, one might assume that Jason himself was a contemporary of this Eupolemus – presumably the historian, and thus also of Judas Maccabeus.[321] If one takes all the viewpoints together, the suggestion of Niese, that Jason spent at least some time in Palestine in those decisive years after 175 BC and wrote his work soon after the death of Judas (May 160) and possibly before Jonathan took over the office of high priest (autumn 152 BC), still has a certain degree of probability (see below, pp. 224ff.). Presumably the intention was to gain some understanding and support in the Greek-speaking Diaspora and the Greek world in general for the Jews who were fighting for the integrity of their sanctuary and their piety. The Maccabean fight for freedom would hardly have been possible without support from outside, especially from Egypt;

the delegations to Rome and Sparta also belong in this context. The fact that Jason of Cyrene wrote contemporary history does not exclude the possibility that he also used written sources, like enumerations of the victorious battles of Judas, which still came from his lifetime, or even of certain political events in the Seleucid kingdom, about whose administration, including the titles and names of officials, he is very well informed indeed.[322] His own observation, narratives of eye-witnesses and access to the archives in Jerusalem gave him the knowledge of events necessary for his work. His predilection for legendary elaborations, especially for the appearances of angels and heavenly figures and for heroic martyrdoms,[323] is conditioned on the one hand by the contemporary style of solemn historiography which used strong colours to excite fear and sympathy,[324] and on the other by his Hasidic piety: the appearances of angels and astonishing miracles play a great role in the book of Daniel, which was written only a short while earlier, and the Essenes were familiar with miraculous healings, prophecies, and above all close connections with angels.[325] Presumably the narratives of the deaths of martyrs testifying to their faith and the atoning effect of their suffering go back to Palestinian models: by combining them with the Hellenistic theme of the *exitus clarorum virorum*, Jason gave them a form that was effective in the Greek-speaking world, and thus became the father of the *martyrium*.[326] 'This synthesis of narrowly orthodox theology and the most powerful rhetoric, which is quite absent from the books of the Bible, gave the work its tremendous success.'[327] Thus, if Jason was in all probability a Jew of the Diaspora – the attempt which has often been made to identify him with Jason son of Eleazar, the second delegate to Rome mentioned in I Macc. 8.17, remains an undemonstrable hypothesis – his work nevertheless points to a very close connection with Palestine, despite its completely Hellenistic form; perhaps it even arose there.[328] Although the writings of the anonymous Samaritan and Eupolemus had a very much simpler form, the content of their work seems to be determined by freer and stronger Hellenistic influences. Despite the rhetorical form of Jason's historical work, it lacks deep philosophical ideas; the echoes of Plato which J. Baer thought that he could find, above all in ch. 7, are not a striking peculiarity, as they were widespread elsewhere in contemporary Palestinian Judaism. On the whole, the author has more of a hostile attitude to Hellenistic civilization. In a strange reversal of the sense of the word, the supporters of the Seleucids are called 'barbarians',[329] and the Jews who are faithful to the law become the citizens of a '*polis*' fighting for the existence of the '*politeia*' given to them by God.[330] On this point the five books of Jason differ considerably from Alexandrian writing which is not too far removed from them in time and has a positive attitude to Hellenistic culture, like the Letter of Aristeas (see above, n. I, 206) and the Apology of Aristobulus (see below, pp. 163ff.). This is a sign that the intellectual climate was in process of changing. The essential point here is that in the encounter between Judaism and Hellenistic culture, the shape and content of a writing did not necessarily have to conform.

Excursus 2: Palestinian-Jewish history writing in the Hellenistic period

It is no coincidence that in the Graeco-Jewish literature associated with Palestine, historical works predominate, whereas in Alexandria 'philosophical-type' writing is more strongly in the foreground. This development finds its climax and conclusion during the first century in the two Jewish-Palestinian historians Justus of Tiberias and Josephus. Of Josephus, who comes from the priestly nobility of Jerusalem, it could be said that a kind of 'priestly' historical writing which can be demonstrated from the Priestly Writer, the work of the Chronicler, Eupolemus, I Maccabees and the anti-Herodian source of Josephus himself[331] comes to an end in his work. Finally, one may also point out that the Greek Peripatetic Nicolaus of Damascus, a friend of Herod and therefore close to him, probably wrote his great universal history of 144 books, in which he also dealt with Jewish history at length and thus formed the main source of Josephus, in Jerusalem at the court of Herod.[332]

The Hebrew-Aramaic literature of the Hellenistic period (see below, pp. 110–15) also shows an intensive interest in the historical tradition of its own people. This is already indicated by the fact that even during the third century – perhaps in the time of the high priest Simon the Just (see below, pp. 271f.) – the Torah of Moses, which was canonically binding, was supplemented by the 'prophetic' writings, to which the 'hagiographies' were attached in their turn (see below, pp. 134f.). This created something like a historical continuity in Israelite history down to Persian times and thus a strong argument for the antiquity and the purity of the Jewish tradition in the controversy with Hellenism. In style and content, I Maccabees deliberately continues the tradition of Kings and Chronicles, and in comparison with the Old Testament text, the great retellings of biblical history, like the book of Jubilees, the Genesis Apocryphon or the later pseudo-Philonic *Liber Antiquitatum Biblicarum*, are very free revisions of the holy history. Even in apocalyptic writings, a peculiar form of 'encoded history' developed, based on *vaticinia ex eventu*; we find it in Dan. 11; I Enoch 85–90 or later in the Assumption of Moses (see below, pp. 183ff., 187ff.). Closely related to the apocalyptic form is the interpretation of Old Testament prophecy in Qumran in relation to an eschatological understanding of history, by use of the *pesher* method.[333] In itself, wisdom may be 'ahistorical', but in the work of Jesus Sirach it is bound up with the history of Israel by its identification with the Torah and through the 'praise of the ancestors' in Sirach 44.1–50.24.[334] The interpretation here of past history in the light of the present, or present history in the light of the saving experiences of the past, gave the Jewish community of believers a support against the manifold influences of the Hellenistic environment. We

already find two significant features of this Jewish history writing in the
Hellenistic period in the work of the Chronicler, which was composed, at least
in its basic form, during the Persian period: an astonishing freedom in the
expansion and adaptation of the received historical tradition to meet the needs
and problems of the present and a stress on direct personal retribution by the
Lord of history. Since in most historical works the eschatological perspective is
either missing or very much in the background, history becomes the place of
judgment.[335] Both features are also expressed in the work of Jason of
Cyrene. He does not set out to write an 'objective' historical report, but to give
a 'theological' interpretation of the events of the most recent past, and thus to
describe God's wonderful work in saving his sanctuary and his people and
punishing evildoers and persecutors.[336] The fact that he could attempt this
in what is externally a completely Hellenistic, highly rhetorical form, is a sign
of the flexibility of the Jewish religion and its capacity for adaptation to a new
intellectual environment. The Jews were the only people of the East to enter
into deliberate competition with the Greek view of the world and of history,
whether they gave their 'historical' works the traditional form of a chronicle,
the cryptic form of an apocalyptic outline of history or even the alien garb of
Hellenistic historiography. That after AD 70 they suddenly broke off from
giving accounts of their history and concentrated entirely on developing a
fundamentally ahistorical *halacha* and *haggada* is a sign of the radical upheaval
which was introduced by the destruction of the second temple and the Jewish
state and the establishment of the Rabbinic claim to leadership in Palestine:
'The Jew no longer created history, but suffered it.'[337]

dd) Greek translations of Jewish writings in Palestine
The work of Jason of Cyrene is at the same time a proof of the close connection
between certain circles of Diaspora Judaism and Jerusalem. The Hasmoneans
attached importance to drawing this connection still closer, because – as with
Herod later – their international significance depended on their influence on
Diaspora Judaism. For this reason alone they must have been interested in a
continuation of Greek studies in Jerusalem. So we find signs of lively translation activity in Jerusalem, with the aim of winning over Jews outside
Palestine, especially in Egypt, to the politics of the new Jewish national state,
and at the same time warding off the competition of the Oniad temple in
Leontopolis.[338] An official 'festal letter' of the Jews in Jerusalem to their
'brothers' in the Egyptian Diaspora from the year 124 BC has been preserved
in II Macc. 1.1–9. It quotes an earlier writing of early 142. Presumably these
were letters which had been translated from Aramaic into Greek in the
Maccabean chancellery.[339] The lengthy 'festal letter' which follows in II
Macc. 1.10–2.18, which is a forgery probably made before Pompey's conquest
of Jerusalem in 63 BC and was possibly also written in Jerusalem,[340] contains
a reference in 2.13ff. to the *temple archive* allegedly founded by Nehemiah and

enlarged by Judas Maccabeus; there is the significant invitation: 'If you need anything now, send (people) to get it.' Here the author presupposes that the Jews in Alexandria had writings with religious and historical content from Jerusalem, and that, as the Jews of Alexandria no longer knew Aramaic, these were at least in part translated into Greek. This is confirmed by the postscript to the Greek book of Esther, in which it is stated that the book was translated in Jerusalem by a Lysimachus son of Ptolemy and that it had been brought to Egypt by the priest Dositheus and his son Ptolemy as a 'festal letter for Purim'.[341] Presumably this translation of the book of Esther was connected with the revision and expansion which distinguishes the Greek form from the Massoretic. The contrast between Jews and Gentiles was made sharper and more profound,[342] the arch-enemy of the Jews, Haman, is described as a 'Macedonian' – a feature which could hardly come from Alexandria, where some Jews were proud to call themselves Macedonians[343] – and God was brought into the centre as an active force by the insertion of prayers, a dream and its interpretation.[344] Finally, the scandal of Esther's marriage with the heathen king, at which the original author had taken no offence, had to be played down. This may be a reason why the book of Esther was not to be found in the library of Qumran.[345] So Esther prays in the additional material (4.17u-y = C 25–29) in a way which represents a clear repudiation of the attitude of the earlier 'court histories' (see above, p. 29ff.):

> Thou hast knowledge of all things; and thou knowest that I hate the splendour of the wicked and abhor the bed of the uncircumcised and of any alien. Thou knowest my necessity – that I abhor the sign of my proud position, which is on my head on the days when I appear in public. I abhor it like a menstruous rag, and do not wear it on the days when I am at leisure. And thy servant has not eaten at Haman's table, and I have not honoured the king's feast or drunk the wine of libations. Thy servant has had no joy since the day that I was brought here until now, except in thee, O Lord God of Abraham . . .

Here a legalistic rigorism has been introduced into the book of Esther which was alien to the original tendency of the work, but which is in many ways akin to the spirit of II Maccabees or Jubilees. In the additions, the translator and reviser Lysimachus son of Ptolemy seems to have used earlier Aramaic or Hebrew models.[346] The addition of the colophon to Esther τῶν ἐν Ἰερουσαλήμ indicates that he was a Palestinian. At the same time the colophon is an indication of the close connection between Hasmonean Jerusalem and the Egyptian Diaspora.[347]

We may reckon that other works, like I Maccabees,[348] were also translated into Greek in Palestine, but here we cannot go beyond suppositions, because only in the case of Esther has a bibliographical note been preserved to that effect. The work of translating and editing the LXX also continued in

Palestine in the first and second centuries AD with Theodotion and Aquila.[349]
The use of the LXX in the anonymous Samaritan and in Eupolemus, together
with the discovery of LXX fragments in Qumran and in the caves used in the
Bar Kochba revolt (see above, n.20), shows that the Greek translation of the
Old Testament also came to be highly prized in Palestine from the second
century BC to the second century AD – in contrast to the sharp criticism of later
Rabbis.[350] On the whole, and above all in the Pentateuch – regardless of the
considerable differences between the various translations of individual books –
the LXX is under the influence of Palestinian tradition, even if it was largely
translated in Alexandria. Those unknown Jews who had the holy tradition of
their people so much at heart and who still had sufficient command of the holy
language to be able to translate the books of the Old Testament into Greek
were probably still closely connected with their mother country, even if the
narrative of the seventy-two Palestinian elders and their precious rolls of the
law from Jerusalem (*Ep. Arist.* 121ff., 176) are to be banished to the realm of
legend. The holy texts were translated as literally as possible, even down to
preserving the Hebrew word order, and more far-reaching influence by Greek
mythology and philosophical speculation was avoided. Individual exceptions
(see below, n.372) only confirm the rule.[351] The prologue and the translation work of the grandson of Jesus Sirach (see below, pp.131ff.) offer a
concrete instance of this link with the Palestinian homeland.

The overall picture of the surviving fragments of Jewish-Hellenistic
literature in Greek from Palestine must inevitably be a one-sided one, because
the number of writings preserved in fragments is limited, and their tendency –
apart from the anonymous Samaritan – is relatively uniform. They served to
strengthen the Jews' religious and national consciousness, to increase the
distance between the non-Jews and the politico-religious influence on the
Diaspora, especially in Egypt.[352] The post-Maccabean situation is evident
here throughout: knowledge of Greek language and literature, indeed training
in rhetoric, were put completely at the service of the defence of the Jewish
tradition against the dangers of Hellenistic civilization. It is also interesting
that the surviving writings, in contrast to Alexandrian Jewish literature and to
the intellectual tradition of Hellenistic cities like Sidon, Tyre, Gadara and
Ashkelon (see above, pp.83ff.), are not philosophical in content, but almost
entirely historical, and have a strong legendary flavour. It is very probable that
there will also have been writing in Jewish Palestine that was more open to
Hellenism, as a counterpart to the nationalistic and progressively more legalistic literature; possibly it will have stemmed from the universalism of the
wisdom literature (see below, pp.127f.). However, because of the victory of the
Maccabees, none of it survives. All we have is fragments of works which – apart
from the anonymous Samaritan – represented a reaction to Hellenistic attempts
at reform; by contrast, the intellectual cultural activity of the friends of
Hellenism which sparked off the reaction can only be inferred indirectly.

4. Summary: The Judaism of Palestine as 'Hellenistic Judaism'

It can be demonstrated from the Zeno papyri that the Greek language was known in aristocratic and military circles of Judaism between 260 and 250 BC in Palestine. It was already widespread at the accession of Antiochus IV in 175 BC and would hardly have been suppressed even by the victorious freedom fight of the Maccabees. Their very desire to influence the Diaspora required the cultivation of the international language. One might almost say that it played the role in Jewish higher society that French played among the German aristocracy at the end of the seventeenth century and after. This is confirmed, among other things, by the large number of Greek loan words in Talmudic literature. Parallel to this ran the adoption of Greek names, which followed in analogy with the Graecizing of Phoenician nomenclature and that of the Egyptian Jews; however, it began somewhat later and can be demonstrated from the end of the third century. It too continued after the Maccabean revolt and even emerged in the family of the Hasmoneans from the second or third generation on.

Language and nomenclature both suggest the infiltration of Greek education. Its influence on the Phoenicians and the Jews in Egypt can be demonstrated considerably earlier; however, we may suppose that it had also penetrated Judea from the second half of the third century on, and in 175 BC this development reached its first climax with the construction of a gymnasium in Jerusalem by the high priest Jason. The process of Hellenization in the *Jewish upper class* then entered an acute phase, the aim of which was the complete assimilation of Judaism to the Hellenistic environment. This was combined with a political aim: the foundation of a Greek *polis* in Jerusalem was intended to strengthen the privileges of the aristocrats friendly to Greece and to disenfranchise conservative circles. Presumably Greek 'education' in Jerusalem not only led to training the ephebes in sports but also had intellectual and literary elements. A Greek school must have existed in Jerusalem as a preparation for the gymnasium and to run alongside it. In later times, too, there are signs of a continuation of Greek education in the Jewish capital, which even included the knowledge of Homer. As a counter-movement to this there developed a broader stratum of scribes, beginning from the scribal group which had long been associated with the temple, whose aim was the instruction of the whole people in the Torah. The culmination of this centuries-long development was the Rabbinate in the second century AD. Even in this movement, however, with its explicitly anti-Hellenistic tendencies, the methods and forms of Greek educational theory were adopted.

Literary and philosophical centres of education developed not only in Alexandria, but also in the Phoenician cities and in individual places in Hellenized Palestine, which produced a whole series of significant poets and philosophers. The greatest influence was exerted by the Stoa, which predominantly went back to founders of Semitic origin; it was the dominant philosophy of the Hellenistic period. At the same time, eclectic mixing of the schools could be seen from the second century BC, to which philosophers of Syro-Phoenician origin contributed.

The penetration of Greek education is confirmed by the beginnings of a Jewish literature in Greek in Palestine, a literature which was above all interested in the Jews' own history. The anonymous Samaritan combined the biblical primal history with euhemeristically interpreted themes from the Babylonian and Greek theogony and made Enoch and Abraham bringers of culture to all the nations, whereas the priest and Jew Eupolemus depicted the Jewish national history with special stress on the sanctuary at Jerusalem. Jason of Cyrene, a Diaspora Jew, narrated the latest events of the Hellenistic reform in an extensive work and presented the struggle of Judas Maccabeus for freedom in the solemn manner of Hellenistic historiography, though in so doing he used a fullness of themes from Hasidic, Palestinian piety. The Hasmoneans attached importance to the circulation of Palestinian Jewish literature in Greek translations outside the mother country in the interest of strengthening the religious and national authority of the liberated, new Jewish state. This led to a certain amount of translation activity in Palestine itself.

On the whole, it emerges that Hellenism also gained ground as an intellectual power in Jewish Palestine early and tenaciously. From this perspective the usual distinction between Palestinian and Hellenistic Judaism needs to be corrected. Here it is not only used misleadingly as a designation of subject-matter and in a false contrast as a geographical concept,[353] but tends to give a mistaken account of the new situation of Judaism in the Hellenistic period. From about the middle of the third century BC *all Judaism* must really be designated '*Hellenistic Judaism*' in the strict sense, and a better differentiation could be made between the Greek-speaking Judaism of the Western Diaspora and the Aramaic/Hebrew-speaking Judaism of Palestine and Babylonia.[354] But even this distinction is one-sided. From the time of the Ptolemies, Jerusalem was a city in which Greek was spoken to an increasing degree. The Maccabean revolt changed little here, and in the New Testament period between Herod and the destruction of AD 70 it must have had a quite considerable minority who spoke Greek as their mother tongue, as Greek inscriptions show. This minority not only consisted of people who had returned from the Diaspora, but also embraced groups of the native aristocracy. Here we come up against the type from which the strongest political, cultural and religious impulses stemmed, the Jews who moved with the same skill in both the traditional Jewish-Aramaic and the alien Greek cultural and linguistic areas. One example of this is offered by the bilingual Greek and Aramaic inscriptions on tombs or ossuaries in Jerusalem.[355] The series of these *Jewish 'Graeco-Palestinians'* begins with the Tobiads, like the tax farmer Joseph and his son Hyrcanus; the later high-priestly Oniads, like Onias III,

Jason and Onias IV, the founder of Leontopolis; the members of the leading priestly nobility like Simon, Menelaus, Lysimachus; and the subsequent high priest Alcimus. It continued in the writer Eupolemus, the grandson of Ben Sira, the later Hasmoneans like Aristobulus Philhellene and Alexander Jannaeus, and their sons. Herod, his family and his supporters, the high-priestly family Boethus brought by him to Jerusalem (see n.154), and other high-priestly families in the New Testament period should be mentioned here. The same is also true of New Testament figures like John Mark (Acts 12.12,25; 13.5, 13; 15.37), Silvanus-Silas,[356] Judas Barsabbas (Acts 15.22, 32) and Menahem, the younger contemporary of Herod Antipas (Acts 13.1). Jews who themselves came from the Diaspora but whose families were closely associated with Palestine and spent a great part of their life there should also be counted among those who belonged to this group of people who had two languages and two cultures, like Jason of Cyrene and later the Levite Joseph Barnabas from Cyprus, the 'cousin' of John Mark (Acts 4.36 etc; cf. Col.4.10), and the Pharisee Saul-Paul from Tarsus.[357] One might also point to the seven 'Hellenists' of Acts 6, though it is uncertain whether they knew Aramaic. Later representatives of this twofold education were Josephus, Justus of Tiberias (= Zadok), who had an excellent rhetorical training, and the house of the patriarchs. The prominent Jewish cemetery of Beth-Shearim in Galilee shows how from the second half of the second century AD Greek influence was almost stronger there than in Jerusalem.[358]

These circumstances make the differentiation between 'Palestinian' and 'Hellenistic' Judaism, which is one of the fundamental heuristic principles of New Testament scholarship, much more difficult; indeed, on the whole it proves to be no longer adequate. We have to count on the possibility that even in Jewish Palestine, individual groups grew up bilingual and thus stood right on the boundary of two cultures. This problem arises not only with Jerusalem, but also with Galilee, which had for a long time had special links with the Phoenician cities; we can ask whether some of the immediate circle of Jesus' disciples were not themselves bilingual. At any rate, two of the twelve, Andrew and Philip, had Greek names (Mark 3.18), and Simon Cephas-Peter, Andrew's brother, later undertook extensive missionary journeys among the Jewish Diaspora of the West, which spoke only Greek.

The differentiation between the (primitive) Palestinian community and the Hellenistic-Jewish community of the Diaspora, especially that of Antioch, which follows from Acts 11.19ff., also needs to be defined more sharply: we must not underestimate the Greek-speaking – and presumably more active – element in the Palestinian communities. Knowledge of Greek was the expression of a higher social standing, better education and stronger contacts with the world outside Jewish Palestine. So we might ask, for example, whether the Gospel of Matthew might not come from such Greek-speaking Jewish-Christian circles in Palestine.[359]

The investigation of the spread of the Greek language, Greek education and culture in the Jewish Palestine of the New Testament faces a new beginning – although the material has grown very considerably in the last decades. In future we must not be influenced so much by the fact that one of the chief witnesses, the Rabbinic tradition, has been preserved only in Hebrew and Aramaic. S. Lieberman has inescapably shown that even here the Hellenistic element and the use of the Greek language often gleams powerfully through. Alongside this, the evidence of Josephus and archaeology, especially inscriptions and papyrus finds, acquire increasing significance.

III

The Encounter and Conflict between Palestinian Judaism and the Spirit of the Hellenistic Age

Particularly in the post-exilic period, Palestinian Judaism produced a rich and many-sided literature which is astonishing, given the smallness, poverty and political insignificance of this ethnic group, even if one presupposes a close contact with the Babylonian and Egyptian Diaspora (see above, pp. 17f.). This literary activity by no means broke off with the change of rule between Alexander the Great and Ptolemy I; on the contrary, in the Hellenistic period it became even more fruitful than before. Nevertheless, to demonstrate direct 'Hellenistic influences' in the literature we now have in Hebrew and Aramaic – or in that which was originally composed in these languages – is extraordinarily difficult.

1. This holds first for the language problem. When foreign – in this case Greek – conceptions were transferred into the language of the Jews, they were considerably altered, as Hebrew and Aramaic had not reached the same high level of abstract reflection as Greek, although they show the beginnings of the formation of abstract concepts in the late wisdom literature. So unless obvious Graecisms or loanwords appear – and this is the case only at a relatively late stage (see above, pp. 6of.) – it is often difficult to say whether a particular idea is developed on a line consistent with Jewish thought or whether alien influences are present.

2. In addition, it is difficult to put a date to those writings, like Koheleth, Job, Proverbs, Song of Songs, Jonah, etc, for which Greek influences have sometimes been claimed. Sometimes scholars differ in dating by several centuries, and sometimes the postulate or the categorical rejection of alien influence and the date proposed are bound up in a circular argument. While Greek 'influence' is not completely impossible if these books are assigned to the fifth and sixth centuries, because of already existing military or trade connections, it is somewhat improbable.[1]

3. Furthermore, in most recent times scholars have increasingly discovered the astonishing connections between the mythology and wisdom of the ancient East and the spiritual world of ancient Greece, in which at this early epoch the Greeks were predominantly the recipients. Oriental influences were not just

limited to the poets of the early period like Homer and Hesiod,[2] but also
affect Ionian natural philosophy and indirectly even Plato and Aristotle.[3]
This fact was well known to the Greeks:

> Thus the mythographer Pherecydes of Syros, to whom Posidonius ascribes
> for the first time the doctrine of the immortality of the soul, is said to have
> possessed 'secret Phoenician books' after 600 BC,[4] and it is reported of
> Pseudo-Democritus and Theophrastus, the pupil of Aristotle (see below,
> p.256), that they translated the book of the Wisdom of Ahikar into
> Greek.[5] Josephus, who in *Contra Apionem* 1,14 designates Pherecydes,
> Pythagoras and Thales as 'pupils (μαθητάς) of the Egyptians and
> Chaldeans' – with some historical justification – shows how much people
> were aware of these connections in antiquity and how even Jewish
> apologetic could make use of them.

We must therefore reckon with the possibility that parallels to Greek conceptions emerge, without it being possible for us to infer a direct dependence,
as these might go back to a *common oriental background*. Furthermore, despite
the unity of the culture of the eastern Mediterranean in the Persian period, we
should bear in mind the possibility that analogous phenomena may have arisen
which are not to be explained by causal derivations and relationships of
dependence, because certain notions simply matured and were expressed quite
independently in different places at the same time.

4. Finally, we should note that the late writings of the Old Testament
canon, the apocryphal and apocalyptic works still extant and the extra-
biblical fragments of the library of Qumran, represent a one-sided selection as
far as our question is concerned, as they were collected and preserved by
circles which saw their task as the repudiation of alien Hellenistic influences.
They found endorsement in the success of the Maccabean revolt, and we can
hardly expect that alien, Hellenistic influences were accepted in awareness of
their origin; on the contrary, new notions found their way into Judaism
precisely in the controversy over and repudiation of alien conceptions, without
those in the circles who accepted them being aware of the fact.

Moreover, to attempt a thorough analysis of the late Hebraic and Aramaic
literature which is followed so to speak without a break by apocalyptic and
Essene, as well as early Rabbinic writing, with the aim of discovering possible
parallels and inferring connections with the Greek intellectual world from
them, would far exceed the scope of this work; and it would only be possible
through close collaboration between Old Testament and Jewish scholarship
and classical philology. We can therefore only present a limited survey here of
the extent to which the relationships of dependence which are constantly
claimed really exist. More important than tracing possible 'influences' is the
attempt to follow certain lines of development in Jewish thought in its controversy with the spiritual forces of the new time.

1. Supposed Greek Influence on the Late Hebrew Literature of the Old Testament Canon

There has constantly been a desire to discover Greek 'influences' in a whole series of late writings of the Hebrew canon. Thus Theodore of Mopsuestia – who contributed some modern-seeming ideas to the historical understanding of the Old Testament – saw Job as an imitation of Greek tragedy,[6] and in more recent times the work has been supposed to be dependent on Euripides[7] or on Aeschylus' 'Prometheus Bound',[8] and even to show some links with the dialogues of Plato.[9] But these hypotheses have rightly met with rejection almost everywhere. The first real imitation of Greek tragedy only came in Alexandria with the Jewish 'tragedian' Ezekiel during the second century BC.[10] In form and theme the book of Job is completely dependent on the ancient East; despite some analogies with themes from Greek tragedy, the contrasts are 'in part of a fundamental nature'.[11] On the other hand, the book of Job shows how, in the thought of the period of the Achaemenides, determined by 'wisdom', intellectual development was preparing to move in the direction of the Hellenistic epoch even without demonstrable Greek influence.[12] In this the most learned book of the Old Testament, we find an express tendency towards the propagation of encyclopedic knowledge, a completely universalist conception of God[13] and, as in the later Koheleth, an individual critical attitude towards the school tradition, stamped as it was by the doctrine of retribution (though not with Koheleth's cool, asseverative scepticism, but presented in passionate form). Its conclusion is neither resignation nor Promethean defiance, nor even a change in God from arbitrariness to righteousness – the speech of God shows God's sovereign right – but the humble submission of Job to God's superior power.[14] This work should not be put too early. It seems best to belong to the fifth or fourth century BC.[15]

A recent Hebrew investigation, following earlier hypotheses, has sought to demonstrate on the basis of a number of parallels, that the author of the Song of Songs was acquainted with the erotic lyrics of the Hellenistic period and especially with the Bucolics of Theocritus.[16] But as F. Dornseiff already recognized, it is more probable that Alexandrian lyric poetry is itself dependent on oriental models, say love poetry from ancient Egypt.[17] This is true still more of the most significant authors of erotic epigrams in the *Anthologia Graeca*, the Palestinian Syrians Meleager and Philodemus of Gadara (see above, pp. 84ff.), who presumably wove popular themes from their homeland into their often very free verse.

M. Friedländer has sought to demonstrate traces of Greek philosophy in the Hebrew wisdom literature, including Job, individual psalms, Prov. 1–9 and Koheleth, but this 'Panhellenism' has generally been rejected with good reason.[18] At best we may say that the Jewish wisdom schools of the pre-Hellenistic period prepared the ground for the penetration and rejection of

Hellenistic civilization after the rule of the Ptolemies by the 'international' and practical-rational character of their teaching:

> If one draws this conclusion, even before the real onslaught of Hellenism on Judaism, the latter had produced in its wisdom teaching an intellectual trend which was related to Greek popular philosophy and at the same time was destined to work against it.

This judgment by Rudolf Kittel at the end of his *History of Israel* is probably an apt expression of the situation.[19] Leaving aside the particular situation of Koheleth (see below, pp. 115ff.), we can nowhere talk of a direct, demonstrable Greek influence on the Hebrew literature that we have before Sirach.

2. The Development of Jewish Literature in the Early Hellenistic Period

Certain *forms of literature* which can be regarded as being typical of the new era can be seen in a number of relatively late writings, some of which belong to apocalyptic literature. But this statement is only true with qualifications. Some of the works are only preserved for us in Greek, though they go back to predominantly Hebrew or Aramaic models. Significantly, these forms of literature emerge both in Palestine and in Alexandria.

First among them is the epistle:[20] e.g. the edict of Nebuchadnezzar (Dan. 3.31–4.34), the *Epistula Jeremiae*, the fictitious festal letter in II Macc. 1.10b–2.18 and the letters of Mordecai and Esther (Esther 9.20–32), together with those of Haman and Artaxerxes in the Greek additions to Esther (after 3.13 and 8.12). The later letters from the Apocalypse of Baruch can also be mentioned.[21] A typical Alexandrian counterpart would be the *Letter of Aristeas*. However, these 'epistles' also imitate Old Testament 'letters'; thus the *Epistula Jeremiae* and the letters of the Baruch group link up to Jeremiah 29, which presumably contains an extended letter of Jeremiah in vv. 1–23 and two further fragments of letters in vv. 24–32.[22] Solomon's correspondence with the kings of Phoenicia and Egypt in the Eupolemus fragment is simply an expansion of the exchange of messages – presumably in the form of letters – between Solomon and Hiram in II Chron. 2.2–15 or I Kings 5.15–23 (see above, pp. 94f.). Thus this new 'genre' at least had some points of contact with the Old Testament.

The narrative romance is another literary form from the Hellenistic period. We meet it in Palestine – where material from the Babylonian Diaspora is used – in Esther, in Tobit and, with strong nationalistic colouring inspired by the Maccabean war of liberation, in Judith. An essential characteristic is the variety of erotic motives.[23] One special case here is the strongly elaborated

Testament of Joseph, which M. Braun has shown to be familiar with the Phaedra legend in the version used in Euripides' *Hippolytus*. Josephus, too, must have known this fictitious version of the Joseph-Potiphar episode and used it (*Antt.* 2, 39–59).[24] The allegorical, novellistic narrative of Joseph and Asenath presumably arose in the Hellenistic Jewish milieu of Alexandria in the first century BC. A further 'romance' from strongly Hellenized Jewish circles in Egypt is the biography of Joseph and Moses by Artapanus, from the second century BC, which still has a striking openness towards syncretistic conceptions and marked aretalogical features.[25] The question is, however, whether the blunt term 'Hellenistic romance' is adequate to give a satisfactory description of the literary character of the works cited, especially as the 'romance' does not just have its origins in Greek literary history, say in history writing, but at least equally goes back to the oriental 'Novelle' which has mostly religious motives. The Greek love romances are all relatively late; the first example of which we have fragments, the romance of Ninus, was composed in the second century BC at the earliest and takes its material from idealized Assyrian history. The romance of the journeys of Iambulus comes from a Syrian or Nabatean of the third century BC.[26] True, the 'Novelle' with erotic themes can already be found in Herodotus, but it clearly points back to Egyptian or Persian sources, or to Asia Minor.[27] If, like Eissfeldt, we describe Esther, Tobit and Judith as 'influenced by Hellenistic romances', we must also do the same for the book of Ruth and the story of Susanna, which are of a related genre, but whose material certainly belongs to the pre-Hellenistic period.[28] Furthermore, the book of Tobit is related to an earlier type of popular wisdom narrative such as we find in the story of the three pages, the romance of Ahikar or in the still earlier Joseph story.[29] Even the book of Esther, as a 'court history' (see above, pp. 29f.), has echoes in this direction.

Even the *aretalogical style of narrative* did not find its way into Alexandrian Jewish literature solely on the basis of Greek or Egyptian models; for the Jews, the description and the praise must have suggested the miracles and the mighty acts of God in history and the present.[30] It is probably hardly a coincidence that the term ἀρεταλογία appears for the first time in the Greek Sirach 36.13,[31] and that the specific conception of the proclamation of the ἀρεταί of God emerges in the Isaiah translation.[32] E. Bickermann points out that the legend of Heliodorus in II Macc. 3 represents a typical aretalogy,[33] and R. Reitzenstein saw in the 'prophetic and missionary story' of the book of Jonah 'the earliest (aretalogy) that we have outside Egypt'.[34] Here he certainly indicates an essential characteristic of this peculiar work, but – against his hypothesis – it should be set towards the end of the Persian period rather than at the beginning of the Hellenistic era.[35] Moreover, it is not the only narrative of this kind; the miracle stories in Dan. 2–6 and above all the Prayer of Nabonidus from Cave 4 at Qumran have an 'aretalogical' character. But as the latter originates in the eastern Diaspora during Persian rule, one cannot speak of the 'aretalogy' without qualification as a 'Hellenistic' genre. The roots of such narratives go far back into the pre-exilic period; one need only think of the Elisha-Naaman narrative in II Kings 5 or of the healing of Hezekiah by Isaiah in II Kings 20.1–11 (= Isa. 38). Even the universal feature of the recognition of the supreme God by the foreign ruler is prefigured in II Kings 5.15–19.[36] The predilection for the romance-like and aretalogical narrative in the Hellenistic period is thus more an expression of oriental influence on the spiritual-religious life of the Greeks than the reverse: 'Something seems to have reawakened among Greeks which facilitates an understanding of oriental religion.'[37]

Furthermore, the fact should not be overlooked that these 'new' literary forms were predominantly used, at least after the Maccabean revolt, for the production of polemic, anti-Hellenistic, tendentious literature. Examples of this are the book of Judith, the additions to Esther and Daniel (see above, pp. 101f.) and – in a completely Hellenistic form – II Maccabees (see above, pp. 95ff.). One might also mention here the *apocalypses* and the testament literature, which on the one hand sought to continue the heritage of the prophets and at the same time had a large number of parallels in the predictive literature of the Hellenistic period.[38]

A typical literary phenomenon of the Hellenistic era which has abundant Greek parallels is the *pseudepigraphon*, which, however, is also not completely absent in the ancient Orient – as e.g. the usually pseudepigraphic royal instructions show.[39] Its accumulation in the Hellenistic period shows that for Jews and Greeks this epoch was a 'post-classical' late period. A work which sought recognition had in Jewish Palestine to relate in aretalogical fashion the great deeds of God and his servants or to take the name and the authority of a spiritually gifted man from earlier times. It was best when the two elements were combined, in which case canonization was still possible, as with the book of Daniel, despite its late origin. The third possibility, which emerged for the first time in Palestine with Ben Sira and Eupolemus (see above, pp. 78f., 92), was to name the author openly: this was above all the rule in Greek-speaking Judaism, whereas in the mother country pseudepigraphical anonymity predominated through its link with the sacred tradition.[40]

Much more significant than the influence of 'Hellenistic' literary forms, which cannot be demonstrated unequivocally in works which were originally written in Hebrew or Aramaic, is the tendency of Jewish literature in the Persian and early-Hellenistic period towards *development*. Here the most significant phenomenon is its *astonishing richness and pluriformity*. Its extent was probably much greater than is suggested by the fragments which we have. This is indicated not least by the large number of fragments of unknown apocrypha from the library of Qumran, which are surely not all the literary products of the Essenes.[41] In addition to the 'official' literature consisting of the Torah of Moses (which was given its final form at the latest in the fourth century BC, before Alexander the Great, since it was taken over by the Samaritans before the final sealing of the schism by the building of the temple on Gerizim),[42] the 'books on the kings, the prophets and David', which according to II Macc.2.13 Nehemiah is said to have had collected in a 'library' in Jerusalem,[43] we find works with explicitly popular traits like Ruth, Esther, Susanna and the Song of Songs, or wisdom works like Proverbs and the book of Ahikar, on which in turn Tobit was dependent and which was therefore probably known in Palestine. We may also presuppose an intellectual and literary exchange with the non-Jewish environment and the Diaspora in Babylon and Egypt. In works like Job and Koheleth a critical reflection could break through the traditional religious view, and in Jonah and the narratives of Daniel – in its original form including the Prayer of Nabonidus – a universalist tendency. Historical works like that of the Chronicler and midrashic works after the fashion of the Genesis Apocryphon and the Book of Jubilees could be reckoned in this many-sided literary production, though the latter are substantially later in their present form (see above, p.99). Finally, collections of liturgical and wisdom hymns should be mentioned, like the Psalm Scroll from Cave 11Q[44] and the special collections from prophetic and apocalyptic circles (see below, pp.176f.). It is astonishing what creative forces were developed in the small and relatively remote Jewish temple state measuring barely more than twenty-four miles across, during the Persian and early Hellenistic period. Morton Smith speaks of 'belles lettres' and sees there 'indications of an educated laity which was in contact with the culture of its environment' and changed its 'literary production with international fashion'.[45] However, there should not be any stress here either on the distinction between priests and laity or on that between sacred and profane literature, especially as there were no fundamentally 'profane' works, and the 'sacral', i.e. priestly-levitical literature, like the Priestly codex and the work of the Chronicler, had an expressly systematic, chronological, i.e. 'rational and scientific' interest.[46] Whether individual works were written before or after Alexander's expeditions is also of secondary importance, as obviously 'Greek' influences are hardly directly demonstrable before Koheleth; rather, we find rational, critical, speculative and universalist tendencies which prepared the ground for the encounter with Hellenistic civilization. In all probability, groups of the priesthood, the Levitical writing schools (see above, pp.78f.) and the lay nobility shared in producing this rich writing. From this perspective we can also understand why from the beginning the Hellenistic rulers made use of the gifted and alert Jews as mercenaries and officials and why the first verdicts of Greek writers on the Jews are completely positive.[47] From the middle of the third century BC – the time of the activity of Zeno in Palestine and first hinted at in Koheleth – a certain division then began gradually to set in. In Palestine, too, an active, aristocratic minority became open to the critical and universalist spirit of early Hellenism, whereas conservative circles, in deliberate antithesis, opposed it by referring to the national tradition, with the help of certain arguments taken from the thought of the new period. The earliest witnesses to this development are the anonymous Samaritan and Ben Sira. But despite the difference in situation, there is no break between the latter and the pre-Hellenistic period; indeed, he regards himself as the legitimate defender of the theological and historical heritage of his people. The striking thing about Jewish literature of the Persian and early Hellenistic period down to the beginning of the second century BC is its *continuity*. That in the period between about 250 BC and the Maccabean revolt a '*liberal trend*' also developed in Jewish Palestinian literature is not improbable, but can only be demonstrated from hints. Beginnings in this direction were already present in the pre-Hellenistic period; further indications might be the critical observation of the second, 'orthodox' redactor in Koh. 12.12: 'Of the making of many books there is no end, and much learning wearies the flesh', or the threat in I Enoch 98.15: 'Woe to you who write down lying and godless words (λόγους πλανήσεως); for they write down their lies that men may hear them and act godlessly towards (their) neighbour' (see above, n. II, 236).

Even the *transition into the Greek-speaking milieu* did not necessarily have to lead to discontinuity. The striking thing in the Septuagint – leaving aside the translations of Proverbs and Job (see below, pp. 162ff.) – was that fundamentally the translators were very little influenced by the Greek spirit. Anyone who was interested in the holy scriptures was no advocate of assimilation.[48] The speculation about hypostatized wisdom which first arose in Palestine was developed further in Alexandria, and from the beginning could display there an affinity to parallel Greek conceptions.

The *crisis under Antiochus IV* first brought a *break in the development* and was followed by the freedom fight which favoured a radicalization of Jewish piety in a way that is not evident before. From the end of the second century BC this process also embraced the Diaspora and grew stronger under Roman rule down to the catastrophe. 'Zeal' became an essential feature of Jewish piety.[49] However, this did not necessarily mean an exclusion of alien influences; on the contrary, Palestinian Jewish apocalyptic from the time of Daniel, which played its part in this radicalization, was no less open to 'syncretistic' tendencies than say wisdom, which is in many ways so different, or the work of Philo. The conservative opposition of the Sadducees, especially in the early period, shows that people were at least partially aware of this fact even in Palestine.[50] Even Pharisaism is based on an unhistorical, 'onto-logical' conception of the law, which was alien to the Old Testament itself (see below, pp. 171ff.), and Old Testament history writing finds its continuation not in the casuistic legal collections of the Mishnah, Tosefta or the Talmuds, nor even in the Rabbinic *midrashim* with their unhistorical thought, but – albeit in the alien garb of Hellenism – in the work of the Palestinian priestly aristocrat and Hellenistic Jew, Josephus. We must now investigate in more detail this development in Jewish thought from the middle of the third century BC.

3. Koheleth and the Beginning of the Crisis in Jewish Religion

Influence from the Greek world of ideas is seen in Koheleth more than in any other Old Testament work. Above all in the earlier period, when the rich comparative material of Egyptian and Babylonian wisdom literature had not yet been discovered and so the special structure of Israelite wisdom had not rightly been recognized, new relations between Koheleth and Hellas were constantly found, despite individual warning voices. 'Koheleth and Greek philosophy' was a standard chapter in the introductions of commentaries.[51] He was seen as a pupil of Epicurus, the Stoa or the hedonists of Cyrene; others supposed the influences of Heraclitus or an immediate dependence on the Greek gnomic thought of a Hesiod or a Theognis. Furthermore, the peculiar form of the work suggested an affinity with the Stoic-Cynic diatribe.[52] However, in the long run all these attempts at derivation could not prove convincing, and it transpired that the decisive parallels were to be sought less in Greece than in the Old Testament itself, in Egypt and in Babylonia.[53] Nor did the examination of alleged Graecisms produce a very satisfactory result; there are some echoes, but nothing that can be regarded with certainty.[54] For this reason, it would seem natural to follow O. Loretz in strictly rejecting any contact with the Graeco-Hellenistic world.[55] But it seems evident that Loretz, who himself wants to exclude Egyptian influences and will only accept Semitic and cuneiform parallels, proceeds with too much violence. This is true primarily of a decisive point, the *question of date*, which he leaves completely uncertain. True, as E. Meyer and K. Galling stressed, one cannot read any direct allusions to individual historical events from Koheleth,[56] but the language, with its strong Aramaic colouring which already paves the way for the Hebrew of the Mishnah,[57] and the whole milieu of the book, suggest a very late date of composition. Thus the work presupposes a long period of peace, in which a man can gather riches and enjoy life; this was hardly possible in Palestine between 350 and 300 BC (see above, pp. 13f.). Furthermore, the indications of a strict, indeed harsh administration, which joined the rich in oppressing the poor, and of an omnipresent power of the king, fit best in the Ptolemaic period.[58] Finally, the manifold references to Egypt, like the form of the work as a royal testament, and the different contacts with the approximately contemporaneous wisdom teaching of the Insiger papyrus, are best explained from this epoch.[59] The *terminus ad quem* is Ben Sira, about 180 BC; he knew the book, and in Cave IV at Qumran fragments of Koheleth have been found which came from a scroll written about the middle of the second century BC.[60] In both cases the work was certainly already in a corrected

form and therefore acceptable to strictly orthodox circles; its origin must
therefore lie at least some decades earlier. This brings us to the period between
270 and 220 BC, when according to the Zeno papyri considerable political and
economic activity was developing in Palestine which could not in the end fail
to make its mark in the intellectual sphere. Thus the majority of scholars, even
if they have rightly rejected a direct dependence of Koheleth on Greek
philosophy and literature, have conceded 'that in ideas and mood the work has
contacts with the spirit of Hellenism'.[61] As a man of his time, the author,
who in his youth was certainly vigorous and ambitious, could hardly close his
mind to the spiritual climate of the age, which brought so many new and
stimulating impressions with it. However, the problem that interests us –
Koheleth and early Hellenism – cannot simply be solved by an enumeration of
parallels. First, the examples adduced from the ancient world are much too
disparate, and, leaving aside the philosophical school altogether, reach from
archaic and aristocratic poets like Hesiod, Theognis and Simonides to such a
late and solitary thinker as Marcus Aurelius;[62] secondly, because of the
'international' spread of wisdom and its universal human themes, the indication of parallels says nothing about their origins. Rather, leaving aside any
hypothetical literary 'dependencies', it could be illuminating to set the thinking
of Koheleth beside the spirit and the atmosphere of early Hellenism by means
of some examples from the New Comedy and Greek epitaphs. However, the
starting point here is an account of the structure of and problems included in
the thought of Koheleth himself, which is critical in the deepest sense.

The first striking thing about him is that in his work we encounter a
wisdom teaching which goes beyond the anonymous matter-of-factness of
earlier wisdom and its unbroken optimism, and find in it the personally
engaged, *critical individuality* of an acute observer and independent thinker.
Thus he may light upon really new insights: 'Within the Old Testament or
Old Testament "wisdom", Koheleth is the first, if I see it rightly, to have
discovered and treated thematically the historicity of existence – *in tormentis.*'[63]
However, as he had a masterly understanding of how to fuse together the
received wisdom tradition and his personal critical analysis of experience, it is
difficult to separate the two and work out any 'biographical' features.[64] On
the other hand, in his writings the foreground is not occupied by the manifold
traditional motives; rather, he transforms them in his extremely individualist
criticism by shattering the traditional world-view of earlier wisdom, denying a
fixed connection between action and result, and proclaiming the absolute
inexplicability of the divine action in nature and history.

Even if we have no more external data about his person than the fact that
as a wisdom teacher he belonged to the well-to-do aristocratic upper class in
Judea and compiled his work in old age as a kind of personal confession,[65]
one can still speak of a marked '*individuality*' of authorship. It is an individuality which emerges with him for the first time among the wisdom

teachers of the Old Testament, and later also appears in a kindred form in Jesus Sirach and is typical for the time of Hellenism. 'Now the individual gains the freedom to live as himself,' for 'the feeling of the unity of the individual with environment and world has given way to the awareness of opposition, independence and self hood.'[66] Significantly, from the middle of the third century we can see an emergence of individual personalities from the tradition of peoples and families, even in Judea.[67] As far as the person of Koheleth is concerned, the most significant thing here is his cool detachment, in which any sense of responsibility for the community of his people is lacking, and which, while noticing injustices in the social sphere, develops no initiative towards setting them right. This distinguishes him on the one hand from the prophets, and on the other from a figure like Marcus Aurelius, with whom he has much in common, especially his fundamentally pessimistic attitude.[68]

The inevitable counterpart to this is *universalism*.[69] True, 'wisdom' had universal features right from the beginning, so that we find no reference to the history of Israel even in Job and Proverbs; only in Sirach are wisdom and the Israelite historical tradition bound together under the impact of the threat of Hellenistic alienation (see below, pp. 136f.) However, Koheleth 'denationalizes' even the concept of God. He avoids – surely deliberately – the divine name Yahweh and instead uses predominantly the expression *hā'elōhîm*; only 8 out of 38 instances are without the article. This consistent terminology is probably meant to express both the universality of his conception of God and its detachment from men.[70] The traditional formula 'under the sun', which had early (probably wrongly) been presumed to be a Graecism[71] and which he uses 27 times, indicates the universality and normativeness of his observations. The terms 'man' and 'children of men' also simply mean men in an all-embracing sense.[72] If practically all references to the history of God with Israel and to the law are lacking in Koheleth, we nevertheless find in him a series of references to the first chapters of Genesis, where, in contrast to Sirach, above all the dark and inexplicable side of God's created world is seen.[73] Gerhard von Rad therefore charges Koheleth with thinking in a 'completely unhistorical' way, though this depends on the way one interprets the term 'history'. One could also say that Koheleth reflects particularly impressively on 'historical' existence (see above, n. 63) in time; it is just that in doing this he excludes a 'salvation-historical' approach.[74]

According to R. Kroeber, this universalist view of God, man and the world corresponds to a new kind of 'knowledge from observation alone, conceivable only in the intellectual atmosphere of Hellenism, philosophic in conception, but quite deliberately practical in realization, along the lines of wisdom teaching, primarily concerned not with knowledge but with a mastery and fulfilment of life'.[75] J. Hempel had already come to a similar conclusion, seeing 'a "Greek" root' in the 'logically consistent thought' of Koheleth, 'quite unoriental in its consistency and power of abstraction'.[76] However, we should not lay excessive emphasis on the contrast between 'Greek' and 'oriental' which is made here and suppose any dependence on the part of Koheleth. The intellectual revolution with which the third century began made more room for new, independent beginnings of thought, though movement in this direction had already begun in the Persian period (see above, pp. 110ff.). Nevertheless, the *critical point of application of his thought* remains the Old Testament.

> What gain (*māh-yitᵉrōn*) does a man have from all his toil at which he toils under the sun? (1.3)

Behind this question of 'gain' – the word appears in the Old Testament only in Koheleth – which keeps being put afresh,[77] is the basic question of the meaning of life. It forms the basic problem of his penetrating urge for knowledge:

> And I applied my mind
> to seek (*lidᵉrōš*) and to search out (*lātūr*) all that is done under heaven (*v.l.* the sun)
> – it is an unhappy business that God has given to the sons of men to be busy with. (1.13)
> I turned my mind to know and to search out (*wᵉlātūr*) and to seek wisdom and the sum of things (*ḥešbōn*), to know the wickedness of folly and the foolishness which is madness.[78]

J. Pedersen wants to see in the *tūr*, which the LXX translates κατασκέψασθαι, an investigation (guetter), 'comme σκέπτεσθαι en sens philosophique'.[79] Even if one must be careful in using the term 'philosophic' – it might be better to speak of a pre-philosophical transitionary stage in his thought[80] – one might say that his striving for knowledge takes new courses. As the last clause of 1.13 shows, in his search for 'wisdom' he quickly comes up against impassable boundaries:

> All this I have tested by wisdom;
> I thought, 'I will be wise';
> but it was far from me.
> That which is, is far off, and deep, very deep;
> who can find it out?[81]

A really valid and permanent 'gain' cannot be found by means of the search for wisdom. Human observation and reflection can at best achieve certain provisional rules of life and counsels. This means that the realm of validity for traditional wisdom is extremely limited. The decisive power in life which ultimately determines everything that happens, the work of God, remains completely impenetrable and therefore cannot be influenced. This is the case not only, as earlier wisdom knew,[82] in natural events, but also in God's conduct towards men. The innocent are oppressed and exploited, and there is no-one to 'comfort' or to take vengeance.

There is a righteous man who perishes in his righteousness,
and there is a wicked man who prolongs his life in his evil-doing.[83]

There is an irresolvable discrepancy between God's universal activity and human demands for righteousness. In contrast to traditional wisdom, for Koheleth the destiny which God has conceived for everyman, be he righteous or wicked, is absolutely inexplicable.[84] In this sense, above all in comparison with earlier optimistic wisdom, one could speak of a scepticism of Koheleth, though this merely doubts human possibilities, and not the reality of God.[85]

This scepticism intensifies to become fatalism, in that Koheleth reflects on the end of human life: neither wisdom nor righteousness, possessions nor descendants, indeed not even reputation can stand before the inexorable *destiny of death*. Although in the traditional view wisdom and folly are as different as light and darkness, the wise man must die like the fool and will eventually be forgotten.[86] Man is no better than the animals (3.19ff.). The sharpness with which Koheleth puts the question of the meaning of human life in the face of the threat of death is unique in the Old Testament; it leads inexorably to the conclusion which stands at the beginning and the end of the work as its key theme: 'Vanity, vanity, all is vanity'.[87] To express man's fate, death, he seven times uses the word *miqre*, which appears only three times elsewhere in the Old Testament with the meaning 'chance', none of them in the wisdom literature.[88] We may therefore reckon that, like *yiterōn*, it is one of those predominantly abstract key terms which Koheleth uses to express certain ideas that are peculiar to him, concepts which are mostly rare elsewhere in the Old Testament and sometimes do not appear again at all. Even if they should come from the Hebrew and Aramaic current in his time, about which on the whole we know very little, they are still an expression of his independent thought which attempted to describe human existence in the world and before God in new concepts, in controversy with traditional wisdom on the one hand and the Hellenistic spirit of the time on the other.[89] Scholars have also attempted to see the word *miqre* as a Graecism and have connected it with $\tau\acute{u}\chi\eta$. Even if such an over-hasty identification has rightly been rejected,[90] we should not overlook the fact that concepts like 'chance' or 'fate' are fundamentally alien to the Old Testament world of ideas; for *miqre* no longer means any particular 'chance', as in the few other passages in the Old Testament, but the fixed unalterable 'destiny of death' which hangs over every man and meets him at the appointed time without reference to his conduct. This is the new element in Koheleth.[91] Alongside he also uses *pega'*, which occurs only once elsewhere in the Old Testament, in the sense of 'chance' and in close connection with 'time' (*'ēt* = LXX $\kappa\alpha\iota\rho\acute{o}\varsigma$):

Again I saw that under the sun
the race is not to the swift,
nor the battle to the strong,

nor bread to the wise,
nor riches to the intelligent,
nor favour to the men of skill,
but time (*'ēt*) and chance (*pegaʿ*) happen (*yiqre*) to them all.
For man does not know his time.
Like fish which are taken in an evil net,
and like birds which are caught in a snare,
so the sons of men are snared at an evil time,
when it suddenly falls upon them.[92]

In the didactic poem 3.1–15, which is of decisive significance for Koheleth,[93] he meditates on the problem of time. To every happening that God brings about he gave a fixed *kairos* (3.1–8), and in the light of its particular *kairos*, all that happens is good (3.11), for all *kairoi* are included in the unalterable *course of God's time*.[94] The difficulty is that the course of God's time (*ʿōlām*) remains completely concealed from man, and so for him God's works are inscrutable:[95]

I know that whatever God does endures for the course of time (*hū' yihye leʿōlām*).
Nothing can be added to it nor anything taken from it;
God has made it so, in order that men should fear before him. (3.14)

Thus for man the whole world becomes an insoluble riddle, and nature and history appear to him as an apparently meaningless circle.[96] Not even love and hate are in man's own hands (9.1). In the last resort, for Koheleth, man no longer has free will. Everything has been laid down by God. The apex of senselessness is the incalculable destiny of death, which affects all men in the same arbitrary way and thus brings all the speculations of earlier wisdom about a just retribution to nothing.[97] On the other hand, the absence of just punishment becomes one of the main reasons for human evil: 'This is an evil in all that is done under the sun, that one fate comes to all; also the hearts of men are full of evil...'[98] Nevertheless, Koheleth sharply wards off any accusation against God such as those made by, say, Job; rebellion would be senseless, for man should not imagine that he can be God's partner in conversation. Towards God's omnipotence there can be only submission:[99]

Whatever has come to be has already been named,
and it is known what man is,
and that he is not able to dispute with one stronger than he.
The more words, the more vanity. (6.10f.)

Similarly, Koheleth does not reject the cult and practices of piety, but considers them with considerable reservation:

For God is in heaven and you upon earth;
therefore let your words be few.[100]

God is far removed from men and is in danger of becoming an impersonal power of destiny. K. Galling points out that 'the "course of time" which God allots to his plan . . . takes on an almost personal character', 'an independence which can be compared with extra-biblical aeon-conceptions'. There is hardly any more room left for prayer, which in the Old Testament forms a bridge to the 'near God'.[101] In addition, God 'loses his moral nature and thus his position as preserver of what exists, as the source of righteousness and the power of life'.[102] Consistently ethical conduct cannot therefore be commended: 'Be not righteous overmuch and do not make yourself over-wise; why should you destroy yourself?' (7.16). All that is left for man, therefore, is a 'resigned' attitude of *'fear of God'*[103] in face of the incomprehensible rule of the divine plan which constantly threatens his life, and contentment with the portion (*ḥēleq*) appointed to him by God. This last is a new conception of Koheleth's, the positive counterpart to the 'destiny of death' (*miqre*).[104] In so far as God gives man his 'portion' in the good things of this world as a gift, man is to use his *'kairos'*, enjoy it and forget tormenting afterthoughts.[105] At one point here a personal feature emerges in the strict picture of the distant God: ' "God is pleased" (*rāṣā*) at the acceptance of this gift.'[106] But even this positive prospect is qualified on two sides. It applies only to what is preferred by God in a fundamentally arbitrary way (2.25f.; 5.18). Those who for unfathomable reasons are put by God on the shadowy side of life have no share in this joy; for them it would be better to be dead or never to have been born,[107] and the 'evil day' of need, sickness and old age which suddenly dawns can bring an end to joy at any time. Only the destiny of death is certain and unavoidable, bringing to an end all joy and toil.[108] 'He receives nothing for his toil.'[109]

In 1925, E. Meyer entitled his chapter about Koheleth 'The Enlightenment' and defined this more closely as 'the Enlightenment stemming from Hellenistic culture'.[110] Twenty-six years later, however, K. Galling entitled his rectoral address on Koheleth *The Crisis of the Enlightenment in Israel*: Koheleth is in sharp critical dispute with the 'theistic enlightenment' of traditional wisdom.[111] But how did this crisis come about? R. H. Pfeiffer does not believe that the ancient oriental background is sufficient to explain it: 'Neither the influence of Egyptian nor Babylonian wisdom would have led Ecclesiastes to criticize orthodox Judaism.'[112] We should ask, rather, whether this 'crisis' was not furthered by the spirit of the time and the new feeling about life in early Hellenism. K. Galling has already pointed out an essential starting point for this critical attitude of Koheleth's: 'It was preceded by a breach with ancestral belief, a breach with the doctrine of retribution.'[113] This breach with faith in the efficacy of the divine righteousness in reward and punishment had already been introduced into Greece a considerable time earlier. The rhetor Thrasymachus took a very critical attitude as early as the end of the fifth century BC: 'The gods do not care about human things, for they overlook the highest good among men, justice. We, on the other hand, see that men make no use of it.'[114] That this was not the opinion of an outsider is shown by his great contemporary Euripides' criticism of traditional belief in the gods, charging the gods with not being in a position to care for righteousness on the earth.[115] Here the criticism goes one stage further, to the conclusion: 'If the gods do shameful things, they are not gods.' Alongside this, however, he can also stress the working of divine righteousness in a conservative way. Through him religious doubt makes its way into wide circles of the people. Over one hundred years later we find similar contradictory expressions in the New Comedy of Menander, which now really reproduces the opinion of the people.[116] Alongside the affirmation of the providence of the gods there are quite opposite accents:

> The gods (help) the bad, but we (although we are good)
> bring nothing good to pass . . .
> No one who is just gets rich quickly.[117]

Here, too, doubt heightens to the point where the question is asked whether the gods can care for men at all.[118] But Menander also makes room for the other possibility, that God alone is responsible for good fortune and misfortune, and that the human character cannot be held responsible for mistakes $(\tau\grave{o}$ $\delta'\dot{a}\tau\upsilon\chi\epsilon\hat{\iota}\nu$ $\mathring{\eta}$ $\tau\grave{o}$ $\mu\grave{\eta}$ $\theta\epsilon\grave{o}s$ $\delta\acute{\iota}\delta\omega\sigma\iota\nu,$ $o\mathring{\upsilon}$ $\tau\rho\acute{o}\pi o\upsilon$ $\delta'\acute{\epsilon}\sigma\theta'\acute{a}\mu\alpha\rho\tau\acute{\iota}\alpha)$; nothing is left for men but to accept the good gifts of the gods $(\tau\hat{\omega}\nu$ $\theta\epsilon\hat{\omega}\nu$ $\tau\grave{o}$ $\sigma\acute{\upsilon}\mu\phi\rho o\nu).$[119] The old view, that Zeus records the actions of men, is mocked by remarks to the effect that Zeus looked at his account books too late or confused the tablets, so that he assigned the punishments inappropriately.[120] Cercidas of Megalopolis in Arcadia, a contemporary of Koheleth (c. 290–220 BC), a politician and poet influenced by Cynic philosophy, put the question of the justice of the gods with biting sharpness:

> What should prevent . . . if anyone should want to ask the question, it is easy for the Godhead $(\theta\epsilon\acute{o}s)$ to bring about anything whenever it comes to mind . . . if one should be the ruin of money, pouring out what he has, or a dross-stain begrimed usurer, ready to perish for gold, that God should drain him of his swine-befouled wealth and give to one feeding frugally? Is the eye of justice $(\delta\acute{\iota}\kappa\eta)$ then as blind as a mole? . . . Does a mist dim the eye of Themis the bright? How can they be held for gods who can neither hear nor see? They say that even the lofty Zeus, the gatherer of lightning, holds the scales in balance and does not incline them. These scales, says Homer, sink when the day of destiny arrives, in favour of mightier men. Why does the balance never incline to my advantage, if it is just? But the Brygians (Macedonians), farthest (of mortals) – clearer words I dare not say – how far they pull down the scales in their favour! To what places or sons of heaven may one then turn to discover how a man may obtain his due portion $(\pi\hat{\omega}s$ $\lambda\acute{a}\beta\eta$ $\tau\grave{a}\nu$ $\grave{a}$ $\xi\acute{\iota}\alpha\nu)$, when the offspring of Kronos, our parent who begat us all, shows himself to be stepfather to one and real father to another? As long as the spirit blows a favourable wind,

honour (Nemesis), you men, whose life is easy. For when the wind turns about and blows in the opposite direction, you will have to spew out your riches and all these gifts of fortune (τύχας) to the last morsel.[121]

Cercidas, who was fundamentally an aristocratic-conservative person – he had a particular reverence for Homer – though very critical of his time, shared with Koheleth a similar social background: the economic activity of the Ptolemaic period brought about increasing prosperity, which, however, was predominantly to the advantage of the upper classes.[122] Both also share an obviously critical attitude towards the naive optimism of traditional religious views, though this went further in the greater emancipation of Greece, and both invite men to a modest enjoyment of life.

We also come across the theme that death comes to both pious and wicked alike, without justification, and the invitation to 'carpe diem' as an expression of the inner thoughts of a wider stratum of the people in Greek epitaphs from the third century BC:

But Hades carries men off without seeing whether they are good or virtuous.[123]
(ἀλλὰ κομίζει Ἀιδης οὐ κακίην οὐδ'ἀρετὴν ἐτάσας)
But if living in the fear of the gods brought its just deserts (εἰ δ'ἦν εὐσεβέων ὅσιος λόγος) my house would never have been visited with such fortune (τύχαις) by my departure.[124]
Truly, the gods take no account of mortals (θεοῖς οὐκ ἔστι βροτῶν λόγος); no, like animals we are pulled hither and thither by chance (αὐτομάτῳ), in life as in death.[125]
The good die before their time, but you always turn suffering away from the wicked.[126]
Rich and poor, wise and foolish, are equal in death: 'For down there in Hades is Thersites, and honoured by none less than Minos himself.'[127]

One consequence is a desperate accusation against the gods: this is expressed openly on the epitaph of Ptolemaic officers in Gaza about 200 BC, which has already been mentioned on several occasions (see above, pp. 15f.):

. . . all that is left for mortal men is to reproach the gods (μέμψασθαι δὲ θεοῖς ἀρκεῖ μόνον ἄνδρα γε θνητόν).[128]

The other possibility is to accept the age-old 'carpe diem', which we have already met in the conversation of Gilgamesh with the harlot and in the Egyptian Song of the Harper,[129] though it also occurs particularly frequently as a popular theme in the Greek tradition:

Remembering that the same end awaits all mortals, enjoy life as long as you live.
This teaching I give, Euodus, to all mortals: do not grudge yourself any good thing. Why do you struggle? Enjoy yourself and so delight in life. For know this well: once you have descended to the drink of Lethe, you will see

no more of those things that are above, once the soul has flown out of this body.[130]

Even if these last examples are relatively late, they go back to an earlier theme that is widespread in the Hellenistic period and which we also find in a Demotic epitaph from the late Ptolemaic period,[131] in Menander, Philetairos, Euripides, Theognis and others.[132]

Significantly, this theme appears on what may well be the earliest known Greek inscription in Jerusalem, the graffito from the tomb of Jason dating from the time of Alexander Jannaeus, which P. Benoit and B. Lifshitz, who supplements it, read in the following way:

εὐφραίνεσθε οἱ ζῶντες

[τ]ὸ δὲ (λοι)πὸ[ν . . .] πεῖν ὅμα φα[γεῖν]

We should probably see Jason as a member of the Sadducean aristocracy. The motto of Koheleth seems to have had further influence in these circles.[133]

In attacking the view that the 'spirit of man goes upwards' (3.21), Koheleth takes up a view which had probably penetrated into Judaism from the Hellenistic world and had made room there for the first beginnings of a hope for eternal life (see below, pp. 196ff.). Both in Euripides and in Greek epitaphs there often appears the conception that after death the human soul mounts to its heavenly dwelling place, the *aether*, the seat of the gods.[134] It was easier for this view to be accepted because of earlier Old Testament ideas that the impersonal breath of life breathed into men by God could be taken back again by him.[135]

However, in the consistency of his criticism of traditional conceptions, Koheleth does not go by any means so far as the popular Greek criticism of the gods, although even there it must be noted that critical comments sometimes appear in the same author side by side with others which take up the traditional piety.[136] So Menander admonishes:

Do not fight against God (μὴ θεομάχει, cf. fr. 673 ζυγομαχεῖν), do not add new misfortune to the matter, bear with what is necessary (fr. 187).

Here one is reminded of the warning in Koh. 6.10 against quarrelling with God in the same way as Job and also of his admonition to observe the golden mean in religious questions:

Be not wicked overmuch neither be a fool; why should you die before your time?[137]

The main difference, however, remains that Koheleth could maintain the reality and omnipresence of God, whereas the polytheistic Greek pantheon had been fundamentally destroyed by criticism, and a very general, impersonal conception of God was maintained only with difficulty. This is already true for the terminology in Euripides and still more for a later period. Even if the old gods had grown pale, people could not renounce the belief 'that a higher power, a guide stood behind the events which befall man . . . People spoke of an unknown god, of the collective of the gods, the abstract θεός τις, θεοί, τὸ θεῖον, τὸ δαιμόνιον. This concept lacked life and credibility and in the end did not mean much more than the course of events.'[138] At an early stage this shadowy conception of God was bound up with the conception of fate, which played a tremendous role among the Greeks even from the time of Homer[139] and for which – unlike the Hebrews – they had an abundance of different expressions.[140] If in early days people still spoke of the 'fate assigned by the gods' (Διὸς αἶσα; μοῖρα θεῶν; δαίμονος αἶσα), the concept later became free from any 'intervention of a higher power' and meant only the 'irrational in human life'.[141] In the Hellenistic period the more neutral *tychē* largely forced out *moira*, the earlier term for fate, as the latter was still associated with the earlier conception of the lot that is a man's due.[142] However, *moira* lived on later as the destiny of death and was usually personified: death became 'the *moira* that is common to all men' and the dead man received his 'lot' from it.[143] Thus *tychē* and *moira* were to some extent used in opposite senses, in the same way as *miqre* and *ḥēleq*. Tyche was already the really popular term for fate in Euripides and still more in the New Comedy.[144] Its identification with the terms αὐτόματον or τὰ προσπίπτοντα shows that it often had a fully secularized sense and simply meant the established course of events.[145] The different forms of time appeared alongside it as further terms for fate and, like καιρός and χρόνος, sometimes even as personified, abstract deities; here, too, the New Comedy and above all the epitaphs offer a series of interesting examples.[146] Time in particular could be closely associated with the destiny of death. Even the concept of the 'aeon' was absolutized under the influence of Plato. It appears as the divine, unalterable, 'total world order' in an Eleusinian inscription of the Augustinian period.[147]

The crisis of Greek religion, briefly sketched out here, which was expressed in the evacuation of the old conceptions of the gods and the replacement of them by the non-committal concepts of fate, and which reached its climax about the third century BC – from that point onwards a religious retrenchment sets in, not least under the influence of oriental religions (see below, pp. 217ff.) – presumably did not fail to make a mark on the thought of Koheleth. At the same time, as is indicated for example by the Insinger papyrus with its constantly recurring stereotyped closing formula, 'Fate and fortune are determined by God', Egyptian wisdom was also occupied with the question of fate,[148] though without achieving the depths reached by Koheleth. Acquaintance with Greek criticism of religion and Greek or Egyptian belief in fate was presumably communicated by Ptolemaic officials, merchants and soldiers, who were not lacking even in Jerusalem (see above, pp. 15f.). *In this way Koheleth encountered not the school opinions of the philosophers, but the popular views of the Greek 'bourgeoisie'.* In a completely individualistic way he fused stimuli from this direction with traditional 'wisdom' and his own observations.

In what follows, we shall attempt to sum up the points in Koheleth's thought in which contacts with the spirit of early Hellenism might be visible:

1. The individuality of his personality breaks through the previous impersonal anonymity of the wisdom tradition despite the use of traditional forms; at the same time, his thought is free from all nationalist limitations and is directed towards the basic questions of human existence.

2. Its unprejudiced, detached observation and its strictly rational, logical thought lead to a radical criticism of the doctrine of retribution in traditional wisdom and thus indirectly attack a cornerstone of Jewish piety. The category of 'righteousness' can no longer be applied to God. Where Koheleth uses it, it has a negative aspect; there is no righteousness on earth, nor does it find the reward that is its due.[149]

3. As a result of this, his conception of God loses its immediate personal relationship to man and threatens to become ossified, for God's action not only is completely incomprehensible to man but every happening is determined by God's 'course of time' ('*ōlām*, 3.14); even love and hate are in his hand (9.1), prayer seems less meaningful, and piety and ethics become a matter of astuteness (5.1ff.; 7.16f.). God is removed far away from man, and in the face of his incomprehensible power Koheleth can only require the fear of God (see above, p. 121, n. 103), though a real relationship of trust between God and man is hardly possible any longer. There is no longer any room either for God's wrath or for his mercy, nor are there any reflections on his commandments, on guilt and forgiveness. Only one more step, and Koheleth's *deus absconditus* becomes impersonal fate.[150]

4. Terms for destiny insinuate themselves between God and man. 'For him the reality of God fades away to become "fate".'[151] The inescapable destiny of death (*miqre*) forms the central point of his thought; its positive counterpart is the 'portion' (*ḥēleq*) of the enjoyment of life assigned – in a fundamentally arbitrary way – by God; however, all is dependent on 'time and chance' ('*ēt wāpega'*, 9.11) and the 'course of time' that stands over against them. Granted, Koheleth avoids a hypostatization of these concepts, but this action happens according to a strict regularity which only God can see (11.5).

5. In the face of God's ordering of time and fate, for man there remains only resignation and a careful *via media* in the practical matters of life. Only the possibility of '*carpe diem*' – here Koheleth takes up a topic that is widely current –, the enjoyment of the portion assigned by God, can give meaning, albeit very limited, to life. In the end this, too, is an attempt at forgetting (5.19), a 'flight before the anguish of death'.[152]

6. In this sense we can rightly speak of a 'questionable bourgeois ideal of education' or a 'bourgeois ethic' in Koheleth.[153] The 'bourgeoisie', i.e. the well-to-do stratum of society who lived off their capital in the form of land or other investments (cf. Koh. 11.1f.), was the really dominant force of the

Hellenistic world, whether Greek or oriental. Rostovtzeff has given a brilliant description of their approach to life, active, yet entirely directed towards security and pleasure, and, despite all its rationalism, basically conservative.[154] In the Ptolemaic monarchy, where the political activity of the 'bourgeoisie' was considerably limited, this activity was predominantly concentrated in the economic sphere. The best example of this is a figure like Zeno, though he himself also had artistic and literary leanings. In the countryside of Palestine this 'bourgeoisie' still had a feudal and aristocratic stamp. The essential feature, however, is that Koheleth at the same time sees through the nihilism of this 'bourgeois' existence, although he himself offers no ethical alternative.

Koheleth stands at the parting of the ways, at the boundary of two times. Under the impact of the spiritual crisis of early Hellenism, his critical thought could no longer make sense of traditional wisdom and, consequently, of traditional piety and the cult. On the other hand, his aristocratic and conservative attitude prevented him from breaking with the religion of his ancestors and identifying God, say, with incalculable fate. For him God is and remains the sovereign law of every happening. He did not even have access to the expedient of newly-developing apocalyptic (see below, pp. 196ff.), which under the influence of Iranian and Greek ideas postulated just recompense after death. So there remained for him only the pessimistic conclusion that human existence with all its toil and its apparent success amounted to nothing. God's unshakable ordinance alone stands fast, though it remains concealed from human understanding.

As is stressed by the writer of the first epilogue (12.9–11), who was probably a personal disciple,[155] Koheleth was a wise man (*ḥākām*) who 'taught the people knowledge'. He mentions the critical weighing (*'izzēn*), studying (*ḥiqqēr*) and arranging (*tiqqēn*) of wisdom sayings (*mešālīm*) by his master, for whom a pleasing form was as important as the truth (*dibᵉrē ḥēpeṣ* and *dibᵉrē 'ᵉmet*). The imagery of the 'ox goad' and the 'firmly fixed nails' may indicate that his teaching had a provocative and deeply penetrating effect. The pupil probably composed this epilogue as a kind of apologia for his teacher, because the latter's work gave rise to fierce controversy soon after his death.[156] As he does not make any theological corrections, but characterizes the work of his master in a matter-of-fact, secular way, he will have shared his master's critical attitude. Presumably Koheleth, who used the weapons of 'wisdom' to fight against traditional wisdom, also founded a school to carry on this critical tradition. The only possible place for these controversies is Jerusalem; suggestions by Dahood and Albright that the work was composed in Northern Palestine or the Phoenician cities are highly improbable.[157] Some linguistic echoes may be explained by the fact that all Palestine was under Phoenician cultural influence after the time of the Persians.[158]

Perhaps a final hypothetical question may be allowed. In what way will the

school of Koheleth have developed ? Surely not in the direction of the writer of
the second epilogue (12.12–14), who in the authoritative tones of the teacher
and at some distance in time from Koheleth warns against the writing of many
books and study, thus probably pointing to a literary productivity and instruction of a heterodox nature, no longer extant, but doubtless thought by him to
be dangerous (see p. 114). His corrective hand is also to be detected in the work
at 11.9c, and presumably also in other places.[159] With his reference in the
closing sentence to the keeping of the *miṣwōt* and to God's judgment, he forms
a bridge to the 'reactionary' wisdom of a Ben Sira, who about 180 BC again
firmly proclaimed the doctrine of retribution in all its massiveness and for the
first time identified 'wisdom' with the law and thus prepared the way for
the end of its universality (see below, pp. 160ff.). The 'orthodox' revision by the
writer of the second epilogue made the work acceptable even to Hasidic circles
who were faithful to the law, so that it could be accepted even into the library
of Qumran and later – albeit with difficulty – be canonized.[160] Certainly the
school which began with Koheleth and was manifested by the writer of the
first epilogue went in another direction. Perhaps a trace of it has been preserved in the writings of the teacher Antigonus of Socho, otherwise unknown,
who flourished about 200 BC and whose chief saying is directed against the idea
of reward (*'Ab.* 1, 3):

> Be not like slaves who serve the master with a view to receiving a reward;
> but be like slaves who serve the master not with a view to receiving a
> reward: and let the fear of heaven be upon you.

That this saying was felt to be offensive at a later date is indicated by the
addition in *'Ab RN* ch. 5: 'that your reward may be twofold in the world to
come'. When Sadduceans and Boethusians were associated with later generations of the pupils of Antigonus, defending the enjoyment of life because they
were without hope for the coming world, historical accuracy may have been
strained, but justification was certainly present.[161] L. Finkelstein suggests
that the school of Koheleth consisted of 'Jewish equivalents of the Athenian
cynics' or 'cynical plebeians'.[162] However, like its master, the school must
rather be sought in the Jerusalem aristocracy, and this finally raises the
question whether under the increasing influence of the Greek spirit, the
criticism of traditional wisdom introduced by Koheleth was not extended
within it to become a criticism of Jewish religion in general. According to the
little that we know of the Hellenistic reform party after 175 BC, it expressed
a sharp criticism of the temple cult and the ritual law, and had such a pale and
universalistic conception of God that it could accept an identification of this
God with the universal heavenly God of the Greeks, Zeus Olympius, or of the
Phoenicians, Ba'al Šāmēm (see below, pp. 296ff.). Is this the end of a development which had been introduced by Koheleth?

Excursus 3: Koheleth and Solomon

The semi-pseudonymity of the work is unique. The name Koheleth probably means 'leader of the assembly' or 'the speaker in the assembly';[163] however, whether it was an official title – say, for an office in the Jerusalem *gerousia* – is uncertain.[164] Additionally, the author presents himself, as 1.12 shows, as 'king over Israel in Jerusalem': the introduction in 1.1, which was added later, shows that by this we can only understand Solomon,[165] the 'prototype of all wisdom teachers'.[166] Here the Deuteronomistic tradition of Solomon as the wise king and writer of poems and sayings (I Kings 5.11ff.) will have had an influence, as will the Egyptian model of the royal testament (see above, note 39). But we should also remember that pseudonymity, which can only be demonstrated in Judaism to any considerable extent after the beginning of the Hellenistic period, was widespread in Greece and especially in the collections of Greek gnomic sayings.[167] Furthermore, from about 300 BC one can speak of a certain accumulation of 'Solomonic writings': the final recension of Proverbs and the Song of Songs are to be put at about the same time as Koheleth, and at best a few decades earlier.[168] The Psalms of Solomon and the Wisdom of Solomon follow about two hundred years later, and the Odes and Testament of Solomon even after that, not to mention the Solomonic writings with a magical content which were in circulation.[169] Thus it is understandable that the Septuagint made the thousand and five songs mentioned in I Kings 5.12 into five thousand.[170] Sirach also shows interest in the 'wise man' Solomon, ascribing to him universal wisdom of international status on the basis of I Kings 5.11:

> How wise you became in your youth!
> You overflowed like a river with understanding (*mūsār*) . . .
> By your songs and proverbs and riddles and parables
> You astounded the peoples.
> Your name reached to far-off islands,
> And they came to hear you.[171]

There is certainly a reference here to the visit of the queen of Sheba, but as the 'islands' often represent the Greek islands,[172] we should also think of Greece. According to a Phoenician tradition, Menelaus is said to have visited Hiram in Tyre after the Trojan war, when he was in the process of marrying his daughter to Solomon.[173] The reason for this emphasis on Solomon in the Hellenistic period was probably the same as that in the presentation of Enoch, Abraham and Moses as the 'first wise men' or the Phoenicians Mochus and Sanchuniaton as 'philosophers' of the pre-Trojan period. The intention was to demonstrate the great age and at the same time the superiority of the national wisdom over against that of Greece. The extent of the 'wisdom' of Solomon was constantly enlarged until it finally embraced the whole of the visible and invisible world, 'the system of the cosmos and the power of the elements' (Wisdom 7.17, cf. 18–21). The Jewish 'Peripatetic' Aristobulus, about 170 BC (see below, n. 378), cites him 'as one of his philosophical predecessors', who went beyond the philosophers of the Peripatetic school in the acuteness with which he expressed himself,[174] and according to Josephus, Solomon 'philosophized' about the whole of nature, though according to the thinking of the Hellenistic period this all-embracing wisdom could only be understood in *a magical* sense.[175] In this way, Solomon took his place alongside Moses in the Hellenistic-Roman world as one of the great wise teachers of secret knowledge long before the first Greek philosophers, comparable with the 'magicians' Zoroaster and Ostanes or the Egyptian Hermes-Thoth. This explains his significance for ancient magic which, according to the witness of Wisdom and Josephus, goes back into the pre-Christian period. The number of astrological, alchemistic, iatromantic and other tractates ascribed to him, quite apart from amulets and magical gems, is almost incalculable.[176] Here was one of the points in which Hellenistic-Roman paganism proved to be extremely interested in Jewish traditions and stretched out a hand to Jewish and pagan syncretism.[177]

Koheleth came before this development and was naturally far removed from its consequences. He chose 'Solomon' as the author of his work because the figure of the wisest and richest king formed an effective foil for his basic thesis of the vanity of human existence. The observations in 1.16 and 2.9, which do not fit the framework very well, show that he himself did not take the pseudonymous garb very seriously. In fact the pseudonymity only applies to 1.12–2.12b; later the individuality of the author breaks through the pseudonymous form. The first epilogue of his pupil, therefore, uses the second designation Koheleth as a proper name for his teacher (12.9). According to O. Eissfeldt, it is perhaps primarily intended to characterize Solomon as an orator.[178] Furthermore, the riches and the wisdom of Solomon form a pendant to the splendour of the Ptolemaic kings, the richest and most learned in the world at that time. Solomon was, so to speak, their Jewish counterpart. The historian Phylarchus, who still lived in the third century BC, reported of Ptolemy II Philadelphus (285–246 BC) an anecdote which by its opposition of towering hybris and pessimistic despair provides an illustration for Koheleth's Solomon:[179]

Ptolemy, the second king of this name in Egypt, despite the fact that he was the most brilliant of all rulers and devoted to education (παιδεία) beyond others, was nevertheless so deceived in his power of judgment and seduced by immoderate luxury that he believed that he would live for ever and asserted that he alone was immortal. When he felt better after an attack of gout which lasted for several days and watched through some windows how the Egyptians were enjoying their simple meal lying in groups on the sand of the river bank (cf. Koh. 5.11, 16), he exclaimed: 'Unhappy man I am, that I cannot become like one of these.'

4. Ben Sira and the Controversy with Hellenistic Liberalism in Jerusalem[180]

a) The personality of Ben Sira, the form of his work and the political and social situation in Jerusalem

Koheleth may be difficult to place, but the time at which Ben Sira's work was written, the intellectual milieu and the personality of its author are easier to establish. By his own testimony in the prologue to the Greek translation, the grandson of the author came to Egypt in the thirty-eighth year of 'king Euergetes' – i.e. Ptolemy Physcon VII Euergetes II (170–164 and 145–117) – and therefore in 132, and translated the work of his grandfather into Greek in a relatively free way, presumably after the death of the king in 117 BC. We may see this work as a testimony to the influence of Palestinian piety on the Jewish Diaspora in Egypt in the Hasmonean period, which may also be observed elsewhere (above, pp. 100f.).[181] The author, whose full name was Joshua b. Eleazar b. Sira,[282] lavishes striking praise in a hymn (50.1–24) on a high priest Simon, presumably Simon II, who according to Josephus (*Antt.* 12, 224, 229, 238; 19, 298) held office at the time of the conquest of Jerusalem by Antiochus III in 199/8 and is also probably identical with Simon the Just mentioned in 'Ab. 1, 2 (see below, pp. 270ff.). As Ben Sira presupposes his death and on the other hand there is no trace yet of the sharpening of the situation in Jerusalem by the deposition of Onias III in 175/4 BC and the erection of a gymnasium (see below, pp. 70ff.), the time of composition will lie somewhere between 190 and 175 BC.[183]

As with Koheleth, we have here a *composite work* which represents the fruits of a lifetime; on the one hand it has a good deal of traditional sayings material, and on the other a whole series of hymnic and didactic poems, e.g. poems about wisdom (1.1–20; 4.11–19; 14.20–15.8; 24.1–34; 51.13–21), hymns to God as the wise creator (see below, pp. 145ff.) and above all the unique 'praise of the fathers' (44.1–49.16). This poem, without parallel in wisdom literature, which previously was 'unhistorical', celebrates the great figures of biblical history. Ben Sira uses a great many poetical forms with skill, stretching from the simply distich of the wisdom saying to the artistic lament and thanksgiving. In this multiplicity he differs quite essentially from earlier wisdom; the multiplicity is an indication of the late form of this Hebrew poetry.[184] Furthermore, it is the poetic passages – as in the case of the later hymns of praise from the Teacher of Righteousness (see n. III, 756) – which express the theological conceptions of the author. Peculiarities in his work which are probably already influenced by Hellenistic usage and which represent an innovation in Hebrew poetry are the titles for individual sections and some transitional passages from one theme to another, or even the mention of his name in 50.27 as a sign of authorship.[185] The fact that he seldom expresses his ideas in independent logia but usually treats definite themes in larger units also represents an innovation in comparison with earlier wisdom.

We know little in detail about his person. He points with obvious pride to his profession as a 'scribe' (sōpēr); for him, lifelong concern with wisdom represents the highest stage that a man can reach:[186] 'Here for the first time appear in Jerusalem scribes who are nothing but scribes.'[187] In the closing hymn which describes his own striving for wisdom from early youth onwards, he invites the 'untaught' to his 'school' and his 'chair' (51.23, 29);[188] we must therefore imagine him as a wisdom teacher giving regular instruction. His admonitions are accordingly often addressed to young men,[189] who were in especial danger from the attractions of Hellenistic civilization. A decisive key concept for him is mūsār, which his grandson reproduces as παιδεία. Here the 'zeal for education' in Jewish wisdom and the Hellenistic world come together.[190] Presumably there were various wisdom schools in the Jerusalem of Ben Sira with different trends, sometimes conflicting with each other. The characterization of the different kinds of teachers might be a reference to this:

> There are wise men who are wise for many,
> and yet are foolish for themselves.
> There are wise men who are hated for their discourse,
> and are excluded from all ( ) enjoyment.
> ( ) There are wise men who are wise for themselves,
> (they learn) the fruit of their knowledge in their life.
> There are wise men who are wise for their people,
> the fruit of their knowledge is trustworthy.
> The man who is wise for himself is filled with enjoyment,
> and all who see him call him happy.
> The man who is wise for his people obtains praise,
> and his name lives for ever.[191]

Thus Ben Sira put his wisdom to the service of his people, perhaps on journeys which he undertook, presumably with a political aim:

> A travelled man knows many things,
> and one with much experience can speak with understanding.
> He that is inexperienced knows few things,
> but he that has travelled acquires much cleverness.
> I have seen many things in my travels,
> and many things have gone by me.
> I have often been in danger of death,
> but have escaped because of these experiences. (34.[G 31.]9–13)[192]

This biographical note is supplemented by the description of the scribe who stands in the service of 'princes' (שרים) and appears before 'rulers' (נדיבים) and thus 'passes through lands and peoples' (39.4, see p. 31 above). Thus the fascinating world of Hellenism was by no means strange to Ben Sira;

we may even conclude from his travels that he had a certain knowledge of Greek. As he often comes to speak of the appearance of the wise man in the council and the assembly of the people,[193] we might assume that sometimes he performed public functions; perhaps he was a judge or counsellor and member of the *gerousia*,[194] and possibly he even belonged to the 'scribes of the temple' mentioned in the decree of Antiochus III (*Antt.* 12, 142; see above, p. 78). It is not clear whether he was himself of priestly or Levitical descent, but unlike Koheleth he had a positive attitude to the temple, the priesthood and the cult; he stressed the inalienable privileges of the priesthood,[195] and above all gave clear expression to his admiration for the Oniad Simon (50.1–24), though after Simon's death the power of the high-priestly family was under severe attack from the intrigues of the Tobiads and events like the Heliodorus affair (see above pp. 24f. and pp. 272f.), and not least by disputes even among his own sons. Ben Sira probably had this threatening situation in mind when he directed a warning against the high-priestly descendants of Phinehas:

> May the Lord give you a wise heart (cf. I Kings 3.9),
> to judge his people in righteousness (supplement M by G);
> so that your goodness is not forgotten
> nor your power to distant generations. (45.26f.)

Following the panegyric on Simon the Just he reiterates:

> May he give you a wise heart,
> and may there be peace between you (!).
> May his grace continue with Simon,
> and may he maintain the covenant with Phinehas,
> which will not be broken by him and his descendants
> as long as heaven stands. (50.23f.)

The following verses may be closely connected with these admonitions:

> Do not seek from the Lord the highest office,
> nor the seat of honour from the king.
> Do not assert your righteousness before the king,
> nor display your wisdom before him.
> Do not seek to become a ruler (MS A מושל),
> lest you do not have the power to remove iniquity;
> lest you be partial to a powerful man
> and thus put a blot on your integrity (G). (7.4–7)

The formulation of these ideas is too concrete and specific for a general wisdom sentence. They would, however, fit Onias III, Simon's successor, well. He was unable to cope with the party struggles and the influence of rich families, and put himself in the wrong by a pro-Ptolemaic policy and the acceptance of a bribe from the Tobiad Hyrcanus in Transjordania, so that he was denounced by his opponents and finally summoned to answer for his conduct to king Seleucus IV Philopator in Antioch, where he was detained.[196] If this interpretation is correct, then Ben Sira's work was finished immediately before the accession of Antiochus IV (Sept. 175 BC). His emphatic plea for the Oniads and for the privileges of the descendants of Aaron and Phinehas shows that these were already being disputed.

In general, Ben Sira shows a considerable *political interest* in a nationalistic Jewish sense, which culminates in a completely this-wordly expectation of salvation for his people.[197] On the other hand, the nationalistic, xenophobic – one might even say anti-Seleucid – attitude of the work is tempered by a caution which probably rests on unfavourable experiences:

Do not set yourself against the current (4.26b) . . .
and do not resist the rulers (מושלים) (27b).
Do not contend with a powerful man,
why should you fall into his hands ? (8.1).

Thus with Sirach two tendencies are in conflict: on the one side political-religious engagement, protest against the arrogance of the liberal aristocracy which was probably already predominantly moulded by the spirit of Hellenism, and on the other side the traditional caution of the wise, which counselled silence and subjection before the powerful.[198]

This tension is to be seen throughout his work, and indeed in his personality. On the one side he is a wisdom teacher who is to a strong degree indebted to the tradition, but on the other side his self-awareness goes beyond that of a mere tradent and assumes *prophetic features*. Thus he concludes the great hymn to pre-existent wisdom, which is identical with the Torah, the hymn which forms the centre and the climax of his work, by comparing it with a channel which is made from a stream and draws off its waters (24.30f.), indeed he himself becomes the 'bearer of light':

I will again make (my) teaching shine forth like the dawn light and I will make it shine afar.
I will again pour out teaching like (thus G, Syr 'in') *prophecy* (G ὡς προφητείαν; Syr ‏ܢܒܝܘܬܐ‎) and leave it to all future generations.[199]

If it pleases God, the *sōpēr* will be filled with the 'spirit of understanding'; he will 'pour forth (ἀνομβρήσει = *hibbaʿ*) words of wisdom' and praise God in hymns.[200] As W. Baumgartner has already shown, Ben Sira uses a variety of prophetic genres, as in the prophecies of the threatening judgment of God (35[G 32].22–26) and the promise of salvation (47.22); the prayer for the redemption of the people (36[G 33].1–22), shaped as a lament, also has prophetic form (cf. v.21). Here we can see a 'quite unique mixture of wisdom and prophecy'.[201] Just as Simon the Just stands at the end of a series of the priestly and royal rulers of Israel, so the author himself concludes the sequence of prophets and wise men of the people:

I was the last on watch (אחרון שקדתי)
and (was) like one who gleans after the grape-gatherers.
By the blessing of the Lord I excelled,
and like a grape-gatherer I filled my wine press.
Consider that I have not laboured for myself alone,
but for all who seek instruction (παιδεία; there is a lacuna in M, presumably *mūsār*).

The concluding statement of this sentence, which is probably directed to the high-priestly family and the *gerousia* (see above, pp. 25f.), makes the prophetic claim particularly clear with a political accent:

Listen to me, you princes of the people (   ),
and attend, you rulers of the community (מושלי קהל).[202]

Here we come up against an inner transformation of the old institution of the *sōpēr*, which was to be significant for the further development of Judaism and also for primitive Christianity. The 'wisdom teacher' becomes the man 'learned in the scriptures', in that his activity is concentrated more and more on the holy scriptures of Israel. Perhaps those conservative and nationalist circles which became more dominant under the high priesthood of Simon the Just awakened interest in the prophetic and historical tradition of Israel in addition to the Torah, which was already widely recognized, and in the controversy with liberal 'Hellenists' furthered the formation of the canon. In any case, for Sirach the 'prophetic writings' from Joshua to the twelve prophets were also an established authority. This is clear from his description of the ideal *sōpēr*:[203]

On the other hand, he who devotes his life to the fear of God (Syr),
and reflects on the *law* of the most high,
will seek out the wisdom of all the ancients,
and will be concerned with the *prophetic* writings (προφητείαις). (38.34cd; 39.1)
. . . .
He will understand (Syr) counsel and knowledge,
and investigate his (i.e. God's) mysteries.
He will reveal instruction (παιδεία) in his teaching,
and will glory in the law of the Lord's covenant. (39.7, 8)[204]

But to study the Torah and the prophetic writings presupposes the 'spirit of understanding' (39.6). So the scribe enters upon the heritage of the prophets – among whom Ben Sira also includes Moses (46.1) – and has to protect this legacy in the onslaughts of the present. From this point the development could go in two directions: either to a new 'prophecy' founded on the inspired interpretation of the law and the prophets, as in Essenism, among the Zealots and in primitive Christianity,[205] or to the institutionalization of exegesis, as

among the Rabbis. The beginnings of this can already be found in Ben Sira
himself, where the prophets are transformed into interpreters and preachers
of the law and proclaimers of the future salvation of Israel by means of a
rationalizing, salvation-historical scheme. The scribe and the prophet 'are no
longer distinguished in principle . . . but merely in degree'.[206] According
to a wisdom collection of psalms of David found in Cave 11 Q, even David
was a *sōpēr* filled with 'an understanding and enlightened spirit' (רוח נבונה
ואורה) and a *ḥākām* who composed all his 4050 psalms and hymns 'in
prophetic inspiration' (בנבואה). There is no fundamental difference between
Palestinian and Alexandrian concepts of inspiration.[207] However, what
marked out the wise men and prophets of Israel's earlier history were their
'heroic' personalities, which manifested themselves above all in astonishing
miracles.[208] At this point the *'praise of the fathers'* is reminiscent of the
glorification of the heroes in Hellenistic times with its biographical genre *de
viris illustribus*.[209] The type of heroic glorification of leaders of the people
and prophets in terms of salvation history, which culminates in an admonition
for the present, is continued in the 'testament' of Mattathias in 1 Macc. 2.49–68.
Another striking feature is the 'principle of succession' (Sir. 46.1; 47.12; 48.12)
by which the continuity of salvation history is guaranteed. For 'successor'
Sirach uses the Aramaic *taḥªlīp*, which is unknown in the Old Testament
(44.17; 46.12; 48.8). Eupolemus, too, gave an exact account of the 'succession'
of kings and prophets in his history work (FGrHist 723 F 2b = Pr. Ev. 9, 30,
1ff. and F.5 = Pr. Ev. 9, 39, 2). Josephus later speaks of τὴν τῶν προφητῶν
ἀκριβῆ διαδοχήν (c. *Ap.* 1, 41), and in *Pirqe 'Aboth* the unbroken chain of
tradents guarantees the authority of the oral Torah ('*Ab.* 1, 1f., see above,
pp. 81f.). The continuity of the tradition, like the idea of inspiration, is meant
to provide rational backing for the ancestral heritage and to support its
authority. Here, too, Ben Sira's *apologetic* attitude is expressed. The holy
literature and history of Israel with its great men and acts is far superior to
non-Jewish, Greek history and literature (44.3–9), and the 'inspired wisdom'
of the *sōpēr* and the prophetic tradition entrusted to him and guided by God is
completely in a position to keep within bounds the threatening influences of
'Greek wisdom', which only rests on human reasoning.

   The tension between a 'criticism of the time' delivered with prophetic
solemnity and traditional wisdom based on observation and experience –
which sometimes appears egotistic – can be seen in Ben Sira's *social 'preaching'*.
He can value riches honestly gained, which guarantee a secure and carefree life,
as much as the modest enjoyment of life; self-incurred poverty and beggary
are hateful to him.[210] Much stronger, however, is his warning against the
dangers of riches and his admonition to a merciful social attitude which
corresponds with the will of God. Here there is, *inter alia*, a decisive difference
from Koheleth, which points towards a changed social consciousness. Ben Sira
gives an impressive description of the power of the rich aristocracy, which

makes unscrupulous use of it.[211] There is thus an unbridgable opposition between poor and rich:

> Every creature loves its like
> and every person his neighbour.
>
> . . . .
> What fellowship has a wolf with a lamb?
> No more has a sinner with a godly man.
> What peace is there between a hyena and a dog?
> And what peace between a rich man and a poor man?
> Wild asses in the wilderness are the prey of lions;
> likewise the poor are pastures for the rich.
> Humility is an abomination to a proud man;
> likewise a poor man is an abomination to a rich one. (13.15–20)
> Do not lift a weight beyond your strength,
> nor associate with a man mightier and richer than you.
> How can the clay pot associate with the iron kettle?
> The pot will strike against it and will itself be broken.
> A rich man does wrong, and he even adds reproaches;
> a poor man suffers wrong, and he must add apologies.
> If you are useful for him he makes you a slave,
> but if you collapse he keeps away from you.
> If you own something, he will live with you,
> he will make you poor and will not come to grief himself. (13.2–5)

However, Ben Sira does not limit himself to a critical description of the *status quo*;[212] he unmistakably utters a warning that the hectic hunt for riches leads a man into sin:

> My son, why do you busy yourself with so many matters;
> if you multiply activities you will not remain guiltless. (11.10)
> He who hunts after money will not remain guiltless,
> and he who loves profit will go astray. (31 [G 34].5)

In his polemic against the 'sacrifices of the lawless' his accusations have an almost prophetic ring.

> Like one who kills a son before his father's eyes
> is the man who offers a sacrifice from the property of the poor.
> The bread of the needy is the life of the poor;
> whoever deprives them of it is a man of blood.
> To take away a neighbour's living is to murder him;
> to deprive an employee of his wages is to shed blood. (34 [G 31].24–27)

He is particularly critical of the merchant, who is presumably often still non-Jewish and whose profession, unlike that of divinely sanctioned agriculture (7.15; 20.28), brings with it extreme danger.

> A merchant can hardly keep from wrong-doing,
> and a tradesman will not be declared innocent of sin.

Many have committed sin for a trifle,
and whoever seeks to get rich will avert his eyes.
As a stake is driven firmly into a fissure between stones,
so sin is wedged in between selling and buying.
If a man is not steadfast and zealous in the fear of the Lord,
his house will be quickly overthrown. (26.29–27.3)[213]

Here we come up against the idea of retribution, which plays a decisive role in all parts of Ben Sira's works (see below, pp. 142ff.). For him, as a member of the well-to-do upper class, it is the basis of social conduct towards those in need.

My son, deprive not the poor of his living,
and do not put desperate eyes to shame

. . . .
Deliver him who is wronged from the hand of the wrongdoer
and do not be fainthearted in judging a case.
Be like a father to orphans,
and instead of a husband to their mother;
you will then be like a son of the Most High
and he will have mercy on you and save you from the pit. (4.1, 9, 10)
The prayer of a poor man goes from his lips to the ears of God,
and his judgment comes speedily. (21.5)[214]

Thus the Jewish social milieu, which Ben Sira depicts in bright colours, on the whole corresponds with the conditions of the early Hellenistic period in Palestine described in the first chapter of this book (see above, pp.47ff.); at the same time, we can see the culmination of the situation on the basis of the partisan struggles in Jerusalem, which was brought about not least by the penetration of the Hellenistic style of life and foreign thought-forms into the Jewish upper class. This starting point gives the whole work of Ben Sira an *apologetic-polemical* basis, which to some degree conflicts with his thought and its indebtedness to traditional wisdom.

b) *Ben Sira's controversy with Hellenistic liberalism*

R. Smend already recognized the decisive tendency of this work clearly: 'Sirach heightens the statement in Prov. 1.7, 9, 10, that the fear of the Lord is the beginning of wisdom . . . by asserting that all wisdom comes from the Lord and that it has been with him from eternity. In these words, which he sets at the head of his work, he formulates a Jewish declaration of war against Hellenism'.[215] In this way the universalistic attitude expressed in earlier Jewish wisdom tradition is necessarily qualified;[216] wisdom and pious observance are identified, and the possibility of a profane wisdom dissociated from piety is excluded. Sirach 1.1 gives a programmatic expression of the main theme of the work, and 1.14 takes it up again to define it more closely *ad hominem*:

To *fear the Lord* is the beginning of *wisdom*,
she is created with the *faithful* (πιστοί) in the womb.

Fidelity is given greater significance by the threat from outside and becomes the *conditio sine qua non* of wisdom.[217] However, Ben Sira goes one stage further in his definition:

All wisdom is the *fear of the Lord*,
and in all wisdom there is the *doing* of the *law*.
But the knowledge of wickedness is not wisdom,
nor is there prudence where sinners take counsel.
There is a cleverness which is abominable,
but there is a fool who merely lacks wisdom.
Better is the God-fearing man who lacks intelligence
than the highly prudent man who transgresses the law. (19.20, 22–24G, T)
A wise man will not hate the *law*,
but he who is hypocritical about it is like a boat in a storm. (33 [G 36].2)

The essential point here is that in Sirach, in contrast to Proverbs, *tōrā* is no longer instruction in general but as a rule the particular *tōrā* of Moses.[218] Thus at the beginning of his work he can set out the basic principle:

If you desire wisdom, keep the commandments (1.26).[219]

In practice, wisdom and the law have become one, and Ben Sira expresses this by putting the great hymn to wisdom (ch. 24), in which this fusion is achieved, in the centre of his work.[220]

As we shall be looking at this hymn later (below, pp. 157f.), we can leave the question whether this notion came from Ben Sira himself or whether he took it over from his tradition; at present the important fact is that with this step 'wisdom' became the exclusive gift of God to Israel. This provided the possibility of repudiating an alien autonomous ideal of wisdom which refused any association with the law; for Ben Sira that meant godlessness. Accordingly, he warns against *false 'striving for wisdom'*:

Seek not what is too difficult for you,
nor investigate what is beyond your power.
Reflect upon what has been assigned to you,
for you do not need what is hidden.
Do not meddle in what is beyond your tasks,
for matters too great for human understanding have been shown you.
For their hasty judgment has led men astray,
and wrong opinion has caused their thoughts to slip. (3.21–24)[221]

R. Smend conjectures that the 'men' (בני אדם) in the last verse refers particularly to the Greeks,[222] and in view of the context we may perhaps concede that he is right. The admonition is directed towards the young, rich aristocrats (3.17f.) who are advised by Sirach to be modest and for whom the free critical questioning of Greek 'wisdom', restricted by no conventions, must have been very attractive. The closing warning against the 'perverse heart', the 'wicked man' who heaps sin on sin and the poison of the mocker, like the admonition at the end to listen to the 'sayings of the wise' (3.26–30), clearly shows the perspective of these verses. Ben Sira illustrates the nature of these impermissible questions by some examples of his own:

> Do not say 'My sin comes from God' (מאל פשעי),
> for he does not do what he hates.
> Do not say, 'It was he who led me astray',
> for he has no need of a sinful man.
> The Lord hates all abominations,
> and does not let evil come upon those who fear him.
> God created man in the beginning (   )
> and gave him his *yēṣer* (the power of distinction in man).
> If you will, you can keep the commandments,
> and to act faithfully (πίστις = אמונה Smend) is to do God's will.
> He has placed before you fire and water;
> stretch out your hand for whichever you wish.
> Before a man are life and death,
> and whichever he chooses will be given to him (15.11–17).[223]

To talk in this almost philosophical way of the *determination or freedom of the human will*, describing the decision to be obedient as אמונה, is something new in Judaism. One is given the impression that in the Jerusalem of Ben Sira – whether as a continuation of the thought of Koheleth (see above, pp. 119ff.) or under the influence of determinist astrology – the freedom of man, and thus the foundation of obedience to the law, was denied. Here and in what follows it may well be that the ideas of some of the wisdom schools which were strongly influenced by Hellenism may be being repudiated. The same themes emerge – though now connected with retribution after death – in the admonitions of I Enoch 98.4–8 (see below, pp.200f.), which are also directed against the liberal upper classes. It is certainly no coincidence that the concept of the 'two ways' (δύο τρίβους 2.12) appears expressly in Sirach for the first time, though it is used in the rather different form of the dichotomy of the sinner, who travels on two ways at the same time.[224] From now onwards the conception gains increasing significance in wisdom literature and in apocalyptic; it should be added that it had certain parallels in the Greek sphere, e.g. in Prodicus' fable of Heracles at the cross roads.[225] The strong stress on the freedom of the will supported the beginnings of a nomistic way of thinking: 'Whoever keeps the law controls his desire' (21.11: G ἐννόημα; Syr ܠܨܝ, M presumably יצר).[226] The term '*yēṣer*' gains its central anthropological significance in the sense of 'character', 'disposition' for the first time in Ben Sira; there is a tendency to think of it primarily as the 'evil impulse', which must be kept in check. Also new is the expression 'flesh and blood' to designate the creatureliness of man in 14.18 and 17.31; in the latter passage, the text of which has not been well preserved, the term is associated with the 'evil impulse' (רע יצר, see Smend, op. cit., 162, following the Syr.; similarly Segal, op. cit., 107). Alongside it appears the 'heart' as the place of thought and conscience (17.6b; 37.13–18). From all this it becomes clear how with the help of his wisdom terminology Sirach is developing the *basic concepts of a theological anthropology*. We meet it again in a strongly dualistic context with the Teacher of Righteousness and the Essenes (see below, pp.218ff.).

The degree to which the question of the freedom of the will occupied Jews in the Hellenistic period – presumably under the influence of the penetration of the ideas of Greek popular philosophy – can be seen on the one hand from the denial of it in Koheleth and later among the Essenes, and from the classification of the Jewish sects by Josephus on the basis of this question. Here too the Pharisees took up the attitude of Ben Sira (see below, pp.219f.). Granted, the latter was also acquainted with the traditional picture of God as the potter (33 [G 36].10–13), but this seems to be an alien body within his general account. Just as the Stoics had difficulties in associating the freedom of man and the denial of any divine responsibility for evil with their deterministic world view, so Ben Sira and later the rabbis found it difficult to relate the divine omnipotence and their picture of man.[227]

Ben Sira had to refute not only denial of free will but also a conception of God which claimed in an almost 'Epicurean' way that God was not concerned with the fate of the individual, thus denying the fundamental dogma of the rational 'theology' of both Judaism and the Stoa, that of *'divine providence'*. Here too the views of his opponents might perhaps rest on a doctrinal development of notions of Koheleth in connection with Hellenistic criticism of religion.[228]

> Do not say, 'I shall be hidden from the Lord,
> and who from on high will remember me?
> Among so many people I shall not be known,
> for what is my soul in the totality of spirits (   )?
> Behold, heaven and the highest heaven,
> the abyss and the earth,
> when he descends on them, they will tremble . . .
> and no mind will reflect on this,
> who will ponder my ways?
> If I sin, no man sees me,
> or if I deceive, quite secretly, who observes it?
> My righteous dealing, who announces it?
> And what is hope? The time is far off.
> This is what those void of understanding think,
> and a simple man thinks like this. (16.17–23)[229]

Wisdom and foolishness are no longer formal criteria, but are exclusively measured by the will of God revealed in the Torah. Even the enlightened sceptic who considers wisdom identified with the law as a prison, fetters and chains, is a fool.[230] Even the problem of the 'delay of salvation' was a disputed question in the Jerusalem of Ben Sira. His prayer for the dawn of the time of salvation – understood in political terms – shows that some of the promises of the prophets were no longer believed because they were thought to have been proved deceptive:

> . . . and fulfil the prophecy (חזון) spoken in thy name.
> Reward those who wait for thee,
>   and let thy prophets be found trustworthy. (36.20f.)

In the dispute of opinions and parties within pre-Maccabean Jerusalem, Ben Sira requires a constant and unequivocal attitude, which for him means fidelity to the law:

> Do not winnow with every wind,
>   nor follow every path.
> Be steadfast in your understanding,
>   and let your speech be consistent. (5.9f.)

The sentence which immediately precedes this shows that his polemic is directed against the aristocracy which is rich and lax in its religious convictions, for whom the faith of the fathers had lost its binding force and who were in danger of falling victim to libertinism:

> Do not set your heart on your wealth,
> nor say, 'I can acquire it.' ( )
> Do not follow your inclination and strength,
> walking according to the desires of your heart.
> Do not say, 'Who will have power over me?',
> for the Lord will surely punish you.
> Do not say, 'I have sinned, and what will happen to me?
> Indeed he is a patient God!'
> Do not say, 'His mercy is great,
> he will forgive the multitude of my sins,'
> for both mercy and wrath are with him,
> and his anger rests on sinners. (5.1–4, 6)[231]

In effect, what we have here is another version of the theme which has already been presented in 16.17ff., that God does not intervene in the life of the individual man. Over against such views, the *doctrine of retribution* occupies a central position in Ben Sira's argument as a basic idea of his work. Even here that 'universal transformation of wisdom in Jewish thought', which according to J. Fichtner derives from the 'controversy with Hellenism', also becomes evident.[232] Corresponding to a widespread basic attitude in the early Hellenistic period (see pp. 54f. above), his opponents had a completely this-worldly, eudaemonistic approach to life, firmly trusting in progress, an approach according to which external success was the decisive factor. Ben Sira counters this with a hardly less eudaemonistic ideology of the law which, while indeed representing a retrogression from the deeper human or theological reflection of a Koheleth or a Job, nevertheless represented a more effective weapon in the ideological struggle.[233] Once 'the theory of a just retribution here on earth' had been 'recognized as an insufficient principle for explaining human destiny' in the books just mentioned, as in Ps. 49 and Ps. 73,[234] the earlier conception in wisdom of the fixed connection between action and consequence also shattered. For Sirach, who was surely not unaware of this crisis in early Israelite wisdom, the old connection was no longer a matter that could be taken for granted.[235] If he nevertheless takes up earlier ideas, while deliberately modifying them, he does so in order to gain a more effective rational starting point for his argument: transgression of the law and apostasy certainly bring punishment from God in this life, while fear of God and obedience to the law lead to all the good things which seem to be worth striving for, even to his opponents: 'honour and praise', 'happiness, joy and a long life', 'well-being and flourishing health' and not least – in contrast to Koheleth – an abiding remembrance after death.[236] Here, too, is the cause of the alleged 'Epicureanism' which I. Lévi wants to discover in Ben Sira.[237] This firm connection between human action and divine retribution runs through the work of Ben Sira like a scarlet thread, and gave it to a large degree its polemic force.[238] While in Proverbs action and consequence are still for the most part directly related, in Sirach God himself appears much more strongly as the author and guarantor of righteous retribution: this is elevated so as to become virtually a theological principle: '*For the Lord is the one who repays*' (כי אלוה תשלומות הוא).[239] We also find this strong stress on divine retribution in two historical works akin to the thought of Ben Sira, first the Chronicler and then that of Jason of Cyrene (see above, p. 97). On the other hand, the criticism of the doctrine of retribution in Sirach's contemporary Antigonus of Socho, who branded counting on divine reward as the attitude of a slave, could be directed against the school of Sirach. Possibly Antigonus was more open to Hellenistic influences; later legend made him the teacher of the founder of Sadduceeism.[240] In any case, we may count on the fact that the doctrine of retribution presented by Sirach did not go undisputed and that like other basic Jewish doctrines in pre-Maccabean Jerusalem it was vigorously contested. It then imposed itself all the more after the Maccabean victory.[241]

The climax of religious criticism in Jerusalem was probably the challenging of the righteousness of Yahweh himself. We find it in the notion that God is fundamentally the cause of sin, and also in the view that God does not care either about the individual or about right and wrong in this world. Both themes are also to be found in the criticism of religion made in the Greek enlightenment after the time of Euripides (see above, pp. 121ff.). However, the criticism of the traditional picture of God was even extended to the question of the perfection of creation, whereas the existence of God was apparently never put in question.[242] On the contrary, even Ben Sirach's opponents spoke of God in their own way and shared in the cult, an attitude which Ben Sira rejected with almost prophetic vehemence.[243]

Ben Sira gives his answer to the question of the perfection of this world in his hymns to creation, which introduce a rational motive not entirely unknown to earlier wisdom, but so far not fixed in any conceptual terms:

> The works of God are all good (cf. Gen. 1.31)
> and they are appropriate for each *purpose* (צורך) in his time. (39.16).

This introduction is the title for a lengthy wisdom hymn about the absolute purposefulness of creation:

> Nothing is small and of no account with him,
> and nothing is incomprehensible and difficult to him.
> No one can say, 'What is this for?',
> for everything has been created for its (necessary) *purpose* (לצרכו הכל כי
> נבחר).
> No one can say, 'This is worse than that',
> for all things prove good in their season (39.20cd, 21).
> To the holy (לתמים, Smend, op. cit., 363) his ways are straight,
> just as they are obstacles to the godless (Smend, op. cit., לזדים).
> From the beginning good things were created for good people,
> just as evil things for sinners.
> Basic to all the needs of man's life
> are water and fire and iron and salt
> and wheat flour and milk and honey,
> the blood of the grape, and oil and clothing.
> All these things are for good to the godly,
> just as they turn into evils for sinners.
> There are winds that have been created for vengeance
>
> . . . .
> (G) in the time of annihilation they pour out their strength
> and calm the anger of their Maker,
> (M) Fire and hail and famine (Smend, op. cit., 365 רעב) and pestilence,
> all these have been created for vengeance;
> wild beasts and scorpions and poisonous snakes
> and the sword that punishes the ungodly with destruction,
> all these things have been created for their *purpose* (לצורכם)
> . . . .
> Therefore from the beginning I have been convinced,
> and have thought this out and left it in writing:
> The works of the Lord are all good,
> and they are adequate for every *purpose* in their time.
> And no one can say, 'This is worse than that',
> for everything is valuable in its season. (39.24–34)

The recapitulation of the theme at the end of a didactic poem, coupled with a personal confession, which is unique in Ben Sira's work, shows how deeply he felt about this doctrine of *the purposefulness of creation* and that it was presumably energetically disputed by his opponents, whom we are perhaps to seek in an 'enlightened', sceptical wisdom school. At the same time, his strong involvement with the doctrine of retribution is manifest, since 'evil is created for the wicked' (על רשע נבראה רעה 40.10). Here we have the clear beginnings of the construction of a theological system, albeit a simple one, such as we can find later to a still greater degree and with a completely different content in Qumran (see below, pp. 219ff.). The term צורך, 'goal, need, use', a *hapax legomenon* in the Old Testament, appears many times in Sirach; like Koheleth before him and the Essene community later, he has a predilection for certain abstract theological key terms.[244] The goal of his concern is rational *theodicy*. Despite the toil and terror of human life, with the inevitable fate of death at its end – significantly all this is described in detail immediately following the theodicy quoted above (40.1–41.4) –, God's creation is perfect in every respect. A pessimistic view of the world and of life was thus by no means unknown to Ben Sira[245] – perhaps he even had to carry on a polemical controversy with a radical version of its consequences – though he comes to a diametrically opposed conclusion: despite all its riddles and its shady side, the world is demonstrably good; man himself is free and on every occasion receives from God only his just deserts. Here the whole theodicy is directed towards man as the ruler of the earth (17.2). Creation serves to sustain him, to reward him and to punish him. So the theme of *purposefulness* appears once again in the last great hymn which, together with the 'praise of the fathers', brings the work to an end. In it he depicts in detail the perfect *harmony* of the 'works of God' (42.15) which in strict regularity[246] follow the order determined by him.

How greatly to be desired are all his works,
and how sparkling they are to see.
All these things live and remain for ever,
and all are obedient for every *purpose*.
All things are *twofold*, one opposite the other,
and he has made nothing incomplete.
One thing changes in value with another,
and who can have enough of beholding his glory?[247]

The later Rabbinic tradition takes up Sir. 38.4, 7f. in its discussion of the purposefulness of the world in *Gen. R.* and further bases the curative power of healing herbs on astrological constellations and 'sympathy' with the stars (see below, pp. 238f.). A fundamental Baraita adds to this: 'Our teachers said: even those things which you regard as being completely superfluous in the world like fleas, gnats and mosquitos, are part of the creation of the world, and the holy one *carries out his purpose through every thing*' (*Gen. R.* 10, 7).

The expansion of Gen. 1.29 by *Targ. Jer.* I ad loc. is on a similar line: God gave man the trees which bring forth no fruit 'for the purpose (לצרוך) of building and heating'. The last consequence of this thinking is that *everything* was made *for the sake of man.*[248]

In addition to the beauty and purposefulness of the world there is its eternal duration, and Ben Sira also believes – perhaps by transforming a sentence of Koheleth (7.13) – that he has discovered an 'ontological structural law' in creation, which he had already discussed in connection with the question of the opposites in creation. This world is not unitary, but has 'paired' structures, i.e. dialectically polar structures, which God has incorporated in it. He distinguished e.g. between festal days and ordinary days, and the same is also true in the case of men:

> As clay in the hand of the potter,
> so that he forms whatever he pleases,
> so men are in the hand of him who made them,
> so that their fate (חלק) is determined.
> Good is the opposite of evil
> and life the opposite of death.
> The good man is the opposite of the sinner
> and light the opposite of darkness.
> Look upon all the works of God:
> they are all *in pairs,* one the opposite of the other (33[G 36].13–15).[249]

Here Ben Sira takes up a traditional picture of prophetic proclamation (Jer. 18.4–6; Isa. 45.9) and draws the 'fate'[250] of men almost with Koheleth's colours. He does, however, bend round the consequence of his statements by reading out of God's free, sovereign activity *a basic structural law of polarity* for creation, which affects the cosmos as well as men. Seen as a whole, both physical and metaphysical evil fit into the purposeful harmony of the work of creation. It is no coincidence that his theodicy had a strong effect on later times.[251]

The contemplation of the works of God in the great hymn to creation which has already been mentioned culminates in a confession which bears almost 'pantheizing' features:

> Further in this vein we will not add,
> let the end of the discourse be '*He is all*'. (43.27)
> וקץ דבר הוא הכל (or even: 'He is the all').

An earlier hymn begins with a statement which could be set above all Ben Sira's theodicy:

> The Lord alone is to be declared righteous.
> κύριος μόνος δικαιωθήσεται (18.2).[252]

The essence of *the divine righteousness* is the possibility of *observing and testing it rationally.* Even if we do not suppose that Ben Sira sets out to strike 'a balance between Jewish faith and the Hellenistic world-view',[253] but recognize that in good faith he believed that he was defending the original intention of the Old Testament revelation, we cannot ignore the fact that particularly in his doctrine of creation and his theodicy a spirit emerges which is related to Hellenistic popular philosophy. The first thing to be noted is his great confidence in the possibility of a rational understanding of the world. The purpose and goal of the world created by God are to be demonstrated with the means of rational argument, even if the full extent of the works of God, like God himself, in the last resort remains immeasurable and unfathomable because of God's boundlessness.[254] There is neither arbitrariness nor even unrighteousness in the conduct of God; he keeps the rules that are manifest to the wise. Rudolf Bultmann may describe the nature of the biblical concept of God in the following way:

> Certainly, the pious Israelite admires and praises the wisdom of God, but he does not see it in the rational cosmic structure. Therefore the conceptions of providence and theodicy, discussed by the Stoic philosophers, are strange to Biblical thinking,[255]

But this is no longer true for Ben Sira and the Rabbis. Certainly Ben Sira knows other sayings taken from the tradition, like 11.14:

> Good things and bad, life and death,
> poverty and wealth, come from the Lord (cf. Isa. 45.7);

however, these are marginal, and the element in the divine action which is perceptibly rational and purposeful in the action of God predominates.

Here we find close contacts with *Stoic* conceptions, since Chrysippus was already concerned to demonstrate the purposefulness of individual phenomena of nature and applied it above all to mankind, who through the Logos is destined to be master of the cosmos. However, in the Stoa the humanitarian and pedagogical tendency was substantially stronger. For Ben Sira, wild beasts and serpents primarily existed to punish the wicked (see p. 144 above on 39.30), but for Chrysippus they were to strengthen human forces and to provide means of healing.[256] Similarly, even the doctrine of retribution was not alien to the Stoa, though its pedagogic and minatory character was stressed even more strongly than in Ben Sira.[257] The remark 'he is all' recalls on the one hand individual passages of the Old Testament like Jer. 23.24 and Ps. 139.7–12, but it also suggests Stoic influence. R. Pautrel points out that before the discovery of the Hebrew text, earlier commentators wanted to delete Sir. 43.27 as a Stoicizing gloss, because 'cette expression a une saveur étrangère'.[258] It is interesting that the earliest Greek witnesses to Jewish belief in God, Hecataeus and Posidonius, interpret him as the 'all-embracing one' ($\tau \grave{o} \ \pi \epsilon \rho \iota \acute{\epsilon} \chi o \nu$ $\dot{\eta} \mu \hat{a} \varsigma \ \dot{a} \pi \acute{a} \nu \tau a \varsigma$, see below, pp. 256f.). It is also significant that Ben Sira has a predilection for the abstract concept of the 'all' (*hakkōl*), which embraces all creation; it is still relatively rare in early Hebrew literature, but appears all the more frequently in literature which is approximately contemporaneous with Ben Sira. Whereas there God is at best called the Creator or the Lord of all, Ben Sira goes a step further and ventures to say: 'He is the all'.[259] Cleanthes' Hymn to Zeus could also have come from the hand of Ben Sira, with some minor alterations.[260]

> It is significant that the Rabbis later singled out pantheistic-type formulas of this kind to retain and made variations on them. Thus Tannaites and Amoreans discussed the fact that while God embraced the sphere of the world (מקומו של עולם), the sphere of the world did not embrace God (ואין עולמו מקומו *Gen. R.* 68, 9n., Jose b. Ḥalaphta), that God 'filled his world' (ממלא את עולמו *Ber.* 10a and *Lev. R.* 4, 8) like the soul the body, and that Moses was the first to recognize that God was present even in the 'empty space of the world' (between heaven and earth: בהללו של עולם *Deut. R.* 2, 26/27).[261]

Ben Sira thus shared with the Stoa the notion 'that the whole world is a single cosmos which is permeated and shaped down to its smallest part (42.22, see n.247 above) by a rational power, deity'.[262] At the same time, though, the idea of the polar structure of creation also has its parallels in Greek thought. It played a considerable role in Heraclitus and from him found entry into the various trends of Greek philosophy. Even the essentially monistic thought of the Stoa did not escape his influence. Here was the notion that the good in the world would not become visible without the evil. Perhaps the views of Ben Sira took a similar direction.[263] Certainly the thought had further currency in the Greek tradition. Possibly we have here a prelude to the dualism of Qumran, albeit still unmythological.[264]

Once we have assumed an analogous development between Jewish wisdom and Stoic philosophy, we can hardly avoid presupposing some popular philosophical influence not only in the opponents of Ben Sira, but also in the thought of Ben Sira himself. In the spiritual climate of the period about 175 BC in Jerusalem, this phenomenon is not surprising. Even a fundamentally conservative scribe like Ben Sira would have to adapt himself to the learned arguments of his time, if only to be heard and understood by his pupils and his opponents in the youth of the aristocracy. Here a number of Stoic conceptions could well have been helpful in his apologetic and polemic statements. Ben Sira could rediscover a number of important elements in Stoic thought: a strict drive towards ethical conduct, an attempt at a balance between human freedom and divine providence, the value of man as God's first creation,[265] the harmony and purposefulness of the world and even the identity of the divine reason of the world (or wisdom) and the moral law that is binding on all men (or the *tōrā* of Moses, see pp.159ff. below), and he could adapt all these statements to Jewish belief. This borrowing was all the easier for him as the

Stoa had grown up on Semitic ground, and had a great deal in common with the thought-world of the Old Testament:

> 'Thus it is certainly not too bold to conclude that the conception of God to be found in Zeno and Chrysippus displays features which have been taken over from the Orient . . .'; of course, 'identification with the *physis* which shapes everything according to immanent laws represents a complete transformation into Hellenistic modes of thought.'[266]

So in one sense the Jewish adoption of Stoic notions from Ben Sira and Aristobulus (see pp. 166ff. below) down to Philo was an oriental interpretation taken back again. Obviously Ben Sira did *not* take over Stoic monism and its identification of God and world. For him God, despite his permeation of the universe, remained the sovereign Creator exalted over his creatures, who is 'greater than all his works' (43.28b). In the last resort the ordering of the world was not oriented by an impersonal, immanent 'world reason' over which man also has control, but by the creative word of God. And the effect of this word is neither arbitrary nor unjust, but purposeful, meaningful and harmonious. Even 'wisdom' (see pp. 159f. below) remained God's property, and it was a free act of his if he filled man at his creation with 'knowledge and understanding' ($\epsilon\pi\iota\sigma\tau\acute{\eta}\mu\eta\nu$ $\sigma\upsilon\nu\acute{\epsilon}\sigma\epsilon\omega\varsigma$ 17.7) or the scribe with the 'spirit of understanding' ($\pi\nu\epsilon\acute{\upsilon}\mu\alpha\tau\iota$ $\sigma\upsilon\nu\acute{\epsilon}\sigma\epsilon\omega\varsigma$ 39.6, see pp. 136f. above). Being in the image of God (17.3) did not yet mean identity of being; man was above all directed towards God's mercy (18.11–14). Nor did Ben Sira surrender the special election of Israel in favour of an 'ideal of world citizenship', although he knew of the incomparable 'glory of Adam' which was surpassed by no man (ועל כל חי תפאדת אדם 49.16). On the contrary, at this very point – from an apologetic situation – we can see a clear constriction in comparison with earlier wisdom:

> He appointed a ruler (שר) for every nation,
> but Israel is the Lord's own portion. (17.17)

On the other hand, we must not overlook the fact that from the second century BC, tendencies were at work in the Stoa to break through the strict monism, and particularly thinkers from Phoenicia and Syria, like Boethus of Sidon and later Posidonius, required the conception of a Godhead separated from the rest of the world and localized in the ethereal sphere. Thus Hellenistic thought came to meet that of Judaism (see above, pp. 110f.).

Furthermore, in Sirach, as in Koheleth, there are a considerable number of 'parallels', or perhaps better, 'echoes', to the Greek gnomic poetry of Theognis, the dramatists, especially Euripides, and comedy. I. Lévi and L. Bigot in particular have drawn attention to this. However, it is no more a question of direct literary dependence than with Koheleth: the comparable themes like the negative verdict on women, the warning against over-hasty friendship, the preservation of the honour of parents, etc, are occasioned by universal human experiences.[267] One thought which already emerged with Koheleth and was rejected (3.20f., see p. 124, n. 134 above), has been given a fixed, almost stereotyped version in Ben Sira:

> All things that are from the earth turn back to the earth,
> and what is from the waters returns to the sea (40.11).

There is a parallel with almost the exact words in Euripides:

> What sprouts from the earth returns to the earth,
> and what has come forth from the 'ether' returns to the firmament of heaven.[268]

Further parallels concern the meaningless of too heavy a death lament[269] or a life without hope, in the face of which death is preferable,[270] and the warning against excessive striving for wisdom.[271] We can hardly talk here of a real 'influence'; the parallels with oriental-Jewish wisdom, say with Proverbs or Ahikar, are incomparably stronger. But in view of the international character of the wisdom tradition in the Hellenistic period, we cannot exclude the possibility of the transmigration of sayings from gnomic Greek thought, tragedy and comedy, by word of mouth.[272] Finally, the influence of Greek conventions can be seen in Sirach's extensive account of dining customs and in his positive attitude towards the doctor, which ran counter to an orthodox rigorism.[273]

Now it would be wrong to attempt, as does R. Pautrel, to explain away the largely anti-Hellenistic tenor of Ben Sira's thought because he takes over certain ideas from the Greek world.[274] It is a frequent phenomenon in religious and intellectual history that one can be influenced by one's opponent precisely in warding off his language and thought-forms. The reason why Ben Sira – with a few exceptions – does not attack non-Jews and pagan polytheism is that his opponents – and pupils – were Palestinian Jews for whom alien thought was a greater danger than pagan cults.

Ben Sira speaks of the *opponents of wisdom* in the rich, traditional language of the wisdom literature. Alongside the fool[275] stand the mocker,[276] the wicked man[277] and finally the 'violent' man, cruel and alienated from God.[278] Here too the supposition is that Sirach is not only repeating formulas, but giving them particular application in his exposed position. True, in mentioning the 'fool' or the 'mocker' he does not have particular people in mind, but we may still assume a polemical reference in individual cases. This may be true, for example, of the collection of sayings about the 'arrogance' (*ga'awā*) of men:[279]

> Do not be violent with your neighbour with any kind of wickedness
> and do not go the way of arrogance.
> Arrogance is hateful before the Lord and before men,
> and oppression is regarded by both as wickedness (10.6f.).

The beginning of arrogance is that a man is stubborn
and departs from his creator in his heart,
for sin is a sea of presumption (*zādōn*)
and its source overflows with transgression.
Therefore God sends his punishment in a wonderful way
and smites it to nothingness.
The Lord casts down the throne of rulers
and sets the oppressed in their place. (10.12–14)
Pride (*zādōn*) was not created for men
nor fierce anger for those born of women. (10.18)

One might feel that the Tobiads, who represented the most powerful group in Jerusalem after the high-priestly family of the Oniads, or the Ptolemaic or Seleucid rulers, were particular embodiments of this 'arrogance'.[280] Ben Sira could not express his criticism directly, but had to clothe it in the form of wisdom discourse to protect himself (see pp. 133f. above).

At one decisive point, however, he does express his view openly.

Woe to you, ungodly men,
who have forsaken the *law* of the Most High God;
When you increase, it is for misfortune,
when you beget children, it is for grief.
When you come to a fall, it is for lasting joy,
when you die, it is for a curse. (41.8, 9)[281]

Wide circles of people seem to have become indifferent to the law and even to have rejected it directly before the beginning of the Hellenistic reform proper; Ben Sira returns to the question on a number of occasions. So he speaks, for example, of the 'clan of apostates' (משפחת בגדים) by whom a city is devastated, whereas it is hallowed by a single God-fearer (16.4). Here, too, it would be reasonable to think of the Tobiads and Simon the Just.[282] The tenor of the admonition also becomes clear in the following sentence, which follows immediately after the warning against 'arrogance' (10.6–18):

What race is worthy of honour? The human race.
What race is worthy of honour? Those who fear the Lord.
What race is despised? Those who transgress the commandments.
Among brothers (their) leader is worthy of honour,
but the one who fears God in the e(yes of God G).
. . . .
It is not right to despise the intelligent poor
nor is it proper to honour any man of violence.
The prince, the counsellor and the judge are honoured,
but none is greater than the one who fears God (10.19–24, text after Segal).

The indirect criticism of prominent families who are lax towards the law illuminates the situation in Jerusalem immediately before the Hellenistic reform. Sirach's often repeated instruction about proper and false shame which immediately follows the lament against apostates shows a similar tendency:[283]

> Of the following things do not be ashamed,
> and do not let partiality lead you to sin:
> of the law of the Most High and his covenant,
> and of rendering judgment to acquit the ungodly (42.1c, 2).

In his portrayal of Abraham – a figure of early Jewish history in whom the Hellenists were particularly interested because of his international significance (see above, pp.90f.) – Sirach, like the Book of Jubilees later, stresses above all that he 'observed the command of the Most High' and entered into the covenant with God by circumcision (44.20). His warning against personal converse or even friendship with the godless is also impressive, presumably because he feared that Hellenistic libertinism would have an attractive influence. This tendency to segregate those faithful to the law then became a typical mark of Jewish piety.[284] Close converse with non-Jews seemed even more dangerous:

> Receive a stranger into your house and he will alienate your way of living
> (השכן זר והזיר דרכיך) and will estrange your family from you. (11.34, cf. v.29)

This is probably an allusion to the frequent contacts of the Jewish Hellenists with non-Jewish friends, by which the confines of Jewish morality and religion which separated Israel from the non-Jewish world were shattered (on this see above, pp.49f., and below, pp.277ff.).

In the prayer for deliverance from the '*goyim*', already mentioned, Sirach emerges from the old wisdom tradition and comes near to the prophetic apocalyptic tradition. He prays for the speedy intervention of divine punishment on the enemies of the people and for the glorification of Israel:

> Deliver us, God of all,
> and cause the fear of thee to fall on all the nations.
> Lift up thy hand against foreign nations,
> and let them see thy might. (36 [G 33]. 1f.)
> Show signs anew and work further wonders,
> make thy hand and thy right arm glorious.
> Rouse thy anger and pour out thy wrath,
> destroy the adversary and wipe out the enemy.
> Hasten the day and remember the appointed time,
> for who can say to thee 'What art thou doing?'
> (G) With the fire of wrath will the survivor be consumed
> and those who do injustice to thy people will meet destruction.
> (M) Hew off the head of the princes of Moab,
> who say, there is no (God?) beside me (36 [G 33]. 6–12).

Here we have an expression of the profound antipathy which Ben Sira has towards the Seleucid oppressors and their Jewish supporters; it also comes out in the threat against the neighbours of Judea, the Samaritans, the dwellers in the coastal plain and the Idumeans (50.25f., cf. Test. Levi 7.2). It is remarkable that, as in later times, Rome is mentioned in a disguised way. One could find a reference to the Tobiads in the prince of Moab; they had great possessions in the Ammanitis, but a reference to the Seleucids and the obligatory ruler cult which was intensified even before the time of Antiochus III is more probable.[285] Ben Sira's *eschatological hope*, which is based on an intensive study of the prophets (see above, pp. 135f.), is still completely this-worldly, and has political and nationalistic colouring; in contrast to Daniel, who comes a little later, there is no hope beyond death, and indeed the idea of the resurrection is perhaps directly repudiated in 38.21.[286] We must not therefore include him among the Hasidim proper, but assign him to that conservative, nationalist-Jewish movement which according to him was represented by the Hasmoneans, and to which many of the later Sadducees approximated.[287] However, any assignation to the later Jewish 'parties' is fundamentally mistaken, as Ben Sira comes *before* these differentiations and still has within his work the various possibilities of the later development of Judaism. Particularly in his attitude to the future, we find in this man, who has so few aggressive features, the attitude which gave later Judaism the strength to overcome the crisis of acute Hellenization in the Maccabean revolt:

Strive even to death for the truth,
And Yahweh will fight for you (4.28).[288]

5. The Encounter between Jewish and Hellenistic Thought in connection with Jewish Wisdom Speculation

a) *Wisdom as a hypostasis in Prov. 8.22ff. and Job 28*

In the latest part of Proverbs, chs. 1-9, which probably came into being in the early Hellenistic period, at the latest, say, by the middle of the third century BC, it has on occasion been supposed that 'the manner in which wisdom and folly are here personified probably betrays Greek influence'.[289] In particular, the independent wisdom hymn Prov. 8.22-31, which was probably worked in at a relatively late stage, speaks of personified wisdom in a unique way which is hard to interpret.[290] Wisdom is described as the primal creation of God, who was present at the creation of the world and its ordering as a playing 'favourite child' – this translation is to be preferred to the interpretation 'master workman'.[291] Alongside Prov. 8.22-31 comes Job 28, probably only a little older, a poem about wisdom, hidden and equally, according to vv. 25-27, present at the creation of the world, which was inserted into the book of Job only at a secondary stage.[292] Here, too, scholars have wanted to discover the influence of Greek thought.[293] In both texts there are possibly two views of the function of wisdom as a hypostasis or as a 'personal entity'.[294] According to Prov.8 it was accessible to the man who earnestly sought it (vv.32–36), but according to Job 28 it was undiscoverable and hidden with God. This conception would point to a more sceptical trend, but it would also correspond to the later apocalyptic conception of the misunderstood wisdom which returned to heaven.[295] Closely connected with Prov.8.22ff. is 9.1ff. immediately following, where wisdom appears as a 'royal hostess'. Here the favourite of God becomes the teacher of men, who sends out her invitation (9.4ff.)[296] and does not allow herself to be put off by her foolish counterpart. Here her appeal has almost the character of revelation (9.3).[297]

However, one should be very careful in supposing that these earliest instances of a Jewish 'wisdom speculation' display Greek 'influences', since in the Greek sphere '*sophia*' appears as a divine, personal entity only at a relatively late stage. This was presumably under oriental and gnostic influence, and comes out more strongly in the Hermetica, in Plutarch and among the Neo-Platonists.[298]

> Granted, Plato speaks at one point of $\sigma o \phi i a$ as the $\beta a \sigma \iota \lambda \iota \kappa \grave{\eta} \ \psi \nu \chi \acute{\eta}$ and the $\beta a \sigma \iota \lambda \iota \kappa \grave{o} s \ \nu o \hat{\nu} s$ of Zeus, as which it represents the cause of all order and all beauty in the world; but even this analogy offers no real parallel; it is too philosophical in form and was never applied to 'wisdom' at a later stage, say by Philo.[299]

In contrast to this, earlier Semitic parallels go back far into the pre-Hellenistic period. There should no longer be any dispute that Jewish wisdom speculation has a mythological background at this point; on the other hand, it remains questionable whether one can construe a unitary primal oriental myth as a starting point.[300] Probably the different impulses and trends run together here.

Thus Albright, Story and H. Donner have pointed to the 'wisdom' of the book of Ahikar from Elephantine which was highly prized by the gods. Its kingdom – the text is unfortunately badly corrupt here – is presumably of everlasting duration and wisdom was exalted to heaven by the 'Lord of the holy ones'. Donner derives this conception from the Egyptian doctrine of *maat*, the hypostatized harmonious ordering of nature and society.[301] However, we cannot exclude the possibility that this '*ḥokmā*' dwelling with God in heaven at the same time represents a transformation of the Semitic mother goddess and goddess of love who had even been set alongside Yahweh as *parhedros* by the Jews at Elephantine, under the name of 'Anatyahu:[302] 'Exclusive Yahwism had repudiated this, but garbed as wisdom the divine woman entered Judaism under the influence of a later syncretism.'[303] Similar 'hypostatizations' can be found elsewhere in the ancient East, especially in Egypt, and on occasion also in Greece, especially in the post-classical period.[304] As parallels from post-biblical Judaism we might mention the hypostatization of the spirit or the various spirits of God,[305] and later forms like the Word of God,[306] the Shekinah and the Metatron.[307] The beginnings of the various personifications of evil[308] and the extension of the doctrine of angels in apocalyptic (see below, pp.231ff.), which goes far beyond the limited conceptions of early Israel, belong in this connection. The remarks by Bousset and Gressmann on the historical reasons for this development are still valid today, and have simply been confirmed by the dominant role of the doctrine of angels in Qumran: 'The trend towards the transcendent and the abstract in Jewish belief in God' favoured the origin of 'middle-beings' which interposed themselves 'between God, who had become distant from the world, and man'.[309] The objections of G. Pfeifer, that there had always been hypostasis-like conceptions in Judaism, but that on the whole they had been rare and that an awareness of God constantly active in the world had always been preserved,[310] cannot conceal the fact that in the Hellenistic period the middle-forms – whether as 'hypostases', like wisdom in Prov.8.22ff., Job 28, etc, or angels, as the boundary is a fluid one[311] – increased in both Palestinian Judaism and that of the Diaspora. At the same time the divine name Yahweh retreated behind more general designations of God (see above, pp.117f. and below, pp.266f.). On the other hand, it is right to note that hypostases 'do not have their place in immediate experience of God . . . but in reflection'.[312] Later wisdom, as we find it in Prov.1–9 or even in Koheleth and Ben Sira, has explicitly reflective character and thus shows the beginnings of systematic theological conceptualization. However, whereas in the sceptical thought of Koheleth the reality of God is concealed behind the unpredictability of the 'plan of the times' and 'destiny' (see above, pp.120f.), in Prov.1–9 the revelation of divine salvation is realized in the personal appeal of 'wisdom', which 'makes the claim to lead to God'.[313] The 'hypostatization' of '*ḥokmā*' as a companion at play by God's side before all the works of creation is intended to provide this invitation with unconditional authority, though it must be noted that its claim also came up against opposition as being an innovation and an alien body in the Jewish tradition. For certain wisdom schools, however, the wisdom of God became a supreme authority and received a function as a '*mediator of revelation*'.[314] The mythological form of individual statements about 'wisdom' may be connected with the fact that they are also intended to ward off the incursion of the worship of foreign mother-goddesses.[315] At the same time, however, we should also consider whether the wisdom whose starting point was the 'fear of Yahweh' (Prov.1.7; 2.5; 9.10) was not also intended in apologetic fashion to prevent the development of an alien wisdom which endangered traditional belief. One indication of this could be the fact that the foreign woman who appears frequently in Prov.1–9 (2.16ff.; ch.5; 6.24ff.; ch.7), and probably also the foolish woman, were already interpreted metaphorically in the Septuagint of Prov.2.16–18 (διδασκαλίαν νεότητος, v.17) as referring to 'foreign wisdom', whereas Clement of Alexandria later

interpreted Prov. 5.3 as Ἑλληνικὴ παιδεία and probably took over this conception from Alexandrian Jewish exegesis.[316] We can also best understand
the wisdom fragment found in Cave 4 of Qumran, which depicts the seductive
arts of the evil woman in the most sombre colours, in the light of this metaphorical interpretation.[317] The counterpart to the foreign seductress was
'wisdom' as a young bride, as she appears in the beautiful love song ascribed
to the young David from 11 QPsᵃ, which has been preserved in Sir. 51.13–20 in
a milder, less passionate form.[318] There is a unique Greek parallel to this:

> In his investigation of Hercules at the parting of the ways,[319] I. Alpers
> draws attention to related features between Prov. 7 and 9, with their
> competing invitations of wisdom and folly, and the fable of Prodicus in
> Xenophon, *Memorabilia* 2, 1, 21–34, and the allegorical figures of *aretē* and
> *kakia* which appear there. Nevertheless, even here dependence is improb-
> able; however, here as elsewhere it is evident that analogous conceptions
> could arise independently of each other in Judaism and in Greece, so that
> there was finally a certain affinity between the two realms.

Literal and metaphorical interpretation of the 'foreign woman' as a counterpart of 'wisdom' need not be completely exclusive. As long as the Phoenician-
Canaanite cult of the mother goddess and goddess of love still represented a
danger to Judaism, the literal interpretation was the obvious one; as from about
the middle of the third century BC criticism of traditional Jewish belief in God
nourished by the Hellenistic spirit and popular philosophy took form, a
metaphorical interpretation was increasingly adopted.

b) Wisdom and the doctrine of creation

An important preparation for the encounter of Jewish wisdom teaching with
Greek thought was that it had become more and more bound up with the
doctrine of creation. Although the Priestly account of creation in Gen. 1.1–2.4
merely represents the introduction to a great historical work with a systematic
and chronological construction, it contains 'the results of concentrated
theological and cosmological reflection'.[320] Its origin can be understood as a
'significant testimony to the first international "scientific" attempts . . . to
investigate the world and all associated with it',[321] and the result can hardly
be understood apart from the systematic work of priestly wisdom schools.
Although it is probably dependent on early Semitic and above all Egyptian
creation narratives,[322] the unknown author has 'created an account of
unique consistency in a strictly ordered construction'. In this way the myth
'appears to be overcome by knowledge, but the knowledge that rests on the
analysis of the world of phenomena is subordinated to the creative power of
God'.[323] From a purely formal point of view, the creation account of Gen. 1
is related to its mythological predecessors in the same way as the philosophical
cosmogonies of the Ionian nature philosophers or Plato's *Timaeus* to their

mythological models.[324] It is 'one of the most rationally consistent parts of the Bible'.[325] If, for instance, as von Rad assumes, 'the conception of a *creatio ex nihilo*' is bound up with the ברא of Gen. 1.1,[326] this is the expression of a reflective capacity for theological abstraction, and it is no coincidence that the explicit formulation first appears in II Macc. 7.28, in a completely Hellenized (see above, pp. 95ff.) form (ὅτι οὐκ ἐξ ὄντων ἐποίησεν αὐτὰ ὁ θεός), although even here one must be careful about introducing the dogmatic formula *creatio ex nihilo*. Even if the later wisdom of the book of Job or Prov. 1–9 differs substantially from the strictly salvation-historical and cultically orientated theology of the Priestly writing, it had in common with that theology a rational tendency towards demythologizing which subjected the sphere of nature to the ordering will of God, seen in unmythical terms.[327] Here the concept of *ḥokmā* was particularly suited to express the rationality of the newly-creating and sustaining activity of God:

Yahweh by wisdom (*beḥokmā*) founded the earth,
by understanding he established the heavens (*bitebūnā*).[328]

This connection of wisdom with the doctrine of creation had a twofold consequence. On the one hand it led to an encyclopaedic treatment of all the phenomena in the world created by God, as they were an expression of the 'wisdom' of God. Here the ordering of creation and the functioning of its offshoots were not, of course, understood as an immanent 'natural' process – this conception was alien to early Jewish wisdom – but as a divine miracle.[329] This was the genuinely Jewish answer to the 'principle of form' of the visible world. We find an early form of this 'natural science' in the book of Job and in Ps. 104, and a later one in apocalyptic speculation, above all in I Enoch, where the whole sphere of history and the heavenly and subterranean worlds are included, thus producing – under heavily foreign influence – a new re-mything (see below, pp. 207ff.). Secondly, the individual who accepted the religious and ethical obligations in the call of *ḥokmā* – 'the fear of Yahweh is the beginning of wisdom' (Prov. 1.7) – received a share in cosmic, divine wisdom. Both consequences necessarily led in the end to an encounter with Hellenistic thought. This can be seen for the first time with Ben Sira, at least in hints.

c) 'Wisdom' in Ben Sira

We shall limit ourselves to those hymns in which Sirach describes wisdom as a 'cosmic hypostasis' or has it speaking in person: 1.1–10 and ch. 24. Unfortunately, neither is extant in its original Hebrew form. Sirach's work, which probably was composed several generations after Prov. 1–9, reflects the intellectual tensions in the Jerusalem of his time (see above, pp. 131ff.). So the general picture which he presents is remarkably ambiguous. On the one hand we find in him the universalistic, optimistic attitude of traditional religion, open to the world, and on the other there is obviously a polemical repudiation of attacks on the threatened faith of the fathers and, in contrast to earlier wisdom, an energetic appeal to the heritage of Israel and its holy history (see above, pp. 135ff.). Thus the mythological background to the *ḥokmā* speculation emerges particularly clearly in the great wisdom hymn of ch. 24, where, as has long been recognized, in the statements made by wisdom about herself (Sir. 24.3–7)[330] there are unmistakable parallels to similar predicative statements in Hellenistic *Isis aretalogies*.[331] In the third century, probably with a certain degree of backing from the state in the Ptolemaic empire,[332] the worship of Isis, together with the Serapis cult, increased considerably. Isis, who had possibly taken over features of early Egyptian Maat, here showed a predilection for the assumption of abstract concepts like δικαιοσύνη, ἐπίνοια, πρόνοια, φρόνησις, etc.[333] That in this form Isis also found a footing in Palestine, in close conjunction with the native Astarte, is shown by the great Isis aretalogy of Oxyrhynchus, which goes back to Hellenistic times. Here her worship in Ptolemais-Acco is attested with the cult name φρονίμη[ν].[334]

> Another whole series of Palestinian and Phoenician cities are mentioned as cult places of Isis: Rhinocolura on the Egyptian border; Raphia, Gaza, Ashkelon, Strato's Tower – thus the tradition seems to go back to pre-Herodian times, and perhaps to the time before the Hasmonean conquests – Dor, Sidon, Berytus, etc. In Sidon she bears the name Astarte, in 'Phoenicia' she is called the Syrian goddess, and in north Syrian Bambyce she is called Atargatis.[335] The cult of Egyptian goddesses was already widespread in the pre-Hellenistic period, and Isis too was not unknown there. In the bronzes discovered at Ashkelon dating from the fourth century, she appears as a small figurine, nursing the child Horus. She later appears as a nurse in the Tannaitic tradition.[336] We have archaeological evidence for the worship of her in the Hellenistic-Roman period from Ashkelon, Gerasa and – from the early Hellenistic period long before the destruction of the city by Hyrcanus about 108 BC – from Samaria.[337] The fragments of bas-relief from the Hellenistic period published by R. A. S. Macalister and I. G. Duncan could point to the worship of Isis-Astarte in Jerusalem under Ptolemaic rule; they were found in a relatively deep, pre-Roman site on the Ophel. They show a headdress similar to that worn by the goddess Hathor, who was identified with Isis, with the disc of the sun between two cows' horns, a triangle (betyl) and ornaments of plants, and could come from circles of Phoenician merchants or the Ptolemaic garrison or its officials. Palestinian goddesses had long tended to take over Egyptian traits.[338]

Thus we cannot exclude the possibility that in the third century BC the Isis cult attempted to penetrate even Jerusalem, and that Jewish wisdom schools transferred predicates of Isis-Astarte, who was then becoming more influential, to divine wisdom in a kind of polemical transformation. If Bubastis was given pride of place in the Isis aretalogies as the holy city of the goddess, it was logical that in Ben Sira Jerusalem should be the place where wisdom descended.[339] The transference was helped by the fact that Isis was regarded on the one hand as creator of the world and on the other as author and guarantor of ethical and legal order and human culture in general.[340] Of course there were fundamental differences which put certain limitations on a transference of predicates from the Isis aretalogies to Jewish *ḥokmā*. The main characteristic difference was that wisdom was not a *parhedros* with equal rights alongside God; she emerged from his mouth – and thus is more to be equated with the creative word of God (24.3) – or appears as his creation (24.8, 9), which serves him and obeys him (24.10f.). Ben Sira presumably took over the echoes of the predicates of the Isis aretalogy from an early wisdom hymn, for in his time the question of the worship of Isis or another female goddess in Jerusalem was hardly an acute one any more. However, we also find, above all in the first hymn to wisdom in Sir. 1.1–20, conceptions which have contacts with popular philosophical thought:

> Wisdom was created before all things
> and prudent understanding from eternity. (1.4)

> προτέρα πάντων ἔκτισται σοφία
> καὶ σύνεσις φρονήσεως ἐξ αἰῶνος

> The Lord himself created wisdom, he saw her and apportioned her (Job 28.27),
> he *poured* her *out* upon *all* his works,
> she dwells in all flesh according to his distribution. (Sir. 1.9, 10a)

> . . . καὶ ἐξέχεεν αὐτὴν ἐπὶ πάντα τὰ ἔργα αὐτοῦ
> μετὰ πάσης σαρκὸς κατὰ τὴν δόσιν αὐτοῦ.

Sir. 24.5f. also points in a more mythological form – presumably taken over from the Isis aretalogy[341] – to this cosmic universality of wisdom:

> Alone I have made the circuit of heaven,
> and have walked in the depths of the abyss.
> In the waves of the sea, in the whole earth,
> and in every people and nation I have gotten a possession.

> γῦρον οὐρανοῦ ἐκύκλωσα μόνη
> καὶ ἐν βάθει ἀβύσσων περιεπάτησα
> ἐν κύμασιν θαλάσσης καὶ ἐν πάσῃ τῇ γῇ
> καὶ ἐν παντὶ λαῷ καὶ ἔθνει ἡγησάμην.[342]

Here wisdom no longer appears, as in Prov. 8.30, as the darling of God, but as a 'power which pervades the whole world, nature and humanity (and not only the Jews)'.[343] Ben Sira was probably no longer aware of the original mythological features in his wisdom hymn in ch. 24, and regarded wisdom more as a kind of '*world reason*' emanating from God, which filled and permeated the whole creation and finds the culmination of its task in making man a rational being (1.9f., 19; cf. 17.7). For him, the working of wisdom and God's creative action formed an inseparable unity. Thus 'wisdom' in Ben Sira could be understood analogously to the Stoic 'Logos', which permeates and shapes the cosmos:

> The universal *law*, which is true wisdom permeating everything, is identical with Zeus, the director of the pervading of all things.[344]
>
> ὁ νόμος ὁ κοινός, ὅσπερ ἐστὶν ὁ ὀρθὸς λόγος διὰ πάντων
> ἐρχόμενος, ὁ αὐτὸς ὢν τῷ Διί, καθηγεμόνι τούτῳ τῆς τῶν
> ὄντων διοικήσεως ὄντι.

However, Ben Sira is not content with the universal interpretation of 'wisdom' as a formative and regulative principle in the world, especially as in this way it could also be acknowledged by the 'enlightened' Jewish circles to whom the national religious tradition of Israel and its law no longer meant anything. He went a decisive step further, and here too Stoic thought could provide him with an analogy: the 'universal law' identical with the Logos which ordered the world harmoniously, at the same time formed the moral norm for human conduct. While it directed the rest of the world in a firmly determined causal way, it directed man endowed with reason by virtue of his free moral decision (see pp. 140f. above), by bringing him 'to live in accord with nature, which means the same thing as living virtuously', for as Zeno already remarked – 'this is what nature drives us to'.[345] In a similar way, Ben Sira identified 'wisdom' as the 'primal image' and the 'principle of order' of the world created by God,[346] which was 'poured out on all (God's) works' (Sir. 1.9), with the firmly delineated moral norm of pious Jews, the Torah communicated exclusively to Israel on Sinai:[347]

> All this is the book of the covenant of the Most High God,
> the law which Moses commanded us,
> as an inheritance for the congregations of Jacob.[348]
>
> ταῦτα πάντα βίβλος διαθήκης θεοῦ ὑψίστου,
> νόμον ὃν ἐνετείλατο ἡμῖν Μωυσῆς
> κληρονομίαν συναγωγαῖς Ἰακώβ.

In this way the many-layered conception of cosmic wisdom, so easily misunderstood, was indissolubly associated with the history of Israel and, conversely, the law which was attacked in Jerusalem in the time of Ben Sira was given a supra-historical and at the same time a rational basis. Granted, with this the universality of the influence of wisdom, which had originally been intended by the hymns of 1.1–9 and 24.3–6, was shattered; but this corresponded to the whole tone of Sirach's work. He therefore bent round even this universalism in a significant way in 1.10 by supplementing

> with all flesh according to his distribution

against its original meaning:

> and he supplied her to those who love him.

ἐχορήγησεν αὐτὴν τοῖς ἀγαπῶσιν αὐτόν.

He does the same sort of thing in 24.6b–8:

> in every people and (every) nation I ruled.

Then follows the change:

> Among all these I sought a resting place;
> I sought in whose territory I might lodge.
> Then the Creator of all things gave me a commandment,
> and the one who created me assigned a place for my tent.
> And he said, 'Make your dwelling in Jacob,
> and in Israel receive your inheritance.'

The violent break is clear in both passages: the originally universal wisdom becomes the possession of a limited number of elect, the people of Israel or the pious devoted to the law. At the same time, an answer was given to the old mythological question whether wisdom sought a dwelling place on earth in vain and so in disappointment returned to her heavenly dwelling: she has found her abiding place on earth in the Torah, which is entrusted to Israel alone.[349]

Whether Ben Sira was the first to make this momentous identification or whether he took over even it from the wisdom school to which he was indebted is hard to say. It certainly marks a climax in the composition of Sirach's collection of sayings which represents the fruits of a lifetime's work (see above, p. 131), and this really indicates that he was presenting ideas which had not long been in general currency. Perhaps the identification was first made in the circle of *sōperīm* around Simon the Just, who as high priest strengthened the national tradition (see above, p. 132f.), a group standing close to Ben Sira. The motto ascribed to Simon in *'Ab.* 1, 2 similarly gives the Torah 'cosmic' significance:

> The world stands on three things: on the Torah and on the (temple) cult and on works of love.[350]

Here the cult and works of love are essentially included in the Torah. But we do not know whether this saying really comes from Simon the Just or his time. The beginnings of an integration of law and wisdom were certainly older; we already have a pointer in this direction in Deut. 4.6, where God's commandments are called the wisdom of Israel over against the nations, and this becomes even more marked in Psalms 1 and 119, which were probably composed in the third century;[351] but a decisive step has still to be taken before the complete identification in Ben Sira. According to von Rad the identification of hypostatized, cosmic wisdom and Torah in Sirach 'has to be regarded as simply a theological conclusion already latent in principle in Prov. 1–9 and now come to maturity'.[352] Without question, there is an inner logic in this development of Jewish wisdom speculation, but we should ask whether a movement in this direction would have developed at all if it had not been furthered by the necessity to ward off foreign influences. We must therefore agree with J. Fichtner, who sees the decisive motive force in the 'controversy with Hellenism':

> Over against Hellenism and its wisdom, a wisdom in Judaism could only assert itself if it approximated to *the* factor which played the decisive role in this struggle on the side of the Jews: *the law* . . . The significance of *ḥokmā* for the shaping of Jewish religion in the struggle against Hellenism and its σοφία is not to be underestimated.[353]

If the rejection of the cult of female deities marked the beginning, the continuation came with the controversy with the Hellenistic 'enlightenment' and its sceptical tendencies. On the positive side, at least at the end of this development, Stoic-type conceptions near to popular philosophy were taken up by Ben Sira. All taken together created that 'powerful conception of world and salvation history'[354] which tenaciously influenced not only the Palestinian *haggada* but also the Alexandrian philosophy of religion and was itself of decisive significance for the development of christology.

d) The Greek translation of Prov. 8.22–31

Understandably, contacts with philosophical thought-patterns increase where the boundary presented by the Greek language is crossed. Although on the whole one can discover only a few echoes of Greek popular philosophy in the Greek translation of the Old Testament, which itself came into being in close conjunction with the Palestinian tradition and in the case of individual books even in Palestine (see pp. 100ff. above),[355] there are some exceptions. Thus G. Gerleman has demonstrated such popular philosophical features in the Greek version of Proverbs.[356] This was presumably composed in the first half of the second century BC and was more strongly subjected to Hellenizing influences than the translation of other books.[357] Above all, according to Gerleman, the translation of the predicates of wisdom in Prov. 8.30 *wā'ehyeh 'eṣelō 'āmōn* by ἤμην παρ'αὐτῷ ἁρμόζουσα shows an approximation to Stoic conceptions: 'Wisdom accommodates, brings into harmony.'[358] In addition, however, the whole Greek translation of Prov. 8.22–31 is illuminating, especially as it deviates from the Hebrew original. Wisdom was created or begotten (ἔκτισέν με 8.22; γεννᾷ με 8.25) as the beginning of the work of God (ἀρχὴν ὁδῶν αὐτοῦ 8.22) and for his works (εἰς ἔργα αὐτοῦ).[359] In that it is present throughout creation, as ἁρμόζουσα it guarantees creation's perfection and purposeful beauty. It is therefore the ground of God's joy (ἐγὼ ἤμην ᾗ προσέχαιρεν 8.30b) and shares in his joy throughout the whole work of creation (καθ' ἡμέραν δὲ εὐφραινόμην ἐν προσώπῳ αὐτοῦ ἐν παντὶ καιρῷ), especially in God's joy at the perfection of his work and at men (ὅτε εὐφραίνετο τὴν οἰκουμένην συντελέσας καὶ ἐνευφραίνετο ἐν υἱοῖς ἀνθρώπων).[360] One could ask whether the conception of wisdom as a kind of *'world soul'* which we already find in Plato's *Timaeus* and which was later taken over and transformed by the Stoa is hinted at here.[361] With the conception of the demiurge as a personal creator God, the Timaeus would inevitably come closer to Jewish thought than the Stoic identification of God and world. As in Jewish wisdom specula-tion, the 'world soul' appears as the first and most excellent creation of the demiurge (γενέσει καὶ ἀρετῇ προτέραν καὶ πρεσβυτέραν), which permeates the universe (διὰ παντὸς ἔτεινεν),[362] surrounding it and guaranteeing rationality and harmony to the corporeal world as an invisible mediatrix (αὐτὴ δὲ ἀόρατος μὲν λογισμοῦ δὲ μετέχουσα καὶ ἁρμονίας ψυχή . . . ἀρίστη γενομένη τῶν γεννη-θέντων).[363] The divine father thus also delighted in the world soul that he had created and in its perfection (ὁ γεννήσας πατήρ, ἠγάσθη τε καὶ εὐφρανθείς);[364] the soul itself is begotten by him as εὐδαίμονα θεόν.[365] The world created by the demiurge through the mediation of the world soul is a κόσμος ἀληθινός and as such 'harmonious and good' (καλῶς ἁρμοσθὲν καὶ ἔχον εὖ).[366]

These conceptions of the world soul and the demiurge influenced not only the Stoa, where it was identified with the Logos,[367] but also Xenocrates, the pupil of Plato, who gave them a more strongly mythological stamp. He set the world soul as a feminine, inferior second principle alongside 'Zeus', 'God the Father', who ruled in heaven as the *nous*: as the mother of the gods (μητρὸς θεῶν) and *dikē*, she is at the same time the 'soul of the universe' (ψυχὴ τοῦ παντός). At a later date, in Plutarch, this Xenocratic world soul is identified with Isis, and R. Henze, the editor of the fragments of Xenocrates, already supposed that Plutarch had taken this identification from his sources. Leisegang with good reason sees in her one of the preludes to |the Gnostic 'Sophia'.[368] We might ask whether wisdom in Wisdom and Philo, which does not have such a strong mythological colouring, is not influenced from this direction.[369] As Plato, among others, also considers the possibility of an evil world-soul (*Laws* 896e–897d), there is also the possibility here of a fall of Sophia.[370]

The unknown translator of Proverbs is probably quite close in time to the first known Jewish 'philosopher of religion', Aristobulus, about 170 BC, who refers to Prov. 8.22ff. and perhaps already presupposes that it has been trans-lated.[371] As Aristobulus expressly stresses that Plato knew Moses' account of creation, even the *Timaeus*, which has the closest contacts with Gen. 1,[372] will not have been unknown to him. Whether and how far the translator of Proverbs knew the *Timaeus* is hard to say. The analogies cited, of course, are in no way sufficient to demonstrate literary dependence; nevertheless we can see how Jewish wisdom speculation and the doctrine of creation grew increasingly close to analogous Greek conceptions. This can be seen for the first time in Aristobulus.

e) Creation and wisdom in Aristobulus, the first Jewish 'philosopher' in Alexandria

At almost the same time as Ben Sira, we find in this Jew from Alexandria a

doctrine of wisdom and of creation which combines inseparably his own
sacred tradition with the thought-forms and ideas of Greek philosophy.
According to II Macc.1.10 he came from a high-priestly family and in later
tradition is called a 'Peripatetic'.[373] A. Schlatter pointed out that the
theological views of Aristotle, his acknowledgment of philosophical monotheism, his doctrine of God as the first unmoved mover and his clear and
moderate ethic might well have influenced a philosophical Jew.[374] But in
Aristobulus we find an explicit eclecticism with influence from no one school,
and moreover the designation 'Peripatetic' was not used as a specific designation
of a school in the Alexandria of his time.[375] N. Walter has recently provided
an impressive demonstration of the authenticity of the fragments of his
writings which have been preserved,[376] which, according to the rather
exaggerated judgment of A. Schlatter, 'are left to us only in a state of complete
ruin'.[377] They derive from an apologetic, didactic work presumably dating
from 175–170 BC, addressed to the young Ptolemy VI Philometor (181–145
BC).[378] They were intended to demonstrate that Jewish doctrine as presented
in the Pentateuch, i.e. the Greek translation of the Mosaic law, represented the
true 'philosophy' and did not contradict philosophically trained reason. Here a
'philosophical' support is provided to the correspondence of 'wisdom' and
piety as taught in the wisdom schools of Judea, with the support of cosmological and psychological arguments. For him, the Jews are basically a nation of
philosophers (see below, pp.255ff.): 'All philosophers agree that men must
have sacred concepts from God; but our αἵρεσις is most principally concerned
with this.' Here Aristobulus employs a term which was commonly used for the
different philosophical schools. A few decades later, the Letter of Aristeas outlines a similar picture of the seventy-two elders from Palestine.[379]

In his thought, Aristobulus proceeds from two basic presuppositions:

1. If men are to understand the 'philosophical', real (φυσικῶς)[380]
meaning of the Pentateuch, they should not 'fall victim to mythological[381]
and human conceptions' (καὶ μὴ ἐκπίπτειν εἰς τὸ μυθῶδες καὶ ἀνθρώπινον
κατάστημα, Euseb., *Pr. Ev.*8, 10, 2). Here Aristobulus is attacking not only the
Greek critics of the law but also its anxiously conservative champions. Here
they are doing him no good service: 'For to those who have neither strength
nor insight, but merely cling to the letter, he (i.e. Moses) does not appear as
anyone who proclaims great things' (τοῖς δὲ μὴ μετέχουσι δυνάμεως καὶ
συνέσεως ἀλλὰ τῷ γραπτῷ μόνον προσκειμένοις οὐ φαίνεται μεγαλεῖόν τι διασαφῶν
8, 10, 5). Rather, one must try to reinterpret all the statements in the Pentateuch
which are offensive because of their anthropomorphic form by allegorical
interpretation, in order to preserve 'the appropriate conception of God' (τὴν
ἁρμόζουσαν ἔννοιαν περὶ θεοῦ 8, 10, 2), as Moses often uses obviously metaphorical concepts to describe physical circumstances (φυσικὰς διαθέσεις 8, 10,
3). Thus when the Pentateuch talks about the 'hands of God' it means his
power; and the 'standing of God' means the existence and immutability of the

world that he has created (8, 10, 7–11). Here Aristobulus takes up the allegorical interpretation of myth from the Stoa or from Alexandrian philologists, though he still uses these methods in a very restrained way.[382] Similarly, the 'descent' of God on Sinai according to Exod. 19.17–20 should not be understood locally, as God is omnipresent (τὴν κατάβασιν μὴ τοπικὴν εἶναι πάντῃ γὰρ ὁ θεός ἐστιν 8, 10, 15).[383] The appearances of fire and the sound of the trumpet were, however, summoned forth by God in a miraculous way without human intervention in order to prove his all-pervading majesty to the Israelites (8, 10, 17).

2. For those 'who can think rightly' (οἷς μὲν οὖν πάρεστι τὸ καλῶς νοεῖν), this law of Moses, understood 'philosophically', is a clear indication of the 'wisdom and divine spirit' of its author (τὴν περὶ αὐτὸν σοφίαν καὶ τὸ θεῖον πνεῦμα 8, 10, 4), who is rightly called a 'prophet'. Greek philosophers and poets are also counted among those who revere him, and have taken over many ideas from him, as a result of which they are marvelled at. For Aristobulus, rationality and inspiration do not exclude each other but belong closely together; they are not in opposition, because they both come from divine wisdom. Here we have the first beginnings of a *doctrine of inspiration* in Alexandrian Judaism, which is essentially different from the later Philonic approach, but is closely connected with corresponding conceptions in Palestinian wisdom, e.g. that of Ben Sira.[384] Because 'right thinking' and the '*pneuma*' are not exclusive, Aristobulus can adduce the '*hieros logos*' of Orpheus and the well-known verses of the Stoic Aratus as witnesses to God's rule over the world.[385] However, the inferiority of these to Moses is shown by the fact that they 'have no holy concepts of God' and therefore must be corrected (13, 12, 7f., see below, p.265). Pythagoras, Socrates and Plato, on the other hand, knew the much earlier Torah which they already had in part in an older translation, and by 'contemplation of the construction of the world, with what care it was created is sustained by God' (τὴν κατασκευὴν τῶν ὅλων συνθεωροῦντες ἀκριβῶς ὑπὸ θεοῦ γεγονυῖαν καὶ συνεχομένην ἀδιαλείπτως . . . 13, 11, 4) were led to the recognition of the truth of the biblical account of creation. There could be an allusion here to the *Timaeus*, as Plato has his doctrine of creation presented to Socrates by the Pythagorean Timaeus. Thus by virtue of its antiquity and the divine wisdom of its prophetic author, the law of Moses is far superior to the doctrines of the Greek wise men and philosophers, who are dependent on it (on this see above, pp.90f., 92).

Here Aristobulus takes up notions which in essence go back to the idea, favoured in the Hellenistic period, of the Egyptian or even Phoenician origin of Greek culture and philosophy, and which we encountered in a Jewish version in the anonymous Samaritan, Eupolemus and the romance writer Artapanus. Even the attempt at a rational or allegorical reinterpretation of offensive passages will not be his own invention; presumably these efforts reached a first climax with him.[386] The Jewish Alexandrian 'philosophy of

religion' which later culminated in Philo, and whose results and methods were
to a large extent taken over by the early church fathers, have their earliest
really tangible representative in him.[387]

In his *doctrine of wisdom and creation* proper, which is unfortunately
preserved only in fragments, we find a unique combination of the resting of
God on the seventh day and the creation of light on the first day with the pre-
temporal being of wisdom according to Prov. 8.22 and certain philosophical
notions:

> God, who created the whole cosmos, also gave us the seventh day for rest,
> because it is wearisome for us all to sustain life. This could in reality
> ($\phi \upsilon \sigma \iota \kappa \tilde{\omega} s$) also be called the first (day and) the begetting of the (spiritual)
> light ($\phi \omega \tau \grave{o} s \ \gamma \acute{\epsilon} \nu \epsilon \sigma \iota s$),[388] in which all is comprehended ($\grave{\epsilon} \nu \ \tilde{\omega} \ \tau \grave{a} \ \pi \acute{a} \nu \tau a$
> $\sigma \upsilon \nu \theta \epsilon \omega \rho \epsilon \tilde{\iota} \tau a \iota$). The same thing could also be transferred to wisdom, as
> all light comes from her ($\mu \epsilon \tau a \phi \acute{\epsilon} \rho o \iota \tau o \ \delta' \ \mathring{a} \nu \ \tau \grave{o} \ a \mathring{v} \tau \grave{o} \ \kappa a \grave{\iota} \ \grave{\epsilon} \pi \grave{\iota} \ \tau \tilde{\eta} s \ \sigma o \phi \acute{\iota} a s \cdot \ \tau \grave{o}$
> $\gamma \grave{a} \rho \ \pi \tilde{a} \nu \ \phi \tilde{\omega} s \ \grave{\epsilon} \sigma \tau \iota \nu \ \grave{\epsilon} \xi \ a \mathring{v} \tau \tilde{\eta} s$); just as some members of the Peripatetic
> school say that wisdom has the role of a lamplighter ($\lambda a \mu \pi \tau \tilde{\eta} \rho o s \ a \mathring{v} \tau \grave{\eta} \nu \ \mathring{\epsilon} \chi \epsilon \iota \nu$
> $\tau \acute{a} \xi \iota \nu$), because those who persevere in following her find that their life
> continues long in a state of rest ($\mathring{a} \tau \acute{a} \rho a \chi o \iota$). But one of our forbears,
> Solomon, said more clearly and more beautifully that it was created before
> heaven and earth (Prov. 8.22f.). Which corresponds with what was said
> beforehand.[389]

The first remarkable thing is the identification of the first and the seventh
days of creation. However, for Aristobulus God was not subject to the ordering
of time. The 'resting of God' on the seventh day did not mean the end of his
work but only the 'fixing of the order of things', and the work of the six days
was to be understood as the establishing of the course of time ($\mathring{\iota} \nu a \ \tau o \grave{v} s \ \chi \rho \acute{o} \nu o \upsilon s$
$\delta \eta \lambda \acute{\omega} \sigma \eta$) and of gradations within the created world (13, 12, 11f.). In this
way Aristobulus attempted to bring the Old Testament conception of the
creation of God in time in accord with the Greek idea of the timeless activity
of God. Not God himself, but only his creation is subject to the course of
time.[390] The individual feast-days which have been established, and above all the
sabbath as a day of rest, appear as symbols of the divine ordering of the world.
The astronomical discussions of the date of the feast of the passover also
suggest a 'cosmic' significance of this feast.[391]

Thus the conception of the seventh day only makes sense when one
recognizes its deeper significance: following Pythagorean, Platonic and Hippocratic number speculation,[392] he interprets it as the principle of the *number
seven* which orders the cosmos. By this 'the whole cosmos, with all its animals
and plants, is moved' ($\delta \iota' \ \grave{\epsilon} \beta \delta o \mu \acute{a} \delta \omega \nu \ \delta \grave{\epsilon} \ \kappa a \grave{\iota} \ \pi \tilde{a} s \ \grave{o} \ \kappa \acute{o} \sigma \mu o s \ \kappa \upsilon \kappa \lambda \epsilon \tilde{\iota} \tau a \iota \ \tau \tilde{\omega} \nu$
$\zeta \omega o \gamma o \nu o \upsilon \mu \acute{\epsilon} \nu \omega \nu \ \kappa a \grave{\iota} \ \tau \tilde{\omega} \nu \ \phi \upsilon o \mu \acute{\epsilon} \nu \omega \nu \ \grave{a} \pi \acute{a} \nu \tau \omega \nu$).[393] The entire natural process,
above all in an organic and physiological respect, is shaped after the structure
of seven, which is for the eye that can see it the proof of the divine
ordering of the world. But Aristobulus does not limit himself to this cosmo-

logical speculation; he goes further and considers its utility for men. The seventh day is to be kept holy 'as a symbol of our "sevenfold Logos", to which we owe our knowledge of human and divine things' (ἔνεκεν σημείου τοῦ περὶ ἡμᾶς ἑβδόμου λόγου ἐν ᾧ γνῶσιν ἔχομεν ἀνθρωπίνων καὶ θείων πραγμάτων 13, 12, 12).³⁹⁴ The 'structure of seven', permeating and ordering the world, is also the basis of human capacity for knowledge and wisdom. Here Aristobulus is evidently taking over the Stoic definition of wisdom. In a similar way, IV Maccabees, which comes from the beginning of the first century AD, describes 'wisdom' in good Stoic fashion as 'the knowledge of divine and human things' (1.16f.), but then qualifies it by defining it as ἡ τοῦ νόμου παιδεία. For Aristobulus, too, right knowledge has ethical consequences, so that he ascribes direct 'saving significance' to the 'sevenfold Logos'. He interprets the apocryphal verse of Homer, 'On the morning of the seventh day we left the floods of Acheron' as a reference to the liberation of men from the 'forget-fulness' which afflicts the soul – λήθη corresponding to Acheron – and evil (κακία) through the 'sevenfold Logos' which corresponds to the truth, from which 'we receive the knowledge of the truth' (γνῶσιν ἀληθείας λαμβάνομεν 13, 12, 15).³⁹⁵ One might suppose that here Aristobulus' thought was completely Greek: right knowledge also leads to right will, as it can rein back the power of the evil forces of the soul. But perhaps, in reality, he did not want to say more than the Palestinian wisdom teachers, that 'wisdom' freed men for right conduct and guided them (cf. 13, 12, 10f.). And the significance of the nine apocryphal verses relating to seven by Hesiod, Homer and Linus, which he quotes presumably from a Jewish-Pythagorean source, lies less in their proof of the authority of the sabbath commandment – this is only the con-sequence – than in their confirmation of the cosmic and spiritual significance of the number seven (13, 12, 13–16). Here we come full circle: the *universal divine structural principle of seven* which, as the 'sevenfold Logos',³⁹⁶ gives men true knowledge, *is identical with wisdom* 'from which all light comes', which according to Solomon, the Jewish wise man, 'was before heaven and earth', which the Peripatetic philosophers compare with a light and which gives the true sabbath rest to those who follow it, by making them ἀτάραχοι (13, 12, 10f.).³⁹⁷ This conjunction of 'wisdom' and 'primal light' is then taken further in Wisdom 7.22–26. By and large, Aristobulus has fused the original Jewish-Palestinian conception of personified 'ḥokmā' as the consort of God at the creation of the world with the biblical account of creation in Gen. 1–2.4a, laying special stress on Gen. 2.1–4a, with conceptions of Greek philosophical cosmology and epistemology, yet without giving up their specific features. Moreover, he does not attach himself to a particular philosophical school, but in a free and eclectic manner uses those ideas which in his view can be reconciled with the Jewish tradition. His understanding of God as being omnipresent, not limited by space or time; his attempt to interpret anthro-pomorphisms and to demonstrate a unitary divine ordering of the cosmos embracing both the world and men, must be understood as a positive effort to adapt the traditional conceptions of the Jewish tradition to the spiritual demands of a new age. If the Jewish community was not to waste away in the isolation it had chosen, but was to assert itself against a superior civilization and go over to a missionary counter-attack, it had to embark on this venture. It is not an insignificant factor that a large number of the ideas which were made explicit in Alexandria had already been prepared for in the Palestinian Jewish tradition.[398] What Ben Sira only hinted at was now made plain: 'wisdom' was comparable with the Stoic Logos, the law of the world or the world-soul. It was the spiritual principle of order and knowledge of the cosmos, recognizable in the number seven and created by the supra-temporal and transcendent God. The individual man shared in this principle by right thinking (8.10.4 $καλῶς νοεῖν$) and the resultant right action; he had to direct his life by it if he was to be happy. It is understandable that in this approach the cosmological-psychological orientation came to overshadow that of salvation history, but as in pre-Christian Jewish understanding 'salvation history' predominantly implied the exclusive limitation of salvation to Israel and its separation from the 'peoples', in the more open circles of the Diaspora a certain reorientation was necessary in the face of the missionary task which went beyond the narrow boundaries of the people. At this point, at a later stage – over against Palestinian and Diaspora Judaism – there set in the penetrating corrective of the eschatological and universal message of primitive Christianity.

The mythological and personal features of wisdom appear less prominent in Aristobulus than in Prov. 8.22, Sir. 24 or later in Wisd. 6.12–8.18 and in Philo (see n. 369 above); we do not even find here the unique connection with Israel, which was achieved in Ben Sira through the identification of wisdom with the law.[399] Its place is taken by the identification of wisdom with the cosmic principle of seven, which had been revealed to Israel in a special way through the sabbath commandment.

This idea, too, essentially goes back to Palestinian foundations. Even in the Priestly writing the sabbath commandment is a universal sign of salvation, which affected the whole of creation; so the Priestly redactor in Exod. 20.11 grounded it in the rest of God, according to Gen. 2.1–4a.[400] According to the book of Jubilees, which originated in Zadokite and Essene circles towards the end of the second century, the sabbath, like the feast of weeks, had been celebrated in the heavenly world long before it had been enjoined on Israel by Moses, as it was regarded as an expression of the heavenly ordering of the world and of time.[401] The 'Apocalypse of the Ten Weeks', which probably derives from the early period of the same movement (I Enoch 93 and 91.12–17), also recognizes a cosmic and noetic significance of the number seven. The great apostasy will begin in the seventh week of the world, and at the same time the elect will be gathered together, who receive 'sevenfold teaching about the whole of creation'.[402] The number seven has similar supernatural significance in the heavenly sabbath liturgy of the seven archangels, published by John Strugnell, where to some extent it represents the basic structure of the whole heavenly liturgy.[403]

Even the notion of the special character of the primal light created on the first day of creation was not unknown in Palestine, nor was the identification of light and wisdom; both appear in Tannaitic-Rabbinic and in apocalyptic literature; however, primal light was not interpreted in noetic and cosmological terms, but eschatologically: God himself has kept it for the time of the Messiah.[404] It is remarkable how in this way Jewish-Palestinian and Pythagorean-Platonic and Stoic conceptions are intermingled in Aristobulus. At that time in Alexandria – and probably also in the wisdom schools of Palestine (see above, pp. 80f. and 171f.) – stimuli from Greek thought were probably not rejected, because in the end they merely demonstrated the superiority of the older Jewish religion. However, while in Palestine after the Maccabean revolt the tendency to spiritual segregation from the non-Jewish world grew stronger in circles faithful to the law, the best forces of the Greek-speaking Diaspora remained more open to their environment. In contrast to the exclusive Zealot limitation of the sabbath commandment to Israel in the book of Jubilees and the later Rabbinic tradition,[405] Aristobulus cites the oldest 'wise men' of Greece as chief witnesses for this 'law of life of the cosmos', and thus makes Pythagoras, Socrates and Plato confessors of an ethical monotheism which they had learnt from Moses. Behind these views there is no weakness which is prepared for assimilation, but a firmly based spiritual and religious self-awareness. Although the thoughts of Aristobulus are preserved for us only in fragments, they suggest 'a bold and clear thinker as their author'.[406] Whereas in Palestine the universality of the old wisdom tradition was constructed in the controversy with Hellenistic liberalism, it was taken further in the Diaspora – albeit in a different form – and even later presented in more or less philosophical garb in works like Ps. Aristeas, the Wisdom of Solomon, Ps. Phocylides, the forged sayings of Menander and Heraclitus. Even if these writings are addressed predominantly to a Jewish public or one that sympathized with Judaism (see above, pp. 69f.), they still raise the supra-national claim to represent true 'wisdom', true philosophy, and are thus at the same time an expression of the missionary expansion of Greek-speaking Judaism of the Hellenistic and Roman period. Thus they represented an ethical monotheism grounded in the doctrine of creation, to which the missionary preaching of the early church could attach itself.

f) Wisdom and Torah in Pharisaic and Rabbinic Judaism

On the other hand, in the Jewish-Palestinian wisdom tradition positions hardened. The identification of cosmic *ḥokmā* and Torah made by Sirach was maintained above all in that branch of the Hasidim from which the Pharisaic movement grew after the separation of the Essenes (see below, pp. 224ff.) in the Hasmonean period, say from the time of Simon and John Hyrcanus I (143–134 or 134–104 BC).[407] Thus in 3.9–4.4, the book of Baruch[408] contains a wisdom psalm, originally in Hebrew, dependent on Sirach 24, which varies the theme of hidden wisdom known from Job 28, to the effect that wisdom remained hidden from the foreign rulers of the nations, the Canaanites and Arab merchants, who are described as 'writers of sayings' (μυθόλογοι) and 'seekers after wisdom', and even from the giants of earlier times. It was communicated only to Israel in the form of the law: only now has it appeared on earth and conversed with men (i.e. Israel).[409]

She herself is the book of the commandments of God
and the law which remains to eternity.

αὕτη ἡ βίβλος τῶν προσταγμάτων θεοῦ
καὶ ὁ νόμος ὁ ὑπάρχων εἰς τὸν αἰῶνα (4.1, cf. Isa. 40.8b).

Granted, even here an earlier universalistic approach shines through, but this is deliberately changed into its opposite: the hymn of wisdom comes to a climax in a call to repentance. Israel must repent and not allow the law, her δόξα, to go to any alien people (4.2f.). We can hardly be mistaken in seeing here polemic against all attempts to discover wisdom among alien nations, too – whether Arabs or Greeks – or to communicate any of Israel's own wisdom, the law, to non-Jews.[410]

Now if wisdom, as the divine, pre-existent ordering of the world, was at the same time identical with the Torah of Israel entrusted to Moses on Sinai, a consequence arose which corresponded in an astonishing way with the Stoic idea of the unity of the world *nomos* and the moral law ordering the life of the individual. To accord with the 'cosmic' significance of the law, the pious man had to put it into practice without omission and without qualification in his everyday life,[411] so that his whole life was directed by it. Of exemplary significance here was the transference of ritual Levitical holiness, which was a matter for the temple and those concerned with temple worship, to the whole life of the faithful, including the laity. The realization of this demand, which was also an Essene ideal (see below, pp.223f.) and goes back to common Hasidic roots, probably led to the foundation of the first Pharisaic *ḥᵃbūrōt*.[412] In one way the whole world was God's sanctuary (ὦ Ἰσραηλ, ὡς μέγας ὁ οἶκος τοῦ θεοῦ καὶ ἐπιμήκης ὁ τόπος τῆς κτήσεως αὐτοῦ Bar. 3.24), and therefore required constant holiness. This idea also contains a mixture of Old Testament, Jewish and Hellenistic-oriental conceptions.[413] As here we are going beyond the temporal limitation of our work, we can only hint at the far-reaching consequences of the identification of wisdom as the ordering of the world and the Torah in a summary way.

The development from Prov. 8.22ff. *via* Sirach 24 to the Septuagint of Proverbs and Aristobulus could be described as a 'process of rationalization'. The same is also true, with qualifications, of the interpretation of wisdom in the Rabbinate.[414] True, hypostatized *ḥokmā* endowed with mythological traits did not disappear completely,[415] but it retreated behind the Torah which in the earliest Tannaitic tradition that we can detect was already regarded as a pre-existent, first creature, standing nearest to God (with reference to Prov. 8.22ff.).[416] 'Wisdom surrendered her cosmic functions . . . to the Torah.'[417] In the parables, above all, the Torah could be called directly 'daughter of God', and here one may see a parallel to the designation of the Logos as the Son of God in Philo.[418] More effective, however, were the conceptions of the role of the Torah in the creation of the world based on Prov. 8.22ff.:

> For R. Akiba, its mediating role was taken for granted and presupposed as a generally recognized teaching tradition: 'Israel is loved, for to her was given an instrument (*keli*) with which the world was created.'[419] R. Hoša'ya from Caesarea, a contemporary of Origen, summed up the different possibilities of interpreting Prov. 8.30: אמון is a 'master builder' ('*ūmān*). The Torah declares: I was the instrument of God's skill (כלי אומנתו של הקב"ה). When a king builds a palace, he does not do it himself, but with the help of 'the knowledge of a master builder' (מדעת אומן). And the master builder in turn considers plans and drawings: in just the same way, 'God looked into the Torah' (מביט בתורה) when he created the world. The beginning of Gen. 1.1 here was interpreted through the *gezērā šāwā* in the light of the *rē'šit darekō* of Prov. 8.22 and the *berē'šit* was understood as *beḥokmā* in the sense of 'through the Torah', with the help of which God created the world.[420] R. Hoša'ya was credited with creative, magic powers because of his doctrine of creation (*Sanh.* 67b).

G. F. Moore has already demonstrated the parallels here to the Platonic-type doctrine of creation in Philo. Whereas there the κόσμος νοητός was created as a spiritual model of the visible creation, among the Rabbis the Torah is the perfect model on which creation is based. Philo uses a similar image. He compares the creator to a king who wants to found a new city and recruits the aid of a master builder who carries everything out according to an exact plan.[421] K. Schubert, who takes this up, stresses that there is a real and deep-rooted analogy between the Torah as understood by the Rabbis and the Philonic Logos.[422] It is hardly likely that the Rabbis are directly dependent on Philo; rather, both will go back to earlier common traditions. In the close connections between Alexandria and Jerusalem in the second and first centuries BC there were many possibilities for mutual influence.[423]

The consequences of this *'ontological' understanding of the Torah*, transposed into the cosmic sphere, were manifold and far-reaching: from the time of Ben Sira, the Torah could be understood as a spiritual light that lightened men;[424] it lasted for ever[425] and was immeasurable;[426] in its absolute significance it was regarded simply as 'the good'.[427] Thus it became the *mediator of creation and revelation between God and the world*. Here the development of a crude doctrine of inspiration or better 'mediation' was a matter of course: 'The whole Torah is from heaven', no verse may be excluded.[428]

In this way, however, its six hundred and thirteen individual commandments and prohibitions received a 'cosmic' significance going beyond the realm of the individual; they were 'materialized forms of expression' of the divine ordinance of creation and salvation.[429] Each individual commandment, indeed each individual consonant possessed absolute importance; each deliberate or unintentional transgression of a commandment, each omission of a letter in copying the Torah meant in principle an attack on the divine structure of the world, formed by the Torah, for 'the Torah is indivisible'.[430]

> When R. Meir came to R. Ishmael (died AD 135) and gave his profession as scribe (of the Torah), the latter required of him the utmost care, 'for if you leave out a single letter or write a single letter too much, you will be found as one who destroys the whole world'.[431] According to R. Simon b. Laqiš (third century), the existence of the world depends on the fact that Israel accepts the Torah; otherwise the world would return to chaos (לתהו ובהו).[432] A Baraita going back to R. Eliezer b. Hyrcanus (c. AD 100) concludes from Jer.33.25: 'If the Torah were not there, heaven and earth would not exist.' Even the laws of heaven and earth (Jer.33.25) are an ingredient of the Torah (*Ned.*32a). R. Bannaya expressed the ultimate consequence (towards AD 200): the world was created for the sake of the Torah (בזכות תורה), a conclusion for which he refers to Prov.3.19 (see above, p.157).[433]

From this there followed with logical consistency both the casuistic securing of the commandments by the oral Torah, the hedge round the law,[434] and the scrupulous fixation of the text.[435] A further necessary development was the unique valuation of the study of the Torah, for only on the basis of constant study was it possible to observe the commandments correctly. The demand for an uninterrupted preoccupation with the Torah was elevated to an extreme form. It comprises the foundations of the tractate *Pirqe 'Aboth*.[436] That it brought the highest reward in the other world was taken for granted. This fact also explains the growing intellectual power of the scribes: they were the only authoritative exponents of the Torah, and as the 'wise men' had the key to the right understanding of it and thus to the mysteries of the present and the future world.[437]

> The significance of the scribe could almost be depicted with expressions which we also find in the thought-world of Hellenistic mysticism. The Torah makes him great and exalts him above all things ('*Ab.*6, 2a). Taking up this statement, and on the basis of an allegorical reinterpretation of Num.21.19, R. Jehoshua b. Lewi (beginning of the third century AD) could say: 'Anyone who occupies himself with the study of the Torah, behold, he goes ever higher. For it is said: 'From the gift (*mimmattānā*) to the heritage of God (*naḥ^ali'ēl*) and from the heritage of God to the heights' (*bāmōt*).

The conception of the absolute authority and sufficiency of the Torah in all the realms of human knowledge had as a consequence the fact that the halachic traditional material of the Pharisaic and Rabbinic schools which arose out of popular custom and the practical tradition of the law had to be derived from the Torah itself with new exegetical methods taken over from Alexandrian philology. Apparent contradictions in the Torah were also removed with this help.[438] The canonical books of the 'prophets' and the 'writings' which were not part of the Pentateuch, and the 'oral Torah', were in the last resort only indirectly authoritative as interpretation of the law given by Moses.[439] Any understanding of history as the sphere of the revelation of the divine salvation was thus excluded. As the Torah contained all wisdom, and the study of it was not to be restricted by any other intellectual occupation, converse with foreign writing not related to teaching, and especially Greek wisdom, was taboo and indeed partly prohibited.[440] Nevertheless, further alien notions flooded into Judaism from a whole variety of sources, from popular philosophical conceptions to the darker levels of popular superstition and magic; indeed, the latter was considerably furthered by the notion of the cosmic significance of the Torah and the unique power of the mysterious name of God which it contained.[441] However, these alien influences were hardly felt to be such; they had already been 'fused' into Jewish thought by translation into the vernacular, and the Rabbis were far from seeing the truth of the Mosaic law confirmed by some evidence from the Greek philosophers, as happened often in Diaspora Judaism, which must be taken to include the Palestinian Josephus, who also claimed to be a Pharisee. The summons to constant study of the law was matched by the obligation of the permanent fulfilment of the commandments; the infinite extension of the casuistic discussion beyond the individual commandments was based on the purpose of making the whole of the everyday conduct of the pious conform with the Torah.

Considered in this perspective, the pious Jew in the Rabbinic tradition was constantly concerned, like the Stoic, 'to live in conformity with the law of the world'. The difference was that he encountered this law not so much as an inner norm but rather in the form of countless individual requirements expressed in minute detail.[442] Yet even the idea that the Torah was 'laid upon' men was not completely alien to the Rabbis. In accordance with their concrete and pictorial way of thinking, it was manifested in the view, demonstrable in various forms from Tannaitic times, that man was made up of 248 members and 365 veins, corresponding to the 248 commandments and 365 prohibitions of the Torah (*Targ. Jer.* 1 on Gen. 1.27). A later Amorean tradition drew from this the practical conclusion: 'Each individual member says to man: I beseech you, do this commandment through me.'[443] In this way there arose the Torah ontology of the learned Rabbis with its 'claim to absolutism . . . [alongside] the philosophical schools of the age, and their attempts to understand the world' (K. H. Rengstorf, *TDNT* 4, 440). Here the ordering of the world and the law conformed with each other to the same extent as in Stoic philosophy.[444]

> Most recently, J. Baer has drawn attention to the analogies between Jewish and Rabbinic thought and Greek philosophy. Thus, for example, he points to the early Mishnah *Sanh.* 4, 5: God 'fashioned all men with the mould of the first man', and sees here a parallel to the conceptions of *eikōn* and *typos* to be found in Philo of Alexandria.[445] One might also refer to the comparison introduced shortly before, according to which the annihilation of a human life is equivalent to the annihilation of a 'complete world' (עולם מלא), whereas the deliverance of a man corresponds to the preservation of a complete world. Here man, as a microcosm, is the image of the macrocosm (see n. III, 499). It is still more significant that Baer relates the Rabbinic understanding of the Torah to the Platonic interpretation of the Logos. Like the Logos in Plato, the Torah is understood as a living organism, comparable to the work of a weaver. Dialectical discussion of it raises the learned man into a higher world. Philo had already interpreted concern for the law – which he identified with the divine Logos – in this sense.[446] Granted, we may not make the Rabbis Platonists, but an analogy is there. Constant and intensive concern with the law as the divine plan of creation brings the soul of those who devote themselves intensively to it near to the divine world. Thus the cosmic understanding of the Torah could become the gateway to Jewish mysticism.

We must therefore ask whether this understanding of the law does not involve a transformation of Old Testament conceptions of the historical revelation of God to his people, a transformation which is hardly less profound than that which took place in Jewish Alexandria with Aristobulus and later with Philo. Certainly the Pharisaic scribes were not aware of the influence of the Hellenistic spirit of the time on their thought and activity, and the Greek 'philosophers' and the 'Epicureans' were regarded as opponents.[447] Nevertheless, this influence was effective not only in combining the divine ordering of the world and personal norms of life through the Torah, but also in the constant, unqualified stress on continuing study as the only certain basis for unobjectionable moral and religious conduct. A teacher-pupil relationship was formed in analogy to the Greek philosophical schools which included the chains of tradition (see pp. 81f. above), the conception of a sacrosanct corpus of holy writings given directly by God or inspired by him, the development of a differentiated exegetical method and finally the adoption of a wealth of foreign views, both in the sphere of cosmology and in that of anthropology and eschatology, where there was any dependence on the legacy of the Hasidim and apocalyptic.[448] In contrast to Diaspora Judaism, which, because of its more exposed position and consequent missionary tendency, never grew weary of stressing the universal validity of the law of Moses in an ethical interpretation,[449] the Rabbis – apart from a very few significant exceptions[450] – stressed the exclusive revelation of the Torah to Israel. The peoples who had once been offered the Torah by God had rejected it.[451] The goal of the education of the whole people in the Torah (see above, pp. 79ff.), which is probably unique in the ancient world, was grounded here also. The Torah was not God's gift to the learned, but for all Israelites. The 'pedagogic' penetration of broader strata of the people which ensued, coupled with growing intellectual isolation from outsiders, was a substantial reason for the preservation of the community of the Jewish people and their religion through all national catastrophes. On the other hand, they lost the sense of the free action of God in history, since its eschatological aspect retreated into the background and was fixed as a 'doctrine of the last things'. The Torah became an 'essentially unhistorical entity'.[452] The moment the Rabbinate achieved its final rule over Palestinian Judaism after Jabneh, the almost thousand-year-old tradition of Israelite and Jewish history writing came to an end. Even apocalyptic literature gradually died out and was replaced by Jewish mysticism. Under the guidance of the Rabbis, the pious Jew found his satisfaction in preoccupation with what for him was the unfathomable Torah, unfathomable because it encompassed God's very wisdom itself.

6. The Hasidim and the First Climax of Jewish Apocalyptic

a) The Hasidim as a Jewish party at the time of the Hellenistic reform

At the beginning of the Maccabean revolt in 167/166 BC we find the 'assembly of the pious' ($\sigma \upsilon \nu \alpha \gamma \omega \gamma \grave{\eta}$ 'Ασιδαίων = '$^a dat$-$h^a s \bar{\imath} d \bar{\imath} m$ or perhaps even $q^e hal$ $h^a s \bar{\imath} d \bar{\imath} m$, I Macc. 2.42) as a clearly defined Jewish party,[453] which resolved to join Mattathias and his sons in the struggle to preserve Jewish belief. The initiative for this alliance presumably came from the Maccabees, who hoped to strengthen their fighting force considerably by the support of this strong group.[454] As the group seems well organized at this time, the period of its origin will lie at least a few years in the past. The name of the Essenes and the history of their origins could give us a hint here. Their designation probably comes from the Aramaic equivalent to the Hebrew $h \bar{a} s \bar{\imath} d$, pious = $h^a s \bar{e}$' absolute, plural $h^a s \bar{e} n$ = Greek 'Εσσηνοί or determinative plural $h^a sayy \bar{a}$ = 'Εσσαῖοι, a hypothesis which is strengthened by Philo's translation of 'Εσσαῖοι as ὅσιοι and the fragment of a letter from the time of Bar Kochba, which probably calls the camp at Qumran the 'fortress of the faithful' (מצד חסידין).[455] This suggests that the Essenes originated from the Hasidim.[456] We can learn a little more about the prior history of the Essenes from the Damascus Document. According to this, the assembly 'of the root of the planting' – i.e. presumably the Hasidim – is said to have taken place in the 'time of wrath', twenty years before the emergence of the Teacher of Righteousness. As the Teacher and his followers most probably separated from the temple in Jerusalem after Jonathan took over the office of high priest in 152 BC, and thus founded the Essene movement proper, we find ourselves putting the closer formation of the 'pious' at about the period between 175 and 170 BC, when the Hellenistic reform in Jerusalem was at its height.[457] Two apocalyptic historical surveys in the book of Enoch, the vision of the beasts, coming from the time of the Maccabees, and composed even before the death of Judas Maccabaeus,[458] and the Ten Weeks' Apocalypse from perhaps a rather earlier date, indicate their formation at this time.[459]

These 'pious' were significant for the religion of Judaism in two ways. First, it has been thought that the author of the earliest real *apocalypses*, the *book of Daniel*, which was composed during the climax of the Maccabean struggle for freedom in 164 BC, before the death of Antiochus IV and the reconsecration of the temple, is to be found in these circles. The *earliest parts of the book of Enoch*, which were composed at about the same time or slightly later, may also have a similar origin. As the discovery of a whole series of Daniel fragments from Cave 4 Q shows, in the case of Daniel we are dealing not just with one book, but, as in Enoch, with a whole cycle, probably backed by a school.[460] Secondly, the Hasidim are looked to as the common *root* of the two most significant religious groups of post-biblical Judaism, the *Essenes*, already mentioned, and the *Pharisees*.[461]

O. Plöger has convincingly demonstrated that the Hasidim have a long history, going back from the closer collaboration born of need into the third century and perhaps even into the Persian period. Perhaps in a way they were opposed to the 'official' Judaism, embodied in the priestly hierarchy and the rich lay aristocracy, who found their satisfaction in the presence of God in cult and Torah and regarded prophetic apocalyptic conceptions with mistrust. In the conventicles of the 'pious', treasured more by the simple people, however, the eschatological tradition of the prophets was handed down and extended.[462] Whereas from the middle of the third century BC a large part of the priestly upper class and the lay nobility fell victim more and more to Hellenistic assimilation – not least 'as a result of the non-eschatological and increasingly aimless attitude'[463] – these groups, hitherto only loosely associated, developed ideas which then suddenly came to light in the period of persecution under Antiochus Epiphanes. Perhaps some references of individual psalms to the *hᵃsîdîm*, like Ps. 149.1 with the *qᵉhal hᵃsîdîm*, are to the conventicles of these 'pious' at an early period, even if we may not assign these psalms to the Maccabean rebellion, as sometimes happened in the past.[464]

> The Hasidim seem to be speaking above all in a wisdom psalm from Cave 11 Q published by J. A. Sanders.[465] The striking thing here is the invitation:
>
> 'Assemble yourself as a community to proclaim his salvation (הַחְבִּירוּ יַחַד לְהוֹדִיעַ יִשְׁעוֹ), and be unceasing in making known his power' (v.4).
>
> According to this psalm, 'wisdom' is no longer an esoteric possession,

but is given for the proclamation of the glory of Yahweh to simple and uneducated people, since the praise of God is as important as sacrifice. Here possession of wisdom is limited to the 'righteous' and the 'assembly of the pious' (קהל חסידים), at whose common meal it is present (vv. 12f.). It cannot be found either among the 'godless' (רשעים) or among the 'proud' (זדים). The reference to the liberation of the humble from the hand of the stranger and to God's judgment on the nations outside Israel[466] clearly demonstrates the threat posed by foreign rule. Language and style still lack the typical Qumran stamp and the parallels to Ben Sira are striking, though the latter lacks the conventicle-like assembly and the almost missionary zeal. The editor is probably right in his characterization of the work as 'perhaps . . . proto-Essenian or Hasidic from the period of the "separation" '.[467] The psalm also shows clearly that the 'pious', too, had *wisdom schools*, in which 'their meditation on the Torah' (שיחתם בתורת עליון v. 14) occupied a central place. In the other non-canonical psalms in this scroll the concept of the חסידים occurs several times. A verse in the Zion hymn points to the apocalyptic element:

Take up a vision (חזון)
(which) was spoken over you
and the dreams of the prophets
(which) were sought out for you.[468]

The intensity of the eschatological hope is also clear in the same psalm:

Great is your hope, Zion,
that (the) salvation and the redemption you long for will come.
Generation upon generation will dwell in you,
the generations of the pious (חסידים) will be your glory,
who wish for the day of your redemption
and look forward to the fullness of your glory.
They suck at the bosom of your glory (Isa. 66.11),
and trip in your glorious streets.
Remember the acts of faith (חסדי) of your prophets
and glorify the works of your pious men (חסידיך).

At the same time, there is evidence of a new conception of man in comparison with the Old Testament, which tends towards a doctrine of redemption and then finds its full expression among the Essenes:

Forgive YHWH my sin,
and cleanse me from my unrighteousness.
Give me the spirit of faithfulness and knowledge,
and do not let me be brought to shame through unrighteousness.
Let *Satan* not rule over me,
nor a spirit of impurity.
Let neither grief nor evil desire (יצר רע, see pp. 140f.)
possess my bones.[469]

It is probable that the conservative nationalist circles which were represented by Ben Sira and later by the family of Mattathias of Modein, who was descended from the lower priesthood, came close to the 'pietistic' Hasidim because of the danger of a Hellenistic alienation. In the 'praise of the fathers', Ben Sira, too, shows an express interest in the prophetic tradition and is the first to presuppose that the 'prophetic canon' has been closed. However, in his writing the main emphasis does not lie on any apocalyptic secret teaching, although he shares in the messianic expectation (see above, pp. 135f.); for him the prophets stand alongside the priests and the god-fearing kings as primarily the great representatives of the national history of Israel.[470] However, this common front was not joined for any length of time; it soon broke up after the raising of the prohibition on the Jewish religion.[471]

An essential characteristic of the 'pious' was their *rigorous strictness in the law*, which was already stressed by the books of Maccabees and which goes far beyond the common sense of a Ben Sira. To understand the law rightly a man needs divine enlightenment, and at the same time the Hasidic teacher of the law receives an almost missionary commission:

Grant me understanding, O Lord, in thy Law,
and lead me in thine ordinances.
That many may hear of thy deeds
and peoples may honour thy glory. (DJDJ IV, 71, col. 24, 8)

The Rabbis later called the 'pious' the 'men of the deed', אנשי מעשה.[472] It is probable that among their members were e.g. those fugitives who would rather be killed than follow the command of the king and desecrate the sabbath.[473] The fact that, unlike the Maccabees, they did not offer resistance on the sabbath at the beginning of the persecution, indicates that they surrendered unconditionally to the will of God revealed in the Torah. So a little later they expected less from their own political action than from the miraculous intervention of God, and strove for a rapid peace treaty after the restoration of religious freedom.[474] In Dan. 11.34b the seer already laments the fact that 'many join themselves to them from flattery' because of the initial success of the Maccabees – the 'little help'. In addition to the rigorous observation of the sabbath, which can be pursued in both the Essene and the Pharisaic tradition,[475] we find a no less strict observation of the food laws. One example of this is provided in Dan. 1.8ff.: neither the fact that Daniel learns the wisdom of the Chaldeans nor that he enters the service of the heathen king causes offence to the Hasidic author of the book, provided that he carefully observes God's commandment and does not take to himself any unclean food.[476] II Maccabees 5.27 (or Jason of Cyrene) reports the same thing of Judas Maccabaeus, who ate only plants in the desert in order to remain pure, and who is portrayed as a member of the Hasidim (14.6, cf. above, pp. 97f.), quite contrary to historical circumstances. A further feature that is maintained with Daniel and the Rabbinic tradition is their great zeal for duty, indeed their devotion to prayer.[477] A final surprising thing in the book of Daniel is the astonishing loyalty shown to the pagan rulers, a fact which cannot be explained solely by saying that earlier narrative traditions were adopted, because of the unitary form of the work.[478] For all their strictness to the law, these 'pious' men allow themselves to be influenced more than other Jewish groups by alien conceptions – as is shown by the many non-Jewish elements in early apocalyptic, as long as the encounter with the alien environment does not lead to a denial of the will of God given in the law.[479] However, the severe crisis caused by the Hellenistic reform attempt brought about a substantial change in this attitude: after the Maccabean revolt the tendency towards spiritual segregation from outsiders grew stronger, whereas on the other hand the Hasidic ideal of piety became dominant for the majority of Palestinian Jews. This strengthening of their spiritual influence ran parallel to a far-reaching split in the Hasidic movement, which was brought about, among other things, by differing attitudes to the new Hasmonean state. The apocalypse with the vision of the beasts is already less positive towards Judas Maccabaeus than the book of Daniel (cf. I Enoch 90.9ff. and Dan. 11.34). After the astonishing success of the sons of Mattathias, such a development could not be long in coming (see below, pp. 290f.). It is very probable that in addition to the Essenes and Pharisees, there were other pietistic and conventicle-like splinter-groups who emerged from the Hasidim but who are unknown to us, combining apocalyptic tendencies with a rigorous view of the law.[480]

The assembling of the 'pious' into a relatively closed community took the form of a *penitential movement*. In retrospect, the Damascus Document describes the situation in the following way:

> And in the age of wrath, three hundred and ninety years after He had given them into the hand of king Nebuchadnezzar of Babylon, He visited them, and He caused a plant root to spring from Israel and Aaron . . . And *they perceived their iniquity and recognized that they were guilty men*, yet for twenty years they were like blind men groping for the way (cf. Dan. 12.4b). And God observed their deeds, that they sought Him with a whole heart, and He raised for them a Teacher of Righteousness to guide them in the way of His heart.[481]

In the vision of the beasts in I Enoch, the newborn lambs, i.e. the Hasidim, call the sheep, i.e. Israel, to repentance, but the latter remain deaf and blind.[482] We also meet repentance for the sin of the people in the penitential prayer inserted in Dan. 9.4–19, which has features akin to a pre-Essene Hasidic liturgy from Cave 4 Q.[483] In the admonitions of I Enoch 91–104, Enoch appears principally as a preacher of repentance and judgment, in some ways comparable to John the Baptist. Finally, the special significance of the term 'repent' in the Essene writings may go back to the Hasidic heritage.[484] This understanding of itself by the movement is also matched by *a radical view of history*: for Israel the present, three hundred and ninety years after the surrender of Judea to Nebuchadnezzar, is a 'time of wrath';[485] for Daniel it appears to be 'a time of trouble, such as there has never been since there was a nation' (Dan. 12.1; cf. 11.36; 8.19 and, in contrast, I Macc. 9.27). But the cause of this lies in the sin of the past, for seventy weeks of years were needed 'to finish the transgression, to put an end to sin, and to atone for iniquity'.[486] According to the later symbolic apocalypse of the beasts (see pp. 187f. below), the return from exile and the establishment of the second temple made no difference to these circumstances, for the sacrifices offered in it were 'tainted and impure'.[487] The Ten Weeks' Apocalypse, which is perhaps still older, is no less abrupt in its judgment on the time after the exile:

> And after that in the seventh week shall an apostate generation arise,
> And many shall be its deeds,
> And all its deeds shall be apostate.[488]

This general verdict – not on a minority of apostates but on the whole development of Israel from the exile, including the temple cult – shows the conventicle-like segregation of the 'pious' from the official cult community, though it did not exclude external recognition. It is best explained from the deep inner crisis in which the Jewish temple state was involved through the influence of Hellenistic forms of living and thinking which had been effective since the third century BC, a crisis which reached its climax after 175 BC. The 'pious' projected their dismay at present conditions in Jerusalem on to the whole of Jewish history since the destruction of Jerusalem, so that this epoch was regarded as a time of apostasy which had now reached its climax and its end with the formation of a penitential movement. For according to the Ten Weeks' Apocalypse, at the end of the seventh week of apostasy 'shall be elected the elect righteous of the eternal plant of righteousness, to receive sevenfold instruction concerning all His creation' (I Enoch 93.10). Thus the conversion of the 'pious' introduces the turn of the ages which begins with the eighth world-week. Here the contrast with Ben Sira becomes particularly clear. In a sharpening of the Chronicler's picture of history, he allows only three pious kings in the pre-exilic period, David, Hezekiah and Josiah, though the Oniad Simon the Just, who died only a short period before, is praised in panegyric fashion.[489] The righteous who 'receive sevenfold instruction' from God probably correspond to the 'wise' (*maśkīlīm*) in Daniel,[490] and are to some degree the vanguard of the eschatological community of salvation. Here we come across the most significant spiritual contribution of these 'pious': in their circles, Jewish apocalyptic reached its first climax.

b) The first climax of Jewish apocalyptic

Jewish apocalyptic did, of course, have a long prehistory, in essentials going back to Ezekiel and Deutero-Isaiah, but it was first given its full form in Daniel and the earliest parts of Ethiopian Enoch. Granted, with some degree of justice Isa. 24–27 has been regarded as the 'earliest apocalypse', but these chapters stand closer in content and in time to the late prophecy of the Old Testament than to Daniel and I Enoch. They may have apocalyptic features, but their form is not homogeneous and they lack a unitary picture of universal history.[491] We shall therefore concentrate above all on the last two works, leaving aside the later Similitudes in I Enoch 37–71, though it is clear that the boundary with the Essene writing which comes a little later is a fluid one (see above, n. 460 and below n. 691).

aa) The universal picture of history in early apocalyptic

Apocalyptic took up the themes provided by Old Testament prophecy, of Yahweh as the Lord of history, his judgment over the peoples, the liberation of Israel and the establishment of the rule of God,[492] and incorporated them in a new universal, world-historical, indeed cosmic framework. In order to systematize and rationalize this drama of world history, writers made use of the widespread conception of predetermined epochs of history. However, the course of world history was not thus made an immanent event with its own laws, but was strictly bound in its individual stages to God's secret *plan*, resolved on by him in freedom, and had its goal in the eagerly awaited time of salvation for Israel or for God's chosen faithful, which was expected to dawn soon.[493]

The materials used to depict these new outlines of 'universal history' culminating in the time of salvation were largely drawn from the mythological conceptions of the Hellenistic oriental environment. Although they were often very different in outward appearance, they did show an astonishing degree of correspondence in certain basic features.[494] An instance of the problems involved here is provided by Dan. 2, where three different themes are combined in Nebuchadnezzar's dream or its interpretation:

It is necessary to be careful in describing themes specifically as 'Hellenistic' or 'oriental', i.e. Babylonian or Persian or even Indian – and this applies to the question of the historical *derivation* of apocalyptic themes in general.[495] These essentially vague designations should not be regarded as fundamental opposites, because the two often run into each other and can often hardly be separated at this late period. This is all the more the case since the question of the *communication* of foreign themes – which must be distinguished from the question of derivation – is neglected. At the expense of a one-sided Iranian and Babylonian derivation,[496] it is probable that mediation through the receptive Greek-speaking Diaspora of Egypt and Syria or Phoenicia has received too little attention. The cultural influence of Alexandria, Antioch and the Phoenician cities probably had greater effect in Jerusalem in the third and second centuries BC than a direct Iranian-Babylonian influence, especially as Babylonia and Iran were similarly under Hellenistic rule from the time of Alexander the Great to the middle of the second century.[497] We must therefore reckon on the possibility that even originally oriental themes were mediated by Hellenistic sources.

1. The background to the giant statue incorporating the history of the four world kingdoms is probably the idea of the representation of the world or, in Daniel, world history, by 'allegorical figures', or its portrayal as a 'microcosm . . . through the picture of a great man'.[498] This idea recurs in ancient astrology, Orphism and the Hermetica, and also in Iran.[499]

2. The notion of the four *metals* of increasingly inferior quality: gold, silver, bronze and iron, as characteristics of the four epochs of history, may go back to the end of the second millennium and have been occasioned by the change from the Bronze Age to the Iron Age. However, its nearest parallel is the portrayal of the ages of the world in terms of metals in Hesiod, in the eighth century BC. In addition, it can be found – albeit in a very late and less precise form – in late Iranian tradition, where a period of steel replaces that of bronze.[500]

3. The interpretation of the dream vision in terms of *four world kingdoms* which are done away with by the rule of God and his people[501] runs parallel to the interpretation of the vision of the beasts in Dan. 7. An unpublished fragment from 4 Q which presumably belongs to the Daniel cycle and probably symbolized the four kingdoms by four trees, mentioning Babylon and Persia, belongs in this context.[502] Test. Napht. 5.8, where 'Assyrians, Medes, Persians, ( ) Syrians' are mentioned as masters of the twelve scattered tribes, and which probably also derives from Hasidic sources, shows that the knowledge of this 'world-historical scheme' was widespread in contemporary Jewish Palestine. This collection also shows the anti-Seleucid attitude adopted (see E. Bickerman[n], *JBL* 69, 1950, 254f). Herodotus (1, 95, cf. 130), and later Ctesias, the physician of Artaxerxes II, already knew the whole scheme of successive world monarchies.[503] The sequence of Assyrians, Medes and Persians is presupposed by Daniel, but for the sake of the scenery he replaces the Assyrian kingdom by the neo-Babylonian.[504] This indicates an originally Persian view of history, but the two historians mentioned above had long made this the common property of the Greek world. This is indicated, for example, by the fact that the scheme was used by Polybius in his portrayal of the lament of the younger Scipio over the ruins of Carthage in 146 BC, where he supplemented it by the Macedonian empire.[505] At an earlier stage, in the first third of the second century BC, two Roman annalists, the otherwise unknown Aemilius Sura and presumably also Ennius,[506] expressed the view that after her victories over Philip of Macedon and Antiochus II, Rome had entered upon the heritage of the Macedonians and thus the four kingdoms of the world.[507]

With the central significance that the historical picture of Dan. 2 – together with Dan. 7 – has for the whole book of Daniel, we may hardly assume that the narrative of the vision of the four kingdoms and their supersession by the kingdom of God was already an independent entity before the origin of the work and was simply taken over by the author. Moreover, not only 7.8, 24 but also 2.43 point clearly to historical events near to the author.[508] Dan. 2 is not a popular miracle story, like the narratives in chs. 3; 5; 6; behind it, as in Dan. 7, there is profound reflection on the 'theology of history'. The story of the four great kingdoms presupposes the end of the history of Israel as an independent nation through its loss of independence and the destruction of Jerusalem; thus the four kingdoms embody the period of the seventy weeks of years as a time of wrath (see above, pp. 179f.) and expiation (Dan. 9.24). One could therefore follow K. Koch and speak of a tripartite division of world history in Daniel:

1. The time of history given by the sacred tradition from the creation of the world to 598 or 587 BC, in the centre of which stands the national history of Israel.

2. The time of the four world kingdoms, which at the same time represents a certain decline, and in which above all the fourth is associated with an extreme heightening of human arrogance, which comes to a climax in the persecution of the faithful. It is followed by:

3. The time of the 'eternal kingdom' after its destruction, in which God's saving plan with his people and with the world is consummated.[509]

Whence do these themes *originate*? It seems likely that the author knew the myth of the four periods of history characterized by the four metals in a simplified popular form, widespread in the Hellenistic period, which essentially goes back to Hesiod. The anonymous Samaritan, who is not too far removed from Daniel, and the earliest Jewish Sibyl also seem to have known Hesiod. On the other hand, there is no possibility of demonstrating an intermediate Babylonian stage for the Iranian myth.[510] The same is true of the replacement of the four world kingdoms by a fifth. It is a very artificial hypothesis to suppose that this conception reached Rome after the victory of Magnesia in 190 BC from groups of Persian settlers in Asia Minor.[511] Its very use by Polybius and others suggests that it was a theme used often in the Greek historiography of the Hellenistic period. The Greeks of the mother country and Asia Minor hated the rule of the Diadochi states just as much as the orientals, and for a short time Rome played the part of the restorer of early Greek freedom for them. The author's detailed knowledge of the history of the Ptolemies and the Seleucids in the third century BC shows that he was familiar with Greek history writing.[512] Even Rome at that time was already in the Jewish field of view, as is clear from the 'ships of Kittim' (11.30) and the contacts made with Rome a little later by Judas Maccabaeus (I Macc. 8), in about 161 BC.

Behind the portrayals of the beasts and the various persons in the judgment scene in Dan. 7, however, there is an abundance of different conceptions, some Babylonian and Iranian, others North Syrian and Phoenician. We need not go into them in detail here.[513] The author (or his school) had a great many possible variations on the pictures and themes to be used, which were not limited by any national or cultural boundaries. All this was used to express the almost 'encyclopaedic' learning of early – Hasidic and Essene – apocalyptic (see below, pp. 207ff.).

> Thus we can easily demonstrate the knowledge of ancient *astral geography* in Dan. 8.2–8, in which the ram represents the star of Persia and the he-goat which attacks him is the star of Seleucid Syria.[514] These and possibly other astral allusions are all the more striking, as in Dan. 2.21ff. the influence of the stars on fate and history is denied, and God's omnipotence is proclaimed. A similar opposition can be found in a still more acute form in Qumran, where astrology is simultaneously rejected and practised (see below, pp. 237ff.).

Typical of the whole of apocalyptic and here especially of Daniel, as of the apocalypses of the symbolic beasts and the weeks (see notes 463–5), which come from the same period and the same circles, are the *vaticinia ex eventu*, describing past or present events of history in the form of a prophecy given in earlier times, in order to strengthen trust in the prophecies of the apocalyptist as a sign of the divine determination of history.[515] At the same time, however, they are also an expression of his political and historical interest. In Daniel they make up a large part of the work, i.e. chs. 2; 7–11, and here attain classical form in the great survey of history in 11.1–39, which then goes over to 'prophecy' in 11.40–12.3. We find *vaticinia* of this kind relatively frequently in the Hellenistic period, especially in Egypt. The most significant is the 'Demotic Chronicle' from the early Ptolemaic period, composed by an Egyptian priest, which claims to come from the time of king Tachus in 360–359 BC, and which proclaims in dark prophecies the further history down to the beginning of Greek rule. Finally it announces the annihilation of Greek foreign rule and the establishment of the national state under a native ruler beloved of Isis:

> Rejoice over the ruler who will be,
> for he will not forsake the law (col. 3, 16).[516]

In addition it claims to be the exposition of obscure oracles which in reality are only a little older; the prophetic interpretation carried out sentence by sentence is reminiscent of the Essene 'prophetic commentaries'. Finally, it has in common with Daniel and the symbolic apocalypse of the beasts the fact that it has in the background a national Egyptian rebellion which has probably just broken out.[517] Probably very close to the time of Daniel is the abruptly anti-Macedonian Potter's Oracle, which is dated by its author back into the Eighteenth Dynasty at the time of king Amenophis:

> According to this, such unspeakable suffering will be inflicted upon the 'girdle-wearers', i.e. the Graeco-Macedonian masters (lines 26, 33, 43, 49, etc.) that the sun will be darkened (16f.). The advent of a 'king from Syria, who is hated by all men' is presumably to be interpreted as Antiochus IV, following Reitzenstein (3f.). The city of the 'girdle-wearers' by the sea, i.e.

Alexandria, is laid waste and becomes a place where fishermen may dry their nets. The god 'Agathos Daimon' (i.e. Knephis-Chnum) abandons Alexandria and returns to Memphis (43ff., 50). Under a king who comes from the east (from the sun?) and from the supreme goddess Isis, Egypt experiences a golden age of abundance, 'so that those who have disappeared and died earlier ask to rise again (from the dead) to share in the good things' (65–71). 'For in the time of the Typhonians (the followers of Typhon-Seth) the sun god was darkened'; but 'he will shine out again when he has brought punishment to the girdle-wearers for their evil and delinquency' (text of the last sentence follows P. Rainer, col. 2, 14f.).[518]

The Messianic features in both prophecies are significant. A further xenophobic fragment of oracle sharply attacks the Jews as 'lawless' (παρά-νομοι); they are to be driven out of Egypt by the 'wrath of Isis'.[519] Manetho had already connected the expulsion of the Jews from Egypt as lepers at the time of Moses with an oracle delivered to the king (Josephus, *c. Ap.* 1, 232ff.). Finally, mention should be made of astrological 'predictions' as they are contained in the standard work of ancient astrology, attributed to king Nechepso and the wise man Petosiris, which arose in Ptolemaic Egypt at about the same time as Daniel. Like Daniel 11, they are concerned, inter alia, with detailed accounts of political events in Egypt and Syria:

> 'When the sun or the moon grow dark in the constellation of the ram, the places of Egypt and Syria will undergo great distress and death; persecution and rebellion will come upon the rulers of those places. And hosts will engage in battle and wreak conflagrations . . .' All the symbolic beasts are treated in this way and continually new catastrophes are forecast.[520]

Significantly, astrological 'prophecies' of a very similar form are also found in Qumran (see below, pp. 237ff.). It is not improbable that Egyptian 'apocalyptic', with its strong national colouring and its anti-Macedonian and xenophobic character, and its Jewish counterpart had a mutual influence on each other.

But the parallels are not only restricted to Egypt. Both O. Eissfeldt and W. Baumgartner point out the numerous mostly anti-Roman oracles from Asia Minor and Syria, for which they assume a strong Iranian influence. A typical example – though from a later period – is the oracle of Hystaspes.[521] However, one must also include in any consideration the Greek *collections of oracles* which flourished afresh under Alexander the Great. Varro knew ten different Sibyls in the first half of the first century BC alone, and others still more.[522]

> According to Suetonius (*Augustus* 31, 1), Augustus, on taking over the office of Pontifex Maximus in 12 BC had over two thousand anonymous oracles (or oracles written by little-known authors) in Greek or Latin collected and burnt; he made a selection only of the Sibylline books. Thus *'political prophecy'* could become a danger to the state. One instance of this is provided by Eunus the slave king from Apamea in Syria in the First

Slave War between 136 and 132 BC in Sicily. He claimed to have received information about the future from the gods in a dream, and indeed that the gods had appeared to him while he had been awake (ἐγρηγορότως θεοὺς ὁρῶν . . . καὶ ἐξ αὐτῶν ἀκούειν τὰ μέλλοντα). Finally, he prophesied in ecstasy and claimed that the Syrian goddess had proclaimed to him that he would become king. In the rebellion which now followed, and which was at first surprisingly successful for Eunus and his followers, the slaves attempted to put into practice a kind of utopian kingdom of social righteousness. The slave revolt of Andronicus in Pergamon after 133 BC also had social-utopian features.[523]

It was an exceptionally skilful move when, about two decades after Daniel, a nationalist Jew of the Egyptian Diaspora mixed his apocalyptic pictures of the future with *vaticinia ex eventu* in the archaic garb of Sibylline prophecy and thus created a successful means of Jewish propaganda.[524] From now on, Jewish apocalyptic could develop its effectiveness in the Diaspora also.

A further example of political 'prophecy' in the Hellenistic sphere is provided by the 'Peripatetic' Antisthenes of Rhodes, a contemporary of the author of Daniel from the first third of the second century BC, in his portrayal of the Roman expedition against Antiochus III. According to him the Syrian cavalry commander Buplagus rose from the dead (ἀνέστη . . . ἐκ τῶν νεκρῶν) and prophesied on the battlefield of Magnesia – like the Pamphylian Er in Plato's Republic (614b) – in hexameters the vengeance of Zeus on Rome. A great host would fall on Italy and bring an end to Roman rule – a prophecy which was confirmed by the oracle at Delphi when the Romans approached it. Still more miraculous were the 'prophecies' of the Roman consul Publius in the camp of Naupactus; they foretold the annihilation of Rome by a tremendous host from the East under a king of Asia. As a *vaticinium ex eventu* he added in prose the further course and outcome of the expedition against Antiochus III and announced his own impending death. Torn to pieces by a wolf, the head, separated from the body, delivered an oracle in verse form at the behest of Apollo and depicted the killing of the Romans who were capable of bearing arms and the exile of the women and children to Asia. Oracles of this kind also played a significant role in the Mithridatic wars and in the Jewish war of AD 66–70. Particularly in the political sphere, Jewish apocalyptic made contact with its environment, adopted ideas from it and in turn influenced it.[525]

Nevertheless, despite all the parallels there is a quite substantial *difference* in the non-Jewish literature of prophecy and oracle in the Hellenistic period. The Egyptian and Greek 'prophecies' as a rule deal with limited periods of time, often without a deeper religious background. Above all, there is no portrayal of world history, no *picture of history* that takes in the whole cosmos, directed towards the realization of the divine plan and the imminent dawn of the future time of salvation. Thus the visions painted in the colours of Hellenistic oriental mythology serve to present world history 'as one and as a whole', in such a way that the whole of history 'is directed from the beginning towards salvation at the end of history'.[526] True, in Daniel universal history is visible only in a particular period – albeit a decisive one – as he did not incorporate primeval times and the national history of Israel and even hints at the time of salvation rather than stating it explicitly (2.44; 7.27; 9.24; 12.1f.). But the fragments of a Daniel apocryphon from 4 Q which embraces world history from the beginning to the consummation, and the apocalypse of the symbolic beasts in I Enoch 85–90, which must have been composed only a little later, before the death of Judas Maccabeus (see above, n.458), both show that a total view of history underlies the partial aspect found in Daniel. According to this, world history is divided into three, or better four epochs: 1. the primeval period from Adam to Isaac (I Enoch 85–89.12), for up to him, the father of the hated Esau and the tribal patriarch Jacob, the history of the nations and that of the chosen people cannot be separated. 2. The history of Israel as God's chosen people from Jacob to the delivery of the people by the 'Lord of the sheep' to the seventy shepherds.

> Here there emerges for the first time the conception of the seventy peoples of the world and their 'guardian angels': Israel is surrendered to their power because of its sin. Perhaps here there was originally the idea of the scattering of the people among the seventy peoples of the world[527] – i.e. likewise a *universal* feature. However, the apocalyptist associated the seventy angels or shepherds of the nations with Daniel's seventy weeks of years (Dan.9), and assigned to each a fixed and determined time span (89.65; 90.5, etc.) Already in Daniel one can see the tendency, noted above, to systematize the course of history. The idea of the angels of the nations is not unknown in Daniel (10.13f., 20). We may follow Bertholet in seeing them as 'dispossessed gods of strange peoples', who like the satraps of the Persian king sometimes fight among themselves and act contrary to the orders of their supreme master, to be punished later by him. The national gods of the pagans are thus given a rational interpretation. T. F. Glasson points out two remarkable parallels to the idea of the angels of the nations: according to Plato, *Laws* 713c/d, Kronos did not set *men* as rulers over the '*poleis*' of men 'but *daimones*, like gods and of better origin', in the same way as herds are led by men and not by animals. In *Critias* 109b/c, the gods divided up the earth and its inhabitants by lot, to rule over men as shepherds over their flocks.[528] H. Gressmann points to the assignation of the peoples by Kronos to different gods, like Attica to Athene and Egypt to Thoth in Philo of Byblos.[529]

The first period of rule in the 23 shepherd periods begins with the conquest of the northern kingdom by Assyria and ends with the return from exile under Cyrus (89.65–71); the second with 12 'shepherds' extends to the end of the Persian kingdom (89.72–77). The third brings about a sharpening of the oppression of Israel, corresponding to the gruesomeness of the fourth beast in Dan.7.7, 23, which incorporates the Macedonian kingdom. It again contains

23 'shepherd periods' down to the change of rule in Palestine from the
Ptolemies to the Seleucids (90.2–6). The fourth, with the last twelve periods,
concerns the Seleucid kingdom. In this last and – as in Daniel – worst period
the Hasidim appear for the first time as 'little lambs', whose 'eyes are opened';
they call to the other sheep, but these do not listen in their deafness (90.6f.).
Only with the appearance of Judas Maccabeus as a 'little goat' with 'a large
horn' who bitterly defends himself against the Macedonian 'eagle' and the
Seleucid 'raven' are the eyes of the sheep opened, and the valiant goats run to
him (90.9–13, see p.179 above). Now follow the real events of the end. First –
as in Dan. 12.1 – Michael comes to the help of the sheep, and then the lord of
the sheep himself, whom Michael had informed of the wickedness practised by
the last twelve shepherds – i.e. in the Seleucid era. The sheep are armed with a
'sharp sword' and wage a last, *holy war* against 'all the beasts of the field'. One
is thus given the impression that the surprising success of Judas against the
various Seleucid armies was regarded by some of the 'faithful' as a prelude to
the final eschatological struggle. Indeed, it seems as if the conception of this
struggle which received its final form in 1 QM was now first developed.[530]
Here, too, is the real difference from Daniel, where God brings in his kingdom
all by himself (see above, p.183). There follows the judgment on the fallen star
angels of Gen.6 (see below, p.232) and the 'blinded sheep', i.e. the countless
apostate Jews (see below, pp.288f.), who are thrown into a fiery sea. The beasts
and the birds subject themselves to the sheep, the sanctuary is purified and
renewed, and all resort to it; the martyrs rise again (cf. Dan.12.2, see below,
pp.196f.), the Diaspora returns, the Messiah is born and finally all the beasts –
not only the sheep or Israel – are changed back into their perfect primal form
of the patriarchal period; they become 'white bulls', like the pious fathers from
Adam to Isaac (90.19–42). Thus at the end of history is restored again what
Ben Sira called the incomparable 'splendour' of Adam and the Essenes the
glory of Adam.[531] The apocalypse ends, taking up the universal prophecies
of salvation from Old Testament prophecy – and despite all the Zealot features
occasioned by the warlike character of the Maccabean period – with a portrait
of salvation for all mankind which breaks the bounds of all national limitations
(cf. I Enoch 10.21).

It is remarkable how, as in Daniel (10.13, 20f.; 12.1) and in various Essene
writings, especially the War Scroll and the newly published Melchizedek
fragment from 11 Q, it is not the Messiah but Michael who plays the role of
an eschatological spokesmen and bringer of salvation.[532] But even he, the
angel who is entrusted with the salvation of Israel and who perhaps goes
back to a depotentiation of the Canaanite-Phoenician God Mikal,[533] is
not the centre of the eschatological drama; this is rather determined by
God's plan for history with his people and all the nations, in which the
eschatological figures of salvation only have limited functions.

The *Ten Weeks' Apocalypse* in I Enoch 93.1–10 and 91.12–17 (see above, n.459) is substantially shorter. It does not display the same abruptly anti-Seleucid attitude as I Enoch 85–90 and was therefore composed perhaps before the beginning of the religious distress and the freedom fight. It is therefore divided more abruptly into ten world weeks, of which seven relate to 'world history' proper. They end with the apostasy of the majority of the people and the illumination of the 'elect righteous'. In the other three the time of salvation develops stage by stage; at its consummation in the tenth week a 'new heaven' (Isa.65.17; 66.22) and 'many countless weeks to eternity in goodness and righteousness' are to be found.

In these parts of I Enoch, which are probably the earliest, the *determinism* and *periodization* of the whole of world history emerges more strongly than in the book of Daniel, which only encompasses one period:

> For everything shall come and be fulfilled;
> and all the deeds of men in their order were shown to me (I Enoch 90.41).

The division of history into epochs, together with a degree of chronological ordering, is already indicated – as a sign of a rational and systematic approach to history – in the *Priestly writing*, which comes from the early Persian period. This, however, finds its culmination in the law giving at Sinai and in the conquest, and does not clearly envisage the establishment of an eschatological kingdom of God.[534] One might perhaps say that Hasidic apocalyptic combined the systematic view of history held in priestly wisdom with an eschatology determined by the prophetic tradition. In its Essene branch in particular, the Priestly and Zadokite element is clearly visible among the Hasidim. A typical example of this is given in the stress on priestly privileges in the Hasidic or early-Essene Testament of Levi, which is composed throughout in apocalyptic style (see below, p.205).[535] It should not therefore be assumed that the whole of the priesthood fell victim to the Hellenistic 'enlightenment'; nor should the opposition between theocracy and eschatology worked out by O. Plöger be made absolute. Possibly the priestly group came more into the foreground among the Essenes and the learned laity of the Hasidic movement among the later Pharisees.

> In the Essene book of Jubilees, the chronological beginnings of P and certain theological insights are elaborated to an ultimate degree of perfection; one need only think of the cosmic significance of the sabbath commandment (see p.168 above). In addition, the 'system' of the weeks of years and Jubilees including the idea of a perfect 'heavenly' ordering of feasts is given an astronomical grounding in the Essene sun-year. On the other hand, the book of Jubilees is closely connected with the Enoch tradition and in its historical framework also incorporates the eschatological consummation, the 'new creation' in the form of prophetic visions for the patriarchs.[536]

In addition, the *differences* between the *early* – Hasidic – forms of *apocalyptic* and its elaboration at a later period should not be overlooked:

1. There are no direct and clear details about the total course of the world such as were very widespread in the astrological speculation of the great world-year, in Iranian eschatology (see below, p. 191), in Jewish apocalyptic from the early first century and in the Rabbinate. It remains uncertain whether they were already in the background as secret teaching. The seventy weeks of years in Daniel encompass only a period, the time of particular temptation after the destruction of Jerusalem, and the ten 'weeks' of I Enoch 93 and 91.12–17 cannot be fixed definitely in chronological terms.[537]

2. The pair of opposites, 'the present aeon' and 'the coming aeon', known to us from the New Testament, are still absent in this form.[538] Certainly there is knowledge of the future and eternal kingdom of God (Dan. 2.44), which will be given to his people (7.18, 22, 27), but this kingdom of God is at the same time already present (3.33; 4.31; 5.21; 6.26f.); the Ten Weeks' Apocalypse and that of the symbolic beasts also show that there was a tendency to divide world history into several periods rather than into two.

3. The Davidic Messiah still hardly plays any part as an eschatological redeemer figure (I Enoch 90.37f.); there is more emphasis on the person of the 'heavenly redeemer' Michael, but even he has only a limited function. God's action itself occupies a central position.

4. There is no real dualism: God is the unqualified Lord over the world and its history. Evil is caused by the disobedience of men (I Enoch 98.4ff.), of the nations as of Israel. The fall of the angels according to Gen. 6.1–4 and the demons who derive from them (I Enoch 15.8ff., see p. 230 below) certainly represent an accentuation, in view of the autonomy of the angels of the nations and the godless world powers, but everything happens with God's will to purify and test his creatures, and especially his people.[539] The conception of a θεὸς τοῦ αἰῶνος τούτου (II Cor. 4.4; cf. Eph. 2.2; John 12.31) would still have been hardly conceivable.

> Significantly, the fallen angels and their rulers Semyasa and Asael cannot work freely on the earth. Rather, Asael is bound by Raphael and brought to a place of punishment in the wilderness, and Semyasa with his companions is fettered by Michael and held in the darkness until the final judgment (I Enoch 10.4–12; cf. chs. 15f.; 18.11–19.3; 21; and the Noah fragment in I Enoch 67). The analogy to the fall of the Titans in Greek myth is closer than Iranian dualism (see below, pp. 230f.); especially as the fallen angels, like Aeschylus' Prometheus, revealed certain cultural benefits and secret knowledge to men.[540]

It was early Essenism with its doctrine of the two spirits, developed under Iranian influence, that brought about a dualistic sharpening of Jewish apocalyptic (see below, pp. 218ff.) and the speculative derivation of evil from one power, in principle anti-godly, though it was created by God.[541] The usual designation of apocalyptic as 'dualistic' needs to be corrected, at least as far as its early forms are concerned. Buber's assertion that 'apocalyptic (eschatological belief) is essentially built on elements of Iranian dualism' must necessarily lead to a distorted picture.[542]

It might be asked how far the apocalyptic *schematization of world history* has its origin or at least its parallels in extra-Jewish sources. Thus Bousset and Gressmann combine the concept ὁ αἰὼν ὁ μέγας[543] which appears in the early angelological book I Enoch 16.1, and I Enoch 18.16; 21.6, where the time of the punishment of certain angels is given as ten thousand years, with the conception of the 'great world year'. Granted, the time of the punishment of these angels probably has another background (see below, p.201), but we must enquire whether and how far the 'great year' was significant for the apocalyptic author of I Enoch. Bultmann goes one step further and sees in the apocalyptic picture of history as it is presented, say, in Daniel, a historicizing transformation of the cosmological myth of the eternal return: 'the cosmic world-year is . . . reduced to the history of the world'.[544]

The conception of the *'great world-year'*, which comes to an end with the meeting of all the comets at their starting point, appears similarly in Greece, Babylonia and India.[545] The earliest direct Greek witness to this is Plato (*Tim.*39c/d), but according to Eudemus, a pupil of Aristotle, it was already taught by the Pythagoreans in conjunction with the doctrine of the eternal return. In view of the fragmentary tradition, it is difficult to say whether Heraclitus knew it, and if so to what degree.[546] Among the Pythagoreans this notion was probably based on their belief in the divinity of the stars and the perfection of their movements. 'The repetition of the circuit of the planets thus necessarily brought about a repetition of historical events on earth.'[547] Alongside the world year Plato also knew the myth of the periodically recurring catastrophes which were caused by the deviations of stars from their courses (*Tim.*22b/23c, cf. *Laws* 676ff.). In addition, in *Statesman* 269c/274[548] the conception of a periodical fall of the world and humanity and their restoration appears. It is brought about by the fact that the demiurge alternately leaves the world to itself, i.e. to its own contrary movement, and then again takes over personal control of its perfect movement. On the other hand, the Pythagorean doctrine of the eternal return is not accepted by Plato (*Republic* 10, 617a). However, according to Censorinus, Aristotle does not seem to have connected the world year and periodically recurring catastrophes with each other.[549] The Stoics, among whom the idea of the eternal return played a decisive role because of their deterministic view of the world and their high valuation of Chaldaean astrology – it was at the same time an expression of the perfection of the world – had it consummated by *ekpyrosis*.[550]

As has been demonstrated in particular by B. L. v. d. Waerden, the conceptions of the world year, the alternating catastrophes for the world and the eternal return – as indeed the whole of Pythagorean mathematics and astronomy – go back to the knowledge of the Babylonian priests and wise men.[551] This is shown *inter alia* by the fact that (Ps.) Berossus also knows the combination of the great world year and the alternating catastrophes of fire and water with astronomical signs. The theme of the burning of the world could therefore derive from Iranian influence.[552] The observations of Babylonian astronomers about the regularity and calculability of heavenly events in the firmament, which were combined with earlier conceptions of the world summer and the world winter and led to the conclusion that all earthly events were also dependent on the strictly regular occurrences in the starry heaven, probably gave impetus to the conception of the world year. Finally, an Egyptian version from the Hellenistic period connected the great year with the sun bird Phoenix.[553]

The first question is whether one can derive all doctrines of world periods from one basic myth – quite apart from the astronomically conditioned conception of the 'great world year', which can be clearly localized. As is the case with other similarly constructed, apparently unitary oriental mythologumena, like primal man, the journey of the soul to heaven (see below, pp. 204f.), the burning of the world or the wisdom myth, it is more probable that certain themes were conceived at different places and at different times, without it being possible to demonstrate mutual dependence. Thus e.g. Hesiod's doctrine of the ages of the world (see above, pp. 182f.) and that of Plato in the *Statesman* show a relatively independent structure which need not have been influenced by Babylonia or Iran. The same is even more true of the picture of history in Jewish apocalyptic. It is certainly possible that the 'great' year was known not only in Hellenistic Judaism – as e.g. in Josephus *Antt.* 1, 106 and probably also in *Sib.* 3, 91f.[554] – but also in the Palestinian Enoch tradition, but the way in which it is transformed only shows the deep gulf between the historical picture of Judaism and the astronomically based, unhistorical doctrine of the world cycles in Babylon and Greece, with their exclusive cosmological orientation. Consequently the Ten Weeks' Apocalypse speaks of the flood in the second week as the 'first end', whereas 'the great eternal judgment takes place' in the tenth week, when – according to I Enoch 18.11; 21.7ff.; 90.24f. – the fallen angels and godless will be punished in the abyss of fire (see below, pp. 201f.). The introduction to the admonitions in 91.6ff. states that – as at the time of the flood – 'unrighteousness will repeat itself for the second time' and God will root out all wickedness and idolatry with fire (see below, pp. 182f.). The conception of alternating catastrophes of water and fire also appears in isolation in the later Jewish tradition.[555] So the 'great aeon' of I Enoch 16.1 could possibly be a Jewish pendant to the great year, though hardly anything is left there of the original Babylonian myth. The course of history is neither based on astronomy nor calculated on the basis of the stars, but rather rests on God's plan, into which Enoch is given insight by the heavenly tables (see pp. 201f. below). Flood and fire are not natural cosmic catastrophes which take an inevitable course, but are punishments determined by God and under his free control. The astronomical book I Enoch 72–82 does not serve as a basis for the apocalyptic picture of history but to explain the Essene sun year of 364 days (see pp. 235f. below). Certain conceptions analogous to the 'great year', like the correspondence between end-time and primal time, or the idea of the ages of the earth, must not be derived from it, but may have their roots in the Old Testament itself.[556] In both instances we have widespread views which are common in antiquity.

A more significant parallel is formed by *Iranian* eschatology with its linear outline of history, which is to be distinguished in principle from the cyclical conception of the great year. This is already attested by Theopompus in the fourth century BC:

> He speaks of several (three or four) successive periods of history, each of three thousand years, in which 'Oromazes-Zeus' and 'Ahriman-Hades' dominate in turn. For further periods of three thousand years the two fight together until, after the victory of Oromazes, Ahriman vanishes and a time of untroubled good fortune dawns for men. The later Iranian tradition records a duration of the world of twelve thousand years, which is divided into different periods of time. Various astrological themes, like the rule of certain zodiacal signs over particular millennia, are taken up, but in every case there stands at the end the victory over evil and the dawn of the time of salvation. Even if one assumes Babylonian astrological influence – say for the Zervanism of the Magusians in Asia Minor and Syria, the linear picture of history is preserved and 'an eternal return' is excluded.[557] Iranian eschatology had a considerable effect in the West on writings like the oracle of Hystaspes and the Chaldean Sibyl.
>
> One interesting example of a Hellenistic-syncretistic mixed form between the astrologically determined conception of the consummation and the new beginning of the 'great year' and the Iranian or Jewish idea of the final dawn of the time of salvation as the consummation of history, conditioned by a Sibylline pattern, is to be found in the fourth Eclogue of Virgil, written about 40 BC. The difficulties of its interpretation are presented not least by the opposition of these two irreconcilable basic themes. However, the '*magnus ab integro saeculorum nascitur ordo*' (l.5, cf. l.12) seems to point clearly to the idea of an eternal return which is supported by astrology.[558]

It is difficult to know whether the Jewish apocalyptic view of history is directly dependent on that of Iran, and if so how far, or whether there is only a far-reaching analogy. First, there are chronological difficulties, as the well-known Iranian 'apocalypses' are relatively late, and in addition there are considerable differences in content. Particularly in the early Hasidic apocalyptic there was no interest in abstract world-periods interpreted in a dualistic form, and astrological regulation of them is even more absent. The seven world weeks of I Enoch 93.1–10 do not stand under the sign of the seven planets as they do in the speculations of the Hellenized Magusians in North Syria and Asia Minor;[559] rather, the history of the world given in the Torah and in the prophets and systematized through the idea of God's plan was interpreted from the perspective of the oppressive present, understood as God's judgment, and there was an extremely intense expectation – in contrast to all astrological-theoretical or mythological-dualistic speculation about the ages of the world – of the imminent dawn of the time of salvation promised by God (Dan. 8.17: *le'et -qēṣ* cf. 19; 11.35, 40ff.; 12.1f.). It would be quite conceivable that the apocalyptic conception of history developed along prophetic and eschatological lines as a continuation of earlier outlines of history, like that in the Priestly writing. Obviously one would have to presuppose a considerable degree of reinterpretation. The history of Israel and the nations was abstracted even more strongly and understood as a whole; it was, moreover, no longer judged from the saving present in the cultus and the law, but in the light of the imminently expected eschaton. In any event, the alien influence in apocalyptic from other religions was not so much in the total view of history as in detail.[560]

Why did this new historical view, and indeed Jewish apocalyptic, come into being? H. Ringgren has rightly suggested that the cause was 'the *difficult situation of the Jewish people in the Hellenistic age*'.[561] It is no coincidence that the first great 'apocalypses' come from the time of the Hellenistic reform and the persecutions and freedom fights that proceeded from it. They were written by the Hasidic 'wise men' – despite the 'almost stifling element of erudition'[562] – primarily as polemical and consolatory writings to strengthen the trust of believers in a 'time of tribulation, such as there never was since there were peoples' (Dan. 12.1). At a time when the temple was desecrated at the hands of Jews (see below, pp. 287ff.) through a foreign cult, when a large number of Jews had turned apostate[563] and the death penalty threatened the faithful, a conservative optimism like that of Sirach, constructed on the basis of God's retribution in this life and the purposefulness of creation, was made impossible. The 'apocalyptic eschatological predetermination' did not 'disappear later with the distresses of the present',[564] because in the eyes of the pious and rigorists, right down to the failure of Bar Kochba's revolt, there was in fact no end to them. Only in the second century AD did Jewish 'apocalyptic' come to an end. Thus the world powers are primarily the 'enemies of God'. The history of Palestinian Judaism between Daniel and Bar Kochba is largely one of blood and tears.

1. The Jewish people, sorely tried, fighting desperately for their sanctuary, their law and the faith of the fathers, now needed a *new interpretation of history* which went beyond the glorification of the past in the 'praise of the fathers' or in the work of the Chronicler[565] and was displayed in God's hidden plan with his people and the powers of the world, to encourage and comfort the oppressed so that they would continue to persevere in an apparently hopeless situation. Understandably, under the experiences of the difficult present, the development of world history was seen in a predominantly negative way: it was in a final crisis immediately before its end. Here there developed that view of the world which O. Spengler characterized by the phrase 'the world as hell' as being typical of 'Arabic' culture under the Hellenistic pseudo-morphosis.

This basic attitude leads from apocalyptic to later gnosticism, fed on oriental and Platonic sources; with it, of course the ultimate unity of creation and history guaranteed by God's plan of salvation collapsed.

2. The desperate-seeming attempt of the apocalyptist to *calculate an imminent end* to the world by continually new suggestions and corrections is to be understood from this situation of extreme crisis:

> The one positive thing that can be said about their calculations is that they were a temporally conditioned expression of faith in the plan of a righteous God for the world, which forms a powerful counterpart to the thoughtless world view of Hellenism with its . . . resignation towards happenings dominated by fate, by Tyche . . .[566]

The *burning expectation of the end* which expressed itself here should not therefore be judged in essentially negative terms. It was the factor which prevented the apocalyptic 'picture of history' from degenerating into mere salvation-historical theory and speculative teaching about the first and last things.

3. If 'the coming of salvation was now no longer bound up with the obedience of the people',[567] because a considerable number of the people had failed in a way that could no longer be made good, so that hardly anything more was to be expected from man's own action, in this desperate situation all hope had to be directed towards the imminent realization of God's *saving plan*. In the situation of crisis, the questionableness of human attempts to create for themselves the presuppositions of salvation were manifest.

4. The *decision of the individual* came more strongly into the foreground because a clear decision between the faith of the fathers and apostasy into a Jewish-syncretistic mixed cult had never been required in this way of any individual in Jewish history. Here, too, we possibly have the stronger emphasis on the individual in the Hellenistic period (see n. III, 66). On the other hand, responsibility for the whole people, who were to be called as a whole to repentance (see above, pp. 179f.), was expressly stressed by the Hasidim, who as a political group joined in fighting for the existence of the people, in contrast to the later separatist Essenes.[568]

5. One final reason why the picture of history finally embraced the whole of *world history* as a *unity* whose central point was Israel is perhaps that the view was a defence against the Hellenistic cosmopolitanism influential in Jerusalem, which wanted to give up what was peculiar to Israel in favour of solidarity with all 'Hellenes' in the *'oikūmenē'*.[569] In this direction the old prophetic idea that the God of Israel is the God of all peoples (Amos 9.7) and the whole of creation was strengthened by a 'historico-theological system' which saw the whole of world history from the perspective of the election of Israel and the imminence of the time of salvation. 'History gains its unity entirely in the light of eschatology.'[570] This attempt at *rationalization* and *systematization* is to be understood analogously to the struggle for a more

rational understanding of creation which becomes visible in Gen. 1–2.4a and later Jewish wisdom (see above, pp. 157ff.). Even the Hasidic wisdom schools could not cut themselves off from this general trend (see below, pp. 207ff.). *Thus the picture of history in apocalyptic is above all a fruit of the Jewish struggle for spiritual and religious self-determination against the invasion of Jerusalem by the Hellenistic spirit.*

bb) Resurrection, immortality and judgment

With the martyrs at the time of the religious distress, who would rather be killed than break God's commandment (see below, pp. 292f.), the immanent doctrine of retribution repristinated by Ben Sira in apologetic fashion inevitably proved to be insufficient. If the God of Israel really was the omnipotent and just Lord of the world, his power could not be limited even by death. So we encounter in early Hasidic apocalyptic the first references to the resurrection, judgment and human fate after death. The problem of theodicy, raised over and again in Israelite wisdom, here sought a new solution. If one leaves aside Isa. 26.19, which is hard to date but is surely earlier,[571] the first clear reference to the resurrection of the dead is in Dan. 12.2, though this is not – as in Isa. 26.19 – in a universal form, but with a vague limitation to 'many', of whom some will awake 'to eternal life' and others 'to eternal shame'. The first group probably refers to those who were true to the faith in earlier times, including the teachers of old times (Dan. 12.13), whereas the second refers to the Jewish apostates.[572] Further references to the resurrection from the same period are to be found in I Enoch 90.33 and the work of Jason of Cyrene, which is close to Palestinian and Hasidic doctrines – and was probably composed not too long after the death of Judas Maccabeus.[573] The indications of the historical origin of resurrection are on the one hand in the direction of Iranian religion, where they are already attested by Theopompus (fourth century BC),[574] while on the other hand conceptions of resurrection communicated by the dying and rising of vegetation deities had certainly been known in ancient Israel for some time.[575]

It is remarkable that the *mode and manner of resurrection* in early apocalyptic witnesses is indicated in very obscure terms. Nothing is said about the form in which the eschatological restitution of men is to take place.[576] Thus in Daniel it is clearly bound up with *astral* themes:

> And those who are wise shall shine like the brightness of the firmament,
> and those who turn many to righteousness, like the stars for ever and ever
> (Dan. 12.3).

As the apocalyptic teachers and admonishers of the people (11.33–35), the 'wise' receive a special share in the heavenly astral glory. Even Isa. 26.19 has an astral component with the 'dew of light'. I Enoch 104.2 takes up this theme again from Dan. 12.2:

Like bright stars (φωστῆρες, cf. Phil. 2.15) in heaven,
you will light up and shine, and the doors of heaven will be opened to you.[577]

Perhaps there is an anticipation here of an idea which was later to be significant among the Essenes, that the pious live in close communion with the angels in the time of salvation: 'stars and angels are often to be regarded as one thing.'[578]

This could be a Jewish version of *'astral immortality'*, which was uncommonly widespread in the Hellenistic period in both philosophy and poetry as in popular belief. Koheleth 3.21 had already rejected the idea that the 'spirit' of man rises 'on high'. F. Cumont attempted to derive the idea of astral immortality, which probably appears in the Greek world for the first time among the Pythagoreans and then later in Plato and his school, from the Maguseans in Asia Minor who were influenced by Iran and Babylon. However, his hypothesis was rightly rejected by M. P. Nilsson. The idea that men will become stars after their death already appears in Aristophanes (*Pax* 832ff.) and on individual Greek epitaphs – a sign of its popular character – and even on a Jewish inscription from Cilicia, though this is late.[579] An epitaph of Antipater of Sidon (see p. 84 above) can combine the concept of ἀν(ά)στασις in the sense of 'rising' directly with the idea of astral immortality:

Blessed for ever the people whom Heraclea raises to the spacious realm of the heavenly clouds

δᾶμος ἀεὶ μακαριστός, ὃς ἄνστασιν (conj. for ἄστεσιν)῾Ηρακλείης
οὐρανίων νεφέων τεῦξεν ἐπ᾽εὐρυάλων (*Anth. Gr.* 7, 748).

Emphasis on the wise in the portrayal of the resurrection is a special feature. It corresponds to the 'metaphysical heightening of the value of education' which can commonly be observed in the Hellenistic period, and is particularly notable in epitaphs.[580] A good example of it is the graffito on the tomb of the famous priest of Thoth, Petosiris, from the middle of the third century BC:

Πετόσειριν αὐδῶ τὸ(ν) κατὰ χθονὸς νέκυν,
νῦν δ᾽ἐν θεοῖσι κείμενον μετὰ σοφῶν σοφό(ν).[581]

Like Homer, the Old Testament knew only the concept of the *underworld* (šᵉ'ōl), in which the dead live a shadow existence; Ben Sira (14.12, 16f.) still shares this view. In the angelological book I Enoch 12–36 (see n. 460 above), there appear for the first time in Judaism – in connection with Enoch's journeys to heaven and to the underworld – detailed portrayals of the mythical kingdom of the dead in the north-west beyond the sea, which have contacts at many points with Greek and Babylonian mythology:

A stream of fire corresponds with Pyriphlegethon, further streams to some degree with the underworld rivers of Styx, Acheron and Cocytus (17.5f.), and even the great ocean into which all the streams flow is there (17.5, 7f.; 18.10). This mythical geography probably rests on a mixture of Greek and

Babylonian elements, as P. Grelot has carefully demonstrated, though he perhaps lays too much stress on the parallels from the Gilgamesh epic. The Greek mythology of the realm of the dead was in popular currency in the Greek world, especially as it derives, *inter alia*, from the portrayal in the *Odyssey* (cf. e.g. 10, 508–15). Presumably Homer was also read in Jerusalem at the time of the foundation of the gymnasium (see pp. 75f.).[582]

There in the west, on a rocky mountain (cf. *Odyssey* 10, 515; 24,11) Enoch is shown the place of the spirits of the souls of the dead (τὰ πνεύματα τῶν ψυχῶν τῶν νεκρῶν).[583] A bright realm with a spring – one is reminded of the Orphic conception of the Elysian fields with the spring of Mnemosyne[584] – is for the 'spirits of the righteous', and two (or three) other dark realms are for the sinners. In the first those who fared well on earth are tormented until the day of judgment; in the other are the sinners who already suffered their punishment while they were still alive. They will not be punished on the day of judgment, but they will not be raised either. Such a division of the realm of the dead, bound up with the conception of a retribution beyond death, is a new idea for Judaism. Only now, as a result of the Hasidim, does there penetrate to the consciousness of further circles of the Jewish people the idea that after death the 'souls' undergo different fates and can be punished or rewarded. This idea had probably been long familiar to the Greek world because of Orphic or Pythagorean doctrines; it occurs both in the philosophers, like Plato and the Stoics, and in the mysteries and in popular belief.[585] At the same time, the influence of Greek anthropology can be seen. The soul is separated from the body and in the resurrection – a conception which as yet does not have a single content – in some circumstances receives it back again. The 'journey to heaven' for the purpose of receiving revelation (see below, pp. 204f.) can now be presented as a separation of the soul from the body.[586] By and large, one receives the impression that the internal consequences of this belief have not always been thought through clearly. In Dan. 12.2 and I Enoch 22 the resurrection is present in a double form, but it remains incomplete and does not apply to all the dead; I Enoch 27 removes the righteous and the damned to Jerusalem: the latter are punished in the valley of Hinnom in the presence of the righteous. Spiritualized and realistic conceptions stand side by side with relatively little connection.[587]

This lack of unity is also shown in the fact that in the Essene wing of the Hasidim the idea of physical resurrection retreated so far into the background that we must ask whether this concept is still appropriate in their case, and whether for them eschatological salvation did not rather consist in the heavenly communion of the exalted spirits with the angels (see below, pp. 223f.). Not only does Josephus stress that they believe in the immortality of the soul, in a place for the blessed and a place of punishment – allegedly after the fashion of the Pythagoreans (see below, pp. 245ff.) – but Jub. 23.30ff. seems to confirm this report:[588]

And at that time the Lord will heal His servants,
And they shall rise up and see great peace,
And drive out their adversaries.
And the righteous shall see and be thankful,
And rejoice with joy for ever and ever,
And shall see all their judgments and all their curses on their enemies.
And their *bones* shall *rest in the earth,*
And their spirits shall have much joy,
And they shall know that it is the Lord who executes judgment
And shows mercy . . .

The statements in the admonition of I Enoch 103.2ff. are similar:

I know this mystery (cf. I Cor. 15.51); for I have read the heavenly tablets
and I have seen the holy books (text follows the Ethiopian) . . . that goodness and joy and honour are prepared and written down for the souls of
those who have died pious (ταῖς ψυχαῖς τῶν ἀποθανόντων εὐσεβῶν). And
their *spirits* (πνεύματα) will rejoice and not perish . . . And you, you
sinners, when you have died, they will say of you: Blessed are the sinners:
they have seen all their days; and now they have died in prosperity and
wealth, and judgment has not been executed on them during their life. You
shall know that their souls will be made to descend to Sheol, and there they
will be in great tribulation.[589]

Alongside this, in the admonitions there are also isolated statements about
the peaceful sleep of the pious in death, from which they will be 'awoken' at
the time appointed by God.[590] Even in the Qumran writings the possibility
of 'resurrection' is intimated only in two passages; otherwise, there is only
mention of 'eternal life', 'eternal joy' and 'eternal salvation', without any
elaboration.[591] There is further mention of the original immortality of
Adam in the Noah fragment I Enoch 69.11 in a way which recalls Wisdom
2.23f.[592] Thus it is understandable that the problem of the Hasidic-Essene
eschatological anthropology is disputed by scholars. Whereas P. Grelot fundamentally rejects the idea that the Essenes knew the concept of resurrection by
reference to the earlier parts of I Enoch and Jubilees, and considers their
views as a prelude to the belief in immortality in Wisdom 2–5,[593] K.
Schubert believed that he could presuppose that they, too, knew it, albeit in a
reduced form compared to later conceptions. The question in the end involves
the definition of the concept of 'resurrection'. Even K. Schubert rejects the
conception 'of a particular resurrection of the flesh' in the sense of 'the
individual bodies of those who have died' and speaks 'only of a new spiritual
and corporeal life', or in more restrained fashion of a resurrection of the soul,
endowed with corporeal functions.[594]

It should be pointed out in this connection that e.g. for Stoic thought the
difference between soul and matter was only a relative one. The soul itself
was merely a 'fine body' (σῶμα) of a substance like fire.[595] Possibly this

feature is connected with their Semitic presuppositions. This connection is also significant for the Pauline conception of the resurrection (I Cor. 15.44, 50; Phil. 3.21).

Thus the Essene doctrine of resurrection still lacks that crudeness which we later find among the Pharisees.[596] Only in the non-Essene similitudes from the first century BC and in the still later IV Ezra and Syrian Baruch does the resurrection emerge in clearer form.[597] The influence of Hellenistic 'eschatology' thus seems to have been stronger in early Hasidic Essene apocalyptic than in the later period, since even for the Greeks the conception of the revivification of the old fleshly body was an idea that was hard to comprehend. Thus it is all the more astonishing that it could find a foothold even in the Greek-speaking Diaspora:

> The fourth Sibylline, which was composed immediately after the destruction of Jerusalem, has the following passage after a description of the judgment by fire which has probably been taken over from the Stoic conception of *ekpyrosis*: 'Then God himself forms men from dust and bones and makes the mortals as they were formerly. And then comes the judgment . . .'[598]

This example also shows how the boundaries between allegedly 'Jewish-Semitic' and 'Hellenistic' forms of conception ran straight through Palestinian Judaism and the western Diaspora. Moreover, as the example of the Essenes shows, a spiritualized form of the individual expectation of salvation after death did not necessarily exclude hope directed to the imminence of the eschaton.

The counterpart to resurrection or eternal life was *judgment*. The earliest apocalypses in Dan. 7.9–14; I Enoch 90.15, 18–26; 91.14f. already described this theme, sometimes with detailed scenery. It involves the godless kingdoms of the world, and especially the last, the seventy angels of the nations, the fallen watchers of Gen. 6, the Jewish apostates, indeed all the 'godless'.[599] In this sense the universal notion of judgment supplements the universal picture of history. However, the individual pictures and conceptions vary considerably. There is no more a fixed 'dogmatic of judgment' than there is a view of resurrection. The visionary images resist being fixed as a system.

The idea of judgment and retribution is expressed most sharply in the admonitions of I Enoch 92–104.[600] Here the godless are threatened in constantly repeated woes with death at the sword of the faithful in the eschatological Holy War, with condemnation in the final judgment, eternal torment in the underworld and annihilation by the fire of judgment. It remains uncertain, however, whether the sinners will be completely annihilated or punished everlastingly.[601]

> The *heavenly books* or *tables* play a special part in the judgment. On them Michael, Enoch or the angels write all the deeds of men, and especially

their sins. The book of those destined to life or death is a theme that is already widespread in the Old Testament, but the conception of heavenly laws or memorial tablets comes from Babylon;[602] however, Greek mythology also knew the theme of the memorandum of Zeus in which the deeds of men were written so that they could be rewarded and punished accordingly.[603] We meet this idea in the Hellenistic period in the prologue of Plautus' *Rudens*, who has taken it over from the new comedy of Diphilus. According to this the stars – in this case Arcturus – observe the evil deeds of men at Jupiter's command in order to note them.[604] This is matched by Diodore's account of the Chaldean astrology of thirty (-six) stars, half of which watch over the places above the earth and half of which watch over those below. Every ten days these messengers change, i.e. one group of stars goes below and another above.[605] A parallel to this appears in I Enoch 100.10: 'Know now that the angels in heaven follow your deeds to note your sin from the sun, the moon and the stars . . .'[606] The idea of judgment thus seems to have been bound up with themes of Babylonian and astral derivation.

The punishment or annihilation of the fallen angels is carried out – following Old Testament and Iranian models – by *fire*, a conception which could at times almost assume the features of a doctrine of *ekpyrosis*.[607]

The mention of the ten-thousand-year time of punishment for the seven stars in I Enoch 18.16; 21.6, which will be 'rolled in the fire', because they transgressed God's commandment and did not rise at the time appointed for them, recalls the ten-thousand-year period of repentance according to the doctrine of the transmigration of the soul in the Pythagoreans and Orphics, which appears e.g. in Plato, *Phaedrus* 248e/249a. In this context the *Phaedrus* also speaks of 'places of punishment under the earth', in which those who come there do 'righteous expiation' (εἰς τὰ ὑπὸ γῆς δικαιωτήρια ἐλθοῦσαι δίκην ἐκτίνουσιν). A. Dieterich, who was the first to point to this context, cites the saying of Heraclitus: '(For) Helios will not overstep his limits, otherwise the Erinnyes, the scourges of fate, will search him out' (fr. 94, Diels).[608] A still more detailed portrayal of the punishments in the underworld is to be found in the Similitudes (I Enoch 53f.), where the plague angels prepare instruments of torture for the fallen '(angel-) hosts of Asasel' and 'the kings and mighty ones of the earth', 'with which to annihilate them'. M. P. Nilsson, who points to this passage, stresses that the nearest parallels come from the portrayals of the places of punishment in the underworld in the Greek tradition, where the punishments for the fallen Titans and the wicked men are mentioned side by side: 'It unfortunately remains the case that hell is a Greek invention.'[609]

Thus it is on the whole evident that Hasidic apocalyptic wisdom not only took over its themes connected with man's fate after death from Iranian or Babylonian mythology, but was also strongly influenced by Greek Orphic conceptions of the beyond. Here the burning problem of a theodicy looked for a new answer. Foreign conceptions need not primarily have been taken over in literary ways; they could also rest on the transference of popular motives, which also happened later with the Rabbis (see above, p. 172). Possibly, too, the Jewish diaspora in Egypt may have been an agent of communication; it was interested in the figure of Orpheus and took over Orphic themes. J. A. Sanders has indicated the possibility that in the Davidic psalm 11 QPs^a 151, Orphic themes were worked over.[610]

The elaboration of apocalyptic doctrines of resurrection, immortality and judgment in Jewish Palestine also explains why the Hellenistic *mystery cults* and their language hardly became influential there – in contrast to Alexandrian Judaism.[611] Since apocalyptic Hasidic piety took up the question of the fate of the individual after death, it answered the basic question of human existence which had burst forth in an elementary way in the Hellenistic period and favoured the spread of the mystery religions from the second century BC onwards. In this way new factors became effective in the religious development of Palestinian Judaism:

1. The already existing tendency to *individualize* piety was quite substantially strengthened: 'Only in the notion of other-worldly retribution does religious individualism find its firm stay and its terse summation.'[612]

2. The question of the *certainty* of eschatological salvation came more strongly into the centre, and with it the problem of the *redemption* of man from the anti-godly powers of sin and death.

3. To the universal consideration of history from an eschatological perspective was added interest in an *anthropology* with a soteriological orientation: why is man subject to sin, and how must he be shaped to obtain eternal salvation? Attempts were made above all in Essenism to give an answer to this question.

cc) Wisdom through revelation

In contrast to Ben Sira, who also claimed 'prophetic inspiration' for himself, though without making it a matter of central importance (see above, pp. 134f.), the apocalyptic Hasidim ground their 'wisdom' in a claim to direct divine revelations, though they put them in the mouths of wise men and prophets of past time. The sober wisdom of the traditional wise men with their observations and reflections could hardly say anything about the all-embracing divine plan for history, the imminent end of the world, resurrection and judgment, angels and the kingdom of the dead; here one could only refer to special divine communications which transcended the usual degree of experience.[613]

This emerges for the first time in concentrated form in *Daniel*, where we find a multiplicity of forms of revelation and supernatural knowledge. Even as a young man Daniel 'had understanding in all visions and dreams' (1.17). In a 'night vision' he discovered the content and the interpretation of Nebuchadnezzar's dream (2.19, cf. 4.16ff.); in 5.24f. he is the only one to read the divine writing on the wall; in 7.1ff., 15 he reports a dream vision the content of which really presupposes a journey to heaven, and the angel who interprets it; in 8.1, 15 he has a vision which is explained by the angel Gabriel; in 9.1ff., 21 Gabriel again appears to him – after penitential prayer and fasting – to interpret to him the seventy years of Jer.25.11f. and 29.10, which he does not understand, as weeks of years; in 10.1ff. he has a final vision, again communicated by an angel, which he experiences while he is awake. In almost all these 'revelations' 'the didactic element is combined with prophecy' in a striking way.[614] Thus Daniel appears – to a much greater degree than the earlier Old Testament prophets – as simultaneously a seer and a wise man. There is deliberate stress here on the extent to which his wisdom surpasses that of the learned Chaldeans (2.1–13; 4.3f.; 5.7f.) – a statement with polemic and apologetic intent in view of the 'international' reputation of the Chaldean wise men and astrologers. Like the Greek Χαλδαῖοι, the designation *kaśśᵉdāyā'* here no longer has a geographical significance, but means 'astrologers' (Dan.2.5, 10; 4.4; 5.7, 11). High praise is given him from pagan lips:

> He is the man in whom is the 'spirit of holy gods' (*'ᵉlāhīn*), in whom 'light and understanding and wisdom' dwell like 'the wisdom of the gods' (5.11, cf. 14), who can solve dreams, riddles and magic problems (*qiṭᵉrīn*) (5.12, 16).

In Daniel's prayer of thanksgiving for the revelation of the king's dream it is made clear that this divine wisdom is the free gift of God:

> Blessed be the name of God for ever and ever,
> to whom belong wisdom and might.
> He gives wisdom to the wise
> and knowledge to those who have understanding;
> he reveals deep and mysterious (things);
> he knows what is in the darkness
> and the light dwells with him.
> To thee, O God of my fathers,
> I give thanks and praise,
> for thou hast given me wisdom and strength. (Dan.2.20–23)

It is no coincidence that the term *rāz* = μυστήριον, which is later so significant at Qumran, appears often for the first time in this context (leaving aside one passage of secular usage in Ben Sira)[615] (2.18f., 27–30, 47): 'But there is a God in heaven who reveals *mysteries*, and he has made known to king Nebuchadnezzar what will be at the end of days.'[616] However, the only one worthy to receive such revelations or to interpret them is the one who brings the necessary disposition. Daniel therefore appears as a '*ḥāsīd*', who only eats pure food and keeps the three times of prayer turned towards Jerusalem, even at the risk of his life (see pp. 178f. below). To show himself worthy of special revelations he fasts and prays intensively and shows his readiness to repent (9.3; 10.2).

The situation is similar in I Enoch. *Enoch* appears as the prototype of the pious wise man of the primal period. The short note about his walking 'with God' and his exaltation in Gen. 5.24 (P) was probably understood to mean that he was the man who stood closest to God; he therefore assumed almost angelic character. A whole series of features of the Babylonian wise men of the primal period were transferred to his figure, which probably derives from the Babylonian primal king Enmeduranki.[617] At the same time he was also a prophet of judgment, who announced the imminent judgment of God to the generation before the flood and the fallen watcher angels. So now he could issue a summons to repentance before the second final judgment, which was imminent.[618] In addition, he was thought to be the bringer of culture who was half human and half belonged to the divine sphere; in this sense he was identified by the anonymous Samaritan with the titan Atlas, the brother of Prometheus: he brought astrology to the Greeks (see above, p. 89). For Sirach, who stresses him twice (44.16; 49.14), he is the great 'pattern of knowledge' as the אות דעת.[619] The Enoch tradition was thus not the exclusive possession of the Hasidic, apocalyptic wisdom teachers; rather, it is possible that the Hellenists in Shechem and Jerusalem developed their own 'Enoch tradition' in the identification with Atlas. He did, however, appear to the apocalyptic speculations of the Hasidic 'wise men' to be the ideal 'mediator of revelation', since he was equally at home in the earthly and the heavenly worlds: according to Gen. Apoc. 2.20f. his lot was 'assigned (with the angels), and they made everything known to him' (cf. Jub. 4.21).

As in Daniel, we find with him an abundance of variable forms of revelation.[620] He receives his wisdom through dreams (13.8; 14.1; 85.1) and visions (1.2; 37.1; 83.1f.; 93.1f.) – the two can hardly be separated –, is introduced by angels into the heavenly mysteries (12.4; chs. 17–27; 72–82; Jub. 4.21), is taken up and experiences an extensive *heavenly journey*, which is at the same time connected with a descent to the kingdom of the dead and the places of punishment (12.1 ἐλήμφθη, 17.1 and chs. 12–36; 71.1ff.).

> Behold, in the vision clouds invited me and a mist summoned me, and the course of the stars and the lightnings sped and hastened me, and the winds in the vision caused me to fly and lifted me upward, and bore me into heaven (14.8).

A spiritualized form in which it is no longer the whole man but the spirit which shares in the journey to heaven is to be found in the Similitudes:

> And it came to pass after this that my spirit was translated
> And it ascended into the heavens (71.1).

The ascent is matched by the return; Enoch is brought back to earth by seven archangels and is set down before the door of his house (81.5). In the context of the journey to heaven the *heavenly tablets* are a particularly important source of revelation (81.1ff.; 93.2; see nn. 602–5 above). On them the whole course of history is inscribed. The esoteric secret knowledge acquired in this way is handed on by Enoch *to his son* Methusalem (76.14; 81.5; 82.1ff.; 83.1; 108.1ff.; see below, p.215); on the other hand he directs his call to repentance and his admonition to all the members of his generation (91.1ff.; cf.91–104). Other fathers and prophets like Noah, Abraham, Levi could also become the bearers of such revelations in the same way as Enoch.[621]

> In the Hasidic or early Essene Aramaic fragment of the *Testament of Levi* there is a description of the way in which after appropriate preparation, purification and penitential prayer Levi receives a vision of heaven in a dream which – according to the secondary version in the Greek text, which is all that we have – takes him through the different heavens. The Geniza fragments of the Testament of Levi, which are probably also Essene, point to further similar visions.[622]

This very theme of the heavenly journey which was so beloved in apocalyptic from the beginning should warn us against viewing apocalyptic one-sidedly and exclusively under the temporal aspect of the imminent expectation of the end, although this latter feature forms its constitutive centre. The spatial conception of the spheres of heaven laid one on top of the other, through which the seer passes in a heavenly vision or a heavenly journey, also has a spceial significance. It belongs just as much to the mythical world-view of the Palestinian Jews as to the conceptual sphere of Hellenistic mysticism. Thus the spatial and the temporal elements cannot be played off against each other (see pp.214f. below).

1. The supposedly great age of these writings was a demonstration of their truth. The *pseudepigraphic form* necessarily became a firm rule for Jewish apocalyptic, since the apocalyptists' unheard-of claim to revelation could only be maintained by reference to those who had been endowed with the spirit in ancient times.[623] This predilection for pseudepigraphy was furthered by the correspondence of primal time and end time. What God had revealed to the spirit-possessed pious of primal times, and these had 'sealed' from profane eyes as secret teaching or had communicated to only a few of the elect,[624] was now made known to the pious of the last time to strengthen their faith. So we find as the predominant recipients of these 'secret doctrines' the fathers from Adam to Moses; the reason why Daniel and Baruch appear alongside them is the parallelism in the situation of judgment, the desecration of the temple and the exile, and the fact that the last period of the history of Israel is beginning, which stands under the sign of dispersion, apostasy and special temptation. On the other hand, Ezra only became an 'apocalyptic prophet' when the view was established that the gift of prophecy in Israel had ceased with him. By contrast, 'apocalyptic pseudonymity' retreated in Qumran and in the early church: the basis for the 'collective authority' in the Essene writings was the spirit at work in the community, whereas Christian apocalyptists like

John of Ephesus and Hermas could write as pneumatic authorities under their own names. It would, however, be over-hasty to conclude from this that the Hasidic apocalyptists no longer considered themselves 'prophets' or the legitimate successors of the prophets. The last prophetic writers, like the author of the prophecies of Trito-Isaiah, Deutero-Zechariah and Malachi, preserved their anonymity and added their writings to prophetic collections that had already been made.[625] The situation of the *late period* had created a new position, similar to that which can also be observed in the Hellenistic environment:

2. The free working of the spirit, without reference to the extant tradition which had already been fixed in writing and had in effect acquired 'canonical' validity, was now impossible. From now on, the 'prophetic self-awareness' was at work not least in the *'inspired' interpretation of prophetic writings which had already been composed.* This is shown by the meditation of Daniel on the seventy 'years' of Jeremiah in Dan. 9.2 and by the exposition of the prophets by the Teacher of Righteousness.[626] We can hardly say here that the apocalyptists no longer regarded themselves as being in possession of the spirit; they simply regarded present inspiration as weaker and therefore referred to the more powerful models of the past.[627] On the other hand, they raised the claim that they understood the prophetic words which they had deciphered better than their very authors, for it was the eschatological present, near to fulfilment, which first put them in a position to interpret the deeper sense of these writings correctly.[628]

3. Prophetic consciousness and the learning acquired by wisdom were now inseparably intertwined. *The wise men acquired prophetic features, and the prophets became inspired wise men.* It should be noted here that for this late period the term 'wisdom' is no less vague, general and therefore disputable than the word 'apocalyptic'.[629] Essentially it could mean the most different forms of learning practised in schools, from the 'Greek wisdom' of the Hellenists (חכמה יוונית, see p. 76 above) to the casuistic distinctions of the *sōperîm* entrusted with the custody of the law, who laid the foundations of Mishnaic law. 'Apocalyptic wisdom' was marked off from other forms of wisdom by the fact that it rested on special revelations of God and therefore was granted only to a few elect. In this respect, the 'apocalyptic' concept of wisdom remained closely bound up with the old conception of wisdom hidden in heaven and beyond man's control.[630] As a consequence of the conjunction of wisdom and prophecy, the great men of the early period from Adam and Enoch down to the last prophets were regarded as both prophets and wise men. The note about David in the psalm scroll of 11 Q portrays David as a 'wise' (חכם) and 'learned' (סופר) man inspired with the prophetic spirit and endowed with particular insight (כאור שמש, cf. Dan. 12.3 and Test. Levi 4.3). The conception in the 'praise of the fathers' (Sir. 44.3–5; cf. 39.1–8, see above, pp. 136f.) is quite similar. The modern approach which wants to derive

apocalyptic one-sidedly from wisdom or prophecy would have been almost incomprehensible to Ben Sira or to the Hasidic apocalyptists.[631]

4. This situation by no means excludes the possibility that, despite its literary form, the apocalyptic literature is derived at least in part from *visions and ecstatic experiences*. There was again a strong interest in such extraordinary experiences in the Hellenistic period, indeed one must suppose that certain methods – like fasts and constant prayer – were developed in order to bring on visionary experiences.[632] The vision and ecstasy thus became the confirmation of the true 'prophetic wise man'.[633] This was also true of the later period. The famous Baraita *Ḥagiga* 14b: 'Four entered paradise (ארבעה נכנסו בפרדם), Ben Azzai, Ben Zoma, Aḥer and R. Akiba . . . ', is to be related not primarily to apocalyptic-gnostic speculations, but to ecstatic experiences. Even the former Pharisee Paul will not have received his ecstatic gift only on becoming a Christian. Certain figures, like Honi the Circle Drawer (first half of the first century BC) and the miraculous healer R. Hanina b. Dosa (*c.* AD 100), indicate the Hasidic apocalyptic components in early Pharisaism, which were only excluded by the stronger institutionalization in the second century AD. The Essene movement also possessed its own 'prophets'.[634]

5. The web of the '*inspired learning*' of the early apocalyptists was stretched widely. If in Daniel it was limited to an exact knowledge of historical events and to the imagery of oriental and Hellenistic mythology, in the Enoch tradition it extends to the whole world, visible and invisible, including earthly and heavenly geography – here the larger world-picture of the Hellenistic period is presented[635] – through astronomy and astrology – rejecting Babylonian Hellenistic astral religion[636] – down to meteorology and medicine.[637] Of course this apocalyptic 'encyclopaedic' wisdom is in no way an end in itself. The cosmological mysteries of I Enoch have a clear eschatological tendency, as they embrace the sphere of God's judgment on angels and sinners as well as God's reward for the righteous. The whole cosmos is in the service of an eschatologically controlled salvation history. Closely connected with this is a second point which E. Sjöberg has noted: 'If one wants to know God in all his glory, one must also know these cosmological mysteries', for 'the glory of God as creator is revealed through them'.[638] This is shown, say, by Enoch's praise at the end of his first great journey through heaven and the world (36.4):

> And when I saw, each time I blessed the Lord of glory . . ., who has done great and glorious wonders to show the greatness of his work to angels and men, so that they may praise his work and his whole creation . . . .

6. On the whole, one can speak of *three stages* in the apocalyptic understanding of wisdom: (*a*) the basic idea, taken over from late Jewish 'wisdom', that only the righteous, i.e. the doer of the law, can be wise: 'None of the wicked shall understand, but the wise will understand' (Dan. 12.10). To 'accept the words of wisdom' means 'to observe the ways of the Most High, to walk in

the way of his righteousness and not to sin with the godless' (I Enoch 99.10). The '*maśkilīm*' (Dan. 11.33, 35; 12.10) are primarily teachers of the law, and the admonitions of I Enoch 92; 94–104 are primarily concerned with concrete obedience. (*b*) In the temptations of the last time the revelations of the ancient men of God and prophets which have hitherto been concealed are opened; they give their explanation of the meaning and the goal of history, the heavenly world, judgment and eternal salvation. But even these revelations, which strengthen the 'pious' in distress and raise them above their unknowing environment, are only provisional and imperfect. (*c*) Perfect wisdom belongs among the eschatological gifts of the time of salvation itself (I Enoch 5.8; 32.3–6; 90.35; 91.10; cf. the Similitudes 48.1f.; 49.1ff.). Of course these three stages are not completely disconnected. The law and the prophets already contain a deeper meaning and need 'study' (דרש, Dan. 12.4b) to discover it. In addition, God's commandments are really taken seriously and rigorously observed only in the circles of the 'pious'. Similarly, the revelation of the eschatological, heavenly mysteries to the beleaguered pious is at the same time the preparation and the foretaste for the communication of perfect wisdom in the time of salvation.[639]

7. The comprehensive apocalyptic striving for knowledge – von Rad speaks of an 'almost hybrid-looking universal gnosis'[640] – only becomes comprehensible when we consider its *historical background*. This conjunction of superabundant learning, rational systematization and a theocentric view of history in an eschatological perspective was something new in the history of the Jewish people. A. Schlatter gives a hint at the reasons for its appearance in his characterization of Daniel, which one might transfer to the Hasidic fathers of apocalyptic in general:

> The Greeks praised knowledge as the highest possession of man, and Daniel took over from them a reverence for the power created by knowledge. So he describes prophecy as a share in divine knowledge, which can even unveil the future. But the Greeks lacked the supreme knowledge, knowledge of the divine will. This was the advantage which raised Israel above the level of the nations.[641]

The Hasidic 'wise men' were even more sharply engaged than Ben Sira in *controversy with Greek wisdom*, which after 175 BC, as the result of the founding of a gymnasium in Jerusalem, had become an acute threat to the continuance of the Jewish religious tradition. The Greek ἐγκύκλιος παιδεία with its logical and systematic force which penetrated the whole cosmos and ordered it, was opposed to a view of the world and history grounded on a divine 'revelation' and 'apocalyptic' in the best sense of the word, which also could claim to be older than any Greek wisdom. The critical 'enlightenment' which filled the Hellenistic world in the third century BC and – as Koheleth shows – came up against analogous streams in Jewish wisdom, had for some time gained influence in the *upper strata* of Jewish society. Its criticism was primarily directed against Israel's special course among the nations, as in its view segregation hampered the economic and cultural development of the people (see below, pp.271f.). Whereas the conventional cultic and legalistic piety of these trends could not put up any adequate resistance, the Hasidic wise men gathered together the forces faithful to the law with their rationally unassailable counter-argument of 'higher wisdom through revelation', created a universal picture of the world and history related to the imminence of the eschaton, in which the election of Israel formed the foundation, and thus laid a decisive basis for the further intellectual development of Palestinian Judaism.

8. If one follows Lagrange and F. M. Abel in designating the world picture of I Enoch as an anachronism in the time of an Erastothenes and a Hipparchus, or with W. Bousset comes to the conclusion that 'all wisdom here is lay fantasy',[642] one overlooks *the pre-scientific character of this wisdom*. Furthermore, the Qumran fragments show that we have both the Enoch tradition and the Testament of Levi in a partially disrupted form, and that in the Aramaic original they were more extensive and more precise.[643] An analysis of the geographical or astronomical parts of I Enoch or the book of Jubilees shows that the 'wise men' were astonishingly familiar with the learning in this area – which presumably was predominantly Babylonian (see pp.183f. above). And as far as their 'philosophy of history' is concerned, hardly any pattern of world history has had greater influence than that of the book of Daniel.[644] Finally, it should be noted that writings like Daniel and the Enoch cycle (excluding the astronomical book) or even presumably Essene works like Jubilees and the Testament of Levi – in contrast to the innermost esoteric writings, which were anxiously kept secret (see below, n.691) – were '*popular books*' written for the wider circles of the 'pious', like the Jewish Sibyllines in the Diaspora, which were intended to support the Jewish mission and which imitated the popular prophetic oracular literature in the Hellenistic period.[645] The esoteric garb here was a deliberate stylistic expedient to arouse the interest of the reader. In the first place, the writings contributed to keeping alive the eschatological expectation of the end down to the rebellion of Bar Kochba, and saw that the views of the Hasidim about the hierarchy and the fall of the angels, resurrection and judgment, the end of the world and the dawn of the time of salvation became common knowledge in the wider circles of Palestinian Judaism in the Hellenistic and Roman period.

9. A general verdict which has been passed on apocalyptic by von Rad and others fails to do it justice because it pays too little attention to its historical setting. The characteristic of 'a fundamentally unhistorical way of thinking'[646] does not apply to it but to its counterpart, the world picture of the Hellenistic period determined by the arbitrary sway of Tyche or by astral determinism. Above all, the speculations on cosmology and the philosophy of history should not lead to a neglect of the '*saving character*' of this wisdom,

which is directed towards the imminent eschaton, as it appears particularly in the closing vision of Daniel and the later admonitions of I Enoch. In the utmost tribulation 'the wise men of the people bring many to understanding (*yābīnū lārabbīm*)', and 12.3, shortly afterwards, shows that this 'insight' was not any mere speculative knowledge: in this way the wise have brought 'many to righteousness' – i.e. to the side of the faithful community and thus to eschatological salvation: they are *maṣᵉddīqē hārabbīm*. This saving character of apocalyptic knowledge then emerges even more clearly a little later, among the Essenes.

Excursus 4: 'Higher wisdom through revelation' as a characteristic of religion in late antiquity

The revival of piety after the collapse of traditional forms of religion in the *polis* and the wave of destructive scepticism in the fourth and third centuries BC have as a typical feature the *personal tie of the individual to particular deities*, a tie which was grounded more strongly than in the earlier period through personal supernatural experiences, dreams, epiphanies, healings, direct instructions from God, etc. The gods who gained great influence in this way early on in the Hellenistic period, because they entered into direct association with their believers and so created a quite personal relationship, included deities like Asclepius and Serapis and Isis, though these are by no means the only ones. A characteristic feature of the latter was that in contrast to the Greek gods they also had power over fate.[647] Especially through dreams, they gave commands to their worshippers and saw that these commands were carried out; they inflicted punishment through sickness and communicated secret knowledge about cures, about the future after death, etc, through revelations. In this way there increased in wide areas of the people an interest in dreams about revelations or visionary, ecstatic experiences, which in earlier days were reserved for individual wise men, seers, kings and poets.[648] If a man did not himself have the capacity for visions, he would at least receive a share in this higher knowledge through reading similar, allegedly 'secret' revelatory writing. The revival of Neo-Pythagoreanism in the first century BC and the success of the mystery religions are to be explained in the light of these tendencies.

This development was prepared for by a '*literature of* revelation'. This partly contained the miraculous experiences of ecstatic wonder-workers, but often also narratives of descents which at least from the classical period were often combined with a 'journey to heaven'.[649] The reason for this was that, as the world-picture changed, people were more and more inclined to transfer the kingdom of the dead to the starry heavens. Homer's *Odyssey* already made rich use of the popular theme of the descent, and it was given a deeper background in the philosophy of religion as Orphic and Pythagorean myths and the doctrine of the soul associated with them were taken over by Empedocles, Plato and others:[650]

'The first literary description of the journey of a man to heaven is that of Parmenides at the beginning of his poem.'[651] On the glowing chariot of the sun, harnessed to heavenly horses, and guided by the Heliades, he goes towards the light. Dike allows him to enter by the door at which the paths of day and night divide. There he receives his revelation from 'Alētheia' (fr. 1, Diels). A. Dieterich derives this large poetic vision from Orphic models, and W. Jaeger saw in it a deliberate borrowing and development of the vision of the call of the Boeotian shepherd Hesiod (*Theogon.* 22ff.), in which the muses revealed the truth to him.[652] In both instances one is reminded of certain Old Testament analogies: in Parmenides of II Kings 2.11 and in Hesiod of Amos 7.15, from about the same period: the latter are 'the two earliest visions which are narrated by the persons who received them'.[653]

Later descriptions no longer have this complete form, but prove to be widespread didactic literature:

Thus Heraclides Ponticus (390–310 BC), a pupil of Plato, combines the themes of a vision, an epiphany of the gods, a descent as a journey to heaven and the revelation of transcendent wisdom in his portrayal of the alleged experiences of Empedotimus. At a lonely spot, Pluto and Persephone appear to him at noon in a garland of light, he is taken up and shown the 'heavenly' Hades on the Milky Way and the three different doors for the dead (see p. 198 above), which divide up into three star-patterns, one leading to the gods in the 'ether' and another presumably to Tartarus. In another work of the author the wonder man Abaris, who comes from the mythical Hyperboreans in the North, asks Pythagoras about his journey to Hades. There were a whole series of such wonder-workers in ancient Greece, whose soul left their body after appropriate preparations; they prophesied the future, healed the sick and turned away disaster, and their experiences were elaborated in romantic fashion by later writers. The effect of these phantasmagoria in the Hellenistic period was considerable. The vision of Empedotimus seems to have influenced Posidonius, Varro and the *Somnium Scipionis*; Clement of Alexandria lists him alongside Zoroaster and Socrates in a catalogue of 'seers'.[654]

When such 'transcendent wisdom' did not come from Greece itself but from barbarian 'philosophers' or from the East, it seemed to be particularly effective:

Thus in the pseudo-Platonic *Axiochus* (first century BC?), the Persian magician Gobryes reports that his description of the astral kingdom of the dead comes from iron tablets – a favourite theme of revelation, see pp. 242f. below – which were brought by the Hyperboreans to Delos in earliest times.[655] This 'revelation literature', which emerged with a serious claim, was mocked by the Palestinian Menippus of Gadara (after 300 BC, see above, pp. 83f.), who among other things wrote a journey to Hades and a journey to heaven, 'testaments' and letters of the gods.[656] Perhaps it was he who, in his *Nekyia* – as it is described later by Lucian in his *Nekyomanteia*, which is dependent on Menippus (ch. 6, ed. A. M. Harmon, LCL 4, 82ff.) – had the door to the underworld opened to him in Babylon by the 'Magi', the pupils and followers of Zoroaster.

Alongside the magicians of Persia, the Egyptian priests were also regarded as dispensers of secret divine wisdom. It was, of course, most effective if one combined Iranian and Egyptian wisdom:

> In the *Physica* of Ps. Democritus (according to Festugière from the first century AD), Democritus travels to Egypt to learn magic and alchemy from the Persian magician Ostanes there. After the latter's untimely death he conjures up his former teacher in order to learn the hiding place of his secret books.[657] According to the introduction to the Pseudo-Clementines, Clement reports how, driven by the question what happens to the soul after death, he goes to Egypt to learn there by means of one of the 'hierophants and prophets', 'whether the soul is immortal'.[658] A Jewish counterpart to this is the conjuring up of the dead by Mambres according to the fragment of the *Paenitentia Ianne et Mambre*.[659]

A threefold intellectual tendency can be seen against the background of these examples from Hellenistic time which have been briefly sketched out:

1. A widespread trend towards the irrational and the mysterious, which could only be discovered by means of supernatural 'revelations'.

2. The attempt in this way to discover the basic questions of human existence, the destiny of the soul after death and the '*sympatheia*' of the individual with the cosmos and its resulting fate.

3. A growing interest in the mysterious, age-old wisdom of barbarian peoples, especially in the East. The '*wise men of the East*', including the Indian Brahmans, the Persian 'Magi', the Babylonian 'Chaldeans' and the Egyptian priests were regarded as special kinds of philosophers and bearers of higher knowledge, from whom answers were sought to questions of life which remained inaccessible to rational thought.[660] This spiritual change, which becomes visible about the beginning of the second century BC and reaches its climax in the second and third centuries AD, inevitably strengthened the self awareness of the spiritual élite of the subject oriental peoples. Their older, religiously shaped 'wisdom' seemed at last to be superior to the rational, logical and systematic thought of their Greek masters. Whether and how far they had been influenced by these very masters was not a question that people asked. Thus Jewish apocalyptic, too, *stands in a wider cultural context as a counter-movement to 'Greek alienation'*, and as such was itself a fruit of the Hellenistic period.

This defensive attitude against Greek language and culture can be seen, for example, in a Hermetic text in which Asclepius appears to king Ammon:[661]

He forbade any translation of the wisdom communicated to him, 'so that these mysteries would not reach the Greeks and the arrogant, impotent and elaborate talk of the Greeks would not destroy the honourable, terse and powerful expression of the words. For the Greeks have . . . empty concepts, with which they can indeed make effective arguments, but in reality the philosophy of the Greeks is just the sound of words (λόγων ψόφος). Of course we do not use (mere) words, but sounds full of efficacy (φωναῖς μεσταῖς τῶν ἔργων).'

Presumably the prohibition against translation is not the decisive element here; indeed in the end value is attached to the fact that the 'Greeks' took over this wisdom.

In the aretalogy of Imuthes Asclepius, therefore, the god could use the punishment of illnesses and epiphanies to convince the lazy translator who feared the superhuman difficulties of a translation that like a prophet (προφητεύων 1.169) he was completing the translation into Greek by virtue of divine inspiration (πληρωθεὶς τῆς σῆς θε[ι]ότητος, 1.164): 'Every Greek tongue will tell your story, and every Greek will honour Imuthes, son of Ptah', ll.198ff.[662]

The decisive thing is rather the absolute superiority of these revelations of the Egyptian god over Greek language, Greek philosophy and Greek religion. In similar fashion the Rabbis on the one hand condemned the translation of the Torah from Hebrew – the language of creation and of the angels – into Greek and Aramaic and then went on to further it. Typical here is the *'bat qōl'* in the translation of the prophets by Jonathan b. Uzziel (Theodotion ?): 'Who is it who has betrayed my secrets to men ?', and the answer, that it was done to God's glory.[663]

The reasons for this *fundamental superiority of the 'prophets of the East'*[664] and their inspired wisdom were given by Festugière with reference to the detailed report of the Egyptian priest and Stoic Chaeremon (first century AD) about the holy life of the prophets and leading priests in the temples of Egypt.[665] He points out that what is said there also applies, with a few changes, to the Jewish Essenes and Therapeutae, the Persian 'Magi' or the Indian Brahmans. Separated from the unclean world, they lead a life of complete self-control in freely chosen asceticism with sparse and ritually pure food, completely devoted to prayer and the praise of God, the observation of heaven, philosophy and the study of holy writings:

For this constant converse with divine knowledge and inspiration (θείᾳ γνώσει καὶ ἐπινοίᾳ) drives away all avarice, damps down the passions and directs life towards wisdom.[666]

The pious ideal of the Hasidim, like the author of the book of Daniel, will not have been too far removed from this attitude. E. Fascher, who describes the 'prophets' of the late Egyptian period as 'scribes, wise men and magicians with a prophetic bent', therefore pointed out the affinity of this 'pseudo-prophecy' to late apocalyptic.[667] One receives the impression that in the

Hellenistic period the forms of religious experience and thought were assimilating to each other over and beyond religious and national limitations. Here 'the prophets of the east' did not remain completely restricted to Egypt. Iranian evidence also indicates similar forms of revelation:

> The oracles of Hystaspes, which have already been mentioned, were presumably composed by a Hellenistic adherent of Iranian religion in the east of the Roman empire between about 100 BC and AD 100. They claim to be a dream of Hystaspes, king of the Medes, i.e. probably the friend and patron of Zarathustra. The dream is interpreted by a boy with prophetic gifts and preserved for posterity (*sub interpretatione vaticinantis pueri ad memoriam posteris tradidit*) – presumably the young Zarathustra himself. It contains references to the appearance of a redeemer figure, the decline of Rome, the annihilation of the godless through Jupiter and the burning of the world. The parallels to Daniel are manifest.[668]

The *astrological* literature also exercised great influence; it made a decisive contribution to the world picture and the religion of educated citizens in late antiquity. First mention should be given here to the fundamental work of Nechepso-Petosiris, which was composed at about the time of Daniel or a little later, and began with a *journey* of the king *to heaven*:

> He noted how the kings and rulers of the early period 'left the earthly behind them to pass through the heaven (οὐρανοβατεῖν) and to take up converse with the immortal souls and divine holy thoughts'. Among other things he describes how, presumably after intensive prayer in the night, he was raised up into the air. A heavenly voice rang out (ἐξήχησεν οὐρανοῦ βοή) and finally a gigantic black figure appeared to him, concealed in a cloak.[669] His conversation partner Petosiris is characterized by Proclus as a trustworthy man who, like Enoch, 'conversed with the manifold classes of gods and angels'. In a letter to the king he admonishes him: 'But on the ground of your wisdom inspired by the divine spirit (⟨διὰ⟩ θεοπνεύστου σου προνοίας) concern yourself over what I have written.'[670] The right interpretation of texts of this kind presupposes the possession of the divine spirit in astrology also.

Here there are quite *similar 'forms of revelation'* to those in apocalyptic. Thus the whole Hermetic astrological literature, the earliest parts of which, according to Festugière, go back to the end of the third or the beginning of the second century BC,[671] claim to be the revelation of the Egyptian God Hermes Thoth. Erastosthenes (275–194 BC) already reported an extensive journey of Hermes through heaven, in which he combined a modern scientific description of heaven and earth with the old Greek star sagas.[672] The astronomer Manilius (about the end of the first century BC) praises him as the author of all holy wisdom: *Tu princeps auctorque sacri, Cyllenie* (= *Mercurius-Hermes*) *tanti.* Even if the poet himself does not understand the divine mysteries, he must describe them at the command of God. Only God himself, though, can give the interpretation.[673] There is an imitation of the entry vision of Nechepso in the later tractate Poimandres of the Corpus Hermeticum (second to third century AD), though it is much more detailed.[674] The heavenly voice (βοή) in Nechepso and CH 1, 4 recalls the *bat qōl* of the Rabbinic tradition.[675] A further detailed journey to heaven which leads through the various heavens up to the opened gates of heaven – also a frequent apocalyptic theme –,[676] behind which the world of the gods opens up and in which finally Helios himself appears and communicates the desired revelation, is contained in the great Parisian magical papyrus. Even the Isis initiation of Apuleius (*Met.* 11, 23, 8) is connected with a journey of the initiate to Hades and to heaven.[677]

A *comparison between Hermes Thoth* in the *Kore Kosmu* and *Enoch* is astonishing. Hermes Thoth, who received the συμπάθεια τοῖς οὐρανοῦ μυστηρίοις from the gods, wrote down all he learned. Part he taught to his son Tat, so that the latter would pass it on to his descendants Asclepius and Hephaestus, and another part he concealed (see pp. 242ff. below). When he had completed his work he ascended to heaven (ἀνέβαινεν εἰς ἄστρα, CH 23,5, cf. 7) and there worked as 'scribe' (ὑπομνηματόγραφος) of the gods (CH 23, 44). The parallels to the Enoch tradition are obvious. Thus it is understandable that Enoch and Hermes Thoth were confused in the early Middle Ages.[678] The transmission of the revealed wisdom from father to son (see above, p. 304), which is so typical of Enoch and the whole 'testament literature', appears here as a constitutive element.[679] With the unique significance of the Egyptian god as *the* 'wise man of primal times', it is understandable why Artapanus identified him with Moses (see above, p. 91, n. II, 262). The Egyptian priests called Moses 'Hermes' διὰ τὴν τῶν ἱερῶν γραμμάτων ἑρμηνείαν.[680]

The problem of the *supplementary interpretation* by a decipherment of a writing regarded as inspired, and the corresponding preparation for it, appears in the letter of the doctor Thessalus to the emperor Claudius. Here one can see an analogy to Dan. 9.2, 24ff.:

According to this, Thessalus discovered in Alexandria an astrological, iatromantic writing of king Nechepso about healing plants and stones under the influence of the Zodiac, but met only with failure in its practical application. So the writing itself seemed to him to be the 'empty vapour of royal folly'. In complete despair and ill will, 'I raised my hands to heaven unceasingly and prayed to the gods to give me the possibility of justifying myself by vision or divine inspiration' (δι' ὄνειρον φαντασίας ἢ διὰ πνεύματος θείου). He came to Thebes, where after three days of fasting an Egyptian priest arranged the epiphany of Asclepius to him. The latter explained to him the incompleteness of Nechepso's information: in addition to noting the time and place for gathering plants it is also necessary to note the changing astral constellations. Thessalus immediately writes down these additional 'revelations' in a new tractate, which he puts in his letter to the emperor.[681]

Finally, mention should also be made of verbal revelation through *'inspired ecstasy'*. We meet it, for example, in the Potter's Oracle, where the prophetic potter falls into ecstasy (ἐξεστ[ηκότως] . . . τῶν φρενῶν fr. 1, 1, 14–15) and, filled with the divine spirit, presents his prophecy to the king (θεοφόρου 1, 15; ἐκ [τοῦ] οὐρα[νοῦ] γνούς 1,16). The description of the prophecies of the consul Publius by Antisthenes is similar: ἐμμανὴς γενόμενος καὶ παράφρων ἀποφθέγγεται πολλά τινα ἐνθουσιωδῶς.[682] Both the Potter and Publius find death in their divine inspiration. Such prophecies *in statu moriendi* recall the Jewish Testament literature.[683] An analogy would be the – historical – fate of the ecstatic prophet of disaster, Jesus son of Ananus, in AD 70 (*Bell*. 6, 300–9). Even the Jewish Sibyl refers to her ecstatic inspiration (3, 810: οἰστρομανής, cf. 816, 818: μαινομένην). Driven by divine necessity (ἀνάγκῃ 3, 296, cf. I Cor. 9.16), she proclaims her prophecy:

> And again the great word of divine revelation (φάτις) entered my breast and bore me up to prophesy the future against that land and the kings (3, 296ff., cf. 490f., 162f.)

Nor is this form of revelation alien to the Enoch tradition, when Enoch as a 'prophet' summons his relatives at the beginning of the admonitions in 91.1:

> for the word calls me, and the spirit is poured out on me to show you everything that will happen to you to eternity.

Finally, Jewish apocalyptic shares with the 'revelation literature' of the Hellenistic world the characteristic of *pseudepigraphy*. This is true of all the Sibylline literature, the Hermetic and Orphic literature, the oracle of Hystaspes, the pseudo-Platonic Axiochus and the writings of Nechepso-Petosiris. The prophetic poem of Lycophron, *Alexandra*, from the third century BC, was presented as a prophecy of Cassandra (see n. 522 above), and the writings of the *physiologos* and alchemist Bolus of Mendes (*c*. 200 BC) partially appeared as the works of Democritus; the *Oracula Chaldaica* in the second century AD appeared as revelations of Hecate. In Rome in 181 BC, books purporting to be by the fabulous second king of Rome, Numa Popilius, were found and immediately burnt by the city praetor, presumably because of their Pythagorean-apocryphal content.[684]

It makes little sense to pursue the details of individual elements – like the heavenly journey – in detail and, as W. Bousset attempted, to construct 'a self-contained oriental view of the heavenly journey of the soul'.[685] We must (see above, p. 205) reckon with the fact that such phenomena appear independently of each other at different places,[686] and they should therefore be interpreted more in terms of the phenomenology and psychology of religion. The examples and parallels mentioned do not on each occasion demonstrate a direct influence on early Jewish apocalyptic by its Hellenistic oriental environment – this is certainly present, but the investigation would have to go into much more detail to demonstrate it in particulars – but only show the relevant spiritual milieu which is typical of the Hellenistic period from the beginning of the second century BC onwards. The common basis is formed by the idea of '*higher wisdom by revelation*'. It characterizes the renewal of the religious feelings of the ancient world under the influence of oriental religions and the suppression of Greek rationalism and religious scepticism, although the new forms of piety – not least as a result of their encounter with the Greek spirit – had taken on a considerable measure of rationality. In the philosophical sphere this new tendency is clear from the end of the second century on in the Syrian Posidonius and in the overcoming of Scepticism within the Academy by his contemporary, the Palestinian Antiochus of Ashkelon (see above, pp. 86f.). Even philosophy now no longer seeks to gain its results 'by the means of academic investigation, but grounds them on positive authorities and higher revelations, and sees its certainty guaranteed only by these'.[687]

Within this total movement, Jewish apocalyptic emerged – alongside astrology – as the *earliest clearly delineated spiritual force*. Its historical effects cannot be ignored, because Christianity too must be included in this context, where according to E. Käsemann 'apocalyptic formed the real beginning of primitive Christian theology'.[688] It could become fruitful in this way because although it had several features in common with the newly emerging Hellenistic-oriental religious development, it in no way surrendered the element of the personal revelation of God to Israel, but rather maintained it in a new universal form – in conformity to its time but at the same time also radical and opposed to Hellenistic cosmopolitanism and cultural optimism. For it, God remains the sovereign Lord of the cosmos and history, of the people Israel whom he has chosen, and of the individual. His judgment and the dawn of the time of salvation which he has promised from the very beginning have become imminent, and a last respite has been granted to the people in which they may prove themselves, together and as individuals. Human history from the creation of the world has been moving towards this climax. The whole cosmos, the nations of the world and the people of God face their last crisis; no one can relieve them of the decision; either men will hearken to the call to repentance issued by the Hasidic 'wise men' and put themselves under the commandment of God given in the Torah, or they will not share in the coming salvation or will forfeit their lives in the coming judgment.[689]

It is understandable that the movement of the Hasidim could not limit themselves to their message amidst the cosmological speculation and speculation about the 'philosophy of history', the struggle after visions by which to acquire divine knowledge; rather, the whole eschatological bent of this movement demanded the solution of a question which the late wisdom of Koheleth and Sirach had raised but could not answer, the question of the significance of a man's life in the face of the divine will, the question of man's salvation and the glory of God. An answer was attempted by the two Jewish groups which evolved from the Hasidim, the Essenes and the Pharisees.

7. Early Essenism[690]

a) The theology of early Essenism

Whereas the early Hasidic apocalypses were addressed to a wider circle of readers and accordingly contained an attractive multiplicity of mythical and legendary elements, the central Essene writings, like the Community Rule, the Hodayot, etc.,[691] are directed towards the smaller circle of the elect members of the Essene community itself and express in part systematic theological statements in extremely concentrated form. They represent a further development of apocalyptic historical thinking, with a tendency on the one hand in the direction of a theodicy – the explanation of the origin and power of evil in the world – and on the other of a soteriologically determined anthropology. In what follows it is impossible to discuss the whole Essene 'theology' *in extenso*, so we shall limit ourselves to a survey, beginning from two well-known central theological texts. The first appears in the Community Rule 1 QS 3.15–4.26; we quote here the first half, down to 4.1:

15 From the God of Knowledge (מאל הדעות) comes all that is and all that
    happens (כול הווה ונהייה). Before ever they existed he established their
16 whole design (לפני היותם הכין כול מחשבתם),/and when, as ordained
    for them, they come into being, it is in accord with his glorious design
    (כמחשבת כבודו) that they accomplish their task, and there is no
17 changing (ואין להשנות). In his hand/are the laws of all things (משפטי
    כול), and he provides them with all their needs. He has created
18 man to govern/the earth and has appointed for him two spirits in
19 which to walk until the time of his visitation: the spirits/of truth and
    falsehood. Those born of truth spring from a fountain of light, but
20 those born of falsehood spring from a source of darkness./All the
    children of righteousness are ruled by the Prince of Light and walk in
21 the ways of light, but all the children of falsehood/are ruled by the
    Angel of Darkness and walk in the ways of darkness. The Angel of
22 Darkness leads all the children of righteousness astray,/ and all their
23 sins . . . are caused by his dominion/in accordance with the mysteries
    of God, until his time. Every one of their chastisements, and every one
    of the seasons of their distress, lies under the rule of his persecution
24 (משטמתו see Jub.)./And all his allotted spirits seek the overthrow of
    the sons of light; but the God of Israel and his Angel of Truth will
25 succour all/the sons of light. And he created the spirits of light and
    darkness and founded every action upon them/(and upon) their (ways)
26 (read ועל דרכיהן) he established every deed (   ). God loves the one
4.1 for all/time and delights in its works for ever. But the counsel of the
    other he loathes, and for ever hates its ways.[692]

This text resembles a catechism and, as J. Becker rightly observes, 'develops an overall theological view in didactic form which outlines with pregnant content and consistent argument a self-contained theological conception which is without parallel in Judaism'.[693] A striking feature is the accumulation of abstract terms which is already prefigured in the late 'wisdom' of Koheleth and Ben Sira, just as Essenism in general is influenced from this direction in its anthropological terminology.[694] We may see here the concern for a systematic, indeed almost 'philosophical' conceptuality which had not appeared earlier in Hebrew thought. This applies, for example, to the pair of concepts 'being and happening' (הוה ונחי(י)ה),[695] which is used elsewhere on a number of occasions in Essene writings. E. Kamlah is probably right when he observes that here 'the Jewish belief in creation' is, among other things, wrestling with an 'understanding of the world which has developed the abstract terms of being and becoming, in other words, Greek. One might translate the . . . sentence by πάντα τὰ ὄντα καὶ τὰ γινόμενα'.[696]

This text forms the didactic heart of the Rule and, as the earliest examples of it are to be found in manuscripts of about 140–120 BC, will have been composed in its original form in about 150–130 BC.[697] It is really an attempt to interpret 'being' and 'happening', i.e. creation and history, in systematic form on a theological basis. The starting point is a terse and precise account of creation. There is no notion of a hypostatized *ḥokmā* as mediator at creation here – nor anywhere else in the Essene writings;[698] its place is taken by the sovereign, perfect knowledge possessed by God himself. The term אל הדעות which appears here is also used elsewhere, always in connection with the idea of predestination.[699] Before the world came into being, God established the whole order of creation and history in an unalterable way through the plans of his thought (מחשבת/ה).[700] Everything is predestined from the very beginning, including the individual human life with its thoughts and actions:

'Before thou didst create them, thou didst know (all) their works for all times. (For without thee) is (nothing) done, and nothing is known without thy will.'[701] God has foreordained the 'lot' of man (גורל), i.e. the realm to which he belongs in relation to the two spirits, from the very beginning of the world, whether for salvation or for damnation. He has 'created the righteous and the godless' (1 QH 4.38).[702]

This conception of the *predestination of the course of history and the fate of the individual* is new in its pregnant form, although it was prepared for both in the apocalyptic picture of history and in Koheleth and, in a weakened form, by Ben Sira. However, the latter, like the Pharisaic movement at a later time, left the postulate of the freedom of the human will and a demonstrable doctrine of retribution juxtaposed and unrelated to the conception of predestination.[703] Josephus is fundamentally right in his report of the difference between Essenes and Pharisees so far as their divergent views of the working of divine *heimarmenē* is concerned – that is, leaving the Stoic terminology aside.[704]

The *two spirits* appear as mediators between God and man, though they are only executive powers of the divine plan. They determine the historical 'sphere of rule' (ממשלה),[705] in which man's ethical and religious existence is to be found, though their spheres partly overlap; thus all the temptations and sins of the 'sons of light' and the tribulations and judgments in history can be regarded as the work of the Angel of Darkness and his spirits.[706] The battle of the two spirits extends to the heart of men, so that man appears as a being divided into parts of light and darkness.[707] God, who, according to the 'mystery' of his prior determination,[708] which even embraces evil, has established this constant struggle for the duration of world history, appoints an end for it at the time he determines, which is imminent. To the spirit of truth, who according to the War Scroll is identified with Michael, the chief angel, he gives final victory over the spirit of evil, or Belial, in an eschatological struggle which embraces the whole cosmos.[709] Thus an exclusively psycho-logical and anthropological interpretation of the two spirits is unjustified,[710] though it is unmistakable that the struggle of the two 'powers' finds its climax and its decision over and in man: the apocalyptic drama concentrates on anthropology, without the cosmic aspect being lost.

The picture of history in 1 QS 3.15ff. is enlarged by a related text:[711]

4 '. . . And they do not know the future mystery (רז נהיה, see 1 QS 11.3f.) and they do not understand past things, nor do they know what will befall them, how their soul (could) be saved in the face of the
5 future mystery./And this shall be a sign for you that these things will come to pass: when the descendants (or ways of birth?) of evil are shut up,[712] wickedness shall vanish in the face of righteousness as
6 darkness vanishes/before the light and vanishes like smoke and is no more. So shall wickedness vanish for ever. But righteousness will be
7 made manifest like the sun as the norm/of the world (תכון תבל), and all those who hold up the marvellous mysteries will be no more. And knowledge shall fill the earth, but folly shall no (longer) be there . . .'

The sign that this prophecy will certainly be fulfilled consists in the contradiction which still dominates all history in the present:

8/9 'Do not all nations/hate wickedness? Yet it is spread abroad by every hand. Does not the knowledge of the truth (שמע אמת?) emerge from the
10 mouth of all nations,/but is there a lip or a tongue which observes it? Which nation loves to be oppressed by a stronger? Who/likes his
11 property to be plundered by wickedness? (But) which nation does not oppress his neighbour? Where is a nation that does not plunder the
12 property (of others)?'

In the fragments of the next column one can detect the hint that in the continuation the old problem of theodicy, the unequal lot of the righteous and the godless, and probably also the unequal distribution of property in this world, will be discussed.

From this we see that behind these apocalyptic outlines there stands a question which occupied post-exilic wisdom after Job, which Sirach sought to solve directly by stress on the doctrine of retribution, but which broke out in a new and elemental way in the terrors of the time of persecution after 167 BC and in the decades-long sufferings of war that followed: this was *the question of the origin, the meaning and the overcoming of evil in history*. As the outline of history in Daniel shows, the answer given to it in apocalyptic Hasidic circles during the climax of the crisis in 164 BC was that with the desecration of the temple and the persecution of those faithful to the Torah, the last time of purification had reached its climax and that the dawn of the time of salvation was imminent (see above, pp. 179f.). This beginning was deepened in Essene circles and an outline of history was developed which bore systematic traits expressing a *'philosophy of history'*: God's plan for the world and for history in which even the spirit of evil is only allotted a limited span of time according to his sovereign will remains an impenetrable 'mystery' for autonomous human reason. God is the sovereign lord over the fate of individual men, over the realm of the two 'spirits', the plan of the times and intervals in history.[713] Man cannot haggle over his fate with God, he must simply accept that he is a blinded sinner in his creaturely weakness and frailty, who has deserved all the trials and torments which he encounters in his historical existence.[714] Here the Essene picture of history and man penetrates deeper than the optimistic and over-simple attitude of Ben Sira and later Pharisaism, who maintain that the pattern of retribution still makes sense (see above pp. 142ff.); however, it does not fall into the impasse of the fatalism of Koheleth (in this connection, it is interesting that the works of both Ben Sira and Koheleth were found in the library of Qumran, see n. II, 60 and n. III, 694). On the contrary, God's righteousness and saving will are demonstrated in the fact that he is preparing an end for the spirit of evil precisely at the point when it has reached its climax, and so 'righteousness' becomes the 'basic order of the world'. The divorce between the will and the action of the peoples is an indication of this aim. Thus the old and ever new question of the origin of evil changes into the question of the saving meaning of history – hidden from sinful man – and at the same time his eschatological liberation from the realm of the spirit of darkness. This Essene picture of history, which has more strongly dualistic features than the earlier Hasidic conceptions, but in the end again overcomes dualism, appears equally in the Community Rule, a large number of hymns, the biblical interpretation and the various 'apocalyptic pictures of history', preserved in fragments and directed towards both past and future. Even the Damascus Document, probably intended for a wider circle of the community, and the book of Jublilees are stamped by it.[715]

This explains the central significance of that group of concepts which probably possessed the greatest importance for Essene theology and the later religious development, and which embraced the concepts of *knowledge, insight and wisdom* (דעת, דעה, שכל, בינה, חכמה, ערמה, etc.) including the related verbs (ידע, שכל, בין). Earlier wisdom traditions may have been influential here, though the terms חכמה and חכם fade well into the background in favour of דעת and שכל.[716] In so far as it corresponds to the 'truth' (אמת),[717] all human knowledge is grounded in the knowledge of God as מקור דעת.[718] Knowledge about the deeper connections in creation and history, about the greatness and the misery of man, come from him alone, and the only wise man is the one to whom God has revealed the mysteries of his knowledge through his spirit.

> For he has displayed his light from the source of his knowledge, so that my eyes have looked on his wonders . . . and the light of my heart on the mystery of future history and eternal being (בר[ז] נהיה והווא עולם) . . . My eyes have looked on the eternal being (בהווא עולם), deep insight which is concealed from men, knowledge and wise thoughts (hidden) from the children of men.[719]

A typical example, the blessing for novices entering the community, shows the meaning of the 'knowledge of being', fundamentally understood in a soteriological way, for the members of the community (1 QS 2.2f.):

> May he bless you with all good things and preserve you from all evil. May he lighten your heart with the insight of life and endow you with eternal knowledge (בדעת עולים).

Year by year the members of the group are classed 'according to the degree of their knowledge and the perfection of their way of life'.[720] Conversely, evil and godlessness always appear also as an expression of misunderstanding and folly.[721] Finally, terms like 'eternal being' and 'eternal knowledge' suggest an assimilation of Essene theological conceptuality to Greek models.

The way to saving knowledge which puts the individual in the realm of the spirit of truth is only open in the community, where in charismatic fashion the Torah and the prophets are interpreted in respect of the divine mysteries of history and a perfect fulfilment of the divine commandments, and are thus disclosed in their deeper meaning.[722] In respect of the apparently 'perfectionist' aspect of the complete fulfilment of the Torah, one might speak of an 'eschatologically radicalized . . . movement of sanctification'.[723] But this is only one side of the community. Whereas in the legal texts 'revelation' is more strongly attached to the interpretation of the Torah and the prophets, in the hymns it appears more in the form of direct inspiration. Of course, there is no unconditional opposition; the chief reason for the difference is the divergent literary form of the statement. Divine revelation is needed, even if one is to be able to know the mysteries of the divine revelation in scripture.[724] Thus alongside the concepts of 'knowledge' and 'understanding' we have such necessary expressions as *'reveal'*, *'enlighten'*, *'appear'* and even *'conceal'* – and above all *'mystery'* (רז) and secret *counsel* (סוד).[725] The hymns in particular portray in ever new variations the incomprehensible miracle of the divine revelation of salvation. It gives man knowledge of his absolute nothingness and complete sinfulness (see above, n.714), leads him to repentance and thus makes him willing to separate himself now, at the end of time, from the *massa perditionis* of apostate Israel and the nations of the world, and enter the holy remnant of the community of the 'children of light' which incorporates the people of God.[726] There his sin is blotted out,[727] his 'knowledge is purified by the truth of the commandments of God',[728] and his way of life is made perfect by the constant practice of obedience. For only in the community is the Torah of God truly expounded and are its demands really fulfilled.[729] Thus man is transposed to the sphere of the spirit of truth, even if there he is still assailed by the 'parts of darkness in him': 'the God of Israel and the angel of his truth help all the sons of light'.[730] In this way the community becomes the *'eschatological community of salvation'*, which has only an external, loose connection with the national association of the people; in other words, it becomes a 'church'. However, the complete 'purification' of man by the spirit of God happens only in the eschaton after the annihilation of the sphere of evil.[731] Rigorous obedience to the law finds its climax in the daily praise of the 'sons of light'. In it is disclosed the perfect harmony of the whole of creation, as it is expressed above all in the ordering of the seasons and the movements of the stars.[732] Moreover they enter into community with the angels of God;[733] for in the *doxology* the world and history reach their goal: the glorification of the divine *kābōd*. In the last resort, creation and the revelation of salvation took place only to the glory of God.[734] The heavenly liturgies or the descriptions of the heavenly Jerusalem are the expression of a contemporizing, proleptic epiphany of eschatological salvation. For the members of the community of salvation, heaven was opened in the praise of God.[735] This did not exclude a future expectation: it was hoped that soon evil would be finally annihilated, that the priestly and the Davidic Messiah would come and that there would be eternal life (see pp. 198f. above). However, the eschatological gifts of salvation were already in the community, if only incompletely.[736] A significant feature here is the restraint in the elaboration of scenes of future judgment and salvation. Here abbreviated themes like 'eternal joy' . . . (I QH 18.15), 'eternal peace' (I QS 2.4) . . . 'eternal light' (I QS 4.8; M.17.6; H.12.15?) or 'light of life' (. . . I QS 3.7) predominate.[737] The pious will share in 'the whole glory of Adam' (I QS 4.23; I QH 17.15; CD 3.20).

Thus on the whole the foundations of an individual *soteriology* and *ecclesiology* are to be seen against the background of a dualism of salvation history and anthropology. However, what happens in and through man for his salvation is not grounded in his own contribution. As he is determined from the beginning either for righteousness or for judgment, 'redemption' by acceptance into the community is grounded exclusively in God's free election.[738]

The early Essene 'theology' which we find in the Rule, the hymns, certain apocalyptic fragments and in parts of the War Scroll,[739] can therefore be regarded as the most impressive theological contribution produced by Judaism in the time 'between the Testaments'.[740] In contrast to the 'creation onto-logy' of Aristobulus and the later 'Torah ontology' of the Rabbis, Essene teaching was concentrated on two apparently divergent focal points, which are, however, in reality closely associated and indeed condition each other: 1. an apocalyptic dualistic interpretation of history which has now – immediately before the end – entered upon its decisive crisis, and 2. an anthropology and ecclesiology directed at the redemption of the individual, according to which God gives man knowledge of his true situation and introduces him into the *vita communis* of the Essene 'community', where alone the Torah is fulfilled: *extra ecclesiam nulla salus.*

b) The Teacher of Righteousness and the crisis caused by the Hellenistic reform

If we pursue our enquiry into the historical causes of the origin of the Essene movement, we come up against the towering figure of its founder, the *Teacher of Righteousness*, who, as has now probably been made sufficiently clear, brought about the final break of the community with the temple in Jerusalem at the time of the Maccabean high priest Jonathan, i.e. between autumn 152 BC and 143 BC – presumably not too long after the appointment of Jonathan as high priest. The secession needed a certain time of preparation, so that the begin-nings of his activity reach back into the decade between 160 and 150;[741] presumably by his prophetic charisma and the compelling authority of his personality[742] he became the leader of a group of Hasidim who were particularly faithful to the law and oriented on the priestly ideal. The strong stress which appears a number of times on the 'sons of Zadok' as the leading group of the Essene movement with its strictly arranged hierarchy also suggests that the leader himself belonged to the Zadokite priestly nobility.[743] As in addition he is hardly likely to have been a young man at the time of the Essene schism – about 150 BC – we are probably best advised to put the year of his birth before rather than after 180 BC; that means that in his youth he will have known of the Hellenistic reform attempt by the Zadokite Jason. We may also assume that as a young member of the priestly nobility he had some degree of Greek education. The son of the last regular high priest, Onias IV, who towards 160 BC founded the Jewish military colony with a temple in Leontopolis in Egypt, is a typical example of the high degree of Hellenization undergone by the Zadokite leaders of the people (see above, pp. 73f. and below, p. 277). Various indications in the hymn 1 QH 5.5–19, which presum-ably comes from the Teacher himself, indicate that for some time he lived abroad among non-Jews and there was in danger of his life. Perhaps he was for a time in Seleucid hands as a prisoner or a hostage. That time also seems to have given him the insights which were fundamental to his later activity.[744] Another personal confession perhaps has a reference to the events during the Hellenistic reform in Jerusalem:

> For I remember my sins
> and the unfaithfulness of my fathers.
> When the wicked rose against thy Covenant
> and the damned against thy word.
>
> (בקום רשעים על בריתך וחלכאים על דברכה)
>
> I said in my sinfulness,
> 'I am cast out of thy Covenant.'
> But calling to mind the might of thy hand
> and the greatness of thy compassion,
> I rose and stood
> and my spirit was established in face of the scourge.[745]

We might ask whether the godless here are not the reform party friendly to the Greeks, and the fathers the Zadokite priestly nobility which – like the majority of the Jewish aristocracy – at first made common cause with the friends of Greece (see below, p.277ff.). In any case, one may assume that the Teacher had come to know Hellenistic civilization and its dangers to the continuance of the Jewish community of religion from his own experience and that the origin of his rigorous doctrine – a radical break with those who required this godless way of life – and the foundation of his self-contained, monastic community with its military discipline are to be understood against the background of that serious inner crisis which had become evident among the Jewish people in the years after 175 BC and which determined their way for the next decades. The beginning of the Damascus Document also connects the appearance of the Teacher directly with the Hasidic movement of repentance which was formed 'in the time of wrath' under Antiochus IV, and other Essene writings, like the later Nahum commentary, the book of Jubilees and the Testament of Levi, mention the king or the events of that time of distress.[746] According to the Habakkuk commentary the new high priest Jonathan confiscated the means 'of the men of violence who rebelled against God', which probably means those Jews of the reform party who sought refuge in the Acra as they had been unfaithful to the faith of the fathers (see p.290 below). Significantly, immediately afterwards the godless (high) priest is himself branded a 'rebel'; i.e., in the eyes of the community his sins were hardly smaller than those of the apostates.[747] Jonathan was not a Zadokite and had illegally obtained the high priesthood from the pagan ruler Alexander Balas, accepting further offices and honours from him. 'There was no better legal basis to his priesthood than to that of Jason or Menelaus.'[748] Political and military success were more important to this man of action than rigorous obedience to the law, and in the prophetic revelations and demands of the

Teacher he could see only a threat to his hard-won power. After the years of deprivation in the guerrilla war and Seleucid oppression, he and his officers probably struggled no less ambitiously for riches and power than the Tobiads and their supporters, who were now driven out and dispossessed.[749] On the other side, in the eyes of the Teacher, the people who were now rejoicing over the Maccabees as liberators had not drawn the one correct consequence from the fearful judgment of God, the abomination of desolation in the temple, the time of persecution and the following tribulations of war, namely serious repentance. Thus they had failed to recognize the threatening signs of the time and had perhaps even delayed the bringing in of the time of salvation. The book of Daniel, the vision of the symbolic beasts and the Ten Weeks' Apocalypse show that the Hasidim had expected the imminent dawn of the time of salvation. Its failure to come, the endless prolongation of the torments of war and the change in the Maccabees from being charismatic leaders of the people to being adaptable real politicians and violent *condottieri* must have been a great disappointment to them. The explanation was ready to hand: the people as a whole had not been worthy of the dawn of the time of salvation, and so it had to be purified by further judgments. Its place was therefore taken by the 'remnant', the Essene community of salvation.[750] Jubilees 23.21ff. stresses this false course of the people after a short description which probably refers to the successful Maccabean revolt:

> And those who have escaped shall not return from their wickedness to the way of righteousness, but they shall all exalt themselves to deceit and wealth, that they may each take all that is his neighbour's, and they shall name the great name (   ), but not in truth and righteousness, and they shall defile the holy of holies with their uncleanness . . . And He will wake up against them the sinners of the Gentiles, who have neither mercy nor compassion.[751]

The apostate Jews and the pagan garrison still occupied the Acra in Jerusalem and Beth Zur and formed a latent threat; only in 141 BC could Simon compel them to surrender – two years after the murder of Jonathan by the Seleucid commander Trypho (I Macc. 13.49–53). But even after that – as the successful siege of Jerusalem by Antiochus VII Sidetes in 135/134 BC shows – the Seleucid danger was by no means ended.[752] In essentials the Teacher had thus forecast the course of the Maccabean Hasmonean dynasty correctly. Its power politics removed it from rigorous obedience to the law and exposed it and the leading strata once again to the seductions of their Hellenistic environment.[753] Its apparently contradictory combination of conservative religious attitudes, political nationalism and a position open to Hellenistic cultural influences, became the basic stance of the *Sadducean nobility*, newly in process of formation, truly devoted to the Hasmoneans for the future, and rich as the result of plunder of war and confiscations.[754] The

Jewish priest and historian Eupolemus (see above, pp. 92ff.) might be cited as a typical representative of them; he was a contemporary of the Teacher of Righteousness. The secular tendency towards power politics strengthened towards the end of the second century BC under John Hyrcanus and his sons to such a degree that even the Hasidic wing, from which the Pharisees grew and which remained loyal to the Maccabees primarily for nationalistic reasons, sharply attacking the Teacher of Righteousness for his separatism, also broke with the Maccabean dynasty and became its most deadly opponent.[755] The complaints which the delegation of two hundred Pharisees brought in the spring of 63 BC to Pompey in Damascus in effect confirm the step which the Teacher of Righteousness had taken about ninety years earlier. They sound like the accusations of II Macc. against Jason and Menelaus: the Hasmonean leaders had 'done away with the ancestral laws' ($\kappa\alpha\tau\alpha\lambda\epsilon\lambda\nu\kappa\acute{o}\tau\alpha\varsigma$ $\tauο\grave{\upsilon}\varsigma$ $\pi\alpha\tau\rho\acute{\iota}ο\upsilon\varsigma$ $\nu\acute{o}\mu\ο\upsilon\varsigma$) and unjustly enslaved the citizens (Diod., 40 fr. 2; Reinach 76f.).

> Conversely, the Sadducean nobility, who, despite all their openness towards a freer life style in their 'official' theological views, remained completely conservative, charged the Essenes and Pharisees with 'alienation' through non-Jewish religious views. The picture of the fronts within Judaism under the aspect of 'Hellenistic influence' remained remarkably broken even after the Maccabean revolt.

The basic views of the early Essene community can hardly be separated from those of their spiritual leader, the Teacher of Righteousness. Their theology, determined by a developed conceptuality, their peculiar form of exegesis and their strict priestly-military organization as a monastic desert community probably all go back to him.[756] His teaching may also be regarded as a fruit of that profound crisis which shook the fabric of the Jewish people to the uttermost after the accession of Antiochus IV and was a consequence of the Hellenistic reform attempt and the secularization of the Maccabean leaders. What the Teacher and his followers felt to be a disastrous development among the Jewish people only left them the possibility of the segregation of a small minority, as the holy remnant and the true Israel.[757] This situation also explains the scrupulous adherence of the Teacher and the community to the *law*. Since the Hellenists in Jerusalem had robbed it of its force and the later Maccabees had refused it radical obedience, the new community had to uphold its demands all the more, interpreting them in a rigorous way. The experience of the overwhelming power of evil, going beyond all traditional forms, in the history of the individual and the people, which raged even in Israel and led the majority of the people astray, together with a deep-rooted prophetic experience of repentance and salvation,[758] gave the founder and his community the basis for their apocalyptic view of history (which has been sketched out above only in a very fragmentary fashion in the sense of a theological answer to the demands of their time).

c) New developments and alien influences in Essene teaching

Now it is strange that in Essene teaching we also find features which appear new in comparison with the Jewish tradition and the Old Testament. In accordance with their dualistic picture of history, the Teacher and his followers advocated an abrupt separation from all the 'sons of wickedness', and included in this not only all the opponents of the community among their own people, but still more all non-Jews. From this perspective they were certainly also the bitterest opponents of any Hellenistic influence. The beginnings of the Jewish reform movement in 175 BC were made under the slogan that separation from non-Jews had to be abandoned.[759] The high priest Jonathan attempted once again to establish closer connections with the godless Seleucids. In the face of these tendencies, the Essenes held the view that only rigorous separation from everything godless could meet the demands of the imminent time of salvation.[760] The desert ideal should probably also be understood in this sense.[761] Thus in Essenism to some extent – as had already happened with the Hasidim – a Jewish *'reform movement'* was opposed to the Hellenistic reform attempt. An indication of this is e.g. the avoidance of any Hellenistic building elements in the site of Ḥirbet Qumran,[762] and the emphatic cultivation of a biblical Hebrew that was as pure as possible, which the community attempted to keep as free as possible from all alien words and which they regarded as 'the language of creation' and of the angels.[763] The same is true of the great library in Qumran, which with the extant remains of over five hundred scrolls (and as 381 of them come from Cave 4, the original number may have been very much higher) formed a spiritual centre of Palestinian Judaism. As some of the scrolls go back to the end of the third century BC and the first half of the second century BC, the library was probably begun at a very early stage.[764] With a touch of exaggeration one could talk of a Jewish 'Atticism' and a Jewish 'Museum'.

All the more astonishing, therefore, are the new spiritual developments and the foreign influences, which we can only indicate by means of a summary:

1. In first place comes the *'intellectualization of piety'* effected by the towering significance of the group of concepts including knowledge, understanding, revelation and mystery.[765] The roots of this already lie in the Hasidic apocalyptic wisdom tradition, in which the 'wise' received insight into the secret plan of God for history and the fate of men after death. In Essenism, because of its anthropological and soteriological tendency, this Hasidic wisdom becomes *'saving knowledge'* to an even greater degree. This is the reason why the Essene texts could sometimes be called 'gnostic'.[766] Whether this was correct is a question of the definition of this term, which is often used loosely. If one begins with the definition of gnosticism which does most justice to its content, using later Christian gnosticism with its complete depreciation of creation and its myth of the ontic identity of the soul with the heavenly

redeemer, the designation is certainly inappropriate. We therefore do best to characterize Essene theology in the light of its historical setting and eschatological expectation as 'apocalyptic',[767] though this term has become wider than in the original context of Hasidic apocalyptic, since the 'apocalyptic' of an Essene character has received strong anthropological and soteriological components. Thus the Essene 'epistemological concepts' mean 'eschatological knowledge of salvation' for both the individual and the community. Here Essenism stands more in the religious stream of the Hellenistic world which was described above by the phrase 'wisdom through revelation'. God discloses the mysteries of his action and his will at the end of time only to those chosen by him in his community of salvation by the spirit.[768] In this sense one can follow K. G. Kuhn in speaking of a 'preliminary form of gnostic thought, planted in the Jewish religion of the law and . . . apocalyptic . . . centuries before the gnostic texts'.[769] The apocalyptic-Essene conception of knowledge anticipates many essential features of that in gnosticism:

> While $\gamma\iota\nu\omega\sigma\kappa\epsilon\iota\nu$ is for the Greeks the cultivated methodical activity of the $\nu o\hat{\upsilon}_S$ or $\lambda\acute{o}\gamma o_S$, fulfilled in science and particularly philosophy, the $\gamma\nu\hat{\omega}\sigma\iota_S$ of the Gnostic, both as process and result, is a $\chi\acute{a}\rho\iota\sigma\mu a$ which is given by God to man. It is thus radically distinguished from rational thought; it is illumination. God is inaccessible to man as such. But he knows men, i.e. the pious, and reveals Himself to them.' Bultmann's definition of gnostic knowledge could, with the alteration of a few terms, be applied word for word to Essenism.[770]

While contacts with ideas and concepts of popular philosophy are probable, as already with Ben Sira, chronology alone makes it impossible that the chief Essene writings have been influenced by any 'gnostic Hellenistic' sources. The origin of the Essene community about 150 BC is too early for this, and in any case it is immediately connected with the Hasidim and early apocalyptic. Influence in the other direction is much more likely, as when Palestinian apocalyptic traditions in the Diaspora met up with Platonic conceptions, e.g. in Wisdom in Alexandria in the first century BC and in Philo. We must therefore reckon with the possibility that Jewish apocalyptic, above all in its Essene form, influenced the development of later Jewish-Christian gnosticism.[771]

2. A further attitude, which goes beyond the framework of the Old Testament, is *dualism* and its limitation by double predestination. This dualism began by being cosmological, but later went on to be historical and anthropological. In principle, the Old Testament pattern of God's sovereign, unlimited omnipotence in nature and history was maintained.[772] However, because evil had been experienced in personal life and in the most recent history of the Jewish people as a concentrated power with apparently a deliberate plan, and there was at the same time a concern to liberate God from the chain of direct causality in the interests of a theodicy, the dualistic doctrine of the two spirits was adopted as a fundamental part of 'angelology'. God's righteousness and

saving will were expressed in the fact that God 'hates the ways of the evil spirit' and will give the final victory to the 'spirit of truth' in the near future.[773] The *Iranian derivation* of this conception has been demonstrated since the fundamental studies of K. G. Kuhn, but Kuhn has at the same time also stressed its Jewish peculiarity, its association with belief in the Creator and its anthropological slant.[774] However, the question of the communication of these Iranian influences remains open. H. Michaud and E. Kamlah have shown that similar dualistic and Iranian traditions also appear in the Hellenistic world, in Philo and Plutarch.[775] Here the latter seems to be going back to reliable sources of the early Hellenistic period, in the fourth century BC, like Theopompus and Eudemus of Rhodes. Because of the great interest which Iranian religion had aroused among the Greeks from the time of Herodotus and Plato, and in view of the considerable interval of time between the Essene community and the end of Persian rule, we might consider the possibility that an Alexandrian Jewish source was involved instead of the Babylonian intermediary which has yet to be demonstrated.[776] This is a real possibility, especially as Alexandrian Judaism apparently knew the Hellenized Zarathustra tradition.[777]

> According to the 'Peripatetic' Hermippus, about 200 BC, the library of Alexandria had at this time writings which were ascribed to Zarathustra, extending to about two million lines – on a conservative estimate eight hundred scrolls. Even if this information is exaggerated, it shows the interest in Iranian religion during the early Hellenistic period.[778]

3. To give clear expression to the omnipotence of God in the face of the tendency towards dualism, stress was laid in strict determinist fashion on the ordering of the world and events within it, even before creation, in '*the plans of God*'. K. Schubert conjectures that 'Platonic influence is unmistakable' here,[779] but one must be careful about these philosophical judgments. C. Schneider seems more correct in pointing to analogies between the creation hymns and the Zeus hymn of Cleanthes.[780] But even here we would be wrong in construing a relationship of dependence. Rather, in the statements about God as creator in the Essene hymns we find the tendency that was also present in Ben Sira and Aristobulus (see pp. 144ff. above). Establishing 'all being and happening' before time is meant to demonstrate the absolute transcendence and superiority of God, corresponding to the spiritual traits of the time, and at the same time to show his care. In striving for a more rational version of the event of creation, Essene theology – like late wisdom in Palestine and Alexandria generally – adopts notions which have contacts with the ideas of Greek philosophy. It is hard to decide here whether we really have 'Hellenistic influence' or whether it is not simply an analogous development. That God's plan relates more to the course of history than to the ordering of the world is not a Greek characteristic. This relationship of Essene theology to

history probably also prevented an identification of God's knowledge or 'plan for the world' with the Torah, in a way that would correspond more with Stoic thought. This, of course, happened with Ben Sira, and later determined Pharisaic and Rabbinic thought. The abrupt *determinism*, too, has some analogy – though one cannot talk in terms of dependence – to the notions of the Stoa where Chrysippus interpreted the Homeric saying Διὸς δ'ἐτελείετο βουλή with reference to the unalterable sway of '*heimarmenē*' or the divine '*pronoia*' which determines not only the external order of the world but also human action. Although man possesses freedom of choice, as a rational being, in the end every event is laid down by fate.[781] In Qumran, too, an appeal was made to the human will, but it was also said that every 'perfect way of life' was the free gift of God (1 QS 11.10f.; see above, n. 738). Finally, as in the Stoa, the Essenes accepted the command only to will what God had resolved for them, even if it led to sorrow and distress.[782] On the other hand, the fundamental difference should not be overlooked. Despite its pre-destinarian basis, what happened in the world did not rest on impersonal fate, which simply expresses strict causality within a world understood along monistic lines,[783] but on God's plan, as the free disposition of his personal transcendent power.

4. *Angelology*, too, serves fundamentally to rationalize the picture of God, although its form looks so mythological to us. It was developed in a system which involved a strict hierarchy. Its significance for Essene theology can be seen in the oath sworn by members of the community which is reported by Josephus, 'carefully to preserve the names of the angels'.[784] However, for the most part individual conceptions were taken over from the traditions of the Hasidim, as is shown by the appearance of individual angels like Gabriel and Michael (see above, pp.188f., 203) in Daniel, and the detailed doctrine about angels in the earliest part of I Enoch. The fact that the same names for angels and similar notions appear again in the Rabbinic tradition shows the common Hasidic root.[785] Thus the doctrine of the two spirits, with a more strongly anthropological bent, was expanded by the doctrine of the 'good and evil angels' taken over from the tradition, and the two were combined into a 'system'. The prince of light was probably identical with Michael, the first of all the angels, to whom Israel was entrusted and who had clearly soteriological traits. 'The angel of darkness' or the 'spirit of evil' represented simultaneously both the head of the fallen angels and all the evil powers.[786] The 'crisis in primeval history' through which the powers of evil became effective on earth was caused by the fall of the watchmen angels according to Gen. 6.1–4, already mentioned several times.[787] The host of 'good angels', on the other hand, was the heavenly counterpart of the eschatological community of salvation, which was very closely connected with it (see pp. 223f. above). At the same time the angels guaranteed that nature would run according to God's will without disruption. The individual phenomena of nature were explained

by the most varied working of very different angels. The late Rabbinic maxim, 'You find that an angel is set above every thing'[788] already applies in essentials to the Essene speculation about angels, where the lowest classes of angel represented little more than personified natural forces.[789] The only disruption in the ordering of the cosmos came from the fall of the heavenly 'watchers', who were also said to be stars; among other things they led men astray into star worship and thus to idolatry in general. Thus a sufficient explanation of the origin of evil was given not only in 'ontological' terms – this came about through the doctrine of the two spirits in connection with that of predestination – but also 'historically'. The demons on earth were regarded as the ghosts of the giants who had emerged from the union of the fallen 'watchers' with the wives of men.[790] There could be a remnant of the Babylonian conception of world ages (see pp. 191f. below) in the idea that the order of heaven will also be destroyed again at the end of the world, 'in the days of sin', so that the moon and individual 'star leaders' will deviate from the order ordained by God. However, it is more probable that this was meant as an aetiological explanation for the deviation of the lunar year and the stellar year from the Essene solar year (see below, pp. 234f.). The Essenes also shared with apocalyptic and the whole Hellenistic environment the widespread conception of a '*sympatheia*' between earthly and heavenly events. Thus on the whole the Hasidic-Essene angel doctrine formed the basis of an attempt at a self-contained explanation of the world and history.

The religious origin of this systematic angelology with its military-sounding hierarchy and an abundance of secret angel names[791] was probably the Old Testament conception of the court of Yahweh; the sudden expansion of angelology in the Persian and Hellenistic period, however, remains a long unsolved riddle. Alleged 'Iranian' origin, often appealed to in such dilemmas, does not bring any clarification.[792] The old idea, widespread throughout the whole of the ancient East and in Hellas, of the stars as living beings (see n. 816 below), and the designation אלים (אלוהים) for the angels, so loved in Qumran,[793] suggests that the angels were essentially gods stripped of their power. In this way conceptions from Canaanite popular religion seem to have been adopted, transformed and systematized. As particular names for individual angels appear for the first time in Daniel and in Tobit, who stands close to Hasidic piety (12.15) – Zechariah knows only the 'angel of Yahweh' as an interpreting angel (1.11, 13; 3.1–10; cf. 2.2, 7; 4.1, etc.), and Job and Ben Sira do not mention any individual angel by name – the formation of names was probably a special development in apocalyptic and Hasidic circles. It was hoped to avoid the danger of polytheistic misinterpretation by representing God himself as the sovereign 'prince of the gods (שר אלים) and the revered king and lord over all the spirits' (1 QH 10.8). The last-mentioned angelic designation (רוחות/רוחים) hints at a spiritualized form of the idea of angels, typical of Hellenistic times; perhaps it was derived from Ps. 104.4;

significantly, it usually means the host of Belial in the War Scroll (cf. I Sam. 16.14).[794]

Thus fundamentally the whole of angelology was an indication that the figure of God had receded into the distance and that the angels were needed as intermediaries between him, creation and man. Now they also became the bringers of his revelations and observed, protected and punished mankind.[795] This strictly-ordered, pyramid-like hierarchical system probably corresponded to a general religious need of the time, as it exercised a profound influence, not only on the Greek-speaking Judaism of the Diaspora and early Christianity, but through them on gnosticism and indeed on the whole of popular religion in late antiquity, as is shown by its significance for magic.[796] Even neo-Platonism could not escape its influence.[797]

Effects of this kind were only possible because analogous tendencies had been at work in the Greek sphere for a long time. T. F. Glasson draws attention to a parallel in Hesiod to the 'watcher angels' in Daniel and I Enoch:[798]

'Three times ten thousand immortal watchers (ἀθάνατοι φύλακες) does Zeus possess on the all-nourishing earth for men, who observe decisions of law and unwholesome deeds and go about the whole earth clothed in air.'[799]

The function of the angels in I Enoch and Jubilees is very similar: 'Therefore we come and make known all sin . . . before the Lord, which is done in heaven and (on) earth and in light and in darkness and everywhere' (Jub.4.6). Attention has already been drawn to a parallel which originally comes from Babylonia (see above, nn.606–8.). However, the heavenly watchers probably come nearest to the ζῷα νοερά in the theogony of Sanchuniaton or Philo of Byblus, who are called Ζοφασημίν, i.e. οὐρανοῦ κατόπται.[800]

The derivation of the demons from the marriages of the fallen angels with human women is also un-Jewish. In Hesiod the spirits of the men of the golden age became 'daimones' (good) and 'watchers of mortal men' in accordance with the 'will of Zeus'.[801] Socrates gives another definition drawn from Greek popular belief in *Apology* 27d: they are 'children of gods, born of nymphs or others'.[802] Xenocrates, the pupil of Plato (see above, p.163), filled the space between the firmament and the earth with such semi-divine 'daimones', who were responsible for the lower forms of religious practice and also for evil. One can find in him a concern similar to that of apocalyptic and Essenism, to bring the forms of popular belief into a system. For Wilamowitz he is 'the real father of Hellenistic spirits and devils'.[803] Chrysippus adopted these views in Stoic teaching, and Posidonius developed them still further. Thus for example he argued that these spiritual beings had a fiery form, a view which also held for Judaism. He conceived the air as being 'inhabited by countless spirits, who are fragments of the fiery primal spirit'. Thus in addition to the supreme deity he accepted divine beings of lower rank as servants of God and helpers of man, who represented a link between

God and the transitory world.[804] Obviously one cannot speak of a
'dependence' of Jewish angelology on Hesiod or Xenocrates; rather, there
were probably analogies between Greek popular belief and that of Asia Minor,
and the climate in the Hellenistic period was favourable to a fusion of them.
The ease with which Jewish and Hellenistic views could be combined is
evident, for example, from the interpretation of the fall of the angels in
Gen. 6.1–4 in Philo, *Gig.* 6ff. (M.1, 263).

5. A further instance of a rational view of the world which was closely
bound up with angelology is to be found in consideration of the *stars* and here
again above all of the *sun*. Reference here was made to ideas which already
occurred in the traditional doctrine of creation in wisdom, and which Ben
Sira had stressed – probably in controversy with Hellenistic liberalism.[805]
Although represented as personal beings, the stars follow exactly the courses
prescribed for them by God, and the regular precision of their movements is
among the mysteries of God's creation.[806] For through the order of their courses
established by God they regulate not only the times of the holy festivals,
which are also celebrated in heaven, and the seasons with sowing and harvest-
ing, but also the epochs of history, which are systematized by division into
jubilees and weeks of years. They are an expression of the orderly course of
history, which guides them to their goal determined by God's plan.[807] If
one leaves aside the disruption as a result of the fall of the angels and the
eschatological shaking of the cosmos, which are included in God's plan,[808]
they – in contrast to men – never transgress the 'laws' given them by God.[809]
In this way they are an expression of the 'reliable order which proceeds from
God's mouth and is a testimony for being' (1 QH 12.9: תכן נאמנה מפי
אל ותעודת חוזה). The degree to which such notions were appropriate for
association with Stoic conceptions is shown by the obedience of the stars,
indeed of the whole cosmos, pictured in 1 Cl.20. H. Bietenhard has already
recognized the difference of apocalyptic from earlier texts like Ps. 104:

> 'The consideration of nature in apocalyptic is to some degree rational; it
> has become more "scientific" and more detached, despite all the fantasy.'
> In this connection he conjectures the 'influx of Greek natural theology into
> late Judaism'.[810]

The *sun* acquires unique significance as the source of light and thus as a
symbol of the divine sphere of light; *its* course – in contrast to that of the
moon – was perfect for ever.[811] The Essene *solar year* of 364 days is
closely connected with this high valuation; the community oriented itself to
this instead of to the official Jewish lunisolar year, and in it the sabbaths and
feasts always fell on the same day in the year. The division of this year could
clearly be seen – in contrast to that of the lunar year – and above all the clash
of commandments between the sabbath rest and the obligation for sacrifice on
great feast days, which had caused such perplexity to the Pharisaic *halacha*

down to Hillel, was abolished.[812] Presumably it was kept functional by intercalation; we have no indication that it was done away with. Rather, certain Essene calendar fragments show that the reckoning of the seasons was kept at Qumran with great exactitude. Thus the calendar, too, is an indication of the *rational tendency* of Essene thought. Its central significance – it was to some degree a shibboleth of 'orthodoxy' – arose from the belief that a life according to the Torah, corresponding to the laws of creation and the course of history, was possible only with the correct calculation of time revealed by God. As its introduction led to a breach with the official cult in Jerusalem and the people as a whole, because the feasts were calculated to be on completely different days, it cannot have been of pre-Essene Hasidic origin. Daniel and the vision of the beasts in I Enoch still give no indication in this direction, whereas Jubilees and I Enoch are of Essene origin. Presumably it came from Ptolemaic Egypt,[813] as the division of the year into four seasons, which was associated with it, follows Egyptian Hellenistic models.[814] This contrasts with the two seasons of Old Testament reckoning; each season consisted of 91 days making 13 weeks and was introduced by intercalary days celebrated as festivals. A direct derivation from Pythagoreanism as conjectured by M. Testuz on the basis of Essene number speculation is, on the other hand, improbable.[815] Possibly this solar year with 365 days had already found entry into Hellenistic circles of Judea during Ptolemaic rule, and had been maintained by the Hasidim or Essenes with a reduction to 364 days, because this could be brought into accord with rigorous observance of the sabbath. Such knowledge of the solar year in Jewish Palestine at the beginning of the second century BC could be indicated by the fact that the feast of Hanukkah was probably attached to a solstice feast already celebrated in Jerusalem by Jews friendly to Greece (see below, pp. 298f., 303).

Belief in the regularity and perfection of the heavenly order, with a philosophical and religious basis, was a common view throughout the Hellenistic world. The roots of the belief may lie in Babylonian astrology (see above, p. 191); however, there is hardly any idea which the Greeks took up early with such enthusiasm, to make it an essential ingredient of their religion and their philosophical thought. We already find it in Pythagoras and later in Plato, his friend Eudoxus of Cnidus and Aristotle; however, it was given its greatest significance in the Stoa through its marriage with 'Chaldean' astrology: the ordered movement of the stars, especially of the firmament, was regarded as an expression of divine perfection and the stars themselves were divine beings.[816] For Philo they were ψυχαί . . . ἀκήρατοί τε καὶ θεαί (*Gig.* 8, M I, 263). This corresponded to both Palestinian apocalyptic and Hellenistic tradition.

In the pseudo-Aristotelian *De mundo*, the writing which with its philosophical monotheism probably comes nearest of all the philosophical works of the Greeks to Jewish belief in God, the divinely perfect ordering of the stars leads to a kind of proof of God.[817] Cicero expresses this view, which was generally held in his time, in a way which comes near to the conceptions of the Essene creation hymns with their stamp from Jewish wisdom: '*nulla igitur in caelo nec fortuna nec temeritas nec erratio nec vanitas inest contraque omnia ordo veritas ratio constantia*' (*De nat. deor.* II, 56).[818]

The Hellenistic 'astral theology' came to completion in '*solar theology*', a 'learned derivation' which was 'dependent on the Stoic explanation of the world'.[819] For Cleanthes, the sun was already τὸ ἡγεμονικὸν τοῦ κόσμου, and in his doctrine of *ekpyrosis* the stars melt into the sun of their own free will. In the Syrian Posidonius it is identified as the 'heart of heaven' and with Zeus.[820] Possibly we have here the notion of the Syrian God of heaven who was later associated with Helios. Even if the Essenes never worshipped the sun as 'divine', the much-discussed report of Josephus in *Bell.*2, 128ff. on their alleged worship of the sun – which in reality probably refers to the Shema prayer before sunrise – shows that the symbolic significance of the sun in Essenism could at least be understood by the non-Jewish observer. In any case, this high estimation corresponded to the trend of the time – particularly outside Judaism.[821]

6. Astral and solar theology could never have gained such significance had it not been for the victorious progress of *astrology* in the Hellenistic era. After the end of the third century it became more and more the spiritually dominant force among the educated. The collapse of old Greek religion in the fifth and fourth centuries BC (see above, pp. 122ff.) and its relegation to a mere belief in fate had inevitably to culminate in astrology, for here there was apparently a possibility of gaining a glimpse into the mysterious working of fate.

The earliest individual horoscopes we have come from Babylon, the earliest from 29.4. 409 BC, the latest from 68 BC.[822] Whereas these horoscopes are still relatively rare, and many learned men from the Babylonian schools of astronomy and mathematics had a sceptical attitude to the astrological practice of omens (according to the evidence of Strabo, 16, 1, 6 [739]), in the second century astrology acquired overwhelming significance in the Hellenistic world of the eastern Mediterranean and also in Rome. O. Neugebauer, who knows it best, comes to the conclusion: 'The main structure of the astrological theory is undoubtedly Hellenistic.'[823]

The central point of this development was Ptolemaic Alexandria, a milieu open to all new spiritual movements.[824] The earliest Egyptian astrological works can be demonstrated from the end of the third century, and the earliest horoscope on papyrus from the beginning of the first century BC. It probably took time for this custom of the learned Alexandrians to penetrate into the simple people and the *chōra*. There is evidence for the first 'Chaldeans' in Rome about the middle of the second century BC. The greatest significance came to be attached to the astrological works under the names of Hermes-

Thoth and Nechepso-Petosiris, which were written in Alexandria before
150 BC.[825]

Significantly, even the *Essene community* could not escape the fascinating
influence of this new 'science'. As the 'community of salvation' was strictly
segregated from alien influences, the adoption of astrological knowledge seems
to have taken place more at the time of its foundation than at a later point of
time. Among others, a number of astrological fragments have been discovered
in Cave IV; J. M. Allegro has published one of them written in secret writing,
which also contains Greek letters.[826]

> Col. II, 5–9: . . . and his bones are long and thin, and his toes are thin and
> long, and he is of the second pillar. His spirit is in the house of light in six
> (parts) and in three (parts) in the house of darkness. And this is the con-
> stellation of his birth (המולד) under which he was born: in the foot of the
> bull (ברגל השור). He will be poor. And this is his beast: (the) bull.
>   Col. III.2–6: 'and his head . . . his cheeks (?) fat . . . his teeth pro-
> minent, the fingers of his hands thick, his legs thick and each very hairy and
> his toes thick and short. His spirit is in the house (of darkness) in eight
> (parts) and one (part) from the house of light . . .'

An Aramaic text published by J. Starcky,[827] which by its orthography
comes from the end of the first century BC, gives a similar but more
thorough physiognomical description of a person expected in the future
with red hair, various striking features like body marks, regular teeth, etc.
During his youth he is without knowledge 'like a lion' . . . 'until the time
of the mystery of the knowledge of the three books'. Thereupon his wisdom
grows immeasurable: 'He will know the secrets of every living thing, all
their plans against him come to an end, the rule (over) all living things will
be great . . . for God has chosen (the time of) his birth . . .' or 'because
he is the elect of God, his birth and the spirit of his breath are (perfect ?)'.

The editor and a further scholar, J. Carmignac, suppose that the last text is
the 'horoscope' of a Messianic personality, presumably the 'prince of the
community' from the family of David. As J. Starcky stresses, there are also
certain contacts with the Messianic picture of the Similitudes of I Enoch.[828]
Common to the two texts is the combination of physiognomical and astrological data. The former belong, as J. Licht rightly observed, in the mantic
sphere. The argument from physique and physical appearance (μορφοσκοπία
and φυσιογνωμία) and peculiarities like body marks (ἐλαία) to ascertain the
character and future of a man was already widespread in the Hellenistic world,
following oriental patterns.[829] In the Essene interpretation it is striking
that a better 'spiritual' constitution also goes with a more ascetic appearance.[830] This does not, however, mean that the astrological details were of
less significance than the physiognomical; it is just that they are less well
preserved because of the fragmentariness of the text. In the Aramaic text, the
מולדה at the end probably indicates the astrological constellation of the date of

birth of the future ruler.[831] The appearance and fate described could only
be inferred from the horoscope. One of the most valuable 'products' of ancient
astrology was the horoscope of a wise 'world ruler' expected in the future.[832]
J. Starcky, the editor, therefore pointed to the correspondence between appearance and physique and constellation of birth, so widespread in astrological
technique, which could even include the '*elaia*'.[833]

The first text presupposes knowledge of the astrological significance of
the *zodiac*:[834] when the person concerned was born, the sun was in eclipse
with a star which was called 'the bull's foot'. This is perhaps identical with the
'kneeling' of the constellation attested by Eratosthenes in the third century
BC.[835] The future was read from the nativity and the mantic interpretation
of physical peculiarities and in addition – according to the first text – the
determination of the inner being was established according to the deterministic
dualistic doctrine of the two spirits. The Community Rule, 1 QS 4.15f., already
stated that the portions of a man in the spirit of light or that of darkness could
be different, and that the two fought together in the hearts of men (4.23).
The significance of the zodiac in the Essene community is confirmed by a
further unpublished fragment from 4 Q, which relates to certain days of the
month:

> 'Le 13 ou le 14 (du mois Tebet) c'est le Cancer.' There follow predictions
> based on an astrological interpretation of thunder: 'S'il tonne dans le signe
> des Gémeaux, terreur et angoisse causée par l'étranger et par . . .' Here
> too the parallels with Ptolemaic astrology are obvious, for example the
> Berlin *Brontologion* of Hermes Trismegistos. In contrast to the Hasidim,
> with the Essenes astrological and apocalyptic predictions of political events
> were combined.[836]

The zodiac also plays a great role in the Essene astrological book (I Enoch
72.13, 19; 75.3) and also in II Enoch (30.6, cf.20.6 [secondary] and 30.3),
which comes from Egypt. Its knowledge and use were then taken for granted
among the Rabbis and the synagogues of the third to sixth centuries AD.[837]
The significance attached in Qumran to these esoteric astrological doctrines is
shown by the fact that they were partly written in cryptic writing. Such a
fragment has the title '(Words) of the instructor to all the sons of the dawn',
and another the title 'Midrash of the words of Moses'.[838] Thus astrological
secret doctrines of this kind, alien to the Old Testament, were traced back to
Moses. This recalls the fact that in the ancient tradition in Pliny, Apuleius,
Celsus, etc., Moses could also appear as a great magician.[839]

It is remarkable that views of this kind from the Hellenistic environment
penetrated the Essene community. However, we should recall the rational
features in Essene theology, which have already been mentioned more than
once. Like the Hasidim, the Essenes could make use of continually new
thought-forms in their controversy with the Hellenistic enlightenment, with
syncretistic tendencies and a retrograde conservatism. Astrology was regarded

as the highest of all 'sciences', and together with manticism it was defended by
the Stoics, especially as both corresponded with Stoic determinism and gave
unsurpassed expression to a basic notion of the attitude of the time, the
'sympathy' of the macrocosm and the microcosm, the world and man.[840]
In addition, they marked the spiritual transformation from the scepticism
which was still predominant in the century after Alexander the Great to a
resurgence of new religious feeling. Astrology, despite its claims to 'science',
expressed the feeling that the deepest mystery of being, that of history and
human fate, was not freely accessible to the approach of the calculations of
reason, but had to be discovered in each single instance by a 'higher' knowledge
oriented on the 'divine' courses of the stars.

That the Hasidic-Essene 'wise men' were engaged in controversy with
such conceptions and that in warding them off they could not altogether escape
them is shown by the fact that they had already taken over Babylonian astronomical and astrological conceptions in the Enoch tradition, though they had
considerably transformed them. The lack of 'compulsion from the stars' was in
fact an essential distinguishing feature between the historical picture of early
Jewish apocalyptic and that of its Hellenistic environment (see pp. 192ff. above).
Presumably interest in astrology was very much stronger among their opponents, the friends of Hellenistic education in Jerusalem. This is shown by the
anonymous Samaritan and the Egyptian Jew Artapanus, who made Enoch-
Atlas or Abraham the inventors and communicators of astrological secret
knowledge (see above, p.91). Jubilees 12.16–18 shows that the Essenes could
produce polemic against the adoption of astrological conceptions:

> According to Jub. 12.16–18, Abraham looks at the sky to discover the rain
> for the coming year (!): 'And a word came into his heart and he said: "All
> the signs of the stars, and the signs of the moon and of the sun (are) all in
> the hand of the Lord. Why do I search them out? If he desires, he causes it
> to rain . . . and if he desires he withholds (the rain), and all things are in
> his hand." '

In this context belongs the view that among the secrets betrayed by the
fallen angels to men all kinds of astrological knowledge were expressly enumerated.[841] But as the astrological fragments show, the Essene attitude was
ambivalent and the insight of Jub. 12 was not maintained. The struggle for
'science' in accord with the times was stronger than that for deeper theological
knowledge.[842] That this division was continued among the Rabbis is
shown by the bitter discussion among the teachers of the second and third
centuries over the question whether Israel was subject to the compulsion of
the stars (*Shab.* 156a/b).

7. The newly-discovered astrological evidence is supplemented by reports
which indicate Essene *manticism* and *magic*. The 'Prayer of Nabonidus'
(which is pre-Essene, stands close to the Daniel narratives and therefore
probably belongs to the Hasidic tradition) has the king of Babylon healed by a

Jewish 'miracle worker' (נוזר),[843] and in the Genesis Apocryphon, Abraham heals the Pharaoh by the laying on of hands and prayer (20.25–30). Daniel, faithful to the law, could assume the office of overseer to all the wise men of Babylon without offence, though this group included all kinds of magicians, interpreters of stars and dreams, etc. (Dan. 2.48, see pp. 203f. above). The sceptical attitude of Sir. 34 (G. 31).1–8 stands in a certain amount of opposition to this. We learn about the Essenes from Josephus:

> There are also those among them who undertake to foretell things to come, by reading holy books, and using several sorts of purification rites, and being perpetually conversant with the discourses of the prophets; and it is but seldom that they miss in their predictions (*Bell.* 2, 159).

The report shows that the Essenes followed the Old Testament prophets in their 'prophecy'. For them the gift of prediction was probably the sign of the possession of the 'prophetic' spirit.[844] But the style of their 'prophecy' differed considerably from Old Testament models by the conjunction of exegesis and rites of purification, and the 'holy books' cannot have been limited to the Torah and the prophets, but must also have included apocalyptic and astrological-mantic writings. The different examples of Essene 'visions of the future' reported to us by Josephus already contain this alien tendency, akin to Hellenistic manticism and dream-interpretation, though, as O. Betz has shown, they are formed from the Old Testament. Thus the Essene Judas as a μάντις prophesied the very day of the death of the Hasmonean Antigonus and gave the exact place where it would take place. His later companion Menahem welcomed the schoolboy Herod as a future king of the Jews, but later gave the king an obscure answer to a question about the length of his reign;[845] and an Essene Simon interpreted the dream of Archelaus in respect of his imminent banishment in a way which recalls Artemidorus' book of dreams.[846] The prophet Agabus would be an early Christian counterpart to these Essene seers (Acts 11.28; 21.10).

Further reports point to the existence of a *mantic-magic medicine* in Essenism:

> They also take great pains in studying the writings of the ancients, and choose out of them what is most for the advantage of their soul and body, and therefore for the cure of distempers they seek out such roots as may be effective and inquire into the (occult) properties (ἰδιότητες) of stones (*Bell.* 2, 136).[847]

Jubilees 10.1ff., 12ff., explains the way in which this Essene medicine is to be understood:

> To prevent the descendants of Noah succumbing to sicknesses caused by the demons, the angels of the presence reveal to Noah 'all the medicines of their disease, together with their seductions, how he might heal them with herbs of the earth. And Noah wrote down all things in a book as we

instructed him concerning every kind of medicine.' He then gives this book to his son Shem.

As the sicknesses were of demonic magical origin, they could only be effectively combatted by a kind of 'white magic' taught by the good angels. Conversely, according to I Enoch 8.3 (presumably from a Noah apocryphon), Semyasa, the leader of the fallen angels, had taught men 'spells and the cutting of roots' as 'black magic'. 'Roots', 'plants' and the 'properties of stones' were used in antiquity as technical terms in a magical iatromantic sense,[848] and frequently also had astrological significance.

> We may therefore imagine the 'Book of Noah' as the same kind of work as that which the doctor Thessalus found in Alexandria as the work of Nechepso, which contained 'cures for the whole body and every ailment in accordance with the zodiac through *stones* and *plants*'.[849] A similar work was also known to the Rabbis; in *Pes.*4.9a, Hezekiah is praised because he concealed the 'book of cures' (ספר רפואות). According to Suidas and Maimonides it was a work of Solomon who, according to Josephus, is said to have composed quite similar writings: 'God granted him to learn the art directed against the demons for the use and the healing of men.' He goes on to describe how in his presence a Jewish exorcist drove out a demon before Vespasian by means of a ring which contained 'a *root* described by Solomon' and with the help of spells composed by Solomon (ἐπῳδάς cf. III Kingdoms 5.12 ᾠδαί).[850]

Thus even Essenism will have had its share in the development of Jewish magic in antiquity. The prohibition against giving away 'the books of the community and the names of the angels' is meant to prevent a magical misuse of their own 'secret knowledge' (Josephus, *Bell.*2, 142). Jewish magic was one of those phenomena in Judaism in which non-Jewish observers were most interested. It is witnessed to us by many ancient writers from the first century AD onwards,[851] and even early gnosticism will not have been uninfluenced by it.[852] Its roots go well back into the pre-Christian Hellenistic period; this is true for the magical Solomon literature[853] and for the travelling Jewish miracle workers. Presumably Clearchus of Soli (first half of the third century BC) met one.[854] Bolus of Mendes, the father of alchemical magical literature, who lived in Alexandria about 200 BC, also seems to have known Jewish magic.[855] Matt.12.27 = Luke 11.19 Q shows that the Pharisees, too, were active as exorcists. The origin and extension of Jewish magic is fundamentally another expression of the feeling of superiority in Jewish religion: men believed that it possessed 'higher' powers, especially in connection with the holy name of God (see below, n. IV 22).[856]

Excursus 5: Secret teaching from primeval times

That the Essenes, despite such apparently strict segregation, were involved in polemical and apologetic controversy with their Hellenistically influenced environment, and that features which seem so strange to us, like astrology, manticism and magic, are to be understood in this context, is shown by the transformation of a widespread travel legend which even found its way into Palestinian Judaism. One of the favourite 'forms of revelation' in the Hellenistic Roman period was the discovery of scrolls, inscriptions or pillars from primeval times. Both the secret Egyptian hieroglyphic inscriptions and the Babylonian cuneiform monuments supported the spread of this frequent theme.[857] The variant which appears probably for the first time in Berossus, that in this way the wisdom of patriarchal times was saved through the great flood, represents a special form:

> According to this Bel-Kronos commanded Xisuthros before the flood to bury all works of writing – i.e. cuneiform tablets – in the sun city of the Siparenes and after the flood to dig them up again and 'deliver them to men'.[858]

In a similar way, the later Ps. Manetho reports that Hermes-Thoth had inscribed his wisdom in hieroglyphics on pillars and that in this way they had survived the flood. However, we also meet it in the Jewish Palestinian tradition in the *Life of Adam and Eve* 49f., in later haggadic works[859] and in Josephus *Antt.* 1, 69–71:

> The sons of Seth, the discoverers of *astronomy*, 'so that their discoveries should not be lost to mankind . . . – for Adam had prophesied the downfall of the universe, once by the power of fire and the second time by violence and abundance of water (see above, n. 552) – erected two pillars, one from tiles and the other from stones, so that if the one made of tiles vanished in the flood, the one of stone would remain to inform men through its inscription . . .'

The same legend appears – in an Essene version – in Jubilees 8.1f., but with a different prelude:

> The grandson of Noah, Kainam, instructed in writing by his father Arpachsad, 'found a writing which former (generations) had carved on the rock, and he read what was thereon, and he transcribed it. And he saw from it that it contained the *teaching of the watchers* in accordance with which they used to observe the omens of the sun and moon and stars in all the signs of heaven. And he wrote it down and said nothing regarding it; for he was afraid to speak to Noah about it lest he should be angry with him on account of it.

In interpreting this passage it should be noted that according to *Antt.* 1, 144 Arpachsad appears as the ancestor of the Chaldeans; the 'wisdom' which Kainam discovered thus presumably laid the foundation for the Chaldean star cult, the practice of omens and magic. According to the Noah fragments from I Enoch, this 'teaching of the watchers' included not only astrology (see above, pp. 237ff.) but metal working, the iatromantic knowledge of plants, of minerals for cosmetics and for colours – an alchemy understood in magical terms probably also appears here[860] – and also, according to another passage, writing on papyrus and all kinds of magic.[861] What other Jewish circles regarded as a positive wisdom tradition deriving from Seth, was rejected in the Essene movement as demonic knowledge coming from the betrayal of divine secrets (I Enoch 16.3) by the fallen angels, and it may be supposed that in effect this included all the wisdom of the pagans and the refined culture of the Hellenistic period. To rob these negative 'revelations' of their force, 'counter-revelations' were given by God on writing and language, the courses of the stars, cures, feasts etc., to Enoch, Noah (see above, n. 621) and Abraham.[862] Thus the dualistic division in history was matched by two opposed streams of revelation and wisdom. When the Essenes were occupied with astrology and iatromantics they believed this to be something fundamentally different from what was happening outside the community in the same area. As a result of their Hasidic heritage, they still maintained an 'encyclopaedic' interest alongside their soteriological and anthropological thought; they wanted to set against the 'demonic' Chaldean, Egyptian or Greek 'wisdom' a more comprehensive, genuine wisdom of their own, encompassing the cosmos and history, and founded on revelation and not on betrayal. It is not to no purpose that the groups of concepts relating to knowledge and understanding lie at the centre of Essene theology. In this sense one could speak of a Hasidic-Essene 'gnosticism', just as Solomon, in a passage related to this way of thinking, Wisdom 7.17ff., says that God has given him $τῶν ὄντων γνῶσιν ἀψευδῆ$:[863] $ὅσα τέ ἐστιν κρυπτὰ καὶ ἐμφανῆ ἔγνων$ (7.21).

(d) The form of the Essene community and the question of Pythagorean influence

New and underivable from the Old Testament Jewish tradition is the form of the Essene community, whether this is the monastic community of Qumran which formed its heart, or the groups of Essene 'tertiaries' living in the cities of Judea.[864] Neither the reference by Morton Smith to the opposition between '*gōlā*' and "*am hā'āreṣ*' at the time of Nehemiah nor the groups of prophets about Elijah and Elisha, the Rechabites nor even the families of priests and Levites are sufficient parallels to explain this formation of groups.[865] It can only be understood in the light of the spirit of a new time, requiring as it did the breaking off of all family ties and the decisive conversion of everyone who wanted to attach himself to the community of salvation. Thus, as H. Bardtke and C. Schneider have shown independently of each other, the nearest parallels to the form of the community are to be found in the law of associations in the Hellenistic period; that is, the external forms of the community and its organization possess typical features of a *private, religious association*, a form of law which neither the Old Testament nor Jewish law knew in this way.[866] This is confirmed and supplemented by B. W. Dombrowski's demonstration that the designation of the Essene community as *hayyahad* in essentials represents a translation of the Greek common-law term τὸ κοινόν. He refers to the κοινόν of the Sidonians in the bilingual inscription from the Piraeus (96 BC ?), and to the κοινόν of the worshippers of Zeus Hypsistos from late Ptolemaic Egypt with their strict disciplinary order. The formation of such associations, partly on the basis of country, partly on the basis of religion, was typical of the Hellenistic period.[867] Here we must remember that the Jewish synagogue communities of the Diaspora had the same legal form, so that it was not unknown to the Jews. Especially in Ptolemaic Egypt, where there were no *poleis* on the Greek pattern in Upper Egypt apart from Alexandria and Ptolemais, the association served to foster patriotic connections and religious interests among the Greeks scattered throughout the country, and the Jews imitated this form of alliance.[868]

Thus the Essenes appear to be the earliest private 'association' in Jewish Palestine known to us. Even after their formation (see above, pp. 175f.), the Hasidim from which they grew were probably not such a strictly organized, self-contained alliance (see above, pp. 176f.), and even the later Pharisaic *hᵃbūrōt*, which probably had the same legal basis, did not have this strict hierarchical organization, despite many similarities.[869] However, presumably the *politeuma* founded by the last Oniad high priest Jason, which was to prepare for the transformation of Jerusalem into a Greek *polis* and provide legal support for the gymnasium, already had the form of an association, albeit with a more public character.[870] We need not make further reference to the individual features which connect the form of the Essene community with the law of associations in the Hellenistic period; they have been convincingly worked out by H. Bardtke and C. Schneider. They begin with the particular honour paid to the person of the founder, continue with the rules laid down for precedence, for the community officials and the full assembly (which was basically responsible for all decisions), with the testing of initiates and the oaths by which they are bound, common meals, the administration of community finance, to which everyone contributes and in which everyone shares, with ethical regulations and a thorough-going system of association law with punishments and the right of exclusion, and end with a common burial place. In particular, 'the legal position of the assembly of members corresponds completely, according to the Community Rule, with that of the Hellenistic association'. By and large, we have here 'a towering example of the appropriation of Hellenistic community thought with all its legal consequences by the Jewish spirit of the second century BC'.[871] On the other hand, the Essene expectation of the imminent end and their certainty that they represented the true Israel produced a self-estimation which is almost without analogy in the Hellenistic world. As a 'union of the everlasting covenant' (יחד ברית עולם), the Essene community of salvation is the only legitimate bearer of the covenant which God concluded with the fathers; they and the 'covenant' are basically identical.[872] We may not therefore assume that the founder of the community and its members were aware that they had chosen a form of community life that was not in the Old Testament; but the very confidence with which they could take over alien forms of organization shows how strongly Hellenistic law and, in conjunction with it, Hellenistic thought-forms, had found their way into Palestinian Judaism.

The only religious or philosophical movement whose strict organization and heightened self-estimation corresponded in any way to the Essene community was that *of the Pythagoreans,* though in the early Hellenistic period and before the blossoming of Neo-Platonism they existed only in individual conventicles without any great influence.[873] Josephus, or probably better his source Nicolaus of Damascus, in *Antt.* 15, 371 described the Essenes as a Jewish pendant to the Greek Pythagoreans (γένος δὲ τοῦτ' ἔστιν διαίτῃ χρώμενον τῇ παρ' Ἕλλησιν ὑπὸ Πυθαγόρου καταδεδειγμένῃ). The close affinity between the two groups was already often assumed in the eighteenth and nineteenth century on the basis of the tradition of Josephus, Philo and Pliny, among others by F. C. Baur, D. F. Strauss and particularly emphatically by the philosopher E. Zeller. Against him A. Hilgenfeld no less emphatically advocated the affinity of the Essenes to Jewish apocalyptic and an early Persian derivation of their ideas.[874] In this century, too, significant scholars like Schürer, F. Cumont and M. J. Lagrange, among others, have conjectured Pythagorean influence; I. Lévy has even devoted a monograph to the relationship between Pythagoreanism and Judaism.[875] After the discovery of the Qumran texts, which shattered all previous views, Dupont-Sommer in particular, and T. F. Glasson, more cautiously, have once again put forward the Pythagorean hypothesis.[876]

That Alexandrian Judaism at the beginning of the second century knew Pythagorean and Orphic doctrines and had a positive view of them is shown by Aristobulus. According to him Pythagoras and Orpheus had been taught by the law of Moses, and in his speculation associated with the number seven he follows both Palestinian and Pythagorean traditions (see pp. 165ff. above). In his life of Pythagoras, the Greek *literatus* Hermippus had already connected the Jews with Greek philosophy in the third century BC.[877] Thus it is possible in theory that the founder of the Essene community knew Pythagorean doctrines. Nevertheless, direct dependence is improbable. The Essene community wanted only to represent the genuine intention of the Torah and the prophetic writings and to defend its own Jewish heritage against all alien influences. Thus these alien influences were accepted only unconsciously or in a polemic apologetic situation. This is also true of the supposedly Pythagorean features. Similarly, the reasons given by Dupont-Sommer for Pythagorean influence do not stand close inspection. The daily evening and morning prayer of the Essenes and Therapeutae were not a cultic veneration of the sun but were made in praise of God as the Lord of creation and of the course of history; the interest in the sun which can without doubt be detected was a result of light symbolism, which was promoted for dualistic reasons.[878] The interpretation of the isolated letter *nun* which appears in 1 QS 10.4 as a reference to the Pythagorean holy number fifty is erroneous, as this is a scribal error – as is shown by other manuscripts of the Rule.[879] A large number of the features said by E. Zeller and others to be typically Pythagorean can be explained by the concern of the community for a life in perfect priestly purity, and a further number are the result of the adoption of the legal form of the Hellenistic religious association. Others, e.g. the secret discipline, were widespread.[880] In addition, we may not overlook the fact that the 'foundations' of both orders had the critical character of rigorous reform movements and that each was stamped by the strong-willed personality of its founder. The critical attitude towards riches and luxury, the sharing of goods and the rejection of money among the Essenes stem, for example, from a radical development of the Hasidic 'ideal of poverty' and from a protest against the hunt for riches which was so typical of the period before and after the Maccabean revolt and which dominated the old and new upper classes.[881] At the same time it is probably to be understood as an anticipation of the eschatological time of salvation.

In view of the instances already cited there can hardly be any more dispute that the Essenes – like the Hasidim before them – adopted and worked over to a considerable degree foreign influences in their Hellenistic environment from Babylonia and Iran and indeed from Ptolemaic Egypt.[882] But they are not typical Pythagoreans. Even the doctrine of the immortality of the soul merely corresponded to a widespread religious opinion in their Hellenistic environment (see pp. 196ff. above). Despite the conjectures of C. Schneider, it remains questionable whether and how far their interpretation of scripture, which was also familiar with simple allegory, was influenced by Alexandria. Certainly allegorical interpretation was widespread among the Stoics for the purpose of interpreting Homer, but it can in fact already be found in ancient Egypt. The Demotic Chronicle offers a typical example; one can be found in Palestine in the apocalyptic interpretation of scripture. The desire to interpret inspired holy scripture in the light of the particular present inevitably led to allegorical interpretation.[883] The starting point of the learning practised by the Essenes was in the Palestinian Hasidic wisdom schools in the first half of the second century BC, in which – as in Ben Sira – we may suppose that there was already some knowledge of 'Greek wisdom' in the sense of popular philosophical views. The Teacher of Righteousness and other learned members of the community probably introduced a certain degree of 'Greek education' into the community at the time of its foundation, which was then used in an apologetic sense. Thus for example the yearly testing of members of the community and their classification according to 'their knowledge and the perfection of their way of life' (1 QS 5.23f.) points to the Greek 'agonistic' ideal of life (see above, p. 67). It is in any case striking that a profound piety and a significant theological anthropology and ecclesiology can go hand in hand with an explicit rational quest for knowledge of an almost encyclopaedic character, which finds its expression in astronomical and astrological interests and in a strict systematic and deterministic division of the course of history. One almost has the impression that various theological outlines with different structures stand side by side,[884] though it is very questionable whether the members of the community were aware of this. Perhaps they were much more strongly under the impression that Essene thought presented a closed theological 'system' of cosmos, history and man under the sign of the glory of God. Despite all the apparent breaks and contradictions, the beginnings of a systematic total view are unmistakable.

If we consider the Essene community against its environment, the essential thing is not the supposed 'Pythagorean' influences, but the fact that Hellenistic observers like Josephus – or Nicolaus of Damascus – could present them as Jewish 'Pythagoreans'. In commenting on a comparison of Essene and Pythagorean eschatology, P. Grelot remarks: 'L'hypothèse de la dépendance étant écartée les parallélismes subsistent.'[885] The ancient reporters like Philo, Pliny the Elder, Solinus, Porphyry and above all Dio Chrysostom presented the Essenes as a *community of 'philosophers'*, who led an ascetic life in the wilderness by the Dead Sea in the service of the knowledge of God, wisdom and the love of man.[886] Thus they belonged to that widespread ideal of wisdom with a religious basis which, according to Festugière, was typical of the 'prophets of the Orient' (see above, n. 664). In one sense the 'Hellenized' interpretation of the Essene order by the various ancient writers was not completely mistaken, for precisely in Essenism, Judaism points beyond the narrow context of Palestine; the retreat into the solitariness of the desert unleashed great religious consequences which had their effects on primitive Christianity, the baptist movements in Transjordania and early gnosticism. The Therapeutae, too, are best explained as an imitation of the Essenes in the Egyptian Diaspora.[887] The very features which disturb us and seem strange to us, like the dualistic doctrine of two spirits, their determinism, the hierarchical angelology, astrology, manticism and magic, aroused attention within and outside Palestine through their speculative scientific character, and in conjunction with the ascetic life of the community occasioned the supposition that the Essenes were Jewish θεῖοι ἄνδρες on Palestinian soil.[888]

8. Summary: Palestinian Judaism between the Reception and the Repudiation of Hellenism

1. and 2. (see pp. 109ff.) The striking thing about the *spiritual situation* of Judaism towards the end of Achaemenidian rule and the beginning of Hellenistic domination is the astonishing *variety* of its literature, which points to a

rich spiritual life within the small community of the Jewish people. The central point of this literary activity was probably provided by the 'wisdom schools', in which very different tendencies come to light. The strongest group was concerned for a fusion of the international wisdom tradition with traditional piety, an attitude which appears, say, in Prov. 1–9 and is continued in the identification of wisdom and law in Ps. 119 and in Ben Sira. Alongside this, however, we find in Job and Koheleth a universalist and critical tendency; another trend, from which later the Hasidim and early apocalyptic literature developed, was particularly indebted to the legacy of the prophetic tradition. This still does not outline the intellectual multiplicity of Judea at that time, however; presumably there were even more substantial differences, which can hardly be brought under a single heading. The feature common to the three main trends that have been mentioned was strictly rational thought, which was expressed, among other things, in a predilection for the formation of abstract terms, and in the beginnings of a certain systematization and establishing of regularity in nature, history and human existence. In this sense one might speak of a 'pre-philosophical' stage of late Jewish wisdom, which displays an affinity to Greek popular philosophy and especially to the Stoa, influenced by the Semitic spirit, which paved the way for the later encounter. Thus the early Hellenistic period produced hardly any break that we can see in the development of Jewish spiritual life; one can rather talk of a continuous development down to the Maccabean period, which did, however, present a certain decline. From the middle of the third century BC we can trace the influence of Greek language and culture even in Judea (see above, pp. 59ff.); from this time onwards a greater differentiation between conservative circles and those friendly to Greece may have set in. All in all, however, during the third century even those circles which observed the law strictly seem to have been open to foreign influences; only on this basis is the development of Hasidic apocalyptic, with its strong syncretistic elements, conceivable in the first half of the second century BC. The positive verdict of the Greeks on the Jews in this early period corresponds to the still open attitude of the latter (see below, pp. 215ff.).

3. In *Koheleth* (see above, pp. 115ff.) about the middle of the third century we can see the critical controversy with the spiritual and religious foundations of traditional school wisdom. Righteousness and thus the meaning of the divine rule of the world is in no way obvious to men; they are helpless in the hands of 'fate', which they cannot understand, which often seems unjust, and yet is determined by God. This fate reveals its arbitrariness above all in death, and before it all human values become questionable. Man's personal relationship to God is reduced to a compliant acceptance of the portion allotted to him by God; prayer and cult become empty, conventional forms. Although it cannot be demonstrated that Koheleth is truly dependent on Greek thought, we can understand his scepticism, with its air of cool resignation, as being to

some extent analogous to the criticism of traditional religion which had burst on the Greek world from the second half of the fifth century BC and had reached its climax in belief in fate in the fourth and third centuries BC. The first epitomist indicates that Koheleth had the effect of founding a school. The lack of further sources leaves open the question whether this school developed in the direction of a sharper criticism of the faith of the fathers and a stronger acceptance of Hellenistic ideas.

4. *Ben Sira* marks the end of this epoch of a first encounter between Judaism and Hellenistic civilization, probably assessed in a predominantly positive way by both sides; at the same time he marks the beginning of a new era, which is characterized by critical repudiation. Writing about 180–175, immediately before the Hellenistic reform attempt, he is involved in a controversy which at heart he does not want and which contradicts his ideal of the *sōpēr*. The controversy is with those groups of the Jerusalem upper classes who as a result of their assimilation to foreign culture had become almost completely alienated from the belief of their ancestors. For him they are apostates from the law and no longer believe that God works meaningfully and recognizably in this world, making demands on individual men. Against these men, with all the massiveness of certainty, Ben Sira puts forward a justification of divine retribution: man is free and receives the reward that is his due. Alongside this – probably under the influence of popular philosophy – there appears the demonstration of a theodicy from creation. The world has been created by God for the sake of man with a deep purposefulness and harmony that can be known; the central point of mankind is Israel, with its unique and miraculous history guided by God. In the law of Moses it has been entrusted with the divine wisdom itself, the power which orders the whole creation. In the threatening situation in Jerusalem Ben Sira came forward with almost prophetic claims: he admonishes the disputatious sons of the high priest Simon, intercedes for the oppressed poor, and in the style of the old prophets prays for the coming of the dawn of national eschatological salvation for Israel.

5. Presumably the most fruitful and most consequential idea of later Jewish 'wisdom' was the conception of hypostatized *ḥokmā*, probably developed as a counterpart to the Canaanite Astarte, who in the Ptolemaic period was identified with Isis. It was understood as the 'mediatrix of creation', and at the same time formed the shaping and fashioning power within creation (see above, pp. 153ff.). In the course of the 'nationalization' of Jewish wisdom it was identified by Ben Sira with the Torah of Moses. In this, its affinity with certain philosophical conceptions became particularly clear, whether these were the Stoic 'world law' or the Platonic 'world soul'. There was a close conjunction of Palestinian wisdom and Greek philosophy in the Jewish wisdom schools of Alexandria, e.g. with *Aristobulus* (see pp. 164ff. above) – a short time after Ben Sira –, who was the first to assert the dependence of the great

Greek philosophers on Moses and with whom 'wisdom' and 'Logos', in conjunction with the number seven, which was equally holy to the Pythagoreans and the Jews, became the principle of the spiritual ordering of the world and at the same time the basis of the knowledge and moral will of the individual. It is significant that in the Alexandrian Jewish wisdom tradition – in analogy to Palestinian wisdom in Ben Sira – the cosmological and individual anthropological interest occupied the central place, whereas the problem of history retreated into the background. In the Palestinian *Pharisaic* tradition, the cosmic character of the law, resting on its identification with divine 'wisdom', gave it a comprehensive ontological significance (see above, pp. 170ff.). Thus it became the centre and goal of Rabbinic life and thought in general. A consequence of this Torah ontology was – as in Alexandria – the loss of historical consciousness, though the Alexandrian Jewish 'philosophy of religion' maintained its missionary task and remained fundamentally open to the Hellenistic environment, whereas Rabbinic Judaism separated itself more and more from the outside world, above all after AD 70.

6. At the beginning of the Maccabean revolt we meet the *Hasidim* (see pp. 175ff. above) as a relatively self-contained group, which presumably closed its ranks as a 'penitential movement' under the impact of the Hellenistic reform. The origins of Jewish *apocalyptic* are to be sought here, where above all there was a desire to preserve the legacy of the prophets (see pp. 180ff. above). Typical of this 'Hasidic' apocalyptic, which becomes visible in Daniel and in the oldest parts of I Enoch, is its view of world history as a unity, the centre of which is occupied by the course of the chosen people Israel and which according to God's plan is hastening towards a speedy end. In the present, last time, human hybris and apostasy are reaching their climax. With this view of history it is fundamentally different from Hellenistic oracle literature and the astrologically based doctrine of world-cycles, although it takes over individual features of them. The problem of theodicy which broke out in late wisdom was solved by the doctrine of resurrection or immortality and retribution after death or at the eschaton. Individual conceptions are still not sharply marked out. The epistemological basis of apocalyptic is the notion of the 'revelation' of special divine 'wisdom' about the mysteries of history, the cosmos, the heavenly world and the fate of the individual at the eschaton, hidden from human reason. Although it was itself strongly shaped by the pressure of late wisdom towards encyclopaedic knowledge, it was radically different from the traditional wisdom which rested on the tradition of the schools, personal observation and experience. Here wisdom and prophecy flowed into one another: the prophet is a wise man and the wise man a prophet. The development of this understanding of wisdom and revelation is to be understood against the background of the reaction of the oriental religions to Greek rationalism. Alongside astrology, Jewish apocalyptic forms the earliest demonstrable counter-movement which could be classified as 'higher know-

ledge through revelation'. Its consummation was probably brought about by the profound crisis of the Jewish people which broke out as a result of the Hellenistic reform and the Maccabean revolt which followed it. On the other hand, no Jewish trend of thought borrowed so strongly from its oriental Hellenistic environment as apocalyptic. The derivation of individual themes is often difficult to elucidate, and it is also often difficult to decide whether we have chance analogies to alien conceptions or real instances of dependence. All in all, however, these alien influences affect the detail rather than the totality of the apocalyptic picture of the world and history, which fundamentally still rests on an Old Testament conception of salvation history.

7. At the end of this development stands the Essene community. It emerged about 150 BC as a result of a division of the 'Hasidim', when the Teacher of Righteousness left the cultic community of Jerusalem with his followers after the appointment of the Maccabean Jonathan as high priest and founded a monastic order with strict discipline and lofty spiritual claims. It considered itself to be the eschatological community of salvation and the holy remnant of Israel. This development represented theological progress over against Hasidic apocalyptic and late wisdom, inasmuch as it was an attempt to give a systematic basis to the apocalyptic picture of history through the deterministic dualistic doctrine of the two spirits. Furthermore, the anthropological elements of the wisdom tradition were here combined into a soteriological anthropology in which the lost and hopeless state of man was shown, and he was told the way, through repentance and acceptance into the community of salvation, to perfect obedience to the law and communion with the heavenly world. In all this the process of salvation was understood as God's unmerited gift. The concepts of knowledge and understanding which occupy a central position in Essene doctrine are thus primarily to be understood in terms of 'saving knowledge'. On the other hand, knowledge is not limited to the anthropological, soteriological sphere. It contains within itself the impulse to grasp the totality of 'being and happening' brought about by God (see above, p.219) – including the heavenly world –, the secrets of history and of human destiny, with the 'scientific' means of its mythical picture of the world. This was brought about by the 'inspired' interpretation of the Torah and the prophets, and also astrology, manticism and the interpretation of dreams. The ordering of the cosmos was explained, in connection with Hasidic apocalyptic angelology, as being through a hierarchy of angels; under Babylonian and Egyptian influence an independent astronomical system was built up based on the solar calculation of time; indeed, there was even a knowledge of horoscopes for determining character and the future, and of iatromantic practices. The demonic wisdom of the rest of the world based on the betrayal of the fallen angels was contrasted with the community's own knowledge, resting on the divine revelation. Penetrating theological reflection and a 'Faustian-gnostic' drive to knowledge which embraced both the visible and the invisible world therefore stand side

by side. In the last aspect in particular, the influence of Hellenistic, syncretistic conceptions is unmistakable.

This attempt at a survey of the development of Jewish thought in the controversy with the Hellenistic spirit of the time from the third to the end of the second century BC in Palestine must necessarily contain gaps, and its dynamics and its riches are only approximately visible. In summary, however, we may draw the following conclusions:

(a) It is clear that the *multiplicity* which was to be observed at the starting point has become even greater. Although the influential Jewish group which pressed for a complete assimilation to the Hellenistic environment had been annihilated in Palestine as a result of the success of the Maccabean revolt, and the validity of the Torah remained unassailed among the Jewish parties which were formed down to the end of the second century, the Jewish people did not succeed in welding themselves into a unity as a result of the victorious war of independence. True, from now on, any movement which criticized the *Torah* in a fundamental way was doomed to failure; however, the question of its authoritative interpretation constantly gave rise to bitter disputes.[889] The religious rigorism kindled by the rejection of the Hellenistic attempt at alienation continued to work as an unsettling element down to the Zealot movement in the first century AD. We may not therefore, regard Palestinian Judaism between 200 BC and AD 70 as a unitary entity under the aspect of the later Rabbinic view of the law, especially as the strongest party, that of the Pharisees, had an internal split.[890] It only became a real unity under great difficulties through the effect of the school of Jabneh and the doctrinal schools of the second century.

(b) Another striking fact is that *Hellenistic oriental influence* was effective even where foreign 'wisdom' was most bitterly repudiated, in Hasidic apocalyptic, among the Essenes and also – to a lesser degree – among the Pharisees. This confirms the observation already made at the end of chapter 2, *that even Palestinian Judaism must be regarded as Hellenistic Judaism.*[891] Its boundaries towards the Diaspora were fluid, and no straight lines can be drawn; the mutual exchange, even in the theological and intellectual sphere, seems to have been extremely vigorous, especially as Jerusalem had become even more a religious and spiritual centre of world Judaism as a result of the deliberate policy of the Hasmoneans and Herod from the second century BC onwards. In Hellenistic-Roman times Jerusalem was an 'international city', in which representatives of the Diaspora throughout the world met together (see above, p.60). Alexandrian wisdom speculation, which we meet for the first time in Aristobulus, evidently had Palestinian origins, and has its later parallels in the 'Torah ontology of the Rabbis': the eschatological expectation of the end and the effectiveness of apocalyptic, on the other hand, cannot be limited to Palestine; it must also have played a significant role in the Diaspora (see below, under *d*).

(*c*) A further essential point is the strong *rational* element which can be traced from Koheleth to Essenism and which is determined by the underlying wisdom thought. Nevertheless, here too a certain 'decline' can be seen. Whereas in Koheleth 'wisdom' still rests entirely on empirical experience and tradition, with which it is engaged in a critical dispute, in Ben Sira we find alongside it the authority of the Torah and the prophetic writings. In Hasidic apocalyptic, on the other hand, the receipt of supernatural revelation stands in the centre. This is meant to be fundamentally superior to the traditional wisdom won from 'primal revelation' and empirical experience[892] and to the rational thought of the Greeks. Finally, among the Essenes this wisdom through 'revelation' becomes saving knowledge in the strict sense, the decisive source of which is 'inspired' exegesis. The tendency to be found in this development runs parallel to the development of religious knowledge and to the struggle for supernatural revelation in the Hellenistic environment, which later finds its climax in gnosticism and in the extension of the mystery religions in Roman times. Concepts like 'reveal', 'mystery' and 'knowledge' are not fundamentally different from analogous concepts in the religious *koinē* of the Hellenistic period.

(*d*) Finally, it is very probable that between the Maccabean revolt and the destruction of Jerusalem the piety of Palestinian Judaism was shaped to a considerable extent by the *apocalyptic expectation of the end*, though this is not so much to be understood schematically as a unitary entity but as a view which contained many nuances. Thus in it salvation in the present and the expectation of salvation in the future do not form exclusive opposites, nor do a temporal conception of the future and spatial conceptions of heaven. This is a point which should be observed in the interpretation of Paul or Hebrews. The great significance of apocalyptic is that it formed a Jewish pendant, based on the historical thought of the Old Testament, to Hellenistic mysticism and the mystery religions. Even in the *early Pharisaic movement*, of which unfortunately we know little, it seems to have played a not insignificant role:

> This is supported by their derivation from the Hasidim (see p. 176 above), the important note in Josephus, *Antt.* 17, 43ff., their bitter struggle against Alexander Jannaeus – we may regard their leader Simeon b. Seṭaḥ as just as much a prophetic figure as a scholar[893] –, the numerous messianic eschatological passages in early Jewish prayers and in Targ. Jer. I,[894] and also the positive attitude of the Shammaite left wing towards the Zealot movement.[895] Finally, this would be the best explanation of why the later Rabbinic tradition had so few reports of the earlier period: they were suppressed, because they contradicted the scepticism of later teachers about messianic expectation which rested on bitter experiences. Possibly this Pharisaic eschatology had even more political and nationalistic colouring on the lines of, say, Ps. Sol. 17, than that of the early Hasidim.

In addition, apocalyptic also seems to have had a considerable influence in the *Diaspora*. The Jewish Sibyllines (from 140 BC) and the Slavonic book of Enoch are a clear sign of this; furthermore, the many works preserved in Christian versions, or at least known through quotations in the church fathers, like the various apocalypses of Baruch and Ezra, the apocalypses of Abraham, Elijah, Moses, Shadrach, Zechariah and Zephaniah, together with the testaments of Adam, Abraham, Isaac, Job, the prayers of Joseph, Jannes and Jambres, Eldad and Modad, to mention only a selection,[896] cannot all have been written in Palestine. Even if they were originally written in Hebrew or Aramaic, people would hardly have gone to the trouble of translating them and other apocalyptic works into Greek had there not been widespread interest in the Diaspora. The mission preaching of primitive Christianity, too, would hardly have become possible without similar apocalyptic tendencies in the Diaspora. There were already Messianic disturbances in Cyrenaica in AD 73, and in the great rebellion of AD 114–117, which involved all the Jews of Egypt and Cyprus as well as the Pentapolis – i.e. all the old Ptolemaic areas – the Jews under their pseudo-Messiah Andreas Lukuas caused the Romans the greatest difficulties.[897] We should not be misled by the fact that in Josephus, who was completely dependent on the imperial favour, and in Philo, the brother of the Jewish Rothschild of his time, the eschatological element is concealed, even if it is not completely absent.[898] The eschatological expectation of the end was above all a matter for the lower classes, who bore the whole burden of an insecure social existence. Without preparation from Jewish apocalyptic literature in Greek, the origin of the later Christian apocalypses is hardly conceivable.

The fact that both early Pharisaism and the Greek-speaking Diaspora knew an intensive eschatological hope with a picture of history to match would finally also explain the apocalyptic foundation of the thought of Paul. The question of the apparent parallels between Paul and Essene literature is often discussed today.[899] The similarity is probably to be derived from the fact that Essenism and Pharisaism, which both went back to the same Hasidic root, shared a whole series of theological views, despite their bitter opposition. The constellation created by the repudiation of the Hellenistic reform and the Maccabean revolt thus was a fundamental influence in determining the religious situation of Palestine in the New Testament period, and had considerable effect on the Diaspora.

IV

The 'Interpretatio Graeca' of Judaism and the Hellenistic Reform Attempt in Jerusalem

There are many aspects to the question of the 'encounter between Judaism and early Hellenism'. In the last chapter we considered it in the theological perspective of Jewish wisdom and early apocalyptic; now, in conclusion, we are to consider it from the standpoint of the Greeks. An attempt will be made to build a bridge towards the 'self-understanding' of those Jewish 'Hellenists' who, between 175 and 164 BC, attempted to dissolve Judaism completely into Hellenistic civilization, but failed because of their own lack of unity and the political obtuseness of Antiochus IV.

1. The Jews as Philosophers, according to the Earliest Greek Witnesses

Down to Posidonius, i.e. as far as the antisemitic movement which set in at the end of the second century BC,[1] the earliest Greek witnesses, for all their variety, present a relatively uniform picture: they portray the Jews as a people of 'philosophers'. From this it is clear that the intellectual 'encounter' between Greeks and Jews did not take place only from the Jewish side, and that the Greeks took an interest in meeting this people with its religion that sounded so 'philosophical'.[2]

Mention should first be made of *Hecataeus of Abdera*, who wrote an idealistic work about Egypt in the time of Ptolemy I, presumably before the end of the fourth century BC, in which he also went into the exodus of the Jews and the priestly state founded by Moses.[3]

> 'He chose the most educated, and those most capable of leading the whole people and made them priests.' He then entrusted them with temple worship, legislation and 'supervision' (φυλακή) of the keeping of the law. 'Thus at no time did the Jews have a king; rather, the leadership of the people was entrusted to those who were best in insight and virtue (τὴν δὲ τοῦ πλήθους προστασίαν δίδοσθαι διὰ παντὸς τῷ δοκοῦντι τῶν ἱερέων φρονήσει καὶ ἀρετῇ προέχειν) among the priests. These they named high priests and regarded them as messengers of the commands of God' (ἄγγελον . . . τῶν τοῦ θεοῦ προσταγμάτων) (§5, 6).

Thus Hecataeus described the Jewish state as a true 'aristocracy' along the lines of the Platonic utopian state. The priests here corresponded to the perfect 'watchmen' or 'regents' in Plato's *Republic*.[4] As he also stresses the Jews' xenophobia, their zeal for war and their just distribution of land, one might suppose that he was already thinking of a comparison with the Sparta that Plato so treasured. Such a comparison was expressed later in the legend of the affinity between Jews and Spartans. This is especially likely as, according to Hecataeus, the forbears of the Spartans, Danaus and Cadmus, emigrated to Greece at the same time as Moses and the Jews came to Palestine (F6, 2). Despite the rationalism that he learnt from Pyrrho, he presents the Jewish picture of God in a positive way. It corresponded to philosophical ideals, following the criticism of polytheism by Xenophanes:

> He (Moses) did not make any kind of picture of gods, as he did not believe that God was in human form; rather, the heaven, which surrounds the earth, was alone God and Lord of all.
>
> Ἄγαλμα δὲ θεῶν τὸ σύνολον οὐ κατεσκεύασε διὰ τὸ μὴ νομίζειν ἀνθρωπόμορ-φον εἶναι τὸν θεόν, ἀλλὰ τὸν περιέχοντα τὴν γῆν οὐρανὸν μόνον εἶναι θεὸν καὶ τῶν ὅλων κύριον (§5).

The fragments of Hecataeus preserved by Josephus, the authenticity of which is disputed, and which depict individual Jews as wise, enlightened men, also show enlightened monotheistic tendencies.[5] Only a short time later there follows the most significant pupil of Aristotle, *Theophrastus*, who in his work 'On Piety' – again probably dependent on Hecataeus – expressly terms the Jews 'philosophers':[6]

> For this whole period – as they are a race of *philosophers* – they discourse on the divine, observe the stars at night, look up to them and call to them in their prayers.
>
> κατὰ δὲ πάντα τοῦτον τὸν χρόνον, ἅτε φιλόσοφοι τὸ γένος ὄντες, περὶ τοῦ θείου μὲν ἀλλήλοις λαλοῦσι. τῆς δὲ νυκτὸς τῶν ἄστρων ποιοῦνται τὴν θεωρίαν, βλέποντες εἰς αὐτὰ καὶ διὰ τῶν εὐχῶν θεοκλυτοῦντες.

As with Hecataeus, we have here the conception that the Jews worship heaven as the highest God, a view which was particularly illuminating for Aristotelian philosophy, as in it the firmament was regarded as an expression of divine perfection (see above, pp. 235f.). This view probably went back through Jewish belief in God to a designation for God, popular in the Persian period, as 'God of heaven'. It was continued in ancient reports about the Jews down to the Roman satirists.[7] According to Bidez/Cumont, Hecataeus and Theophrastus were dependent in turn on Democritus, but this supposition is extremely questionable, as we have no indication that Democritus made any statements about the Jews.[8]

A little later, and quite independent of this line of tradition, is a report in the *Indica* of *Megasthenes*, who was ambassador of Seleucus I Nicator to India between 304/3 and 292 BC: [9]

> Everything that was taught among the ancients about *nature* is also said among the *philosophers* outside Greece, first among the Indians by the Brahmans, and then in Syria by the so-called *Jews*.
>
> ἅπαντα μέντοι τὰ περὶ φύσεως εἰρημένα παρὰ τοῖς ἀρχαίοις λέγεται καὶ παρὰ τοῖς ἔξω τῆς Ἑλλάδος φιλοσοφοῦσι, τὰ μὲν παρ' Ἰνδοῖς ὑπὸ τῶν Βραχμάνων, τὰ δὲ ἐν τῇ Συρίᾳ ὑπὸ τῶν καλουμένων Ἰουδαίων.

As Megasthenes gives a detailed account of Brahman 'philosophy' and here again presents their doctrine of the origin of the world and of nature with Stoic elaborations, we may assume that he also knew some basic teachings of the Jews and interpreted them in a similar way. *Clearchus of Soli*, a pupil of Aristotle, is in turn dependent on him; in what is surely a fictitious account he describes the meeting of Aristotle with a Jewish 'wise man' in Asia Minor and makes the master himself give the following report:

> 'It would be too tedious to report it all, but those features which call for admiration (θαυμασιότητα) and show 'love of wisdom' (φιλοσοφίαν) deserve to be mentioned. Here I will give the impression of telling . . . wonders, which are like dreams (θαυμαστὸν ὀνείροις ἴσα) . . . By origin the man was a *Jew* from Coele Syria. These are descendants of the *philosophers* in India (ἀπόγονοι τῶν ἐν Ἰνδοῖς φιλοσόφων).
>
> Among the Indians, it is said, the philosophers are called Calani, but among the Syrians, taking the name of the area, they are called Jews. For the territory in which they live is called Judea (see above, pp. 20ff.). The name of their city is very exceptional: Jerusalem . . . This man had friendly dealings with many and travelled from the interior of the land to the coast. He was a *Greek* not only in his language but also in his soul. As he visited the same places during our stay in Asia and held converse with us and some other learned men, he tested their wisdom (πειρώμενος αὐτῶν τῆς σοφίας). As one who had met with many educated men, however, it was rather he who contributed from his (intellectual) store.' Thus far the quotation from Clearchus. Josephus adds: 'This is what Aristotle said in Clearchus, and moreover he treated the great and marvellous duration and moderation of the Jew in the life that he leads (πολλὴν καὶ θαυμάσιον καρτερίαν τοῦ Ἰουδαίου ἀνδρὸς ἐν τῇ διαιτῇ καὶ σωφροσύνην διεξιών)'.[10]

Since Clearchus in his writing 'On Sleep' deals above all with 'para-psychological phenomena' which are meant to demonstrate the independence of the soul over against the body, H. Lewy assumes that the Jew whose wisdom is praised so highly by Clearchus' Aristotle is identical with a miracle worker who appears alongside other witnesses in this writing of Clearchus'. With a wand, this man made the soul of a youth depart from him and return again, and moreover needed no sleep, but was nourished by the rays of the sun. Lewy argues that since such magical practices cannot be attributed to a Jew in the second half of the fourth century BC, this must be a pure fantasy.[11]

Now despite the many miraculous things with which Clearchus deals in his tractate, it remains open whether the Jew is to be identified with this particular hypnotizer. It is, however, probable that he too had 'supernatural' gifts, perhaps the art of interpreting dreams, which Posidonius ascribed to the Jews one hundred and fifty years later. It is also almost certain that here we have a stereotyped theme of Hellenistic literature, the encounter of a Greek with a 'barbarian philosopher', in which the non-Greek partner shows his superiority. Thus Aristoxenus of Tarentum, a pupil of Aristotle who claims, among other things, that Pythagoras was a pupil of Zoroaster, asserts that in Athens Socrates met with an Indian philosopher who was far superior to him by virtue of his knowledge of divine things. The counter-movement of oriental religions thus began on this basis.[12] However, the Prayer of Nabonidus, the Daniel narratives and the work of Artapanus, which was composed at most a century later (see above, n. II, 262), show that in the first half of the third century BC, when Clearchus composed his tractate, there may very well have been Jewish miracle workers. H. Lewy overlooks the fact that – apart from the nonsensical information about the Indian Calani, which represents an elaboration of the statements of Megasthenes – the account also contains information which is to be taken completely seriously, like the Hebrew name of Jerusalem in contrast to the form Hierosolyma, which is customary else-where, and the name of the province Judea. This points to an encounter with a Palestinian. Why should Clearchus not have known a Jewish miracle-worker coming from Palestine, whom he then introduces into his tractate as partner in a conversation with Aristotle?

Still in the third century BC, the Alexandrian biographer Hermippus, who also gave himself out to be a 'Peripatetic' (see pp. 163f. above), asserted that Pythagoras had 'imitated the opinions of the Jews and Thracians and had transferred them to himself' (τὰς Ἰουδαίων καὶ Θρᾳκῶν δόξας μιμούμενος καὶ μεταφέρων εἰς ἑαυτόν), a view which was not only readily taken up by the Alexandrian Jews, but also handed on further by the Greeks.[13] Only the Maccabean revolt and the bitterness fostered thereafter on both sides, together with the increasing Alexandrian antisemitism in the second half of the second century – a reaction to the political and military influence of the Jews in Ptolemaic Egypt after the time of Philometor – put an end to this positive presentation of the Jews.

Nevertheless, amazement at the founder of the Jewish religion and the original teaching of Moses continued in the Syrian Posidonius of Apamea (c. 135–50 BC). As E. Norden and I. Heinemann have demonstrated in-dependently, following T. Reinach, R. Reitzenstein and J. Geffcken,[14] his report is contained in the positive portrait of Moses given by Strabo, though their view has again been disputed recently.

According to Strabo, Moses, an Egyptian priest, went with his followers to Judea, because he was not content with Egyptian religion. 'Neither the

Egyptians nor the Libyans had a correct view of the deity, when they portrayed it like wild beasts or cattle; but even the Greeks, who formed their gods in human shape, were wrong. For only this one being is God, which embraces us all, earth and sea, and which we call heaven, world and the nature of being (εἴη γὰρ ἓν τοῦτο μόνον θεὸς τὸ περίεχον ἡμᾶς ἅπαντας καὶ γῆν καὶ θάλατταν, ὃν καλοῦμεν οὐρανὸν καὶ κόσμον καὶ τὴν τῶν ὄντων φύσιν). Now how could anyone with understanding dare to form a picture of this being that was like any of the things with us? Rather, the making any kind of picture has to be abandoned; one must mark off a holy precinct and here in a worthy cult-place establish worship without images. Incubation must also be used, both for one's own help and for that of others. The person who lives morally and in righteousness may always expect good of God, whether as a gift or as a sign, but not the others.' There follows an account of the foundation of Jerusalem by Moses in the Jewish hills. By the renunciation of weapons and proper worship – a clear attack on the Hasmonean policy of force – he also wins over a large number of those living in the country. 'His followers remained for a time following the same customs, for they were righteous and truly god-fearing men. But afterwards superstitious (δεισιδαιμόνων, see n. 30 below) and ambitious men succeeded to the status of the priesthood. The consequence of the superstition was that now the withholding of the enjoyment of certain foods . . . the circumcision of men and the excision of women and other such practices were adopted. The rule of the powerful led to a policy of exploitation. For the apostates damaged their own and the adjoining territory, and those who remained true to the rulers seized alien land and subjected a large part of Syria and Phoenicia.[15]

The last part of this report clearly alludes to the struggles within Judaism in connection with the Hellenistic reform attempt and the subsequent Maccabean revolt, followed by the Hasmonean expansion. It is remarkable here that the origin of an 'apostasy' within Judaism is grounded on the later introduction of superstitious customs, like food laws and circumcision. Perhaps this detail – as E. Bickermann supposed – is connected with the views of the radical reformers in Jerusalem after 175 BC, who believed that the originally good legislation of Moses had been falsified by 'superstitious' additions:[16] 'The commandment is ambivalent; it is either from the gods or from men.' Posidonius also knew that the reform attempt brought only misfortune to the Jews and to neighbouring territories.[17] At the same time, this theory fitted admirably into his own ideas of the good lawgivers and founders of olden times and the later decline, which he discusses in connection with his report on the Jews: 'For this is so natural, and is common to both Greeks and barbarians.'[18] Another striking feature is his account of the Jewish doctrine of God, in which he himself is again probably dependent on Hecataeus of Abdera. However, he expands this portrayal of the worship of 'heaven which embraces the earth' (see above, p. 256) in a Stoic fashion: the Phoenician and Syrian conception of Ba'al Šāmēm could well stand behind his picture of God (see below, pp.296f.). For him the conception of God held by the Jewish lawgiver and the philosophers is the same: 'The God of Moses is the God of Posidonius.'[19] These connections also explain, in part, why the philosopher who parted company with contemporary Judaism could still exercise such profound influence, partly indirectly but more indirectly through the diatribe, on Jewish philosophy of religion.[20] Even *Varro* (116–27 BC) is dependent on Posidonius' reports of the God of Moses. We have several indications from Augustine, and in one instance from J. Lydus:

> '*Varro . . . deum Iudaeorum Iovem putavit, nihil interesse censens quo numine nuncupetur, dum eadem res intellegatur.*' Augustine supplements this statement: '*nos autem Iovem colimus, de quo ait Maro: "Iovis omnia plena (Eclog. 3, 60)." Id est omnia vivificantem spiritum. Merito ergo et Varro Iovem opinatus est coli a Iudaeis, quia dicit per prophetam, coelum et terram ego impleo (Jer.23.24)*'.[21]

The way in which Augustine combines the quotation from Jeremiah and the quotation from Virgil, shaped by the famous verse of Aratus from the beginning of his *Phainoumena*, with Varro's statement about the Jews, shows that there were points of contact between certain Old Testament/Jewish conceptions of God and Stoic views. On occasion these made possible the Stoicizing of the Jewish concept of God and the Judaizing of the Stoic concept (see p.148f. above). Varro also knew – presumably from Posidonius – the Jewish divine name Iao: he says it is given in the 'secret writings of the Chaldeans', i.e. in the syncretistic Jewish magical literature; its magical significance must therefore already have been known at the beginning of the first century BC.[22] Finally, like Hecataeus and Posidonius, he praises the fact that in worshipping God the Jews have no images:

> *dicit etiam antiquos Romanos plus annos centum et septuaginta deos sine simulacro coluisse. 'Quod si adhuc, inquit, mansisset, castius dii obseruarentur.' Cui sententiae suae testem adhibet inter cetera etiam gentem Iudaeam.*[23]

The writing περὶ ὕψους presumably comes from the first half of the first century AD, from the hand of an unknown rhetorician who was possibly a pupil of the Palestinian Theodore of Gadara (c. 30 BC), and also refers very positively to the 'lawgiver of the Jews' (θεσμοθέτης):

> He was no insignificant man, especially as he had a worthy conception of the power of the deity and described it well, yet at the very beginning of his law he wrote 'God said'; and what did he say? 'Let there be light, and there was light; let the earth be, and it was.'

Thus he represents Moses as the recipient of divine laws in the middle of a series of quotations from Homer, indeed he puts him above Homer, since Moses – in contrast to the Homeric theomachy – gave worthy expression to the divine activity.[24] About a century later the Hermetica then fused the account of creation with Platonic philosophy.[25]

2. The Identification of the God of Judaism with Greek Conceptions of God

However, this positive verdict on the Jews in early writings and the identification of their concept of God with the philosophical monotheism of, say, the Stoa, had its dangers. If Hecataeus, Manetho and Posidonius were struck by the segregation of the Jews from foreign peoples as a special peculiarity, and if this peculiarity later became an irremovable stumbling block,[26] the Greeks must similarly have found the exclusiveness of the Jewish conception of God strange and presumptuous. As the *'interpretatio graeca'* of foreign gods shows, they had long been ready to accept alien forms of the divine into their pantheon, and no exception was made even for the gods of Palestine. For the most part, the new masters gave the old Semitic gods Greek names;[27] in more exceptional cases they paid due reverence to them in their old form.[28] But where they raised themselves through philosophically-trained thought beyond the naive polytheistic nature religion of the simple people and regarded the 'spiritual' Jewish worship of God, devoid of images, with goodwill, there was nevertheless no understanding of the way in which this religion was anchored in the law in a way which excluded all other forms of religious practice, and was inseparably bound up with the Jewish people and its history. According to Josephus, *c. Ap.* 2, 258, the rhetorician Apollonius Molon (ambassador from Rhodes to Rome in 81 BC) criticized the fact that 'we do not accept those who put forward other conceptions of God (ὅτι μὴ παραδεχόμεθα τοὺς ἄλλαις προκατειλημμένους δόξαις περὶ θεοῦ)'.[29] Thus even before the emergence of Christianity, there was never an intensive concern on the part of non-Jews with the Jewish history written in the Septuagint. Rather, the charge of superstition was never far away,[30] and the history and law of the Jews were presented in the utmost distortion even by capable and critical historians like Tacitus.[31] Even Posidonius showed clearly that he rejected the Jewish religion practised in his time as superstition. The universal religious attitude of learned men which developed in the Hellenistic period through *'theocrasy'* regarded *the different religions as in the end only manifestations of the one deity*.[32] Thoughtful Greeks like Hecataeus, and later Posidonius, may have acknowledged Jewish belief in its unfalsified form to be a high stage of spirituality, and Greek philosophy with an interest in religion had long been on the way to monotheism,[33] but they found the claim of Jewish religion that it embodied the one revelation of the one God, to the exclusion to all else, to be inacceptable. In their view the – relative – truth of even the Jewish faith could be expressed only in a *universal* way without national and historically conditioned limitations.

We find this attitude in a polemically heightened and late, but typical, form in Celsus (second half of the second century AD):

'[They] thought that there was one God called the Most High (᾿Υψιστον), or Adonai, or the Heavenly One (Οὐράνιον), or Sabaoth, or however they like to call this world (τόνδε τὸν κόσμον), and they acknowledged nothing more . . . It makes no difference whether one calls the supreme God (τὸν ἐπὶ πᾶσι θεόν) by the name ['Zeus'] used among the Greeks, or by that, for example, used among the Indians, or by that among the Egyptians.' In another place, referring to Herodotus I, 131, he asserts: 'It makes no difference whether we call Zeus the Most High (᾿Υψιστος), or Zen, or Adonai, or Sabaoth, or Amoun like the Egyptians, or Papaeus like the Scythians. Moreover, they (the Jews) would certainly not be holier than other people because they are circumcised; the Egyptians and Colchians did this before they did.'[34]

The same idea appears in a more positive form at about the same time in the saying of the oracle of Claros preserved by Cornelius Labeo, which identified Iao as the highest deity with Hades, Zeus, Helios and Dionysus Iao as the embodiment of the four seasons.[35] The conception of such a 'theocrasy', which combines the most different gods in one deity and regards the names that have been given to them in history as 'noise and smoke', was nothing new for educated Greeks; it goes far back into the pre-Christian Hellenistic period. We find it as early as Terentius Varro, who has already been mentioned, in the first half of the first century BC. For him, Iao and Jupiter formed one deity, 'nihil interesse censens quo nomine nuncupetur'.[36] The fact that this is no chance phenomenon, but a fundamental approach in which Varro was following the learned world of his time and in which he was dependent on his oriental teachers, the Stoicizing Platonist Antiochus of Ashkelon and the Platonizing Stoic Posidonius of Apamea, is attested to – again via Augustine – by Varro himself:

Hi omnes dii deaeque sit unus Iupiter, sive sint, ut quidam volunt, omnia ista partes eius sive virtutes eius, sicut eis videtur, quibus eum (sc. Iovem) placet esse mundi animum, quae sententia velut magnorum multumque doctorum est.[37]

The scholiast Servius points out that here we have a doctrine of the Stoa which passed over into the general consciousness of antiquity: et sciendum Stoicos dicere unum esse deum, cui nomina variantur pro actibus et officiis.[38] In essentials this idea probably goes back to Zeno, the Graeco-Phoenician founder of the Stoa: 'There exists one God and spirit and fate and Zeus, who is also named with many other names.'[39] One may add that Orphic circles also propagated similar ideas from a relatively early period and expressed them in a series of hymns. This 'monotheizing' tendency and the strict way of life practised by Orphic conventicles with their esoteric, didactic house-worship devoid of sacrifice early aroused the interest of Jewish circles in Egypt who, as Aristobulus and Artapanus show, made Orpheus a witness to the truth of the Mosaic law.[40]

This tendency towards theocrasy, which grew continually in the Hellenistic period and was furthered by popular philosophy, did not remain without consequences even for Judaism. One example of this is provided by the earliest account of the appearance of Jews in Rome in 139 BC, which has been preserved for us by the Roman compiler Valerius Maximus:

Cn. Cornelius Hispalus praetor peregrinus. M. Popilio Laenate, L. Calpurnio consulibus, edicto Chaldaeos citra decimum diem abire ex urbe atque Italia iussit, levibus et ineptis ingeniis fallaci siderum interpretatione quaestuosam mendaciis suis caliginem inicientes. Idem Iudaeos, qui Sabazi Iovis cultu Romanos inficere mores conati erant, repetere domos suas coegit.[41]

It is hard to decide here whether we simply have a change of 'Iao Sabaoth' into 'Iupiter Sabazius' by the unknown annalist and informant of Valerius Maximus,[42] or whether, as is supposed by F. Cumont, R. Reitzenstein, A. D. Nock, etc.,[43] syncretistic Jews were already seeking to propagate their mixed cult from Judea and Asia Minor in Rome at that time. There are some features which support the latter possibility. At the same time or slightly earlier, a Jewish delegation sent by Simon the Maccabee, coming from Jerusalem, was honoured in Rome by the Senate and was able to obtain from the Roman consul Lucius (Calpurnius Piso?) a number of commendatory letters to those Hellenistic states which had a Jewish Diaspora, letters which among other things asked for the delivery of fugitive members of the Hellenist party to the high priest Simon. R. Reitzenstein calls attention to the possibility that an expulsion of heterodox Jews from Rome followed as the result of this Palestinian embassage. E. Bickermann supposed that the Jews immigrated via Southern Italy and were sent back there again.[44] We know further that two thousand Jewish families from the Babylonian Diaspora were settled as cleruchs in Phrygia by Antiochus III before 200 BC. After the peace of Apamea in 188 BC, these Jews came under Pergamene rule, which furthered the cult of Sabazius, who was native to Phrygia and was closely associated with Rome.[45] Furthermore, at a relative early stage Jewish-pagan mixed cults developed in Asia Minor in which, *inter alia*, the designation 'hypsistos', beloved of both Jews and Gentiles, occupied a central position (see below, nn. 264-6). In general, pre-Maccabean Judaism was more open to its non-Jewish environment than after the religious distress and the struggle for freedom which followed. Its effects also extended to the Diaspora, especially as the Hasmoneans sought to exercise their influence there (see above, pp. 100f.).

Whatever events may stand behind the note of Valerius Maximus, it shows how the Jewish God could be regarded by the Romans – and probably not only by them – as a kind of Zeus-Jupiter with an oriental orgiastic flavour. A parallel to this is the identification of Yahweh-Iao and Dionysus which keeps recurring in ancient writers. It perhaps played a certain role in the religious policy of Ptolemy IV Philopator towards the Jews after his victory at Raphia in 217 BC.[46] We later find references to it in Tacitus, Plutarch, the oracle of Claros (see above, n.35) and Johannes Lydus. An identification with other deities, e.g. Kronos-Saturn, may also have taken place, but we cannot trace it any longer.[47]

However, we find this tendency to 'theocrasy' including the Jewish God not only among the Greeks but also in one or two particular Jewish witnesses. Thus two Jewish inscriptions from the Ptolemaic period are to be found in Redesīeh in Apollonopolis Magna (Edfu) in Upper Egypt:

> God be praised, Theodotus (son of) Dorion, a Jew, saved from the sea.
> Θεοῦ εὐλογία | Θε(υ)όδοτος Δωρίωνος | ᾽Ιουδαῖος σωθεὶς ἐκ πε/λ(άγ)ους
> Ptolemy, son of Dionysius, a Jew, thanks God.
> ᾽Ευλογεῖ τὸν θεὸν | Πτολεμαῖος | Διονυσίου | ᾽Ιουδαῖος.[48]

These come, however, not from some synagogue but from a temple to *Pan*, in which there are also a great many non-Jewish inscriptions, which were probably affixed by members of a Ptolemaic garrison. Significantly, these pagan inscriptions, which all run in the same way, mention the God – Pan Euhodos – by name,[49] whereas the two Jews speak only of 'Theos' in general terms. Nevertheless, 'Pan', as the universal God, was for them presumably identical with the God of the Jews. The grandson and translator of Ben Sira could likewise say, following the spirit of his time: τὸ πᾶν ἐστιν αὐτός (Sir. 43.27b; see above, pp. 146, 147).

The Letter of Aristeas shows that this tendency towards an assimilation of the Jewish concept of God to the Greek, universalist conception of God was to be found not only among Jews in a remote garrison in Upper Egypt, but also in circles who cannot be suspected of syncretism or assimilation. Here the alleged writer of the letter of King Ptolemy II Philadelphus explains the universal Jewish conception of God:

> Since, as I have been at pains to discover, the God who gave them their law is the God who maintains your kingdom. They worship the same God – the Lord and Creator of the Universe, as all other men, as we ourselves, O king, though we call him by different names, such as Zeus or Dis. This name was very appropriately bestowed upon him by our first ancestors, in order to signify that He through whom all things are endowed with life and come into being, is necessarily the ruler and lord of the Universe (Ps. Aristeas 15/16).

> . . . τὸν γὰρ πάντων ἐπόπτην καὶ κτίστην θεὸν οὗτοι σέβονται, ὃν καὶ πάντες, ἡμεῖς δὲ, βασιλεῦ, προσονομάζοντες ἑτέρως Ζῆνα καὶ Δία· τοῦτο δ᾽οὐκ ἀνοικείως οἱ πρῶτοι διεσήμαναν, δι᾽ὃν ζωοποιοῦνται τὰ πάντα καὶ γίνεται, τοῦτον ἁπάντων ἡγεῖσθαί τε καὶ κυριεύειν.

Even if the Jewish author of the letter puts the speech in the mouth of a

Greek, the view presented here is astonishing. It clearly takes up a position on two fronts. On the one hand it goes against the Jewish radicals, who demanded a complete break with Greek education and culture and for whom all non-Jews were reprehensible, and on the other hand it shows the kind of judgment clear-sighted Greeks might make about the faith of the Jews in the face of growing Greek prejudice about the Jewish religion.[50] The author asserts that philosophically educated Greeks – as the Stoic etymology of $\Delta \acute{\iota} a$ and $Z\tilde{\eta}\nu a$ shows[51] – had long had a genuine monotheism. Granted, he later attacks idolatry, but his judgment on it is milder than that in other contemporary Jewish works. It is a sign of apostasy resting on folly and ignorance, which moreover is to be found in a more reprehensible form among native Egyptians than among Greeks.[52] Over against this, Judaism appears as the true 'philosophy' of ethical monotheism, with which clear-sighted Greeks, too, can only agree. In essentials, at this point the earlier judgment of individual Greek writers about the Jews as 'philosophers' is taken up and given the status of a principle: 'Judaism is a combination of a universal philosophy with the idea of monotheism.'[53] This provides the aim of the work: 'the synthesis between Judaism and Hellenism'.[54]

We can see that this is not the view of an individualist, but a relatively widespread attitude, from the way in which Aristobulus, a little earlier, quotes the Jewish Testament of Orpheus and the verses of Aratus. In their original form these also contained the names 'Dis' or 'Zeus', but they are replaced in Aristobulus by 'Theos' for special reasons.[55]

> We have interpreted the passage as necessary by removing the names 'Dis' and 'Zeus' which occur in the poems, since their meaning relates to God. That is why we express them in this way. We believe it right to attach this to the questions already raised. For all philosophers agree that one must have holy concepts of God, and this is something with which our community is most concerned.
>
> Καθὼς δὲ δεῖ, σεσημάγκαμεν περιαιροῦντες τὸν διὰ τῶν ποιημάτων Δία καὶ Ζῆνα · τὸ γὰρ τῆς διανοίας αὐτῶν ἐπὶ θεὸν ἀναπέμπεται, διόπερ οὕτως ἡμῖν εἴρηται . . . πᾶσι γὰρ τοῖς φιλοσόφοις ὁμολογεῖται διότι δεῖ περὶ θεοῦ διαλήψεις ὁσίας ἔχειν, ὃ μάλιστα παρακελεύεται καλῶς ἡ καθ' ἡμᾶς αἵρεσις
> Euseb., *Pr. Ev.* 13, 12, 7f., GCS 43, 2, 195, ed. Mras.

Here Aristobulus agrees with the author of Ps. Aristeas in granting that when the Greek poets and philosophers speak of 'Zeus', they mean the true God. Yet at the same time he displays a critical attitude. He will not himself countenance this terminology, and will certainly not adopt it himself, since as a Jew he must take more care than any philosopher to use 'pure concepts' for God. Presumably he saw in the use of 'pagan' names for God the danger of falsifying his own picture of God. From this discussion we may conclude that at about the time when Yahweh was identified with Olympian Zeus in Jerusalem, in Greek-educated circles of Jews in Alexandria there were reflections on the problem of the relationship between the God of Israel and the 'Zeus' of the philosophers. The Palestinian, priest, Pharisee and Hellenist Josephus, who about two hundred and fifty years later incorporated the Letter of Aristeas into the twelfth book of his *Antiquities*, did not, on the other hand, find anything to object to in the formula, but repeated it in a slightly altered form:

> They (the Jews) and we revere the God who has ordered all things, by naming him in an etymologically correct way (ἐτύμως) Zeus (Ζῆνα) and giving him his name on the basis of the fact that he breathes life (ζῆν) into all creatures (*Antt.* 12, 22).

Contra Apionem above all shows that Josephus' conception of God was not too far removed from the spiritual breadth of Ps. Aristeas:

> I will not now describe how the wisest men of the Greeks were taught by that man (Moses) how to think about God, but they have testified to God's nature in a fine and seemly way. For Pythagoras, Anaxagoras, Plato and the philosophers of the Stoa who followed them, like almost all philosophers, seem to have thought in this way about the nature of God.[56]

For Josephus, as for Aristobulus and for Ps. Aristeas, the God of the philosophers is fundamentally also the God of Israel.

Clearly, this was not the predominant attitude of Judaism towards conceptions of God current in the world of Greek culture. The negative, separationist tendency was very much stronger. But even here, Hellenistic forms of criticism of religion were used, like Euhemerism, which we find both in Palestine and in the Diaspora, as in the anonymous Samaritan (see pp. 88ff. above) and in individual instances also in the Rabbinate. It can also be found in the earliest Jewish Sibyl, about 140 BC (3, 110–158), which makes use of Hesiod's *Theogony* interpreted along the lines of Berossus, in Artapanus, Ps. Heraclitus ch. 3, the Samaritan Theodotus, Philo and again in Josephus.[57] Even the 'demonological' explanation of pagan religions, beloved in apocalyptic circles, is not solely of Jewish origin, and has its analogies in Hellenistic thought.[58] Both these forms of criticism and the identification of the God of the philosophers with the God of the Bible were later taken over by the Christian apologists and the early church fathers. The syncretistic combination of Iao with pagan deities, on the other hand, lived on in the popular religion of the magical papyri.[59]

The refusal of the overwhelming majority of the Jewish people – even in the Diaspora[60] – to allow a transference of non-Jewish divine names – and thus also conceptions of God – to the God of Israel by theocrasy led relatively early to a unique consequence, connected with the growing suppression of the original divine name Yahweh-Iao and the mystery attached to it. As the abstract and universal terms used to replace it often, as with 'Kyrios', did not have any specific religious significance in the Greek world[61] or, like 'Theos', were too impersonal and weak[62] – Greek religion understood the term

'Theos' in a quite different way from Jewish, in an impersonal, predicative sense – the view emerged that the God of the Jews was 'nameless'. This amounted to a debasement. We meet this notion for the first time in the writing of the Samaritan community (or the 'Sidonians' in Shechem) to Antiochus IV in 166 BC (*Antt.* 12, 261, see n. 234 below). When this characterization appeared in the works of Graeco-Roman writers hostile to the Jews, the Jews made a virtue out of necessity and argued that the true God had to be nameless.[63] The alleged worship of 'heaven' already attested by Hecataeus, which was later changed by the satirist Juvenal into worship of the clouds, may be connected with this 'namelessness' in Jewish worship of God. Aristophanes had already characterized the indefinite worship of God by Socrates in a similar way. The last conclusion in this direction which went on to affect Christians was the charge of 'atheism'.[64]

We might ask whether these problems were not limited to the Greek-speaking Diaspora, leaving Jewish Palestine untouched. But the very reference to the 'nameless' God of the Samaritans shows that this is not the case. On the contrary, the problem of theocrasy between the God of Zion and the conceptions of God in the Hellenistic oriental environment became acute for the first time in Jerusalem, in the reform attempt by the Jewish Hellenists between 175 and 163 BC. The tendency towards 'theocrasy' was indissolubly bound up, for the Jews, with the pressure towards assimilation.

3. The Hellenistic Reform Attempt in Jerusalem and its Failure

(a) The Tobiads and Oniads

The reforms of Ezra and Nehemiah certainly repressed the influence of the religiously lax aristocratic circles who, for economic and cultural reasons, were likely to become assimilated to their non-Jewish neighbours, including the 'semi-Jewish' Samaritans, but they could not remove it altogether. From the middle of the third century BC there suddenly re-emerges an influential group with quite similar tendencies, the family of the Tobiads.[65] We find their supreme chief, the feudal lord Tobias, in the Zeno papyri, as the commander of a Ptolemaic cleruchy in the Ammanitis.[66] According to Josephus he was married to the sister of the high priest Onias II (*Antt.* 12, 160); presumably he was the most powerful man in Jewish society next to the high priest.

> He was very probably a descendant of the 'Tōbiyyā with whom the (high) priest 'Elyāšīb had intermarried and who had already made difficulties for Nehemiah by his great influence as an 'Ammonite official'.[67] It is hard to decide whether this Tobiah was a Judaizing Ammonite at the time of Nehemiah or a real Jew; he certainly did not come from a priestly family, as was sometimes supposed.[68] His name is a good Jewish one, and in the third century the family had become completely Judaized and according to Josephus lived principally in Jerusalem (*Antt.* 12, 160).

On his visit to the citadel of Tobias in the Ammanitis in April/May of 259 BC, Zeno bought a seven-year-old slave girl called Sphragis. Tobias' steward, a Greek Nicanor from Cnidos, signed for the sale. Although at least one Jewish witness, '. . . son of Ananias' and also a soldier of Tobias, was present at the sale (l. 17), there is no evidence of any concern for Jewish sensibilities. Following the style of the time, the dating is given with reference to the priests of Alexander the Great and the divine ruling couple (θεῶν ἀδελφῶν, ll. 2, 13).[69] The reference to the θεοὶ ἀδελφοί may pass, as the agreement itself was concluded between two Greeks, but the correspondence between Tobias and the *dioikētēs* Apollonius which developed as a result of Zeno's visit shows a very lax view of the law on the part of the brother-in-law of the high priest himself. In one letter whose whole form expresses the attitude of the Jewish feudal lord,[70] he writes to the minister:

> If all goes well with you and all your company, and all else (goes) according to your (wishes), many thanks be to the *gods* (πο]λλὴ χάρις τοῖς θεοῖς, p. 2).

Certainly the letter, composed in unobjectionable Greek, is the work of the Greek secretary of the feudal lord, but Tobias, who determined its tone, was responsible for the content. It is no coincidence that a similar formula appears in Jewish letters from the military colony at Elephantine, which was under syncretistic influence.[71] The introduction is matched by the content of the letter: Tobias is sending on a eunuch and four slaves between seven and ten years old, of whom two were uncircumcised. As he expressly stresses their qualities as house slaves, one might assume that they had grown up for at least some time in his possession. So Tobias already seems to have been rather lax about the circumcision commandment, which also included slaves belonging to the house.[72] It became a stumbling-block in Jerusalem eighty years later (see above, n. II, 138, and below, p. 289). The sale of Jewish slaves abroad in pagan territory was also strictly forbidden for a Jew, at least in the post-Maccabean period.[73] It is significant how the indifference of Tobias to the Jewish law emerges in the few reports that we have of him. One could compare his attitude with that of Herod – who did, however, have to pay more attention to his environment, and its faithfulness to the law.[74]

We learn more from Josephus about the brilliant career of his son Joseph and his grandson Hyrcanus.[75] This report of Josephus must be used with care, but it is partly confirmed by the Zeno papyri and the archaeological investigations at 'Araq el Emir. We need not go into detail here about the reasons for the rapid rise of Joseph to become general tax farmer of 'Syria and Phoenicia', or at least for Palestine (see above, pp. 98f.).

> Josephus' chronology, which puts the whole story in the time after the conquest of Palestine by Antiochus III, should be corrected. This contradicts its content, which is exclusively oriented towards the Ptolemaic royal house. The temporal sequence proposed by Tcherikover and others

comes nearer to reality.[76] According to it, the refusal of Onias II to pay tribute falls into the time towards the end of the third Syrian war, when Seleucus II Callinicus undertook an at first successful counter-thrust to the south as a result of which Orthosia and Damascus went over to his side in 242/41 and were able to assert themselves successfully. However, his real attack on Palestine failed, and he made peace approximately on the basis of the *status quo* (cf. Dan. 11.9). The visit of Ptolemy III Euergetes to Jerusalem after the third Syrian war, reported by Josephus in *c. Ap.* 2, 48, is perhaps connected with the new ordering of circumstances there. The twenty-two years during which Joseph occupied the office of general tax farmer (*Antt.* 12, 186) would then best be placed in the period between about 239 BC and 217 BC, when Ptolemy Philopator presumably reordered the administration on his lengthy visit to the province after the victory at Raphia (see above, p. 8). The successful mission of Hyrcanus, the youngest son of Joseph, to Egypt to celebrate the birth of the successor to the throne could then perhaps be transferred to 210 BC, when Ptolemy V Epiphanes was born. Hyrcanus then was probably given supreme command over the cleruchy in Transjordania to protect the border against the Arabs, and incurred the enmity of his family in Jerusalem as a result.[77]

The romance about the Tobiad Joseph and his sons was probably composed in Alexandria in the second half of the second century BC. On the one hand it contains such gross errors that one must assume that a considerable space of time had elapsed since the events described, but on the other hand it has such exact information that it is probable that it used good sources, like a family chronicle of the Tobiads. One might suppose a Hellenized Jew to have been the author, one who had not been occupied with the religious renewal movement after the Maccabean revolt.[78] The tendency of the work is completely secular, with a nationalist bias (*Antt.* 12, 175–185), and it is therefore most comparable to the book of Esther in its Hebrew form. A central position is occupied by the fabulous success of its hero at the court of Ptolemy and especially at the royal table, together with delight at the extraordinary riches there. The regulations about purity and about the eating of food that play so great a role in the narratives of Daniel – which also takes the form of a court history – and Tobit, simply do not exist for the author.[79] The law is only given a marginal mention on two occasions: in the case of Joseph, when he is involved in an affair with a dancer in Alexandria, and in the case of Hyrcanus, when he praises the king for his generosity.[80] Nevertheless, even the Tobiad romance has its slant. In conclusion, it says of the death of Joseph:

A noble and generous man who led the Jewish people from poverty and miserable circumstances to a brighter way of life.[81]

ἀνὴρ ἀγαθός . . . καὶ μεγαλόφρων καὶ τὸν τῶν Ἰουδαίων λαὸν ἐκ πτωχείας καὶ πραγμάτων ἀσθενῶν εἰς λαμπροτέρας ἀφορμὰς τοῦ βίου καταστήσας.

Here we have a chief theme of the Jewish Hellenists, which matches their programme as it is sketched out in I Macc. 1.11: only close economic, political and cultural contact with the non-Jewish Hellenistic environment can improve the situation of the Jews in Palestine. Joseph is therefore glorified as the bringer of economic and cultural progress, who opened the door for backward and isolated Judea to enter the great world and introduced a higher standard of life for the people.[82] Here the narrator has transferred features of the great namesake of Joseph, who likewise found his fortune in Egypt, to the Tobiad,[83] though he leaves aside any religious motive. Thus the Tobiad narrative presents a court history in completely Hellenized form (see pp. 29ff. above). The darker foil against which the brilliance of Joseph shone out brightly was his uncle the high priest Onias II, who embodied conservative backwardness and was said to have brought his people to the brink of disaster through his ambition and the stubbornness of old age. He therefore rightly lost financial and political representation of the people to the king, the προστασία τοῦ λαοῦ (12, 161), to his wiser nephew and counterpart.[84]

One striking feature is that the young Joseph equips himself for his first journey to Alexandria with money which he has borrowed from friends in *Samaria*. The Tobiads seem to have maintained good relations with their kin in the northern tribes even in the third century BC, as at the time of Nehemiah and their ancestor Tobiah. This was an attitude which was opposed to the abruptly anti-Samaritan tendency of religious circles in Jerusalem. Religious indifference and friendship with the Samaritans apparently belonged together.[85]

In addition, Joseph and his family became the first Jewish bankers,[86] with a variety of capital interests and a slave as steward (οἰκονόμος) in Alexandria. The narrative mentions a reserve of three thousand talents deposited there (*Antt.* 12, 200). Generous bribes to the king and his friends saw that good relations with the court were not affected. In this way Ptolemaic 'high finance' had found an entry even into Jerusalem.[87] In this sense the Tobiads were 'Philhellenes and business men of the regular new Hellenistic type' (Rostovtzeff, *CAH* 7, 160), and under their influence the style of life in Jerusalem altered. Ben Sira is evidently in dispute with the new spirit that they introduced (see above, pp. 150f.).

At the same time, there is an indication of a split within the leading stratum of Judea, which made a decisive contribution to the later conflict under Antiochus IV: the struggle for power between the Tobiads and the high-priestly Oniads. The family of the high priest – as is shown by its last representatives Jason and Onias IV – was by no means untouched by Hellenistic influences (see above, pp. 73f. and below, n. 132), but as the Tobiads could constrict and endanger the position of the high priest through their support at the Ptolemaic and later at the Seleucid court, the latter had to seek stronger support from conservative circles. During his period of twenty-two years as general tax farmer, the Tobiad Joseph will have been the real holder of power in Jerusalem. However, he lost this office – perhaps after Raphia in 217 BC – and finally, towards 210 BC (?), the dispute between his son Hyrcanus and his older brothers came out into the open. At this point Simon II, 'the Just', the energetic son of the high priest Onias II, probably succeeded with the help of active religious groups which would include, e.g., a man like Ben Sira, in building up his position of power and again obtaining a strong position as high priest:

> He protected his people against plunder
> and fortified his city against the enemy (Sir. 50.4).

The right of *prostasia*, in the sense of the political representation of the people to the Seleucid king, was now probably again in the hand of the high priest. In the struggle against the pro-Ptolemaic Hyrcanus, who was asserting himself on the family's ancestral possession in Transjordania with the help of the military colony there, and was probably attempting to find a foothold in Jerusalem, too, he was a welcome colleague for the other sons of Joseph, who were now representing the interests of the Seleucids.[88] Although Jerusalem had suffered severely in the fifth Syrian war because of a twofold change of occupation and the bloody internal party struggles (see above, pp. 9f.), the final victory of Antiochus III at Paneion showed that Simon had estimated political developments correctly. The king showed his gratitude in the decrees preserved in Josephus, which were probably negotiated as 'royal marks of favour', through a Jewish delegation in Antioch (II Macc. 4.11). At the same time they may be regarded as the personal success of Simon II. They confirm the right of the Jews to live according to their ancestral laws, i.e. the Torah and the oral legal tradition associated with it (πολιτευέσθωσαν δὲ πάντες οἱ ἐκ τοῦ ἔθνους κατὰ τοὺς πατρίους νόμους, *Antt.* 12, 142). These laws were not, of course, laid down in detail, but complete internal autonomy was granted. Finally, the *gerousia* and the temple personnel including the 'scribes' (see p. 26 above) were completely freed from taxes, a tax remission for three years was proclaimed and the 'tribute' of the province of Judah was reduced by a third (see p. 28 above). The king also contributed generously to sacrifice and the restoration of the temple.[89]

> If the very first decree goes to meet the cultic and legal interests of the conservative circles under the leadership of Simon II, 'the Just', the second decree, which was probably formulated by the priests with the authorization of the king himself, shows this tendency to a still stronger degree. The 'ancestral law' is specified at a point which also affected non-Jews: the import of the meat and hides of unclean animals and even their breeding is prohibited, and only the flesh of pure animals, which have been slaughtered in traditional 'kosher' fashion, may be eaten. These ritual regulations must have restricted the economic significance of the city as a mercantile centre, for which the Tobiads strove, since foreign merchants would avoid a place with such restrictive regulations as far as possible. Thus the decree probably

has an indirect point, directed against the economic strength of the Tobiads.[90]

However, the development introduced by the Tobiad Joseph could not be halted. After the death of Simon II, a breach seems to have come about between the conservative and presumably weak Onias III and his brother Jason, who had a more marked leaning towards the Hellenists. Various references of Ben Sira indicate that the power of the high priest was seriously threatened (see p. 133 above). Presumably the similarly pro-Seleucid sons of Joseph could find a hearing in the court of Antioch more easily, in the long run, than the high priest, by virtue of their riches and their freedom from all the restrictive regulations of the law. In addition, the political constellation altered. The defeat of Antiochus III by the Romans at Magnesia and the weakening of the Seleucid kingdom by the oppressive peace of Seleucus IV Philopator (187–175 BC) allowed the Ptolemaic party to become strong again, and the high priest himself probably adopted a different political course. There was probably the hope of a re-conquest by the Ptolemies (see above, p. 10). One indication of this is provided by the *Legend of Heliodorus*: according to this Onias III fell out with the financial administrator of the temple (II Macc. 3.4), Simon, the priestly delegate of the Tobiads,[91] over the 'market administration' in Jerusalem – perhaps in connection with limitations on trade made in order to preserve the ritual purity of Jerusalem. Thereupon Simon denounced the high priest to Apollonius, son of Thraseas, the *stratēgos* of Coele Syria and Phoenicia, for having illegitimately concealed money in the temple (II Macc. 3.5f.). In the legendary report which now follows, Onias III makes his defence before the royal chancellor Heliodorus, who had hastened to Jerusalem, that it was only a question of 'some deposits belonging to widows and orphans, and also some money of Hyrcanus, son of Tobias, a man of very prominent position' (3.10f.). According to this, Onias seems to have been in a close business relationship with the Tobiad Hyrcanus in Transjordania, who had been such a vigorous supporter of the Ptolemies before the conquest of Palestine by Antiochus III, and presumably reverted to this position after Magnesia. That political accusations were also involved here – probably because of Ptolemaic tendencies – is indicated by the fact that Onias, again on the prompting of Simon, was compelled a little later to defend himself in Antioch, and was not able to return again.[92] At the same time, there seems to have been unrest and bloodshed in Jerusalem itself (II Macc. 4.3). The murder of the king by Heliodorus and the surprising accession of Antiochus IV Epiphanes, who had returned from Rome, created a completely new situation.

Excursus 6: Hyrcanus in Transjordania

According to Josephus, Hyrcanus constructed for himself an independent sphere of rule beyond the Jordan, in which he could assert himself against his brothers and the Arabs. He remained unmolested even by Antiochus III and Seleucus IV – presumably he subjected himself to them formally. Only when Antiochus IV Epiphanes came to power, and Hyrcanus feared that he would come into his grasp, did he put an end to his life (*Antt.* 12, 229–236). Hyrcanus' ambition was not, however, sated by his struggles with the Arabs and his brothers; he built a mighty palace (βᾶρις) from white stone, which he adorned with giant figures of animals. This last report has been confirmed by archaeological evidence: the building of Hyrcanus is identical with the monumental ruins of Qasr el-ʿAbd at ʿAraq el-Emir in the Wadi eṣ-Ṣir.[93] H. C. Butler, who undertook the first thorough investigations of the ruins with the Princeton University Expedition, clearly recognized its Hellenistic-oriental mixed style and dated it at the beginning of the second century BC, though he left open the possibility of an earlier date going back to the time of Ptolemy II Philadelphus (285–247).[94] He also decided the question which had been discussed for long beforehand, whether it was a fortress, a palace or a temple, in favour of a temple – with certain reservations.[95] E. Littmann, who edited the inscriptions on the same expedition, supported the interpretation that it was a temple even more emphatically,[96] and supposed that Josephus had kept silent about its character as a temple. This hypothesis was taken up later by Vincent,[97] who connected the site with the Ammonite 'Birta' of the Zeno papyri, and believed that the military colony of Tobias, in spite of its Jewish commander, had had a pagan temple here. H. Gressmann also believed the site to be a sanctuary, but he ascribed its foundation to Hyrcanus, whom he believed to have made messianic claims.[98] As it was thought improbable that a pagan or Jewish-schismatic temple would have been built in Tobiad territory, the palace hypothesis found an increasing number of supporters, despite the archaeological evidence unfavourable to it.[99] Partly the question was left unanswered, and a new more thorough archaeological investigation was looked for.[100] Here Watzinger pointed to kindred forms in Alexandria, Miletus and Samothrace. Albright attempted to solve the question with a compromise proposal: Hyrcanus wanted to build a mausoleum to the Tobiad family.[101] O. Plöger took Butler's observations further and conjectured a lake sanctuary in Egyptian style which served the military colony as a temple.[102] The excavations which P. W. Lapp carried out from 1961 in three stages were able to bring a certain amount of clarity into the dispute.[103] The first and most important result was to confirm Josephus' dating: all the buildings investigated, the Qasr itself, remains in the village of ʿAraq el Emir and the so-called smaller 'square building' between the caves and the Qasr, point to the early second century BC. It is thus as impossible to make an identification with the 'Birta' of the Tobias of the Zeno papyri as it is to assume that there was a special temple for the military colony.[104] A further important point which was seen by Butler but interpreted wrongly is the fact that the site at Qasr could not be properly completed. The lion frieze, the capitals of the pillars and the bosses on the stones are unequally finished. Hyrcanus did not succeed in completing his work.[105] The investigations also made the temple hypothesis more likely, and Lapp was able to build on the fundamental work of Amy.[106] The latter investigated a large number of Syrian temples from the Roman period and in so doing established a series of common structural elements. Chief among them were the tower-like corner rooms, which flank the entrance halls set on the narrow sides. In at least one of these rooms is a staircase leading to the towers, galleries or terraces. Hyrcanus' building also contains these typical forms.[107] So the excavator comes to the conclusion: 'The Qasr emerges as a unique example of the old Syrian temple type in the Hellenistic period.'[108] The cultic impression is further strengthened by the monumental lion frieze, though this has only rough-hewn animal capitals in the interior and the figures of two eagles; a similar impression is given by the size of the rectangular building (5′ 10″ by 4′ 9″) with its large basilica-like inner room supported by half pillars, a great staircase in the front left tower room, and by two doors east and south of the Qasr, together with the moat that surrounds the whole.[109] In addition to the pictures of animals already mentioned, the bas-relief of a great (6′ 10″ by 4′ 10″) predator was found, half lion and half leopard, which was probably intended to serve as the gargoyle for a spring and was elaborated on the basis of Greek models.[110] On the other hand, it is significant that portrayals of human beings are not found. The prohibition against images in Exod.20.4, which gained such great significance in the post-Maccabean period,[111] existed only to a limited degree for the builder; the dependence of the whole building even down to details on Hellenistic-Alexandrian and Syrian-oriental models is obvious.

There remains the question of the purpose of this temple site. It can hardly have been a pagan temple, as the building was in the centre of the neighbourhood which Hyrcanus himself used as a residence with its caves and its halls, and to which he gave the name 'Tyrus'.[112] The most probable thing is that Hyrcanus wanted to make the Qasr into *a temple to compete with Jerusalem*, a parallel to the sanctuaries of Elephantine, Leontopolis and Gerizim.[113]

> Probably at about the same time as the foundation of Leontopolis, the synagogue at Antioch also took on temple-like functions to which 'the successors of Antiochus IV' – presumably Demetrius I Soter, 162–150 BC – bequeathed the bronze vessels taken by Antiochus from the temple. Later kings also bequeathed valuable gifts to the growing community, with which 'the sanctuary was adorned' (τὸ ἱερὸν ἐξελάμπρυναν).[114] Presumably the Ptolemies, like the Seleucids, sought to make 'central sanctuaries' in their sphere of rule independent of 'apostate' Jerusalem, for the use of the Jews. Of course these efforts remained without real success.

Presumably Hyrcanus also saw a danger in the fact that his Jewish supporters were still cultically bound to the temple in Jerusalem, which was dominated by supporters of the Seleucids. The Deuteronomic command for centralization of the cult (Deut. 12) was still not strong enough to exclude centrifugal forces, even in Judea. How much this situation changed in the two centuries after the Maccabean period is shown by the fact that after the destruction of the temple in AD 70 no Jewish group attempted to erect a substitute temple anywhere else.[115] Nor should one overlook the fact that the animal figures gave the building something of a syncretistic stamp. Watzinger points out that the eagle figure is a symbol of the supreme Syrian goddess of heaven; possibly there is also a hint of this in Dan. 9.27b.[116] There seems to have been no dominant concern to establish any demarcation from Syrian non-Jewish cults in these circles which were open to Hellenistic civilization. In this context, reference might also be made to certain syncretistic influences among the military colonists in Elephantine, who were also gathered round a 'separatist temple'. That such tendencies were not completely lacking even in Judea could be indicated by the much-discussed Jehud coins, with a divine image on the winged chariot in the form of Triptolemus, which presumably comes from the late Persian or pre-Ptolemaic Diadochi period.[117] With the religious laxity of the Tobiads and the Greek education of Hyrcanus as stressed by Josephus (see above, p. 59), the spirit in which the reform attempt was made in Jerusalem presumably came to the fore.

According to Josephus, Hyrcanus is supposed to have ruled only seven years in Transjordania, 'the whole period of Seleucus' reign over Syria' (*Antt.* 12, 234). This is obviously incorrect, as Seleucus IV reigned for twelve years (187–175 BC), so that the seven years are probably to be interpreted in a different way. Hyrcanus must have begun to rule over the Transjordanian cleruchy and the region belonging to it substantially earlier (after 210 BC?, see p. 269 above). The complex of buildings realistically depicted by Josephus in 'Araq el Emir, which in addition to its monuments embraced a moat, great halls, parks and the excavation of caves (*Antt.* 12, 230–233),[118] will have taken more than seven years to build. As Hyrcanus (according to II Macc. 3.11) continued to maintain good relations with the high priest Onias III down to the end of the reign of Seleucus IV (see above, p. 272), so that he deposited considerable sums of money in the temple in Jerusalem, it can hardly be assumed that he would already have begun to build a competing temple at this point. However, when immediately after the accession of Antiochus IV Jason drove his brother Onias III from the office of high priest, and the sanctuary thus probably came into the hands of the pro-Seleucid party, i.e. his brother, who was hostile to him, Hyrcanus may have felt the necessity to erect a schismatic sanctuary, though he was unable to complete it. In 173 BC the last Oniad, Jason, also lost the high priesthood and fled to the Ammanitis, i.e. – as Momigliano already conjectured – to Hyrcanus.[119] From there, in 168 BC – about seven years after the accession of Antiochus IV – Jason attacked Jerusalem, but could not assert himself in the long run and had to retreat to Transjordania (II Macc. 5.5–9, see below, pp. 280f.). Now the rule of Hyrcanus probably collapsed as a result of the retributive attack of the king; Hyrcanus, who had grown old, committed suicide and Jason fled to the Nabateans and then to Egypt and Sparta.[120] Thus the seven years would be best put in the rule of Hyrcanus during the reign of Antiochus IV, and perhaps refer to the time it took to build the temple proper.

The report in I Macc. 5.13 that the Jews οἱ ὄντες ἐν τοῖς Τουβίου were attacked by the Syrians living round about and enslaved or killed shows that there were other anti-Seleucid, Jewish strongpoints in the area beyond the Jordan which went back to the Ptolemaic cleruchy of Tobias, while according to II Macc. 12.17, Judas rushed to the help of τοὺς λεγομένους Τουβιανοὺς Ἰουδαίους in their fortress (Χάραξ).[121] The Jews, probably descended from the former Ptolemaic cleruchies of the Zeno papyri (ἐν τῇ Τουβίου, CPJ I, 123, no. 2d, 16), had their own cavalry, and at least some of them had Greek names. Thus two cavalry officers Sosipater and Dositheus (II Macc. 12.19, 24 and 35: Δωσίθεος δέ τις τῶν Τουβιηνῶν)[122] gave powerful support to Judas Maccabaeus.[123] Consequently the struggle on the side of the Maccabees against the Seleucids must have been determined by more than religious motives; at the same time it can be seen against the background of the old political opposition between the Ptolemaic and the Seleucid party in Palestinian Judaism.

A figure like Hyrcanus seems to have adopted a very sovereign position against the Jewish religious tradition, though he did not become an apostate from Jewish faith. So all sorts of hypotheses have been associated with his person. H. Gressmann believed that messianic claims were made about him, on the basis of which he entered the Rabbinic tradition as the dying Messiah b. Joseph.[124] J. Klausner even made him the author of Koheleth, with reference to Koh. 2.4–10,[125] and O. Plöger attributed ambitious political plans to him: he envisaged the establishment of a neutral, independent buffer state between Egypt and Syria similar to the Nabatean kingdom.[126] Finally Tcherikover, following Momigliano, sought to understand Hyrcanus as one of the typical adventurer figures of the early Hellenistic period and points to Plutarch's accounts of the lives of Eumenes, Demetrius Poliorcetes and Pyrrhus.[127] But we find the best parallels to Hyrcanus in contemporary Judaism itself. Like his father Joseph, he is certainly a sign of the rise of sovereign individual personalities who go beyond the bounds of tradition. But in this capacity he stands in that extensive series of deliberate and vigorous figures whom we meet so often among the Jewish rulers and scholars, teachers of the law, founders of sects and apostates of the Hellenistic and Roman period: they include the Hasmoneans from Judas to Alexander Jannaeus, the Teacher of Righteousness and Simeon b. Seṭaḥ, Antipater, Herod and Agrippa I, Hillel and Shammai, Philo and Tiberius Julius Alexander, Simon bar Giora, Josephus and Johanan b. Zakkai, Akiba and Bar Kochba. They and many others are an expression of the overflowing vital and spiritual force of the Jewish people which produced its greatest historical influences in those centuries.

(b) The Hellenistic reform in Jerusalem down to the erection of the Acra at the beginning of 167 BC

The preliminaries to the Maccabean revolt and its deeper causes were described exhaustively in E. Bickermann's masterly monograph and the work of V. Tcherikover; in what follows, therefore, we are not so much concerned to give a comprehensive account as to attempt to concentrate on points where scholars still come to conflicting results.[128]

By travelling to Antioch, Onias III had played into the hands of his opponents in Jerusalem. His brother Jeshua-Jason, who probably had automatically taken over his position,[129] went over to the 'Hellenistic' side and – presumably soon after the accession of Antiochus IV in September/October 175 BC – bought the high priesthood with their support, together with the authority to prepare for the transformation of Jerusalem into a Greek *polis*. Suspicions of leanings towards the Ptolemies on the part of Onias III and a voluntary increase of the tribute to 360 talents and a 'special payment' of 80 talents were probably reason enough for Antiochus IV to make a change of high priests.[130] The position of the new king was still not fully assured; he needed money and reliable supporters, since those circles who were friendly towards the Ptolemies seemed to him (according to a report of Porphyry) at first to have refused him recognition.[131] The retreat of Onias III to the sanctuary of a shrine of Apollo and Artemis of Daphne suggests that he was not as 'zealous for the law' as Jason of Cyrene made out. The degree to which the Oniads were stamped with the spirit of Hellenism is shown not only by the new high priest Jason but also by Onias IV, the son of the deposed Onias III and the founder of the schismatic temple of Leontopolis.[132] The king readily acceded to the wishes of the Jerusalem aristocracy and their new head for preparations to found the new *polis* 'Antioch in Jerusalem', since this served to establish the multinational Seleucid state. One cannot speak of a deliberate policy of Hellenization on the part of the Seleucids or Antiochus IV, but it was useful when orientals adopted Greek customs and became Hellenes. Furthermore, he attached importance to stable conditions on his southern border in the face of the revanchist Egyptians. Not least, this royal mark of favour was honoured with an additional one hundred and fifty talents. Thus it is easy to understand that during his reign the king granted similar rights to a further eighteen cities, including Babylon.[133]

The initiative here clearly came from the Hellenists in Jerusalem, who presumably had the majority of the priests and lay nobility, who in practice held all power in their hands, on their side (I Macc. 1.11: ἀνέπεισαν πολλούς, cf. Dan. 11.23).

They had a threefold aim:

1. A way was to be opened for the extension of Hellenistic civilization and customs, which had previously been hindered by the religious prejudices of conservative groups. The limitations which the latter placed on unrestricted economic and cultural exchanges with the non-Jewish environment were to be abolished (I Macc. 1.11, see above, pp. 72ff. and below, p. 300).

2. To this end the 'reactionary' conservative groups had to be deprived of their political power, so that they could no longer exercise their influence to carry through limiting, legalistic and ritual regulations, as had happened under Simon the Just.

3. The prerequisite for this was the repeal of the 'letter of freedom' promulgated by Antiochus III, as this grounded the internal ordering of the Jewish 'ethnos' solely on the traditional 'ancestral laws' and gave a legal basis to the defenders of the traditional theocracy. These aims could be most easily achieved by *the transformation of Jerusalem* – and thus of the whole Jewish ethnos in Judea – *into a Greek 'polis'*. As the bestowal of citizenship of the proposed *polis*, and admission to the gymnasium and ephebate, were under the control of Jason and his friends, those faithful to the law, who probably relied for the most part on the poorer classes in the city and on the country populace, were deprived of their power and reduced to the status of perics (see pp. 74f. above). True, the temple liturgy with its sacrifices continued in the usual way, and the law of Moses was by no means officially repealed, remaining valid largely as a popular custom, but the legal foundations were removed from the Jewish 'theocracy'. Political order and policy were no longer determined by the Torah and the authoritative interpretation of it by priests and *sōperīm*; in the future they were to be based on the constitutional organs of the new *polis*, the '*dēmos*', i.e. the full citizens, the *gerousia* and the magistrates appointed by them. This inevitably resulted in a lowering of the status of the priestly nobility, and a sign of the strength of the desire within the priestly aristocracy to adopt Greek customs is the fact that this consequence was taken into account. The most powerful lay family, the Tobiads, will on the other hand have welcomed the tendency, as the fact that they were not of priestly descent had been a hindrance to them in earlier struggles for power. The considerable relaxation of the law, which was no longer a binding norm, was evidenced in the fact that individual Jewish ephebes, presumably because of the participation of foreigners in contests in the gymnasium, underwent epispasm (see above, n. II, 135). The unsuccessful sacrifice for the Tyrian Heracles can also be regarded as a sign of the tendency towards assimilation in the development as a whole.[134]

Revolutionary innovations of this kind in a city like Jerusalem, which so far had only become Hellenized in a relatively superficial way, did of course take a number of years. Consequently we should not reject out of hand Bickermann's suggestion that the citizens of the new 'Antioch' formed themselves into a kind of association preparatory to the foundation of the city proper. Its centre would have been the gymnasium, and the high priest Jason was at the same time both gymnasiarch and archon (see above, p. 73, n. II, 129). At least in the city, the Hellenists seem to have found considerable support among the landowners, merchants and craftsmen; there was probably the expectation of an economic boom and perhaps even of the right for them to mint their own coinage.[135] When the king visited Jerusalem about two and a half years after Jason's institution, he was welcomed 'magnificently by Jason and the city (population), and ushered in with a blaze of torches and with shouts' (II Macc. 4.22). Whether, as V. Tcherikover assumes, this visit of its '*ktistēs*' officially constituted the new *polis*, and the time of preparation was over, does, of course, remain completely uncertain.[136]

This development sounds positive, but a short time later it was abruptly broken off. About three years after the appointment of Jason as high priest, towards the end of 172 or the beginning of 171 BC, Menelaus, the brother of Simon the 'financial administrator of the temple' and perhaps his successor,[137] succeeded in purchasing the office of high priest from Antiochus IV by the offer of an increase in tribute of three hundred talents. This step might not have meant much for the king, who was behind in his payments to Rome and therefore took money where he could get it. In the Greek world priestly office was frequently purchased, and even city magistrates were appointed in a steady succession. Moreover, as '*ktistēs*' Antiochus could claim the right to bestow by favour the decisive office in the city founded under his name.[138] However, it was a momentous decision for Jerusalem. As an Oniad, Jason came from the family of the Zadokites, who had occupied the office of high priest for centuries in hereditary succession; with Menelaus, a non-Zadokite from the priestly family of Bilga became high priest for the first time.

The Greek codices at II Macc. 3.4 read 'Benjamin' throughout, and according to this Menelaus and Simon would have been of non-priestly descent, but this is improbable. The original reading Balgea is preserved in Old Latin and Armenian manuscripts.[139] This tradition is supplemented by the old Mishnah that the priestly clan of Bilga was excluded from offering sacrifice for all time (לעולם) because of its conduct in the religious distress under Antiochus IV: 'Its ring of slaughter is closed and its niche is shut up' (*Sukkah* 5, 8c). A Baraita explains this punishment in two ways: according to one view, Miriam had become apostate from the priestly order of Bilga, had married a Greek officer, desecrated the altar and blasphemed God. According to the other, the order of Bilga allowed itself to be deterred from exercising priestly office. Both reasons probably conceal a more severe charge which alone could match the uniqueness and magnitude of the punishment, namely, the chief responsibility for the desecration of the temple in 167 BC. According to S. Klein, the priestly order of Bilga still bore the name יונית, i.e. 'the Greek', in the time of Eleazar Kalir (seventh century AD).[140]

According to the report of Josephus, which goes back to Seleucid sources,

Menelaus was backed by the Tobiads, who through the fall of Jason had finally driven the hated Oniads from their dominant position.[141] Presumably Menelaus and Simon were related to the Tobiads, and were their willing tools. Jason fled to Hyrcanus in the Ammanitis, and his opponents thought that they were finally in possession of power in Jerusalem.

However, it was precisely these events which led to the failure of the Hellenistic reform attempt in Jerusalem. The upper class, who had supported the programme of progressive assimilation in view of their friendship towards the Greeks, was split, and it was obvious for the supporters of Jason again to turn towards the conservative religious circles who for long had maintained more of a negative attitude towards the experiment of 'Antioch in Jerusalem'. The basis of those in favour of a progressive Hellenization of the city thus shrank to a minority which could only sustain itself through the constant support of the Seleucids. The situation was aggravated by the fact that Menelaus could only produce the sums required by the king with the help of recourse to the temple treasury. This inevitably made the majority of the inhabitants of Jerusalem, whether they were favourable towards assimilation or conservative, particularly bitter towards him, and while he was away in Antioch to bring the king at least some of the payment, his brother Lysimachus, his representative, was killed by an angry mob although he had a considerable bodyguard – II Macc. 4.40 speaks, probably with some exaggeration, of three thousand men. Menelaus for his part succeeded in murdering Onias III, who could have been dangerous to him in Antioch, with the help of a high Seleucid official.[142] Despite the complaints of three members of the *gerousia* in Jerusalem, Antiochus, who was holding an investigation in Tyre into the events at Jerusalem, took the side of Menelaus and had three councillors executed. Here, too, the Tobiad agent had taken care to influence the king by bribing the officials involved. 'His alliance with the government rested on the solid basis of a mutual financial interest.'[143] It was only logical, when the king visited Jerusalem for the second time on his return from his first Egyptian campaign, that he entered the sanctuary, stole the cultic vessels and thoroughly plundered the temple: 'he had all the gold stripped off' (I Macc. 1.22). In all, about 1800 talents are said to have come into his hands.[144] Possibly Menelaus had again been in arrears with payment of tribute, but the plundering of sanctuaries had almost become a regular custom of the Seleucids after the time of Antiochus III, who had lost his life in an unsuccessful attack on the temple of Bel in the Elymais. Polybius, a contemporary, says of Epiphanes himself: ἱεροσυλήκει δὲ καὶ τὰ πλεῖστα τῶν ἱερῶν (31, 4, 9 = 30, 26, 9). For the Hellenistic ruler this may have appeared an obvious expression of his unlimited power to rule, but in the eyes of his oriental subjects it was unforgivable sacrilege.[145]

The harvest came up in the next year, when Antiochus was held in check by C. Popilius Laenas, and Jason, on the basis of a rumour of the death of the king, fell on Jerusalem with a thousand men from the Ammanitis and forced Menelaus back into the citadel (II Macc. 5.5–7; see p. 275f. above). According to the Seleucid source worked over in Josephus, *Bell.* 1, 31 and *Antt.* 12, 239, he was supported by the majority of the people and finally drove Menelaus and the Tobiads out of the city. They fled to the king – presumably to Egypt – and asked for his support. Jason could not cope with an attack by the Seleucid army, so he fled, probably before Antiochus reconquered the city, into the Ammanitis and then through the Nabateans to Egypt. The vengeance of the king and his Jewish supporters was harsh; the city was ruled under martial law, a considerable number of its inhabitants were killed, and others sold as slaves.[146] Tcherikover's view that Jason had already been driven out by a third Jewish party, the plebeian Hasidim who were faithful to the law, and that these had incurred the punishment of the king, has no support in the sources, and misunderstands the attitude of the 'pious', who certainly did not resort to armed revolt on their own initiative.[147] It is, however, worth noting the interpretation in *Bell.* 1, 32, which in a Seleucid perspective states that the king 'occupied the city with force and killed a large number of Ptolemy's supporters'. The old constellation of parties from the struggles of the time of Antiochus III was also revived in this unrest. The Jews will also have been considerably encouraged from Egypt in the Maccabean revolt which broke out a little later.

To support the Tobiads, the Phrygian Philip remained behind with a garrison, but they too were less than masters of the situation, so that at the beginning of 167 BC an army had to be sent to Judea for the second time. Its commander, the '*mysarch*' Apollonius, took a hard line. He occupied Jerusalem on a sabbath,[148] again made use of martial law, razed the city walls and erected in the city of David – presumably south of the temple hill – a large and well-fortified citadel, the so-called 'Acra'.[149] Non-Jewish military settlers were put in it as a garrison: 'And they stationed there a sinful people, lawless men . . . Because of them the residents of Jerusalem fled and (the city) became a dwelling of strangers' (I Macc. 1.34, 38; cf. 3.36). For the next decades the 'Acra' was to form the firm support for Seleucid power in Judea. In this way Jerusalem and Judea were also subjected to the usual form of punishment for a rebellious city or province in antiquity: the property of the pro-Ptolemaic supporters of the Oniads, and indeed of all those who took part in Jason's rebellion, was confiscated and divided among the military colonists and the supporters of the Tobiads.[150] Presumably the 'Acra' simply continued the tradition of the 'Antioch in Jerusalem', though it produced a substantial redeployment of the citizenry. The numerous enemies of Menelaus probably lost their rights as citizens, and part of the population fled into the desert. This '*anachōrēsis*' was a favourite means of passive resistance in antiquity.[151] The foreign cleruchs took the place of the 'rebels', and as a result the city lost its purely Jewish character and became a 'Jewish-pagan colony'[152] with mixed population. Judea was its territory, and its inhabitants, 'the ethnos of the Jews', became for the most part citizens without rights. Of course it went into a state of smouldering rebellion, and the task of the Jewish-Gentile population of the Acra – 'the sons of the Acra'[153] – will not least have been the military one of 'pacification'. In this sense we must concede the justice of Tcherikover's thesis: 'It was not the revolt which came as a response to the persecution, but the persecution which came as a response to the revolt.'[154] However, by way of qualification to Tcherikover one must say that it was less the 'pious' than the pre-Ptolemaic Oniads who stood behind the beginnings of the revolt. Nor can one talk of an organized rebellion before the intervention of the Maccabees, which only came about after the religious decrees. It will above all have been a matter of '*anachōrēsis*' into the wilderness and the refusal to pay taxes which went with it; active guerrilla warfare will only have been a secondary matter. The supreme authority in the Acra will not have been the usual magistrates of the *polis*, of whom we have no account, but a royal 'commissar' (ἐπιστάτης), the Philip who has already been mentioned.[155] Afterwards, as before, Menelaus too will have had decisive significance (II Macc. 5.23; cf. 11. 29ff.; 13.3f.); he was the head of the Jewish 'ethnos' and high priest.[156] That the Acra itself was still regarded as a Seleucid '*polis*' long after Jerusalem had returned to Jewish hands is shown by the charges of the ambassador of Antiochus VII Sidetes to Simon the Maccabee in 139 BC:

'You hold control of Joppa and Gazara and the citadel in Jerusalem; they are *cities of my kingdom* (πόλεις τῆς βασιλείας μου). You have devastated their territory, you have done great damage in the land.' Simon defends himself – in particular with respect to the Acra – with the argument of legitimacy: 'We have neither taken foreign land nor seized foreign property, but only the inheritance of our fathers, which at one time had been unjustly taken by our enemies.'[157]

The nearest parallel to the military colony in the Acra is the settlement of Macedonian colonists in Samaria by Alexander the Great or Perdiccas after the Macedonian commander there had been murdered by the Samaritans. However, the Samaritans remained strictly separated from the settlers in Samaria and founded Shechem as a new centre. One city which was inhabited by Jewish and 'Greek' citizens from the beginning and at the same time became the metropolis of a large stretch of Jewish territory was Tiberias, founded by Herod Antipas. The situation was similar in Sepphoris-Auctocratoris, which he re-established.[158]

The temple, too, headed by Menelaus as high priest, became the common property of the new Jewish-pagan citizenry. The bitter hostility with which the restless Jewish country population watched new developments in Jerusalem left no retreat open for the Tobiads and their supporters to a compromise peace with their Jewish compatriots. If they wanted to assert their leadership in Jerusalem and Judea, the only possibility left open to them was the vigorous application of force, and at the same time close collaboration with the non-Jewish cleruchies which had been settled in the Acra to support them. Here the goal of complete assimilation and the abolition of the barriers between Jews and non-Jews had in practice been completely achieved, though hardly in the way that the Jewish Hellenists had expected in 175 BC.

(c) The edict of religion, the king and the Jewish apostates

The establishment of the Acra in early 167 BC and the occupation of the temple by its mixed, Jewish-Gentile populace, made the question of a Jewish-syncretistic mixed cult in the sanctuary an acute one, even before the prohibition of the Jewish religion. According to I Macc.1.37, 39, the 'holy precinct' had already been desecrated and 'laid waste like a desert' ($\dot{\eta}\rho\eta\mu\dot{\omega}\theta\eta$ $\dot{\omega}s$ $\ddot{\epsilon}\rho\eta\mu\rho s$) by the penal expedition of Apollonius. This probably meant that the *tamid* offering had been stopped at least from then on. Daniel, too, hints at this by putting the cessation of the *tamid* offering – which was certainly not ordered personally by Antiochus – at the beginning of this wickedness practised against the sanctuary: 'Forces from him shall appear and profane the temple and fortress, and shall take away the continual burnt offering.'[159] However, the legendary Baraita of Miriam from the priestly order of Bilga (from which Menelaus also came), who apostatized and married a Seleucid officer, shows that the extreme Hellenists under Menelaus had lost any interest in sacrifice according to the law:

> When the heathen entered the temple, she came and struck (*b. Sukk.*56b) against the corner of the altar with her sandal and said to him: 'Wolf, wolf, you have squandered the riches of Israel (לוקם לוקם אתה החובתה ממון ישראל) and do not stand up for her in the time of her need!' The uselessness of the *tamid* offering could not be expressed more vividly. The age of this legend is shown by the fact that it was later transferred to Titus.[160]

The cohabitation of Jewish and non-Jewish military settlers was nothing new in itself; we already find it in the third century in Egypt and in the cleruchy of Tobias, but it never amounted to a cultic community (see above, pp.15f., nn.I, 83–94). Thus it would have been conceivable in theory, even now, that the pagan settlers erected their own sanctuaries – indeed the Ptolemaic and Seleucid officials and soldiers or the Phoenician merchants in Jerusalem may already have had their own private house cults.[161] So when the sanctuary on Zion was opened to the non-Jewish cleruchs, who were of mixed nationality in origin,[162] and the worship of the God of the Jews was assimilated to the cult of the supreme Semitic God of heaven, we may assume that the initiative for the assimilation came from the Jewish minority of the Tobiads and their supporters. Fundamentally the unsuccessful sacrifice for Heracles already represented a beginning in this direction (see above, pp.73f., 279f.).

This tendency was substantially sharpened – though not initiated – by new measures which I Macc. 1.41f. describes in the following way:

> Then the king wrote to his whole kingdom that all should be one people and that each should give up his customs (ἐγκαταλιπεῖν . . . τὰ νόμιμα αὐτοῦ). All the Gentiles accepted the command of the king.

For I Maccabees this command, allegedly directed at the whole Seleucid empire, formed the basis of the royal decree prohibiting the Jewish religion, which immediately followed. This, too, is said to have gone out to the whole kingdom (1.51).[163] The historical value of this report is of course considerably disputed. Whereas earlier historians attached decisive importance to it,[164] E. Bickermann declared that it was unhistorical,[165] and even his critic I. Heinemann, who holds that I. Macc. 1.41 describes a circular letter, 'which commended certain ordinances as desired by the king', had to concede that 'the reporter takes a great deal on'.[166] The statements in Daniel about the religious politics of Antiochus IV would support an initiative of this kind on the part of the king:

> He shall give no heed to the gods of his fathers, or to the one beloved by women; he shall not give heed to any other god, for he shall magnify himself above all. He shall honour the god of fortresses instead of these; a god whom his fathers did not know he shall honour with gold and silver, with precious stones and costly gifts. He shall deal with the strongest fortresses by the help of a foreign god.[167]

Of course, this description presented in dark prophetic style could, like I Macc. 1.41, be written from a very limited Jewish perspective. The Hasidic author could hardly have had the possibility of informing himself about the religious policy of the king throughout the Seleucid realm; rather, so far as the present was concerned, his attention was totally directed towards the terrifying situation in Judea. The 'god of fortresses' is therefore not, as R. H. Charles and others suppose, Jupiter Capitolinus, to whom the king built a temple in Antioch,[168] but the 'god of the Acra', worship of whom was also transplanted by the apostates and their Seleucid confederates into the larger fortified areas. A newly discovered inscription from Scythopolis consecrated to 'Zeus Akraios', the Zeus of the summit of the mountain of the Acra, is a more likely explanation of the origin of the term.[169] As all that the Jewish renegades and the foreign military settlers did to compel worship of him happened with royal legitimation, Antiochus IV necessarily became the real author, in the eyes of the apocalyptist, of the persecution which now began. This happened particularly because for the apocalyptic picture he was a much more effective anti-godly projection than say the apostate Menelaus. On the other hand, a comparison of royal 'religious politics' with the statements in I Macc. 1.41ff. and Dan. 11.37f. does not produce a unitary picture which could be cited in support.

The author of Daniel could best draw certain conclusions from royal coinage and from the partial change of imagery from the traditional Apollo to the Olympian Zeus, who appeared as a throned figure on the reverse of coins from 173/2, and from 169/8 BC replaced the royal head with a bearded portrait of him on Antiochene mintings.[170] However, one should not overestimate the numismatic evidence for Zeus Olympius, as at the same time a minting also appeared with the portrait of Apollo on one side and a standing Apollo Citharoides on the reverse. Nor can the approximation of the portrait of Zeus to the features of the king himself, which is so often maintained, really be established.[171] Moreover, in the nearest mint at Acco-Ptolemais from 170–168 BC, Judea still exclusively minted coins with the royal portrait on the front and seated Apollo on the reverse, and these continued at least in part from 168 to 164 BC. The portrait of Zeus did not appear on the coins coming from there at all.[172] The imperial coins minted in Tyre also seem to have carried only the traditional Apollo as an image.[173] Finally, as E. Bickermann rightly stresses, the evidence of the local copper mintings allowed for the first time by Antiochus IV in various cities stands in contradiction to the allegedly uniform religious policy of the king; alongside the obligatory royal portrait, these places for the most part had representations of their manifold local deities and cult symbols. The Phoenician cities even added legends in their vernacular, and thus stressed their own national tradition. Precisely at this point signs of a striving towards independence become visible, which later made a substantial contribution to the downfall of the Seleucid empire.[174]

The reason why Daniel lays so much stress on the heaven-storming hybris of the king[175] could, on the other hand, also be because of his reaction to the king's policy on coinage. The king was the first Seleucid ruler to have his full title, elaborated by epithets from the emperor cult,[176] *ΒΑΣΙΛΕΩΣ ΑΝΤΙΟΧΟΥ ΘΕΟΥ ΕΠΙΦΑΝΟΥΣ*, to be minted on coins. This happened from 173/2 BC, and from 169/8 *ΝΙΚΗΦΟΡΟΥ* was also added. But even here there was not complete uniformity.[177] The application of the Samaritans to the king in 166 BC mentions the epithet Θεὸς Ἐπιφανής (*Antt.* 12, 258), but the answer to it has only the short form Βασιλεὺς Ἀντίοχος (12, 262) which was usual in royal documents; furthermore, it was also used in most of the local mintings.[178] As Ben Sira, Daniel and Judith show, now for the first time the Jews took up polemic against the Hellenistic emperor cult, although they had certainly already known it for some time.[179] On the other hand, it cannot by any means be said that the king identified himself directly with Zeus Olympius.[180] This diverse picture which already emerges from the evidence of coinage about the royal favouring of Zeus Olympius also emerges in the other reports:

Thus he completed the temple of Zeus Olympius in Athens,[181] left incomplete by the Pisistratids, and probably made over a splendid curtain to the temple of Zeus in Olympia,[182] though at the same time he generously demonstrated his reverence for Apollo of Delos.[183] Polybius does not therefore speak of a preference of the king for Olympian Zeus, but says in general terms that he exceeded all the Hellenistic kings in his tokens of reverence for the gods (ἐν ταῖς πρὸς τοὺς θεοὺς τιμαῖς) – towards the cities of the Greek motherland (Polyb.26, 1, 10). He had the temple of Apollo in Daphne, the 'chief sanctuary of the royal house',[184] extended and put there a copy of the statue of Zeus made by Phidias of Olympia;[185] in the spectacular 'pompē' of Daphne he had representations of 'all the gods or divine beings named or worshipped by men' presented (Polyb. 30, 25, 13); 'the number of images of the gods could not be counted'. We have evidence for the worship of Olympian Zeus in the second half of the second century BC in Scythopolis and perhaps in Samaria, where there was a close association with the emperor cult;[186] and at a later date for Dura Europos[187] and for Gerasa, which, since it also had the name 'Antioch on the Chrysoroas', could have been founded by Epiphanes.[188] According to the Phoenician historian Dio, 'Zeus Olympius' had long had a temple in Tyre, and in Philo of Byblos the 'Zeus of the Greeks' was identified with 'Ba'al Šāmēm'.[189] However, worship of Zeus in Syria is evidently *older* than Antiochus IV. Thus there is evidence of the cult of Zeus Olympius, Zeus Coryphaeus, Apollo and the emperor cult in the priestly lists from Seleucia in Pieria under Seleucus IV.[190] According to a legend connected with the founding of Seleucia in Pieria, the founder of the dynasty, Seleucus I Nicator, who was probably a model for Antiochus IV in many things, had shown reverence to the famous Baal of Mount Kasion as Zeus Kasios.[191] He was already called Seleucus 'Zeus Nicator', and his son Antiochus I 'Apollo Soter'; it should be noted here that with the Seleucid kings, including Antiochus IV, divine epithets changed according to time and place.[192]

Thus from the beginning Zeus and Apollo were 'the two chief gods of the Seleucids', and presumably very closely connected with the emperor cult.[193] However, we cannot speak either of a unitary religious policy of the first Seleucids or of a deliberate attitude over the emperor cult. Traditionally, the religious interests of the Ptolemies seem to have been decidedly greater.[194] Thus in his only sporadic, and therefore certainly not over-emphatic, predilection for Olympian Zeus, and in his foundations of cities, Antiochus IV may be taking up an earlier tradition of the first Seleucids; as he was a person who was indifferent to religion, this will have been on purely political grounds.[195] Possibly he had the ideal of a syncretistic 'imperial cult' which would unite the worship of the Semitic-Iranian God of heaven and the Greek Zeus, but he did not advance this consistently, nor did he achieve a success comparable to Ptolemy I and the introduction of the cult of Serapis.[196] His concerns in this direction ultimately live in historical memory only because of the failure of the reform attempt in Jerusalem.

The decree of I Macc.1.41 and the picture drawn by Dan.11.37ff. of the religious attitude of the ruler are therefore primarily *determined by the narrow Palestinian perspective* from which they are presented, and can only be accepted with very considerable qualifications. If there is nevertheless a desire to maintain the historicity of the decree, then it can only be regarded as 'an expression of loyalty which was originally meant to be quite innocuous',[197] commending in a quite voluntary way the introduction of the worship of Zeus Olympius, identified with the supreme Semitic God of heaven, in connection with the emperor cult. It is improbable that such a decree was issued to the whole empire. E. Meyer already proposed that I Macc. 1.41f. should be understood as a rewritten formula from the royal prohibition proper,[198] and F. M. Abel pointed to the parallels to the decrees directed to the whole empire in Dan. 3.4ff. and 6.8ff., which similarly have a 'religious political' character.[199] Thus this could be a theme of legendary Jewish patriotic literature. In making it the starting point for his criticism of E. Bickermann, I. Heinemann is on very uncertain ground.

As a result, the chief reason for the second royal degree which immediately followed and which prohibited the practice of the Jewish religion in the region of Judea – despite the evidently false note in I Macc. 1.51a, the Diaspora was not affected[200] – commanding the consecration of the temple to 'Zeus Olympius' (cf. I Macc. 1.44ff. and II Macc. 6.1ff.) can no longer be given as an initiative of the king in the context of his alleged 'Hellenization policy'.[201] Nor is Tcherikover's thesis, that the religious edict of the king was issued because the Jews faithful to the law were already in open rebellion against Seleucid rule,[202] adequate in this form. In the first place, explicit religio-political measures to subject unruly populaces are without parallel in antiquity, and in the second place we must ask who informed the king about the religious situation in Judea to the effect that the rebellion of the Jews could not be put down by the usual means of sheer force, but only by a completely unique prohibition of religion. Neither the king nor his 'friends', who were certainly very little interested in the Jews, will have conceived such unusual ideas, which presuppose a knowledge of conditions within Judaism. *This gives greatest probability to Bickermann's view that the impulse to the most extreme escalation of events in Judea came from the extreme Hellenists in Jerusalem itself.*[203]

The Jewish religion was the only religion in the East and in the Hellenistic world in which the worship of foreign gods was fundamentally regarded as apostasy and could be punished with death.[204] In the acute tension which had long been present in Jerusalem between those faithful to the law and the 'antinomians', the antipathy of the extreme Hellenists, forming a hopelessly small minority yet sure of the support of the king, towards their conservative opponents was no less intensive than the 'zeal' of a Mattathias in issuing a summons to follow Phinehas and kill the apostates.[205] Why should not the apostates, turning the regulations of the Old Testament upside down, break the faithfulness of their opponents to the law by threatening them with death? The fully assimilated Jewish renegades knew well enough that their rule in Jerusalem could in the end only be ensured by rooting out the traditional

Jewish religious attitude by force, since it was impossible for those who were faithful to the law to be reconciled with the apostates because of the uncompromising character of the Jewish religion. The foundation of the Acra gave them a firm legal basis: the law obligatory for all was no longer the Torah of Moses, as it had been once in the decree of Antiochus III, but the legal ordinances of the new *polis* permitted by Epiphanes – including their religious clauses.[206]

Furthermore, *even the sources themselves* in various ways *point directly to the decisive role of the Jewish Hellenists*, although they tend to exaggerate the co-operation of the king. We should draw attention here first to Dan.9.27: *wehigᵉbbîr bᵉrît lārabbîm šābūaᶜ 'eḥād*, which is best translated, without a textual emendation, 'He will make strong a covenant for the many, a week (of years) long'. The word 'covenant' will be meant to express the close community of interest between the king and the extreme Hellenists, 'the many', who, from the appointment of Menelaus at the end of 172 or the beginning of 171 BC down to the time of the author, about 165 BC, held sway in Jerusalem for about seven years, i.e. a week of years, and according to I Macc. 1.11 wanted to conclude a covenant with the Gentiles (διαθήκην μετὰ τῶν ἐθνῶν).[207] There is a further reference immediately before the report of the foundation of the military colony and the desecration of the sanctuary: 'He (Antiochus IV) shall turn back (from Egypt) and shall give heed to those who forsake the holy covenant': *wᵉšāb wᵉyābēn ᶜal-ᶜōzᵉbē bᵉrît qōdeš*.[208] Jerome explains this, following Porphyry: '*postquam eum de Aegypto pepulerunt Romani, indignans contra Testamentum sanctuarii, et ab his invitatus sit qui derelinquerant Legem Dei et se caeremoniis miscuerant ethnicorum.*'[209] According to Josephus, this primarily involved the Tobiads. A further important indication is the corresponding judgment on their agent Menelaus as the real person responsible for the persecution and thus for the rebellion of the Jews:

According to II Macc. 13.3ff., Menelaus came with Antiochus V Eupator and Lysias to Judea in 163 BC and also attempted to be restored to his office in Jerusalem, which was in the hands of the Maccabees. 'When Lysias informed the king that this man was to blame for all the trouble' (αἴτιον τῶν κακῶν εἶναι πάντων), the king ordered them to take him and kill him. Independently of this, the same man counsels the king in Josephus, *Antt.* 12, 384: 'That he should kill Menelaus if he wanted to give the Jews peace and not to make any more trouble for himself, as Menelaus had caused the disturbance *by convincing* his father (Antiochus IV) *to compel the Jews to give up their traditional worship of God.*' τὸν Μενέλαον ἀνελεῖν, εἰ βούλεται τοὺς Ἰουδαίους ἠρεμεῖν καὶ μηδὲν ἐνοχλεῖν αὐτῷ. τοῦτον γὰρ ἄρξαι τῶν κακῶν, πείσαντ᾽ αὐτοῦ τὸν πατέρα τοὺς Ἰουδαίους ἀναγκάσαι τὴν πάτριον θρησκείαν καταλιπεῖν. After the report of his execution there follows the significant characterization of the high priest (12, 385): 'and so that he himself could rule, he compelled the people to transgress their own laws': καὶ ἵνα αὐτὸς ἄρχῃ τὸ ἔθνος ἀναγκάσαντα τοὺς ἰδίους παραβῆναι νόμους.

We may also apply these verdicts to the Tobiads standing behind Menelaus; nor is there any reason to doubt these clear statements of two completely independent sources.[210] II Maccabees 5.23 describes the high priest immediately before the invasion of Apollonius and the foundation of the Acra in the same way:

> He lorded it over his fellow citizens worse than the others (i.e. the Seleucid commanders) did, filled with malice ($\dot{a}\pi\epsilon\chi\theta\hat{\eta}$ . . . $\delta\iota\dot{a}\theta\epsilon\sigma\iota\nu$) against his Jewish fellow citizens.[211]

Thus Menelaus and the Tobiads who supported him appear as the authors of the edict of persecution. Presumably, by furnishing appropriate information, they caused the king to prepare the decree for the extermination of the Jewish religion by force in the summer of 167 BC, soon after the erection of the Acra, and it was then brought to Jerusalem by an 'Athenian senator'.[212] Possibly this decree was part of the constitution of the newly established *polis* with Jewish-Gentile citizenship. Even if one assumes that an earlier royal initiative – still in essentials voluntary – stands behind I Macc. 1.41f., this would not be a contradiction. For according to 1.43, '*many* from Israel' ($\pi o\lambda\lambdao\grave{\iota}$ $\dot{a}\pi\grave{o}$ $\,{}^{\prime}I\sigma\rho a\acute{\eta}\lambda$) had already assented to the religious custom of the new *polis* and to the form of worship furthered by the king ($\epsilon\mathring{v}\delta\acute{o}\kappa\eta\sigma a\nu$ $\tau\hat{\eta}$ $\lambda a\tau\rho\epsilon\acute{\iota}\dot{a}$ $a\mathring{v}\tauo\hat{v}$) *before* any use of force, 'sacrificing to idols and profaning the sabbath'. This note, that *many* followed the Hellenistic reform, appears in the sources many times. I Macc. 1.11 itself says in connection with the 'programme' of assimilation to the non-Jews that the Hellenists succeeded in convincing 'many' (see above, p. 72). The fact that at that time Jewish ephebes attempted to remove the marks of their circumcision means that they had already broken with the law completely (I Macc. 1.15, see above, p. 278).

> Jubilees 15.33f. designates the omission or removal of the marks of circumcision, which was apparently practised by many people in the Maccabean period, as a breach of the covenant, and makes specific reference to these events. It is evasion of God's command and blasphemy, which conjured up his anger, so that they 'will be driven out and exterminated from the earth'. This could be a reference to the later fate of the apostates, who were either put to death or fled abroad.

I Maccabees 1.52 attests that as a consequence of the royal prohibition of religion, '*many* of the people, everyone who forsook the law, joined them' (i.e. overseers from the Acra appointed in the royal decree). In Modein 'many came from Israel' to sacrifice before the royal officials (2.16). One can hardly follow Tcherikover in his attempt[213] to interpret this phrase to the higher praise of the Maccabees in the sense of 'much enmity, much honour'. Alcimus, who later became high priest, was charged with having '*voluntarily* polluted himself in the time of the revolt' ($\dot{\epsilon}\kappa o\upsilon\sigma\acute{\iota}\omega s$ $\delta\grave{\epsilon}$ $\mu\epsilon\mu o\lambda\upsilon\mu\mu\acute{\epsilon}\nu o s$ $\dot{\epsilon}\nu$ $\tauo\hat{\iota} s$ $\tau\hat{\eta} s$ $\dot{a}\mu\iota\xi\acute{\iota} a s$ $\chi\rho\acute{o}\nuo\iota s$), so that he could no longer be considered for service at the altar. Nevertheless, the Hasidim who were faithful to the law accepted him as high priest; presumably the candidates by this time were very few.[214] In the case of the councillor Razis, on the other hand, it was expressly stressed that at that time he had decided for Judaism ('Ιουδαϊσμός, see above, pp. 1f.) and had interceded for it vigorously (II Macc. 14.37f.), because this was a rare exception – at least among those inhabitants of Jerusalem who had not fled. Dan. 11.32 also shows that the Jewish Hellenists did not shrink from the ultimate consequence of complete apostasy: 'He shall seduce with flattery those who violate the covenant: *waḥᵃnîp baḥᵃlaqqōt*.[215]

> The form in which the royal 'seduction' led to apostasy is shown in 11.39b: 'Those who acknowledge the strange god he shall magnify with honour. He shall make them rulers over many and shall divide the land for a price.' While those who were faithful to the law were dispossessed as rebels, the apostates received their property, to be worked on by disenfranchised elements of the population who, perhaps like the Syrian fellahin, were to be kept under in a state of semi-slavery.[216] The same procedure was repeated after the death of Judas in 160 BC, when the victorious general Bacchides deliberately supported 'the lawless ones in the hill country of Israel' and the 'godless men', and made them 'masters of the country' (I Macc. 9.23ff.). Of course when Jonathan, the brother of Judas, was made high priest by Alexander Balas in 152 BC, he reversed the position and 'plundered and collected the riches of the men of violence who had rebelled against God' (ויגזול ויקבוץ הון אנשי חמס אשר מרדו באל).[217]

Here we can see at the same time the strong social background of events in Judea.

As a result of the surprising military successes of Judas Maccabaeus in the battles from the end of 167 BC to the beginning of 164 BC, which to a large extent amounted to a *civil war* between those faithful to the law and the apostates,[218] the prohibition of the observance of the Jewish law was repealed by a document from the king (or his son?) in March 164 BC, after lasting not quite three years. Here again Menelaus appears as an ambassador. Perhaps he was sent by Lysias to Antioch, so that he could present the failure of his politics of force in person and salvage what could be salvaged. Lysias himself, who also dealt directly with the rebels (II Macc. 11.14ff.), seems to have had a less favourable attitude towards the Hellenists and their policy of imposing religion by force.[219] But the counter-movement launched by Menelaus and his supporters could no longer be stopped. Towards the end of 163 BC the son of Epiphanes, Antiochus V Eupator, also had to withdraw officially from jurisdiction over the Acra – which Judas had already won back in 164 BC – and hand it over to the Jews.[220] Of course the Jewish apostates could not return into the community of the Jewish people and its religion. Unlike Alcimus, who could still become high priest although he had seriously compromised himself with the Hellenists, they were bound to the Gentile military settlers on the Acra for better or worse. They probably refused to make a real peace treaty with their own people because it was known that they had been the ultimate authors of the religious distress. The exclusion of the priestly order of Bilga from sacrifice 'for all time' likewise points in this direction (see above, pp. 279f., 283f., nn. IV, 139f., 160).

Even after the repeal of the religious ordinances, the Jewish *renegades in the Acra* remained a constant political threat. When Judas began to besiege the Acra at the beginning of 163 BC, some of the garrison broke out through the ring of besiegers and 'a mob of wicked men from Israel joined forces with them' to complain to Antiochus V Eupator about their rebellious fellow-countrymen:

> How long will you fail to do justice and avenge our brethren? We were happy to serve your father, to live by what he said and to follow his commands. For this reason the sons of our people besieged the citadel and became hostile to us . . . Unless you quickly prevent them . . . you will not be able to stop them.[221]

When Jonathan later had a free hand as a result of the struggle between Alexander Balas and Demetrius I, built the walls of Jerusalem again and forced the garrison of the Acra to give up their hostages, the foreign military settlers (ἀλλογενεῖς) fled to the smaller fortresses in Judea, 'each to his own land'. 'Only in Beth Zur did some remain who had forsaken the law and the commandments, for it served as a place of refuge' (I Macc. 10.14). Even now, the Jewish apostates were still in a position to hold the fortress of Beth Zur against the Maccabees, although to some extent they had been left in the lurch by the non-Jewish military settlers. A little later a deputation from this side, 'pestilent men from Israel, lawless men', sought to complain about Jonathan to Alexander Balas, but were rejected by him because he needed Jonathan's help (I Macc. 10.61). The same scene was repeated in 145 BC before Demetrius II: when Jonathan began to besiege the Acra, again some lawless men, who hated the people, made complaints against him. He had to answer before the king, but was able to change his mind with presents (11.20ff.). Twenty-six years had gone by after the erection of the citadel when on 4.6.141 Simon succeeded in getting the Acra into his hands by starvation and after the assurance of a free passage out; he also succeeded in conquering Beth Zur (I Macc. 13.49–51; 14.7).[222] Only now did the Jewish apostates cease to be a danger to the people. The suggestion in the letter of protection from the consul L. Calpurnius Piso for the Jewish embassy to Rome that a whole series of Greek states should hand over Jewish fugitives to the high priest Simon 'so that he might punish them according to the law' may refer above all to Jewish apostates who had fled abroad (I Macc. 15.21ff.).

In the thirty-four years between the beginning of the Hellenistic reform and its final liquidation by the expulsion of the Seleucid garrison and the

Jewish apostates from the Acra and from Beth Zur, Palestinian Judaism had been given a profound impression which still continued its effect even in New Testament times. One can hardly understand the desperate zeal with which the Jewish people continued to fight for the unqualified validity of the law and for their sanctuary, and branded any criticism of the law as apostasy, unless one notes that for more than three decades they had to defend themselves in Jerusalem – the Acra on the hill south of the temple, the site of the old city of David, was in the true sense of the word a thorn in the flesh – with the utmost vigour against a minority whose chief aim was the abolition of the law of Moses and complete assimilation to the Gentile environment.

(d) 'Zeal against the law', the new worship of God and the ideology of apostasy

If the royal decree on the prohibition of the Jewish religion goes back to an initiative on the part of radical 'reform Judaism',[223] we must be able to find points of contact in the edict and in the way in which it was carried out. I Maccabees 1.44–51 has some indications of its content; I Macc. 1.52–54 and II Macc. 6.6–11 describe the consequences of its execution. Granted, I Maccabees, which was written towards 100 BC, gives only a very superficial, one-sided description of events in Judea. Nevertheless, in the religious ordinances and their execution two fundamental tendencies can be seen which certainly have a historical background:

1. The chief aim was the complete *abolition of the law* of Moses, its commandments and prohibitions, with particular note of the repeal of the most noticeable regulations, e.g. the hallowing of the sabbath, the festivals, circumcision, the impurity of certain kinds of meat, etc. These were all regulations which had the character of a confession of Judaism. The aim was for the Jews to 'forget the law and do away with all their holy ordinances' (I Macc. 1.49). For this reason all the scrolls of the law were destroyed which people could get their hands on, and the very possession of the law was made punishable by death (1.56f.). There were individual instances of martyrdom, but the greatest sacrifice was probably in the massacre of those who had fled to the desert on the sabbath, during the time that those who were faithful to the law did not defend themselves on this day.[224] Just as the Maccabees, at least at the beginning of their struggle for freedom, were directed by 'zeal for the law', one could say that the Jewish apostates were directed by a 'zeal against the law'.

2. Closely connected with this was a thoroughgoing *reform of the cultus* which affected not only the sanctuary attached to the Acra but the whole Jewish 'ethnos' in Judea. The abolition of the 'burnt offerings, sacrifices and drink offerings' (1.45) prescribed by the law sanctioned a situation which had probably existed only since the invasion of Apollonius (see above, nn. 159f.). The same thing might be said of the abolition of the regulations to protect the sanctity of the temple and the priesthood (1.46). Even women could enter the

inner court of the sanctuary which had previously been closed to them.[225] The abolition of the deuteronomistic cult centralization was of decisive significance here: 'altars, holy precincts and chapels' were to be erected even in the country, so that the populace who lived a long way from the now desecrated sanctuary could be compelled to observe the new cult (vv. 47, 54b). People were not content with offering incense on the streets in Jerusalem, but 'sacrificed before the doors of the houses' (v. 55): 'Every Jew was to be compelled to the new belief.'[226] Thus behind the edict there was an explicit 'zeal for conversion', and at the same time a well-thought-out plan which presupposed a knowledge of the Jewish law that was to be abolished. For precisely what the law had forbidden was now deliberately ordained. Circumcision, largely practised among Egyptians, Arabs and Syrians, was now prohibited for Jews, and against a widespread Semitic custom pigs were sacrificed, because the rejection of this animal was characteristic of those Jews who were faithful to the law.[227] Thus the royal edict brought 'not only the abolition of the previous law but the introduction of a new one',[228] which in many points represented a reversal of the old. What was prohibited there, now became an obligation. Strict consistency in the abolition of the law, the 'reform' of the cult and the adoption of what were considered 'Greek customs' ($\tau\grave{\alpha}$ $\dot{'}E\lambda\lambda\eta\nu\iota\kappa\acute{\alpha}$, II Macc. 6.9; 11.24) were probably neither the work of the king nor that of the royal chancellor in Antioch, since these lacked the basic requisite, knowledge of the 'superstition' which was to be rooted out. Behind all this stand rather the 'resolute' Jewish reformers who, according to I Macc. 1.11, had already striven in 175 BC to make an alliance with the nations round about and who now believed, on the basis of the extremely acute political and social situation, that they could introduce complete assimilation and remove the strict orthodox opposition, as they wished, by a violent solution. The king was certainly pleased to be convinced by these Jewish '*zealots against the law*',[229] who had taken his side against the majority of their fellow-countrymen, even in plundering the temple. He gave them his full approval and support against the orthodox who, according to the accounts of their opponents, were rebels inclined to revolution and friends of the Ptolemies. In this way the reformers could come forward in the name of the king, as their proposals were backed by a royal edict, and royal officials and soldiers were the executive instruments of their concerns.

As E. Bickermann has shown in detail,[230] an indirect proof of this interpretation of events was the quite different course matters took in *Samaria*. The royal officials also began to make difficulties for the Samaritans, because of the often obscure border line between the Samaritan and the Jewish population and the Samaritans' almost identical religious customs,[231] especially as Judea and Samaria were presumably an administrative unit under a *meridiarch* with his seat in Samaria.[232] At the beginning of 167 BC a royal commissar, Andronicus, was appointed for both Jerusalem and for the

Samaritans (II Macc. 5.23). In 166 BC the latter finally asserted in a deputation to the king – in which they described themselves as 'Sidonians in Shechem'[233] – that while they observed the sabbath, they had nothing to do with the charges raised against the Jews, especially since, as Sidonians, they were not related to them. They asked not to be molested by royal officials and they wanted to name their sanctuary on mount Gerizim, long anonymous (12.259: ἱδρυσάμενοι δὲ ἀνώνυμον ἐν τῷ Γαριζείν . . . ὄρει ἱερόν), after 'Zeus Xenios' (thus II Macc. 6.2; Josephus, Antt. 12, 261, 263 has 'Zeus Hellenios').[234] The king listened to their ambassadors in the company of his friends and granted their wish 'not to be involved in the charges laid against the Jews', i.e. recognized that they were not rebels like the Jews faithful to the law. He was satisfied with the fact that the 'supreme God' worshipped on Gerizim could in the future also be named 'Zeus', as a demonstration that 'they wanted to live according to Greek custom' (Antt. 12, 262f.). There was thus no more a question of the abolition of their way of life in accordance with the Torah of Moses than there was of a 'reform' of the cult on Gerizim, which was probably as much in accordance with the Torah as previous worship on Mount Zion. In Shechem the Torah of Moses and the religious customs associated with it, like the observance of the sabbath, continued to be valid, while in Jerusalem they were prohibited on penalty of death, and this policy was forcibly carried out. Antiochus IV was probably interested very generally in a 'Hellenization' of his oriental subjects, but not in the concrete details, the alteration of religious customs and laws. The Samaritans kept their law and cult – leaving aside the voluntary naming of the temple on Gerizim, which made sense only to the Greeks; even Ps. Aristeas allows the God of the Bible to be called Zeus (see above, pp. 264f.) – although they were no less different from their heathen neighbours than the Jews.[235] Thus if the persecution in Judea was regional and limited to the 'ethnos' of the Jews, it seems reasonable to suppose that it was initiated by the local authorities.[236] The real reason for the harshness of the edict of religion lay not so much in giving a Greek name to the God on Zion but in the attempt at a radical elimination of the law, 'zeal against the law' and the introduction of completely new cult forms. In contrast to the extreme Hellenists in Jerusalem, no one among the Samaritans had thought to do away with law and cult, and so here the king proposed no changes.

E. Bickermann has also made a brilliant analysis of the *new form of worship* forced on the Jewish populace.[237] The naming of the temple in Jerusalem after 'Zeus Olympius' (II Macc. 6.2) in no way meant the introduction of Greek cult-forms, for until a late and presumably unhistorical report from Porphyry there is no sign that an anthropomorphic cult image of the god was erected in the temple.[238] The 'abomination of desolation' erected in the temple on the 15 Chislev (6 December) 167 BC[239] represented, rather, a second altar set on the great altar of burnt offerings, which perhaps had the significance of a massebah or a betyl, a sacred stone widespread in the Phoenician-Syrian environment; 'this object was as much a place as an object of worship'.[240] Possibly the same altar had an inscription or a pictorial representation. According to Philo of Byblos, betyls as 'ensouled stones' were an invention of the god 'Uranus', the son of 'Elyon Hypsistos'.[241] The sanctuary itself was changed into a *sacred grove* with trees after the destruction of the gates, and the temple buildings proper stood empty.[242] Both the planting of trees and the massebah represented a direct opposition to Deut. 16.21f. The altars and groves made in country areas were to some degree offshoots of the great precinct on Zion with its holy stone on the old altar of burnt offering. 'In this way the cult places of the new worship corresponded to the old Semitic type of sanctuary which was a place for sacrifice among trees, surrounded by a wall and open to the skies.'[243] The most famous and most venerable Palestinian and Syrian sanctuaries still had this form in Hellenistic times, for example on Mount Kasion near Seleucia, in Mamre, the old Abraham sanctuary near Hebron, and above all on Carmel, where as early as the time of Elijah and Ahab, Yahweh and the Tyrian Baal had struggled for supremacy.[244] The archaic form of worship there is described by Tacitus: '*nec simulacrum deo aut templum – sic tradidere maiores –: ara tantum et reverentia*' (*Hist.*2, 78). Here the old Semitic and the old Greek usages met. On the summits of Olympus, Mount Ida on Crete and other mountains sacred to Zeus, there was also likewise just a simple altar; even on the magnificent acropolis of Pergamon, Zeus – in contrast to the other gods who had temples – declared himself content with an altar, albeit of gigantic dimensions.[245] There is also a good deal of evidence for the veneration of sacred stones in Greece, as throughout the Mediterranean; Pausanias 7, 22, 4 reports that once all the Greeks revered unworked stones instead of images of gods.[246]

Herodotus reports a partially comparable, apparently 'archaic' form of worship among the Persians: 'It is not customary among them to construct idols, temples and altars. They even assert that anyone who does this is a fool. They do not believe, it seems to me, that the gods have human form, as among the Greeks. They are accustomed to sacrifice to Zeus on the summits of mountains and designate the whole firmament Zeus.'[247] Numa Pompilius, the pious philosophical king of primeval Rome, also worshipped gods without images or a temple: '*nondum tamen aut simulacris aut templis res divina apud Romanos constabat*', and Zeno of Citium declared in his first work that it was senseless to build temples and consecrate images to the gods.[248]

Thus the new cult of the Jewish renegades and their Seleucid confederates on Zion could claim to be 'universal', archaic – proof of age was at the same time proof of truth – and rational. It corresponded to what the colonists in the Acra knew and at the same time matched 'the religion of the philosophers'.[249]

In one way it anticipated Stephen's enlightened, polemic thesis in Acts 7.48: ἀλλ' οὐχ ὁ ὕψιστος ἐν χειροποιήτοις κατοικεῖ.

According to the contemporary judgment of the book of Daniel, this new form of worship was concentrated on the 'alien god', the 'god of fortresses', the occupant of the Acra (see above, nn. 167–8). This is certainly an apocalyptic symbol for the fact that the temple in Jerusalem was named after *Zeus Olympius* (τὸν ἐν Ἱεροσολύμοις νεὼ καὶ προσονομάσαι Διὸς Ὀλυμπίου, II Macc. 6.2), though in the Hellenistic period Olympius was merely a 'synonym for heaven' (*GM*, 96). There is no mention of the worship of other gods – leaving aside the emperor cult associated with that of Zeus Olympius, which was obligatory and had existed even before Antiochus IV (see above, nn. 190–3). True, according to II Macc. 6.7, the Jews 'were compelled to walk in the procession in honour of Dionysius, wearing garlands of ivy', but there is no mention of any way in which 'Dionysus' was related to 'Olympian Zeus' and his cult on Zion. E. Bickermann's term 'the gods of the Acra' (*GM*, 111–116) is in some contradiction to the statements of Daniel and I Maccabees which, as Tcherikover rightly stresses, saw 'a monotheistic policy' in the propagation of the new cult (*HC*, 182). The late report of Malalas that Athene was worshipped alongside Zeus Olympius – Bickermann sees the Semitic Allat behind her – has hardly any value as a source, in view of the confused reports about events under Antiochus IV by the Byzantine chronographer.[250] So it remains very questionable whether we may suppose that there was the cult of a divine triad in Jerusalem such as was later worshipped in Heliopolis Baalbek.[251] The 'monotheizing tendency' in the reports of Daniel and I Macc. about the reform in Jerusalem does not have its cause in any uniformity as a religious policy of the king – such a policy can only have been a marginal one – nor in the fact that the Jews faithful to the law, who were monotheists, interpreted events in Judea in this way.[252] They would have slated an obvious and crude polytheism such as can be found in Kings, say, in Manasseh (II Kings 21.1–18), just as sharply. But the central feature of their polemic is the prohibition of the law, the persecution of those faithful to the law and the desecration of the sanctuary by new cultic forms contradictory to the law. The impression given by I Macc. and Daniel, that what was happening was an attempt to make religion uniform throughout the empire and to propagate the 'foreign god' to whom the king was particularly devoted, is not of course completely without historical background. It presumably comes from the religious propaganda of the reformers in Jerusalem itself, who emphatically appealed to the king in support of their innovations.

It has long been recognized by most scholars that the various designations which apply to the 'abomination of desolation' in Daniel: 8.13 *happeša' šōmēs*; 9.27 *šiqqūṣim mᵉšōmēs* and *'al-šōmēs*; 11.31 *haššiqqūṣ mᵉšōmēs* and 12.11 *šiqqūṣ šōmēs*, represent in the first word a distortion of *ba'al* and in the second of *šāmēs*, and thus reproduce a Semitic name for the god worshipped in the

'Acra'.[253] Baʿal Šāmēm, or in his Aramaic form Beʿel Šemīn, was destined to gain influence in the Hellenistic period as a god who – at least in his later form – 'ruled the whole world', and at the same time 'stood in a particularly intimate relationship to the individual worshipper'.[254] He corresponded to both the individualistic and the universalistic tendencies of the epoch (see above, pp. 116f. and 210f.). We can trace worship of him from the beginning of the first millennium BC down to the middle of the second century AD; it extended from Sardinia and Carthage to Armenia, East Mesopotamia and Arabia. In the earlier period he was worshipped above all in the *Phoenician sphere of influence*, and there Philo Byblius attests the identification of him with Zeus (and Helios): τοῦτον (sc. τὸν ἥλιον) γάρ (φησίν) θεὸν ἐνόμιζον μόνον οὐρανοῦ κύριον Βεελσάμην καλοῦντες, ὅ ἐστι παρὰ Φοίνιξι κύριος οὐρανοῦ, Ζεὺς δὲ παρ᾽ Ἕλλησιν.[255]

Presumably he is also identical with the 'Zeus Olympius' who, according to Menander and Dio, two writers who describe Phoenician history from the second century BC, had a sanctuary in Tyre as early as the time of king Hiram, said to be friend and father-in-law of Solomon.[256] Evidence for him increases from the first century BC onwards and relates above all to the Arabian-Syrian-Mesopotamian borders, from the Nabateans, via the Hauran and the Ṣafa, Palmyra, Dura Europos, Haran and Nisibis to the inscriptions of Hatra. Whether this sudden extension of worship of him 'was zealously furthered by the (Seleucid) royal house and all who were close to it or attached importance to its good opinion' (Eissfeldt, op. cit., 2, 178) is, however, questionable. It is much more likely that the development was determined by the religious need of the time, with the supreme god of heaven or the sun god of the monotheism of late antiquity as its final stage.[257] In Babylonian Uruk, the heavenly god Anu suddenly came strongly into the foreground for reasons which have hitherto been unexplained; he occupied the highest place in the pantheon, but early had played only a small part as a *deus otiosus*.[258] It is significant for Judea that as in Idumean Marisa or Samaritan Shechem the aristocracy who were friendly to the Greeks were in close economic and cultural contact with the *Phoenicians*, who had had a dominant role in Palestine from the Persian period onwards and who also played an important role as communicators of Hellenistic civilization. One need only think of their participation in festivals in Tyre, of the anonymous Samaritan or the Jewish 'historian' Eupolemus, according to whom the golden pillar given by Solomon to Hiram was set up in the temple of Zeus Baʿal Šāmēm.[259] Thus for the Hellenists in Jerusalem Baʿal Šāmēm was probably the universal god of heaven of the Phoenicians, who were a model for them here, as in so much else.

Of course we do not know whether the Jewish renegades gave the god on Zion this unaccustomed name. It may have been enough for the Seleucid military settlers to have worshipped him under the name known to them to arouse the polemic of the apocalyptist. In the Persian period, the Jews had readily allowed the official designation of Yahweh as the God of heaven to be used, although at that time it implied identification with the Persian Ahura Mazda and, willy nilly, with the Semitic Ba'al Šāmēm,[260] and precisely in the early Hellenistic period, when the name of Yahweh had become 'unmentionable', the related designation (*'el*) *'elyōn* = ($\theta\epsilon\grave{o}s$) $\H{v}\psi\iota\sigma\tau\sigma s$ enjoyed great popularity in both Jerusalem[261] and in Shechem,[262] although in the Phoenician pantheon it represented a deity almost identical with Ba'al Šāmēm,[263] and the corresponding Greek $\H{v}\psi\iota\sigma\tau\sigma s$ was a widespread epithet of Zeus.[264] Significantly, the designation 'Hypsistos', which appears particularly often in the early evidence from the Diaspora,[265] became the starting point for Jewish-Gentile mixed cults in Asia Minor and on the Black Sea.[266] Whether it was the 'highest' God or, as in Persian times and later, the 'God of heaven' or the 'Lord of heaven', i.e. Ba'al Šāmēm or 'Zeus Olympius' who was worshipped on Zion, for the radical reformers these were *all simply different names for the one, all-embracing deity.* Thus they could assent to the official designation for the sanctuary on Zion – which perhaps had been regarded for a long time as anonymous, as in Shechem[267] – without further ado: the precinct and the altar were consecrated to a universal god of heaven. This conception is thus astonishingly close to what was said of the God of the Jews by Hecataeus, Theophrastus, Posidonius and Varro (see above, pp.256ff.): $\mathring{a}\lambda\lambda\mathring{a}$ $\tau\grave{o}\nu$ $\pi\epsilon\rho\iota\acute{\epsilon}\chi\sigma\nu\tau\alpha$ $\tau\grave{\eta}\nu$ $\gamma\mathring{\eta}\nu$ $\sigma\mathring{v}\rho\alpha\nu\grave{o}\nu$ $\mu\acute{o}\nu\sigma\nu$ $\epsilon\mathring{\iota}\nu\alpha\iota$ $\theta\epsilon\acute{o}\nu$. In this sense one can also speak of a 'Hellenization' of the new form of worship as a result of 'theocrasy' – despite the 'old Semitic' form of the new cult on Zion (see above, pp.261ff.).

It remains questionable whether other gods were also worshipped, and if so how far – whether the new cult can be designated 'polytheistic', as by E. Bickermann (*GM*, 116). It was certainly 'syncretistic', but the sources do not really speak of 'polytheism' proper; the one-sided stress on the 'alien god' in Daniel rather suggests the opposite. In the case of the one exception, the celebration of the feast of Dionysus in II Macc.6.7, we might ask whether 'Dionysus' appears here as an independent deity alongside Zeus Olympius – in this connection E. Bickermann thinks of the Nabatean Dusares[268] – or whether we should regard him as a 'manifestation' of the same god. According to two inscriptions published by B. Lifshitz, in Scythopolis, where there is similarly parallel attestation to the cult of Dionysus and that of Zeus Olympius, at a later date Zeus was on the one hand worshipped as 'Zeus Akraios', as a god of heaven or of the mountains, and perhaps in Dionysian form as 'Zeus Bacchus'.[269] The god Sabazius, who was possibly identified with the Jewish God at an early stage (see above, pp.263f. nn. 45–47), was associated with both Zeus and Dionysus.[270] J. Wellhausen conjectured that the procession in honour of Dionysus should be combined with the consecration of the addition to the altar on 25 Chislev, which was both celebrated as a winter solstice festival and, after the purification of the temple and the reconsecration of the sanctuary by the Maccabees, had a further life in a different form as the 'feast of lights' ($\phi\hat{\omega}\tau\alpha$, *Antt.* 12, 325).[271]

> 'It can be doubted whether Dionysus, in whose honour the feast at Jerusalem was instituted, was so very different from Zeus Olympius. The "Lord of heaven" (Belsamin) corresponds to both the former and the latter, but he could also be regarded as an equivalent to the "God of heaven", the name the Jews gave to their ancient God Yahweh.'[272]

Also in favour of this interpretation would be the fact that according to II Macc. 14.33 Nicanor threatened to destroy the temple and erect a temple to Dionysus in its place: this was presumably because the God on Zion could also be brought into connection with Dionysus.[273] Unless II Macc. 6.4 is a piece of traditional polemic, the reference there to feasting and debauchery may perhaps be connected with the feast of Dionysus and the monthly feast of the king's birthday. The character of such feasts is evidenced by the Bacchanalia displayed twenty years earlier in Rome.[274]

E. Bickermann was subjected to the sharpest criticism for his attempt to explain the 'cultural' background to the Hellenistic reform, the *ideology of persecution*.[275] Both I. Heinemann and V. Tcherikover saw the 'Hellenists' merely as the representatives of a decadent aristocracy who were concerned only with riches, power and a luxurious life. As with the *Graeculi* of the Orient', it was said that 'there is no trace of a serious, painful struggle between Hellenistic knowledge and Jewish piety'.[276] This, however, is to present an impermissible simplification of the historical position. Not only can we point to a whole series of significant philosophers and other learned men in the second and first centuries in the Phoenician coastal cities from Laodicea on the Sea through Sidon, Tyre and Ptolemais to Palestinian Ashkelon, but even an inland city like Gadara in Transjordania has a significant tradition of Greek education which reached back into the third century BC (see above, pp. 83ff.). The many-sided literary production of the Palestinian Judaism of the Persian and Hellenistic period, for which the learned upper classes are above all responsible, contradicts the general thesis that the aristocracy who inclined towards Hellenism in the first third of the second century BC were without any intellectual interest. In view of the strength of the forces which, even under Jason, had a very positive attitude towards a reform, and the concerns for the reception of Greek language and civilization going back well into the third century, it would be extremely improbable if the reformers could not have grounded their criticism of the law and the tradition in the intellectual sphere also – and possibly even have put it into writing.

Here E. Bickermann begins from the maxim already quoted several times which, according to I Macc. 1.11, represented the 'programme' of the Hellenists: 'Let us go and make a covenant with the Gentiles round about us, for since we separated from them many evils have come upon us.' Here the traditional view is certainly maintained that disaster in history is punishment for the wrong conduct of the people, but its content is turned upside down: the catastrophe of past history has been caused not by imitation of the Gentiles and their idolatry, but by separation.[277] The ἀπάνθρωπόν τινα καὶ μισόξενον βίον of the Jews had already struck their earliest chronicler Hecataeus, and became one of the chief causes of ancient antisemitism.[278] According to Eratosthenes (275–194 BC), 'xenophobia' was a typical characteristic of the barbarians: κοινὸν μὲν εἶναι τοῖς βαρβάροις πᾶσιν ἔθος τῆς ξενηλασίας.[279] The ideal of the educated, which became common property as a result of the Stoa, was not segregation in a national religion with separatist customs, but world citizenship:[280] μίαν, ξένε, πατρίδα κόσμον ναίομεν cried the Palestinian Meleager of Gadara to his readers (see above, pp. 84f., n. II, 209). The tolerant apologetic author of Ps. Aristeas, for whom the Zeus of the philosophers was identical with the God of Israel (see above, pp. 264f.), had great difficulties in making the segregation of the Jews comprehensible. He was only able to do so by portraying the Jews – again in accordance with an ideal of his time – as 'philosophers', who remained aloof from all external matters to 'devote their whole life to the study of the divine rule'.[281] The reformers may have felt not only the political catastrophes of the past but also the economic, political and intellectual isolation of the Jewish 'ethnos' to have been a 'punishment' for their segregation: once the Tobiad Joseph had succeeded in breaking through it, the conservative circles had erected new protective walls as a counter-measure.[282] True, one could follow I. Heinemann in objecting that these trends present in the time of Jason had nothing to do with the later persecution, which was solely the work of Antiochus.[283] But according to the account in I Macc. I, the events in Jerusalem represented a *consistent escalation* which had been hastened and heightened to the level of armed revolt by party disputes in the city, the political ineptitude of the king, the deposition of Jason, the plundering of the temple and above all the growing resistance of those faithful to the law. The 'zeal against the law' and the 'zeal for the law' finally beat up against one another and led to a bitter civil war.

Bickermann's view that the Hellenists believed 'that there had been a primeval time when separation was unknown', and that they thus 'applied to their own people ideas from the Greek enlightenment' (*GM*, 128) is an illuminating one. He refers to the theories of Posidonius about the great lawgivers of primeval times and the later distortion which he believed to have happened in the history of the Jews, namely, that the good and simple legislation of Moses had been falsified at a later period by superstitious and forceful priests who by separatist regulations had changed the simple and truthful worship of God intended by the founder into something quite different.[284] Of course, here one can only bring forward tentative hypotheses, as the sources say nothing about the deeper reasons for the reform. Posidonius (*c.* 135–51/50 BC) wrote his treatise on the Jews probably about a hundred years later, after the conquest of Jerusalem by Pompey in 63 BC, but the theory of the perfection of primeval times and a later decline was a widespread one. It already appears in Hesiod and – in another form – in the Yahwist and in the Priestly codex. Ideas of this kind are likely (see n.14 above). According to Tacitus, too, or the sources on which he drew, the ritual commandments which brought about the segregation of the Jews only entered the nature of the Jewish state, constituted in this way, after Moses, by the annexing of bad elements from neighbouring peoples (*Hist.*5, 4f). One could ask whether this theory of the perversion of the originally good legislation of Moses did not perhaps derive from the Jewish Hellenists.

Possibly in some aristocratic families in Jerusalem there was still a dim awareness that in its present form the law was not as old as all that and was not the work of Moses alone. The continuance of such critical ideas in Palestinian Judaism is indicated by the Mishnah *Sanh.*10, 1, which was written during the early controversy with the Sadducees at the beginning of the first century BC. This states that no one will have a share in the future world who asserts, 'There is no Torah from heaven' (i.e. from God). Philo, too, reports much criticism of the Torah in Greek-educated and predominantly Jewish circles in Alexandria, 'who disregard kinsmen and friends, who transgress laws in which they were born and brought up, who undermine ancestral custom which cannot rightly be censured, and fall away from it' (*Vit.Mos.*1, 31, M2, 85). In another passage he attacks those 'who proclaim their displeasure with the constitution made by the fathers and express incessant censure and complain against the law', talking about the ludicrous fables ($\mu\hat{v}\theta o\iota$) in the Pentateuch.[285] We must imagine that the criticism of the law made by the 'enlightened' aristocracy in Jerusalem took an analogous form. It is further conceivable that influence was exerted not only by those wisdom schools in Jerusalem which worked towards an association of '*ḥokmā*' with the national tradition and its identification with the Torah, but also those which maintained the international and rational character of wisdom and in view of their starting point had a more open attitude towards the Greek enlightenment. It must remain an open question whether Koheleth should be associated with an earlier stage of this trend. Nevertheless, it is not improbable that there are contacts between him and criticism of religion in the early Hellenistic period; an 'enlightened' interpretation of this independent wisdom teacher would be at least as possible as a later correction in a traditional orthodox direction (see above, pp.127ff.). So it is conceivable that in pre-Maccabean Jerusalem there was a broad, influential stream which rejected the constricting limitations of the ritual law as 'superstition', which unwillingly associated with pious convention as long as conservative groups were in the ascendancy, but which were only waiting for the moment when they could throw off the yoke of the law. Sirach's open polemic against those who 'put the law to shame' and those who 'abandon the law of the Most High' shows that the battle was fully joined in his own time. The 'praise of the fathers' could be intended to glorify the history of the faith of his people, looked on critically by the Hellenists, through its great figures, and the universal picture of history in apocalyptic, which does, however, have the history of Israel at its centre, is perhaps (among other things) also an answer to certain 'cosmopolitan' trends in the Jewish metropolis (see above, pp. 136f.). Of course, for the 'reform Jews', not only was the history of Israel essential, but so also were those features which gave occasion to glorify the fathers of primal times, like Abraham and Moses, as '*prōtoi heuretai*' and true citizens of the world, features which we have encountered in the anonymous Samaritan, Eupolemus, Artapanus, Cleodemus Malchus and others (see above, p. 91, n. II, 262 and pp. 73f., n. II, 135). The idea of the primal affinity between the Spartans and the Jews through Abraham, the marriage of a daughter of Hiram of Tyre to Solomon and the legends about the golden pillar given by Solomon and placed in the temple of Ba'al Šāmēm in the city, or about the contest of riddles between the two, may also come from these circles (see above, p. 72, n. II, 262, and p. 94, n. II, 287). *Abraham* above all seems to have been of interest to them, especially as the most remarkable reports about him were current: Berossus had already mentioned him; he was said to have joined friendship with the Pergamenes and to have ruled for a certain time as king of Damascus. He is also said to have gone to Egypt to hear the priests there and to compare his views about the gods with theirs.[286] This is not to say that these scattered reports all come from the 'Hellenists' in Jerusalem from the time about 175 BC, but they show that in early Hellenistic Judaism there was a view of Abraham and the other fathers which in its cosmopolitan breadth fundamentally differed from the one which Ben Sira puts in the foreground:

> He kept the law of the Most High
> And was taken into covenant with him;
> he established the covenant in his flesh,
> and when he was tested he was found faithful (44.20).

The climax of this presumably antithetical picture of Abraham oriented on the law comes in the book of Jubilees, according to which Abraham already fulfilled all the essential commandments of the Torah before Moses (see above, pp. 91, 168). In extreme opposition to this is a report, albeit a late one, that in the fifth century AD the Samaritan Marinus justified his transition to Neo-Platonism on the grounds that his fellow Samaritans had all departed from the original teaching of Abraham because of later innovations ($\kappa\alpha\iota\nu\sigma\tauo\mu\iota\alpha\nu$).[287] The parallel to Posidonius' theory of the decline is striking. Might not the Jewish Hellenists similarly have sought the ideal of a 'natural', original patriarchal religion, not yet falsified by superstitious usages? Unfortunately the lack of sources prevents us from giving a definitive answer.

One might also perhaps draw certain conclusions for the 'conception of God' among the 'reformers' from Ben Sira's polemic. In 16.17–23 he attacks

those who believe that God cannot care about the individual and that there is
no obvious righteous retribution; in 15.11–17 he turns to those who assert that
there is no freedom of decision, and that man's wrong conduct rather comes
from God himself (see above, pp. 140f.). His theodicy, which is meant to
demonstrate the perfection of creation, even including evil, and its purposefulness for men (see above, pp. 144ff.), is probably directed against views to the
opposite effect. Was a conception of God perhaps predominant among the
Hellenists in which the omnipotence of God and the incalculability of fate
coincided, so that the all-embracing 'heavenly God' was in effect identical
with the compulsion of the stars ? Again one could cite the anonymous Samaritan and Artapanus (see above, pp. 89ff.), and also the Essenes (see above,
pp. 237ff.), for the strong interest of Jewish circles in astrology. F. Cumont and
H. Gressmann have also pointed out the strong astral features in Baʿal Šāmēm
or the supreme Semitic God of heaven in the Hellenistic period.

> The distance between the human and the divine was always much greater
> among the Semites, and astrology could only contribute to stressing it still
> more strongly, by giving it a didactic basis and a scientific garb.[288]

Thus the consecration of the addition to the altar on 25 Chislev 167 BC
would be understood 'as the solstice festival of the hated Belsamin', which
lived on after the Maccabean victory as the feast of lights and the consecration
of the temple.[289] It seems most improbable that the supporters of unqualified
assimilation imitated the still relatively primitive forms of Arabian-Nabatean
assimilation – here E. Bickermann contradicts his own views to some extent.
Rather, the models for them were the 'progressive' Phoenician cities, which
were able to combine national tradition and unqualified acceptance of Hellenistic civilization. Towards the middle of the second century BC, the opinionated
Stoic Boethus of Sidon taught there that the world and God were not identical,
but that the latter had his place in the perfect firmament: θεοῦ τὴν ἀπλανῶν
σφαῖραν. Presumably he was also influenced by the conception of the
Semitic supreme God of heaven in the astral sphere,[290] a view in which
Semites and Greeks agreed. If the 'apostates' accepted certain apparently
polytheistic forms – as e.g. the emperor cult or the worship of Dionysus, this
was because as 'enlightened' Hellenists they believed themselves to be in a
position to 'interpret' the different forms of religion rationally.

These hypotheses cannot amount to more than 'suggestions for the ideology
of apostasy'. Unfortunately the defeated party has left behind no direct source
as to the deeper motives of their 'reform attempt', which came to a conclusion
in a bloody persecution.

4. Summary: The Reform Attempt, its Failure and the Far-reaching Consequences of the Jewish Counter-reaction

Jewish worship of God, without images, spiritual and appearing rational to the Greeks, aroused the positive interest of a number of Greek writers in the Jews in the early Hellenistic period. They regarded the Jew as a special kind of barbarian 'philosopher', a notion which was taken up by the Jews with a Greek education, say, in Alexandria – but probably not only there – and put to their own ends. On the other hand, the exclusive claim to truth of the Jewish religion and the segregation of the Jews from their non-Jewish environment, furthered by the ritual commands of the law, had to an increasing degree a negative effect. From this there developed the charge of 'superstition', intolerance, indeed of 'impiety', and among serious ancient history writers this even led to the severest distortions of Judaism. The God of the Jews was partially interpreted in a philosophical sense – as say with Hecataeus, Posidonius and Varro, by being identified with the heavens or the cosmos, but another way was to identify him, through theocrasy, with other deities like Sabazius, Dionysus or Zeus, a process which was not always rejected out of hand even by Jews.

The most dangerous development was the attempt by a part of the Jewish aristocracy to approximate Jewish belief in God and the cult on Zion in a syncretistic way to its Hellenistic environment in Jerusalem itself, under Antiochus IV, by violent means. Whereas alien influences were at work unconsciously with Ben Sira, the Hasidim and Essenism, here there was a consistent and open tendency towards complete Hellenization. Presumably the tendencies towards assimilation in Judea had a long history behind them, and go well back into the third century BC. Probably the most powerful Jewish lay family, the Tobiads, already had very close contacts with the Greeks in the middle of the third century BC: the Tobiad Joseph became chief tax farmer under the Ptolemies and worked for a closer economic and cultural contact with the non-Jewish environment. However, for the moment the vigorous conservative high priest Simon the Just succeeded in suppressing the influence of his sons. Thus the struggle for power of the high-priestly Oniads and the Tobiads forms the historical background to the real reform attempt in Jerusalem after the accession of Antiochus IV in 175 BC. While the liberal Tobiad Hyrcanus built up the Ptolemaic cleruchy of his grandfather Tobias in the Ammanitis into a semi-independent territory and finally managed to erect a schismatic Jewish sanctuary with a syncretistic flavour, in Jerusalem the aristocracy in favour of reform gained the upper hand through the deposition of Onias III, and with the king's help prepared to change Jerusalem into a Greek *polis* by the building of a gymnasium and the establishment of a list of citizens. The expulsion of the last Oniad, Jason, from his office and his replacement with Menelaus, who was closely associated with the Tobiads, gave full power to the reformers, but as their support was limited, it made them even more dependent on the favour of the Seleucid ruler who – in exchange for his services – laid his hands on the temple treasures. After an abortive attempt at revolt by Jason and in view of the hostile attitude of the simple, conservative populace, the radical reformers with Menelaus at their head advised the king to abolish by royal edict the Jewish law, from which they had long been alienated and towards which they were hostile (as it gave support to their opponents). To support them, Seleucid cleruchs were settled in the newly-built Acra south of the temple, and together they formed the citizens of the new *polis*. The decree obtained from the king formed the basis of the compulsory abrogation of the law and the persecution of those faithful to it. The cult in the temple was also 'reformed' in syncretistic fashion, presumably following the example of the more strongly Hellenized Phoenicians. As maller altar on the great altar of burnt offering formed the real cultic centre on Zion within a temple courtyard changed into a 'holy precinct'. Honour was given above all to the 'supreme God of heaven', interpreted in a syncretistic and universalistic way. He was identified with Ba'al Šāmēm of the Phoenicians and Zeus Olympius of the Greeks. Presumably the radical reformers were influenced by the ideas of the Greek enlightenment, and perhaps they sought to restore the original 'reasonable' form of worship of the deity without 'superstitious' falsification. At the same time they sought the complete dissolution of the characteristics of Judaism and its consistent assimilation to its Hellenistic oriental environment. As a result of their victorious revolt and the continuing weakening of the Seleucid empire, the Maccabees succeeded in warding off the deadly threat, and after struggles lasting for decades achieved national independence through the edict of Demetrius II in 142 BC (I Macc. 13.31–42). The Acra fell a year later. Of course a severe 'collective trauma' remained, despite the victory, and this had a decisive influence on the further course of Jewish history.

The controversy in Jerusalem after 175 BC, which reached its climax between 167 and 164 BC, was a *struggle over the law*. The Jewish renegades wanted to reverse by violence the course which the Jewish people had pursued since the exile. However, those who were faithful to the law – as is shown by both the book of Daniel and the first chapters of I Maccabees – did not refer one-sidedly to the Torah;[291] they used a more comprehensive term from salvation history: they defended 'the holy covenant'.[292] Among the fathers of Jewish apocalyptic there was still a lively awareness that the history of God with his people rested on a 'covenant' the most important part of which was, of course, the law.[293] So the attack on the law let loose by the renegades' hate of it – one can speak directly of a 'zeal against the law' – aroused a corresponding counter-reaction, 'zeal for the law', and as a result the further spiritual development of Judaism was in a remarkable way associated with the Torah. The Pharisees, who were primarily involved in this development, are in a direct line from the Hasidim of the Maccabean period who formed the intellectual élite of the Jewish struggle for freedom (see above, pp. 175ff.); about fifty years later, in the time of Hyrcanus, they parted company with the Hasmoneans because the latter would not accept their legal casuistry and additional oral tradition. Significantly, a considerable element of the people went over to their side even at this stage, not least because as a result of the institution of the synagogue they had become the teachers of the simple populace and had deeply anchored in them the aggressive pattern of 'zeal for the law'.[294] We should not overlook the significance of the crisis after 175 BC, which only to a limited degree came to an end with the official return of the temple at the end of 163 BC and dragged on until the conquest of the Acra in 141 BC. It was particularly important for the future history of Judaism and indirectly for the origin of Christianity. It gave a new direction to the political and intellectual development of the Jewish people in many respects.

1. The *extreme sensitivity* of Palestinian Judaism towards even an apparent usurpation of power over the law and the sanctuary which is demonstrated in the Essene attacks on Jonathan and the Pharisaic criticism of John Hyrcanus,[295] and which was expressed in wild mass demonstrations under Alexander Jannaeus, Herod and Archelaus and the Roman procurators,[296] is a fruit of this newly awakened '*zeal*'. One might see it as an almost anarchical feature which on the one hand made it extraordinarily difficult for the Jews to be governed by their own or by foreign rulers, and which at the same time was directed against the people themselves, because it made unitary action in times of political need almost impossible, since the disputing groups kept accusing each other of 'apostasy from the law'. This anarchic radicalism, especially in Palestinian Judaism, which however also extended in the Roman period to the Diaspora and found an expression in the intensive national eschatological expectation of the future (see pp.254f.), is one of the chief causes of the incessant series of rebellions in Judea and the great catastrophes of AD 66–70, 116–117 and 132–135. The moderate forces were too weak to restrain these developments. Among the themes which developed in apocalyptic in the time of persecution under Antiochus IV is the figure of the 'final tyrant' or 'Antichrist', and the notion that the holy city and the temple or part of it will be 'trampled down' by the Gentiles. Thus it was natural to judge the Roman rule in the light of this pattern, and for the Jews always to persecute the 'apostates' in their own ranks.[297]

2. The tendency towards segregation from non-Jews, which had been strengthened by the attempt at assimilation by force, coupled with the political expansion of the Hasmoneans in Palestine and the political and military ascendancy of the Jews under the later Ptolemies,[298] led to ancient '*antisemitism*'. Positive judgments were displaced by negative ones: the change can clearly be seen in Posidonius. Antiochus IV was the political model of the new antisemitism. A similar interpretation of his actions against the Jews is to be found in Posidonius, Apion, Porphyry,[299] and above all in Tacitus:

> Rex Antiochus, demere superstitionem et mores Graecorum dare adnisus, quominus taeterrimam gentem in melius mutaret, Parthorum bello prohibitus est (*Hist.* 5, 8, 2).

This one-sided and tendentious account of the motives of Antiochus IV may have spurred on later Roman emperors to similar anti-Jewish measures. Perhaps this motive already had its effect with Caligula and his attempt to set up his image in the temple at Jerusalem, and possibly also with Vespasian and Titus in respect of the destruction of the temple and the introduction of the *fiscus Judaicus* in favour of Jupiter Capitolinus. Be this as it may, it certainly influenced Hadrian in his prohibition of circumcision and his founding of Aelia Capitolina, and in the erection of temples of Jupiter Capitolinus on Zion and on Gerizim. He then responded to the revolt of Bar Kochba – following the example of Antiochus IV – with the prohibition of the practice of the Jewish law.[300]

3. The persecution and the victorious Maccabean revolt had aroused not only strong religious but also *political forces* – the two can hardly be separated in ancient Judaism. The conquest of Samaria, large parts of Transjordania and all the 'Greek' cities of the coastal plain except Ashkelon, the forcible conversion of the Itureans in Galilee and the Idumeans in the south, must have seemed a miracle to the Jews under foreign rule, and it is understandable that John Hyrcanus could assume charismatic messianic features as a successful commander and high priest.[301] In this way, a tremendous strengthening of Jewish national consciousness came about in Palestine. Despite its expansion and to a degree its missionary successes, the Jewish religion remained primarily a 'national' religion, and for most people the eschatological hope had strong political colouring. The loss of freedom after 63 BC was therefore felt all the more severely. The constant attempts to regain it resulted from the fact that foreign rule was felt to be a threat to obedience to the law, and there was a belief in a repetition of the 'Maccabean miracle'.[302] Even the Jewish mission had its political side: according to Esther 8.17, after the royal edict 'many people accepted Judaism (M *miteyahªdīm*, LXX περιετέμνοντο), for fear of the Jews had fallen upon them', and in Judith 14.6–10 the Ammonite Achior comes to believe in the God of Israel and has himself circumcised when Judith shows him the head of Holofernes, 'and he was reckoned in the house of Israel'. This *connection between nation and religion*, probably unique among the ancient 'missionary' religions, gave Judaism its tremendous strength in the Diaspora, but with few exceptions, say in Adiabene, prevented really extensive missionary success, although in the more open, Greek-speaking Diaspora attempts were made to rob this element of its force. In antiquity, to become a Jew was never simply a religious action; it was always also a political decision: on his conversion the Gentile became a member of the Jewish 'ethnos'.[303] It is understandable that the Roman state regarded the Jewish mission as a danger and often tried to limit it.[304] Jerusalem became the antipodes for Rome, even for the Jews of the Diaspora and the full proselytes, who were closely tied to Jerusalem by the didrachm tax, and the holy land was the real centre of the world. Paul's struggle against circumcision and the law

was not least a 'betrayal of Judaism' in the eyes of his Judaistic opponents because of its 'ethnic political consequences'.[305]

4. True, in the mother country of Judaism a brake was put on the manifest *syncretistic tendencies* which led towards an assimilation to paganism,[306] but in Samaria, in Transjordania[307] and still more in the Greek-speaking Diaspora, they continued to have an effect. We find evidence for Jewish-pagan mixed cults in various inscriptions from Asia Minor, e.g. on the Sambatheion in Thyatira and the worshippers of the God 'Sabbatistēs' in Cilicia, as also in the 'synhodos Sambathikē' in Egyptian Naucratis, the Hypsistos worshippers in the kingdom of the Bosphorus and the later Hypsistarians in Asia Minor. Although this evidence only begins with the time of Augustus, the small number of Jewish pre-Christian inscriptions outside Egypt suggests an earlier date for this mixed cult.[308] The way in which scholars differ in their assessment of it – partly purely Gentile, partly Jewish – is an indication of its ambivalent character, which makes it impossible in practice to distinguish between Judaizing pagans and paganizing Jews.[309] Reports like Acts 19.3ff.; Rev. 2.9 and the false teachers in Colossae may point to the existence of Jewish syncretistic groups of this kind.[310] Philo attests that there were Greek-educated Jews who robbed the law of its literal meaning by radical allegorization, and others who criticized it sharply.[311] Moreover, in his writing, in III Maccabees and in epigraphic sources we find a whole series of references to Jewish apostates.[312] Thus the first beginnings of gnosticism probably developed in heterodox Jewish Samaritan groups. A Jewish antinomianism could also have continued its influence here. Finally, the broad field of Jewish magic must also have led to open syncretism.[313] Thus the Hellenistic environment represented a certain danger, though its effects should not be over-estimated. In warding off the 'reform attempt', the Judaism of Palestine and the Diaspora had found a firm centre in the law which, despite all alien influences and an astonishing multiplicity, at least enabled it to present a relatively closed front to the outside world. This is in fact confirmed by later antisemitic evidence. In addition, a strengthened national self-awareness provided a further effective protection.

5. The failure of the attempt of the Hellenistic reformers to abolish the Torah by force in effect *fixed* intellectual development *on the Torah*. There were presumably preliminaries to the struggle for the law; Ben Sira refers to them, and they are probably also expressed in the 'basic programme' of *'Ab.* 1, 1b: '. . . Set up many schools, put a hedge round the law', regardless of whether this statement comes from before the Maccabean period or after it. This development is sometimes characterized in a derogatory sense as *'nomism'* – mistaking the historical necessity for it. In accordance with the spirit of the Hellenistic period it had a strong rational element which found expression, among other things, in an almost arithmetical idea of reward and in the 'Torah ontology' sketched out on pp. 170ff. above. We find this con-

centration on the Torah both in Pharisaism and in Greek-speaking Judaism, say in Josephus and Philo. But it found its most pregnant expression – in an eschatological context – among those groups whose characteristic H. Braun has described with the concept of '*sharpening of the Torah*'.[314]

6. This fixation meant that any fundamental theological criticism of the cult and the law could no longer develop freely within Judaism. This is also true of the attempt to abolish, for intrinsically religious reasons, the exclusive limitations which pious Jews had imposed as a protection against the 'despisers of the law' among their own people, the Samaritans and the non-Jews, for the sake of the universal character of the salvation conveyed in the message of the prophets. Equally intolerable was a fundamentally critical consideration of their own history and especially the giving of the law, as this is expressed say in Mark 10.5ff.; Acts 7.35–53; or Gal. 3.19ff. Undertakings of this kind were inevitably misunderstood in analogy to the Hellenistic reform attempt as an attack on the supreme articles of Israelite faith or even as apostasy to paganism. Here is the profound tragedy of the reaction of Judaism to the primitive Christian movement which developed from its midst. Jesus of Nazareth, Stephen, Paul came to grief among their own people because the Jews were no longer in a position to bring about a creative, self-critical transformation of the piety of the law with its strongly national and political colouring. The small Jewish Christian community could only maintain itself in Palestine by strict observance of the Torah – and even then only with great difficulty. The charge of apostasy to Hellenistic syncretism still has its influence on Jewish interpretation of Paul, even today.[315] The apostle appears as a 'Diaspora Jew who had become alienated from the faith-ideas of the fathers'.[316] This is to fail to see that the apologetically rigidified understanding of the Torah, which no longer measures up to the message of the prophets, was irreconcilable at that time with the universal eschatological claim of the gospel, and had to be broken.

7. By and large, Judaism had its greatest influence on world history in the Hellenistic-Roman epoch. This included the reception and reworking of Greek thought side by side with self-assertion against alienation; the foundation of a national state after four hundred years of foreign rule, and the inner strength to withstand the new catastrophes which brought that state to an end and led to the final 'dispersion'. We may regard this as an expression of the incomparable *vitality and dynamism* of the Jewish people. Both its freedom fight against the Seleucids and its bitter struggle with Rome are probably unique in the ancient world. However, 'this dynamism' developed most strongly in the religious sphere. This happened in a world-wide mission which was likewise without analogy, and then in the new force which burst the framework of a nationalistic legalism which had grown too narrow with its prophetic and eschatological appeal: the primitive Christianity which grew out of Judaism.

SUMMARY AND CONCLUSION

As is the rule in complex historical circumstances, our account of the first encounter between Judaism and Hellenism in Palestine has not produced a uniform, easily understandable, uncontradictory picture, which could be summed up in a schematic judgment. It is not possible to say that Palestinian Judaism, leaving aside the interlude under Antiochus IV, which was speedily remedied, maintained a straight course through the Hellenistic period untouched by the alien civilization and completely faithful to the Old Testament tradition. Still less can it be claimed that it was completely permeated by the Hellenistic spirit and fell victim to syncretism, betraying its original task. The truth lies between the extremes.

It is evident that as early as the third century BC an encounter between Hellenistic civilization and the Jewish upper classes took place which was probably more intensive than our scanty sources indicate to us. The Zeno papyri and the earliest Greek reports about the Jews on the one hand, and the Tobiad romance, the anonymous Samaritan and similar literary fragments, together with the polemic of Ben Sira on the other hand, all indicate this. So the significance of one hundred years of predominantly Ptolemaic rule for the internal development of Palestine cannot be set too highly. However, this process of Hellenization did not affect all the Jewish population in the same way. Following the character of the new civilization in the conquered areas of the East as being a civilization for the aristocrats and more well-to-do citizens, it had an open and direct influence only on the relatively narrow, but normative stratum of the priestly and lay nobility and the prosperous city population. These took delight in a freer, more expensive style of life and in freer thought. In these circles, perhaps in connection with a 'wisdom school' which was influenced by the Greek 'enlightenment' and had a hostile attitude to the received tradition, the law was increasingly criticized as being a hindrance to economic and cultural development. This development culminated in the violent 'reform attempt' depicted in the last chapter, which, however, came to grief on the resolute resistance of the majority of the population.

However, even the traditional wisdom schools in which 'wisdom' and 'Torah' were identified, probably in repudiation of the antinomian tendencies mentioned above, came near to some of the ideas of a popular Stoicism, as is shown by the example of Ben Sira. In this sense the manifest adoption of philosophical ideas in Alexandria, which emerges for the first time with

Aristobulus, simply represents a continuation of tendencies which were already at work in Palestine, albeit in a less marked form. At that late period there was an alliance between oriental Jewish wisdom and Greek popular philosophy. Common to both was their rational, empirical character, their universalist tendency, their interest in the divine ordering of the cosmos and their marked anthropological and ethical perspective. This is confirmed, among other things, by early Greek verdicts on the Jews as 'philosophers'.

The draughts of the new spirit were to be felt not only in the realm of the pro-Hellenistic upper class and in late wisdom, but at the very point where the bitterest defensive action was being fought against the destructive forces of Hellenism, among the Hasidim. With their rigorist fidelity to the law, they wrote the first apocalypses and thus exercised a most tenacious influence on the further religious development of ancient Judaism, but even they reveal a 'syncretistic' influence fed from many sources. The spirit of a disruptive enlightenment was countered by an encyclopaedic wisdom, superior to all purely human wisdom, which was based on a divine revelation that unveiled all the mysteries of the cosmos and of history. These 'faithful' formed a spiritual bulwark in the battle against the Hellenistic reformers and their Seleucid allies, yet a little while later their radical wing turned no less sharply against the successful Hasmonean dynasty which, after its victory, could not escape the hated alien form of life. Under the 'Teacher of Righteousness' this Hasidic group of 'Essenes' separated from the bulk of the people and formed a strictly organized community with a virtually monastic character, which, however, despite its abrupt rejection of all that was un-Jewish, had its nearest analogy as an organization in the Greek association. Even it was strongly influenced by the Hellenistic oriental environment, though at the same time, with astonishing attempts at systematic thought, it produced the most significant theological statements between Deutero-Isaiah and the New Testament. Even Pharisaism, the second branch of the Hasidim, developed – as a continuation of Ben Sira's identification of wisdom and Torah – a kind of 'Torah ontology' which has parallels to the thought of Philo. Here is a confusing, many-sided picture of changing types of reception and reaction which none of the different, partially opposed groups in Palestinian Judaism could avoid. Even where people thought themselves to be oriented to the Torah alone – indeed precisely among such people – an abundance of alien influence was accepted, often without the fact being noticed. Thus the spirit of the new period worked on each of the different Jewish groups in another form again, and in this way Palestinian Judaism underwent a profound transformation during the Hellenistic era in a relatively continuous development down to 175 BC. For this reason, the distinction between 'Palestinian' Judaism and the 'Hellenistic' Judaism of the Greek-speaking Diaspora, which has been customary for so long, now becomes very questionable. Strictly speaking, for the Hellenistic-Roman period the Judaism of the mother country must just as much be included under the heading 'Hellenistic Judaism' as that of the western Diaspora. This statement applies not only to external cultural influences, but even in the religious sphere – indeed, particularly there. For 'Palestinian' Judaism also shared in the 'religious *koinē*' of its Hellenistic oriental environment. This is true, *inter alia*, of the idea of a 'natural revelation' which appears even before wisdom, the knowledge of God from the purposefulness and perfection of the natural order, and especially the stars; it is true of the idea of divine providence and retribution in the life of the individual and above all after his death, the expectation of a future realm of peace, the existence of heavenly hypostases and redeemer figures, angels, demons and spirits of the dead, the significance of astrology, manticism and magic, the forms of supernatural revelation of divine wisdom through dreams, visions, journeys through heaven and the underworld, ecstatic or inspired discourse or holy scriptures given by God. Jewish Palestine was no hermetically sealed island in the sea of Hellenistic oriental syncretism.

Of course Judaism both inside and outside Palestine retains a dominant central feature in the form of the *Torah*, despite its confusing multiplicity. Indeed, the Torah gained this absolute significance precisely through the struggle for spiritual self-affirmation. Ben Sira declared that the Torah was identical with wisdom, but for the reformers in Jerusalem it was the embodiment of superstition and folly, against which they finally fought with brute force. In so doing, however, they simply aroused the 'zeal for the law' among those faithful to the Torah on which their party came to grief. Thus the controversy with Hellenism made the Torah the centre point of Judaism, though of course not only in Alexandria, but also in the Rabbinic 'Torah ontology', it was interpreted in a 'Hellenistic rationalist' way. It became more and more the only, exclusive medium of revelation, and all other forms of revelation were derived from it and formed to a certain extent its interpretation. There may have been hopeless disputes over the right interpretation of the law, but it was still the expression of the unity of the Jewish people, by which it was distinguished from all other peoples. At the same time, even in the Greek-educated circles of the Diaspora, the law gave a guarantee of religious and national cohesion, while its ethical monotheism provided a feeling of superiority over the Hellenistic cults.

A second fruit of the controversy with Hellenism was *hope for the future*, which among the simple populace usually took the form of an imminent eschatological expectation. This was hope, for the whole people, of the rule of God or the messianic kingdom, and for the individual, of resurrection or immortality. The whole of world history, according to God's plan, would find its goal in the time of salvation, which was expected to come in the near future. At the same time, eschatology formed the only regulative force by which the omnipotence of the Torah, dominating the present and anchored in the cosmos, could possibly be limited.

In the Hellenistic period, say from the second half of the second century BC, Judaism was well on the way towards becoming a *world religion* as a result of the rapid extension of the Diaspora and a partially very active mission – the success of the Maccabean period had also raised its self-awareness in this respect. The anxious and zealous fixation on the letter of the Torah which we meet in Pharisaism was, of course, in manifest opposition to this. Even in Greek-speaking Judaism there was only a slightly greater freedom towards the law here; the allegorical interpretation did not do away with the literal sense, and the concrete commands and prohibitions remained unqualifiedly in force even in Philo. Moreover, after the Hasmonean rule the influence of the Palestinian mother country and its piety also grew in the Diaspora. Even the eschatological hope among the people was predominantly interpreted in a nationalistic sense as the expectation of a Jewish world-kingdom (Acts 1.6). Under this lay a defensive attitude which was largely justified, brought about by the trauma of the Hellenistic reform and the unexpected national expansion of the Hasmoneans, their sudden collapse after the intervention of Pompey and the subsequent Roman rule. The almost complete fusion of religion and nationalism not only prevented any assimilation, but at the same time gave the Jewish minority, particularly in the Diaspora, a political importance which even the Roman rulers after Caesar had to take seriously. A universal missionary consciousness could not really develop freely in the face of this elemental impulse towards national self-preservation. The large number of semi-proselytes standing between Judaism and paganism in the New Testament period, who could not take the last step towards complete association with the Jewish people (*c. Ap.* 2, 183), although out of conviction they followed the Jewish faith and its monotheism supported by a profound ethical consciousness, shows the insoluble dilemma of the Jewish religion in ancient times. As it could not break free from its nationalist roots among the people, it had to stoop to constant and ultimately untenable compromises. This is where the reaction of the primitive church with its prophetic spirit, growing out of Judaism, set in. The first step in this direction was the early Christian mission among the hated Samaritans, which was presumably carried out by members of the Greek-speaking Jewish-Christian group who were driven out of Jerusalem (Acts 8.4ff.). A little later followed the mission towards the non-Jews in Antioch (Acts 11.19ff.). At this point, though in a very different way from the reform attempt after 175 BC, the door really was thrown open to the 'nations'.

With Jesus' prophetic and eschatological message of the imminence of the kingdom of God, and the kerygma of the primitive community which took that message further – its revolutionary consequences were recognized above all by the group of 'Hellenists' in Jerusalem who were familiar with the self-contradictory nature of the Jewish mission – the protective attitude of Judaism over against its environment, which had been developed in the controversy

with Hellenism and was most strongly expressed by the absolutized place of
the Torah, was shattered in pieces. Christology took the place of 'Torah
ontology' as an expression of the free and sovereign saving revelation of God in
history, which no longer recognized national or historically conditioned
limitations. Thus particularly in view of the especially active, Greek-speaking
Jewish-Christian community in Jerusalem and later in Antioch, primitive
Christianity is to be seen as an eschatological and revolutionary movement
within Judaism itself in which the 'salvation-historical' task of the people of
God on the basis of the 'fulfilment of time' and in expectation of the imminent
end of the world was fulfilled by national self-surrender for the nations of the
world (cf. Gal. 3.28; 4.4). That it was misunderstood from the Jewish side at
that time as a new sect urging apostasy from the law and assimilation is
indirectly the last and most grievous legacy of those Jewish renegades who,
between 175 and 164 BC, attempted to do away with the law and 'make a
covenant with the people round about'. The zeal for the law aroused at that
time made impossible all attempts at an internal reform of the Jewish religion
undertaken in a prophetic spirit, as soon as the nerve centre, the law, was
attacked.

VOLUME TWO

INTRODUCTION

1. II Macc. 2.21; 8.1; K. G. Kuhn, *TDNT* 3, 364; M. Hengel, *ZNW* 57, 1966, 179f.

2. For the first time in Theophrastus, see R. Laqueur, *Hellenismus*, 1925, 22 n. 8, cf. Diogenes of Babylon, SVF 3, 214, no. 24. Cf. W. Jaeger, *Das frühe Christentum*, 1963, 3, 81; H. Preisker, *Ntl. Zeitgeschichte*, 1936, 5f.

3. Laqueur, op. cit., 27f. n. 9.

4. Ibid., 4ff., 21 n. 1; G. Droysen, *Johann Gustav Droysen* I, 1910, 69 n. 1; cf. F. Meinecke, *HZ* 141, 1930, 261.

5. See the introduction to Vol. 1 of *Geschichte des Hellenismus*, 1836, 4f. Italics mine.

6. Preface to Vol. 2 of *Geschichte des Hellenismus*, 1843; reprint ed. E. Bayer, Tübingen 1953, Vol. 3, xxii, cf. xvii.

7. F. Meinecke, 'Johann Gustav Droysen', in *Staat und Persönlichkeit*, 1933, 110; cf. *HZ* 141, 1930, 262.

8. J. G. Droysen, *Historik*, ed. R. Hübner, 1937, 319 (Foreword to *Grundriss der Historik*, 1868). Cf. also Jaeger, op. cit., 2f., 80 n. 5.

9. Bousset/Gressmann, 483: 'However, Hellenism is not a unity, but a combination of all possible forms and interpenetrating influences'; V. Grönbech, *Der Hellenismus*, 1953, 15: 'In Hellenism the horizon is enlarged, there are no walls which round off experience as a whole and provide firmness for thought', cf. 13–17. Similarly H. Preisker, op. cit., 11.

10. S. J. Kaerst, *Geschichte des Hellenismus* I³, 110ff., 138ff.; 2², 272; H. Bengtson, *GG*³, 285ff., reckons the Hellenistic period from 360 BC, from about the accession of Philip II of Macedon.

11. Cf. F. Altheim, *Weltgeschichte Asiens* 2, 1948, 147: 'The Hellenic character of the Stoics of Phoenician origin was a direct continuation of the self-Hellenization of Western Asia, which had already taken place before the conquest of Alexander' (see Vol. I, pp. 32ff., 61f.).

12. For the first view see e.g. W. Schubart, *Verfassung und Verwaltung des Ptolemäerreiches*, AO 35, 1937, Vol. 4, 4: 'Hellenism brings and is an extension of the Hellenic character', and H. Herter in *Das Neue Bild der Antike* 1, 1942, 334–55, cf. 336ff. For the pseudomorphosis between 'ancient' and 'Arab culture' see O. Spengler, *The Decline of the West*, 1926, 209ff., and on this H. Jonas, *Gnosis und spätantiker Geist* 1, ²1954, 73f. Cf. also Preisker, op. cit., 6–12.

13. Views differ over the proportions of Greek and oriental influence in the religious sphere. Whereas R. Reitzenstein, *Die hellenistischen Mysterienreligionen*, ³1927, 2f., and F. Cumont, *Die orientalischen Religionen*, ⁴1959, xiiif., etc. over-

stress the oriental side, it is almost completely denied by C. Schneider, *ARW* 36, 1939, 300–47, and in his *Geistesgeschichte des Antiken Christentums*, 2 vols., 1954. M. P. Nilsson, *GGR*² 2, 5ff. occupies a middle position and stresses that the permanent share of Greek religion, despite all the transformations, should not be underestimated.

14. E. Schürer, *Geschichte des jüdischen Volkes im Zeitalter Jesu Christi*, ³˒⁴1901–1909, 3 vols. (cited as Schürer); F. M. Abel, *Histoire de la Palestine*, Tome I, *De la conquête d'Alexandre jusqu'à la guerre Juive*, 1952 (cited as *HP*); V. Tcherikover, *Hellenistic Civilization and the Jews*, tr. S. Applebaum, 1961 (cited as *HC*).

15. Bousset/Gressmann, *Die Religion des Judentums im späthellenistischen Zeitalter*, ³1926; A. Schlatter, *Geschichte Israels von Alexander d.Gr. bis Hadrian*, ³1925 (cited as *GI*³).

16. M. Rostovtzeff, *The Social and Economic History of the Hellenistic World*, 3 vols., 1941 (cited as *HW*); M. P. Nilsson, *Geschichte der Griechischen Religion*, Vol. I, ²1955; Vol. II, ²1961 (cited as *GGR*²).

I

Early Hellenism as a Political and Economic Force

1. Cf. Diodore 20, 113; 21, 5; W. W. Tarn, *CAH* 6, 502; 7, 76ff., 701f.; E. R. Bevan, *History of Egypt*, 1927, 37; P. Jouguet, *L'impérialisme Macédonien*, 1926, 183; Volkmann, *PW* 23, 1623f.; H. H. Schmitt, *Untersuchungen zur Geschichte Antiochos' d.Gr.*, Historia-Einzelschriften 6, 1964, 35; É. Will, *Histoire politique du monde hellénistique* 1, 1966, 68ff. W. Otto, *Beiträge zur Seleukidengeschichte*, AAM 34, 1928, 78 n.2, believes that Ptolemy was summoned back because of unrest in Cyrene. For the hypothesis that Palestine and Coele Syria originally belonged to the Seleucid empire see J. Beloch, *APF* 2, 1902, 229–37, and Tcherikover, *HC*, 53f.; F. M. Abel, *HP* 1, 42, and B. Niese, *GGMS* 1, 387, conjecture a Seleucid rule until at least 295 BC. Bouché-Leclerq, *Histoire des Lagides* 1, 154, and E. Meyer, *UAC* 2, 3, even go down to the murder of Seleucus I in 281 BC. The report of Sulpicius Severus, II, 17, 4f. (ed. C. Halm, CSEL 1, 73), that Seleucus imposed an annual tax of 300 talents on the Jews, does not prove anything, as he has no knowledge of any Ptolemaic rule in Palestine. It could be a Ptolemaic tax or one imposed later by Seleucus IV (see below, pp.28f.). Nor is there evidence for the foundation of cities by the Seleucids in Coele Syria and Palestine in the third century BC. However, the Seleucids never gave up their claim, see Polybius 5, 67.

2. Eusebius, *Chron.*, ed. Helm, GCS 7, 127f.: *Samaritarum urbem vastat*. On this cf. P. Jouguet, op. cit., 188f., and Tcherikover, *HC*, 424 n. 42; 451, n. 101. In that case the city would have been destroyed three times within 35 years. B. Niese, *GGMS* 1, 355 and W. W. Tarn, *CAH* 7, 78, doubt the historicity of the episode. For the role of Demetrius to 286 see H. Bengtson, *GG³*, 374ff.

3. The strategic significance of Coele Syria for the Ptolemies is already stressed by Diodore on the basis of Hieronymus of Cardia, 18, 43, 1. For the Jewish mercenaries see Vol.I, pp.15f.

4. 'Syria and Phoenicia' was the official Ptolemaic designation of the province: see W. Otto, AAM 34, 1928, 37; U. Wilcken, *APF* 12, 1937, 223; H. Bengtson, *Die Strategie in hellenistischer Zeit* 3, 1952, 166 n.1, and Tcherikover, *HC*, 423 n.36; 428 n.55; CPJ 1, 5 n.13. Perhaps in this way the Ptolemies wanted to express a claim to all Syria. The designation appears even in Seleucid documents, see V. H. Landau, *IEJ* 16, 1966, 59 III, 14 (Ḥepzibah).

5. See Vol.I, pp.39ff. They key work on Zeno and his relationship with Apollonius is M. Rostovtzeff, *A Large Estate in Egypt in the Third Century BC*, 1922, esp. 16–41; see also the introduction by C. C. Edgar to PMichZen. 5–50. Archaeological details are given, *inter alia*, by P. Viereck, *Philadelphia*, Morgenland 16, 1928. On the decisive role of the Greeks in the economic development of

Egypt see C. Préaux, *Les Grecs d'après les archives de Zénon*, 1947 (lit.). For conditions in Palestine, which can also be discovered from the Zeno correspondence, see L. H. Vincent, *RB* 29, 1920, 161–202; G. M. Harper, *AJP* 49, 1928, 1–35; V. Tcherikover, 'Palestine under the Ptolemies', *Mizraim* 4/5, 1937, 9–90 (especially 11ff. on Zeno's journey) and *HC*, 60–72; M. Rostovtzeff, *HW* 1, 340–50.

6. P. Rainer, no. 24552 Gr., ed. H. Liebesny, 'Ein Erlass des Königs Ptolemaios II. Philadelphos über die Deklaration von Vieh und Sklaven in Syrien und Phönizien', *Aeg* 16, 1936, 257–88 = SB no. 8008. Cf. Rostovtzeff, op. cit., 1, 350ff.

7. For the administration and economic development of Ptolemaic Palestine see Vol. I, pp. 18ff., 39ff. For the chronology of the Ptolemies see A. E. Samuel, *Ptolemaic Chronology*, MBPAR 43, 1962.

8. Tcherikover, *HC*, 59.

9. See B. Niese, *GGMS* 2, 127ff., 134f., 151ff.; Bouché-Leclerq, *Histoire des Séleucides*, 66ff., 78ff., 104f.; W. W. Tarn, *CAH* 7, 702ff., 711ff., 718f.; Volkmann, *PW* 23, 1650f., 1654f., 1669ff.; H. Bengtson, *GG*³, 394–9. There are only fragmentary traditions about the three wars. Even the dates are not completely certain, cf. H. Bengtson, op. cit., 395 n. 4: 274–272/71; 260 (259) – 253 (op. cit., 397 n. 4) and 246–241 BC; É. Will, op. cit., 1, 127ff., 208ff., 221ff.

10. F. M. Abel, *HP* 1, 45, 48f.; W. Otto, AAM 34, 1928, 242 n. 1; Volkmann, *PW* 23, 1651, 1671.

11. K. D. Schunk, *VT* 9, 1959, 192ff., sees an allusion in Koh. 4. 13ff. to the preliminaries to the third so-called Laodicean war. As he needs violent textual emendations for his thesis, this is improbable: see H. W. Hertzberg, *Der Prediger*, 1963, 117; see also below, n. III, 56.

12. For the course of the boundary see W. Otto, op. cit., 37ff., who gives a critical discussion of the hypotheses of U. Kahrstedt, *Syrische Territorien in hellenistischer Zeit*, AGG 19, 2, 1927, 14ff. His assumption was confirmed by H. Seyrig, *Syria* 28, 1951, 212f. For the information from the Zeno papyri see in detail Tcherikover, *Mizraim* 4/5, 1937, 32–6, and *HC*, 61 and 428 n. 56; F. M. Abel, *Géographie* 2, 129. For variations see H. H. Schmidt, op. cit., 35f., though he puts the boundary too far to the south: Damascus seems to have belonged to the Ptolemies for most of the time, see Tcherikover, *Mizraim*, 34f.

13. Polybius 5, 45, 10–46, 6; F. M. Abel, *HP* 1, 72. For the geographical details see F. W. Walbank, *A Historical Commentary on Polybius* 1, 1957, 577f.; for the political situation of Antiochus III, who had to struggle with internal difficulties, see É. Will, *REG* 75, 1962, 71–129; id, *Histoire politique* 2, 14ff.

14. Polybius 5, 61–66, 68–71; on this see F. W. Walbank, op. cit., 1, 587–97; F. M. Abel, *HP* 1, 5–79; Tcherikover, *HC*, 73f. and 54; Volkmann, *PW* 23, 1680ff; É. Will, op. cit., 2, 23ff. For the change of sides on the part of Theodotus see E. Bevan, *History of Egypt*, 224f.; in addition, Panaitolus, friendly officers and, a year later, the *hyparch* of Galilee (?), Keraias, the Thessalian commander Hippolochus and the commandant of Abila, Nicias, came over to Antiochus' side (5, 70f).

15. 5, 86, 10; as a friend of the Romans, Polybius has a certain anti-Seleucid attitude; cf. 5.71: the Arabs changing sides. For the contradiction in Polybius see

Tcherikover, *Mizraim* 4/5, 1937, 56. For the pro-Seleucid attitude of the Arabs see Altheim-Stiehl, *Die Araber in der Alten Welt* 1, 1964, 75, 77. They still supported Antiochus III at Magnesia, Appian, *Syr.* 32.

16. See F. M. Abel, *HP* I, 77, 79 n. 1; on Gaza see E. Meyer, *UAC* 2, 122, and Tcherikover, *HC*, 96. For the Jews it was decisive that the Tobiad Joseph was tax farmer for Coele Syria: see Vol. I, pp. 27f. The quotation is from Polybius 5, 71, 11.

17. Polybius 5, 79–87; on this see W. F. Walbank, op. cit., 1, 607–16; cf. III Macc. 1.1–7; P. Jouguet, op. cit., 251–5; F. M. Abel, *RB* 48, 1939, 225–30. For the effects of Raphia on internal politics see W. W. Tarn, *CAH* 7, 731. Cf. also below, n. 301.

18. H. Gauthier and H. Sottas, *Un Décret trilingue en l'honneur de Ptolémée IV*, 1925. The best preserved Demotic inscription is particularly important: pp. 35ff., ll. 15–25. In almost four months, the king seems to have spent three weeks on hostile Seleucid territory. Polybius 5, 87, 6 speaks of a three-month stay and confirms the joy of the liberated subject peoples: 5,86, 87; on this see W. Otto, AAM 34, 1928, 80–5. The conjecture of the editor, based on a doubtful reading, that a certain Eleazar had risen against the Egyptians (op. cit., 36, l. 23, see the commentary, 54ff.) is untenable. See W. Otto, op. cit., 81f.; Tcherikover, *HC*, 434f. nn. 95 and 97, against P. Jouguet, op. cit., 253 and F. M. Abel, *HP* I, 83 n. 5. See H.-J. Thissen, *Studien zum Raphiadekret*, 1966, 60ff.

19. Joppa-Jaffa: B. Lifshitz, *ZDPV* 78, 1962, 82f.; Marissa: Bliss/Macalister, *Excavations in Palestine* 1898–1902, 62f., and the supplementary information in Clermont-Ganneau, *CRAI* 1900, 536–41; cf. also SEG 7, 326 = Polybius 5, 61, 9, from the neighbourhood of Tyre.

20. The report has legendary elaborations and has been assimilated to the legend of Heliodorus in II Macc. 3. Perhaps we may see the characterization of Heliodorus, 'and his heart became proud', in Dan. 11.12 as an allusion to inconsistencies which III Macc. takes up. On his reverence for Dionysus and his identification with him see Volkmann, *PW* 23, 1689f. and below, n. IV, 43.

21. Josephus, *c. Ap.* 2, 48. Josephus exaggerates for apologetic reasons.

22. See H. H. Schmitt, op. cit., 85; É. Will, op. cit., 2, 34ff., and n. 301 below.

23. On the downfall of the Ptolemaic empire and the successes of Antiochus III see H. Bengtson, *GG*³, 406f., 414f.; cf. Volkmann, *PW* 23, 1684f. On the change of throne in Egypt and the ensuing confusion see Bouché-Leclerq, *Histoire des Lagides* I, 335–50. H. W. Hertzberg, *Der Prediger*, 1963, 50ff. would see in Koheleth 8.2ff. an allusion to the pro-Seleucid tendencies under Philopator and in 10.16f. an allusion to the child Epiphanes. But these can equally well be themes of wisdom. We can hardly date Koheleth from this (see n. III, 56 below). For the date of the deaths see A. E. Samuel (n. 7 above), 108ff.

24. We are very much less well informed over the fifth Syrian war than over the fourth. Cf. Volkmann, *PW* 23, 1694f.; M. Holleaux, *Études d'épigraphie et d'histoire grecques* 3, 1942, 318–35 = *Klio* 8, 1908, 267–81; É. Will, op. cit., 2, 101f. On the siege of Gaza see Polybius 16, 22a.

25. *In Dan.* 11.14, Migne *PL* 25, 562. E. Täubler, *JQR* 37, 1946/47, 1–30,

125–37, gives an interpretation of Dan. 11.14 and the quotation from Porphyry, but his theory of a messianic revolt is untenable. The attempt to consider the '*pārīṣē*' with the Hasidim and Pharisees as 'members of a chain' (26) stands historical connections on their head. Daniel gives a negative verdict on the 'men of violence': see Tcherikover, *HC*, 78f. and 436 n. 108.

26. Josephus, *Antt.* 12, 135.

27. Polybius 16, 18; *Antt.* 12, 32; B. Niese, *GGMS* 2, 578f. For the siege of Sidon see Jerome, *in Dan.* 11, 15, 16, *PL* 25, 563 = FGrHist 260 F 46.

28. Provisional report by Y. Landau, *RB* 69, 1962, 406; final text in *IEJ* 16, 1966, 54–70 (58–60). A similar ordinance from Ptolemaic Egypt may be found in the Alexandrian *dikaiōmata*, PHal I, ll. 166–85 (pp. 98ff.). According to Polybius 5, 83, 3, Ptolemy was commander in the army of the fourth Ptolemy in 219 BC, but later went over to Seleucid service, see H. Volkmann, *PW* 23, 1762 no. 42.

29. Josephus, *Antt.* 12, 133, 136, 138; cf. Polybius 16, 39, 3ff.

30. *In Dan.* 11.14, *PL* 25, 563 = FGrHist 260 F 45. Jerome gives Scopas as its originator; in Jerome's view Scopas was besieged in Jerusalem by Antiochus III with the help of the Jews. Thus he connects the sieges of Sidon and Jerusalem.

31. Josephus, *Antt.* 12, 129f., 139.

32. *Antt.* 12, 138–144: in the form of a letter to Ptolemy, the *stratēgos* of Coele Syria. For literature see R. Marcus, *Josephus* 7, LCL, 743–61. Its authenticity was already argued for by E. Meyer, *UAC* 2, 127 n. 21; a thorough investigation was made by E. Bi(c)kerman(n), *REJ* 100, 1935, 4–35; cf. *Inst.*, 136f., 195 and *GM*, 51–3; but cf. the critical comments by K. Galling, *OLZ* 42, 1939, 227; further A. Alt, *ZAW* 57, 1939, 283ff., according to whom there are two edicts here, one about the restoration and resettlement of Jerusalem and the other about privileges for temple, cult personnel and *gerousia*, and about tax relief for the people; see also F. M. Abel, *HP* 1, 89ff., and Tcherikover, *HC*, 76ff., 438ff. For the whole see also Vol. I, pp. 28f., 270ff. Cf. the granting of privileges to the temple of Pluto in Nysa by Seleucus I in C. B. Welles, *Royal Correspondence*, 1934, 54ff.; the decree of Antiochus I in favour of Erythrae, OGIS 223 = C. B. Welles, op. cit., 78ff.; the thanksgiving of Antiochus III at Amyzon, op. cit., 165ff., cf. 171f.; his letter to Ilion about the preservation of 'ancestral privileges' (ll. 3f. ἃ δι] ἁ προγόνων προϋπηργ[μένα, op. cit., 175ff., and the edict in favour of a city on the Hellespont, SEG 2, 663, ll. 9ff. ἠξίωσεν τὸν βασιλέα ἀποδοθῆναι τούς τε νό[[μους καὶ τὴν πάτριον πολιτείαν καὶ ἱερὰ τὰ τεμέ/νη, including care of the sanctuary and freedom from tax for three years.

33. II Macc. 4.11. On the concept of royal φιλάνθρωπα cf. I Ezra 8.10, the promise to the Galilean peasants of Beth Anath, PSI 554, 34f., and H. Kortenbeutel, *PW Suppl* 7, 1032ff.

34. H. Zucker, *Studien zur jüdischen Selbstverwaltung im Altertum*, 33ff.; R. Marcus, op. cit., 73 n. b; Tcherikover, *HC*, 49 and 422 nn. 29, 30, assumes that Alexander the Great had already confirmed 'autonomy' for the Jews, cf. *Antt.* 11, 338.

35. H. H. Schmitt, op. cit., 96, 99.

36. Not only the Jews in Palestine supported him; Jewish mercenaries elsewhere were at his service, see below, nn. 90–92.

37. See M. Holleaux, *CAH* 8, 165: a few months after the siege of Sidon a Roman delegation visited him. As Rome needed a free hand against Philip V, at first he did not find the engagement of Antiochus with Egypt particularly unattractive, but after the victory over Macedon in 197 BC Rome regarded the Seleucids as her most dangerous adversaries in the East. Forces were then at work to destroy her rule. For the politics of Antiochus III after the conquest of Palestine, see O. Plöger, *Theocracy and Eschatology*, 1968, 1ff.

38. Jerome, *in Dan.* 11.17, *PL* 25, 564, cf. Appian, *Syr.* 5; Josephus, *Antt.* 12, 154; Polybius 18, 51, 10. On this see B. Niese, *GGMS* 2, 639, and E. Meyer, *UAC* 2, 124f., with the right dating. The report of Josephus, *Antt.* 12, 155, that the income of Coele Syria was divided between the two rulers, is unhistorical, see H. Bengtson, *GG³*, 469 n. 1, and *Die Strategie* 2, 1944, 161 n. 2.

39. M. Holleaux, *CAH* 8, 222–34; É. Will, op. cit., 2, 177f.; Polybius 21, 45; cf. Dan. 11.18.

40. Bouché-Leclerq, *Histoire des Séleucides*, 221ff.; for the date of his death see H. H. Schmitt, op. cit., 1f.; cf. Dan. 11.19.

41. Jerome, *in Dan.* 11.20, *PL* 25, 565, see on this Bouché-Leclerq, *Histoire des Lagides* 1, 396–9; W. Otto, AAM NF 11, 1934, 23f., and Volkmann, *PW* 23, 1697f. The decree of Cairo of the year 23 (= 182 BC) mentions the victory of an Aristonicus before the Syrian coast at Aradus; see G. Daressy, *Receuil de Travaux relat. à la Philol. et l'Archéol. Egypt. et Assyr.* 33, 1911, 6f.

42. Rostovtzeff, *HW* 2, 695ff., certainly stresses that despite the peace of Apamea and other setbacks, the riches of Syria were hardly affected; but the attempts at confiscating temple treasuries suggest that the Seleucids had trouble in producing any large sums of actual money: see Vol. I, pp. 28f., 280, n. IV, 145.

43. II Macc. 3.4ff.; 4.1ff.; and Dan. 11.20; on this see A. Schwarz, *MGWJ* 63, 1919, 225; E. Meyer, *UAC* 2, 132 n. 2, 136ff.; E. Bi(c)kerman(n), *AIPHOS* 7, 1939–44, 5–40, whose thesis, that the temple of Jerusalem did not have any income of its own and had to be supported by the king, who supervised the finance, is questionable. There are criticisms in Tcherikover, *HC*, 157ff., 465 n. 12; Rostovtzeff, *HW* 2, 1278ff., 1282, and 3, 1630 nn. 205 and 206, who demonstrates that there were very probably temple banks in the Hellenistic period. Similarly, N. Q. Hamilton, *JBL* 83, 1964, 365–72. A *dioikētēs* Heliodorus appears as the recipient of a royal letter on the Ḥephzibah inscription of 195 BC, see *IEJ* 16, 1966, 61 l. 34.

44. On these figures and their rule see W. Otto, *Die Geschichte der Zeit des 6. Ptolemäus*, AAM NF 11, 1934, 21, 24ff.; O. Mørkholm, *Antiochus IV of Syria*, Classica et Medievalia 22, 1961, 32–43.

45. For the sixth Syrian war see W. Otto, op. cit., 23ff.: the declaration of war was made by Egypt: Diodore 30, 15, cf. Livy 42, 29; see op. cit., 42. Supplements and corrections in Volkmann, *PW* 23, 1705–11. For the problem of dating see T. C. Skeat, *JEA* 46, 1960, 91–94; 47, 1961, 107–12. There is hardly justification for the hypothesis of three expeditions of Antiochus IV, thus F. Heichelheim, *PW Suppl* 7, 33f., more cautiously H. Bengtson, *GG³*, 482; see E. Bi(c)kerman(n), *ChrEg* 27, 1952, 396–403; cf. Tcherikover, *HC*, 473 n. 19; Volkmann, op. cit., 1705. For the plundering of the temple treasury see nn. IV, 144–6. Cf. O. Mørkholm, *Antiochus IV*, 1966, 64–101.

46. Evidence from antiquity in Volkmann, *PW* 23, 1710.

47. On the sacking of Jerusalem see II Macc. 5.5–23. For the dating see E. Meyer, *UAC* 2, 155ff.; Bickermann, *GM*, 160–8; Tcherikover, *HC*, 187ff. = late summer 168 BC, after the second expedition, see II Macc. 5.1, against W. Otto, op. cit., 66 n. 3, and Volkmann, *PW* 23, 1709 = after the first expedition in 169 BC. For Hyrcanus see *Antt.* 12, 236. Further see Vol. I, pp. 272ff., 280f. According to Dan. 11.28, 30 the king probably also came to Jerusalem on this punitive expedition, see Tcherikover, *HC*, 186, 473f. n. 20 and Abel/Starcky, *Macc.*, 252, on II Macc. 5.11ff.; O. Mørkholm, op. cit., 142f.

48. See Porphyry, FGrHist 260, F 56 = Jerome, *in Dan.* 11, 44f., *PL* 25, 573; cf. H. Seyrig, *Syria* 28, 1951, 219; against him O. Mørkholm, op. cit., 122ff.

49. E. Bi(c)kerman(n), *From Ezra to the Last of the Maccabees*, 1962, 73; cf. e.g. the differing translation of Deut. 26.5 in LXX or Jub. 46.6f., 11, 13f., on the oppression of the Israelites by Pharaoh in Egypt.

50. Two examples of divergent views on this question: 'We have no information about Hellenism in Jerusalem during the Egyptian period. In that time it does not seem to have been a general and penetrative influence there. It only became a danger for Palestinian Judaism in the Syrian period' (J. Wellhausen, *Israelitische und jüdische Geschichte*, [8]1921, 227). 'Friendship with the Greeks was quite common in Jerusalem and Judea, particularly in the first hundred years after Alexander, under Ptolemaic rule' (G. Kittel, *Die Religionsgeschichte und das Urchristentum*, repr. 1959, 47). We believe that Kittel's view is nearer to historical reality.

51. For resistance to the Hellenistic ruling classes see S. K. Eddy, *The King is Dead*, 1961, passim; for Iran, cf. 65–100, for Egypt, 271–94.

52. M. Launey, *Recherches sur les Armées hellénistiques* I, 1949, 3f.: 'Le monde hellénistique est pour une bonne part demeuré un monde militaire.' This is also true for the later Roman period.

53. Personal communication from Dr Y. Aharoni, who excavated Tell 'Arad, cf. now *IEJ* 16, 1966, 2–5. For what is presumably a Greek settlement on the coast from the same period see J. Naveh, *IEJ* 12, 1962, 98f.

54. H. Bengtson, *GG*[3], 76 (esp n. 2), 98; F. K. Kienitz, *Die politische Geschichte Ägyptens von 7 bis 4 Jahrhunderts vor der Zeitwende*, 1953, 12, and on this Herodotus 2, 152: Ionians and Carians in the service of Psammetichus I; cf. also Kienitz, op. cit., 144ff.

55. J. D. Quinn, *BASOR* 164, 1961, 19f.; cf. Strabo, 13, 2, 2 (617), and Alcaeus, fr. 50, ed. Diehl.

56. H. W. Parke, *Greek Mercenary Soldiers from the Earliest Times*, 1933, 4ff., 59f., 105ff., 165–9; F. K. Kienitz, op. cit., 70ff.; the attacks of the Athenians on Egypt and the Phoenician coast; 89ff.: the camp of Akē and the expedition of Iphicrates; for the rebellion of Sidon and the consequences for Judea see op. cit., 101f., 181ff.; cf. also G. Hölscher, *Palästina in der persischer und hellenistischer Zeit*, QFAGG 5, 1903, 35, 46ff.; Schürer, 3, 6 n. 11. Probably Jews were by then transplanted to Hyrcania on the Caspian Sea, and perhaps Jericho was affected as well as Jerusalem. For archaeologically demonstrable effects on Palestine see D. Barag, *BASOR* 183, 1966, 6–12. According to G. Hölscher, the historical

nucleus of the later legend of Judith is to be found here. For 'Aṭliṭ see C. N. Johns, *QDAP* 2, 1933, 56; Watzinger, *DP* 2, 9. For the conquest of Egypt see F. K. Kienitz, op. cit., 105ff., 115f.

57. For Alexander's army see W. W. Tarn, *Alexander the Great* 2, 1948/50, 135–69. For the siege of Tyre and Gaza see Arrian, *Anab.* 2, 16–27, and Curtius Rufus, *Hist. Alex.* 4, 8–29, and on it F. M. Abel, *RB* 43, 1934, 528ff.; 44, 1935, 34ff.; *HP* 1, 3–10. The convulsions of the two sieges probably had an effect on the prophetic saying Zech. 9.1–8: K. Elliger, *ZAW* 62, 1949–50, 63–115; M. Delcor, *VT* 1, 1951, 110–24. For the defection and punishment of the Samaritans see Curt. Ruf., *Hist. Alex.* 4, 34; Eusebius, *Chron.*, GCS, ed. Helm, 7, 123, and on this F. M. Abel, *RB* 44, 1935, 56ff.; R. Marcus, *Josephus* 6, LCL, 1958, 523ff.; also the great new papyrus discovery of which there is a provisional report in F. M. Cross, *BA* 26, 1963, 110–21; cf. *HTR* 59, 1966, 201–11 and the report by P. W. Lapp on the renewed investigation of the death cave, *RB* 72, 1965, 405ff.

58. See G. E. Wright, *HTR* 55, 1962, 357–66; id., *Shechem*, 1964, 175ff. Now traces of the first Samaritan temple on Gerizim seem to have been found; see E. F. Campell, *BA* 28, 1965, 21; the report *RB* 72, 1965, 419f.; R. J. Bull, *BASOR* 180, 1965, 39ff.; Bull/Wright, *HTR* 58, 1965, 234–7.

59. For Jewish tradition on Alexander see J. Gutman, *EJ* 2, 204ff.; R. Marcus, op. cit., 512–31; see E. Bickerman(n), *RB* 59, 1952, 44; F. Pfister, *Alexander der Grosse in den Offenbarungen*, 1956, 8f.; 24ff.

60. For the armies of the Diadochi see M. Rostovtzeff, *HW* 1, 144–9; for the military assembly see H. Bengtson, *GG*[3], 427 n. 1.

61. Rostovtzeff, *HW* 2, 1203, 1232–5; 3, 1625 n. 180; see also Jax-Thraede, *RAC* 5, 1182ff.

62. J. Kromayer and G. Veith, *Heerwesen und Kriegführung der Griechen und Römer*, 1928; for Graeco-Macedonian tactics, 79ff., 113ff., 141ff.; the phalanx, 132ff.; techniques of siege, 244; cf. Rostovtzeff, op. cit., 2, 1082–4.

63. For mercenaries in Hellenistic times see G. I. Griffith, *The Mercenaries of the Hellenistic World*, 1935, and above all M. Launey, op. cit., passim.

64. H. Bengtson, *GG*[3], 430f., 435f.; for the military colonies in Egypt see J. Lesquier, *Les institutions militaires de l'Égypte sous les Lagides*, 1911, 30–66; M. Launey, op. cit., 1, 41ff.; Rostovtzeff, op. cit., 1, 284–7; they did not settle there in groups according to their units, but in villages scattered over the country.

65. M. Launey, op. cit., 2, 724–812, esp. 748ff., 776f., 780ff.; and Rostovtzeff, op. cit., 1, 25f.

66. For the size and composition of Hellenistic armies see M. Launey, op. cit., 1, 7–18; for the Seleucid army see E. Bi(c)kerman(n), *Inst.*, 51–100; for native troops see 58ff.; military settlements, 78–83; also M. Launey, 1, 49ff.

67. F. M. Abel, *RB* 44, 1935, 559–81; *HP* 1, 22–43.

68. *C. Ap.* 1, 209–11 = *Antt.* 12, 3–6 (Agatharchides, FGrHist 86 F 20) and Appian, *Syr.* 50. The dating is disputed: Eusebius, *Chron.*, GCS, ed. Helm, 7, 125, puts the conquest at 322 BC; F. M. Abel, *RB* 44, 1935, 576f., and HP, 21, conjectures 312 BC; Tcherikover, *HC*, 55–58, probably rightly suggests 302 BC.

69. Eusebius, *Chron.*, op. cit., 132, 128; on this see Tcherikover, *HC*, 103f. For Gerasa see C. B. Welles in C. H. Kraeling, *Gerasa*, 1938, 423 no. 137: in-

scription of the third century AD, and on it, A. H. M. Jones, *The Cities of the Eastern Roman Provinces*, 1937, 238f., 447, and Tcherikover, *HC*, 448 n.77, against C. H. Kraeling, op. cit., 29. Seleucus I was honoured as '*ktistēs*' in a similar way in Roman Dura in the second and third centuries AD, see M. Rostovtzeff, *Dura Europos and its Art*, 1938, 10, 58f., and *HW* 1, pl. LI. However, a Gerasene coin published by H. Seyrig, *Syria* 42, 1965, 25–8, indicates Alexander the Great as '*ktistēs*'.

70. J. Beloch, *APF* 2, 1902, 233, also includes Scythopolis (but see below, n.75), Gadara and Hippos among early Macedonian foundations. Perhaps one should also add Anthedon (Boeotia), Apollonia and Arethusa (Chalcidice) in the coastal plain. But a Hellenization of earlier place names could also have taken place as a result of homonymity: Tcherikover, *HC*, 98: Peḥal-Pella; Apollonia (present-day 'Arsuf'), because the Phoenician Rešeph-Apollo was worshipped there, see below, n.IV, 27.

71. Rostovtzeff, *HW* 1, 346f. see also A. Schlatter, *GI*³, 19f.

72. J. W. Crowfoot et al., *Samaria-Sebaste, Reports 1931–1933*, Vol. 1, 1942, 24: on the round tower, 'the finest monument of the Hellenistic age in Palestine'. On the later fortress see 1, 28ff. On the walls of Philotheria see *RB* 63, 1956, 89, and M. Avi-Yonah, *Ten Years of Archaeology in Israel*, 1958, 58.

73. On Beth Zur see O. R. Sellers, *The Citadel of Beth Zur*, 1933, 10, 22; Watzinger, *DP* 2, 24ff.; R. W. Funk, *BASOR* 150, 1958, 8–20, who puts the first fortress in the Ptolemaic period on the basis of new excavations, see 14 nn.5, 15. For Tell 'Arad see *RB* 70, 1964, 566; for 'Engedi see below, n.354.

74. Tcherikover, *Mizraim*, 43f., *HC*, 91f., 99, 100f., 102. For Arsinoe see Tcherikover, *Die hellenistische Städtegründungen*, PhilSuppl 19, 1, 1927, 66f.; A. H. M. Jones, op. cit., 242; F. M. Abel, *HP* 1, 58. Cf. S. S. Weinberg, *IEJ* 21, 1971, 86ff., on Tell Anafa.

75. The name Σκύθων πόλις appears for the first time in Polybius 5, 70; cf. also the gloss Judg. 1.27 LXX; Judith 3.10 and II Macc. 12.29; on this M. Avi-Yonah, *IEJ* 12, 1962, 123–36. The founding date of 254 BC is, however, improbable. See also A. H. M. Jones, op. cit., 242.

76. The Macedonian nobility was already completely Hellenized at the time of Alexander, but this extended to the peasant populace only in the third century, see W. W. Tarn, *CAH* 7, 197, and Tarn-Griffith, *Hellenistic Civilization*, 63.

77. H. Liebesny, *Aeg* 16, 1936, 258f., r. col. ll.12–15 = SB 8008, on this 274; cf. Tcherikover, *HC*, 63; Rostovtzeff, *HW* 1, 340f.

78. Tcherikover, *Mizraim*, 36–8; cf. H. Zucker, *Studien zur jüdischen Selbstverwaltung im Altertum*, 1936, 31.

79. Gaza: P. Roussel, *Aeg* 13, 1933, 145–51 = SEG 8, 269; on this F. M. Abel, *RB* 49, 1940, and *HP* 1, 54f. Sidon: E. Bickerman(n), *Inst.*, 88ff., and Rostovtzeff, *HW* 3, 1401 n.137 and plates XIX, 2 and LVII.

80. OGIS 2, 592.

81. Cf. *Antt.* 12, 131–133. For the citadel see Neh. 2.8; 7.2; Ps. Aristeas 100ff.; II Macc. 4.12; it lay on the north side of the temple: L. H. Vincent, *Jérusalem de l'Ancien Testament* 1, 1954, 193 n.1, 215, 232f.; H. Zucker, op. cit., 32, conjectures no garrison, but does not go into the problem of the citadel: positive verdict in M. Smith, *Hellenismus*, Fischer-Weltgeschichte 6, 1965, 266.

82. II Macc.4.28f., 49; 5.22, 24 and F. M. Abel, *HP* 1, 275. Cf. Vol. I, pp. 282f.

83. PCZ 59003 = CPJ 1, 118–120 no. 1. For miscegenation see Tcherikover, *Mizraim*, 52f.; see also Vol. I, p. 63. For the religious significance of this phenomenon see C. Schneider, *ARW* 36, 1939, 328ff.

84. *C. Ap.* 1, 192ff.: the mutiny of Jewish troops in Babylon, cf. *Antt.* 11, 339: summons to the Jews to military service. Samaritan troops are said to have been settled by Alexander in the Egyptian Thebais, *Antt.* 11, 321–45. However, the attempts of Josephus to connect the Jewish mercenaries with a supposed grant of Macedonian citizenship to the Jews in Alexandria are an apologetic expedient: *c. Ap.* 2, 35, 42, 71f.; *Bell.* 2, 487ff.; on this see CPJ 1, 14, esp. n. 38. The scepticism of M. Launey, op. cit., 1, 542, and Tcherikover, *HC*, 272f., towards Jewish mercenaries under Alexander is too great. Cf. Curtius Rufus, *Hist. Alex.* 4, 6, 31, after the conquest of Gaza: *namque etiam secundis atterebantur tamen copiae, devictarum gentium militi minor quam domestico fides habebatur.* Alexander used 'barbarian' auxiliaries, albeit with reservations. Moreover the Jews had an old mercenary tradition.

85. *Antt.* 12, 7f.; *Ps. Arist.* 12, 35f.; according to this Ptolemy I took a large number of Jewish prisoners into his army; cf. also *c. Ap.* 2, 44: the establishment of Jewish military colonies in Egypt, Libya and the Cyrenian pentapolis. These reports are confirmed by papyrological and epigraphical evidence: see Schürer 3, 40–53: e.g. the presumably military 'Jewish camp', 42f., and the prosopography in M. Launey, op. cit., 2, 1232–35, 1242ff.; further CPJ 1, 11ff., 15, 17, and nos. 18–32, pp. 147–78. No. 18 (260 BC) shows a Jewish soldier, Alexander son of Andronicus, in completely Greek surroundings, cf. on this M. Launey, op. cit., 1, 544f. We later come across Jewish officers: CIJ 2, 370f., no. 1443 = OGIS 96 and 2, 438, no. 1531. For the Jewish garrisons in Egypt going back to the sixth century BC, above all at Elephantine, see E. G. Kraeling, in the introduction to *The Brooklyn Museum Aramaic Papyri*, 1953, 27–48, 76–117 and *RGG*[3], 2, 415–8, cf. also Jer. 41.16ff.; 43.8ff.; 44.1ff. The danger of assimilation was already great at that time: Jer. 44.15ff. On the great P. Cowley 81 (in A. Cowley, *Aramaic Papyri of the Fifth Century BC*, 1923, 190–9), which comes from the end of the fourth century and gives a survey of the distribution of Jews in Egypt at this time, see the new edition by J. Harmatta, *Acta Antiqua* 7, 1959, 337–409 and esp. 404ff.; cf. J. T. Milik, *Aeg* 40, 1960, 79–81; a Jewish officer Ješebiah in el Hibeh. F. Uebel, *Die Kleruchen Ägyptens*, AAB 1968, 3, see index 420, s.v. ʼΙουδαῖος.

86. For Cyrenaica see *Antt.* 14, 114ff., according to Strabo (Cyrene); Procopius, *De aed.* 6, 2, 22, ed. H. B. Dewing, LCL 7, 370 (Boreion), S. Applebaum, *ScrHieros* 7, 1961, 39ff., 46ff. (Teucheira) and SEG 16, 931 (= CIG 3, 5361) and 17, 823 (Berenice); cf. Schürer 3, 52ff., 79ff. The great Jewish Diaspora goes back to the Ptolemaic military colonies: see M. Hengel in: *Festgabe für K. G. Kuhn*, 1971, 182f.

87. In themselves the Ptolemaic mercenaries were an internationally mixed company, see M. Launey, op. cit., 2, 1116–267. The Samaritans can hardly be distinguished from the Jews because of the similarity of their names, op. cit., 1, 554. However, there was a place in the Fayum called 'Samaria', which was

probably founded by Samaritans, though later it had a mixed population including Jews, Macedonians and Cilicians; there was a gymnasium there founded by a Cilician officer (see below, n. II, 63): O. Guéraud, P. *ENTEYΞEIΣ*, 1931, 20ff. no. 8 = SB 7245; on this see Schürer 2, 51 n. 58; F. Heuchelheim, *Die auswärtige Bevölkerung*, Klio Beiheft 18, 1925, 67 n. 10, 70f.; M. Launey, op. cit., 1, 547; 2, 841, 846f., 850f. etc.; Rostovtzeff, *HW* 3, 1394f. n. 121; 1588 n. 23; CPJ 1, 158ff. no. 22, 1. 6. For the Idumeans see M. Launey, op. cit., 1, 556ff.; 2, 974ff., 1235f.; Arabs: op. cit., 1, 560f.; 2, 124f.; Syrians: 1, 536, 539f.; 2, 1231; there were indeed many Syrians in Egypt, see F. Heichelheim, op. cit., 71, but these came as slaves and private persons, see also Vol. I, pp. 41f.

88. *Bell.* 1, 190; 7, 421ff.; *Antt.* 13, 287; 14, 131; *c. Ap.* 2, 49: from the time of Ptolemy VI Philometor. The temple in Leontopolis was founded about 160 BC; on this U. Kahrstedt, AGG NF 19, 2, 1927, 132–45; Tcherikover, *HC*, 275–83; CPJ 1, 44–6; see Vol. I, pp. 274f.

89. M. Launey, op. cit., 1, 90ff.

90. *Antt.* 12, 119 under Seleucus I, cf. *c. Ap.* 2, 39, and Antiochus II for the Ionian cities, *Antt.* 12, 125; see also M. Launey, op. cit., 1, 551f. For Hellenistic influence on the Jews in Babylonia, see J. Neusner, *A History of the Jews in Babylonia* 1, 1965, 10ff. For a Samaritan Eumenes son of Demetrius in Iran see L. Robert, *CRAI* 1967, 295f.

91. On this I. Lévy, *Mélanges H. Grégoire, AIPHOS* 10, 1950, 681–8. It is quite possible that Jewish mercenaries fought among the lightly armed troops of Antiochus I, see E. Meyer, *UAC* 2, 36 n. 1, cf. also J. Neusner, op. cit., 12f.

92. On this see the letter to Zeuxis, *Antt.* 12, 147–53; see below, n. IV, 45, 150.

93. See E. Bi(c)kerman(n), *Inst.*, 70ff., and *GM*, 55.

94. See CPJ 1, 27ff.: Greek names; 30: Greek language (see Vol. I, pp. 22ff.); Jewish 'Macedonians', see CPJ 1, 13–15, cf. 175f. no. 30 and CPJ 2, 5f. no. 142.

95. FGrHist 726 F 3, 4, 7 (= Eusebius, *Pr. Ev.* 9, 23); cf. Josephus, *Antt.* 2, 238–53.

96. FGrHist 264 F 6, 6 (Diodore 40, 3). For overpopulation see Philo, *Vit. Mos.* 2, 232.

97. M. Launey, 1, 42f. The Jerusalem ossuary inscriptions from the first century BC and the first century AD show that there were a large number who returned from the Diaspora to Jerusalem. For the problem see also E. R. Bevan, *Jerusalem under the High Priests*, 1904, 43.

98. Tcherikover, CPJ 1, 44ff. and *HTR* 51, 1958, 81.

99. Dan. 7. 7. Translation follows A. Bentzen, *Daniel*, ²1952, 48; cf. also 7. 19, 23 and 2. 33, 40. The fourth kingdom is of iron and crushes everything; 8. 5ff.: the goat which overcomes the ram. Here Daniel has made use of earlier traditions, at least in part, see A. Bentzen, op. cit., 33, and M. Noth, *The Laws in the Pentateuch*, 1966, 194–214. Cf. also K. Koch, *HZ* 193, 1961, 19: the picture 'comes from the experience which the orientals apparently had of their Greek rulers'.

100. Zech. 9. 13 and 10. 3–5. War traditions also appear elsewhere in Deutero-Zechariah: 12. 2–9; 14. 1–3, 12–14. Perhaps Zech. 14. 2 is a reminiscence of the conquest of Jerusalem by Ptolemy I. Cf. also II Chron. 26. 15, the 'invention' of skilful machines of war by Uzziah, which is probably meant to demonstrate the greater antiquity of Jewish techniques of war.

101. On the question whether Roman or Hellenistic techniques of war are used in the War Scroll see J. v. d. Ploeg, *Le rouleau de la guerre*, 1959, 7ff. Perhaps the special Hebrew military expressions, many of which are difficult to interpret, go back to Jewish mercenaries in Hellenistic armies or the experiences of the Maccabean wars. See already J. G. Février, *Semitica* 3, 1950, 53–9, and K. M. T. Atkinson, *BJRL* 40, 1957–58, 272–97. There was, however, no direct dependence on Leontopolis, as A. supposes. See also M. H. Segal, *ScrHieros* 4, 1958, 138–43, and C. H. Hunzinger, *RGG*³ 4, 944f.: middle of the second century BC. The Roman period is in any case too late. For the complicated history of the tradition of 1 QM see J. Becker, *Das Heil Gottes*, 1964, 43ff., 74f., and P. v. d. Osten-Sacken, *Gott und Belial*, 1969.

102. E. Bi(c)kerman(n), *Inst.*, 7, 11f., 201ff.; H. Bengtson, *GG*³, 427f.

103. H. Bengtson, *MusHelv* 10, 1953, 170ff.

104. F. K. Kienitz, op. cit., 105ff., 109ff.

105. Op. cit., 118–21. The economy and administration of Egypt were disrupted by the constant state of war with Persia and internal unrest; cf. M. Rostovtzeff, *A Large Estate in Egypt*, 1922, 3f.; *HW* 1, 255ff.; E. Bevan, *History of Egypt*, 1927, 132f. This does not exclude the possibility that Cleomenes, Alexander's governor, and the first Ptolemies followed the old ordinances, see W. Schur, *Klio* 20, 1925/26, 270–302; F. Heichelheim, *Historia* 2, 1953–54, 129–35, and H. Volkmann, *PW* 23, 1633ff., on Ptolemy I; J. Vogt, *Chiron* 1, 1971, 153ff.

106. For the philosophical and religious bases see Rostovtzeff, *CAH* 7, 113f., and *HW* 1, 267ff.; 3, 1379 n.83, lit.; cf. also the collection of texts in W. Schubart, *APF* 12, 1936, 1–26, and the fundamental article by E. R. Goodenough, 'The Political Philosophy of Hellenistic Kingship', *YCS* 1, 1928, 55–104, and B. Kötting, *RAC* 6, 851ff. (lit.).

107. C. B. Welles, *JJurPap* 3, 1949, 40–4; on Hecataeus of Abdera see also F. Jacoby, *PW* 7, 2761ff., and below n.IV, 3. He presents the ideal of the βασιλεὺς εὐεργέτης, 'the enlightened despot'.

108. For the discussion of this question see H. Volkmann, *PW* 23, 1632.

109. For Egyptian administration and the special position of the king see Rostovtzeff, *CAH* 7, 113ff.; *HW* 1, 267ff.; 3, 1378ff.; W. Schubart, AO 35, 4, 1937, 19ff., 34ff.; H. Bengtson, *GG*³, 433; *MusHelv* 10, 1953, 161–77, and *Strategie* 3, 1952, passim; also C. B. Welles, op. cit., 21–47 (lit.), who lays too much stress on the adoption of the old traditions of the pharaohs. For criticism see H. Bengtson, *MusHelv* 10, 1953, 177. On Ptolemy I Soter see H. Volkmann, *PW* 23, 1635f.; on Ptol. II Philadelphus, 1658, 1662ff.

110. Rostovtzeff, *HW* 1, 269.

111. See R. Seider, *Beiträge zur ptolemäische Verfassungsgeschichte*, 1938, 43–75.

112. For the relationship between the Greeks and the Egyptians in Ptolemaic state service see W. Peremans, *Vreemdelingen en Egyptenaaren in vroeg-ptolemaeisch Egypte*, 1943; A. E. Samuel, *Proceedings of the 12th International Congress of Papyrologists*, 1970, 443ff.; C. B. Welles, op. cit., 505ff.

113. See H. Bengtson, *Strategie* 3, 32ff.; H. Volkmann, *PW* 23, 1677; also see PColZen 2, 120. This is probably the reason for the assignment of the tax-

farming contract for 'Syria and Phoenicia' to the Tobiad Joseph; see Vol. I, p. 27, and the hypothesis of H. Bengtson, op. cit., 3, 170, on the change of administration in the province.

114. See the instance from the second century BC cited by E. Bevan, op. cit., 137ff. = U. Wilcken, *UPZ* I, 150–71, no. 14; cf. also H. Bengtson, *MusHelv* 10, 1953, 163f.

115. For the distribution of land in Egypt see C. Préaux, *L'économie royale des Lagides*, 1939, 459–91; Rostovtzeff, *HW* I, 276–91; 3, 1380–5.

116. For taxation see C. Préaux, op. cit., 297ff., 302ff., 307ff., etc., above all 450ff.; cf. U. Wilcken, *Griechische Ostraka* I, 1899, 512–630, and Mitteis-Wilcken, *Grundzüge und Chrestomathie der Papyruskunde* I, 1, 1912, 169–85, and the selection of texts in I, 2, 231ff., 256ff., 264ff., 280ff., 284 (P. Revenue, ed. Grenfell, cols. 36f.) and 296ff. (cols. 1–22). Further Rostovtzeff, *CAH* 7, 136–42 and *HW* I, 273, 279, 283, 305, 313, 316; 3, 1396 n. 125 lit. For the monopoly of trade see below, n. 272.

117. Rostovtzeff, op. cit., 1, 316–20; cf. the concrete instances in P. Viereck, *Philadelphia*, Morgenland 16, 1928, 41ff. However, no clear conclusion has been reached as to the question of the Egyptian situation, cf. H. Volkmann, *PW* 23, 1631, lit. and 1665; see also Vol. I, pp. 38f.

118. H. Bengtson, *MusHelv* 10, 1953, 175.

119. Tcherikover, *Mizraim*, 7ff. Cf. A. Alt, *Kleine Schriften* 2, 402f.

120. H. Zucker, *Studien zur jüdischer Selbstverwaltung*, 1936, 30; H. Bengtson, *Strategie* 3, 168ff., and Rostovtzeff, *HW* I, 344, against Tcherikover, op. cit., 38f., and *HC*, 61f.; see also P. M. Fraser, *JEA* 46, 1960, 101 no. 37: a *stratēgos* in Caria, where none had been known for a long time. The financial administrator appears in P. Rainer, inv. 24552, ed. H. Liebesny, *Aeg* 16, 1936, 258ff. (= SB 8008), col. 2.18: τοῦ διοικοῦντος τὰς κατὰ Συρίαν καὶ Φοινίκην προσόδους. According to F. M. Abel, *HP* I, 60, he was a direct subordinate of the *dioikētēs* in Alexandria. Polybius 5, 40, 1 mentions Theodotus as ὁ τεταγμένος ἐπὶ Κοίλης Συρίας and by this means his office as *stratēgos*; according to 5, 87, 6 Philopator appointed Andromachus as στρατηγός in the province after Raphia. See now the Ḥephzibah inscription, Y. H. Landau, *IEJ* 16, 1966, 59: Ptolemy (son of Traseas) as '*stratēgos*' in 'Syria and Phoenicia' (ll. 14f.) in 201 BC and his subordinate '*dioikētēs*', ll. 5, 22.

121. PCZ 59004, 59008, 59698 (?); PSI 366, 403, 495, 612, 616; the as yet unpublished P.Lond inv. 2358 B and 1931 (inv. 2661); also Polybius 5, 61, 5: the seat of the *stratēgos* Theodotus, cf. 62.2; 71.2; Antiochus III wintered there; Ps. Arist. 115: founded by Philadelphus, cf. *Dig.* 65, 1, 3. For the significance of Ptolemais see also F. M. Abel, *HP* I, 53f., and B. Spuler, *PW* 23, 1884. With 11 mentions, Ptolemais appears most frequently in the Zeno papyri; Gaza has 9 and Sidon 6. For the minting of coinage in Ptolemais see B. V. Head, *Historia Numorum*, 1912, 793f. For the history of the place see also Tcherikover, *HC*, 92, 443 n. 11.

122. H. Liebesny, *Aeg* 16, 1936, 258ff. (= SB 8008), col. 1.3–2.1; for the changing designations of the administrative areas see E. Bi(c)kerman(n), *Inst.*, 197f.; the designation '*nomos*' which appears in I Macc. 10.30 is likewise of Ptolemaic origin. A. Schalit, *König Herodes*, 1969, 187ff., is a fundamental study.

123. A. H. M. Jones, *The Cities of the Eastern Roman Provinces*, 1937, 241, 448 n. 19, and *The Greek City from Alexander to Justinian*, 1940, 20; Rostovtzeff, *HW* 3, 1402 n. 142. Double forms also occurred: Ps.Aristeas 107: 'Samareitis', cf. I Macc. 10.30; 11.28, 34, and Eupolemus, FGrHist 723 F 33. For 'Judaia' and 'Galilaia' see also G. Hölscher, QFAGG 5, 1903, 76ff., who however puts the Graecizing of the province too late. A Zeno papyrus (CPJ 1, 124, no. 2e = PCol-Zen 1, 2) still knows the form 'Galila'; Hecataeus, end of the fourth century, see Vol. I, pp. 18f. (FGrHist 264 F 6, 2 = Diodore 40, 3), probably already knew the form 'Ioudaia', similarly Clearchus of Soli in *c.Ap.* 1, 179, in the first half of the third century BC; cf. Schürer, 2, 2 n. 2.

124. U. Kahrstedt, *Syrische Territorien*, AGG NF 19, 2, 1927, 52.

125. The titles could in part be exchanged, see PCZ 59341: a '*stratēgos*' and an '*oikonomos*' in Calynda; similarly in Thera: OGIS 59 ll. 4, 9 and 110. l. 5; cf. also Rostovtzeff, *HW* 3, 1398f. n. 129. For Jerusalem and Samaria in the Seleucid period see *Antt.* 12, 261: the '*meridiarch*' Apollonius, and Nicanor, who was responsible for the royal exchequer. According to the Tobiad romance, *Antt.* 12, 220, Ptolemy wrote in favour of Hyrcanus to all '*hēgemones*' and '*epitropoi*' in the province: III Ezra 4.47, 49 has a royal missive directed to all '*oikonomoi*' and '*toparchai*' in the Persian empire and moreover – probably in ascending order – to the '*stratēgoi*' and satraps. For the whole see also R. Seider, op. cit., 67. Cf. also Y. H. Landau, *IEJ* 16, 1966, 59 l. 14: an οἰκονόμος and a [. . .]ου πρ[ο] εστηκώς . . .

126. PCZ 59016 for Cyprus: OGIS 102 for Crete.

127. See H. Liebesny, op. cit., 257 col. 1.18. For κωμαρχία in the later Herodian sense see A. Schalit (n. 122 above), p. 214. There were still '*kōmogrammateis*' in Judea in this period, an institution which probably goes back to the Ptolemaic period: *Bell.* 1, 479 = *Antt.* 16, 203, and on this A. Schlatter, *GI³*, 391 n. 25. Cf. also the Nabatean *stratēgoi* in Madeba, 37 BC, CIS 2, 196 = RES 674 and on this W. Schrottrof, *ZDPV* 82, 1966, 197ff.; also Y. H. Landau, op. cit., 58, on the villages of the *stratēgos* Ptolemy at Scythopolis.

128. Idumea was already an '*eparchy*' or '*satrapy*' under Antigonus, i.e. in the fourth century (Diodore 19, 95, 2 and 98, 1, according to Hieronymus of Cardia), see Tcherikover, *Mizraim*, 40. We see here how the Persian designation was taken over from the Greek. For Marisa see also n. II, 32.

129. PCZ 59015 verso; on this see F. M. Abel, *RB* 33, 1924, 566–74, and *HP* 1, 67; G. M. Harper, *AJP* 49, 1928, 23–6; Tcherikover, *Mizraim*, 40–2, and *HC*, 65f. The correspondence is preserved in Zeno's records. An explanation for the demand of a second purchase price is perhaps that the Idumeans knew a regulation similar to Deut. 23.16, see F. M. Abel, *HP* 1, 67. PCZ 59804 probably reports the successful recapture of the slaves.

130. CPJ 1, 129 no. 6 = PCZ 59018; on this G. M. Harper, op. cit., 22f.; Tcherikover, *Mizraim*, 42f., and HC, 65.

131. H. Liebesny, op. cit., 259, col. 2, 21f.: the law on the farming-out of tax; 1.25, royal letter; 1.3, 8, 33; 2.1: '*prostagma*' and 1.6f., 26, 30f.: '*diagramma*'; cf. Tcherikover, *HC*, 428 n. 59, and Rostovtzeff, *HW* 1, 340.

132. Gaza, PColZen 1, 11 no. 3 and as a supplement PCZ 59804: Tyre, PCZ 59093; on this Tcherikover, *Mizraim*, 60ff.

133. H. Liebesny, op. cit., 257, col. 1, 17ff.; on this Rostovtzeff, *HW* 1, 340ff.

134. PSI 554, col. 1, 14; the criticism of Rostovtzeff, *HW* 3, 1403 n. 149, of the interpretation of the passage by Tcherikover, *Mizraim*, 46–8, is hardly justified. We can hardly expect exact juristic distinctions between κτῆμα and γῆ ἐν δωρεᾷ from the writer of the letter in Galilee: κτῆμα could simply mean 'vine planting' (see Vol. I, p. 39).

135. Rostovtzeff, *HW* 1, 345; the expression already indicated that this could be no 'finance official' in the sense of a state officer as is supposed by F. Preisigke, *Fachwörterbuch*, 1915, 115, and Tcherikover, *Mizraim*, 46. These were private persons who had contracted for the tax returns of a village, and who were employed in a supervisory capacity by the fiscal authorities.

136. *Antt.* 12, 155, 169, 175ff.; the division of taxes between Ptolemy V Epiphanes and Antiochus III is, however, unhistorical; the events belong in the time of Ptolemy III Euergetes (see above, n. 38 and n. IV, 76). Josephus' account shows that this was a real increase. Of the figures given, the first, 8000 talents, is by no means too high, see below, nn. 199–202, but the second is; see Rostovtzeff, *HW* 2, 1152; Tcherikover, *HC*, 460 n. 42, differs; C. Préaux, *Économie*, 425 n. 1, is cautious. For the whole subject see also M. Rostowzew, *Geschichte der Steuerpacht*, PhilSuppl 9, 1904, 360ff., and *HW* 1, 340f.; 3, 1400 n. 132; also A. H. M. Jones, *The Cities*, 240, 448 n. 18. Taxes of the Ptolemaic cities of Asia Minor were probably also administered in similar fashion, see PCZ 59036f.: Halicarnassus, and OGIS 1, 55: Telmessus in Lycia, both from the time of Ptolemy V Epiphanes, about 200, see Rostovtzeff, *HW* 1, 336–8, and 3, 1399 nn. 131, 131a, see also R. Seider, op. cit., 65.

137. See H. Liebesny, op. cit., 258f., cols. 1, 29 and 2, 25; Ps.Arist. 26; see Rostovtzeff, *HW* 1, 321, 350, 411f.; 3, 1392f. n. 118, 1402f. n. 146, 1419f. n. 208.

138. Diodore 18, 39, 5; and on this W. Schmitthenner, *Saeculum* 19, 1968, 31ff.

139. For the legal and economic position over the royal land see M. Rostowzew, *Studien zur Geschichte des römischen Kolonats*, APF-Bh 1, 1910, 246ff., and for the Ptolemaic possessions 278ff., see also *HW* 1, 269, 277-80, 336, 346. For Palestine see J. Herz, *PJB* 24, 1928, 105f., and Tcherikover, *Mizraim*, 47ff. Cf. also Y. H. Landau, *IEJ* 16, 1966, 66 n. 14, and M. Hengel, *ZNW* 59, 1968, 20ff.

140. Alt, *Kleine Schriften* 2, 1953, 390–5. For the royal possessions of the Persian period in Syria ('Pardes') see Neh. 2.8; Xenophon, *Anab.* 1,4,10; Diodore 16, 41, 5b: Sidon. Further instances in Tcherikover, *HC*, 432 n. 75; cf. also Posidonius, FGrHist 87 F 68 = Athen. 1,28D: Persian vineyards in Damascus.

141. CPJ 1, 118ff., no. 1 = PCZ 59003, and on this Tcherikover, *Mizraim*, 48. For the balsam plantations see Vol. I, pp. 44ff.

142. Cf. J. Kaplan, *RB* 62, 1955, 92ff.: it could be a matter here of cleruchs settled on royal land. The whole new situation of agricultural settlements fits the economic activity of the early Ptolemaic period, see Vol. I, pp. 83ff. A large store centre discovered 12 miles east of Jaffa could have been the centre of a domain: see *RB* 69, 1962, 406f.; this would fit the observation of A. Alt, op. cit., 2, 382 n. 4, on the character of this area as royal land on the basis of Neh. 6.2. Perhaps

the border at 'Pēgai', later Antipatris, suggested in PSI 406, marks the transition from city territory of Joppa to royal land, see Tcherikover, *Mizraim*, 40, 86n. 89, and *HC*, 433 n. 85.

143. See F. M. Heichelheim in T. Frank, *An Economic Survey of Ancient Rome* 4, 1940, 145 n. 19 lit.

144. For taxation under the Seleucids see Vol. I, pp. 28f.; for the Roman period see O. Michel, *TDNT* 8, 93ff., and also the survey of literature, 88; see also M. Hengel, *Die Zeloten*, 1961, 132–45.

145. Rostovtzeff, *HW* 1, 350 and 2, 1116f.; cf. E. Bickerman(n), *From Ezra to the Last of the Maccabees*, 1962, 52f. This policy favoured the tendency towards Hellenization in the indigenous aristocracy, see Vol. I, pp. 49ff.

146. See the schedule and the prohibition against the sale of σώματα λαϊκὰ ἐλεύθερα, H. Liebesny, op. cit., 258f., cols. 1, 34ff. and 2, 17ff.; on this *Antt.* 12, 7f. The Ḥephzibah inscription calls both the Palestinian population at Scythopolis and Egyptian fellahin λαοί, see Y. H. Landau, *IEJ* 16, 1966, 59, ll. 12, 26 and forbids their expulsion (or abduction).

147. Ps.Aristeas 12–14, 19–27; cf. U. Wilcken, *APF* 12, 1937, 221; A. Wilhelm, *APF* 14, 1941, 30–5, and W. L. Westermann, *AJP* 59, 1938, 1–30. On the problem of welfare under the Ptolemies see W. L. Westermann, 'The Ptolemies and the Welfare of their Subjects', *AHR* 43, 1937/38, 270–87, and Rostovtzeff, *HW* 3, 1377f., lit. Especially on Ptolemy II see also W. Peremans, *RBPH* 12, 1933, 1005–22; W. L. Westermann has too favourable an assessment of the situation of the native-born population; the 'welfare' of the king was conditioned less by humanitarian motives than by economic considerations. See Vol. I, p. 38.

148. Tcherikover, *Mizraim*, 54f., supposes that the Ptolemaic regime was milder in Palestine than in Egypt and made room for the struggles of the cities and *ethnē* for independence, but sees that they made a systematic attempt to introduce Egyptian methods of administration here as well. The result is that he finds 'an ambiguous picture'; similarly Rostovtzeff, *HW* 1, 340–51, who also wants to draw a distinction between conditions in the province of 'Syria and Phoenicia' and those in Palestine. This is impossible on geographical grounds, as Palestine formed the nucleus of this province (346ff.).

149. On the '*poleis*' in Palestine see Schürer, 2, 95–222; A. Schlatter, *GI³*, 12ff., 385ff.; A. H. M. Jones, *The Cities*, 1937, 227–95; *The Greek City*, 1940, 14ff., 79ff.; V. T(s)cherikov(w)er, *Die Hellenistischen Städtegründungen*, Phil-Suppl 19, 1927, 64–81; *Mizraim*, 43ff.; *HC*, 90–116, 441–3; M. Avi-Yonah, *QDAP* 5, 1936, 139–93 (Roman period); F. M. Abel, *HP* 1, 51–60. Cf. also A. Alt, 'Hellenistische Städte und Domänen in Galiläa', op. cit., 384–95, and H. Bietenhard, *ZDPV* 79, 1963, 24–58.

150. See Vol. I, pp. 14f. and n. 70.

151. *Antt.* 14, 75, 88 = *Bell.* 1, 156, 166; on this A. H. M. Jones, *The Cities*, 258f., 454f., and Schürer, 1, 299; 2, 101ff.

152. Cf. A. Alt, op. cit., 2, 393ff., on Philotheria and the later Seleucid foundations of Antiocheia and Seleuceia north of Lake Gennesaret. On the other hand, in the Ptolemaic period Scythopolis was not only a *politeuma* but a real *polis*. Josephus, *Antt.* 12, 183, tells against the view expressed by M. Avi-Yonah,

IEJ 12, 1962, 129. That the Ptolemies founded no new free *poleis* in their territory applies only to Egypt; see A. H. M. Jones, *The Cities*, 302ff. Above all, the cities on the Phoenician coast seem to have changed themselves into '*poleis*' at an early stage: on this, see Tcherikover, *Mizraim*, 44.

153. See O. Eissfeldt, *PW*, 2 R. 7, 1895f., and H. Gressmann,*PW*, 2 R. 2, 2224f.: Tyre became a democratic *polis* on the Greek pattern presumably in 275 BC and Sidon at the latest in 262/1, after the death of Philocles: cf. E. Bi(c)kerman(n), *Mélanges Dussaud* 1, 1939, 97f.

154. In Carian Calynda in 247 BC, two royal officials were at work, see Edgar, ad loc., 67. A letter of the *dioikētēs* is said to be addressed to the '*oikonomos*', the '*boulē*' and the '*dēmos*' (PCZ 59341). Thus royal officials and the organs of city administration worked together. Cf. also Rostovtzeff, *HW* 1, 335, and R. Seider, op. cit., 63ff., and above, n. 125.

155. So E. Bi(c)kerman(n), *RevPhil* 65, 1939, 337f. Moreover there is also a difference between the cities which had long been autonomous and the royal 'foundations' in 'Syria and Phoenicia'.

156. 16, 2, 2 (C 749): ἔνιοι δὲ τὴν Συρίαν ὅλην εἴς τε Κοιλοσύρους καὶ Σύρους καὶ Φοινίκας διέλοντες τούτοις ἀναμεμίχθαί φασι τέτταρα ἔθνη· Ἰουδαίους, Ἰδουμαίους, Γαζαίους, Ἀζωτίους, cf. Ps.Aristeas 107, 117, and Sir. 50.25f. The Samaritans are not included; Josephus speaks of the '*ethnos*' of the Samaritans only for a later period (*Antt.* 17, 20; 18, 85). Perhaps the עם אינו of Sir. 50.25 (cf. also Deut. 32.21) is to be understood to mean that after their revolt against Alexander these were added to the territory of the new military colony of Samaria (see also below, n. 158) and received the legal status of an *ethnos* only after Pompey. In the correspondence with Antiochus IV, too, they do not call themselves '*ethnos*', but 'Sidonians in Shechem', on this see below n. IV, 233. This view would in part go against A. Alt, op. cit., 2, 403f. n. 8.

157. For the Jews as an '*ethnos*' see E. Bi(c)kerman(n), *Inst.*, 164f.; A. Alt, op. cit., 2, 401f. and Tcherikover, *HC*, 88.

158. *C.Ap.* 2, 43, according to Ps.Hecataeus: Alexander 'added Judea' to the territory. The report is hardly historical in this form. The new boundary was presumably only drawn under Demetrius II in 145 BC: see I Macc. 10.30, 38; 11.34. For the extent of the province of Jehud see the map *BHHWB* 2, 1299. G. Hölscher, *QFAGG* 5, 1903, 46ff. and 67ff., supposes that the Jews under Artaxerxes III Ochus had lost the Jericho valley to the Edomites, but bases his view on late, questionable sources; cf. on the other hand I Macc. 9.50: Jericho under the citadel of Judea. See also Schürer, 2, 1ff., and A. Alt, *Kleine Schriften* 2, ²1959, 346–62, 347: 'Still almost two centuries after the end of Persian rule the Jewish-Samaritan border was where it had been drawn in the time of Nehemiah'; cf. the survey by K. Galling, *PJB* 36, 1940, 47ff. Probably the Jewish area of settlement in the north-west or north-east extended beyond the narrower boundaries of the province.

159. H. Zucker, *Studien zur jüdischen Selbstverwaltung im Altertum*, 1936, 32, and Tcherikover, *HC*, 59. The construction by Bo Reicke, *The New Testament Era*, 1969, 48, is unhistorical.

160. Both Hecataeus (Diodore 40, 3 = FGrHist 264 F 6, 3ff.) and Ps. Aristeas (e.g. 84ff., the term '*ethnos*' for the Jews does not occur here) describe

Judea as a temple state. See also Tarn/Griffith, *Hellenistic Civilization*, 138ff. (140), 210, and H. Bengtson, *Strategie* 2, 1944, 7f.: the temple states in Asia Minor. Clearchus of Soli still knew the correct name ʽΙερουσαλημην, Josephus, *c.Ap.* 1, 179. Eupolemus, FGrHist 723 F 2, 11, similarly knows both designations and derives the Graecized form from ἱερὸν Σολομῶνος. Philo, *Spec. leg.* 36; *c.Flacc.* 46, etc., uses ἱερόπολις.

161. Bi(c)kerman(n), *Inst.*, 172ff.; Rostovtzeff, op. cit., 1, 505–7. The later conflicts are for a large part connected with the limitation of these freedoms.

162. W. Otto, *Priester und Tempel im hellenistischen Ägypten* 1, 1905/8, 75: the governing officials never took part in the purely priestly administrative apparatus of the temple, but 'exercised a very intensive supervision'. See also 2, 42ff., 81ff., 287, 289f.; C. Préaux, op. cit., 48, 480; Rostovtzeff, op. cit., 1, 281ff.; 3, 1383f. n.90. For 'epistates' or 'archiereus' see W. Otto, op. cit., 1, 39f., 45, 409f.; Préaux, op. cit., 480, and Rostovtzeff, op. cit., 1, 282.

163. R. Seider, op. cit., 59–63.

164. On this see P. W. Lapp, *BASOR* 172, 1963, 22–35, esp. 31ff.; supported by F. M. Cross, *HTR* 59, 1966, 209.

165. Perhaps one might better speak of a division into three in the Persian period: governor, high priest, prince: K. Galling, *Studien zur Geschichte Israels im persischen Zeitalter*, 1964, 162f.

166. On this see W. F. Albright, *BASOR* 148, 1957, 28–30: the high priest Hezekiah mentioned by Ps.Hecataeus (*c.Ap.* 1, 187–9), who at the age of 66 was brought by Ptolemy I to Egypt and whose business experience is stressed, could have been such a temple treasurer. His name perhaps also appears on the Jehud coins published by O. R. Sellers, *The Citadel of Beth Zur*, 1933, 73f.; on the reading see E. L. Sukenik, *JPOS* 14, 1934, 178–84. Possibly the Jehud coins were minted in the interregnum between the death of Alexander in 323 and the final occupation of Judea by Ptolemy I in 301 BC .In no way do they fit the third century (against G. Garbini, in Y. Aharoni, *Excavations at Ramat Raḥel, Seasons 1959 and 1960*, 65), as the Ptolemies kept the monopoly of coinage strictly in their own hands: on this see Vol. I, pp. 36f., and n.275. The two stamps with the double inscription *yhwd* + Hebrew proper name described by N. Avigad (and Y. Yadin, *IEJ* 7, 1957, 146–53) could come from the same period (after 333 BC); cf. a third find in Y. Aharoni, *Ramat Raḥel, Seasons 1961/62*, 44. The far more numerous *pḥw'* stamps (with *yhwd* or Hebrew proper name or both), cf. Y. Aharoni, loc. cit. and P. W. Lapp, op. cit., 33, on the other hand indicate the Persian period; the *pḥw'* is probably to be identified with the *peḥāh*, the local satrap in Jerusalem. *peḥāh* is not translated in LXX either by *epistatēs* or *prostatēs*, but with more political and military designations, see Hatch-Redpath 3, 257c, and the related concepts like 'eparchos', Ezra 5.3, 6; 6.6, 13; 8.36; Neh. 2.7, 9; 'satrapēs', III Bas. 10.15; 21 (20). 24; II Chron. 9.14; 'toparchēs', Isa. 36.9; 'hēgemōn', Jer. 28 (51), 23 etc.; cf. also K. Galling, *Studien zur Geschichte Israels im persischen Zeitalter*, 1964, 182f.

167. On this see Tcherikover, *HC*, 465 n.11; F. M. Abel, *Macc.*, 317; A. Mannzmann, *KP* 1, 142; cf. also SEG 16, 801, a high priest and *agoranomos* in Byblos; Y. H. Landau, *'Atiqot* 2, 1959, 186f., the same office in 129/8 BC in Joppa.

168. The title '*prostatēs*' appears above all in the Egyptian priesthood; see W. Otto, op. cit., 1, 45, 362; 2, 81–111; E. Bi(c)kerman(n), *AIPHOS* 7, 1939–44, 7ff.; F. M. Abel, *HP* 1, 116 and *Macc.*316f. ad loc.; in II Chron. 24.11 the finance official of the high priest, '*pāqīd*', is rendered '*prostatēs*' in LXX. Tcherikover, *HC*, 464f. n. 10 would derive the title from Neh. 11.11, the 'prince in the house of God'; there, however, it is applied to the high priest ,see W. Rudolph, *Esra und Nehemiah*, 1949, 185. Cf. also the προστάτες in the Egyptian synagogues, CIJ 2, 1441, 1447. The title is to be distinguished from the προστασία τοῦ λαοῦ of the high priest, see Vol. I, p. 27, n. 183, against A. Momigliano, *AttiAcc.Torino* 67, 1931/32, 188ff. For the later leading temple officials see J. Jeremias, *Jerusalem in the Time of Jesus*, 1969, 160–81.

169. P. W. Lapp, op. cit., 23ff.; for the dating see 25: third quarter of the third century BC; on the collection of taxes see 30 and 34; cf. say Neh. 13.12. However, the star is not so widespread as a high-priestly symbol, as is assumed by Lapp, with reference to F. M. Cross, *The Ancient Library of Qumran*, 1958, 112. CD 7.19 and T. Levi 18.3 are typically Qumranite instances, and far more messianic passages can also be cited which are based on Num. 24.17: see e.g. Bill. 1, 76f. and M. Hengel, op. cit., 245f. The star perhaps goes back to Greek models, see F. M. Cross, *HTR* 59, 1966, 209 n. 29.

170. A. Alt, op. cit., 2, 401, assumes that there was no royal land in Judea (and Samaria) as the dwelling place of an '*ethnos*'. However, there remains the question what happened to the pre-exilic royal domains (on this see K. Galling, *BRL*, 339). Thus the fortress-like sites from the Persian-Hellenistic period in Ramat Raḥel (*RB* 69, 1962, 403, and 70, 1963, 573) and in Engedi with its balsam plantations (*RB* 70, 1963, 575f., see Vol. I, pp. 44ff.) could indicate such domains. Even the existence of temple land – e.g. on the basis of gifts – cannot be excluded. Perhaps *Pes.*57a Bar. of Abba Ša'ul, first century AD, gives a reference to Jericho.

171. N. Avigad, *IEJ* 8, 1958, 118f.

172. E. Préaux, op. cit., 49: 'lorsque les rois absorbent les domaines sacrés, il leur faut payer le culte'. For the payment of expenses falling due in the temple by foreign rulers see Ezra 6.4f., 8f.; 7.20ff.; cf. II Chron. 31.3ff.; II Macc. 2.13: the library of Nehemiah with the letters of the (Persian) kings about sacrifice (ἀναθήματα); Josephus, *Antt.* 12, 140ff.: Antiochus III; II Macc. 3.2f.: Seleucus IV; I Macc. 10.44: Demetrius I; Philo, *Leg. ad C.* 157: Augustus; on this see E. Bi(c)kerman(n), *AIPHOS* 7, 1939–44, 6ff., and K. Galling, *ZDPV* 68, 1949–51, 134–42: the kings of the time as patrons. However, against Bickermann, it is improbable that the rulers bore the entire costs of the sanctuary, and the temple otherwise had no other sources of income. Royal control was essential; see above, n. 43.

173. So L. Koole, *OTS* 14, 1965, 395.

174. For the earlier stages of the *gerousia* in the Persian period see E. Meyer, *Die Entstehung des Judentums*, 1896, 132ff.: 'die Vorgänger des späteren Synhedrions, der γερουσία'; E. Schürer 2, 238ff.; Poland, *PW*, 2R. 4, 1346ff., and E. Lohse, *TDNT* 7, 86off.; cf. Neh. 2.16; 4.8.13; 5.7; 7.5: haḥōrīm weḥasseganīm; Ezra 5.5, 9; 6.7f., 14: śābē yehūdāyē; 10.8: haśśārīm wehazzeqēnīm, cf. 10.14, 16: rāʾšē hāʾābōt, cf. Neh. 8.13. For more general comments on the *gerousia* see H.

Zucker, op. cit., 29, 32ff., though he puts it too early, and H. Mantel, *Studies in the History of the Sanhedrin*, 1961, 49ff., who wants to put the 'Sanhedrin' dominated by the Pharisees far too early, in the time of Jose b. Joezer, before 160 BC.

175. A. Cowley, *Aramaic Papyri of the Fifth Century*, 1923, 112, no. 30, l. 18.

176. *Antt.* 12, 142, cf. 138: the *gerousia* and the people went out to meet the king: καὶ μετὰ τῆς γερουσίας ἀπαντησάντων, cf. also E. Bi(c)kerman(n), *REJ* 100, 1935, 8f. In Sir. 33 (G 30). 27, the *gerousia* could be meant by the קהל מושלי and in 7.14 by the עדת שרים.

177. On this see J. L. Koole, *OTS* 14, 1965, 391; K. Schubert, *Die Religion des nachbiblischen Judentums*, 1955, 210 n. 7. The beginnings of the Mishnah may have developed from the legal decisions of the *gerousia* or its authorities and from the traditions of the temple scribes in the Hellenistic period. Cf. J. Baer, *Zion* 27, 1962, 117–55.

178. Against E. Lohse, *TDNT* 7, 862; cf. E. Schürer 2, 238: 'An aristocratic senate in Jerusalem . . . can only be demonstrated definitely in the Greek period.' A. Alt, *Kleine Schriften* 2, 1953, 402, is correct: as a result of the disappearance of the governor appointed by the great king, who in the fourth century BC presumably came from the native aristocracy (on this see K. Galling, *Studien zur Geschichte Israels im persischen Zeitalter*, 1964, 182 on Neh. 11.24), the nobility could extend its influence more strongly, and by means of the *gerousia* receive a share in government. For the *gerousia* in the Greek states, and especially Sparta, see V. Tcherikover, *HC*, 466 n. 22; M. Hadas, *HCu*, 272f., and J. Miller, *PW* 7, 1264–8. For the affinity see Vol. I, pp. 72f. Rhodes also had an aristocratic constitution, see Strabo 14, 25 (652/3) and Rostovtzeff, *CAH* 8, 633f.; *HW* 2, 684f.; and in the Macedonian settlement of Laodicea on the Sea in North Syria there is evidence of an aristocratic council of elders in 175 BC, see P. Roussel, *Syria* 22, 1942/3, 29ff. = IGLS 1261.

179. II Macc. 4.44: three men are sent to the king ὑπὸ τῆς γερουσίας cf. Tcherikover, *HC*, 162.

180. See Vol. I, pp. 277f.; later Jerusalem never became a '*polis*' in the Greek sense, see V. A. Tcherikover, *IEJ* 14, 1964, 61–78.

181. I Macc. 12.6 = Josephus, *Antt.* 13, 166; cf. also II Macc. 1.10, the fictional letter to Alexandria on the consecration of the temple: ἡ γερουσία καὶ ᾽Ιούδας . . . II Macc. 11.27, letter of Antiochus V: τῇ γερουσίᾳ τῶν ᾽Ιουδαίων καὶ τοῖς ἄλλοις ᾽Ιουδαίοις, and Judith 4.8; 11.14; 15.8. II Macc. 14.37; I Macc. 11.23; 12.35; 13.36; 14.20 speak of πρεσβύτεροι.

182. E. Schürer 2, 242ff.; E. Lohse, op. cit., 860ff.

183. J. Baer, *Israel among the Nations*, 1955, 63. M. Hadas, *HCu*, 75, cf. also 276: 'modeled on Greek patterns'.

184. *Antt.* 12, 158ff.: the history is elaborated in favour of the Tobiads: the low sum of twenty talents is meant to stress the ambition of Onias; the king's ambassador plays the intermediary between Joseph and Ptolemy. The whole description of the development of the conflict, the conversation with the high priest, the assembly of the people, the reception by the king in Memphis are fictitious scenes. The threat itself (cf. I Macc. 3.36 and Rostovtzeff, *HW* I, 348) and the increase in taxation are realistic. On this see Josephus, *Bell.* 2, 405.

185. In *Antt.*12, 161, Josephus made the high priest point out the duties associated with the προστασία τοῦ λαοῦ. Onias replied that he was not in a position to represent the people to the crown. Thereupon Joseph held a popular assembly and went before the king as προστάτης (τοῦ πλήθους). According to the later account of Josephus, 'prostasia' was bound up with the office of the high priest, see *Antt.*20, 238, 244, 251. However, after the battle of Actium Herod took it to himself by a popular resolution: *Bell.*1, 395 = *Antt.*15, 160. Cf. also Diodore 40 fr.2 (Reinach 76): The Hasmoneans had received 'prostasia' over the Jewish people, who had hitherto been free, from the Roman senate. The ראש חבר היהודים on the coins of John Hyrcanus (Schürer 1, 269) probably corresponds to the title προστάτης. See also Vol.I, p.25, and n.168 above, and below, n.IV, 84. The report in Hecataeus (FGrHist III A 264, fr.6.5f. = Diod.40, 3, 6) that the prostasia' was always given to the noblest priest, is also a consequence of his idealistic picture of the Jews (see Vol.I, pp.255f.) and has only limited historical value; in reality, it went by heredity. The same is true – pace H. Zucker, *Studien zur jüdischen Selbstverwaltung*, 1936, 32 n.1 – of the report of Ps.Aristeas on the Jewish priestly state. B. Mazar, *IEJ* 7, 1957, 138, cf. also S. Gandz, *JQR* 31, 1941, 383–404, is right.

186. *Antt.*12, 175ff., 182f., 224; cf. H. Volkmann, *PW* 23, 1677.

187. Josephus, *c.AP.*2, 48, see also Vol.I, pp.268f.

188. In Telmessus in Lycia, Euergetes changed the Lycian royal land, some of which had been given by his father as a gift and some of which he had expropriated himself, 'into a kind of *dynasteia* or vassal kingdom', which he handed on to a relation. His first measure was a substantial reduction of tax: Rostovtzeff, *HW* 1, 336f. On the other hand, the '*dioikētēs*' of his father Apollonius probably fell out of favour after the death of Philadelphus, and his property was confiscated: M. Rostovtzeff, *A Large Estate in Egypt*, 1962, 20, and P. Viereck, *Philadelphia*, Morgenland 16, 1928, 67; however, see R. Seider, op. cit., 45.

189. See H. Volkmann, *PW* 23, 1673f.

190. *Antt.*12, 224; on this see H. Zucker, op. cit., 32; see also J. L. Koole, *OTS* 14, 1965, 394.

191. On the kinds of tax see E. Bi(c)kerman(n), *Inst.*, 111ff.; Rostovtzeff, *HW* 1, 464ff.

192. *Antt.*12, 142f.; for what follows see A. Mittwoch, *Bibl* 36, 1955, 352–61. For freedom from tax: *Antt.*12, 151 (Antiochus III to Zeuxis); I Macc. 10.29f. = *Antt.*13, 52 (Demetrius I); *Antt.*15, 303 and 17, 25 (Herod); cf. Antiochus I, OGIS 223, and Antiochus III, SEG 2, 663 (see above, n.32).

193. A. Mittwoch, op. cit., 360, conjectures *inter alia* in the *nōgēš* of Dan. 11.20 a reference to increased taxation; the report of Sulpicius Severus (see above, n.1) about a tax laid on the Jews by Seleucus Nicator of 300 talents could also refer to Seleucus IV Philopator. Cf. also Bickermann, *GM*, 55; *Inst.*, 108; and Tcherikover, *HC*, 459 n.39.

194. II Macc. 4.8f., and also a once-for-all payment of 80 talents and 150 for the transformation of Jerusalem into a *polis*; for the 300 talents see I Macc. 11.28 and A. Mittwoch, op. cit., 353.

195. For war reparations see B. Niese, *GGMS* 2, 758; for the delay in

payment see II Macc. 8.10, 36; Livy 42, 6, 6; Sulpicius Severus 2, 19, 6, CSEL 1, 75, ed. Halm; on this E. Bickermann, *GM*, 67.

196. II Macc. 4.24, cf. 27ff., 39; for the temple see I Macc. 10.42 and J. Pirenne, *RIDA* 1, 1954, 225.

197. A. Mittwoch, op. cit., 354; similarly Bi(c)kerman(n), *Inst.*, 131ff.; Rostovtzeff, *HW* 1, 468, supposes that taxes to this level 'were traditional in Judaea'.

198. A. Mittwoch, op. cit., 360f.; cf. I Macc. 8.18.

199. For the Ptolemaic duties see C. Préaux, *Économie*, 371–9. With imported goods they could be up to 50% of the value.

200. Rostovtzeff, *HW* 2, 1152; see above, n. 136.

201. See FGrHist 260 F 42 = Jerome, *in Dan.* 11.5, *PL* 25, 560. On this see Rostovtzeff, *HW* 2, 1150ff., especially 1155: the total income of Alexander is said to have been 30,000 talents, that of Antigonus 11,000. The exploitation of the Ptolemaic administration seems to have been the most effective.

202. Herodotus 3, 91: Egypt paid 700 talents and 120,000 *artaboi* of grain, cf. K. Galling, *Studien zur Geschichte Israels im persischen Zeitalter*, 1964, 172: the basic income from taxation in Macedonia under the Antigonids amounted to only a little over 200 talents, see Tarn/Griffith, *Hellenistic Civilization*, 62; on the whole question see Rostovtzeff, *HW* 2, 1143–59. For the devaluation of money and increase in income see Tarn/Griffith, op. cit., 112f., 120f., and Rostovtzeff, *HW* 1, 165f., cf. 2, 712f. and 2, 1159ff.: 'New Sources of Wealth'.

203. See M. Hengel, *Die Zeloten*, 329 n. 4. Cf. A. Schalit (above n. 122), 256ff.

204. FGrHist III C 726 fr. 2, 2; 3,4 (Eusebius., *Pr.Ev.* 9, 23 and 27).

205. For Agatharcides see Vol. I, p. 14 and n. 67 above; on this cf. H. Willrich, *Judaica*, 1900, 99f., and B. Schaller, *ZNW* 54, 1963, 30 n. 70. F. M. Abel, *RB* 44, 1935, 575ff., and *HP* 1, 31f., on the other hand rightly supposes that Ptolemy changed his attitude towards the Jews. Ps. Hecataeus has a completely positive assessment of it, see above, n. 84.

206. The work comes from Alexandria; its date is disputed. E. Bickermann, *ZNW* 29, 1930, 280–98, puts it between 145 and 127 (100) BC because of certain formulas of the style used by the Ptolemaic chancery and other details; W. W. Tarn, *The Greeks in Bactria and India*, 1938, 424f. at 100 BC; cf. M. Hadas, *Aristeas*, 1951, 54, etc.; see, on the other hand, Schürer 3, 612f.; S. Jellicoe, *JTS* 12, 1961, 266 n. 5 (before 168 BC), and A. Pelletier, *Lettre d'Aristée*, 1962, 57f. There is still no trace in the letter of the more critical attitude towards Hellenistic culture furthered by the Maccabean revolt and of the Alexandrian antisemitism which arose towards the end of the second century BC. On the other hand the names seem to presuppose the Maccabean revolt: the names of Mattathias and his five sons given in I Macc. 2.2 appear particularly frequently, see the index in A. Pelletier, op. cit., 318f. Thus the letter probably was written between 150 and 130 BC. For the tendency of this work directed to Greek-speaking Jews see M. Hadas, *Aristeas to Philocrates*, 1951, 20, 60, and V. Tcherikover, *HTR* 51, 1958, 59–85. The model for princes goes back to a philosophical writing *Peri Basileias*, written in the third century, see W. W. Tarn, op. cit., 414–36 (425ff.). For this style of literature see E. R. Goodenough, *YCS*

1, 1928, 58ff.; Rostovtzeff, *HW* 3, 1346; M. Hadas, *HCu*, 25, 293 n. 7; P. Hadot, *RAC* 8, 555–632.

207. *Antt.* 12, 171ff., 176ff., 185, 207, 214ff.

208. On this see CPJ 1, 17–19, 194ff., 244f.

209. Dan. 1.17; 2.48ff.; 3.30; 6.2ff., 29. For the term 'court history' see W. Baumgartner, *TR* NF 11, 1939, 131f.

210. See R. Meyer, *Das Gebet des Nabonid*, BAL 107, 3, 1962, 13–52; cf. also 107, where the author stresses that 'the so exceptionally positive and sympathetic description of the foreign ruler' hardly fits the militant attitude of the Essenes.

211. See A. Bentzen, *Daniel*, ²1952, 6, 29ff., 37f., 39. The legends 'arose in the Hellenistic period and were probably first transmitted by word of mouth' (6). This view was also confirmed by linguistic investigation: see W. Baumgartner, *Zum AT und seiner Umwelt*, 1959, 104ff., 107, 110; see also n. III, 460 and n. III, 508 below.

212. A. Bentzen, op. cit., 45, 47: the whole of ch. 3.31–4.34 is a proclamation of the 'converted' great king. Cf. also W. Baumgartner, *RGG*³ 2, 28 and R. Meyer, op. cit., 109ff.

213. Tobit 1.10–22 (cf. Dan. 1.8–20). In Tobit the 'court history' is only a framework: on its connection with the story of Ahikar see 2.10; 11.19 and 14.10ff., and Altheim/Stiehl, *Die aramäische Sprache unter den Achaemeniden*, 192ff. For the time of composition see R. H. Pfeiffer, *History of NT Times*, 1949, 265, 274f. and O. Eissfeldt, *The Old Testament. An Introduction*, 585: after 200 but before the Maccabean revolt. The place of origin is probably Palestine, even if the material comes from the east.

214. For the time and place of its composition see H. Bardtke, *Das Buch Esther*, 1963, 252–5: end of the third century BC in Palestine.

215. For Esther and the 'Hellenistic romance' see R. Stiehl, *WZKM* 53, 1957, 6–9, and Altheim/Stiehl, op. cit., 195–201; also Eissfeldt, *The Old Testament*, 507, and H. Bardtke, op. cit., 253, who also wants to include Daniel in the 'genre of the Hellenistic romance'. However, an 'aretalogical Novelle' would better fit Dan. 1–6 and the LXX additions (see Vol. I, pp. 111ff.). For Tobit see M. Hadas, *HCu*, 206: 'A romance, based on the oriental story of Ahikar but influenced in form by Hellenistic practice.' On the whole, see Vol. I, pp. 110–15.

216. Cf. 3.7; 4.42; 4.60. The derivation of the narrative is disputed. W. Rudolph, *Esra und Nehemia*, 1949, pp. v–x, follows R. Laqueur in supporting a Greek derivation, but R. H. Pfeiffer, op. cit., 250–7, conjectures an Aramaic-Persian source on the basis of studies made by C. Torrey. More substantial is the affinity with the Ahikar tradition and the wisdom background pointed out by Pfeiffer. An oriental (Persian-Indian) derivation is also conjectured by A. Schalit, *BJPES* 13, 1946/7, 119–28. F. Zimmermann, *JQR* 54, 1963, 182ff. strengthens the arguments for an originally Aramaic form.

217. 4.53; this Hellenizing tendency is probably to be attributed to the translator.

218. For the relationship of Esther and Daniel to the story of Joseph see L. A. Rosenthal, *ZAW* 15, 1895, 278–90, and 17, 1897, 125–8; cf. also H. Bardtke, op. cit., 302f., 323f., 373, and M. Gan, *Tarbiz* 31, 1961, 144–9. For the

relationship of the story of the Tobiads to the Joseph story see H. Willrich, *Die Juden und Griechen vor der makkabäischen Erhebung*, 1895, 94, 100; cf. e.g. Gen. 41.43 and *Antt.* 12, 172, or the theme of the hostile brothers, 12, 202. The starting point for these 'court histories' is the good relationship of the Jews to their Persian overlords; apart from the Joseph story, the pre-exilic tradition does not know this genre. For the oriental basic motif see E. Meyer, *UAC* 2, 39 n. 1, on Koh. 4.13f.

219. For the dating of the translation see E. Bickerman(n), *JBL* 63, 1944, 346ff.: 78/77 BC; Altheim/Stiehl, *Aramäische Sprache*, 210–3: about 130 BC. On the other hand, the book of Esther is put too late, op. cit., 201ff., and R. Stiehl, *WZKM* 53, 1957, 18ff., and E. Bickerman(n), op. cit., 355. The book is too secular for the time of the Maccabean revolt and later. The translation made in Jerusalem (see E. Bickerman(n), op. cit., 355f., 361ff., and *PAAJR* 20, 1951, 101–33; 114ff.) therefore enriched the work in a religious and a polemic direction; see Vol. I, p. 101. The addition to Daniel of Bel and the Dragon, on the other hand, merely shows a polemical rationalist tendency against idolatry (cf. Ps. Hecataeus in *c.Ap.* 1, 192, 201ff.). He is loyal to the pagan king.

220. Cf. *b.Sanh.* 43a; *Sota* 49b: of Jesus; *Gittin* 14b.

221. See M. Hengel, *Die Zeloten*, 1961, 309 n. 1.

222. For Ptolemaic Egypt see CIJ 2, nos. 1432, 1440–4, 1449 and CPJ 3, 164, no. 1532a. The very much more numerous synagogue inscriptions from Roman Byzantine times have dedications to the rulers in only two instances, see CIJ, no. 927, and the newly discovered synagogue inscription in Ostia, F. M. Squarciapino, *Archaeology* 16, 1963, 203, both from the time of Septimius Severus, who was relatively friendly towards the Jews.

223. Josephus, *c.Ap.* 1, 192, 201ff.

224. So under Euergetes and Philopator a certain Dositheus son of Drimylus, cf. III Macc. 1.3 and CPJ 3, 230ff., no. 127: in 244 BC he was '*hypomnēmatographos*' of the king, in 222 priest of Alexander and of the divinized Ptolemies. In 217 he is said to have saved the life of the king before Raphia; see A. Fuks, *JJurPap* 7/8, 1953/54, 205–9. In Roman times it was the Rabbi Elisha b. Abuya ('Aḥēr) and the famous Tiberius Julius Alexander, the nephew of Philo. A further Ptolemaic instance in O. Mørkholm, *Classica et Medievalia* 22, 1961, 39f.

225. Koh. 5.7f.; 8.2ff.; 9.17; 10.4f.; 10.16–20.

226. Sir. 36 (G 33). 1–22; 10.8ff., 14ff.; see Vol. I, pp. 152f.

227. Sir. 39.4; cf. 34 (G 31). 9ff.; on this see E. Bickerman(n), *From Ezra to the Last of the Maccabees*, 1962, 62.

228. H. Gressmann, *Vorträge der Bibliothek Warburg 1922/23*, 1926, 173f.

229. See I. L. Seeligmann, *The Septuagint Version of Isaiah*, 1948, 81.

230. Schürer 2, 139 n. 182, and F. M. Heichelheim, *ZRGG* 3, 1951, 251–3. For Phoenician trade connections with the West according to Ezek. 27 see P. Rüger, *Das Tyrusorakel, Ez 27*, typescript diss. Tübingen, 60ff., 66ff., 74f.; for import statistics see 22f. and for dating 118ff. However, it seems more probable that the list is of Phoenician origin, as at this time Jewish trade was little developed and the Phoenicians dominated the coastal area (see below, n. 252).

231. *Orat.* 4, 7. Isaeus lived in Athens c. 420–350 BC; cf. Schürer 2, 141 n. 195, and F. M. Abel, *HP* 1, 19. For the Greek *mercenaries* see Vol. I, pp. 12ff.

232. *Orat.* 52, 20, where on the basis of Harpocration, ed. Dindorf, 1853, 1, 19 and 2, 23, Ἄκην is to be read for Θράκην; see Schürer, loc. cit.

233. So e.g. in Meṣad Hashavyahu, between Ashdod and Jaffa, as early as the end of the seventh century BC; see J. Naveh, *IEJ* 12, 98–113. There may also have been a settlement in ʿAṭliṭ; see C. N. Johns, *QDAP* 2, 1933, 41ff., and on this Watzinger, *DP* 2, 8f. For the Greek settlement Al-Mina in Northern Syria see Rostovtzeff, *HW* 1, 85–8, and 3, 1326 n. 19.

234. Schürer 3, 98–100; see *KAI*, 53–66; Dittenberger, *Syll.*³ 1, no. 185; CIS I, 1, 114. For the earlier period see T. J. Dunbabin, *The Greeks and their Eastern Neighbours*, 1957, 24ff., 35ff.; see also Vol. I, p. 43 and n. I, 337.

235. Schürer 2, 68f.; see also Vol. I, pp. 37, 42f. The Athenian comic poet Hermippus (*c.* 425 BC) mentions among other things the import of fine wheat meal and dates from Phoenicia and incense from Syria: Athen. I, 27f/28a; see H. Bengtson, *GG*³, 200. Cf. also Herondas 2.16 (beginning of the third century): grain from Acco to supply the famine on Cos.

236. *British School of Archaeology in Jerusalem Bulletin* 4, 1924, 42f.

237. According to the Eshmunazar inscription (specially for Sidon), CIS I, 1, 13 l. 19 = KAI 14 and Ps. Skylax: see K. Galling, *Studien*, 196–204. The Palestinian coast at that time received a whole series of new harbours: see K. Galling, *BRL*, 264. Pliny 5, 69 still speaks of 'Jope Phoenicum', and according to Strabo 16, 2, 21 (756) the whole coast from Orthosia to Pelusium is called Φοινίκη: cf. also 2, 33 (760).

238. On the earlier discoveries see J. H. Iliffe, *QDAP* 2, 1933, 15–26. Newer discoveries (without any claim to completeness): (*a*) in the *coastal plain*: *IEJ* 1, 1950/51, 212f.: Tell Qasilé at the mouth of the Yarkon; *IEJ* 6, 1956, 259 = *RB* 64, 1957, 242: Jaffa; *IEJ* 8, 1958, 97: Ḥirbet al-Muqamma = Ekron; op. cit., 133f.: Tell Abu-Zeitun, Yarkon valley; *IEJ* 9, 1959, 110f.: Zephat, south-west of Dor; *RB* 62, 1955, 90: Bat-Yam, south of Jaffa (cf. already *AJA* 51, 1952, 142); *RB* 70, 1963, 584: Strato's Tower; *QDAP* 2, 1933, 47: ʿAṭliṭ; *QDAP* 4, 1935, 5, 16f.: Tell Abu-Ḥawam (near Haifa). (*b*) *Inland*: O. Sellers, *The Citadel of Beth Zur*, 1933, 41; O. Tufnell, *Lachish* III, 1953, 58f., 131; *IEJ* 14, 1964, 125f.: ʿEngedi; *IEJ* 6, 1956, 137; Ramat Raḥel (near Jerusalem); *BASOR* 83, 1941, 24f.; Tell en Naṣbeh = Mizpah; *BASOR* 161, 1961, 52 and 169, 1963, 38: Balātah = Shechem; J. W. Crowfoot, *Samaria-Sebaste* 3, 1957, 210ff.; *BASOR* 173, 1964, 43f.: two lecythoi from the middle of the fifth century BC from Tell Taʿannek. In general see C. Clairmont, *Berytus* 11, 1954/55, 85–139, and 12, 1956/58, 1–34, though Palestine is treated in rather a niggardly way. J. M. Myers, *ZAW* 74, 1962, 178–85, also gives a survey of trade relationships between Greece and Palestine from the seventh/sixth century with special reference to pottery.

239. D. von Bothmer, *BASOR* 83, 1941, 26.

240. J. Meshorer, *ʿAtiqot* 3, 1961, 185 pl. xxviii, 6; G. E. Wright, *BASOR* 144, 1956, 19f.

241. For the distribution of Attic coins and imitations of them in Syria and Palestine see Rostovtzeff, *HW* 1, 88f., and 3, 1324 n. 16, and the earlier literature there; W. Schwabacher, 'Geldumlauf und Münzprägung in Syrien von 6 u. 5 Jahrhunderten v. Chr', *Opuscula Archaeologica* 6, 1960, 139–49; R. Loewe, *PEQ* 87, 1955, 141–50, and B. Kanael, *BHHWB* 2, 1250f. For the so-called

Philisto-Arabian imitations from Palestine see G. F. Hill, *Catalogue of the Greek Coins of Palestine*, 1914, lxxxiiff., 176ff., pl.xix; for the Jehud coins see E. L. Sukenik, *JPOS* 14, 1934, 178–87, and 15, 1935, 341–3; A. Reifenberg, *Ancient Jewish Coins*, ²1947, 5–9. Six instances in all are known. A new one with lilies and an eagle has been published by J. Meshorer, *IEJ* 16, 1966, 217–19. For the Hebrew loanword *darkᵉmōnīm* see Ezra 2.69; Neh. 7.69ff., where in view of the context it must mean gold and drachmae, i.e. darics; see R. de Vaux, *Ancient Israel*, 1961, pp.207f.

242. *Alexander Marx Jubilee Vol.*, ES, 1950, 65; similarly K. Galling, *Studien*, 101; D. Schlumberger, *L'Argent Grec dans l'empire Achéménide*, Paris 1953, 9ff.: the situation in Egyptian finds is similar.

243. Op. cit., 25.

244. Rostovtzeff, *HW* 3, 1325 n.17; J. H. Iliffe, *QDAP* 4, 1934, 182–6; Watzinger, *DP* 2, 5, 10. The excavator Flinders Petrie, *Beth Pelet* I, 1930, 14 (no.42, pll.xliv–vi), put the bed about 850 BC, so at first also Watzinger, *DP* 1, 110; see, however, the correction 2, 10. For the bronze vessels, see Petrie, op. cit. (no.43, pl.xlvii), and Watzinger, *DP* 2, 5.

245. Watzinger, loc. cit., esp. n.3.

246. See the collection in A. Ciasca, *OA* 2, 1963, 63; for literature on the sites see pp.51–8. They are Tell ed-Duwēir (Lachish); Tell Sandaḥannah (Marisa); Tell eṣ Ṣāfi; Tell Gat; Achsib: all these places in the Shephelah; Macmish (plain of Sharon); Tell Abu Ḥawam (Haifa); Tell et Tiyur (as yet unpublished); Beth Shean; Ḥarayeb (near Sidon); cf. also Watzinger, *DP* 2, 5f., and O. Negbi, *IEJ* 14, 1964, 187–9, who distinguishes between terra cottas of Western Greek and of Syro-Palestinian-Eastern types; in one case (pl.42a) he demonstrates importation from Rhodes. The strong Greek influence is confirmed by the find of twenty statuettes and two hundred terra cottas at Tell Ṣippor from the fourth century BC: O. Negbi, '*Atiqot* 6, 1966.

247. M. H. Chéhab, *Les Terres cuites de Harayeb*, BMB 10, 1951/52, passim, esp. 156ff.

248. N. Avigad, *IEJ* 10, 1960, 90–6 (95 n.12); A. Ciasca, op. cit., 53ff. and 63.

249. J. H. Iliffe, *QDAP* 5, 1936, 61–8, pll.xxix–xxxiv; above all in the Horus-Harpocrates figures, pl.xxix and the two priests pl.xxxii.

250. C. N. Johns, *QDAP* 2, 1933, 41–104 (cit. 41); cf. Watzinger, *DP* 2, 7–9. From 470/60 BC onwards Greek sculptors were at work in Sidon, who developed anthropoid sarcophagi following Greek models of a new type; see K. Galling, *ZDPV* 79, 1963, 142ff., 145 n.2, and in detail E. Kukahn, *Anthropoide Sarkophage in Beyrouth*, 1955, 15–22: the sarcophagi have 'the closest connections' with the 'mixed style' of the north Phoenician terra cottas (16). A climax of this Graeco-Phoenician art is the Alexander sarcophagus of Abdalonymus, who was named king of Sidon by Alexander in 332: see M. Hadas, *HCu*, 225f., and M. Bieber, *The Sculptor of the Hellenistic Age*, 1961, 272ff. (lit.)

251. Marisa: OGIS, 593, see also Vol.I, pp.293f.; Shechem, *Antt.* 11, 344 and 12, 257ff.; cf. on this Rostovtzeff, *CAH* 7, 191 and *HW* 3, 1401 n.137, and M. Delcor, *ZDPV* 78, 1962, 36ff.; see also below n.IV, 233. For Rabbath Ammon see Vol.I, p.41.

252. On this see K. Galling, *Die Bücher der Chronik, Esra, Nehemiah*, ATD

12, 1954, 16, who ascribes this passage to the 'second Chronicler' about 200 BC.

253. For the agricultural ideal see below, n.413; cf. Ps.Aristeas 107f., 112f.; Josephus, *c.Ap.* 1, 60 and G. Boström, *Proverbiastudien*, LUÅ, 1935, 59–69, 79–82; G. Hölscher, SAH Ph. h. Klasse 34, 1944/48, 3, 17f.; R. de Vaux, *Ancient Israel*, 1961, 72ff.; see Vol. I, p. 138. Cf. on this Cicero, *De Officiis* 1, 150f.

254. Tcherikover, CPJ 1, 15f.; J. Harmatta, *Acta antiqua* 7, 1959, 337–409 (378ff.).

255. Hos. 12.8; Ezek. 16.29; 17.4; Job 40.30; Prov. 31.24; Zeph. 1.11 and Isa. 23.11 are probably already directed against the Phoenicians as merchants.

256. Zech. 14.21; the passage is most probably to be understood in the light of Neh. 13.16ff. and the decree directed against alien merchants in *Antt.* 12, 145f. This does not exclude an additional reference to the Samaritans (so K. Elliger, *Kleine Propheten* II, ATD 1950, 175); see below, n. IV, 233, their description of themselves as 'Sidonians from Shechem'.

257. G. Boström, op. cit., 51–98: 'Trade is a contract which brings in its train alien culture and certainly also alien religion' (92), cf. also 95: his rejection is a 'reaction against Canaanism'.

258. For the Jewish view of 'Arab' caravan trade, see Gen. 37.25; Isa. 21.13; Ezek. 27.20ff.; 38.13; Job 6.19; Bar. 3.23; Ps.Aristeas 114. For the position of Judea see E. Täubler, *Tyche*, 1926, 121–4, and K. Galling, *BRL*, 262.

259. See Vol. I, p. 33, and above, n. 239: Beth Zur, Ramath Raḥel (Beth Kerem?); Mizpah. For Jerusalem see Macalister-Duncan, 'Excavations on the Hill of Ophel', *PEFA* 4, 1926, 187f.

260. Loc. cit., figs 197/8 and 201.

261. Neh. 3.5; 4.3; 6.10–19; 13.28; Josephus, *Antt.* 11, 302f., 306ff.; 12.168. For the 'liberal' group see K. Galling, *Studien*, 157, 164f.; M. Smith, *Fischer Weltgeschichte*, Vol. 5, ed. H. Bengtson, 1965, 362ff., 366ff.

262. Rostovtzeff, *HW* 2, 1018ff., 1026ff., 1238ff.; Tarn/Griffith, *Hellenistic Civilization*, 239ff.

263. Cf. also F. K. Kienitz, op. cit., 144f. The Egyptian king Tachus already allowed himself to be advised by the Attic *stratēgos* Chabrias on the financing of his expedition to Palestine, op. cit., 96f., 119f., cf. 175ff. The description given above follows Rostovtzeff, *HW* 1, 255–422 on essential points, also making use of C. Préaux, *L'économie royale des Lagides*, 1939.

264. Tarn/Griffith, *Hellenistic Civilization*, 179.

265. This claim did not exclude private property: see Rostovtzeff, *HW* 1, 273; 3, 1380 n. 84; C. Préaux, op. cit., 459ff.; it was, however, substantially limited, op. cit., 533–57.

266. Rostovtzeff, *HW* 1, 272; cf. also C. B. Welles, *JJurPap* 3, 1949, 23.

267. See H. Bengtson, *MusHelv* 10, 1953, 162: the years between 323 and, say, 260 BC, the beginning of the Zeno papyri, are decisive for the organization of Ptolemaic rule, but almost completely unknown to us.

268. On P. Cowley 81: J. Harmatta, *Acta Antiqua* 7, 1959, 394ff., 397f.

269. See E. Leider, *Der Handel von Alexandria*, Diss. 1934, 17ff.: trade with Syria and Arabia, and W. Schubart, *RAC* 1, 271ff., 278ff.

270. *HW* 2, 1164ff.; see above, nn. 201/2.

271. For Egyptian agriculture see M. Schnebel, *Die Landwirtschaft im*

hellenistischen Ägypten, 1927, I, *Der Betrieb des Landes,* 1925, passim; see especially the summary, 355ff.; C. Préaux, op. cit., 117–52 (especially on the growing of grain); and Rostovtzeff, *HW* 1, 274–87; 3, 1380–9 (lit.). For growing of wheat see J. Harmatta, op. cit., 396, and *HW* 1, 359–62; 1404f.; for technical and economic progress in Hellenistic times see 2, 1180–1200; 3, 1615–20; cf. PCZ 59195 and 19430: the testing of Milesian and Arabian sheep: for Apollonius as 'minister of agriculture' see R. Seider, op. cit., 47ff.

272. The extent of the monopoly cannot be established clearly because of the limited nature of the sources. The bases are P. Revenue, ed. Grenfell, cols. 38–72, new ed. J. Bingen, SB Bh 1, 1952, and P. Tebt. 703. An introduction can be found in Mitteis/Wilcken, *Grundzüge und Chrestomathie der Papyruskunde,* 1912, I, 1, 239–58, and the selection of texts in II, 2, 348ff.; for their derivation see A. Andreades, *Mélanges Maspero* 2, 1934–37, 289–95; C. Préaux, op. cit., see Index 'Monopole', 615, and the summary 429ff.; Rostovtzeff, *HW* 1, 302–13 and 3, 1388–91.

273. Rostovtzeff, *HW* 1, 313ff.

274. See M. Rostovtzeff, *A Large Estate,* 1922, 140: 'Almost no branch of economic life was closed to these revenue farmers and concessionaires.'

275. For the bank monopoly see P. Revenue, cols. 73–8, see also Mitteis/Wilcken, op. cit., I, 2, 212ff.; on the policy on coinage and banking, C. Préaux, op. cit., 267–97; Rostovtzeff, *HW* 1, 398–407; 2, 1292f.; 3, 1416–8. PCZ 59021 is especially important for the monopoly on coinage, see op. cit., 1416f., lit. For Alexander's monetary policy see D. Schlumberger, op. cit., 27ff.

276. A. Rowe, *The Topography and History of Beth Shean,* 1930, 45; G. M. Fitzgerald, *Beth-Shean, Excavations 1921–23,* 1931, 51ff., pl. 41; see also F. M. Abel, *HP* 1, 53, 56, 57, and O. R. Sellers, *BA* 25, 1962, 89f.

277. Rostovtzeff, *HW* 1, 249–398; especially on trade with Syria and Palestine see Tcherikover, *Mizraim* 15–24, and Vol. I, pp. 42f. On the old Phoenician trade connections with southern Arabia according to Ezek. 27 see P. Rüger, op. cit., 82ff., 86ff., 96–103. On the 'incense route' see 108ff.

278. PCZ 59536; 59009 and the supplement Vol. 4, 285; 59011, col. 1. 15 (in l. 10 Joppa is mentioned and in l. 8 the property of Apollonius in Beth Anath, see Vol. I, pp. 39f.); PSI 628 and 678; cf. Strabo 16, 3, 2 (766); 16, 4, 19 (778); Diodore 2, 49, 1–33, 46; Pliny, *Hist. nat.* 12, 52ff. The significance of aromatic trade for the prestige of Egypt is shown by its role in the *'pompē'* of Philadelphus: Athen. 5, 201a; see also H. Kortenbeutel, *Der aegyptische Süd- und Osthandel,* 1931, 16ff.; E. Leider, op. cit., 4, 51ff.; Tcherikover, *Mizraim,* 25–9; C. Préaux, op. cit., 362–6; Tarn/Griffith, *Hellenistic Civilization,* 244–9; Rostovtzeff, *HW* 1, 387f.; 2, 1243ff.; and 3, 1414 n. 185 lit.; G. W. v. Beek, *BA* 23, 1960, 70–95 and on Gerrha especially F. Altheim, *Weltgeschichte Asiens* 2, 1948, 43f.

279. ·Διοδώρου τοῦ ἐπὶ τῆς λιβανωτικῆς: PSI 628 (to be supplemented by PCZ 59009 and the addition Vol. 4, 285), see U. Wilcken, *APF* 8, 1927, 277; A. Willrich, *APF* 10, 1932, 239, and C. Préaux, op. cit., 363 n. 6.

280. PCZ Vol. 4, 285 on 59009; cf. Tcherikover, *Mizraim,* 78 n. 35. The Nabateans are also mentioned: PSI 406.

281. F. M. Abel, *RB* 46, 1937, 373–91, and *HP* 1, 34–7; see Diodore 2, 48, 1–6; 19, 94–100.

282. W. W. Tarn, *JEA* 15, 1929, 9–25; M. Rostovtzeff, *Caravan Cities*, 1932, 24–8, 56–61; F. Altheim, *Weltgeschichte Asiens* I, 158f.; and Altheim/Stiehl, *Die Araber in der Alten Welt* I, 1964, 65–79. See Diodore 3, 43, 4–5.

283. Polybius 5,71, 1, 4; 79, 8; 82, 12; 85, 4; see above, n. 15.

284. I Macc. 5.25; 9.35; II Macc. 5.8.

285. Strabo 16, 4, 21, 26 (779, 783f.). On the Nabateans see J. Starcky, *BA* 18, 1955, 84–106, and R. Dussaud, *La pénétration des Arabes en Syrie avant l'Islam*, 1955, 21–61; Nabatean kings can be demonstrated from about 170 BC (II Macc. 5.8: Aretas I). Aretas III, *c.* 87–62 BC, gave himself the surname Philhellene (op. cit., 54).

286. Rostovtzeff, *HW* 1, 359f.; 2, 1249; H. Bengtson, *GG*³, 437.

287. Theocritus 14, 58ff. Cf. Ps.Aristeas 124.

288. Herondas, *Mim.* I, 26–32; cf. Athen. 5, 203 c/d; and Teles, ed. Hense, 1889, p. 29, 6; see Rostovtzeff, *HW* 1, 407ff.

289. See Vol. I, p. 15 and n. I, 79 = Peek, *Griechische Grabgedichte*, 1960, no. 162, ll. 9f.

290. Tarn/Griffith, *Hellenistic Civilization*, 201. Hauck/Kasch, *TDNT* 6, 319ff., miss the problem, as the article only refers to the critical voices of a few Cynic-Stoic philosophers against riches.

291. F. Heichelheim, *Die auswärtige Bevölkerung im Ptolemäerreich*, Klio Bh 18, 1925, 36ff.; immigration was particularly strong from Athens and its surroundings and the Aegean islands: 47ff., 55ff.: see also E. R. Bevan, *A History of Egypt*, 1927, 83ff.: W. Schubart, BhAO 10, 1927, 10–21; W. Peremans, *Vreemdelingen*, 1943, 21ff.: the political position of the Greeks; 74f.: the relationship between Greeks and Egyptians in the administration; 86ff., 171f.: social status; 135ff.: the distribution of professions; Rostovtzeff, *HW* 1, 323f., 407ff.; 2, 1077–95; 3, 1394f. n. 121, lit. A. Świderek, *JJurPap* 9/10, 1955/56, 365–400, gives a detailed description of the private economic activity of the Greeks in the Zeno papyri.

292. See Schürer 3, 70f.

293. Rostovtzeff, *HW* 1, 421f.; cf. 2, 1076.

294. Op. cit., 2, 1181, 1183f., 1193f. The Georgics of Bolus of Mendes were probably the best known; op. cit., 2, 1183 and 3, 1616 n. 136 (see also below, n. III, 848); cf. F. Susemihl, *Geschichte der griechischen Literatur in der Alexandrinerzeit* I, 1891f., 829ff.; F. Heichelheim, *Wirtschaftsgeschichte des Altertums* 2, 1938, 1108ff. n. 49 lit.: Varro, *De re rust.* I, 1, 8 enumerates fifty Greek writers occupied with Georgics, etc. The Hellenistic period brought a climax of ancient empirical 'sciences', see O. Neugebauer, *The Exact Sciences in Antiquity*, ²1957, 1ff.

295. Title of ch. 3 in J. Kaerst, *Geschichte des Hellenismus* 2, ²1926, 146–67: the decisive turning point was brought with 'the organizational idea of the division of work' (157), which, however, antiquity was not able to combine with independence and freedom of initiative (167).

296. PCZ 59329 ll. 15ff.; PSI 421, 514, cf. 602, 637, 667; see also C. C. Edgar, Introduction to PMichZen, 26ff., 43ff. Zeno, for example, not only worked for Apollonius but at the same time increased his own property as owner of a vineyard and of baths, as a tax farmer and moneylender. Cf. C. Préaux, *Les Grecs en Égypte d'après les archives de Zenon*, 1947, 59ff., 65ff., 81ff.; also A. Świderek,

op. cit., 370ff., and W. Peremans, 'Ptolemée II Philadelphe et les Indigènes égyptiens', *RBPH* 12, 1933, 1005–22: J. Bingen, *Proceedings of the 12th International Congress of Papyrologists*, 1970, 35ff.

297. M. Rostovtzeff, *A Large Estate*, 1922, 85, see also 72ff., 77ff., etc.

298. C. Préaux, op. cit., 83. On the attitude of the king and his officers towards the *laoi* see Rostovtzeff, *HW* 1, 1098ff., and W. L. Westermann, *AHR* 43, 1936, 281ff.; for '*philanthrōpia*' see W. Schubart, *APF* 11, 1935, 9ff.; cf. also the model for the king, Ps.Aristeas 208, 265, 290, and in addition, H. Bolkestein, *Wohltätigkeit und Armenpflege im vorchristlichen Altertum*, 1939, 391f., who sees a typical instance of this *philanthrōpia* in the 'care' of the Ptolemies for their subjects.

299. PColZen 2, 16ff., no.66, 18, 21.

300. U. Wilcken, *APF* 14, 1941, 154f., following UPZ 1, 7, 13; 8, 14; 15, 17f.

301. On this see P. Jouguet, 'Les Lagides et les Indigenes', *RBPH* 2, 1923, 419–45, and *L'histoire politique et la papyrologie*, 1934, 93ff.; C. Préaux, *ChrEg* 11, 1936, 522–52, and F. Uebel, *APF* 17, 1960, 147–62 on a papyrus fragment which reports on a ταραχὴ Αἰγυπτίων in the Thebais between about 175 and 145 BC.

302. On these two possibilities see Tcherikover, *CPJ* 1, 43f. Cf. also the assertions of Josephus about the '*isopoliteia*' of the Alexandrian Jews: *c.Ap.*2, 35; *Antt.*12, 8. On Antioch and Asia Minor see above, n.90.

303. PSI 324, 325.

304. P. Lond 1948 (inv.2661) of 6 Xanthikos (8.5) 257 BC. The letter was written four days before the letter of Tobias and two years after the journey of Zeno. The correspondence between Alexandria and Palestine seems to be lively.

305. PSI 594, col.3, 17; cf. also 554; PCZ 59004, col.1, 4; 59011 col.1, 8; cf. Tcherikover, *Mizraim*, 45–8, and *HC*, 67 and 431 n.73. On the site see A. Alt, *PJB* 22, 1926, 55–9, and F. M. Abel, *Géographie* 2, 265. The *stratēgos* Ptolemy son of Traseas had a domain from a royal gift at Scythopolis. It included a number of villages, see Y. H. Landau, *IEJ* 16, 1966, 58ff., 66ff., and M. Hengel, *ZNW* 59, 1968, 20f.

306. For the length of the stay see Tcherikover, *Mizraim*, 11–13, and the introduction to PLond 1930, about to be published; for the route of the journey and geographical detail see also 57ff., 84 n.80, 87 n.97 and *HC*, 430 n.70. The lists of rations are important: PCZ 59004, col.1, cf. *CPJ* 1, 121f., no.2a; PCZ 59005 = *CPJ* 1, 122, no.2b; PLond 1930 (inv.2358 A) in part in *CPJ* 1, 123f. no.2d. For the 'Birta' of Tobias see PCZ 59003 (SB 6709) = *CPJ* 1, 118ff., no.1. For the identification of individual places see F. M. Abel, *RB* 32, 1923, 409ff.; 33, 1924, 566ff.; 36, 1927, 145ff., 474ff.; A. Alt (in the report on documents, see U. Wilcken, *APF* 7, 1924, 293) and J. Herz, *PJB* 24, 1928, 107f. n.4, have a critical discussion of the hypotheses of Abel. For a reference see PSI 322. For the whole see Table I, pp.206f. below. Cf. S. Mittmann, in: *Archäologie und Altes Testament* (Festschrift K. Galling), 1970, 199–210.

307. PCZ 59012. Report on the duty on wares in Pelusium; according to the unpublished PLond inv.2358b Zeno sent presents from Ptolemais to Pelusium, see Tcherikover, *HC*, 432 n.80.

308. PCZ 59016; 59006, 59015; 59537; PSI 322.

309. PCZ 59008 col.3; 59016.

310. PLond 1931 (inv.2326) of 25 Audenaios (= 10.2), 258 BC.

311. CPJ I, 122, no.2b = PCZ 59005 cf. also 2a = PCZ 59004.

312. For what follows see Tcherikover, *Mizraim*, 57–67; Apelles: PCZ 59006, 26, and 59004, 27, on this U. Wilcken, *APF* 8, 1927, 276; Callicrates: PCZ 59006, 22, 39: two Greeks from his entourage, on this see U. Wilcken, loc. cit., and W. Otto, AAM 11, 1934, 25 n. 3; cf. OGIS 1, 26 and PZenMich 147f. no. 100. Dionysodorus: 59006, 38, 65; 59093, 8; PCorn 1, 7, 40, 59 etc.; PCZ 59263. Ariston: PCZ 59006, 46; 59052, 9 PLond inv.2358b and the introduction by Edgar to PCZ 59029.

313. Rostovtzeff, *A Large Estate*, 1922, 26f., assumes a predominantly private commission, cf. also *CAH* 7, 120, 135; on the other hand, Tcherikover, *HC*, 63, rightly stresses the official character of this journey, even though some private business was also undertaken on it.

314. Hauran: see above, n.309; aromatic trade, n.309 above; for the caravan trade see PColZen 1, 3–10, no.2; a caravan of Apollonius moved to and fro between Gaza and Sidon and Sidon and Galilee. If PCZ 59015 were better preserved, it would give us a closer look into Apollonius' involvement in the aromatic trade.

315. See Vol.I, pp.8, 14f., 34. The report of Polybius 5, 71, 1–10 shows that 'Philadelphia Rabbath Ammon' was built into a strong fortress especially against the Arabs. Cf. also M. Rostovtzeff, *Caravan Cities*, 1932, 58–62.

316. The letters of Tobias: PCZ 59075/6 = CPJ 1, 125–9, nos.4 and 5. For the later activity of agents from Palestine and Phoenicia see PCZ 59057, 59077, 59093, 59292; 59537, 59804; PSI 406, 444, 494, 495, 594, 616, 628; PCorn 1, 224f.; see also Tcherikover, *Mizraim*, 15, 67.

317. For trade between Palestine and Egypt in general see Rostovtzeff, *HW* 1, 346, 384f.; 3, 1413f. n.184 lit; especially on the slave trade see Tcherikover, *Mizraim*, 16ff., and *HC*, 68f.; for the limitation of slavery in Egypt, Rostovtzeff, *HW* 1, 321f.; 3, 1393f., n. 119; for slavery in Ptolemaic Egypt in general see also W. L. Westermann, *The Slave Systems of Greek and Roman Antiquity*, 1955, 28, 30f.

318. PCZ 59015 (see Vol.I, pp.21f.) and perhaps 59804; PCZ 59076a and b = CPJ 1, 125f., no.4. Cf. also PCZ 59003 = CPJ 1, 118f., no.1.

319. PCZ 59292, and on this in detail Tcherikover, *Mizraim*, 68ff.

320. PSI 406, and on this op. cit., 17f. and 74 n.10; cf. also Herondas 2, 16: the export of prostitutes from Tyre to Cos. For the situation of Pēgai see Josephus, *Antt.*13, 261; A. Alt, *ZDPV* 45, 1922, 220–3, and Tcherikover, *HC*, 433 n.85.

321. PCZ 59015, 59537: the slaves have escaped as they were badly treated by the addressee (Zeno?) in Marisa (l.4); 59804 (= PColZen no.3 and PSI 602); cf. also Sir.33 (G 30). 40.

322. Harsh treatment: Sir.23.10; 33 (G 30). 33f.; 42.5. Positive: 4.30 (G); 7.20f.; 10.25; 33 (G 30). 39ff. For the Greek attitude see J. Vogt, *Sklaverei und Humanität*, 1965, 37ff., 68ff., 83ff.

323. For the slaves from Palestine or 'Syria' see PCZ 59011, 22; 59077; PSI 648; PColZen 2, 92ff. no.87; PCorn 1, 223ff.; it is hard to say whether the Syrians in the great list PCZ 59292, 52, 464, 472, PCol Zen 2.109ff. no.93, and

PZenMich 49 are slaves or paid workers. The slave girl Sphragis bought by Zeno in the Ammanitis was perhaps occupied in the Fayum as a wool spinner according to PCZ 59145, see CPJ 1, 121, l. 5. For the Jewish slave girl see PCorn 1, 160ff. = CPJ 1, 132f. no. 7; and PCorn 1, 198 (see Introduction p. 1). Cf. Ps.Aristeas 12–14, 23; of course the number 100,000 is exaggerated, see W. L. Westermann, op. cit., 28.

324. PCZ 59241, 59292, 611, 59367, 59710, 41, 66; PSI 393 and Vol. 6, p. xiii = CPJ 1, 134–45, nos. 9–14. For the Syrian villages see PCZ 59404, 59497, and Tcherikover, CPJ 1, 4 nn. 12 and 14. Σύρος was a favourite name for a slave, Liddell/Scott, 1732.

325. See above, n. 146.

326. M. Mitsos, *Archaiologike Ephemeris 1952*, ed. 1955, 194–6, and D. M. Lewis, *JSS* 2, 1957, 264–6. On this F. Bömer, *Untersuchungen über die Religion der Sklaven* II, AAMz 1960, 24ff. In 136–132 BC the Syrian slave Eunus, inspired by the Syrian goddess, led his fellow slaves in revolt, see J. Vogt, *Sklavenkriege*, AAMz 1957, 27ff.

327. Because of its prose form Joel 4.4–8 is often regarded as a later insertion, see A. Weiser, *Das Buch der 12 kleinen Propheten* I, ATD 24, 1949, 107, and Robinson-Horst, *Die 12 kleinen Propheten*, ³1964, 67. It is less probable that it should be put before Alexander at about 520 BC, as is attempted by J. M. Myers (*ZAW* 74, 1962, 190, 195). For the inscription of Ma'in see Altheim/Stiehl, *Araber* I, 75.

328. CIJ 1, 512ff., no. 710 and 709; cf. 711: a Jewish freeing, 119 BC.

329. R. Helm, *PW* 16, 888; M. Hadas, *HCu*, 110f.; see Vol. I, pp. 83f.

330. PSI 324, 325; cf. Tcherikover, *Mizraim*, 20f., and *HC*, 69f., 434 n. 88, lit.; see also OGIS 56.17: Under Euergetes grain was imported from 'Syria and Phoenicia' and Cyprus during a famine. For Syrian wheat see A. Thompson, *APF* 9, 1930, 207–13 (PCZ 59155). It remains uncertain whether the large quantity of wheat and barley which Zeno is said to have delivered according to PLond 1931 (inv. 2326) shortly before his return to Ptolemais was grain imported from Egypt or from the Palestinian hinterland. Certainly there were also great granaries in Ptolemais, as being the most important Ptolemaic centre of administration.

331. PCZ 59/12; 59015 recto; 59077; on this see Tcherikover, *Mizraim*, 22, and C. Préaux, *Économie*, 85ff. The Revenue Laws (col. 52.25ff. = Mitteis/Wilcken, *Grundz*. I, 2, 256f.) already distinguish between 'Syrian' and foreign oil.

332. PSI 594 cf. 554; Tcherikover, *Mizraim*, 23.

333. PCZ 59012, 59013, 59014; PSI 594; PColZen 1,3ff., no. 2; Tcherikover, *Mizraim*, 23f., cf. also the still unpublished PLond inv. 2358B with a list of 'gifts' of Zeno's which he left behind in Ptolemais; it contains an abundance of food from Chian wine to Syrian honey.

334. Rostovtzeff, *HW* 1, 366ff., 263f.; Tarn/Griffith, *Hellenistic Civilization*, 252, 257; K. Galling, *BRL*, 199, 360, see also R. Giveon, *IEJ* 13, 1963, 20–9, and E. Leider, *Der Handel von Alexandria*, 14ff., 49ff. For local production of glass, etc., see Tell Anafa: S. S. Weinberg (n. 74 above), 99ff.

335. PCZ 59012; see on this Tcherikover, *Mizraim*, 24f. Apollonius supported his own merchant fleet for transport on the Nile and to Palestine; a captain Heraclides travelled there in his service: PCZ 59012; 59013; 59804; cf. also

59002 and PSI 322 and 594: the small boats easily got up the Nile as far as Memphis; see Tcherikover, HC, 432 n. 79.

336. PSI 616.

337. For the role of Rhodes in the third century in trading with the Ptolemaic empire see Rostovtzeff *HW* 1, 225ff., and 3, 1370ff.; among other things gifts of Sidonian notables were sent to the *dioikētēs* in Alexandria through their agents from Rhodes, see PRyl 554 = C. C. Edgar, *BJRL* 18, 1934, 111f. n. 1 and PMichZen 3. For merchants from Ashkelon in Rhodes, Delos, Athens, etc., from the third century BC, see Schürer 2, 124f. The earliest report of a Jewish diaspora is contained in the writing of the Roman senate of 139 BC which lists a series of cities and islands in the Aegean alongside Rhodes and Delos: I Macc. 15.16–24; the number of Jews in this area must therefore have been relatively large. For Delos see Rostovtzeff, *HW* 1, 230ff., and P. Roussel, *Délos Colonie Athénienne*, 1916, 86ff.: lists of ephebes with mentions of their homes in Ashkelon, Tyre, Sidon, Damascus. In the second century BC there appear Gerrhaeans, Minaeans and Nabateans. See also the sanctuaries of the gods of Ashkelon and Jamnia in A. Plassart, *Exploration archéologique de Délos*, vol. 11, 1928, 278ff., 285ff. For the Jews see P. Roussel, op. cit., 94f., the discovery of the earliest known Jewish synagogue (first century BC), and on this M. Hengel, *ZNW* 57, 1966, 151 n. 53, and the Jewish prayers for vengeance from the neighbouring island of Rheneia, see A. Deissmann, *Light from the Ancient East*, 1927, 413–24, c. 100 BC. In general on the Jews in the Aegean see Schürer 3, 56f., and Juster 1, 188f. From the island of Cos we have the dedicatory inscription of an Abdaeus from Gerasa to Helios about 200 BC and a Nabatean-Greek bilingual inscription of 68 BC. There was also a Jewish community here, according to I Macc. 15.23: see O. Eissfeldt, *Kleine Schriften* 2, 1963, 309–12.

338. M. Smith, in *Fischer Weltgeschichte* 6, 1965, ed. P. Grimal, 255.

339. J. P. Peters and H. Thiersch, *Painted Tombs in the Necropolis of Marisa*, 1905, 9ff.: the epitaph, op. cit., 12, 36, 38 = OGIS 593 and Schürer 2, 4f. n. 8, is important: Ἀπολλοφάνης Σεσμαίου, ἄρξας τῶν ἐν Μαρίσῃ Σιδωνίων ἔτη τριάκοντα καὶ τρία καὶ νομισθεὶς | πάντων τῶν καθ' αὑτὸν χρηστότατος καὶ φιλοκειότατος, ἀπέθανεν δὲ βιώσας ἔτη ἑβδομήκοντα καὶ τέσσαρα ἐν . . . Apollophanes was 'archōn' of the *politeuma* of Sidon. A Philothion terms herself 'Sidonia' (Peters/Thiersch, 66) and so does an Eikonion (F. M. Abel, *RB* 34, 1925, 275). For the names see Vol. I, 61f. The feudal way of life is shown, among other things, by the hunting scene depicted by Rostovtzeff, *HW* 1, pl. lviii (Peters/Thiersch, pl. vi). The '*hipparch*' Ananus (?) on a leopard hunt could be a Jewish (?) officer of the garrison; for the name see the index to Josephus, ed. B. Niese, 1955, 7, 9; for the picture see n. II, 235.

340. Tcherikover, *HC*, 100. For the cult of Melkart Heracles and Asteria see Clermont-Ganneau, *RAO* 7, 1906, 147–55, and F. M. Abel, *RB* NS 5, 1908, 568–77. See also above, pp. 14, 41.

341. On this see Table 2, pp. 208f. below. It is based on the following publications: 1. G. A. Reisner–C. S. Fisher, *Harvard Excavations at Samaria, 1908–1910* 1, 1924, 252ff.; J. W. Crowfoot, etc., *Samaria-Sebaste. Reports, 1931–33*, 1953, 3, 45ff.; 3. O. Sellers, *The Citadel of Beth Zur*, 1933, 70f., and R. W. Funk, *BASOR* 150, 1958, 8–20; 4. G. M. Fitzgerald, *Beth-Shean Excavations 1921–1923*, 1931,

51ff. (for the most part from a find of coins); 5. O. R. Sellers, *BA* 25, 1962, 87–96 (partly from treasure, partly *in situ*); 6. O. Tufnell, *Lachish* III, 1953, 412ff.; the coins here show clearly that the place flourished in the Persian period and lost significance in Hellenistic times; 7. C. C. McCown, etc., *Tell en Nasbeh* I, 1947, 174, 275; 8. B. Mazar et al., '*Ein-Gedi*, 1963, 81f.; 9. Y. Aharoni, *Excavations at Ramath Raḥel, Seasons 1959 and 1960*, 1962, 93f., and *Seasons 1961 and 1962*, 1964, 107–15; 10. L. A. Sinclair ,*AASOR* 34/35 (1954/56), 1960, 36. The collection is by no means complete, especially as important earlier excavations like R. A. S. Macalister, *Gezer* I, 1912, 267, and Bliss/Macalister, *Excavations in Palestine*, 1902, 68 (Marisa), provide no usable survey of coins. For the problem see already Sellers/Albright, *BASOR* 43, 1931, 10. There is still no overall survey of Balāṭah Shechem.

342. Jars from Rhodes were found in the coastal plain in almost every early Hellenistic excavation: see J. H. Iliffe, *QDAP* 2, 1933, 155, earlier literature; C. A. Johns, *QDAP* 3, 1934, 151: 'Aṭliṭ; *IEJ* 9, 1959, 274: Ptolemais Acco; *RB* 70, 1963, 584; Strato's Tower; *RB* 69, 1962, 406f.: Tirat Yehuda: *RB* 67, 1960, 397: Tell Mor; M. Dothan, *IEJ* 14, 1964, 88: Ashdod; *QDAP* 9, 1942, 131ff.: Petra; O. R. Sellers, op. cit., 41ff., 52: Beth Zur; Bliss-Macalister, op. cit., 131f.: Marisa; R. A. S. Macalister, op. cit., 2, 251ff., and *QDAP* 4, 1934/35, 200: Gezer; Macalister-Duncan, *PEFA* 4, 1926, 191ff., 203; Jerusalem-Ophel *c*. 3–400 jars, probably from the garrison of the Acra, see also Crowfoot-Fitzgerald, *PEFA* 5, 1927, 86ff.: Tyropoeon valley, Jerusalem; Toombs-Wright, op. cit., 45: Shechem; Reisner-Fischer, op. cit., 1, 310ff.; J. W. Crowfoot, *Samaria-Sebaste* 3, 380; *RB* 63, 1956, 79 = *ADAJ* 3, 1956, 79ff.: Tell Dothan; G. M. Fitzgerald, op. cit., 44ff.: Scythopolis; B. Maisler, etc., *IEJ* 2, 1952, 166, 22f.: Philotheria; *IEJ* 5, 1955, 211: Beth Shearim. For Transjordania see E. Olavarri, *RB* 71, 1965, 93: Aroer. This enumeration necessarily remains incomplete. For trade from Rhodes, especially with wine and oil, see Rostovtzeff, *HW* 1, 225ff.; 2, 676ff.; 3, 1485 n.93, 1486 n.97, 1488 n.109.

343. Dan.1.8; cf. S. Lieberman, *Hellenism*, 150, and E. Bickerman(n), *RIDA* 5, 1958, 140.

344. The fact that the post-biblical Talmudic tradition mentions a great many more herbs than the Old Testament, see G. Dalman, *Arbeit und Sitte in Palästina* 2, 1932, 264–302, cf. also Schürer 2, 78f., and K. Galling, *BRL*, 84, may at least be because new plants were introduced into Palestine in the Hellenistic period; see also the examples cited by Rostovtzeff, *HW* 2, 1163–8, and F. Heichelheim in T. Frank, *An Economic Survey of the Roman Empire*, 4, 130ff.

345. Theophrastus, *Hist. plant.*, 9, 6, 1; cf. 2, 6, 8; 9, 7, 1: by the lake of about 300 stadia, in which the reed grows from which aromatics are gained; this is perhaps Lake Gennesaret, though the size is much nearer that of the Dead Sea, cf. Strabo 16, 12, 16 (755).

346. Diodore 2, 48, 9 = 19, 98; Strabo 16, 2, 41 (763): the term 'paradise' and the 'great profit' also appears here; Pompeius Trogus in Justin, *Epit.*36, 3 (Reinach 225); Jos., *Antt.*4, 100; 14, 54; *Bell.*1, 138; 4, 469. For Jericho see also Schürer 1, 380–2 n.37. For Engedi see Josephus, *Antt.*9, 7, cf. Pliny, *Hist. Nat.*5, 73; *Shab.*26a on Jer.52.16 and B. Mazar et al., '*Atiqot* 5, 1966, 8f.

347. Justin, op. cit.,: *Opes genti ex vectigalibus opobalsami crevere*; cf. Horace, *Epp.*2, 184 (Reinach 247). In the Talmudic tradition אפובלסמין is a loanword which is often used, see S. Krauss, *Talmudische Archäologie* 1, 1910, 234ff., and *Griechische und Lateinische Lehnwörter* 2, 1898f., 99; I. Löw, *Die Flora der Juden* I, 1, 1926, 299–304.

348. Strabo 17, 1, 15 (800).

349. Josephus, *Bell.*1, 361; *Antt.*15, 96; cf. Plutarch, *Antonius* 36 (Reinach 148).

350. Zoar: I. Löw, op. cit., I, 1, 301; Scythopolis: Aristides, *Or.*48 = 2,470 Dindorf = 36 cuneiform, p. 82; Lake Gennesaret: Strabo 16, 2, 16 (755), cf. also S. Krauss, *Archäologie* I, 688 n.254; Ber.43a (Bar.); Egypt: Dioscorides, *Mat. med.*1, 18 (Reinach 134f.), Dioscorides goes back to the same source as Pliny, i.e. Theophrastus; Arabia: Diodore, 3, 46, 2; Strabo 16, 419 (778); Pausanias 9, 28, 3, *et al.*

351. Pliny, *Historia naturalis* 12, 111–23.

352. At the time of Alexander balsam was already weighed out at twice its weight in silver and often faked: Theophrastus 9, 6, 4 = Pliny 12, 117.

353. According to K. Reinhardt, 'Poseidonios über Ursprung und Entartung', *Orient und Antike* 6, 1928, 60–75, the description of the Dead Sea in Strabo goes back to Posidonius, but the account of the balsam plantations to an unknown source.

354. B. Mazar, '*Ein Gedi, Archaeological Excavations 1961/62*, 1963, 6ff.,11ff., 62ff. ET in '*Atiqot* 5, 1966, 39–44, 51f., stratum III and the coins. Cf. also the third season, B. Mazar and I. Dunayewsky, *IEJ* 14, 1964, 123ff.

355. The restrictions on the plantations probably come from the time of Jewish rule, to keep the price high; balsam also acquired religious significance, see *Antt.*14, 54: the juice issues out at dawn in the direction of Jerusalem; the use of a stone knife to cut the bark (see Pliny 12, 115 and Tacitus, *Hist.*5, 6, against the earlier report of Theophrastus) is also probably to be understood in religious terms. *Taan.*27a (Bar.) mentions that twelve of the twenty-four priestly watches lived in Jericho; this probably means a settlement on Hasmonean royal land. *Shab.*26a and *Ber.*43a both indicate royal supervision over the processing. In addition there was also balsam 'from the house of the Rabbi', i.e. perhaps from a domain of the patriarch in Galilee, which might go back to a royal gift; cf. also Solin 35, 5 (Reinach 339): the Romans again extended the plantations considerably and also used the hillsides as a result of artificial irrigation at Engedi. This could already go back to Ptolemaic times.

356. Diodore 2, 48, 6–8 = 19, 98–100, 3; in 100,1 Hieronymus is explicitly mentioned as commander of the unsuccessful undertaking and a later historian. Further reports on the Dead Sea are to be found in Aristotle, *Meteorol.*2, 3, 39 (Reinach 6f.); Strabo 16, 2, 42 (763f.), following Posidonius: Pomp. Trogus in Justin, *Epit.*36.3 (Reinach 256); Pliny, *Hist.nat.* 12, 72f., etc., see Reinach, index 366; Asphaltide. For the economic significance of the acquisition of asphalt for the Ptolemies see R. J. Forbes, *Studies in Ancient Technology* 1, 1955, 27–30, 98ff.; P. C. Hammond, *BA* 22, 1959, 40–8. The Essenes of Qumran also seem to have procured asphalt at a later date: see R. de Vaux, *L'Archéologie et les manuscrits*, 1961, 68f.

357. A. Schlatter, *GI*[3], 23, 393 n.31; Theophrastus, *Hist. plant*, 4, 8, 4; Josephus, *Bell*. I, 130 = *Antt*. 14, 33: a place 'Papyrus' near Jericho.

358. A. Kaplan, *RB* 62, 1933, 90f., 98.

359. *RB* 69, 1962, 406f.; see above, n. 142.

360. M. Dothan, *RB* 67, 1960, 397, and *BIES* 24, 1960, 120ff.; Dor: Claudius Iolaus, FGrHist 788 F. 2; Gezer: see Macalister, *Gezer* I, 223f., and the interpretation by Watzinger, *DP* I, 101, and K. Galling, *BRL*, 154.

361. P. W. Lapp, *BA* 28, 1965, 8, and O. R. Sellers, op. cit., 16ff.; cf. *RB* 72, 1963, 399.

362. Sheep-rearing and weaving also had an upsurge in Egypt in the Ptolemean period. For example, there was a special Syrian woollen cloth ($\sigma\nu\rho\iota\alpha\iota$) which was used in the army. The wool industry in Palestine was important, because originally Egypt produced almost nothing but linen, see Rostovtzeff, *HW* I, 308, and 3, 1390 n. 108; cf. also V. Edgar, PMichZen 37 and 74 no. 13; PColZen I, 55ff., 61ff., nos. 15 and 17; PSI 854 and PCZ 39484; also C. Préaux, *Économie*, 106ff.

363. For Engedi see B. Mazar, *'Ein-Gedi*, 12ff., see above, n. 354. For Damascus see Strabo 16, 2, 16 (755), on which see H. Bietenhard, *ZDPV* 79, 1963, 47f., who suggests Gerasa. For Jericho see Diodore 2, 48, 4 (Reinach 72).

364. L. V. Rachmani, *RB* 67, 1960, 403 and Z. Ron, *IEJ* 16, 1966, 33–49, 111–22; for the date, 113.

365. See 1 QH 8.21–26 and R. de Vaux, *RB* 66, 1959, 230–7 and *L'Archéologie*, 61ff., 67ff.; a refined irrigation system of great technological skill has been found there; it partially served industrial ends, dyeing or the cultivation of fish; for the possibility of gardening see *RB* 66, 1959, 254, and *L'Archéologie*, 48, 59, 67ff., above all with dates; cf. Pliny, *Hist. nat.* 5, 73, and 13, 44 and Reinach 372, index: Palmiers. Even here a coin of Ptolemy II was found, *RB* 66, 1959, 248f.; for Galilee, Jericho and the Hauran see K. Galling, *BRL* 4, 84, 535f., and S. Krauss, *Talmudische Archäologie* 2, 1911, 164ff.; the Talmudic tradition speaks of artificial irrigation as an obvious arrangement; cf. G. Dalman, *Arbeit und Sitte in Palästina* 2, 1932, 230ff., and R. J. Forbes, *Studies in Ancient Technology* 2, 1955, 9, 37.

366. F. M. Abel, *Géographie de la Palestine* II, 476f., 373: presumably identical with *migdal nūnayyā* (fish-tower) = Magdala.

367. M. Avi-Yonah, *Geschichte der Juden im Zeitalter der Talmud*, 1962, 20ff.

368. O. R. Sellers, op. cit., 18–20; R. de Vaux, *L'Archéologie*, 12f., 22, 63ff., 68, 98; cf. W. R. Farmer, *TZ* 11, 1955, 295–308; 12, 1956, 56–8.

369. K. Galling, BRL, 403: first of all probably the beam press and in the later Hellenistic period the screw press, following on the invention of the screw (Archytas of Tarentum, 394 BC); cf. Rostovtzeff, *HW* I, 364ff.; 2, 1190, and R. J. Forbes, op. cit., 2, 38 and 133ff.

370. K. Galling, *BRL*, 387 (Matt. 18.6); cf. R. J. Forbes, op. cit., 2, 144; it was already known in Greece about 300 BC.

371. Dalman, op. cit., 2, 230; S. Krauss, op. cit., 2, 166; R. J. Forbes, op. cit., 2, 37ff.

372. K. Galling, *BRL*, 428; cf. Rostovtzeff, I, 364.

373. For the Hippodamian city plan see K. Galling, *BRL*, 499; H. Bengtson,

*GG*², 444 (lit.). For Palestine see Watzinger, *DP* 2, 11f.: Marisa; 26: Samaria. Moreover, we also find it in Damascus (see J. Sauvaget, *Syria* 26, 1949, 339ff., 355ff.) and perhaps in Philotheria, see B. Maisler, etc., *IEJ* 2, 1952, 166ff. For wall technique and house building see K. Galling, *BRL*, 373f. and 271f., and Watzinger, *DP* 2, 25ff.; cf. J. Kaplan, *RB* 70, 1963, 578: Joppa; also G. E. Wright, *BASOR* 148, 1957, 24: Shechem; B. Maisler, loc. cit.: Philotheria (cf. *RB* 62, 1955, 87). For the whole see Rostovtzeff, *HW* 2, 1051; 3, 1587 nn. 19, 20 lit. For loan words see Vol. I, pp. 60f.

374. For Egypt see R. J. Forbes, op. cit., 2,27; for the growth of the population in Egypt see Rostovtzeff, *HW* 2, 1136ff.

375. J. P. W. Lapp, *Palestinian Ceramic Chronology*, 1961, 230.

376. Josephus, *Antt.* 12, 160, 164; see also Vol. I, pp. 267f.

377. CPJ 1, 122ff., no. 2b (= PCZ 59005); 2c (= PCZ 59802, 2,18): 2d (= PLond 1930, ll. 49, 175). In this long list an ostler of Tobias appears as a member of the company six weeks before the visit to the Ammanitis. Thus Tobias supported the expedition from the beginning. A further Tobias is mentioned in the unpublished PLond inv. 2378 fr. 1 verso; even if this is an Egyptian list, as Tcherikover stresses in his publication of a fragment, CPJ 1, 146 no. 17, we cannot exclude the possibility that there is an allusion here to the Jewish sheikh, e.g. to slaves who come from him.

378 See above, n. 30.

379. PColZen 1,3ff., no. 2, col. 3,22, cf. p. 9 (= CPJ 1, 124 no. 2e); for the present see PCZ 59508.

380. CPJ 1, 127f., no. 3 (= PJand Giessen, inv. 413).

381. A. Kuschke, *ZAW* 57, 1939, 40ff., 44ff., 49f.; E. Bammel, *TDNT* 6, 888ff.; C. van Leeuwen, *Le développement du sens social en Israel avant l'ère chrétienne*, 1955, 117–52.

382. H. Bolkestein, *Wohltätigkeit und Armenpflege im vorchristlichen Altertum*, 1939, 129: 'It is never stressed or commended that one should accept the lot of the poor'; cf. 114f., 118, 241ff., 248ff. The Greeks therefore had no word for alms: 114, 213. For the role of slavery: 463f.; for conduct towards the poor in Israel: 38ff. and 401ff.; see also W. Schwer, *RAC* 1, 691ff., and Bolkenstein/Kalsbach, *RAC* 1, 698ff. For the oriental parallels, only some of which are adduced by Bolkestein, see E. Bammel, op. cit., 6, 891 nn. 48–50 and 892 n. 53.

383. Neh. 5.1–5; on this W. Rudolph, *Esra und Nehemia*, 1949, 129ff. ad loc.

384. Neh. 13.10–14; cf. 10.38a and the addition 38b–40, together with 12.44f. The charges of Nehemiah here are again directed against the 'supervisors' (סגנים), on which see M. Smith, *Fischer-Weltgeschichte* 5, ed. H. Bengtson, 1965, 363. The preference for Levites rather than priests continues in the work of the Chronicler, see W. Rudolph, *Chronikbücher*, 1955, xxii: the Levites become above all communicators of the right teaching: Neh. 8.12; II Chron. 17.7ff.; 30.22; 35.3 etc. K. Galling, *Die Bücher der Chronik, Esra, Nehemia*, ATD 12, 1954, 11, counts on the possibility that the editor of the work of the Chronicler, the 'second Chronicler', came from 'Levitical circles'; for his dating see 15ff.: the time of the edict, Antiochus III, c. 197 BC.

385. The legal claim of the Levites to the tithe goes back to P (Num. 18.21, 24ff.). O. Eissfeldt, *Erstlinge und Zehnten im AT*, BWAT 22, 1917, 115ff., 131

conjectures that the transfer to the priests was made as early as the time of Sirach (Sir. 7.31; 35 (G 32). 10f.; 45.20f.); the objections of B. Schaller, *ZNW* 54, 1963, 23 n.48a, do not refute this assumption. Judith 11.13 and Jub.32.15, which both probably reflect an established custom, regard delivery to the priests as a matter of course. The archaizing Tobit 1.6–8 cannot be adduced as a counter-proof, especially as here there is a tendency to increase the tithe, see Eissfeldt, op. cit., 119ff., 123. The strongly pro-Levite tendency of the Chronicler probably presupposes tensions between the priestly nobility and the Levites – these continued until the destruction of the second temple, see Josephus, *Antt.* 20.216ff. – and the question of the tithe will have been one of the main points at dispute. Perhaps the resolution of this question in favour of the priests goes back to the vigorous high priest Simon the Just. It is certainly no coincidence that Sirach often speaks of the priests (7.29, 31; 50.1, 12, 24) but never of the Levites.

386. For the relationship with Samaria see M. Smith, *Fischer Weltgeschichte* 5, ed. H. Bengtson, 1965, 367, 369ff. For the family of Sanballat see F. M. Cross Jr, *BA* 26, 1963, 120f., and K. Galling, *Studien*, 208f.; for the Tobiads see Vol. I, pp. 27f., 267f.

387. *Antt.* 12, 160, 222.

388. See above, nn. 256/7; for Sirach see below, n. III, 284.

389. Josephus, *c.Ap.* I, 187: . . . ἔτι δὲ καὶ λέγειν δυνατὸς καὶ τοῖς περὶ τῶν πραγμάτων, εἴπερ τις ἄλλος, ἔμπειρος see above, n. 166.

390. For the books of Chronicles see K. Galling, *Die Bücher der Chronik, Esra, Nehemia*, ATD 12, 1954, 8ff. (for the redactor, the 'second Chronicler', 10ff., 14–17) etc., above n. 384 and *RGG*³ 1, 1804f.; cf. also W. Rudolph, op. cit., viiif., xviiiff. To show the legitimacy of the sanctuary in Jerusalem over against the Samaritans and the Diaspora which was developing above all in Egypt, the author of the Chronistic work idealized the picture of Jewish history and stressed the temple cult as the manifestation of the saving presence of God. For the interest of the 'second Chronicler' in the Diaspora see K. Galling, op. cit., 16; cf. Ezra 7.25: Ezra's authority concerns all the Jews beyond the Euphrates.

391. O. Plöger, *Theocracy and Eschatology*, 1968, 26ff., 42, 46ff.; see also Vol. I, pp. 175ff.: the Hasidim.

392. Diodore 40,3, fr. 13,9 (Reinach 19f.).

393. Pss. 9.13, 19; 10.2, 9, 17; 25.16ff.; 35.10; 37.14, 16; 40.15–18; 69.20–30; 86.1, 14 etc.; see E. Bammel, *TDNT* 6, 891f., and J. J. Stamm, *TR* 23, 1955, 55ff.

394. It is significant that the Aramaizing form ʿᵃnāwīm has a completely religious note, see E. Bammel, op. cit., 6, 892f.: 'The description of a movement of ʿᵃniyyīm or humble pious and humble, called ʿᵃnāwīm in Aramaic, has thus made its way primarily or secondarily into the Psalms.' In the late, perhaps Hasidic Ps. 149, the ʿᵃnāwīm and the kᵉhal-ḥᵃsīdīm have become completely identical (see Vol. I, pp. 175f.).

395. Prov. 1.13, 17, 19; 3.31; 4.17 (cf. 11.26, 28).

396. Isa. 24.2; 26.5f.; Zech. 10.3ff.; 11.4ff., 15ff.; 13.7ff.: against the high priests.

397. Koh. 5.9f.; cf. 6.7ff. The whole section 5.9–6.9 deals in effect with the use and uselessness of riches.

398. Koh. 4.1; cf. 3.16; 8.10; 9.16.

399. Koh. 5.7f., see below, n. III, 58. See the acutely ironic exegesis of this passage in *Mek.Ex.*17.14 (Lauterbach 2, 150).

400. Koh. 5.11f., 16 (18); 6.1ff., 6ff.; cf. 4.4; the 'competition': Sir. 11.10–19, cf. 13.24f.; 14.3f.; 21.8; 31 (G 34). 3ff., cf. Menander, fr. 624 (Kock), see also 621, 665, 539, 301, 281, and H. L. Ginsberg, *Studies in Koheleth*, 1950, 44.

401. F. Hauck–W. Kasch, *TDNT* 6, 323f.; Prov. 2.10; 3.16f.; 8.18; 10.15; 11.16; 13.8, 11; 14.20; 19.4; 22.4; Koh. 2.24f.; 3.12; 7.12; 9.7ff.; Sir. 10.30; 19.1ff.; 44.1–8, etc; see also below, n. III, 210.

402. Prov. 6.6–11; 10.4f.; 12.24, 27; 14.25; 20.13; 21.17; 23.21 etc.; Sir. 18.32f.; 25.2f.; 40.28–30; for the conceptions in Greece see H. Bolkestein, op. cit., 174ff., 282ff.

403. E. Bammel, *TDNT* 6, 893; Prov. 11.28; 18.10ff.; 28.6, 11; for post-biblical and especially Rabbinic Judaism see Bill. 1, 818ff., 822ff., 826ff.; H. Bolkestein, op. cit., 401ff.; F. Hauck–W. Kasch, op. cit., 323f.; E. Bammel, op. cit., 899ff.

404. Sir. 26.29–27.3; cf. 31 (G 34). 5f. and 11.10ff., 34 (see Vol. I, p. 152); on Antiochus III see *Antt.* 12, 145f., and below, n. IV, 90.

405. S. L. Ginzberg, *On Jewish Law and Lore*, 1955, 79ff., and M. Hengel, *Zeloten*, 205ff., 208.

406. Tcherikover, *IEJ* 14, 1964, 61–78; cf. also E. Bickerman(n), *JBL* 63, 1944, 356: legally Jerusalem was not a *polis*.

407. Timochares, see FGrHist 165 = Eusebius, *Pr.Ev.*9, 35 (Reinach 53), also R. Laqueuer, *PW*, 2R. 6, 1258; for Xenophon or the anonymous Samaritan see FGrHist 849 = Eusebius, *Pr.Ev.*9, 36 (Reinach 54), in both instances according to Alexander Polyhistor. The figure of over 50 stadia from Ps. Hecataeus, according to *c.Ap.*1, 197, is a complete exaggeration, whereas Josephus, *Bell.*5, 159, speaks of a total extent, including the wall of Agrippa I encompassing the suburbs, of 33 stadia. The main growth of the city would thus come in the Hellenistic period; see also F. M. Abel, *HP* 1, 96f., and B. Niese, *GGMS* 3, 222, 224.

408. Cf. also II Kings 11.18–20; 14.21; Zech. 12.7; 14.14; for the time before the Maccabean revolt see Vol. I, pp. 282f.; for the time between Herod and AD 70 see M. Hengel, op. cit., 335, 371 n. 1.

409. M. Weber, *Gesammelte Aufsätze zur Religionssoziologie* 2, 1921, 400.

410. From the latest part of the collection (1.1–9.18), see Prov. 2.16ff.; 5; 6.24ff.; 7; cf. also 9.13ff.: folly as a seductress, and 22.14; 23.27, also the fragment from 4 Q ed. J. M. Allegro, *PEQ* 96, 1964, 53–5. According to G. Boström, *Proverbiastudien*, 1935, 42–52; 103–55, the strange woman is to be referred to the wives of foreign merchants settled in Judea: the temptation of adultery was accompanied by that of idolatry. Cf. Vol. I, pp. 155f.

411. Prov. 5.3ff.; 7.10ff.; cf. also the older sayings 20.1ff.; 21.17; 23.29–35; 31.4f.; Koh. 2.10, 24f.; this probably presupposes people who seek enjoyment of life without God, cf. also 3.13; 5.17ff.; 6.7ff.; 8.15ff.; 9.7ff.; 10.16, 19; 11.9f.; Sir. 31 (G 34). 25–33 (G 35). 13 presumably presupposes the customs of Greek feasts, see A. Schlatter, *GI*[3], 21, and 392 n. 28; see also Sir. 9.9ff.; 19.2; 23.16ff.; 26.8; 32 (G 35). 4–8.

412. *Antt.* 12, 186ff., 209ff., 231; see Vol. I, pp. 269f.

413. See G. Boström, op. cit., 53–102, esp. 64ff., 78ff.; cf. Prov. 24.30–34; 27.23–27; Sir. 7.15; 20.28; Koh. 2.4f.; 5.8; Test. Iss. 3–6 and above, n. 253.

414. Rostovtzeff, *HW* 2, 1125f.; for the Graeculi of Rome see Cicero, *Orat.* 1, 22; *Tusc.* 1, 35, 86, and J. Jüthner, *Hellenen und Barbaren*, 1923, 63, 137 n. 15.

415. Athen. 12, 527e/f (FGrHist 87 F 10) par. 5, 210 e/f; see also the extravagance of the 'royal camps' in Syria: 15, 692c. Luxury was much greater in Egypt and Syria, as in the Magna Graecia of southern Italy and Sicily, than in the sparse motherland; cf. Plato, *Epist.* 326b and *Republic* 404d = Athen. 12, 527 c/d; see also S. K. Eddy, *The King is Dead*, 1961, 209. There is a Jewish confirmation in Ps. Aristeas 108ff.

II

Hellenism in Palestine as a Cultural Force
and its Influence on the Jews

1. For the origin and distribution of the *koinē* see A. Deissmann, *RE* 7, 630ff.; L. Rademacher, SAW 224, 5, 1947, 6ff., 14ff.; cf. also H. Bengtson, *GG*[3], 352, 447, 444 (literature) and F. Altheim, *Die Weltgeltung der griechischen Sprache*, NBGAW 1, 1964, 315–32. Cf. J. N. Sevenster, *Do you know Greek?*, 1968.

2. Reference may be made, as just one example, to the Greek treaties found in Kurdistan, a long way from any considerable Greek settlement, dating from the first century BC: E. Minns, *JHS* 35, 1915, 22–65, cf. also the release of slaves with a dedication to Serapis from Gorgan on the north-eastern corner of the Caspian Sea, 281–61 BC, see L. Robert, *Hellenica* 11/12, 1960, 85–91.

3. Liddell-Scott, [9]1940, 536; R. Laqueur, *Hellenismus*, 1925, 22ff. n.8; J. Jüthner, *Hellenen und Barbaren*, 1923, 39f., 47.

4. W. Spiegelberg, *Die demotische Urkunden des Zenonarchivs*, Demot. Studien 8, 1929: 25 documents of which 9 are bilingual. For the Jewish evidence see the early Ptolemaic inscriptions CIJ 2, nos. 1424, 1425, and on them Tcherikover, CPJ 1, 3 n.8. CIJ 1, 1534, 1536 on the other hand are only from the Byzantine period. Still more striking is the find of papyri, on which see L. H. Feldman, *Jewish Sociological Studies* 22, 1960, 217. P. Nash, see CPJ 1, 107f., is a unique exception.

5. Joppa and Marisa; see Vol. I, p.8 and n.I, 19; Ḥephzibah near Scythopolis: see above, n.I, 28; the religious inscriptions in Ptolemais: M. Avi-Yonah, *IEJ* 9, 1959, 1–12; Y. Landau, *IEJ* 11, 1961, 118–26; Scythopolis and Samaria: R. Mouterde, *MUSJ* 17, 1933, 180–2; J. W. Crowfoot, *Samaria* 1, 1942, 37 no. 13; Marisa: Clermont-Ganneau, *CRAI* 1900, 536ff.; epitaphs in Gaza; see Vol. I, p. 15 and n.I, 79; Marisa: see below n. 32: here there are also some Aramaic inscriptions among the many Greek ones, see F. M. Abel, *RB* 34, 1925, 267–79; in Shechem (second to first century BC), see R. J. Bull, *BASOR* 180, 1965, 32ff. For the graffiti see the love poem from Marisa, Vol. I, pp. 83f. and below, n. 192; further examples, Peters and Thiersch, op. cit., 48 nos. 16, 17; 60, 72: the inscription of a curse against Simon the Maccabee in Gezer: CIJ 1, 225 no. 1184 and no. 1183, the bilinguals on the boundary of Gezer from the first century AD. Cf. also SEG 20, 1964, 389, and the Greek inscriptions from Tell Anafa on Lake Huleh (second century BC), *IEJ* 19, 1969, 250ff., and S. S. Weinberg, *IEJ* 21, 1971, 108f.

6. For Phoenician bilingual inscriptions see CIS I, 1 nos. 45, 89, 95, 114–20, 122 = KAI 39, 42, 53–6, 58, 59, 47; RÉS 3, 1212, 1213, 1215 = KAI 41, 60. The bilingual inscriptions come above all from Cyprus, Athens, Rhodes, Malta, etc.; in the home country itself there are predominantly purely Phoenician

inscriptions: RÉS 3, 800, 1204, 1205, 1211 Lapethos (Cyprus) = KAI 17, 19, 43, and the inscription of the Hellenistic period from the temple of Melk Astart in M. Dunand, *Oumm el-'Amed*, 1962, 181ff.: sixteen Phoenician inscriptions from the third to second century BC and only one small Greek fragment. However, the temple was in a country area (pp.233, 240). For bilingual coins see G. F. Hill, *Catalogue of the Greek Coins of Phoenicia*, 1910, cvif.: Sidon; cxxxiii: Tyre, and H. Seyrig, *Syria* 28, 1951, 225–8: even a Greek text could be reproduced in Phoenician writing.

7. CPJ 1, 125ff. nos.4 and 5 = PCZ 59076, 59075 of 12.5.257 BC; see also the editor, C. C. Edgar, on the passage, 1, 97: 'The letter is written in a beautiful large hand, no doubt by a Greek scribe.' For the treaty see CPJ 1, 118ff., no. 1; see below, n.IV, 69.

8. See Vol.I, p.27: a Jewish tax farmer Simon in Upper Egypt in the second century BC was, however, illiterate: CPJ 1, 222, no.107, though he had quite subordinate local significance.

9. Josephus, *Antt.*12, 191, 196f.

10. Josephus, *c.AP.*1, 176–81; on this see Vol.I, pp.257f.

11. Ps.Aristeas 121: ἀλλὰ καὶ τῆς τῶν Ἑλληνικῶν ἐφρόντισαν οὐ παρέργως κατασκευῆς.

12. Ibid.: τοὺς ἀρίστους ἄνδρας . . . ἅτε δὴ γονέων . . . ἐνδόξων.

13. I Macc.8; 12.1–23; 14.16–24 etc.

14. H. Hegermann in *UU* 1, 301ff.

15. Cf. I Macc.15.15–24; II Macc.1.1–9; Esther 10.31 LXX; Sir., Prologue LXX; cf. V. Tcherikover, CPJ 1, 46; *ScrHieros* 7, 1961, 26; M. A. Beek, *OTS* 2, 1942, 142f.

16. For the inscriptions see CPJ 2, 244–339, and Bagatti/Milik, *Gli Scavi del 'Dominus Flevit'* I, 1958, 70–99.

17. See L. Y. Rahmani, etc., *'Atiqot* 4, 1964, 1–40; for the inscription see P. Benoit, 39, and the further supplementation by B. Lifshitz, *RB* 73, 1966, 248–55, see also below, n.III, 133, and more recently P. Benoit, *IEJ* 17, 1967, 112f.

18. Cant.3.9; see on this Köhler/Baumgartner, *Lexicon*, 79; and F. Rundgren, *ZAW* 74, 1962, 70–72; Dan.3.5, 7: $qît^er\bar{o}s$ = κίθαρις — κίθαρα; Dan.3.5, 10, 15 $p^esant\bar{e}r\hat{\imath}n$ and 3.7 $p^esant\bar{e}r\hat{\imath}n$ = ψαλτήριον; Dan.3.5, 15 $s\bar{u}mp\bar{o}n^ey\bar{a}$' = συμφωνία; Dan.3.7, 10, 15 $sabb^ek\bar{a}$' = σαμβύκη, according to Athen.4, 175d a 'Syrian invention'; the Aramaic form could be original here; on this see A. Bentzen, *Daniel*², 28 on 3.5ff. and Köhler/Baumgartner, op. cit., 1103, 1113, 1119, 1125. Fohrer, *Introduction*, 1970, 319, also wants to derive *'ētūn* in Prov.7.16 from ὀθόνη, linen garment, but the replacement of θ by ṭ is not very probable. Cf. M. Wagner, *Die lexicalische und grammatikalische Aramaismen*, BZAW 96, 1966, 153 and n.19.

19. For Qumran see S. Segert, *Qumranprobleme*, ed. H. Bardtke, 1963, 317f.: merely some Greek proper names are mentioned: 1 QH 4.16 perhaps means Greek. For the loanwords in *koinē* see L. Rademacher, op. cit., 24.

20. DJDJ III, *Les petites Grottes de Qumran*, ed. M. Ballet, etc., 1962, 142ff., and the survey by C. Burchard, *Bibliographie zu den Handschriften*, 1965, 328f.: five Greek MSS from Qumran. Among other things a fragment of the Letter of Jeremiah, only preserved in Greek, has been found (7 Q 2); on this see Vol.I,

p. 228 and n. III, 763, cf. O. Eisfeldt, *The Old Testament*, 594f. (lit.); P. W. Skehan, *BA* 28, 1965, 89ff., and Vol. I, pp. 100ff.: 'Translation activity in Palestine'.

21. CD 14.9f., cf. *Sanh.* 17a end.

22. See S. Krauss, *Griechische und Lateinische Lehnwörter in Talmud*, two vols., 1898f.; by way of supplement see G. Zuntz, *JSS* 1, 1956, 129–40, and H. B. Rosen, *JSS* 8, 1963, 56–72; cf. also S. Lieberman, *Greek in Jewish Palestine*, 1942, passim, and B. Lifshitz, *ZDPV* 78, 1962, 78ff., and *RB* 72, 1965, 520–38.

23. Schürer 2, 59–84, see also S. Krauss, *Lehnwörter* 2, 623ff., the survey of areas where Greek (and Latin) loanwords can be demonstrated in the literature of the Talmud, through I. Löw.

24. DJDJ III, 246f., no. 84 ἔξεδρα; 247, nos. 88f.: ζυγόν or ζυγόω; 248 no. 104: περίστυλον; 251 no. 128: ἀλόη; 253 no. 149 στατήρ. Greek consonants were also used as numerals, see E. Ullendorf, *VT* 11, 1962, 227f. For Greek letters in the cryptic writing of the Essene horoscope see below, n. III, 826.

25. *Sheb.* 10.3ff., and on this Schürer 2, 427f.; M. Jastrow, *Dictionary* 2, 1218, puts forward a false derivation. The word comes from Greek law, see D. Correns, *Schebiit*, Giessener Mischna, 1960, 150; F. Preisigke, *Wörterbuch* 2, 390.

26. For Strato see Schürer 2, 134, and 3, 100; Fiehn and Obst, *PW*, 2R. 4, 273f. There were three Phoenician princes of this name: 1. a king of Sidon at the time of Artaxerxes II Mnemon (404–358), see Dittenberger, *Syll.*³ 1, no. 185; 2. a prince of Aradus; 3. a king of Tyre, the two last at the time of Alexander the Great; presumably the Phoenician name was ʿAbdʿaštart and Strato was the Greek form. Cf. further K. Galling, *ZDPV* 63, 1961, 70ff. on Ezra 4.17: possibly the Tripolis founded from the three Phoenician cities of Sidon, Tyre and Aradus already had its Greek name at the time of Ezra.

27. Josephus, *Antt.* 11, 303; on this see G. E. Wright, *BASOR* 144, 1956, 15: quotation from a letter of W. F. Albright to Wright; on the name itself see W. Pape, *Wörterbuch der griechischen Eigennamen* 2, 1863ff., 1001/2 = CIG 882 and 1710; F. Preisigke, *Namenbuch*, 1922, 234, and also PHambZen no. 105; PCZ 59335 (?) and 59676, 13.

28. See H. Gressmann, *PW*, 2R. 2, 2224f.; cf. also Rostovtzeff, *CAH* 7, 92, 190f., and Dittenberger, *Syll.*³1, nos. 390 and 391.

29. PCZ 59009, see Tcherikover, *Mizraim*, 52.

30. See Repert. Epigr. Sem. 3, 1212, 1215 = KAI 41, 60; CIS 1, 115, 116, 122, cf. 117; = KAI 54, 53, 47, 55; see A. H. M. Jones, *The Greek City from Alexander to Justinian*, 1940, 36, and C. Clermont-Ganneau, *RAO* 3, 1000, 145ff.

31. CPJ 1, 125 no. 3: 'The conflation may serve as evidence of the religious syncretism of the epoch.' Marisa: Peters and Thiersch, op. cit., 71 no. 57.

32. Only a small number of the graves can be dated. The family of Sesmaius-Apollophanes can be traced through four generations, though the last relatively certain date refers to the year 201 of the Seleucid era = 112 BC, i.e. shortly before the conquest of the city by John Hyrcanus (F. M. Abel, *RB* 34, 1925, 275 no. 11; the reading of no. 14 = 210 Seleucid era is, as Abel himself says, very uncertain). Thus we may put the earliest tombs at least 100 to 120 years earlier (see Peters and Thiersch, op. cit., 76). This would be matched by the reading ZP

= 107 Seleucid era = 206/5 BC in tomb no. 29, thus M. J. Lagrange, *CRAI* 1902, 503f.; cf. Schürer 2, 5 n. 8, and A. Schalit, *ASTI* 2, 1962, 146 n. 16; Peters and Thiersch, op. cit., 54f., read IZP = 117 Seleucid era = 196/5 and discuss the possibility of XP = 160 Seleucid era = 153 BC; the second oldest datable tomb is from the year 188 BC: see the demonstration, op. cit., 77. The time of the origin of the tombs towards the end of the third century BC would also correspond to the inscription of Philopator after the battle of Raphia: see above, n. I, 19 and the elements of Alexandrian style in the tomb paintings. For the names of the tomb inscriptions see Peters and Thiersch, op. cit., 37–71, and Add. 2–4, esp. nos. 1, 3, 9–13, 20, 23, 28–32, 50, 52, 53, 57, 58. On 'Sarya' see Josephus, *Antt.* 10, 149f., 160, and A. Schlatter, *Die hebräische Namen*, BFCT 17, 1913, Vol. 3, 105f. For the Idumean god Kos see more recently T. C. Vriezen, *OTS* 14, 1965, 330–53, esp. 333, and Josephus, *Antt.* 15, 253; he was identified with Apollo, see below n. IV, 27.

33. *RB* 34, 1925, 269f., see also already W. Moulton, *AJA* 19, 1915, 63–70, and in general also E. R. Goodenough, *Jewish Symbols* 1, 1953, 72ff.

34. A. Schalit, *ASTI* 1, 1962, 110ff.: an indication of this is the complete destruction of Marisa by the Parthians after the flight of Herod, *Antt.* 14, 364 = *Bell.* 1, 269.

35. R. J. Bull, *BASOR* 180, 1965, 33; for the inscription of Simonides see Toombs/Wright, *BASOR* 161, 1961, 45, and G. E. Wright, *Shechem*, 1964, 183.

36. J. Harmatta, *Acta Antiqua* 7, 1959, 383ff. One exception is perhaps col. A l. 10: Haggai son of Diaphorus (*dyprs*).

37. CPJ 1, 148ff. no. 18; 151ff. no. 19; 157ff. no. 21; 188ff. no. 22. For what follows see Tcherikover, CPJ 1, 27ff., and *HC*, 346f., 523f. and already L. Fuchs, *Die Juden in Ägypten*, 1924, 143ff.

38. CPJ 1, 28.

39. CPJ 1, 28 nn. 69 and 70; *HC*, 523 n. 6.

40. CPJ 1, 228f. no. 126, cf. CIJ 2, no. 1425. For the theophorous names see also the prosopography CPJ 3, 170: Apollonius, etc., Artemidorus; 172: Demetrius (cf. also the Jewish chronographers in Alexandria towards the end of the third century BC), Dionysius; 173: Dosarion (Dusares); 176: Heliodorus, Heracleides; 181: Isidorus, etc.

41. Dan. 1.7 and esp. 4.5; on this see A. Bentzen, *Daniel²*, 21: it is, however, improbable that we have a condemnation of foreign names here; rather, this is merely a feature of historicizing realism. Daniel bears his pagan names without objections, so to speak as second names.

42. Tcherikover, *HC*, 523 n. 5; see also the prosopography CPJ 3, 173f., 176f. For the release in Delphi see above, n. I, 328.

43. CIJ 2, 366f. no. 1440, and CPJ 3, 164 no. 1532a (SB 8939); M. Hengel, (n. I, 86 above), 157ff.

44. *Antt.* 12, 189, 189–95, etc.: the name appears in the Genesis Apocryphon for an official of Pharaoh: 20, 8, 21, 24. Cf. J. Neusner, op. cit., 11 n. 2: presumably it was originally a designation of descent, 'from Hyrcania', on this see above, n. I, 56.

45. See P. Kleinert, *ThStKr* 82, 1909, 503f.; I. Heinemann, *MGWJ* 82, 1938, 159; E. Bickerman(n), *HTR* 54, 1951, 153–65; see below, n. III, 161.

46. I Macc. 12.16; 14.22, 24; 15.15; cf. *Antt.* 13, 169; 14, 146, the resolution of the senate cited here probably belongs to the time of Simon. According to I Macc. 8.17 the above mentioned Jason perhaps already went as an ambassador to Rome under Judas. By some scholars he is identified with Jason of Cyrene, see below, n. III, 328.

47. II Macc. 4.11 and I Macc. 8.17.

48. II Macc. 12.19, 24, and probably also 35; on this see below, p. 276.

49. Esther 10.31 LXX, see also below, nn. III, 341–4. Cf. E. Bickermann, *JBL* 63, 1944, 348f.

50. Ps. Aristeas 47–50. Cf. the Hasmonean delegations, *Antt.* 13, 260; 14, 248.

51. Schürer, I, 255, 257ff., 273ff., 284f.: in the case of Aristobulus the Hebrew name is only preserved through coins, and in the case of Antigonus (*Bell.* 1, 64, 71–80 = *Antt.* 13, 276ff., 301–14) is no longer preserved at all.

52. On this see W. R. Farmer, *NTS* 4, 1958, 149, and M. Hengel, *Zeloten*, 177.

53. For the frequency of the name see already G. Hölscher, 'Zur jüdischen Namenskunde', in *Vom alten Testament, K. Marti z. 70 Geburtstag gewidmet*, 1925, 155; his observation is confirmed by Bagatti/Milik, *Gli scavi del 'Dominus Flevit'* I, 1958, 76f., and the statistics, 108. Cf. also J. A. Fitzmeyer, *HTR* 56, 1963, 1–5.

54. H. I. Marrou, *Histoire de l'éducation dans l'antiquité*, 1948, 139.

55. J. Jüthner, *Hellenen und Barbaren*, 1923, 25ff., and M. Hadas, *HCu*, 12ff.

56. Isocrates, *Panegyr.* 4, 50. The interpretation of the passage in Jüthner, op. cit., 34f., turns it into the opposite. Cf. H. C. Baldry, *The Unity of Mankind*, 1966, 69f.

57. J. Kaerst, *Geschichte der Hellenismus* I, ²1917, 140.

58. In Strabo 1, 4, 9 (66f.); cf. M. Mühl, *Die antike Menschheitsidee*, 1928, 54f.; very similarly Plutarch, *De Alex. fort.* 6 (329 C/D).

59. H. I. Marrou, op. cit., 144.

60. M. Launey, *Recherches sur les armées hellénistiques* 2, 1950, 813; cf. M. Hadas, *HCu*, 59f., and L. Robert, *CRAI* 1968, 416ff., 454ff.

61. For the institution of the gymnasium in newly-won territory see M. Launey, op. cit., 2, 813–74; Rostovtzeff, *HW* 2, 1058–60; H. I. Marrou, op. cit., 148–64, esp. 154ff.; M. P. Nilsson, *Die hellenistische Schule*, 1955, 83–98, and specially on the buildings, J. Delorme, *Gymnaseion*, 1960, 136ff., 198ff., 459–79.

62. M. Launey, op. cit., 2, 869–74; Rostovtzeff, *HW* 2, 1060f.; M. P. Nilsson, op. cit., 83f.

63. M. Launey, op. cit., 2, 836–68; Rostovtzeff, *HW* 2, 1058f., 1082; 3, 1588f. lit.; M. P. Nilsson, op. cit., 85ff.; J. Delorme, op. cit., 90, 137ff., 199ff. Even in the village of Samareia in the Fayum there is evidence of a gymnasium about 221/20 BC: see above n. I, 87. We already find individual reports in the Zeno papyri: PSI 340; 418, 7; 391, 7, 21: the feast of 'Hermeia' in the gymnasium of Philadelphia. For the gymnasia of the larger Egyptian villages see F. Zucker, *Aeg* 11, 1931, 485–96. For the Hellenistic elementary schools see H. I. Marrou, op. cit., 200–22, and M. P. Nilsson, 34f., 42ff.; for the school papyri see the index of R. A. Pack, *The Greek and Latin Literary Texts from Greco-Roman Egypt*, 1952, 82–92; in all ninety papyri from the third to the seventh century AD, for their

distribution see M. P. Nilsson, op. cit., 16. For the literary papyri, see below, n. 70. For the school papyrus from the third century BC see Pack, op. cit., 89, no. 2068 = O. Guéraud–P. Jouguet, *Un livre d'écolier du IIIe siècle*, 1938.

64. M. P. Nilsson, op. cit., 83.

65. M. Launey, op. cit., 2, 865ff.; M. P. Nilsson, op. cit., 85ff., 90ff.; the exclusion of natives in Roman times is probably also connected with the poll-tax obligations of the non-Greek populace. Cf. also H. Brunner, *Altägyptische Erziehung*, 1957, 27, 29.

66. W. Peremans, *Vreemdelingen*, 1943, 173–99.

67. M. P. Nilsson, op. cit., 34ff., who here attacks the division by H. I. Marrou, op. cit., 152ff.; the latter puts the ephebate, as in Athens, between the ages of 18 and 20. For military training and conscription into the army see M. Launey, op. cit., 2, 815ff., 836f., and H. I. Marrou, op. cit., 157, 500f. nn. 13 and 14; it occurred particularly in Egypt.

68. For the associations and the office of gymnasiarch see H. I. Marrou, op. cit., 158, 163ff., 502ff., and M. P. Nilsson, op. cit., 53ff., 75ff.; the centre of public life: op. cit., 78ff.; J. Delorme, op. cit., 352ff., 441ff., 443; the buildings came increasingly to the centre of the Hellenistic cities.

69. H. I. Marrou, op. cit., 165, 168f.; M. P. Nilsson, op. cit., 43ff.

70. H. I. Marrou, op. cit., 214ff.; M. P. Nilsson, op. cit., 46ff., 49ff. For Homer see H. I. Marrou, op. cit., 226ff.; M. P. Nilsson, op. cit., 61, 80; M. Hadas, *HCu*, 61, see also R. A. Pack, op. cit., 29–44, nos. 412–962; of the 2368 literary papyri enumerated in the catalogue, 371 are *Iliad* texts and 109 relate to the *Odyssey*; in addition there are about 70 paraphrases and philological aids, i.e. in all about 550 Homerica. For the Ptolemaic period cf. especially C. H. Roberts, *MusHelv* 10, 1953, 267f. For the other 'canonical' classics see H. I. Marrou, op. cit., 227f. For the school book see O. Guéraud/P. Jouguet, op. cit., ll. 155–61, 131–9; 115–29.

71. *Iliad* 6, 208 = 11, 784; on this see H. I. Marrou, op. cit., 38. Posidonius gave this saying to Pompey as a motto on his departure: Strabo 11, 1, 6 = FGrHist 87 T 8.

72. M. P. Nilsson, op. cit., 81.

73. M. Hadas, *HCu*, 60/61. For the conservative form of the instruction see C. H. Roberts, op. cit., 264f., for Egypt; C. Welles, *Aeg* 39, 1959, 26ff., for Dura Europos.

74. L. Dürr, *Das Erziehungswesen im AT und im Alten Orient*, 1932, 22ff., 74ff. Only the young nobility or kings' sons knew training in sports = war: 18f., 70f.

75. M. Hadas, *HCu*, 68.

76. M. P. Nilsson, op. cit., 61ff.; J. Delorme, op. cit., 339ff., 347, etc.

77. J. Delorme, op. cit., 352: 'Athlétisme et religion se confondent dans les gymnases depuis les origines.'

78. M. Launey, op. cit., 2, 853ff. (lit.); M. P. Nilsson, op. cit., 64ff., 67ff., 71ff.; J. Delorme, op. cit., 340ff. The gymnasium in the place 'Samaria' in the Fayum was also dedicated to Ptolemy II (Philadelphus): O. Guéraud, *P. Εντευξεις*, 1931, no. 8, 3f., and on this, op. cit., 139f., and above n. 1, 87. H. Kortenbeutel, *APF* 12, 1937, 44–53, gives a further example.

79. Education at the gymnasium was a presupposition for citizenship in a number of Hellenistic cities, see E. Bickermann, *GM*, 62 n. 3, cf. also CPJ 2, 27f. no. 150, ll. 2ff.: the petition of the Alexandrians to Augustus *c.* 20/19 BC for the preservation of the purity of the ephebate and citizenship. For the difficulty of acquiring citizenship see Tarn/Griffith, *Hellenistic Civilization*, 84f. and 221f.

80. Josephus, *Antt.* 12, 126; cf. 16, 27–60. For religious misdemeanours in the Greek *polis* see E. Fascher in *Abraham unser Vater, Festschrift für O. Michel*, 1963, 78–105, and W. Nestle, *RAC* 1, 735–40.

81. Josephus, *c. Ap.* 2, 65.

82. See III Macc. 2.30f.; cf. 3.21; see also below, n. IV, 46.

83. CIJ 2, 15 no. 749.

84. For the lists of ephebes in Iasus and in Corone in Messenia see L. Robert, *REJ* 101, 1937, 85f., and *Hellenica* 3, 1946, 100f. (= IG V, 1, no. 1398, 91f.); also in Cyrene; SEG 20, 740, 3: Ἰησοῦν Ἀντιφίλωι (first century BC), 741, 48f.; twice Ἐλεάζαρος (third/fourth century AD); in Sardes (second century AD); CIJ 2, 19 no. 755. For the whole matter see Tcherikover, *CPJ* 1, 39 n. 99; 41 and 75ff.; S. Applebaum, *ParPass* 19, 1964, 291–303.

85. This would correspond to the open attitude of the patriarchs from the house of Hillel towards Greek education and culture or even the later attitudes of the Jewish congregations towards the prohibition of images, see below, n. II, 158.

86. Ps.Aristeas 3, 272, 285, cf. 43, 46, 207 and on this V. Tcherikover, *HTR* 51, 1958, 66f., 81.

87. Cf. e.g. *Spec. leg.* 2, 230 (M 2, 298); *De somn.* 69 (M 2, 631), 129ff. (M 2, 640); on this see L. H. Feldman, *JewSocSt* 22, 1960, 224ff.

88. *Antt.* 12, 119f., cf. *c.Ap.* 2, 39 and *Bell.* 7, 43f., on this Tcherikover, *HC*, 516 and E. Bickerman(n), *From Ezra to the Last of the Maccabees*, 1962, 53 and 89 n. 47.

89. S. Applebaum, *Tarbiz* 28, 1958/59, nos. 3, 4, XIII (Summary), see Hebrew T. 424f.; cf. already a similar suggestion in Wolfson, *Philo* 1, 79f. The existence of special Jewish gymnasia is extremely improbable, on this see also L. H. Feldman, *JewSocSt* 22, 1960, 225f.

90. See L. Robert, *Nouvelles Inscriptions de Sardes*, Iᵉʳ fasc., 1964, 54ff., nos. 13–19, and D. G. Mitten, *BA* 29, 1966, 64f. (quot.); cf. the inscription above, n. 84.

91. CPJ 2, 36ff. no. 153, esp. col. V, 92f. The question of citizenship had been disputed long before, see 2, 25ff. nos. 150/151; on this V. Tcherikover, CPJ I, 59–78, esp. 73f.

92. See H. I. Marrou, op. cit., 156f., 332.

93. For this ideal of education see op. cit., 252f., 330, 336, 538f. nn. 2–5. The significance was fleeting, see in detail H. Fuchs, *RAC* 5, 366ff., and especially on Philo, 389f.

94. W. W. Tarn, *The Greeks in Bactria and India*, 1938, 34–70 and esp. 40f.: the majority of scholars migrated from the Seleucid empire; see also Rostovtzeff, *CAH* 7, 195; *HW* 2, 1084f.; M. P. Nilsson, *GGR²* 2, 39.

95. W. Schubart, *RAC* 1, 271–83, and with particular reference to the museum, E. A. Parsons, *The Alexandrian Library*, 1952, 53ff., 84ff., see also

N. Walter, *Der Toraausleger Aristobulos*, 1964, 41 n.2, and J. Schwartz, *ZPapEp* 1, 1967, 197ff.

96. The various fragments can be found in FGrHist 722; for his work see I. Freudenthal, *Hellenistische Studien*, 1875, 35–82, who stresses his dependence on Palestinian exegesis, and Schürer 3, 472–4; Y. Gutman, *The Beginnings of Jewish–Hellenistic Literature* 1, 1958, 132–9; cf. also M. Hadas, *HCu*, 94f.; N. Walter, op. cit., 43, and H. Hegermann, *UU* 1, 318f. Josephus, who quotes him in *c.Ap.* in connection with the discussion of the extreme antiquity of the Jewish tradition (1, 218), confuses him with Demetrius of Phaleron – probably he knew him only from the collection of excerpts in Alexander Polyhistor.

97. Freudenthal, op. cit., 82–174; Schürer 3, 474ff., 497ff.; Y. Gutman, op. cit., 1, 221–61 and 2, 9–143.

98. Schürer 3, 505–603, and on Aristobulus N. Walter, op. cit., 150ff.

99. So in P. Dalbert, *Die Theologie der hellenistisch-jüdischen Missionsliteratur*, 1954, 8, 18ff., etc.; see already M. Friedländer, *Geschichte der jüdischen Apologetik*, 1903, and Bousset–Gressmann, 80f.

100. So S. Baron, *A Social and Religious History of the Jews*, ²1952, 197f.; Tcherikover, *Eos* 48.4, 1956 (= *Symb.*, R. Taubenschlag, III), 169–93, and *HTR* 51, 1958, 59ff.

101. This could be true e.g. of Eupolemus and the anonymous Samaritan; see also V. Tcherikover, *Eos*, 48.3, 1956, 187; not everything that is termed 'Jewish Alexandrian literature' need come from Alexandria.

102. For what follows cf. E. Bickermann, *GM*, 59–65.

103. J. Delorme, op. cit., 136f.

104. II Macc. 4.9–14 and I Macc. 1.14f.; cf. Josephus, *Antt.* 12, 251.

105. *Bell.* 1, 422; cf. 2, 560.

106. R. Savignac, *RB* 25, 1916, 576–9. According to E. Bi(c)kerman(n), *Mélanges Dussaud* 1, 1939, 96 n.8, it falls in the year 25 BC.

107. F. M. Abel, *RB* NS 5, 1908, 568–77.

108. J. Delorme, op. cit., 218f.

109. Soloi in Cilicia: OGIS 230 from the time of Antiochus III; Laodicea on the Sea: 163 BC, see J. Delorme, op. cit., 199; Babylon, 111/10 BC, and Seleucia on the Eulaius = Susa *c.* 100–50 BC, see B. Haussoullier, *Klio* 9, 1909, 352–63; Rostovtzeff, *HW* 2, 1061 and SEG 7, 3, 39, cf. 11–14. Especially on Babylon see OGIS 253 and Bengtson, *GG*³, 482 n.3; see below n. IV, 133. Both places were at that time under Parthian rule. All the gymnasia mentioned of course point back to a much earlier time; cf. further M. Launey, op. cit., 2, 873f.

110. IG XI, 2. no. 203, 68: on this and on what follows see M. Launey, op. cit., 2, 871f.

111. Le Bas/Waddington, *Voyage archéologique* II, 3, 1847ff., no. 1866a, newly edited by E. Bi(c)kerman(n), *Mélanges Dussaud* I, 1939, 91–9. The statue going with the inscription was erected by a Cretan Timocharis.

112. Le Bas/Waddington, op. cit., no. 1866c, see also E. Bi(c)kerman(n), op. cit., 96f.

113. IG² II, 2, no. 2314, 21; 2316, 51f.; cf. also 960, 16: the Sidonian Dionysius won the young men's pankration at the Athenian Theseia in 142 BC.

114. IG² II, 2, no. 2315, 27; cf. VII no. 417, 40: a Tyrian in Oropus.

115. IG² II, 2 no. 2313, 50: Ἐπίνικος Θάλωνος Πτολεμαιεὺς ἀπὸ [Φοινίκης . . .?], cf. 965, 50.

116. IG VII, no. 1760, 21, at the end of the second century BC.

117. For the double name see *Antt.* 12, 139.

118. II Macc. 4.9, and on it see E. Bickermann, *GM*, 59ff., and following him F. M. Abel, *Macc.* 331f. The petition (ἔντευξις) of Jason did not lead immediately to the foundation of the new *polis* 'Antiochia in Jerusalem', thus Tcherikover, *HC*, 404ff., but it served to prepare for it; see below, pp. 277ff.

119. See above, n. I, 224; see Vol. I, pp. 268ff.

120. See W. H. Roscher, *Lexikon* 1, 1409 on Europa; according to Lucian, *Dea Syr.* 4, there was a temple of Europa-Astarte in Sidon. For Andromeda see Roscher, op. cit., I, 345–8: the connection between her and Joppa is old and can already be found in the time before Alexander in Ps. Skylax, C. Müller, *GGM* 1, 565. The whole material is in F. M. Abel, *HP* 1, 271f.

121. Roscher, *Lexikon* 2, 824–93, cf. already Herodotus 2, 49. The claim to cultural superiority is expressed e.g. by a coin from Tyre which depicts how Cadmus gives the alphabet to the Greeks, op. cit., pl. 7, on this see Herodotus 5, 57–9. The inscription edited by E. Bickermann (see above, n. 111) expressly stresses the delight of the Thebans of Cadmus at the victory of their mother city Sidon (νίκαις εὐκλέα μητρόπολιν); cf. Achill. Tat. 1, 1. ed. R. Hercher, *Erot.script.gr.* 1, 1856, 37 and Josephus, *c.Ap.* 1, 10–13.

122. E. Bi(c)kerman(n), *Mélanges Dussaud* 1, 94: Hellanicus (fifth century BC), FGrHist 4 F 36; according to Arrian, *Anab.* 2, 24, 2, there was an 'Agenoreion' in Tyre as early as 332 BC.

123. FGrHist. 264 F 6, 4 (Diod. 40, 3); Herod. 1, 65, 2.

124. I Macc. 12.6–23 (10.20); II Macc. 5.9; Josephus, *Antt.* 12, 226f., cf. 13, 166f. The starting-point is the letter of king Areus to Onias II. As Areus I, who is the only possible author, fell as early as 265 BC, a defence of the authenticity of this letter is difficult. The suggestion by Y. Gutman, op. cit., I, 108–11, that the initiative came from the Spartans who had learned from Hecataeus of the common exodus of Jews and Daneans from Egypt, is improbable; similarly M. S. Ginsburg, *ClassPhil* 29, 1934, 117–22, and F. M. Abel, *Macc.*, 231–3 and *HP* 1, 41. M. Hadas, *HCu*, 87, rightly observes: 'Claims of relationship . . . were not proffered by the Hellenes but by the non-Hellenes.' The correspondence of Jonathan with the Spartans, on the other hand, may be genuine. It shows that some ideas of the Hellenists continued to influence the Maccabees; see E. Bickermann, *PW* 14, 786 and below, n. 286. The origin of the affinity is probably to be sought in the Jewish Hellenistic mythographers like Cleodemus Malchus, who had the sons of Abraham by Keturah migrating to Libya (i.e. Cyrene), where they met up with the children of Heracles (FGrHist 727). The report of Hecataeus, mentioned above, of the emigration of the Daneans under Cadmus and the Jews under Moses from Egypt could also have been a cause (FGrHist 264, 2, Diod. 40,3; fr. 25, Diod. 1, 28, 2). Cf. further the note of Claudius Iolaus (Reinach 215 = FGrHist 788 F 4) on the derivation of the name Judea from a certain Οὔδαιος Σπάρτων ⟨εἷς⟩, i.e. one of the men sown by Cadmus in Thebes; on this see A. Schlatter, *GI³*, 15. Only fragments of this remarkable literature have

been preserved. As the Hellenists in Jerusalem were most interested in the legend, it will also have arisen there. E. Bickermann, *PW* 14, 786, supposes that it arose in the first quarter of the second century BC. Later, reference to the laws and the xenophobia of the Spartans probably became a theme of Jewish apologetic. Josephus makes rich use of it: *c.Ap.*2, 130, 172, 225–31, 259f., 271. A parallel which probably comes from the Jewish military settlers in Phrygia, who came under Pergamene rule after the peace of Apamea (*Antt.* 12, 147–53, see below, n. IV, 45), is the alleged friendship between Jews and Pergamenes in the time of Abraham: *Antt.* 14, 255.

125. SEG 2, 330; A. H. M. Jones, *The Greek City*, 1940, 50, 311 n. 68. The construction of such affinities was a widespread phenomenon of great political significance in Hellenistic times, see E. Bi(c)kerman(n), *Mélanges Dussaud* 1, 1939, 95f., and *RHR* 115, 1937, 207.

126. E. Bickermann, *PW* 14, 786.

127. I. Heinemann, *MGWJ* 82, 1938, 146.

128. F. M. Abel, *HP* 1, 112f.

129. Cf. E. Bickermann, *GM*, 63 n. 4: the high priest and gymnasiarch in the temple city of Ma in Cappadocia; G. de Jerphainion/L. Jalabert, *MUSJ* 5, 1911/12, 316 no. 10: ἀ[ρ]χιερέως καὶ γυμνασιάρχου.

130. II Macc. 4.12; on this see E. Schuppe, *PW* 19, 1, 1119–24.

131. The acropolis probably means the citadel at the north-eastern corner of the temple, see above, n. I, 81.

132. II Macc. 4.14; on this see A. Wilhelm, SAW 214, 4, 1932, 45, and L. Robert, *Études Anatoliennes*, 1937, 290 n. 50. According to A. Wilhelm, op. cit., 46, and L. Robert, the μετέχειν τῆς ἐν παλαιστρῇ παρανόμου χορηγίας refers to the distribution of oil and other things necessary for use in the gymnasium; see also Abel/Starcky, 243 ad loc.

133. II Macc. 4.18–20; on this F. M. Abel, *Macc.*, 335 ad loc. For the foundation of festivals see Arrian 2, 24, 6 and 3, 6, 1: ἐν Τύρῳ αὖθες θύει τῷ Ἡρακλεῖ καὶ ἀγῶνα ποιεῖ γυμνικόν τε καὶ μουσικόν.

134. FGrHist 723 I 2, 34, 16; see on this below n. 287.

135. Op. cit., 727; on this see E. Bi(c)kerman(n), *RHR* 115, 1937, 205. The reasons why Freudenthal, *Hellenistische Studien*, 1875, 130–6, wants to make him a Samaritan, and A. Schlatter, *GI*³, 409 n. 100, wants to make him a pagan Syrian are not compelling; cf. Schürer 3, 481, and B. Wachholder, *HUCA* 34, 1963, 87 n. 27.

136. Jub. 3.31 on Gen. 3.21.

137. Josephus, *Bell.* 2, 123; cf. also CD 12.16, where possibly the incomprehensible שמו should be emended to שמן; see E. Lohse, *Die Texte aus Qumran*, 1964, 286 n. 78.

138. I Macc. 1.15; *Antt.* 12, 242, cf. Jub. 15.33f.; Ass.Mos. 8.3 and Philo, *Migr.Ab.* 92f. (M 1, 450). According to Herodotus 2, 104, the Phoenicians did not introduce circumcision into Greece; in Egypt it was limited more and more to the priests. Cf. E. Bi(c)kerman(n), *RHR* 115, 1937, 219f.; I. Lévy, *Semitica* 5, 1955, 17; F. Stummer, *RAC* 2, 159f. For epispasm at a later period see Martial 7, 35; 'Ab. 3, 11; J. Juster 2, 284 n. 4; Bill. 4, 33f. Perhaps the gymnasium text CPJ 3, 117 no. 519, ll. 18ff. also refers to a Jew who performed epispasm. For the

rejection of circumcision by the Greeks see already Herodotus 2, 37, cf. R. Meyer, *TDNT* 6, 78.; see also below, n. IV, 72.

139. Jewish–Hellenistic writers like Cleodemus Malchus, Artapanus, the older Philo, the earliest Sibyl, the tragedian Ezekiel, the translator of the book of Job or the anonymous Samaritan and his compatriot Theodotus knew Greek mythology and the language of the Greek poets. We may presuppose the same thing, though to a lesser degree, even in Jerusalem, see Vol. I, pp. 88ff. For Homer see Vol. I, pp. 75f.

140. Tcherikover, *HC*, 166f., cf. on the other hand the statement to the opposite effect, 193.

141. Tcherikover, *HC*, 163f., 165.

142. Josephus, *Antt.* 12, 164 ἐκκλησία; I Macc. 5.16; 14.28; see also Schlatter, *GI³*, 401 n. 26.

143. Rostovtzeff, *HW* 2, 1060f.

144. The significance of the reforms introduced by Jason in 175 BC are underestimated by I. Heinemann, op. cit., 145ff., and Tcherikover, *HC*, 166f., because they overlook the fact that at that time there was no division between religion and politics as we understand them. On the other hand, the brief observation by A. Alt, *Kleine Schriften* II, ³1964, 402f., 403 n. 1, is correct. Political aims necessarily had religious consequences. For the problem see M. Hengel, *Die Zeloten*, 1961, 147.

145. On this see M. Noth, *History of Israel*, ²1960, 361ff., and Vol. I, pp. 267ff

146. According to Menander and Laitus, two Phoenician history writers about 200 BC, Menelaus visited Tyre at the same time as king Hiram married his daughter to Solomon, after the conquest of Sparta: see FGrHist 784 F 1 = Tatian, *Adv. Gr.* 37.

147. The charge of the Sadducees is refuted by R. Johanan b. Zakkai (c. AD 1–80). The המירם was corrupted by later copyists to מירם מירון; Fr.E 1/152 of the Taylor-Schechter Collection in Cambridge, however, still reads המררם, see G. Lisowsky, *Yadayim*, Giessener Mischna VI, 11, 1956, 74, 91; cf. also *j. Sanh.* 28a l. 18 (R. Akiba), and B. Heller, *MGWJ* 76, 1932, 330–4; R. Meyer, *Hellenistisches in der Rabbinischen Anthropologie*, 1937, 138f.; J. Neusner, *A Life of R. Yohanan b. Zakkai*, 1962, 49.

148. See S. Lieberman, *Hellenism in Jewish Palestine*, 1950, 105–14.

149. See Eusebius, *Pr. Ev.* 13, 12, 14, and on it N. Walter, TU 86, 1964, 151ff., who rightly does not suppose a direct falsification by Aristobulus but the adoption of such verses from Jewish Pythagorizing circles, cf. 166ff. The 'monotheistic' interpretation of Homer, with reference to *Iliad* 2, 204, in Ps. Justin, *Coh. ad Gen.* 17, may go back to Jewish models.

150. *Sib.* 3.419ff.; in 414–30 we have an old oracle, see Pausanias 10, 12, 2, from Alexander Polyhistor, which was interpolated by the Jewish author, see A. Kurfess, *Sibyllinische Weissagungen*, 1951, 9, 296. For the dating of the third Sibylline see Rzach, *PW*, 2R. 2, 2127ff. For Josephus, see *c. Ap.* 2, 256, and for reference to Plato, H. I. Marrou, op. cit., 112; see also E. Norden, AAB Kl. f. Sprachen, 1954, no. 1, 9. There is a further example of apologetic usage in *Antt.* 7, 67, possibly a gloss which goes back to the association of *c. Ap.* 1, 173 (quot. Choerilus of Samos) with Homer, *Odyss.* 5, 283; on this see Thackeray/Marcus,

Josephus 5, LCL, 394. For the view of Meleager of Gadara that Homer was a Syrian, see n.212, cf. 213.

151. G. Glockmann, *Klio* 43–45, 1965, 270–81 (lit.).

152. Josephus, *Antt.*12, 186f.; see below n.III, 423.

153. *Sota* 49b, see also Bill.4, 411 (BQ 82b), Bar. The Josephus parallel *Antt.* 14, 25–28 probably follows Nicolaus of Damascus. For dating see Schürer 1, 294. For the later addition of the curse see R. Meyer, op. cit., 136.

154. *Antt.*13, 318, on this, against Schürer 1, 275, see E. Meyer, *UAC* 2, 277 n.1. A little later, the Nabatean king Aretas III bore the title 'Philhellene', as did Arsaces VII and other Parthian kings, see Schürer 1, 275 n.1 and 733.

155. *Antt.*15, 373: he went 'to (the house of) the teacher's', probably hardly a Jewish *bēt sēper* but 'Herod's tutor in Greek studies', see Thackeray/Marcus, *Josephus* 8, LCL, 181 n.g., against W. Otto, *PW Suppl.*2, 17; the passages cited there about his being brought up with the Hasmonean princes, *Bell.*1, 215; *Antt.*14, 183 and 15, 18, do not exclude Greek instruction, but imply it. For his later studies see the report of Nicolaus in his autobiography, FGrHist 90 F 135; on this Otto, op. cit., 105. According to this 'Herod had full command of the Greek language', i.e. because he had learned it in Jerusalem in his youth. For the education of his sons see *Antt.*16, 242ff.: the royal tutors Gemellus and Andromachus, on which see W. Otto, op. cit., 87, cf. also 106, 109; cf. also B. Wacholder, *Nicolaus of Damascus*, 81ff.: Greek authors in Herod's library.

156. See *Antt.*15, 320ff.; 17, 78: Joazar son of Boethus: 17, 164, 339 (the son of Simon); see also 18, 3, 26 and *Bell.*2, 55: Eleazar son of Boethus. Simon son of Boethus also seems to belong to this family (*Antt.*19, 297f.), and the same is true of Matthias son of Boethus (*Bell.*5, 527), despite the objections of Niese. The members of this high-priestly family formed the Sadducean group of Boethuseans, see R. Meyer, *TDNT* 7, 42f., 45f.; for the legendary riches of this family see the Rabbinic traditions about Martha from the house of Boethus, J. Jeremias, *Jerusalem in the Time of Jesus*, 1969, 194f.

157. *Vita* 13–16.

158. On this see Billerbeck 4, 407ff.; R. Meyer, *Hellenistisches*, 139ff.; B. Lifshitz, *ZDPV* 78, 1962, 77ff. For the patriarch and Libanius see M. Avi-Yonah, *Geschichte der Juden im Zeitalter der Talmud*, 1962, 228, and H. Mantel, *Studies in the History of the Sanhedrin*, 1961, 241f., 251f.

159. Cf. e.g. I Chron.2.55: Jabesh as the dwelling-place of the families of the *sōperīm*, though the exegesis of this is disputed; see W. Rudolph, *Chronikbücher*, 1955, 25.

160. Cf. already Deut.33.10; further Hecataeus in Diodore 40, 3,6 (Reinach 17) and FGrHist 264 F 5: they function as judges in all difficult situations and are also responsible for the 'maintenance of law and custom'; cf. II Chron.34.13; Sir.45.17; Test.Levi 13.2ff. For the older wisdom schools see L. Dürr, *Das Erziehungswesen im Alten Testament und im Antiken Orient*, MV(Ä)G 36, 2, 1932, 110f.; W. Baumgartner, *TR* 5, 1933, 269f.; see also K. Galling, *Die Krise der Aufklärung in Israel*, Mainzer Universitätsreden 19, 1952, 6ff., 10ff.: the 'wisdom school' in Jerusalem goes back to the time of the monarchy, indeed to Solomon. On teaching and judgment see R. de Vaux, *Ancient Israel*, 1961, 353–5. For what follows see R. Meyer, *Tradition und Neuschöpfung*, BAL 110, 2, 1965, 33–43.

161. E. Bickerman(n), *From Ezra to the Last of the Maccabees*, 1962, 68ff., cf. also H. Brunner, *Altägyptische Erziehung*, 1957, 29ff.

162. J. Fichtner, *Die altorientalische Weisheit in ihrer israelitisch-jüdischer Ausprägung*, 1933, 35, 46ff.; W. Baumgartner, op. cit., 283f. For the Levites see II Chron. 17.8f.; 19.8, 11; 23.7f.

163. Above all from the beginning of the Hellenistic period: for Solomon see Vol. I, pp. 129f.; on David see 11 QPs^a DavComp, ed. J. A. Sanders, *The Psalms Scroll*, DJDJ IV, 91ff., see also Vol. I, p. 135f.

164. On this see I. Lévi, *L'Ecclésiastique*, 1901, Vol. 2, lxxxiiiff., and R. Pautrel, *RSR* 51, 1963, 535; see also Vol. I, pp. 116f.

165. Sir. 51.23, 29. R. N. Whybray, *Wisdom in Proverbs*, 1965, 90f. already sees in Prov. 9.1 a reference to the house of the wisdom teacher. Moore, *Judaism* 1, 41 n. 2, supposes – probably wrongly – a reference in Sir. 39.6; cf. also R. H. Pfeiffer, *History of New Testament Times*, 374. The beginnings of the synagogue are probably hinted at in the work of the Chronicler, see the reading of the law in Neh. 8.1–12 and Ezra 7.25, which reports the appointment of scribes for legal decisions and instructions in the law, and on this K. Galling, *ZDPV* 72, 1956, 167f. For the earliest synagogue inscriptions in Egypt see CIJ 2, 366f., and CPJ 3, 164 no. 1532a, from the time of Ptolemy III Euergetes, 246–222 BC. The word 'teaching house' appears for the first time in Ben Sira; for its significance in the later period see J. Levy, *Wörterbuch* 3, 34f. For the seat of the teacher see the synagogue of Delos, E. L. Sukenik, *Ancient Synagogues*, 1934, 61, and Goodenough, *Symbols*, 2, 74f.; also the so-called *cathedra* of Moses (Matt. 23.2), in Chorazin and Hammath near Tiberias, see Sukenik, op. cit., 57ff., may go back to the y^{e}šībā of the teacher. For the whole matter see M. Hengel (above n. I, 86), 157–84.

166. See his praise of the scribes, 38.24–39.11 and 51.13–29, his hymn to wisdom formed from a wisdom hymn attributed to David with an invitation to the foolish attached. For a preliminary stage see 11QPs^a Sir, DJDJ IV, 79ff.

167. *'Ab.* I, 1; on this see L. Finkelstein, *The Pharisees* 2, ^{3}1962, 580, cf. 576; see also N. Morris, *The Jewish School*, 1937, 12.

168. Sir. 38.25ff., presumably taken over from the wisdom tradition; on this see the satire on the various professions and the praise of the scribe in the teaching of Heti son of Duauf, *ANET*^{2}, 432ff., and in some contrast to that Sir. 37.23 (M). Ben Sira may stand at a point of transition, and the urgent invitation to the fool, 51.23ff., perhaps reflects his real intention.

169. Cf. *Bell.* 3, 252; *Vita* 8ff.; *Test. Levi* 13, 2–6; *Yoma* 3, 11: the priestly family tradition about the incense; on this, J. Jeremias, *Jerusalem in the Time of Jesus*, 25. Cf. also *Shekalim* 6, 1.

170. DJDJ IV, 64 col. 18, 3, 4f., 15f. For the text see below, n. IV, 466. Cf. also 71 col. 24, 9, and Dan. 11.33; 12.3b; see Vol. I, pp. 176ff.

171. W. F. Albright, *From the Stone Age to Christianity*, 1940, 355; see also E. Bi(c)kerman(n), *RB* 59, 1952, 53f.; A. Schlatter, *GI*^{3}, 61: 'Access to knowledge was open to everyone and not associated with priestly birth.'

172. *'Ab.* I, 4, 6; for R. Jose b. Joezer see *Gen. R.* 65, 22 = Bill. 2, 263.

173. See R. Meyer, op. cit., 36f.

174. E. Bickerman(n), op. cit., 44–54; cf. K. H. Rengstorf, *TDNT* 4, 439ff.,

esp. 440. The anecdotes about the early teachers of the law are collected in K. Schlesinger, *Die Gesetzeslehrer*, 1936, and J. Neusner, *The Rabbinic Traditions about the Pharisees before 70* I, 1971, 24–183.

175. *Yoma* 35b Bar; cf. however, J. Jeremias, *Jerusalem in the Time of Jesus*, 112, against Schürer 2, 380. For the tradition see J. Neusner, op. cit., 1, 258f.

176. Bill. 1, 563b; *Derek Ereṣ Zuta* 41, and other instances.

177. Josephus, *Bell.* 2, 119; *Antt.* 18, 11, cf. *Vita* 12, on which see R. Meyer, op. cit., 43f. n. 3.

178. See K. H. Rengstorf, *TDNT* 4, 421ff., 429ff., cf. A. Schlatter, *GI³*, 62. The word תלמיד appears only in I Chron. 25.8, that is, very late in the OT; the word רב does not appear at all with the meaning 'teacher'. On this see M. Hengel, *Nachfolge und Charisma*, 46ff.

179. M. Hadas, *HCu*, 79f.; cf. N. Morris, op. cit., 40, 74; J. Baer, *Zion* 13/14, 1958/59, 139ff.; D. Daube, *The New Testament and Rabbinic Judaism*, 1956, 151ff.

180. For Hillel see W. Bacher, *Die Agada der Tannaiten* I, ²1903, 1ff. and on the question of Alexandrian influence on Rabbinic exegesis see D. Daube, *HUCA* 22, 1949, 239–64; E. E. Hallewy, *Tarbiz* 29, 1959/60, 47–55; 31, 1961–62, 157–69; 264–80. Cf. already S. Lieberman, *Hellenism in Jewish Palestine*, 1950, 47–82, esp. 53ff.; R. Meyer, op. cit., 81f., and G. Mayer, *RAC* 6, 1196ff., with an abundance of parallels from Hellenistic Roman rhetoric.

181. *j.Keth.* 32c, 4; see G. F. Moore, op. cit., III, 104 n. 92, and critically Schürer 2, 493f.; E. Ebner, *Elementary Education*, 1956, 38f., 45, sees here a reference to the first elementary school in Jerusalem. However, this certainly goes back to the scribal school of the temple.

182. BB 21a (third century AD); on this see S. Krauss, op. cit., 200f., and the detailed discussion in E. Ebner, op. cit., 39ff. The time immediately before the outbreak of the Jewish war was probably inappropriate for such a school reform in view of the chaotic situation in Judea, and moreover it is questionable whether the high priest, who was close to the Sadducees (cf. *Antt.* 20, 199, about his friend Ananus son of Ananus) and married to one of the richest families in Jerusalem (*Yeb.* 6.4), was interested in educating the people on a broad basis and the strengthening of the Pharisees which would result from it. The time of Hyrcanus I, who was indeed originally a friend of the Pharisees (*Antt.* 13, 289), with its nationalist expansion and compulsory conversion of non-Jewish neighbours to Judaism (*Antt.* 12, 257), would be more appropriate for an intensification of school policy.

183. A. Schlatter, *GI³*, 59; according to *Shab.* 1.3 the synagogue servants functioned as children's teachers.

184. I QSa 1.6–8, see DJD 1, 109 and E. Lohse, *Die Schriften von Qumran*, 1964, 46. Cf. also Jub. 19.14; cf. 11.16.

185. *Antt.* 4, 211; *c.Ap.* 2, 204, cf. also 2, 178 and 1, 60. For the Diaspora see IV Macc. 18.10ff.; Philo, *Leg. ad C.* 115, 120 and II Tim. 3.15; Luke 2.46ff. might also be mentioned.

186. *jMeg.* 73d, 23ff., cf. Bill. 2, 150 and 662 (par.).

187. *CIJ* 2, 332f. no. 1404.

188. Prohibition of the non-Jewish teacher, S. Krauss, op. cit., 218, T. 'AZ

3, 2 (1.463). For the role of the Bible, op. cit., 220; for the book of Leviticus, op. cit., 235, cf. A. Schlatter, *GI*³, 60, 402 n.77.

189. Op. cit., 227; see *Gen.R.* 65.20. According to *Ruth R.*2.13, he was a friend of R. Meir; cf. also *Ex.R.* 13, 1 and *Ḥag.* 15b. The identification of the אבנימוס of Rabbinic tradition and Oenomaus is very probable, despite the doubt of H. J. Mette, *PW* 17, 2249ff., as both come from the same period; see also W. Bacher, *Die Agada der Tannaiten* 2, 31.

190. *HC*, 115. For what follows see also F. M. Abel, *HP* 1, 278–81, and Schürer 2, 53–5.

191. See above, n. I, 79 and n. III, 111; cf. also E. Bi(c)kerman(n), *Mélanges Dussaud* 1, 93.

192. Peters/Thiersch, *Painted Tombs*, 1905, 56–60, no.33 = SEG 8, 244 (lit.); in detail, W. Crönert, *RheinMus* 64, 1909, 433–48; cf. also U. von Wilamowitz-Möllendorf, *Griechische Verskunst*, 1921, 344f. For pledging the cloak see M. Dahood, *Bibl* 42, 1961, 359–66. For dating see Peters/Thiersch, op. cit.: 'The script resembles that of the papyri at the end of the third century', against this W. Crönert, op. cit., 433f.: *c.* 150 BC. The graffito reproduced in op. cit., 447, from Marisa (see R. A. S. Macalister, *CRAI* 1901, 109), belongs in the same milieu. The same is true of the obscure verse (Peters/Thiersch, op. cit., 60 no.34), which is also said to have metric form, see Crönert, op. cit., 438f. According to Ulpian in Athen. 15, 697c, the whole of Phoenicia was full of these (Locrian) songs. On this see S. A. Cook, *The Religion of Ancient Palestine*, 1930, 205, and F. Altheim, *Weltgeschichte Asiens* 2, 153f. The magical interpretation of the poem in R. A. S. Macalister, *A Century of Excavation in Palestine*, 1925, 322ff., is improbable; similarly the explanation by H. Lamer, *ZDPV* 55, 1932, 56–67.

193. See P. Maas, *JHS* 62, 1942, 33–8, see 36 col. II, 4; Bliss/Macalister, *Excavations in Palestine, 1898–1902*, 156ff., 175, and S. A. Cook, *The Religion of Ancient Palestine*, 200f.; on the dating see op. cit., 201 n. 1.

194. Schürer 2, 161 n.262. For interpretation see P. Perdrizet, *RevArch* 35, 1899, 49f.: 'ville lettrée'. The epigram itself seems to date from post-Christian times.

195. Strabo 16, 2, 29 (759).

196. For Menippus see R. Helm, *PW* 16, 888–94; F. Susemihl, *Geschichte der griechischen Literatur in der Alexandrinerzeit* 1, 1891f., 46f.; Schmid/Stählin, *GGL*⁶ II, 1, 88–90, cf. also 53, 56; M. Hadas, *HCu*, 110f., and Überweg/ Praechter, *Philosophie des Altertums* 12, 1925, 13f.ˣ lit.

197. Diogenes Laertius 6, 95, 99–101; Aulus Gellius, *Noct.Att.*2, 18, 6f.

198. F. Dornseiff, *Antike und Alter Orient* 1, ²1959, 244. M. Hadas, loc. cit., cf. P. Wendland, *Die hellenistisch-römischer Kultur*, 1912, 77f. The influence of Menippus is evident in Varro's Menippean satires, Petronius, Seneca's *Apocolocyntosis*, etc. For the oriental background see F. Altheim, op. cit., 2, 154.

199. Diogenes Laertius 6, 101; cf. Lucian, *Icaromenippus*, ed. A. M. Harmon, LCL 2, 267ff.

200. Op. cit., II, 1, 189 n. 5; cf. also R. Reitzenstein, *Hellenistische Wunder- erzählungen*, 16, 18ff. Journeys to heaven and to the underworld also occurred in Alexandrian literature of the third and second century BC, see Vol. I, pp. 210ff.

Cf. also Diog.Laertius 6, 102, which according to K. von Fritz, *PW* 15, 794, is to be transferred to Menippus.

201. M. Hadas, op. cit., 111; F. Dornseiff, op. cit., 1, 234f.; cf. Lucian, *Bis accus.* 33, LCL 3, 146. R. Merkelbach, *Roman und Mysterium*, 1962, 333f., sees in the prose metre the form of presentation of the early aretalogies.

202. See R. Helm, *Lucian und Menipp*, 1906, 14ff., 19ff., 8off., 343ff.

203. *Anth.Gr.*7, 417, 3 and 418, 6; on Meleager see Geffcken, *PW* 16, 481–8; Susemihl, op. cit., 2, 555–7; Schmid/Stählin, op. cit., II, 1, 326f.; *Anth.Gr.*, ed. H. Beckby, 1957, Vol.1, 35ff.; M. Hadas, *HCu*, 111f. A clear edition of all the epigrams of both poets with an excellent commentary can be found in A. S. F. Gow – D. L. Page, *The Greek Anthology, Hellenistic Epigrams* 1, 1965, 11–34 and 214–53.

204. E. Schwartz, *PW* 1, 2513; Susemihl, op. cit., 2, 551ff. Meleager gave him his own epigram: 7, 428.

205. *Anth.Gr.*, ed. H. Beckby, Vol.1, 37; cf. also M. Hadas, *HCu*, 112. The only contact with Judaism is significantly the mention of a Jewish rival: *Anth.Gr.* 5, 160.

206. *Anth.Gr.*7, 417, 1–6; translation following H. Beckby; similarly 418, 1f.

207. *Antt.*13, 356, 396; *Bell.* 1, 86.

208. See R. Philippson, *PW* 37, 2444, though he wrongly wants to put Gadara near Ashkelon. Cf. also Gow/Page, op. cit., 2, 607: 'a city of poets and philosophers'.

209. *Anth.Gr.*12, 256, cf. 59; 7, 418, 428; probably the Tyrian coin inscription Τύρου ἱερᾶς καὶ ἀσύλου lies in the background; see G. F. Hill, *Catalogue of the Greek Coins of Phoenicia*, 1910, cxxxiiiff., 233ff. The designation 'holy' for Jerusalem appears on coins of the Jewish rebellion of AD 66–70, cf. M. Hengel, *Die Zeloten*, 1961, 121. On the other hand the Samaritan Theodotus calls Shechem ἱερὸν ἄστυ, FGrHist IIIc 732.

210. For the origin of the idea of the world citizen in Cynicism see Diog. Laert.6, 63: Diogenes, and 6,93: Crates; cf. Tarn/Griffith, *Hellenistic Civilization*, 79f.; M. Hadas, *HCu*, 15ff. This apolitical and individualist conception is connected with the Stoic notion of the 'world state'; see J. Mewaldt, 'Das Weltbürgertum in der Antike', *Die Antike* 2, 1926, 177–90, and M. Mühl, *Die antike Menschheitsidee*, 1928, 49ff. The negative version seems to be older, see Xenophon, *Mem.*2.1, 13: Aristippus to Socrates: 'I am a stranger everywhere.'

211. *Anth.Gr.*7, 419, 5ff.; 'Audonis', conjectured by Scaliger from אדוני.

212. Athenaeus 4, 157b; cf. M. Hadas, *HCu*, 83: the wise man Calasaris in the *Ethiopiaca* of Heliodorus similarly asserts that Homer was begotten of Hermes-Thoth in Thebes (3, 14, cf. 2, 34). Phoenician or Syrian descent was also claimed for Thales and Pythagoras: Clem.Alex. 1, 62, 2–4, GCS Stählin/ Früchtel, 2, 39, and Herodotus 1, 170.

213. *Anth.Gr.*16, 296, 5–9; cf. in general 292–304.

214. Diogenes Laertius 7, 29.

215. R. Philippson, *PW* 19, 2444–82; cf. Susemihl, op. cit., 2, 267–78, 561; Überweg/Praechter, op. cit., 439, 444, 134[x] lit. For his personality see Cicero, *in Pis.*70: '*Est non philosophia solum, sed etiam ceteris studiis . . . perpolitus.*'

216. E. Zeller, *PhGr* III, 1[4], 284ff., 385 n.1; Überweg/Praechter, op. cit.,

436,438,134[x] lit. For the so-called 'Syrian Epicureans' see W. Schmid, *RAC* 5, 758f.

217. W. Peek, *Griechische Grabgeschichte*, 1960, no. 201.

218. *c.* 200–130 BC, see W. Crönert, *Der Epikureer Philonides*, SAB, 1900, 2, 942–59, cf. 953 cols. 29/30; cf. also R. Philippson, *PW* 20, 63ff.; E. R. Bevan, *CAH* 8, 498f., and W. Schmid, loc. cit. He edited the letters of Epicurus.

219. Strabo 16, 2, 24 (757): Mochus was presumably an old Phoenician mythographer like Sanchuniation. For fragments on him see FGrHist 784. As the *Iliad* was regarded as the earliest monument to Greek culture, 'before the Trojan wars' meant 'earlier than the earliest Greek tradition'; on this see the arguments of Josephus, *c.Ap.* 1, 11f.

220. On this see K. Thraede, *RAC* 5, 1207ff.; cf. Diogenes Laertius, 1,3: the rejection of claims to a higher antiquity for 'barbarian' philosophers, and the learned statements to the contrary effect by Josephus, *c.Ap.* 1, 6–14; Clem. Alex., *Srom.* 1, 66ff., 74ff., GCS Stählin/Früchtel 2, 41ff., 47ff. Cf. below, index s.v. 'Inventor'.

221. Von Arnim, *PW* 3, 601–3, and SVF 3, 265f.; E. Zeller, *PhGr* III, I[4], 47 n. 1, cf. *Kleine Schriften*, 1910, 1346; J. F. Dobson, *ClassQ* 8, 1914, 88–90; M. Pohlenz, *Die Stoa* 1, ³1964, 185; 2, 94f.; cf. also Diog. Laert. 7, 143, 148, and on this below n. IV, 290; see the polemic against *ekpyrōsis* bound up with this view in Philo, *Aet. mundi* 78–84 (M2, 502–4).

222. Stephen of Byzantium, *Ethnika*, ed. A. Meineke, 1849, 132, under 'Askalon'; the source is probably Herennius Philo of Byblos. For Antiochus see also Strabo 16, 2, 29 (759).

223. For Sosus see Schürer 2, 53 n. 121; M. Pohlenz 1, 249; 2, 98 and 129.

224. Überweg/Praechter, op. cit., 470ff., 142[x], for earlier literature; A. Lüder, *Die philosophische Persönlichkeit des Antiochus von Askalon*, 1940; M. Pohlenz, op. cit., 1, 249–53; 2, 129f.; G. Luck, 'Der Akademiker Antiochos', *NoctRom* 7, 1953. His brother Aristos also had a philosophical education, op. cit., 15. A. Wlosok, *Laktanz und die philosophische Gnosis*, AAH, 1960, 2, 50f.

225. For the influence of Plato in the Hellenistic period see M. Hadas, *Journal of the History of Ideas* 19, 1958, 3–13, and *HCu*, 72ff.; H. J. Krämer, *Der Ursprung der Geistmetaphysik*, ²1967.

226. A. Lüder, op. cit., 59ff.; see Cicero, *de Fin.* 5, 14, etc.

227. See P. Wendland, *Die hellenistisch-römische Kultur*, 1912, 71.

228. Strabo 16, 2, 24 (757), on which see Gercke, *PW* 3, 603f.; von Arnim, *PW* 5, 715.

229. Von Arnim, *PW* 8, 508.

230. Von Arnim, *PW* 1, 2516 and 2, 2146.

231. Diogenes: Diog. Laert. 7, 41, cf. von Arnim, *PW* 5, 777 and M. Pohlenz, op. cit., 2, 91; Apollonius: von Arnim, *PW* 2, 146 and M. Pohlenz, op. cit., 2, 98.

232. J. Kaerst, *Hellenismus* 2², 111ff. For Semitic influence see M. Pohlenz, 'Stoa und Semitismus', *NJWJ* 2, 1926, 257–69, and *Die Stoa*, ³1964, Zeno: 1, 22f. and 2, 14; see Diogenes Laertius 7, 3, 30 (see Vol. I, p. 72) = *Anth. Gr.* 7, 117; Cicero still called him *poenulus*, *de Fin.* 4, 56; Chrysippus: M. Pohlenz, *Stoa* 1, 28 and 2, 17, his father Chrysippus came from Tarsus. Cf. also U. von Wilamowitz-Moellendorf, *Der Glaube der Hellenen* 2, ³1959, 297ff., and M. Hadas, *HCu*, 106ff.

233. M. Pohlenz, op. cit., 1, 46f.: the Stoic conception of the structure of language is determined by Semitic sensibility, 1, 68f.: the nature which is identical with the Logos is not understood in a mechanical way, as with Epicurus, but as 'the living, all directing deity'. Behind this there could be a 'new feeling of life', the 'idea of a transcendental creator god'. 65f.: the corporeality of the soul and the deity is un-Greek, but has Old Testament parallels. 100: the 'new feeling of life' can be seen in the fact that man becomes the sole purpose for the creation of the world; everything is created for his sake (see Vol. I, pp. 145f., Ben Sira), 107f.: the fatalism furthered by the unrestricted sway of *heimarmenē* is not Greek, but oriental, like Chaldrean astrology (see Vol. I, pp. 236ff.), which was furthered by the Stoa; see also op. cit., 1, 164f.

234. J. Bidez, 'La Cité du Soleil chez les Stoiciens', *Bull. Acad. roy. Belg.*, classe des lettres, 18, 1932, 244–94; on this see M. P. Nilsson, GGR^2 2, 259 n. 2. R. P. Festugière, *Révélation* 2, 266 n. 1, has a critical attitude towards the 'oriental' features in the Stoa, but his verdict here is too one-sided.

235. For the tomb paintings of Marisa see Peters/Thiersch, op. cit., 86ff. and the plates; E. R. Goodenough, *Jewish Symbols* 1, 1953, 68ff., and 3, plates 7–16. Parallels to Alexandrian art can be seen from, say, a comparison of the representations of animals with the illustrations in B. R. Brown, *Ptolemaic Paintings and Mosaics and the Alexandrian Style*, 1957, pl. 44, 1 and 2; see also Rostovtzeff, *HW* 1, pl. lviii, and in comparison the hunting theme on the Calabrian gilt key, pl. liv: 'Without doubt both were made by Alexandrian artists or artists trained in Alexandria.' Cf. above n. I, 339.

236. B. Wacholder, *HUCA* 34, 1963, 112f.: 'It may be assumed that the so-called Hellenizers produced their own literature, now lost.' See Vol. I, p. 114.

237. See Vol. I, pp. 268f.

238. FGrHist 724 = Eusebius, *Pr.Ev.* 9, 17; 18, 2. The most important investigations are J. Freudenthal, *Hellenistische Studien*, 1875, 82–103, esp. 86f.; Schürer 3, 482; Y. Gutman, *The Beginnings of Jewish–Hellenistic Literature* 2, 1963, 95–108; B. Wacholder, *HUCA* 34, 1963, 83–113, and N. Walter, *Klio*, 43/45, 1965, 282–90. Bousset/Gressmann, 21 n. 2, would nevertheless assign the fragment to Eupolemus; cf. A.-M. Denis, *Introduction*, 1970, 261f. lit.

239. See J. Freudenthal, op. cit., 85f., 91f., 96, and B. Wacholder, op. cit., 104. The translation of Ἀργαριζίν (cf. Deut. 27.4 Samarit.) by ὄρος ὑψίστου and the assertion that Abraham met Melchizedek there clearly point to it. Cf. id., *HTR* 61, 1968, 458ff., and H. G. Kippenberg, *Garizim und Synagoge*, 1971, 80ff.

240. See already J. Freudenthal, op. cit., 96: not in Egypt, but in 'one of the Syro-Phoenician Greek cities'. However, a direct derivation from Samaria is more probable. This is also indicated by his acquaintance with the Palestinian Haggada and the Enoch tradition, see B. Wacholder, op. cit., 98f., 109, 112: 'remnants of a work written in Samaria circa 200 BCE'; cf. N. Walter, op. cit., 283f.

241. For Berossus see already J. Freudenthal, op. cit., 94, and P. Schnabel, *Berossus*, 1923, 67ff.; on the other sources see Y. Gutman, op. cit., 1, 100f. and B. Wacholder, op. cit., 88, 90f. The formulas in F 1, 9: Βαβυλωνίους γὰρ λέγειν and Ἕλληνας δὲ λέγειν already point to the use of Greek and Babylonian sources.

242. J. Freudenthal, op. cit., 83; B. Wacholder, op. cit., 87f. nn. 30 and 32; critical remarks in N. Walter, 284ff.: the use of the Hebrew text remains uncertain.

243. F. 1, 9. According to Greek tradition Atlas discovered astrology, see B. Wacholder, op. cit., 96 n. 83, and Roscher, *Lexikon* 1, 707f. Cleanthes, SVF 1, 125 no. 549, mentions him in connection with Homer, *Od.* 1, 52, περὶ τῶν ὅλων φρονοῦντος. We also find the combination of Babylonian and Greek mythology in Philo of Byblos (AD 54–142), see FGrHist 790 F 2. For Enoch and the angels see Gen. Apoc. 2.19ff.; I Enoch 106.13; Jub. 4.21: 'And he was with the angels of God six jubilees of years, and they showed him everything that is on earth and in heaven . . . and he wrote it all down.' For the astrological revelations of Enoch see Jub. 4.17; I Enoch 72–82 and *Antt.* 1, 68ff.: the descendants of Seth invent 'science of the heavenly bodies'; see below, nn. III, 859–62; on this see also the astrological text in R. Reitzenstein, *Poimandres,* 183 n. 2. For the Babylonian origin of the Enoch tradition see below n. III, 617. M. Gaster, *The Asatir,* 1927, 9–27, draws attention to an abundance of parallels between the anonymous Samaritan and the Samaritan book Asatir; see 6.18, Enoch and astronomy, on this, op. cit., 37f.

244. F 1.2, 9 and F 2: the killing of the godless 'giants' mentioned in F 2 refers to the flood and corresponds to 1.2. B. Wacholder, op. cit., 94, overlooks this identification of Noah and Nimrod = Bel-Kronos, which necessarily follows from the text. It comes about because the anonymous Samaritan identifies the γίγαντες of Gen. 6.4 and the γίγας of 10.9. There was also speculation in the Jewish haggada whether Noah might not be descended from the sons of God; see Gen. Apoc. 2.16 and I Enoch 106.8. Even the Rabbis knew of extremely peculiar attempts at identification: thus Shem and Melchizedek (Bill. 3, 692), and Phinehas and Elijah (M. Hengel, *Die Zeloten,* 1961, 167ff.), were regarded as one person. M. Gaster, op. cit., 38f. differs.

245. Berossus: see P. Schnabel, op. cit., 68f. (cf. on the other hand 246) and FGrHist 680 F 1.7ff.; Bel appears here as God and creator of the world. For the foundation of Babylon by Bel see Abydenos, who goes back to Berossus: FGrHist 685 F 1. According to Ctesias Babylon was built by Semiramis, the wife of Ninus, the son of Bel: FGrHist 688 F 1b = Diodore 2, 7, 2, cf. also Wacholder, op. cit., 91f., 102, and N. Walter, op. cit., 289.

246. Sib. 3, 97 = 161, and Hesiod, *Theog.* 421ff. Castor of Rhodes (first century BC) already knows of a battle of Bel against the Titans: FGrHist 250 F 1. For the dependence of the Sibyl on the anonymous Samaritan see *Oracula Sibyllina,* GCS ed. J. Geffcken, 53 (on 3, 97) and 59 (on 3, 218). For the whole see B. Wacholder, op. cit., 90–3. The theogony of Hesiod is in turn of oriental origin, see below, n. III, 2.

247. Op. cit., 93 n. 68, and the examples cited by J. Geffcken, op cit., 53.

248. B. Wacholder, op. cit. 99: 'By identifying Noah with Kronos or Belus, Pseudo-Eupolemus apparently was satisfied that he had undermined the polytheistic creed.' For the genealogy see F 1.9: Chum the ancestor of the Ethiopians is also said to have been called 'Asbolus' by the Greeks; for attempts at interpretation see P. Schnabel, loc. cit., and B. Wacholder, op. cit., 95. The name 'the ruddy' is probably derived from the colour of his skin.

249. R. Laqueur, *PW*, 2.R. 3, 1225f., and FGrHist 256 F 2; critical remarks in F. Jacoby, FGrHist II B p.835 (Comm.).

250. See FGrHist 732 F 1 = Eusebius, *Pr.Ev.*9, 22; Epiphanius, *Panar.*55, 2, 1, GCS Holl, 2, 326.

251. F 1, 3: εὐγενείᾳ καὶ σοφίᾳ πάντες ὑπερβεβηκότα . . . ἐπί τε τὴν εὐσέβειαν ὁρμήσαντα εὐαρεστῆσαι τῷ θεῷ.

252. The stress on the tenth generation after the flood also appears in Berossus, FGrHist 680 F 6 = Josephus, *Antt.*1, 158, and in *Sib.*3, 108ff. The additional contradictory statement about a birth of Abraham in the thirteenth generation is probably to be excluded, following Jacoby, as a gloss: B. Wacholder, op. cit., 100, differs.

253. Perhaps Χαλδαικὴ (τέχνη?) refers to manticism and visions of the future, see R. Reitzenstein, *Die hellenistische Mysterienreligionen*, ³1927, 155f. According to *Asatir* 2,6, see M. Gaster, op. cit., 198, Enoch received the 'book of signs' (ספר האותות) from Adam.

254. We may see here a sign of friendliness towards the Seleucids: in contrast to Babylonia, Armenia never belonged to the Seleucid kingdom. This would also have prevented a fight between Abraham and his own kinsmen. Genesis Apoc.21.23 mentions 'Arioch of Kptwk' (= Cappadocia) among the kings.

255. F 1, 5: ξενισθῆναί τε αὐτὸν ὑπὸ πόλεως ἱερὸν ᾿Αργαριζίν.

256. For the punishing of Pharaoh (1, 7), see Gen.Apoc.20.17; Josephus, *Antt.*1, 162–5 and *Gen.R.*41, 2; *j.Keth.*31d, 33ff.; *Asatir* 6, 10–26; see B. Wacholder, op. cit., 109, and M. Gaster, op. cit., 250ff.

257. F 1, 8: we also find the same report in Artapanus, FGrHist 726 F 1 = Eusebius, *Pr.Ev.*9, 18, 1, and Josephus, *Antt.*1, 166–8. In contrast to the anonymous Samaritan, Abraham here goes first to Egypt and remains there twenty years; only then does his journey to Syria take place: here the Palestinian and Egyptian view of affairs stand side by side.

258. Herodotus 2, 3, 1; 77, 1; 160, 2, cf. 54ff.: the oracles come from Egypt; 81: the Orphic and Dionysian mysteries are Egyptian, cf. below n.273.

259. For the problem see A. Kleingünther, *ΠΡΩΤΟΣ ῾ΕΥΡΕΤΗΣ*, *PhilSuppl* 26, 1, 1933, though he deals only with the pre-Hellenistic period; further in K. Thraede, *RAC* 5, 1192–1278. For the Jewish tradition see op. cit., 5, 1243ff., and Bousset/Gressmann, 72ff.; see also Vol.I, pp.29, 86, 92, 129f., 165f.

260. *Antt.*12, 258, 260, 162: the Samaritans called themselves officially οἱ ἐν Σικίμοις Σιδώνιοι. On this see n.IV, 233.

261. For the border unrest in Palestine see *Antt.*12, 156; for the disputes in Alexandria see 2, 10, 12 and 13, 74–9, and on this H. Graetz, *Geschichte der Juden*, ⁵1905, 651f., who cites Rabbinic and Samaritan sources. Cf. also N. Walter, *Der Toraausleger Aristobulus*, TU 86, 1964, 38f. n.7. *Antt.*12, 168 shows that the connections between Jews and Samaritans nevertheless did not break off completely; see also Smith, *Der Hellenismus*, Fischer-Weltgeschichte 6, ed. P. Grimal, 1965, 254f.

262. FGrHist 726 F 3, 3 (Eusebius, *Pr.Ev.*9, 27): Musaeus, the teacher of Orpheus 3, 6: Moses receives godlike honour (ἰσοθέου τιμῆς) and is named

Hermes (= Thoth) because of his ἑρμηνεία of the ἱερὰ γράμματα, 3, 4, 9, 12: the introduction of animal cults by Moses. 3, 32: the earth is identified with Isis. In addition Moses is also the inventor of artificial irrigation, war machines and philosophy (3, 4). Nevertheless, Artapanus is not a polytheist, see his account of the activity of God: 3, 21f., 23ff., 38. His whole work, which is probably a romantic aretalogy, see M. Hadas, *HCu*, 96ff., expresses a strong nationalist feeling, see I. Heinemann, *PW* 16, 367. The epic fragment of Theodotus, FGrHist 732 (Eusebius, *Pr.Ev.*, 9, 22) identifies Hermes in a euhemeristic way with 'Sikimios', the king of Shechem. According to Philo Byblius (FGrHist 790 F 1, 23 = Eusebius, *Pr.Ev.* 1, 9, 23), on the other hand, the Phoenician Taut was the inventor of writing, called by the Egyptians 'Thōuth' and the Greeks 'Hermes'.

263. See N. Walter, *Klio*, 43/45, 1965, 289f.

264. Theophrastus already attributed to the Jews a predilection for astrological studies: fr. 151 Reinach, see Vol. I, pp. 256f. This report from the end of the fourth century BC may still rest on invention; in later times the interest is manifest. The Jewish Alexandrian tradition ascribes astrological knowledge above all to Abraham. Artapanus, FGrHist 726 F 1 = Eusebius, *Pr.Ev.* 9, 18, 1; Orpheus in Aristobulus: *Pr.Ev.* 13, 12, 5 = Clem.Alex, *Strom.* 5, 132, 2; Josephus, *Antt.* I, 158, 167f.: in general see also Wisdom 7.18 and Philo, *Spec.Leg.* I, 13, 89–92. Vettius Valens, *Anth.* 2, 28f., ed. Kroll 96, and Firmicus Maternus, had an astrological writing ascribed to Abraham: *Math.* 4, 17, 3; 4, 18, 1 etc. For the rabbis see *'Ab.* 3, 15; *T.Qidd.* 5, 17 (l. 343) = BB 16b, Eleazar of Modaim (*c.* AD 80–135): 'Our father Abraham had astrological knowledge in that all the kings of the east and west came early to his gate (to ask counsel of him)', Bill. 3, 451. For the whole question see A. Schlatter, *GI*³, 397 n. 48. However, we also find the opposite view, that Abraham had broken with astrology: Jub. 12. 15–17; Sib. 3, 221–7; J. Geffcken, op. cit., 59, sees here a polemic against (Ps.)-Eupolemus; Philo, *De Abr.* 69ff.; *De Migr.Abr.* 178ff., 184ff.; *Quis Rer.Div.Her.* 96–9, etc. For the Rabbinic tradition on it see Bill. 2, 403f. and 3, 212f.; *Shab.* 156a and *Gen.R.* 44.10, 12 on 15.15 Bar. in connection with a journey to heaven: 'The rabbis said: (God spoke to Abraham): You are a prophet and not an astrologer (אסטרו־לוגום).' Presumably there is polemic here against the widespread view of Abraham as an astrologer. According to Samaritan tradition, Adam was already introduced to astrology, see J. C. H. Lebram, *VT* 15, 1965, 193 n. 5, cf. *Asatir* 1, 22 = M. Gaster, op. cit., 192; for the whole matter cf. also N. Walter, op. cit., 226f. n. 5. For Enoch see above n. 243. For the role of astrology in Essenism and apocalyptic see Vol. I, pp. 236ff.

265. Cf. Gen.Apoc. 21.15–20, the journey of Abraham round Arabia, on which see R. Meyer, *Das Gebet des Nabonid*, BAL 107, 3, 1962, 76ff. Nicolaus of Damascus and Pompeius Trogus, in Justin, *Epit.* 36, 2 (Reinach 252), report that Abraham ruled in Damascus for some time. *Antt.* 14, 255 could suggest a saga of Abraham's journey to Asia Minor, see also above, n. 124.

266. According to Demetrius, FGrHist 722 F 2 = Eusebius, *Pr.Ev.* 9, 29, Moses' wife, the 'Ethiopian woman' Zipporah, also stemmed from Abraham by Keturah. The postscript to Job(LXX) makes Job a great-grandson of Esau and thus one of the descendants of Abraham; the same is true with his friends Eliphaz, king of the Temanites, and Zophar, king of the south Arabian Mineans;

Gen.36.10, 15, 33f. LXX suggest such genealogies, see Freudenthal, op. cit., 136ff., and Schlatter, *GI*³, 74, 76. According to Cleodemus Malchus, FGrHist 727 = Josephus, *Antt.* 1, 240f., the sons of Keturah are said to have given their names to Assyria and Africa (cf. Gen.25.4). The Sophacians are said to have sprung from the marriage of Heracles to the granddaughter of Abraham. Even the Spartans refer to their common descent from Abraham in the forged letter of Areus to Onias: I Macc. 12.19–23 and *Antt.* 12, 226f.; on this see n. 124. Sir.44.19, 21 also knows of the universality of the descendants of Abraham: 'to give them a possession from sea to sea and from the river (Euphrates) to the ends of the earth.' For the Rabbinic tradition of Abraham as the 'heir of the world' see Bill.3, 209.

267. FGrHist 723 (Eusebius, *Pr.Ev.* 9, 25, 4; 9, 30); on this see J. Freudenthal, op. cit., 82–129; Schürer 3, 474–7; Y. Gutman, op. cit., 2, 73–94; J. Giblet, *ETL* 39, 1963, 539–54.

268. The information follows from the chronological details in F 4 = Clem. Alex., *Strom.* 1, 141, 4, according to which Eupolemus reckoned 5149 years from Adam to the fifth year of Demetrius I; on this see F. Jacoby, *PW* 6, 1226. Bousset/Gressmann, 20 n.2, come to a rather later date, after 145 BC. Like Demetrius, see above n.96, Eupolemus also has chronographical interests in demonstrating the greater antiquity of the Jewish tradition.

269. J. Freudenthal, op. cit., 127. His thesis found general acceptance, see Schmid/Stählin, *GGL*⁶ II, 1, 589. F. Jacoby, op. cit., 1227ff., and FGrHist 723 T 1; N. Bentwich, *Hellenism*, 1919, 92. F. Baron, *A Social and Religious History* 1, 185f.; E. Bickerman(n), *A. Marx Jubilee Volume*, 1950, 164f.; F. M. Abel, *Macc.*,153, on I 8.17. Only H. Willrich, *Juden und Griechen*, 1895, 157f., opposed it. The *terminus a quo* would be the translation of Chronicles into Greek. This was already available to the grandson of Ben Sira after 117 BC; see H. J. Cadbury, *HTR* 48, 1955, 223f. It could already have been translated about the middle of the second century. Literature in A. M. Denis, *Introduction*, 1970, 252ff.

270. J. Freudenthal, op. cit., 109; F. Jacoby, *PW* 6, 1229: 'His style is miserable, his vocabulary scanty and the construction of sentences clumsy.'

271. J. Freudenthal, op. cit., 107; J. Giblet, op. cit., 547.

272. F 1 after Clem.Alex, *Strom.* 1, 153, 4: γραμματική; more generally Eusebius, *Pr.Ev.* 9, 25, 4: γράμματα. For the communication of the alphabet by the Phoenicians to the Greeks see Herodotus 5, 57–59, and A. Kleingünther, op. cit., 60ff., see also n.121 above; cf. also Y. Gutman, op. cit., 2, 81f., and P. Wendland, *Die hellenistisch-römische Kultur*, 1912, 198 n.1.

273. Plato, *Phaedrus* 274c–d, cf. R. Hanhart, *VT* 12, 1962, 143 n.1. For Hecataeus see Diodore 1, 16, and on this I. Heinemann, *PW* 16, 368, and F. Jacoby, *PW* 7, 2766. The basis for these views can already be found in Herodotus' account of Egypt, cf. 2, 49, 54ff., 58, 77. For the verdict of Hecataeus cf. F. Jacoby, *PW* 7, 2760: 'Egyptomania', which did, however, have a political background, the demonstration of the power of Ptolemy I. For Hermes Thoth see above n.262.

274. See *Antt.*1, 166–8: Abraham as teacher of knowledge (see also Vol.I, pp.90f.), *c.Ap.*1, 168, 279, 281: Moses as teacher of the Greek philosophers, similarly already in the second century BC Aristobulus, *Pr.Ev.*8, 10, 3f.: the

pagan poets made great borrowings from Moses, cf. 13, 12, 1ff.: Plato, Pythagoras and Socrates as disciples of Moses: on this see N. Walter, op. cit., 27f., 44ff.; J. Jeremias, *TDNT* 4, 850; L. H. Feldman, 'Abraham the Greek Philosopher', *TAPA* 59, 1968, 156, and below pp. 165f., 167ff.

275. F 4 after Clem Alex., *Strom.* 1, 141, 4; on this see A. v. Gutschmid, *Kleine Schriften* 2, 1890, 193f., and N. Walter, op. cit., 47f.

276. J. Freudenthal, op. cit., 118; Y. Gutman, op. cit., 1, 94; see FGrHist 688 F 5 = Diodore 34, 1. Cf. Josephus, *Antt.* 11, 5: Cyrus' edict rested on a reading of the prophet Jeremiah.

277. Eupolemus sees the kingdom of Judah completely in the light of the situation of the Maccabean period: cf. I Macc. 5.9f., 14f., 52, 55ff.; II Macc. 12.30.

278. Cf. II Macc. 2.4ff. and *Vita proph.*, ed. T. Schermann, *Propheten und Apostellegenden*, TU 31, 3, 1907, 83. The legend persisted among the Rabbis that Josiah had hidden the ark: see L. Ginzberg, *Legends of the Jews*, 1911ff., 3, 48 and 4, 19 n. 112.

279. For Pharaoh Uaphres see Y. Gutman, op. cit., 2, 88; cf. Jer. 51.30 LXX. For Suron see Freudenthal, op. cit., 108 and 208. Sidon is also included in the kingdom of the Phoenician partner – to the greater glory of Solomon.

280. Freudenthal, op. cit., 110, 210; Y. Gutman, op. cit., 1, 86; P. Wendland, op. cit., 198; 'both pairs of letters are composed in the conventional forms of Hellenistic epistolary style.'

281. For the 'Phoenicians' in Palestine see Vol. I, pp. 32ff., 61f.; cf. also Sir. 46.18 G in contrast to M.

282. F 2b = Eusebius, *Pr.Ev.* 9, 30, 3, 4, 7. There is a remarkable coincidence between the extension of the Davidic kingdom in Eupolemus and the promise to Abraham and the following journey of the patriarch from the Taurus mountains to the Erythrean sea in Gen. Apoc. 21.8–19.

383. F 2b = Eusebius, *Pr.Ev.* 9, 33: the names of the Ptolemaic and Seleucid administrative units have probably been preserved here, see Vol. I, pp. 20f.

284. Antiochus III: see OGIS 230.5; 237.12; 239.1; 240.1; 245. 18, 40; 249.2; 250.2; 746.1. Antiochus VII Sidetes: OGIS 255.1, 2; 256.2, 3; the formula is rare with the Ptolemies, see e.g. Ptolemy III Euergetes: OGIS 54.1ff.

285. F 2 = Eusebius, *Pr.Ev.* 9, 34, 9, cf. *Midd.* 4, 6; MQ 9a; see J. Freudenthal, op. cit., 118. Cf. also Josephus, *Bell.* 5, 224, and D. Sperber, *JQR* 54, 1964, 251f.

286. According to the otherwise unknown Phoenician historian Dio, cf. *Antt.* 8, 147 and O. Eissfeldt, *Kleine Schriften* 2, 1963, 174.

287. F 2 = Eusebius, *Pr.Ev.* 9, 34, 16; cf. 33 and 34, 1; see Vol. I, pp. 296ff.

288. An otherwise unknown Theophilus, FGrHist 733 = Eusebius, *Pr.Ev.* 9, 34, 19, reports that Solomon sent Hiram, his father-in-law, a statue of his daughter, and the golden pillar served as a case for it. Herodotus had already reported a golden pillar, though this stood in the temple of Heracles (2, 44): the writers of Phoenician history, Menander of Ephesus, FGrHist 783 F 1 = Josephus, *c.Ap.* 118, and Dio, FGrHist 785 F 1 = Josephus, *c.Ap.* 1, 113, tell both of the close contacts between the two kings, e.g. the exchange of riddles, and of the erection of a golden pillar in the temple of Zeus. According to Laitus and

Menander, FGrHist 784 F 1b = Clem.Alex., *Strom.* 1, 114, 2, Solomon married the daughter of Hiram at a time when Menelaus was visiting Tyre after the destruction of Troy.

289. P. Dalbert, *Die Theologie*, 1954, 42.

290. F 1 = Eusebius, *Pr.Ev.*9, 25, 4: Moses is said to have been the first to have written down the law of the Jews.

291. A. Schlatter, *GI*[3], 187–92. Cf. also Bousset/Gressmann, 21 n.2. The report of the building of the temple by Solomon is irreconcilable with the Gerizim tradition; on this see J. C. H. Lebram, *VT* 15, 1965, 207.

292. For elements held in common by the Samaritan and Jewish traditions see J. Jeremias, *TDNT* 7, 89ff., and J. C. H. Lebram, op. cit., 167; cf. M. Gaster, *The Asatir*, 61–124.

293. A. Schlatter, *GI*[3], 191.

294. Cf. FGrHist 724 F 1 = Eusebius, *Pr.Ev.*9, 17, 3 with FGrHist 723 F 1.

295. K. D. Schunck, *Die Quellen des I u. II Makkabäerbuches*, 1954, 70ff., would also ascribe to Eupolemus the composition of the Hebrew Judas source which he finds in I Macc., a hypothesis which it is impossible to prove.

296. O. Eissfeldt, *The Old Testament*, 580f. For the work of Jason see the basic article by B. Niese, *Hermes* 35, 1900, 268–307, 453–527, esp. 299ff.; also Schürer 3, 482–9; J. Moffatt in Charles, *Apocrypha* I, 125ff.; R. H. Pfeiffer, *History of New Testament Times*, 1949, 506–18; Funaioli, *PW* 9, 778–80; F. M. Abel, *Maccabees*, xxxiiif.; Abel/Starcky, 17ff.; Tcherikover, *HC*, 381–90. Full details now in J. G. Bunge, *Untersuchungen zum zweiten Makkabäerbuch*, Diss. Bonn 1971.

297. For the rhetorical style of the work see B. Niese, op. cit., 300: 'Jason must have written in a luxuriant style with poetic phrases and all kinds of unusual word-formations', see also 303; F. M. Abel, *Macc.*, xxxvif.: R. H. Pfeiffer, op. cit., 518, and E. Bickermann, *GM*, 147: 'the only example of this literary genre, of which otherwise no works have been preserved complete'.

298. Cf. the table of contents and the characterization of the work of Jason by the epitomator: II Macc.2.19–25, 28–30. According to this the epitome covers the whole work of Jason; see B. Niese, op. cit., 305; R. H. Pfeiffer, op. cit., 509f.; F. M. Abel, *Macc.*, xliiif.; K. D. Schunck, op. cit., 120f.: possibly Jason reported down to the death of Judas. The conjecture of E. Meyer, *UAC* 2, 456f., and A. Schlatter, *GI*[3], 121, that the work went down to the elevation of Jonathan to be high priest or even to Simon is unfounded.

299. For the epitome see R. H. Pfeiffer, op. cit., 519ff.; according to him 2.19–32; 15.37–39 and probably 4.17; 5.17–20; 12–17 come from the epitomator. We may add the introductory letters (on which see Vol.I, pp.110f.) and the mention of Mordecai's day in 15.36. The problem of ch.7 is difficult, as here the king himself appears, in contrast to the historical framework. Possibly we also have a revision here or even the insertion of an additional martyr haggada by the epitomator (cf. B. Niese, op. cit., 305). The other martyrdoms, cf. 6.10f., 18–31; 14.37–46, on the other hand, probably come from Jason. On the whole the tendency of the work of Jason and the epitome itself will have been the same (see B. Niese, loc. cit.).

300. Cf. e.g. II Macc.3.4; 4.12, 19f., 28, 41, 49; 12.34, 40; 13.21; 14.24f., 38.

301. B. Niese, op. cit., 304; Schürer 3, 484f.; F. Jacoby, FGrHist, Comm. on 182, II B p.606; F. M. Abel, *Macc.*, xliff. (with J. Moffatt in R. H. Charles, *Apocrypha* 1, 123f., he assumes a rather later point of origin, after 130 BC); Abel/Starcky, 17, 34; Tcherikover, *HC*, 385f.

302. E. Meyer, *UAC* 2, 457f.; E. Bickermann, *PW* 14, 793, cf. 796 and *GM*, 18, 34, 147, 150; his view of a 'Seleucid source' is followed by R. H. Pfeiffer, op. cit., 516; cf., however, the criticism of Tcherikover, *HC*, 385f.

303. K. D. Schunck, op. cit., 36ff., 59ff., 116ff., and the collection of sources, 126.

304. Op. cit., 122ff.; on this cf. also II Macc. 2.13f.

305. Op. cit., 97–109; but Schunck regards the second letter 11.23–26 as inauthentic; see, however, E. Bickermann, *PW* 14, 789f.; *GM*, 174, 181; Tcherikover, *HC*, 214ff., 388f.; R. Hanhart, *Zur Zeitrechnung des I und II Makkabäerbuches*, BZAW 88, 1964, 71f.

306. Sachs/Wiseman, *Iraq* 16, 1954, 202–12, and on this J. Schaumberger, *Bibl* 36, 1955, 423–34; Abel/Starcky, op. cit., 35ff., and R. Hanhart, op. cit., 71, 82 etc.: the Macedonian and Antiochene calculation from autumn 312 was used in I Macc. for political and secular dates and the Babylonian reckoning from 1 Nisan 311 BC for cultic and priestly ones.

307. J. Schaumberger, op. cit., 428f.; Abel/Starcky, 38. The sequence in II Macc. 9; 10. 1–9 is correct; the positioning of I Macc. 6.1–13 a long way after 4.36–61 is not. R. Hanhart, op. cit., 81, attempts to mediate by putting the death of the king between 14 and 17.12.164 BC in order to justify I Macc. at least relatively, but this is unjustified. The king did not die in the neighbourhood of Babylon, but in Tabae (Gabai ?), on the Persian/Median border (see B. Niese, *GGMS* 3, 218, and Weissbach, *PW*, 2R. 4, 1840f. = Polyb.31, 9), which was about 350–400 miles from Babylon as the crow flies.

308. See the comparison of events between I and II Macc. in Hanhart, op. cit., 75. In contrast to this, however, the death of Antiochus and the reconsecration had already been deliberately made into a unity by Jason by the addition of 10.9. The investigation of W. Mölleken, *ZAW* 65, 1953, 205–28, on the date of the appointment of Alcimus shows that even I Macc. did not work in a chronologically unobjectionable fashion: it was not 161 BC but 163; cf. II Macc. 14.3, 7 and *Antt.* 12, 385. I Maccabees 7.12–18 and 20–24 belong in the structure after I Macc. 6.58ff.; see also M. Smith, *Der Hellenismus*, Fischer-Weltgeschichte 6, 384 n.370.

309. On this see Abel/Starcky, op. cit., 18–25, and R. H. Pfeiffer, op. cit., 513ff., 515: 'His theology is distinctly Palestinian rather than Jewish–Hellenistic.' According to R. H. Charles, *Eschatology*, reprinted 1963, 277f., the eschatology of II Macc. belongs in the second century BC because of its affinity with I Enoch 83–90.

310. Refusal of self-defence on the sabbath: 6.11; 8.25ff.; 15.1–6, cf. Jub. 50.1 and CD 10.17ff.; see also 11.15ff.; 12.6f. and Vol. I, p.178.

311. II Macc. 5.27; cf. also 6.18ff.; also see Dan. 1.8; Judith 10.5; Tobit 1.10f., etc.; we find a related situation in Asc.Isa. 2.8–11.

312. 12.44; 14.46 (7.9, 11, 14, 23); cf. Dan. 12.2; I Enoch 25.5; 27.3; 90.32f.; 91.10. For the immortality of the soul see on the other hand Wisd. 1.15; 2.23ff.

etc.; IV Macc. 14.5f.; 16.13, etc., and Volz, *Eschatologie*, 231ff., 266f. and R. H. Pfeiffer, op. cit., 514. For the intercession for the departed faithful see 15.12ff.; cf. I Enoch 39.5 and O. Betz, *Der Paraklet*, 1963, 56ff.

313. On this see below n. 325.

314. For the theme of the holy war in II Macc. see M. Hengel, op. cit., 278f.

315. R. Hanhart, op. cit., 74 n. 33, and I. L. Seeligmann, *The Septuagint Version of Isaiah*, 1948, 94, in connection with the murder of Onias III, II Macc. 4.30–38.

316. On this see M. P. Nilsson, *GGR* 2², 198ff., and R. Laqueur, *PW*, 2R. 6, 1191f. He lived about 356–260, first in Sicily and later in Athens. In contrast to the widespread scepticism of the early Hellenistic period he stresses direct retribution by the gods in his history writing in an almost archaic way. His love of omens and oracles is also striking. The report preserved by Diodore 20, 70, of the murder of Ophellas and the adoption of his army by the tyrant Agathocles is typical: on the same day the latter lost his son and his army. He gives a similar report on the date of the conquest of Tyre by Alexander, Diodore 13, 108 = FGrHist 566 F 106: it fell on the same day and at the same hour on which the Carthaginians had stolen the statue of Apollo in Gela in 406 BC and had sent it back to Tyre. Even Polybius can sometimes refer to divine retribution, despite his enlightened attitude: 1, 84, 10 and 18, 54, 10. Later Plutarch deals with the problem in a positive way in *De sera numinis vindicta*. Cf. below n. 336.

317. Cf. 2.19, 22; 3.38f.; 5.19ff.; 14.13, 31, 35f.; 15.18. Even pagan kings reverenced the temple: 3.2f.; 5.16; 13.23; cf. 9.16. God intervenes directly, to protect the temple and punish those who sin against the sanctuary: 3.24–40; 9.5ff., 16; 13.6–8; 14.33f.; and 15.32–35. The work has two new temple feasts as its climax: the reconsecration, 10.1–8, and the celebration of the victory against Nicanor, 15.36f.; however, this order might only go back to the epitomator, see E. Bickermann, *PW* 14, 793.

318. Brothers of Judas are mentioned just once as subordinate commanders: in 10.20 there is a report of the treachery of the men of Simon and in 14.17 Simon suffers a defeat. For Onias III see 3.1ff.; 4.2, 33–38 and above all his appearance with Jeremiah – both were regarded as martyrs – in the vision in 15.12ff. The only indirect reference to the rank of Judas is 14.26.

319. See R. H. Pfeiffer, op. cit., 515.

320. 14.6; cf. 5.27, and in contrast to this I Macc. 2.42; 7.13. O. H. Steck, *Israel*, 260f. n. 5, stresses the connections with the conception of suffering in Ps.Sol.

321. Tcherikover, *HC*, 384f. On this see the similar observation in Mark 15.21 and M. Dibelius, *From Tradition to Gospel*, reprinted 1971, 182f.

322. B. Niese, op. cit., 294f.; E. Bickermann, *PW* 14, 793 and GM, 147.

323. In 2.21 the epitomator counts as a special characteristic of the work of Jason τὰς ἐξ οὐρανοῦ γενομένας ἐπιφανείας. For details see 3.24–39 (on this see E. Bickermann, *AIPHOS* 7, 1939–44, 21ff., 37f.); 5.1–4 (on this see the omens before the outbreak of the Jewish war according to the 'eye-witness' Josephus, *Bell.* 6, 297ff.); 10.29f.; 11.8; 15.12–16; and the prayers of II Macc. 11.6 and 15.22f. For the martyrdoms see 6.18 – 7.42; 14.37–46.

324. E. Bickermann, *GM*, 147; cf. also B. Niese, op. cit., 301f. and F. M. Abel, *Macc.*, xxviif. and the contemporary examples cited there.

325. Dan. 3.25, 28; 9.22; 10.5ff., 13ff., 20ff.; 12.1. For Qumran see Vol. I, pp. 188f. n. III, 773, and Vol. I, 231, cf. J. T. Milik, *Ten Years of Discovery*, 1959, 87. The epiphanies in II Macc. are apocalyptic conceptions of angels presented in a fundamentally Hellenistic form.

326. Cf. e.g. Asc. Isa. 5.2–14; also the various martyrdoms of the prophets in the *Vita prophetarum*, ed. T. Schermann, TU 31, 3, 1907: 51, Amos; 60, Micah; 74f., Isaiah; 81f., Jeremiah, also *Gen. R.* 65, 22, the martyrdom of Jose b. Joezer. For the expiatory effect of suffering see II Macc. 7.33, 37f. Cf. G. F. Moore, *Judaism* 1, 546ff., and M. Hengel, *Zeloten*, 273. The 'confession narratives', say in Dan. 3 and 6, are a prelude to the history of the martyrs, see M. Smith, Fischer Weltgeschichte, Vol. 6, ed. P. Grimal, 1965, 270. For the *exitus clarorum virorum* see R. Reitzenstein, *Hellenistische Wundererzählungen*, 37f.; M. Hadas, *HCu*, 177ff., and A. Ronconi, *RAC* 6, 1258–68 lit. The starting point here is the report of Plato on the death of Socrates. Cf. also I. Baer, *Zion* 23/24, 1958/59, 20f.

327. E. Bickermann, *PW* 14, 792.

328. A. Geiger, *Urschrift und Übersetzungen der Bibel*, 1857, 226, and J. Freudenthal, op. cit., 129, regarded Jason as a Palestinian. L. Herzfeld, *Geschichte des Volkes Israel*, 1855, 445f., wanted to bring out the connection with I Macc. 8.17. Tcherikover, *HC*, 385, is more cautious. On the one hand we have to take seriously the express derivation of Jason 'from Cyrene', while on the other hand the close connections with Palestine cannot be ignored.

329. I. Baer, op. cit., 20f., 161. We must not overlook the fact that both *creatio ex nihilo* and the resurrection of the body are hardly Platonic notions, despite some echoes of Platonic concepts in II Macc.; cf. below n. III, 326, and R. H. Pfeiffer, op. cit., 515; e.g. it is not chance that the concept of the wisdom of God is absent, and also retreats into the background in Qumran in contrast to the position in Sirach and Wisdom: see Vol. I, p. 221. For condemnation of Greek culture see 4.7–20; 5.15–26; 6.1–9; 14.38; cf. 11.24f. For the opponents of Judas and his followers Jason has a rich arsenal of insults, see R. H. Pfeiffer, op. cit., 513f.; for 'barbarians' or 'barbarian' see 2.21; 4.25; 5.22; 10.4; cf. also 4.47; 7.4: Scythians.

330. πολίτης: II Macc. 4.5, 50; 5.6, 8, 23; 9.19; 15.30 cf. 14.37. πολιτεία: 4.11; 8.17; 13.14; cf. 6.1; 11.25. The term πατρίς is very frequent: 4.1; 5.8f., 15; 8.21, 33; 13.3, 10, 14; 14.18. IV Macc. is again dependent on this 'political terminology' (cf. 3.20; 8.7; 17.9). The term Ἰουδαϊσμός, used for the first time, also belongs in this context, see II Macc. 8.1; 14.38; cf. 2.21 and IV Macc. 4.26.

331. On this see G. Hölscher, *PW* 9, 1982, 1992f. However, Hölscher brings the 'predecessors' of Josephus too close to him, 1993. On this see W. Otto, *PWSuppl* 2, 10–12. For Justus of Tiberias see Schürer 1, 58–63; F. Rühl, *RheinMus* 71, 1916, 289–308, and Schmid/Stählin, *GGL⁶* II, 1, 601f. He seems to have been a highly educated writer with rhetorical training who wrote a history of the Jewish kings from Moses to the death of Agrippa II in AD 100, see Schürer 1, 61 and Rühl, op. cit., 292. In style and presentation his work was superior to that of Josephus, see *Vita* 40.

332. B. Wacholder, *Nicolaus of Damascus*, 52ff.: it was his aim to incorporate a relatively 'objective' account of Jewish history (in contrast to other Greek historians) into the total framework of his world history and thus also to stress the international standing of his master and friend Herod. 'Nicolaus' full account of Biblical history contained Jewish apologetics mixed with Hellenistic embellishments', op. cit., 56.

333. On this see O. Betz, *Offenbarung und Schriftforschung in der Qumransekte*, 1960, 77ff., 83ff., 86.

334. On this see J. Fichtner, *TLZ* 76, 1951, 146–150, and W. Baumgartner, *TR* 5, 1933, 283f., and Vol. I, pp. 289f.

335. For the two traits in the work of the Chronicler see E. Bickerman(n), *From Ezra to the Last of the Maccabees*, 1962, 20–31; here Bickerman draws parallels with Greek history writing: 'The Chronicler, like Hecataeus of Miletus or Herodotus, gives such information concerning the past as appears to him most probable, and corrects the sources in conformity with his own historical standards' (22). For the doctrine of retribution see pp. 24ff.; cf. here the express quotation from Deut. 24.16 in II Chron. 25.4. For the theological background to the historical view of the Chronicler see G. von Rad, *Das Geschichtsbild des chronistischen Werkes*, 1930, passim and D. Rössler, *Gesetz und Geschichte*, ²1962, 38ff.

336. R. H. Pfeiffer, op. cit., 512: 'Jason is much more interested in theology than is the author of I Maccabees.' For the doctrine of retribution see loc. cit.; cf. 4.38, 42; 5.9f.; 7.19, 35; 8.33; 13.5–8; 15.31–35 and above all 9.8–28: Antiochus IV dies through being eaten by worms, the manner of death of the enemy of God: see P. Wendland, *Hellenistisch–römischer Kultur*, 1912, 330 n. 6; it also appears as early as Herodotus 4, 205. Cf. also the excursus of the epitomator in 6.12–16. See also above, n. 316.

337. N. N. Glatzer, *Geschichte der talmudischen Zeit*, 1937, 11; cf. also D. Rössler, *Gesetz und Geschichte*, ²1962, 20f.

338. On this see U. Kahrstedt, *Syrische Territorien in hellenistischer Zeit*, AGG, NF 19, 2, 1927, 137–45; E. Bickermann, *ZNW* 32, 1933, 253f.; M. A. Beek, *OTS* 2, 1943, 121–32, 141ff., whose transposition of the foundation of the temple in Leontopolis to 270 BC is surely incorrect. Tcherikover, *HC*, 279f., on the other hand, puts it too late, at 145 BC. Onias IV fled to Alexandria after the naming of Alcimus in 163 (?) BC and will have founded the temple and the military colony in Leontopolis a little later; cf. *Antt.* 12, 387f.; 13, 62–73; 20, 236.

339. On II Macc. 1.1–9 see E. Bickermann, op. cit., 233–54; M. A. Beek, *OTS* 2, 1943, 138–43, against R. H. Pfeiffer, op. cit., 508. 1.1–9 would be quite incomprehensible as an edificatory work of Alexandrian epistolography.

340. According to E. Bickermann, op. cit., 234, the work comes from the time around 60 BC; for its origin in Jerusalem see his short note in *JBL* 63, 1944, 357. N. Walter, op. cit., 17 and 18 n. 2, conjectures that it originated in Alexandria. In any event the legend 2.1ff. is Palestinian and also appears in Eupolemus, see above n. 278; the miracle of fire in 1.19ff. is probably of Iranian origin. C. C. Torrey's hypothesis of an original Aramaic version, *ZAW* 20, 1900, 225–42, and *JAOS* 60, 1940, 119–50, is unconvincing; the same is true of the defence of the authenticity of the letter by Abel/Starcky, op. cit., 27ff. However, the objections

to a late date in Abel, *Macc.* 289, are worth considering. After the loss of independence, such influence on the Jews in Egypt hardly seems to make sense any longer. The question of the origin of the epitome is closely connected with this. Bunge (n. 296), 56ff. posits a genuine work with some interpolations.

341. See E. Bickerman(n), *JBL* 63, 1944, 339–62, and by way of supplement and correction, R. Marcus, *JBL* 64, 1945, 269–71, and P. Kahle, *The Cairo Geniza*, ²1959, 213 n. 1.

342. Cf. 3.13d (B 4); 10.3g (F 7); for the tendencies of the Greek book of Esther see above all E. Bickermann, *PAAJR* 20, 1951, 101–33, and O. Eissfeldt, *The Old Testament*, 591f. It is improbable that these abruptly anti-Greek expansions were only added in Alexandria at a later date (thus Hautsch, *PW*, 2R. 2, 1600f.). Josephus had access to the additions in *Antt.* 11, 184–296.

343. 8.12k (E. 10); 9.24; for the Macedonians in Alexandria see above, n. I, 94. Altheim/Stiehl, *Die aramäische Sprache unter den Achämeniden*, 210–3, want to put this expansion in 130 BC on the basis of the Parthian successes in the east of the Seleucid kingdom.

344. 1.11 (A 11); 4.17a–z(C); 5.1aff. (D 1ff.); 8.12d, q, r, t (E 4, 16, 17, 20); 10.3a (F 1). The dream at the beginning and its interpretation at the end of the book, like the edict of the great king, are also meant to strengthen the religious components of the book (against O. Eissfeldt, op. cit., 591f.), cf. II Macc. 15.11ff. and 9.13ff.

345. Cf. e.g. Jub. 30.7ff., 14ff., and on this M. Hengel, op. cit., 192f.

346. See O. Eissfeldt, *The Old Testament*, 802: 'B and E were written originally in Greek . . . , ACD and F presuppose . . . a Hebrew or Aramaic original'. Similarly R. H. Pfeiffer, op. cit., 308ff.

347. See E. Bickermann, op. cit. (n. 341 above), 335ff.

348. E. Bickermann, *GM*, 145 and *JBL* 63, 1944, 357: the slavishly literal translation suggests that this was carried out in Palestine.

349. For later redactional or translation work on the LXX during the first and second centuries AD in Palestine see D. Barthélémy, *Les Devanciers d'Aquila*, SVT 10, 1963, 15ff., 148ff., 271f. He conjectures that the LXX redactor Theodotion was identical with Jonathan b. Uzziel, the pupil of Hillel, to whom the Prophet Targum was later falsely ascribed. *Meg.* 3a could contain a reference to his translation of Daniel (op. cit., 150f.), see also below, n. III, 663. Both his translation work and the later translation activity of Aquila presuppose the tendency to religious influence and control on the Diaspora which already begins in the Hasmonean period. For Theodotion see S. Lieberman, *Greek in Jewish Palestine*, 1942, 17ff., and M. Smith, *BJRL* 40, 1957/58, 482 n. 3; for the work of the Palestinian redactors of the LXX in general see E. Bickerman(n), *Alexander Marx Jubilee Volume* I, 1950, 164. Finally see the general comment by B. Lifshitz, *RB* 72, 1965, 521.

350. See Billerbeck 4, 414 w, x; R. Hanhart, *VT* 12, 1962, 144f.

351. On this see already Z. Frankel, *Vorstudien zur Septuaginta*, 1841, 8ff., 105ff., 185ff., and *Über den Einfluss der palästinischen Exegese auf die alexandrinische Hermeneutik*, 1851. For the same problem see also J. Freudenthal, *Hellenistische Studien*, 1873, 65ff. and P. Katz, *ZNW* 47, 1956, 210f. Palestinian and Alexandrian exegesis had a mutual influence on each other, see Vol. I, pp.

169, 171ff. The influence of Hellenistic mythology (on this see H. A. Redpath, *AJT* 9, 1905, 34f.) and philosophy on the LXX as a whole is small: see J. Freudenthal, *JQR* 2, 1889/90, 205–22; E. Zeller, *PhG*⁶ III, 2, 274ff.; R. Marcus, 'Jewish and Greek Elements in the Septuagint', in *L. Ginzberg Jubilee Volume*, 1945, 227–45; cf. also R. Hanhart, *VT* 12, 1962, 139–62, and E. Bickerman(n), *PAAJR* 28, 1959, 11f., especially on the language. On the other hand, Bickermann defends with good reason the existence of an official translation of the Pentateuch under Philadelphus, pp. 7ff., 13ff. For the uniqueness of the LXX in the Hellenistic–Roman period see 38.

352. J. Freudenthal, *Hellenistische Studien*, 129, presupposes a lengthy and perhaps permanent stay of the author in Jerusalem on the basis of the description and glorification of Jerusalem in four books by the older Philo (FGrHist 729). It is impossible to move beyond conjecture in view of the small number of fragments which have been preserved. The assumption of M. Hadas, *HCu*, 100, that the work of the Jewish tragedian arose in Jerusalem (see below, n. III, 10), is pure speculation.

353. See H. F. Weiss, *Klio* 43–45, 1965, 307 n. 3.

354. In this sense Bousset/Gressmann, 2–5, already speak of 'Hellenistic Judaism'; cf. also W. G. Kümmel, *Heilsgeschehen und Geschichte, Gesammelte Aufsätze*, 1965, 15 and 377, and G. Pfeiffer, *Ursprung und Wesen der Hypostasenvorstellungen im Judentum*, 1967, 95 n. 427: 'The Judaism of that time is always Hellenistic Judaism – sometimes more, sometimes less.'

355. Cf. CIJ 2, 261ff., no. 1256: the Nicanor inscription; 1266; 1282; 1393; 1337–41; 1344; 1350 (cf. 1351–4); 1366; 1372–4; 1378; see also the indications of a homeland in 1283: Bethel and 1372ff.: Scythopolis. Further bilingual inscriptions in P. B. Bagatti/J. T. Milik, *Gli Scavi del Dominus flevit*, I, 1958, Stud. bibl.frans. 13, 1958, 84 no. 13 ab; 97f. no. 37. On the whole, Hebrew–Aramaic and Greek inscriptions alternate at random. Cf. also R. de Vaux, *RB* 65, 1958, 409, and N. Avigad, *IEJ* 12, 1962, 1–12, a family tomb with Greek inscriptions, two of them bilingual, and E. M. Meyers, *Jewish Ossuaries*, 1971, 48ff.

356. Acts 15.22, 27, 32 etc.: I Thess. 1.1; II Cor. 1.19 etc. For the form of the name see W. F. Arndt and F. W. Gingrich, *A Greek–English Lexicon of the New Testament*, 1957, 758.

357. Cf. Phil. 3.4; cf. Gal. 1.13f.; on this see G. Bornkamm, *RGG*³ 5, 167, on the 'bilingual character of the family 'and its stay in Jerusalem.

358. On this see B. Lifshitz, *ZDPV* 78, 1962, 77ff.

359. The conjecture of W. G. Kümmel, *Introduction to the New Testament*, 1966, 84, that it is difficult to assume composition in Palestine for linguistic reasons therefore needs to be examined carefully again. Presumably the author of the First Gospel was a multilingual 'Graeco–Palestinian'; cf. also J. Jeremias, *ZNW* 50, 1959, 270–4 = *Abba*, 1966, 255–60.

III

The Encounter and Conflict between Palestinian Judaism and the Spirit of the Hellenistic Age

1. Phoenicia had long had strong economic and cultural connections with the Aegean; considerable artistic and economic influence is noticeable there even before Alexander's expedition. The question is, however, whether one can suppose an influence extending to ideas, or even a literary influence. The Greek mercenaries in the service of the Jewish, Egyptian, Babylonian and Persian kings might be involved as intermediaries (see Vol. I, pp. 12ff., 32ff., 61f. and nn. II, 26–7).

2. See e.g. W. Baumgartner, 'Israelitisch-griechische Sagenbeziehungen', *Zum AT und seiner Umwelt*, 1959, 145–78, esp. 171ff.; also the investigations by C. Gordon, 'Homer and the Bible', *HUCA* 26, 1955, 43–108, and *Before the Bible*, 1962 (though these are disputed; further literature, ibid., 303ff.); F. Dornseiff, 'Hesiods Werke und Tage und das alte Morgenland', *Antike und Altes Orient*, [2]1959, 72–95; F. Dirlmeier, 'Homerisches Epos und Orient', *RheinMus* 98, 1955, 18–37; P. Walcot, 'Hesiod and the Didactic Literature of the Near East', *REG* 75, 1962, 13–36; the collection *Éléments Orientaux dans la Religion Grecque Ancienne*, 1960; M. C. Astour, *Hellenosemitica*, 1965, who deals with the many-sided mythological and historical connections between the Aegean and the Semitic Orient in the second millennium BC.

3. See U. Hölscher, 'Anaximander und die Anfänge der griechischen Philosophie II', *Hermes* 81, 1953, 385–418, and the supplementation and correction by O. Eissfeldt in the collected volume *Éléments Orientaux*, cited above, pp. 3ff., 14; also H. Schwabl, in op. cit., 41 n. 1 and *PW Suppl.* 9, 1484, 1505ff., 1513ff.: Thales (cf. U. Hölscher, op. cit., 388f., and above n. II, 212); 1515ff.: Anaximander. No direct dependence of Plato on the East has been demonstrated, although he uses oriental (e.g. Egyptian) traditions (see *Timaeus* 21e ff.) and there was speculation at an early date about visits supposed to have been made by him to Egypt, Phoenicia and Babylonia, see T. Hopfner, *Orient und griechische Philosophie*, BhAO 4, 1925, 7ff.; cf. J. Kerschensteiner, *Plato und das Orient*, 1945, passim, against W. Jaeger, *Aristoteles*, [2]1955, 133ff.; but see W. Baumgartner, op. cit., 175 n. 4. On the interest of Plato in his old age in Egyptian and Syrian (Chaldean) astronomy see also E. des Places, *MUSJ* 37, 1960/61, 201–5, lit., on the basis of *Epinomis* 986e–987d, and cf. on this Theophrastus on the Jews: see Vol. I, pp. 256f. A member of the Academy was himself a 'Chaldean' (op. cit., 203 n. 4). Now see above all M. L. West, *Early Greek Philosophy and the Orient*, 1971.

4. Diels, *Vorsokratiker* 1, 44 fr. 2 and K. v. Fritz, *PW* 19, 2025ff., and in detail M. L. West, op. cit., 1–75.

5. F. Dornseiff, *Echtheitsfragen in der Antik-Griechischen Literatur*, 1939, 26; see also E. Schürer 3, 255f., 251f.

6. L. Pirot, *L'oeuvre exégétique de Théodore de Mopsueste*, 1913, 131–4; the author, '*paganica scientia esse eruditus*', imitated the pagan = Greek tragic poets (132f. n. 3); see also J. M. Vosté, *RB* 38, 1929, 390–3. This conjecture was taken up by R. Lowth, *Praelectiones de sacra Poesi Hebraeorum*, 1753 (non vidi). C. Kuhl, *TR* 21, 1953, 204–306, gives a survey of more recent attempts to connect Job with the Greek tradition.

7. See above all H. M. Kallen, *The Book of Job as a Greek Tragedy*, 1918 (repr. 1959), 19ff.; cf. M. Hadas, *HCu*, 136ff., and C. G. Montefiore, *HTR* 12, 1919, 219–24.

8. N. Schmidt, *The Message of the Poets*, Vol. 7, see *The Message of the Bible*, 1907, 76ff., 87ff., 91ff.; M. Jastrow, *The Book of Job*, 1920, 177ff., 185ff. is critical; J. J. Slotki, *ExpT* 39, 1927/28, 131–4, presupposes 'a careful study of the Prometheus Bound' by the author of Job (134). W. A. Irwin, *JR* 30, 1950, 90–108, gives a more restrained ·verdict: it is not impossible that the author knew Aeschylus, but analogies do not amount to dependence; see also C. J. Lindblom in *Dragma Martino P. Nilsson*, 1939, 280–7, and H. G. May, *ATR* 34, 1952, 240–6, both of whom rightly observe that in Job, as opposed to Prometheus, the solution does not come from a change on God's side, but through the subjection of Job. A. Alvarez de Miranda, *Anthologia Annua* 2, 1954, 207–37, gives a detailed comparison. C. Kuhl, op. cit., 306, comes to the conclusion: 'We must consider more than before the question whether the poet of Job was familiar with the tragedy of Aeschylus.' F. M. Heichelheim, *ZRGG* 3, 1951, 253 n. 3, believes that the poet of Job could have come to know Greek tragedy perhaps about 460 BC, when the Athenians settled in Dor (see above, n. I, 280). However, all this is very improbable. At best there remain certain analogies between late wisdom and Greek thought.

9. K. Fries, *Das philosophische Gespräch von Hiob bis Platon*, 1904, who at the same time refers to earlier models of 'philosophical dialogue' in the *Iliad*, Egypt, etc. O. Holtzmann, in B. Stade, *Geschichte des Volkes Israel* 2, 1888, 348–51, transfers the book of Job to the Ptolemaic period: 'Without doubt (!) we have here a Hebrew imitation of the philosophical dialogue in Plato'; cf. also N. Schmidt, op. cit., 80, 84. Even N. Peters, *Das Buch Job*, 1928, 58, sees parallels to the ideas of Greek poetry and poesy and will not exclude the possibility of acquaintance; cf. on the other hand M. Jastrow, op. cit., 181: 'Perhaps in a very general way one may conjecture that a wave of rationalism spread over the ancient Orient in the fifth and succeeding centuries.'

10. In Eusebius, *Pr.Ev.* 9, 28f., GCS VIII, 1, 524–38, ed. Mras.

11. G. Fohrer, *Das Buch Hiob*, 1963, 47.

12. On the question of Job and 'wisdom' see H. Gese, *Lehre und Wirklichkeit*, 1958, 1ff. and 74ff.

13. R. H. Pfeiffer, *Introduction to the OT*, 1948, 679, terms the unknown author 'the most learned man up to his time known to us', see also H. Richter, *ZAW* 70, 1958, 1–20. Even R. H. Pfeiffer, who rejects any dependence of Job on Greek models and – probably wrongly – believes that it was composed about 600 by an Edomite (op. cit., 678–83), stresses the peculiarity of Job's conception of

God (op. cit., 703): 'Job's theology is more akin to the Greek than to the Israelite notion . . . the function and attributes of the Deity in Job indicate that the author conceived his God primarily as a cosmic force, not as the patron God of a nation.' G. von Rad, *Old Testament Theology* 1, 417, speaks of the 'theological boundary situation' of the work, see also P. Humbert, 'Le modernisme de Job', *SVT* 3, 1955, 150–61, esp. 164. Like Koheleth, Job has also been corrected for doctrine by the addition of the speeches of Elihu: see G. Hölscher, *Das Buch Hiob*, ²1952, 6f.

14. G. Fohrer, op. cit., 552–7. The 'speech of God' in Job 38–40.14, however, expresses far more God's absolute sovereignty than his 'saving, blessing concern' (G. von Rad, op. cit., 1, 418). God's omnipotence is the demonstration of his righteousness, not of his concern.

15. See the survey in C. Kuhl, op. cit., 314ff.: 700–200 BC; G. Fohrer, op. cit., 42f.: fifth to third century BC, cf. O. Eissfeldt, *The Old Testament*, 470: the fourth century seems most likely to be right. G. Hölscher, op. cit., 7f., puts it relatively late, between 400 and 200 BC.

16. M. Rosler, אשכולות (*ΣΧΟΛΙΑ*) *Commentationes de Antiquitate Classica* 1, 1954, 33–48; H. Graetz, *Schir Ha-Schirim*, 1871, 67ff.; N. Schmidt, op. cit., 229ff., and C. Gebhardt, *Das Lied der Lieder*, 1931, 19ff., already put forward a similar view; the last mentioned made a special comparison with the mimes among the *Idylls* of Theocritus; see, however, the criticism of K. Budde, *ChrW* 45, 1931, 957–60. Cf. also M. Hadas, *Journal of History of Ideas* 19, 1958, 5, and *HCu*, 159ff., over against C. Schneider, *Gnomon* 33, 1961, 308. For further examples see W. Rudolph, *Das Buch Ruth, Das Hohe Lied*, 1962, 117.

17. F. Dornseiff, *ZDMG* 90, 1936, 593f.; cf. e.g. Philodemus, *Anth.Gr.* 5, 132, and Song of Songs 7.1–7.

18. M. Friedländer, *Griechische Philosophie im Alten Testament*, 1904, passim; objections are, however, raised by W. Swart, op. cit. (n. 52 below), and E. Sellin, *Die Spuren griechischer Philosophie im Alten Testament*, 1905, 17ff., though the latter will not exclude some traces of 'influences of Greek culture and life style' in Prov. 1–9 and Job 28; 29.18 (Phoenix saga, see below, n. 553); there is also a critical survey in P. Heinisch, 'Griechische Philosophie und AT', *Biblische Zeitfragen* 6/7, 1913, 15ff.

19. *Geschichte des Volkes Israels*, 1929, III, 2, 733. Cf. also Bousset/ Gressmann, 497 n. 2.

20. K. Galling, *BRL*, 121; O. Eissfeldt, *The Old Testament*, 22–4; Fohrer, *Introduction to the Old Testament*, 85.

21. For the additions to Esther and the festal letter from II Maccabees see Vol. I, pp. 101f.; on *Ep. Jer.* see O. Eissfeldt, op. cit., 594f., and R. H. Pfeiffer, *A History of NT Times*, 429f. For the Baruch literature see Syr. Bar. 78ff., and cf. the so-called 'remains of the Sayings of Baruch', trans. in Riessler, *Altjüdisches Schrifttum* 6, 17ff. (912); 7,23ff. (914f.).

22. W. Rudolph, *Jeremia*, ²1958, 166ff., and O. Eissfeldt, *The Old Testament*, 22f.; for the Baruch literature see also Jer. 36.4f., 32. The edict of Nebuchadnezzar in Dan. 3.31ff. could have as a model the various edicts of the Persian kings in Ezra 1.2ff.; 4.17ff.; 5.6ff.; 6.3ff.; cf. also Dan. 6.26ff.; the aretalogical style can

already be found in the Prayer of Nabonidus (see below, n.36). Cf. also the legendary letter of Elijah, II Chron. 21.12–15.

23. O. Eissfeldt, op. cit., 38; especially on Esther see R. Stiehl, *WZKM* 53, 1957, 6–9; Fohrer, op. cit., 253f.; see also already Bousset/Gressmann, 495f.

24. M. Braun, *History and Romance in Graeco-Oriental Literature*, 1938, 44–93; cf. M. Hadas, *HCu*, 153ff. For Josephus see M. Braun, *Griechischer Roman und Hellenistische Geschichtsschreibung*, 1934, 23–117. The version of *T.Jos.* is the earlier, which would suggest a non-Christian, Jewish origin for the work; see the discussion in O. Eissfeldt, op. cit., 40ff.

25. For Joseph and Asenath see now C. Burchard, *Untersuchungen zu Joseph und Aseneth*, 1965, 140ff.: first century BC; perhaps the eirenic character of the work indicates that it was composed in pre-Roman, Ptolemaic times, when the relationship between Jews and non-Jews in Egypt was not so tense. For Artapanus see above, n.II, 262, and M. Hadas, *HCu*, 172.

26. For the origin of the romance see K. Kerényi, *Die griechische orientalische Romanliteratur . . .*, ²1962, 206–28; cf. 24ff., 44ff., 229ff.; see also R. Merkelbach, *Roman und Mysterium in der Antike*, 1962, 333ff.: 'Greek and oriental elements were mixed in the ancient romance . . . the external form of the romance is essentially Greek'. For the romance of Ninus (P. Ber. 6926 A) see in F. Zimmermann, *Griechische Romanpapyri*, 1936, 13–35; cf. also 36–40 = P.Ox 1826, the son of king Sesonchis. On Iambulus see W. Kroll, *PW* 9, 681ff., and F. Altheim, *Weltgeschichte Asiens* I, 155ff.

27. Herodotus 9, 108–13: Xerxes and the wife of Masistes; 2, 111: the blind Pherus; 2, 121: the treasure house of Rampsinit; 1.8–13: Gyges and Candaules; on this see also W. Aly, *PW* 17, 1174ff.

28. Quotation from Eissfeldt, op. cit., 38; on Ruth and Susanna see op. cit., 477ff., 589f.; cf. also Fohrer, op. cit., 250, and R. H. Pfeiffer, op. cit., 449ff. Even if the last version of the narratives possibly goes back to Hellenistic times, the material is older. The Daniel of the Susanna narrative still emerges as the type of the wise judge, according to Ezek. 14.14, 20, and not as the Babylonian and Persian official of the Daniel legends.

29. The narrative cycle about the fortune and misfortune of the wise Croesus in Herodotus could also be included among the 'wisdom narratives'; it comes from the milieu of Asia Minor and Persia: see I, 29–35, 86–91; 3, 36. For the Egyptian milieu of the Joseph 'Novelle' see G. von Rad, *The Problem of the Hexateuch*, 1966, 293ff.

30. For the aretalogy in the Jewish milieu see E. Bi(c)kerman(n), *AIPHOS* 7, 1939–44, 34 n.1, and M. Hadas, *HCu*, 170ff.

31. As a translation of *hōd* (in M v.19); cf. also Symmachus, Ps.29 (30). 6 in Origen, *Hexapla*, ed. Field, 2, 130.

32. Isa.42.8; 43.21; 63.7 as a translation for *tehillā*, cf. also Hab.3.3 and in the NT I Peter 2.9 and II Peter 2.3. For Alexandrian Judaism, cf. Philo, *Vit.cont.* 26.

33. Op. cit., 34ff.

34. R. Reitzenstein, *Hellenistische Wundererzählungen*, ²1963, 35.

35. O. Eissfeldt, op. cit., 405; Fohrer, op. cit., 442.

36. For the same feature in the book of Daniel see Dan.2.46ff.; 3.28ff.; the whole creed-like edict 3.31–4.34; 5.29; 6.25ff.; for the prayer of Nabonidus see

R. Meyer, *Das Gebet des Nabonid*, BAL 107, 3, 1962, first publication by J. T. Milik, *RB* 63, 1956, 407–15.

37. W. Aly, *PW Suppl*, 6, 15, cf. also Crusius *PW* 2, 670, and A. Kiefer, *Aretalogische Studien*, Diss. 1929, there 2ff., the evidence for the terms ἀρεταλογία and ἀρεταλόγος, also 38ff. for a collection of aretalogies; see, however, the critical comments in W. Aly, op. cit., 13ff. R. Merkelbach, *Roman und Mysterium*, 1962, 333–6, derives the Greek romance from the Isis aretalogy. A collection of texts with comments in V. Longo, *Aretalogie nel mondo Greco*, I, 1969.

38. A. Bentzen, *Daniel*, ²1952, 11; see Vol. I, pp. 272ff., nn. 516–25; 193f.

39. On this see H. Gese, *RGG³* 6, 1578f.

40. For pseudepigraphy see also Vol. I, pp. 205f., 216. In Alexandria the names of authors are known to us only from fragmentary works preserved through Alexander Polyhistor. The anonymous or pseudonymous work is by far the most predominant in Palestine. J. Lebram, *VT* 15, 1965, 215, sees in the mention of the author's name a typical characteristic of wisdom literature and points to Prov. 25.1; 30.1; 31.1, and to the Samaritan Marqah in the third or fourth century AD. But Prov. 25.1 names two well-known kings of the pre-exilic period and 30.1; 31.1 very old Ishmaelite wisdom teachers from outside Israel. The rule was in fact anonymity or pseudonymity, as is shown by Koheleth (see Vol. I, 129f.) and Prov. 1–9. Ben Sira and the naming of authorities in the Rabbinic tradition are, however, a parallel to Marqah. The naming of authorities emerges for the first time from Simon the Just, i.e. it is a phenomenon of the Hellenistic period, see Vol. I, pp. 81f. Cf. W. Speyer, *Die literarische Fälschung im Altertum*, 1971, 15ff., 150.

41. On this see the provisional observation by R. Meyer, op. cit., 7f.

42. For the background to the schism see Josephus, *Antt.* 11, 302ff., 306ff., 324ff. The Torah was possibly introduced among the Samaritans by the son of the Jewish high priest, Manasseh, who went over to them. See also above, n. I, 58.

43. As in this enumeration the canonical books which were largely established about 60 BC, the approximate time of composition of the forged letter, are not included (see Sirach, Prologue 8ff., and Josephus, *c.Ap.* I, 37ff.), and furthermore the decrees of the (Persian) kings on sacrifice are mentioned, this note seems to have a historical background, see Abel, *Macc.*, 307ff.

44. Ed. J. A. Sanders, *The Psalm Scroll*, DJDJ IV, 1965, 53–93.

45. M. Smith, *Fischer Weltgeschichte*, Vol. 5, 1965, 365; cf. R. H. Pfeiffer, *Introduction to the OT*, 1948, 655, and M. Hadas, *HCu*, 23: 'A new literature arose to answer the needs of ordinary people.'

46. We also find this chronological interest in the first known Jewish teacher in Alexandria, the chronographer Demetrius, at the time of Ptolemy IV Philopator, 222–204 BC, see Vol. I, p. 69. The Palestinian Hellenist Eupolemus based himself above all on Chronicles in his historical work, see Vol. I, pp. 94ff.

47. See Vol. I, pp. 256ff. The self-awareness of the Jews at the beginning of the Hellenistic period is reflected in the anecdotes of Ps. Hecataeus in Josephus, *c.Ap.* I, 187ff., 192f., 201ff.

48. On this see the comments of R. Hanhart about the character of the LXX as a translation, *VT* 12, 1962, 158ff., esp. 161: the LXX appeared as 'something completely heterogeneous over against Hellenism'. R. Marcus, 'Jewish and

Greek Elements in the Septuagint', *L. Ginzberg Jubilee Volume*, 1945, 239f. argues emphatically, among other things, that the deletion of certain anthropomorphisms from the Hebrew text in the LXX, which was apparently done on the basis of Greek influence, took place in parallel fashion in the Targums. Further, see Vol. I, p. 102 and below, n. 372.

49. M. Hengel, *Zeloten*, 154–234; see Vol. I, pp. 292ff., 306f.

50. R. Meyer, *TDNT* 7, 49: 'a strand of belief . . . which was not interwoven into ongoing dogmatic development. It may thus be described as conservative' (see Vol. I, pp. 226f.).

51. K. Galling, *TR* NF 6, 1934, 361.

52. A critical survey of earlier attempts to interpret Koheleth in the light of Greek philosophy is to be found in P. Kleinert, *ThStKr* 56, 1883, 761–82, and 82, 1909, 493–529; see also W. Swart, *De invloed van der griekschen Geest op de boeken Sprewken, Prediker, Job*, 1908, 23–106. For Epicurus see already Jerome, *in Eccl.*, on 9.7, *PL* 23, 1072; clearly in Voltaire, see O. Loretz, *Qoheleth und das Alte Orient*, 1964, 49 n. 1; further earlier commentators there, who wanted to see K. as an Epicurean; cf. also M. Hadas, *HCu*, 17. Both Epicurean and Stoic influence is assumed more frequently: see W. F. Albright, *From the Stone Age to Christianity*, 1940, 352; M. Hadas, *HCu*, 140ff.; John Bright, *A History of Israel*, rev. ed., 1972, 452 n. 39, who assumes only indirect influence. For the relationship to the Stoa see E. Zeller, *PhGr*[6] III, 2, 301–7, and the literature in O. Loretz, op. cit., 50 n. 37. For the Cynics and Cyrenaicans see L. Levy, *Das Buch Qoheleth*, 1912, 12ff.; for Heraclitus, E. Pfleiderer, *Heraklit*, 1886, 256–69; for Theognis and Greek gnomic poetry, H. Ranston, *Ecclesiastes and the Early Greek Wisdom Literature*, 1925, and the criticism by K. Galling, op. cit., 363ff.; cf. also *PW* 22, 1831. H. W. Hertzberg, *Der Prediger*, 1963, 59f., would concede the possibility of an indirect acquaintance of Koheleth with Theognis. For the Cynic-Stoic diatribe see P. Kleinert, *ThStKr* 82, 1909, 508, etc., and the criticism of O. Loretz, op. cit., 32f., 55f. As the diatribe only developed as a genre in the third century BC (see W. Capelle, *RAC* 3, 994ff.), Koheleth can hardly have made use of it. J. Pedersen, *RHPR* 10, 1930, 333–44; H. J. Blieffert, *Weltanschauung und Gottesglauben im Buche K.*, Diss. 1938, 84–8, and R. Gordis, *Kohelet*, 1951, 51ff., also reject any direct dependence of Koheleth on Greek philosophy. On the other hand, in view of the international character of wisdom, we need not exclude an acquaintance with Greek sayings wisdom, which does not have to be a literary one. For a fundamental investigation, see now R. Braun, *Koheleth und sein Verhältnis zur literarischen Bildung und Popularphilosophie*, Diss. Erlangen 1971.

53. On this see W. Baumgartner, *TR* NF 5, 1933, 262ff., 281ff.; K. Galling, op. cit., 366f., and *ZAW* 50, 1932, 293ff.; here above all there are Egyptian parallels; R. Kroeber, *Der Prediger*, 1963, 48ff., 59ff., and – very one-sidedly – O. Loretz, op. cit., 53ff., 90ff. For the themes in Koheleth deriving from Old Testament wisdom literature see the collection by K. Galling, *ZAW* 50, 1932, 293, and O. Loretz, op. cit., 196ff. F. Dornseiff, *ZDMG* 89, 1935, 246ff., puts forward the possibility that the relationships between Greek thinking and Koheleth go back to early connections between the ancient East and Greece.

54. L. Levy, op. cit., 13ff., noted a number of Graecisms; critical comments

78

Chapter III

in K. Galling, *TR* NF 6, 1934, 362f.; R. Gordis, op. cit., 358 n. 3; O. Loretz, op. cit., 45ff. Suggestions of Graecisms are indicated by W. Svart, op. cit., 98ff., and H. W. Hertzberg, op. cit., 56; O. Eissfeldt, *The Old Testament*, 498f.; R. H. Pfeiffer, *Introduction to the OT*, 1948, 729, and Fohrer, op. cit., 340. Cf. R. Braun (n. 52).

55. Op. cit., 56. As Loretz considers neither the personality of the author nor the period in which he is writing, and rejects the possibility of alterations by the writer of the epilogue (40, 144, 166ff., 296ff.), he comes to an exaggerated, apologetic view of the whole which does not do justice to the tensions and depths of the work. G. Hölscher, *Geschichte der israelitischen und jüdischen Religion*, 1922, 182, doubts that there is any Graeco–Hellenistic influence in Koheleth. But as he wants to reduce the influence of Hellenism in the third and second centuries BC in Palestine and the Orient in general to a minimum, and can hardly continue to maintain this general attitude, his judgment is prejudiced.

56. E. Meyer, *UAC* 2, 39 n. 1; K. Galling, *TR* NF 6, 1934, 357. Nevertheless, F. Dornseiff, op. cit., 248, on 9.13–16; H. W. Hertzberg, op. cit., 50ff., on 8.2ff. and 10.4ff., 16; and K. D. Schunck, *VT* 9, 1959, 192–201 on 4.13–16, have again seen concrete allusions to individual historical events. They misunderstand the 'parabolic character' of these instances, see K. Galling, loc. cit., cf. *ZAW* 50, 1932, 286f., and *RGG*[3] 5, 513. The attempt by A. D. Corré, *VT* 4, 1954, 416–8, on 2.3, to demonstrate in Koheleth, by means of a textual emendation, an attempt to remove the marks of circumcision for which there is evidence in the time of the reform in Jerusalem after 175 BC, is misguided; see also O. Eissfeldt, *The Old Testament*, 498–500.

57. H. W. Hertzberg, op. cit., 28ff.; R. Kroeber, op. cit., 28; relatively speaking, Koheleth has the most Aramaisms among the books of the Old Testament; cf. M. Wagner, *Die lexikalischen und grammatikalischen Aramaismen*, BZAW 96, 1966, 142, 145f.

58. Striving for riches: 4.8; 5.10ff., 18; 6.2; 7.11 (see also Vol. I, pp. 49ff.). For the Ptolemaic administration and the oppression of the poor: 5.7; 'in the province' (*meḏīnā*), cf. 4.1 and 7.7. The textually difficult 5.8 could indicate the interest of the Ptolemaic kings in agricultural produce (see above, n. I, 399). The agricultural undertakings of 'Solomon', 2.4ff., with parks (*pareḏēsīm*, Persian loanword, Vol. I, p. 44), domains, artificial irrigation (see above, n. I, 363–5), would also fit best in the Ptolemaic period; cf. E. R. Bevan, *History of Egypt*, 1927, 78. On the power of the king see 8.2ff.: K. Galling, *ZAW* 50, 1932, 294f., and *Die 5 Megilloth*, HAT 18, 1940, 79, sees here the ὅρκος βασιλικός of the Ptolemies. The question remains whether in this textually difficult passage we should not follow H. W. Hertzberg, op. cit., 50f., 163ff., in seeing a warning against apostasy, which was always an acute possibility, since in the third century Palestine was in the centre of the tension between Ptolemies and Seleucids. However, the passage gives no help towards a more exact dating. Rostovtzeff, *HW* 1, 350, refers to the work of informers under the Ptolemies in connection with 10.20.

59. P. Humbert, *Recherches sur les sources égyptiennes*, 1929, 107ff., already saw Egyptian parallels, but he exaggerates in supposing that Koheleth was composed in Egypt (113) and has a knowledge of Demotic (124). For the royal

testament see K. Galling, *ZAW* 50, 1932, 298f., cf. O. Eissfeldt, *The Old Testament*, 499, and the literature given in notes 1 and 2. The objections of O. Loretz, op. cit., 57ff., will not hold. For Pap.Insinger see K. Galling, *TR* NF 6, 1934, 366f.; O. Loretz, op. cit., 84ff.: and R. Kroeber, op. cit., 53, 57f.: 'The contents and the imagery of the two works have so many points of contact that we must assume some literary acquaintance. However, statements on the same subject are often diametrically opposed.' For a translation see A. Volten, *Das demotische Weisheitsbuch*, Analecta Aegyptica II, 1941. B. Gemser, *SVT* 7, 1960, 102–28, points to certain parallels between Koheleth and the equally late Egyptian *Teaching of Onchsheshonqy*, cf. especially 125f.; see also O. Loretz, op. cit., 86ff. On the whole, however, Koheleth's thinking goes its own way: 'As far as content is concerned, the belief and thought of this material are so completely fused together that it always clarifies and enriches, but never defines' (R. Kroeber, op. cit., 56).

60. R. Kroeber, op. cit., 64f., 67ff.; H. W. Hertzberg, op. cit., 46ff.; O. Eissfeldt, *The Old Testament*, 491, lit.; 683 n.18.

61. R. Kroeber, op. cit., 47, cf. the enumeration in n.9; for the names cited there see also W. Zimmerli, *Die Weisheit des Predigers Salomo*, 1936, 28 n.2. O. Eissfeldt, *The Old Testament*, 498; W. Rudolph, *Vom Buche Kohelet*, 1959, 16f.: 'It cannot be denied that this whole way of thinking only became possible in the time of Hellenistic world culture . . . an important testimony to the historical controversy between Judaism and Hellenism.' More cautiously K. Galling, *RGG*[3] 5, 513: 'There can be no question of real Graecisms. So we may affirm only a degree of affinity with Hellenistic views.'

62. See Vol.I, pp.115f. and n.52 above; E. Meyer, *UAC* 2, 35; on Marcus Aurelius see H. J. Blieffert, op. cit., 92–94; cf. also W. Rudolph, op. cit., 17. H. L. Ginsberg, *Studies in Kohelet*, 1950, 43f., cites a whole series of parallels from the Hellenistic period, above all from Menander. R. Braun (n.51 above) has the largest collection of parallels.

63. K. Galling, *ZTK* 58, 1961, 1.

64. Cf. K. Galling, *ZAW* 50, 1932, 280f.: 'I statements and Thou addresses' are 'concretizations of wisdom'; see, however, id., *Prediger Salomo*, HAT 18, 1940, 48: even if they should not be 'evaluated in autobiographical terms', they are still 'confessions'. In that Koheleth works out his opposition to the 'school tradition' through ' "broken" sentences' (op. cit., 47), we are at the same time given a picture of his personality; the I discourse keeps breaking through the stylistic form of the wisdom tradition and can become a personal confession; see R. Kroeber, op. cit., 35, on K. Galling's question, *ZAW* 50, 1932, 280. For the personality of Koheleth see also R. T. Gordis, op. cit., 77–86.

65. For his Palestinian home see H. W. Hertzberg, *ZDPV* 73, 1957, 113–24, and *Der Prediger*, 1963, 42ff.; for the social milieu of his origin see K. Galling, op. cit., 284: 'The state order he finds there is the feudal aristocracy', see also R. Kroeber, op. cit., 23f.

66. P. Wendland, *Die hellenistich–römische Kultur*, 1912, 45, 47f.; cf. also M. P. Nilsson, *GGR* 2[2], 294, 300; M. Hadas, *HCu*, 22ff. For Koheleth's 'individualism' cf. R. T. Gordis, op. cit., 75: 'No other book within the Bible . . . (is) as intensely personal as Koheleth . . . individual in content and

unique in expression'; see also K. Galling, loc. cit., 'aristocratic individualism'.

67. Tcherikover, *HC*, 159; the best example is the family history of the Tobiads and Oniads, see Vol. I, pp. 268ff.

68. For a comparison with the prophets see A. Lauha, *SVT* 3, 1955, 185; on Marcus Aurelius see H. J. Blieffert, op. cit., 92ff. His verdict on the state is also fundamentally negative and restrained: 8.9, 11.

69. Tarn/Griffith, *Hellenistic Civilization*, 2: '. . . the particularism of the Greek city state . . . was being replaced by universalism and its corollary, individualism'; see also P. Wendland, loc. cit.; individualism is matched by cosmopolitanism, cf. 35ff. For the conjunction of the two in Koheleth see H. J. Blieffert, op. cit., 90f.

70. R. Kroeber, op. cit., 130f.; cf. K. Galling, HAT 18, 1940, 47: 'sometimes one is almost tempted to say "deity".'

71. Cf. on the other hand K. Galling, *TR* NF 6, 1934, 362ff., who is followed by the modern commentators. R. Braun (n. 52 above) now differs.

72. K. Galling, HAT 18, 1940, 53: 'the universal human anthropology which "wisdom" largely has.' For 'under the sun' see O. Loretz, op. cit., 180; however, this formula was surely not repeated by Koheleth 'just for the sake of the sound'; rather, it is intended to underline the universality of his observations. Alongside 'men' appear other typical figures: the wise man, the fool, the king, the rich man, the righteous man and the wicked man (7.15; 9.2); the woman (7.26), etc.; they are typified manifestations of mankind.

73. Cf. 5.14–16 with Gen. 3.17–19; 3.20b and 12.7a with Gen. 2.7, 19 and 3.19, also 3.11 and Gen. 1.13. Further instances in H. W. Hertzberg, op. cit., 227–30, cf. W. Zimmerli, *Prediger*, ATD 16/1, 1962, 137f.; 12.1 (245) has, however, a disputed text, see below, n. 108. The name Israel is only mentioned in 1.12 in connection with the alleged royal status of the author; a legal regulation appears in 5.3–5, but the two in no way figure in the author's perspective.

74. G. von Rad, *Old Testament Theology* I, 1962, 455.

75. R. Kroeber, op. cit., 26f.

76. J. Hempel, *Die althebräische Literatur*, 1934, 191, followed by H. J. Blieffert, op. cit., 91.

77. Cf. 2.11; 3.9; 5.15; 10.10 (textually difficult), 11; cf. H. J. Blieffert, op. cit. 99, 'the question with which Koheleth approaches his consideration of the world and of life'.

78. 7.25; text following Hertzberg, op. cit., 137, 142. For the interpretation of *ḥešbōn*, which is equally strange, see K. Galling, HAT 18, 1940, 77: 'In the end he wants to settle with wisdom.'

79. J. Pedersen, *RHPR* 10, 1930, 331 n. 12.

80. E. Bickerman(n), *HTR* 54, 1951, 162; see also Vol. I, pp. 104f., 219f.

81. 7.23f., cf. already 1.17f., 8, 16f.; cf. above, n. 72.

82. Cf. Prov. 30.1–4; Job 36.26ff.; 37.14ff.; 38.1ff.; see already Isa. 40.12–14 and Ps. 139.6, 7.

83. 4.1 and 7.15, cf. 3.16; 5.7; 8.10, 14.

84. 2.26: *ḥōte'* is here to be translated 'failure', see 7.26; 3.11; 7.13f.; 8.16f.; 9.1ff.; 11.5: here an earlier theme of wisdom (Ps. 139.13ff.; Job 10.9–13) is used

to demonstrate the incomprehensibility of God's activity. For the whole see H. Gese, in: *Les Sagesses du proche-Orient ancien,* 1963, 149: 'World history is incomprehensible and all knowledge of it is delusion.'

85. On this see J. Pedersen, op. cit., 344.

86. Cf. the typical 'broken sentence' 2.12a–17, which begins with an apparent confirmation of traditional views in vv. 13f. and ends in inexorable consistency with the despair of v. 17; cf. K. Galling, HAT 18, 1940, 57: 'It shows the invasion of *new* insights which shake Koheleth.' Righteous and wicked: 9.2ff., cf. 7.15. For the meaninglessness of riches and posterity see the next sentence 2.18–23; cf. 4.8; 5.14; for reputation and memory see 1.9–11; 2.16; 9.5f.; on this see O. Loretz, op. cit., 225ff.

87. 1.2 and 12.8: all in all, *hebel* appears 23 times; for its significance see W. Zimmerli, op. cit., 13f. n.2, and above all O. Loretz, op. cit., 218–46.

88. 2.14, 15; 3.19 (3 times); 9.2f. In the sense of chance, see I Sam.6.9; 20.26; Ruth 2.3; for the concept see R. Kroeber, 55f.; H. J. Blieffert, 20f.; and H. Gese, op. cit., 143f.

89. On this see R. Kroeber, op. cit., 41. The category also includes *hōlēlōt sikᵉlūt* (μανία) *ra'yōn* and *rᵉ'ūt; ḥešbōn, kišrōn* or even terms which occur elsewhere in the OT but are used in a stereotyped way in Koheleth, like *hebel* and *'āmāl;* on both see H. Gese, op. cit., 139 n.1; *ḥēleq* and *'ēt* (see Vol. I, p. 126). In general Koheleth has a typical vocabulary and a characteristic style; see the detailed investigations of O. Loretz, op. cit., 166–217.

90. E. Meyer, *UAC* 2, 37 n.1, and O. Eissfeldt, *The Old Testament,* 498, point to τύχη; on the other hand, K. Galling, *TR* 6, 1934, 362; O. Loretz, op. cit., 46, but see n.5: *tychē* can also be used *ad malam partem.*

91. This fact is noted too little by R. Kroeber, op. cit., 55; see, however, F. Nötscher, *Vom Alten zum Neuen Testament,* 1962, 13f., and below, n.148. Cf. also H. Gese, op. cit., 143f.

92. 9.11f.: *pega'* appears only once elsewhere in the OT, see I Kings 5.18; it is synonymous with *miqre;* cf. also its appearance in the sayings of Ahikar: A. Cowley, *Aramaic Papyri,* 1923, 215, l. 89.

93. On this see K. Galling, 'Das Rätsel der Zeit im Urteil Kohelets (Koh. 3.1–15)', *ZTK* 58, 1961, 1–15, and H. Gese, op. cit., 148ff. According to Gese (n.1), the 'beginning of the main part of the book of Koheleth' is to be found at 3.1–15, and the author always keeps returning to it: 3.17; 8.5f., 9; 9.11.

94. 3.14a and 11a. The latter passage is difficult textually. The interpretation by H. Gese, op. cit., 150, is preferable to that of K. Galling, HAT 18, 1940, 62, cf. also *ZTK* 58, 1961, 5ff., in that it requires no complicated alteration of the text. On the other hand, the translation of *'olām* as 'course of time' (K. Galling, followed by H. Gese) is infinitely preferable to the attempts at interpretation by H. W. Hertzberg, op. cit., 96. For the quite different 'plan of time' of the Jewish philospher Aristobulus in Alexandria about 80 years after K., see Vol. I, pp. 166f.

95. Cf. 3.17b, 22b; 6.10–12; 7.10, 14b, 24, 29; 8.5b–8.17; 9.12; 10.14; 11.2, 5f.

96. See the introductory poem 1.3–11 and on it H. Richter, *ZAW* 70, 1958, 19, with special reference to 5–7: 'Here nature is considered neither on its own

account nor to introduce the praise of Yahweh. These observations are meant to consolidate and demonstrate a philosophical theory.' On this cf. also 1.15; 7.13; 11.3.

97. 2.12a–17; 9.1–6; 3.18–21; cf. 7.2; 8.9; 9.10.

98. 9.3; cf. 8.11: here related to the power of the state.

99. H. Gese, op. cit., 150: in this 'Koheleth is a faithful pupil of old wisdom'.

100. 5.1b, cf. also 4.17–5.6 and 7.16–18.

101. K. Galling, *ZTK* 58, 1961, 13; cf. also *Die Krisis der Aufklärung in Israel*, 1952, 17.

102. A. Lauha, op. cit., 186.

103. 3.14; 5.6; there could be additions in 7.18 and 8.12f., see K. Galling, HAT 18, 1940, 74f. and 80; 12.13 is a correction added by the epitomist. For the positive significance of the 'fear of God' see H. Gese, op. cit., 150; cf., however, also the more restrained judgment of K. Galling, *ZTK* 58, 1961, 14.

104. 3.22; 5.17; 9.9; see on this H. J. Blieffert, op. cit., 21, and R. Kroeber, op. cit., 56, 127.

105. This constantly recurring summons of Koheleth is the positive side of his interpretation of life: only here can he see a limited meaning for human life; cf. 2.24; 3.12f.; 3.22; 5.17ff.; 8.15; 9.7–9; 11.9. The motif of self-forgetfulness in 5.19 is significant.

106. H. Gese, op. cit., 151; for God's good pleasure see 9.7. The account by H. Gese is perhaps too positive; 'striving after wind' and 'nothing to be gained' also come at the end of 2.1–11, and the joy given by God is realized in forgetting the latent problem of life (5.19).

107. Cf. already 2.26b (and on this above, n. 84); 4.1–4; 6.3–6; cf. also 5.18f.: the summons to enjoy life is only meaningful to someone to whom God has given the outward possibilities; it is considerably limited by the crude social contrasts prevailing at that time. Koheleth speaks 'under the protection of money' (7.12); cf. R. Kroeber, op. cit., 24.

108. In 9.12b; 11.8b; 12.1 we should probably follow K. Galling in reading *bōrᵉkā*, HAT 18, 1940, 88. For the rejection of hope for life after death see 3.21f.; 9.4ff., 10b.

109. 5.14, in the light of this, even 'delight in toil' (2.24; 3.13; 5.17), etc., becomes a questionable intermediary solution; cf. already 2.11 as a consequence of 2.10.

110. *UAC* 2, 35f. For the 'Hellenistic enlightenment' see W. Nestle, *RAC* I, 938ff.

111. *Die Krisis der Aufklärung in Israel*, 1952, 12ff.

112. R. H. Pfeiffer, *Introduction to the Old Testament*, 1948, 730. However, the further interpretation of Koheleth by the author is unfortunate: we certainly cannot speak of 'the first attempt to make a synthesis of Judaism and Hellenism'; this is an inadmissible simplification. The same time is also true of the attempt of O. Loretz to explain Koheleth merely from a 'general Semitic background'.

113. K. Galling, *ZAW* 50, 1932, 291.

114. K. Oppenheimer, *PW*, 2R. 6, 586.

115. M. Nilsson, *GGR²* I, 772f.; the following quotation: fr. 292; on this and what follows see also Festugière, *Révélation* 2, 161–8, who shows how the

philosophical enlightenment shattered naive popular belief and changed the conceptions of the gods.

116. M. P. Nilsson, op. cit., 2, 196: cf. fr. 379; 515; 516: God is good; 818.

117. *Kolax*, 26f., 42, cf. also 33. The text has considerable gaps, see Menander, ed. F. G. Allison, LCL, 1964, 384ff.; on the same question see also frs. 335, 386.

118. *Epitrepontes*, 875ff., 880ff. (LCL, 116ff.): the gods cannot be bothered with details, and so they have given each man 'character' as a watcher; cf. also fr. 759: 'I sacrificed to gods who were not concerned about me'; fr. 245: God cannot be influenced, otherwise he would not be God.

119. M. Nilsson, op. cit., 2, 197; fr. 425, cf. frs. 482, 483: the incapability of the *nous*; *tyche* rules everything.

120. Op. cit., 196f.: cf. already Euripides fr. 506 (Nauck²): it is impossible for Zeus to write down the unjust deeds of men, they are too many.

121. Op. cit., 193f.; text see POx 8, 1911, 1082, and Herodes, *Cercidas*, ed. A. D. Knox, LCL 1961, 194ff. For the personality of Cercidas see Gerhard, *PW* 11, 294ff.

122. See Vol. I, pp. 50f. cf. also Rostovtzeff, *HW* 2, 1148f. An economic decline in Greece began from the end of the third century onwards.

123. W. Peek, *Griechische Grabgedichte*, 1960, no. 139: Alexandria, third century BC.

124. Op. cit., no. 151, 9: Samos, second to first century BC (?).

125. Op. cit., no. 308, 7f.: Cyprus, second to third century AD; cf. also 352,1f.: bad reward for piety, and 326,9.

126. Op. cit., no. 288,5: Thrace, second century AD. Coupled with this is the charge against 'Phthonos', the personified envy of the gods; cf. 352.

127. *Anth.Gr.* 7, 727, cf. 740 and IG XIV, no. 2131.

128. Peek, op. cit., no. 162, 13. Cf. Antipater of Sidon, *Anth.Gr.* 7, 427.

129. On this see O. Loretz, op. cit., 78 (cf. also 83, the conversation of the man weary of life), and 117; however, it is incomprehensible that Loretz, 134, should want to see a 'forerunner' of Koheleth in parts of the Gilgamesh epic, while pushing Egyptian (and Hellenistic) 'parallels' to one side. This and similar topics are too general for one to construct relationships of dependence from them.

130. W. Peek, op. cit., no. 371, second to third century AD, Pisidia, and 465, 17ff., second to third century AD from Corcyra; cf. also 248, 479, 480; also the many instances from Asia Minor in L. Robert, *RevPhil* 17, 1943, 182f.

131. A. Erman, 'Zwei Grabsteine griechischer Zeit', *Festschrift für E. Sachau*, 1915, 107–11, and here above all the last, the inscription of the priest consort Taimhotep of 42 BC, 108ff.

132. Menander, fr. 410, and LCL, 432 (Demianczuk, Suppl. Com. 58); cf. also the interesting fragment 481: man should treat the period of his life as a 'feast'. Philetairos (middle comedy), fr. 7, ed. Kock, CAF 2, 232; Euripides, *Alcestis* 788f.; Theognis, *Eleg.* 1, 567–70, 753–6, 1047f. Further examples from Greek and Latin poetry in R. H. Pfeiffer, *The Joshua Bloch Memorial Vol.*, 1960, 63f.; F. Dornseiff, *ZDMG* 89, 1935, 244f., who also refers to Menippus of Gadara (see Vol. I, pp. 83f.) and to the parting words of the ghost of Darius in Aeschylus, *Persae* 840f., and M. P. Nilsson, *opuscula selecta* 3, 1960, 173f.

= *GGR*[2] 2, 662 n.2: tomb of Vincentius and the epitaph of Sardanapalus according to Cicero, *Tusc.* 5, 101 = *Anth.Gr.*7, 325. Old Testament – Jewish parallels: Isa.22.13; Sir.14.11–19, cf. I Cor.15.32. 'The summons *carpe diem* rings out through all times and all peoples in view of the transitoriness of man', see R. Kroeber, op. cit., 49, and the Chinese example cited there. The theme of Koheleth 4.2ff. (6.3f.): better dead than alive, or *better never born*, is also a universal one: cf. Jer.20.13ff.; Job 3.1ff.; Sirach 30.17, see below, n.270; but also Euripides, frs. 285 and 833, ed. Nauck[2]; Theognis, *Eleg.*425ff.; Herodotus 7, 46, 2ff.; further examples in O. Loretz, op. cit., 233 nn.75–7; K. Galling, HAT 18, 1940, 65, and F. Dornseiff, op. cit., 246: it goes back to old wisdom communicated by Silenus to the Phrygian king Midas; see also Eitrem, *PW* 15, 1527ff.: 'A confession of an ancient pessimistic view of life as old as it is comfort-less.' This view is said also to have been widespread among barbarian peoples: see Herodotus 5, 4 and Strabo 11, 11, 8 C 519/20 = Euripides 449 (ed. Nauck[2]). A similar direction is taken by W. Peek, op. cit., no.274, 3–6, and 333; *Anth.Gr.* 9, 359, ll.9f., and 360, ll.9f., and Menander, frs. 14, 169; cf. 223, 534: better dead than living, better an animal than a man. On the whole matter see H. Diels, 'Der antike Pessimismus', *Schule und Leben* 1, 1921, 8ff., 18ff. For Epicurus' criticism of this attitude see Diogenes Laertius 10, 125f.

133. P. Benoit, '*Atiqot* 4, 1964, 39; *IEJ* 17, 1967, 112/3, and B. Lifshitz, *RB* 73, 1966, 248–55. Many instances from Greek tomb epigraphy can be found there.

134. M. Nilsson, *GGR*[2] 1, 194 n.1; 2, 279f., further see below n.579; E. Rohde, *Psyche* 2, 1961, 257 n.3; Euripides, *Suppl.*1140; *Electra* 59; fr. 971, Nauck[2], cf. also fr. 481; see further W. Peek, op. cit., no.12, 5: αἰθὴρ μὲν ψυλὰς ὑπεδέξατο, σώμ[ατα δὲ χθῶν] τῶνδε, Athens 435 BC, for those fallen at Potidea; no.74: Piraeus, 350 BC; 218, 3b: Ephesus, first century BC (?); 250, 2/3 century AD; cf. 296; 381, 8; 391, 4; on this see H. W. Hertzberg, op. cit., 112: 'a view which has found its way into Judaism from Hellenism'. Doubted by Koheleth, it was later a firm rule for Sirach: 40.11, see Vol.I, p.149; cf. also Dan.12.3 and below, n.579.

135. Koh.12.7; Ps.90.3; 104.29f.; Job 34.14.

136. The tragic or comic poets already found this to be necessary because the various views circulating among the people had to be expressed on the stage and the view of the author retreated into the background. The traditional, all-seeing deity who 'assigns to each man his portion of fate' *([νέ]μει δ'ἑκάστῳ τὴν καταίσιον μοῖραν)* in his time appears in a poem ascribed to Cercidas (Herodes, *Cercidas*, ed. A. D. Knox, LCL 1961, 237, *Cercidea* ll.100ff.); cf. also M. Nilsson, *GGR*[2] 2, 200 (192), while from time to time divine retribution appears in the otherwise completely 'enlightened', rationally thinking Polybius (cf. e.g. 1, 84 and 18, 54, 10f., see above n.II, 316).

137. Koh.7.17, cf. 16–18. Koheleth does not draw the consequences from his revolutionary insights, that 'an attitude of *medio tutissimus ibis* commends itself' in the realm of practical life, see K. Galling, HAT 18, 1940, 75; see also Vol.I, pp.126f.: like Menander (cf. e.g. fr. 531), he praises a completely 'bourgeois morality', cf. K. Galling, *ZAW* 50, 1932, 292.

138. M. Nilsson, *GGR*[2] 1, 813, cf. 774.

139. Op. cit., 361ff.; cf. also S. Eitrem, *PW* 15, 2453ff.

140. See the collection by S. Eitrem, *PW* 15, 2449.

141. M. Nilsson, *GGR*² 1, 366, 774.

142. Op. cit., 2, 201ff.

143. The conjunction of *moira* and the destiny of death is already introduced in Homer, see M. Nilsson, *GGR*² 1, 362f., and S. Eitrem, *PW* 15, 2455; later, *moira* appears above all on epitaphs, see op. cit., 2475f., and W. Peek, op. cit., no. 97, 3: τῆς κοινῆς μοίρας πᾶσιν ἔχει τὸ μέρος, Eleusis, fourth century BC, similarly 468, 5; cf. also 152, 12; 158, 1; 209 etc.; see the index, 367 and 373.

144. M. Nilsson, *GGR*² 1, 774; 2, 202f.; S. Eitrem, *PW* 15, 2465, and G. Herzog-Hauser, *PW*, 2.R. 7, 1654 and 1657f.; 'in the face of its régime, human spirit and human foresight are completely powerless'; cf. also Menander, fr. 355; it acts ἀσυλλόγιστον; fr. 598: all things are only lent out by it; 483: τύχη κυβερνᾷ πάντα. For the epitaphs, see the index in W. Peek, op. cit., 367 and no. 95: it is stronger than all hope (Attica, fourth century BC), cf. 198, 6.

145. M. Nilsson, *GGR*² 2, 203; G. Herzog-Hauser, *PW*, 2.R 7, 1658; in addition to the instances cited there see also Menander, fr. 291: ταὐτόματόν ἐστιν ὡς ἔοικέ που θεός . . ., and 460, 4.

146. According to Palladas, *Anth.Gr.* 10, 52, ed. Beckby 3, 502, Menander also described the *kairos* as a 'god', see Weissbach, *PW* 10, 1508. For *chronos* see Menander, fr. 538: all the treasures of the world can avail nothing against time; the underworld is the common lot of all mortals; 593: time and human character bring astonishing and wonderful things to pass. Diphilus, fr. 83, Kock, CAF 2, 569, calls it a 'grey-haired deceiver'. The epitaph on those who fell at Chaironea is well known, W. Peek, op. cit., no. 15 (338/7 BC): [ὦ Χρόν]ε, παντοίων θνητο[ῖς πανεπίσκοπε δαῖμον (= *Anth.Gr.* 7, 245); cf. 164: 'All-seeing time has separated me from them and with it . . . the fates have assigned me . . . this lot', Egypt (second century BC); 260: 'I did not receive this life as my own . . . I borrowed it from time and now return it to time as to my creditor' (Lydia, second century AD), further in A. B. Cook, *Zeus* II, 2, 859ff. A unique personification of time can be found in the letter of Mara bar Serapion, which perhaps comes from the end of the first century AD (ed. Cureton, *Spicilegium Syriacum*, 1855, 48 (76)). Time (ﺯﺑﻧﺍ) appears here as the decisive concept of fate: fettered Mara is asked by a friend why he is laughing and he replies: 'I am laughing at time because without having borrowed evil from me it is repaying me.' On this see J. A. Montgomery, *HTR* 31, 1938, 148.

147. M. Nilsson, *GGR* 2², 348, cf. also 499; cf. Dittenberger, *Syll.* 3, no. 1125. For αἰών as a fixed attribute of God in Aristotle see H. Leisegang, *PW*, 2R. 3, 1030; see also A. D. Nock, *HTR* 27, 1934, 78–99, who rejects the usual Iranian derivation and with Philo Byblius supposes a Phoenician origin (86f.), see FGrHist 790 Fr 2 = *Pr.Ev.* 1, 10, 7.

148. A. Volten, *Das demotische Weisheitsbuch*, 1941, 165 (5, 11); 174 (7, 19), etc.; see also S. Morenz and D. Müller, *Untersuchungen zur Rolle des Schicksals in der ägyptischen Literatur*, AAL, Ph. hist. Kl. 52, 1, 1961, 29ff., 35f., and F. Nötscher, op. cit., 27ff., who points out that the concept of fate gains significance in Egypt in the later period. In Hellenistic times – probably in contrast to the Greek view that even the gods cannot master fate – different deities, above all

Isis, are described as 'master (mistress) of fate', see Morenz/Müller, op. cit., 30f.
R. Kroeber, op. cit., 53 (cf. also S. Morenz, *Ägyptische Religion*, 1960, 72ff., 80),
sees above all a connection between conceptions of fate in Egypt and Koheleth,
which he contrasts with the Greek conception of fate. There are certainly
differences here, but it is remarkable that in Koheleth – in contrast to the rest
of the OT – a whole series of concepts of fate emerge. The confident word of the
suppliant in Ps. 31.16 is no longer spoken by Koheleth, because he has only a
broken relationship to prayer: 5.1.

149. 3.16; 5.7; 7.15. The resigned conclusion follows in 7.16.

150. H. W. Hertzberg, op. cit., 236: 'God becomes a fate . . .'; K. Galling,
ZAW 50, 1932, 292: 'a belief bordering on fatalism'.

151. Loc. cit., cf. 288: 'With "fate" the question of God becomes acute for
the *Jew* Koheleth: providence? retribution? *tychē*? *anankē*?'

152. Op. cit., 290.

153. Op. cit., 292.

154. Rostovtzeff, *HW* 2, 1105, 1108, and especially 1116ff.: 'a class of men
who had achieved by their efforts or inherited from their parents a certain
degree of prosperity, and lived not on the income derived from their manual
labour but from the investment of their accumulated capital in some branch of
economic activity' (above all from land-owning). See also the description by
H. L. Ginsberg, *Studies in Koheleth*, 1950, 44.

155. K. Galling, HAT 18, 1940, 89: 'In it a pupil presents the achievement
of his master'; cf. also H. W. Hertzberg, op. cit., 219: 'An apologia is given here
for Koheleth', and R. Kroeber, op. cit., 157. For a reference to the 'acuteness,
penetration and indeed annihilating effect of Koheleth's wisdom', see W.
Zimmerli, *Prediger*, ATD 16/1, 1962, 249.

156. H. W. Hertzberg, op. cit., 219f., cf. also 237: 'He formed a school and
had opponents.'

157. M. Dahood, *Bibl* 33, 1952, 30–52; 39, 1958, 302–18; cf. W. F. Albright,
SVT 3, 1955, 15.

158. We have already encountered this influence many times; see Vol.I,
pp.32ff., 61f., 71ff., 87f., 90ff., 93f., 296ff.

159. W. Zimmerli, 'Die Weisheit des Predigers Salomo', *Aus der Welt der
Religion* 11, 1936, 16 n.2, and ATD 16/1, 1962, 250; for the problem of the
further additions see E. Meyer, *UAC* 2, 38f. As Koheleth often introduces the
views of his opponent, traditional wisdom, so to speak as a quotation, it becomes
difficult to recognize them. K. Galling, *RGG*[3] 5, 512, still ascribes 3.17 (so
probably instead of 16, see HAT 18, 1940, 49); 7.28–8.1; 7.18b; 8.5, 12f. to the
writer of the second epilogue. O. Loretz, op. cit., 290ff., would recognize only
one epilogue writer and also rejects all revision. The epilogue does not go
'beyond what has already been said in the book of Koheleth' (297). In the
perspective of this apologetic attitude we can hardly expect a real understanding
of the author of this work, who stands 'at the farthest frontier of Yahwism'
(G. von Rad, op. cit., I, 458).

160. See the difficulties in the canonization of the book, R. Kroeber, op. cit.,
69ff.; the remarks by O. Loretz, op. cit., 302ff., who also wants to deny these
difficulties, are incorrect. Certainly the definitive discussion in *Yad.* 3, 5cd took

place in the second century AD, but the reference of R. Simeon b. Joḥai to the controversy over this question between the schools of Hillel and Shammai indicates that the discussion lasted for several generations, for the school of Shammai ceased to exist in practice after AD 70.

161. For Antigonus of Socho see E. Bickerman(n), *HTR* 54, 1951, 153–65; W. F. Albright, *From the Stone Age to Christianity*, 1940, 351, would see Stoic influence in him. The impersonal concept 'heaven' is said to be an expression for '*heimarmenē*'. John Bright, *A History of Israel*, 1959, 401, speaks similarly of Stoic influence. This is surely going too far. As elsewhere in post-biblical Judaism, the term 'heaven' is meant to represent the divine name, see below, n. IV, 260. On '*Ab RN* 5 (rev. ed., Schechter, 13ab), see also R. Meyer, *TDNT* 7, 41. L. Levy, op. cit., 42–45, regards the late note as historical and makes 'Zadok or Boethus', the alleged founder of Sadducaism, the author of the book of Koheleth. We know nothing about Zadok, but (Simon son of) Boethus was the Alexandrian appointed by Herod to be high priest in Jerusalem; see above n. II, 156). A parallel tradition appears in Ps.Clem., *Recog.* 1, 54, GCS 2.39, ed. Rehm; on this see T. Caldwell, *Kairos* 4, 1962, 108f.

162. L. Finkelstein, *The Pharisees* I, ³1962, 230, 235. He believes that Koheleth is thus in a critical tradition which derives from Job. Quite apart from the fact that the difference between Job and K. is very great (on this see A. Lauha, op. cit., 183–91), the sociological classification seems to be very improbable.

163. O. Eissfeldt, *The Old Testament*, 492. Cf. Vol. I, p. 130.

164. R. Kroeber, op. cit., 3, would regard the name 'as a proper name . . . derived from an office'. However, it is improbable that מלך should be understood as 'councillor' – following W. F. Albright, *SVT* 3, 1955, 15 n. 2. The same is true of the interpretation by H. L. Ginsberg, *SVT* 3, 1955, 148f., as 'property owner'. For the '*gerousia*' in Jeruslem see Vol. I, pp. 25f.

165. Thus K. Galling, HAT 18, 1940, 47, and H. W. Hertzberg, op. cit., 52ff. O. Loretz, op. cit., 154, doubts whether the author intended an identification with Solomon. However, 'king over Israel in Jerusalem' in 1.12 hardly permits any other conclusion.

166. J. A. Sint, *Pseudonymität im Altertum*, 1960, 139; see above n. II, 160, and below n. 853. For the pre-exilic wisdom tradition, in Israel, which probably goes back to the time of Solomon, see A. Alt, *Kleine Schriften* II, ³1964, 90–9, and R. N. Whybray, *Wisdom in Proverbs*, 1965, 20ff. (lit.).

167. J. A. Sint, op. cit., 140ff.; see also W. F. Albright, *From the Stone Age to Christianity*, 1940, 78: deliberate forgeries are rare in the ancient East before the Ptolemaic period.

168. O. Eissfeldt, *The Old Testament*, 483, 490. Obviously there were even older collections current under the name of Solomon, cf. Prov. 10.1 and Ps. 72.1; 127.1.

169. Cf. J. A. Sint, *Pseudonymität*, 154; Bousset/Gressmann, 495; E. Lohse, *TDNT* 7, 459ff. For the magic literature current under the name of Solomon, see K. Preisendanz, *PW Suppl* 8, 660ff.

170. A similar productivity of 4050 psalms was also ascribed to his father David: DJDJ IV, 91ff.

171. Sir. 47.14, 17, 16, see M. Segal, *Sēfer Ben Sīrā*, ²1958, 226. Verse 16 is only preserved in LXX.

172. Cf. I Kings 5.14 and 10.1, where the 'islands', however, do not appear. For the significance of Greece or the Aegean see Dan. 11.18; cf. also Isa. 11.11; Ezek. 27.3, 6; perhaps this reference of Sirach comes from Ps. 72.10.

173. Menander of Ephesus and Laitus, see FGrHist 784 F1, see Vol. I, pp. 75 and 94f.

174. Eusebius, *Pr.Ev.* 13, 12, 11a, on the basis of Prov. 8.22ff. (see Vol. I, pp. 166f.); quoted N. Walter, *Der Thoraausleger Aristobulus*, TU 86, 1964, 32 n. 2. Solomon appears here as the second great Jewish 'philosopher' alongside Moses.

175. *Antt.* 8, 44: ἐν πάσαις ἐφιλοσόφησε. The tradition of Solomon as a magician was developed in Palestine; it derives from I Kings 5.12f. Josephus already knows a considerable magical literature under his name, *Antt.* 8, 45; cf. also Syr.Bar. 77.25 and Ps.Philo 60, 2, ed. Kisch 261: *'nascetur de lateribus meis qui vos domabit'*, *David in Citharismus contra daemonium Saulis*, on this see K. Preisendanz, op. cit., 663; the original text of the Testament of Solomon probably also originated in Palestine, see op. cit., 688, 690. Rabbinic evidence in Bill. 4, 533ff.

176. See K. Preisendanz, *PW Suppl* 8, 662–704, cf. also Schürer 3, 418f.; F. Pfister, *PW* 19, 1451f.; P. Festugière, *Révélation* 1, 20ff., 41, 145f., 152ff., 200, 339.

177. For Jewish and especially Essene magic see Vol. I, pp. 239ff.

178. O. Eissfeldt, *The Old Testament*, 493.

179. FGrHist 81 F 40 (Athen. 12, 536e), on which see E. R. Bevan, *A History of Egypt under the Ptolemaic Dynasty*, 1927, 78.

180. For the Hebrew text (M) see M. S. Segal, *Sefer Bēn-Sīrā*, ²1958 (Hebr.), and R. Smend, *Die Weisheit des Jesus Sirach hebräisch und deutsch*, 1906; id., *Die Weisheit des Jesus Sirach erklärt*, 1906; and on 33.4 – 34.1 see I. Levi, *REJ* 92, 1932, 139–45; on 15 and 16.1–9 see J. Schirrmann, *Tarbiz* 27, 1958/59, 440–3, and on 39.27–44.17 the new fragments ed. Y. Yadin, *The Ben Sira Scroll from Masada*, 1965. For the Greek text (= G) see *Sapientia Jesu filii Sirach*, ed. J. Ziegler, 1965, Vol. XII, 2 of the Göttingen edition of the Septuagint. For the Syriac text (Syr) see *Libri VT apocryphi Syriace*, 1861, ed. P. de Lagarde; I am grateful to Dr Rüger for a series of observations on textual criticism, see also his book, *Text und Textform im hebräischen Sirach, Untersuchungen zur Textgeschichte und Textkritik des hebräischen Sirachfragmente*, BZAW 112, Berlin 1970.

181. The date of the translation is almost universally acknowledged, see Schürer 3, 216; N. Peters, *Das Buch Jesus Sirach*, 1913, xxxiff., and O. Eissfeldt, *The Old Testament*, 597; cf. also H. J. Cadbury, *HTR* 48, 1955, 219–25.

182. The names vary, see 50.27 and the colophon 51.30 (M), the Prologue and the title of the Greek translation and the Syriac text. The decisive thing is that the grandson renders the name of his grandfather 'Jesus' in the prologue; 50.27 is to be corrected from here; see Schürer 2, 215f., and Oesterley/Box, in R. H. Charles, *Apocrypha and Pseudepigrapha* I, 291f.

183. Oesterley/Box, op. cit., I, 293; R. H. Pfeiffer, op. cit., 367; O. Eissfeldt, *The Old Testament*, 597. The suggestion of N. Peters, op. cit., xxxiv–xxxvii,

174–171 BC, i.e. after the beginning of the reforms in Jerusalem, has a false assessment of the situation of the book.

184. For the genres of the work see W. Baumgartner, *ZAW* 34, 1914, 161–98. Cf. also W. Jenni, *RGG*[3] 3, 654.

185. Titles in G: 20.27; 23.7; 24.1; 30.1, 16; 44.1; 51.1; in M: 31.12 (G 34.12); 41.14; 44.1. Transitions: 42.25 to 43.1; 43.33 to 44.1; and 49.16b to 50.1; on this see I. Lévi, *L'Ecclésiastique* I, 1898, xxv, cf. 50, and L. Bigot, *DTC* IV, 2, 1920, 2047. For the literary form influenced by Hellenism see also A. Schlatter, *GI*[3], 100.

186. 38.24 – 39.11; cf. 1.24b; 8.8f.; 24.30ff.; 37.26; 44.10–15.

187. A. Schlatter, *GI*[3], 97.

188. Sir.51. 13–30. The first half of the hymn appears in an earlier form in 11 QPsDav, ed. J. N. Sanders, DJDJ IV, 1965, 79ff. We see here how Ben Sira shaped earlier forms.

189. See the frequent address 'my son': 2.1; 4.20; 6.18, 23 (G, Syr.), etc.; on this G. F. Moore, *Judaism* I, 38: 'The inclination to adopt Hellenistic civilization was nowhere stronger . . . than among the young aristocrats, who were sent to school to him.' Similarly I. Heinemann, *MGWJ* 82, 1938, 159.

190. R. Smend, 'Griechisch-Syrisch-Hebräischer Index' to *Weisheit des Jesus Sirach*, 1907, 176f.; the Greek translation uses the term even more often. Cf. Vol. I, pp. 65ff.

191. 37.19–26, text follows V. Hamp, *Sirach*, Echterbibel, 1951, 98f. Brackets indicate secondary expansions.

192. For the text in vv. 12 and 13 see V. Hamp, op. cit., 90. One might think, say, of an embassage to Antioch as in II Macc. 4.11.

193. 4.7; 15.5; 21.17; 38.33; 39.10.

194. Judge: 38.33, cf. 4.9, 15; 10.1f., 24; counsellor of the ruler, 11.1; 13.9; 20.27; 39.4; see W. Baumgartner, op. cit., 162.

195. 7.29ff.; 35 (G 32). 6ff.; description of Aaron, 45.6–22; of the covenant of Phinehas, 45.23–26; the defence of priestly privileges, 45.13, 18; the hymn to Simon the Just, 50.1–21. On the other hand, the Levites are not mentioned, see above, n. I, 385.

196. Cf. II Macc. 3.4ff., 11; 4.1ff.; see also Vol. I, pp. 10f., and further, pp. 271f. The view of A. Schlatter, *GI*[3], 94f., that he does not go into the political circumstances of his time, is hardly correct, cf. e.g. 10.8, 14, 16ff.; 16.4ff. He just cannot speak openly.

197. 17.17; 35 (G 32). 22ff.; 36 (G 33). 1–22; 50.25f.; cf. also 48.24f.; 49.10; 50, 4. In 10.22 he counsels foreigners and non-Jews to the fear of God, i.e. to turn to Judaism.

198. Cf. 4.7; 7.14; 8.10f., 14; 9.13; 13.9–13; 26.5: fear of calumny and popular unrest; see also R. H. Pfeiffer, op. cit., 371, on 1.22–24, and V. Tcherikover, *HC*, 148: 'in several places in his book we feel that behind this humility lies a feeling of fear of the powerful rather than respect for authority'.

199. 24.32f., cf. R. Smend, *Die Weisheit des Jesus Sirach erklärt*, 224; we should probably also read ויבא instead of ויבע in the closing saying 50.27c, thus Smend, op. cit., 494f.; N. Peters, op. cit., 436, and W. Baumgartner, op. cit. 186. Cf. also the reference to Isa. 55.1 in Sir. 51.25.

200. 39.6, cf. 18.29. For *hibbi'a* cf. 16.25 and 50.27d, see also W. Baumgartner, loc. cit.

201. Op. cit. 186–9 (quot. 186/7).

202. 33 (G 30). 16, 25–27 (text follows V. Hamp, op. cit., 88). The 'overseers of the community' might be a reference to the *gerousia*.

203. J. L. Koole, *OTS* 14, 1965, 374–92, esp. 386ff., and E. Jacob in *Mélanges bibliques A. Robert,* 1957, 289f.

204. For the text see V. Hamp, op. cit., 103f. J. Koole, op. cit., 376, points out that with reference to the Torah the verb שׁרִד means the exposition of the law, see 32 (G 35). 14f. – against it, probably wrongly, G. Mayer, *RAC* 6, 1195.

205. For Essenism see Vol. I, pp. 222f., 239f.; for prophecy in Judaism see R. Meyer, *TDNT* 6, 812ff., and M. Hengel, op. cit., 236ff.

206. R. Meyer, *TDNT* 6, 816f., on the Rabbinic conception of prophecy; for Ben Sira, see J. Koole, op. cit., 381.

207. J. S. Sanders, DJDJ IV, 92: 11 QPs^a Dav. Comp., col. 27.4 and 11; for Ben Sira's conception of inspiration see also J. L. Koole, op. cit., 382f., who refers to Ps.Aristeas, and Philo, *Vit.Mos.* 2.40 (M 1.140). Cf. also inspiration in Aristobulus, a little later, Vol. I, p. 165; also Wisdom 7.7, 15, 27, etc.

208. See in the 'praise of the fathers': 45.2 Moses; 45.19 Aaron; 46.4 Joshua; 46.15ff. Samuel; 47.3 David; 48.3ff. Elijah; 48.12f. Elisha; 48.20, 23 Isaiah; 49.8 Ezekiel; 49.14 Enoch; on this see E. Jacob, op. cit., 290f., and on the 'praise of the fathers', R. T. Siebeneck, *CBQ* 21, 1959, 411–28.

209. Cf. E. Jacob, op. cit., 290: 'ce genre de l'éloge des individus est une nouveauté dans l'AT'; see also R. T. Siebeneck, op. cit., 413f.; R. Pautrel, *RSR* 51, 1963, 541f. Greek biography reached a climax in the third century BC under Peripatetic influence, with Hermippus, Satyrus and Sotion. From the latter, between 200 and 170 BC, come the διαδοχαὶ τῶν φιλοσόφων, see Münzer, *PW*, 2R. 3, 1235ff. For examples by way of biography see A. Lumpe, *RAC* 6, 1229–57.

210. Estimation of riches: 10.27; 13.24; 25.3; 40.18 (G), cf. also 33 (G 30). 28–32; self-incurred poverty 18.31–19.1; 26.28; 25.2f., cf. also 40.28–30; further instances in R. H. Pfeiffer, op. cit., 390f. For fear of poverty in the Rabbinate, see Bill. 1, 818ff.

211. 8.2, 12; 9.13; 13.9–13. For the social climate in Sirach see V. Tcherikover, *HC*, 145ff., and R. Smend, op. cit., xxv; see Vol. I, pp. 49ff.

212. Cf. also 13.22f.; 5.1ff.; 8.14.

213. Cf. 14.4f.; 20.9–12; 21.8 and 11.29, where רוכל does not mean 'calumniator' but the itinerant, foreign merchant; see N. Peters, op. cit., 102, and G. Boström, *Proverbiastudien,* 70. For the rejection of the merchant in Judea see Vol. I, pp. 34f.; for the agricultural ideal see above, n. I, 413. Similarly Panaitios, according to Cicero, *De offic.* 1, 150f.

214. Cf. 3.17, 30f.; 5.1–8; 7.11, 32; 10.23; 29.8; 35 (G 32). 15ff., etc. R. H. Pfeiffer, op. cit., 390, is right here when he speaks of the 'self-interest' of the advice of Ben Sira.

215. R. Smend, *Die Weisheit des Jesus Sirachs erklärt,* xxxiii, cf. also R. H. Pfeiffer, op. cit., 371f. R. Pautrel, op. cit., 545, attacks Smend, but overlooks the fact that Ben Sira is not taking a position over against the non-Jews but against his contemporaries infected by the Hellenistic spirit of the time. For the Rabbinic

interpretation of Sir.3.21f. in terms of '*merkābā*' speculation see H. W. Weiss, *Untersuchungen zur Kosmologie des hellenistischen und palästinischen Judentums*, 1966, 80. For the anti-Hellenistic position of Sirach see A. Sisti, *RivBibl* 12, 1964, 215–56.

216. O. Eissfeldt, *The Old Testament*, 598: 'Much more strongly than in Prov. or even in [Koheleth] the element of universal and general human interest retreats behind the specifically Jewish.' For the fundamental difference between Sirach and Proverbs see J. Fichtner, *Die Altorientalische Weisheit*, 1933, 82–94, 125ff., and E. G. Bauckmann, *ZAW* 72, 1960, 33–63, who unfortunately go too little into the reasons for this change. J. Fichtner, op. cit., 127, speaks in general terms of the 'controversy with Hellenism'.

217. The group of terms πίστις, πιστός, (ἐμ)πιστεύειν = האמין; נאמן, אמונה plays a key role, albeit in a wider context, see R. Smend, index 189f.; cf. above all 1.27; 2.8, 10, 13; 4.16; 15.15, where we should follow G in reading אמונה; see R. Smend, *Die Weisheit des Jesus Sirachs erklärt*, 143, and an addition in M and Syr to Hab.2.4 is referred to (15.15c): 'If you trust him, you will live'. Cf. further 34 (G 31). 8; 36.21; 40.12 (G); 44.20: Abraham; 45.4: the אמונה of Moses; 46.15 Samuel, see Smend, op. cit., 445; 48.22: Hezekiah. Significantly the group of concepts appears even more frequently in the translation. On this see A. Schlatter, *Der Glaube im NT*, ⁴1927, 16ff.

218. The same is the case with the term *miṣwā*; see E. G. Bauckmann, op. cit., 36ff., 48f. J. Fichtner, op. cit., 93f., wants to understand some passages (32[G 35].15; 33 [G 36].2; 37.12: 'not impossible'; 32 [G 35].17, 18, 23f.: 'certain'), where the concepts seem to be indeterminate, in 'a hochmatic significance'. However, all these passages seem to refer to the *tōrā* of Moses in a concrete sense. Ben Sira deliberately transformed the older wisdom tradition at this point, and his grandson was not wrong in translating the indeterminate *tōrā* or *miṣwā* with *nomos*, see op. cit., 94; cf. also R. H. Pfeiffer, op. cit., 381ff.

219. Cf. 15.1b: 'He who keeps to the law acquires it (wisdom)', and on the other hand 15.7: 'The unholy do not acquire it . . . it is far from the mockers.' Cf. further 6.37; 21.11f.; 23.27b; 34 (G 31). 8; 33 (G 36). 2 and 43.33.

220. Cf. 17.11; 38.34cd and 39.1.

221. For the text see H. P. Rüger, op. cit., 34f.; cf. 43.28: God is greater than man's capacity for comprehension; see below, n.271.

222. Op. cit., 31; N. Peters, op. cit., 34, also wants to include 'exaggerated Jewish speculation', but the context makes such an anti-apocalyptic position improbable; cf. also the אדם and אנוש in 35 (G 32). 24.

223. For the text see H. P. Rüger, op. cit., 75ff.; cf. 17.7b: 'He teaches them good and evil', see 27.8: anyone who strives after righteousness acquires it, cf. Aeschylus, *Agamemnon* 1497ff., 1505ff. Here Ben Sira develops ideas from Deut.30.15, 19.

224. For the conception before Sirach see Ps.1 and Jer.21.8, cf. Sir.15.17; after Sirach see I Enoch 91.18; T. Asher 1.3, 5–7; Slavonic Enoch 30.15; Hermas, *Mand.* 12, 3, 4. Cf. Bill. I, 461f., and W. Michaelis, *TDNT* 5, 57f. For polemic against the split see Sir.1.28; 5.14; 6.1. Cf. also Ps.119.113. As a Greek parallel see Theognis 910ff.

225. Xenophon, *Mem.* 2, 1, 21–34, on which see I. Alpers, *Hercules in Bivio*,

diss. 1912, 9ff., and W. Michaelis, *TDNT* 5, 43ff. According to Persius, *Sat.* 3, 56f., the doctrine of the two ways is derived from Pythagorean tradition; cf. P. Wendland, *Hellenistisch-römischer Kultur*, 85f.

226. Cf. Sir. 15.14; 27.6; 37.3: יצר רע, see R. Smend, op. cit., 327, after the Syriac; presumably also 17.31 (G) after Gen. 8.21, see R. Smend, op. cit., 162; on 23.2 see R. Smend, op. cit., 304; cf. also the retrotranslations by Segal. For *yēṣer* in Ben Sira and later see R. H. Pfeiffer, op. cit., 393, and Bousset/Gressmann, 403ff.; see esp. '*Ab.* 4, 1 and *Kidd.* 30b Bar.: the law as a 'means of salvation' against the '*yēṣer*' which has similarly been created by God. For the Rabbis see Bill. 4, 466–83, and Moore, *Judaism* 1, 479–83; 3, 146f. The concept also has great significance as an anthropological term in Qumran, above all in the Ḥodayot; see Kuhn, *Konkordanz*, 92f.

227. Cf. also 11.14; 18.6; 42.21; on this R. H. Pfeiffer, 393f. For the comparison with the Stoa and Chrysippus' defence against the charges of his opponents, that Stoic determination leads to loss of freedom, see M. Pohlenz, *Stoa* 1, 104ff. and 2, 60; see also R. Pautrel, op. cit., 542.

228. Obviously this 'depersonalization' of God is in contradiction to the whole of the OT with the possible exception of Koheleth; however, we find it in the Greek enlightenment: see Vol. I, pp. 124f. We find an analogous situation to Ben Sira, say, in the controversy of Socrates with Aristodemus, who believed that the gods were not concerned with men and that therefore it was useless to worship them (Xenophon, *Mem.* 1, 4). The argument of Socrates on the basis of the purposefulness of the world created by the demiurge and here again especially of man formed by the divine '*pronoia*' is often quite near to the rational argument of the son of Sira about the purposefulness of creation. Later the Stoa caused the doctrine of divine providence, which overlooks nothing and is concerned for every man, to be acknowledged widely. For Ps.Arist. 210 it is τὸ τῆς εὐσεβείας . . . κατάστημα. It was also a basic feature of the theological views of Josephus, cf. his polemic against the Epicureans, in connection with the prophecies of Daniel, *Antt.* 10, 278, who 'drive *pronoia* from the life of men and assert that God is not concerned with what happens in the world', see also *c.Ap.* 2, 180 and *Antt.* 2, 24; 4.47, and on this A. Schlatter, *Wie sprach Josephus von Gott*, BFCT 14, 1910, 50. For divine providence and care in the Stoa see M. Pohlenz, op. cit., 2, 98–101, who assumes that this feature is to be derived from the founder's Semitic belief in providence.

229. For the text in 16.17d see V. Hamp, op. cit., 43.

230. 21.18f., see Smend, op. cit., 193f. according to the Syriac; cf. 6.24ff., 29.

231. For the text in 5.1, 2, see R. Smend, op. cit., 48: M has expansions, in v. 3 read כחי. For the text of vv. 4 and 6 see H. P. Rüger, op. cit., 13, 35ff.

232. Op. cit., 127.

233. This 'eudaemonistic understanding of the law' in Ben Sira is a chief starting point of criticism: see D. Michaelis, *TLZ* 83, 1958, 606; E. G. Bauckmann, op. cit., 50ff. Of course the term 'eudaemonistic' is inappropriate for earlier wisdom – on this see H. Gese, *Lehre und Wirklichkeit in der älteren Weisheit*, 1958, 7–11, and *RGG*³ 6, 1578 – however, one can use it for Ben Sira.

234. J. Fichtner, op. cit., 74.

235. This objection must be made to O. Kaiser, op. cit., 59. K. Koch, *ZTK*

52, 1955, 37ff., shows that the doctrine of retribution found a way into the LXX; one may add Ben Sira, who was virtually contemporaneous with it, as a Palestinian witness. The early oriental notion of order was no longer unaffected even in earlier Israelite wisdom, see H. Gese, op. cit., 33–50 and especially 45ff.; for its real transcending by Job see pp. 74ff.

236. See already the programmatic introductory verses 1.11ff., 18f.; cf. also the praise of the fear of God in 40.18ff. For remembrance after his death see 39.9–11, cf. 37.26 and 41.11; see on the other hand the pessimistic judgment of Koh. 2.16.

237. I. Lévi, op. cit., 2, lxf.; see on the other hand W. O. E. Oesterley in R. H. Charles, *Apocrypha* I, 269.

238. In what follows there is only an incomplete selection of allusions to retribution: 2.8; 3.14f., 31; 4.10, 13, 28; 5.7f.; 6.16; 7.1–3; 9.11f.; 10.13f.; 11.17, 21f., 26 (G); 12.2, 6; 15.13; 16.11–13; 17.23; 18.24; 20.18, 26; 21.10; 23.8, 11, 14, 25–27; 26.28; 27.24–29; 28.1; 33 (G 36). 1; 38.15; 39.25–30; 40.10; 41.6ff.; 46.6–10 etc. For the connection between retribution and the end of life see 11.26–28; 1.13; 7.36; 28.6; 41.9; cf. Ps. 73.17ff.

239. 35 (G 32). 13, cf. 12.6b: '. . . he exercises retribution on the wicked'; 17.23: 'Later he raises himself up and takes retribution on them and pours it upon their head'; cf. 35 (G 32). 24.

240. '*Ab*. 1, 4. For Antigonus see above, n. 161. O. S. Rankin, *Israel's Wisdom Literature*, 1954, 99–109, conjectures that the idea that man must do good for its own sake goes back to Stoic influences.

241. Thus e.g. J. Becker, *Das Heil Gottes*, 1964, 19–35, though he overlooks the fact that in this late period the Old Testament pattern of action and consequence cannot be presupposed without interruption, even if the formulas still continue. Punishment and reward are wholly directed towards God's judgment and retributive action.

242. Theoretical atheism was almost completely unknown in antiquity, see W. Nestle, *RAC* I, 866–8; E. Sandvoss, *Saeculum* 19, 1968, 312–29. Ps. 14 (53) might already be understood in a similar sense to Sir. 16.17ff.

243. Cf. 15.9, 10 and on it R. Smend, op. cit., xxv, also 34 (G 31). 21ff.; 35 (G 32). 5, 14f., see Vol. I, pp. 137f.

244. In the OT only II Chron. 2.15. For its significance in Ben Sira see R. Smend, *Die Weisheit des Jesus Sirach* (Hebrew and German), 77: need, necessity: 15.12 (in MS A, MS B חפץ); 32 (G 35). 2; 38.1, 12; (time of) need: 8.9; 10.26; use: 13.6; 32 (G 35). 17; 37.8; purpose: 39.16, 21, 30, 33; 42.23 (in the creation hymns).

245. For the knowledge of Koheleth in Ben Sira see the comparison in H. W. Hertzberg, *Der Prediger*, 1963, 46ff.; e.g. the theme of *carpe diem*: 14.11; 30.14ff.

246. 16.26ff. (following the Syriac, see V. Hamp, op. cit., 44); 42.15, see Y. Yadin, op. cit., 26; 43.10. The term for the 'natural order' is *ḥōq*, see below, n. 809.

247. 42.22–25. The reconstruction of this important verse has been considerably simplified by the Masada scroll, see Y. Yadin, op. cit., 27f. Previously, v. 22 was preserved only in the Greek and the Syriac, the order of the verse was disrupted and the text partially corrupt. In 23b, however, נשמע is to be read instead of נשמר with M, G and Syr, against the Masada Text, whereas in v. 24 Y.

Yadin is to be followed in his addition following 33 (G 36). 15. We thus arrive at the following text:

הלוא כל מעשין נחמד[ים]   עד ניציץ וחזית מראה
הכל חי ועו[מ]ד לעד   [ול']כל צרך הכל נשמר(ונשמע.1)
כלם [שנים שנים זה] לעמת זה   ולא עשה מחם שוא
זה על זה חלף טובם   [ו]מי ישבע להביט הודם

248. IV Ezra 8.44; cf. also the two parables *Sanh.* 108a and *Gen.R.* 28.6, in Bill. 3, 249d. This statement is usually limited to saying that the world was created for the sake of Israel, as an embodiment of the new humanity, see op. cit., 3, 248.

249. For the text see I. Lévi, *REJ* 92, 1932, 140f.; for v. 13b see V. Hamp, op. cit., 88, whereas v. 14d is to be retained despite its absence in G and Syr.

250. Like Koheleth (see Vol. I, pp. 119ff.), Ben Sira also has different terms for fate; e.g. חלק: 33.13d; 41.4 (here for the destiny of death) and חק, 38.22; 41.13, also for the destiny of death.

251. On this see O. S. Rankin, op. cit., 28–35. For the 'polarity' see the Habdala prayer in W. Staerk, *Altjüdische liturgische Gebete*, ²1930, 26 and Hermas, *Mand.* 8, 1.

252. R. Smend, op. cit., 163, reads δίκαιος with the Syriac (וכא) and some MSS, cf. also K. Ziegler, op. cit., ad loc.

253. So D. Michaelis, *TLZ* 83, 1958, 606.

254. 43.28–32; cf. 11.4b and 18.4–7. These are early wisdom themes which Ben Sira takes over from the tradition.

255. R. Bultmann, *History and Eschatology*, 1957, 96. In the same way Ben Sira and later Judaism know the idea of 'training and education', see Vol. I, pp. 132f.

256. M. P. Nilsson, *GGR*² 2, 258–62, and M. Pohlenz, *Stoa* 1, 94ff., 98ff.; 2, 55f. Cf. e.g. Chrysippus' definition of God in SVF 2, 305 fr. 1021 = Diog. Laert. 7, 147: θεὸν δὲ εἶναι ζῷον ἀθάνατον λογικὸν ἢ νοερόν τέλειον (see M. Pohlenz, loc. cit.) ἐν εὐδαιμονίᾳ, κακοῦ παντὸς ἀνεπίδεκτον, προνοητικὸν κόσμου τε καὶ τῶν ἐν κόσμῳ . . . εἶναι δὲ τὸν μὲν δημιουργὸν τῶν ὅλων καὶ ὥσπερ πατέρα πάντων κοινῶς τε καὶ τὸ μέρβος αὐτοῦ τὸ διῆκον διὰ παντῶν . . . see also Vol. I, pp. 159f.

For anthropocentric teleology see M. Pohlenz, op. cit., 1, 99; 2, 56f. and cf. Chrysippus, SVF 2, 168 fr. 527; 342 fr. 1118; 332 fr. 1150 = Philo, *De prov.* 2, 74, and fr. 1152.

257. See M. Pohlenz, op. cit., 1, 98, 101; 2, 57; cf. SVF 2, 337f., fr. 1175/6; 339 fr. 1180. For retribution in the Greek world outside the Stoa see also n. II, 317; for doubts about it see Vol. I, pp. 121ff.

258. R. Pautrel, op. cit., 543.

259. The term is relatively frequently in Chronicles and Koheleth; it appears for the first time with reference to God's creation in Jer. 10.16 = 51.19, cf. also Koh. 3.11; 11.5 and Ps. 119.91, and without the article in Isa. 44.24. Also in 11 Q Ps. 151 A, ed. J. A. Sanders, DJDJ IV, 54f.; V, 4; Gen.Apoc. 20.12f. and 'Ab. 4, 22. For Sirach see 36 (G 33). 1: אלהי הכל cf. 45.23c (without article); 39.21, 34: all things created by God. In the sense of 'the universe', 43.27, 33; 51.12d (M): יוצר הכל and presumably also 18.1 and 24.8: ὁ κτίστης ἁπάντων.

260. SVF 1, 121ff., fr. 537: almost all these features can be found in Ben Sira:

l.4 language (and thought) of man: 17.6; ll.5f., 38 invitation to the praise of his works: 38.14; 43.30; ll.7f., willing obedience of creation: 16.28; 39.31; 42.23; 43.7f.; ll.10f. lightning; 39.29; 43.13; l.12 reason or wisdom of God: 1.4ff.; 24; l.13 the lights of heaven; 43.2ff., 8ff.; ll.14f. God's omnipotence works through his word; 43.15bc; 43.26b; ll.17f. does not cause evil: 15.11–20; ll.28ff. against avarice: see Vol. I, pp.137f.; ll.32ff. God's demonstration of himself to man: 36 (G 33). 5, 22b. Similar features in common can also be found in the creation hymns of Qumran: see below, n.780.

261. For Rabbinic testimony to the ubiquity of God see S. Schechter, *Some Aspects of Rabbinic Theology*, 1909, 26ff.; cf. below n.383.

262. M. Pohlenz, op. cit., 1, 72.

263. Heraclitus B, fr. 10, Diels 1, 152ff., following (Ps.) Aristotle, *De mundo* 5, 396b; cf. A fr. 22 = 1, 149 and C fr. 1 §15ff. = 1, 186ff. (Hippocrates, *De victu*). For the Stoa see above all Chrysippus, SVF 2, 335 fr. 1169, on the relationship between good and evil, and on it M. Pohlenz, op. cit., 1, 100. For the Stoics, being was only existent in relation to another – opposing – being, see op. cit., 1, 69f.

264. For the polarity in later Jewish speculation of a cabbalistic stamp see M. Segal, op. cit., 212, who points to the Sefer Jezira and Midrash Temura, see the translation in M. J. bin Gorion, *Sagen der Juden. Von der Urzeit*, 1913, 29–32 and 352 no. 5.

265. The picture of man in Ben Sira is remarkably variable; 17.1–23 is relatively positive, cf. also the praise of the fear of God in 40.18ff.; 18.8ff. is more negative; cf. also the stress on the fall in 25.24 and 40.1ff.; 41.1ff. on tribulation and death in human life. On the whole, the positive features predominate, and the optimism of old wisdom continues here. This is the decisive difference from Essene anthropology, see Vol. I, pp.219f., 221f.

266. M. Pohlenz, op. cit., 1, 108; cf. 69; further Vol. I, p. 87, nn. II, 233f.

267. Lévi, op. cit., 2, lxivff.; Bigot, op. cit., IV, 2, 2047f.; Ehrhardt, *HTR* 46, 1953, 61f.

268. Euripides, *Chrysippus*, fr. 839, 8ff., Nauck[2]; cf. *Suppl.* 532; *Orest.* 1086; and on this I. Lévi, op. cit., 2, lxv.

269. Sir. 38.20f., cf. Sophocles, *Electra* 137ff.; Euripides, *Androm.* 1270f.

270. Sir. 30.17, cf. Aeschylus, *Persae* 750f.; Euripides, *Troiades* 632; *Hecuba* 377; Theognis 181f.; cf. above, n.132.

271. Sir. 3.20–26 (see Vol. I, p. 139); Euripides, *Bacc.* 393ff.; *Medea* 1224.

272. Further instances in L. Bigot, op. cit., 2048; cf. 7.11 and Theognis 155–8; 9.7f. and Aristophanes, *Nub.* 996f., see also Herodotus 1, 8; 11.14 and Theognis 165f.; 11.17ff. and Theognis 903ff.; 12.3f., 7, 10f. and Theognis 955f., 101f.; 31 (G 34). 26 and Theognis 499–502.

273. 31 (G 34). 12–32 (G 35). 13, esp. 32.1ff. and 38.1–15, cf. II Chron. 16.12 and R. and M. Hengel, *Medicus viator, Festschrift für R. Siebeck*, 1959, 332f., 335f.; cf. also N. Bentwich, *Hellenism*, 1919, 89f.

274. R. Pautrel, op. cit., 545; cf. also R. H. Pfeiffer, op. cit., 372.

275. *nābāl* 4.27; 21.22; 50.26 etc.; *pōtā* 8.17; 42.8; k[e]*sīl* 20.13; 42.8.

276. *lēṣ* 3.28; 8.11; 13.1 etc.; 15.8 'it (wisdom) is far from the mockers' is typical.

277. *rāšāʿ* 5.6; 8.10; 12.6; 13.17; 16.6; 40.10 etc.; *zēd* 11.9; 39.24 (following Smend); *anᵉšē zādōn* 11.14; 15.7; cf. 13.24 and 40.15.

278. (*ʾiš*) *ḥāmās* 10.23; 13.12; 32 (G 35). 18 etc.; *ʾakᵉzārī* 8.15; 35 (G 32). 22; *ḥonēp* 16.6; 41.10.

279. For the word group גאה :גאון :גאות see 10.6–18; 11.30; 13.20; 16.8; 23.8; 25.2, cf. in G ὑπερηφανία, ὕβρις etc. 21.4; 22.22; 27.15, 28; see further 7.17 against the *ʾᵉnōš rimmā*.

280. 'Overweening violence' (חמם גאוה) is mentioned in 10.8 as a reason for change of rule; this could refer to the change of rule in Palestine in 198 BC and to the loss of Asia Minor after Magnesia in 190 BC; perhaps the death of Ptolemy IV Philopator in 203 BC is mentioned in the following verses, see R. Smend, op. cit., 93. A. T. Olmstead, *JAOS* 56, 1936, mentions further historical possibilities. 21.4 might also refer to the party struggle in Jerusalem and to the dispute in the Tobiad family: 'violence and pride lay waste a city (text follows Smend, op. cit., 189f.) and the house of the overweening is devastated.'

281. The warning against apostasy also appears elsewhere: 2.3 from Yahweh; 4.19 from wisdom (= the law); 28.39; 29.17 (text following Smend, op. cit., 260), from the creator (cf. also 10.12); see also the 'praise of the fathers': 46.11; 47.23; 48.16, and above all 49.4ff., where the threat of the present has probably strengthened the negative judgment on the past: 'Apart from David, Hezekiah and Josiah they all acted wickedly and left the law of the Most High . . . They gave their power to the stranger and their honour to another people' (text following Smend, op. cit., 469f.).

282. Cf. 21.4 (see above, n.280); 11.9b: 'Do not take part in the dispute of the wicked (זדים)', could refer to partisan struggles in Jerusalem.

283. Cf. on the whole question 41.16–42.8; also 4.21; 'there is a shame which leads to sin . . .'; 4.26a; 20.22f. A few years later, Jewish ephebes performed epispasm in order to remove their circumcision: I. Macc. 1.15, see above n. II, 138, and Vol. I, p.289. On the warning against transgression of the law see also 2.7, 15; 17.14; 26.28c.

284. Cf. 6.17 (G); 9.16; 11.9; 12.14: 'Anyone who goes about with the wicked stains himself with his sin'; 13.1: 'Anyone who attaches himself to the mocker learns his mode of conduct', cf. also 13. 17f. and 22.13. This attitude was later normative for Essenes and Pharisees; the latter gave it its name. For the Christian community see I Cor. 5.11; for the rabbis see Bill. 2, 510ff.

285. M. P. Nilsson, *GGR*² 2, 168f., and E. Bi(c)kerman(n), *Inst.*, 254ff. For the naming of Moab see Isa. 25.10, which is also hard to interpret.

286. Cf. 10.11; 14.11f., 16; 16.30; 17.1, 27f.; 28.6; 38.21; 40.1, 11; 41.4, 10f.; 44.9. 2.9c and 17.26b have been expanded by the Greek glossator to indicate hope in eternal life, see J. Fichtner, op. cit., 70. 48.11 also originally contained no kind of reference to eternal life. Unfortunately the Hebrew text is illegible; for its later alterations see R. Smend, op. cit., 461f.; cf. O. Kaiser, op. cit., 63 n.3, and O. S. Rankin, op. cit., 208. Ben Sira's eschatological hope at no point goes beyond what is indicated in the Old Testament, cf. 36.22 and 48.10. For a possible rejection of the resurrection see G. Widengren, *SVT* 4, 1956, 227.

287. Apart from the doctrine of immortality there is no speculation about the heavenly world and no halachic casuistry. The concrete individual command-

ments are hardly mentioned. For 'Sadduceeism' in Ben Sira see Oesterley/Box, 1, 282f.; G. F. Moore, *Judaism* 1, 44, and H. Duesberg/P. Auvray, op. cit., 18: 'présadducéisme'. His difference even from the Hasidim is unmistakable. In any case, it is impossible to follow L. Finkelstein, *Pharisees*[3] 2, 589, and read 'neo-Hasidism' out of him. He is free from any Hasidic pietistic anxiety and prudishness, cf. 32 (G 35). 1; 38.1ff., and on it R. Smend, op. cit., xxvi; perhaps the omission of Ezra from the 'praise of the fathers' is a consequence of this non-Hasidic attitude, see H. H. Schaeder, *Esra der Schreiber*, 1930, 37.

288. Text following G; see Smend, op. cit., 45, against Segal, op. cit., 27. Cf. also the description of Phinehas and Elijah, 45.23f. and 48.1ff. For zeal in the Maccabean period see M. Hengel, *Zeloten*, 154ff.

289. O. Eissfeldt, *The Old Testament*, 473; cf. also Fohrer, *Introduction*, 319. R. N. Whybray, *Wisdom in Proverbs*, 1965, 106, puts Prov. 1–9 in the Persian period, but this is probably too early; the period between 330 and 250 BC is more likely. In connection with the time of origin we should note that Koheleth is presumably arguing against the optimism and the doctrine of retribution which we find in Prov. 1–9.

290. Cf. also Prov. 1.20–33; 3.13–26; 4.7ff.; 7.4ff.; 9.1ff. and personified folly, 9.13–18. M. Friedlander, *Griechische Philosophie im AT*, 1904, 77–89, and R. Kittel, *Geschichte des Volkes Israel* III, 2, 1929, 731, conjecture a Greek background as well as Babylonian and Persian influence; E. Sellin, *Geschichte des israelitisch-jüdischen Volkes* 2, 1922, 180f.; see also the literature given in P. Heinisch, op. cit., 31f.; W. Schencke, *Die Chokma in der jüdischen Hypostasenspekulation*, 1912, 78f., and K. Schubert, *Die Religion des nachbiblischen Judentums*, 1955, 15f.

291. The translation of *'āmōn* in 8.30 is largely disputed: the traditional interpretation *'āmān* = master workman (LXX, Syr, V, Rabbis, see Bill. 2, 356) is put forward, *inter alia*, by H. Ringgren, *Word and Wisdom*, 1947, 102–4; J. de Savignac, *VT* 12, 1962, 212f., and H. F. Weiss, op. cit., 191. One could refer to 3.19 for it, but the whole context of 8.22, according to which wisdom is not actively engaged in creation, tells against it. The explanation by G. Gerleman, *OTS* 8, 1960, 26f., that this interpretation arose under Stoic influence (= δημιουργός), is illuminating. The interpretation *'āmōn* or *'emūn* (?), favourite child, darling, is therefore to be preferred; see B. Gemser, *Sprüche Salomos*, [2]1963, 46 (further interpretations are given there); G. Fohrer, *TDNT* 7, 491, and H. Gese, *RGG*[3] 6, 1576. The secondary explanation 'master workman', 'mediator in creation', is less mythological and more rational (against H. F. Weiss, op. cit., 192f.).

292. G. Hölscher, op. cit., 67; G. Fohrer, *Das Buch Hiob*, 1963, 392ff., and *TDNT* 7, 490; even if wisdom here appears less as a person and rather 'as a thing', this hymn has the same historical background as personified wisdom in Prov. 8; Sir. 1 and 24; cf. e.g. Job 28.27 and Sir. 1.9. In no case should one talk at this early stage of a 'gnostic myth' (thus loc. cit.), see against this also H. Conzelmann, *The Future of Our Religious Past*, ed. James M. Robinson, 1971, 232 n. 16.

293. For Job 28 and Prov. 8 see W. Eichrodt, *Theology of the Old Testament* 2, 1967, 83f. Job 15.7f. could represent a preliminary stage of personified wisdom,

where the wisdom that is with God is connected with the first man; see on this
H. Ringgren, op. cit., 89ff.

294. The question whether this is the hypostatization of a divine characteristic, a mythical person or merely a poetical expression is also disputed. The idea
of the hypostasis is argued for by H. Ringgren, op. cit., 104; H. Donner, *ZÄS* 82,
1958, 9f., but against him are R. Marcus, *HUCA* 23, 1, 1950/51, 167ff.; B.
Gemser, op. cit., 48; R. B. Y. Scott, *VT* 10, 1960, 223, and R. N. Whybray, op.
cit., 103, 'the poetic personification of an attribute of Yahweh'. However, all
three interpretations flow into each other and have their limited justification, see
H. Conzelmann, op. cit., 232: 'The statements made by or about Wisdom actually
do reflect so many shades of meaning that every attempted explanation can be
supported by some texts. The denial of any mythical derivation, to be sure,
leaves entirely too many statements unexplained.' The essential point is that this
is not an 'abstract principle', see H. Gese, loc. cit.

295. R. H. Pfeiffer, *History of New Testament Times*, 1949, 253, sees in
Prov. 8 a direct attack on the view of Job 28 about the inaccessibility of wisdom.
A similar opposition emerges, among other things, between the magicians'
answer to Nebuchadnezzar in Dan. 2.11 and the praise of Daniel in 2.20ff., cf.
also I Enoch 42 and 91.10, on which see Vol. I, pp. 202ff. Cf. further von Rad,
Old Testament Theology 1, 451, and 2, 306f. The offence caused by Job 28 is
mitigated by the addition of v. 28. Cf. also n. 349 below.

296. Cf. virtue, SVF 3,508: *omnibus patet, omnes admittit, omnes invitat.*

297. B. Gemser, op. cit., 51f. (quot.). Here too we can hardly follow H. F.
Weiss, op. cit., 194f., in reading a share of wisdom in the creation of the world
out of 9.1.

298. See H. Leisegang, *PW*, 2.R. 3, 1026f., and Höfner in Roscher, *Lexikon* 4,
1212–4: it appears now and again as a poetic personification, see Aristophanes,
Birds, 1320; also Nauck², *Frag.trag. adesp.* 130 (Diodore 31, 30, 3): an appeal to
Wisdom as a goddess; and Euripides, *Med.* 843: in the train of Cypris: τᾷ Σοφίᾳ
παρέδρους πέμπειν Ἔρωτας, παντοίας ἀρετᾶς ξυνεργούς. The scene possibly goes back to
oriental influences. In Priene and Ephesus, Wisdom was represented as an
allegorical figure with other similar concepts. All in all, the evidence for a
personified wisdom in the pre-Christian period is small. Even Athene, most
appropriate for the attribute of wisdom, while named φρόνησις (see Leisegang,
op. cit., 1028, and von Arnim, SVF 4, 7) by Democritus and the Stoics and
receiving σοφία (*Protag.* 321d) and φιλοσοφία (*Critias* 109c) from Plato, is never
directly identified with σοφία in the pre-Hellenistic period. Cf. also Justin, *Apol.* 1,
64, 5: the Stoics designate Athene as τὴν πρώτην ἔννοιαν and daughter of Zeus, who
created the world ἐννοηθέντα . . . διὰ λόγου. J. R. Harris, *BJRL* 7, 1922/23, 56–72,
would derive Wisdom 18.15ff. *inter alia* from this Stoic conception of Athene.
However, the Justin passage could already be influenced by the Gnostics, see
H. Leisegang, op. cit. For the 'world soul' of the philosophers and of 'wisdom'
see Vol. I, pp. 163f.

299. *Phileb.* 30b–d, and see W. L. Knox in *Judaism and Christianity*, 2, 1932,
73f.: Knox draws from this the conclusion that Philo, too, had not read the
Philebus, but that his knowledge of Plato was largely derived from Posidonius.

300. Against U. Wilckens, *TDNT* 7, 508f., and *Weisheit und Torheit*, 1959,

190–7; cf. also the criticism by H. Conzelmann, op. cit., 232f. Perhaps a sharper distinction should be drawn between 'mythological background' and 'mythological origin'; the most recent investigation by R. N. Whybray, *Wisdom in Proverbs*, 1965, 103ff., which again asserts in apologetic terms that there is no 'mythological origin for wisdom' in Prov. 8.22ff., and that the terms discussed are 'metaphorical not mythological', does not take matters further. There can be no question that Prov.8.22ff. represents the starting point for the later speculation of Sirach, Wisdom and Philo, and if the hymn of 8.22ff. was composed for the purpose of warding off alien influences and, as a result, features of the strange goddess (Astarte, Isis, etc.) were transferred to wisdom, 'mythological influence is still present'; see the author's assent to Boström's theses, op. cit., 90.

301. A. Cowley, *Aramaic Papyri*, 1923, 215, 'Words of Ahikar' ll. 94 and 95; see also W. F. Albright, *AJSL* 36, 1920, 285; W. Baumgartner, *TR* 5, 1933, 287; C. I. K. Story, *JBL* 64, 1945, 333–7; H. Donner, op. cit., 12ff.; cf. also the assent of S. Morenz, *Ägyptische Religionen*, 1960, 133.

302. A. Cowley, op. cit., 147, no.44, 3: the oath of Menahem son of Sallum by 'Yahu the God, the temple and Anatyahu'; cf. 70 no.22, 125: "Anatbethel'. Albright, op. cit., 258ff., had already drawn attention to a Semitic goddess 'of life and wisdom' of the Ishtar type. In *SVT* 3, 1955, 7, the same author stresses that 'the wisdom cosmogony in VIII, 22ff. is full of obvious Canaanite reminiscences', see also *From the Stone Age*, 1940, 368f., and G. Boström, *Proverbiastudien*, LUÅ 30, 1934, no.3, 14. G. Pfeifer, *Ursprung und Wesen der Hypostasenvorstellungen im Judentum*, 1967, inconsistently rejects the influence of Canaanite–Phoenician conceptions (79), but then conjectures that a feminine deity of the type of 'Anatyahu or the queen of heaven of Jer.44.17 (102, cf. 27f.) might be of Canaanite origin. For the term *qnh* in Prov. 8.22 and the context see W. A. Irwin, *JBL* 80, 1961, 136ff., 'the imagery here is not the creation but birth of wisdom'.

303. G. Hölscher, op. cit., 69.

304. On this see H. Ringgren, *RGG³* 3, 504–6, and M. P. Nilsson, *opuscula selecta* 3, 1960, 233–42, and *GGR²* 1, 812ff. Cf. already H. Usener, *Götternamen*, ³1948, 364–75.

305. On this see Bousset/Gressmann, 347ff.; cf. also H. F. Weiss, op. cit., 211ff. The doctrine of the spirits at Qumran is a new stage which was surely not developed without alien influences, see Vol. I, pp. 220f. Cf. also H. Gese, *RGG³* 6, 1576: '. . . in which it comes very close to the concepts of *rûaḥ* and *dābār*'.

306. For the word of God see H. Ringgren, op. cit., 157ff.: apart from Aristobulus (see below, n.396) and Wisdom 18.15f., it is relatively rare as a hypostasis in Jewish writing; it only gains significance in Philo and in part is a substitute for 'wisdom', For the Rabbis see the long excursus in Bill. 2, 302–33. The tendency to hypostatization and divinization in the Greek tradition emerges much more strongly with the term '*logos*' than with '*sophia*', see H. Leisegang, *PW* 13, 1021ff. See in detail now H. F. Weiss, op. cit., 216–82, who stresses that the 'word' has no explicit creative function in Palestinian Judaism.

307. For Metatron see G. F. Moore, *HTR* 15, 1922, 55f.; Bill., Index 4, 1249. For the later identification with Enoch see L. Ginzberg, *Legends* 1, 140, and 5, 162f. n.61.

308. Bousset/Gressmann, op. cit., 331–42; G. von Rad, *TDNT* 2, 71ff.; W. Foerster, *TDNT* 2, 75ff., and 7, 151ff. Basically, what we have here is the negative side of the doctrine of spirits and angels starting from I Kings 22.19ff.; see also Vol. I, pp. 220ff., 231f.

309. Op. cit., 319, 342f., cf. also 357: hypostasis speculation as one of the foundations of christology. The objection made by R. N. Whybray, op. cit., 104, overlooks the fact that Prov. 8.22ff. or chs. 1–9 are not the only sources for hypostatized wisdom. Job 28 and Sir. 24, *inter alia*, can be added. This is a relatively wide tradition. The tendency to make the divine absolutely transcendent and to introduce intermediary beings was also to be found in Hellenistic, Platonizing philosophy of religion, see A. Wlosok, *Laktanz*, AAH 1960, 2, 53, 56ff.

310. G. Pfeifer, op. cit., 66f.

311. See e.g. the text published by A. S. van den Woude, *OTS* 14, 1965, 358, in which in ll. 10 and 16 Melchizedek (Michael?) is mentioned in connection with the *'elohīm* of Ps. 82.1 and Isa. 52.7; the doctrine of the two spirits in 1 QS 3.18ff. also goes beyond the bounds of traditional angelology. In Philo, on the other hand, mention can be made of the hypostasis of the Logos *(ἀρχ)άγγελος*: *Conf.ling.* 146 (M 1, 427); *De somn.* 239 (M 1, 656); *Quis.rer. div.* 205 (M 1, 501) etc.

312. G. Pfeifer, op. cit., 16.

313. G. von Rad, *Old Testament Theology* 1, 443.

314. For the formation of wisdom schools in post-exilic Israel see above, pp. 78ff., and J. C. H. Lebram, *VT* 15, 1965, 227ff., who regards the 'Levitical schools' as being above all 'the representatives of *ḥokmā* in Palestine' (229); he points to possible tensions between the returning Golah and the schools existing in the country. For wisdom as 'a divine mediator of revelation' see G. von Rad, op. cit., 1, 441, and H. Gese, *RGG*³ 6, 1576.

315. H. Ringgren, *Word and Wisdom*, 1947, 134, and *RGG*³ 3, 506; see also Bostrom, op. cit., 102–55 and, in agreement, G. von Rad, op. cit., 1, 443f.: 'wisdom personified largely received blood and life from her more sensual opposite, Astarte, the goddess of love' (444); see also W. L. Knox, *St Paul and the Church of the Gentiles*, 1939, 57.

316. On this see M. Friedländer, op. cit., 73ff.; R. Kittel, op. cit., 3, 732; R. Reitzenstein, *Das mandäische Buch des Herrn der Grösse*, SAH 1919, no. 12, 54ff., though his historical classification is too fantastic; see the polemic by G. Boström, op. cit., 16–32. For Clem.Alex., see *Strom.* 1, 29, 6, GCS 2, 18.

317. J. M. Allegro, *PEQ* 96, 1964, 53–55 = 4 Q 184 (DJDJ V, 82ff.) and J. Strugnell, *RQ* 7, 1969/71, 263ff. J. Carmignac, *RQ* 5, 1964/66, 361–74, supposes that a competing sect is meant here. The literal interpretation of the 'strange woman', presented by Boström, op. cit., 42ff., and above all the 'cultic interpretation' associated with it, 103–55, need not be the only possibility. For the theme see H. Ringgren, *Word*, 134ff.; however, it appears extraordinarily frequently in Prov. 1–9.

318. DJDJ IV, 79ff. The very artificial acrostic hymn was taken into his collection by Ben Sira in a considerably altered, extended version. For the theme see also Sir. 15.2f.; Prov. 5.18f.; Wisdom 8.2ff.

319. I. Alpers, *Hercules in Bivio*, diss. 1912, 62f.; see W. Michaelis, *TDNT* 5, 55 n.36. Allegorical interpretation of Prov.7 and 9 can no longer be excluded after the discovery of the fragment about the wicked woman in 4 Q. The fable then emerges later in the Rabbinic tradition; see Bill.4, 408f.: *Koh.R.* 1, 14. R. Abba b. Kahana (beginning of the fourth century AD).

320. G. von Rad, *Old Testament Theology* 1, 141.

321. S. Hermann, *TLZ* 86, 1961, 418; cf. also H. Schwabl, *PW Suppl* 9, 1498f.

322. G. von Rad, op. cit., 143; S. Herrmann, op. cit., 418ff.

323. S. Hermann, op. cit., 423, 424; see also C. F. von Weizsäcker, *The Relevance of Science*, 1964, 42ff.: 'If it is a work of scholarship, it belongs to theology' (46).

324. On this see H. Schwabl, op. cit., 1513ff., 1539ff. G. von Rad, op. cit., 1, 141f., rightly indicates that the creation story of P does not look for a 'cosmological primal principle' like the Ionian natural philosophers, but connects everything with the 'personal creative will of Yahweh'. On the other hand, genuine analogies appear in the *Timaeus*, see Vol.I, p.163.

325. C. F. von Weizsäcker, op. cit., 52.

326. G. von Rad, op. cit., 1, 142; for *creatio ex nihilo*, see H. W. Weiss, op. cit., 11–17: the Old Testament presuppositions; 69ff. in Philo; 73f. in II Macc.7.28; 86ff. in the Rabbis; 119ff. in apocalyptic; 129ff. the Samaritans. There is a summary at 165ff.: the conception was not present from the beginning, 'but must first have established itself in the controversy with Gentile myth and . . . philosophical thought' (66); cf. 174.

327. On this see G. von Rad, op. cit., 1, 450ff.

328. Prov.3.19; cf. Job 38–42; Ps.104.24; 136.5; see also the hymn to Yahweh, the wise creator, in 11 Q Ps^a, DJDJ IV, 89ff. For the creation traditions in Ben Sira see Vol.I, pp.144ff. Cf. already Jer.10.21 = 51.15. For the whole see J. Fichtner, *Die altorientalische Weisheit*, 1933, 111f. For the difference from Prov.8 see H. W. Weiss, op. cit., 189. A parallel conception is the notion that the world was 'built up' by the spirit, Judith 16.14. G. Pfeifer, op. cit., 98, already conjectures Stoic influence here.

329. Ps.139.14; Job 5.9ff.; 9.8ff.; 37.14 etc., and on it see G. von Rad, *Old Testament Theology* 1, 449.

330. Sir.24.1, 2 characterizes this self-predication as an explicit aretalogy with reference to wisdom's praise of itself (αἰνέσει ψυχὴν αὐτῆς and twice καυχήσεται).

331. Thus for the first time W. L. Knox, *JTS* 38, 1937, 230–7, who rightly characterizes the historical context: 'a startling affinity to a Syrian Astarte with features of Isis' (235), see further *St Paul and the Church*, 59ff.; H. Ringgren, op. cit., 144f., and in detail H. Conzelmann, op. cit., 234–43. As the Isis aretalogies in the form preserved for us and also the propaganda for Isis 'of the many names' in her syncretistic transformation are products of the Ptolemaic era from the beginning of the third century BC at the earliest (see A. D. Nock, *Conversion*, 1933, 48f., and R. Harder, *Karpokrates von Chalkis und die memphitische Isispropaganda*, AAB 1943, no.14.45ff.), a connection between the Isis aretalogies and Proverbs, which probably arose in the first half of the third century at the

Chapter III

latest, is still uncertain. The texts appear in W. Peek, *Der Isishymnus von Andros*, 1930; R. Harder, op. cit., 18ff., gives a reconstruction of its context. Other important passages are Diodore 1, 27, 4, the epiclesis of Isis, POx 11.1380, and the hymns of Isidorus (first century BC), SEG 8, 548–51. Cf. also Kore Kosmou in Hermes Trismegistos 23, 64ff. = CH4, 21ff., and Apuleius, *Met.* 11, 5; on this see also M. Nilsson, *GGR²* 2, 626ff. n. 5 and H. Conzelmann, op. cit., p.230 n. 5. For identification with earlier Egyptian goddesses see Roeder, *PW* 9, 2091f., 2096 (Plutarch, *Isis et Osiris* 56, 374b), and S. Morenz, op. cit., 279. Cf. J. Bergman, *Ich bin Isis*, 1968.

332. State support is of course heavily qualified by P. M. Fraser, *Opuscula Atheniensia* 3, 1960, 1–54, 21ff., but a complete denial is unjustified.

333. Goddess of righteousness: see Roeder, *PW* 9, 2129, and Waser, *PW* 5, 565; ἐπίνοια see POx 11, 1380, ll. 60f.; πρόνοια loc. cit., ll. 43f., cf. Apuleius, *Met.* 11.18; *dea providens*; φρόνησις POx 11, 1380, l.44, cf. 123f. and Plutarch, *Isis et Osiris*, 2, 353 A/B and 60, 375 D, where Isis is elevated to be the goddess of knowledge and her name is derived from οἶδα and ὄν. See also her connections with the 'world soul', n.368 below. Cf. further R. Reitzenstein, *Poimandres*, 1904, 44, on Isis as goddess of wisdom; A. Wlosok, *Laktanz*, AAH 1960, 2, 95f. n. 103 and 56f., nn.32, 33; R. Merkelbach, *Roman und Mysterium*, 1962, 6 n. 1 and 97 n. 1: Isis as *'providentia'*.

334. POx 11, 1380, ll. 116/7, cf. SEG 8, 548 l.18 and Dittenberger, *Syll³.*, 1132, and Drexler in Roscher, *Lexikon* 2, 500. For Isis-Sophia in Aristides see Bergman, op. cit., 35 n.2.

335. POx 11, 1380, 93–97: Rhinocolura, Dor, Tower of Strato, Ashkelon, Raphia; 98: Gaza; 100f.: Bambyce; 106f.: Phoenicia; 116f.: Berytus, Sidon. Cf. also S. Herrmann, 'Isis in Byblos', *ZÄS* 82, 1958, 48–55, and P. Roussel, *Syria* 22, 1942/43, 21ff.: the private sanctuary of Serapis and Isis in Laodicea on the Sea in Northern Syria, 175 BC.

336. Bronze discovered at Ashkelon, see J. H. Iliffe, *QDAP* 5, 1936, 64, 66f., 68; cf. also the Palestinian terra cottas with the picture of a mother and child from the Persian/Hellenistic period in A. Ciasca, *OA* 2, 1963, 45–63, esp. 51 n. 1, and O. Negbi, *'Atiqot* 6, 1966, 10 pls. 1 and 2. For 'nurse' see T.AZ 5.1 (l.468), and b. AZ 43a, see below, n.IV, 57.

337. Ashkelon, see Schürer, 2, 31, and M. R. Savignac, *RB* NS 2, 1905, 426–9, with the features of a city goddess (Tyche); Gerasa: Schürer, 2.40, and the inscription in C. H. Kraeling, *Gerasa* 1938, 382, no.15 (143 AD); Hauran (Kanatha); Schürer, 2, 47; Samaria: J. W. Crowfoot etc., *Samaria-Sebaste* 1957 3, 37, no.13 = SEG 8.93, presumably already the third century BC. Cf. L. Vidman, *Sylloge*, 1969, 180ff.

338. Macalister/Duncan, 'Excavations on the Hill of Ophel', *PEFA* 4, 1926, 159ff., 'provisionally we may ascribe it to the time of Ptolemaic domination'. On this see S. A. Cook, *The Religion*, 67, and the illustration, pl.XIV. For Isis and Hathor see H. Gressmann, *Vorträge der Bibl. Warburg*, 1923/24, 1924/25, 182ff., and Roeder, *PW* 9, 2092, 2120, etc.; see also the Astarte with ram's horns as the royal headdress according to Philo Byblius, FGrHist 26 F 2.31 = Eusebius, *Pr.Ev.* I, 10, 31. An illustration of this is given by a representation of Isis with the Horus child and a Phoenician dedication 'to ʿAštoret', from about the fourth

century BC, *CRAI* 1904, 472–5. In general on the old and beloved 'Egyptian type' representation of Palestinian goddesses see S. A. Cook, op. cit., 125f.

339. Sir.24.10f., cf. POx 1380, 5f., 37; Diod. 1, 27, cf. Andros, ll. 3, 25; Cyme 11; Ietica 8; Gomphoi 5 (ed. W. Peek, op. cit.).

340. W. Peek, op. cit., 122, Cyme, ll. 4, 16, etc.; 123ff., Ietica, ll. 3, 13, 28, 35, 38 etc.; line 32 = 28 shows how much legal order and knowledge hang together: the distinction between good and evil comes from Isis; cf. also SEG 8, 548, l. 6.

341. Cf. above all PSI 844, which was shown to be an Isis aretalogy by E. Heitsch, *MusHelv* 17, 1960, 185–8.

342. Read ἡγησάμην with Sin., Syr., Lat., instead of ἐκτησάμην. H. Conzelmann, op. cit., 238f., calls attention in this context to the prediction of Isis as ruler of the earth, which frequently emerges in this context.

343. W. Schencke, op. cit., 27, who sees a prelude to this in Prov. 8.15 and the wisdom of the animals, 6.6ff.; 30.24ff. Cf. also H. F. Weiss, op. cit., 196ff.

344. Zeno according to Diogenes Laertius 7, 88 = SVF 1, 162; cf. U. Wilckens, *Weisheit*, 239. Similarly Cicero, *Republic* 3, 33: *Est quidem vera lex recta ratio . . . diffusa in omnes.*

345. Diogenes Laertius 7,87 (cf. already 86) = SVF 1, 552; on this see M. Pohlenz, *Die Stoa* I, 1959, 114f. The identification of the κοινὸς λόγος ὃς διὰ πάντων with the κοινὸς νόμος which men are to follow also appears in the Cleanthes hymn SVF 1, 1222, no. 537, lines 8, 20. Cf. Cicero, loc. cit., *quae vocet ad officium iubendo.*

346. H. F. Weiss, op. cit., 196f.

347. K. Schubert, *Judaica* 9, 1953, 67f.; *Die Religion des nachbiblischen Judentums*, 1955, 14ff. and J. L. Koole, *OTS* 16, 1965, 377, which point to Cicero, *De natura deorum* 2, 14, 37 (after Chrysippus, see SVF 2, 1153): *Ipse autem homo ortus est ad mundum contemplandum et imitandum.* See also already W. L. Knox, *St Paul*, 60.

348. Sir.24.23, cf. already 8b, 10f. and 1.10b; on this see Vol. I, pp. 148f. All the preceding statements are included in the stressed πάντα: see G. F. Moore, op. cit., I, 264 n. 1. It is extremely improbable that Sir. 24.23ff. is a later interpolation, as W. L. Knox, op. cit., assumes.

349. Cf. already Ahikar, Vol. I, p. 154, and above n. 302; Job 28; the model for Bar. 3.15–32 (see Vol. I, pp. 170f.) and the interspersed I Enoch 42. See also U. Wilckens, *TDNT* 7, 508f., though he overstresses the significance of this 'myth'. A considerable number of the passages cited by him do not appear in this context.

350. It is, however, questionable whether this identification was a 'commonplace in his times', as G. F. Moore, op. cit., I, 265, supposes; op. cit., I, 268, he sees in the motto of Simon from '*Ab.* I, 2 an anticipation of the later idea that the world was created for the sake of the Torah, see *Gen.R.* I, 10; 12, 2 etc. But here the formula is substantially different. Cf. also J. Goldin, *PAAJR* 27, 1958, 43–58, esp. 53ff. The identification of עולם and world, which can only be demonstrated later, is a disruptive element.

351. In Ps. 119 there is also talk of apostasy (vv. 118f., 158), neglect of the commandments (126, cf. 110, 113, 139) and oppression of those faithful to the law (121, 143, 150f., 157, 161); this could already be a hint at the conflict which has been fully developed in Ben Sira; the psalm will therefore come from the

second half of the third century, when the free-thinking party of the Tobiads were already in power (see Vol. I, pp. 267ff.), cf. also A. Deissler, *Ps.* 119, Münchener Theologische Studien 11, 1955, 283ff., 289, 'a degree of closeness to the epoch of Ben Sira'. The second half of the third century therefore appears more probable than the first half, which he supposes. H. W. Wolff, *EvTh* 9, 1949/50, 385, conjectures the milieu of Ptolemaic rule for Ps. 1.

352. *Old Testament Theology* I, 445.

353. Op. cit., 127f. Author's italics.

354. G. von Rad, loc. cit.

355. J. Freudenthal, *JQR* 2, 1889/90, 205–22; E. Zeller, *PhGr*⁶ III, 2, 274ff., and R. Marcus, *L. Ginzberg Jubilee Vol.*, 1945, 237ff.

356. G. Gerleman, *OTS* 8, 1950, 15–27, and *Studies in the Septuagint III, Proverbs*, LUÅ I, 52, 1956, no. 3: for the special form of this translation see 15: the use of Greek metre, cf. also 29 on Prov. 19.15: ἀνδρογύναιον and on this Plato, *Symp.* 139e, and Philo and the late Palestinian *haggada*, see Bill. 4, 405, 410f., and 1, 801f.; cf. already J. Freudenthal, *Hellenistische Studien*, 68f.

357. G. Gerleman, *Studies*, 59ff., defends a relatively early date against Thackeray with good reasons, and with reference to the affinity with the book of Job puts the LXX in the middle of the second century BC. Cf. also Vol. I, pp. 155f. for the metaphorical interpretation of Prov. 2.16 LXX.

358. G. Gerleman, *OTS* 8, 1950, 26, and *Studies*, 57; similarly already G. Bertram, *ZAW* 54, 1936, 162: 'its all-embracing activity arises through the harmony in creation . . .'; the interpretation of G. Pfeifer, op. cit., 27, 'I was betrothed to him', is extremely improbable; here one would have to expect the middle or passive, see Liddell-Scott, *Lexicon* 243: perhaps, however, ἁρμόζουσα is to be understood intransitively, as an object is missing: 'I was in harmonious community with him'; this would also correspond to the idea of the world soul.

359. M has 'as the earliest of his works': *qedem mipeʿālāy*.

360. Prov. 8.30c, 31: M mentions only the 'delight' (*šaʿašūʿīm* or *šaʿašuʿay*) of 'wisdom' and not the joy of God. The originality of LXX LA here is questionable. For the joy of God in creation cf. Targ. Jer. II Gen. 2.2.

361. For the Platonic world soul and the origin of the *Timaeus* see U. von Wilamowitz-Mollendorf, *Platon*, ⁵1959, 464ff., 480f., and R. P. Festugière, *Révélation* 2, 94,102ff.; cf. also H. Schwabl, *PW Suppl*, 9, 1539f. It already appears in the *Statesman*, 269d: ζῷον ὂν καὶ φρόνησιν εἰληχὸς ἐκ τοῦ συναρμόσαντος αὐτὸ κατ᾽ἀρχάς, cf. also *Philebus* 30a. The Platonic conception is fundamentally different from all Jewish interpretations of wisdom, but there were certain starting points in common.

362. Plato, *Timaeus* 34c, 4f. and 34b, 3f.

363. *Tim.* 36e/37a.

364. *Tim.* 37c, 7, cf. also Aristotle, *Eth. Nic.* 1154, 25f.

365. *Tim.* 34b, 8f.

366. *Tim.* 40a, 5; 41b, 1; see R. P. Festugière, op. cit., 2, 110.

367. For the world soul in the Stoa see M. Pohlenz, op. cit., I, 77, 215f.; there it is identified with the Logos and even called God, see e.g. Cleanthes, SVF I, 111, no. 495: τὴν δὲ ψυχὴν δι᾽ ὅλον τοῦ κόσμου διήκειν, ἧς μέρος μετέχοντας ἡμᾶς ἐμψυχοῦσθαι. Here there is an analogy to the spirit of God in Judaism; cf. also 1,

120, no. 532. Further instances, op. cit., index 4, 166. For the problem see also J. Moreau, *L'âme du monde de Platon aux Stoiciens*, 1939.

368. R. Heinze, *Xenokrates*, 1891, fr. 15, p. 164, cf. 35ff., 72ff., and Plutarch, *Isis and Osiris* 45–60, 396A–375D and on it R. Heinze, op. cit., 31–77; cf. further H. Leisegang, *PW*, 2.R 3, 1027, and now in detail H. J. Krämer (above n. II, 225), 21–126.

369. Cf. Wisd. 7.22b, 25f.; 8.1, 3; 9.4; for Philo see above all J. Pascher, *Der Königsweg*, 1931, 60–105, and following it, U. Wilckens, *Weisheit und Torheit*, 1959, 142–57. The derivation of gnostic 'Sophia' from an 'ancient Near Eastern myth' (op. cit., 194f.), following W. Bousset, sees only one side of this complex of tradition. Cf. on it G. Quispel, *Eranos Jahrbuch* 22, 1953, 208, 'it must always be remembered that for the Gnostic, Sophia represented something like the *anima mundi* and had contacts with Greek ideas about the world soul; this world soul attracted every possible metaphor and comparison from Hebrew literature to itself like a magnet.'

370. J. Kaerst, *Geschichte des Hellenismus* 2, ²1926, 221, supposes a dualistic Iranian influence here, cf. also *Statesman* 269e/270a.

371. Eusebius, *Pr.Ev.* 13, 12, 11; see below, n. 389.

372. *Pr.Ev.* 13, 11, 4; see Vol. I, pp. 165f. There are already certain echoes in the LXX translation of Gen. 1, cf. the rendering of *tōhū wābōhū* by ἀόρατος καὶ ἀκατασκεύαστος, and the formlessness of Platonic matter, *Tim.* 51a, 7: ἀνόρατον. . . . καὶ ἄμορφον or 30a.5: εἰς τάξιν ἤγαγεν ἐκ τῆς ἀταξίας, cf. E. Zeller, *PhGr⁶* III, 1, 275 n. 1; also the καλὰ λίαν of Gen. 1.31 and the constant stress on the perfect beauty of the Platonic creation, see 29a; 41b; 68c; 92c; see *Statesman* 273b: πάντα καλά; on the rest of God see 42c; for the creation of time and the stars: 37c; 40bff. Whereas in Gen. 1.26f. and 5.1 man was created κατ'εἰκόνα θεοῦ, according to *Tim.* 92c, 7, the universe filled with living being is itself εἰκὼν τοῦ νοητοῦ. Cf. F.-W. Eltester, *Eikon im Neuen Testament*, 1958, 17ff., 27ff.; for its use as a loan word in the Rabbis, see L. Baeck, *Aus drei Jahrtausenden*, 1958, 153 n. 2. However, in no case do we have deliberate allusions; in part they were also suggested by the original text. Even in Ex. 3.14, the translation of *'ehyeh 'ªšer 'ehyeh* by ἐγώ εἰμι ὁ ὤν, one cannot follow Morton Smith, *BJRL* 40, 1957/58, 474, in speaking of 'clear Platonism' (similarly M. Hadas, *HCu*, 50); see already the restrained judgment of J. Freudenthal, *JQR* 2, 1889/90, 220, who conjectures Stoic influence. More important than this supposed philosophical borrowing by the translator of the Pentateuch before the middle of the third century BC – the legend of Aristeas probably has a historical background, as it already appears in Aristobulus (*Pr.Ev.* 13, 12, 2), cf. N. Walter, *Aristobulus*, 88ff., and E. Bickerman(n), *PAAJR* 28, 1959, 2f. – were the later effects of these points of contact, for it could be argued from them that Plato had known the work of Moses. Galen provides a critical comparison between Plato's demiurge and Moses in the second century AD: R. Walzer, *Galen on Jews and Christians*, 1949.

373. Clem. Alex., *Strom.* I, 72, 4; Περιπατετικός, cf. Eusebius, *Chron.*, GCS, ed. Helm, 7, 139, and *Pr.Ev.* 9, 6, 6; 13.11, 3, 12; cf. also 8.9, 38; critical remarks on this in N. Walter, op. cit., 10ff., lit. For II Macc. 1.10 see op. cit., 16ff. More weight should probably be attached to this note, cf. Ps.Hecataeus in Josephus, *c.Ap.* 1, 187–9 on the Jewish high priest Hezekiah, see above, n. I, 389, and

Jerome, *De viris illustribus* 11, Migne *PL* 23, 658f., on Philo. Cf. J. G. Bunge (see n. II, 296) 67ff.

374. A. Schlatter, *GI*³, 82ff., cf. 408 n. 99. For Aristotle's acknowledgement of philosophical monotheism see e. g. *Met.* 1076a, 3f. with the quotation from Homer, *Iliad* 2, 204, and his positive verdict on Xenophanes, *Met.* 986b, 21–24. Theophrastus and Clearchus, pupils of Aristotle, showed special interest in the Jews, see Vol. I, pp. 256ff.

375. The name did not necessarily mean membership of the Aristotelian school in Alexandria of the third to first centuries BC, but also 'a literary historian, a biographer or perhaps even a scientific writer . . . who presented an artistic popular account', see K. O. Brink, *PW Suppl* 7, 904. This would describe Aristobulus, with his eclectic exegetical work. The quotation from Anatolius in Eusebius, *HE* 7, 32, 17–18, indicates interests in astronomy and the calendar. The designation need not therefore be a construction of Clem.Alex. on the basis of *Pr.Ev.* 13, 12, 10 = *Strom.* 5, 96, as N. Walter, loc. cit., thinks. Clement may already have found the designation in the tradition at his disposal, like that of Philo as a Pythagorean (*Strom.* 2, 100, 3).

377. A. Schlatter, *GI*³, 407 n. 96, cf. BFCT 1, 5, 1897, 163f. It does not seem to me so certain that Aristobulus' writing was included in Clement and Eusebius in an unabbreviated form, as N. Walter, op. cit., 27 n. 1; 34 n. 6; 97ff., etc. supposes. The indubitable difficulties in translation and interpretation in *Pr.Ev.* 13, 12, 9–16 are perhaps connected with the abbreviations of an epitomator. The view of Schlatter, op. cit., that other quotations had been given a short allegorical commentary as well as *Pr.Ev.* 13.12, 14, l. 4, is not completely erroneous. N. Walter, op. cit., even supposes that alterations were made to the work of Aristobulus in connection with the Jewish–Orphic poem (op. cit., 103–15). However, his hypothesis of a complete substitution is not convincing.

376. Here the investigation by N. Walter has brought clarity, after R. Keller, *De Aristobulo Judaeo*, diss. Bonn 1948, 19–78, had already shown his affinity with the *koinē* of Polybius, Diodore (who is himself in turn dependent on earlier Hellenistic sources) and the Ptolemaic papyri. N. Walter, op. cit., 7ff., 264ff., gives a survey of the fragments. The most important are: F. 2 = *Pr.Ev.* 8, 10, 1–17; F. 3 = 13, 12, 1f.; F. 4 = 12, 3–8; F. 5 = 13, 12, 9–16 (12, 10, 11 = 7, 14, 1) = Eusebius GCS ed. Mras 8, 1, 451–4, and 8, 2, 190–7. Also a fragment from Anatolius in Eusebius, *HE* 7, 32, 17f.

378. For the dating see E. Bickerman(n), *PAAJR* 28, 1959, 3 n. 3, with reference to Eusebius, *Chron.*, GCS, ed. Helm 7, 139. The writing is directed solely to king Ptolemy VI (Philometor); however, he was sole ruler only between 176 and 170 BC. Before that he had to share the rule with his mother, later with his brother and sister, or with his sister alone. He received the surname Philometor in 179/78 BC. The didactic, personal address to the king would best fit the young king, born 186 or 184/3 BC. For the form of a didactic writing from a wise man to a king see Festugière, *Révélation* 1, 324ff. The occasion for the writing, which presupposes questions from the king, will hardly have been the Samaritan–Jewish religious conversation according to *Antt.* 13, 74–9 (thus A. Schlatter, *GI*³, 82), especially as the name Aristobulus does not appear here. Possibly the apology of Aristobulus was, however, caused by the events in

Jerusalem after 175 BC, as this made the question of the relationship between Hellenistic education and the Mosaic law a topical one. At that time, too, there were still illusions about a possible reconquest of Judea. The characterization of Aristobulus as διδάσκαλος of king Ptolemy in the fictitious letter II Macc. 1.10 would also fit a young king. It is less probable, as N. Walter, op. cit., 16–26, supposes, that the designation of Ptolemy as Philometor was only introduced by Clem. Alex. (*Strom.* 1, 150, 1 and 5, 97, 7) on the basis of II Macc. 1.10. Rather, the forger of II Macc. 1.10ff. has introduced the well-known personality of Aristobulus as a prominent addressee of the letter, because it was known that he had written a didactic letter to the young Philometor. N. Walter nevertheless arrives at a remarkably similar dating: op. cit., 24 and 123 n. 2: the middle of the second century BC, cf. also Schmid/Stählin, *GGL*[6] II, 1, 603f. Aristobulus shares with his contemporary Polybius (*Athen.* 2, 35c) the first appearance of the name Philadelphus for Ptolemy II (*Pr.Ev.* 13, 11, 2; Mras 2, 191), which is significant for dating. For Philadelphus and Philometor see H. Volkmann, *PW* 18, 1645 and 1702ff. In view of this hostility to the Jews, a dating of the work under Ptolemy VIII Lathyrus (Philometor II), 116–108 and 88–80 BC (see A. Gercke, *PW* 2, 919), is improbable.

379. *Pr.Ev.* 13, 12, 8; cf. *Ps.Arist.* 31: the law is φιλοσοφώτερον, 200f.: the philosophers at the court of the king recognize the greater knowledge (συνιέναι πλέον) of the seventy-two elders; cf. also 235.

380. The term appears in this sense in Aristobulus, cf. in addition to *Pr.Ev.* 8, 10, 2 also 13, 12, 9 and 8, 10, 3: φυσικὰς διαθέσεις cf. also Ps. Aristeas 171: φυσικὴ διάνοια τοῦ νόμου.

381. For the rejection of the 'myth' see also a little later Ps.Aristeas 168: καὶ οὐδὲν εἰκῇ κατατέτακται διὰ τῆς γραφῆς οὐδὲ μυθωδῶς; also the polemic against the Greek inventors of myths, 137 and 322. Cf. on this N. Walter, op. cit., 100; Philonic examples, op. cit., 135 n. 4; for the problems, G. Stählin, *TDNT* 4, 777–86.

382. For Aristobulus' method of exegesis and its models see N. Walter, op. cit., 124–49; also E. Stein, *Die allegorische Exegese des Philo von Alexandrien*, 1929, 6–12, and R. P. C. Hanson, *Allegory and Event*, 1959, 41ff. E. Stein already recognized that in Aristobulus we have the earliest form of Alexandrian allegorical exegesis; according to him 'it does not go beyond the framework of Palestinian, anti-anthropomorphic allegory' (op. cit., 7). Thus Aristobulus is more restrained in using allegorical methods even than Aristeas and Philo. N. Walter, op. cit., 138, therefore follows J. Freudenthal (*Hellenistische Studien*, 1874f., 67) in speaking of a 'Hellenistic midrash'.

383. The omnipresence of the divine 'dynamis' (thus *Pr.Ev.* 13, 12, 7) is also said to be shown by the Orphic hymn and the quotation from Aratus: see 13, 12, 6, l. 4: πάντη δὲ θεοῦ κεχρήμεθα πάντες. We find this thought taken further in the mission preaching of Judaism and early Christianity, e.g. in Acts 17.27f., see J. C. Lebram, *ZNW* 55, 1964, 221–43, and E. Haenchen, *The Acts of the Apostles*, 1971, 516 (lit.), 524f. However, the conception has an Old Testament, Palestinian component: Jer. 23.23f.; Amos 9.2ff.; Ps. 139.8–10; Isa. 6.3, cf. Sir. 43.27 and Vol. I, p. 146; it also appears among the Rabbis, see Vol. I, p. 148. Here there is a close contact with Stoic ideas. Because there already was this

background, similar quotations could be taken over from Greek poets; cf. also Vol. I, pp. 167f. The 'descent of God' is also reinterpreted in *Mek.Ex.* 19, 20 (L. 2, 224).

384. See Vol. I, pp. 134ff. Judaism and Hellenism also come close to each other in the conception of the 'prophets' as men inspired by the spirit and the notion of 'inspired writings' which develops from this. At the end of this movement we have the theory of 'absolute inspiration' in Philo and the Rabbis, see Bousset/Gressmann, 149f. On this see H. Kleinknecht, *TDNT* 6, 339ff., esp. 343: Plato as the founder of the 'secular Greek notion of inspiration'; F. Baumgärtel, *TDNT* 6, 362: the spirit as the cause of ecstasy and ecstatic speaking in the Old Testament, and W. Beider, *TDNT* 6, 374f.: Philo with Moses as 'prototype'. Aristobulus seems to stand on a similar level in his conception of inspiration to the Palestinian *sōperīm*, which is essentially distinct from the later almost mechanical conceptions. A comparison between Philo and Ben Sira shows that there was no difference in principle between Alexandrian and Palestinian conceptions of inspiration, see P. Katz, *ZNW* 47, 1956, 209–11. Further see Vol. I, pp. 202ff.: 'Wisdom through revelation', and pp. 210f.

385. *Pr.Ev.* 13, 12, 5, 6. N. Walter, op. cit., 114, etc., supposes that the Orphic poem was inserted later: see above, n. 377.

386. A. Schlatter, *GI*³, 81f., rightly supposes that the 'theological movement' which appeared with Aristobulus was already 'in full flood'. N. Walter, op. cit., 39f., considers the possibility that Aristobulus 'was one of the learned men of the Museion'.

387. This group of ideas becomes the firm possession of Jewish and Christian apologetic, see K. Thraede, *RAC* 5, 1242ff. However, Aristobulus and his contemporaries, and indeed Jewish apologetic in general, do not know the later Christian polemical idea of the 'theft of the philosophers'; this first appears in Tatian, op. cit., 1251.

388. For the conception of the creation of the 'noetic' light in Philo see K. Schubert, *Judaica* 9, 1953, 72ff., cf. *Op.mundi* 20 and 31: the 'spiritual' light was the seventh thing to be created, it is an '*eikōn*' of the divine Logos; in detail, A. Wlosok, *Laktanz*, 85ff., 88ff.: the Logos is 'a pneumatic substance of light'. W. L. Knox, *St Paul*, 69 n. 4, points to Isis as 'the light of men' according to CIG 3724. For Palestinian instances see below, nn. 404 and 424. Cf. also n. 820 below.

389. *Pr.Ev.* 13, 12, 9–11, Mras 2, 195; cf. Clem.Alex., *Strom.* 6, 16, 138: here we find the central significance of the concept of wisdom which can be replaced by the 'seven' or the 'Logos'. For the whole matter see N. Walter, op. cit., 65ff., who rightly stresses that in comparison with Philo, Aristobulus represents 'a much less developed stage in Jewish Alexandrian philosophy' (82f.); cf. also A. Schlatter, BFCT 1, 5, 1897, 174ff.

390. For the pagan question why God did not keep the sabbath and what he did after the six days' work, see the reports in the early Rabbinic tradition given in W. Bacher, *Agada der Tannaiten* 1, ²1903, 79.

391. See Anatolius in Eusebius, *HE* 7, 32, 17f., see also below, n. 813.

392. N. Walter, op. cit., 73, and on the verses about seven, 150–71. Evidently there was already a Jewish Pythagoreanism in Alexandria before Aristobulus, see

also below, n.877. For the Greek sources of the speculation involving the number seven see op. cit., 156 n. 1 and 168 n. 1, supplemented by K. Ziegler, *PW* 24, 226ff., and on Philolaus 238ff., together with the controversy over the pseudo-Hippocratic writing about seven, περὶ ἑβδομάδων, ed. W. H. Roscher, *Die hippokratische Schrift von der Siebenzahl*, Studien zur Geschichte und Kultur des Altertums VI 3, 4, 1913 (lit. in Überweg/Praechter, *Philosophie des Altertums*, ¹²1926, 41!). Also more recently W. Burkert, *Weisheit und Wissenschaft*, 1962, 445f., 448ff., see also the index, 495, under 7. For the anthropological significance of the Hebdomas cf. SVF 3, 83, 764. Thus for Aristobulus and Philo there were sufficient points of contact in Old Testament and Greek tradition for their speculation on the number 7. In Philo this is then continued in abundance, cf. *Op.mundi* 100ff. (M 24): *Quis rer. div.* 170 (M 487); 216 (M 503), where the Hebdomas is in part personified.

393. *Pr.Ev.* 13, 12, 13, cf. Clem. Alex., *Strom.* 5, 14, 107; 6, 16, 141f.

394. On this see N. Walter, op. cit., 68–81; cf. also A. Schlatter, *GI*³, 85f.: the ἕβδομος λόγος is not to be understood as the Stoic power of seven, but as a cosmic principle; however, this does not exclude the possibility that this cosmic principle becomes effective also in human thought and action as a psychic force. The parallel to the Stoic definition of σοφία as ἐπιστήμη θείων καὶ ἀνθρωπίνων πραγμάτων shows that Stoic conceptions are involved here, see N. Walter, op. cit., 84f. n.4 (= von Arnim, SVF 2, 35f. and 1017); but see the Pythagorean parallel, op. cit., 164 n.4.

395. For the interpretation of this difficult passage see A. Schlatter, BFCT 1, 5, 1897, 164f., and N. Walter, op. cit., 75–78, cf. the more developed speculation in Philo, *Leg.all.* 1, 16–19 (M 46/47). The idea of the sevenfold Logos also appears in the gloss Sir. 17.5.

396. In Aristobulus, along with the tragedian Ezekiel, who probably also belongs in the second century BC (see Eusebius, *Pr.Ev.* 9, 29, 8a, GCS Mras 1, 530, l. 18, we have the earliest evidence for the beginnings of a 'Logos theology' in Alexandria, see A. Schlatter, op. cit., 168. However, the Logos is not yet understood as a divine hypothesis, as in Wisdom 18.14ff. and in Philo; it is rather an expression of the divine activity; *Pr.Ev.* 13, 11, 3 states that the world according to Gen. 1 was created through θεοῦ λόγος, which should not, of course, be regarded as ῥητὸν λόγον but as ἔργων κατασκευάς. At best there is a beginning of hypostatization in the fact that the Logos was bound up with hypostatized wisdom in the 'regularity of seven'. N. Walter, op. cit., 80f., pays too little attention to the decisive role of 'wisdom'.

397. The ἀτάραχοι is here to be understood as an interpretation of the 'day of rest'. For the problem of the 'Peripatetic' concept of '*ataraxia*' after Aristobulus see N. Walter, op. cit., 11. n.10. It need not unconditionally be understood along the lines of Stoic apathy, but simply as the 'rule of reason', see P. Wilpert, *RAC* 1, 845, and Aristotle, *Eth.Nic.* 1125b, ll.33–35: βούλεται γὰρ ὁ πρᾶος ἀτάραχος εἶναι καὶ μὴ ἄγεσθαι ὑπὸ τοῦ πάθους, ἀλλ' ὡς ἂν ὁ λόγος τάξῃ, οὕτω . . . χαλεπαίνειν. For the (noetic) 'primal light' and sabbath allegory see A. Wlosok, op. cit., 174f.

398. For the ubiquity of God see Ben Sira, Vol. I, pp. 146ff. There are the beginnings of a concept of the supratemporality of God in Ps. 90.41; 102.27 and in the eschatological prospects of Amos 9.13; Isa. 60.19f.; Zech. 14.7 and the

apocalyptic view of the end of the time determined by the stars, which is based on them, cf. *Sib.*3, 81–90; II Enoch 65.7, and for Palestine I Enoch 72.1 and Jub. 50.5. Nevertheless, probably the greatest difference between Palestinian thought and Jewish Alexandrianism lay in the transformation of the view of time; on this cf. G. von Rad, *Old Testament Theology* 2, 99ff. and T. Boman, *Hebrew Thought compared with Greek*, 1960, 129ff. The predominantly cosmological and psychological thinking made understanding of history retreat under the aspect of time experienced as salvation and judgment.

399. Against W. L. Knox, *St Paul*, 62 n.2.

400. Cf. Exod. 31.12–17; on this see N. Walter, op. cit., 170f., cf. R. de Vaux, *Ancient Israel*, 480ff., and G. von Rad, op. cit., 1, 148.

401. Jub. 1.10, 14; 2.1ff., 18ff., 31ff.; cf. 50.6ff. The reckoning of jubilees is a transference of the high estimation of the seven-day pattern to the chronology of world history in general, cf. 1.26, 29; 50.1–5. For the heavenly celebration of the rest of the feasts see 6.18ff.; the feasts of weeks, tabernacles and passover were entered on tables in heaven, 16.29; 49.8. For the Essene solar year, see below, nn. 813/4. A regular sympathy between cosmic order and human life was also known in Palestine, especially in Essenism. Cf. also S. Aalen, op. cit., 152ff.

402. I Enoch 93.9f., cf. 91.16 from the same apocalypse and Isa. 30. 26b, and the explanatory gloss.

403. The number seven appears fourteen times in the fragment of nine lines; see J. Strugnell, *SVT* 7, 1960, 322 = 4Q Sl 39 I, 1.17–26: for further examples of the 'heavenly' significance of the number seven see op. cit., 328f.; cf. also H. Bietenhard, *Die himmlische Welt im Urchristentum und Spätjudentum*, 1951, see index under 'Sieben'.

404. See above, n.388 and below n.424. For the Rabbinic conception of primal light see K. Schubert, *Judaica* 9, 1953, 73f.; S. Aalen, *Licht und Finsternis*, 1951, 262ff.; H. J. Schoeps, *Urgemeinde, Judenchristentum, Gnosis*, 1956, 46ff., and Billerbeck 4, 960ff. For the apocalyptic identification of light and wisdom see Syr.Bar. 54.13 and S. Aalen, op. cit., 175ff. The conception is probably dependent on the idea of the perfect light of the divine revelation which was widespread in Qumran, see O. Betz, *Offenbarung und Schriftforschung*, 1960, 111–4. Passages like Ps. 36.10 probably stand in the background. Cf. also the designation of David as 'wise man and light like the light of the sun', DJDJ IV, 92 = col. 27.2 (11 QPs^a DavComp).

405. For the limitation of the sabbath day, by which the whole earth is blessed, to Israel, see Jub. 2.31f.; cf. later Sanh. 58b = Bill. 1, 362; Simeon b. Laqiš about AD 250: 'If a non-Jew celebrates the sabbath, he deserves death', and on it M. Hengel, op. cit., 204.

406. A. Schlatter, *GI*³, 407.

407. On this see R. Meyer, *Tradition und Neuschöpfung im antiken Judentum*, BAL 110, 2, 1965, 44ff., cf. *Antt.* 13, 171f.

408. On this see R. H. Pfeiffer, *History of New Testament Times*, 417ff.: 180–100 BC; for Sirach 24 and Bar. 3.9 – 4.4 see op. cit., 418, and O. C. Whitehouse in Charles, *Apocrypha* I, 570f.

409. Bar. 3.23, 38; see on this U. Wilckens, *Weisheit und Torheit*, 1959, 167ff.

410. M. Hengel, op. cit., 210, 204 n.4: *Sanh.* 59a par. *S.Deut.* 33, 4 § 345.

411. R. Meyer, op. cit., 42, 44; for the ideal of purity see 22f.

412. Op. cit., 23ff.; cf. also 43ff.

413. Cf. also the Zealots, *Bell.* 5, 458f., and on them M. Hengel, op. cit., 312, and Michel/Bauernfeind, *Fl. Josephus, De Bello Judaico* II, 1, 269 n. 185; *Bell.* 5, 212f., 217ff.; *Antt.* 3, 122ff., 179ff., and above all 8, 107. Also Philo, *Plant.* 126; *Somn.* 1, 149; 2, 248 etc. I Kings 8.27 and Isa. 66.1ff. probably lie in the background. For Greek parallels, above all from Stoicism, see E. Norden, *Agnostos Theos*, 1912, 22 (Panaitios); H. Wenschkewitz, *Angelos* 4, 1932, 87f.; G. Schrenk, *TDNT* 3, 238 (Posidonius, Seneca); oriental parallels are in G. Boström, *Proverbiastudien*, 1935, 8f. Jewish–Rabbinic examples in J. Weill, in T. Reinach, *Flavius Josephus* 1, 184 n. 3 on *Antt.* 3, 180. Also Targ. Isa. 40.22 and 66.1ff., cf. *Ber.* 8a: the temple of God is where the *halacha* is learnt. This is a typical view, in which Orient and Hellenism meet.

414. R. Meyer, op. cit., 84: the suppression 'of mystic tendencies . . . in favour of a nomistic rationalism'. For what follows see also H. F. Weiss, op. cit., 283–300.

415. Cf. e.g. *Ex.R.* 15, 22: there were three primal elements before creation: water, fire and the *rūaḥ*: 'the *rūaḥ* became pregnant and bore *ḥokmā*'. Here we have an explicit 'gnostic terminology'. According to Rab (beginning of the third century AD), the world was created by ten spiritual principles, headed by *ḥokmā*. R. Abin (about AD 300) saw the Torah as the (incomplete) 'counterpart' of 'higher wisdom': *Gen.R.* 17, 3 and 44, 17, see H. F. Weiss, op. cit., 289f., and L. Baeck, *Aus drei Jahrtausenden*, 1950, 153 n. 1. There was probably fear of the invasion of gnostic thought through the expansion of such speculations, and therefore they were restrained by a prohibition, see Bill. 1, 977f. and 2, 307; *M. Ḥag.* 2, 1 and *T. Ḥag.* 2, 1, 7 (ll. 233f.); dualistic suggestions were above all strictly condemned: see O. Betz, in *Abraham unser Vater, Festschrift für O. Michel*, 1963, 41f., and H. F. Weiss, op. cit., 79–86; for polemic against dualism see 324ff.

416. See *S.Deut.* 11, 10 § 37, Bill. 3, 256: the Torah is loved by God more than all things (חביבה מכל), for according to Prov. 8.22f. it is created before all; cf. also *S.Deut.* 32, 6 § 309; 31, 14 § 317 and *Pes.* 54a Bar.: the seven things created before the creation of the world, headed by the Torah; scriptural proof follows through Prov. 8.22; cf. Bill. 2, 353f. and 4, 435f., and G. F. Moore, op. cit., 1, 266.

417. H. F. Weiss, op. cit., 289.

418. Bill. 2, 355f.; *Sanh.* 101a Bar.; cf. further *Ex.R.* 30, 5; 33, 1; *Lev.R.* 20, 10; *Deut.R.* 8, 7; *Cant.R.* 8, 11 § 2. For wisdom as the daughter of God in Philo see *De fug. et inv.* 50 (M 533), further in Leisegang, *PW*, 2.R. 3, 1033, and for the Logos as son of God, *PW* 13, 1074f.; cf. also K. Schubert, *Judaica* 9, 1953, 76.

419. *'Ab.* 3, 14, cf. R. Eleazar b. Zadok, *c.* AD 100, according to *S.Deut.* 11, 22 4 48.

420. *Gen.R.* 1, 1 and on it Bill. 2, 356f., where there are wider parallels. According to *Tanch. B. Berešit* § 5 fol. 2b (Bill. 3, 257), the tradition already comes from R. Jehuda b. 'Il'ai, about 150. Cf. Moore, op. cit., 1, 266ff.; K. Schubert, op. cit., 72, and O. Betz, op. cit., 37; L. Baeck, op. cit., 162ff., and H. F. Weiss, op. cit., 294–300. The same conjunction of Gen. 1.1 and Prov. 8.22

appears in Targ. Jer. I on Gen. 1.1 where 'in the beginning God created' is interpreted as 'through wisdom God created' (בחוכמא ברא יי). In the newly discovered Targum Neofiti I, Gen. 1.1 sounds even more archaic, see A. Diez Macho, *SVT* 7, 1959, 232: מלקדמין בחוכמא ברא ממרא דיהוה, cf. H. F. Weiss, op. cit., 197f. For the connection of Prov. 8.22 with the Torah see Moore, op. cit., 3, 82 N. 32: 'References . . . could be multiplied almost indefinitely'. Presumably the conception of the mediation of wisdom (Torah) at creation ultimately lies behind statements like I Cor. 8.6; Heb. 1.2, 10, where Christ takes the place of wisdom.

421. Moore, op. cit., 1, 267: cf. Philo, *Op. mundi* 15–25 (M 4), cf. Plato, *Tim.* 27dff.; cf. also W. L. Knox, 'Pharisaism and Hellenism', in *Judaism and Christianity* 2, 1937, 75ff., and H. F. Weiss, op. cit., 284, who points to the Platonic 'original – image speculations' and to *Tim.* 28a 5ff. Cf. L. Wächter, *ZRGG* 14, 1962, 36–56.

422. K. Schubert, op. cit., 74ff., cf. *Die Religionen des nachbiblischen Judentums*, 1955, 18ff. According to *Op. mundi* 20 and 24/5, the spiritual original of this world has its place in the reason *(λόγος)* of God.

423. See *j. Hag* 77d ll. 35ff. on the foundation of a school in Alexandria by Jehuda b. Tabai, who had fled there, at the beginning of the first century BC, par. *Sanh.* 107b; similar remarks are made of Joshua b. Perahya, *Sota* 47a; cf. also the colophon to Greek Esther and the Sirach prologue, see Vol. I, pp. 101ff. Further indications in H. F. Weiss, *Klio* 43–45, 1965, 322f.

424. On this see S. Aalen, *Die Begriffe Licht und Finsternis*, 1951, 183ff., and Bill. 2, 357. The conception already occurs in Sir. 45.7 and Bar. 4.2, and in the apocalyptic literature at IV Ezra 14.20f.; Syr. Bar. 59.2, etc., e.g. Test. Levi 14.4; 19.1; *S. Num.* 6, 25 § 41 on the basis of Prov. 6.23: 'A light (*nēr*) is the commandment and instructions (*tōrā*) is a light'. We also find it in Alexandria, see Wisd. 18.4: for Israel's sake, God has 'given the unfading light of the law to the world'. See also *Mek. Ex.* 19, 1 (L. 2, 220): 'The Torah is fire, was given out of the fire, and is comparable with fire'. Further in H. F. Weiss, *Kosmologie*, 87, on the conjunction of the light of creation and the Torah, *Gen. R.* 3, 1 and 3, 5 and the speculations of Rabbi about the seven books of the Torah, *S. Deut.* 10, 35 § 87. All this recalls Aristobulus and Philo.

425. Thus already in the wisdom hymn Bar. 4.1 (see Vol. I, p. 170); cf. also I Enoch 99.2; IV Ezra 9.37; Syr. Bar. 48.47; 77.15; Josephus, *c. Ap.* 2, 277: ἀθάνατος διαμένει; Philo, *Vit. Mos.* 2, 14 (M 2, 136). Numerous Rabbinic instances in Bill., 1, 245ff. and 4, 1ff. True, it was said that in the world to come the prophets and hagiographers and even certain commandments and prohibitions would become immaterial, but this would at most change the forms of expounding the Torah; that would itself remain valid as a pre-existent communication of God's self. In some places the view persisted that God himself (cf. Isa. 51.4) or the Messiah would expound it in a new perfect way. On this see also H. J. Schoeps, *Paul*, 1961, 172ff.; W. D. Davies, *Torah in the Messianic Age*, JBL Monograph Series 7, 1952, 50ff., 85ff. People could perhaps talk of certain alterations in the form of the Torah, as the structure of this world would be changed in the new aeon. True, there were some beginnings towards the doctrine of a 'new Torah' in the messianic age, but this view was never clearly expressed,

still less generally recognized. See op. cit., 85f. For the Torah as the 'ordinance of the created' in pre-rabbinic Judaism see M. Limbeck, *Die Ordnung des Heils*, 1971.

426. See *Pea* 1, 1a, cf. also Bill. 1, 961.

427. With reference to Prov. 4.2, hinted at by R. Akiba in *'Ab.* 3, 14. *'Ab.* 6, 3, 'But there is nothing good outside the Torah', cites the same passage. See also *S. Deut.* 11, 17 § 43. Further in Bill. 1, 809 and 3, 238.

428. Cf. *Sanh.* 99a and the Mishnah *Sanh.* 10, 1 that goes with it; see also *S.Deut.* 1, 65 and R. Akiba, *S.Deut.* 14, 7 § 102, and the discussions in *S.Num.* 15, 31 § 112. Bill. 4, 435–51, gives an abundance of instances; the Pentateuch comes directly from God and was either taught directly to Moses or dictated or given to him to copy. There is 'inspiration' in the strict sense only among the 'prophets' and 'writings', cf. 3, 238 on Rom. 7.14. Ps.Arist. 177, 313 also knows of a direct divine origin for the law; similarly Josephus, *c.Ap.* 1, 37; on Essenism see O. Betz, *Offenbarung und Schriftforschung*, 1960, 6ff., 14ff.

429. K. Schubert, *Judaica* 9, 1953, 78. For the significance of the individual commandments see D. Rössler, *Gesetz und Geschichte*, ²1962, 16f., and Bill. 1, 900f.; 4, 438f.; cf., however, the corrections by H. F. Weiss, op. cit., 287f.

430. E. Käsemann, *New Testament Questions of Today*, 1969, 56.

431. *Erub.* 13a Bar. according to Bill. 4, 130. Cf. *'Ab.* 6, 3.

432. *Shab.* 88a par. AZ 3a, 5a, see H. F. Weiss, op. cit., 285.

433. *Gen.R.* 1, 4. For the whole question see H. F. Weiss, loc. cit., par., n. 2, cf. *Ass.Mos.* 1, 12 and above, n. III, 248.

434. For the permanence of each individual letter and each word of the Torah see Bill. 1, 244f., 247ff. For the hedge round the Torah see already the 'men of the great synagogue', *'Ab.* 1, 1 and later Akiba, *'Ab.* 3, 13b. Further in Bill. 4, 439ff. and 1, 691ff. Cf. Chrysippus, SVF 2, 38: logic as a wall round the garden of ethics.

435. Ps.Aristeas already requires that the text of the Torah shall be transmitted as accurately as possible, see 30ff., 176ff., and on them A. Pellétier, *Lettre d'Aristée*, 1962, 119f. Similarly Josephus, *c.Ap.* 1, 29; cf. G. Maier, *RAC* 6, 1199ff.; J. Freudenthal, *Hellenistische Studien*, 75ff., and R. P. C. Hanson, *Allegory and Event*, 1959, 11ff. For the rules to be observed by the scribe see Bill. 4, 126ff. S. Lieberman, *Hellenism in Jewish Palestine*, 1950, 20–46, above all points to parallels between the text-critical work of the *sōpᵉrim* and the Alexandrian philologists.

436. See *'Ab.* 2, 8b; 2, 16; 3, 2b., 3f., 6f. and the whole of ch. 6; *Pe'a* 1, 1b etc.; see Moore, op. cit., 2, 239–47 and 3, 192f., and *Bill.* 2, 185, 273; 4, 488a, etc. The question of the relationship between studying the law and doing it is judged in different ways; however, there was a tendency to rate studying higher, as the presupposition for doing the law.

437. Cf. Luke 11.52; Matt. 23.13 and Bill. 1, 923, and the authority to bind and to loose, which applies even for heaven itself; 1, 736ff., 742ff. Even those learning to be scribes were held in high respect, see K. H. Rengstorf, *TDNT* 4, 435.

438. For the Rabbinic interpretation of scripture see E. L. Dietrich, *RGG*³ 5, 1515ff. (lit.), and F. Maass, *ZTK* 52, 1955, 129–61. For Alexandrian influence see

G. Maier, *RAC* 6, 1195ff.; J. Freudenthal, *Hellenistische Studien*, 75ff., and R. P. C. Hanson, *Allegory and Event*, 1959, 11–36. For dependence on Alexandrian philology see above, n.433 and n.II, 180.

439. Bill. 1, 246f.; 4, 439f.; 443ff.; 446ff.; there were divergent views on the nature of the revelation of the prophetic and hagiographical writings.

440. Bill.4, 406ff., 411ff. T.AZ 1, 20 (l.461) is typical: the command to be constantly occupied with the Torah left no time for learning Greek. See also S. Lieberman, *Greek in Jewish Palestine*, 1942, 16, 24, and *Hellenism*, 100–14; also R. Meyer, *Hellenistisches in der rabbinischer Anthropologie*, 1937, 136ff. There was obviously also a liberal attitude among the nobility, as in the family of the patriarch, see op. cit., 140, and S. Lieberman, *Greek*, 17ff., 20ff., cf. above, n.II, 158. We must also distinguish between the widespread knowledge of Greek (see Vol.I, pp.59ff.) and concern with Greek literature. That the higher social strata protested against Rabbinic rigorism is clear, e.g., from the strongly Hellenistic influence on the tombs of prominent Jews in Beth-Shearim, see Goodenough, *Jewish Symbols* 1, 89–102, etc. On the other hand, a comparison of Jewish epitaphs from Leontopolis in Egypt from the turn of the century and Jewish catacomb inscriptions in Rome from the second to fourth centuries AD shows a degree of isolation: see Frey, CIJ 2, nos.1451–64, and 1, nos.1–529. Still, it is significant that we have no Jewish Greek writings which have not been rescued by being taken over by the church. The Graeco–Jewish tradition was radically segregated within Judaism.

441. Bill.4, 405f. and 408f.: J. Freudenthal, op. cit., 67–74; R. Meyer, op. cit., passim; cf. also *Tradition und Neuschöpfung*, BAL 110, 2, 1965, 35f., where he ascribes the adoption of these Hellenistic oriental doctrines to the Pharisaic wise men. Perhaps their beginnings already go back to Hasidic apocalyptic circles; see Vol.I, pp.178f. Further material in S. Lieberman, *Hellenism*, 180–93: 'The Natural Science of the Rabbis'. For Jewish magic see below, n.851. The elaborate demonology is typical of the abundance of syncretistic influences – in contrast to the restraint of the Old Testament, see Bill.4, 501–35, and Trachtenberg, op. cit., 25–77.

442. Rom.2.14f. is put from the standpoint of a Diaspora Jew standing in this mission situation: see O. Michel, *Der Brief an die Römer*, [12]1963, 78ff. For the Rabbis, on the other hand, the six Adamitic and the seven Noachic commandments were firmly framed *miṣwōt*, not inner norms, see Bill.3, 36ff. There is evidently Hellenistic influence in the view that God taught the Torah to the pre-existent souls on Sinai (Bill.1, 342ff.) or even to the embryo (op. cit., 3, 90). There is reference here to a kind of anamnesis. For the pre-existence of souls see R. Meyer, *Hell.*, 49ff., 62f.; according to *Lev.R.*34, 3, this can already be demonstrated with Hillel. However, for a contrary view see E. Sjöberg, *TDNT* 6, 379: second century AD.

443. *Pesiq.*101a, see Bill.1, 901e, cf. *Makk.*23b, Bar. *Erub* 53b, Bill.2, 687; 3, 448 and 'ARN 16, Bill. 4,472b. The Torah must therefore be treated primarily as a unity, see A. Nissen, *NovTest* 9, 1967, 253ff. and M. Limbeck (above n.425), passim.

444. Cf. also *c.Ap.*2, 168ff., where Josephus describes the dependence of Greek philosophy from Pythagoras to the Stoics on the teaching of Moses. The

only difference between Moses and the philosophers is, according to him, that they addressed themselves to very few people, whereas Moses was the law giver of a whole people, because in him word and action were completely in accord. Here the Pharisaic programme of the realization of the law in everyday life and the education of the people in the Law exerts its influence. For Pharisaism and the Stoa see also J. Bergmann, in *Judaica, Festschrift H. Cohen*, 1912, 145–66, and A. Kaminka, *REJ* 82, 1926, 233–52. Paul, too, hardly received the Stoic features in his teaching through direct contact with Stoic philosophers in Tarsus, thus M. Pohlenz, *ZNW* 62, 1949, 69, but from the teaching of the Greek-speaking synagogue.

445. J. Baer, *Zion* 23/24, 1958/59, 22f.; cf. also L. Baeck, *Aus drei Jahrtausenden*, 1958, 152ff., see *Gen.R.* 17, 5 and 44, 17, and εἰκών in Talmudic literature.

446. J. Baer, op. cit., 141–60. English summary II/III.

447. See inter alia *Lam.R.*, introduction II: Balaam and Oenomaus (of Gadara, see above, n. II, 187) are the greatest 'philosophers'. Controversies with 'philosophers' were reported particularly of R. Gamaliel II, who was himself open towards Greek culture (see above, n. II, 158): see AZ 3.4; b. AZ 54b; further in Bacher, op. cit., 1, 76ff.; *Gen.R.* 1, 9; cf. also *Gen.R.* 11, 6f.; 20, 4f.; T.AZ 6.7 (l. 469); *T.Sebu* 3.6 (ll. 449f.) and the survey in S. Krauss, *Lehnwörter* 1, 446f. The designation 'Epicurean' already appears in the Mishnah, *Sanh.* 10, 1b and '*Ab.* 2, 14a, and probably means Jewish 'liberalism'; on this see A. Marmorstein, *REJ* 54, 1907, 181–93; cf. S. Krauss, op. cit., 2, 107f.; W. L. Knox in *Judaism and Christianity* 2, 74, and E. Bi(c)kerman(n), *RB* 59, 1952, 47 n. 4. The term may stem from the controversy between Sadducees and Pharisees in the first century AD. Cf. also Josephus, *Antt.* 10, 277f. and Acts 17.18.

448. R. Meyer, *Hell.*, 15–133 passim; W. L. Knox, op. cit., 76ff.; see also J. Baer, *Zion* 23/24, 1958, 3–34; 141–65.

449. For the universality of the law as the future 'world law' see *Sib.* 3, 757f., cf. 772; see also the Jews as bringers of salvation, Rom. 2.17ff.; *Sib.* 3, 194f., 582ff. For the success of the Jewish mission see Philo, *Vit.Mos.* 2, 17–31 (M 2, 13) and Josephus, *c.Ap.* 2, 123, 281ff.; see also Moore, *Judaism* 1, 323–53; F. Hahn, *Mission in the New Testament*, 1965, 21ff.; Bousset/Gressmann, 80–85; for the later period M. Simon, *Verus Israel*, 1946, 315–55: the attitude of the Rabbis was not uniform (318ff.); cf. also the postscript, 1964, 482ff., lit.

450. Cf. e.g. Hillel, '*Ab.* 1, 12b, and *Sanh.* 31a Bar.; his grandson Simeon b. Gamaliel and *Lev.R.* 2, 9 on 1, 2, or the conversion of the royal house of Adiabene to Judaism, *Antt.* 20, 17–96. After AD 70, however, interest in the gaining of proselytes notably faded among the Palestinian teachers, according to Bill. 1, 924ff. With Antoninus Pius' edict of toleration *c.* 139/40 AD, proselytism was forbidden in practice, as circumcision was allowed only to Jews, see J. Juster, *Juifs* 1, 254ff. However, the Roman authorities were generous, see M. Simon, op. cit., 325ff. For the dispute whether proselytes would be accepted in the days of the Messiah see Bill. 1, 927b and 929; and K. G. Kuhn, *TDNT* 6, 737f. lit.

451. See *Mek.Ex.* 20, 2 (L. 2, 234ff.). The Gentiles could not observe the seven Noachic commandments, much less the Torah (236). Further instances in Bill. 3, 38f. Even in the messianic period the subject Gentiles will not be taught

the Torah by the Messiah, but merely a selection of thirty commandments, see W. D. Davies, op. cit., 76f., following *Gen.R.*98.9; however, this is a late special view. The Rabbis do not seem to have been specially concerned with the question of the nations and their relationship to the Torah in the messianic period.

452. D. Rössler, *Gesetz und Geschichte*, ²1962, 42. True, the apocalyptic traditions were not excluded, but conserved and domesticated.

453. Cf. I Macc. 7.13 and II Macc. 14.6f., and later Ps. Sol. 16: συναγωγαὶ ὁσίων. The view of K. D. Schunck, *Die Quellen der 1. u. 2. Makk.*, 60f., that in I Macc. 2.42, Sin. etc. should be followed in reading συναγωγὴ Ἰουδαίων is extremely improbable; the same is true of the hypothesis of L. Gulkowitsch, *Die Entwicklung des Begriffs Ḥasid im A.T.*, Acta et Comm. Univ. Tartuensis B 32, 4, 1934, 29, that this means the 'whole people fighting for religious freedom'. In understanding *ḥᵃsīdīm* to mean only pious Jews in a general sense, M. Schlössinger, *JE* 6, 251, M. Burrows, *The Dead Sea Scrolls*, 1955, 274, and J. O. Dell, *RQ* 3, 1961/62, 257, overlook the clear statement in the text. The same is true of R. Meyer, *TDNT* 7, 39 n. 27 (also in *Tradition und Neuschöpfung*, BAL 110, 2, 1965, 16), who conjectures 'quite disparate groups of Jews'. Against this rightly O. Plöger, *Das Buch Daniel*, 1965, 30: 'characterized as a fixed community'. Cf. also K. Schubert, *Die Gemeinde vom Toten Meer*, 1958, 33ff., and Abel/Starcky, 56–9; W. Grundmann in *UU* 1, 220–34, and in detail O. H. Steck, *Israel und das gewaltsame Geschick*, WMANT 23, 1967, 205ff.

454. O. Plöger, *Theocracy and Eschatology*, 1968, 7f.; cf. the testament of Mattathias, 1 Macc. 2.67, and *Antt.* 12, 284. However, it is less probable that they were the authors of the armed rebellion against the Hellenists, as Tcherikover, *HC*, 196ff., supposes.

455. For the derivation see Schürer 2, 655; cf. R. Meyer, *TDNT* 7, 39 n. 27, and *Tradition*, 17f. G. Vermes, *RQ* 2, 1959/60, 427ff., gives a survey of the various attempts at interpretation. However, his own derivation from אסיא, 'healer', is to be rejected. For Philo, *Quod omnis* 91 (M 2, 459); for the letter from the time of Bar Kochba see DJD II, 1961, 163 no. 45, 6. Dr Rüger points out that the Peshitto often renders *ḥāsīd* with ܚܣܝܐ; cf. Deut. 33.8; I Sam. 2.9; Micah 7.2; Ps. 16.10; 18.26; Prov. 2.8.

456. See already S. Wagner, *Die Essener*, 1960, 85–88, the derivations in the eighteenth century; further Jackson/Lake, *The Beginnings of Christianity* 1, 1920, 87–9; Bousset/Gressmann, 457, and Oesterley, *Hist.* 2, 316f. Cf. also K. Schubert, op. cit., 36ff.

457. CD 1.5–12 (quot. Vol. I, pp. 179f.). For the planting see Isa. 60.21 and I Enoch 93.5, and directly for Qumran 1 QS 8.5; 11.8; 1 QH 6.15; 8.6ff. R. H. Charles, *Apocrypha* 2, 800, ad loc., points to the Hasidim. For the appointment of the teacher see G. Jeremias, *Der Lehrer der Gerechtigkeit*, 1963, 71ff., 76. For the root of the 'planting' see below, n. 741; similarly J. T. Milik, *Ten Years of Discovery*, 1957, 58f., and Abel/Starcky, 56–9, who see the foundation of 'Antioch' in Jerusalem as the cause of the formation; cf. also O. Plöger, *Theocracy*, 116.

458. I Enoch 83–90; cf. above all 90.6–19: Michael helps Judas, then comes the end; on this see Charles, op. cit., 2, 170f., 257, and *The Book of Enoch*, ³1950, 54, 59f.; S. B. Frost, *Old Testament Apocalyptic*, 1952, 173ff.; K. Schubert, *BZ*

NF 6, 1962, 192 n.56. The visions certainly belong to the Maccabean period; in the time of Hyrcanus I the pious no longer glorified the Maccabees in this way (90, 9ff.). A fragment of the vision was found in Qumran, see J. T. Milik, op. cit., 33, and C. Burchard, *Bibliographie* 2, 1965, 333f. Cf. J. T. Milik, *HTR* 64, 1971, 358f., 164 BC.

459. I Enoch 93.1–10 and 91.12–17; cf. especially 93.10; on this R. H. Charles, *Apocrypha* 2, 171, and *Enoch*, LIII, 228ff. As all references to a persecution are lacking here, it could go back to a time immediately before the religious troubles. Rowley's objections, op. cit., 83, do not exclude this possibility.

460. For Daniel see O. Plöger, op. cit., 1off., 26, and *Daniel*, 30; H. Ringgren, *Israelite Religion*, 1966, 333ff.; M. Noth, *History of Israel*, 370; L. Finkelstein, *The Pharisees*, ³1962, 1,154f.; 2, 592; A. Jaubert, *La notion d'Alliance*, 1963, 74f.; cf. also E. W. Heaton, *Daniel*, 1956, 24 – however, on pp. 2off., 42ff., he puts Daniel too near Ben Sira; for criticism see N. W. Porteous, *Daniel*, 1965, 15f., and D. S. Russell, *The Method and Message of Jewish Apocalyptic*, 1964, 16, 49. For the dating of Daniel see A. Bentzen, op. cit., 8, and E. Bickermann, *GM*, 144: he knows neither the consecration of the temple nor Antiochus IV's expedition to the East. The *terminus ad quem* is therefore 165 BC; the *terminus a quo* is the end of 167, as he presupposes the 'little help' of the Maccabean revolt. For the apocryphal fragments of Daniel from 4Q see J. T. Milik, *RB* 63, 1956, 411–5.

For I Enoch see R. H. Charles, *Enoch*, XLIIff.; D. S. Russell, op. cit., 51ff.; O. Eissfeldt, *The Old Testament*, 617ff., and K. Schubert, *BZ* NF 6, 1962, 190 n. 53. With the exception of chs. 83–90 and 93.1–10 + 91.12–17 (see below, nn. 463–4), the following sections are probably pre-Essene and Hasidic: the angelological book 12–36 and perhaps parts of an earlier Noah book, cf. 6–11; 54–55.2; 65–69.25; 106f., which is presumably presupposed in Jub.10.13; 21.10 and 7.25ff. For the admonitions 91–104 see below, n.600. The astronomical book, 72–82, is certainly Essene, see below n.806. The *Similitudes* – or the earlier Noah interpolations – probably come only from the first half of the first century BC, as 56.5 presupposes the Parthian invasion. Apart from the Similitudes, all the parts of I Enoch are attested at Qumran in Cave 1 Q (Noah) and 4 Q, see C. Burchard, op. cit., 2, 333f. According to P. Grelot, *RSR* 46, 1958, 18f., Jub.4.17–22 presupposes all the parts of I Enoch except the Similitudes. As the *Book of Jubilees* is itself in turn named in the Damascus document, which was probably written in the first half of the first century BC (16.3f.), and appears nine times in the Qumran fragments (see Burchard, op. cit., 2, 333, and O. Eissfeldt, op. cit., 608), it is probably of Essene origin; we may follow M Testuz in putting it at the end of the second century BC, *Les idées religieuses*, 1960, 33, 39. The pre-Essene dating of Jubilees by A. Jaubert, op. cit., 86ff., and O. H. Steck, op. cit., 158f., is unconvincing because of 23.16–26, which indicates further development in the late Maccabean period (see Vol. I, p.226). On the other hand, the kindred Genesis Apocryphon seems older, perhaps even pre-Maccabean, because of its less rigorous and more generous attitude. For further similar fragments from Qumran see O. Eissfeldt, op. cit., 661ff. The borderline between Essene and Hasidic tradition is often difficult to determine, as one runs into the other. For a thorough study of I Enoch, see now J. T. Milik (above, n.458), 333–78.

461. For the connection between Hasidim and Pharisees see above all R. Meyer, *Tradition*, 18ff.; cf. W. Grundmann, *UU* 1, 269.

462. O. Plöger, op. cit., 23f., 26ff., 44–52. However, the opposition to the cultic ideal of 'theocracy' is drawn too sharply, see the criticism of R. Tournay, *RB* 68, 1961, 444f.; probably the conflict only became really acute with the Hellenization of the priestly aristocracy from the second half of the third century on. L. Finkelstein, op. cit., see Index 2, 980, takes the Hasidim well back into the post-exilic period, cf. also the preface to the third edition, LXVff. The term 'Hasidean' calls for a differentiation, as is shown by the distinction between 'early Hasideans', CXff., and 'New Hasidim', 2, 593, which is not explained further; in addition, too little notice is taken of the apocalyptic and Essene literature, and the sociological background is over-emphasized. Finally, there is hardly a difference between the pious of the early period and the later Pharisaic party, see already the reviews by R. Meyer, *OLZ* 44, 1941, 70ff., and P. Winter, *RQ* 4, 1963/4, 592ff. On the other hand, we must acknowledge that Finkelstein is right in arguing that the development of apocalyptic and the *halacha* must not be derived from any fundamental opposition (XLIXf.). The best example is provided by Jub. (and Test.Levi), which is closely related to the Enoch cycle; but Finkelstein, CIIff. and 2, 641ff., puts it too early. One could also point to the *halacha* in CD and the fragment of an Essene *halacha* published by J. M. Allegro, *JSS* 6, 1961, 71–73, whereas on the other hand a number of apocalyptic speculations can be seen among the Pharisees; see Vol. I, pp. 353f. and the abundance of evidence in M. Zobel, *Gottes Gesalbter*, 1938; for the problem see J. Klausner, *The Messianic Idea*, 1955, 391ff., cf. W. G. Kümmel, *Heilsgeschehen und Geschichte*, 1965, 450. The fundamental opposition between the 'apocalyptic' and the Pharisaic conception of the law stressed by S. B. Frost, op. cit., 125f., does not exist in this way. The Hasidim and later the Essenes differed from the Pharisees precisely in their more rigorous *halacha* which could be achieved only by segregation, or in common life. The form, and not the content of the so-called 'apocalypses', is the reason why they contain no *halacha*. Cf. now A. Nissen, *NovTest* 9, 1967, 260ff.

463. O. Plöger, *Theocracy*, 44ff. (quotation 45).

464. For the rejection of the possibility of 'Maccabean' psalms see P. R. Ackroyd, *VT* 3, 1953, 131f.; H. J. Kraus, *Psalmen* 1, 1960, XVII, 550f., and 2, 966, and O. Eissfeldt, *The Old Testament*, 447f. In Ps. 149, where the 'pious' are mentioned several times, see vv. 1, 5, 9; as this psalm already appears to be late because of its position in the psalter, one might perhaps assume that it arose in 'pre-Hasidic' circles in the third century BC.

465. DJDJ IV, 64ff., 11 QPsᵃ 154. Cf. D. Lührmann, *ZAW* 80, 1968, 87–98.

466. Here מִיד זֹרְ[י]ם should probably be read as a Hebrew equivalent to the Syriac text ܣܛ ܐ̈ܠ ܢ̈ܦܣܐ see M. Noth, *ZAW* 48, 1930, 6; Ps. 2.34. Whereas in the new scroll it appears as a psalm of David, it is ascribed to Hezekiah in the Syriac version.

467. J. A. Sanders, DJDJ IV, 70.

468. Op. cit., 77 col. 19, 7, 13; 86 col. 22, 3, 6; for the vision see 87 col. 22, 13f.; cf. 22.5.

469. Op. cit., 86 col. 22, 2–6; 77 col. 19, 13–16. 'Śāṭān' is here to be under-

stood not in a cosmic dualistic sense but as in I Chron. 21.1, see also below, n.
541. For the whole, cf. D. Flusser, *IEJ* 16, 1966, 194–205, who indicates the
parallel in the Aramaic prayer of Levi, J. T. Milik, *RB* 62, 1955, 400, col. I, 17,
and later Jewish prayers. Ps. 119.133b could represent a preliminary stage.

470. Cf. Sir. 46.1, 13; 48.1ff.; 48.22; 49.7f.; cf. also the similar statements
about the judges in 46.12 and the twelve minor prophets in 49.10b: see also
Vol. I, pp. 136f. The formation of the prophetic canon could have been completed by conservative nationalist circles at the time of Simon the Just, cf. O.
Plöger, op. cit., 24f., say about 200 BC.

471. See already I Macc. 7.12ff.; for the breach between Maccabees and
Essenes see Vol. I, pp. 224ff. The Pharisees were the last to break with the new
dynasty, see Vol. I, pp. 227f.

472. Cf. I Macc. 2.42: πᾶς ὁ ἑκουσιαζόμενος τῷ νόμῳ. For the 'men of action' see
Sukk. 5.4; cf. S. Safrai, *JJS* 16, 1965, 15, and K. Schubert, op. cit., 33. The term
could significantly also mean the 'miracle worker', see *Sota* 9, 15m; cf. also n. 885
below.

473. I Macc. 2.29–38; see on this O. Plöger, op. cit., 8, and L. Finkelstein,
op. cit., 1, 156: for the Hasidim, self defence on the sabbath was 'a moral
revolution'. Further in M. Hengel, op. cit., 293f.

474. I Macc. 7.12ff. The underestimation of the Maccabean revolt in Dan.
11.34a also goes in this direction, cf. 2.34, 45; 8.25c and on it A. Bentzen, op. cit.,
87: the author 'builds on Isa. 10.5ff.'. The efficacy of the wise man as a teacher of
the people is more essential: 11.33; 12.3. On this A. Bentzen, op. cit., 83, and
M. Noth, *History of Israel*, 370; cf. also the role of the συναγωγὴ γραμματέων᾽ I
Macc. 7.12, which are to be distinguished from the 'Hasidim', see O. Plöger, op.
cit., 8, though they stand very near to them.

475. Cf. Jub. 50.12f.; 1 QM 2.8f. and the qualifications in CD 10. 14ff. For
the early Hasidim חסידים הראשנים in the Rabbinic tradition see S. Safrai, *JJS* 16,
1965, 15–33, though he puts their beginning too late (20f.). According to the
Rabbinic tradition, they had a *halacha* of their own which among other things
prohibited the killing of scorpions and snakes on the sabbath and thinking of
work on the sabbath (*Shab.* 121b and 150b). They limited marital intercourse to
Wednesday, in order to avoid a birth on the sabbath if possible (*Nidda* 38a/b
Bar.). According to Essene teaching, Wednesday was the day of the creation of the
stars and thus of time. A further characteristic feature – corresponding to their
tendencies – seems to have been their altruistic 'philanthropy', see S. Safrai, op.
cit., 22ff. Hasidic rigorism continued to exercise its influence for a long time in
Pharisaism, but it aroused the protests and mockery of the later Rabbis.

476. Cf. Jud. 10.5; 12.1ff.; and Tob. 1.10.

477. Dan. 6.11f., and for the Rabbinic evidence about the extreme devotion of
the Hasidim at prayer, *Ber.* 5, 1 and 32b, see S. Safrai, op. cit., 25, and W.
Grundmann, *UU* 1, 220, 222; cf. also Bill. 1, 405k; however, they come from a
much later time.

478. By and large the unity of the work predominates, see O. Eissfeldt, *The
Old Testament*, 518, and *ZAW* 72, 1960, 143; also O. Plöger, *Theocracy*, 16, and
Daniel, 25ff.

479. Cf. O. Plöger, *Theocracy*, 26ff., 49ff. This relative openness to the world

even among circles faithful to the law is typical for the pre-Maccabean situation. The same is also true for Ben Sira. The counterpart to this is the post-Maccabean, Essene book of Jubilees. D. S. Russell, op. cit., 19f., derives these alien influences from people who returned from the Diaspora and were actively involved in religion.

480. Cf. O. Plöger, op. cit., 8f.: the difference between the groupings among the pious which soon developed. The conventicles of Jewish 'pious' who were not established as parties are probably very significant for later Palestinian Judaism. Groups like this could have produced writings which have not been found in Qumran, like the Similitudes of Enoch (chs. 37–71), the Testaments of the Twelve Patriarchs apart from Levi and Naphtali (see Burchard, op. cit., 1, 334f.), the *Assumptio Mosis* and perhaps even the Ascension of Isaiah. We might consider whether they did not later produce men like John the Baptist and Bannus, Josephus, *Vita* 11; cf. W. Grundmann, *UU* 1, 228f.

481. CD 1.5–11. For the Hasidim as a penitential movement see W. Grundmann, *UU* 1, 220. For the time of their foundation see H. Stegemann, *Die Enstehung der Qumrangemeinde*, Diss. Bonn 1971, 242ff.: *c.* 172/1 BC.

481. I Enoch 90.6; cf. also Dan. 9.24; 11.33–35. Jub. 1.22ff. and 23.26 speaks similarly of eschatological repentance in Israel; cf. also II Macc. 12.42f.; 13.12, which are also permeated by hasidic piety.

482. Ed. M. Baillet, *RB* 68, 1961, 195–250; cf. esp. cols. 5 and 6, pp. 207ff. and 224f. Col. 5 has contacts above all with Dan. 9.7 and 16. The editor sees in the liturgy 'une relique de la piété assidéenne' (250); he is followed by K. G. Kuhn, *RQ* 4, 1963/64, 168f. On this cf. O. H. Steck, *Israel*, 113ff.; 208 etc., who also counts Bar. 1.15ff. and the prayer of Azariah among the Hasidic penitential prayers.

484. For Enoch as a preacher of repentance see H. L. Jansen, *Die Henochgestalt*, 1939, 12, 60ff.; for Qumran see K. G. Kuhn, *Konkordanz*, 217f.; especially the verb שוב in the Qal as a participle; see also 237 תשובה and the addenda, *RQ* 4, 1963/64, 229.

485. G. Jeremias, op. cit., 158ff.; the 390 years come from Ezek. 4.5; they are to be understood as an apocalyptic number and should not be evaluated chronologically. See H. H. Rowley, in *Mélanges Bibliques André Robert*, 1957, 341–53.

486. Dan. 9.24; i.e. the whole period from the beginning of the exile is a time of judgment which now comes to an end with the time of persecution, cf. O. Plöger, *Daniel*, 140.

487. I Enoch 89.73; cf. 90.28. Probably a generalization of Mal. 1.7.

488. I Enoch 93.9. On this see R. H. Charles, *Enoch*, 231: 'the period from the Captivity to the time of the author. It is an apostate period.'

489. Sir. 49.4; 50.1–21. O. Plöger rightly points out that there is not even any eschatological interpretation of the present tribulation in I Macc. 9.27, see *Theocracy*, 17f.

490. Dan. 11.33, 35; 12.3, 10. In Daniel the *maśkīlīm* is a fixed term for a group which proved itself as teachers and martyrs in the persecution. They will be identical with the Hasidic 'élite', cf. O. Plöger, *Theocracy*, 17, and *Daniel*, 165. The term lived on in Qumran as a technical term for the 'instructors' in the community, see K. G. Kuhn, *Konkordanz*, 134.

491. It probably comes from the late Persian period or the time of Alexander; for it as the earliest apocalypse see S. B. Frost, op. cit., 143. The question of the unity and dating of the whole work and its individual parts are, however, disputed, see Fohrer, *Introduction*, 369f.; Eissfeldt, *The Old Testament*, 324ff. The period of peace during Ptolemaic rule can hardly come into account; the time of the fourth and fifth Syrian wars under Antiochus III is probably too late, as Sir. 48.24f. already presupposes Deutero- and Trito-Isaiah, i.e. the whole of the work bearing Isaiah's name. J. Lindblom, *Die Jesaja-Apokalypse Jes. 24–27*, 1938, 63ff., with the agreement of W. Baumgartner, *TR* 11, 1939, 225, wants to see the resurrection (26.15–19) as an addition from about 145 BC, as the general resurrection is later than the qualified form of Dan. 12.1. But the Isaiah scroll of 1 Q makes this improbable. The possibility of an earlier insertion, say about the beginning of the second century, is on the other hand not completely impossible (but see n. 571 below). In any case, the apocalypse is fully developed for the first time in Daniel and I Enoch, see H. Ringgren, *RGG*[3] 1, 464, and *Israelite Religion*, 332f.; W. Baumgartner, *RGG*[3] 2, 29f.; H. H. Rowley, *The Relevance of Apocalyptic*, [2]1947, 16.

492. For the development of prophetic eschatology before the rise of apocalyptic see G. Fohrer, *TLZ* 85, 1960, 401–20.

493. Especially on Daniel see A. Bentzen, *Daniel*, [2]1959, 29; M. Noth, *The Laws in the Old Testament*, 1966, 194ff.; K. Koch, *HZ* 193, 1961, 7ff.; for apocalyptic in general see D. Rössler, *Gesetz und Geschichte*, [2]1962, 55ff., for 'salvation as the goal of history', 60ff. There is criticism of Rössler in M. Limbeck (above, n. 425), 63ff. etc.

494. K. Koch, op. cit., 7: the 'multiplicity of modes of approximation'.

495. For the ambiguity of the term 'oriental' and the possibility of mis-understanding it see C. Colpe, *Die religionsgeschichtliche Schule*, 1961, 28ff.

496. This applies e.g. to A. von Gall, op. cit., 83–162; Bousset/Gressmann, 502ff., and above all E. Meyer, *UAC* 2, 51ff., and 58–120, who want to argue almost exclusively for Iranian influences and (55f.) in contrast to Bousset/Gressmann – wrongly – reject any influence from Babylonian astrology and religion. The historical problem cannot be solved by one-sided derivations. See the critical remarks of Bo Reicke, *RGG*[3] 3, 881ff.; T. F. Glasson, *Greek Influence in Jewish Eschatology*, 1961, passim, and the Iranist J. Duchesne-Guillemin, *Ormazd et Ahriman*, 1963, 71–84: 'En somme, dans l'évolution du judaïsme postexilique, l'influence iranienne sûrement établie paraît moindre que celle de l'hellénisme.' (83) See also his critical comparison in *The Western Response to Zoroaster*, 1958, 56ff., and *La Religion de l'Iran Ancien*, 1962, 257–64. Cf. H. D. Betz, *ZTK* 63, 1966, 391–409.

497. W. W. Tarn, *The Greeks in Bactria and India*, [2]1951, and E. Meyer, *Blüte und Niedergang des Hellenismus in Asien*, 1925, passim. A. Falkenstein, *Topographie von Uruk I, Uruk in der Seleukidenzeit*, 1941, 2ff., 5f., 7f. Although the old forms were preserved, an 'extraordinary breakthrough' took place here, 'caused by a penetrating religious transformation'. For the mingling of themes in the Hellenistic period see F. Cumont, *RHR* 104, 1931, 93, on the Iranian Magusians in Northern Syria and Asia Minor: 'Ce système est né de la combinaison de vieilles traditions mazdéennes avec l'astrologie babyloniennne, et

quand l'hellénisme eut conquis l'orient, la doctrine chaldéo-persique s'adapta a la cosmologie stoïcienne.'

498. A. Bentzen, op. cit., 27, cf. W. Baumgartner, op. cit., 213; K. Koch, op. cit., 9.

499. J. Festugière, *Révélation* 1, 92ff., 141 (= CCAG 6, 1903, 83). Plato already speaks in *Tim.* 32c of τοῦ κόσμου σῶμα composed of four parts. For Iranian examples see A. Goetz, *Zeitschrift für Indologie und Iranistik* 2, 1923, 60–98, and 167–77, who conjectures an Iranian influence on Orphism, and the Hippocratic writing *Peri hebdomadōn*, see above n. 392, as indeed on Jewish Adam speculation. Cf. e.g. *Targ. Jer.* I on Gen. 2.7, the creation of Adam from the 'dust of the sanctuary', the four winds and all the waters of the world: man is the image of the universe.

500. Hesiod, *Erga* I, 109–201, 156–73, who also inserts a 'heroic age'; cf. also I Enoch 52; see below, n. 559. For the Iranian parallels see Dinkart 9.8 = 4.181 E. W. West, *Pahlavi Texts*; Brahman Yašt 1.3 = 1.192 West and 2.14 = 1.198 West, and on it E. Meyer, *UAC* I, 190ff., and A. von Gall, *Basileia*, 1926, 126ff. However, these reports come from very late sources, which are hardly older than the ninth century AD; the age of the tradition lying behind them is hard to ascertain. Cf. also F. Cumont, *RHR* 104, 1931, 50ff.; Reitzenstein/Schaeder, *Studien zum antiken Synkretismus*, ²1965, 45f., 57, and 223, 228; also A. Bentzen, op. cit., 29, and K. Koch, op. cit., 8f. According to Servius' scholion on the fourth eclogue of Virgil, the Cumean Sibyl also seems to have known the division of world empires according to ages of kinds of metal: '*saecula per metalla divisit, dixit etiam quis quo saeculo imperaret*'; see E. Norden, *Die Geburt des Kindes*, 1924, 15 n. 1.

501. In argument with O. Procksch and M. Noth, *The Laws in the Old Testament*, 1966, 215ff., C. R. W. Brekelmanns, *OTS* 14, 1965, 305–29, has convincingly demonstrated, using all the material from Qumran, that in Dan. 7 the 'people of the saints of the most high' means Israel, and not the angelic 'host'. Therefore the eternal kingdom in Daniel is to be understood as the rule of the people of God – perhaps in conjunction with the angels (cf. 7.14, 27).

502. J. T. Milik, *RB* 63, 1956, 411 n. 2.

503. FGrHist 688 F 1–8 = predominantly Diodore 2, 1–34.

504. M. Noth, op. cit., 26of. The replacement of the Assyrian kingdom by that of the Medes is likewise presupposed in the *vaticinium ex eventu* represented as a prophecy of the dying Tobit, see J. J. Lebram, *ZAW* 76, 1964, 328–31.

505. Appian, *Punica* 132 = Polybius 38, 22; Polybius is said to have been an eyewitness of this scene as a teacher and companion of Scipio; cf. M. Noth, op. cit., 200.

506. J. W. Swain, *ClassPhil* 35, 1940, 1ff.; on this W. Baumgartner, *TZ* 1, 1945, 17–22. For the gloss in Velleius Paterculus 1,6, 6 on Aemilius Sura see T. Mommsen, *RheinMus* 16, 1861, 282f., who already stresses his dependence on the scheme of Ctesias.

507. This notion became a firm tradition, see Dionysus of Halicarnassus (second half of the first century BC), *Antt. Rom.* 1, 2, 2–4; Tacitus, *Hist.* 5, 8, 2, in a sketch of Jewish history; for further Graeco–Roman writers see J. W. Swain, op. cit., 13ff., and by way of supplement H. Fuchs, *Basler Zeitschrift für*

Geschichte und Altertumskunde 42, 1943, 49, 50 n. 37. In Sib. 4.49–192 a Jewish author takes over the scheme of the five monarchies including Rome, the fiery judgment and the Nero *redivivus* coming from the east to make an end (shortly before AD 80).

508. Dan. 2.43 presupposes both in marriages between the Seleucid and Ptolemaic dynasties mentioned in 11.6, 17. The latter, between Ptolemy V and Cleopatra I, the daughter of Antiochus III, took place in 194/3. The answer to the much-discussed problem of the 'unity' of the work is therefore that the author went back to an old narrative collection of 'court stories' (see above, n. 1, 211), which probably included the framework of ch. 2 and chs. 4–6, but worked it over thoroughly to give his work as much unity as possible, an aim in which he succeeded, see above, n. 478. E. Bickerman, *Four Strange Books of the Bible*, 1967, 61ff., differs.

509. K. Koch, op. cit., 28.

510. Hesiod's myth was common property in the Greek-speaking world, see Seeliger, in Roscher, *Lexikon* 6, 375–429; T. F. Glasson, *Greek Influence in Jewish Eschatology*, 1961, 2f., and J. Duchesne-Guillemin, *Ormazd et Ahriman*, 1953, 78. For its use in Plato, who varies it in a number of ways, see J. Kerschensteiner, *Platon und die Orient*, 1945, 161ff. For the supposed Babylonian derivation see W. Bousset, *Die Himmelsreise der Seele*, ARW 4, 1901, 243ff. = reprint 52ff.; Bousset/Gressmann, 505, who conjecture the influence of planet speculations; W. Baumgartner, *Zum AT und seiner Umwelt*, 1959, 158–60, and supplement, 177 (lit.), passes too positive a judgment on the investigations of R. Reitzenstein (Reitzenstein/Schaeder, op. cit., 57ff., see above, n. 500). We should rather suppose that this *very* late Iranian tradition was influenced by Hesiod or the popular Hellenistic tradition. There were Greek politicians and men of letters at the Persian court from the fifth century onwards. The objections of M. P. Nilsson and Wilamowitz (see W. Baumgartner, op. cit., 159, nn. 5, 6) were therefore justified. While there are 'still no direct pieces of evidence' for Babylon, we cannot postulate an origin from there. See also Kerschensteiner, op. cit., 166ff., on Dan. 2, and in general 178ff. For the anonymous Samaritan and the Sibyl see Vol. I, pp. 88ff.

511. Thus J. W. Swain, op. cit., 4; cf. W. Baumgartner, *TZ* 1, 1945, 18; M. Noth, op. cit., 201 n. 16, is more restrained. The most bitter opponents of the Macedonian Diaspora were not the orientals – the Parthians, from the end of the third century east of the Caspian Sea, only penetrated further towards Media after 160 BC, see H. Bengtson, *GG*³ 401f., 484ff. – who in the third century BC still did not have much military significance, but the smaller Greek states like Pergamon, Rhodes, Sparta, the Achaean alliance and the Aetolians, who at first welcomed the repulsion of the empires of the Diadochi in Greece and Asia Minor. However, the rule of Rome rapidly altered the situation. It is still impossible to demonstrate that the theory of the four empires was developed 'from the oriental opposition against Greek rule', as W. Schottrof, *RGG*³ 6, 1633f. conjectures. This indefinite oriental 'opposition' must be given further definition. True, there were anti-Greek oracles in Egypt and anti-Roman oracles in Asia Minor and Greece which were concerned with the question of world rule (see Vol. I, pp. 184–6); however, we cannot talk of a general 'oriental' scheme of

world empires. For the whole question see H. E. Stier, *Roms Aufstieg zur Weltmacht und die griechische Welt*, 1957, passim.

512. Dan. 11.1–30a gives a picture of history without any mistakes over the relationships between Ptolemies and Seleucids; it merely omits Antiochus I, 281–261 BC. Here it probably goes back to a non-Jewish source, cf. Fohrer, op. cit., 477 n.23; O. Eissfeldt, *The Old Testament*, 519f.; O. Plöger, *Daniel*, 158f.

513. W. Baumgartner, op. cit., 214–22; A. Bentzen, op. cit., 57–67.

514. F. Boll, *Sphaera*, 1903, 297 and on this F. Cumont, *Klio* 9, 1909, 263–73. Cf. R. Eisler, *ΙΗΣΟΥΣ ΒΑΣΙΛΕΥΣ* 2, 1930, 646f., 661f., who also conjectures astral elements in Dan. 7; also W. Baumgartner, op. cit., 142ff.; A. Bentzen, op. cit., 69, and A. Caquot, *Semitica* 5, 1955, 10ff., who wants to derive the beasts of Dan. 7.1ff. from the beast symbols of the Egyptian Dodekaoros, the counterpart of the zodiac: cf. F. Boll, op. cit., 295f. According to Cumont this astral, geographical scheme goes back to the Persian period, but was well known about 200 BC in Egypt. The version in Dan. 8.2ff., in which Syria appears as conqueror of the Persians, could only have arisen after the firm establishment of the Seleucid empire. The reference in Ammianus Marcellinus 19,2, 2 according to which Sapor II, ruler of the Sassanides, wore the image of a golden ram as a headdress, probably goes back to this conception; the constellation of the ram was regarded in the Hermetic literature as κεφαλή . . .τοῦ κόσμου, see Festugière, *Révélation* 1, 141 n.3 = CCAG 6, 1903, 83. For the astral terminology see also Dan. 12.3.

515. For the problem see E. Osswald, *ZAW* 75, 1963, 27–44, where there is a list of the numerous *vaticinia* in Jewish apocalyptic. Cf. also the Daniel apocryphon, J. T. Milik, *RB* 63, 1956, 413f.

516. C. C. McCown, *HTR* 18, 1925, 387–411; H. Gressmann, *Der Messias*, 1929, 417–45. G. Lanczkowski, *Altägyptischer Prophetismus*, 1960, 3–9. These Egyptian predictions for the most part go back to earlier Egyptian tradition. For the Demotic Chronicle, ed. by W. Spiegelberg, *Die sogenannte demotische Chronik*, Demotische Studien 7, 1914, see E. Meyer, *Ägyptische Dokumente aus der Perserzeit*, SAB 1915, 286–304, and *UAC* 2, 187; A. von Gall, op. cit., 77ff.; F. K. Kienitz, *Die Politische Geschichte Ägyptens*, 1953, 136ff.; E. Osswald, op. cit., 42f.

517. On this see W. Spiegelberg, op. cit., 5ff., 9.

518. The most complete version is now to be found in POx 22, 2332, 1954, ed. C. Roberts, 89–99; the earlier P. Rainer is in G. Manteuffel, *De opusculis graecis*, 1930, 99ff. no. 7, on which see A. von Gall, op. cit., 69ff.; H. Gressmann, *AOT*², 49ff. and Reitzenstein/Schaeder, op. cit., 38ff., the Iranian origin of which, asserted by F. Altheim, *Weltgeschichte Asiens* 2, 174ff., is to be denied. The earlier Demotic prophecy of the lamb is akin to it, see H. Gressmann, op. cit., 425, and *AOT*², 48f., and G. Lanczkowski, op. cit., 5. For the dating of the Potter's Oracle see R. Reitzenstein, op. cit., 51; the objections against it by C. Roberts, op. cit., 93, are not very convincing, cf. his concession, 98, on l. 30; the basic material of the oracle may be much older and go back into the third or even the fourth century BC. The characterization by the editor shows its affinity with Jewish apocalyptic: 'The prophecy is a medley of legend, history and apocalyptic fantasy . . .' It is controlled by 'its idea of a period of general disaster followed

by a period of utopian prosperity', and 'its strongly nationalist and xenophobic sentiment'. Cf. also H. Gressmann, *JTS* 27, 1926, 242ff, and *Der Messias*, 422ff. Further literature in M. P. Nilsson, *GGR*² 2, 111. New editions by L. Koenen, *ZPapEp* 2, 1968, 178–209.

519. CPJ 3, 119ff. no. 520 = PSI 982, and on it C. Roberts, op. cit., 89 n. 4. For the 'wrath of Isis' (l. 9) cf. Chairemon in Josephus, *c.Ap.* 1, 289f. The fragment certainly goes back to the Hellenistic period. Cf. also PSI 760, a further similar oracle of this genre = = G. Manteuffel, op. cit., 107ff., no. 8. For the sources and their influence see L. Koenen, *Proceedings of the 12th International Congress of Papyrologists*, 249ff.

520. CCAG 7, 1908, 129–51; quot. 132 according to the *Excerpta Monacensia*. For this and similar 'calendars of disaster' see J. Freundorfer, *Die Apokalypse*, BSt 23, 1, 1929, 87–123, who indicates the parallel between Syr.Bar. 27 and CCAG 7, 226ff. on p. 122. According to Lactantius, *Inst. div.*, *Epit.* 68, CSEL, ed. S. Brandt, 19, 760, cf. H. Windisch, *Die Orakel des Hystaspes*, 1929, 44, Hermes Trismegistos, the author of astrological wisdom, was mentioned alongside the Sibyllines and Hystaspes as prophet of the end of the world; cf. also op. cit., 84: the renewal of the world in the Hermetic tractate Asclepius of Ps. Asclepius chs. 24–6 = CH 2, 326ff.

521. W. Baumgartner, op. cit., 140; O. Eissfeldt, *The Old Testament*, 150ff.; cf. also E. Osswald, op. cit., 28, 33. For the Iranian apocalypses see F. Cumont, *RHR* 103, 1931, 29–96, and esp. 64ff., on the 'apocalypse' of Hystaspes, and Bidez/Cumont, *Les mages hellénisés* 1, 1938, 215–23 and 2, 359–77; F. Altheim, *Weltgeschichte Asiens* 2, 174–84; H. Windisch, op. cit., passim, cf. 70: between 100 BC and AD 100 and G. Widengren, *Die Religionen Irans*, 1965, 199–207, though he puts it too early.

522. M. P. Nilsson, *GGR*² 1, 721, 793f.; 2, 109ff. A typical instance of Hellenistic Sibylline literature is Lycophron's Alexandra, which after 197 BC in Alexandria foretold the rise of Rome and the decline of Macedonia, see above all 1226–80 and 1436–50, ed. A. W. Mair, LCL 1955, the introduction, pp. 308–14, and S. Josifović, *PW Suppl* 11, 888–930. For the Sibyls see Rzach, *PW*, 2R. 2, 2073ff., 2103ff. and M. P. Nilsson, *GGR*² 2, 109f., 481f.; for Varro see Lactantius, *Div. Inst.* 1, 6ff., 8ff., CSEL 19,21, cf. Rzach, op. cit., 2076. K. Kerényi, *Klio* 29, 1936, 1–35, supposes very early influence of Persian chiliasm on the Greek Sibyls. In the time of Alexander the Great these were given a new impetus, see J. Wolff, *Archiv für Kulturgeschichte* 24, 1934, 312–25, esp. 316ff. The fourth eclogue of Virgil is also strongly influenced by Sibylline poetry: see l. 4 and on it E. Norden, *Die Geburt des Kindes*, 1924, 15f. nn. 1, 2, and K. Kerényi, op. cit., 1ff.

523. For Eunus see Posidonius, FGrHist 87, F 108e = Diodore 2, 5–7, and on it Altheim-Stiehl, *Araber* 1, 8off.; R. Eisler, ΙΗΣΟΥΣ ΒΑΣΙΛΕΥΣ 2, 723ff.; J. Vogt, *Sklavenkriege*, AAMz 1957, 1, 27ff., 31ff., and *Sklaverei und Humanität*, 37ff., who draws parallels with the Maccabean revolt (43). For Andronicus see op. cit., 43ff., 61–68.

524. On this see Schürer 3, 555f.; Rzach, op. cit., 2128f., and A. Kurfess, *Sibyllinische Weissagungen*, 1951, 289ff.; M. P. Nilsson, *GGR*² 2, 112f. The earliest Jewish Sibyl (3, 97–294, 573–623, 652–829) was composed a little after

Daniel, about 140 BC; whether it follows an older 'Chaldean' Sibyl is questionable: against A. Kurfess, in Hennecke-Schneemelcher-Wilson, *New Testament Apocrypha* 2, 703ff. (lit.).

525. FGrHist 257 F 36 III, according to Phlegon of Tralles. For Antisthenes see E. Schwartz, *PW* 1, 2537. Cf. also H. Windisch, op. cit., 52ff.; H. Fuchs, op. cit., 5ff., 29ff.; M. P. Nilsson, *GGR*[2] 2, 110ff. For later anti-Roman prophecy see H. Windisch, op. cit., 55ff. and H. Fuchs, op. cit., 8ff., 30ff.: here the third Sibylline stands in the first place, cf. 179ff., 350ff., 652ff. For the time of Vespasian see M. Hengel, op. cit., 234f.

526. D. Rössler, op. cit., 68f. The criticism of A. Nissen, *NovTest* 9, 1967, 270ff. is irrelevant at this point.

527. For the seventy nations which probably emerged from the interpretations of Gen. 10, see *Targ. Jer.* I on Gen. 11.7f., and on Deut. 32.8f., where the LXX shows the relationship of angels to nations without giving any number. It is questionable whether Sir. 17.17 alludes to the angels of the nations; *śar* there could still simply mean rulers, cf. Judg. 8.23. The idea clearly occurs at Jub. 15.30ff. and Heb. Test. Napht. 8ff., see Bill. 3, 48ff. For the seventy languages, see *Sota* 7, 5c. Cf. D. S. Russell, op. cit., 244ff., and Moore, *Judaism* 1, 226f.

528. A. Bertholet in *Oriental Studies . . . C. E. Pavry*, 1933, 34–40 (quot. 35); A. Bentzen, op. cit., 78f., and T. F. Glasson, op. cit., 70f.

529. FGrHist 790 F 2 = Eusebius, *Pr.Ev.* 1, 10, 32, 38, and on it H. Gressmann, *Der Messias*, 217f., cf. also 246f., 326, 504.

530. For this theme of the holy eschatological war see M. Hengel, op. cit., 277ff.

531. Sir. 49.16; see Vol. I, p. 149. For Qumran see 1 QS 4.23; 1 QH 17.15; CD 3.20.

532. For Michael in the apocalypse of the beasts see 87.2; 88.3 (cf. 9.1; 10.11f.; 20.5); 89.61, 68ff., 76; 90.14, 20, 22; on this see R. H. Charles, *Enoch*, 1912, 201. Here Michael is given the role of a heavenly scribe, like the Egyptian Thoth (Hermes), see H. Gressmann, *Der Messias*, 405, or the Babylonian Nabu, which Enoch probably takes over in a rather later form; see I Enoch 12.3ff.; 15.1; 92.1; and still later is ascribed to Metatron (see above, n. 307): *Hag.* 15a; *Pesikt.R.* 5 (ed. Friedmann 22b), see Bill. 3, 701; *Targ. Jer.* I on Gen. 5.24, see Bill. 3, 744f., etc. For the role of Michael in general see W. Lueken, *Michael*, 1898, passim; for Michael in Qumran above all 1 QM 9.15f.; 17.6f.; and Y. Yadin, *The Scroll of the War*, 1962, 235ff.; cf. O. Betz, *Der Paraklet*, 1963, 63ff., 103ff., 112f., and the Melchizedek text, which is unfortunately very fragmentary, ed. A. S. van der Woude, *OTS* 14, 1965, 354–73, and M. de Jonge – van der Woude, *NTS* 12, 1966, 301–8. Michael (-Melchizedek) here comes close to the form of a heavenly redeemer. Cf. J. T. Milik, *RB* 79, 1972, 85ff. (4 Q 'Amram).

533. A. Bentzen, op. cit. 79, who points to Graham/May, *Culture and Conscience*, 1936, 108. For Mikal, who was worshipped above all in Scythopolis-Beth-Shean, see S. A. Cook, *The Religion of Ancient Palestine*, 1930, 99f., 128f. He also seems to have been worshipped as Reseph-Mikal and Apollo Amyclos on Cyprus; see the bilingual inscription CIS I no. 89, cf. 86 n. 13, B. 5, and 91; 93.5; 94.5. Further in W. Röllig, *WM* 1, 298f. The name would then be

approximated to one of the usual Jewish theophorous angel names by the introduction of an aleph. The possible derivation from the root יכל, 'be superior, conquer', would fit the character of Michael well.

534. For the historical view of P see K. Elliger, *ZTK* 49, 1952, 121–43. Composed in the Babylonian exile as a 'comforting and admonitory testimony' (143), it had a similar function to Daniel during the religious distress; see Vol. I, pp.194f. See also Fohrer, op. cit., 183f., and J. Hempel, *PW* 22, 1947f. G. von Rad, *Theologie des Alten Testaments* 2, ⁴1965, 329, points to Num. 14.21 as a possible eschatological passage (this comment is not in the English translation): however, as in Ps. 72.19 and Isa. 6.3, what we have here will be an uneschatological cultic formula. Von Gutschmid (in T. Nöldeke, *Untersuchungen zur Kritik des AT*, 1869, 40ff.) felt that on the basis of the chronology of P he could work out a total duration of 4000 years for the world and A. von Gall, op. cit., 208, 276, derived this from Iranian apocalyptic and put its end at 164 BC, but these are very uncertain hypotheses.

535. Cf. the fragment from the Bodleian, R. H. Charles, *The Greek Versions*, 1908, 246 ll. 7f. (v. 6) = *Apocrypha and Pseudepigrapha* 2, 364, and further P. Grelot, *RB* 63, 1956, 391–406; DJD I, 87–91 = 1 QT Levi, see also below, n. 622. For a discussion of the dating, see O. H. Steck, *Israel*, 150ff., though he does not make sufficient distinction between Test. Levi and the other testaments, which (apart from Test. Naphtali) were not found in Qumran, see Eissfeldt, *The Old Testament*, 634f.

536. Jub. 1.26, 29; 4.26; 5.12; 23.27–31; I Enoch 72.1; 1 QS 4.25; 1 QH 11.13; 13.12; cf. Isa. 42.9; 43.19; 48.6. The 'new creation' affects men and the world in the same way.

537. For details of the total duration of the world see Ass. Mos. 1.2 and 10.12: 5000 years; II Enoch 33.1: 6000 years; Ps. Philo 28.2: seven thousand years. Further in P. Volz, *Eschatologie*², 143f.; Bill. 4, 986ff.; M. Zobel, op. cit., 69ff., A. von Gall, op. cit., 275ff., whose derivation from the Iranian doctrine of the periods of the world (see Vol. I, p. 193) is questionable.

538. G. Dalman, *Words of Jesus*, 1902, 147ff.; P. Volz, op. cit., 65; A. von Gall, op. cit., 272ff., though like Bousset/Gressmann, 243ff., he pays too little heed to the temporal differentiation.

539. See Dan. 9.24; 11.32, 35; I Enoch 89.59f., 74ff.; 90.6ff., 18ff. On this see also P. Volz, op. cit., 87f.

540. Aeschylus, *Prometheus* 454–505, and I Enoch 7 and 8; 69.8ff., see Vol. I, pp. 242f.; cf. T. F. Glasson, op. cit., 62ff. It should, of course, be noted that the doctrine of the fall of the Titans, based on Hesiod's theogony, is probably of ancient oriental origin: see above, n. 2.

541. On this see H. Ringgren, *Israelite Religion*, 313ff. Of course Job 1.6ff.; 2.1f.; and Zech 3.1ff. already knew Satan as accuser, but in both instances he is in the service of God and not yet thought of as the embodiment of evil. Even in I Chron. 21.1 he is not yet an 'independent counterpart of God', see W. Rudolph, *Die Chronikbücher*, 1955, 142f. Nor is there likely to be any influence from Persian dualism here. Only the Essene writings develop a many-sided, hierarchically arranged doctrine of the powers hostile to God, see W. Foerster, *TDNT* 7, 152–6, though he makes too much of a distinction between the 'spirit of wicked-

ness' (see Vol. I, pp. 220f.) and the fallen angels according to Gen. 6. More recent fragments from Qumran show the connection quite clearly. As with Michael, the names could change, see e.g. J. M. Allegro, *ALUOS* 4, 1962/63, 3–5. Here the Iranian influence is evident, see below, n. 776.

542. M. Buber, *Kampf um Israel*, 1933, 61; he is followed by H. L. Jansen, *Die Henochgestalt*, 76f., and P. Vielhauer, in Hennecke-Schneemelcher-Wilson, *New Testament Apocrypha* 2, 594f.

543. Bousset/Gressmann, 498; but cf. G. Dalman, *Words of Jesus*, 1902, 149, 'of course one can hardly get anywhere' with the term.

544. R. Bultmann, *History and Eschatology*, 26.

545. On this see M. Eliade, *The Myth of the Eternal Return*, 1945, esp. 86ff., 134ff.; B. L. v. d. Waerden, *Hermes* 80, 1952, 129–55; B. Sticker, *Saeculum* 4, 1953, 241–9. Seeliger gives the Graeco–Roman material in Roscher, *Lexikon* 6, 426–30.

546. M. Eliade, op. cit., 87f.; B. L. v. d. Waerden, op. cit., 129ff.; for Heraclitus see op. cit., 132f.

547. B. Sticker, op. cit., 245.

548. For the *Statesman* myth see J. Kerschensteiner, op. cit., 101–4, who rejects Iranian dualistic influence even here.

549. For the text of Censorinus, *De die natali* 18.11, see B. L. v. d. Waerden, op. cit., 133f.; Seeliger, in: Roscher, *Lexikon* 6, 428f.

550. Seeliger, in: Roscher, *Lexikon* 6, 427f., and M. Pohlenz, *Stoa* 1, 79f., 96; 2, 45ff. Cf. e.g. the astronomical reckoning of the great year at 1, 753, 005 years in Rhetorius, *Quaest. astrol. ex Antiochi Thesauris excerptae*, CCAG 1, 1898, 163, see B. L. v. d. Waerden, op. cit., 137, which is dependent on the Babylonians, cf. P. Schnabel, *Berossus*, 1923, 176.

551. B. L. v. d. Waerden, op. cit., 138ff.; according to v. d. Waerden, the Indian conceptions of the world year, about which Megasthenes reported *c.* 300 BC, are of Babylonian origin, see O. Stein, *PW* 15, 311f.

552. For (Ps.) Berossus, see Seneca, *Nat. quaest.* 3, 39 and P. Schnabel, *Berossus*, 1923, 266f., no. 37 and 94ff. = FGrHist 680 F 21; cf. on this Bousset/ Gressmann, 502f.; F. Cumont, *Die orientalische Religionen*, ⁴1959, 161f., and H. L. Jansen, op. cit., 78f. For Iranian influence on the theme of the burning of the world see the mythical representation of the doctrine of the burning of the world in the 'Mysteries of the magi' in Dio Chrysostom, 36, 39ff., text and commentary in Bidez/Cumont, op. cit., 2, 142ff. For interpretation see F. Cumont, *RHR* 104, 1931, 42ff.; M. Pohlenz 2, 45ff., and B. L. van der Waerden, op. cit., 147f., who assumes strong Babylonian influence. For the Sibyl and the oracle of Hystaspes according to Justin, *Apol.* 20, 1, see H. Windisch, op. cit., 26–33. Cf. also R. Mayer, *Die biblischen Vorstellungen vom Weltenbrand*, 1956, 1–79, and F. Lang, *TDNT* 6, 931ff. In the Hellenistic period the notion of the burning of the world was held only in a strongly syncretistic form, and as R. Mayer, op. cit., 78, rightly stresses, all themes of the burning of the world need not be derived from Iran.

553. Cf. A. Rusch, *PW* 20, 414f., and G. Hölscher, *Das Buch Hiob*, ²1952, 73ff.

554. *Sib.* 3, 1–92 is the conclusion of the lost second Sibylline and comes from the first century AD.

555. For the 'great year' in I Enoch see H. L. Jansen, *Die Henochsgestalt*, 1940, 76ff., though he stresses its significance too much. For catastrophes of fire and water see Josephus, *Antt.* 1.69–71, and *Vit.Ad. et Ev.*, 49–50; cf. also the rejection of this doctrine in Eleazar of Modaim (second century AD), *Zeb.* 116a and par., see P. Volz, op. cit., 336. For the notion of the judgment of fire see below, n. 607.

556. For the distinction between the 'two ages' and the correspondence of the beginning and end of time see G. Fohrer, *TLZ* 86, 1960, 402ff., 411ff., 415ff.; it is already hinted at in Old Testament prophecy; cf. also P. Volz, op. cit., 113f., 359f., 370, 383ff., 388ff. For the age of the earth see Syr.Bar. 85.10; IV Ezra 5.50–55; 14.10, 16; cf. e.g. Ps. 102.27f., or even the diminution of lifespan according to the historical picture of P in the primal period. The idea appears in Lucretius, *De rerum natura* 2, 1144–74, on a materialistic basis. For Posidonius see Vol. I, pp. 259ff.

557. FGrHist 115 F 65 = Plutarch, *Is.et.Osir.* 47; cf. also F 64 on the resurrection, see Vol. I, pp. 196ff.; on this Bidez/Cumont, op. cit., 2, 72, 78f.; A. von Gall, op. cit., 124ff.; B. L. v. d. Waerden, op. cit., 145–9. For the later Maguseans and their astral eschatology see F. Cumont, *RHR* 104, 1931, 26–96, and for Iranian-type syncretistic apocalyptic in the Hellenistic Roman period, H. Windisch, op. cit., 14, 26ff. G. Widengren, *Iranisch-semitische Kulturbegegnung*, 1960, 53 n. 183, already assumes Zervanite influence for the source of Theopompus, but there is no mention of this in the partly obscure fragment. For the questionability of his hypothesis see R. C. Zaehner, *Zurvan*, 1955, 20ff.

558. E. Norden, *Die Geburt des Kindes*, [4]1958, 8ff. For Iranian influences see K. Kerényi, *Hermes* 29, 1936, 1–35; H. Gressmann, *Der Messias*, 462–78, conjectures Babylonian ones. H. Windisch, op. cit., 60f., gives an interesting indication of a possible acquaintance of Virgil with the Jewish doctrine of the Messiah, op. cit., 60f. For the inner contradiction see K. Bucher, *PW*, 2R. 8, 1196: 'According to the Sibylline conception, one finds oneself . . . in a final state; according to the Pythagorean . . . of the great year, in a beginning state.' Cf. also H. Hommel, *Theologia viatorum* 2, 1950, 210ff.

559. F. Cumont, *RHR* 104, 1931, 44ff., 58ff. A parallel to the astrologically coloured teachings of the Maguseans might be found in the later Similitudes (I Enoch 52), with the hills of the six metals; perhaps there were originally seven (cf. 52.8), each of which indicated a planet. On this see the guide of Mithras, Origen, *c.Cels* 6.22, GCS 2, 92, ed. Koetschau, and on it W. Bousset, *Die Himmelsreise der Seele*, reprinted 1960, 52f. However, all astrological significance has been removed from I Enoch 52.

560. For a reference back to earlier outlines of history see G. von Rad, *Old Testament Theology* 2, 319f., and D. S. Russell, op. cit., though for P he takes over the thesis of von Gutschmid and Nöldeke (see above, n. 534). Against this, however, is the fact that a duration of four thousand years for the world is disproportionately short, and does not appear again with the later reckonings of 5–7000 years. G. Fohrer, *TLZ* 85, 1960, 401–20, shows how much the historical picture of apocalyptic is dependent on post-exilic prophecy. Apocalyptic is 'the modern form' of this prophetic eschatology (420).

561. H. Ringgren, *RGG*[3] 1, 464.

562. O. Eissfeldt, *The Old Testament*, 528.

563. Dan. 11.30, 32a; I Enoch 90.7, 26; 93.9. Cf. already the polemic of Ben Sira Vol. I, pp. 151f., and the reports of the books of Maccabees about the 'lawless' and the apostates, see below, pp. 289ff.

564. P. Vielhauer, in Hennecke-Schneemelcher-Wilson, op. cit., 592f.; cf. against this G. F. Moore, *Judaism* 1, 28, 'which from the days of Antiochus IV to those of Domitian had apparently revived in every crisis of the history'.

565. Cf. K. Galling, *Studien zur Geschichte Israels im persischen Zeitalter*, 1964, 184: 'the crisis in world view and the political crisis of the second century tears apart . . . the historical picture of the (second) Chronicler'.

566. A. Bentzen, op. cit., 10. For the calculation of the end see Dan. 7.25; 8.14; 12.7, 11f.

567. R. Bultmann, op. cit., 31.

568. Cf. Dan. 11.32b, 33, 35; I Enoch 90.6–19.

569. For 'world citizenship' in the Hellenistic period see the Palestinian Meleager of Gadara, Vol. I, pp. 85f. and n. II, 210. The first point in the reform programme in Jerusalem was the abolition of restrictions against the non-Jews, see Vol. I, pp. 73ff., 277f. The Hellenistic Jew Philo of Alexandria took up the notion of the 'world citizen' again, but considerably changed the emphasis by making the advocate of Jewish monotheism the 'world citizen' and thus demonstrating the missionary claim of Jewish belief to represent the true 'world religion', see *Opif. mund.* 3 (M 1, 1): the one who lives according to the 'law'; 142 (M 1, 34): Adam; *Conf. ling.* 106 (M 1, 420): Moses; cf. *de Jos.* 29 (M 2.46), etc. For the conception of the *'oikūmenē'* see J. Kaerst, *Die antike Idee der Oekumene*, 1903, and *Geschichte des Hellenismus* 2², 270ff.: 'There arose the idea of a cultural world which finds its basis in the generally reasonable character of this world' (272); cf. also F. Gisinger, *PW* 17, 2140f., and O. Michel, *TDNT* 5, 157ff.

570. H. G. Gadamer, *RGG*³ 2, 1490.

571. On this see above, n. 491. G. Widengren, *SVT* 4, 1957, 228f., conjectures in Isa. 26.19 influence from the old Semitic conceptions of the life-giving power of dew; the context is also supposed to point to the Canaanite–Israelite New Year feast, cf. H. Riesenfeld, UUÅ 1948, no. 11, 6ff., 9ff. G. Fohrer, *TR* 28, 1962, 361, on the other hand, rejects any conception of the resurrection for Isa. 26.19.

572. For the various attempts at interpretation see B. J. Alfrink, *Bibl* 40, 1959, 355–71, though his own interpretation, which supposes only the eternal death of the sinner, cannot be convincing. O. Plöger, *Daniel*, 171, is right.

573. For the disputed passage I Enoch 90.33, R. H. Charles, *Enoch*, 215, and K. Schubert, *BZ* NF 6, 1962, 192. For Jason see Vol. I, p. 96, and n. II, 309, 312.

574. For Theopompus see FGrHist 115 F 64, following Diogenes Laertius 1.9 and Aeneas of Gaza (fifth century AD); cf. also F 65 conclusion and Bidez/ Cumont, op. cit., 2, 68, 70. On this A. von Gall, op. cit., 149f.; on the other hand, Herodotus 3, 62 can hardly be produced as evidence. The Gathas do not know the resurrection, but only the later Avesta, see *Yašt* 19, 11, 89, ed. H. Lommel, 1922, 177, 185, and *Bundahishn* 30, 7 = E. W. West, *Pahlavi Texts* 1, 123, on which see A. von Gall, op. cit., 105ff., 108ff.; cf. also Bousset/Gressmann, 510

n.3. Possibly the Jewish/Christian hope in the resurrection has for its part influenced the Iranian, see C. M. Edsman, *RGG*³ 1, 691.

575. Cf. Hos. 6.2. and on it Robinson/Horst, *Die Zwölf kleinen Propheten*, 1964, 25; Ezek. 37.1–14, and on the whole matter, W. Baumgartner, *Zum AT und seiner Umwelt*, 1959, 124–46; H. Riesenfeld, op. cit., passim, and G. Widengren, op. cit., 226ff. But the notion of resurrection was not completely alien even to the Greeks. In addition to their acquaintance with dying and rising gods from the near East, there was knowledge of the resurrection of individual dead by a special miracle or for the purpose of revelation, see Vol. I, p. 186 and the myth of Er, Plato, *Republic* 10, 614bff., which served the later church fathers as proof for the resurrection, see Ganschinietz, *PW* 10, 2413f.; Philostratus, *Vit. Apoll.* 4, 45 = P. Fiebig, *Antike Wundergeschichten*, 1911, 26, and the resurrections performed by Asclepiades, Pliny, *Hist. nat.* 7,124, and Apuleius, *Flor.* 19 = op. cit., 18f., cf. A. Oepke, *TDNT* 1, 369. I. Lévy, *La Légende de Pythagore*, 255f., and following him T. F. Glasson, op. cit., 26ff., point out that the Pythagorean-Orphic metempsychosis could also be understood as an analogy to the notion of the resurrection. However, this idea of the 'infinite circle of the generations' (see M. P. Nilsson, *GGR*² 1, 695) with its completely individualistic form of a life after death, could not be taken over by Jewish eschatology, which remained *continually oriented on the continuation of the people*; on the other hand, the Rabbis could later take up the idea of the pre-existence of souls, see Vol. I, p. 173, n. 440. This also explains the question raised by W. Bousset, *Die Himmelsreise der Seeler*, reprinted 1960, 68, why there is no migration of souls in Jewish and Iranian eschatology.

576. For the Jewish resurrection hope in the early period see P. Volz, *Eschatologie*², 230ff., 237ff.; Bousset/Gressmann, 269ff., who at 270f. rightly point to the 'great obscurity' in the earlier parts of I Enoch. See also K. Schubert, *BZ* NF 6, 1962, 177–214, and especially for the Essenes, *WZKM* 56, 1960, 154–67; with special reference to I Enoch, P. Grelot, *RQ* 1, 1958/59, 112–31.

577. Text follows C. Bonner, *The Last Chapters of Enoch in Greek*, Studies and Documents, 8, 1937, 71, cf. Syr. Bar. 51.10ff.

578. P. Volz, op. cit., 400, cf. 399–401, and A. Dupont-Sommer, *REG* 62, 1949, 80–87, on Wisdom 3.7.

579. F. Cumont, *Lux perpetua*, 1949, 142–288; see on the other hand M. P. Nilsson, *opuscula selecta* 3, 250–65, and *GGR*² 2, 278ff., 491ff.; cf. already Plato, *Tim.* 41d/e: the number of human souls corresponds to the number of stars; one is assigned to each star. For Koheleth 3.21 see above, n. 134; cf. Sir. 40.11. For the Jewish inscription see CIJ 2, 43f., no. 788, cf. also I Enoch 100.10: the angels observe men from the stars. Further in E. Bickerman(n), *Syria* 44, 1967, 145ff.

580. H. I. Marrou, *Histoire de l'Education dans l'Antiquité*, 1948, 146f., cf. 495 n. 7. See also Virgil, *Aen.* 6, 661ff., and in comparison with it the Orphic description of the underworld. M. Treu, *Hermes* 82, 1954, 30ff.

581. W. Kroll, *PW* 16, 2164f. The mausoleum of the priest itself comes from the middle of the fourth century, but already shows elements of Greek style. See M. Rostovtzeff, *HW* 1, 82, and pl. XII. Cf. the epitaph of the priestess of Isis,

Dionysia from Megalopolis, second to third century AD: ἀστρ'ἔβα, ὡς ἀνόσως ᾤχετ'ἐς ἡμιθέους, Peek, *Griechische Grabgedichte*, no.317 l.13 and the inscription from Smyrna, first to second century AD, with Hermes as spokesman and guide: οἰκεῖν ἐν μακάρεσσι κατ' οὐρανὸν ἀστερόεντα, χρυσείοισι θρόνοισι παρήμενον ἐς φιλότητα. For an analogous reward for the righteous statesman see Cicero, *Republic* 6, 13.

582. Cf. *Odyssey* 4, 561f.; 10, 513ff.; 24, 11f. and on it already A. Dieterich, *Nekyia*, 1893, 218: further R. H. Charles, *Enoch*, 38, 'full of Greek elements', and T. F. Glasson, op. cit., 8–19. Though it is directed rather too one-sidedly towards the Babylonian hypothesis, the comparison in P. Grelot, *RB* 65, 1958, 33–69 is fundamental; cf. above all 68. As he assumes a Phoenician or Syrian mediation, Greek influence could have been at work here. Above all, reward and punishment in the underworld is hardly of Babylonian origin. For the parallels between the Greek and Babylonian descriptions of the underworld see already Ganschinietz, *PW* 10, 238ff.

583. I Enoch 22; Greek text in R. H. Charles, *Enoch*, 298 (v.3 quot.). Unfortunately the text is partially corrupt, see Bousset/Gressmann, 270. A distinction between '*pneuma*' and '*psychē*' is impossible, see P. Grelot, *RQ* 1, 1958/9, 116. The interpretations of T. F. Glasson, op. cit., 14ff., and K. Schubert, *WZKM* 56, 1960, 159, and *BZ* NF 6, 1962, 192, following H. H. Rowley, *The Relevance of Apocalyptic*, ²1947, 83, are unconvincing. The school of Shammai knew the tripartite division of the underworld, *T.Sanh.* 13, 3 (1.434), see Bill. 4, 1178, and J. Baer, *Zion* 25, 1960, 5ff., who believes that this Pharisaic teaching was influenced by Orphism and conjectures an origin in the Maccabean period. For its continued influence in Judaism, see R. Mach, *Der Zaddik in Talmud und Midrash*, 1957, 177ff.

584. M. P. Nilsson, *GGR*² 2, 237ff., 240; for the Orphic gold leaves as passes for the dead see O. Kern, *Orphicorum fragmenta*, ²1963, 104ff., fr. 32a; cf. also S. Eitrem, *PW* 15, 2267f., and Ganschinietz, *PW* 10, 2402f.

585. The Greek conceptions are already very old; see E. Rohde, *Psyche*² 1, 289ff.: Eleusis; 2, 208ff.: 274ff., Pindar and Plato; 366ff.: popular belief and mysteries. Cf. also the collection of material in L. Ruhl, *De mortuorum iudicio*, RGVV 1903, II 2, 34ff., passim, and M. P. Nilsson, *GGR*² 1, 672ff., 688ff.: Eleusis and Orphism; 815–26: the classical period and Plato; 2, 239ff.: in the Hellenistic period, cf. e.g. Ps.Plato, *Axiochus* 371a ff. (see Vol.I, p.211, and n.654), and on it F. Cumont, *CRAI* 1920, 272–85. For the Stoa see M. P. Nilsson, *GGR*² 2, 59f., and F. Cumont, *Lux perpetua*, 113ff.; cf. Zeno, SVF 1, 40, no.147 = Lactantius, *Inst.div.*7.20: *Esse inferos . . . et sedes piorum ab impiis discretas: et illos quidem quietas et delectabiles incolere regiones, hos vero luere poenas in tenebrosis locis*'; cf. Tertull., *De anima*, ch. 54. For the mysteries see M. P. Nilsson, op. cit., 2, 350, 367, and F. Cumont, op. cit., 235–74. For popular belief see W. Peek, *Griechische Grabgedichte*, 1960, index 371, see under 'Stätte (Haus) der Frommen'; cf. also no.209, third to second century BC: isles of the blessed and judgment of the dead, and 216, second century BC: request to the doorkeeper of Hades to show the way to the abode of the pious.

586. P. Grelot, *RQ* 1, 1958/59, 119ff., and D. S. Russell, op. cit., 149ff.

587. See e.g. I Enoch 5.7–9: long life in the time of salvation, cf. 25.6, and on it T. F. Glasson, 29ff.

588. On this see P. Grelot, *RQ* 1, 1958/59, 122f., and K. Schubert, *WZKM* 56, 1960, 159, and *BZ* 6, 1962, 193, though his interpretation is not grounded in the text. For Essene eschatology according to Josephus see *Bell.* 2, 154-9, and *Antt.* 18, 18, which has strongly Platonizing colouring. As P. Grelot, op. cit., 113ff., 127ff., demonstrated, Josephus could have based himself on the eschatological conceptions of the older parts of I Enoch and Jubilees. For further literature on the problem of the resurrection among the Essenes, see K. Schubert, *WKZM* 56, 1960, 154f., nn. 3-5, and the supplement, *BZ* 6, 1962, 202 n. 83; cf. also P. Grelot, op. cit., 123 n. 25.

589. Text following C. Bonner, op. cit., 63f. On p. 8, line 3, however, the Ethiopian should be followed in reading τῶν ἁγίων or τὴν ἁγίαν and not ἀναγκαίαν. Cf. also 102.4ff.

590. I Enoch 91.10; 92.3; 100.5.

591. Cf. 1 QH 6.29f., 34f.; 11.10-14, and on this K. Schubert, *WKZM* 56, 1960, 155ff., and *BZ* NF 6, 1962, 202ff. For the eschatological terminology of salvation see Vol. I, pp. 223f.; cf. on it J. Becker, *Das Heil Gottes*, 1964, 69f., on 1 QH 7.14f.

592. P. Grelot, op. cit., 117.

593. P. Grelot, op. cit., 123: 'elle suppose l'immortalité de l'âme ou de l'esprit . . .; elle exclut la résurrection du corps.'

594. K. Schubert, *BZ* 6, 1962, 204, and *WZKM* 56, 1960, 158f.

595. M. Pohlenz, *Stoa* 1, 86, 93; 2, 50 cf. the definition SVF 2, 218 no. 780 according to Galen ψυχή ἐστιν—κατὰ δὲ τοὺς Στωϊκοὺς σῶμα λεπτομερὲς ἐξ ἑαυτοῦ κινούμενον and 2, 217 no. 773: πνεῦμα . . . ἔνθερμον καὶ διάπυρον, cf. also the Platonist Heracleides Ponticus in the fourth century BC, who named the soul an αἰθέριον σῶμα; see Daebritz, *PW* 8, 476, 26ff. According to Eratosthenes, the soul always possessed a body, but there were degrees of fineness, see Wilamowitz/Möllendorf, *Der Glaube der Hellenen* 2, 525f. Cf. also L. Ginzberg, *Legends* 1, 140. In the transformation of Enoch to Metatron his body becomes 'a heavenly fire' = III Enoch 15 (ed. Odeberg).

596. K. Schubert, *BZ* 6, 1962, 208ff., and P. Volz., op. cit., 234ff., 250; Bill. 4, 815f. (*Gen.R.* 14, 5), 948 (*Gen.R.* 95, 1), 1173 (*Sanh.* 91b and *Koh.R.* 1, 4): the resurrection with bodily failings, cf. also R. Mach, op. cit., 195ff.

597. I Enoch 51.1-3; 61.5; 62.14f.; IV Ezra 7.32, 75-101; Syr. Bar. 50.2ff.; 51.1ff. etc.

598. *Sib.* 4, 180f., translation follows A. Kurfess, *Sibyllinische Weissagungen*, 1951, 120. Cf. also Ps.Phocylides 102-8, ed. J. Bernays, 1856, the prohibition of the cutting of corpses, and the Apocryphon Ezekiel in Epiphanius, *Panarion* 64, 70, 5, GCS, ed. Holl, 31, 2, 515, ll. 24ff., see P. Volz, op. cit., 244. Josephus, *Bell.* 2, 163, has a Hellenizing correction of the Pharisaic doctrine of the resurrection, cf. also *Antt.* 18, 14 and *c.Ap.* 2, 218. For the later Rabbinic conceptions of the ascent of the soul after death, which are similarly borrowed from the Hellenistic-oriental environment, see R. Mach, op. cit., 181ff.

599. Various features are common, others seem to be contradictory, see Dan. 7.11 and I Enoch 90.18, 25: the annihilation of the godless powers and the judgment of fire; Dan. 7.9a and I Enoch 90.20a: setting up the thrones for the judgment court. In I Enoch 90.21 the seven archangels are mentioned as helpers

at the judgment; they are perhaps related to the group presupposed in Dan. 7.10c, 22. Daniel 7.10c = I Enoch 90.20b: opening of the books, cf. Dan. 12.1 and I Enoch 89.61ff., 70f.; 90.17; 97.6. Dan. 7.11, 21, on the other hand, reveals a significant difference: here the fourth kingdom is annihilated in a miraculous way without human intervention, and the 'power' and the 'kingdom' are given to Israel, whereas in I Enoch 90.19; 91.12, Israel receives the sword for the eschatological war of annihilation; cf. also Dan. 9.27 and 11.45. This opposition was to remain effective in Jewish apocalyptic down to the time of the great rebellions against Rome. It also remains obscure who is to take part in the 'resurrection to judgment', or whether this in fact takes place: cf. Dan. 12.2; I Enoch 90.26, 32, cf. 22.11, 13; 27.2. In general on the conception of judgment see Bousset/Gressmann, 257ff.

600. For dating see R. H. Charles, *Enoch*, LIIIf. (probably too late), rightly against this O. Eissfeldt, *The Old Testament*, 619, and O. H. Steck, *Israel*, 154 n. 4: pre-Essene, i.e. before about 150 BC; cf. also K. Schubert, *BZ* 6, 1962, 196f. Two fragments were found in Qumran, see C. Burchard, op. cit., 2, 33f.; chs. 105 and 108 are secondary, see C. Bonner, op. cit., 4. Cf. now J. T. Milik (above n. 458), 360ff.

601. Death at the hands of the faithful: 95.3; 96.1; 98.10, 12; 99.16; 100.1ff. Punishment in the underworld: 97.10; 99.14; 100.4ff.; 102.11. Final judgment: 96.8; 97.1, 5ff.; 98.9; 104.5. 103.8 suggests permanent punishment in hell, cf. 22.11; 27.2. The formula which probably derives from Isa. 48.22; 57.21, that the godless 'have no peace' *'ēn šālōm* = οὐκ ἐστιν χαίρειν is also typical; cf. I Enoch 94.6; 98.11, 16; 99.13; 102.3; 103.8 and on the fallen angels (οὐκ ἐστιν εἰρήνη), 12.5f.; 13.1; 16.4; see P. Volz, op. cit., 320f.

602. On this, including the Old Testament parallels, see Bousset/Gressmann, 258 and P. Volz, op. cit., 303f. They are inscribed either with the names of those marked out for life or death or with the deeds of men. However, the two things can be associated in the judgment scenes, see above, n. 599. The theme is especially frequent in the apocalypse of the symbolic animals, where Michael brings the book, and in the admonitions; see 89.61ff., 70f., 76f.; 90.17, 20; 97.6; 98.7, 8; 104.7; 108.10. The tables of the law and the tables of fate, which appear above all in the strongly deterministic Essene writings, are a special conception. See Jub. passim, but also I Enoch 81.1f.; 93.1–3, and on it R. H. Charles, *Enoch*, 91f. on 47.3; P. Volz, op. cit., 290ff. and F. Nötscher, *Vom Alten zum Neuen Testament*, 72–9. In Qumran, 1 QS 10.6, 8, 11; 1 QH 1.24; 1 QM 12.3 and CD 20.19 presuppose this idea, cf. also M. Testuz, *Semitica* 5, 1955, 38 ll. 3 and 5, and J. Starcky, *RB* 63, 1956, 66. The strong emphasis on predetermination points back to Babylonian astral religion, see H. L. Jansen, op. cit., 46f., 68, 75; F. Nötscher, 180 n. 48. However, the tables now serve as an expression of the unmovable will of God and no longer have any direct astral significance. Cf. now M. Limbeck (n. 425 above), 58ff.

603. Cf. e.g. Euripides, fr. 506, Nauck², and also the collection in L. Ruhl, *De mortuorum iudicio*, RGVV 103, 11, 2, 101ff., and M. P. Nilsson, *GGR*² 2, 196f., and there n. 5: supplements to L. Ruhl; see also G. H. Maccurdy, *JBL* 61, 1942, 218ff., with reference to the later Testament of Abraham.

604. Plautus, *Rudens*, prol. 9ff., and on it E. Fraenkel, *ClassQ* 36, 1942, 10–14;

H. Windisch, op. cit., 86: 'one of the finest testimonies to pagan piety', and M. P. Nilsson, *GGR²* 2, 276.

605. Diodore 2, 30f., see M. P. Nilsson, loc. cit.

606. Cf. I Enoch 98.6–8; 104.7; Jub.4.6 and II Enoch 19.5.

607. For the judgment of fire see Dan.7.11; I Enoch 10.6; 18.15; 21.7; 90.24, 26; 91.9; 100.7, 9; 102.1. Further examples in P. Volz, op. cit., 314f., 318f., 323f., 335f.; F. Lang, *TDNT* 6, 937. Behind this stand Old Testament pictures, cf. Zeph.1.18; 3.8; Deut.32.22, etc., see F. Lang, op. cit., 6, 935ff. We should therefore assume no general dependence on old Persian conceptions but at best a certain general influence, see R. Mayer, *Die biblischen Vorstellungen vom Weltenbrand*, 1956, 19ff., 99ff., 114ff., and esp. 125f. and 135. Cf. also the criticism of M. P. Nilsson, *GGR²* 2, 557f. I Enoch 1.5ff., and in Essenism 1 QH 3.29–36; 6.17ff.; Jub.9.15, and Hippolytus, *Philos.*9, 27, GCS Wendland 3, 260f., come near to the conception of *ekpyrosis*. For the annihilation of evil by fire in Qumran see 1 QS 4.13; 1 QpHab 10.5, 12f. The *ekpyrosis* theme is even stronger in the later Sibyls, see 2, 196ff., 252ff.: the Iranian ordeal by fire; 286ff.; 3, 80ff.; 4, 172ff., etc., see P. Volz, op. cit., 335; Bousset/Gressmann, 281f. See also above, n.552.

608. A. Dieterich, *Nekyia*, 219f., cf. 117ff.; cf. also E. Rohde, *Psyche* ²2, 179 n.3; T. F. Glasson, op. cit., 27; and Bousset/Gressmann, 244; cf. e. g. Virgil 6, 580ff.: the Titans go to the deepest abyss of Tartarus.

609. M. P. Nilsson, *GGR²* 2, 558, cf. 550ff., 234f., 242 with reference to the description of the tortures in Lucretius, 3, 1012ff.; Virgil, *Aen.*6, 661ff., cf. A. Dieterich, op. cit., 195ff., 199ff., and M. Treu, *Hermes* 82, 1954, 42ff.

610. DJDJ IV, 54ff., 61ff., and especially 62ff., cf. also already *ZAW* 75, 1963, 73–85; see below, n.IV, 40, and M. Hengel (above I, n.86), 165.

611. For the influence of the mystery religions see the polemical translation Deut.23.18 and Num.25.3 LXX, cf. also Ps.105.28 LXX and Wisd.12.3f.; 14.15, 22ff.; III Macc.2.30 and on it N. A. Dahl, *Das Volk Gottes*, ²1963, 105 and G. Bornkamm, *TDNT* 4, 814; also O. S. Rankin, *Israel's Wisdom Literature*, reprinted 1954, 209ff., and in detail, though rather one-sided, L. Cerfaux, *Le Muséon* 37, 1924, 28–88. Philo above all takes up the terminology of the mysteries to a considerable degree at a later stage, see Wolfson, *Philo* 1, 1948, 43ff., and A. Wlosok, *Laktanz*, AAH 1960, 2, 74ff., 97ff., who presupposes these views in the Alexandrian Jewish community. A closer acquaintance with the mystery cults can be noted in Palestinian Judaism in the Rabbinic period, see S. Lieberman, *Hellenism in Jewish Palestine*, 1950, 119ff. J. Lebram, *VT* 15, 1965, 211f., points to the 'language bordering on that of the mystery cults' in Marqah.

612. Bousset/Gressmann, 291, cf. 298.

613. G. von Rad, *Theologie des Alten Testaments* 2, ⁴1965, 319: apocalyptic goes 'far beyond the claims of older wisdom', it is based on 'charismatic authorization' (passage not in the English translation), cf. H. P. Müller, 'Mantische Weisheit und Apokalyptik', *Congress Volume*, SVT 22, 1972, 268–93.

614. A. Bentzen, op. cit., 43.

615. Sir.8.18; according to V. Hamp, the LXX version is to be preferred in 12.11c; cf. also H. P. Rüger, *Text und Textform*, 1970, 51 n.28. The foreign

word *rāz* (= μυστήριον), deriving from the Iranian, appears outside Daniel and the Qumran literature only in the Apocrypha and in the Greek parts of I Enoch 8.3; 16.3; 103.2; 104.12 and Tobit 12.7, 11; Judith 2.2; Wisdom 2.22; 6.22; 14.15, 23. Its emergence is an indication of the changed intellectual situation of the Hellenistic period. For Qumran see below, n.725, cf. also G. Bornkamm, *TDNT* 4, 813ff.

616. In Daniel we still find the old idea that the king receives divine revelations by virtue of his office, cf. Gen.41.1ff.; Dan.4.2ff.; 5.5; Herodotus 1, 34, 38f., 108, 209; 3, 30, 64; 7, 12–19; Josephus, *Antt.* 17, 345ff.; Cicero, *De div.* 1, 23, 46, cf. also the Hytaspes oracle, Vol.I, pp.185f. For the interpretation of dreams in Judaism, especially in Qumran, see Vol.I, p.240.

617. O. Plöger, *RGG*³ 3, 22; cf. P. Grelot, *RSR* 46, 1958, 15; D. S. Russell, op. cit., 112.

618. H. L. Jansen, op. cit., 22–81; cf. also B. Wachholder, *HUCA* 34, 1963, 95–99, and P. Grelot, op. cit., 5–26; 181–210.

619. P. Grelot, op. cit., 180f.

620. Cf. E. Sjöberg, *Der Menschensohn im äthiopischen Henochbuch*, 1946, 104ff.

621. For Noah see the fragments of a Noah apocryphon in I Enoch 6–11; 65–69.25; 106f. Cf. Jub. 10.13 and the fragment of a Noah book 1 Q 19, DJD 1, 84ff., 152; on Abraham see Jub. 21 and 22 and the Testament of Abraham, in its Christian revision, ed. M. R. James, *Anecdota apocrypha*, Texts and Studies II, 2, 1892, and G. H. Maccurdy, *JBL* 61, 1942, 213–26. For the Testament of Levi see n.623, cf. the fragment of a Testament of Naphthali with apocalyptic content, C. Burchard, *Bibliographie* 2, 334. Even fragments of a 'vision of Amram', the father of Moses, have been preserved. It is almost impossible to distinguish between the genres of apocalypses, testaments and midrash-like works such as Jubilees. The apocalypses contain paraenetic and midrash-like narrative passages, and as a 'prophetic' genre (see below, n.667), the testament literature clearly as its eschatological parts. In the midrash works, on the other hand, smaller 'testaments' and 'apocalypses' have been incorporated. The extent and variety of this kind of literature can hardly be put high enough in view of the fragments from Qumran and the reports of the church fathers, see C. Burchard, op. cit., 333–6, the summary report *RB* 63, 1956, 60f., 65f., and below n.895; it must have had a wide readership.

622. J. T. Milik, *RB* 62, 1955, 400, cols. I and II, and on them R. H. Charles, *The Greek Versions*, 246 col. a l. 10 (v.7), and T. Levi 2ff.; further apocalyptic examples of journeys to heaven in D. S. Russell, op. cit., 166, cf. W. Bousset, *Die Himmelsreise der Seele*, reprinted 1960, 7ff., and G. Bertram, *RAC* 6, 28–34 (see Vol.I, pp.214f.).

623. On this see D. S. Russell, op. cit., 127–39. However, pseudepigraphy applies to a large part of Jewish literature with a religious content, see Vol.I, p.112, and occurs also in the astrological and prophetic revelation literature of the Hellenistic environment, see Vol.I, p.206.

624. Cf. Dan.8.26; 12.4, 9; cf. I Enoch 104.10–13. In I Enoch, handing on to the firstborn predominates, see Vol.I, p.204, cf. below, n.679. See also IV Ezra 14.38 and 14.42–47.

625. Cf. D. S. Russell, op. cit., 418f.; against P. Vielhauer, in Hennecke-Schneemelcher-Wilson, op. cit., 595.

626. Cf. K. Elliger, *Studien zum Habakkukkommentar*, 1953, 156f.; O. Betz, *Offenbarung und Schriftforschung*, 1960, 80ff., 137; D. S. Russell, op. cit., 187–94, and R. Meyer, *TDNT* 6, 820f.

627. A similar tendency appears in Hellenistic philosophy: the Platonist Antiochus of Ashkelon took *'veteres sequi'* as his motto at the beginning of the first century BC, and thus laid the foundation for traditionalist eclecticism (see Vol. I, p. 87 and n. II, 224–6).

628. A similar distinction, merely 'of degree', existed between the prophets and the 'wise men' in Rabbinic views, see R. Meyer, *TDNT* 6, 816ff.

629. G. von Rad, *Old Testament Theology* 2, 300ff., critical observations on the term apocalyptic. For 'wisdom' see H. Gese, *RGG*³ 6, 1577: '. . . as there was no unitary term wisdom in the ancient East'; see also 1578: 'the boundary between wisdom poetry and scientific literature cannot be marked out clearly'.

630. See Vol. I, pp. 153f. and nn. 293, 301: hidden wisdom in Ahikar. In I Enoch, 84.3 and ch. 42, which is not original in its present place, point to this wisdom hidden with God; cf. also the praise of wisdom in Aramaic Test. Levi, see R. H. Charles, *The Greek Versions*, 256, col. c. = *Apocrypha and Pseudepigrapha* II, 366. It becomes an eschatological gift for the elect, cf. I Enoch 5.8; 90.10; 104.12; cf. 37.4; 49.1; 51.3; 99.10. For the apocalyptic concept of wisdom see U. Wilckens, *Weisheit und Torheit*, 1959, 65f., 160ff., and *TDNT* 7, 503f. See also details in A. Théocharis, *La sagesse dans le Judaïsme Palestinien de l'insurrection maccabéenne*, Strasbourg 1963, typescript dissertation, and H.-P. Müller (above n. 613), 280ff.

631. Cf. the contrast in the derivation of apocalyptic between G. von Rad, op. cit., 2, 300ff., who bases it on 'wisdom', and H. H. Rowley, *The Relevance of Apocalyptic*, ³1950, 11–50, who sees it as the continuation of prophecy. The historical connection with the latter has been shown by O. Plöger, *Theocracy and Eschatology*, 27ff., and passim, and G. Fohrer, *TLZ* 85, 1960, 401–20; cf. also D. S. Russell, op. cit., 75–103. However, with the historical development there is an unmistakable difference between apocalyptic thought and the great prophets of the pre-exilic period and the exile. The temporal interval of at least three to four hundred years and the changed historical and cultural situation in the Persian and Hellenistic period must be noted here, not the least of whose determinative influences was the growing significance of the wisdom literature.

632. Dan. 9.3; 10.3, at the same time an expression of penitence. For the widespread 'ecstatic fasts' see P. R. Arbesmann, *Das Fasten*, RGVV 21, 1929, 97ff., and J. Behm, *TDNT* 4, 927f., 930; cf. IV Ezra 5.13, 19f., etc.; Syr.Bar. 9.2; 21.1ff., etc. Cf. also the drink of prophecy in IV Ezra 14.39ff., which might hint at drugs.

633. D. S. Russell, op. cit., 164–73; cf. also G. Widengren, *Literal and Psychological Aspects*, UUÅ 1948, 10, 108ff., on the 'heavenly journey' of Enoch in comparison to Ezekiel. For the influence of 'mantic wisdom' see H. P. Müller, op. cit., 275ff.

634. See W. Bousset, *Himmelsreise*, 14ff.; Bousset/Gressmann, 356f., 398f.; Moore. *Judaism* 1, 413; R. Meyer, *TDNT* 6, 820. For the Essene 'prophets' see

Vol. I, pp. 239ff. For 'mystical' experiences of doctrines of the first and second centuries AD in connection with 'secret doctrine' see Bill. 1, 603f. For the early Rabbinic miracle-workers, see A. Guttmann, *HUCA* 20, 1949, 363–406, and R. Phinehas b. Jair: *jDemai* 21d/22a.

635. Cf. I Enoch 17–36; Jub. 8.11–9.15; 10.26–36; Gen. Apoc. 21; on this see G. Hölscher, *Drei Erdkarten*, SAH phil. hist. Kl. 34, 1944/48, 29, 33 and 57–73, where above all the Greek influences in Jub. are pointed out. For the earlier Babylonian wisdom tradition see P. Grelot, *RQ* 1, 1958/59, 124ff., and *RB* 65, 1958, 33ff.; for 'geographical instruction' in the Jewish wisdom schools in Jerusalem see also K. Galling, *Die Krisis der Aufklärung in Israel*, 1950, 10. According to the fragments of I Enoch 30–32 from Cave 4Q, published by J. T. Milik, *RB* 65, 1958, 70ff., Enoch travels into the spice-producing lands of the south and east (Arabia Felix and India ?) and over the Erythrean sea (cf. Gen. Apoc. 21.17ff.) to paradise in the East. The report shows some familiarity with the spice trade and the origin of individual ingredients, and makes use of themes from the Hellenistic utopian travel romance (Iambulus, Euhemerus); cf. K. Kerényi, *Die griechisch-orientalische Romanliteratur*, ²1962, 45ff.

636. For astrology see Vol. I, pp. 236ff. For the rejection of astral religion see Jub. 12.16f.; I Enoch 80.7; Dan. 2.20ff., on which see A. Bentzen, op. cit., 25.

637. Meteorology, I Enoch 34.36; Jub. 2.2ff.; for medicine see Vol. I, pp. 240f.

638. E. Sjöberg, *Der Menschensohn im äthoipischen Henochbuch*, 1946, 110.

639. For later 'research in the Torah' among the Essenes see O. Betz, *Offenbarung*, 19–35. H. W. Kuhn, *Enderwartung und gegenwärtiges Heil*, 1966, 145–52, argues that these forms of knowledge are completely unconnected in apocalyptic.

640. See his *Theologie des Alten Testaments* 2, ⁴1965, 321.

641. A. Schlatter, *GI²*, 109f.

642. M. J. Lagrange, *Le Judaïsme*, 1931, 79, and F. M. Abel, *HP* 1, 284; Bousset/Gressmann, 184.

643. J. T. Milik, *RB* 63, 1956, 60; cf. also *RB* 65, 1958, 75f.: detailed systematic work in describing the journeys of Enoch and the better comprehensibility and ordering in the extant fragments of the astronomical book, which comes to light on the basis of the fragment of 77.3 and other fragments. Cf. *HTR* 64, 1971, 338ff., 343ff.

644. F. C. Burkitt, *Jewish and Christian Apocalypses*, 1914, 7: 'in Daniel there is a philosophy of universal history', cf. also K. Koch, *HZ* 193, 1961, 31, 'a sketch of a universal history – the first in the history of the world'.

645. The term is not to be understood in W. Bousset's pejorative sense as a non-scribal 'literature of a strongly lay character', see *Die jüdische Apokalyptik*, 1903, 9; cf. Bousset/Gressmann, 184, 211f., and still more abruptly *ARW* 18, 1915, 151: 'literature which often displays the character of a minority sect.' The alliance of 'piety with learning' did not take place only in the Herodian period but even before the Maccabean revolt, as a defence against Hellenistic influence. The apocalypses were written by the Hasidic '*sōpᵉrīm*' for a wider audience. Daniel is the best example of this. With their archaizing style, their historical and geographical knowledge and their knowledge of Greek mythology, the Sibyllines

also presuppose a considerable degree of learning. P. Vielhauer ought to accept as true of apocalyptic, 594f., what he rightly says about the Sibyllines in Hennecke-Schneemelcher-Wilson, op. cit., 600f. The Ten Weeks' Apocalypse, for instance (see n.459 above), has the character of a pamphlet.

646. G. von Rad, *Old Testament Theology* 2, 303f.

647 For Asclepius see W. Fauth, *KP* 1, 644ff., and M. P. Nilsson, *GGR*² 2, 186, 188 n.6, 223ff., 336f. E.g. Aelius Aristides had such a complete personal relationship to Asclepius in the second century AD (op. cit., 561f.). For Serapis (and Isis) see op. cit., 2, 121ff., 124ff., 128ff., 224: healings and aretalogies. Cf. also H. Bell, *JEA* 34, 1948, 87–94, and A. D. Nock, *Conversion*, 36ff., 49ff. E.g. the Zoilus letter from the Zeno correspondence is typical, PCZ 59034 = A Deissmann, *Light from the Ancient East*, 1927, 152–61. For Isis and Serapis as lords of destiny see S. Morenz/D. Müller, AAL 52, 1, 1960, 30f. Further instances of a quite personal relationship with a god – albeit from Roman times – are provided by the inscriptions on the temple of the god Mandulis-Aion in Talmis in Nubia, see A. D. Nock, *HTR* 27, 1934, 53–78, and Festugière, *Révélation* 1, 46ff. The vision of Maximus is typical, A. D. Nock, op. cit., 63 l.9: ἐνθεασάμενος ἀνε(πάην): 'I had a vision and found rest for my soul.' For the problem see in detail A. J. Festugière, *Personal Religion among the Greeks*, 1954, 53f., 68ff., 85ff., 122ff., and for the Ptolemaic empire, M. T. Lenger, *Proceedings of the Twelfth International Congress of Papyrologists*, 255ff.

648. H. Gese, *RGG*³ 6, 1575: 'special revelations' are exceptions in ancient oriental wisdom. In the Hellenistic period 'these exceptions become the rule'. A good example of this is offered by the diary-like accounts of dreams of the *katochos* Ptolemy in the Serapeion in Memphis. On 2 June 159 BC the god Ammon appeared to him, at his request, with two other deities. Another time he turned to Isis and Serapis for a manifestation and a little later had the epiphany of the (good) daimon Knephis, who announced to him his imminent release, see U. Wilcken, *UPZ* 1, 353f., no.77, col.2, 22–31 and 1, 360, no.78, ll.22–45; on this see Festugière, *Révélation* 1, 51. For the great significance of epiphanies for the revivification of the cult in the Hellenistic period see F. Pfister, *PW Suppl* 4, 295ff., 298ff.; for the question of the authenticity of experiences see 316. The liberation of the Jewish slave Moschus son of Moschion in Oropus in Attica on the ground of a command of the healing gods Amphiaraus and Hygieia communicated by an incubation dream also belongs in this context (first half of the third century BC), see Vol. I, p.42, and n.I, 326. The incubation dream was already regarded highly in classical Greece in individual sanctuaries like Epidaurus, see E. Roos, *Opuscula atheniensia* 3, 1960, 55–97, and E. R. Dodds, *The Greeks and the Irrational*, 1951, 110ff.

649. Ganschinietz, *PW* 10, 2395–2430; cf. also E. Rohde, op. cit., 2, 90ff.

650. M. P. Nilsson, *GGR*² 1, 452ff., 688ff., 815–26; 2, 231ff.; also – with qualifications – W. Bousset, *Die Himmelsreise der Seele*, reprinted 1960, 59ff. See also E. R. Dodds, op. cit., 140ff.: the original forms come from shamanist culture.

651. A. Dieterich, *Eine Mithrasliturgie*, ed. O. Weinreich, ³1923, 197.

652. Op. cit., 197–200; W. Jaeger, *Die Theologie der frühen griechischen Denker*, 1953, 110ff. Cf. G. Bertram, *RAC* 6, 30f.

653. F. Pfister, *RAC* 4, 971.

654. Wilamowitz-Moellendorf, *Der Glaube der Hellenen* 2, ³1959, 524ff.; E. Rohde, op. cit., 2, 94 n. 1; on his influence: 2, 320 n. 1 and Clem.Alex., *Strom.* 1, 133, 2, GCS 2, 82, Stählin-Früchtel. Cf. also M. P. Nilsson, *GGR*² 2, 240f., and H. Lewy, *HTR* 31, 1939, 214f. For parallel phenomena see Rohde, op. cit., 2, 90ff., and Nilsson, op. cit., 1, 615ff.

655. 371a, see M. P. Nilsson, *GGR*² 2, 41f.

656. R. Helm, *PW* 15, 888–94.

657. Festugière, op. cit., 1, 224, 228f., and Bidez/Cumont, op. cit., 1, 198ff., 210f.; 2, 311–21, esp. 317 n.6.

658. Ps.Clem., *Hom.* 1, 5, GCS 1, 24, ed. Rehm, cf. on this F. Boll, *ZNW* 17, 1916, 139–48, who points to the parallels to Lucian and the Thessalus letter (see below, n.681). Lucian, *Philopseudes* 33ff., LCL 3, 370ff., offers a satire on the Egyptian secret sciences.

659. Text in M. Förster, *Archiv für das Studium der neueren Sprachen* 108, 1902, 15–28, German in Riessler, *Altjüdische Schrifttum*, 496. For necromancy, which especially flourished in the Hellenistic period, see T. Hopfner, *PW* 16, 2218–33.

660. Festugière, op. cit., 1, 6–18: 'Le déclin du rationalisme', though this does not begin with the empire but from the second century BC, cf. Tarn/ Griffith, *Hellenistic Civilization*, 351ff.: the problem of fate drove men to astrology, and to escape the compulsion of the stars 'there were three main lines . . . Gnosis, magic and the eastern mystery-religions'.

661. CH 16, 2, cf. Festugière, op. cit., 1.26f. Cf. also Philo Bybl., FGrHist 790 F 2, 10, 8 on the erroneous Greek divine names based on wrong translations. Cf. C. Préaux, *ChrEg* 42, 1967, 369–83.

662. POx 11, 1381: the aretalogy on Asclepius-Imuthes: the text is also in G. Manteuffel, op. cit., 86ff., cf. Festugière, op. cit., 1, 52ff., and A. D. Nock, *Conversion*, 86ff.; see further SB 7470 and on the Hermetica, Iamblichus, *De myst.* 8,4.

663. *Meg.*3a, cf. also *Tractate Soperim* 1, 7; on the other hand *Meg.*9a Bar., see Bill.4, 414v–x, is positive. For Jonathan b. Uzziel and Theodotion see above, n. II, 349. Among other things, the Prophet Targum was ascribed to him. Cf. the punishment for an illegitimate translation, Ps.Arist. 314f.

664. Festugière, op. cit., 1, 17–44: (ch.2) 'Les prophètes de l'Orient'. Cf. M. P. Nilsson, *GGR*² 2, 527ff.

665. Op. cit., 1, 28ff.

666. FGrHist 618 F 6 = Porphyry, *De abst.*4, 6. Cf. on this Festugière, *REG* 50, 1937, 476ff., and A. Wlosok, *Laktanz*, AAH 1960, 2, 55f.

667. E. Fascher, ΠΡΟΦΗΤΗΣ, 1927, 94f.

668. Lactantius, *Divin. Inst.* 6, 15, 19, CSEL 19, 1, 634, ed. Brandt; on this see H. Windisch, op. cit., 46ff., and F. Altheim, *Weltgeschichte Asiens*, 2, 180f. The gift of sight was often ascribed to youths, see P. Courcelle, *RAC* 3, 1237, 1241f.

669. See the fragments in E. Riess, *Phil.Suppl.* 6, 1891–93, 322 fr. 1 = Vettius Valens 6, 1, and the text reconstruction in R. Reitzenstein, *Poimandres*, 1904, 4f., cf. *Mysterienreligionen*, 189f., and W. Kroll, *PW* 16, 2160ff. For the type of these 'heavenly journeys' see A. Wlosok, *Laktanz*, AAH 1960, 2, 34ff.,

who points out the influence of these conceptions on Philo. Cf. also G. Bertram, *RAC* 6, 31.

670. E. Riess, op. cit., 380 fr. 33: ἀνὴρ παντοίαις τάξεσι θεῶν καὶ ἀγγέλων συναλισθείς, and less emphatically Vettius Valens 6.1, ed. Kroll 242,17: τὰ θεῖα μοι προσομιλεῖν.

671. Op. cit., 1, 77. The earliest Hermetic-astrological evidence is the fragment of the *Salmeshiniaka* preserved in POx 3, 126ff., no. 465, which still has similarities with Babylonian texts, see W. Kroll, *PW Suppl* 5, 843ff., and W. Gundel, *PW*, 2.R 3, 2424. The Latin translation of an extensive astrological work of Hermes coming from the time of the Ptolemies (second century BC) was edited by W. Gundel: *Neue astrologische Texte des Hermes Trismegistos*, AAM NF 12, 1936. Its original version is probably only a little earlier than the work of Nechepso, see also O. Neugebauer, *The Exact Sciences in Antiquity*, ²1957, 68f., and Festugière, op. cit., 1, 112ff.

672. Knaack, *PW* 6, 388, see E. Hiller, *Erastosthenis carminum reliquiae*, 1872, 38–65, fr. 15–19, and J. U. Powell, *Collectanea Alexandrina*, 1925, 61ff.; cf. A. Wlosok, op. cit., 36 n. 111, and Manilius 2, 115: revelation through exaltation.

673. *Astronomica*, ed. Wageningen, 1, 30, cf. 4, 436–40: '*sed mihi per carmen fatalia iura ferenti / et sacros caeli motus ad iussa loquendum est; / nec fingenda datur, tantum monstranda figura; ostendisse deum nimis est, dabit ipse sibimet / pondera.*'

674. CH 1, 1, cf. R. Reitzenstein, *Poimandres*, 1904, 12ff., and Festugière, op. cit., 1, 314, who points to I Enoch 12.1 and Rev. 1.10; 4.2, etc., as parallels.

675. See on this R. Meyer, *TDNT* 6, 817f., and n. 242; Bill. 1, 125ff. It appears as the most extreme abbreviation of a divine epiphany reduced to an audition, the starting point of which is the heavenly sanctuary. It is meant to replace the lack of prophetic inspiration: *T. Soṭa* 13, 2 (l. 318), cf. on this A. Guttmann, *HUCA* 20, 1947, 367ff.

676. PGM 4, 625, cf. I Enoch 14.15; 104.2; T. Levi 5.1; Acts 7.56; Rev. 4.1; III Macc. 6.18; on this W. C. van Unnik, *Festschrift E. Haenchen*, BZNW 30, 1964, 269–80; F. Lentzen-Deis, *Bibl* 50, 1969, 301–27.

677. PGM 1, 88–98 no. 4, 475–750, cf. Dieterich/Weinreich, op. cit., passim, and Festugière, op. cit., 1, 315. For Apuleius see M. P. Nilsson, *GGR²* 2, 633ff., and M. Dibelius, *Botschaft und Geschichte* 2, 1956, 48ff. *Gen.R.* 44, 12 (on 15.5) reports a 'heavenly journey' of Abraham related to Plato, *Phaedrus* 247b/c, as a tradition of R. Joḥanan (third century AD), to give a basis for the rejection of astrology (see above, n. II, 254), see L. Baeck, op. cit., 149f.

678. Festugière, op. cit., 1, 334 n. 7, cf. 137 n. 8: the tractate ascribed simultaneously to Enoch and Hermes, *De XV herbis lapidibus et figuris*, and on it F. Pfister, *PW* 19, 145 and L. Thorndike, *A History of Magic* 1, 1923, 340f. Cf. Hermes as an intercessor and guide on the heavenly journey, above, n. 581.

679. On this Festugière, op. cit., 1, 332ff., and *RB* 48, 1939, 52: it is a matter of a secret 'paradosis'. This is the very earliest form of the wisdom tradition and at the same time has an esoteric character; cf. e.g. the Ahikar romance ed. A. Cowley, *Aramaic Papyri*, 1923, 212, cols. I and II: Ahikar and his ungrateful adopted son Nadin. Cf. D. Langen, *Archäische Ekstase*, 1963, 16f.,

for prehistoric shamanism. Jub. 7.38f.; Test.Benj. 10.2–6 are typical. On this see L. Dürr, in *Heilige Überlieferung, Festschrift I. Herwegen,* 1938, 1–20.

680. FGrHist 726 F 3, 6 = Eusebius, *Pr.Ev.,* cf. Hecataeus, FGrHist 264 F 25 = Diodore 1, 16, 1.

681. CCAG 8, 3, 1912, 134ff., cf. Festugière, *RB* 48, 1939, 45–77; *Révélation,* 1, 56ff. The authenticity of the letter is doubted. Against R. Reitzenstein, *Mysterienreligionen,* [3]1927, 127ff., and with H. Diller, *PW,* 2.R 6, 181f., and M. P. Nilsson, *GGR*[2] 2, 532 n. 5, we should probably assume a pseudepigraphon.

682. G. Manteuffel, op. cit., 100, and FGrHist 257 F 36 III, 6; see above, n. 525. Cf. also F. Pfister, *RAC* 4, 97f. This form cannot by any means be described as typically Greek. For a related phenomenon in the Old Testament see G. Widengren, UUÅ, 1948, no. 10, 96, 113ff., cf. e.g. II Kings 3.15; 9.11; Hos. 9.7; Jer. 29.26; see also above, n. 384. Ps.Longinus, *De sublim.* 13, 2; 16, 2, transfers it to the orator.

683. In the hour of death (and in sleep), when the soul is parted from the body, a man receives special gifts of insight, see Cicero, *De div.* 1, 30, 63f., with reference to Posidonius; cf. P. Courcelle, *RAC* 3, 1237. This is the historical background to the 'prophetic' testament literature, see also E. Stauffer, *RAC* 1, 30f.

684. J. A. Sint, *Pseudonymität im Altertum,* 1960; K. Latte, *Römische Religionsgeschichte,* 1960, 269ff.; W. Speyer, *Die literarische Fälschung im Altertum,* 1971.

685. *Die Himmelsreise der Seele,* reprinted 1960, 67; cf. on the other hand the justified criticism of Dietrich/Weinreich, op. cit., 186ff., 191ff. R. Reitzenstein, *Mysterienreligionen,* 223ff., also supposes Iranian derivation. O. Eissfeldt, *The Old Testament,* 620, favours Egypt. However, the phenomenon is too widespread for a one-sided geographical conclusion to be reached, see n. 686.

686. The apocalyptists believed that they were dependent on Old Testament models like Ezek. 3.14; 8.3; 11.1 and II Kings 2.11f., as I Enoch 14.8 and 70.2 show; see G. Widengren, op. cit., 102ff. It is less probable that they were aware how different they were from the prophecy of the Old Testament in the theme of the heavenly journey, their description of the kingdom of the dead and of paradise, and even in their view of history. 'Inspired exegesis' offered a possibility of reading a new meaning into the old texts. Of course the phenomenon of the heavenly journey and the visit to the underworld is very old, like that of prophetic ecstasy, and presumably goes back to prehistoric times. See D. Langen, *Archäische Ekstase,* 1963, 15ff., 23f., 65; cf. also E. R. Dodds, op. cit., 140ff., see above, n. 650. The one thing typical of the Hellenistic period is that interest in such experiences was aroused on a broad basis, even in Judaism.

687. P. Wendland, *Die hellenistisch-römische Kultur,* 1912, 159ff.; A. Wlosok, op. cit., 53ff.

688. *New Testament Questions of Today,* 102, cf. 137, 'apocalyptic as the mother of Christian theology'.

689. See the fine formulation by P. Stuhlmacher, *Gerechtigkeit Gottes bei Paulus,* 1965, 147 (cf. K. Koch, *HZ* 193, 1961, 31): 'If God is the basis and author of history, then man resting on the faithfulness of God is its goal.'

690. We begin from an assumption, almost universally accepted, that the

community of Qumran is identical with the Essenes; on this see P. Wernberg-Møller, *The Manual of Discipline*, 1957, 19 n.2 lit.; A. Dupont-Sommer, *The Essene Writings from Qumran*, 1961, 39–67, and K. G. Kuhn, *RGG³* 5, 745.

691. The 'central writings' are 1 QS, 1 QH and 1 QM, the *pᵉšārīm* and a series of fragments with typical terminology like 1 Q 27 (see n.711). Their basic ideas probably go back to the founder himself, the Teacher of Righteousness, even if some of them, like the *pᵉšārīm*, in fact arose later. Their frequency in the library is also striking, see C. Burchard, op. cit., 2, 337ff., 341. 1 QM could be the Essene revision of a Hasidic-apocalyptic writing from the Maccabean period; see above, n.I, 101. For the problem see n.739 below.

692. For the text see E. Lohse, *Die Texte aus Qumran*, 1964, 11f. English version follows G. Vermes, *The Dead Sea Scrolls in English*, 1962, 75f., with some alterations.

693. J. Becker, *Das Heil Gottes*, 1964, 84.

694. See Vol.I, pp.140f., and 221. For the relationship of the Rule to the language of wisdom literature see P. Wernberg-Møller, *The Manual of Discipline*, 1957, 16f.; for Ben Sira see M. R. Lehmann, *RQ* 3, 1961/62, 103–16, and J. Carmignac, *RQ* 3, 1961/62, 209–18. So far two Koheleth fragments and a fragment of Sirach have been found in Qumran itself, see A. Muilenberg, *BASOR* 135, 1954, 20–8, and C. Burchard, op. cit., 2, 328f.; cf. also J. Strugnell, *RB* 63, 1956, 57f., and DJDJ III 75ff. (2 Q 18).

695. For the expression see Wernberg-Møller, op. cit., 68 n.48; cf. 1 QS 11.4, 11; 1 QM 17.5, and similarly also CD 2.10. (ה)הוא appears only in 1 QS 11.5 and 1 QH 12.9; נהי(י)ה (niph. היה, cf. נהיוה = events, Sir.42.18; 48.25): 1 QS 10.5; 11.9; 1 QM 17.5; 1 QH 11.14; 13.12, etc.

696. E. Kamlah, *Die Form der katalogischen Paränese im NT*, 1964, 44 n.1.

697. Fragments of 12 (11 ?) copies of the Rule are known, see C. Burchard, op. cit., 2, 337f.; see on this J. T. Milik, *RB* 63, 1956, 60f.; 67, 1960, 410–16, and K. G. Kuhn, *TLZ* 85, 1960, 652. The attempt of Wernberg-Møller, op. cit., 18, 20f., to put it in the first half of the second century BC is on the other hand too early. Apart from Col.V (see J. T. Milik, op. cit., 412), no essential variants in tradition have so far been found. Thus – against J. Becker, op. cit., 59, 84 – the dualism of the catechesis cannot be regarded as a teaching which only found its way in after the founder of the community: see also below, n.739. The dating by J. Becker, op. cit., 42, already makes this questionable.

698. This feminine hypostasis of God probably seemed to be too mythological; it did not correspond to the strict outline of Essene theology. The hypothesis of C. Colpe, *KP* 2, 832, that in 1 QS 3.15; 11.11 דעת is 'mediatrix of creation', is unjustified. 'God's knowledge' has no independent function that can be detached from God. Together with the call into the community of salvation it has, however, become a decisive concept for salvation as a gift of God: 1 QS 11.5–8.

699. Cf. 1 QH 1.26; 12.10; fr. 4.15; cf. 4 QSl 40.24, 2, ed. J. Strugnell, *SVT* 7, 1960, 336. See on this J. Becker, op. cit., 85 n.2. Sir.42.40 already says that God possesses all דעת, but does so without drawing the ultimate predestinarian consequence.

700. (מחשבת) מחשבה in the LXX is usually rendered διαλογισμός (cf. also

Sir. 13.26) or λογισμός; Isa. 55.9: διανόημα; 55.7 βουλή. In the sense of God's plan before creation see 1 QS 11.11, 19; 1 QH 4.13; 11.7; 18.22, cf. fr. 20; on this F. Nötscher, *Zur Terminologie der Qumrantexte*, 1956, 53. In Sir. 43.23 it means the plan of creation. For the obvious Hellenistic influence in Rabbinic terminology – which stands near to that of Qumran – see L. Wächter, *ZRGG* 14, 1962, 37ff.

701. 1 QH 1.7f., cf. 13.8–10; 15.13f., 17–19; 1 QS 11.10f., 17f. Cf. further 1 QM 13.14f.; CD 2.7f. and 1 QH 9.29f. (cf. Gal. 1.15). The formula בטרם בראתם or בט "ט היותם is typical of predestinarian thought, see 1 QH 1.10, 19, 28 and J. M. Allegro, *ALUOS* 4, 1962/63, 3 Doc. I, 2 = 4 Q 180 1, 2 (DJDJ V, 77); also J. Strugnell, *RQ* 7, 1969, 171, 252. These statements should not in any event be weakened down to a mere prescience, as happens with F. Nötscher, *Vom Alten zum Neuen Testament*, 1962, 46f., 51ff., and *Terminologie*, 173ff. God's omnipotence and righteousness are fundamentally identical as 'the demonstration of the creative power of God who has made all the world only for his glory', see P. Stuhlmacher, *Gerechtigkeit Gottes bei Paulus*, 1965, 166; on this see Vol. I, pp. 223ff.

702. Cf. 1 QS 2.2, 5; 3.24; 4.24, 26 etc. 1 QH 3.22, 27; 7.34; 1 Q 34bis 3.1, 2 = DJD 1, 153; 1 QSb 4.26 = op. cit., I, 126; on this see also F. Nötscher, op. cit., 169ff., who also weakens the predestinarian meaning here.

703. Cf. Koh. 3.14, to which again Sir. 18.6 refers, though in a weaker sense; see also 42.21. The stress on the freedom of the will is essentially stronger in Ben Sira and can be explained from his cultural situation, see Vol. I, pp. 140f.; as Pharisaic instances see Ps. Sol. 9.7–9 (4.5) and R. Akiba in 'Ab. 3, 15. Further in Bill. 1, 583; 4, 7; Bousset/Gressmann, 405, and R. Mach, *Der Zaddik in Talmud und Midrasch*, 1957,41ff.

704. *Bell.* 2, 162f.; *Antt.* 13, 171f. (probably dependent on Nicolaus of Damascus); 18, 12ff., 18. See also G. F. Moore, *HTR* 22, 1929, 371–89; G. Maier, *Mensch und freier Wille*, 1971.

705. The term is related to מלכות, see J. Becker, op. cit., 79, 98f.

706. See 1 QS 3.21–24, and the duties of the novices, 1.17f., 23. Cf. 2.19.

707. See 1 QS 4.24–26; this conception also underlies the horoscopes at Qumran, see Vol I, pp. 236ff.

708. The phrase 'mystery(ies) of God' relates above all to the predestinarian plan of God which he realizes in history: see e.g. 1 QS 11.19. It comprises both the 'mystery' of the annihilation of evil at the end of time (1 QS 4.18; 1 QM 3.9, etc.) and also the 'mystery' of the effectiveness of evil in history, which is equally laid down by God: 1 QS 3.23; 1 QM 16.11–16; 17.9; cf. 14.9 and above all 1 QH 5.36; the interpretation of the passage by F. Nötscher, op. cit., 47, distorts its meaning. In his predestinarian 'mystery' God has determined that sinners alter 'God's work' (presumably the ordering of feast times, cf. Dan. 7.25) through their transgressions. For the concept of the mystery see also E. Vogt, *Bibl* 37, 1956, 247–57, and J. Hempel, *Die Texte von Qumran*, NGG 1961, no. 10, 363f.; cf. also above n. 615 and below n. 725.

709. For the two spirits see 1 QS 3.18ff.; 4.9, 21–29; they are identical with the spirits of light and darkness, 3.25 cf. 3.20; cf. also 1 QM 13.10–14; 17.5ff. (Michael) and CD 5.18; for Belial see 1 QS 1.17f., 24; 2.5, 19; the War Scroll and CD passim. The developed angelology is closely connected with the

doctrine of the two spirits, see Y. Yadin, *The Scroll of the War*, 1962, 229–42, and M. Mansoor, *The Thanksgiving Hymns*, 1961, 77–84, cf. also Vol. I, p. 231, n. 786. For Belial see also K. Galling, *RGG*³ 1, 1025f. For the final overcoming of evil see 1 QS 3.18; 4.18ff.; 1 QH 3.19–36; 1 QM passim and M. Mansoor, op. cit., 90f.

710. P. Wernberg-Møller, *RQ* 3, 1961/62, 413–41, put forward a purely anthropological interpretation without a cosmic background; see on the other hand the justified objections of H. G. May, *JBL* 82, 1963, 1–14; cf. already O. Betz, *Offenbarung*, 143ff.

711. 1 Q 27, see DJD I, 103, col. 1; cf. A. Dupont-Sommer, op. cit., 327, and J. Hempel, op. cit., 305; the translation follows J. Becker, op. cit., 94, with alterations. The apocalyptic text published by J. M. Allegro, op. cit. (above, n. 701), and the fragment from DJD I, 154, 1 Q 34bis 3, 2, where the historical failure of man is also described, are related.

712. For imprisonment in the underworld see also 1 QH 3.17f.; 1 QS 4.13; 2.7f.; cf. I Enoch 22 and Vol. I, pp. 198f.

713. For the mystery of history see O. Betz, *Offenbarung*, 82–7. For קץ see F. Nötscher, *Terminologie*, 167ff.; עת and מועד also appear alongside it.

714. For creatureliness see 1 QH 1.21; 3.23f.; 10.3–5; 11.3; 12.31f.; 1 QS 11.21f. This group of ideas comes from wisdom, see Wernberg-Møller, *Manual*, 155, cf. Job 4.19; 10.9; Koh. 3.20; Sir. 17.1; Wisd. 7.1; 9.15; 'Ab. 3, 1. However, inextricably bound up with man's creatureliness is his complete fallenness in sin, see the abundance of instances in Mansoor, op. cit., 59–62; cf. also K. G. Kuhn, *ZTK* 49, 1952, 200–22; O. Betz, *Offenbarung*, 120–6; J. Becker, op. cit., 109–14 and 137–48. As in Paul, the association of creatureliness and sinfulness is expressed in the term *bāśār*, see op. cit., 112: 'All men are sinners, because they are *bāśār*', cf. also J. Hempel, op. cit., 357ff.

715. For the Damascus document see K. G. Kuhn, *TLZ* 85, 1960, 652; *RGG*³ 5, 749: 'the rule for the "worldly" lay brotherhoods . . . who form individual communities scattered through the country.' For the book of Jubilees see its mention in CD 16.3f.: it is similarly of Essene origin, see above, n. 460.

716. F. Nötscher, *Terminologie*, 38–79, gives a survey of the terms. For the hymns see especially M. Mansoor, op. cit., 65–74. דעת/דעה appears most frequently with 62 times; there follow שכל with 27; בינה with 25; on the other hand חכמה is used only 13 times; see K. G. Kuhn, *Konkordanz*, and the supplement, *RQ* 4, 1963/64, 175–234, on the individual terms. The stratification in terminology is probably connected with a greater emergence of noetic-reflective knowledge. The old term 'wisdom' no longer did justice to the stronger differentiation of revealed 'knowledge'. For 'knowledge' in the community hymns see H. W. Kuhn, *Enderwartung*, 154ff.

717. Cf. e.g. 1 QS 9.17: 'true knowledge' and 1 QH 9.10; 10.20, 29. With אמת (the term appears 133 times in the Concordance and the supplement), the ethical practical significance of the reference to God predominates; cf. F. Nötscher, *Vom Alten zum Neuen Testament*, 112–25; O. Betz, *Offenbarung*, 53–59, and especially for the community hymns, J. Becker, op. cit., 155–60. This word, which is central to Essene theology, encompasses the whole range of divine revelation: what God does, communicates and demands is אמת.

718. 1 QS 10.12; 11.3; 1 QH 2.18; cf. 1 QH 5.26; 8.6; God has given the Teacher the source of knowledge in his heart.

719. 1 QS 11.3f., 5f.; cf. 1 QH 1.21–23, 26–28; 3.20–23; 4.27f., 30 etc.

720. 1 QS 5.20–24: alongside this the 'perfection of conduct' is also tested, cf. 1 QSa 1.17.

721. Cf. 1 QS 4.10, 24; 10.22; 1 QH 1.37; also 1 Q 34bis 3, 2 in DJD I, 154: the failure of man to understand, on which see F. Nötscher, *Terminologie*, 51f.

722. O. Betz, *Offenbarung*, 6ff., 16ff., 54, 73ff., 155–82. E.g. the hymn 1 QM 10.10ff. shows the connection between teaching the law and direct revelation.

723. C. Burchard, *KP* 2, 378; cf. also P. Seidensticker, *Studii biblici Francisci, Liber annuus* 9, 1958–59, 158ff., 167ff.

724. O. Betz, *Offenbarung*, 110–49; cf. above all 1 QH 12.11b–13 and on this op. cit., 119f.

725. For reveal (גלה) see op. cit., 6ff.; the past participle niphal נגל or נגלות appears above all in the Community Rule; in the hymns, on the other hand, we find mostly the finite verb. 1 QH 1.21; 6.4; 11.17, etc.; also הודיע 1 QH 4.27; 7.27; 1 QpHab 7.4, etc.; for enlighten (האיר) see 1 QS 2.3; 4.2; 1 QH 3.3; 4.5, 27 etc.; light up, appear (הופיע) 1 QH 4.6, 23; 9.31 etc. רז is of central importance, as it already is in Daniel (see above, n.615): it appears 55 times, while סוד appears 43 times, 28 of them in the hymns; see F. Nötscher, *Terminologie*, 71–7, and above, n.708. Alongside this we find the verbs חבא: 1 QS 4.6; 1 QH 5.11–25; 9.24, and סתר: partly as a finite verb, 1 QS 11.6; 1 QH 5.26, etc., partly as a past participle niphal נסתרות 1 QS 5.11; 1 QH fr. 55.1; CD 3.14. For the affinity of this 'understanding of illumination' with that of Philo see A. Wlosok, *Laktanz*, AAH 1960, 2, 110f. and n.113.

726. For membership of the community see 1 QS 1.1–2.18, the great liturgy for new members; also 5.7ff., 6.20–24. 'Willingness' to enter is expressed above all in the group of terms נדיב נדב and conversion by the frequently used שיב (see above, n.484). For the community as a remnant see 1 QH 6.8; 1 QM 13.8; 14.8f., see J. Becker, op. cit., 62f. For separation from the *'massa perditionis'* see 1 QS 1.26–3.6 and 5.11–20.

737. For the forgiveness of sins in the community see 1 QS 3.7–9; 11.14f.; 1 QH 4.37; 7.29ff.; 11.10f., cf. especially 16.12 and fr. 2.13: through the holy spirit. The verbs כפר and מהר מהר are essential.

728. 1 QS 1.12; on this see O. Betz, *Offenbarung*, 58, 133f.

729. Op. cit., 54: 'The members of the sect call themselves "men of truth", because they are "doers of the Torah" ', on 1 QpHab 7.10–12. For the rigorous fulfilment of the law see 1 QS 1.5, 8, 15; cf. also the entry oath 5.8ff. Any transgression is strictly dealt with, even by complete exclusion. The struggle for perfection can be seen in formulas like תום דרך or הלך תמים, or similar ones, see 1 QS 1.8, 13; 2.2; 5.24; 8.10, 18, 21; 11.2, 11 etc. This corresponds to the Greek τέλειος, see already Sir.44.17 M and G.

730. 1 QS 3.22f., cf. 11.12ff.; 1 QH 1.32; 4.30f.

731. 1 QS 4.20–23; on this see O. Betz, *Offenbarung*, 131ff. In this way man receives back the כבוד אדם, see the 'glory of Adam' in Sir.49.16 and n.531 and Vol.I, p.223. For the annihilation of the sons of darkness see the term כלה, cf.

1 QS 2.15; 5.13; 1 QH 6.19; 1 QM 1.5, 10 etc.; the ideas of imprisonment in the underworld and of the judgment of fire appear often, see above, n. 607.

732. For the constant praise of God and for accord with the orbits of the stars see 1 QS 10.1–17, 23; cf. also 1 QH 12.1–12 with reference to the sun. This is probably the particular background for the difficult passage *Bell*. 2, 128, see Vol. I, p. 236. For 1 QH 1.27–31, Bergmeier/Pabst, *RQ* 5, 1964–65, 435–9, have pointed to part of a hymn on the creation of language for the praise of God by the community in connection with the creation hymn of col. 1; see also 1 QH 11.4, 33, and cf. already O. Betz, *Offenbarung*, 83 n. 5.

733. For community with the angels of God see 1 QS 11.7f.; 1 QH 3.19–23; 6.12–14; 11.10–14; fr. 2, 10; 1 QSb 4.26 and 1 Q 36.1, 3 = DJD I, 126, 138. The presence of the angel in the War Scroll is brought out, see above all 1 QM 10 10; 12.1–4, and on this Y. Yadin, op. cit., 240ff. It is typical of the anticipation of salvation that in the hymnic texts it is often impossible to say whether the statements refer to the present or the future: on this see A. Dupont-Sommer, op. cit., 102 n. 2: 'The earthly Community is in communion with the whole angelic and celestial world'. Cf. H. W. Kuhn, *Enderwartung*, 66–73.

734. The statements about the כבוד of God are many and varied: (*a*) in connection with God's plan and creation, see 1 QS 3.16; 1 QM 14.14; 1 QH 1.9f.; 7.24; 9.26; 10.12; 18.22; fr. 2.4f.; cf. 2.16 (see already Isa. 43.7 and later '*Ab*. 6.11); (*b*) God's judgment: I QH 2.24f., cf. 1 QS 4.18; 1 QM 4.6, 8; 12.7, 10; (*c*) God's saving revelation happens for the sake of his 'honour': 1 QH 6.14; 7.15; 4 QDibHam 3.4, see M. Baillet, *RB* 69, 1961, 202, a doxology which probably goes back to the Hasidim (see above, n. 483); 1 Q 34bis 3.1, 6f. = DJD I, 153: 'for we praise thy name in eternity . . . for to that end thou hast created us.' Cf. also 1 QS 10.9ff.; 1 QH 3.23; 10.10f.; 11.4–6: the constant praise of God. For the whole matter see also J. Becker, op. cit., 126–37: 'praise brought about by God'. For his thesis that the hymns formed the daily liturgy of the community cf., however, the critical objection of E. Cothenet, *RQ* 5, 1964/65, 272, on the basis of C. H. Hunzinger's reference in *TLZ* 85, 1960, 152. We cannot overestimate the abundance of the liturgical material and the liturgy of the community; cf. also J. Hempel, op. cit., 315, and P. Stuhlmacher, op. cit., 160ff.

735. E.g. the angelic liturgies published by J. Strugnell in *SVT* 7, 1960, 322f., 336f., or the descriptions of the heavenly Jerusalem in 1 Q 32 = DJD I, 134f.; 2 Q 24 = DJDJ III, 84–89, and 5 Q 15, op. cit., 184–93; on this G. Jeremias, *Der Lehrer der Gerechtigkeit*, 1963, 245ff., and J. Hempel, op. cit., 324f. Cf. also the Hasidic/pre-Essene (?) book of Noah, I Enoch 69.24: the 'food' of all natural forces consists in the praise of God. See now H. W. Kuhn, *Enderwartung*, passim.

736. On this F. Nötscher, *Terminologie*, 149–67; M. Mansoor, op. cit., 84–92.

737. J. Hempel, op. cit., 361f.

738. This already follows from the doctrine of predestination, see J. Becker, op. cit., 70f., on the personal hymns of the Teacher; 122f. on the closing hymn of the Rule, cf. 1 QS 11.2, 11–13; 149ff. on the community hymns, cf. also P. Stuhlmacher, *Gerechtigkeit Gottes*, 162. Significantly terms for reward are almost completely absent in respect of God. For 'election' the verb בחר and the noun בחיר are essential; 1 QS 4.22; 8.6; 9.14; 11.7, 16; 1 QH 2.13; 14.15; 15.23, etc.

H. Braun, *Spätjüdisch-häretischer Radikalismus* 1, 1957, 41–7, reaches a false conclusion because he does not use the Hodayoth. It is not the case that 'man himself offers obedience' (47). Everything that man does is God's work and gift. The early Essene writings – as Josephus stresses in contrast to Pharisaism – knew no synergism.

739. Even if we are dealing here with texts which display a certain 'history of tradition', we can still regard them as typical of basic Essene teaching of the early period. The strict discipline and closed nature of the community makes the juxtaposition of different deliberately contradictory 'theologies' very improbable; the attempts of J. Becker (and similarly H. W. Kuhn) to argue this on the basis of analyses in 1 QS, 1 QM and 1 QH, op. cit., 39–59, are unconvincing. Obviously the Rule or even the War Scroll show a certain literary development, and they are composed of different units, hymns, catechetical instruction, liturgical formulas or legal statements; it is, however, misleading to assume from the different stress laid on certain subjects, like predestination or dualism, that these views only found their way into the community later and that the Teacher of Righteousness had not shared in them (op. cit., 59ff., 74, 84, 189, and see below, n.756). Predestination and dualism are then again (!) weakened in the Damascus document, which arose in the first half of the first century (op. cit., 181f.). The supposed theological differences are predominantly caused by the different forms of the individual literary units. One cannot expect any statements about the theology of history in halachic legal definitions, nor any fundamental statements about the creation and consummation of the world in individual hymns of an almost 'biographical' character. It is misleading if these differences are made oppositions and are played off against each other. It is true that the Damascus document, the additions to the Rule 1 QSa and Sb and the *pešārīm*, which come from the first half of the first century, indicate a certain development of the doctrines of the community. They are therefore noted less. On the other hand, the remembrance of the Teacher of Righteousness plays a special role there.

740. P. Stuhlmacher, op. cit., 148: 'The heart of late Jewish apocalyptic theology'.

741. On this G. Jeremias, op. cit., 63ff., 68–71, 74ff., 161ff. Jonathan was the only high priest to be killed by *Gentiles*; see above all 4 QpPs 37.4, 10 (in H. Stegemann, *RQ* 4, 1963, 245, and E. Lohse, op. cit., 274); cf. also 1 QpHab 9.1ff., 10ff. The Teacher is at the same time the founder, op. cit., 65f., 141ff., 165f., see above all 4 QpPs. 37.2, 16; CD 1.10f. and also J. Hempel, op. cit., 338f. and above, n.691. For dating see also J. T. Milik, *Ten Years of Discovery*, 1957, 67ff., and in agreement K. G. Kuhn, *RGG*³ 5, 745f., and W. Grundmann, *UU* 1, 234ff., 248f. Archaeological and palaeographical evidence also allows this dating; see R. de Vaux, *L'archéologie et les manuscrits de la mer morte*, 1961, 4, 90, cf. also H. Bardtke, *Die Sekte von Qumran*, 184–98, and *TR* 29, 1963, 269ff.: in all, five Seleucid copper coins from the reigns of Antiochus III, IV and VII have been found. For the chronology of this period, R. Hanhart, *Zur Zeitrechnung*, BZAW 88, 1964, 59ff., 94f.: the Maccabean Judas was killed in April/May 160 BC, the high priest Alcimus, who was already appointed by Antiochus V Eupator in 163 BC (see below n.IV, 142) died in May 159; in 157 Bacchides launched a new attack which was followed by a truce. Jerusalem remained in the hands of the enemy, and

Jonathan lived in Michmash as a 'judge': I Macc. 9.70–73. He functioned for the first time as high priest at the Feast of Tabernacles in October 152. Cf. H. Stegemann (n. 481 above), 242ff.; J. Starcky, *RB* 70, 1963, 481ff.; and I Macc. 10.1–21.

742. For the prophetic charisma of the Teacher see G. Jeremias, op. cit., 81, 141, etc.; cf. O. Betz, *Offenbarung*, 88–92, 98f.

743. Cf. 1 QS 5.2, 9; 1 QSa 1.2, 24; 2.3; Sb 3.22; 4 Qflor 1.17; J. M. Allegro, *JBL* 77, 1957, 354, and E. Lohse, *Die Schriften*, 258; cf. also R. Meyer, *TDNT* 7, 39f. For the Teacher as priest see 4 QpPs 37 ed. H. Stegemann, *RQ* 4, 1963, 250, 252 = 2.19 and 3.15; E. Lohse, op. cit., 270, 272; on this see G. Jeremias, op. cit., 147f. For the Hellenistic leanings of the Zadokite priestly nobility see G. Molin, *Saeculum* 6, 1955, 273.

744. In 5.5 supplement עם with נכרי, the lower part of which can still clearly be recognized on the photograph; cf. Dupont-Sommer, op. cit., 214, and G. Jeremias, op. cit., 218 n.2; see further l.8: 'In the dwelling place of the stranger (מגור) with many fishers . . . and with hunters for the sons of wickedness': this could be a reference to the Jewish-Seleucid opponents of the Maccabees, e.g. the garrison of the Acra; cf. the description of them in I Macc. 1.36. 1 QH 5.17 is also important: 'The godless of the nations (רשעי עמים) made haste against me with their tribulations.' For the Teacher's knowledge of revelation in this period see 5.9, 11: the oppressors (Gentile or apostates from Judaism) did not recognize the significance of his teaching. For the Jewish prisoners see I Macc. 1.32; II Macc. 5.24, and above all the taking hostage of Jewish sons of eminent families by the garrison of the Acra, 157 BC, who were only returned in 152 BC: I Macc. 9.53 and 10.6, 9. For banishment cf. also J. T. Milik, op. cit., 53, and J. Carmignac, *RQ* 2, 1959/60, 209.

745. 1 QH 4.34–36. For the terminology of 'covenant' see Dan. 11.30, 32 and I Macc. 1.15, 63; 2.20, 27, 50; Jub. 23.19, see Vol. I, p. 305 and n. IV, 292. The term 'plague' (*nega‘*) appears in the Essene literature as a particular punishment from God: 1 QS 3.14, 22; 4.12; 1 QH 1.18, 32f.; 9.10, 12; 11.8, etc. Many members of the Jerusalem aristocracy had compromised themselves in the time of persecution after 173: thus the Zadokite Alcimus, II Macc. 14.3; unobjectionable conduct was therefore a particular merit: 14.38; see also Vol. I, p. 289.

746. CD 1.1–10; for the time of wrath see l.5; for the expression see G. Jeremias, op. cit., 159f.; cf. I Macc. 1.64; 3.8 and II Macc. 8.5; also 1 QH 3.28 and fr. 1.5; it is the beginning of the end time. Cf. further 4 QpNah 1.5b. E. Lohse, op. cit., 262; T. Levi 14–16 and Jub. 3.31; 15.33; 23.19f.; 30.7ff. The Bilga affair is also an example of this, see Vol. I, pp 279f, 283f. Further instances in H. H. Rowley, *Jewish Apocalyptic and the Dead Sea Scrolls*, 1957, 30 n. 49.

747. 1 QpHab 8.11, cf. 16. The conjecture of G. Jeremias, op. cit., 40f., that it could possibly be Gentiles, is unjustified; there is separate mention later of the 'riches of the nations', which the godless priest likewise takes to himself. For the term 'rebel' (מרד) cf. Josephus 22.16, 18f., 29 and Dan. 9.5, 9. These are the Jewish apostates who above all came from the rich property-owning upper class and who are mostly termed ἄνομοι or ἀσεβεῖς in I Macc.; cf. e.g. 2.44; 3.5f.; 7.5; etc., see Vol. I, pp. 288ff.; for the question see also 10.7–14, 61.

748. M. Smith in *Der Hellenismus*, Fischer-Weltgeschichte 6, ed. P. Grimal,

1965, 266. He rightly bore his title at the beginning of his rule – presumably as 'judge' in Michmash, 157–152 BC (see I Macc. 9.73): 'but when he had gained rule over Israel' (1 QpHab 8.8–10) – i.e. after he had become high priest in autumn 152 (I Macc. 10.15–21), 'he lifted up his heart and forsook God'. Alexander Balas made him 'friend of the king' and later *'meridiarch* and *stratēgos'* (10.59–65), i.e. a Seleucid official and dignitary, and honoured him in other ways also (10.20, 64, 88). The embassies to Rome and Sparta (I Macc. 12.1–24) also lie on the same line; here significantly the 'blood affinity' with the Spartans through Abraham was stressed (12.10, 21); this probably goes back to an invention of the friends of the Greeks in Jerusalem (see Vol. I, pp. 72f.). Cf. the apt brief characterization in E. Bickermann, *GM*, 87f.

749. 1 QpHab 8.10ff.; 12.9. In 9.4ff. the Hasmoneans generally are attacked; cf. also Jub. 23.21. For the alleged self-indulgence of the godless priest see 1 QpHab. 11.13f. C. Schneider, in *Qumran-Probleme*, ed. H. Bardtke, 1963, 303, sees here – probably wrongly – a 'Hellenistic tyrant pattern'. For the godless priest generally see G. Jeremias, op. cit., 36–77.

750. This remains a hypothesis, though a likely one. For parallel situations in the later period see M. Hengel, op. cit., 127–32.

751. 23.16 corresponds to the apostasy in the post-exilic period: I Enoch 91.9. Jub. 23.19f. refers to the Maccabean revolt, see M. Testuz, *Jubilés*, 167; 23.21ff. then alludes to the failing of the Maccabees.

752. *Antt.* 13, 236–48; *Bell.* 1, 61ff. and Posidonius according to Diodore 34 fr. 1 = FGrHist 87 F 109 (Reinach 56ff.), see also Schürer 1, 259ff. According to *Antt.* 13, 249f., Antiochus VII compelled the Jews to military service against the Parthians.

753. For the Hellenization of the Hasmonean ruling house see Vol. I, p. 76 and M. Smith, op. cit., 265f. The tombstones and monuments erected by Simon for his brothers and parents in Modein were completely influenced by Hellenistic style (I Macc. 13.25–30 and *Antt.* 13, 211f.); see Watzinger, *DP* 2, 22f., and F. M. Abel, *Macc.*, 239ff.

754. For the Sadducees see R. Meyer, *TDNT* 7, 43ff., though he puts too much emphasis on the conservative side and too little on the social-cultural side. In *Antt.* 13, 171–3, Josephus puts the origin of the three Jewish parties in the time of Jonathan. A typical example of the aristocratic, Hellenized milieu of early Sadduceeism is the tomb of Jason from the time of Alexander Jannaeus, see above, n. II, 17.

755. Among the opponents of the Teacher were those who came from his own Hasidic camp (1 QH 2.31ff.; 4.6ff.; 5.22ff.; 6.19, 21f.; 1 QpHab 5.9–12: the house of Absalom), but who did not want to follow him in secession. The Pharisaic movement began from them, see F. M. Cross, *The Ancient Library of Qumran*, 1958, 107 n. 66, cf. also J. Carmignac, *RQ* 2, 1959/60, 220f., and W. Grundmann, *UU* 1, 244f. For the apostasy of the Pharisees from John Hyrcanus and the later Essene criticism of the Pharisees in CD and the *pᵉšārīm* see R. Meyer, *Tradition und Neuschöpfung,* BAL 110, 2, 1965, 44f., 61ff., against G. Jeremias, op. cit., 79–126.

756. The teaching of the Teacher should certainly not be restricted to the personal confessional hymns in 1 QH (see G. Jeremias, op. cit., 168–244, and

J. Becker, op. cit., 50ff., 58ff.) and their predestination and dualism. Becker in effect involves his assertion in a circular argument, as he has already based it on his principle of selection and his interpretation of the hymns. Belial does not just mean 'evil' and not a personal figure (4.10, 12f.; 5.38f.; 6.21; 7.3 etc.), nor can one refuse the Teacher authorship of the personal hymns 3.19–36 and above all the portion 4.29–5.4 (pp. 52, 54). The 'mysteries of God' or 'sin' in 4.27 and 5.36 are as predestinarian as God's counsel and 'plan' (4.13) or 'lot' (6.13f., cf. also 4.38). It is impossible to see why the Teacher – with a change of style – could not have also composed the creation and community hymns. For the whole matter see also above, n. 739.

757. Possibly the abrupt breach with Jerusalem (see 1 QpHab 11.4ff.) was later moderated, see *Antt.* 18, 18f.; *Bell.* 5, 145; *Vita* 10.

758. Cf. 1 QH 2.6ff.; 3.3ff., 19ff.; 4.34ff.; 5.8ff. (see Vol. I, p. 225.

759. I Macc. 1.11; see Vol. I, pp. 72f. and below, pp. 277ff.

760. The Teacher is God's instrument for separation: 1 QH 7.12. This concerned all 'men of wickedness', Jews and still more Gentiles, see above all the verb בדל: 1 QS 5.1, 10, 18; 8.13; 9.14, 20; 1 Q 34bis 3, 2, 6, DJD 1, 154; CD 6.14 etc. The abrupt rejection of everything non-Jewish can be seen above all in the War Scroll and the book of Jubilees, which was presumably intended for a wider circle.

761. Cf. e.g. the interpretation of Isa. 40.3 in 1 QS 8.13f.; 9.20; cf. also 4 QpPs 37.3,1 (ed. E. Lohse, op. cit., 272); 1 QM 1.2 and M. Hengel, op. cit., 255ff.

762. R. de Vaux, *L'archéologie et les manuscrits*, 1961, cf. also P. W. Lapp, *Palestinian Ceramic Chronology*, 1961, 229: the absence of foreign pottery in Qumran. On the other hand, see the Hellenistic tomb of the Maccabees at Modein, n. 753 above.

763. Jub. 12.25, cf. 3.28 and the Hebrew Test. Napht. 8.4–6, ed. Charles, *Greek Versions*, 242f., and the old Bar. *Ḥag.* 16a. Cf. S. Segert, 'Die Sprachenfrage in der Qumrangemeinschaft', in *Qumranprobleme*, ed. H. Bardtke, 1963, 316ff., 328f.: according to this a biblical Hebrew was used in liturgy, doctrine and all the official writings of the community, which had no Greek and very few Aramaic loanwords. The few Greek LXX manuscripts (see Vol. I, pp. 60f.) were probably used for the private education of novices from the Greek-speaking Diaspora. The Aramaic writings are to a considerable degree of non-Essene origin (322f.). The unavoidable Aramaic influence was limited to syntax and pronunciation, and attempts were made to counter even this by the use of vowel pointing. In contrast to the view expressed by Segert, 329, the Essenes were probably interested in preserving classical biblical Hebrew; however, we should not imagine that they used any modern philological methods.

764. F. M. Cross, op. cit., 32f., and *JBL* 74, 1955, 147–72, esp. 163ff.; cf. also R. de Vaux, op. cit., 75ff.; P. W. Skehan, *BA* 28, 1965, 87–100, and H. Bardtke, *TR* 30, 1964, 303ff. For the plan of the library see K. G. Pedley, *RQ* 2, 1959/60, 21–41, cf. also M. Smith, op. cit. (above, note 748) 269, for the whole period: 'classicism is characteristic of this whole literature.'

765. J. Hempel, op. cit., 349. This process, which begins from wisdom, continues with the Rabbis, see K. H. Rengstorf, *TDNT* 4, 402ff.; he sees Greek influence at work here.

766. K. G. Kuhn, *ZTK* 47, 1950, 203–5; K. Schubert, *TLZ* 78, 1953, 502, 506; *Die Gemeinde vom Toten Meer*, 1958, 65ff.; H. Bardtke, *Die Handschriftenfunde*, 1953, 114, 166; H. J. Schoeps, *ZRGG* 6, 1954, 276–9; H. Grässer, *TR* 30, 1964, 176, see also the survey in n. 3. Against such an overhasty use of the terms 'gnostic' or 'gnosis' for Essene theology see the rightly critical Bo Reicke, *NTS* 1, 1954/55, 137–41; F. Nötscher, *Terminologie*, 39ff.; M. Burrows, *The Dead Sea Scrolls*, 1956, 252–60; M. Mansoor, op. cit., 66f., and J. Hempel, op. cit., 315. The designation '(pre)gnostic' applies mostly to the concept of knowledge, see below, nn. 769/70, not to dualism.

767. However, it is impermissible to set apocalyptic and anthropology over against each other in an irreconcilable opposition and reduce apocalyptic to the 'demonstration of an apocalyptic plan of history, astronomy, etc.' (see H. Conzelmann, *NTS* 12, 1966, 233). This close connection between anthropological and apocalyptic thought also appears again in IV Ezra, a work which similarly arose from a deep crisis in Judaism. For the term 'apocalyptic', see E. Käsemann, *New Testament Questions of Today*, 109 n. 1. For the term 'gnosis' see K. Wegenast, *KP* 2, 831, and C. Colpe, *RGG*³ 2, 1648ff.

768. The conception of inspiration which we have already encountered in Ben-Sira, the Hasidim and Aristobulus (see Vol. I, pp 134ff.) is also developed among the Essenes in an apocalyptic context. Like those endowed with the spirit in ancient Israel (1 QS 8.16; CD 2.12; 6.1; 7.17; Jub. 15.14, etc.), the Teacher and his community have also received the spirit, see 1 QH 12.11–13; 13.18f.; 14.13, and see H. W. Kuhn, *Enderwartung*, 136ff.

769. K. G. Kuhn, *ZTK* 47, 1950, 204; cf. 203: 'the gnostic "concept of knowledge" is present here'. See also above, n. 725 and H. W. Kuhn, op. cit., 142ff.

770. R. Bultmann, *TDNT* 1, 694. Cf. R. Reitzenstein, *Hellenistische Mysterienreligionen*³, 68f., and H. Gressmann, *ZKG* 41, 1922, 179; 'Gnosticism is the innermost essence of apocalyptic.'

771. For the time and place of Wisdom see Eissfeldt, *The Old Testament*, 601f. For Platonic influence see I. Heinemann, *Poseidonios' metaphysische Schriften* 1, 1921, 139ff.; for the Jewish background to early gnosis see below, n. IV, 313.

772. Cf. e.g. I Sam. 19.9; I Kings 22.20ff.; Amos 3.3–8; Isa. 45.7.

773. 1 QS 4.1; cf 1 QH 14.25; 15.19; 17.24. From this arises the command to hate 'all sons of darkness': 1 QS 1.10; cf. 10.20f. The tendency to relieve God of direct responsibility for evil through two 'servants' can be seen in the dualistic text in Philo, *Quaest. in Ex.*, 1, 23, translated by R. Marcus, LCL, *Philo Suppl.* 2, 32ff., which is related to 1 QS 3.13–4.26.

774. K. G. Kuhn, *ZTK* 49, 1952, 296–313; Dupont-Sommer, *Nouveaux aperçus*, 1953, 157–72; J. Becker, op. cit., 96ff. P. v. d. Osten-Sacken (I, n. 101 above), 130f., differs.

775. Philo, loc. cit. (above, n. 773); Plutarch, *Is. et Os.* 47 (369f–370c). On this H. Michaud, *VT* 5, 1955, 137–47; E. Kamlah, *Die Form der katalogischen Paränese*, 1964, 39ff., 50ff., 57ff., 163ff.; cf. J. Duchesne-Guillemin, *Indo-Iranian Journal* 1, 1957, 96–99, and *RAC* 4, 344–6, and A. Wlosok, AAH 1960, 2, 107–11. For Plutarch see Bidez/Cumont, op. cit., 2, 7–8, and T. Hopfner,

Über Isis und Osiris 2, 1940f., 201–11; further literature in E. Kamlah, op. cit., 57 n. 1 and 59 n. 4. For Philo it is important that he knew the Persian magi and compares them with the Essenes, *Quod omnis* 74 (M 2, 456). J. Schoeps, *ZRGG* 6, 1954, 277, calls attention to a further dualistic text in Ps.Clem., *Hom.* 15, 7, 4, ed. Rehm, GCS, 215. However, it is different from 1 QS 3.16ff. in the fact that, following an Iranian pattern, it leaves man a free choice between the two 'kingdoms'.

776. Plutarch's closing section on the Iranian system of world ages, the overcoming of evil (= Hades) and the time of salvation comes from Theopompus, who is himself possibly dependent on Eudoxus of Cnidus, the friend of Plato (see R. Laqueur, *PW*, 2R. 3, 2213). See also FGrHist F65 and 64; cf. above, n. 574. For the interest of the early Hellenistic writers of the fourth century BC in Iranian teaching see E. Meyer, *UAC* 2, 69ff., who conjectures Eudemus of Rhodes as Plutarch's second source (second half of the fourth century BC), see also 2, 73, 83, 91, the prologue to Diogenes Laertius, chs. 8, 9, and Damascius, *De prim. princ.* 125, text in Bidez/Cumont, op. cit., 2, 69, and on it, op. cit., 1, 18ff., 62ff. For the early academy and Aristotle cf. also W. Jaeger, *Aristoteles*, ²1955, 133–38, 438, and Bidez/Cumont, op. cit., 1, 11ff. The following reasons would support a Jewish–Alexandrian source for the doctrine of the two spirits of 1 QS: (*a*) That – as E. Kamlah, op. cit., 58f., observes – in 1 QS 3.19 and in Plutarch the two powers arise from light and darkness respectively, whereas according to *Bundahishn* 1, 21f. (trans. E. W. West, *Pahlavi Texts*, 1, 8) they are without beginning. (*b*) That neither in Plutarch nor in 1 QS can a syncretizing Babylonian or Asia Minor intermediary stage be demonstrated, as is elsewhere the case in the mediation of Iranian conceptions, cf. Michaud, op. cit., 143, see also Bousset/Gressmann, 481. Zervanite influences are also absent, as E. Kamlah, op. cit., 55 n. 3 and 70, stresses against Michaud, op. cit., 144f., and Duchesne-Guillemin, op. cit., 96ff.; Zervanism can only be demonstrated with any certainty in the third century AD, as the Eudemus quotation in Damascius is not unambiguous, see R. C. Zaehner, *Zurvan*, 1955, 20ff. (*c*) According to Kamlah, op. cit., 167, we have 'an early stage of the adoption of the cosmological myth in anthropology' in the doctrine of the two spirits, which is to be put between the later form in Philo and the report of Plutarch, which stands near to the original Iranian form and goes back to Greek, well-informed sources of the fourth century BC. Philo and 1 QS – in contrast to Iranian teaching, which stresses the freedom of decision – combine the complete independence of man with his acquiescence in his own decision. (*d*) It is striking that the clear abstract form of 1 QS 3.13–4.24 makes it relatively easy to translate into Greek, see C. Schneider, op. cit., 301, and cf. E. Kamlah, op. cit., 44 n. 1. Perhaps Philo, *Quaest. in Ex.* 1, 23, contains a more developed anthropological or cosmological form of the Jewish–Alexandrian source of 1 QS 3.13ff., which for its part is in turn dependent on the fourth-century Greek reports on Iranian religion. (*e*) Finally, the form of the doctrine of the two ways in Barn. 18, which according to Kamlah, op. cit., 211f., stands nearer (by contrast with 1 QS) to the original Iranian dualism, points back to an earlier version which is best located, as Barnabas itself, in Alexandria. As the designation of the devil as 'the black one' shows, Barnabas has an independent, Hellenistic–Jewish version of salvation-historical, ethical dualism (cf. Barn. 4.9; 20.1).

777. E.g. the identification of Zarathustra-Zaratos with Ezekiel according to Clem.Alex., *Strom.* 1, 15, 70, 1, and on this Bidez/Cumont, 2, 36, a report which possibly goes back to Alexander Polyhistor (first half of the first century BC), see op. cit., 1, 42; F. Jacoby, FGrHist IIIa, Comm. on 273 F 94, pp. 294–8, who assumes an addition by Clement, is, however, sceptical. Jewish interest in Zarathustra is combined with interest in Pythagoras, who was regarded as his pupil and, according to Aristobulus (see Vol. I, pp. 165f.), even went to be taught by the Jews; cf. also n. 877 below. Other identifications are Zarathustra-Nimrod, Ps.Clem., *Hom.* 9, 4f., GCS, Rehm 133, and on this H. J. Schoeps, *Aus frühchristlicher Zeit*, 1950, 19–24, 32, 132; and in the treasure cave that goes back to Jewish tradition, see Bidez/Cumont, op. cit., 1, 43ff.; 2, 50ff., 121; and Zarathustra-Balaam, -Baruch or -Daniel, op. cit., 1, 47ff.; 2, 129–35, though these are only in late Syrian sources. Cf. J. Neusner, *Numen* 12, 1965, 66–9.

778. Bidez-Cumont, op. cit., 1, 85ff. (87); 2, 9 fr. B 2.

779. K. Schubert, *Die Religion des nachbiblischen Judentums*, 1955, 17f.; in addition he also presupposes Stoic themes.

780. C. Schneider, op. cit., 310f., who sees a 'Stoic supplementation of the Old Testament idea' in the community's picture of God as it is expressed, e.g., in 1 QH 10.8f. There are a number of analogies to the Cleanthes hymn, see von Arnim, SVF 1, 121f. no. 537: the established order of creation in respect of the stars and natural forces: ll. 8–14, cf. 1 QH 1.9ff.; 12.5ff.; nothing happens without God: ll. 16f., cf. 1 QH 1.20; 12.10f.; 1 QS 11.11, 18; God gave language: l.5, cf. 1 QH 1.27ff.; negative verdict on mankind: ll.23ff., cf. 1 QH 1.26f.; liberation of man from his weakness, ll. 33ff. and 1 QH 1.31ff. However, it is significant that, in contrast to Essenism, 'what the wicked have shattered in their vanity' is exempted from the divine causation. On the whole, however, it is clear how closely the philosophical monotheism of the Greeks and the Jewish belief in creation approached each other despite their fundamental differences – even if one may not speak of a dependence; see also above, n. 260.

781. For Stoic determinism, see M. Pohlenz, *Stoa* 1, ³1964, 103–6, and 2, 58ff. For the Homer quotation see Chrysippus, SVF 2, 269, no. 937. Cf. also Manilius, *Astron.* 4, 14: *'Fata regunt orbem certa stant omnia lege'*, the later astrological version.

782. 1 QS 9.23b–26: 'Find pleasure in all that is done through him (i.e. God)' (24); cf. 10.12f., 15f.; Josephus, *Antt.* 13, 172 and 18,18; further Philo, *Quod omnis* 84 (M 2, 458): God causes only good, evil does not come from him. This is probably to be understood as complete surrender to God's will. The Stoics similarly recognized the purposeful divine *pronoia* in unswerving fate and affirmed it, see M. Pohlenz, op. cit., 1, 100f., 106; 2, 56f., 61f., and the fine Cleanthes verse handed down through Epictetus, SVF 1, 118 no. 527.

783. M. Pohlenz, op. cit., 1, 101f.; 2, 58, and the definition of *heimarmenē* by Chrysippus, SVF 2, 293 no. 1000; also the etymological interpretation SVF 2, 265 no. 918.

784. *Bell.* 2, 142, and on it see Michel/Bauernfeind, op. cit., 1, 436 n. 66. Outside I Enoch names of angels appear above all in 1 QM 9.15f.; 17.6f.; cf. also the angel liturgy, ed. J. Strugnell, *SVT* 7, 1960, 336, which, however, significantly does not give the names of the seven archangels mentioned. Perhaps, as with the

divine name, there were hesitations about speaking the holy names of the angels, as they could be misused in magic. A glimpse at the abundance of names of angels is afforded by the conclusion of the book of astronomy, I Enoch 82.10–20, which is surely Essene (see above, n.460 and below n.806).

785. For Daniel and I Enoch see Vol.I, pp.187ff. For Rabbinic angelology see Bill.3, 412–6, 437ff., 581–3, 818–20, and – including apocalyptic – H. Bietenhard, *Die himmlische Welt im Urchristentum und Spätjudentum*, 1951, 101–42; J. Michl, *RAC* 5, 60–97, cf. 201ff., and 243–58; for matters in common between the Rabbis and the Essenes, see Y. Yadin, op. cit., 229–42, and especially 237ff. For Essene angelology see O. Betz, *Der Paraklet*, 1963, 51ff., 60ff., 66ff., 113ff., and M. Mansoor, op. cit., 77–84. For its rich vocabulary see J. Strugnell, *SVT* 7, 1960, 331ff.

786. For the role of Michael in Daniel and the early parts of I Enoch see Vol.I, pp.188f. In Qumran (above, n.709) this 'soteriological' role of Michael appears at 1 QM 17.6f.; cf. Y. Yadin, op. cit., 235f., and O. Betz, op. cit., 60–9; see also A. S. van der Woude, *OTS* 14, 1965, 354–73. The names 'spirit of truth' (1 QS 3.19), 'Prince of light' (1 QS 3.20; cf. CD 5.18), 'angel of his truth' (1 QS 3.24) and Michael were probably interchangeable. The same is also true of the 'spirit of wickedness' (3.19; 4.9),' angel of darkness' (3.20f.), Belial (see K. G. Kuhn, *Konkordanz*, and Jub.1.20; 15.33) and Mastema (Jub.10.8; 11.5, 11; 17.16, etc.; cf. 1 QS 3.24). Here too there is a 'multiplicity of intermediate beings', see above, n.493. Cf. now J. T. Milik, *RB* 79, 1972, 77ff.

787. This doctrine runs through I Enoch and Jubilees like a scarlet thread; cf. the Hasidic (see above n.465), angelological book I Enoch 6–36; 54f., 64, 68f., 86–88 etc.; Jub.4.22; 5.1ff.; 7.21ff.; 8.3ff.; 10.1ff.; 11.5ff.; 16.3ff.; 18.9ff.; etc.; Gen. Apoc.2.4ff.; 1 QM 14.15; CD 2.1ff., and the text published by J. M. Allegro, *ALUOS* 4, 1962/63, 3f. Doc.I = 4 Q 180 (DJDJ IV, 77ff.); cf. also J. Michl, op. cit., 80f.

788. Bill.3, 818; *Midr.Teh.* on Ps.104 § 3, 220b, ed. Buber; cf. also II Enoch 19.4f., especially version B, R. H. Charles, *Apocrypha and Pseudepigrapha* 2, 441.

789. Jub.2.2; I Enoch 60.12–21 (Noah fragment); 75; 80 (astronomical book).

790. I Enoch 18.13ff.; 21.6ff.; 86–88; 90.21. The fallen angels are stars. For the end time see I Enoch 102.2 and above all 80.4–6; however, the text here is partially corrupt, see R. H. Charles, *Apocrypha and Pseudepigrapha* 2, 245, ad loc.; on this see also O. Betz, op. cit., 47f. For the demons see I Enoch 15.8ff.; 16.1; Jub.10.1ff., 5. For the stars as heavenly beings see already Judg.5.20; Job 38.7; for the danger of star worship see Deut.4.19; 17.3; Jer.8.2; 19.13, etc. For the anthropological interpretation of angelology and demonology see the early Baraita *Ḥag.*16a, which probably goes back to Hasidic tradition.

791. I Enoch 75 and 82.4ff., from the Essene astronomical work. For the continuing influence of these views see H. J. Schoeps, *Aus frühchristlicher Zeit*, 1950, 38–81, cf. 56ff. on demonology. Here the close connection between Jewish apocalyptic and Hellenistic syncretistic views in the Pseudo–Clementines becomes particularly clear. For the military order of angels among the rabbis see R. (Simeon b.) Laqiš, *Ber.*32b (third century AD).

792. For the Old Testament court of Yahweh see C. Cooke, *ZAW* 76, 1964,

22–47; for its supposed Iranian origin see Bousset/Gressmann, 320ff., cf. D. S. Russell, op. cit., 258ff. Individual Babylonian and early Persian influences like Tob. 3.8, 17 are possible, but hardly of decisive significance, see J. Michl, *RAC* 5, 64, 77f. The late tradition of R. Simeon b. Laqiš (third century AD), *jRH* 56d, 56ff., that the Israelites brought the names of the angels with them from Babylon, does not have any historical value. According to F. Cumont, *RHR* 72, 1915, 163f., angelology is a phenomenon which belongs as much to 'paganisme sémitique' as to Judaism, though the strongest influence was exercised by Jewish angelology.

793. I QM 1.10f.; 14.15 (for the fallen angels); 15.14; 17.7; 4 QMa 13 (see C. H. Hunzinger, *ZAW* 69, 1957, 135); I QH 7.28; 10.8; 19.3; fr. 1.3, 10; I Q 22.41 = DJD I, 95; 5 Q 13.1, 6 = DJDJ III, 182; and the two angelological texts 4 Q Sl 39 I, 1, 18, 21, 26 (J. Strugnell, *SVT* 7, 1960, 322) and 4 Q Sl 40, 2 (op. cit., 336); there and in van der Woude, *OTS* 14, 1965, 358 l. 10: אלוהים as a plural = angels, cf. also l. 14. In 4QpHos 2.6 = J. M. Allegro, *JBL* 78, 1959, 146, on the other hand, אלים probably means 'gods'. The term is relatively rare in the OT, see the comparison with the gods in Exod. 15.11; Ps. 29.1; 89.7; and Ps. 82.1b, quoted in the text mentioned above together with Dan. 11.36, which is used in the Qumran texts. Cf. also J. Strugnell, op. cit., 331f. According to Philo Bybl., FGrHist 790 F 2, 10, 20, the σύμμαχοι Ἥλου (i.e. of El Kronos) in Phoenicia were called 'Ἐλωείμ. The inferiority of the angels was expressed by their creation on the first day; see Jub. 2.21; cf. already Job 38.7. The later apocalyptic (Sl. Enoch 39, see Charles, 2, 447) and Rabbinic tradition (Targ. *Jer.* on Gen. 1.26 and elsewhere, see Bill. 4, 1085c, 1128p) transfers the creation of the angels to the second day. In addition, a *creatio continua* of angels appears in Bill. 1, 977 = *Gen.R.* 78, 1. Behind this there is probably a certain depotentiation of the angels.

794. Cf. I QS 3.24f.; I QM 10.12; 13.2, 4, 10f.; 14.10; 15.14; I QH 1.10f.; רוחות דעת 3.22f.; 8.12; 13.8; 14.11. Cf. J. Strugnell, op. cit., 332f. Further instances in Bousset/Gressmann, 321 n.3.

795. J. Michl, *RAC* 5, 71f.; see Vol. I, pp. 154f.

796. Op. cit., 5, 102ff., and on Philo 82f.,; cf. also F. Cumont, *RHR* 72, 1915, 167f.; for the magical texts see also M. O. Nilsson, *opuscula selecta* 3, 136ff.

797. J. Michl, *RAC* 5, 57ff.; F. Cumont, op. cit., 170ff. Cf. the '*nocentes angeli*', Asclep. 25.

798. For the watchers see Dan. 4.10, 14, 20 (עירין): I Enoch 1.5; 12.2, 3; 20.1 (ἐγρήγοροι). The fallen angels were also given this description, I Enoch 10.9, 15, etc.; Jub. 4.22, etc.; see Bousset/Gressmann, 322 n.2, cf. also CD 2.18; Gen. Apoc. 2.1, 16. Cf. J. T. Milik, *RB* 79, 1972, 77ff.

799. Hesiod, *Erga* 252f.; see T. F. Glasson, op. cit., 69f.

800. Philo Byblius, FGrHist 790 F 2.2 = Eusebius, *Pr.Ev.* I, 10, 2; Bousset/Gressmann, loc. cit., point to Ezek. 10.12.

801. Hesiod, *Erga* 122f.; cf. T. F. Glasson, op. cit., 59.

802. Op. cit., 58ff. Glasson also points to the fall of the angels and the analogy of the fall of the Titans, op. cit., 62ff. See on this above, n. 540.

803. U. von Wilamowitz-Mollendorf, *Platon*, 51959, 579. Cf. also R. Heinze, *Xenokrates*, 1892, 78–123; on this see M. P. Nilsson, *GGR*² 2, 254f., 259f., and

Andreas, *PW Suppl* 3, 296. Especially on Posidonius see op. cit., 298; K. Reinhardt, *PW* 22, 647ff. (the system of forces) and on the demonology bound up with the problem of the post-existence of the soul, 779ff.; also M. Pohlenz, op. cit., 1, 96, 230f.; 2, 54, 116f. F. Cumont, op. cit., 167f., already supposed a strong influence of Posidonius on the angelology of later Hellenistic syncretism.

804. M. Pohlenz, op. cit., 1, 230.

805. Cf. Ps. 19.1–7; Sir. 16.26ff.; 42.15ff.; 43.1–10; Bar. 3.34f.; etc.

806. 1 QS 10.1ff. (though individual details are different to interpret); 1 QH 1.9–12: מאורות לרזיהם (11) and on it see F. Nötscher, *Terminologie*, 73; 1 QH 12.4–11, and above all the astronomical book I Enoch 72–82, of which four extensive Aramaic fragments have been discovered in Cave 4, see J. T. Milik, *Ten Years of Discovery*, 33; one has been published in *RB* 65, 1958, 76. For a dating of hardly later than 150 BC see O. Eissfeldt, *The Old Testament*, 620. According to this, the stars are subordinated in strict military division to the archangel Uriel: 72.1; 74.2; 75.1, 3; 82.4, 7, 10f. etc., cf. also Y. Yadin, op. cit., 239f. See also H. Bietenhard, op. cit., 25: 'These chapters of I Enoch probably provide the most scholarly and accurate astronomical teaching from late Judaism that we have.'

807. 1 QS 10.3–8; 1 QH 1.24; 12.5; 1 QM 10.15; Jub. 2.9; I Enoch 82.15ff.; cf. also Jub., Introduction; 1.26, 29; 4.30, see also n.536 above.

808. See I Enoch 9.4–11 and the '*pēšer* on all times that God made', ed. J. M. Allegro, *ALUOS* 4, 1962/63, 3f., which begins: 'Before he created them he established their works', and then narrates the fall of the angels. Cf. Jub. 1.29; 6.35 etc.

809. 1 Q 32bis 3, 2, 2 (DJD I, 154); I Enoch 41.5ff.; 43.2 and Test.Napht. 3.2; cf. already Ps. 148.6; Sir. 16.28; 43.9f.; Ps.Sol. 18.10. For חוק as 'natural law' see 1 QS 10.1, 6; 1 QH 1.10; 12.5; 1 QM 10.12, etc.; cf. I Enoch 72.3; 73.1; 82.9. תכן, ordering, has a similar significance: 1 QS 10.5, 6f. (חוק תכונם); 1 QH 12.5, 8f.; 1 QpHab 7.13; 1 Q 27.1, 1, 6 (DJD I, 103). Here, too, wisdom conceptions of creation stand in the background, see Jer. 31.36; Job 38.33 (*huqqōt šāmayim*). The difference from earlier wisdom consists above all in the fact that the Essenes believed that they could see 'law' and 'order' in the movement of the stars on the basis of divine revelation – as e.g. their astronomical book shows.

810. H. Bietenhard, op. cit., 270. Cf. M. Limbeck (see n. 425 above), passim.

811. 1 QS 10.1ff.; 1 QH 8.22; 1 QH 12.4ff.; in a transferred sense also 1 QS 11.3f.; 1 QSb 4.27f.; 1 QH 4.5, 23; 1 Q 27. 1, 1, 6f. (DJD I, 103); cf. Jub. 2.9; 4.21; I Enoch 72; 73.3–8; see espec. 72.35: 'The great light which from eternity to eternity is called sun'; 37: 'As it rises, so it sets, and does not cease and does not rest, but runs day and night in its chariot, and its light is seven times brighter than the moon'; translation follows G. Beer in Kautzsch, *Apoc.* 2, 280. F. M. Cross, *The Ancient Library*, 77 n. 123, points to an unpublished prayer at sunrise. For alleged sun worship according to *Bell.* 2, 128 see below, n. 821. For the depreciation of the moon cf. Jub. 6.36 and I Enoch 74.12ff.

812. Moore, *Judaism* 2, 78f.

813. Cf. 1 QS 10.3–8; 1.14ff.; CD 6.18ff.; Jub. 6.32ff.; I Enoch 78–80 and DJDJ IV, 92, col. 27 (see below). The discussion and literature is almost boundless; see the brief survey in H. Cazelles, *Bibl* 43, 1962, 202–12. A. Jaubert,

Le Date de la Cène, 1957, 13–75, 142–49, and as a corrective *NTS* 7, 1960/61,
1–22, and following her, J. T. Milik, *Ten Years of Discovery*, 107–13 (see also
the reconstruction of the calendar there), trace it back to the exile. It is said to
have been abolished for the temple first by the Hellenistic party, and to have
been replaced by the secular lunisolar calendar. However, this is extremely
improbable, see E. Kutsch, *VT* 11, 1961, 39–47. K. G. Kuhn, *TLZ* 85, 1960,
654–8, and *ZNW* 52, 1961, 65–73, argues that it was incapable of functioning and
was later done away with. On the other hand, E. Kutsch, op. cit., and A. Strobel
have convincingly argued that it could function, and have argued for a Hellenistic-
Egyptian derivation, see *ZNW* 51, 1960, 87–95; *TLZ* 86, 1961, 179–84; *RQ* 3,
1961/62, 395–412 and 539–43. 'The sun calendar developed by the Essenes is in
the last resort merely the special expression of an older and more widespread
Hellenistic-Egyptian calendar tradition' (405), cf. G. Molin, *TLZ* 78, 1953, 654.
The Alexandrian Aristobulus knew this calendar tradition: A. Strobel, *ZNW* 51,
1960, 92, and *RQ* 3, 1961/62, 410 (see above, n. 391). The fragment of the
mišmārōt of 4 Q with a concordance between the Essene and the traditional
calendar, published by J. T. Milik, *SVT* 4, 1957, 24ff., and E. Vogt, *Bibl* 39,
1958, 72–7, likewise presupposes that it functioned. This fact is confirmed by the
new discovery of an Essene hymn scroll for the sabbath sacrifice from Masada,
which is similarly arranged on the Essene calendar, see Y. Yadin, *IEJ* 15, 1965,
105–8. For the problem see also A. R. C. Leaney, op. cit., 80–107. For the
rational character of the calendar reckoning in Jubilees (i.e. of the Essene
calendar) see already E. Bickermann, *From Ezra*, 62f.: its author 'succumbs to
the seduction of the Greek penchant for rationalism.' 11 Q DavComp = DJDJ
IV, 92, col. 27.6, also presupposes this calendar and may therefore be an Essene
addition to the older Hasidic psalm scroll. Cf. now M. Limbeck (above n. 425),
134ff.

814. According to I Enoch 75.1, the four intercalary days, one at the
beginning of each season, were not included in the reckoning of twelve thirty-day
months. Cf. Jub. 6.29f., see also J. T. Milik, *Ten Years of Discovery*, 107ff., and
A. Strobel, *RQ* 3, 1961/62, 406ff. I Enoch 72.12ff. differs: at the end of the
quarter there is a month of 31 days. Like the Egyptian year, the Essene year
began with the spring equinox on a Wednesday, on which, according to Essene
doctrine, the stars and thus also time itself were created. In the Egyptian year of
365 days, too, the intercalary days, the *epagomeni*, were not counted as part of the
year. Whereas according to I Enoch 75, special 'chiliarchs' were set over the four
intercalary days, in Hellenistic Egypt the five intercalary days were regarded as
the birthdays of the five chief Egyptian gods, see A. Strobel, op. cit., 408 n. 47,
and Dittenberger, *PW* 5, 2671. For the reckoning of the year see also A. Dupont-
Sommer, *RHPR* 35, 1955, 89. The charge that opponents celebrated the 'festivals
of the Gentiles' on the basis of their lunisolar calendar, 4QpHos 2.15, see J. M.
Allegro, *JBL* 78, 1959, 146, cf. Jub. 6.35, was in essence also true of the Essenes
themselves.

815. M. Testuz, *Les idées religieuses*, 1960, 134ff., cf. also A. R. C. Leaney,
op. cit., 88f., and Vol. I, pp. 245ff.

816. M. P. Nilsson, *GGR²* 1, 839–43; 2, 268ff.; for the Stoa see M. Pohlenz,
op. cit., 1, 82f., 96; 2, 48. For the astronomy of the classical Greek period and its

religious evaluation see W. Burkert, *Weisheit und Wissenschaft*, 1962, 278ff.; see 328ff. for the music of the spheres and 335ff. for astral immortality; on this, Vol. I, pp. 196f.

817. Ps.-Aristotle, *De mundo* 391b, 10ff.; 392a, 5ff.; 397a, 5ff.; 399a, 18ff.; for the writing see below, n. IV, 36. Cf. the quite Jewish-sounding CH 5.3–7.

818. Boll/Gundel, *Sternglaube und Sterndeutung*, ⁴1931, 89f., cf. 19ff.

819. M. P. Nilsson, *GGR*² 2, 510, cf. 273, following F. Cumont, *Die orientalische Religionen*, ⁴1959, 122ff., whose Chaldean–Syrian hypothesis as to their origin he does, however, reject.

820. Cleanthes, SVF 1, 112 no. 499; 1, 114 no. 510. For Posidonius, K. Reinhardt, *PW* 22, 692–6, 779f.; cf. also M. Pohlenz, op. cit., 1, 162, 223f., 229. For the origin and development of the sun religion see M. P. Nilsson, *GGR*² 2, 273, 507ff., and *opuscula selecta* 2, 1952, 462–504; however, the sun calendar is earlier than he supposes. Its centres were Egypt and Syria, and its expansion was favoured by the solar calendar. Philo, too, accorded the sun great significance as an image of the Logos and a symbol of God, see A. Wlosok, *Laktanz*, 89–93; see above nn. 388 and 424 on light symbolism.

821. Cf. *Bell.* 2, 148; Lucian, *Salt.* 13 (LCL 5, 23) on the Indians and Pliny, *Hist. nat.* 28, 69, on the Magi. For the Therapeutai see Philo, *Vit. cont.* 89 (M 2, 530) and 27 (M. 2, 475). Directing prayers to the rising sun was felt by the Rabbis to be offensive, according to the early Mishnah *Sukk.* 5.4d (cf. Ezek. 8.16), see A. R. C. Leaney, op. cit., 75ff. Greeting the sun by a gesture was a widespread custom, see M. P. Nilsson, op. cit., 465, cf. already Plato, *Apol.* 26d; *Symp.* 220d; *Laws* 10, 887e. For the historical problem see also Michel/Bauernfeind, op. cit., 1, 432 n. 44, and A. R. C. Leaney, 77ff. The interpretation by Dupont-Sommer, *RHPR* 35, 1955, 87f., which argues for an Essene sun cult, is to be rejected; see against this P. Seidensticker, *Studii biblici Francisci Liber annuus* 9, 1958/59, 155, cf. *Ber.* 9b Bar. The Essene direction of prayer eastwards, and not westwards, towards the temple, remains striking, but see Dan. 6.11.

822. A. Sachs, *JCS* 2, 1948, 271–90, and above all 6, 1952, 49–75: nineteen horoscopes from the period mentioned. For the dating of all horoscopes found down to the Arabian period see O. Neugebauer/H. B. van Hoesen, *Greek Horoscopes*, 1956, 161ff.; see also 205ff., lit. Cf. further W. and H. G. Gundel, *Astrologoumena*, Sudhoffs Archiv, Bh. 6, 1966, 366, index s.v. Horoskop.

823. O. Neugebauer, *The Exact Sciences in Antiquity*, ²1957, 170f.

824. For the whole matter, see M. P. Nilsson, *GGR*² 2, 268ff. (lit.), and *opuscula selecta* 3, 552–62. For the significance of Hellenistic Egyptian astrology see Boll/Gundel, op. cit., 23ff.; Tarn/Griffith, *Hellenistic Civilization*, 346, and F. Cumont, *L'Egypte des astrologues*, 1937, 13ff. and passim. In Greece itself the earliest evidence goes back to the sixth/fifth centuries BC, see W. Capelle, *Hermes* 60, 1925, 373–95, and B. L. v. d. Waerden, *AfO* 16, 1952/53, 225ff. Cf. W. and H. G. Gundel, op. cit., 9ff., 75ff.

825. For the earliest evidence of Egyptian astrology see above, n. 671. For Italy and Rome see K. Latte, *Römische Religionsgeschichte*, 1960, 275.

826. J. M. Allegro, *JSS* 9, 1964, 291–4; see also J. Carmignac, *RQ* 5, 1964/65, 199–206, and J. Licht, *Tarbiz* 35, 1965, 18–26. For the unpublished texts see also J. Allegro, *The Dead Sea Scrolls*, ²1964, 126f.

827. J. Starcky, in *Mémorial du Cinquantenaire*, 1964, 51–66; see also Carmignac, op. cit., 206–17, and J. Licht, op. cit. For the dating see J. Starcky, op. cit., 54 n. 1, following F. M. Cross. J. A. Fitzmyer, *CBQ* 27, 1965, 348–72, conjectures a Noah text.

828. J. Starcky, op. cit., 51, 60f., 64ff.; J. Carmignac, op. cit., 217.

829. J. Licht, op. cit., 21ff.; see T. Hopfner, *PW* 14, 1287f., and J. Schmidt, *PW* 20, 1064ff. The Greeks occupied themselves with physiognomical character studies after the Sophists, and these were furthered especially in the Stoa, op. cit., 1070ff.; see also M. Pohlenz, 1, 226f.; 2, 113f. Thus there was a link between astrology and manticism on the popular level: J. Schmidt, *PW* 20, 1066. Physiognomical omens were already known in Babylonia, see F. R. Kraus, *Die physiognomischen Omina der Babylonier*, MVÄG 40, 1935, H. 2, but these were concerned less with character than with predicting the future. On the other hand, the short, pregnant type of text we have here is relatively closely related to them, see the instances in op. cit., 61ff. The frequent mention of body marks (ἐλαία), see J. Starcky, op. cit., 52; 1, 1, 2, in the positive sense and 1, 2, 2 in the negative, on the other hand, points to a mantic interpretation as was offered in the Ptolemaic period e.g. by the mantic Melampus in a writing περὶ ἐλαίων τοῦ σώματος, see Raeder, *PW* 15, 399.

830. J. M. Allegro, *The Dead Sea Scrolls*, ²1964, 127.

831. J. Carmignac, op. cit., 214f.; the Hebrew המולד in col. 2, 8 of the first text is to be understood in a similar way, cf. J. Starcky, op. cit., 60ff., who points to the astrological significance of the Greek equivalent γένεσις, op. cit., 62 n. 2.

832. W. Gundel, *Neue astrologische Texte*, AAM NF 12, 1936, 84 l. 31: 'et ipsos reges ostendit cosmocratores'; ll. 33f.: 'et ipse sapiens fit in sermone et sapientia et gloria mirabilis'; cf. 73 ll. 22ff and 75 ll. 19ff., 41: the future God-king: 'ostendunt et ipsum regem deum existentem hominem humanitatis particem', according to a Hermetic work from Ptolemaic Alexandria, cf. also op. cit., 353 (lit.). It was strictly forbidden in imperial Rome on political grounds to make horoscopes on members of the imperial family, see A. Bouché-Leclercq, *L'Astrologie Grecque*, 1899, 560f., and T. Mommsen, *Römisches Strafrecht*, 1899, 584f. Matthew 2 is also to be understood against this background.

833. J. Starcky, op. cit., 65, cf. CCAG 12, 1936, 173ff., or Hippolytus, *Philos.* 4, 6, 15–26 GCS, ed. Wendland 3, 39, 48ff.: the definition of the physical form of those born under different constellations.

834. For the zodiac see B. L. v. d. Waerden, *AfO* 16, 1953, 216–30, and as a corrective, O. Neugebauer, op. cit., 140f. Its Babylonian origin is now definitely established; it dates from about 400 BC. Its early introduction into Greece in the 58th Olympiad, 548–545 BC, by Anaximander is legendary; Eudoxus of Cnidus, in the middle of the fourth century BC, knew it well, albeit in a rather different form. It was introduced in Egypt in the early Hellenistic period. The famous representation in Dendera is a mixture of Babylonian and Greek elements, op. cit., 228ff. Knowledge of it is generally presupposed in Hermetic astrology from the beginning of the second century BC.

835. For the constellation of Taurus see Bouché-Leclercq, op. cit., 132ff.; W. Gundel, AAM NF 12, 1936, 53 l. 20, 182ff. and *PW*, 2.R., 5, 53ff. For Erastothenes (third century BC) see *Catasterismorum reliquiae*, ed. C. Robert, 1913, 112;

cf. also Aratus, *Phain.* 515, and Virgil, *Georg.* 1, 217. It was originally the sign of the spring equinox, but had to surrender its place to the ram, B. L. v. d. Waerden, op. cit., 221. For the characterization of one born under the sign of Taurus see e.g. CCAG 12, 1936, 175f.

836. J. T. Milik, *Ten Years of Discovery*, 42, and J. M. Allegro, op. cit., 126; cf. on this CCAG 7, 1908, 226ff., and the fragments from Nechepso-Petosiris, op. cit., 132ff., see above, n. 520.

837. According to II Kings 23.5, Manasseh is already said to have worshipped the *mazzalōt*, i.e. particular constellations (according to *Ber.* 32b and *Shab.* 75a, Taurus) or planets; Jewish wisdom of a later period also knew of an abundance of constellations, as is shown by Job 9.9 (presumably a later gloss, see G. Hölscher, *Das Buch Hiob*, ²1952, 28) and the speeches of Elihu, Job 38.31ff. In 38.32 the Targ interprets *mazzārōt* as שטרי מזליא = sign of the zodiac; Hölscher, op. cit., 95, on the other hand conjectures 'Hyades' (in the constellation of Taurus). For a later knowledge of the zodiac see Josephus, *Bell.* 5, 214, 217, and Philo, *Spec.Leg.* 1, 87 (M 2, 87); *Vit.Mos.* 2, 123 (M 2, 153) etc.; for the Rabbis see *Bill.* 4, 1046, 1048f.; for the synagogues and Judaism in general see Goodenough, *Symbols*, index 1, 298, and in the wider historical context 8, 167ff., 195ff., 207ff., though the conclusions that he draws are misleading. For the constellations in the Old Testament see M. A. Beek, *BHHWB* 3, 1867, lit.

838. J. T. Milik, *RB* 63, 1956, 61; cf. Dupont-Sommer, *The Essene Writings*, 338.

839. *Hist.nat.* 30, 1, 11 (Reinach 282); Trogus Pompeius = Justin, *Epit.* 36, 2 (Reinach 253) and Numenius (Reinach 175) = Eusebius, *Pr.Ev.* 9, 8. Further below, n. 851.

840. 'Its once compelling power on men's dispositions rested on its scientific nature', M. P. Nilsson, *GGR*² 2, 276–81 (278); see also F. Cumont, *Die orientalische Religionen*, 153ff., 157ff. For its significance in the Stoa, see A. Bouché-Leclerq, op. cit., 28–34; with the inclusion of manticism also M. Pohlenz, op. cit., 1, 106ff., 171f. At first it was the only school of philosophy to take a positive attitude. Chrysippus considered the still relatively primitive art of the Chaldeans as a support for his teaching, op. cit., 2, 62, SVF 2, 277 no. 954, 15–20. Rejection by Panaitios, who was influenced by Carneades, was an exception. Its validity was strengthened by Posidonius, see K. Reinhardt, *PW* 22, 653ff., 691, 792ff., and *Kosmos und Sympathie*, 1926, see index under Astrologie and Mantik; also W. and H. G. Gundel (n. 822 above), 102f.

841. I Enoch 8.3: ἀστρολογίας; τὰ σημειωτικά; ἀστεροσκοπίαν; σεληναγωγίας.

842. Cf. already Isa. 47.13; Dan. 2.19–23 and *Sib.* 3, 221, 227ff.; cf. also Vol. I, pp. 193ff., and 302f. For Jewish astrological pseudepigrapha see Gundel (n. 822 above), 51ff.

843. Text in J. T. Milik, *RB* 63, 1956, 408; for the term '*gāzer*' see R. Meyer, *Das Gebet des Nabonid*, BAL 107, 3, 1962, 24f.; it has the sense 'determiner of fate', i.e. astrologer or haruspex: Dan. 2.27; 4.4; 5.7, 11.

844. Michel/Bauernfeind, op. cit., 1, 439 n. 83, and in detail O. Betz, *Offenbarung*, 99–108.

845. Judas: *Bell.* 1, 78–80 = *Antt.* 13, 311–13, and on it O. Betz, op. cit., 99ff. The prediction of the death on the same day and the exact detail of the place,

though wrongly interpreted, are without Old Testament parallel; the nearest parallels would perhaps be Jer. 28.16f. and Ezek. 11.13 (on which see G. Fohrer, *ZAW* 78, 1966, 36f., who points to the magic background); Menahem: *Antt.* 15, 372–9, and on it, op. cit., 102ff.; see the reference to I Sam. 16.1ff. and II Sam. 7.14. That Herod later asked Menahem about the length of his rule shows that he saw him as a kind of soothsayer. Cf. also the prediction of a German prisoner about Agrippa I, *Antt.* 18, 195–202, and the prophetic gift in Josephus himself, *Bell.* 3, 351ff.; 399–408 and *Vita*, 208ff.; it rests on knowledge of scripture and his priestly descent.

846. *Bell.* 2, 111f. = *Antt.* 17, 345–8, and on it see op. cit., 104ff.; here the Joseph narrative of Gen. 41.17–24 is a clear model, but the interpretation of the dream also takes up the themes of ancient interpretative practice, see the interpretation of the ox in Artemidorus, *Oneirocrit.*, ed. R. A. Pack, 1963, 1, 39 (p. 46); 2, 12 (p. 121), and the torn-off ears of corn indicating disaster, 5, 81 (p. 322). The interpretation of dreams had already developed into an almost stereotyped technique in Ptolemaic Egypt in the third century, following ancient Egyptian tradition, see A. Volten, *Demotische Traumdeutung*, 1942, 43ff.: 'In the Demotic book of wisdom, magic, healing and the interpretation of dreams go in parallel. All three arts are of divine origin' (43). Above all in the Serapis cult the interpretation of dreams was developed into a fixed technique, see above, nn. 647–8, cf. H. Bell, *JEA* 34, 1948, 95f. We find it already in the Zeno papyri, PCZ 59034, 59426; PSI 435. It was particularly beloved in Hasidic circles in Palestine, see Dan. 1.17; 2; 3.31–4.34; II Macc. 15.11–16; additions to Esther 1.1aff.; 10.3aff., LXX; here the border with visions was fluid. For criticism of dreams see Sir. 34.1ff., and among the Rabbis (R. Me'ir) see A. Oepke, *TDNT* 5, 233f., but even with the latter – as elsewhere in the ancient world – it played a great role, see E. Ehrlich, *ZNW* 47, 1956, 133–45, on the assumption of a common (Hellenistic–Egyptian ?) source, 143ff.

847. For magical interpretation see E. Zeller, *PhGr*[5] III, 2, 333f.; A. Dieterich, *Abraxas*, 1891, 145; A. Dupont-Sommer, *SVT* 7, 1960, 246–61; 'cette médecine essénienne était tout imprégnée de magie . . .' (246), cf. also Tarn/Griffith, *Hellenistic Civilization*, 353, on *Bell.* 2, 142; G. Vermes, *RQ* 2, 1959/60, 440ff., and D. Flusser, *IEJ* 7, 1957, 107ff. See the apotropaic psalms in J. P. M. v. d. Ploeg, *Festgabe K. G. Kuhn*, 1971, 128ff.

848. Ancient superstition about plants and stones with a medical and astrological trend is a limitless field: T. Hopfner, 'Lithika', *PW* 13, 747–68; W. Kroll, 'Kyraniden', *PW* 12, 127–34; E. Pfister, 'Pflanzenaberglaube', *PW* 19, 1446–56. In addition there is the healing art of 'Iatromathēmatikē', influenced by astrology, which already plays a great role in Nechepso-Petosiris (see above, nn. 669–81), cf. E. Riess, op. cit., 378–80, frs. 27–32, and W. Kroll, *PW* 9, 802–4; see also Bouché-Leclerq, op. cit., 518–34, and Boll/Gundel, 139ff. For the whole matter see Festugière, op. cit., 123–85, and Bidez/Cumont, op. cit., 1, 188–98. Writings of this kind were current partly under the names of Hermes, Democritus, the Persian Ostanes, and even Solomon (cf. Wisdom 7.20; *Antt.* 8, 44ff., and Ganschinietz, *PW Suppl* 8, 664, see above, nn. 175/6). Chief author of this magical-medicinal literature on the basis of '*sympatheia*' was the neo-Pythagorean Bolus (Democritus) of Mendes, *c.* 250–150 BC in Alexandria, see

J. M. Wellmann, *PW* 3, 676f., and *Die ΦΥΣΙΚΑ des Bolos Demokritos*, AAB 1928, no. 7; Festugière, op. cit., 1, 224–38, with critical qualifications by J. H. Waszink, *RAC* 2, 502–8, cf. also F. Jacoby, FGrHist IIIa, 263, comm. 24ff., and W. Kroll, *Hermes* 69, 1934, 228–32. In particular, the attempt of Wellmann, op. cit., 6, 9f., to demonstrate a direct dependence of the Essenes on Bolus and stamp them neo-Pythagoreans, is very unconvincing, see Vol. I, pp. 245f.

849. CCAG VIII, 3, 1912, 135 l. 13, see Vol. I, pp. 215f. Cf. also A. J. Festugière, *RB* 48, 1939, 69ff., for the prayers to the 'Lord of the world' to be spoken at the gathering of plants, some of which show Jewish influence. For the Rabbis see n. 441 above.

850. Josephus, *Antt.* 8, 46–9. For the 'Book of Healings', see A. Wünsche, *Aus Israels Lehrhallen* 3, 201–12; Schürer 3, 419f.; cf. Ganschinietz, *PW Suppl* 8, 665f.

851. Cf. Acts 8.9, 11; 13.6, 8; 19.13ff.; cf. Trogus Pompeius (first century BC) = Justin, *Epit.* 36, 2 (Reinach 253); Pliny, *Hist. nat.* 30, 10f. (Reinach 282), who derives it from Egyptian magic, see M. Wellmann, AAB 1928, no. 7, 64; Juvenal 6, 542 (Reinach 291f.); Apuleius, *Apol.* 90 (Reinach 335f.); Lucian, *Tragopodagra* 173 (Reinach 159), cf. also *Philopseudes* 16; Celsus, in Origen, *c.Cels.* 1, 26, cf. 5, 6; GCS 1, 77; 2, 5f. ed. Koetschau; Justin, *Dial.c.Tr.* 85, 3, and Iren., *Haer.* 2, 6, 2; on this see Schürer, 3, 407–20; and O. Eissfeldt, *Kleine Schriften* 1, 150–71; cf. S. Baron, *A Social and Religious History of the Jews*, ²1960, 15–23; L. Thorndike, *A History of Magic* 1, 348–58; Goodenough, *Symbols* 2, 155–95, and M. Simon, *Verus Israel*, 1948, 394–429. Further see above, n. 441 and below, n. IV, 22. For magic in Palestine see also Vol. I, pp. 83f.; cf. the amulets II Macc. 12.40, and on them K. Galling, *BRL* 29. For Jewish exorcisms, see Bill. 4, 533ff.h, cf. e.g. *Shab.* 67a. For the magical gems with Jewish influence see C. Bonner, *Studies in Magical Amulets*, 1950, 26ff.

852. Thorndike, op. cit., 1, 360–84, and M. Wellmann, op. cit., 54–62; cf. also J. H. Waszink, *RAC* 2, 507f. Cf. e.g. the portrait of the Simonian, Hippolytus, *Philos.* 6.20, GCS 3, 148, ed. Wendland, and the fictional report about Simon Magus, Ps.Clem., *Hom.* 2, 32f.; 5,4; GCS, ed. Rehm 49, 94, and on it H. J. Schoeps, *Aus frühchristlicher Zeit*, 1950, 249–54; further Irenaeus, *Haer.* 1, 13, on the gnostic Marcus.

853. Festugière 1, 339f.; Ganschinietz, *PW Suppl* 8, 663ff.

854. Josephus, *c.Ap.* 1, 176–83, and on it H. Lewy, *HTR* 31, 1938, 209ff., 222ff. and Vol. I, pp. 257f.

855. M. Wellmann, op. cit., 9, 12ff. Bolus is said to have appealed to the Jewish magician Dardanus (see III Kingd. 5.11 LXX and above all Josephus, *Antt.* 8, 43, cf. Pliny, *Hist.Nat.* 30, 9; Apuleius, *Apol.* 90); cf. R. Reitzenstein, *Poimandres*, 163 n. 4; Festugière, op. cit., 1, 317 n. 3, and with more restraint W. Kroll, *PW Suppl* 6, 25f.; A. Herrmann, *RAC* 3, 593f.; Bidez/Cumont, op. cit., 2, 13 n. 20.

856. G. Fohrer, *ZAW* 78, 1966, 25–47, points to certain magical and mantic features in the Old Testament prophets. Despite Deut. 18. 9ff.; Lev. 20.6, the magical element emerges much more strongly in the Judaism of the Hellenistic period. For the Rabbinic exorcists see Bill. 4, 534f.; for the miracle workers of the early Rabbinic period see A. Guttmann, *HUCA* 20, 1947, 374–88. E.g. the

miracle worker R. Phinehas b. Jair made use of magical practices: *Demai* 22a, about AD 200. For Moses as a magician among the non-Jews see J. G. Gager (below n. IV, 2), 134–61.

857. Festugière, 1, 319–24, cf. 211f. and 230 n. 6, and *RB* 68, 1939, 46; also Bidez/Cumont, op. cit., 1, 285, see index under 'Stèles'. For Axiochus see above n. 655. With respect to Phoenicia see S. A. Cook, *The Religion of Ancient Palestine*, 1925, 161ff., and Philo Byblius, FGrHist 790 F 1.26, and E. Amélineau, *RHR* 21, 1890, 285.

858. FGrHist 680 F 4.14f., cf. Abydenos, FGrHist 685 F 3; on this, H. L. Jansen, *Die Henochgestalt*, 28ff., cf. also W. Bousset, *ZNW* 3, 1902, 44; Bousset/ Gressmann, 492f.; S. A. Cook, op. cit., 163. For the theme, W. Speyer, *Bücherfunde*, 111ff.

859. Ps.Manetho, FGrHist 609 F 25, cf. also Zosimus in Syncellus 1, 23, ed. Dindorf, and on it Reitzenstein, *Poimandres*, 1904, 139. There is a connection between the Hermetic Egyptian and Babylonian tradition in the Hermetic Cyranides, see M. Wellmann, 'Marcellus v. Side', *Phil. Suppl* 27, 2, 1934, 14, where the origin of this ἀρχαϊκὴ βίβλος is derived from a 'Syrian' stele on the Euphrates; for a further parallel see in the *Korē Kosmū*, CH 23, 67 (end): for protection from the demons in the sky. For Jewish haggadic parallels see M. J. bin Gorion, *Die Sagen der Juden, Von der Urzeit*, 1913, 155ff., 356.

860. On this Festugière, op. cit., 1, 223; the mention of 'metal' and the παντοίους λίθους καὶ τὰ βαφικά in I Enoch 8 correspond to similar lists in old alchemical literature. However, the influence of the βαφικά of Bolus of Mendes on I Enoch, as conjectured by Festugière, is improbable. Still, conversely the ancient alchemists and Hermetists seem to have known some of the Enoch literature, and here again the doctrine of the fall of the angels, see Festugière, 1, 255ff. The magical character of angelic wisdom can again be seen in the interpretation of Ps.Clem., *Hom.* 8,14,2, Rehm GCS 127 μαγευθεῖσιν λίθοις, which depends on I Enoch. For the Egyptian origin of alchemy see Bidez/Cumont, op. cit., 1, 198ff.

861. I Enoch 7; 8; 69.8–12. Cf. Ps.Philo 25.10ff. (pp. 182f. Kisch).

862. Cf. Jub. 4.17ff., 21ff.; 10.12; 12.22ff., 27ff.; 21.10, cf. on this P. Grelot, *RSR* 46, 1958, 15f. Ps.Clem., *Hom.* 8, 14, Rehm GCS 127, is directly dependent on I Enoch and Jubilees, see H. J. Schoeps, op. cit., 13f. (lit.). The view that astrology and magic came from the fallen angels had an influence in the early church, see Boll/Gundel, 104f.; cf. e.g. Tertullian, *De idol.* 9. Here the reaction – in contrast to the Essenes – was predominantly negative. Cf. Bouché-Leclerq, op. cit., 614ff., and W. Gundel, *RAC* 1, 828f.; id. and H. G. Gundel (n. 822 above), 318ff., 332ff.

863. Cf. also the portrayal by Johanan b. Zakkai of this all-embracing wisdom, which itself contained 'the conversation of serving angels and demons': *Sukka* 28a Bar., Bill. 4, 535. We find the same thing already in Hillel, *Tractate Soperim* 16, 9.

864. The Damascus document is probably directed against them, see above, n. 715, cf. also *Bell.* 2, 160f.: the ἕτερον Ἐσσηνῶν τάγμα which did not renounce marriage. For the dwelling of Essenes in Jewish cities see *Bell.* 2, 124, and Philo, *Hypoth.* 11, 1 (M 2, 632), cf. also Michel/Bauernfeind, 1, 432 n. 40, and

the numerical details in *Antt.* 18, 20 and Philo, *Quod omnis* 75 (M 2, 457): 4000 or more than 4000 members. They probably go back to the same source.

865. For the *'gōlā'* see M. Smith, *NTS* 7, 1960/61, 347–60; for the groups of prophets and priestly clans see L. Rost, *TLZ* 80, 1955, 1–8; for the Rechabites see already Nilus of Ancyra and the Suidas Lexicon in A. Adam, *Antike Berichte über die Essener*, Kleine Texte 182, 1961, 57, 59 and H. J. Schoeps, *Theologie und Geschichte des Judenchristentums*, 1949, 235f., 247ff.

866. H. Bardtke, *TLZ* 86, 1961, 93–104, and C. Schneider, *Qumranprobleme*, ed. H. Bardtke, 1963, 305–9. E. Koffmann, *Bibl* 42, 1961, 433–42; 44, 1963, 46–61, has to concede this situation – against his will – see 434ff. on the term יחד, which the Old Testament does not know in this sense. The term probably appears for the first time with this meaning in 11 QPs^a 154 = DJDJ IV, 64, col. 18, 1, see Vol.I, pp. 176f. Cf M, Delcor, *RQ* 6, 1967/69, 401–25.

867. *HTR* 59, 1966, 293–307; KAI 60; Roberts/Skeat/Nock, *HTR* 29, 1936, 39–88, and the κοινόν of Mareatos, P. M. Fraser, *JEA* 15, 1964, 85 no. 14, 6, named after the person of the founder. Further instances in Tcherikover, *CPJ* 1, 6f.

868. CIJ 2, 366f. no. 1440, the synagogue inscription of Schedia near Alexandria from the time of Ptolemy III; from the same period CPJ 3, 164 no. 1532a from Arsinoe, and CPJ 1, 248 no. 134; CPJ 1, 239ff. no. 129: the earliest mention of a Jewish synagogue in the Fayum, in 219 BC, cf. also Schürer 3.97ff., and Tcherikover, *HC*, 296–332; *CPJ* 1, 6–10. See on this Ps.Aristeas 310: the Jewish *politeuma* in Alexandria: CIG 3, 5361 = SEG 16, 931: the Jewish *politeuma* in Berenice; the designation *'synhodos'* for a Jewish community in Carian Nysa: L. Robert, *Hellenica* 11/12, 1960, 261f.: the *politeuma* of the Idumeans in Memphis, OGIS 737.

869. H. Bardtke, op. cit., 95 n. 12. E. Ziebarth, *Das griechische Vereinswesen*, 1896, 130, sees the Essenes as a Greek association, with reference to Philo.

870. Cf. II Macc. 4.9ff.; I Macc. 1.14; H. Bardtke, op. cit., 96; E. Ziebarth, op. cit., 110f., 112, see Vol.I, pp. 72ff., pp. 277f.

871. H. Bardtke, op. cit., 102, 104.

872. 1 QS 5.5f.; cf. 1.8, 16; 2.10, 12; 3.11f.; 5.7f., 18ff. and often, see A. Jaubert, *La notion d'alliance*, 211ff., and W. Grundmann, in *UU* 1, 254f.

873. K. von Fritz, *PW* 24, 218f., 267f., 269: the Pythagorean movement hardly had any great significance in the Hellenistic period between 250 and 50 BC; it existed above all in literature and perhaps in small conventicles. For its influence on Judaism, see below, n. 877. Cf. H. Thesleff, *An Introduction to the Pythagorean Writings*, 1961.

874. S. Wagner, *Die Essener in der wissenschaftliche Diskussion*, 1960, 156ff., 162ff., 165ff. For E. Zeller see *PhGr*⁵ III, 2, 308–77.

875. S. Wagner, op. cit., 226, and the survey by A. Dupont-Sommer, *RHPR* 35, 1955, 76f. For details see Schürer 2, 670, 678; F. Cumont, *CRAI* 1930, 99–112; M. J. Lagrange, *Le Judaisme*, 1931, 326; I. Lévy, *La Légende de Pythagore*, 1927, 264–93; id., *Recherches esséniennes et pythagoriciennes*, 1965, 57ff.; M. Wellmann, op. cit., 5ff., following Bolus Democritus, see above, n. 848.

876. A. Dupont-Sommer, *Nouveaux Aperçus*, 1953, 154ff., and *RHR* 35, 1955, 75–92; T. F. Glasson, *Greek Influence*, 49ff., cf. also M. Hadas, *HCu*, 194f.

877. According to Josephus, *c.Ap.* 1, 163ff.; cf. Origen, *c.Cels.* 1, 15 (Reinach 39 and 40 n. 2), and on this Schürer 3, 625. As the views borrowed by Jews and Thracians according to *c.Ap.* are very strange, these may be allusions from comedy, see R. Rohde, *RheinMus* 26, 1871, 562. However, the whole tradition seems to be older, and could go back to Hecataeus of Abdera. Isocrates, *Busiris* 11, already reports that Pythagoras brought the basis of his philosophy from Egypt; this corresponds to a theme which became increasingly popular from the time of Herodotus: see T. Hopfner, *Orientalische und Griechische Philosophie*, BhAO 4, 1925, 11 n. 2 and 12f.; J. Kerschensteiner, *Platon und die Orient*, 1945, 1ff., and for the historical background K. von Fritz, *PW* 24, 186, 198f. The romancer Antonius Diogenes (Reinach 159), writing even before Lucian (second century AD), has Pythagoras learning the interpretation of dreams and magic among Egyptians, Arabs, Chaldeans and Hebrews. It is interesting that from the time of Aristotle's pupil Aristoxenus, Pythagoras and Zoroaster were connected, see Bidez/Cumont, op. cit., 1, 33ff., cf. 103ff.; 2, 35ff. fr. B 25–27; W. Burkert, op. cit., 127f. n. 18. This could be one of those places where Iranian dualistic conceptions found their way into the Hellenistic West.

878. For *Bell.*2, 128, see Vol. I, p. 236. For evening and morning prayer see 1 QS 10.10, and for the Therapeutae, Philo, *Vit.cont.* 37 (M 2, 475).

879. Dupont-Sommer, op. cit., 89; cf. on the other hand E. Lohse, op. cit., 36 n. e and the variants 4 QSb + D in J. T. Milik, *RB* 67, 1960, 415.

880. E. Zeller, op. cit., 365ff.: the Essene concern presented here 'to gain a higher holiness through an ascetic life' is connected with the priestly and Levitical ideal of purity and the desire for community with the heavenly world, cf. e.g. 1 QM 7.6f. The arcane discipline is part of the character of oriental wisdom, cf. e.g. O. Neugebauer, *Astronomical Cuneiform Texts* 1, 1955, 12, no. 135 (N) and 180 (S) with the stereotyped formula: 'The informed may show it to the informed; the uninformed shall not see it. (It belongs) to the forbidden things of Anu, Enlil . . .' or Ahikar, col. 7, 96–99, etc., ed. Cowley, *Aramaic Papyri*, 215. For the whole problem see also the critical remarks of G. Molin, *Saeculum* 6, 1953, 280; R. de Vaux, *VT* 9, 1959, 404f.; P. Grelot, *RQ* 1, 1958/59, 127, and in detail P. Seidensticker, op. cit., 150–75.

881. For Essene communism in property see Josephus, *Bell.*2, 122, 127; *Antt.*18, 20, 22; Philo, *Quod omnis* 76f. (M 2, 457); Pliny, *Hist.nat.* 5,73 (Reinach 272); 1 QS 1.11–13; 6.19. For the self-designation אביונים see K. G. Kuhn, *Konkordanz*, 1. It was this sharing of property that aroused the attention of the ancient world, because echoes were found here of certain philosophical doctrines of the ideal state or the golden age, see W. Bauer, *PW Suppl* 4, 410ff. Michel/Bauernfeind, op. cit., 1, 432 n. 38, point to Ezek. 44.28 and Test.Levi 2.12, according to which the priests may have neither 'possession' nor 'heritage', as God himself represents their 'heritage' and 'possession'.

882. For Egypt see G. Molin, *TLZ* 78, 1953, 653–6.

883. C. Schneider, op. cit., 305; cf. also M. Smith, *BJRL* 40, 1957/58, 483. For allegory see O. Betz, *Offenbarung*, 176ff., cf. E. Zeller, op. cit., 327ff. For ancient Egyptian allegory see H. Gressmann, *Die Umwandlung der orientalischen Religionen*, Vorträge d. Bibl. Warburg, 1924/25, 193, and F. Daumas, *Mémorial Gélin*, 1961, 203–11. A simple kind of allegory can already have been practised

in pre-Essene priestly exegesis, as is stressed by G. Mayer, *RAC* 6, 1209, following K. Elliger, *Studien zum Habbakkukkommentar*, 1953, 126.

884. This tension arose above all because the Essenes on the one hand took over the whole Hasidic view of history and the doctrine of the fall of the angels, etc., while they maintained the theological views of their founder without reconciling them with the new teaching. In any case, we cannot apply modern systematic standards.

885. *RQ* 1, 1958/59, 127.

886. The texts are collected in A. Adam, op. cit.; Philo 1ff.; Josephus 26ff.; Pliny and Dio 38f.; Hippolytus 41ff.; cf. also Suidas 59; for Solinus and Porphyry see Reinach 205, 341.

887. Their name could arise from a 'translation' of the Aramaic *'ās(s)ayyā* = θεραπευταί, 'skilled in healing, miracle worker', arising on the basis of a false etymological explanation of 'Εσσαῖοι; cf. G. Vermès, *RQ* 2, 1959/60, 435–43, and Jastrow, *Dictionary*, 93.

888. Cf. e.g. Festugière, *REG* 50, 1937, 476ff., where attention is drawn to the parallels between the Pythagorean-type report of Chairemon (see above,n.666) on the Egyptian priests, the description of the Brahmans in Philostratus, *Vit. Apoll.*3, 10–80, the Persian magi and the Essenes. For the '*theios anēr*' see R. Reitzenstein, *Mysterienreligionen*, ³1927, 25ff., 237ff., 298, and L. Bieler, ΘΕΙΟΣ ANHP, two vols., 1935f., who discusses the Old Testament phenomena in 2, 1–36. The *iš-'elōhīm* of I Kings 17.18, 24; 20.28; II Kings 1.9ff.; 4.7, etc., is the Old Testament counterpart, see op. cit., 2, 24f. R. Bultmann, *The Gospel of John*, 1971, 102 n.1, seeks to distinguish the Essene prophetic gift from the type of the '*theios anthrōpos*'. However, among the Essenes there were not only prophets but interpreters of dreams, healers and astrologers; they were at the same time ascetics and illuminati and were in contact with the angels and the heavenly world. Their superhuman behaviour under Roman torture, *Bell.*2, 152f., also belongs in this context; cf. *Mart.Isa.*5, 14, and M. Hengel, op. cit., 274. The difference lay not in the outward manifestation but in the theological interpretation. Judaism knew no direct apotheosis of the charismatic, see M. Hengel, *Nachfolge und Charisma*, 30.

889. R. Meyer, *Tradition und Neuschöpfung*, BAL 110, 2, 1965, 60ff., on the Essene criticism of the Pharisees, as the latter 'tone down and dissolve' the law. For the differences between the Pharisees and Sadducees on the validity of oral paradosis for law and eschatology see Josephus, *Antt.*13, 294ff.; 18, 16, and R. Meyer, *TDNT* 7, 49ff.; 8, 28ff.

890. In the old contrast which emerges between the presentation of ancient Judaism in Bousset/Gressmann (pp.40ff.) and G. F. Moore, *Judaism*, the Qumran texts seem to strengthen the case for Bousset/Gressmann. This is not meant to belittle the significance of the Rabbinic tradition, but it should be realized that it was subjected to a good deal of 'censorship', see M. Smith, *BJRL* 40, 1957/58, 487. For the division of the Pharisees into Hillelites and Shammaites see M. Hengel, *Zeloten*, 206ff., cf. 89ff.

891. Cf. E. Grässer, *TR* 30, 1964, 176: the alternative 'Hellenistic' or 'Palestinian' has finally proved to be completely misleading, see also n.4. For the whole see Vol.I, pp.103ff.

892. H. Gese, *RGG*[3] 6, 1575: this does not exclude individual 'special revelations' like Job 4.12–21, 'though there are also exceptions here'.

893. *Antt.* 13,288–99, 372–83, 400ff. For Simeon b. Seṭaḥ see Schürer 1, 279f., 289f., and the Rabbinic legends collected in K. Schlesinger, *Die Gesetzeslehrer*, 1936, 39–62. For him as the possible 'lying prophet' of the Damascus document (cf. CD 1.14f.; 8.13; 19.26; 20.15), see R. Meyer, *Tradition*, 63f.

894. Jewish prayers: see P. Volz, op. cit., 51ff. For the Palestinian Targum see *Targ. Jer.* I on Gen. 29.11 = Bill. 4, 877; on Ex. 4.13; 6.18; 40.9–11 and Num. 25.12 = Bill. 4, 463; on Num. 24.17 = Bill. 3, 383c; cf. also M. Hengel, *Zeloten*, 167.

895. M. Hengel, op. cit., 89ff., 204–11, 293, 340f. K. Schubert wrongly doubts the significance of the apocalyptic expectation of the end for the Pharisees in his review, *WZKM* 58, 1952, 259f.; R. Meyer, op. cit., 55ff., 69, is correct. Cf. also M. Hengel, *Nachfolge und Charisma*, 27, 62f.

896. Schürer 3, 357–69; P. Volz, op. cit., 50f.; D. S. Russell, op. cit., 66.

897. Schürer 1, 662–6; V. Tcherikover, *CPJ* 1, 86–92, and the papyrus texts, 2, 225–60.

898. Philo, *De virt.* 77 (M 2, 388); *Praem. et poen.*, passim, and especially 95ff., 164ff. (M 2, 423f., 435f.); *Vit. Mos.* 2, 288 (M 2, 179). For Josephus, M. Hengel, *Zeloten*, 245. A. Wlosok, *Laktanz* 2, AAH 1960, 111, points out that 'dualistic, specifically Jewish traditions emerge more strongly in Philo, where he goes back to the community understanding'.

899. From the abundance of literature cf. e.g. K. G. Kuhn, *ZTK* 49, 1952, 200–22; P. Stuhlmacher, *Gerechtigkeit Gottes*, 1965, 145ff., 217ff., 228ff.; J. Becker, *Das Heil Gottes*, 1964, passim, esp. 238–79. R. Bultmann, in discussing Albert Schweitzer's *The Mysticism of Paul the Apostle*, 1931, judges his term 'eschatological gnosis' (op. cit., 74) appropriate (DLZ, 3.F. 2, 1931, 155); with equal justification this term could already be transferred to 'Essene theology', indeed to Hasidic apocalyptic from the time of Daniel. The *maśkīlīm* of Dan. 11 were already concerned with saving knowledge, with respect to the woes of the last time.

IV

The 'Interpretatio Graeca' of Judaism and the Hellenistic Reform Attempt in Jerusalem

1. On this see I. Heinemann, *PW Suppl* 5, 3–43. The earliest account that is hostile to the Jews has nationalistic Egyptian colouring and comes from Manetho, see FGrHist 609 F 10 = *c.Ap.* 1, 223–53, still from the beginning of the third century BC; later writers like Chairemon and Apollonius Molon, at the beginning of the first century BC, are dependent on him. In the Seleucid sphere an anti-semitic tendency can first be noted after Posidonius (see op. cit., 26f. and 30ff.). For the later period see M. Simon, *Verus Israel*, 1948, 239–45, and *Post-Scriptum*, 1964, 489ff., lit.

2. A. Schlatter, *GI³*, 28, and W. Jaeger, *JR* 18, 1938, 127–43 = *Scripta minora* 2, 1960, 169–83, and *Diokles v. Karystos*, 1938, 134–53; Y. Gutman, *The Beginnings of Jewish–Hellenistic Literature* 1, 1958, passim; J. G. Gager, *Moses in Greco–Roman Paganism*, 1972.

3. FGrHist 264 F 6 = Diodore 40,3 (Reinach 14ff.), on his person see F. Jacoby, *PW* 7, 2750ff. He probably received his information through Jews who had emigrated from Palestine to Egypt. For his utopian description of the Jewish state see W. Jaeger, *JR* 18, 1938, 136–43, and *Diokles*, 144–52; F. Jacoby, *PW* 7, 2765f. Y. Gutman, op. cit., 1, 39–73, also stresses the utopian-idealistic character of his work; F. Jacoby wrongly attacks him, op. cit., and FGrHist IIIa, Comm. on no. 264, pp. 46ff. For the religio-political characterization see M. P. Nilsson, *GGR²* 2, 285f.; perhaps leaning to some degree on Sparta, which Plato estimated so highly: for the Spartans and the Jews see Vol. I, pp. 72f.

4. Cf. *Republic* 414b; for the piety of the guardians, 383b; 421a: φύλακες δὲ νόμων, cf. *Laws* 754d.

5. See *c.Ap.* 1, 186–189: the sagacity and ability of the high priest 'Hezekiah' (see Vol. I, p. 49); 1, 200–205: the Jewish archer Meshullam free of any superstition. For the authenticity see F. Jacoby, op. cit., 66f.; B. Schaller, *ZNW* 54, 1953, 20ff.

6. FGrHist 737 F6 = Reinach 8; on this see W. Jaeger, *JR* 18, 1938, 131ff., and *Diokles*, 134ff. J. Bernays, *Theophrasts Schrift über die Frömmigkeit*, 1866, 109ff., the real discoverer of this 'source', regarded it as the earliest known Greek account of the Jews; however, W. Jaeger has shown the probability that it is dependent on Hecataeus' *Aegyptiaca*. He is also followed by O. Regenbogen, *PW Suppl* 7, 1515, and Y. Gutman, op. cit., 1, 74ff. Against this see A. D. Nock, *Essays on Religion* 2, 1972, 601f., and M. Stern, *Kirjath Sepher* 46, 1970/71, 99.

7. W. Jaeger, *Diokles*, 147; *JR* 18, 1938, 133, who points out the connection of these conceptions with the natural philosophical thought of the Greeks, of Anaximander, Xenophanes, Democritus and Aristotle. Cf. also Nilsson, *GGR²* 1, 839ff.; 2, 253ff., and *HTR* 33, 1940, 11f. = *opuscula selecta* 3, 1960, 36ff. For the

'God of heaven' see below nn. 262–6. For the worship of 'heaven' by the Jews see Strabo (and n. 15) from Posidonius; Petronius, fr. 37 (Reinach 266), and Juvenal, *Sat.* 6, 545 and 14, 96 (Reinach 292); see below nn. 64, 260.

8. Bidez/Cumont, op. cit., I, 240–2; the report of Hecataeus and Theophrastus on the Jews is too positive to be brought into conjunction with the derivation of religion from human fear in Democritus; the nearest feature would be the positive judgment of fr. 30, Diels 2, 15, on the worship of God by the first wise men. Cf. the judgment of Philo of Byblos on Hecataeus and the Jews, FGrHist 790 F 9 = Origen, *c.Cels.* 1, 15. Bidez/Cumont overlook the political background of the writing activity of Hecataeus.

9. FGrHist 737 F 8 = Clem. Alex., *Strom.* 1, 72, 5 (Reinach 13); on this see W. Jaeger, *JR* 18, 1938, 132 n.14, and *Diokles*, 141f.; Y. Gutman, op. cit., 1, 89ff. For his person see O. Stein, *PW* 15, 231ff.; for his Stoic interpretation of Indian 'philosophy', 259ff. and esp. 262. Cf. further Diog.Laert. 1, 9 on the common derivation of Jews and Brahmans from the 'Magi'.

10. In Josephus, *c.Ap.* 1, 176–82 (quot. 179–81) from a writing of Clearchus in dialogue form, περὶ ὕπνου. On this see W. Jaeger, *JR* 18, 1938, 130ff., and *Diokles*, 138ff.; in detail H. Lewy, *HTR* 31, 1938, 205–35. Presumably Peripatetic circles held the view that the Jews were a kind of learned priestly caste among the Syrians, like the Brahmans in India. Clearchus is probably dependent on the *Indica* of Megasthenes, which was written towards 290 BC, in the same way as Theophrastus is dependent on the *Aegyptiaca* of Hecataeus, though his picture of the Jews will also have been shaped by his own experience with them; on this see also Y. Gutman, op. cit., 1, 91ff. Clearchus was still a personal pupil of Aristotle, but he had strong Platonizing tendencies: see W. Kroll, *PW* 11, 580ff. L. Robert, *CRAI* 1968, 447–54, differs.

11. H. Lewy, op. cit., 209ff., 222ff.; cf. already A. v. Gutschmid, *Kleine Schriften* 4, 1893, 587f.

12. H. Lewy, op. cit., 218ff.: Eusebius, *Pr.Ev.* 11, 3, 8, GCS VIII, 2, 9, Mras.

13. On this see above n. III, 877. The view of Hermippus already seems to have been influenced by some old Palestinian *halachoth*: see S. Safrai, *JJS* 16, 1965, 31 n.73, with reference to S. Lieberman.

14. See already Reinach's conjecture, 89; R. Reitzenstein, *Zwei religionsgeschichtliche Fragen*, 1901, 77 n.2; J. Geffcken, *Zwei griechische Apologeten*, 1907, XI n.5; in more detail I. Heinemann, *MGWJ* 63, 1919, 113–21; E. Norden, *Festgabe f.A.v. Harnack*, 1921, 292–8, and K. Reinhardt, 'Posidonius über Ursprung und Entartung', *Orient und Antike* 6, 1928, 5–34: 'Moses as prehistoric founder', cf. also *PW* 22, 638f. Further cf. F. Jacoby, FGrHist IIC 87, Comm. 196ff.; I. Heinemann, *Poseidonios' metaphysische Schriften* 2, 1928, 72ff. A. D. Nock (n.6 above), 860ff., takes the *via media* in controversy with W. Aly, *Strabonis Geographica* 4, 191ff.; criticism in J. G. Gager (n.2 above), 44ff.

15. Strabo 16, 2, 35–37 (C 760/61) = FGrHist 87 F 70 (Reinach 99f.). Translation, with small alterations, follows E. Norden, op. cit., 292f.

16. Strabo 16, 2, 38: for the whole see E. Bickermann, *GM*, 130. The objection by I. Heinemann, *MGWJ* 82, 1938, 156, that the theory of a retrogression only arose after the Maccabean revolt, with Posidonius, is untenable; the theory is probably older and goes back to Stoic conceptions, see M. Pohlenz,

op. cit., 1, 42, or the notion of the golden age in the Peripatetics Theophrastus and Dicaearchus, see O. Regenbogen, *PW Suppl.*7, 1514 (lit.). Its basis can already be found in Hesiod. Cf. also Vol. I, p. 300.

17. Strabo 16, 2, 37: οἱ μὲν γὰρ ἀφιστάμενοι τὴν χώραν ἐκάκουν καὶ αὐτὴν καὶ τὴν γειτνιῶσαν.. In my view, the 'apostates' are the Jewish reform party, and the whole passage is a reference to the Jewish 'civil war' from 167 BC to the capture of the Acra in 141, which was carried on by the 'reformers' with considerable help from the Seleucids. However, Posidonius shows that even from the Seleucid side a negative judgment was passed on it at a later stage; cf. Vol. I, p. 288f. The abrupt rejection of the Maccabean policy of expansion by Posidonius can be seen in Diodore 44 fr. 1 = FGrHist 87 F 109 = Reinach 56ff.

18. Strabo 16, 2, 38, on which see G. Rudberg, *Forschungen zu Posidonius*, 1918, 51ff., and above all K. Reinhardt, *Poseidonius über Ursprung* . . ., 16ff., 56f. For the concept of God in Posidonius see also I. Heinemann, *Poseidonius*, 2.43ff. A similar concept of God appears in the romance of Iambulus, see Vol. I, p. 111, and n. III, 26, among the inhabitants of the wonder island in the Indian ocean: Diodore 2, 59, 2: σέβονται δὲ θεοὺς τὸ περιέχον πάντα καὶ ἥλιον καὶ καθόλου πάντα τὰ οὐράνια.

19. K. Reinhardt, op. cit., 14.

20. For his influence on Wisdom and Philo see I. Heinemann, op. cit., 1, 136ff. (Wisdom) and 1, 70, 73 n. 3, 133; 2, 286f., 433f., 471f.; see also *Philons griechische und jüdische Bildung*, ²1962, index 592. For the Areopagus speech, see E. Norden, *Agnostos Theos*, ⁴1956, 20ff.; M. Pohlenz, *ZNW* 42, 1949, 70ff., and, *Stoa* 1, 403f.; see also the newest survey of the literature by J. Lebram, *ZNW* 55, 1964, 221 n. 1.

21. Augustine, *De consens. evang.* 1, 22, 30 and 23,31, *PL* 34, 1055f. = Varro, fr. 1, 58b, ed. Agahd, JbPhilSuppl. 24, 1898, 163; on this see E. Norden, *Festgabe Harnack*, 298ff.; *Agnostos Theos*, 1912, 61. Cf. Vol. I, p. 262.

22. J. Lydus, *De mens.* 4,53 (ed. Wünsch 109f.), on which see E. Norden, op. cit., 58ff. According to Diodore 1, 94 (Reinach 70), too, Moses received his laws from the god Iao. Even here K. Reinhardt, op. cit., 58f., and E. Norden, *Festgabe Harnack*, 300, presume a dependence on Posidonius, who for his part perhaps in turn goes back to Hecataeus. For knowledge of the divine name Iao in the Hellenistic sphere and above all in the magical papyri, see Ganschinietz, *PW* 9, 698–721; A. Vincent, *La Religion des Judéo-Araméens*, 1937, 37–45; O. Eissfeldt, *Kleine Schriften* 1, 1962, 150–71, and Goodenough, *Symbols* 2, 192f. Septuagint fragments from a Leviticus manuscript presumably of the first century BC were found in Cave 4 Q bearing the divine name ΙΑΩ, see O. Eissfeldt, *The Old Testament*, 707. This easily explains how it could also be known in non-Jewish circles.

23. Augustine, *Civ. Dei* 4, 31 = Varro, fr. 59, ed. Agahd, op. cit., 164; cf. E. Norden, *Festgabe Harnack*, 298.

24. Ps. Longinus, *De sublim.* 9, 9; on this cf. Schürer 3, 631, who supposes that the quotation comes from the writing of the rhetorician and alleged Jew Caecilius of Calacte, which is attacked by the unknown author. But this hypothesis is very improbable. For the dependence of the author on Theodore of Gadara, in whom some Jewish background is supposed, see Aulitzky, *PW* 13, 1415ff. E. Norden,

AAB Kl. f. Spr., 1954, no.1, presupposes knowledge of Philo. Cf. W. Bühler, *Beiträge zur Erklärung der Schrift von Erhabenen*, 1964, 34f., who stresses that the designation of Moses as θεσμοθέτης refers to the divine reception of the law.

25. C. H. Dodd, *The Bible and the Greeks*, 99–242; *The Fourth Gospel*, 32f., 38.

26. For Hecataeus see FGrHist 264 F 6, 4 = Diodore 40,3 (Reinach 17), see Vol. I, pp. 18f. and pp. 255f.; cf. also Manetho (first half of the third century BC), following *c.Ap.* 1, 239; also the anti-Jewish councillor of Antiochus VII Sidetes in Posidonius, FGrHist 87 F 109, following Diodore 34 fr. 1 (Reinach 56); Apollonius Molon (first half of the first century BC), according to *c.Ap.*2, 148: ἀθέους καὶ μισανθρώπους, cf. 258; Lysimachus of Alexandria (first century BC), according to *c.Ap.* 1, 309; Apion (first half of the first century AD), according to *c.Ap.*2, 121; Tacitus, *Hist.*5, 5: *adversus omnes alios hostile odium*. Further instances in I. Heinemann, *PW Suppl* 5, 20, cf. *MGWJ* 82, 1938, 166, and F. M. T. de Liagre Böhl, *Opera minora*, 1953, 117ff. The otherness and xenophobia of the Jews also appears in Esther 3.8 and in the Greek expansions (see Vol. I, pp. 101f.): 3.13d, e (B 4f.), cf. III Macc. 3.24, and on it E. Bi(c)kerman(n), *PAAJR* 20, 1951, 127. For the whole thing see also Vol. I, pp. 152f. and below, pp. 300, 306f.

27. This is already true for the time before Alexander, see Herodotus 1, 105, the Astarte of Ashkelon as *Aphrodite Urania*, and also the interesting inscription of an Ashkelonite on Delos as thanksgiving for being saved from pirates, ed. by Clermont-Ganneau, *CRAI* 1909, 308 = *ZDPV* 36, 1913, 233: Ἀστάρτηι Παλαιστίνηι Ἀφροδίτηι Οὐρανίαι. The Baal of Carmel already appears in Ps. Skylax before 345 BC as *Zeus:* (Κάρμελος) ὅρος ἱερὸν Διός, see C. Müller, *GGM* 1, 79, and K. Galling, *Studien zur Geschichte Israels*, 1964, 197, 203. He was later identified with the Zeus of Heliopolis-Baalbek: see below, n. 244. The Baal of Tabor was worshipped as 'Zeus Atabyrios' long before Alexander in Rhodes, on Sicily and in the Crimea, see O. Eissfeldt, *Kleine Schriften* 2, 1963, 29–54 (32f.). After Alexander this idea became common property. The Idumean Cos and the Phoenician Rešeph were transformed into *Apollo*, and for that reason the Apollo cult was probably so strongly represented in Marisa, Adora (see Vol. I, pp. 61f.) and in many places on the coastal plain, see Schürer 2, 5ff., 31, 35f., 133; S. A. Cook, *Religion*, 113f., 129, 203ff. Even the Idumean mercenaries in Egypt worshipped their Kos there as Apollo, see OGIS 737 and F. Zucker, AAB 1937, 1938, no. 6, 15. The cult of *Heracles* was also a favourite in Palestine, helped on by the old identification with the Tyrian Melkart, see Schürer 2, 31, 35, 39ff.; S. A. Cook, op. cit., 69, 135ff., 168f.; cf. C. N. Johns, *QDAP* 2, 1933, 45. His cult was significant in Gaza and Acco-Ptolemais (see Schürer 2, 56f.: foundation legends) and in Rabbath-Ammon-Philadelphia, where there was perhaps a Tyrian colony (see above, n. I, 340), see F. M. Abel, *RB* NS 5, 1908, 568–77, and *HP* 1, 58; cf. Clermont-Ganneau, *RAO* 8, 1924, 121–5, and S. A. Cook, op. cit. 165. *Dionysus* also achieved great significance; possibly his cult was helped on by the Ptolemies, as they traced their descent from him; see Schürer 2, 35, 38, 44f., 55, 56; S. A. Cook, op. cit., 194ff. Scythopolis-Nysa and Damascus were specially associated with Dionysus by their foundation legends. Among other things, the Nabatean Dusares was identified with Dionysus, see below, n. 269. On the whole question see Schürer 2, 27–47; S. A. Cook, op. cit., passim, and esp. 153–225;

T. Klausner, etc., *RAC* 1, 1066–1101, on the Hellenization of the various local Palestinian-Syrian Baals. For the problem see E. Bi(c)kerman(n), *Journal of the Warburg Institute* 1, 1937/38, 189ff.; *GM*, 95f.; D. van Berchem, *Syria* 44, 1967, 73ff., 307ff.

28. Cf. e.g. the dedicatory inscription to Hadad and Atargatis in Acco Ptolemais from the second century BC made by Diodotus son of Neophthalmus, presumably a Greek with his family, see M. Avi-Yonah, *IEJ* 9, 1959, 1–12. In AD 105/6, two slaves in Berytus could still dedicate an altar to Atargatis, who was called at the same time Artemis, Venus Heliopolitana and Dea Syria, see SEG 14, 824. For the extension of the cult of Atargatis-Astarte (and of Hadad) in the Greek world see P. Lambrechts/P. Noyen, *NClio* 6, 1954, 258–77; cf. also W. Fauth, *KP* 1, 1401ff.

29. For Apollonius Molon see W. Schmid, *PW* 2, 141ff. In contrast to his contemporary Posidonius he was hostile to philosophy. He had no comprehension of the 'philosophical' components of Jewish thought.

30. Agatharcides of Cnidos (second century BC), according to *c.Ap.* 1, 208ff.; Cicero, *pro Flacc.* 67 (Reinach 238): *barbara superstitio;* similarly Quintilian, *Inst. orat.* 3, 7, 21 (Reinach 284); see also the judgment on the later development of Jewish religion until it became δεισιδαιμονία in Posidonius, Vol. I, p. 259.

31. Tacitus, *Hist.* 5, 2–5, cf. I. Heinemann, *PW Suppl* 5, 36ff., and generally on the treatment of biblical history in Graeco-Roman writers, Liagre-Böhl, op. cit., 105ff. The starting point of this anti-Jewish Graeco-Roman history writing is Manetho, see *c.Ap.* 1, 227–87, and also Apollonius Molon, FGrHist 728 F 1 = Eusebius, *Pr.Ev.* 9, 19 (Reinach 60f.), according to Alexander Polyhistor.

32. On this M. P. Nilsson, *GGR²* 2, 294ff., 573ff., and *HTR* 56, 1963, 101–20; cf. also Tarn/Griffith, *Hellenistic Civilization,* 339f., and J. Kaerst, *Geschichte des Hellenismus* 2, ²1926, 198ff., 233ff.

33. M. P. Nilsson, *GGR²* 2, 296ff., 569ff.; M. Pohlenz, *Die Stoa* 1, 96f.; for the first beginnings in Xenophanes, Anaxagoras, etc., see W. Jaeger, *Die Theologie der frühen griechischen Denker,* 1953, 50ff., 197f., 209f. For the whole matter see E. Zeller, *Die Entwicklung des Monotheismus bei den Griechen, Vortr. u. Abhandlungen* 1, ²1875, 1–29. This development found a climax in the first century AD in the pseudo-Aristotelian writing *De mundo,* which in individual points comes very near to the Jewish belief in creation, see M. P. Nilsson, op. cit., 2, 297ff. n. 1, lit., and *HTR* 56, 1963, 102ff. Wilamowitz-Moellendorf, *Der Glaube der Hellenen* 2, ³1959, 450f., supposes that the influence of Posidonius lies behind this 'decisive monotheism'. J. Bernays even thought of Tiberius Julius Alexander, nephew of Philo and apostate, as author, whereas Bergk ascribed the writing of Nicolaus of Damascus, friend of Herod; on this see E. Zeller, *Kleine Schriften* 1, 1910, 332f., 345f. and H. Strohm, *MusHelv* 9, 1952, 137–75. Cf. also above n. III, 817.

34. Origen, *c.Cels.* 1, 24 and 5, 41 (45), ed. H. Chadwick, 1953, 23f., 297 (299); cf. also 5, 34. For what follows see above all M. P. Nilsson, *HTR* 56, 1963, 101–20.

35. Macrobius, *Sat.* 1, 18, 19f., see also Reinach 70 n. 1 and R. Reitzenstein, *Die hellenistische Mysterienreligionen,* ³1927, 148ff.; cf. Ganschinietz, *PW* 9, 708; A. D. Nock, *Conversion,* 1933, 111f.; M. P. Nilsson, *GGR²,* 477f.; Goodenough,

Symbols 2, 207, and H. Kusch, *RAC* 3, 432ff. Cf. also Julian the Apostate, *Ep.* 89a (154f. Bidez).

36. See above n. 21; cf. also Augustine, *De civ. Dei* 4, 9 = Varro fr. I 58a, ed. Agahd, op. cit., 163; see on this E. Norden, *Festgabe A. von Harnack*, 1921, 299. The *Antiquitates rerum humanarum et divinarum* were probably composed between 60 and 50 BC, see H. Dahlmann, *PW Suppl* 6, 1178, 1230.

37. Augustine, *De civ. Dei* 4, 11 = Varro, fr. I 15a, Agahd; cf. also 7.13 = Varro, fr. I 15c, Agahd, op. cit., 149: '(*Ad Iovem) ceteri referendi sunt . . . cum hic ipse sint omnes, sive quando partes eius vel potestates existimantur . . .*', on which see M. P. Nilsson, *HTR* 56, 1963, 107f. Antiochus of Ashkelon was the direct teacher of Varro; he probably knew Posidonius indirectly, as he was very indebted to the Stoa generally, see H. Dahlmann, *PW Suppl* 6, 1174f.

38. Servius, *ad Aen.* 4, 638 (1, 574, ed. Thilo), cf. *ad Georgica* 1, 5; see M. P. Nilsson, op. cit., 108f.; similarly also Cicero, *De nat. deor.* 2, 28, 71: '*deus pertinens per naturam cuiusque rei, per terras Ceres, per maria Neptunus, alii per alia, poterunt intellegi qui qualesque sint.*' The common source also seems to be Posidonius here, but the basic idea is even older; see M. Pohlenz, op. cit., 1, 96f. and 2, 97, and I. Heinemann, *Poseidonius* 2, 135–43.

39. Zeno, SVF 1, 28 no. 102, according to Diog.Laert. 7, 135; cf. also Chrysippus SVF 2, 269, lines 13ff. no. 937; 305 no. 1021; 315 no. 1076 according to Philodemus of Gadara, see also M. P. Nilsson, *GGR*² 2, 258.

40. M. P. Nilsson, *GGR*² 2, 427ff., and *HTR* 56, 1963, 103ff. Cf. above all O. Kern, *Orphicorum Fragmenta*, ²1963, 90–93 frs. 21 and 21a = Plato, *Laws* 716a/716a, and on this see K. Ziegler, *PW* 18, 1359ff. For Aristobulus see Vol. I, pp. 165ff.; for Artapanus, who makes Moses–Musaeus the teacher of Orpheus and thus transposes the usual relationship, see above n. II, 262. Furthermore see the 'Testament' of Orpheus in its various recensions in O. Kern, op. cit., 255–65 = nos. 245–7. No. 248 = Clem.Alex., *Strom.* 5, 125, 1, should not now be included among them, but it is equally of Jewish origin. For the 'Testament' see N. Walter, *Aristobulos*, TU 86, 1964, 103–15, 184ff., 202–61, who does not accept that it derives from the original Aristobulus, and K. Ziegler, *PW* 18, 1398ff. P. Gurob, no. 1 = O. Kern, op. cit., 101ff., no. 31, which comes from the third century BC, shows the early emergence of Orphic and Dionysiac mysteries in Ptolemaic Egypt, cf. M. P. Nilsson, op. cit., 2, 244f. For the encounter with Jewish see M. Hengel in *Festgabe K. G. Kuhn*, 1971, 165.

41. Valerius Maximus, epit. of Julius Paris 1, 3, 3, ed. Kempf 16/17 = Reinach 258f.; cf. the shorter epitome of Nepotianus: '*Iudaeos quoque, qui Romanis tradere sacra sua conati erant, idem Hispalus exterminavit arasque privatas e publicis locis abiecit.*' This too could refer to a mixed Jewish-syncretistic cult, cf. I Macc. 1.55 and R. Reitzenstein, *Mysterienreligionen*, 105: 'Both exoduses complemented one another.' In detail, E. Bickerman(n), *RIDA* 5, 1958, 144–53.

42. Schürer 3, 58f.; E. Meyer, *UAC* 2, 264 n. 3; 3, 460; Ganschienietz, *PW* 9, 714. H. Leon, *The Jews of Ancient Rome*, 1960, 3f., conjectures a confusion of Sabbath-Sabazius; cf. further H. Vogelstein, *History of the Jews in Rome*, 1940, 10, 14. The view of J. B. Frey, *RSR* 20, 1930, 273f., cf. Leon, op. cit., 4, that it was nothing to do with Jews, is quite improbable. K. Latte, *Römische Religionsgeschichte*, 1960, 275, remains undecided.

43. F. Cumont, *CRAI* 1906, 63–79; cf. *Musée Belge* 14, 1910, 55–60, and *Die orientalische Religionen*, 58ff., 231 n.60, 316 n.25; R. Reitzenstein, op. cit., 104ff.; see also H. Gressmann, *ZAW* 43, 1925, 16ff., and 'Jewish Life in Ancient Rome', in *Jewish Studies in Memory of J. Abrahams*, 1927, 171f.; H. Lietzmann, *The Beginnings of the Early Church*, 1937, 161f.; O. S. Rankin, *The Origins of the Festival of Hanukkah*, 1930, 126ff., 142ff.; R. McL.Wilson, *The Gnostic Problem*, ²1964, 11f. M. P. Nilsson, *GGR*² 2, 661–7, also gives a good survey.

44. I Macc. 15.15–24, esp. v.16. Doubt about the authenticity of the letter is hardly justified, as K. D. Schunck, *Die Quellen*, 32–6, shows. For dating see Schürer 1, 250ff.; E. Meyer, *UAC* 2, 264; F. M. Abel, *Macc.*, 267: L. Calpurnius Piso, 139 BC; E. Bickermann, *GM*, 175, and Abel/Starcky, 207, differ: L. Caecilius Metellus, 142 BC. The senate decision of *Antt.* 14, 145–8, falsely dated by Josephus, belongs in this context. For Reitzenstein, see op. cit., 106f. n. 1, cf. Bickerman(n), *RIDA* 5, 1958, 146.

45. *Antt.* 12, 147–53: the letter to Zeuxis. On its authenticity see A. Schalit, *JQR* 50, 1960, 298–318, see also Schürer 3, 12f., and G. Kittel, *TLZ* 69, 1944, 11. For the furthering of the cult of Sabazius in the Pergamene kingdom see Schaefer, *PW*, 2 R.1, 1544, and F. Cumont, *Orient.Rel.*, 193, 314 n.4; cf. OGIS 331 ll.34, 4g. In 132 BC, Attalus III made over his kingdom to the Romans by testament. About eighty years after the first appearance of Jews in Rome, Cicero again attests the great influence of Jews from Asia Minor in the metropolis, see *pro Flacco* 66–69 (Reinach 237–42), cf. also the Sabazius inscription of Elian(os) Eisr(aelites), J. Keil/A v. Premerstein, 'Bericht über eine 2. Reise in Lydien', *DAW* 54, 1911, no.218, and on it G. Kittel, op. cit., 16. For the question see also E. Bickerman(n), *RIDA* 5, 1958, 148ff., though he interprets these 'Jews' in too orthodox a sense.

46. Cf. III Macc. 2.29f. Even if III Macc., which arose about the turn of the first century BC, is legendary, see V. A. Tcherikover, *ScrHieros* 7, 1961, 1–21, it contains good historical material, as is shown by its report on the battle of Raphia (see Vol.I, pp.8f.). The great interest of Philopator in the Dionysus cult is indisputable, see M. P. Nilsson, *GGR*² 2, 161f., and especially on the important Berlin papyrus (BGU VI, 1211 verso = SB 7266), op. cit., 162 n.2, lit. The earlier material has an extensive account but is too one-sided, see P. Perdrizet, *RevEtudAnc* 12, 1910, 216–47; cf. also F. J. Dölger, *Antike und Christentum* 2, 1930, 103f., and J. Tondriau, *Aeg* 26/27, 1946/47, 84–95, and 30, 1950, 57, 66. Also Tarn/Griffith, *Hellenistic Civilization*, 212f.; T. A. Brady, *The Reception of the Egyptian Cults by the Greeks*, 1935, 25, and Volkmann, *PW* 23, 1689f. Further details above, n.III, 611.

47. Tacitus, *Hist.* 5, 5, rejects the identification; similarly J. Lydus, *De mens.* 4, 53 (Wünsch 109, 111); Plutarch, *Quaest.conv.* 4, 6 (Reinach 142–7), on the other hand, is positive. On this F. Cumont, op. cit., 314 n.7. Possibly this identification is closely connected with the mixed cult of Sabaoth-Sabazius, see M. P. Nilsson, *GGR*² 2, 662f., and R. Reitzenstein, op. cit., 105ff., 146ff., though his conclusions go much too far, whereas Liagre-Böhl, op. cit., 120f., makes too little of the connections; cf. also IIMacc. 14.33 and Vol. I, p. 299. The alleged connections between the Jewish God and *Adonis*, see H. Gressmann, *ZAW* 43, 1925, 17; cf. N. A. Dahl, *Das Volk Gottes*, ²1963, 105, and O. Rankin, op. cit.,

187ff., *Attis*, see R. Reitzenstein, op. cit., 145f., and F. Cumont, op. cit., 231 n. 60, and *Osiris*, see Reitzenstein, *Poimandres*, 1904, 182ff., hardly have any real foundation. The idea that the Jews worshipped *Kronos-Saturn*, see Tacitus, *Hist.* 5, 4, and Lydus, *De mens.* 4, 53 (Wünsch 110), may have been caused above all by their hallowing of the Sabbath, the day of Saturn (see Tibullus, *Eleg.* 1, 3, 17f. = Reinach 247); of course, it may also be connected with the identification of the God of the Jews with the supreme Semitic god of heaven: H. Gressmann, op. cit., 19, 21, cf. also Philo Byblius, FGrHist 790 F 2 = *Pr.Ev.* 1, 10, 16: Kronos = 'El, son of 'Uranus' and grandson of 'Hypsistos', see Vol. I, pp. 297f. See also I. Heinemann, *PW Suppl* 5, 31.

48. OGIS 73, 74 = CIJ 2, 445 nos. 1537–8; cf. Schürer 3, 50, and Tcherikover, *HC*, 352.

49. OGIS 70–72 and 37; on this see the survey on the inscriptions in the temple by W. Schwarz, *JbPhil* 153, 1896, 145–70. For Pan as the universal deity, especially in Egypt, see F. Brommer, *PW Suppl* 8, 1005. Cf. also CH 5, 11 and 12, 22f.

50. For the general attitude of the Letter of Aristeas see V. A. Tcherikover, *HTR* 51, 1958, 59–85; cf. CPJ 1, 37, 42f. and *HC*, 351, though he stresses too one-sidedly that the letter is only directed to Jews. We may include all Greeks interested in Judaism.

51. Chrysippus, SVF 2, 305 no. 1021 = Diog. Laert. 7, 142; 312 no. 1062f.; 315 no. 1076, according to Philodemus of Gadara.

52. Ps. Arist. 135–138. Similarly Wisdom 13.1ff. finds the (Greek) worship of stars and elements preferable to the Egyptian worship of animals in 15.14ff.

53. V. A. Tcherikover, *HTR* 51, 1958, 71, cf. Ps. Arist. 235, 256; see also Vol. I, pp. 90, 164.

54. Tcherikover, op. cit., 70. Possibly the Jewish self-awareness at this point takes up the early Greek judgment of, say, a Hecataeus, see F. Jacoby, *PW* 7, 2765f.

55. The probably original recension contained in Ps. Justin, *De monarch.* 2 = O. Kern, op. cit., 256ff. no. 245, shows that the name Zeus appeared in the Jewish Testament of Orpheus (see l. 16). The criticism made by E. Norden, *Agnostos Theos*, 122, of Aristobulus because of this alteration of the name is unfounded. He does not follow the methods of other Jewish 'forgers'. N. Walter, op. cit., 101, rightly rejects any claim that Aristobulus is 'dependent' on Ps. Aristeas, cf. also 110ff.

56. *c.Ap.* 2, 168, cf. 160–163, 188f., 221, 237, following the translation of Exod. 22.27 LXX, which deliberately diverges from the Hebrew wording, similarly *Antt.* 4.207. Cf. *c.Ap.* 2, 255ff.: Plato's knowledge of God corresponds to that of the Jews. For Josephus' universalist view of God, with relatively few nationalistic limitations, which is probably also conditioned by his political fate, see A. Schlatter, *Wie sprach Josephus von Gott*, BFCT 14, 1910, 49–55, 68, and G. Delling, *Klio* 43–45, 1965, 263–9. For Philo see *De prov.* II, 91, the cry 'By Zeus!'.

57. For Euhemerism generally see M. P. Nilsson, *GGR²* 2, 283ff.; for Judaism see A. Schlatter, *GI³*, 199, 424 n. 185; Bousset/Gressmann, 305; K. Thraede, *RAC* 6, 882ff.; see also Vol. I, pp. 89f. For the Rabbis see the identification Eve = Isis and Joseph = Serapis (Osiris), AZ 43a Bar.; perhaps this is dependent on the designation of Joseph as Osarsiph and leader of the

Hyksos by Manetho, *c.Ap.* 1, 238, 250, 265, 286, see Liagre-Böhl, op. cit., 110; cf. also G. Kittel, *Die Probleme des palästinischen Spätjudentums*, 1926, 168–94, and S. Lieberman, *Hellenism in Jewish Palestine*, 137 n. 87. Firm. Mat., *Err. prof. rel.* 13, 2, interprets Serapis as *Σάρρας παῖς* = Joseph.

58. Bousset/Gressmann, 305f.: it appears in early apocalyptic: I Enoch 19.1; 99.7; in Essenism: Jub. 11.3f.; 19.28; 22.16f.; and also in the Diaspora, Deut. 32.17; Ps. 95.5; 105.37 LXX; Sib. 3, 547, 554; fr. 1, 22, ed. Kurfess 68, and I Cor. 10.20. Cf. also H. J. Schoeps, *Aus frühchristlicher Zeit*, 73ff. For the Greek parallels see above, n. III, 803.

59. Cf. Preisendanz, PGM 1, 300: *ἄγγελε πρῶτε [θε]οῦ Ζηνὸς μεγάλοιο 'Ιάω*, cf. 5, 471ff.; 3, 76ff.: Iao Mithra: 3, 211: *πύρινον Διὸς ἄγγελον θεῖον 'Ιαώ*, 4, 1000, 1010: 'Iao, Bal, Bal', etc.; see also Goodenough, *Symbols* 2, 191, 194f., 200f., 205f., etc., and L. H. Feldman, *JewSocStud.* 22, 1960, 233f.

60. Jewish syncretistic mixed cults seem to have come into being more intensively in the Judaism of Asia Minor and the Bosphorus, see above n. 45, 47 and below, n. 265.

61. W. Foerster, *TDNT* 3, 1049: before the first century BC there is hardly any evidence for the address 'Kyrios' or 'Kyria' for a god or goddess. It appears relatively early in the Isis cult as an expression of personal association with the deity, see n. III, 647. Cf. already the hymn to Demetrius Poliorcetes, Duris, FGrHist 76 F 13, p. 142, 12.

62. Wilamowitz-Möllendorf, *Der Glaube der Hellenen* 1, 17, cf. M. P. Nilsson, *GGR*² 1, 812 ff.

63. On this see E. Bickermann, *GM*, 92–6; *RHR* 115, 1937, 211ff.; *Journal of the Warburg Institute* I, 1937/38, 187–96. Cf. already E. Norden, *Agnostos Theos*, 25–62, cf. 83ff. and 115–24; see also below, n. 234.

64. For Hecataeus, Theophrastus and Strabo/Posidonius see Vol. I, pp. 255ff.; cf. also Petronius, fr. 37 (Reinach 266); Celsus in Origen, *c.Cels.* 5, 6, GCS, Koetschau 2, 5f.; on the *Clouds* see Juvenal, *Sat.* 14, 97 (Reinach 292). For Socrates see Aristophanes, *Clouds* 228ff., 253f., 264f. etc. For the alleged 'godlessness' of the Jews see Manetho, *c.Ap.* 1, 239; Apollonius Molon, *c.Ap.* 2, 79, 148, 258 (see n. 26 above); Posidonius, FGrHist 87, F 109, 2 = Diodore 34 fr. (Reinach 57): *ἀσεβεῖς καὶ μισουμένους ὑπὸ τῶν θεῶν*; Lysimachus, *c.Ap.* 1, 309ff.; Pliny, *Hist. nat.* 13, 4, 46: '*gens contumelia numinum insignis*'. Cf. also the *ἀνόσιοι 'Ιουδαῖοι* in Egypt, CPJ 2, 84 no. 157, ll. 43, 49f. (l. 78 *ἀσεβεῖς*); 2, 93 no. 158a col. 6, 14; and from the time of the revolt in AD 116–7: 2, 238 no. 438 l. 4; 2, 248 no. 443 col. 2, 4f. In the charge of *ἀθεότης* made against Fl. Clemens and Fl. Domitilla at the time of Domitian (Dio Cassius 67, 14, Reinach 195f.), it remains open whether the *τὰ τῶν 'Ιουδαίων ἔθη* is a conversion to Judaism or to Christianity. On the other hand see the defence made by Josephus against the charge of *asebia* which comes from about the same time, see G. Delling, *Klio* 43–45, 1965, 265f.

65. A summary of the earlier literature is given by R. Marcus, *Josephus* 7, LCL, 1943, 767f.; see further J. Regner, *PW*, 2 R. 6, 1629ff.; J. E. Bruns, *Scripture* 7, 1955, 2–5; B. Mazar, *IEJ* 7, 1957, 137–45; S. Zeitlin, *The Rise and Fall*, 1964, 60–7; M. Stern, *Tarbiz* 32, 1962, 35–47; V. Tcherikover, *HC* 70ff., 126–42, 458ff.

66. CPJ 1, 115ff., 118ff. no. 1; see above, n. I, 306. The citadel is certainly to be sought in the environs of 'Araq el Emir (Wadi eṣ-Ṣir) in Transjordania, where the inscription טוביה in Aramaic has been preserved over two caves: CIJ 2, 105 no. 868 (lit.). It is no longer possible to decide from which 'Tōbiyyā' the inscription comes, see G. Dalman, *PJB* 16, 1920, 34f. Possibly it is an epitaph, see K. Galling, *Die Welt des Orients* 2, 1, 1954, 4. For the position of the *birta* see B. Mazar, op. cit., 141 n. 21.

67. Neh. 2.10, 19; 4.1; 6.1ff. etc.; see above all 6.17ff. and 13.4ff. Possibly he was a Persian governor in the Ammonite region, see H. Gressmann, SAB 1921, 665, and A. Alt, *Kleine Schriften* 2, 341.

68. B. Maisler (= Mazar), *Tarbiz* 12, 1940/41, 109–23, and *IEJ* 7, 1957, 142ff., 227ff., and V. Tcherikover, *HC*, 430 n. 71, conjecture that the Tobiads were entirely of Jewish descent and that their family goes well back into the pre-exilic period. On the other hand, the challenging of the purity of Israelite descent in the family of Tobiah, Ezra 2.60 = Neh. 7.62, speaks against this, and cf. W. Rudolph, *Esra und Nehemia*, 1949, 24. H. Gressmann regards the Tobiads as 'rich semi-Jews living in Ammon', op. cit., 666; similarly E. R. Bevan, *A History of Egypt*, 1927, 72f., and L. Finkelstein, *HTR* 36, 1943, 31. Priestly descent is conjectured by B. Maisler-Mazar, *Tarbiz* 12, 1940–41, 116, and *IEJ* 7, 1957, 230f., 234f.; S. Zeitlin, op. cit., 62f., and *PAAJR* 4, 1932–33, 215–9; cf. also V. Tcherikover, *GC*, 126, 156.

69. CPJ 1, 119ff. no. 1. Nicanor of Cnidos is described in l. 14 as τῶν περὶ Τουβίαν just as in l. 4 Zeno belongs to τῶν περὶ 'Απολλώνιον; that is, Tobias had not only Macedonian (cf. ll. 7 and 18) and Jewish soldiers in his cleruchy – the 'Persians', on the other hand, are not to be understood in an ethnic sense (ll. 17f., cf. CPJ 1, 13f., 51; 2, 187 no. 417, 5ff., etc.) – but also Greeks in his personal service. Possibly Nicanor was also at the same time an agent of Apollonius, see Rostovtzeff, *HW* 3, 1403 n. 149.

70. CPJ 1, 125ff. no. 4 (PCZ 59076), see Vol. I, p. 59; on this cf. H. Gressmann, op. cit., 664: the greeting says 'that Tobias moves on the same foot as Apollonius'.

71. See the collection in A. Vincent, *La Religion des Judéo-Araméens*, 1937, 92f., cf. also P. Cowley 21, 2, which was written from Jerusalem, and on it E. G. Kraeling, *The Brooklyn Museum Aramaic Papyri*, 1953, 84, and P. Grelot, *VT* 4, 1954, 352ff. As in the Tobias letter this is a 'formule de politesse', though it indicates a degree of generosity. The Book of Ahikar, in which the God 'Šamaš' appears, did not cause any offence. For the letter of Tobias see Tcherikover, CPJ 1, 127 n. 4 and *HC*, 71; cf. also J. Klausner, *Hist.* 2, 130, and W. Schubart, *AO* 35, 2, 1937, 9.

72. R. Meyer, *TDNT* 6, 77. In the post-exilic period the commandment about circumcision was intensified, see Gen. 17.12ff. (P); Exod. 12.43ff. and Jub. 15.13f.; on this J. Jeremias, *Jerusalem in the Time of Jesus*, 348f. Tobias particularly stresses the fact that two slaves are not circumcised, as these were more valuable in the eyes of the Greeks, because the Greeks regarded circumcision as being reprehensible, see R. Meyer, op. cit., 6, 78 ll. 13ff. Possibly they were intended for use in Egypt as prostitutes, see Tcherikover, *Miz.*, 18, cf. Joel 4.3.

73. For the prohibition of the sale of Jewish slaves to non-Jews see CD

12.10f.; cf. the bitterness of the people against Herod in *Antt.* 16, 2ff. because he had Jewish criminals sold abroad as slaves. See also Jeremias, op. cit., 350 n. 7, with reference to *Git.* 4.6 and *S.Deut.* 23, 16, § 259.

74. On this see M. Hengel, op. cit., 325ff.; cf. e.g. his sacrifice in the Capitol, *Antt.* 14, 388 = *Bell.* 1, 285.

75. Joseph: *Antt.* 12, 157–85, 224; Hyrcanus and his brothers: *Antt.* 12, 186–222; 228–36.

76. The source of Josephus itself seems to contradict this arrangement: in 12, 158 it mentions Ptolemy III Euergetes (246–21 BC); despite Niese (app. ad.loc.), the name is hardly a gloss, but reproduces the original historical situation. For dates see Tcherikover, *HC*, 130f.; S. Zeitlin, *PAAJR* 4, 1932–33, 179, and *The Rise and Fall*, 60; above all, M. Stern, *Tarbiz* 32, 1962, 35–47. R. Marcus, *Josephus* 7, LCL, 82c arrives at a later dating under Euergetes. For the third Syrian war see F. M. Abel, *HP* 1, 48ff., and Vol. I, p. 7. The impossibility of the dates in Josephus is not noted sufficiently by E. Cuq, *Syria* 8, 1927, 143–62; J. Regner, *PW*, 2 R. 6, 1929ff., and Bo Reicke, *The New Testament Period*, 1969, 48. Josephus' note in *Antt.* 12, 224 that the tax farmer Joseph died at the time of Seleucus IV (187–75 BC) is valueless, as immediately after that Josephus speaks of the death of Onias II, the father of Simon the Just, who at that time had already been dead for thirty or forty years. Joseph probably died before the change of rule in Palestine.

77. *Antt.* 12, 196ff., 221f., 228ff. The establishment of Hyrcanus in 'Araq el Emir in the sphere of the old Ptolemaic cleruchy of his grandfather in the Ammanitis was possible only with the support of Ptolemaic authority, because of the superior power of his brothers.

78. Tcherikover, *HC*, 141f.; H. Willrich, *Die Juden und Griechen*, 1895, 99, rightly seeks for the author in Egypt and contrasts him with those Jewish writers who, like Ps.Aristeas, 'could not discourse enough on the intimate friendship of the legitimate high-priestly family with the royal house'. Of course, both he and A. Bücher, *Die Tobiaden und Oniaden*, 1899, 88, 95, are wrong in assuming a Samaritan source (100).

79. Cf. Dan.1 and the prayer of Esther, LXX 4.17, and on it A. Büchler, op. cit., 85 and Tcherikover, *HC*, 460 n.44. Cf. on the other hand the compromise in Ps.Aristeas 182–186, 293f.

80. *Antt.* 12, 187ff., 206: here Hyrcanus compares God and the king.

81. *Antt.* 12, 224; cf. already the characterization in 12, 160.

82. Tcherikover, *HC*, 134, 140.

83. In many respects the Joseph narrative imitates the 'court histories', see above, n. I, 218.

84. See the description of the Tobiad Joseph in *Antt.* 12, 161, 167, and on the other hand the negative picture of Onias II: 158, 161f., 171. It is less probable that Onias gave away the '*prostasia*' of his own free will. See also above, n. I, 185.

85. *Antt.* 12, 168, cf. also Josephus, *Antt.* 11, 306–12; cf. J. D. Purvis, *JNES* 24, 1965, 88–94, see also Vol. I, p. 49, and n. I, 183. However, *Antt.* 12, 156 reports boundary struggles between Samaritans and Jews in the third century BC. Cf. also the hate of Ben Sira in 50.26b and Test.Levi 6.4ff.; 7.2. On the other hand,

the good relations of Herod with the Samaritans should be noted, M. Hengel, op. cit., 331 n. 4. The primitive Christian mission in Samaria in Acts 8.1ff. must also have been felt to be an affront.

86. A. Schlatter, *Die Theologie des Judentums nach dem Bericht des Josephus*, 1932, 270.

87. *Antt.* 12, 184, 199f., 203, 208. For the presents see 12, 185f., 208; cf. already the letter of Tobias to Ptolemy II and the dispatch of valuable animals which is connected with it, CPJ 1, 178f. no. 5 = PCZ 59075.

88. *Antt.* 12, 221f., 229: after the death of Joseph the majority of the Jewish population followed the older sons of Joseph and the high priest Simon II, see Tcherikover, *HC* 80f., 154; see also Vol. I, p. 9, on the party struggles in Jerusalem according to Dan. 11.14.

89. For the identification of Simon II and 'the Just' of *'Ab.* I, 1, against Josephus, *Antt.* 12, 43, 157, see G. F. Moore, *Judaism* 1, 34ff., and 'Simeon the Righteous', in: *Israel Abrahams Memorial Vol.*, 1927, 348–64. He is followed by R. Marcus, *Josephus* 7, LCL, 732–6 (lit.); the conjecture already appears in L. Herzfeld, *Geschichte des Volkes Israel* 2, 1855, 377. Cf. also L. Finkelstein, *The Pharisees*[3] 2, 575ff., 581, 583, though his picture is too romantic. He makes Simon 'the leading exponent of Hasidean doctrine'; similarly Tcherikover, *HC* 125. In view of the scanty accounts about him, such conclusions are misguided. He probably strengthened Jewish self-awareness against Hellenistic influences by a nationalist policy, see Sir. 50.1–24, and Vol. I, pp. 133ff. The general Hasidic criticism of the leading priests is also directed against him.

90. *Antt.* 12, 138–44 and see on this Vol. I, pp. 9f., and n. I, 32 and 33 lit; Vol. I, pp. 28f., and n. I, 192. For the priestly edict (12, 145f.) see E. Bi(c)kermann, *Syria* 25, 1496–48, 67–85, and in criticism Tcherikover, *HC*, 84f. For the matter see *M. Kelim* 1, 8. Neh. 13.15–22 would be a parallel case.

91. He was the brother of Menelaus who later became high priest, see Vol. I, pp. 279f.; cf. also above, n. I, 43 and n. I, 167/8.

92. II Macc. 4.1–6; the account has strongly apologetic features. See Tcherikover, *HC*, 156ff., and above all O. Plöger, *Theocracy*, 5. For the external political situation see Vol. I, pp. 10f.

93. Almost directly on the line between Jericho and Amman, 29 km east of Jericho and 17 km west of Amman: see P. W. Lapp, *BASOR* 165, 1962, 16. The ruins were discovered in 1818 by two English naval officers: C. L. Irby and J. Mangles, *Travels in Egypt and Nubia, Syria and the Holy Land*, reprinted 1852 (I had no access to the first edition of 1844).

94. *Syria, Princeton University Archaeology Expedition* 1904/5, Div. II, Sect. A, 1919, 1–25. For the dating see 16f. Earlier literature is also cited there; cf. also the survey of literature in M. Weippert, *ZDPV* 79, 1963, 165–9.

95. Butler, op. cit., 17: however, only extensive excavations could produce complete certainty.

96. Op. cit., Div. III, sect. A., 5ff.

97. *RB* 29, 1920, 198ff.

98. SAB 1921, 665ff., see below, n. IV, 124.

99. E. Meyer, *Ursprung* 2, 134 n. 1; H. Willrich, *APF* 7, 1924, 64; G. Ricciotti, *History of Israel* 2, [2]1958, 210; Bo Reicke, *The New Testament Era*,

47, 51, and above all Jewish scholarship: Tcherikover, CPJ 1, 116, and *HC*, 430 n.69; J. Klausner, *Hist.*2, 141f.; B. Mazar, *IEJ* 7, 1957, 141.

100. A. Momigliano, op. cit., 174f.; Watzinger, *DP* 2, 14f.

101. *Archaeology of Palestine*, ³1954, 149.

102. *ZDPV* 71, 1955, 75f. Here Plöger points to the Ma'bed of 'Amrit and Lucian, *Dea Syria* 46.

103. *BASOR* 165, 1962, 16–34, and 171, 1963, 5–39.

104. *BASOR* 165, 1962, 34, and 171, 1963, 24: 'Any attempt to alter Josephus' date for the Qasr was misguided'; see also 37ff.

105. See already Butler, *Syria*, 11 and 19, and on this P. W. Lapp, *BASOR* 171, 1963, 24f.: 'The extent to which the Qasr was left unfinished, presumably at the death of Hyrcanus, is difficult to determine.'

106. *BASOR* 171, 1963, 29f., and on this R. Amy, 'Temples à escaliers', *Syria* 27, 1950, 82–136; cf. A. Alt, *Kleine Schriften* III, ²1959, 100–15. F. M. Cross, *HTR* 59, 1966, also assents.

107. Lapp, op. cit., points especially to the temple of Dmeir near Damascus (Amy, op. cit., 83ff.), Slem (op. cit., 87ff = Butler, *Syria*, 356) and Eṣ-Ṣenamen (op. cit., 91f. = Butler, *Syria* 316); one could also add the temple of Mousmieh (op. cit., 94) and the temple of Del at Palmyra (op. cit., 99), together with the front of the temple of Ba'al-Šāmem in Ši which Amy does not mention (Butler, *Syria*, 375); cf. also the survey in Amy, op. cit., 122. He also mentions the parallel of Qasr (123), but although it is in fact the only 'civil monument', cannot decide for the temple hypothesis. For the reconstruction of Qasr see also M. J. B. Brett, *BASOR* 171, 1963, 39–45.

108. *BASOR* 171, 1963, 30.

109. See Butler, *Syria*, 5, 11, 14, 16; Butler discovered one of the eagle figures on the second gate. Cf. also P. W. Lapp, *BASOR* 171, 1963, 29f. For contacts with the ancient 'basilica' see E. Langlotz, *RAC* 1, 1232f., cf. 1234f. on the Syrian temples.

110. D. K. Hill, *BASOR* 171, 1963, 45–55.

11. Cf. on this the eagle episode at the temple of Herod or the destruction of the palace in Tiberias in AD 66 because of its representation of animals; see M. Hengel, op. cit., 105ff., 195ff.

112. *Antt.*12, 231, 233: the caves were used to live and sleep in as well as for banquets; at the same time they were places of refuge. 'Tyrus' is probably to be derived from the Hebrew *ṣwr* (= Aram. *bīrtā*), fortress, citadel, and is contained in the place name Wadi eṣ-Ṣir: see CPJ 1, 116. One of the halls was discovered by P. W. Lapp right next to the village of 'Araq, and a further one is probably identical with the 'square building' already investigated by Butler and excavated by Lapp: see *Syria*, 22ff., and *BASOR* 171, 1963, 33ff. For the caves with their two Tobias inscriptions see above, n.66.

113. Thus already E. Littmann, *Syria*, Div. III n.5ff. A. Spiro, 'Samaritans, Tobiads and Judahites', *PAAJR* 20, 1951, conjectures on the basis of indications in Ps.Philo 22.1ff.; 38.1–4 that schismatic services were held earlier by the Tobiads in Transjordania, as in the temple on Gerizim (314f.), although otherwise he can adduce no evidence. That the Tobiad family had already split into a Transjordanian branch and a Jerusalem branch in the middle of the third

century or even in the fourth, the former maintaining good relations with the Samaritans, contradicts Josephus' report (315 n.72); similarly adventurous hypotheses can be found on pp. 336f. Spiro overlooks the late date of the writing, see M. Hengel, *Die Zeloten*, 169 n. 1, and O. H. Steck, *Israel*, 173ff.

114. Josephus, *Bell.* 7, 44f.; cf. E. Bickerman(n), *Byzantion* 21, 1951, 73ff., 82.

115. This development is to be traced *inter alia* back to the institution of the synagogue and its worship. The Theudas affair in Rome shows how zealously the Rabbis in Palestine took care to see that no cultic temple functions were transferred to the Diaspora: Bill. 3, 23. On the other hand, pagans could worship 'the supreme God' in altars, see E. Bickermann, *RIDA* 5, 1958, 137–64. Cf. M. Hengel in *Festgabe für K. G. Kuhn*, 1971, 156ff.

116. Op. cit., 2.14f. Cf. also A. Bentzen, *Daniel*, ²1952, 68, on 9.27b. See below, n. 241.

117. On this see A. Vincent, *La Religion des Judéo-Araméens d'Éléphantine*, 1937, 562ff. passim; for the Jehud coins see the excellent illustration in S. A. Cook, *Religion*, pl. xxxii; the reading Yahu (47f.) is false, see above, n. I, 241; the correct interpretation is יהד, by E. L. Sukenik, *JPOS* 14, 1934, 178ff. Cf. also H. Gressmann, *AOB²*, nos. 362f., 365. Any overinterpretation is, however, to be rejected.

118. For the halls and caves see n. 112 above; the terraces of the gardens and the dam of the reservoir can still be seen.

119. II Macc. 4.26f., see A. Momigliano, op. cit., 193; G. Ricciotti, op. cit., 2, 212f., 220; cf. also Abel, *Macc.*, 339.

120. II Macc. 5.9f.; cf. 1.7. See Vol. I, pp. 72f. For the suicide of Hyrcanus see *Antt.* 12, 236, though this has been given the wrong date by Josephus or his source – the Tobiad narrative – see Momigliano, op. cit., 185, and Ricciotti, op. cit., 223; Tcherikover, *HC*, 468 n. 37, on the other hand presupposes the death of Hyrcanus and simply conjectures a continuance of a pro-Ptolemaic attitude in the Ammanitis.

121. The interpretation of these passages was disputed. Jews from the land of Tob have frequently been conjectured here, see Judg. 11.3 and II Sam. 10.6 (see here, however, LXX as a proper name), thus Wellhausen, *Israelitische und jüdische Geschichte*, ⁸1921, 240 n. 1; H. Gressmann, SAB 1921, 669; E. Meyer, *UAC* 2, 134 n. 1, and Abel, *Macc.*, 93, and *Géographie* 2, 1938, 10: the present eṭ-Ṭaiyibeh between Bostra and Der'a. D. Baly, *The Geography of the Bible*, 1957, 288, suggests Tob in northern Gilead 20 km east of Scythopolis, where there is a second eṭ-Ṭaiyibeh. According to Jehoshua b. Lewi (third century AD), it is identical with Susitha Hippos: *jSheb.* 36c, 51ff., see S. Zeitlin/S. Tedesche, *The First Book of Maccabees*, 1950, 112. The location thus remains completely uncertain. Only the information in the Zeno papyri takes us further, see nn. 122–3.

122. A well attested and presumably original reading, see R. Hanhard, *Macc. liber II*, Septuaginta IX, 2, 1959, 101, on 12.35; see appendix and F. Abel, *Macc.*, 440ff., and Abel/Starcky: Δωσίθεος δέ τις τῶν Τουβιανῶν ἔφιππος, cf. the cavalry in the cleruchy of Tobias, CPJ 1, 119 no. 1, 6f., 13, 19 τῶν Τουβίου ἱππέων κληροῦχος; also the later Jewish 'cavalry', which Herod settled in the Trachonitis: *Antt.* 15, 34ff.; 16, 281ff. etc., and on this M. Hengel, op. cit., 30 n. 1 and 368. For the text of II Macc. 12.35 see also P. Katz, *ZNW* 51, 1960, 16.

123. See above all H. Willrich, *APF* 7, 1924, 63f. B. Niese, *GGMS* 3, 226 n. 1 already put forward the same view; similarly L. H. Vincent, *RB* 29, 1920, 188 n. 5, and especially A. Deissmann, *Byzantinisch-Neugriechische Jahrbücher* 2, 1921, 276f. He stresses that the endings in I Macc. 5.13 and II Macc. 12.17 indicate 'belonging to a person'; cf. further S. Klein, *BJPES* 3, 1936, 115; J. Klausner, *Hist.* 1, 126f.; B. Mazar, op. cit., 139 and Abel/Starcky, 53, 121, 296. For I Macc. 5.13, cf. above all CPJ 1, 122, nos. 2b–2d.

124. SAB 1921, 668, 670ff.; see on the other hand J. Klausner, *The Messianic Idea*, 489.

125. *Hist.* 2, 141 n. 58 and 230f.

126. *Theocracy*, 5.

127. *HC*, 461 n. 50.

128. E. Bickermann, *GM*, passim, and V. Tcherikover, *HC*, 152–203. For Bickermann see the reviews of K. Galling, *OLZ* 42, 1939, 225–8; F. M. Abel, *RB* 47, 1938, 441–6; J. A. Montgomery, *JBL* 59, 1940, 308f.; M. Burrows, *JR* 18, 1938, 219–21, and J. Bonsirven, *RSR* 28, 1938, 612–4. Apart from a few individual critical comments, these are on the whole positive. I. Heinemann, *MGWJ* 82, 1938, 145–72, is more critical. The wild polemic of S. Zeitlin, *JQR* 31, 1940, 199–204, is quite beside the point.

129. Tcherikover, *HC*, 466 n. 17; cf. II Macc. 4.29; also *Antt.* 11, 306.

130. II Macc. 4.7–9; cf. Dan. 11.21f.; cf. Vol. I, pp. 279f.

131. FGrHist 260 F 49, according to Jerome, in *Dan.* 11, 21f. Antiochus was in Athens on the way back from Rome when he was surprised by the news of the death of his brother and was only able to drive out the usurper Heliodorus with the help of Eumenes II of Pergamon, see Appian, *Syr.* 45 and OGIS 248; also M. Zambelli, *Riv di Filol. e di Istruzione classica* 38, 1960, 363–89. For the date of the accession see Sachs/Wiseman, *Iraq* 16, 1954, 204, 208f.; R. Hanhart, op. cit., 55f.; between 3 and 22.9. 175 BC. E. R. Bevan, *CAH* 8, 498, following the note of Porphyry, suggests that the negative judgment in Dan. 11.21 was shared by wide circles in Coele Syria. Cf. O. Mørkholm, *Antiochus IV of Syria*, 1966, 38ff.

132. II Macc. 4.33. The description of Onias III in II Macc. 3.16ff., 33f.; 4.1f.; 15.12 is 'hagiography', see Vol. I, p. 97, and n. II, 318. For the question of historicity see Tcherikover, *HC*, 469 n. 40 and M. Stern, *Zion* 25, 1960/61, 1–15 lit. In his 'hagiographic' account of Onias III, Jason of Cyrene would never have invented the high priest's stay in the pagan sanctuary of Daphne. However, the Oniads were not orthodox in the strict sense, see already H. A. Redpath, *AJT* 9, 1905, 43; Tarn/Griffith, *Hellenistic Civilization*, 214, and L. Finkelstein, *The Pharisees*, ³1962, 585. The argument of I. L. Seeligmann, *The Septuagint Version of Isaiah*, 1948, 94, which R. Hanhart, op. cit., 87, follows, basically contradicts the author's own view. S. Krauss, *REJ* 45, 1902, 30f., draws attention to a Rabbinic tradition about Daphne in Antioch as one of the three places of the Israelite exile (*jSanh.* 29c, 63f., R. Šemuel b. Naḥaman, c. AD 300).

133. Tcherikover, *HC*, 179, 471 n. 5, and *Hellenistische Städtegründungen*, PhilSuppl 19, 1, 1927, 176ff., and A. H. M. Jones, *The Cities of the Eastern . . .*, 25off., 452 n. 31. Thus after a long pause, as only two foundations of his father in Asia Minor are know, Antiochus IV again took up the policy of the first Seleucids, see H. H. Schmitt, *Untersuchungen zur Geschichte Antiochus d. Gr.*, 1964, 104.

An inscription from Babylon, OGIS 253, names Antiochus IV κτίσ[του] τῆς πόλεως and σωτῆρος τῆς 'Ασίας, see W. W. Tarn, *The Jews in Bactria and India*, 1938, 194f., who conjectures that Antiochus had selected Babylon as a future capital, 187ff. Cf. also Rostovtzeff, *HW* 2, 1049, and 3, 1586 n. 17, who associates the inscription with the building of the Greek theatre in the city, and the elaborations by M. Zambelli, op. cit., 374ff. The gymnasium there probably also belongs in this context, see above, n. II, 109. In contrast to the first Seleucids, this is mostly a matter of transferring the city rights to Hellenized cities, e.g. in Cilicia, and not of new settlements. It was mostly bound up with the granting of rights for coinage (see below, n. 135). The 'autonomy' of these cities also released centrifugal forces which weakened the unity of the empire. Cf. O. Mørkholm, op. cit., 115ff., 138.

134. The contrast between Bickermann, *GM*, 59ff., and Tcherikover, *HC*, 159ff., 404ff., should probably be resolved as follows: the disputed phrase τοὺς ἐν 'Ιεροσολύμοις 'Αντιοχεῖς ἀναγράψαι in II Macc.4.9c should probably be translated as Bickermann translates it, 'make a list of the Antiochenes in Jerusalem'. The listing thus also represented the selection of Jerusalemites who would be likely to be citizens of the projected *polis*. In *HC*, 161, Tcherikover also stresses that not all 'hewers of wood and drawers of water' were entered on the city lists. Bickermann, however, takes too little notice of the fact that this '*koinon*' or '*politeuma*' (cf. also H. Bengtson, *Die Strategie* 2, 1944, 175 and *GG*³, 483), or the '*symbiosis*' between it and the old Jerusalem only had a transitory character, in the sense of preparing the *dēmos* for the *polis* that was to be founded. The parallels given by Bickermann from inscriptions on coins about the 'Seleucids in Gaza' and the 'Antiochenes in Ptolemais' (op. cit., 62 nn. 1, 2) do not relate to *politeumata*, but to the *dēmoi* of real *poleis*, see Tcherikover, *HC*, 443 n. 12, and 447 n. 51; cf. Bi(c)kermann himself, *Inst.*, 231, 234; also L. Kadman, *The Coins of Akko Ptolemais*, 1961, 18, 43f.; see SEG 12, 511, the reverencing of the Antiochenes ad Cydnum (Tarsus) by the Antiochenes ad Pyramum (Magarsus) *c.* 140 BC and Schürer, 1, 157: the 'Antiochenes' of Hippos. Tcherikover, *HC*, 407, also points out that the terms *politeuma, koinon*, etc., were used above all for ethnic groups, as for the Caunians in Sidon,OGIS 592, the Jews in Berenice, see SEG 16, 931; cf. also the *koinon* of the Sidonians in the Piraeus, KAI 60; the Sidonians in Marisa, OGIS 593 (see Vol.I, pp.43 and 62); the Hellenes in the iron mines of Nicipolis. L. Robert, *Hellenica* 11/12, 1960, 288f., etc. Note also the sequence in II Macc.4.9: 1. gymnasium; 2. ephebate; 3. list of citizens. Thus the gymnasium and the ephebate formed the basis for the constitution of the city. Josephus, *Antt.*12, 240, also indicates the goal: καὶ τὴν 'Ελληνικὴν πολιτείαν ἔχειν. For the formation of religious groups, like associations, in contemporary Judea, see Vol.I, pp.243f., and nn.III, 866–8.

135. Antiochus IV granted a whole series of cities the right to coin their own copper, see E. Bickermann, *Inst.*, 231ff., who lists 14 places.

136. *HC*, 164f.; for the dating, 468 n.26; cf. also Abel/Starcky, op. cit., 244f. W. Otto, *Zeit des 6. Ptolemaers*, AAM NF 11, 1934, 15ff., and H. Volkmann, *PW* 23, 1704, conjecture 175/74. In principle we must reckon with the possibility that the *polis* was not fully constituted before the erection of the Acra. We have no indication of new magistrates or of the '*dēmos*'. It remains doubtful whether the

gerousia in II Macc. 4.44 formed the senate of the new *polis*. It is very improbable that the bodyguard of Lysimachus, numbering about 3000 men (4.40), represented the *dēmos* (Tcherikover, *HC*, 162). Cf. O. Mørkholm, op. cit., 138f.

137. Thus F. M. Abel, *HP* I, 116.

138. For the sale of Greek priestly offices to the highest bidders in the Hellenistic period see M. P. Nilsson, *GGR*² I, 732 n. 5, and F. Sokolowski, *JJurPap* 3, 1949, 139; cf. also the threat of Lysias, II Macc. 11.2f., and on this Tcherikover, *HC*, 170f. For the dating see R. Hanhart, op. cit., 63 nn. 14, 88.

139. On this see de Bruyne, *Les anciennes traductions latines*, Anecdota Marcdsolana 4, 1932, X, 118f. His conjecture was accepted by R. Hanhart, *Maccabaeorum liber II*, Septuaginta IX, 2, 1959, 26, 34 and 55 on 3.4: Σίμων δέ τις ἐκ τῆς Βαλγεα φυλῆς. For the priestly order of Bilga see Neh. 10.9; 12.5, 18; I Chron. 24.14. The term φυλή, which is unusual for LXX, may be connected with the fact that the Egyptian priesthood was divided into φυλαί, see W. Otto, ·*Priester und Tempel* 1, 23ff. The reading was adopted by E. Bickermann, *GM*, 65 n. 1, though he altered his view again in *AIPHOS* 7, 1939–44, 8 n. 22; Tcherikover, *HC*, 403f.; F. M. Abel, *Macc.*, 316; Abel/Starcky, 234; G. Jeremias, *Der Lehrer der Gerechtigkeit*, 70 n. 6. H. H. Rowley gives a survey of the various earlier interpretations in *Studia Orientalia J. Pedersen*, 1953, 303–15, but himself rejects the reading Balgea = Bilga on inadequate grounds.

140. *T.Sukk.* 4, 28 (l. 200), and on this the commentary by S. Liebermann, *Tosephta Ki-Fshutah*, part IV, 1962, 277f.; par. *jSukk.* 55d; 40ff. and *bSukk.* 56b; cf. also Josephus, *Bell.* 6, 280, and on Kalir, S. Klein, *Die Barajta des 24 Priesterabteilungen*, 1909, 70ff., and *MGWJ* 73, 1929, 73. For marriage between priests and pagan women see T. Levi 14.6: all this was a consequence of assimilation.

141. II Macc. 4.23–32. On this cf. *Antt.* 12, 237ff. Josephus distorts the situation for apologetic reasons when he makes Menelaus the third son of Simon II and brother of Jason for the sake of a legitimate high-priestly succession. The reason for the deposition of Jason is said to have been the anger of the king. The account in *Bell.* 1, 31 and *Antt.* 12, 237–41 is uninfluenced by II Macc., which Josephus did not know, and probably goes back via Nicolaus of Damascus to a Seleucid source, in which the intervention of the king was explained by the revolt of the Jews which had taken place earlier, cf. Tcherikover, 170ff., and Bickermann, *GM*, 150, 163f. and 166f.

142. II Macc. 4.27–38. Presumably Dan. 9.26a; 11.22; I Enoch 90.8 refer to this, see E. Meyer, *UAC* 2, 150 n. 1; A. Bentzen, op. cit., 75, 77, 81; O. Plöger, *Daniel*, 134 on Dan. 9.26a and 141, 163; in detail R. H. Charles, *Daniel*, 1929, 246f. For the historicity of the murder of Onias III see above, n. 130. Only 4.36–38 is unhistorical, presenting the vengeance of the king on Andronicus as a consequence of the slaying of the former high priest. This has probably been influenced by the report of the retribution for the murder of the nephew and co-regent of Epiphanes, Antiochus son of Seleucus IV; see Diodore 30, 7, 2f.; Johannes Antiochenus, FHG, Müller, 4, 558 fr. 58, and the Seleucid list, ed. Sachs/Wiseman, *Iraq* 16, 1954, 208f. verso 12: the execution of the (co-)regent of Antiochus on the king's orders in August 170 BC; cf. E. Bi(c)kerman(n), *Inst.*, 19, 218; R. Hanhart, op. cit., 63 n. 15; 74 n. 33; 88, and Abel/Starcky, 248, who

conjectures the extremely improbable killing of two nephews. No argument
against the historicity of sanctuary at Daphne can be derived from this. Perhaps
Jason of Cyrene reported both murders, which lay about a year apart, and the
epitomator effectively abbreviated them. As is shown by *Antt.* 12, 387, correcting
Bell. I, 33 and 7, 423, the temple in Leontopolis was founded by Onias IV, the
son of the murdered man, after the nomination of Alcimus as high priest
(probably already under Eupator in 163 BC, see II Macc. 14.3, 7: *Antt.* 12, 385f.,
and W. Molleken, *ZAW* 65, 1953, 213ff.). The conjectures of I. L. Seeligmann
are not very convincing, op. cit., 91ff. Jason never would have glorified the
founder of a schismatic temple.

143. E. Bickermann, *GM*, 67; cf. II Macc. 4.24, 27ff., 32, 39ff., 50: Menelaus
remained in power because of the πλεονεξία τῶν κρατούντων and Sulpicius Severus,
2, 19, 6, CSEL I, 75, ed. Halm, on *Antt.* IV: *cogebatur pecunias rapto quaerere
neque ullam praedandi causam omittere.* Cf. O. Mørkholm, op. cit., 139f.

144. II Macc. 5.21. Josephus, *c.Ap.* 2, 83, demonstrates that this first
plundering took place during peacetime: *egestate pecuniarum ad hoc accessit, cum
non esset hostis et super nos auxiliatores suos et amicos adgressus est.* Cf. Dan. 11.28
and *Antt.* 12, 246, though the Seleucid source combines the plundering of the
temple and the repression of the revolt which took place a year later, see Bickermann, *GM*, 160f.

145. For the plundering of sanctuaries after Antiochus III see B. Niese,
GGMS 3, 89, 215, 218; W. Otto, AAM NF 11, 1934, 78 nn. 1, 2; F. Altheim,
Weltgeschichte Asiens 2, 49f.; E. Bickermann, *GM*, 66f.; *Inst.*, 121f.; H. H.
Schmitt, op. cit., 102, 107 n. 1. Obviously the contradictory reports about the
proceedings of Antiochus IV against the sanctuary of 'Artemis' or Nanea in the
Elymais (II Macc. 1.13, cf. 9.2ff. and I Macc. 6.1) are of little historical value, see
W. W. Tarn, *The Greeks in Bactria and India*, 214, 463ff., and the supplement in
the second edition, 530. But as the parallel accounts in Polybius 31, 9 (11) and
Appian, *Syr.* 66, show, they have a real background, which can only be re-
constructed with difficulty, see Rostovtzeff, *HW* 2, 695f. and 3, 1489 n. 115. The
temple of Diana in Hierapolis (see Granus Licinianus, ed. M. Flemisch, 1914, 5)
and the Egyptian sanctuaries were also plundered, see W. Otto, op. cit., 79 n. 2,
and H. Volkmann, *PW* 23, 1710. The view of H. L. Jansen, *Die Politik Antiochos'
IV*, 1943, 33, that Antiochus merely wanted to destroy the financial basis of the
anti-Seleucid party, however, seems less probable. Measures of this kind served
to break up the empire, not to consolidate it.

146. For dating see above, n. I, 47. Tcherikover, *HC*, 186, 473 n. 20, has
demonstrated with reference to Dan. 11.28, 30 that the king carried out the
capture and punishment of Jerusalem in person in the late summer of 168 BC, cf.
II Macc. 5.11–23 and *Antt.* 12, 246f., and that this punitive expedition is not
identical with the action of Apollonius (see I Macc. 1.29ff.); cf. already B. Niese,
GGMS 3, 231f., and also Abel/Starcky, 63, 252ff. The dating for Apollonius'
undertaking in I Macc. 1.29, two years after the plundering of the temple in 169
BC = spring 167 BC, supports this result. The detail would match II Macc.
5.24ff. At the end of 168 BC the king probably terminated the semi-independent
rule of Hyrcanus in the Ammanitis. Cf. O. Mørkholm, op. cit., 141f., 192f. and
above n. I, 48.

147. *HC*, 187f., 192, 196f. The Hasidim were not a social class but a religious movement. H. Stegeman (above n. III, 481) connects their formation with the murder of Onias III.

148. II Macc. 5.24ff.; cf. I Macc. 1.29ff. For the old theme of the capture of Jerusalem on the sabbath see M. Hengel, op. cit., 293. J. Wellhausen, *NGG* 1905, 129, already conjectured that the Jews rebelled again after the departure of the king and made the second punitive expedition of Apollonius necessary.

149. I Macc. 1.33ff., cf. Dan. 11.29 LXX and on this E. Bickermann, *GM*, 70ff., and *Inst.*, 85; Tcherikover, *HC*, 189f., 194. For the dispute over the site of the Acra see L. H. Vincent, *RB* 43, 1934, 205–36, and *Jérusalem de l'Ancien Testament* I, 176–92, and against him, rightly, W. A. Shotwell, *BASOR* 176, 1964, 10–19: on the south-east and not on the west hill, the extent cannot be determined further without new discoveries.

150. Cf. Dan. 11.39b (and on this below, nn. 215–7); I Macc. 3.36, the commission of the king to Lysias and the threat of Ptolemy III, *Antt.* 12, 159. For the Ptolemaic military colonies in Palestine see Vol. I, pp. 14ff., cf. the settling of two thousand Jewish military colonists from Babylonia in disturbed Phrygia by Antiochus III, *Antt.* 12, 147ff., and by Herod in the Trachonitis, see above, n.122; cf. E. Bi(c)kerman(n), *Inst.*, 85f.

151. I Macc. 1.38; II Macc. 5.27 and the invitation to return, 11.29ff.; on this Tcherikover, *HC*, 192, 475 n. 27; cf. also *Antt.* 12, 261, and on this I. Heinemann, op. cit., 168, and Preisigke/Kiessling, *Wörterbuch*, 1, 113 and 4, 149.

152. E. Bickermann, *GM*, 73, cf. 80: 'Jewish-pagan *polis*'. Cf. Josephus, *Antt.* 12, 252.

153. See the fast roll, H. Lichtenstein, *HUCA* 8/9, 1931/32, 286f., 327, and I Macc. 4.2, cf. 4.41; 6.18; 10.7; 11.41; 13.21, 49: οἱ δὲ ἐκ τῆς ἄκρας ἐν Ἰερουσαλήμ. For their military role see E. Bickermann, *GM*, 71 n. 3.

154. Op. cit., 191, similarly 201. However, Tcherikover puts too much stress on the Jewish preparedness to fight before the beginning of the religious distress. There can be no question of a generally organized rebellion of the Hasidim.

155. II Macc. 5.22; cf. 6.11 and 8.8. For the title see F. M. Abel, *Macc.*, 355, and E. Bi(c)kerman(n), *Inst.*, 162f., 163 n. 5.

156. E. Bickermann, *GM*, 75f. O. Mørkholm, op. cit., 145, 156.

157. I Macc. 15.28, 33, cf. F. M. Abel, *RB* 35, 1926, 518ff.; *Macc.*, 271; *HP* 1, 123, and M. Smith, *Der Hellenismus*, Fischer-Weltgeschichte 6, 1965, 259.

158. E. Bickermann, *GM*, 73, 79. For Samaria see Vol. I, p. 14, n. I, 69. For Tiberias see *Antt.* 18, 36ff.; *Vita* 32ff., and G. Hölscher, *PW*, 2. R.6, 779f. In contrast to Sepphoris, Tiberias had from the beginning a Greek constitution and the right to make its own coinage, see G. F. Hill, *Catalogue of Greek Coins of Palestine*, xiff., xiiiff. For Sepphoris see *Antt.* 18, 27, cf. Schürer 2, 210ff. The city did not take part in the Jewish revolt of AD 66, unlike its hinterland Galilee, and thus aroused the hate of the Galileans, *Vita* 38f.

159. Dan. 11.31. For the expression $z^e r\bar{o}'\hat{\imath}m$ = military forces, cf. 11.15, 22.

160. *T. Sukk.* 4, 28. Text following S. Lieberman, *Tosephta Ki Fshutah*, 1962, IV, 277f. par.bab. 56b; j55d. For the transference to Titus see 'ARN 1, ed. Schechter, 4.

161. See Vol. I, p. 158, and n. III, 338 on the Isis cult; cf. already I Kings 11.4.

In the post-Maccabean period the Jews were extremely sensitive on this point, see M. Hengel, op. cit., 222. There may be a certain pagan influence among the Jewish military settlers in Phrygia, see above, n.45.

162. Tcherikover, *HC*, 194, naturally assumes that these were 'local Syrian troops', but cf. 188. Of course, there also seem to have been Cypriots (II Macc.4.29) and men from Asia Minor (cf. 5.24, mysarch; 5.22, Phrygian) among the occupation forces in Jerusalem. According to Polyb.31, 3, 3f., the army in Daphne displayed a varied mixture of people, cf. I Macc.6.29 and *Antt*.12, 366; on this see F. Altheim, op. cit., 2, 96. For reasons of security it was a favourite practice to use military settlers from remote areas, and in addition Syrian soldiers had a reputation for being unreliable, see above n.I,87. Of course the assumption that 'Greek colonists' or a 'Macedonian garrison' were settled there (U. Wilcken, *PW* I, 2472), is still more improbable. The derivation of the military settlers remains an open question.

163. I Macc.1.44–64, cf. II Macc.6.1–11; Dan.11.31–35.

164. E. R. Bevan, *The House of Seleucus* 2, 1902, 155; *CAH* 8, 507f., 622; W. Otto, AAM NF 11, 1934, 85, who wants to explain the edict psychologically through the immoderation of the king; W. W. Tarn, on the other hand, depicts him positively, op. cit., 183ff.; similarly F. Hampl, *Gnomon* 15, 1939, 622. E. Meyer, *UAC* 2, 143f., supposes that I Macc.1.41f. reproduces the intention of the king rightly, but that no decrees were needed outside Jerusalem because the rest of the empire followed his efforts at Hellenization voluntarily. Further earlier literature is given by I. Heinemann, *MGWJ* 82, 1938, 161. H. Herter also follows his negative judgment on E. Bickermann in E. Kiessling, *Der Hellenismus in der deutschen Forschung 1938–48*, 1956, 63f. But cf. O. Mørkholm, op. cit., 132 n.53; 146 n.36.

165. E. Bickermann, *GM* 127; cf. already B. Niese, *GGMS* 3, 233 n.2: 'An improbable exaggeration without any evidence from elsewhere.'

166. I. Heinemann, op. cit., 162f. Here he stresses the difference between the decree in I Macc.1.41f. to the 'whole empire' and 1.44 'by messengers to Jerusalem and the cities of Judea', though he overlooks the fact that according to 1.51 this too was regarded as being 'for his whole empire'.

167. Dan.11.37–39a. In the last half-verse we should read '*am* '*elōah nēkār* instead of '*im* . . . with most of the commentators, Bickermann, *GM*, 173; Tcherikover, *HC*, 474 n.24. W. Baumgartner, *TR* 11, 1939, 206f., criticizes E. Bickermann for 'dismissing' Dan.11.37f., and treating I Macc.1.41f. 'rather too lightly'. He is followed by A. Bentzen, op. cit., 82. The question is whether the apocalyptist can really draw an objective picture of the supposed 'religious policy' of the king.

168. R. H. Charles, *Daniel*, 1929, 316, referring to Livy 41, 20, 9; cf. also I. Heinemann, op. cit., 163 n.38, and F. M. Abel, *HP* I, 125. The building of the temple is connected with his pro-Roman tendencies, see F. Reuter, *Beiträge zur Beurteilung des Königs Antiochus Epiphanes*, 1938, 38f. According to Granus Licianus, ed. M. Flemisch, 1914, 5, he erected colossal statues to Jupiter Capitolinus and Zeus Olympius; see also n.185 below.

169. E. Bickermann, *GM*, 115f. E. Meyer, *UAC* 2, 159 n.1, already described '*elōah mā'uzzīm*' as an 'unsolved riddle'. For the inscription see B. Lifshitz,

ZDPV 77, 1961, 186ff., and H. Seyrig, *Syria* 39, 1962, 207f.; cf. also A. B. Cook, *Zeus* II, 2, 871 n. 3 and index. Whereas there is also evidence for Zeus Olympius in Scythopolis, at Seleucia in Pieria Zeus Olympius and Zeus Coryphaeus were associated, see below, n. 190.

170. See now O. Mørkholm, *Studies in the Coinage of Antiochus IV of Syria,* 1963, 11ff. The real change began with the second series of mints established by Antiochus in 173/172 BC. The traditional representations of Apollo on the *omphalos* and other themes did, however, continue, even if the Zeus motif predominated. At first the royal portrait was always on the obverse, and it grew more strongly stylized with time: 56ff. As the form of the seated Zeus was very similar to that of Apollo, the change was not very striking.

171. Op. cit., 24ff., 31ff., 34. For the Zeus portrait see 58ff. The false supposition of an approximate portraiture was very widespread, and great importance was attached to it, see E. R. Bevan, *CAH* 8, 508; H. Thiersch, NGG 1932, H. 1, 69f.; M. Rostovtzeff, *Mélanges Dussaud* 1, 1939, 294; F. M. Abel, *HP* 1, 128; A. Bentzen, op. cit., 83; E. Pax, *RAC* 5, 846, and L. Cerfaux/J. Tondriau, *Le Culte des Souverains,* 1957, 243f.

172. O. Mørkholm, op. cit., 44ff. These particular mintings were more widespread in Palestine. See also E. Bickermann, *GM*, 116 n. 2. Mørkholm investigated only the mintings of Antioch and Ptolemais. For conservative minting in the East see G. le Rider, *Suse sous les Séleucides,* 1965, 62ff., 37ff., and O. Mørkholm, *Museum Notes* 16, 1970, 31ff.

173. E. T. Newell, *The First Seleucid Coinage of Tyre,* 1921, 21, 25ff., and *The Seleucid Coinage of Tyre,* 1936, 12ff.

174. E. Bickerman(n), *Inst.*, 228ff., 231ff. The bilingual coinage begins in 169/68, at a time when the 'Hellenization attempt' in Jerusalem was moving towards its climax. Under Antiochus VII Sidetes in 139 BC, the Seleucids did not grant the right of coinage to the '*polis* Antioch in Jerusalem', but to the Jewish '*ethnos*' under Simon the Maccabee, though use was first made of this right by his son John Hyrcanus, cf. I Macc. 15.6 and B. Kanael, *BHHWB* 2, 1251.

175. Dan. 7.8, 20; 8.10, 24; 11.36. The 'he speaks great things' could refer to the divine epithets which distinguish his coins completely from those of his predecessors.

176. O. Mørkholm, *Coinage,* 68ff. Possibly Antiochus was influenced by the model of his father-in-law Ptolemy V Epiphanes (204–180 BC) in adopting the title Epiphanes. Together with Cleopatra I, Antiochus' sister, he had this title on inscriptions: OGIS 95, 97–100: see Cerfaux-Tondriau, op. cit., 240. Cf. also F. Taeger, *Charisma* 1, 1957, 318: 'There can be . . . no doubt that Epiphanes proclaimed to the world without concealment his claim to be God and thus no longer recognized the limitation wh:ch hitherto had been respected by all the kings of his house from the time of Soter.' For the significance of the designation 'Epiphanes', which was adopted at about the same time by the kings of the Bactrian kingdom in the East, see F. Pfister, *PW Suppl* 4, 306ff. This simultaneous emergence is perhaps also a sign of the general religious change which begins in Hellenistic world with the second century BC; see Vol. I, pp. 217f. Cf. O. Mørkholm, *Antiochus,* 113, 131f.

177. O. Mørkholm, *Coinage,* 68f.; E. Bi(c)kerman(n), *Inst.*, 240f.; F. Taeger,

op. cit., 1, 318f. The surname 'Nikephoros' appears by itself with a whole series of gods and goddesses, among them Zeus, see F. Münzer, *PW* 7, 310ff. Antiochus IV probably adopted it following the designation of the first Seleucid as Nicator, see on this H. Seyrig, *Syria* 20, 1939, 298f. The title never appears in inscriptions, but only on the later coins. His successors maintained these and similar divine epithets, despite their vanishing force.

178. E. Bickerman(n), *Inst.*, 231, 233.

179. Dan. 3.1ff.; 4.17, 19; 6.8; Judith 3.8, cf. 6.2, and the change of mind of the dying Epiphanes, II Macc. 9.12; on this see F. Taeger, op. cit., 1, 434ff. For Egypt, see Cerfaux/Tondriau, op. cit., 218ff. In this respect, too, the attitude of post-Maccabean Judaism was increasingly sharpened; see M. Hengel, op. cit., 103–11. Presumably Sir. 36 (G 33). 12 already contains a reference, see Vol. I, p. 152.

180. O. Mørkholm, *Coinage*, 74; *Antiochus*, 130f. The alleged identification of Antiochus IV with Zeus was stressed above all by W. W. Tarn, op. cit., 191; see on the other hand already A. D. Nock, *HTR* 45, 1942, 209 n. 82 = *Essays* 2, 755. Later Herod modelled the statue of the emperor in the temple of Augustus in Caesarea on the Zeus Olympius of Phidias, *Bell.* 1, 414.

181. Polyb. 26, 1, 11; Livy 41, 20, 8: Granus Licinianus, ed. M. Flemisch, 1914, 6; Velleius Paterculus 1, 10, 1. This happened in connection with rich gifts to all the Greek cities, cf. Livy 41, 20, 5ff.; on this see F. Reuter, op. cit., 41f.; a certain 'ruler's vanity' also lies behind it. Cf. O. Mørkholm, *Antiochus*, 58f.

182. Pausanias 5, 12, 4, cf. also A. Pelletier, *Lettre d'Aristée*, 1962, 145 n. 3.

183. OGIS 249–51, cf. Polybius 26, 1, 11; O. Mørkholm, op. cit.

184. M. P. Nilsson, *GGR*² 2, 165.

185. Ammianus Marcellinus 22, 13, 1, and on this A. B. Cook, *Zeus* II, 2, 1940, 1188ff. However, it is improbable that this statue was meant to represent Antiochus.

186. For Scythopolis see the inscription in A. Rowe, *The Topography and History of Beth-Shean* 1, 1930, 44 = SEG 8, 33, with a mention of the priests of Zeus Olympius and the emperor cult, and its expansion by R. Mouterde, *MUSJ* 17, 1933, 180f., who compares it with the even more damaged inscription from Samaria, see G. A. Reisner etc., *Harvard Excavations at Samaria, 1908–10* 1, 1924, 250 = SEG 8.96. He expands the latter as a testimony to the worship of Zeus Olympius and the ruler cult in Samaria. As the name of the ruler has been carved out and put in again later, at least in Samaria, Mouterde supposes that the inscriptions arose at the time of Demetrius II Nicator, 145–140 and 129–25 BC. It is not so completely certain that this cult was founded by Antiochus IV; as in Seleucia, it could be much older, see M. Rostovtzeff, *JHS* 55, 1935, 60f. There is still evidence of Zeus Olympius in Scythopolis under Caracalla, see Watzinger, *DP* 2, 20f. H. Thiersch, 'Ein hellenistischer Kolossalkopf aus Beisan', NGG, 1932, 52–76, presumes the head found there as part of a colossal statue from the Hellenistic period to be a youthful statue of Zeus approximated to Alexander the Great in the style of Dionysus, who is particularly closely associated with Scythopolis-Nyssa; however, it is meant to represent Antiochus IV himself. For these hypotheses see, however, the criticism by Watzinger, *DP* 2, 21, and O. Mørkholm, op. cit., 63f. B. Lifshitz, *ZDPV* 77, 1961, 186–90, published an

inscription from the year AD 156 in honour of Zeus Akraios, perhaps a variant of Zeus Olympius, and a further one for Zeus Bacchus, a contamination of Zeus and Dionysus, see of course the criticism of his reading in H. Seyrig, *Syria* 39, 1962, 207–11, and L. Robert, *REG* 75, 1962, 207.

187. M. Rostovtzeff, *Mélanges Dussaud* 1, 294f., and *Dura Europos and its Art*, 1938, 59f.; also the short note by F. E. Brown, *AJA* 45, 1941, 94. Cf. also O. Eissfeldt, *AO* 40, 1941, 108, 114, 120f., 126f., and *Kleine Schriften* 2, 180f. The city itself was a foundation of Seleucus I. There were a whole series of deities here who could be identified with Baʿal Šāmēm/Zeus Olympius. However, the later 'Zeus Megistos' is most likely to be the one in question: a Zeus Olympius temple probably stood under his temple alongside the citadel of the city.

188. C. H. Kraeling, *Gerasa*, 1938, 373–82: Zeus Olympius is by far the most frequently mentioned god there, see nos. 2–7, 10, 13, 14. The earliest inscription comes from AD 22/23. For the Antiochenes on the Chrysoroas see 461f., no. 251, and on the foundation by Antiochus IV, 30f. This does not exclude a first foundation by Perdiccas, see Vol. I, p. 14, and n. I, 69. Cf. also O. Eissfeldt, 'Tempel und Kulte', AO 40, 1941, 16–20, who supposes that an earlier Semitic god like Hadad or Baʿal Šāmēm stood behind Zeus as in Baalbek, Palmyra and Dura. According to *Kleine Schriften* 2, 1963, 310ff., the dedication to Helios from about 200 BC, made by a Gerasene on Cos, is also to be referred to Baʿal Šāmēm.

189. Josephus, *c.Ap.* I, 113, 118 and *Antt.* 8, 147; Philo Byblius, FGrHist 790 F 2, 7 = Eusebius, *Pr.Ev.* I, 10, 7; on this see O. Eissfeldt, *Kleine Schriften* 2, 1963, 174.

190. OGIS 245 = IGLS 3, 1184, cf. also 1185.

191. I. Malalas, ch. 8, pp. 199ff., ed. Dindorf, cf. Strabo 16, 2, 5 (750), and Appian, *Syr.* 58; see Adler, *PW* 10, 2265. The narrative has features akin to the legend of the founding of Antioch which was conneced with Zeus Bottiaeus. An Iranian sanctuary on mount Silpion in Antioch, where Antiochus IV later erected a temple of Jupiter Capitolinus, was regarded as a sanctuary of 'Zeus Keraunios', see A. B. Cook, *Zeus* 3, 1940, 1187f. E. Bi(c)kerman(n), *Inst.*, 250f., and Abel/Starcky, 69f. Presumably this and similar sanctuaries took up the old cults of the local baals. Further see below, n. 244. For the divine epithets of the early Seleucids see E. Bi(c)kerman(n), *Inst.*, 243ff.; M. P. Nilsson, *GGR*² 2, 166f., and the inscription mentioned in n. 190 above.

192. For the ruler cult of the Seleucids in general see E. Bi(c)kerman(n), *Inst.*, 236–57; Cerfaux/Tondriau, op. cit., 229–40; F. Taeger, op. cit., I, 309ff., and M. P. Nilsson, op. cit., 167–71; cf. *JHS* 55, 1935, 56–66. Antiochus III had already made particular efforts to organize the emperor cult in a circular communication of which one copy was found in Phrygia and another in Susa, see M. P. Nilsson, op. cit., 168 n. 7; F. Taeger, op. cit., I, 314ff. Presumably since his time the *polis* and the military colony had had at least one priest for the gods of the dynasty and one or two for the *progonoi* and the reigning ruler, see M. Rostovtzeff, *JHS* 55, 1935, 61. For the ruler cult of the later Seleucids see the inscription in honour of Antiochus VII Sidetes and his consort Cleopatra Thea *c.* 130/129 BC in Ptolemais, ed. Y. H. Landau, *IEJ* 11, 1961, 118–26, and B. Lifshitz, *RB* 70, 1963, 75–81.

193. M. P. Nilsson, op. cit., 167f.

194. For the ruler cult among the Ptolemies see op. cit., 154–65; F. Taeger, 1, 287–308; Cerfaux/Tondriau, op. cit., 189–218 and H. Volkmann, *Historia* 5, 1956, 448–55, who shows how the increasing Hellenization of the Phoenician cities in Cyprus was expressed in it. For Palestine see the inscriptions in Joppa and Marisa after the victory of Ptolemy IV at Raphia in 217 BC; B. Lifshitz, *ZDPV* 78, 1962, 82–4, with a priest of the ruler cult and M. L. Strack, *APF* 2, 1902, 544 = Clermont-Ganneau, *CRAI* 1900, 536–41, and on this F. M. Abel, *HP* 1, 82f. The ruler cult was a fixed institution in Palestine long before Antiochus IV.

195. E. R. Bevan, *CAH* 8, 498f., cf. above, n. II, 218.

196. The comparison with the Serapis cult and Ptolemy I is therefore unjustified; against Rostovtzeff, *Dura Europos*, 36f.; *HW* 2, 704, and A. Bentzen, op. cit., 82. O. Mørkholm, *Antiochus*, 131ff., is rightly restrained.

197. K. Galling, *OLZ* 42, 1939, 228.

198. E. Meyer, *UAC* 2, 158; he is followed by A. D. Nock, *HTR* 45, 1952, 209f.

199. F. M. Abel, *Macc.*, 19, cf. Abel/Starcky, op. cit., 91. See also Esther 3.8–15 and III Macc. 3.12–30. 2.18f. shows that I Macc. 1.41f. follows the style of the author. J. G. Bunge, *Untersuchungen zum zweiten Makkabäerbuch*, 1971, conjectures an invitation to the *pompē* in Daphne.

200. E. Bickermann, *GM*, 120ff., and the unconvincing objections of I. Heinemann, op. cit., 169. In any case, II Macc. 6.8 is to be regarded as an exception, regardless of whether Πτολεμαίων = Πτολεμαιέων means the inhabitants of Ptolemais, with the Lucianic recension, Vulg., Arm. and Syr., or Ptolemy the *stratēgos* of Coele Syria with Alex. Πτολεμαίου (cf. 8.8). This edict, too, had local character and concerned only the 'neighbouring Greek cities'. The Jews in Syria, Antioch and Babylon remained unaffected, cf. J. Neusner, *A History of the Jews in Babylonia* 1, 1965, 13.

201. The much-disputed assessment of the king and his policy (see F. Reuter, op. cit., passim; F. Hampl, *Gnomon* 15, 1939, 619–23, and H. E. Stier, *Roms Aufstieg zur Weltmacht*, 1937, 16f.) thus contributes little to an assessment of events in Judea. Worth noting is C. A. Kincaid's remark in *Oriental Studies for C. E. Pavry*, 1933, 209f., that by descent Epiphanes was as much a Persian as a Macedonian. The most recent assessment of the king by F. Kiechle, *Geschichte in Wissenschaft und Unterricht* 14, 1963, 159–70, is too one-sidedly positive.

202. Tcherikover, *HC*, 196ff.

203. O. Plöger, *Theocracy*, 2–9, comes near to Bickermann's view; cf. also T. H. Gaster, *Evidence* 4, 1952, H. 29, 27–33; W. F. Albright, *From the Stone Age to Christianity*, 1940, 353; John Bright, *A History of Israel*, ²1972, 420ff.; M. Smith, *Hellenismus*, Fischer-Weltgeschichte 6, 1965, 257ff., and K. Galling, *RGG*³ 3, 982. See now O. Mørkholm, *Antiochus*, 145ff.

204. This was already true for the pre-exilic period and in part even in the Northern Kingdom; see K. Galling on I Kings 18.40 in *Geschichte und Altes Testament*, *A. Alt zum 70 Geburtstag*, 1953, 122ff.; cf. also I Macc. 2.58.

205 I Macc. 2.24–28, 50, 54, 58; see also M. Hengel, *Zeloten*, 152ff.

206. E. Bickermann, *GM*, 73, 80.

207. Cf. O. Plöger, *Daniel*, 135 ad loc., though he conjectures 'covenant' as

subject, which makes an interpretation difficult. Cf. also Theodotion ad loc.:
καὶ δυναμώσει διαθήκην πολλοῖς. For the many, cf. I Macc. 1.43 and Vol. I, p.
289.

208. Dan. 11.30b and on it R. H. Charles, op. cit., 307: 'On his return to
Antioch, Antiochus kept up communication with the apostate Jews. It was not
Antiochus that took the initiative in the attempt to hellenize the nation.' For
what follows see E. Bickermann, *GM*, 26ff.

209. Jerome, in *Dan.* 11, 30, *PL* 25, 568. Cf. the Greek source of Josephus,
Bell. I, 32, where the 'sons of the Tobiads' ask Antiochus 'to use them as guides
on his attack against Judea'. *Antt.* 12, 241 connects this report with I Macc. 1.11ff.,
according to which the Tobiads tell the king that 'they want to abandon their
ancestral laws and the way of life prescribed in them, and to follow the royal
laws and adopt the Greek way of life'.

210. Josephus did not know II Macc. (see above, n. 141); Jason of Cyrene
and the Greek source of Josephus, or better of Nicolaus of Damascus, thus go
back independently to a historical circumstance which cannot simply be explained
away as 'fiction', as is attempted by I. Heinemann. The deliberately gruesome
execution of Menelaus, see II Macc. 13.4ff., and on it F. M. Abel, *Macc.*, 451,
shows that he was really regarded as the chief author of the hopeless situation in
Judea. Cf. also Dan. 3.32 LXX and Eth. En. 90.16, 26.

211. For the hostility of Menelaus and his supporters to the Jewish people,
see II Macc. 4.39ff., 50: πολιτῶν ἐπίβουλος; 5.15: as a 'traitor to the law and the
nation' he led Antiochus IV into the temple and handed its treasures over to him;
cf. also 13.3. As I Macc. and Dan. mention neither Menelaus nor the Tobiads,
but speak only in general terms of apostates, it is only possible to obtain from
them limited illumination on the true background of the reform.

212. II Macc. 6.1, cf. I Macc. 1.44: the king sent 'letters by messenger'. No
conclusion can be drawn from the person of the messengers to the origin of the
edict and its real author. For the name see J. G. Bunge (n. 199 above), 473, and
M. Stern, *Kirjath Sepher* 46, 1970/1, 99.

213. Tcherikover, *HC*, 478 n. 38.

214. II Macc. 14.3. Cf. on the other hand I Macc. 7.12ff. Those who lapsed
as a result of direct threats seem to have been so many that they were no longer
regarded as incriminated. For Alcimus as high priest see also n. 142 (end).

215. On this see R. H. Charles, op. cit., 308f.: for *ḥᵃlaqqōt*, 'flatteries', cf.
11.21, 34. The apostates and the king had very many interests in common, cf. I
Macc. 2.18. Perhaps Ass. Mos. 5 is also a reference to these circumstances in
Jerusalem.

216. This indicates express social components, which Tcherikover, *HC*,
168ff., 192ff., 197ff., etc., rightly stresses; it was prepared for by tension at the
time of Ben Sira, Vol. I, pp. 137f., cf. pp. 49ff., and for the 'Syrian' population
see Vol. I, pp. 21ff., 41f. H. Kreissig, *Studii Clasice* 4, 1962, 143–75, puts forward
this side in an extremist way, interpreting the Maccabean revolt in a dogmatic
Marxist fashion.

217. I QpHab 8.11: this certainly means Jews. 'Revolt against God' only
makes sense if they are in question (see above, n. III, 747). On the other hand,
9.4f. points to the successful Maccabean wars of conquest. Cf. already I Macc.

6.24, where the turning point is already indicated, and 9.73: καὶ ἠφάνισεν τοὺς ἀσεβεῖς ἐξ ᾽Ισραηλ.

218. Tcherikover, *HC*, 212f.; O. Mørkholm, *Antiochus*, 149ff.; O. Plöger, *Aus der Spätzeit des Alten Testaments*, 134ff.; cf. I Macc. 2.44, 46f.; 3.5, 8, 15; 4.2; 6.21ff.; 7.5; cf. Jub. 23.20ff.

219. E. Bickermann, *GM*, 83, and F. M. Abel, *HP* 1, 140f. Tcherikover, *HC*, 482f. n. 23, on the other hand, supposes that the writing comes from the king's son, the later Antiochus V Eupator, as Antiochus IV would have been out of touch in the East, cf. also E. Meyer, *UAC* 2, 216ff. In that case Lysias would be the author here. The view of Tcherikover, *HC*, 215ff., 483 n. 24, that Lysias would have dealt only with the Hellenists, is, however, hardly tenable. Presumably the report of the fast roll for the 28 Adar, see H. Lichtenstein, op. cit., 279 and 350, means the offer of peace.

220. The letter II Macc. 11.22–26, which of course also comes from the imperial administrator Lysias. The reference to the death of the king stresses that here a concluding line is intended to be drawn under a mistaken policy. The execution of Menelaus also corresponds with this, see above, n. 210; cf. also II Macc. 13.19–26 and I Macc. 6.48–63. Tcherikover, *HC*, 236ff., supposes that with the return of the temple the Acra came to an end as a *polis* and the military colony was dissolved, but this is contradicted by I Macc. 15.28, cf. above, n. 157; cf. also I Macc. 10.12. Bacchides even strengthened the settling of foreigners at a later date, see I Macc. 9.23ff. and 10.13f., and thus gave new support to the apostates.

221. I Macc. 6.18, 21–27. This complaint to Lysias and Antiochus V shows that the Seleucids began to get tired of the Jewish Hellenists. According to 9.57–71 they later asked Bacchides to help, but after setbacks he made peace.

222. Cf. also I Macc. 11.41; 13.21 and the fast roll for the 23 ᾽Iyyār, H. Lichtenstein, op. cit., 286f. and 327.

223. For the term see E. Meyer, *UAC* 2, 120–66, esp. 144f., and W. Kolbe, *Beiträge zur syrischen und jüdischen Geschichte*, 1926, 150.

224. I Macc. 1.57, 61ff.; cf. 2.29–38; II Macc. 6.9–11, 18ff.; cf. Dan. 11.33, 35. Later accounts probably tended to exaggerate, cf. e.g. Ass. Mos. 8.

225. Cf. II Macc. 6.4 and the fast roll for 23 Marḥeśwān, H. Lichtenstein, op. cit., 273, 337. It is, however, questionable whether sacral prostitution was introduced into the temple (against Bickermann, GM, 114). II 6.4 could be simply a reference to some omission in the sanctuary. Cf. Josephus, *Bell.* 4, 560ff.; Test.Levi 14.6, see below, n. 275.

226. E. Bickermann, *GM*, 119.

227. Op. cit., 118. There seems to have been an aversion to circumcision for a long time among the 'enlightened' Jews, see above, n. 68 and n. II, 138. For pursuit and omission of circumcision see I Macc. 1.15, 60; 2.46; II Macc. 6.10. For the sacrifice of pigs see I Macc. 1.47; cf. II Macc. 6.5 and Josephus, *Antt.* 12, 253, the martyrdom of Eleazar, II Macc. 6.18ff.; 7.1, cf. also Posidonius, FGrHist 109,4 (Reinach 58), and on it Abel/Starcky 75f. For the prohibition of pork see Lev. 11.7; Deut. 14.8; cf. Isa. 65.4. In Greece, sacrifices of pigs were made almost exclusively to the chthonic deities, see Orth, *PW*, 2R. 2, 811ff.; in Ptolemaic Egypt, according to the Zeno papyri, they appear in offerings on the

feasts of Arsinoe and in the Demeter cult, see C. Préaux, *L'Économie royale des Lagides*, 222, cf. Rostovtzeff, *HW* 1, 292, 358; details from de Vaux in *Von Ugarit nach Qumran, Festschrift O. Eissfeldt*, 1958, 250–65, and P. R. Arbesmann, *Das Fasten*, RGVV 21, 1929, 41–5. The Phoenicians above all rejected the sacrifice of pigs; use of them was rare throughout the orient. Cf. D. v. Berchem, *Syria* 44, 1967, 86ff., 99f., and Sil. Ital., *Pun.* 3, 21ff.

228. E. Bickermann, *GM*, 119, cf. R. de Vaux, op. cit., 261.

229. F. Kiechle, *Geschichte in Wissenschaft und Unterricht* 14, 1963, 168, speaks of an 'anti-Mosaic zealotism'. M. Avi-Yonah, *IEJ* 21, 1971, 169, conjectures the building of a temple of Zeus on the west hill.

230. For the request of the Samaritans and the king's answer see *Antt.*12, 257–64 and E. Bi(c)kerman(n), *RHR* 115, 1937, 188–221; *GM*, 123–6, who has shown its authenticity, already argued by B. Niese, *Hermes* 35, 1900, 520. For the earlier literature see R. Marcus, *Josephus* 7, LCL, 774.

231. According to I Macc. 11.34, the three toparchies belonging to Samaria were oriented on Jerusalem and were annexed to Judea by Demetrius II; cf. also the unhistorical report of Ps.Hecataeus, *c.Ap.*2, 43; A. Alt, *Kleine Schriften* 2, 346–62; H. G. Kipperberg, *Garizim und Synagoge*, 1971, 85ff.

232. H. Bengtson, *Die Strategie* 2, 1944, 170f.; cf. E. Bickermann, *GM*, 123 n.4.

233. E. Bickermann, *RHR* 115, 1937, 204ff., interprets the term 'Sidonian' as being a better expression for 'Phoenician' and this in turn for 'Canaanite'; cf. e.g. Gen. 10.15: Canaan as the father of Sidon, and the Tyrian coins from the time of Antiochus IV with the inscription 'Tyre, metropolis of the Sidonians' (לצר אם צדנם), see B. V. Head, *Historia numorum*, ²1911, 800, and Bickermann's further instances. The LXX often translates 'Canaan' or 'Canaanite' by 'Phoenician' or 'Phoenicia', see Exod. 6.15; Josh. 5.1, 12; Job 40.30. On the other hand, Isa. 23.2 renders *ṣīdōn* as Φοινίκη; Deut. 3.9 *ṣīdōnīm* as Φοίνικες; Susanna 56 θ: σπέρμα Χαναάν; ὁ: Σιδῶνος (ed. J. Ziegler). In *Antt.*11, 344, the Samaritans present themselves to Alexander as 'Sidonians in Shechem': in Strabo 16, 2, 34 (760) the inhabitants of Samaria and Galilee, Jericho and Philadelphia are regarded as a mixture of Egyptian, Phoenician and Arabian tribes, whereas the Jews descend from the Egyptians. Over against this M. Rostovtzeff, *CAH* 7, 191f., and *HW* 3, 1401 n.137, and M. Delcor, *ZDPV* 78, 1962, 36ff. point to the 'Sidonians in Marisa', (see above n. I, 339 and n. II, 32). However, the two are not mutually exclusive. From the Persian period Sidonians and Tyrians were the dominant political and cultural forces in Palestine; presumably the Sidonians had a trading colony in Shechem as they did in Idumean Marisa. When the Sidonians ran into trouble, the Samaritans fell in behind them, especially as they could construct a relationship with them on the basis of being 'Canaanites', and as Sidonians could have a better standing with the Greeks. The remarks about the temple do of course show – against Delcor – that not only the small Sidonian *politeuma* but the whole 'ethnos' of Samaritans stood behind the *hypomnēma*. The close connection between Samaritans and Phoenicians is already demonstrated by the Abraham tradition in the anonymous Samaritan (see Vol. I, pp. 88ff.). Cf. H. G. Kippenberg (n.231 above), 74–85.

234. For the naming of the 'anonymous' sanctuary see above, n. 63 and

below, n. 267; also E. Bi(c)kerman(n), *RHR* 115, 1937, 212f., and M. Delcor, *ZDPV* 78, 1962, 39, who both stress that the majority of the Semitic gods were in effect 'anonymous' to the Greeks and were therefore particularly suitable for an *'interpretatio Graeca'*. 'Zeus Hellenios' (on this see Jessen, *PW* 8, 176f.) is probably secondary to 'Zeus Xenios'. J. A. Montgomery, *The Samaritans*, 1907, 77 n. 11, wanted to derive the name from גר, the first two radicals of *gᵉrizzīm* (cf. the equally incorrect etymology in the anonymous Samaritan, see above, n. II, 239). S. A. Cook, *Religion*, 188, and O. Eissfeldt, *Kleine Schriften* 2, 196, n. 2, connect it with the *baʿal bᵉrīt* of Judg. 9.4; M. Delcor, op. cit., 40f., points to the rejection of strange gods in Gen. 35.4 and Josh. 24.23; on the other hand the Sidonians invoked 'a god of hospitality'. However, the whole Samaritan 'ethnos' is involved here. Evidently the distinction is from the Zeus Olympius of Zion, and furthermore a reference to the hospitality offered to Abraham on his visit to Gerizim could also be present (ξενισθῆναι, see the anonymous Samaritan, FGrHist 724 F 1, 5 = Eusebius, *Pr.Ev.* 9, 17, 5). Furthermore, as a rule 'Zeus Xenios' is associated with 'Zeus Hikesios' or 'Philios', and appears as the merciful god of the weak, the alien and those who look for protection, see A. B. Cook, *Zeus* II, 2, 1097 n. 1, 1101f., 1177 n. 2, and M. P. Nilsson, *GGR²* 1, 419; cf. Homer, *Odyssey* 6, 207f. πρὸς γὰρ Διός εἰσιν ἅπαντες ξεινοί τε πτωχοί τε, cf. 9, 269f. Thus biblical reminiscences could underlie it; cf. Deut. 10.17–19 and Ex. 22.20–23.

235. The god worshipped and his cult remained the same, see E. Bi(c)kerman(n), *RHR* 115, 1937, 214f., cf. *GM*, 90ff., cf. already J. A. Montgomery, op. cit., 78: the Samaritans did not have any radical Hellenist party like the Jews. The interpretation of the offering in I. Heinemann, op. cit., 167f., overlooks the decisive point of the continuing validity of the law in Samaria. Readiness 'to live according to Greek custom' is noticeably lacking from the Samaritan message and appears only in the royal letter to Nicanor, which rests merely on a personal impression of the king on the basis of his conversation with the Samaritan deputation in the 'circle of his friends'. The king thought tranquillity and the regular payment of tax in Samaria (*Antt.* 12, 261) more important than a real 'reform'. In Judea it was not the 'cultural concern' of the king (I. Heinemann, op. cit., 169) but the Jewish renegades who hindered a compromise of this kind.

236. E. Bickermann, *GM*, 126.

237. Op. cit., 90–116; cf. also O. Eissfeldt, *Kleine Schriften* 2, 171–98, and Tcherikover, *HC*, 195.

238. Jerome, *in Dan.* 8.5, *PL* 25, 536: '*in templo dei simulacrum statuit*' and 11.31, *PL* 25, 569, where the '*Antiochi statuas*' are added. Cf. E. Bickermann, *GM*, 102f., 105 n. 1. H. H. Rowley defends the exhibition of a divine image with inadequate reasons in *Studia Orientalia J. Pedersen*, 1953, 310ff. (lit.). The obscure note in *Taan.* 4, 7 and 28b (Gemara), which cites Dan. 12.11, have no value as sources. On the other hand, we must assume that statues of the king were displayed in the sanctuary, see E. Bickermann, *GM*, 104 n. 1.

239. I Macc. 1.54, cf. Dan. 8.13; 9.17; 11.31; 12.11. For the term see F. M. Abel, *Macc.*, 38f. For the date see R. Hanhart, op. cit., 64. The various details about the half week of years up to the outbreak of the imminent end (see Vol. I, pp. 194f.) should not, however, be used to 'correct' the exact dating of I Macc.

Hanhart, op. cit., 83f., puts Daniel about a year too late and overlooks the fact that it does not know anything about the departure of the king for the East at the end of 166 BC (see above, n. III, 460).

240. I Macc. 1.54, 59: τὸν βωμόν, ὃς ἦν ἐπὶ τοῦ θυσιαστηρίου, cf. *Antt.* 12, 253 and I Macc. 4.43, the purification of the sanctuary: καὶ ἦραν τοὺς λίθους τοῦ μιασμοῦ εἰς τόπον ἀκάθαρτον and on this E. Bickermann, *GM*, 105ff. (quot. 109); cf. F. M. Abel, *Macc.*, 29: O. Eissfeldt, *Kleine Schriften* 2, 195 n. 10; O. Plöger, *Daniel*, 126, and Abel/Starcky, 66ff. Cf. also K. Galling, *RGG*³ 1, 254: 'an additional altar, perhaps after the fashion of the stone *ḥammanīm*', i.e. the altars of incense in the old cult, cf. II Chron. 14.4; 34.4, 7; Lev. 26.30 and *BRL*, 20. For the 'sacred stones' cf. also 16f. and *RGG*³ 6, 348ff., together with S. A. Cook, op. cit., 160f.: a royal betyl on an altar, surrounded by a precinct sealed off by a hall of pillars. For instances of the massebah altars see K. Galling, *Der Altar*, 1924, 67f. and pll. 13, 37–42; for the basic original connection of masseboth and altars see 58f. The most widespread form of altar, the horned altar, is a further development of the massebah altar, 65–7.

241. One might imagine here the representation of an eagle, the symbolic creature of Zeus and Ba'al Šāmēm, or the winged sun; see on this A. Bentzen, op. cit., on Dan. 9.27b, following O. Eissfeldt, *FF* 18, 1942, 298f. = *Kleine Schriften* 2, 431ff.; cf. also op. cit., 2.179f., and the eagle representations of the Tobiad Hyrcanus at Qasr el-'Abd, see above, n. 109. For a betyl with a pictorial representation see e.g. H. Seyrig, *Syria* 40, 1963, 17–19, with Helios, the zodiac and the four winds. An altar of Ba'al Šāmēm, with pictorial representations, was found in Philadelphia, see below, n. 255.

242. E. Bickermann, *GM*, 109ff. For the destruction of the gates and the plantings in the temple precinct see I Macc. 4.38. The gates seem to have been destroyed by Jewish apostates, see their punishment by burning in II Macc. 8.33, cf. also 1.18. Possibly the 'temenos' was separated off by a partition, see H. Lichtenstein, op. cit., 273f. and 337. For the plantings see the plantings in honour of 'Kronos Kyrios' in Abila at the time of Lysanias, R. Savignac, *RB* NS 9, 1912, 536, and for 'Zeus Kronos' in Phoenician Arados see R. Savignac, *RB* 25, 1916, 579, and additionally L. Robert, *Mélanges Dussaud* 2, 1939, 729–31, at the behest of the 'supreme god': ὁ πάντων ἐναργέστα[τος θεός . . .

243 E. Bickermann, *GM*, 111. Cf. Ps. Hecataeus, *c.Ap.* 1, 199, but without the hedge!

244. Loc. cit.; see also above, nn. 27, 191. For the old hill sanctuaries of Canaanite and Phoenician origin, cf. O. Eissfeldt, *Kleine Schriften* 2, 43–51, with reference to Philo Byblius, FGrHist 790 F 2, 9 = Eusebius, *Pr.Ev.* 1, 10, 9: Kasion, Lebanon, Antilebanon and 'Brathy', presumably 'Atabyrion Tabor'. For *Mount Kasion* see O. Eissfeldt, *Baal Zaphon, Zeus Kasios*, Beiträge zur Religionsgeschichte des Altertums 1, 1932, 30ff., and M. H. Pope, *WM* 1, 256ff. For his cult in the Hellenistic period see A. B. Cook, *Zeus* II, 2, 981ff., see there figs. 880–4, the coins of Seleucia which presumably depict the betyl sacred to Zeus Kasios. According to O. Eissfeldt, op. cit., 32, it had the significance of an omphalos in the sense of the 'navel of the world', cf. the same significance of Zion according to Jub. 8.19. Significantly there seems to have been no temple on the summit itself, but probably only an altar. An epigram ascribed to the emperor

Hadrian, *Anth.Gr.*6, 332, ed. Beckby 1, 620, names Zeus Kasios in the universal sense 'Lord of the immortals', whom the 'Lord of men', Trajan, reverenced. For *Carmel* see O. Eissfeldt, *Kleine Schriften* 2, 135–49, and K. Galling in *Geschichte und Altes Testament, A. Alt zum 70 Geburtstag*, 1953, 105–25, who point out that the independent Baal of the mountain should not be immediately identified with Melkart or with Ba'al Šāmēm, the gods of Tyre. He was identified with the Zeus of Heliopolis-Baalbek only in Roman times, probably because the area belonged politically to the territory of Ptolemais, see M. Avi-Yonah, *IEJ* 2, 1952, 118–24; cf. W. Röllig, *WM* 1, 270, 272.

245. A. B. Cook, *Zeus* I, 102f., 117f., 124. E.g. the cult of Zeus Atabyrios on Rhodes, Sicily and in the Crimea shows that Zeus and Baal were already identified at a very early stage, see above n. 27. Cf. further, op. cit., II, 2, 890ff., the multiplicity of mountain cults of Zeus in Greece and Asia Minor, and 980ff. for the Hellenistic period in Cilicia, Cyprus, Syria, Phoenicia and Palestine; see also D. v. Berchem (n. 227), 97f.

246. M. P. Nilsson, *GGR²* 1, 201–7, and W. Fauth, *KP* 1, 806: betylolatry was particularly widespread in the West-Semitic, Arabian area. Cf. also the verdict of Dio Chrysostom, 12, 61 (cf. 53), on the mountain, tree and stone worship of the barbarians.

247. 1, 131, and on this see G. Widengren, *Die Religionen Irans*, 1965, 124f.

248. Tertullian, *Apol.*25; see E. Bickermann, *GM*, 132 n. 2. See also K. Latte, *Römische Religionsgeschichte*, 1960, 150 n. 1. For Zeno see SVF 1, nos. 264–7.

249. E. Bickermann, *GM*, 132f.; see above all 133 n. 3 (lit.).

250. J. Malalas, ed. Dindorf, 1831, 207, and on this E. Bickermann, op. cit., 112f., and *Byzantion* 21, 1951, 63–83. The Athene note could even be 'l'imagination d'un sacristain'.

251. For this triad see H. Seyrig, *Syria* 10, 1929, 314–56.

252. So Tcherikover, *HC*, 187.

253. This connection was discovered by E. Nestle, *ZAW* 4, 1884, 284, on the basis of the translation of 'Zeus' Olympius in II Macc. 6. 2 by the Peshitto with

ܗܡܘܒܚܠ ܐ݂ܠ ܕܒܝ݂ܟܠ݂ܬܐ and of 'Zeus Xenios' with ܕܒܝ݂ܟܠ݂ܬܐ ܢܘܡܪܘܐ ܗܡܘܒ

see *Libri Veteris Testamenti apocryphi Syriace*, ed. P. de Lagarde, 1861, 227. Details in O. Eissfeldt, *Kleine Schriften* 2, 171–98, especially 191f.

254. Op. cit., 2, 180, cf. 183.

255. FGrHist 790 F 2.7 = Eusebius, *Pr.Ev.* 1, 10, 7. For the dissemination of Ba'al Šāmēm see O. Eissfeldt, op. cit., 2, 169–83; cf. also 'Tempel und Kulte', *AO* 40, 1941, 79f., 90ff.; R. Dussaud, *La Pénétration des Arabes en Syrie*, ²1955, 46, 57ff.: Nabateans; 98–101: Palmyra; on this especially also J. Fevrier, *La Religion des Palmyréniens*, 1931, 103ff., 120ff.; for Hauran see D. Sourdel, *Les Cultes du Hauran*, 1952, 19–31. Also W. Röllig, *WM* 1, 273; M. Höfer, *WM* 1, 425, 427f., 429f., and W. Fauth, *KP* 1, 793f. The most important epigraphic evidence is printed in KAI. Phoenician inscriptions are no. 4, 3, the Jeḥimilk inscription, middle of the tenth century BC, and Vol. 2, 6f.; 26 n. II. 18, Karatepe, 720 BC; 78, 2 Carthage, third century BC ?; 64, 1 Sardinia, c. third century BC; for the West, cf. 'balsameni' Plautus, *Poen.* 1027. Aramean inscriptions are no. 202

A 3, 11ff. B 23 *c*. 800 BC, inscription of king ZKR of Hamath; 266, 2, *c*. 700 BC, letter of a Palestinian vassal king to Pharaoh Necho II; 259, 3, Cilicia, fifth to fourth century BC; 241 and 244–8, all from Hatra in the north-west of Assyria, first and second century AD. A Ba'al-Šāmēm temple was also discovered there, op. cit., 2,294. See also the altar dedicated to Ba'al-Šāmēm, the sun and the moon from Amman, the old Rabbath-Ammon-Philadelphia, between the first and the third centuries AD with eagle, bull and bosom with garland of rays, *RB* 69, 1962, 85f., and cf. on this the Phoenician altar discussed by F. Cumont, *Syria* 8, 1927, 163–8. For Palmyra see P. Collart, *Mélanges K. Michalowski*, 1966, 325–37, also J. Texidor, *Syria* 45, 1968, 358f.

256. Menander, FGrHist 783 F 1 = Josephus, *c.Ap.* 1, 118 (only Zeus), and Dio 785 F 2 = Josephus, *c.Ap.* 1, 113, and *Antt.* 8, 147.

257. On this see M. P. Nilsson, *GGR*² 2, 513ff., 707f. In the time of the empire Ba'al-Šāmēm finally became *Jupiter summus exsuperantissimus*, see F. Cumont, *Orientalische Religionen*, 117f., 174f.; *ARW* 9, 1906, 236–336; and *Syria* 8, 1927, 164ff. Cf. also J. Kaerst, op. cit., 2², 216f.

258. A. Falkenstein, *Topographie von Uruk, I, Uruk zur Seleukidenzeit* 2, 1941, cf. 8f.; see also S. Morenz, *RGG*³ 3, 331.

259. For Marisa, see Vol. I, pp. 34, 43, 62f.; for Shechem, above, n. 233; for the influence of Phoenician culture see Vol. I, pp. 32ff., 71f.; for the anonymous Samaritan pp. 88f. and for Eupolemus 93f.

260. 'God of heaven', see Ezra 1.2; 5.11f.; 6.9; Neh. 1.4, 5; 2.4, 20. Only Gen. 24.7 is pre-exilic. The term is still widely used into the Hellenistic period, see Dan. 2.18f., 37, 44; I Enoch 106.5; Tobit 10.11; Judith 5.8; 6.19; and on this A. Bentzen, op. cit., 22, and in detail, A. Vincent, *La Religion des Judéo-Araméens*, 1937, 100–42. From the evidence from Elephantine see esp. P. Cowley 30.15 יהו מרא שמיא, see also Tobit 10.11 sin. ὁ κύριος τοῦ οὐρανοῦ. For the identification of the designation of God with Ahura Mazda see 116ff., on Ba'al-Šāmēm, 119ff. A tendency to theocrasy among the various gods of heaven was already to be found among the Achaemenides, on this see also G. Lanczkowski, *Saeculum* 6, 1935, 227–43, esp. 231ff. According to E. G. Kraeling, *The Brooklyn Museum Aramaic Papyri*, 1953, 84, the 'God of heaven' in Elephantine became above all an 'official divine designation'. The word 'heaven' by itself could also become a periphrasis of the divine name, see Dan. 4.23; Matt. 21.25; Luke 15.18, 21; Bousset/Gressmann, 314; Bill. 1, 862ff.

261. The term appears in the Old Testament above all in the Psalms, but apart from that it is not very frequent. It is therefore all the more striking that it is often used in Ben Sira, see R. Smend, *Griechisch-syrisch-hebräischer Index*, 1907, 236, and still more often in G than in M; it also occurs in Dan. 3.26, 32; 4.14, 21f., 29; 5.18, 21; 7.25; cf. the plural 7.18, 22, 25, 27; Gen.Apoc. 12.7; 20.12, 16; 21.2, 20; 22.15, 16, 21; Jub. 7.13; 13.16, 19; 16.27; 20.9; 21.20, 22ff. etc.; I Enoch 9.3; 10.1; 77.1; 94.8; 98.7; 99.3, 10; 100.4; 101.1, 6; Judith 13.18; Tobit 1.4, 13 and the psalm scroll from 11 Q, DJDJ IV, 64 col. 18, 1, 6f., 12; 87 col. 22, 15; 91 col. 27, 11. On the other hand the term retreats in the main Essene writings, see K. G. Kuhn, *Konkordanz*, 164. In the title of the high priest see RH 18b and *Antt.* 16, 163, cf. E. Bickerman(n), *RIDA* 5, 1958, 147 n. 29. See now G. Bertram, *TDNT* 8, 613ff.

262. See the anonymous Samaritan, FGrHist 724 F 1,5 = Eusebius, *Pr.Ev.* 9, 17, 5: Abraham is received by Melchizedek as a guest in the city of ἱερὸν Ἀργαριζίν, ὃ εἶναι μεθερμηνευόμενον ὄρος ὑψίστου, cf. Gen. 14.19. On this E.Bi(c)-kerman(n), *RHR* 115, 1937, 211f. and *GM*, 91f. This tradition persisted after the transformation of Shechem into the Roman colony Flavia Neapolis. Marinos of Neapolis still speaks in the fifth century of Διὸς ὑψίστου ἁγιώτατον ἱερόν ᾧ καθιέρωτο Ἀβράμος on Gerizim. Damascius, *Vit. Isid.*, in Photius, *Bibl.* 345b Bekker; cf. also F. Cumont, *PW* 9, 445.

263. Philo Byblios, FGrHist 790 F 2.15 = *Pr.Ev.* I, 10, 15: Ἐλιοῦν καλούμενος ὕψιστος, cf. A. B. Cook, *Zeus* II, 2, 886f.; M. H. Pope, *WM* I, 283f., and Mesnil du Buisson, *MUSJ* 41, 1965, 6–9, 24–27. The relationships between the 'Lord of heaven' and the 'supreme God' are old: in a bilingual Phoenician-Hittite inscription from Karatepe *c.* 720 BC, KAI 26 A III, 18f., בעל שמם ואל קן ארץ appear side by side, whereas in Gen. 14.19 (אל עליון קנה שמים וארץ), the god of heaven Elyon and the creator of the earth El are linked in a union, see R. O'Callaghan, *Archiv. Orientální* 18, 1/2, 1950, 361ff. The Eighteen Benedictions show in the first petition that this formula also remained alive in Judaism, see W. Staerk, *Altjüdische Gebete*, KlT 58, 1930², 11, 14. In the inscription of Hatra from the second century AD, KAI 244, 3, on which see A. Caqot, *Syria* 40, 1963, 15f., בע(ל) שמין קנה די רעא, on the other hand Beʻel Šemin as the supreme God of heaven is at the same time the omnipotent creator or 'possessor' of the earth. Further in F. Cumont, *PW* 9, 445f., and *Orientalische Religionen*, 117, 225. The Palmyrene bilingual inscription (*[Διὶ ὑ]ψίστῳ καὶ ἐπηκόῳ* לבעלשמין רבא ו(ר)חמנא) is illuminating J. Cantineau, *Revue d'Assyrologie* 27, 1930, 35; on this see J. G. Février, *La Religion des Palmyréniens*, 126f., and the dedications to the anonymous god 'Zeus Hypsistos'. See also the Phoenician inscription on Arados, SEG 14, 823, AD 208 following the reading of R. Mouterde, *MUSJ* 31, 1954, 334: *[θε]ῷ ὑψίστῳ οὐρανίῳ ὑ<π>[αι]θρα ὁ βωμὸς ἐκτίσθ[η]* and the inscriptions from Byblos in E. Schürer, *SAB* 1897, I, 210. The original close connections of "ʾēl ʻelyôn" with the Phoenician 'baʻal' are stressed by R. Lack, *CBQ* 24, 1962, 44–64, cf. p. 47, the evidence from Ugarit where the epithet "ʻly" is applied to 'bʻl'. On p. 53 there, two further Phoenician inscriptions appear in Greek from the Roman period. The inscription in n. 91 is of course to be altered following R. Mouterde (see above); 'Mithra' is not mentioned here. R. Rendtorff, *ZAW* 78, 1966, 282, 291, agrees.

264. A. B. Cook, *Zeus* II, 2, 875–90. The evidence mounts especially in the Aegean, Asia Minor and Syria, see the details in Nock/Skeat/Roberts, *HTR* 29, 1936, 39–88; cf. M. P. Nilsson, 56, 1963, 101ff. Newer instances in SEG 16, 185; 19, 225, 226, 748, 847, 852; 20, 10, 724. The inscriptions are predominantly post-Christian and it is often difficult to distinguish between the purely pagan, those with Jewish influence and those which are Jewish. The Jewish instances are often the earlier ones, and in part come from the time immediately before the Christian era. Cf. also E. Bickerman(n), *RIDA* 5, 1958, 153ff., and L. Robert, *Anatolia* 3, 1958, 112–20; *CRAI* 1968, 594.

265. See the collection of literary evidence (outside Josephus and Philo) in R. Marcus, *PAAJR*, 1931/32, 1932, 115, and the pre-Christian Jewish inscriptions from Egypt, CIJ 2, nos. 1433, 1443, 1532; Acmonia in Phrygia no. 769;

Delos, CIJ 1, nos. 727–30, and the prayer for vengeance from Rheneia *c.* 100 BC, no. 725. Even in the Roman period, 'Hypsistos' does not seem to have been the official designation of God in dealings with non-Jewish rulers, see Philo, *Leg. ad C.* 157 (M 2, 569), 278 (586), 317 (592); *Antt.* 16, 163; Tacitus, *Hist.* 5, 5, *unumque numen . . . summum illud et aeternum*, Julian the Apostate to the Jews, *Epist. et leges*, ed. Bidez-Cumont, 134 = Lydus, *De mens.* 4, 53: τὸν ναὸν τοῦ ὑψίστου. In synagogue usage, on the other hand, the phrase fell into the background because of the danger of a syncretistic misunderstanding, so the term does not appear at all in the inscriptions in Rome. Even in the NT it is relatively rare; Mark 5.7 and Acts 16.17 are perhaps typical – in the mouth of demon-possessed pagans! Cf. also M. Hengel, in *Festgabe K. G. Kuhn*, 1971, 167 n. 43: 175 n. 46.

266. E. Schürer, *Die Juden im bosporanischen Reich*, SAB 1897, 1, 200–25; A. B. Cook, *Zeus* II, 2, 884f.; M. P. Nilsson, *GGR*² 2, 662ff., and E. R. Goodenough, *JQR* 47, 1956, 221–44, who conjectures that the Bosporus inscriptions come from true Jewish communities. For the syncretistic character of the term see also H. Gressmann, *ZAW* 43, 1925, 16ff., and in *Jewish Studies in Memory of J. Abrahams*, 172, and R. McL. Wilson, *The Gnostic Problem*, 1964, 12f., 24. The later 'Caelicolae' in North Africa point in a similar direction, see A. Torhoudt, *RAC* 2, 817ff., and M. Simon, *RHPR* 26, 1946, 108ff.

267. E. Bickermann, *GM*, 92ff.; see above, n. 63 and n. 234.

268. GM, 113; cf. Herodotus 3,8 and Arrian, *Anab.* 7, 20. For Dusares see T. Klauser, *RAC* 1, 1087; C. Colpe, *KP* 2, 184f.; D. Sourdel, op. cit., 59–68. It is, however, questionable whether the Nabateans were the models for the Jewish Hellenists in 167 BC; moreover, he could be connected with Baʿal-Šāmēm, see op. cit., 28f., 64.

269. *ZDPV* 77, 1961, 186–90; however, the reading is not completely certain, see above, n. 186, and M. Stern (see n. 212 above), 99.

270. Schäfer, *PW*, 2 R.1, 1542; M. P. Nilsson, *GGR*² 2, 660ff.

271. Cf. also II Macc. 10.7: thyrsos staffs (lulab?) at the consecration of the temple, and II Macc. 1.9: the designation 'feast of tabernacles in Chisleu'. For the whole see J. Wellhausen, NGG 1905, 131f.; cf. E. Meyer, *UAC* 2, 209 n. 5; W. O. E. Oesterley, *History of Israel* 2, 307; in detail O. S. Rankin, *The Origins of the Festival of Hanukkah*, 1930, passim; cf. also T. Gaster, *Evidence*, 4 Jg, H. 28, 1952, 31ff. The objection that the celebration of a solstice would have been impossible for the Jews with their luni-solar calendar (see S. Aalen, *Die Begriffe Licht und Finsternis*, 1951, 130–50), is refuted by the existence of the Essene solar calendar. This too probably goes back to an original form of 365 days, perhaps used by the Hellenists, cf. Dan. 7.25: the king altered 'times and law'. The Jewish festal calendar was of course most effectively superseded by a new reckoning of the year from the angels, see Vol. I, p. 235, and below, n. 289.

272. J. Wellhausen, NGG 1905, 131. Cf. M. Avi-Yonah (n. 229 above), 169.

273. For the identification of Iao and Dionysus see above, nn. 46f. For the historical problem see Tarn/Griffith, *Hellenistic Civilization*, 338ff.: 'Far the most important Greek god of the age outside Greece was Dionysus.' He was identified with many gods, not only with Sabazius but also with Serapis, who similarly stood near to Zeus. Typical of the philosophically-based theocrasy is

the definition ascribed to Pythagoras and reminiscent of the Stoic etymology of Zeus, of Dionysus as Διὸς νοῦς or ἡ τοῦ κόσμου ψυχή, in Lydus, *De mens.* 4, 51, Wünsch 108, cf. already Cleanthes, SVF 1, no. 546, and 'the Stoics', SVF 2, no. 1093. Cf. also E. Bickerman(n), *RIDA* 5, 1958, 149f.

274. II Macc. 6.7f.: σπλαγχνισμόν. For the Bacchanalia see K. Latte, *Römische Religionsgeschichte*, 1960, 270ff. Cf. the Bacchantes in Antipater of Sidon (middle of the second century BC), *Anth.Gr.* 9,603, and the musicians in Marisa, Peters/Thiersch, *Painted Tombs*, p. xvi = Goodenough, *Symbols* 2, no. 14.

275. See the superscription in E. Bickermann, *GM*, 134–6, and all the fifth chapter, 117–39.

276. I. Heinemann, op. cit., 159, cf. V. Tcherikover, *HC*, 185.

277. E. Bickermann, *GM*, 128ff. The stylization of the passage is perhaps dependent on Jer. 44.17; cf. I. Lévy, *Semitica* 5, 1955, 16.

278. Hecataeus of Abdera, FGrHist 264 F 6.4 = Diodore 40, fr. 3, who, however, excuses it through the expulsion (ξενηλασία) experienced by the Egyptians.

279. According to Strabo, 17, 1, 19 (802). Cf. above, n. 26.

280. M. Mühl, *Die antike Menschheitsidee*, 1928, 46f., and passim; H. C. Baldry, *The Unity of Mankind*, 1966; Tarn/Griffith, *Hellenistic Civilization*, 79f.; and M. Hadas, *HCu*, 11–19. For the ideal of the world state in Zeno see SVF 1, no. 262: πάντας ἀνθρώπους ἡγώμεθα δημότας καὶ πολίτας.

281. Ps.Aris. 141, cf. 139–69. Cf. Vol. I, pp. 29f.

282. Cf. *Antt.* 12, 244 and on it Vol. I, pp. 52, 271ff.

283. Op. cit., 146ff., 156ff.

284. With this comprehensive thinker it is hardly credible that the teaching of Posidonius on the Jews 'simply rests on ignorance', as I. Heinemann, op. cit., 157 assumes. Behind his account there is a bias, especially as he also attacks alleged Jewish 'superstition' elsewhere, see Vol. I pp. 259f., nn. 14–20, and Seneca, *Epist.* 95, 47 (Reinach 263f.), on which see I. Heinemann, *Poseidonios* 1, 1920, 119, who derives the polemic against the Jewish use of sabbath lights from this. Rhodes, the place of his activity, had a Jewish colony in the first half of the first century, see above, n. I, 337; at the same time the anti-Semitic rhetorician Apollonius Molon worked with him there, though he did not imitate the latter's hostile presentation (see above, nn. 29, 64).

285. *Conf. ling.* 2f. (M 1, 404); for the whole matter see I. Heinemann, *Philons griechische und jüdische Bildung*, 1962, 454ff., and H. A. Wolfson, *Philo* 1, 1948, 82ff.; see also below, n. 311.

286. Josephus, *Antt.* 1, 158–61, cf. 165–9; 159–60, comes from Nicolaus of Damascus and seems to be taken from earlier sources. His contemporary Trogus Pompeius, see Justin, *Epit.* 36, 2 (Reinach 251), also knew it. For the Pergamenes see above, n. 128. For the whole, A. Büchler, *Die Tobiaden und Oniaden*, 1899, 131. Of course his general assignment of these Abraham traditions to Samaritan sources has apologetic motivations. Cf. also L. H. Feldman, *TAPA* 59, 1968, 145–56.

287. Damascius, *Vit. Isidor*, following Photius, *Bibl.* 345b, ed. Bekker, cf. e.g. Eusebius, *Demonstr.Ev.* 1, 5, GCS, ed. I. A. Heikel, 6, 20: Christianity is the renewal of the old pre-Mosaic religion which was lived by Abraham, the friend of God; in Marinus this would then be neo-Platonism.

288. F. Cumont, *Die orientalischen Religionen*, 118, cf. 116ff. For the rise of astrology from the second century BC see Vol. I, pp. 236ff.

289. H. Gressmann, *Die hellenistische Gestirnreligion*, BAO 5, 1925, 19, cf. also in *Jewish Studies in Memory of I. Abrahams*, 1927, 172.

290. SVF 3,265 no. 3, cf. 2: Βόηθος τὸν αἰθέρα θεὸν ἀπεφήνατο, on this see F. Cumont, *Syria* 8, 1927, 163–5, the evidence adduced in connection with two Phoenician altars, from the *Somnium Scipionis*, Cicero, *De re pub.*, 6.17, and Agartharcides of Cnidos, also *ARW* 9, 1906, 331ff., e.g. the definition of 'Sabaoth' as a demiurge over the planets in Lydus, *De mens.* 4, 53, 111 Wünsch, and *Sib. fr.* 3, 3 πανυπέρτατος, cf. 12, 132. For Boethus, see above, n. II, 221.

291. In Daniel the term is relatively rare, 6.3 and 7.25, with the exception of the originally independent penitential prayer, 9.4f., 10f., 13. Cf. also I Macc. 1.49, 52, 57; 2.26f., 42, 48, 50, 58, 64, 67f., etc.

292. Dan. 11.28, 30, cf. 9.4; 11.32. In 9.27 (see Vol. I, p. 288, and n. IV, 207) the 'holy covenant' probably refers to the 'covenant' of the king with the apostates. See also I Macc. 1.15, 63; cf. 1.57, the law as the 'books of the covenant', 2.20, 27, 50; 4.10; II Macc. 7.36; 8.15. On the whole matter see A. Jaubert, *La notion d'alliance dans le Judaïsme*, 1963, 73ff., 77ff. The idea of the covenant founded on the divine election lived on above all among the Essenes (1 QS 4.22), see op. cit., 182ff.

293. Op. cit., 80f. H. J. Schoeps, *Paul*, 1961, 213ff., stresses the original connection between law and covenant, but overlooks the fact that the idea of the covenant was suppressed by the ontology of the Torah not only in the Greek-speaking Diaspora but also among the Rabbis.

294. Josephus, *Antt.* 13, 171ff., 288ff.; see also M. Hengel, *Die Zeloten*, 154ff., 181ff., 190ff., 211ff., 229ff. This zeal is given its final point by its eschatological character, 233f.

295. Josephus, *Antt.* 13, 288–98; cf. *Kidd.* 66a. For the Essenes, see Vol. I, pp. 224–7.

296. For Alexander Jannaeus see *Antt.* 13, 372–6, 379–83; for Herod, Archelaus and the procurators see M. Hengel, op. cit., 107–110, 196, 326ff., 332ff., 348f.

297. Op. cit., 204ff., 229ff. For Antichrist see op. cit., 309ff.; for the temple 190 n. 3, 4, and 211ff., 215ff.

298. *Antt.* 13, 254ff., 274–81, 324ff., 356ff., 393ff. For the position of the Jews in Egypt see *Antt.* 12, 387ff.; 13, 284ff., 349, 354ff.; 14, 99 and *c. Ap.* 2, 64, see also Vol. I, pp. 15ff., and Tcherikover, CPJ 1, 19–25.

299. For Posidonius, see above, n. 17; for Apion see *c. Ap.* 2, 80f.; for the fragments from Porphyry's work 'Against the Christians' preserved in Jerome's commentary on Daniel see FGrHist F 49–58. For the Hellenistic-antisemitic assessment of Antiochus IV see also E. Bickermann, *GM*, 21ff.

300. Schürer 1, 674ff.; N. N. Glatzer, *Geschichte der talmudischer Zeit*, 1937, 38ff. See already Sidetes, the counsellor of Antiochus VII, following Posidonius (Reinach 56).

301. *Antt.* 13, 299 = *Bell.* 1, 68f., cf. on this E. Bammel, *TLZ* 79, 1954, 352–6.

302. The degree to which the victory of the Maccabees lived on among the people is shown by the relatively numerous memorial days from this period in

the fast scroll, see H. Lichtenstein, *HUCA* 8/9, 1931/32, 273–90, cf. also M. Hengel, op. cit., 176ff.

303. The best instance of this is the conversion to Judaism of the ruling house in Adiabene, the members of which fought against the Romans in the defence of Jerusalem, see *Antt.*20, 17–96 (cf. also *Gen.R.*46, 10); *Bell.*2, 388, 520; 6, 356. Seneca's judgment on the Jewish mission is typical (according to Augustine, *Civ.Dei* 6.10, Reinach 262f.): '*victi victoribus leges dederunt*', cf. Juvenal 14, 100 (Reinach 292). For the whole matter see also K. G. Kuhn, *TDNT* 6, 730–45. The complete proselyte was 'in every respect an Israelite', *Yeb.*47b: בישראל הוא לכל דבריו. After AD 70 the *fiscus Judaicus* was levied from every circumcised Jew, even the proselytes. Intrinsically a punitive tax for the rebellious 'ethnos' of the Jews (see Suetonius, *Domitian* 12, 2: *posita genti tributa*), it also affected the Jews as a 'religious association', see J. Juster, 2, 282ff., and Tcherikover, *CPJ* 1, 8off. The two could not be separated. For the Jewish mission in general and for the later period see M. Simon, *Verus Israel*, 1949, 315–55, who stresses that in contrast to the full proselytes the *metuentes* were never completely recognized: 'ils restent sur le parvis comme des catéchumènes permanents' (323, 331). Cf. also 327: 'Se convertir au judaïsme, c'est rompre avec le monde.'

304. This is one of the background reasons for the frequent expulsion of the Jews from Rome, see Valerius Maximus, above n. 41, and H. Leon, *The Jews of Ancient Rome*, 1960, 17ff., together with Domitian's sharp measures against the Jews, op. cit., 33ff. For the indirect prohibition of proselytism through the maintaining of the prohibition against circumcision by Antoninus Pius see J. Juster, 1, 266ff.; Moore, *Judaism* 1, 351f., and K. G. Kuhn, *TDNT* 6, 738f. For the political power of Diaspora Judaism see H. Hegermann, *UU* 1, 302f.

305. He defends himself against this charge in Romans 9.1ff., see on this O. Michel, *Der Brief an die Römer*, ¹²1963, 223: 'The synagogue regards him as "apostate" and 'heretic" '; i.e. for them he was comparable with the apostates in Jerusalem under Antiochus IV.

306. Cf. however, also for Judea *Sanh.*10, 1; *T.Sanh.*13, 5 or *Sanh.*111b Bar.: 'those who want to cast off the yoke of heaven', and the detailed discussion of apostasy in the Talmudic tradition: K. Kohler and R. Gottheil, *JE* 1, 12f.

307. For Samaria see figures like Dositheus (possibly two of this name), Simon Magus and Menander, who exercised a notable influence on the development of gnosticism, see already A. Hilgenfeld, *Die Ketzergeschichte des Urchristentums*, 1884, 155ff., 163ff., 187ff.; for the more recent discussion see R. McL. Wilson, *ZRGG* 9, 1957, 21–30; T. Caldwell, *Kairos* 3, 1962, 105–17; K. Beyschlag, *ZTK* 68, 1971, 395–426. For Transjordania see e.g. the origins of the Mandeans, C. Colpe, *RGG*³ 4, 711f.; K. Rudolph, *Die Mandäer* 1, 1960, 52ff.; 246–55, and the summary by S. Schulz, *TR* 26, 1960, 314ff., 318f., 323, 325f., 334; also the sect of the Elkesaites, who presumably stem directly from the Jewish baptist movement and were only 'Christianized' superficially when they penetrated into the West, see J. Thomas, *Le mouvement baptiste*, 1935, 140ff. Syncretistic-gnostic groups could also be contained in the catalogues of Jewish sects in Justin, *Dial. c. Tryph.* 80, 2, and Hegesippus in Eusebius, *HE* 4, 22, 7.

308. Tcherikover/Fuks, *CPJ* 3, 45ff., cf. also R. McL. Wilson, *The Gnostic*

Problem, ²1964, 9–17. The survey by H. Gressmann, *ZAW* 43, 1925, 1–32, is still fundamental. For Asia Minor see G. Kittel, *TLZ* 69, 1944, 16.

309. Whereas Tcherikover, loc. cit., suggests purely pagan groups, who imitated Jewish customs, Goodenough believed the Hypsistos worshippers in the kingdom of the Bosporus to be Jews, see above n. 266. Cf. M. Hengel, *Festgabe K. G. Kuhn*, 1971, 173ff., 179.

310. See on this G. Bornkamm, *Das Ende des Gesetzes*, 1952, 139–56.

311. For Philo see above, n. 285; for the 'allegorists' see *Migr.Ab.* 89ff. (M 1, 450), cf. also his polemic against apostasy to the mystery religions, *Spec.leg.* 1, 319–25 (M 2,260f. on Deut. 23.17 LXX).

312. III Macc. 1.3; 2.30f.; 7.10f., 15, cf. also CIJ 2, nos. 742, 749 and CPJ 3, no. 475, and Schürer 3, 49. On the whole these remain exceptions, see Tcherikover, *HC* 352ff.

313. R. McL. Wilson, *The Gnostic Problem*, ²1964, passim, see esp. 172–255. Cf. G. Quispel, *Eranos Jahrbuch* 22, 1953, 195–234 in connection with Codex Jung, p. 112; *EvTh* 14, 1954, 474–84; O. Betz, in *Abraham unser Vater, Festschrift für O. Michel*, 1963, 24–43, and the articles by A. Böhlig, 'Mysterion und Wahrheit', *AGSU* 6, 1968, 80–111, 149–61, on the texts from Nag Hammadi; K. Rudolph, *Kairos* 9, 1967, 105–22. For Jewish magic see Vol. I, pp. 241f.

314. H. Braun, *Spätjüdisch-häretischer und frühchristlicher Radikalismus*, 1957, I, 17, 32f., 73, 99; 2, 3 etc.; cf. also M. Hengel, *Zeloten*, 229ff.

315. E.g. J. Klausner, *From Jesus to Paul*, 1944, 450ff., 496ff., 528ff., 600ff. L. Baeck, *Aus drei Jahrtausenden*, 1958, 47ff.; L. Baeck, *Paulus, die Pharisäer*, 1961, 19ff., 131ff., and H. J. Schoeps, *Paul*, 1961, 149ff., 213ff., 259ff. Cf. on the other hand W. G. Kümmel, *Heilsgeschehen und Geschichte*, 1965, 169–91 and 441f., 450, 453f.

316. H. J. Schoeps, op. cit., 261.

TABLE I

Palestinian and Phoenician Places and Regions according to the Zeno Papyri, see J. Herz, *PJB* 24, 1928, 98ff.

	PCZ	PSI	PColZen	Others
Gaza/5	(59001 Gazaios) 59009/93 59537	322–616		
Gazaiōn limēn/4 (Strabo 759)	59006/59813	863g (602)	2	
Skēnai/2			2,6	PLond 1930, 34
Ashkelon/2	59012(?) 59010			
Iopē/3	59011/93	406		
Pēgai/1		406		
Stratonos Pyrgos/1	59004			
Ptolemais/12	59004/8 59689(?) lines 11, 25	366/403 406/495 612/616		PLond inv. 2358b, 2 PLond 1931
Tyre/3	59011/59093 59558 (59666 Hendylus, son of Dio, Tyrian)			
Sidon/6	59010/59093 59672/59281		2	PZenMich 3 (PRyl, 554 Abdemoun of Sidon)
Tripolis/1		495		
Heraclea in Phoenicia	59088 see L. H. Vincent, *RB* 29, 1920, 178			
Plains of Masyas/1	59093			
Idumaea/1	59015			
Marisa/3	59006/15 59537			

	PCZ	PSI	PColZen	Others
Adoreos/1 (Adora)	59006			
Hierosolyma/2	59004/5			
Ericho/1	59004			
Galila/1			2	
Bait(i)anata/4	59004/11	594(554)		PLond 1948
Cydisus/1	59004			
(Nabataioi)		406		
(Moabitĕs)	Vol. 4, 285 on 59009			
Ammanitis/1	59003			
Rabbatammana/2		406(?): ἐξ ᾽Αμμώνων 616		
Birta/2 (of Tobias)	59003			
Abella/2 (Abila)	59004			PLond 1930, 171
Surabit/2 (Sorabitt)	59004			PLond 1930, 175f.
Lakasa	59004			
Noĕ	59004			
Eitoui	59004			
Hauran	59008	406		
Damascus	59006 Dionysus from D.			
Syria	59672	648 slaves 324/5 grain		PZenMich 2 PCorn I EPColZen 66, 2, 11

TABLE II

Early Hellenistic Coins from Palestinian Excavations: see notes I, 341

	1 Samaria 1908/10	2 Samaria 1931/3€	3 Beth Zur 1931+57	4 Scytho-polis 1921/23	5 Shechem	6 Tell ed Duweir	7 Tell en Nasbe	8 Engedi	9 Ramath Raḥel	10 Tell el-Ful	Total
Before Alexander	1	—	} 10	—	1	5	1	—	—	—	} 24
Alexander the Great	1	—		—	1	4	—	—	—	—	
Total	2	—	10	—	2	9	1	—	—	—	24
Ptol. I 305–285(3)	17	4	6	1	12	1	—	—	—	—	41
II 285(3)–246	31	48	35	20	30	6	4	2	1	3	180
III 246–221	3 }	6	5	—	1	—	—	—	—	—	22
IV 221–204	1 }	—	1	—	3	2	—	—	—	—	
V 204–200(181)	1	—	2	—	11	—	—	—	—	—	14
VI 181–145	—	—	—	—	—	—	—	—	—	—	—
Ptolemaic coins to which no exact date can be assigned (mostly Ptol. II)	12	22	10	—	—	7	—	—	—	—	51

	1 Samaria 1908/10	2 Samaria 1931/33	3 Beth Zur 1931+57	4 Scytho-polis 1921/23	5 Shechem	6 Tell ed Duweir	7 Tell en Nasbe	8 Engedi	9 Ramath Raḥel	10 Tell el-Ful	Total
Total	65	80	59	21	57	14	4	2	1	—	308
Seleucids before 200	1 (Ant. I. gold)	—	—	—	—	1 Sel. I 1 Ant. I	—	—	—	—	3
Ant. III (221) 200–187	20	18	10	—	7	6	1	1	2	—	65
Sel. IV 187–175	1	—	2	—	—	—	—	—	—	—	3
Ant. IV 175–164	46	34	110	—	3	3	1	—	—	—	197
Ant. III or IV, no exact assignation	—	—	14	—	—	—	—	—	—	—	14
Total	68	52	136	—	10	11	2	1	2	—	282
Others	1 Aradus 208 BC	—	—	—	—	1 Side 300 BC	—	—	2 Sophene Armenia	—	4
Total	1	—	—	—	—	1	—	—	2	—	4

ABBREVIATIONS

To save space, titles of books cited in the notes are often referred to in abbreviated form after the first mention of them; such abbreviations are not listed here, but can easily be clarified with the use of the bibliography.

AAB	Abhandlungen der königlich Preussischen (after 1945/46 Deutschen) Akademie der Wissenschaften zu Berlin
AAH	Abhandlungen der Heidelberger Akademie der Wissenschaften
AAM	Abhandlungen der Bayerischen Akademie der Wissenschaften, München
AAL	Abhandlungen der Sächsischen Akademie der Wissenschaften, Leipzig
AAMz	Abhandlungen der Akademie der Wissenschaften . . ., Mainz
(A)ASOR	(Annual of the) American Schools of Oriental Research
ADAJ	Annual of the Department of Antiquities of Jordan
Aeg	Aegyptus, Rivista Italiana di Egittologia e di Papirologia
AfO	Archiv für Orientforschung
AGG	Abhandlungen der Gesellschaft der Wissenschaften, Göttingen
AGSU	Arbeiten zur Geschichte des Spätjudentums und Urchristentums
AHR	American Historical Revue
AIPHOS	Annuaire de l'Institut de Philologie et d'Histoire Orientales et Slaves
AJA	American Journal of Archaeology
AJP	American Journal of Philology
AJSL	American Journal of Semitic Languages and Literatures
AJT	American Journal of Theology
ALUOS	Annual of the Leeds University Oriental Society
ANET²	Ancient Near Eastern Texts, ed. J. B. Pritchard
AnthGr	Anthologia Graeca
AO	Der Alte Orient
AOB²	Altorientalische Bilder, ed. H. Gressmann
AOT²	Altorientalische Texte, ed. H. Gressmann
APF	Archiv für Papyrusforschung
ARW	Archiv für Religionswissenschaft

ASTI	*Annual of the Swedish Theological Institute in Jerusalem*
ATD	Das Alte Testament Deutsch
ATR	*Anglican Theological Review*
BA	*The Biblical Archaeologist*
BAL	Berichte über die Verhandlungen der Sächsichen Akademie . . . zu Leipzig
BASOR	*Bulletin of the American Schools of Oriental Research*
BBB	Bonner Biblische Beiträge
BFCT	Beiträge zur Förderung Christlicher Theologie
BGU	Ägyptische Urkunden aus den königlichen Museen zu Berlin: Griechische Urkunden I–VIII, 1895–1933
BhAO	Beiheft zu Der Alte Orient
BHHWB	*Biblisch-Historisches Handwörterbuch*, ed. B. Reicke and L. Rost
BHT	Beiträge zur historischen Theologie
Bibl	Biblica
BIES	*Bulletin of the Israel Exploration Society*
Bill	*Kommentar zum Neuen Testament aus Talmud und Midrasch*, ed. H. L. Strack and P. Billerbeck
BJPES	*Bulletin of the Jewish Palestine Exploration Society*
BJRL	*Bulletin of the John Rylands Library*
BKAT	Biblisches Kommentar, Altes Testament
BMB	*Bulletin du Musée de Beyrouth*
BRL	*Biblisches Reallexikon*, ed. K. Galling
BSt	Biblische Studien
BWA(N)T	Beiträge zur Wissenschaft vom Alten (und Neuen) Testament
BZ	*Biblische Zeitschrift*
BZAW	Beihefte zur Zeitschrift für die Alttestamentliche Wissenschaft
BZNW	Beihefte zur Zeitschrift für die Neutestamentliche Wissenschaft
CAF	Comicorum Atticorum Fragmenta
CAH	*The Cambridge Ancient History*
CBQ	*Catholic Biblical Quarterly*
CCAG	Catalogus codicum Astrologorum Graecorum
CH	Corpus Hermeticum
ChrEg	*Chronique d'Égypte*
ChrW	*Christliche Welt*
CIJ	Corpus Inscriptionum Judaicarum
CIS	Corpus Inscriptionum Semiticarum
ClassPhil	*Classical Philology*
ClassQ	*Classical Quarterly*
CPJ	Corpus Papyrorum Judaicarum
CRAI	*Comptes Rendus de l'Académie des Inscriptions et Belles-Lettres*
CSEL	Corpus Scriptorum Ecclesiasticorum Latinorum

DAW	Denkschriften der Kaiserlichen Akademie der Wissenschaften in Wien
DJD(J)	Discoveries in the Judaean Desert (of Jordan)
DP	C. Watzinger, *Denkmäler Palästinas*
EJ	*Encyclopaedia Judaica*
ET	English translation
ETL	*Ephemerides Theologicae Lovanienses*
EvTh	*Evangelische Theologie*
ExpT	*Expository Times*
FF	*Forschungen und Fortschritte*
FGrHist	Fragmente der Griechischen Historiker, ed. F. Jacoby
FHG	Fragmenta Historicorum Graecorum, ed. C. Müller
FRLANT	Forschungen zur Religion und Literatur des Alten und Neuen Testaments
G	Greek text
GCS	Die Griechischen Christlichen Schriftsteller der ersten 3 Jahrhunderte
GG³	H. Bengtson, *Griechische Geschichte*
GGL⁶	W. Schmid and O. Stählin, *Geschichte der Griechischen Literatur*
GGM	Geographi Graeci Minores, ed. C. Müller
GGMS	B. Niese, *Geschichte der griechischen und makedonischen Staaten*
GGR²	M. P. Nilsson, *Geschichte der Griechischen Religion*
GI³	A. Schlatter, *Geschichte Israels*
GM	E. Bickermann, *Der Gott der Makkabäer*
HAT	Handbuch zum Alten Testament
HAW	Handbuch der Altertumswissenschaft
HC	V. Tcherikover, *Hellenistic Civilization and the Jews*
HCu	M. Hadas, *Hellenistic Culture*
HNT	Handbuch zum Neuen Testament
HP	F. M. Abel, *Histoire de la Palestine*
HTR	*Harvard Theological Review*
HUCA	*Hebrew Union College Annual*
HW	M. Rostovtzeff, *The Social and Economic History of the Hellenistic World*
HZ	*Historische Zeitschrift*
IEJ	*Israel Exploration Journal*
IG	Inscriptiones Graecae
IGLS	Inscriptions Grecques et Latines de la Syrie, ed. L. Jalabert and E. Mouterde
Inst	E. Bickerman(n), *Institutions des Séleucides*
JAOS	*Journal of the American Oriental Society*
JBL	*Journal of Biblical Literature*
JbPhil	Jahrbücher für classische Philologie
JCS	*Journal of Cuneiform Studies*
JE	*The Jewish Encyclopedia*

JEA	*Journal of Egyptian Archaeology*
JewSocSt	*Jewish Social Studies*
JHS	*Journal of Hellenic Studies*
JJS	*Journal of Jewish Studies*
JJurPap	*Journal of Juristic Papyrology*
JPOS	*Journal of the Palestine Oriental Society*
JQR	*Jewish Quarterly Review*
JR	*Journal of Religion*
JSS	*Journal of Semitic Studies*
JTS	*Journal of Theological Studies*
KAI	H. Donner and W. Röllig, Kanaanitische und aramäische Inschriften
KAT	Kommentar zum Alten Testament
KEKNT	Kritisch-exegetischer Kommentar über das Neue Testament
KP	*Der Kleine Pauly*
LCL	Loeb Classical Library
LUÅ	Lunds Universitets Årsskrift
M	Hebrew text
MBPAR	Münchener Beiträge zur Papyrusforschung und antiken Rechtsgeschichte
MGWJ	*Monatsschrift für Geschichte und Wissenschaft des Judentums*
MUB = MUSJ	*Mélanges de (la Faculté Orientale de) l'Université Saint-Joseph, Beyrouth*
MusHelv	*Museum Helveticum*
MVÄG	Mitteilungen der Vorderasiatisch(-Ägyptisch)en Gesellschaft
NBGAW	Neue Beiträge zur Geschichte der Alten Welt
NClio	*La Nouvelle Clio*
NF(NS)	Neue Folge (new series)
NGG	Nachrichten von der Gesellschaft der Wissenschaften zu Göttingen
NJWJ	*Neue Jahrbücher für Wissenschaft und Jugendbildung*
NoctRom	*Noctes Romanae*
NovTest	*Novum Testamentum*
NTS	*New Testament Studies*
OA	*Oriens Antiquus*
OGIS	W. Dittenberger, Orientis Graeci Inscriptiones Selectae
OLZ	*Orientalische Literaturzeitung*
OTL	Old Testament Library
OTS	*Oudtestamentische Studiën*
P (CZ; Corn; Ox; Si; etc.)	See bibliography on papyrus collections
PAAJR	*Proceedings of the American Academy for Jewish Research*
ParPass	*La Parola del Passato*
PEFA	*Palestine Exploration Fund Annual*
PEQ	*Palestine Exploration Quarterly*

PG	J. P. Migne, *Patrologia*, Series Graeca
PGM	Papyri Graecae Magicae
PhGr[6]	E. Zeller, *Philosophie der Griechen*
Phil	Philologus
PJB	*Palästinajahrbuch*
PL	Migne, *Patrologia*, Series Latina
PW	*Paulys Realencyclopädie der classischen Altertumswissenschaft*
PW, 2R	Second row, beginning with letter R
PW Suppl	Supplementary volumes
QDAP	*Quarterly of the Department of Antiquities in Palestine*
QFAGG	Quellen und Forschungen zur Alten Geschichte und Geographie
RAC	*Reallexikon für Antike und Christentum*
RAO	*Revue d'Assyriologie et d'Archéologie Orientale*
RB	*Revue Biblique*
RBPH	*Revue Belge de Philologie et d'Histoire*
RE	*Realencyklopädie für protestantische Theologie und Kirche*
REG	*Revue des Études Grecques*
REJ	*Revue des Études Juives*
RES	Répertoire d'épigraphie sémitique
RevArch	*Revue Archéologique*
RevPhil	*Revue Philologique*
RGG[3]	*Die Religion in Geschichte und Gegenwart*
RGVV	Religionsgeschichtliche Versuche und Vorarbeiten
RheinMus	*Rheinisches Museum für Philologie*
RHPR	*Revue d'Historie et de Philosophie Religieuses*
RHR	*Revue de l'Histoire des Religions*
RIDA	*Revue Internationale des Droits de l'Antiquité*
RivBibl	*Rivista Biblica*
RQ	*Revue de Qumran*
RSR	*Recherches de Science Religieuse*
SAB	Sitzungsberichte der Deutschen (Preussischen) Akademie der Wissenschaften zu Berlin
SAH	Sitzungsberichte der Heidelberger Akademie der Wissenschaften
SAW	Sitzungsberichte der Österreichischer Akademie der Wissenschaften in Wien
SB	Sammelbuch griechischer Urkunden aus Ägypten, ed. F. Preisigke, F. Bilabel and E. Kiessling
SBT	Studies in Biblical Theology
SC	Sources Chrétiennes
ScrHieros	*Scripta Hierosolymitana*
SEG	Supplementum epigraphicum Graecum
StTh	Studia Theologica cura ordinum theologorum Scandinavicorum edita
SUNT	Studien zur Umwelt des Neuen Testaments

SVF	Stoicorum veterum fragmenta
SVT	Supplements to *Vetus Testamentum*
Syr	Syriac text
T	Tosephta, ed. M. S. Zuckermandel
TAPA	*Transactions and Proceedings of the American Philological Association*
TDNT	*Theological Dictionary of the New Testament*
TLZ	*Theologische Literaturzeitung*
TR	*Theologische Rundschau*
ThStKr	*Theologische Studien und Kritiken*
TU	Texte und Untersuchungen zur Geschichte der altchristlichen Literatur
TZ	*Theologische Zeitschrift*
UAC	E. Meyer, *Ursprung und Anfänge des Christentums*
UUÅ	Uppsala Universitets Årsskrift
UU	J. Leipoldt and W. Grundmann, *Umwelt des Urchristentums*
UPZ	U. Wilcken, *Urkunden der Ptolemäerzeit*
VT	*Vetus Testamentum*
WM	*Wörterbuch der Mythologie*, ed. H. W. Haussig
WMANT	Wissenschaftliche Monographien zum Alten und Neuen Testament
WUNT	Wissenschaftliche Untersuchungen zum Neuen Testament
WZKM	*Wiener Zeitschrift für die Kunde des Morgenlandes*
YCS	Yale Classical Studies
ZAW	*Zeitschrift für die Alttestamentliche Wissenschaft*
ZÄS	*Zeitschrift für Ägyptische Sprache und Altertumskunde*
ZDMG	*Zeitschrift der Deutschen Morgenländischen Gesellschaft*
ZDPV	*Zeitschrift des Deutschen Palästina-Vereins*
ZNW	*Zeitschrift für die Neutestamentliche Wissenschaft*
ZPapEp	*Zeitschrift für Papyrologie und Epigraphik*
ZRGG	*Zeitschrift für Religions- und Geistesgeschichte*
ZTK	*Zeitschrift für Theologie und Kirche*

BIBLIOGRAPHY

Titles of works cited in abbreviated form in the notes are given in full here, but articles from encyclopedias and dictionaries, etc. (*PW, RAC, RGG, TDNT, KP*), are not listed in detail.

I SOURCES

1. *Old Testament and Jewish Sources*

(*a*) *Pseudepigrapha and Jewish-Hellenistic literature*
Adam, A., *Antike Berichte über die Essener*, Kleine Texte 182, Berlin 1961.
Aristeas, Letter of: A. Pelletier, *Lettre d'Aristée à Philocrate*, SC 89, Paris 1962.
Asatir: M. Gaster, *The Samaritan Book of Moses*, London 1927.
Assumptio Mosis: C. Clemen (ed.), *Die Himmelfahrt des Mose*, Kleine Texte 10, Berlin 1904.
Baruch Apocalypse (Syr.): M. Kmosko (ed)., *Liber Apokalypseos Baruch filii Neriae*, Patrologia Syriaca I, 2, Paris 1907.
Charles, R. H., *The Apocrypha and Pseudepigrapha of the Old Testament*, Vols. I and II, Oxford 1913, reprinted 1963.
Daniel: J. Ziegler (ed.), *Susanna, Daniel, Bel et Draco*, Septuaginta, Soc.Litt.Gott. XVI, 2, Göttingen 1954.
Enoch, Ethiopian (= *I Enoch*): R. H. Charles, *The Book of Enoch*, Oxford ²1912.
Ezra Apocalypse: ed. B. Violet, Vols. I and II, GCS 18/32, Leipzig 1910/24.
— C. Bonner, *The Last Chapters of Enoch in Greek*, Studies and Documents 8, London 1937.
Josephus, Flavius: B. Niese (ed.), *Opera*, Vols. I–V, Berlin ²1955.
— H. St J. Thackeray, R. Marcus and L. H. Feldman (eds.), LCL I–IX, London 1926–65.
— T. Reinach (ed.), Vols. I–IV, *Antiquités*, French translation by J. Weill and J. Chamonard, Paris 1900ff.
— O. Michel and O. Bauernfeind (eds.), *De bello Judaico*, Vols. I and II, 1, edited and with a German translation, Darmstadt 1959, 1963.
Kautzsch, E., *Die Apokryphen und Pseudepigraphen des Alten Testaments*, Vol. II, *Die Pseudepigraphen des Alten Testaments*, Tübingen 1900.
Maccabees: W. Kappler (ed.), *Maccabaeorum liber 1*, Septuaginta, Soc.Litt.Gott., Vol. IX, 1, Göttingen 1936.
— W. Kappler and R. Hanhart (eds.), *Maccabaeorum libri 2-3*, Septuaginta, Soc.Litt.Gott., Vol. IX, 2, Göttingen 1965.

— Bruyne, D. de, *Les anciennes traductions latines des Machabées*, Anecdota Maredsolana 4, 1932.

Philo of Alexandria: L. Cohn and P. Wendland, *Opera quae supersunt*, Vols. I–VII, Berlin 1896–1930.

— *Philo Supplement, Questions and Answers on Genesis/Exodus*, ET by R. Marcus, Vols. I and II, LCL, 1953.

Pseudo-Philo: G. Kisch (ed.), *Liber Antiquitatum Biblicarum*, Notre Dame, Indiana 1949.

Pseudo-Phocylides: J. Bernays (ed.), *Ueber das Phokylideische Gedicht*, Berlin 1853.

Riessler, P., *Altjüdisches Schrifttum ausserhalb der Bibel*, Augsburg 1928.

Schermann, T., *Propheten- und Apostellegenden*, TU 31, 3, Leipzig 1907.

Sibyllines: A. Kurfess, *Sibyllinische Weissagungen*, text and German translation, Berlin 1951.

— J. Geffcken (ed.), *Die Oracula Sibyllina*, GCS 8, Leipzig 1902.

Sirach: J. Ziegler (ed.), *Sapientia Jesu Filii Sirach*, Septuaginta, Soc.Litt.Gott., Vol. XII, 2, Göttingen 1965.

— Segal, M. S., *Sefer Ben-Sira*, Jerusalem ²1958 (in Hebrew).

— Smend, R., *Die Weisheit des Jesus Sirach*, Berlin 1906 (Hebrew and German).

— Lévi, I(sraël), 'Un nouveau fragment de Ben Sira', *REJ* 92, 1932, 136–45.

— Schirrmann, J., 'A New Leaf from the Hebrew Ecclesiasticus', *Tarbiz* 27, 1958–59, 440–3.

— Yadin, Y., *The Ben Sira Scroll from Masada*, Jerusalem 1965.

— Syriac translation: P. A. de Lagarde (ed.), *Libri Veteris Testamenti apocryphi Syriace*, 1861.

Testaments of the Twelve Patriarchs: R. H. Charles, *The Greek Versions of the Testaments of the Twelve Patriarchs*, Oxford 1908.

Wisdom of Solomon: J. Ziegler (ed.), *Sapientia Salomonis*, Septuaginta, Soc.Litt. Gott., Vol. XII, 1, Göttingen 1965.

(b) *Qumran texts*

Allegro, J. M., 'Messianic References in Qumran Literature', *JBL* 75, 1956, 174–87.

— 'Fragments of a Qumran Scroll of Eschatological Midrāšîm', *JBL* 77, 1958, 350–4.

— 'A Recently Discovered Fragment of a Commentary on Hosea from Qumran's Fourth Cave', *JBL* 78, 1959, 144–7.

— 'An Unpublished Fragment of Essene Halakhah', *JSS* 6, 1961, 71–3.

— 'Some Unpublished Fragments of Pseudepigraphical Literature from Qumran's Fourth Cave', *ALUOS* 4, 1962–3, 3–5.

— 'The Wiles of the Wicked Woman, a Sapiental Work from Qumran's Fourth Cave', *PEQ* 96, 1964, 53–5.

— 'An Astrological Cryptic Document from Qumran', *JSS* 9, 1964, 291–4.

The Dead Sea Scrolls from St Mark's Monastery, Vol. 1: *The Isaiah Manuscript and the Habakkuk Commentary*, ed. M. Burrows, New Haven 1950.

— Vol. II: *The Manual of Discipline*, New Haven 1952.

The Dead Sea Scrolls of the Hebrew University, ed. E. L. Sukenik, Jerusalem 1955 (1 QM and 1 QH).

DJD I, *Qumran Cave I*, ed. D. Barthélemy, J. T. Milik, et al., Oxford 1955.

DJD II, *Les Grottes de Murabba'ât*, ed. P. Benoit, J. T. Milik and R. de Vaux, Oxford 1961.

DJDJ III, *Les 'petites Grottes' de Qumrân*, ed. M. Baillet, J. T. Milik and R. de Vaux, Oxford 1962.

DJDJ IV, *The Psalms Scroll of Qumrân Cave 11*, ed. J. A. Sanders, Oxford 1965.

DJDJ V, *Qumran Cave 4, I (4Q 158–186)*, ed. J. M. Allegro with the collaboration of A. A. Anderson, Oxford 1968.

A Genesis Apocryphon, ed. N. Avigad and Y. Yadin, Jerusalem 1956.

Lohse, E., *Die Texte aus Qumran*, Darmstadt 1964 (Hebrew and German).

Milik, J. T., 'Le Testament de Lévi en Araméen', *RB* 62, 1955, 398–406.

— ' "Priere de Nabonide" et autres écrits d'un cycle de Daniel', *RB* 63, 1956, 407–15.

— 'Hénoch au pays des aromates', *RB* 65, 1958, 70–7.

Sanders, J. A., 'Ps. 151 in 11QPss', *ZAW* 75, 1963, 75–85.

— 'The Non-canonical Psalms in 11 QPsᵃ', *ZAW* 76, 1964, 57–75.

Starcky, J., 'Un texte messianique araméen de la grotte 4 de Qumran', in: *Mémorial du Cinquantenaire de l'École des langues orientales anciennes de l'Institut Catholique de Paris*, 1964, 51–66.

Stegemann, H., 'Der Pešer Psalm 37 aus Höhle 4 von Qumran', *RQ* 14, 1963, 235–70.

Strugnell, J., 'The Angelic Liturgy at Qumran', *Congress Volume Oxford 1959*, SVT 7, 1960, 318–46.

Testuz, M., 'Deux fragments des manuscrits de la Mer Morte', *Semitica* 5, 1955, 37–8.

Vermes, G., *The Dead Sea Scrolls in English*, Harmondsworth ²1965.

Woude, A. S. van der, 'Melchisedek als himmlische Erlösergestalt in den neugefundenen eschatologischen Midraschim aus Qumran Höhle XI', *OTS* 14, 1965, 354–73.

(c) Rabbinic texts

Aboth de Rabbi Nathan, ed. S. Schechter, Wien 1887 (*AbRN*).

Lichtenstein, H., 'Die Fastenrolle', *HUCA* 8/9, 1931/32, 257–351.

Mekilta de Rabbi Jischmael, ed. J. Z. Lauterbach, Vols. I–III, Philadelphia 1949 (*Mek.Ex.*).

Midrasch Rabbah über die 5 Bücher der Tora und die 5 Megillot, Vols. I and II, ed. R. J. Grassman and M. S. Weisberg, reprinted New York 1952.

Midrash Rabbah, ET ed. H. Freedman and M. Simon, Vols. I–X, London 1951.

Midrasch Tehillim, ed. S. Buber, Wilna 1892.

The Mishnah, ed. H. Danby, Oxford 1933.

Siphre on Num. and Deut.: Sifre d'be Rabh, ed. M. Friedmann, 1866, reprinted New York 1948.

Talmud Babli, Vols. I–XII, Wilna 1895–1908.

The Babylonian Talmud, ET ed. I. Epstein, London 1935–48.

Talmud jeruschalmi, reprint of the Krotoschiner Ausgabe, New York 1949.

Targum Jeruschalmi I: Targum Pseudojonathan, ed. M. Ginsburger, Berlin 1903.

Tosephta, ed. M. S. Zuckermandel, Pasewalk 1881.

Tosephta Ki-Fshutah, ed. S. Lieberman, Vol. IV, New York 1962.

2. *Christian Sources*

Novum Testamentum Graece, ed. E. and E. Nestle and K. Aland, Stuttgart
    [25]1963.

Clement of Alexandria, Vol. I, *Protrepticus and Paedagogus*, ed. O. Stählin,
    GCS 12, Leipzig 1936.

— Vol. II, *Stromata* I–VI, ed. O. Stählin–L. Früchtel, GCS 52 (15), Berlin
    [3]1960.

— Vol. III, *Stromata* VII–VIII etc., ed. O. Stählin, GCS 17, Leipzig 1909.

Epiphanius, *Panarion Haer.*, Vols. I–III, ed. K. Holl, GCS 25, 31, 37, Leipzig
    1915–33.

Eusebius, *The Ecclesiastical History*, ed. H. J. Lawlor and J. E. L. Oulton,
    Vols. I and II, London 1927–28.

— Vol. VIII, 1, 2, *Praeparatio evangelica*, ed. K. Mras, GCS 43, 1, 2, Berlin
    1954–56.

— Vol. VI, *Demonstratio evangelica*, ed. I. A. Heikel, GCS 23, Leipzig 1913.

— Vol. VII, *Die Chronik des Hieronymus*, ed. R. Helm, GCS 47 (24, 34), Berlin
    1956.

Hennecke, E.–Schneemelcher, W.–Wilson, R. McL., *New Testament Apocrypha*,
    Vol. II, London 1965.

Hippolytus, *Refutatio omnium haeresium (Philosophumena)*, ed. P. Wendland,
    GCS 26, Leipzig 1916.

Irenaeus, *Adversus haereses*, ed. W. W. Harvey, Vols. I and II, Cambridge 1857.

James, M. R., *Anecdota Apocrypha*, Texts and Studies II, 2, London 1892.

Jerome, *Liber de viris illustribus*, Migne *PL* 23, 631–766.

— *Commentarius in Ecclesiasten*, Migne *PL* 23, 1061–1174.

— *Commentarii in Danielem*, Migne *PL* 25, 491–584.

Justin Martyr, *Die ältesten Apologeten*, ed. E. J. Goodspeed, Göttingen 1914.

(Ps.-) Justin, *Coh.ad Gent. in Justini opera*, ed. J. C. T. v. Otto, Corpus Apologe-
    tarum Christianorum, Vol. III, Jena 1879.

Lactantius, Vol. 1, *Divinae Institutiones*, ed. S. Brandt, CSEL 19, Wien
    1890.

Origen, *Contra Celsum*, ed. H. Chadwick, Cambridge 1953.

— *Hexaplorum quae supersunt*, ed. F. Field, Oxford 1875.

Photius, *Bibliotheca*, ed. I. Bekker, Vols. I and II, Berlin 1824f.

Pseudo-Clementines, I. *Homilien*, ed. B. Rehm and I. Irmscher, GCS 42,
    Berlin 1953.

— II. *Recognitionen in Rufins Übersetzung*, ed. B. Rehm and F. Paschke, GCS 51,
    Berlin 1965.

Sulpicius Severus, *Chronica*, ed. C. Halm, CSEL 1, Wien 1866.

Syncellus Chronographia, ed. W. Dindorf, Corpus scriptorum historiae Byzan-
    tinae, Bonn 1829.

Tertullian, *Opera*, Corpus christianorum, Vols. I and II, Turnhout 1954.

3. Graeco-Roman Secular Writers and Collected Editions

Achilles Tatius, *Erotici scriptores graeci*, ed. R. Hercher, Vol. I, Leipzig 1858.

Aelius Aristides, *Orationes*, ed. B. Keil, Vol. II, Berlin 1897.

Aeschylus, *Tragedies*, Vols. 1 and 2, LCL, London 1922, 1926.

Alcaeus, *Lyra Graeca*, Vol. 1, ed. J. M. Edmonds, LCL, London 1922.

Anthologia Graeca, Vols. 1–5, ed. W. R. Paton, LCL, London 1916–18.

— *The Greek Anthology, Hellenistic Epigrams*, ed. A. S. F. Gow and D. L. Page, Vols. I and II, Cambridge 1965.

Appian, *Historia Romana*, Vols. 1–4, ed. H. Withe, LCL, London 1912f.

Apuleius, *Metamorphoses*, ed. S. Gaselee, LCL, London 1915.

Aratus, ed. G. R. Mair, LCL, London ³1960.

Artemidorus, *Oneirocriticon*, ed. R. A. Pack, Leipzig 1963.

Arnim, J. von, *Stoicorum veterum fragmenta*, Vols. I–IV, Stuttgart ²1964.

Arrian, Vol. 1, *Alexandri anabasis*, ed. A. G. Roos, Leipzig 1907.

Aristotle, *Works*, ed. J. A. Smith and W. D. Ross, Vols. 1–12, Oxford 1908–52.

Athenaeus, *The Deipnosophists*, Vols. 1–7, ed. C. B. Gulik, LCL, London 1927–41.

Catalogus codicum Astrologorum Graecorum, Vols. I–XII, ed. F. Cumont, F. Boll, W. Kroll, Paris 1898ff. (CCAG).

Censorinus, *De die natali*, ed. F. Hultsch, Leipzig 1867.

Cercidas, ed. A. D. Knox, LCL, London ⁴1961.

Cicero, *Scripta quae manserunt omnia*, ed. Marx, Strobel et al., Leipzig 1914ff.

Corpus Hermeticum, Vols. I–IV, ed. A. D. Nock and A. J. Festugière, Paris 1954–60 (CH).

Corpus iuris civilis, Vol. I (Digests), ed. P. Krüger and T. Mommsen, Berlin ¹⁵1928.

Curtius Rufus, *Historiae Alexandri Magni*, ed. E. Hedicke, Leipzig 1919.

Diels, H. – Kranz, W., *Die Fragmente der Vorsokratiker*, Vols. I–III, Zürich – Berlin ¹¹1964.

Demosthenes, *Orationes*, Vol. III, ed. W. Dindorf and F. Blass, Leipzig 1907.

Dio Chrysostom, *Orationes*, ed. G. de Budé, Leipzig 1906.

Diodorus Siculus, Vols. 1–11, ed. C. H. Oldfather et al., LCL, London 1936–47.

Diogenes Laertius, Vols. 1 and 2, ed. R. D. Hicks, LCL, London ⁵1959.

Dionysius of Halicarnassus, Vols. I–IV, ed. A. Kiessling, Leipzig 1860–70.

Erastosthenes, *Catasterismorum reliquiae*, ed. C. Robert, Berlin 1913.

— *Carminum reliquiae*, ed. E. Hiller, Leipzig 1872.

Firmicius Maternus, *Matheseos libri VIII*, ed. C. Sittl, Leipzig 1894.

(Aulus) Gellius, *Noctes Atticae*, Vols. 1–3, ed. I. C. Rolfe, LCL, London 1954ff.

Granus Licinianus, *quae supersunt*, ed. M. Flemisch, Leipzig 1914.

Gundel, W., *Neue astrologische Texte des Hermes Trismegistos*, AAM ph.-hist.Kl. NF 12, 1936.

Harpocration, *Lexicon in decem oratores Atticos*, ed. W. Dindorf, Vols. I and II, Oxford 1953.

Heliodorus, *Aethiopiaca*, ed. I. Bekker, Leipzig 1855.

Herodotus, Vols. 1–4, ed. A. D. Godley, LCL, London 1921–24.

Herondas, ed. A. D. Knox, LCL, London ⁴1961.

Hesiod, ed. H. G. Evelyn-White, LCL, London ⁹1964.

Homer, *Iliad*, Vols. 1–2, ed. A. T. Murray, LCL, London 1924–25.

— *Odyssey*, Vols. 1–2, ed. A. T. Murray, LCL, London 1919.

Isaeus, *Orations*, ed. E. S. Forster, LCL, London 1927.

Isocrates, *Works*, ed. G. Norlin, LCL, London 1928–45.

Jacoby, F., *Die Fragmente der Griechischen Historiker*, Vols. I–III with commentary volumes, Leiden 1923ff. (FGrHist).

Julian Apostate, *Epistulae, leges*, ed. I. Bidez and F. Cumont, Paris 1922.

Kern, O., *Orphicorum Fragmenta*, Berlin ²1963.

Kock, T., *Comicorum Atticorum Fragmenta*, Vols. I–III, Leipzig 1880–88 (CAF).

Livy, *Works*, Vols. 1–13, ed. B. O. Foster, F. G. Moore, E. T. Sage and A. C. Schlesinger, LCL, 1914–51.

(Ps.) Longinus, *De sublimitate*, ed. A. O. Prickard, Oxford 1906.

Lucian of Samosata, Vols. 1–7, ed. A. M. Harmon, LCL, London 1913ff.

Lucretius, *De rerum natura*, Vols. I–III, ed. Cyril Bailey, Oxford 1947.

Lycophron, *Alexandra*, ed. A. W. Mair, LCL, London ³1955.

Lydus, J. Laurentius, *Liber de mensibus*, ed. R. Wünsch, Leipzig 1898.

Malalas, I., *Chronographia*, ed. W. Dindorf, Corpus scriptorum historiae Byzantinae, Bonn 1831.

Manilius, *Astronomicon*, Vols. I–V, ed. A. E. Housman, London 1903–30.

Martial, *Epigrams*, Vols. 1 and 2, ed. W. A. Ker, LCL, London ⁶1961.

Menander, ed. F. G. Allison, LCL, London ⁴1964.

Müller, C. and T., *Fragmenta Historicorum Graecorum*, Paris 1841–72 (FGH).

Muller, C., *Geographi Graeci minores*, Vol. I, Paris 1860 (GGM).

Nauck, A., *Tragicorum Graecorum fragmenta*, Hildesheim ³1964.

Pausanias, *Descriptio Graeciae*, Vols. I–III, ed. F. Spiro, Leipzig 1903.

— *Description of Greece*, Vols. 1–5, ed. W. H. S. Jones et al., LCL, London 1918–35.

Peek, W., *Griechische Grabgedichte*, Darmstadt 1960.

— *Der Isishymnus von Andros*, Berlin 1930.

Plato, *Works*, Vols. I–V, ed. I. Burnet, Oxford 1900ff.

Plautus, *Comoediae*, ed. G. Goetz and F. Schoell, Leipzig 1913ff.

Pliny the Elder, Vols. 1–10, ed. H. Rackham et al., LCL, London 1938–62.

Plutarch, *De Iside et Osiride* and *De Alexandri magni fortuna aut virtute*, in Plutarch's *Moralia*, Vols. 4 and 5, ed. F. C. Babbit, LCL, London ³1962.

Polybius, Vols. 1–6, ed. W. R. Paton, LCL, 1922–27.

Powell, J. U., *Collectanea Alexandrina, Reliquiae minores poetarum Graecorum aetatis Ptolemaicae 323–146 ante Christum*, Oxford 1925.

Procopius, *De aedificiis*, ed. H. B. Dewing, LCL, London 1940.

Reinach, T., *Textes d'auteurs Grecs et Romains relatifs au Judaïsme*, 1895, reprinted Hildesheim 1963.

Riess, E., *Nechepsonis et Petosiridis fragmenta magica*, PhilSuppl 6, 1891–93.

Servius in Vergilii Carmina Commentarii, ed. G. Thilo and H. Hagen, Vols. I and II, Leipzig 1881–1884.

Sophocles, ed. A. C. Pearson, Oxford 1924.

Stephen of Byzantium, *Ethnika*, ed. A. Meineke, 1849, reprinted Graz 1958.

Strabo, Vols. 1–8, ed. H. L. Jones, LCL, London 1917–32.
— *Strabon von Amaseia, Strabonis Geographica*, Vol. 4, ed. W. Aly, Bonn 1957.
Tacitus, *Annals*, ed. H. Furneaux, Vols. I and II, Oxford 1896–1907.
— *Histories*, ed. G. G. Ramsay, London 1915.
Teles, ed. O. Hense, Leipzig 1889.
Theocritus, ed. M. M. Edmonds, *The Greek Bucolic Poets*, LCL, London 1960.
Theognis, ed. E. Diehl and E. Young, Leipzig 1961.
Theophrastus, *Historia plantarum*, ed. T. Eresius and F. Wimmer, Vratislavia 1842.
Valerius Maximus, ed. C. Kempf, Leipzig 1888.
Varro, *De re rustica*, ed. H. Keil and G. Goetz, Leipzig 1912.
— R. Agahd, *M. Terentii Varronis antiquitates rerum divinarum*, JbPhilSuppl 24, 1898.
Velleius Paterculus, ed. C. Stegmann, Leipzig ²1933.
Vettius Valens, *Anthologiae*, ed. W. Kroll, Berlin 1918.
Virgil, *Opera*, ed. F. A. Hirtzel, Oxford 1900.
Xenophon, *Anabasis*, Vols. 2 and 3, ed. C. L. Brownson, LCL, London 1921–22.
— *Memorabilia*, ed. E. C. Marchant, LCL, London 1925.

4. Inscriptions, Papyri, Coins and Other Sources

Abel, F. M., 'Inscriptions de Transjordanie et de Haute Galilée', *RB* NS 5, 1908, 568–77.
Bonner, C., *Studies in Magical Amulets*, London 1950.
Cantineau, J., 'Inscriptions Palmyréniennes', *Revue d'Assyriologie* 37, 1930, 27–51.
Caquot, A., 'Nouvelles Inscriptions Araméennes de Hatra(V)', *Syria* 40, 1963, 1–16.
Clermont-Ganneau, C., 'Une dédicace a Astarté Palestinienne découverte à Délos', *CRAI* 1909, 307–17.
Corpus inscriptionum Semiticarum, I, 1–3 *Inscriptiones Phoeniciae*, 1887–90; II, 1–3 *Inscriptiones aramaicae*, 1889f., Paris.
Cowley, A., *Aramaic Papyri of the Fifth Century BC*, Oxford 1923.
Daressy, G., 'Un Décret de l'an XXIII de Ptolémée Épiphane', *Receuil de travaux relatifs à la philologie et l'archéologie Égyptiennes et Assyriennes* 33, 1911, 1–8.
Dittenberger, W., *Orientis Graeci Inscriptiones Selectae*, Vols. I and II, Leipzig 1903–05 (OGIS).
— *Sylloge Inscriptionum Graecarum*, Vols. I–IV, Leipzig ³1915–24.
Donner, H., and Röllig, W., *Kanaanäische und Aramäische Inschriften*, Vols. I–III, Wiesbaden 1962–64 (KAI).
Edgar, C. C., 'A New Group of Zenon Papyri', *BJRL* 18, 1934, 111ff.
Erman, A., 'Zwei Grabsteine griechischer Zeit', *Festschrift E. Sachau z. 70. Geburtstag*, ed. G. Weil, Berlin 1915.
Frey, J. B., *Corpus Inscriptionum Iudaicarum*, Vols. I and II, Rome 1936 and 1952.

Gauthier, H., and Sottas, H., *Un décret trilingue en l'honneur de Ptolemée IV*, Cairo 1925.

Guéraud, O., and Jouguet, P., *Un livre d'écolier du IIIe siècle avant J.C.*, Cairo 1938.

Guéraud, O. see also P. *ENTEYΞEIΣ*.

Head, B. V., *Historia numorum*, London ²1911.

Hill, G. F., *Catalogue of the Greek Coins of Phoenicia*, A Catalogue of the Greek Coins in the British Museum, London 1910.

— *Catalogue of the Greek Coins of Palestine*. A Catalogue of the Greek Coins in the British Museum, London 1914.

Inscriptiones Graecae, ed. Preussische Akademie der Wissenschaften, Berlin 1873ff. (IG).

Jalabert, L., and Mouterde, R., *Inscriptions Grecques et Latines de la Syrie*, Vols. I–V, Paris 1929ff. (IGLS).

Jerphainon, G., and Jalabert, L., 'Taurus et Cappadoce III, Inscriptions', *MUSJ* 5, 1911/12, 304–28.

Kadman, L., *The Coins of Akko Ptolemais*, Corpus Nummorum Palaestinensium, I, 4, Jerusalem 1961.

Landau, Y. H., 'A Greek Inscription from Acre', *IEJ* 11, 1961, 118–26.

— 'A Greek Inscription found near Hefzibah', *IEJ* 16, 1966, 54–70.

Le Bas, P., and Waddington, H., *Voyage archeologique en Grèce et en Asie Mineure*, Vol. II, *Inscriptions*, Paris 1847–73.

Liebesny, H., 'Ein Erlass des Königs Ptolemaios II. Philadelphos über die Deklaration von Vieh und Sklaven in Syrien und Phönikien (PER Inv. Nr. 24552 gr)', *Aeg* 16, 1936, 257–88.

— 'Ergänzungen zur Publikation', op. cit., 289–91.

Lifshitz, B., 'Sur le culte dynastique des Séleucides', *RB* 70, 1963, 75–81.

— 'Der Kult des Zeus Akraios und des Zeus Bakchos in Beisan (Skythopolis)', *ZDPV* 77, 1961, 186–90.

— 'Beiträge zur palästinischen Epigraphik', *ZDPV* 78, 1962, 64–8.

— 'Notes d'épigraphie Palestinienne', *RB* 73, 1966, 248–55.

Littmann, E., in: *Publications of the Princeton University Archaeological Expedition to Syria 1904–1905*, Div. IV A, *Nabatean Inscriptions*, Leiden 1914.

Lommel, H., *Die Yašt's des Avesta*, Göttingen 1927.

Maas, P., 'The Philinna Papyrus', *JHS* 61, 1941, 33–38.

Manteuffel, G., *De opusculis Graecis Aegyptiae papyris, ostratis, lapidibusque collectis*, Warsaw 1930.

Meshorer, J., 'An Attic Archaic Coin from Jerusalem', *'Atiqot* 3, 1961, 185.

— 'A New Type of YHD Coin', *IEJ* 16, 1966, 217–9.

Milik, J. T., 'Lettre araméenne d'el-Hibeh', *Aeg* 40, 1960, 79–81.

Minns, E. H., 'Parchments of the Parthian Period from Avroman in Kurdistan', *JHS* 35, 1915, 22–65.

Mitsos, T. M., "Ἐπιγραφαὶ ἐξ Ἀμφιαρείου', *Archaiologikē Ephemeris 1952* (appeared 1955), 167–204 (194–6).

Mørkholm, O., *Studies in the Coinage of Antiochus IV of Syria*, Hist.filos. Meddeleser udgivet af det kong. Danske Videnskabernes Selskab 40, 3, Kopenhagen 1963.

Mouterde, R., 'Bibliographie', *MUSJ* 17, 1933, 180–2.
— Review, *MUSJ* 31, 1954, 333–4.
Neugebauer, O., *Astronomical Cuneiform Texts*, Vols. I–III, London 1955.
Newell, E. T., *The First Seleucid Coinage of Tyre*, Numismatic Notes and Mono-
graphs 10, 1921.
— *The Seleucid Coinage of Tyre*, Numismatic Notes and Monographs 73,
1936.
Papyri Graecae Magicae, ed. K. Preisendanz, Vols. I and II, Berlin 1928 (PGM).
PCZ, *Zenon Papyri*, ed. C. C. Edgar, Vols. I–IV = *Catalogue General des
Antiquités Égyptiennes du Musée du Caire*, Vols. 79, 82, 85, 89, Cairo 1925–40.
— *Zenon Papyri*, Vol. V, ed. O. Guéraud and P. Jouguet, Publications de la
Société Fouad, I de Papyrologie, Textes et Documents, Cairo 1940.
PColZen, *Zenon Papyri, Business Papers of the Third Century dealing with
Palestine and Egypt*, Vols. I and II, ed. W. L. Westermann and E. S.
Hasenoehrl et al., New York 1934, 1940.
PCorn, *Greek Papyri in the Library of the Cornell University*, ed. W. L. Wester-
mann, New York 1926.
P. *ΕΝΤΕΥΞΕΙΣ*, *ΕΝΤΕΥΞΕΙΣ*, ed. O. Guéraud, Publications de la Société
Royale Égyptienne de Papyrologie, Textes et Documents I, Cairo 1931.
P. Hal., *Dikaiomata, Auszüge aus alexandrinischen Gesetzen*, Verordnungen in
einem Papyrus des philol.Sem. der Univ.Halle, ed. from Graeca Halensis,
Berlin 1913.
P. Haun., *Papyri Graecae Haunienses*, ed. T. Larsen, fasc. 1, Kopenhagen 1942.
PMichZen, *Zenon Papyri in the University of Michigan Collection*, ed. C. C.
Edgar, Ann Arbor 1931.
POx, *Oxyrhynchus Papyri*, ed. B. Grenfell, A. S. Hunt, et al., London 1898ff.
P. Revenue Law, ed. B. P. Grenfell and J. P. Mahaffy, Oxford 1896.
— ed. J. Bingen, in SB-Bh 1, 1952.
PRylands, ed. C. H. Roberts and E. G. Turner, *Catalogue of the Greek and Latin
Papyri in the John Rylands Library*, Manchester, Vol. IV, 1952.
PSI, *Pubblicazioni della Società Italiana, Papiri Greci et Latini*, ed. G. Vitelli
et al., Vols. IV–VI, 1917–20.
P. Tebt., *The Tebtunis Papyri*, Vols. I–III, 2, ed. A. S. Hunt, J. G. Smyly et al.,
London 1902–37.
Reifenberg, A., *Ancient Jewish Coins*, Jerusalem ²1947.
Robert, L., 'Inscriptions Grecques de Phénicie et d'Arabie', *Mel. Syriens offerts
à M. René Dussaud*, Vol. II, 729–38, Paris 1939.
— 'Voyages épigraphiques en Asie Mineure', *RevPhil* 17, 1943, 170–201.
— 'Épitaphe de Nicopolis', *Hellenica* 11/12, 1960, 283–96.
— 'Inscription Hellénistique d'Iran', ibid., 85–91.
— 'Bulletin Épigraphique', *REG* 75, 1962, 207.
— *Nouvelles Inscriptions de Sardes*, Iᵉʳ Fascicule, Paris 1964.
Roussel, P., 'Épitaphe de Gaza commémorant deux officiers de la garnison
ptolémaïque', *Aeg* 13, 1933, 145–51.
— 'Décret des Péliganes de Laodicée sur Mer', *Syria* 22, 1942–43, 21–32.
Sachs, A. J., and Wiseman, D. J., 'A Babylonian King-List of the Hellenistic
Period', *Iraq* 16, 1954, 202–12.

Sammelbuch griechischer Urkunden aus Ägypten, ed. F. Preisigke, F. Bilabel and E. Kiessling, Vols. I–V, 3, 1915ff. (SB).

Savignac, R., 'Une visite à l'île de Rouad', *RB* 25, 1916, 565–92.

— 'Découverte d'une statue à Ascalon', *RB* NS 2, 1905, 426–9.

— 'Texte complet de l'inscription d'Abila relative à Lysanias', *RB* NS 9, 1912, 533–40.

Schwarz, W., 'Die Inschriften des Wüstentempels von Redesiye', *JbPhil* 42, 1896, 145–70.

Sellers, O. R., 'Coins of the 1960 Excavations at Shechem', *BA* 25, 1962, 87–96.

Spiegelberg, W., *Die sogenannte Demotische Chronik*, Demotische Studien 7, Leipzig 1914.

— *Die demotischen Urkunden des Zenonarchivs*, Demotische Studien 8, Leipzig 1929.

Tcherikover, V. A., and Fuks, A., *Corpus Papyrorum Judaicarum*, Vols. I–III, Cambridge, Mass. 1957–64 (CPJ).

Uebel, F., 'Ταραχη τῶν Αἰγυπτίων', *APF* 17, 1960, 147–62.

Volten, A., *Das demotische Weisheitsbuch, Studien und Bearbeitung*, Analecta Aegyptiaca II, Kopenhagen 1940.

— *Demotische Traumdeutung, P. Carlsberg XIII and XIV verso*, Analecta Aegyptiana 3, Kopenhagen 1942.

West, E. W., *Pahlavi Texts*, Parts I and IV = *The Sacred Books of the East*, 5 and 37, Oxford 1880 and 1892.

Wilcken, U., *Griechische Ostraka aus Aegypten und Nubien*, Vols. I and II, Leipzig-Berlin 1899.

— *Urkunden der Ptolemäerzeit*, Vol. I, Berlin-Leipzig 1922ff. (UPZ).

Zimmermann, F., *Griechische Roman-Papyri und verwandte Texte*, Quellen und Studien zur Geschichte und Kultur des Altertums und des Mittelalters 2, Heidelberg 1936.

II DICTIONARIES, LEXICA AND COMPOSITE WORKS

Ancient Near Eastern Texts, ed. J. B. Pritchard, Princeton ²1955 (*ANET*).

Arndt, W. F. – Gingrich, F. W. – Bauer, W., *A Greek-English Lexicon of the New Testament*, Cambridge 1957.

Biblisch-Historisches Handwörterbuch, ed. Bo Reicke and L. Rost, Göttingen 1962 (*BHHWB*).

Encyclopedia Judaica, Vols. I–X, Berlin 1928–1934 (*EJ*).

Gressmann, H., *Altorientalische Texte zum Alten Testament*, Berlin-Leipzig ²1926 (*AOT²*).

— *Altorientalische Bilder zum Alten Testament*, Berlin-Leipzig ²1927 (*AOB²*).

Hatch, E. and Redpath, H., *A Concordance to the Septuagint*, Vols. I and II, 1897, reprinted Graz 1954.

The Jewish Encyclopedia, ed. I. Singer, Vols. I–XII, New-York – London 1901–07 (*JE*).

Der Kleine Pauly, Lexikon der Antike, ed. K. Ziegler and W. Sontheimer, Stuttgart 1964ff. (*KP*).

Köhler, L., and Baumgartner, W., *Lexicon in Veteris Testamenti libros*, Leiden 1953.

Kuhn, K. G., *Konkordanz zu den Qumran-Texten*, Göttingen 1960.

— 'Nachträge zur Konkordanz zu den Qumran-Texten', *RQ* 4, 1963/64, 163–234.

Levy, J., *Wörterbuch über die Talmudim und Midraschim*, Vols. I–IV, reprinted Darmstadt 1963.

Pape, W., *Wörterbuch der griechischen Eigennamen*, Braunschweig 1863ff.

Paulys Realencyclopädie der classischen Altertumswissenschaft, new edition by G. Wissowa, W. Kroll et al., Stuttgart 1893ff.; 2. R., 1914ff. (*PW*).

Preisigke, F., *Fachwörterbuch des öffentlichen Verwaltungsdienstes Ägyptens*, Göttingen 1915.

— *Namenbuch*, Heidelberg 1922.

Preisigke, F., and Kiessling, E., *Wörterbuch der griechischen Papyrusurkunden*, Vols. I–IV, Heidelberg – Marburg 1924ff.

Realencyclopädie für protestantische Theologie und Kirche, ed. A. Hauck, Leipzig ³1896–1913 (*RE*).

Reallexikon für Antike und Christentum, ed. T. Klauser, Stuttgart 1950ff. (*RAC*).

Die Religion in Geschichte und Gegenwart, ed. K. Galling et al., Tübingen ³1957–62 (*RGG³*).

Roscher, W. H., *Ausführliches Lexikon der griechischen und römischen Mythologie*, Leipzig (and Berlin) 1884–1937.

Theological Dictionary of the New Testament, ed. G. Kittel and G. Friedrich, translated by G. W. Bromiley, Grand Rapids, Michigan 1964ff. (*TDNT*).

Wörterbuch der Mythologie, ed. H. W. Haussig, Part I, *Die Mythologie der alten Kulturvölker*, Vol. 1: *Götter und Mythen im Vorderen Orient*, Stuttgart 1965 (*WM*).

III SECONDARY LITERATURE

Aalen, S., *Die Begriffe 'Licht' und 'Finsternis' im Alten Testament, im Spätjudentum und im Rabbinismus*, Skrifter utg. av det norske Videnskaps-Akademi, Oslo 2, 1951, 1.

Abel, F. M., 'La liste géographique du papyrus 71 de Zénon', *RB* 32, 1923, 409–15.

— 'Marisa dans le Papyrus 76 de Zénon et la traite des esclaves en Idumée', *RB* 33, 1924, 566–74.

— 'Tombeaux récemment découverts à Marisa', *RB* 24, 1925, 267–75.

— 'Topographie des Campagnes Machabéennes', *RB* 35, 1926, 510–31.

— Review of PCZ I and PSI IV, *RB* 36, 1927, 145–7.

— Review of PCZ II, op. cit., 475–6.

— 'Alexandre le Grand en Syrie et en Palestine', *RB* 43, 1934, 528–45; *RB* 44, 1935, 42–61.

— 'La Syrie et la Palestine au temps de Ptolémée Iᵉʳ Soter', *RB* 44, 1935, 559–81.

— 'L'expédition des Grecs à Pétra en 312 avant J.-C.', *RB* 46, 1937, 373–91.

— *Géographie de la Palestine*, Vol. II, Paris 1938.

— Review of E. Bickermann, *Der Gott der Makkabäer*, RB 47, 1938, 441–6.
— 'Les confins de la Palestine et de l'Égypte sous les Ptolémées', RB 48, 1939, 207–36; 531–48; RB 49, 1940, 55–75; 226–39.
— *Les Livres des Maccabées*, Paris ²1949 (*Macc.*).
— *Histoire de la Palestine*, Vols. I–II, Paris 1952 (*HP*).
Abel, F. M., and Starcky, J., 'Les Livres des Maccabées', *La Sainte Bible . . . de Jérusalem*, Paris 1961.
Ackroyd, P. R., 'Criteria for the Maccabean Dating of OT Literature', *VT* 3, 1953, 113–32.
Adcock, F. E., *The Greek and Macedonian Art of War*, Berkeley 1957.
Aharoni, Y., 'Excavations at Ramat Raḥel 1954', *IEJ* 6, 1956, 137–57.
— *Excavations at Ramat Raḥel. Seasons 1959 and 1960*, Rome 1962 (G. Garbini, 'The Dating of Post-Exilic Stamps', 61–8),
— Excavations at Ramat Raḥel', *BA* 24, 1961, 98–118.
— *Excavations at Ramat Raḥel, Seasons 1961 and 1962*, Rome 1964.
— 'Hebrew Ostraca from Tell Arad', *IEJ* 16, 1966, 1–7.
Albright, W. F., 'The Goddess of Life', *AJSL* 36, 1919/20, 258–94.
— *From the Stone Age to Christianity*, New York ²1957.
— 'The Judicial Reform of Jehoshaphat', *Alexander Marx Jubilee Volume* (English Section), New York 1950, 61–82.
— 'Some Canaanite-Phoenician sources of Hebrew Wisdom', in *Wisdom in Israel and the Ancient Near East*, SVT 3, 1955, 1–15.
— 'The Seal Impression from Jericho and the Treasurers of the Second Temple', *BASOR* 148, 1957, 28–30.
— *The Archaeology of Palestine*, Harmondsworth 1960.
Alfrink, B. J., 'L'idée de Résurrection d'après Dan. XII, 1.2', *Bibl* 40, 1959, 355–71.
Allegro, J., *The Dead Sea Scrolls*, Harmondsworth 1964.
Alpers, I., *Hercules in Bivio*, Diss. Göttingen 1912.
Alt, A., *Kleine Schriften zur Geschichte des Volkes Israel*, Vols. I and II, München 1963 and 1964.
— 'Zu Antiochos' III. Erlass für Jerusalem', *ZAW* 57, 1939, 283–5.
— 'Pegai', *ZDPV* 45, 1922, 220–3.
— 'Beth Anath', PJB 22, 1926, 55–9; APF 7, 1924, 293.
Altheim, F., *Weltgeschichte Asiens im griechischen Zeitalter*, Vols. I and II, Halle/Saale 1947/48.
— 'Die Weltgeltung der griechischen Sprache', *Neue Beiträge zur Geschichte der Alten Welt* 1, 1964, 315–32.
Altheim, F.-Stiehl, R., *Die aramäische Sprache unter den Achämeniden*, Vol. I, Frankfurt 1963.
— *Die Araber in der Alten Welt*, Vols. I and II, Berlin 1964/65.
Alvarez de Miranda, A., 'Jób y Prometeo', *Anthologia Annua* 2, 1954, 207–37.
Amélineau, E., 'Les traités gnostiques d. Oxford II', *RHR* 21, 1890, 261–94.
Amy, R., 'Temples à escaliers', *Syria* 27, 1950, 82–136.
Andréades, A., 'De l'origine des Monopoles Ptolémaïques', *Mélanges Maspero II Orient Grec, Romain et Byzantin* (Mémoires de l'Institut Français d'Archéologie . . . I, 67), Cairo 1934–1937, 289–95.

Applebaum, S., Review of V. Tcherikover and A. Fuks, CPJ I, *Tarbiz* 28, 1958/59, 418–27, Summary XIII/XIV.
— 'The Jewish Community of Hellenistic and Roman Teucheira in Cyrenaica', *ScrHieros* 7, 1961, 27–52.
— 'Jewish Status at Cyrene in the Roman Period', *Par Pass* 19, 1964, 291–303.
Arbesmann, P. R., *Das Fasten bei den Griechen und Römern*, RGVV 21, 1929.
Astour, M. C., *Hellenosemitica. An Ethnic and Cultural Study in West Semitic Impact on Mycenaean Greece*, Leiden 1965.
Atkinson, K. M. T., 'The Historical Setting of the "War of the Sons of Light and the Sons of Darkness"', *BJRL* 40, 1957/58, 272–97.
Avigad, N., 'A New Class of Yehud Stamps', *IEJ* 7, 1957, 146–53.
— 'New Light on the MSH Seal Impressions', *IEJ* 8, 1958, 113–19.
— 'Excavations at Makmish 1958. Preliminary Report', *IEJ* 10, 1960, 90–6.
— 'YEHUD or HA'IR', *BASOR* 158, 1960, 23–7.
— 'A Depository of Inscribed Ossuaries in the Kidron Valley', *IEJ* 12, 1962, 1–12.
Avi-Yonah, M., 'Map of Roman Palestine', *QDAP* 5, 1936, 139–93.
— 'Mount Carmel and the God of Baalbek', *IEJ* 2, 1952, 118–24.
— *Ten Years of Archaeology in Israel*, Jerusalem 1958.
— 'Syrian Gods at Ptolemais-Accho', *IEJ* 9, 1959, 1–12.
— *Geschichte der Juden im Zeitalter des Talmud*, Studia Judaica 2, Berlin 1962.
— 'Scythopolis', *IEJ* 12, 1962, 123–36.

Bacher, W., *Die Agada der Tannaiten*, Vol. I, *Von Hillel bis Akiba*, Strassburg 1903.
Baeck, L., *Aus drei Jahrtausenden*, Tübingen 1958.
— *Paulus, die Pharisäer und das Neue Testament*, Frankfurt 1961.
Baer, J., *Israel among the Nations*, Jerusalem 1955 (in Hebrew).
— 'On the Problem of Eschatological Doctrine during the Period of the Second Temple', *Zion* 23/24, 1958/59, 3–34; 141–65 (in Hebrew).
— 'The Historical Foundation of the Halakha', *Zion* 27, 1962, 117–55 (in Hebrew).
Bagatti, B.-Milik, J. T., *Gli Scavi del 'Dominus Flevit'*, I. *La necropoli del periodo romano*, Pubblicazioni dello Studium Biblicum Franciscanum No. 13, Jerusalem 1958.
Baillet, M., Milik, J. T., etc., 'Le Travail d'édition des fragments manuscrits de Qumrân', *RB* 63, 1956, 49–67.
Baldry, H. C., *The Unity of Mankind in Greek Thought*, Cambridge 1966.
Baly, D., *The Geography of the Bible, A Study in Historical Geography*, London 1957.
Bammel, E., "Ἀρχιερεὺς προφητεύων", *ThLZ* 79, 1954, 351–6.
Bardtke, H., *Die Handschriftenfunde am Toten Meer*, Berlin ²1953.
— *Die Sekte von Qumran*, Berlin 1958.
— 'Die Rechtsstellung der Qumran-Gemeinde', *ThLZ* 86, 1961, 93–104.
— *Das Buch Esther*, KAT XVII 5, Gütersloh 1963.
— 'Qumran und seine Funde', *ThR* 29, 1963, 261–92; 30, 1964, 281–315.

Baron, S. W., *A Social and Religious History of the Jews*, Vols. I and II, Philadelphia ²1952.

Barthélemy, D., *Les Devanciers d'Aquila*, SVT 10, 1963.

Bauckmann, E. G., 'Die Proverbien und die Sprüche des Jesus Sirach', *ZAW* 72, 1960, 33–63.

Baumgartner, W., 'Die literarischen Gattungen in der Weisheit des Jesus Sirach', *ZAW* 34, 1914, 161–98.

— 'Die israelitische Weisheitsliteratur', *TR* NF 5, 1933, 258–88.

— 'Ein Vierteljahrhundert Danielforschung', *TR* NF 11, 1939, 59–83; 125–44; 201–28.

— 'Zu den vier Reichen von Daniel 2', *TZ* 1, 1945, 17–22.

— *Zum Alten Testament und seiner Umwelt*. Collected articles, Leiden 1959.

Becker, J., *Das Heil Gottes. Heils- und Sündenbegriffe in den Qumrantexten und im Neuen Testament*, SUNT 3, Göttingen 1964.

Beek, M. A., 'Relations entre Jérusalem et la Diaspora égyptienne au 2ᵉ siècle avant J.-C.', *OTS* 2, 1943, 119–43.

Beek, G. W. v., 'Frankincense and Myrrh', *BA* 23, 1960, 70–95.

Bell, H. J., 'Popular Religion in Graeco-Roman Egypt. I, The Pagan Period', *JEA* 34, 1948, 82–97.

— 'Graeco-Egyptian religion', *MusHelv* 10, 1953, 222–37.

— *Cults and Creeds in Graeco-Roman Egypt*, Liverpool 1955.

Beloch, J., 'Die auswärtigen Besitzungen der Ptolemäer', *APF* 2, 1902, 229–56.

Bengtson, H., *Die Strategie in der hellenistischen Zeit*, Vol. I, 1937; II, 1944; III, 1952 = MBPAR 26, 32, 36.

— 'Die ptolemäische Staatsverwaltung im Rahmen der hellenistischen Administration', *MusHelv* 10, 1953, 161–77.

— *Griechische Geschichte von den Anfängen bis in die römische Kaiserzeit*, HAW III, 4, München ³1964 (*GG*³).

Bentwich, N., *Hellenism*, Philadelphia 1919.

Bentzen, A., *Daniel*, HAT I 19, Tübingen ²1952.

Berchem, D. van, 'Sanctuaires d'Hercule – Melqart, Contribution à l'etude de l'expansion phénicienne en Mediterranée', *Syria* 44, 1967, 73–109, 307–38.

Bergmaier, R.-Papst, H., 'Ein Lied von der Erschaffung der Sprache', *RQ* 5, 1964/65, 435–9.

Bergman, J., *Ich bin Isis*, Acta Universitatis Upsaliensis, Historia Religionum 3, 1968.

Bergmann, J., 'Die stoische Philosophie und die jüdische Frömmigkeit', *Judaica, Festschrift zu H. Cohens 70. Geburtstag*, Berlin 1912, 145–66.

Bernays, J., *Theophrasts Schrift über die Frömmigkeit*, Berlin 1866.

Bertholet, A., *Der Schutzengel Persiens*, Oriental Studies in Honour of Cursetji Erachji Pavry, London 1933, 34–40.

Bertram G., 'Die religiöse Umdeutung altorientalischer Lebensweisheit in der griechischen Übersetzung des AT', *ZAW* 54, 1936, 153–67.

Betz, H. D., 'Zum Problem des religionsgeschichtlichen Verständnisses der Apokalyptik', *ZTK* 63, 1966, 391–409.

Betz, O., *Offenbarung und Schriftforschung in der Qumransekte*, WUNT 6, Tübingen 1960.

Betz, O. *Der Paraklet*, AGSU 2, Leiden 1963.
— 'Was am Anfang geschah, Das jüdische Erbe in den neugefundenen Koptisch-gnostischen Schriften', in *Abraham unser Vater, Festschrift f. O. Michel*, AGSU 5, Leiden 1963, 24–43.
Bevan, E. R., *The House of Seleucus*, Vols. I–II, London 1902, reprinted 1966.
— *Jerusalem under the High Priests*, London 1904, reprinted 1952.
— *A History of Egypt under the Ptolemaic Dynasty*, History of Egypt IV, London 1927.
Beyschlag, K., 'Zur Simon-Magus-Frage', *ZTK* 68, 1971, 395–426.
Bi(c)kerman(n), E., 'Die Datierung des Pseudo-Aristeas', *ZNW* 29, 1930, 280–98.
— 'Ein jüdischer Festbrief vom Jahre 124 v. Chr. (II. Macc. 1, 1–9)', *ZNW* 32, 1933, 233–54.
— 'La Charte séleucide de Jérusalem', *REJ* 100, 1935, 4–35.
— 'Un Document relatif à la persécution d'Antiochus IV Épiphane', *RHR* 115, 1937, 188–221.
— *Der Gott der Makkabäer*, Berlin 1937 (*GM*).
— 'Anonymous Gods', *Journal of the Warburg Inst.* 1, 1937/38, 187–96.
— *Institutions des Séleucides*, Bibliothèque historique 26, Paris 1938 (*Inst.*).
— 'La Cité Grecque dans les Monarchies hellénistiques', *RevPhil* 65, 1939, 335–49.
— 'Sur une inscription grecque de Sidon', *Mélanges Syriens offerts à M. R. Dussaud*, Vol. I, Bibliothéque Archéologique et Historique 30, Paris 1939, 91–9.
— 'Héliodore au Temple de Jérusalem', *AIPHOS* 7, 1939–44, 5–40.
— 'The Colophon of the Greek Book of Esther', *JBL* 63, 1944, 339–62.
— 'Une proclamation Séleucide relative au Temple de Jérusalem', *Syria* 25, 1946–48, 67–85.
— 'Some Notes on the Transmission of the LXX', *Alexander Marx Jubilee Vol.* (English section), New York 1950, 149–78.
— 'The Maxim of Antigonus of Socho', *HTR* 54, 1951, 153–65.
— 'Notes on the Greek Book of Esther', *PAAJR* 20, 1951, 101–33.
— 'La chaîne de la Tradition Pharisienne', *RB* 59, 1952, 44–54.
— 'Sur la chronologie de la Sixième Guerre de la Syrie', *ChrEg* 27, 1952, 396–403.
— 'The Altars of the Gentiles', *RIDA* 5, 1958, 137–64.
— 'The Septuagint as a Translation', *PAAJR* 28, 1959, 1–39.
— *From Ezra to the Last of the Maccabees, Foundations of Post-biblical Judaism*, New York 1962.
— 'Sur la théologie de l'art figuratif . . .', *Syria* 44, 1967, 131–61.
— *Four Strange Books of the Bible*, New York 1967.
Bidez, J., 'La Cité du Monde et la Cité du Soleil chez les Stoïciens', *Bulletin de l'Académie royale de Belgique Classe des Lettres*, 5. Ser. 18, 1932, 244–94.
Bidez, J.-Cumont, F., *Les Mages Hellénisés*, Vols. I and II, Paris 1938.
Bieber, M., *The Sculpture of the Hellenistic Age*, New York ²1961.
Bieler, L., ΘΕΙΟΣ ANHP, Vols. I and II, Wien 1935f.

Bietenhard, H., *Die himmlische Welt im Urchristentum und Spätjudentum*, WUNT 2, Tübingen 1951.

— 'Die Dekapolis von Pompeius bis Trajan', *ZDPV* 79, 1963, 24–58.

Bigot, L., Article 'Ecclésiastique', *Dictionnaire de Théologie Catholique* IV, 2, 2028–54.

(Strack, H. L.)-Billerbeck, P., *Kommentar zum Neuen Testament aus Talmud und Midrasch*, Vols. I–VI, München 1922–61 (Bill.).

Bingen, J., 'Grecs et Égyptiens d'après *PSI* 502', *Proceedings of the Twelfth International Congress of Papyrology*, American Studies in Papyrology 7, Toronto 1970, 35–40.

Bliffert, H. J., *Weltanschauung und Gottesglaube im Buch Kohelet*, Diss. Rostock 1938.

Bliss, F. J., and Macalister, R. A. S., *Excavations in Palestine*, London 1902.

Bömer, F., *Untersuchungen über die Religion der Sklaven . . .*, AAMz 1960, No. 1.

Bolkestein, H., *Wohltätigkeit und Armenpflege im . . . Altertum*, Leipzig 1939.

Boll, F., *Sphaera*, Leipzig 1903.

— 'Das Eingangsstück des Ps.-Klementinen', *ZNW* 17, 1916, 139–48.

— *Sternglaube und Sterndeutung*, ed. W. Gundel, Leipzig ⁴1931.

Boman, T., *Hebrew Thought compared with Greek*, London and Philadelphia 1960.

Bonsirven, J., Review of E. Bickermann, *Der Gott der Makkabäer*, 1937, *RSR* 28, 1938, 612–4.

Boström, G., *Proverbiastudien*, LUÅ, NF Avd. 1, Vol. 30, No. 3, Lund 1935.

Bothmer, D. v., 'Greek Pottery from Tell en-Naṣbeh', *BASOR* 83, 1941, 25–30.

Bouché-Leclercq, A., *L'Astrologie Grecque*, Paris 1899.

— *Histoire des Lagides*, Vols. I–III, Paris 1903.

— *Histoire des Séleucides*, Vols. I and II, Paris 1913f.

Bousset, W., 'Die Himmelsreise der Seele', *ARW* 4, 1901, 136–69, 229–73. Reprinted, Reihe Libelli 71, Darmstadt 1960.

— 'Die Beziehungen der ältesten jüdischen Sibylle zur chaldäischen Sibylle . . .', *ZNW* 3, 1902, 23–49.

— *Die jüdische Apokalyptik*, Berlin 1903.

— 'Zur Dämonologie der späten Antike', *ARW* 18, 1915, 134–72.

Bousset, W.-Gressmann, H., *Die Religion des Judentums im späthellenistischen Zeitalter*, HNT, Tübingen ³1926, reprinted 1966.

Brady, T. A., *The Reception of the Egyptian Cults by the Greeks (330–30 BC)*, The University of Missouri Studies 10, 1935.

Braun, H., *Spätjüdisch-häretischer und frühchristlicher Radikalismus*, Vols. I and II, BHT 24, Tübingen 1957.

Braun, M., *Griechischer Roman und hellenistische Geschichtsschreibung*, Frankfurter Studien zur Religion u. Kultur der Antike, Vol. VI, 1934.

— *History and Romance in Graeco-Oriental Literature*, Oxford 1938.

Braun, R., *Kohelet und sein Verhältnis zur literarischen Bildung und Popularphilosophie*, Theol. Diss. Erlangen 1971, BZAW 130, 1973.

Brekelmans, C. H. W., 'The Saints of the Most High and their Kingdom', *OTS* 14, 1965, 305–29.

Brett, M. J. B., 'The Qasr el-'Abd, A Proposed Reconstruction', *BASOR* 171, 1963, 39–45.

Bright, J., *A History of Israel*, London and Philadelphia ²1972.

Brown, B. R., *Ptolemaic Paintings and Mosaics and the Alexandrian Style*, Monographs on Archaeology and Fine Arts VI, Cambridge, Mass. 1957.

Brunner, H., *Altägyptische Erziehung*, Wiesbaden 1957.

Bruns, J. E., 'The Davidic Dynasty in Post-Exilic Palestine', *Scripture* 7, 1955, 2–5.

Buber, M., *Kampf um Israel*, Berlin 1933.

Budde, K., 'Neuestes zum Hohenliede', *ChrW* 45, 1931, 957–60.

Bühler, A., *Die Tobiaden und Oniaden im 2. Makkabäerbuch und in der verwandten jüdisch-hellenistischen Literatur*, Wien 1899.

Bühler, W., *Beiträge zur Erklärung der Schrift vom Erhabenen*, Göttingen 1964.

Bull, R. J., et al., 'The Fifth Campaign at Balâtah', *BASOR* 180, 1965, 7–41.

Bull, R. J.-Wright, G. E., 'Newly Discovered Temples on Mt Garizim in Jordan', *HTR* 58, 1965, 234–7.

Bultmann, R., *The Gospel of John. A Commentary*, Oxford 1971.

— *History and Eschatology*, Edinburgh 1957.

Bunge, J. G., *Untersuchungen zum zweiten Makkabäerbuch*, Phil. Diss. Bonn 1971.

Burchard, C., *Untersuchungen zu Joseph und Aseneth*, WUNT 8, Tübingen 1965.

— *Bibliographie zu den Handschriften vom Toten Meer*, Vols. I and II, BZAW 76, 1957, and 89, 1965.

Burkert, W., *Weisheit und Wissenschaft, Studien zu Pythagoras, Philolaos und Platon*, Erlanger Beitr. z. Sprach- und Kunstwissenschaft 10, 1962.

Burkitt, F. C., *Jewish and Christian Apocalypses*, Schweich Lectures 1913, London 1914.

Burrows, M., Review of E. Bickermann, *Der Gott der Makkabäer*, *JR* 18, 1938, 219–21.

— *The Dead Sea Scrolls*, London and New York 1955.

— *More Light on the Dead Sea Scrolls*, London and New York 1958.

Butler, H. C., *Publications of the Princeton University Archaeological Expeditions to Syria in* 1904/05 . . ., Division II, 'Ancient Architecture in Syria, Section A, Southern Syria', Part I, 1–25, Leiden 1919 (Butler, *Syria*).

Cadbury, H. J., 'The Grandson of Ben Sira', *HTR* 48, 1955, 219–25.

Caldwell, T., 'Dositheos Samaritanus', *Kairos* 4, 1962, 105–17.

Cambridge Ancient History, ed. J. B. Bury (et al.), Vols. VI–IX, Cambridge 1927ff. (*CAH*).

Campbell, E. F., 'Archaeological News from Jordan', *BA* 28, 1965, 17–32.

Capelle, W., 'Spuren der Astrologie bei den Griechen', *Hermes* 60, 1925, 373–95.

Caqot, A., 'Sur les quatre Bêtes de Daniel VII', *Semitica* 5, 1955, 5–13.

Cardauns, B., 'Juden und Spartaner, Zur hellenistisch-jüdischen Literatur', *Hermes* 95, 1967, 317–24.

Carmignac, J., 'Les éléments historiques des "Hymnes" de Qumrân', *RQ* 2, 1959/60, 205–22.

— 'Les Rapports entre l'Ecclésiastique et Qumrân', *RQ* 3, 1961/62, 209–18.

— 'Les Horoscopes de Qumrân', *RQ* 5, 1964/66, 199–217.

— 'Poème allégorique sur la Secte rivale', *RQ* 5, 1964/66, 361–74.

Cazelles, H., 'Sur les origines du calendrier des Jubilés', *Bibl* 43, 1962, 202–12.

Cerfaux, L., 'Influence des mystères sur le Judaïsme alexandrin avant Philo', *Le Muséon* 37, 1924, 28–88.

Cerfaux, L.-Tondriau, J., *Le culte des souverains dans la Civilisation Gréco-romaine*, Tournai 1957.

Charles, R. H., *A Critical and Exegetical Commentary on the Book of Daniel*, Oxford 1929.

— *Eschatology*, reprinted New York 1963.

Chéhab, M. H., *Les Terres Cuites de Kharayeb*, BMB 10, 1951/52.

Ciasca, A., 'Un deposito di statuette da Tell Gat', *OA* 2, 1963, 45–63.

Clairmont, C. 'Greek pottery from the Near East', *Berytus* 11, 1954/55, 85–139; 12, 1956/58, 1–34.

Clermont-Ganneau, C., 'Séance du 19 Oct. 1900', *CRAI* 1900, 536–41.

— 'Les Phéniciens en Grèce', *RAO* 3, 1900, 142–7.

— 'L'Héracleion de Rabbat-Ammon Philadelphie et la déesse Asteria', *RAO* 7, 1906, 147–55.

Clermont-Ganneau, C., and Macalister, M., 'Mitteilung des M. Clermont-Ganneau', *CRAI* 1901, 108–10.

Collart, P., 'Aspects du culte de Baalshemên à Palmyre', *Mélanges offerts à Kazimierz Michalowski*, Warzawa 1966, 325–37.

Colpe, C., *Die religionsgeschichtliche Schule*, FRLANT 78, Göttingen 1961.

Conzelmann, H., 'Paulus und die Weisheit', *NTS* 12, 1966, 231–44.

— 'The Mother of Wisdom', in *The Future of Our Religious Past*, ed. James M. Robinson, London and New York 1971, 230–43.

Cook, A. B., *Zeus, A Study in Ancient Religion*, Vols. I–III, Cambridge 1914–1940.

Cook, S. A., *The Religion of Ancient Palestine in the Light of Archaeology*, Schweich Lectures 1925, London 1930.

Cooke, G., 'The Sons of (the) God(s)', *ZAW* 76, 1964, 22–47.

Corré, A. D., 'A Reference to Epispasm in Koheleth', *VT* 4, 1954, 416–18.

Cothenet, E., Review of J. Becker, *Das Heil Gottes*, 1964, *RQ* 5, 1964/66, 272.

Crönert, W., 'Der Epikureer Philonides', SAB 1900, 942–98.

Crönert, W. (and Wünsch, R.), 'Das Lied von Marisa', *RheinMus* 64, 1909, 433ff.

Cross, F. M., Jr, 'The Oldest Manuscripts from Qumran', *JBL* 74, 1955, 147–72.

— *The Ancient Library of Qumran and Modern Biblical Studies*, London and Garden City, NY 1958.

— 'The Discovery of the Samaria Papyri', *BA* 26, 1963, 110–21.

— 'Aspects of Samaritan and Jewish History in Late Persian and Hellenistic Times', *HTR* 59, 1966, 201–11.

Crowfoot, J. W., and Fitzgerald, G. M., 'Excavations in the Tyropoeon Valley, Jerusalem 1927', *PEFA* 5, 1927, London 1929.

Crowfoot, J. W., Crowfoot, G. M., Kenyon, K. M., *Samaria Sebaste, Reports of the Works of the Joint Expedition in* 1931–1933, Vols. I–III, London 1942–57.

Cumont, F., 'Jupiter summus exsuperantissimus', *ARW* 9, 1906, 323–36.
— 'Les Mystères de Sabazius et le Judaïsme', *CRAI* 1906, 63–7.
— 'La plus ancienne géographie astrologique', *Klio* 9, 1909, 263–73.
— 'Les Anges du Paganisme', *RHR* 72, 1915, 159–82.
— 'Les Enfers selon l'Axiochos', *CRAI* 1920, 272–85.
— 'Deux autels de Phénice', *Syria* 8, 1927, 163–8.
— 'Esséniens et Pythagoriciens', *CRAI* 1930, 99–112.
— 'La fin du monde selon des mages occidentaux', *RHR* 104, 1931, 29–96.
— *L'Égypte des Astrologues*, Bruxelles 1937.
— *Lux Perpetua*, Paris 1949.
— *Oriental Religions in Roman Paganism*, reprinted New York and London 1956.
Cuq, E., 'La condition juridique de la Coelé-Syrie au temps de Ptolémée V
    Épiphane', *Syria* 8, 1927, 143–62.
Cureton, W., *Spicilegium Syriacum*, London 1855.

Dahl, N. A., *Das Volk Gottes*, Darmstadt ²1963.
Dahood, M., 'Canaanite-Phoenician Influence in Qoheleth', *Bibl* 33, 1952,
    30–52.
— 'Qoheleth and Recent Discoveries', *Bibl* 39, 1958, 302–18.
— 'To pawn one's cloak', *Bibl* 42, 1961, 359–66.
Dalbert, P., *Die Theologie der hellenistisch-jüdischen Missionsliteratur unter
    Ausschluss von Philo und Josephus*, Theologische Forschung 4, Hamburg 1954.
Dalman, G., 'Die Tobia-Inschrift von 'arāḳ el-emīr und Daniel 11, 14', *PJB*
    16, 1920, 33–35.
— *Arbeit und Sitte in Palästina*, Vol. II, *Der Ackerbau*, BFCT II 27, Gütersloh
    1932.
— *The Words of Jesus*, Edinburgh 1902.
Daube, D., 'Rabbinic Methods of Interpretation and Hellenistic Rhetoric',
    HUCA 22, 1949, 239–64.
Daumas, F., 'Littérature prophétique et exégétique égyptienne et commentaires
    esséniens', *Mémorial A. Gélin*, ed. A. Barucq et al., Le Puy, 1961, 203–11.
Davies, W. D., *Torah in the Messianic Age and/or the Age to Come*, JBL Monogr.
    Ser. 7, 1952.
Deissler, A., *Ps. 119*, Münchner Theologische Studien 11, 1955.
Deissmann, A., 'Tubias', *Byzantinisch-Neugriechische Jahrbücher* 2, 1921, 275–6.
— *Light from the Ancient East*, London 1910 (*LAO*).
Delcor, M., 'Les allusions à Alexandre le Grand dans Zach. IX 1–8', *VT* 1, 1951,
    110–24.
— 'Vom Sichem der hellenistischen Epoche zum Sychar des Neuen Testa-
    mentes', *ZDPV* 78, 1962, 34–48.
— 'Repas cultuels esséniens et thérapeutes, thiases et ḥaburoth', *RQ* 6, 1967/69,
    401–25.
Delling, G., 'Josephus und die heidnischen Religionen', *Klio* 43–45, 1965,
    263–9.
Delorme, J., *Gymnasium, Étude sur les Monuments consacrés à l'éducation en
    Grèce (des origines à l'Empire romain)*, Bibliothèque des Écoles françaises
    d'Athènes et de Rome 196, Paris 1960.

Denis, A. M., *Introduction aux Pseudépigraphes grecs d'Ancien Testament*, Leiden 1970.

Dibelius, M., *From Tradition to Gospel*, reprinted Cambridge 1972.

— *Botschaft und Geschichte*, Vol. II, Tübingen 1956.

Diels, H., 'Der antike Pessimismus', *Schule und Leben* 1, 1921.

Dieterich, A., *Abraxas*, Leipzig 1891.

— *Nekyia*, Leipzig 1893.

— *Eine Mithrasliturgie*, reprint of the third enlarged edition, ed. O. Weinreich, 1923, Darmstadt 1966.

Diez Macho, A., 'The recently discovered Palestinian Targum: its Antiquity and Relationship with the other Targums', SVT 7, 1959, 222–45.

Dirlmeier, F., 'Homerisches Epos und Orient', *RheinMus* 98, 1955, 18–37.

Dobson, J. F., 'Boethus of Sidon', *ClassQ* 8, 1914, 88–90.

Dodds, E. R., *The Greeks and the Irrational*, Sather Classical Lectures 25, Berkeley-Los Angeles 1951.

Dölger, F. J., 'Die Gottesweihe durch Brandmarkung', *Antike und Christentum* 2, 1930, 100–6.

Dombrowski, B. W., 'היחד in 1 QS and τὸ κοινόν, An Instance of Early Greek and Jewish Synthesis', HTR 59, 1966, 293–307.

Donner, H., 'Die religionsgeschichtlichen Ursprünge von Prov. Sal. 8', *ZÄS* 82, 1958, 8–18.

Dornseiff, F., 'Hesiods Werke und Tage und das alte Morgenland', *Phil* 89, 1934, 397–415 = *Antike und Alter Orient*, ²1959, 72–95.

— 'Das Buch Prediger', *ZDMG* 89, 1935, 243–9.

— 'Ägyptische Liebeslieder, Hoheslied, Sappho, Theokrit', *ZDMG* 90, 1936 = *Antike und Alter Orient*, ²1959, 189–202; 589–601.

— *Echtheitsfragen antik-griechischer Literatur*, Berlin 1939.

— *Antike und Alter Orient*, *Kleine Schriften* I, Leipzig ²1959.

Dothan, M., 'Excavations at Tell Mor 1959' (in Hebrew), *BIES* 24, 1960, 120–32.

— 'Ashdod, Preliminary Report on the Excavations in Seasons 1962/63', *IEJ* 14, 1964, 79–95.

Droysen, G., *Johann Gustav Droysen*, Berlin 1910.

Droysen, J. G., *Geschichte des Hellenismus*, Vol. I, Hamburg 1836.

— *Geschichte des Hellenismus*, ed. E. Bayer, Vols. I–III, Tübingen 1952/53.

— *Historik*, ed. R. Hübner, München and Berlin 1937.

Duchesne-Guillemin, J., *Ormazd et Ahriman*, Paris 1953.

— 'Le Zervanisme et les Manuscrits de la Mer Morte', *Indo-Iranian Journal* 1, 1957, 96–9.

— *The Western Response to Zoroaster*, Oxford 1958.

— *La Religion de l'Iran Ancien*, Mana 1, III, Paris 1962.

Dürr, L., *Das Erziehungswesen im Alten Testament und in antiken Orient*, MV(Ä)G 36, 2, 1932.

— 'Heilige Vaterschaft . . .', in: *Heilige Überlieferung*, *Festschrift I. Herwegen*, Münster 1938.

Duesberg, H.-Auvray, P., 'Le Livre de l'Ecclésiastique', *La Sainte Bible . . . de Jerusalem*, Paris ²1958.

Dunand, M., and Duru, R., *Oumm el-'Amed. Une ville de l'époque hellénistique aux Échelles de Tyr*, Études et Documents d'Archéologie IV, Vols. I and II, Paris 1962.

Dunbabin, T. J.. *The Greeks and their Eastern Neighbours*, London 1957.

Dupont-Sommer, A., 'De l'Immortalité astrale dans la "Sagesse de Salomon" (3, 7)', *REG* 62, 1949, 80–7.

— 'Nouveaux Aperçus sur les Manuscrits de la Mer Morte', *L'orient Ancien Illustré* 5, Paris 1953.

— 'Le problème des influences étrangères sur la secte juive de Qoumrân', *RHPR* 35, 1955, 75–94.

— 'Exorcismes et Guérisons dans les écrits de Qoumrân', SVT 7, 1960, 246–61.

— *The Essene Writings from Qumran*, Oxford 1961.

Ebner, E., *Elementary Education in Ancient Israel during the Tannaitic Period* . . ., New York 1956.

Eddy, S. K., *The King is Dead. Studies in the Near Eastern Resistance to Hellenism 334–31 BC*, Lincoln 1961.

Edgar, C. C., 'A new letter of Apollonios the Dioiketes', *APF* 11, 1935, 218–19.

Ehrlich, E. L., 'Der Traum im Talmud', *ZNW* 47, 1956, 133–45.

Eichrodt, W., *Theology of the Old Testament*, Vols. I and II, London and Philadelphia 1961 and 1967.

Eisler, R., *ΙΗΣΟΥΣ ΒΑΣΙΛΕΥΣ ΟΥ ΒΑΣΙΛΕΥΣΑΣ*, Vols. I and II, Heidelberg 1929–30.

Eissfeldt, O., *Erstlinge und Zehnten im AT*, BWAT 22, Leipzig 1917.

— *Baal Zaphon, Zeus Kasios und der Durchzug der Israeliten durchs Rote Meer*, Beiträge zur Religionsgeschichte des Altertums 1, Halle 1932.

— *Tempel und Kulte syrischer Städte in hellenistisch-römischer Zeit*, AO 40, 1941.

— *Der Gott Karmel*, SAB Kl. f. Sprachen . . . No. 1, 1953.

— *The Old Testament: An Introduction*, Oxford 1965.

— *Kleine Schriften*, Vols. I–III, Tübingen 1962–1966.

Éléments Orientaux dans la Religion Grecque ancienne, Colloque de Strasbourg 22–24 Mai 1958, Paris 1960.

Eliade, M., *The Myth of the Eternal Return*, London 1954.

Elliger, K., 'Ein Zeugnis aus der jüdischen Gemeinde im Alexanderjahr 332 v. Chr.', *ZAW* 62, 1949/50, 63–115.

— *Das Buch der zwölf Kleinen Propheten II*, ATD 25, Göttingen 1950, ⁵1964.

— 'Sinn und Ursprung der priesterlichen Geschichtserzählung', *ZTK* 49, 1952, 121–43.

— *Studien zum Habakuk-Kommentar vom Toten Meer*, BHT 15, Tübingen 1953.

Eltester, F.-W., *Eikon im Neuen Testament*, BZNW 23, Berlin 1958.

Falkenstein, A., *Topographie von Uruk*, I, *Uruk in der Geschichte der Seleukidenzeit*, Berlin 1941.

Farmer, W. R., 'The Economic Basis of the Qumran Community', *TZ* 11, 1955, 295–308; 12, 1956, 56–8.

— 'Judas, Simon and Athronges', *NTS* 2, 1958, 147–55.

Fascher, E., 'Der Vorwurf der Gottlosigkeit in der Auseinandersetzung bei

Juden, Griechen und Christen', in: *Abraham unser Vater, Festschrift f. Otto Michel*, AGSU 5, Leiden 1963, 78–105.

Feldman, L. H., 'The Orthodoxy of the Jews in Hellenistic Egypt', *JewSocSt* 22, 1960, 215–37.

— 'Abraham the Greek Philosopher', *Transactions and Proceedings of the American Philological Association* 59, 1968, 145–56.

Festugière, A. J., 'Sur le "de vita Pythagorica" ', *REG* 50, 1937, 470–94.

— 'L'expérience religieuse du médecin Thessalos', *RB* 48, 1939, 45–77.

— *La Révélation d'Hermès Trismégiste*, Vols. I–IV, Paris 1950–54.

— *Personal Religion among the Greeks*, Sather Classical Lectures 26, Berkeley-Los Angeles 1954.

Février, J. G., *La Religion des Palmyriennes*, Paris 1931.

— 'La Tactique Hellénistique dans un Texte de ʿAyin Fashka', *Semitica* 3, 1950, 53–9.

Fichtner, J., *Die altorientalische Weisheit in ihrer israelitisch-jüdischen Ausprägung*, BZAW 62, Giessen 1933.

— 'Zum Problem Glaube und Geschichte in der israelitisch-jüdischen Weisheitsliteratur', *TLZ* 76, 1951, 145–50.

Fiebig, P., *Antike Wundergeschichten*, Kleine Texte 79, 1911.

Finkelstein, L., 'Pre-Maccabean Documents in the Passover Haggadah, Additional Note D: The Tobiads', 31–3, 'Additional Note E: The Family of the High Priest Menelaos', 33–4, *HTR* 36, 1943.

— *The Pharisees*, Vols. I and II, Philadelphia ³1962.

Fischer Weltgeschichte, Vol. V, *Griechen und Perser*, ed. H. Bengtson; Vol. VI, *Der Hellenismus und der Aufstieg Roms*, ed. P. Grimal, Frankfurt 1965.

Fitzgerald, G. M., *Beth-Shan Excavations 1921–1923, The Arab and Byzantine Levels*, Publications of the Palestine . . . Section, Vol. III, Philadelphia 1931.

Fitzmyer, J. A., 'The Name Simon', *HTR* 56, 1963, 1–5.

— 'The Aramaic "Elect of God" Text from Qumran Cave IV', *CBQ* 27, 1965, 348–72.

Flusser, D., 'Qumrân and Jewish Apotropaic Prayers', *IEJ* 16, 1966, 194–205.

Förster, M., 'Das lateinisch-altenglische Fragment der Apokryphe von Jannes und Jambres', *Archiv f. d. Studium der neuen Sprachen* . . . 108, 1902, 15–28.

Fohrer, G., 'Die Struktur der alttestamentlichen Eschatologie', *TLZ* 85, 1960, 401–20.

'Zehn Jahre Literatur zur alttestamentlichen Prophetie (1951–1960), XIII, Verkündigung und Botschaft der Propheten', *TR* 28, 1962, 335–62.

— *Das Buch Hiob*, KAT 16, Gütersloh 1963.

— 'Prophetie und Magie', *ZAW* 78, 1966, 25–47.

— *Introduction to the Old Testament*, London and Philadelphia 1970.

Forbes, R. J., *Studies in Ancient Technology*, Vols. I and II, Leiden 1955.

Frank, T., *An Economic Survey of the Roman Empire*, Vol. II: H. Heichelheim, 'Roman Syria', Baltimore 1940.

Fraenkel, E., 'The Stars in the Prologue of the Rudens', *ClassQ* 36, 1942, 10–14.

Frankel, Z., *Vorstudien zu der Septuaginta*, Leipzig 1841.

Frankel, Z., *Über den Einfluss der palästinischen Exegese auf die alexandrinische Hermeneutik*, Leipzig 1851.

Fraser, P. M., 'Bibliography, Graeco-Roman Egypt, Greek Inscriptions 1959', *JEA* 46, 1960, 95–103.

— 'Two Studies on the Cult of Sarapis in the Hellenistic World', *Opuscula Atheniensia* III, Lund 1960, 1–54.

Freudenthal, J., *Hellenistische Studien*, Vols. I–III, Breslau 1875–79.

— 'Are there Traces of Greek Philosophy in the Septuagint ?', *JQR* 2, 1889/90, 205–22.

Frey, J. B., 'Les communautés Juives à Rome', *RSR* 20, 1930, 269–97.

Friedlander, M., *Geschichte der jüdischen Apologetik*, Zurich 1903.

— *Griechische Philosophie im Alten Testament*, Berlin 1904.

Fries, K., *Das philosophische Gespräch von Hiob bis Platon*, Tübingen 1904.

Frost, S. B., *Old Testament Apocalyptic: Its Origins and Growth*, London 1952.

Fruin, R., 'Studien in de joodsche Geschiedenis na 333', *Nieuw Theologische Tijdschrift* 24, 1935, 101–10.

Fuchs, H., *Der geistige Widerstand gegen Rom*, Berlin 1938.

Fuchs, L., *Die Juden Ägyptens in ptolemäischer und römischer Zeit*, Wien 1924.

Fuks, A., 'Dositheos Son of Drimylos: A Prosopographical Note', *JJurPap* 7/8, 1953/54, 205–9.

Funk, R. W., 'The 1957 Campaign at Beth-Zur', *BASOR* 150, 1958, 8–20.

Gager, J. G., *Moses in Greco-Roman Paganism*, JBL Monograph Series 16, 1972.

Gall, A. V., *ΒΑΣΙΛΕΙΑ ΤΟΥ ΘΕΟΥ*, Heidelberg 1926.

Galling, K., *Der Altar in den Kulturen des alten Orients*, Berlin 1925.

— 'Kohelet-Studien', *ZAW* 50, 1932, 276–99.

— 'Stand und Aufgabe der Kohelet-Forschung', *TR* NF 6, 1934, 355–73.

— *Biblisches Reallexikon*, HAT I, 1, Tübingen 1937 *(BRL)*.

— 'Die syrisch-palästinische Küste nach der Beschreibung bei Pseudo-Skylax', *ZDPV* 61, 1938, 66–96 = *Studien zur Gesch. Isr.*, Tübingen 1964, 185–209.

— Review of E. Bickermann, *Der Gott der Makkabäer*, *OLZ* 42, 1939, 225–8.

— 'Judäa, Galiläa und der Osten im Jahre 164/3 v. Chr.', *PJB* 36, 1940, 33–47.

— 'Prediger Salomo', *Die Fünf Megilloth*, HAT I, 18, Tübingen 1940.

— 'Königliche und nichtkönigliche Stifter beim Tempel von Jerusalem', *ZDPV* 68, 1951, 134–42.

— 'Kronzeugen des Artaxerxes', *ZAW* 63, 1951, 66–74.

— *Die Krisis der Aufklärung in Israel*, Mainzer Universitätsreden 19, 1952.

— 'Der Gott Karmel und die Ächtung fremder Götter', in: *Geschichte und Altes Testament*, Festschrift f. A. Alt, BHT 16, Tübingen 1953.

— *Die Bücher der Chronik, Esra, Nehemia*, ATD 12, Göttingen 1954.

— 'Die Grabinschrift Hiobs', *Die Welt des Orients* II, 1, 1954, 3–6.

— 'Erwägungen zur antiken Synagoge', *ZDPV* 72, 1956, 163–78.

— 'Das Rätsel der Zeit im Urteil Kohelets (Koh 3, 1–15)', *ZTK* 58, 1961, 1–15.

— 'Eschmunazar und der Herr der Könige', *ZDPV* 69, 1963, 140–51.

— *Studien zur Geschichte Israels im persischen Zeitalter*, Tübingen 1964.

Gan, M., 'The Book of Esther in the Light of the Story of Joseph in Egypt', *Tarbiz* 31, 1961, 144–9.

Gandz, S., 'The Hall of Reckonings in Jerusalem', *JQR* 31, 1940/41, 388–404.

Gaster, T. H., 'La Révolte des Macchabées', *Evidence* 4, Vol. 29, December 1952, 27–33.

Gebhardt, C., *Das Lied der Lieder*, Berlin 1931.

Geffcken, J., *Zwei griechische Apologeten*, Leipzig and Berlin 1907.

Geiger, A., *Urschrift und Übersetzungen der Bibel in ihrer Abhängigkeit von der inneren Entwicklung des Judenthums*, Breslau 1857.

Gemser, B., 'The Instruction of 'Onchsheshonqy and Biblical Wisdom Literature', SVT 7, 1960, 102–28.

— *Sprüche Salomos*, HAT I, 16, Tübingen ²1963.

Gerleman, G., 'The Septuagint Proverbs as a Hellenistic Document', *OTS* 8, 1950, 15–27.

— *Studies in the Septuagint* III, *Proverbs*, LUÅ I, 52, 1956, No. 3.

Gese, H., *Lehre und Wirklichkeit in der alten Weisheit. Studien zu den Sprüchen Salomos und dem Buche Hiob*, Tübingen 1958.

—' Die Krisis der Weisheit bei Koheleth', in: *Les Sagesses du Proche Orient Ancien. Travaux du centre . . . d'histoire des religions de Strasbourg*, Paris 1963, 139–51.

Gibbert, J., 'Eupolème et l'historiographie du Judaïsme hellénistique', *ETL* 39, 1963, 539–54.

Ginsberg, H. L., *Studies in Koheleth*, Texts and Studies of the Jewish Theological Seminary of America, New York 1960.

— 'The Structure and Contents of . . . Koheleth', in: *Wisdom in Israel and in the Ancient Near East*, SVT 3, 1955, 138–49.

Ginsburg, M. S., 'Sparta and Judaea', *ClassPhil* 29, 1934, 117–22.

Ginzberg, L., *The Legends of the Jews*, Vols. I–VII, Philadelphia 1909–55.

— *On Jewish Law and Lore*, Philadelphia 1955.

Giveon, R., 'A Ptolemaic Fayence Bowl (b. Mishmar ha-'Emeq)', *IEJ* 13, 1963, 20–9.

Glasson, T. F., *Greek Influence in Jewish Eschatology, with Special Reference to the Apocalypses and Pseudepigraphs*, London 1961.

Glatzer, N. N., *Geschichte der talmudischen Zeit*, Berlin 1937.

Glockmann, G., 'Das Homerbild der altchristlichen Literatur', *Klio* 43–45, 1965, 270–81.

Glueck, N., 'Explorations in Eastern Palestine III', *AASOR* 18/19, 1937–39.

Götze, A., 'Persische Weisheit in griechischem Gewande', *Zeitschrift für Indologie und Iranistik* 2, 1923, 60–8, and 167–77.

Goldin, J., 'The Three Pillars of Simeon the Righteous', *PAAJR* 27, 1958, 43–58.

Goodenough, E. R., *The Political Philosophy of Hellenistic Kingship*, YCS 1, 1928, 55–104.

— *Jewish Symbols in the Greco-Roman Period*, Vols. I–XI, New York 1953ff. (Bollingen Series XXXVII).

— 'The Bosporus Inscriptions to the Most High God', *JQR* 47, 1957, 221–44.

Gordis, R., *Koheleth–The Man and his World*, Texts and Studies of the Jewish Theological Seminary of America, New York 1951.

Gordon, C. H., 'Homer and Bible: The Origin and Character of East Mediterranean Literature', HUCA 26, 1955, 43–108.

— *Before the Bible*, London 1962.

Gorion, M. J. bin, *Die Sagen der Juden*, (I) *Von der Urzeit*, Frankfurt 1913.

Grässer, E., 'Der Hebräerbrief 1938–1963', *TR* 30, 1964, 138–236.

Graetz, H., *Geschichte der Juden*, Vol. III, ed. M. Braun, Leipzig [5]1905.

Graham, W. C., and May, H. C., *Culture and Conscience*, Chicago 1936.

Granier, F., *Die makedonische Heeresversammlung, Ein Beitrag antiken Staatsrechts*, MBPAR 13, 1931.

Grelot, P., 'Études sur le "Papyrus Pascal" d'Éléphantine', *VT* 4, 1954, 349–84.

— 'Notes sur le Testament Araméen de Lévi', *RB* 63, 1956, 391–406.

— 'La Légende d'Hénoch dans les Apocryphes et dans la Bible', *RSR* 46, 1958, 5–26; 181–210.

— 'La géographie mythique d'Hénoch et ses sources orientales', *RB* 65, 1958, 33–69.

— 'L'Eschatologie des Esséniens et le Livre d'Hénoch', *RQ* 1, 1958/59, 113–31.

Gressmann, H., 'Die ammonitischen Tobiaden', SAB 1921, 663–71.

— 'Das religionsgeschichtliche Problem des Ursprungs der hellenistischen Erlösungsreligion II', *ZKG* 41, 1922, 154–80.

— 'Die Umwandlung der orientalischen Religionen unter dem Einfluss hellenistischen Geistes', *Vorträge der Bibliothek Warburg 1923–1924*, 1924/25, 170–95.

— *Die hellenistische Gestirnreligion*, BhAO 5, 1925.

— 'Die Aufgaben der Wissenschaft des nachbiblischen Judentums', *ZAW* 43, 1925, 1–32.

— *Der Messias*, FRLANT NF 26, 1929.

— 'Foreign Influences in Hebrew Prophecy', *JTS* 27, 1926, 241–54.

— 'Jewish Life in Ancient Rome', in: *Jewish Studies in Memory of Israel Abrahams*, New York 1927, 170–91.

Griffith, G. I., *The Mercenaries of the Hellenistic World*, London 1935.

Grönbech, V., *Der Hellenismus. Lebensstimmung Weltmacht*, Göttingen 1953.

Gulkowitsch, L., *Die Entwicklung des Begriffes Ḥāsīd im Alten Testament*, Acta et Commentationes Universitatis Tartuensis, B 32, 4, 1934.

Gundel, W. and H. G., *Astrologumena*, Sudhoffs Archiv Beiheft 6, 1966.

Guthe, H., *Die griechisch-römischen Mächte des Ostjordanlandes*, Das Land der Bibel II, 5, 1918.

Gutman, Y., *The Beginnings of Jewish Hellenistic Literature* (in Hebrew), Jerusalem I, 1958; II, 1963.

Gutschmid, A. v., *Kleine Schriften*, ed. F. Ruhl, Vols. II and IV, Leipzig 1890 and 1893.

Guttmann, A., 'The Significance of Miracles . . .', HUCA 20, 1947, 363–406.

Hadas, M., *Aristeas to Philocrates*, Jewish Apocryphal Literature, New York 1951.

— *The Third and Fourth Books of Maccabees*, Jewish Apocryphal Literature, New York 1953.

— 'Plato in Hellenistic Fusion', *Journal of the History of Ideas* 19, 1958, 3–13.

— *Hellenistic Culture, Fusion and Diffusion*, New York 1959 (*HCu*).

Haenchen, E., *The Acts of the Apostles*, Oxford 1971.

Hahn, F., *Mission in the New Testament*, SBT I, 47, London 1965.

Hallewy, E. E., 'Biblical Midrash and Homeric Exegesis', *Tarbiz* 31, 1961/62, 157–69, 264–80 (in Hebrew).

— 'The Writers of the Aggada and the Greek Grammarians', *Tarbiz* 29, 1959/60, 47–55 (in Hebrew).

Hamilton, N. Q., 'Temple Cleansing and Temple Bank', *JBL* 83, 1964, 365–72.

Hamilton, R. W., 'Excavations at Tell Abu Hawan', *QDAP* 4, 1934/35, 1–69.

Hammond, P. C., 'The Nabataean Bitumen Industry at the Dead Sea', *BA* 22, 1959, 40–8.

Hampel, F., Review of F. Reuter, *Beiträge zur Beurteilung des Königs Antiochos Epiphanes*, *Gnomon* 15, 1939, 619–23.

Hanhart, R., 'Fragen um die Entstehung der LXX', *VT* 12, 1962, 139–62.

— *Zur Zeitrechnung des 1. und 2. Makkabäerbuches*, BZAW 88, 1964.

Hanson, R. P. C., *Allegory and Event*, London 1959.

Harder, R., *Karpokrates von Chalkis und die Memphitische Isispropaganda*, AAB ph.-hist. Kl. 1943, No. 14.

Harmatta, J., 'Irano-Aramaica, zur Geschichte des frühhellenistischen Judentums in Ägypten', *Acta Antiqua* 7, 1959, 336–409.

Harper, G. M., Jr, 'A Study in the Commercial Relations between Egypt and Syria in the Third Century BC', *AJP* 49, 1928, 1–35.

Harris, J. R., 'Athena, Sophia and the Logos', *BJRL* 7, 1922/23, 56–72.

Haussoullier, B., 'Inscriptions grecques de Babylone', *Klio* 9, 1909, 352–63.

Heaton, E. W., *The Book of Daniel*, Torch Commentary, London 1956.

Heichelheim, F. M., *Die auswärtige Bevölkerung im Ptolemäerreich*, Klio-Beiheft 18, Leipzig 1925.

— 'Roman Syria', in: T. Frank, *An Economic Survey of Ancient Rome*, Vol. IV, Baltimore 1938, 121–257.

— 'Ezra's Palestine and Periclean Athens', *ZRGG* 3, 1951, 251–3.

— 'Recent Discoveries in Ancient Economic History', *Historia* 2, 1953/54, 129–35.

Heinemann, I., 'Poseidonios über die Entwicklung der jüdischen Religion', *MGWJ* 63, 1919, 113–21.

— *Poseidonios' metaphysische Schriften*, Vols. I and II, Breslau 1921, 1928.

— 'Wer veranlasste den Glaubenszwang der Makkabäerzeit?', *MGWJ* 82, 1938, 145–72.

— *Philons griechische und jüdische Bildung*, reprinted Darmstadt 1962.

Heinisch, P., *Griechische Philosophie und Altes Testament*, I, *Die palästinischen Bücher*, Biblische Zeitfragen 6/7, 1913.

Heitsch, E., 'PSI 844, ein Isishymnus', *MusHelv* 17, 1960, 185–8.

Heinze, R., *Xenokrates*, Leipzig 1892.

Heller, B., 'Ein Homerisches Gleichnis im Midrasch', *MGWJ* 76, 1932, 330–4.

Helm, R., *Lucian und Menipp*, Leipzig-Berlin 1906.

Hempel, J., *Die althebräische Literatur und ihr hellenistisch-jüdisches Nachleben*, Handbuch der Literatur-Wissenschaft, Vol. XXII, Potsdam 1934.

— *Die Texte von Qumran in der heutigen Forschung*, NGG I ph.-hist. Kl. 1961, No. 10.

Hengel, M., *Die Zeloten*, AGSU 1, Leiden 1961.

— 'Die Synagogeninschrift von Stobi', *ZNW* 57, 1966, 145–83.

— *Nachfolge und Charisma*, BZNW 34, 1968.

— 'Proseuche und Synagoge. Jüdische Gemeinde, Gotteshaus und Gottesdienst in der Diaspora und in Palästina', *Tradition und Glaube. Festschrift für K. G. Kuhn*, Göttingen 1971, 157–84.

Hengel, R. and M., 'Die Heilungen Jesu und medizinisches Denken', *Medicus Viator, Festschrift f. R. Siebeck*, Tübingen 1959, 331–61.

Herrmann, S., 'Isis in Byblos', *ZÄS* 82, 1958, 48–55.

— 'Die Naturlehre des Schöpfungsberichtes', *TLZ* 86, 1961, 413–24.

Herter, H., 'Hellenisches und Hellenentum', *Das neue Bild der Antike* 1, ed. H. Berve, Leipzig 1942, 334–55.

Hertzberg, H. W., 'Palästinische Bezüge im Buche Kohelet', *ZDPV* 73, 1957, 113–24.

— *Der Prediger*, KAT XVII, 4, Gütersloh 1963.

Herz, J., 'Grossgrundbesitz in Palästina im Zeitalter Jesu', *PJB* 24, 1928, 98–113.

Herzfeld, L., *Geschichte des Volkes Israel*, Vols. I–III, Nordhausen 1855–57.

Hill, D. K., 'The Animal Fountain of 'Arâq el-Emîr', *BASOR* 171, 1963, 45–55.

Hölscher, G., *Palästina in der persischen und hellenistischen Zeit*, QFAGG 5, 1903.

— *Geschichte der israelitischen und jüdischen Religion*, Giessen 1922.

— 'Zur jüdischen Namenskunde', in: *"Vom Alten Testament"*, *K. Marti zum 70. Geburtstag gewidmet*, BZAW 41, 1925, 148–57.

— *Drei Erdkarten, Ein Beitrag zur Erderkenntnis des hebräischen Altertums*, SAH ph.-hist. Kl. 34, 1944–48, 3. Abhandlung, published 1949.

— *Das Buch Hiob*, HAT I, 17, Tübingen ²1952.

Hölscher, U., 'Anaximander und die Anfänge der griechischen Philosophie', *Hermes* 81, 1953, 257–77; 385–418.

Holleaux, M., *Études d'épigraphie et d'histoire grecques*, Vol. III, *Lagides et Séleucides*, Paris 1942.

Holtzmann, O., 'Das Ende des jüd. Staatswesens und die Entstehung des Christentums', in: B. Stade, *Geschichte des Volkes Israel*, Vol. II, Berlin 1888.

Hommel, H., 'Vergils "messianisches" Gedicht', *Theologia Viatorum* 2, 1950, 182–212.

Hopfner, T., *Orient und griechische Philosophie*, BhAO 4, 1925, 7ff.

— *Plutarch über Isis und Osiris*, Vols. I and II, Prague 1940f.

Humbert, P., *Recherches sur les sources égyptiennes de la littérature sapientiale d'Israël*, Memoires de l'Université de Neuchâtel 7, 1929.

— 'Le Modernisme de Job', in: *Wisdom in Israel and the Ancient Near East*, SVT 3, 1955, 150–61.

Hunzinger, C. H., 'Fragmente einer älteren Fassung des Buches Milḥamā aus Höhle 4 von Qumrān', *ZAW* 69, 1957, 131–51.

— 'Aus der Arbeit an den unveröffentlichten Texten von Qumrān', *TLZ* 85, 1960, 151–2.

Iliffe, J. H., 'Pre-Hellenistic Greek Pottery in Palestine', *QDAP* 2, 1933, 15–26, plates V–IX.
— 'A Tell Fār'a Tomb Group Reconsidered', *QDAP* 4, 1934, 182–6, plates LXXXIX–XCI.
— 'A Hoard of Bronzes from Askalon', *QDAP* 5, 1935, 61–68, plates XXIX–XXXIV.
Irby, C. L., and Mangels, J., *Travels in Egypt and Nubia, Syria and the Holy Land including a Journey round the Dead Sea and through the Country East of Jordan*, London 1852.
Irwin, W. A., 'Job and Prometheus', *JR* 30, 1950, 90–108.
— 'Where shall Wisdom be Found ?', *JBL* 80, 1961, 133–42.

Jackson, J. F., and Lake, K., *The Beginnings of Christianity* I, 1–5, London 1920–30.
Jacob, E., 'L'histoire d' Israël vue par Ben Sira', *Mélanges bibliques rédigés en l'honneur de A. Robert*, Paris 1957, 288–95.
Jaeger, W., *Diokles von Karystos*, Berlin 1938.
— 'Greeks and Jews', *JR* 18, 1938, 127–43 = *Scripta Minora* 2, 1960, 169–83.
— *Die Theologie der frühen griechischen Denker*, Stuttgart 1953.
— *Aristoteles*, Berlin ²1955.
Jansen, H. L., *Die Henochgestalt*, Skrifter utgitt av det norske Videnskapsakademi i Oslo 1939.
— *Die Politik Antiochus IV*, Skrifter utgitt av det norske Videnskapsakademi i Oslo 1943.
Jastrow, M., *The Book of Job*, Philadelphia and London 1920.
Jaubert, A., *La Date de la Cène*, Paris 1957.
— 'Jésus et le Calendrier de Qumran', *NTS* 7, 1960/61, 1–22.
— *La Notion d'Alliance dans le Judaïsme . . .*, Patristica Sorbonensia 6, Paris 1963.
Jellicoe, S., 'Aristeas, Philo and the Septuagint Vorlage', *JTS* 12, 1961, 261–71.
Jeremias, G., *Der Lehrer der Gerechtigkeit*, SUNT 2, Göttingen 1963.
Jeremias, J., *Jerusalem in the Time of Jesus*, London and Philadelphia 1969.
Johns, C. N., 'Excavations at 'Aṭlīṭ 1930–31', *QDAP* 2, 1933, 41–104.
Jonas, H., *Gnosis und spätantiker Geist*, Vol. I: *Die mythologische Gnosis*, FRLANT 51, Göttingen ²1954.
Jones, A. H. M., *The Cities of the Eastern Roman Provinces*, Oxford 1937.
— *The Greek City from Alexander to Justinian*, Oxford 1940.
Jonge, M., and de Woude, A. S. v. d., '11 Q Melchizedek and the New Testament', *NTS* 12, 1965/66, 301–26.
Jouguet, P., 'Les Lagides et les indigènes Égyptiens', *RBPH* 2, 1923, 419–45.
— *L'impérialisme Macédonien et l'hellénisation de l'Orient*, Évolution de l'humanité 15, Paris 1926.
— 'L'histoire politique et la papyrologie', *MBPAR* 19, 1934, 62–101.
Jüthner, J., *Hellenen und Barbaren*, Das Erbe der Alten, NF 8, 1923.
Juster, J., *Les Juifs dans l'empire Romain, leur condition juridique, économique et sociale*, Vols. I and II, Paris 1914 (Juster).

Kaerst, J., *Die antike Idee der Oekumene in ihrer politischen und kulturellen Bedeutung*, Leipzig 1903.

— *Geschichte des Hellenismus*, Vol. I, ³1927; Vol. II, ²1926, Berlin.

Käsemann, E., *New Testament Questions of Today*, London and Philadelphia 1969.

Kahle, P. E., *The Cairo Geniza*, Oxford 1959.

Kahrstedt, U., *Syrische Territorien in hellenistischer Zeit*, AGG NF ph.-hist. Kl. XIX, 2, Berlin 1926.

Kaiser, O., 'Die Begründung der Sittlichkeit im Buche Jesus Sirach', *ZTK* 55, 1958, 51–63.

Kallen, H. M., *The Book of Job as a Greek Tragedy*, reprinted New York 1959.

Kaminka, A., 'Les rapports entre le rabbinisme et la philosophie stoïcienne', *REJ* 82, 1926, 233–52.

Kamlah, E., *Die Form der katalogischen Paränese im Neuen Testament*, WUNT 7, Tübingen 1964.

Kaplan, J., 'Exploration Archéologique de Tel-Aviv-Jaffa', *RB* 62, 1955, 92–9.

Katz, P., 'The Old Testament Canon in Palestine and Alexandria', *ZNW* 47, 1956, 191–217.

Keil, J. and Premerstein, A. v., *Bericht über eine zweite Reise in Lydien . . .*, DAW ph.-hist. Kl. 54, 2, 1911.

Keller, R., *De Aristobulo Judaeo*, Diss. typescript, Bonn 1948.

Kerényi, K., 'Das persische Millienium im Mahābharata, bei der Sibylle und Vergil', *Klio* 29, 1936, 1–35.

— *Die griechisch-orientalische Romanliteratur in religionsgeschichtlicher Beleuchtung*, Darmstadt 1962.

Kerschensteiner, J., *Platon und der Orient*, Stuttgart 1945.

Kiechle, F., 'Antiochos IV . . .', *Geschichte in Wissenschaft u. Unterricht* 14, 1963, 159–70.

Kiefer, A., *Aretalogische Studien*, Diss. Freiburg 1929.

Kienitz, F. K., *Die politische Geschichte Ägyptens vom 7. bis zum 4. Jh. vor der Zeitwende*, Berlin 1953.

Kiessling, E., *Der Hellenismus in der deutschen Forschung 1938–1948*, Wiesbaden 1956.

Kincaid, C. A., 'A Persian Prince—Antiochus Epiphanes', *Oriental Studies in Honour of Cursetji Erachji Pavry*, London 1933, 209–19.

Kippenberg, H. G., *Garizim und Synagoge*, Religionsgeschichtliche Versuche und Vorarbeiten, Berlin and New York 1971.

Kittel, G., *Die Probleme des palästinischen Spätjudentums und das Urchristentum*, BWANT 3, 1, Stuttgart 1926.

— *Die Religionsgeschichte und das Urchristentum*, Gütersloh 1931.

— 'Das kleinasiatische Judentum in der hellenistisch-römischen Zeit', *TLZ* 69, 1944, 9–20.

Kittel, R., *Geschichte des Volkes Israel*, Vol. III, 2, Stuttgart 1929.

Klausner, J., *Historiyah šel habbayit haššenī*, Vols. I–IV, Jerusalem ⁴1954 (*Hist.*).

— *The Messianic Idea in Israel*, New York 1955.

Klein, S., *Die Barajta der vierundzwanzig Priesterabteilungen*, Diss. Heidelberg, Kirchhain 1909.

— Review of P. Kahle, *Masoreten des Westens*, *MGWJ* 73, 1929, 69–73.

— 'Notes on the History of Large Estates in Palestine', *BJPES* 3, 1936, 110–16 (in Hebrew).

Kleinert, P., 'Sind im Buche Kohelet ausserhebräische Einflüsse anzuerkennen?', *ThStKr* 56, 1883, 761–82.

— 'Zur religions- und kulturgeschichtlichen Stellung des Buches Koheleth', *ThStKr* 82, 1909, 493–529.

Kleingünther, A., *ΠΡΩΤΟΣ ΕΥΡΕΤΗΣ*, PhilSuppl 26, 1, 1933.

Knox, W. L., 'The Divine Wisdom', *JTS* 38, 1937, 230–7.

— *Pharisaism and Hellenism in Judaism and Christianity*, Vol. II, *The Contact of Pharisaism with other Cultures*, London 1937, 61–114.

— *St Paul and the Church of the Gentiles*, Cambridge 1939.

Koch, K., 'Gibt es ein Vergeltungsdogma im AT?' *ZTK* 52, 1955, 1–42.

— 'Spätisraelitisches Geschichtsdenken am Beispiel des Buches Daniel', *HZ* 193, 1961, 1–32.

Koenen, L., 'Die Prophezeiungen des "Töpfers"', *ZPapEp* 2, 1968, 178–209.

— 'The Prophecies of a Potter: A Prophecy of World Renewal Becomes an Apocalypse', *Proceedings of the Twelfth International Congress of Papyrology*, American Studies in Papyrology 7, Toronto 1970, 255–61.

Koffmann, E., 'Rechtsstellung und hierarchische Struktur des יחד von Qumran', *Bibl* 42, 1961, 433–42.

— 'Die staatsrechtliche Stellung der essenischen Vereinigungen', *Bibl* 44, 1963, 46–61.

Kolbe, W., *Beiträge zur syrischen und jüdischen Geschichte*, BWAT NF 10, Stuttgart 1926.

Koole, J. L., 'Die Bibel des Ben Sira', *OTS* 14, 1965, 374–96.

Kortenbeutel, H., *Der ägyptische Süd- und Osthandel in der Politik der Ptolemäer und römischen Kaiser*, Diss. Berlin 1931.

— *ΓΥΜΝΑΣΙΟΝ und ΒΟΥΛΗ*, *APF* 12, 1937, 44–53.

Kraeling, C. H. (ed.), *Gerasa, City of the Decapolis*, New Haven 1938.

Kraeling, E. G., *The Brooklyn Museum Aramaic Papyri*, New Haven 1953.

Krämer, H. J., *Der Ursprung der Geistmetaphysik. Untersuchungen zur Geschichte des Platonismus zwischen Platon und Plotin*, Amsterdam ²1967.

Kraus, F. R., *Die physiognomischen Omina der Babylonier*, MVÄG 40, 1935(2).

Kraus, H. J., *Psalmen*, Vols. I and II, BKAT 15, Neukirchen 1960.

Krauss, S., *Griechische und lateinische Lehnwörter in Talmud, Midrasch und Targum*, Vols. I and II, Berlin 1898–99.

— 'Antiochia', *REJ* 45, 1902, 27–49.

— *Talmudische Archäologie*, Vols. I–III, Leipzig 1910–12.

Kreissig, H., 'Der Makkabäeraufstand, zur Frage seiner sozialökonomischen Zusammenhänge und Wirkungen', *Studii Clasice* 4, 1962, 143–75.

Kroeber, R., *Der Prediger*, Schriften und Quellen der Alten Welt 13, Berlin 1963.

Kroll, W., 'Bolos und Demokritos', *Hermes* 69, 1934, 228–32.

Kromayer, J. and Veith, G., *Heerwesen und Kriegführung der Griechen und Römer*, HAW IV, 3, 2, München ³1928.

Kümmel, W. G., *Heilsgeschehen und Geschichte, Gesammelte Aufsätze 1933 bis 1964*, Marburger theologische Studien 3, 1965.
— *Introduction to the New Testament*, London and New York ²1974.
Kuhl, C., 'Neuere Literarkritik des Buches Hiob', *TR* 21, 1953, 163–205; 257–317.
Kuhn, H. W., *Enderwartung und gegenwärtiges Heil*, SUNT 4, 1966.
Kuhn, K. G., 'Πειρασμός-ἁμαρτία-σάρξ im Neuen Testament und die damit zusammenhängenden Vorstellungen', *ZTK* 49, 1952, 200–22.
— 'Die in Palästina gefundenen Texte und das Neue Testament', *ZTK* 47, 1950, 192–211.
— 'Die Sektenschrift und die iranische Religion', *ZTK* 49, 1952, 296–316.
— 'Zum heutigen Stand der Qumranforschung', *TLZ* 85, 1960, 649–58.
— 'Zum essenischen Kalender', *ZNW* 52, 1961, 65–73.
Kukahn, E., *Anthropoide Sarkophage in Beyrouth*, Berlin 1955.
Kuschke, A., 'Arm und reich im Alten Testament, mit besonderer Berücksichtigung der nachexilischen Zeit', *ZAW* 57, 1939, 31–57.
Kutsch, E., 'Der Kalender des Jubiläenbuches und das Alte und das Neue Testament', *VT* 11, 1961, 39–47.

Lack, R., 'Les Origines de Elyon . . .', *CBQ* 24, 1962, 44–64.
Lagrange, M. J., 'Deux Hypogées Macédo-Sidoniens à Beit-Djebrin (Palestine)', *CRAI* 1902, 497–505.
— *Le Judaïsme avant Jésus Christ*, Paris 1931.
Lambrechts, P., and Noyen, P., 'Recherches sur le culte d'Atargatis dans le monde grec', *NClio* 6, 1954, 258–77.
Lamer, H., 'Der Kalypso-Graffito in Marissa', *ZDPV* 54, 1931, 59–67.
Lanczkowski, G., 'Die Entstehung des antiken Synkretismus', *Saeculum* 6, 1955, 227–43.
— *Altägyptischer Prophetismus*, Ägyptologische Abhandlungen 4, 1960.
Landau, Y. H., 'A Stamped Jar Handle from Jaffa', *'Atiqot* 2, 1959, 186–7.
Langen, D., *Archäische Ekstase und asiatische Meditation mit ihren Beziehungen zum Abendland*, Schriftenreihe zur Theorie und Praxis der Psychotherapie, Vol. III, Stuttgart 1963.
Lapp, P. W., *Palestinian Ceramic Chronology*, ASOR, Publications of the Jerusalem School, Archaeology Vol. III, 1961.
— 'Soundings at 'Araq el-Emir (Jordan)', *BASOR* 165, 1962, 16–34.
— 'The 1961 Excavations at 'Araq el-Emir', *ADAJ* VI/VII, 1962, 80–9.
— 'The Second and Third Campaigns at 'Arâq el-Emîr', *BASOR* 171, 1963, 8–39.
— 'Ptolemaic stamped Handles from Judah', *BASOR* 172, 1963, 22–35.
— 'Tell el-Fûl', *BA* 28, 1965, 2–10.
Laqueur, R., *Hellenismus*, Schriften der hessischen Hochschulen, Universität Giessen, Vol. 1, 1924.
Latte, K., *Römische Religionsgeschichte*, HAW V, 4, München 1960.
Lauha, A., 'Die Krise des religiösen Glaubens bei Kohelet', *SVT* 3, 1955, 183–91.
Launey, M., *Recherches sur les armées hellénistiques*, Bibliothèque des Écoles françaises d'Athènes et de Rome 169, Vols. I and II, Paris 1949/50.

Leaney, A. R. C., *The Rule of Qumran and its Meaning*, London 1966.
Lebram, J. C. H., 'Der Aufbau der Areopagrede', *ZNW* 55, 1964, 221–43.
— 'Die Weltreiche in der jüdischen Apokalyptik. Bemerkungen zu Tob. 14, 4–7', *ZAW* 76, 1964, 328–31.
— 'Nachbiblische Weisheitstraditionen', *VT* 15, 1965, 167–237.
Leeuwen, C. v., *Le développement du sens social en Israël avant l'ère chrétienne*, Assen 1955.
Lehmann, M. R., 'Ben Sira and the Qumran Literature', *RQ* 3, 1961/62, 103–16.
Leider, E., *Der Handel von Alexandria*, Diss. Hamburg 1935.
Leipoldt, J., and Grundmann, W. (eds.), *Umwelt des Urchristentums*, I. *Darstellung des neutestamentlichen Zeitalters*, Berlin 1965 (*UU*).
Lenger, M. T., 'Ordonnances divines et *prostagmata* dans l'empire des Ptolémées', *Proceedings of the Twelfth International Congress of Papyrology*, American Studies in Papyrology 7, Toronto 1970, 255–61.
Lentzen-Deis, F., 'Das Motiv der "Himmelsöffnung" in verschiedenen Gattungen der Umweltliteratur des Neuen Testaments', *Bibl* 50, 1969, 301–27.
Leon, H. J., *The Jews of Ancient Rome*, Philadelphia 1960.
Lesquier, J., *Les institutions militaires de l'Égypte sous les Lagides*, Paris 1911.
Lévi, I(sraël)., *L'Ecclésiastique* I, Paris 1898; II, Paris 1901, Bibliothèque de l'école des hautes études, Sciences religieuses, 10, 1, 2.
Lévy, I(sidore)., *La Légende de Pythagore de Grèce en Palestine*, Bibl. de l'école des hautes Études, Sciences hist. et phil. 250, Paris 1927.
— 'Notes d'Histoire hellénistique sur le second Livre des Maccabées', *Mélanges H. Grégoire = AIPHOS* 10, 1950, 681–99.
— 'Les deux Livres des Maccabées et le Livre Hébraïque des Hasmonéens', *Semitica* 5, 1955, 15–36.
— *Recherches esséniennes et pythagoriciennes*, Geneva and Paris 1965.
Levy, L., *Das Buch Qoheleth, Ein Beitrag zur Geschichte des Sadduzäismus*, Leipzig 1912.
Lewis, D. M., 'The First Greek Jew', *JSS* 2, 1957, 264–6.
Lewy, H., 'Aristotle and the Jewish Sage according to Clearchus of Soli', *HTR* 31, 1938, 205–35.
Liagre-Böhl, F. M. T. de, *Opera minora*, Groningen 1953.
Licht, J., 'Legs as Signs of Election', *Tarbiz* 35, 1965, 18–26 (in Hebrew).
Lieberman, S., *Greek in Jewish Palestine*, New York 1942.
— *Hellenism in Jewish Palestine*, New York 1950.
Lietzmann, H., *The History of the Early Church*, Vol.I., *The Beginning of the Christian Church*, London ³1953.
Lifshitz, B., 'L'Hellénisation des Juifs de Palestine', *RB* 72, 1965, 520–38.
Limbeck, M., *Die Ordnung des Heils*, Düsseldorf 1971.
Lindblom, C. J., *Die Jesaja-Apokalypse, Jes. 24–27*, LUÅ, NF Avd. I, 34, No. 3, 1938.
— 'Job and Prometheus', *Dragma Martino P. Nilsson*, 1939, 280–7.
Löw, I., *Die Flora der Juden*, Alexander Kohut Memorial Foundation IV, Vol. I, 1, Wien-Leipzig 1926.
Loewe, R., 'The Earliest Biblical Allusion to Coined Money', *PEQ* 87, 1955, 141–50.

Longo, V., *Aretalogie nel mondo Greco*, I, *Epigrafi e Papiri*, Genova 1969.
Loretz, O., *Qoheleth und der Alte Orient*, Freiburg 1964.
Luck, G., *Der Akademiker Antiochos*, Noctes Romanae 7, 1953.
Lueder, A., *Die philosophische Persönlichkeit des Antiochos von Askalon*, Diss. Göttingen 1940.
Lührmann, D., 'Ein Weisheitspsalm aus Qumran (11Q Psᵃ XVIII)', *ZAW* 80, 1968, 87–98.
Lueken, W., *Michael*, Göttingen 1898.

Maass, F., 'Von den Ursprüngen der rabbinischen Schriftauslegung', *ZTK* 52, 1955, 129–61.
Macalister, R. A. S., *The Excavation of Gezer*, Vols. I–III, London 1912.
— *A Century of Excavation in Palestine*, London 1925.
— *Excavations on the Hill of Ophel, Jerusalem 1923-25*, *PEFA* IV, 1926.
Macurdy, G. H., 'Platonic Orphism in the Testament of Abraham', *JBL* 61, 1942, 213–26.
Mach, R., *Der Zaddik in Talmud und Midrasch*, Leiden 1957.
Maier, G., *Mensch und freier Wille, Nach den jüdischen Religionsparteien zwischen Ben Sira und Paulus*, WUNT 12, Tübingen 1971.
Maisler, B. (see also B. Mazar), 'The house of Tobias', *Tarbiz* 12, 1940/41, 109–23 (in Hebrew).
— 'The Excavations at Tell Qasîle', *IEJ* 1, 1950/51, 61–76; 194–218.
Maisler, B., et al., 'The Excavations at Beth Yeraḥ (Khirbet el Kerak) 1944–46', *IEJ* 2, 1952, 165–73; 218–29.
Mansoor, M., *The Thanksgiving Hymns*, Studies on the Texts of the Desert of Judah, Vol. III, Leiden 1961.
Mantel, H., *Studies in the History of the Sanhedrin*, Cambridge, Mass. 1961.
Marcus, R., 'Divine Names and Attributes in Hellenistic Jewish Literature', *PAAJR 1931/32*, 1932, 43–120.
— 'Jewish and Greek Elements in the Septuagint', *Louis Ginzberg Jubilee Volume* I, New York 1945, 227–45.
— 'Dositheus, Priest and Levite', *JBL* 64, 1945, 269–71.
— 'On Biblical Hypostases of Wisdom', *HUCA* 23, I, 1950/51, 157–71.
Marmorstein, A., 'Les Épicuriens dans la littérature talmudique', *REJ* 54, 1907, 181–93.
Marrou, H. I., *Histoire de l'éducation dans l'antiquité*, Paris 1948.
Masson, O., 'Quelques noms sémitiques en transcription Grecque à Délos et à Rhénée', *Hommages A. Dupont-Sommer*, Paris 1971, 61–73.
May, H. G., 'Prometheus and Job', *ATR* 34, 1952, 240–6.
— 'Cosmological Reference in the Qumran Doctrine of the Two Spirits and in Old Testament Imagery', *JBL* 82, 1963, 1–14.
Mayer, Rudolf, *Die Biblische Vorstellung vom Weltenbrand*, Bonner Orient. Studien, NS 4, 1956.
Mazar, B. (see also Maisler, B.), 'The Tobiads', *IEJ* 7, 1957, 137–45; 229–38.
— et al., '*Ein-Gedi, Archaeological Excavation 1961/62*, Jerusalem 1963.
Mazar, B., and Dunayevsky, I., '"En-Gedi, Third Season of Excavations', *IEJ* 14, 1964, 121–30.

Mazar, B., Dothan, T., and Dunayevsky, I., "En-Gedi, The First and Second Season of Excavations', 'Atiqot 5, 1966, 1–100.

McCowan, C. C., 'Hebrew and Egyptian Apocalyptic Literature', HTR 18, 1925, 357–411.

— Tell en-Naṣbeh, Vol. I, Archaeological and Historical Results, Berkeley-New Haven 1947.

Meinecke, F., 'Johann Gustav Droysen', HZ 141, 1930, 249–87.

— Staat und Persönlichkeit, Berlin 1933.

Merkelbach, R., Roman und Mysterium in der Antike, München and Berlin 1962.

Mewald, J., 'Das Weltbürgertum in der Antike', Die Antike 2, 1926, 177–89.

Meyer, E., Die Entstehung des Judenthums, Halle 1896.

— 'Ägyptische Dokumente aus der Perserzeit, 1, Eine eschatologische Prophetie . . .', SAB 1915, 286–304.

— Ursprung und Anfänge des Christentums, Vol. II, Stuttgart 1925 (UAC).

— 'Blüte und Niedergang des Hellenismus in Asien', Kunst und Altertum 5, Berlin 1925.

Meyer, M. A., History of the City of Gaza, Columbia University Oriental Studies V, 1907.

Meyer, R., Hellenistisches in der rabbinischen Anthropologie, BWANT IV, 22, 1937.

— Review of L. Finkelstein, The Pharisees, Vols. I and II, 1938, OLZ 44, 1941, 70–2.

— Das Gebet des Nabonid, BAL 107, 3, 1962.

— Tradition und Neuschöpfung im antiken Judentum, BAL 110, 2, 1965, 7–88.

Meyers, E. M., Jewish Ossuaries, Reburial and Rebirth, Biblica et Orientalia 24, Rome 1971.

Michaelis, D., 'Das Buch Jesus Sirach als typischer Ausdruck für das Gottesverhältnis des nachalttestamentlichen Menschen', TLZ 83, 1958, 602–8.

Michaud, H., 'Un Mythe Zervanite dans un des Manuscrits de Qumran', VT 5, 1955, 137–47.

Michel, O., Der Brief an die Römer, KEKNT, Göttingen ¹²1963.

Milik, J. T., 'Le travail d'édition des manuscrits du Désert de Juda', SVT 4, 1957, 17–26.

— Ten Years of Discovery in the Wilderness of Judaea, London 1959.

— Review of P. Wernberg- Møller, The Manual of Discipline . . . with attached textual variants, of the Rule, RB 67, 1960, 410–6.

— 'Problèmes de la littérature hénochique à la lumière des fragments araméens de Qumran', HTR 64, 1971, 333–78.

— '4 Q Visions de 'Amram et une citation d'Origène', RB 79, 1972, 77–97.

Mitteis, L.-Wilcken, U., Grundzüge und Chrestomathie der Papyruskunde, Vols. I–II, Leipzig-Berlin 1912, reprinted Darmstadt 1963.

Mitten, D. G., 'A New Look at Ancient Sardis', BA 29, 1966, 38–68.

Mittmann, S., 'Zenon in Ostjordanland', Archäologie und Altes Testament, Festschrift für Kurt Galling, Tübingen 1970, 199–210.

Mittwoch, A., 'Tribute and Land-Tax in Seleucid Judaea', Bibl 36, 1955, 352–61.

Mölleken, W., 'Geschichtsklitterung im 1. Makkabäerbuch (Wann wurds Alkimus Hoherpriester?)', ZAW 65, 1953, 205–28.

Mørkholm, O., 'Eulaios and Lenaios', *Classica et Mediaevalia* 22, 1961, 32–43.
— *Antiochus IV of Syria*, Classica et Mediaevalia, Dissertationes VII, København 1966.
— 'The Seleucid Mint at Antiochia on the Persian Gulf', *The American Numismatic Society, Museum Notes* 16, 1970, 31–44.
Molin, G., 'Hat die Sekte von Khirbet Qumrân Beziehungen zu Ägypten?', *TLZ* 78, 1953, 653–6.
— 'Qumrân – Apokalyptik – Essenismus', *Saeculum* 6, 1955, 244–81.
Momigliano, A., 'I Tobiadi nella prehistoria de moto Maccabaico', *Atti della reale Accademia della scienze di Torino* 67, 1931/32, 165–200.
Mommsen, T., *Römisches Strafrecht*, Leipzig 1899.
— 'Mamilius Sura, Aemilius Sura . . .', *RheinMus* 16, 1861, 282–4.
Montefiore, C. G., Review of H. M. Kallen, *HTR* 12, 1919, 219–24.
Montgomery, J. A., *The Samaritans*, Philadelphia 1907.
— 'The Highest, Heaven, Aeon, Time etc. in Semitic Religion', *HTR* 31, 1938, 143–50.
— Review of E. Bickermann, *Der Gott der Makkabäer*, *JBL* 59, 1940, 308–9.
Moore, G. F., 'Intermediaries in Jewish Theology', *HTR* 15, 1922, 41–61.
— 'Simeon the Righteous', in: *Jewish Studies in Memory of Israel Abrahams*, New York 1927, 348–64.
— 'Fate and Free Will in the Jewish Philosophies according to Josephus', *HTR* 22, 1929, 371–89.
— *Judaism*, Vols. I–III, Cambridge, Mass. ²1954.
Moreau, J., *L'âme du monde de Platon aux Stoïciens*, Paris 1939.
Morenz, S., 'Das Tier mit den vier Hörnern', *ZAW* 63, 1951, 151–4.
— *Ägyptische Religion*, Die Religionen der Menschheit 8, 1960.
Morenz, S., and Müller, D., *Untersuchungen zur Rolle des Schicksals in der ägyptischen Religion*, AAL 52, 1, 1960.
Morris, N., *The Jewish School from the Earliest Times to the Year 500 of the Present Era*, London 1937.
Moulton, W., 'An Inscribed Tomb at Beit Jibrin', *AJA* 19, 1915, 63–70.
Mühl, M., *Die antike Menschheitsidee in ihrer geschichtlichen Entwicklung*, Erbe der Alten 14, 1928.
Müller, H.-P., 'Mantische Weisheit und Apokalyptik', in: *Congress Volume Uppsala 1971*, SVT 22, 1972, 268–93.
Muilenburg, J., 'A Qoheleth Scroll from Qumran', *BASOR* 135, 1954, 20–8.
Myers, J. M., 'Some Considerations bearing on the Date of Joel', *ZAW* 74, 1962, 177–95.

Naveh, J., 'The Excavations at Meṣad Ḥashavyahu', *IEJ* 12, 1962, 89–113.
Negbi, O., 'A Contribution of Mineralogy and Palaeontology to an Archaeological Study of Terracottas', *IEJ* 14, 1964, 187–9.
— 'A Deposit of Terracottas and Statuettes from Tel Ṣippor', *'Atiqot* 6, 1966.
Nestle, E., 'Der Greuel der Verwüstung', *ZAW* 4, 1884, 248.
Neugebauer, O., *The Exact Sciences in Antiquity*, Providence ²1957.
Neugebauer, O., and Hoesen, H. B. van, *Greek Horoscopes*, Philadelphia 1959.

Neusner, J., *A Life of Rabban Yohanan b. Zakkai*, Studia Post-Biblica 6, Leiden 1962.
— *A History of the Jews in Babylonia*, I, Studia Post-Biblica 9, Leiden 1965.
— 'Note on Barukh Ben Neriah', *Numen* 12, 1965, 66–9.
— *The Rabbinic Traditions about the Pharisees before 70*, Vols. I–III, Leiden 1971.
Niese, B., 'Kritik der beiden Makkabäerbucher nebst Beiträgen zur Geschichte der Makkabäischen Erhebung', *Hermes* 35, 1900, 268–307; 453–527.
— *Geschichte der griechischen und makedonischen Staaten*, Vols. I–III, 1893/1903, reprinted Darmstadt 1963 (*GGMS*).
Nilsson, M. P., *Die hellenistische Schule*, München 1955.
— *Opuscula selecta* III, 1960, Skrifter utg. Svenska inst. Athen II, 3.
— *Geschichte der Griechischen Religion*, Vols. I and II, HAW V, 2, 1, 2, Munchen ²1961 (*GGR²*).
— 'The High God and the Mediator', *HTR* 56, 1963, 101–20.
Nissen, A., 'Tora und Geschichte im Spätjudentum', *NovTest* 9, 1967, 241–77.
Nock, A. D., *Conversion*, London 1933.
— 'A Vision of Mandulis Aion', *HTR* 27, 1934, 53–104.
— 'Roman Army and Religious Year', *HTR* 45, 1952, 187–252.
— *Essays on Religion and the Ancient World*, Vols. I and II, Oxford 1972.
Nock, A. D.–Skeat, T. S. – Roberts, C., 'The Gild of Zeus Hypsistos', *HTR* 29, 1936, 39–88.
Nöldeke, T., *Untersuchungen zur Kritik des Alten Testaments*, Kiel 1869.
Nötscher, F., *Zur theologischen Terminologie der Qumran-Texte*, BBB 10, 1956.
— *Vom Alten zum Neuen Testament, Gesammelte Aufsätze*, BBB 17, 1962.
Norden, E., *Agnostos Theos*, Leipzig 1913, reprinted Darmstadt 1956.
— 'Jahve und Moses in hellenistischer Theologie', *Festgabe f. A. v. Harnack*, Tübingen 1921, 292–301.
— *Das Genesiszitat in der Schrift vom Erhabenen*, AAB, Kl.f. Sprachen 1954, No. 1.
— *Die Geburt des Kindes*, 1924, reprinted Darmstadt ³1958.
Noth, M., 'Die fünf syrisch überlieferten apokryphen Psalmen', *ZAW* 48, 1930, 1–23.
— *History of Israel*, London ²1960.
— *The Laws in the Pentateuch and Other Essays*, Edinburgh 1966.

O'Callaghan, R., 'An Approach to Some Religious Problems of Karatape', *Archiv Orientálni* 18, 1/2, 1950, 354–65.
O'Dell, J., 'The Religious Background of the Psalms of Solomon', *RQ* 3, 1961/62, 241–57.
Oesterley, W. O. E., *A History of Israel*, Vol. II, reprinted Oxford 1951.
Olavarri, E., 'Sondages à 'Aro'er sur l'Arnon', *RB* 72, 1965, 77–94.
Olmstead, A. T., 'Intertestamental Studies', *JAOS* 56, 1936, 242–57.
Orlinsky, H. M., Review of M. Hadas, *Aristeas to Philocrates* 1951, *Crozer Quarterly* 29, 1952, 201–5.
Osswald, E., 'Zum Problem der *vaticinia ex eventu*', *ZAW* 75, 1963, 27–44.
Osten-Sacken, P.v.d., *Gott und Belial*, SUNT 6, Göttingen 1969.

Otto, W., *Priester und Tempel im hellenistischen Ägypten*, Vols. I and II, Leipzig 1905–08.

— *Beiträge zur Seleukidengeschichte des 3. Jahrhunderts v. Chr.*, AAM 34, 1, 1928.

— *Zur Geschichte der Zeit des 6. Ptolemäers*, AAM NF 11, 1934.

Otto, W., and Bengtson, H., *Zur Geschichte des Niederganges des Ptolemäerreiches*, AAM NF 17, 1938.

Pack, R. A., *The Greek and Latin Literary Texts from Greco-Roman Egypt*, Ann Arbor 1952.

Parke, H. W., *Greek Mercenary Soldiers. From the Earliest Times to the Battle of Ipsus*, Oxford 1933.

Parsons, E. A., *The Alexandrian Library*, Amsterdam 1952.

Pascher, J., *Η ΒΑΣΙΛΙΚΗ ΟΔΟΣ, Der Königsweg zu Wiedergeburt und Vergöttung dei Philon von Alexandreia*, Studien zur Geschichte und Kultur des Altertums 17, 3f., Paderborn 1931.

Pautrel, R., 'Ben Sira et le Stoïcisme', *RSR* 51, 1963, 535–49.

Pedersen, J., 'Scepticisme israélite', *RHPR* 10, 1930, 317–70.

Pedley, K. G., 'The Library at Qumran', *RQ* 2, 1959–60, 21–41.

Perdrizet, P., 'Le fragment de Satyros sur les Dèmes d'Alexandrie', *Annales de la Fac. des lettres de Bordeaux 4ᵉ sér., Revue des Études Anciennes* 12, 1910, 217–47.

— 'Syriaca', *RevArch* 35, 1899, 34–53.

Peremans, W., 'Ptolémée II. Philadelphe et les indigènes égyptiens', *RBPH* 12, 1933, 1005–22.

— *Vreemdelinge en Egyptenaaren in Vroeg–Ptolemaeisch Egypte*, Recueil des travaux publiés par les Membres des Conférences d'Histoire et de Philologie, 2ᵉ série 43ᵉ fasc., Louvain 1943.

Peters, J. P., and Thiersch, H., *Painted Tombs in the Necropolis of Marissa*, London 1905.

Peters, N., *Das Buch Jesus Sirach oder Ecclesiasticus*, Exegetisches Handbuch zum Alten Testament 25, Münster 1913.

— *Das Buch Job*, Exegetisches Handbuch zum Alten Testament 21, Münster 1928.

Petrie, Flinders et al., *Beth–Pelet* I, London 1930; II, 1932.

Pfeifer, G., *Ursprung und Wesen der Hypostasenvorstellungen im Judentum*, Arbeiten z. Theol. I, 31, Stuttgart 1967.

Pfeiffer, R. H., *Introduction to the Old Testament*, New York 1948.

— *History of New Testament Times*, New York 1949.

— 'Hebrew and Greek Sense of Tragedy', *The Joshua Bloch Memorial Volume*, New York 1960, 54–64.

Pfister, F., *Alexander d. Gr. in den Offenbarungen der Griechen, Juden, Mohammedaner und Christen*, Deutsche Akademie der Wissenschaften zu Berlin, Schriften der Sektion f. Altertumswissenschaft 3, 1956.

Pirot, L., *L'oeuvre exégétique de Théodore de Mopsueste*, Rome 1913.

Pirenne, J., 'Les institutions du peuple hébreu V', *RIDA* 1, 1954, 195–255.

Places, E. des, 'Platon et le ciel de Syrie', *MUSJ* 37, 1960/61, 201–5 (*Mélanges R. Mouterde*).

Plassart, A., *Exploration archéologique de Délos*, Vol. II, *Les sanctuaires et les cultes du mont Cynthe*, Paris 1928.

Ploeg, J. P. M. v. d., *Le rouleau de la guerre*, Studies on the Texts of the Desert of Judah, Vol. II, Leiden 1959.

— 'Un petit touleau de psaumes apocryphes (11Q PsAp³)', *Tradition und Glaube, Festgabe K. G. Kuhn*, Göttingen 1971, 134–64.

Plöger, O., 'Hyrkan im Ostjordanland', *ZDPV* 71, 1955, 70–81.

— *Theocracy and Eschatology*, Oxford 1968.

— *Das Buch Daniel*, KAT 18, Gütersloh 1965.

— 'Die Feldzüge der Seleukiden gegen den Makkabäer Judas', *Aus der Spätzeit des Alten Testaments*, Studien, Göttingen 1971, 134–64.

Pohlenz, M., 'Stoa und Semitismus', *NJWJ* 2, 1926, 257–69.

— 'Paulus und die Stoa', *ZNW* 42, 1949, 69–104.

— *Die Stoa*, Vols. I and II, Göttingen ³1964.

Porteous, N. W., *The Book of Daniel*, OTL, London 1965.

Préaux, C., 'Esquisse d'une histoire des révolutions égyptiennes sous les Lagides', *ChrEg* 11, 1936, 522–52.

— *L'économie royale des Lagides*, Bruxelles 1939.

— *Les Grecs en Égypte d'après les archives de Zénon*, Bruxelles 1947.

— 'De la Grèce classique a l'Égypte hellénistique. Traduire ou ne pas traduire', *Chronique d'Égypte* 42, 1967, 369–83.

Purvis, J. D., 'Ben Sira and the Foolish People of Shechem', *JNES* 24, 1965, 88–94.

Quinn, J. D., 'Alcaeus 48 (B 16) and the Fall of Ascalon', *BASOR* 164, 1961, 19–20.

Quispel, G., 'Der gnostische Anthropos und die jüdische Tradition', *Eranos-Jb.* 22, 1953, 195–234.

— 'Christliche Gnosis und jüdische Heterodoxie', *EvTh* 14, 1954, 474–84.

Rad, G. v., *Das Geschichtsbild des chronistischen Werkes*, BWANT 54, Stuttgart 1930.

— 'The Joseph Narrative and Ancient Wisdom', in: *The Problem of the Hexateuch and other Essays*, Edinburgh 1966, 292–300.

— *Old Testament Theology*, Vols. I and II, Edinburgh 1962, 1965.

Radermacher, L., Κοινή, SAW ph.-hist. Kl. 224, 5, 1947.

Rahmani, L. Y. – Avigad, N. – Benoit, P., 'The Tomb of Jason', *'Atiqot* 4, 1964, 1–40 (in Hebrew).

Rankin, O. S., *The Origins of the Festival of Hanukkah*, Edinburgh 1930.

— *Israel's Wisdom Literature. Its Bearing on Theology and the History of Religion*, reprinted Edinburgh 1954.

Ranston, H., *Ecclesiastes and Early Greek Wisdom Literature*, London 1925.

Redpath, H. A., 'Mythological Terms in the LXX', *AJT* 9, 1905, 34–45.

Reicke, Bo, 'Traces of Gnosticism in the Dead Sea Scrolls ?', *NTS* 1, 1954/55, 137–41.

— *The New Testament Era*, London 1965.

Reinhardt, K., *Kosmos und Sympathie*, München 1926.

— *Poseidonios über Ursprung und Entartung*, Orient und Antike 6, 1928.

Reisner, G. A., Fisher, C. S., et al., *Harvard Excavations at Samaria 1908 to 1910*, Vol. I, Cambridge, Mass. 1924.

Reitzenstein, R., *Zwei religionsgeschichtliche Fragen*, Strassburg 1901.

— *Poimandres*, Leipzig 1904.

— *Das mandäische Buch des Herrn der Grösse*, SAH ph.-hist. Kl. 1919, No. 12.

— *Die Hellenistischen Mysterienreligionen*, ³1927, reprinted Darmstadt 1956.

— *Hellenistische Wundererzählungen*, 1906, reprinted Darmstadt 1963.

Reitzenstein, R., and Schaeder, H. H., *Studien zum antiken Synkretismus*, 1926, reprinted Darmstadt 1965.

Reuter, F., *Beiträge zur Beurteilung des Königs Antiochos Epiphanes*, Diss. Münster 1938.

Ricciotti, G., *History of Israel*, Vol. II, New York 1955.

Richter, H., 'Die Naturweisheit des Alten Testament im Buche Hiob', *ZAW* 70, 1958, 1–20.

Rider, G. le, *Suse sous les Séleucides et les Parthes. Les trouvailles monétaires et l'histoire de la ville*, Paris 1965.

Riesenfeld, H., *The Resurrection in Ezekiel XXXVII and in the Dura-Europos Paintings*, UUÅ 1948, No. 11.

Ringgren, H. *Word and Wisdom*, Lund 1947.

— *Israelite Religion*, London 1966.

Robert, L., 'Un Corpus des Inscriptions Juives', Review by J. B. Frey of CIJ I and II, *REJ* 101, 1937, 73–86; *Hellenica* 3, 1946, 90–108.

— 'Encore une Inscription Grecque de l'Iran', *CRAI* 1967, 281–96.

— 'De Delphes à l'Oxus. Inscriptions nouvelles de la Bactriane', *CRAI* 1968, 416–57.

— 'Reliefs votifs et cultes d'Anatolie', *Anatolia* 3, 1958, 103–36.

— 'Trois oracles de la Théosophie et un prophète d'Apollon', *CRAI* 1968, 568–99.

— *Études anatoliennes*, Études Orientales V, 1937.

Roberts, C. H., 'Literature and Society in the Papyri', *MusHelv* 10, 1953, 264–79.

Robinson, T. H., and Horst, F., *Die Zwölf Kleinen Propheten*, HAT I, 14, Tübingen ³1964.

Rössler, D., *Gesetz und Geschichte*, WMANT 3, Neukirchen ²1962.

Rohde, E., *Psyche*, ²1898, two vols. reprinted in one, Darmstadt 1961.

Rohde, R., 'Die Quellen des Iamblichus in seiner Biographie des Pythagoras', *RheinMus* 26, 1871, 554–76.

Ron, Z., 'Agricultural Terraces in the Judean Mountains', *IEJ* 16, 1966, 33–40 and 111–22.

Roos, E., 'De incubationisritu per ludibrium apud Aristophanem detorto', *Opuscula Atheniensia* III, Lund 1960, 55–98.

Roscher, W. H., *Die hippokratische Schrift von der Siebenzahl in ihrer vierfachen Überlieferung*, Stud. z. Gesch. u. Kultur des Altertums VI, 3, 4, 1913.

Rosén, H. B., 'Palestinian *KOINH* in Rabbinic Illustration', *JSS* 8, 1963, 56–72.

Rosenthal, L. A., 'Die Josephsgeschichte mit den Büchern Ester und Daniel verglichen', *ZAW* 15, 1895, 278–84.

— 'Nochmals der Vergleich Ester, Joseph-Daniel', *ZAW* 17, 1897, 125–8.

Rosler, M., in *'Eṣkolot (ΣΧΟΛΙΑ) Commentationes de Antiquitate Classica*, ed. M. Schwabe and I. Gutman, Jerusalem 1, 1954, 33–48.

Rost, L., 'Gruppenbildungen im AT', *TLZ* 80, 1955, 1–8.

Rostovtzeff (Rostowzew), M., *Geschichte der Steuerpacht in der römischen Kaiserzeit bis Diokletian*, PhilSuppl 9, 1904, 331–512.

— *Studien zur Geschichte des römischen Kolonates*, APF Bh 1, 1910.

— *A Large Estate in Egypt in the Third Century BC*, Madison 1922.

— *Caravan Cities*, Oxford 1932.

— *'ΠΡΟΓΟΝΟΙ'*, *JHS* 55, 1935, 56–66.

— *Dura-Europos and its Art*, Oxford 1938.

— 'Le Gad de Doura et Seleucus Nicator', *Mélanges Syriens, offerts à M. René Dussaud*, Vol. I, Paris 1939, 281–95.

— *The Social and Economic History of the Hellenistic World*, Vols. I–III, Oxford 1941.

Roussel, P., *Délos, colonie athénienne*, Bibliothèque des écoles françaises d'Athènes et de Rome, fasc. III, Paris 1916.

Rowe, A., *The Topography and History of Beth-Shan*, Publications of the Palestine Section of the Museum of the University of Pennsylvania, Vol. I, Philadelphia 1930.

Rowley, H. H., *The Relevance of Apocalyptic*, London ³1950.

— 'Menelaus and the Abomination of Desolation', *Studia Orientalia J. Pedersen*, Kopenhagen 1953, 303–15.

— 'The 390 Years of the Zadokite Work', *Mélanges Bibliques André Robert*, Paris 1957, 341–53.

— *Jewish Apocalyptic and the Dead Sea Scrolls*, London 1957.

Rudberg, G., *Forschungen zu Poseidonios*, Skrifter utgifna af K. Humanistika Vetenskaps-Samfundet i. Uppsala, 20: 3, Uppsala 1918.

Rudolph, K., 'Randerscheinungen des Judentums und das Problem der Enstehung des Gnostizismus', *Kairos* 9, 1967, 105–22.

Rudolph, W., *Esra und Nehemia*, HAT I, 20, Tübingen 1949.

— *Chronikbücher*, HAT I, 21, Tübingen ²1955.

— *Jeremia*, HAT I, 12, Tübingen ²1958.

— *Vom Buch Kohelet*, Münster 1959.

— *Das Buch Ruth, Das Hohe Lied*, KAT XVII, 1–2, Gütersloh 1962.

Rüger, H. P., *Das Tyrusorakel Ez. 27*, typewritten dissertation, Tübingen 1961.

— *Text und Textform im hebräischen Sirach, Untersuchungen zur Textgeschichte und Textkritik der hebräischen Sirachfragmente*, BZAW 112, Berlin 1970.

Rühl, F., 'Justus von Tiberias', *RheinMus* 71, 1916, 289–308.

Ruhl, L., *De Mortuorum iudicio*, RGVV II, 2, 1903, 33–105.

Rundgren, F., ' "appiryol" Tragsessel, Sänfte', *ZAW* 74, 1962, 70–2.

Russell, D. S., *The Method and Message of Jewish Apocalyptic*, London 1964.

Sachs, A., 'A Classification of the Babylonian Horoscopes', *JCS* 2, 1948, 271–90.

— 'Babylonian Horoscopes', *JCS* 6, 1952, 49–75.

Safrai, S., 'Teaching of Pietists in Mishnaic Literature', *JJS* 16, 1965, 15–33.

Sauvaget, J., 'Le Plan antique de Damas', *Syria* 26, 1949, 314–58.

Savignac, J. de, 'La Sagesse en Proverbes VIII, 22–31', *VT* 12, 1962, 211–15.

Schalit, A., 'The Date and Place of the Story about the Three Bodyguards of the King in the Apocryphal Book of Ezra', *BJPES* 13, 1946–47, 119–28.

— 'The Letter of Antiochus III to Zeuxis regarding the Establishment of Jewish Military Colonies in Phrygia and Lydia', *JQR* 50, 1959/60, 289–318.

— 'Die frühchristliche Überlieferung über die Herkunft der Familie des Herodes', *ASTI* 1, 1962, 109–60.

— *König Herodes*, Studia Judaica, Vol. IV, Berlin 1969.

Schaller, B., 'Hekataios von Abdera über die Juden, Zur Frage der Echtheit und der Datierung', *ZNW* 54, 1963, 15–31.

Schaumberger, J., 'Die neue Seleukiden-Liste BM 35 603 und die makkabäische Chronologie', *Bibl* 36, 1955, 423–35.

Schencke, W., *Die Chokma (Sophia) in der jüdischen Hypostasenspekulation*, Vidensskapselkapets Skrifter II Hist.-Fil.-Kl. 1912 No. 6, Kristiania 1913.

Schlatter, A., 'Die Beṇē pariṣim bei Daniel 11, 14', *ZAW* 14, 1894, 145–51.

— *Das neugefundene hebräische Stück des Sirach. Der Glossator des griechischen Sirach*, BFCT 1, 5/6, 1897.

— *Wie sprach Josephus von Gott?*, BFCT 14, 1, 1910.

— *Die hebräischen Namen bei Josephus*, BFCT 17, 3, 1913.

— *Geschichte Israels von Alexander d. Gr. bis Hadrian (GI³)*, Stuttgart ³1925.

— *Der Glaube im Neuen Testament*, Stuttgart ⁴1927.

— *Die Theologie des Judentums nach dem Bericht des Josefus*, BFCT 2. R., 26, Gütersloh 1932.

Schlesinger, K., *Die Gesetzeslehrer*, Berlin 1936.

Schlumberger, D., *L'argent grec dans l'empire achéménide*, Paris 1953.

Schmid, W.-Stählin, O. (–Christ, W.v.), *Geschichte der Griechischen Literatur*, HAW VII, 2; Vol. I, München 1920 (*GGL⁶*).

Schmidt, N., *The Message of the Poets = The Message of the Bible*, Vol. VII, New York 1907.

Schmitt, H. H., *Untersuchungen zur Geschichte Antiochos' des Grossen und seiner Zeit*, Historia Einzelschriften H. 6, Wiesbaden 1964.

Schmitthenner, W., 'Über eine Formveränderung der Monarchie seit Alexander d. Gr.', *Saeculum* 19, 1968, 31–46.

Schnabel, P., *Berossos und die babylonisch-hellenistische Literatur*, Leipzig-Berlin 1923.

Schnebel, M., *Die Landwirtschaft im hellenistischen Ägypten*, Vol. I, *Der Betrieb der Landwirtschaft*, MBPAR 7, 1925.

Schneider, C., 'Die griechischen Grundlagen der hellenistischen Religionsgeschichte', *ARW* 36, 1939, 300–47.

— Review of M. Hadas, *Hellenistic Culture* 1959, *Gnomon* 33, 1961, 306–8.

— 'Zur Problematik des Hellenistischen in den Qumrantexten', *Qumranprobleme*, ed. H. Bardtke (for fuller title see S. Segert), Berlin 1963, 299–314.

Schoeps, H. J., *Theologie und Geschichte des Judentums*, Tübingen 1949.

— *Aus frühchristlicher Zeit*, Tübingen 1950.

— 'Das gnostische Judentum in den Dead Sea Scrolls', *ZRGG* 6, 1954, 276–9.

— *Urgemeinde, Judenchristentum, Gnosis*, Tübingen 1956.

— *Paul*, London 1961.

Schottroff, W., 'Horonaim, Nimrim, Luhith und der Westrand des Landes Ataroth', *ZDPV* 82, 1966, 162–208.

Schubart, W., 'Bemerkungen zum Stile hellenistischer Königsbriefe', *APF* 6, 1920, 324–7.

— *Die Griechen in Ägypten*, BhAO 10, 1927.

— 'Das hellenistische Königsideal nach Inschriften und Papyri', *APF* 12, 1936, 1–26.

— *Die religiöse Haltung des frühen Hellenismus*, AO 35, 2, 1937.

— *Verfassung und Verwaltung des Ptolemäerreichs*, AO 35, 4, 1937.

Schubert, K., 'Der Sektenkanon von En Feshcha und die Anfänge der jüdischen Gnosis', *TLZ* 78, 1953, 495–506.

— 'Einige Beobachtungen zum Verständnis des Logosbegriffs im frührabbinischen Schrifttum', *Judaica* 9, 1953, 65–80.

— *Die Religion des nachbiblischen Judentums*, Freiburg-Wien 1955.

— *Die Gemeinde vom Toten Meer*, München – Basel 1958.

— 'Das Problem der Auferstehungshoffnung in den Qumrantexten und in der frührabbinischen Literatur', *WZKM* 56, 1960, 154–67.

— 'Die Entwicklung der Auferstehungslehre von der nachexilischen bis zur frührabbinischen Zeit', *BZ* NF 6, 1962, 177–214.

— Review of M. Hengel, *Die Zeloten*, *WZKM* 58, 1962, 258–60.

Schürer, E., 'Die Juden im bosporanischen Reiche und die Genossenschaften der σεβόμενοι θεὸν ὕψιστον ebendaselbst', SAB 1897, I, 200–25.

— *Geschichte des jüdischen Volkes im Zeitalter Jesu Christi*, Vols. I–III, Leipzig 1901–1909 (Schürer).

Schulz, S., 'Die Bedeutung neuer Gnosisfunde für die neutestamentliche Wissenschaft (3)', *TR* 26, 1960, 301–34.

Schunck, K. D., *Die Quellen des I. und II. Makkabäerbuches*, Halle 1954.

— 'Drei Seleukiden im Buche Kohelet?', *VT* 9, 1959, 192–201.

Schur, W., 'Zur Vorgeschichte des Ptolemäerreiches', *Klio* 20, 1925/26, 270–302.

Schwabacher, W., 'Geldumlauf und Münzprägung in Syrien im 6. und 5., Jahrhundert v. Chr.', *Opuscula Archeologica* 6, Lund 1950, 139–49.

Schwabl, H., 'Die griechischen Theogonien und der Orient', in: *Éléments Orientaux dans la Religion Grecque ancienne, Colloque de Strasbourg 22–24 mai 1958*, Paris 1960.

Schwartz, J., 'Die Rolle Alexandrias bei der Verarbeitung orientalischen Gedankenguts', *ZPapEp* 1, 1967, 197–217.

Schwarz, A., 'Die Schatzkammer des Tempels in Jerusalem', *MGWJ* 63, 1919, 227–52.

Scott, R. B. Y., 'Wisdom in Creation: the *'āmōn* of Proverbs VIII 30', *VT* 10, 1960, 213–23.

Seeligmann, I. L., *The Septuagint Version of Isaiah*, Leiden 1948.

Segal, M. H., 'The Qumran War Scroll and the Date of its Composition', *ScrHieros* 4, 1958, 138–43.

Segert, S., 'Die Sprachenfrage in der Qumrangemeinschaft', in: *Qumranprobleme, Vorträge des Leipziger Symposions über Qumranprobleme v. 9.–14. 10. 1961*, ed. H. Bardtke, Dt. Ak. d. Wiss. in Berlin, Schriften der Sektion Altertumskunde 2, Berlin 1963, 315–39.

Seidensticker, P., 'Die Gemeinschaftsform der religiösen Gruppen des Spätjudentums und der Urkirche', *Studii Biblici Franciscani*, Liber Annuus 9, 1958–59.

Seider, R., *Beiträge zur ptolemäischen Verwaltungsgeschichte*, Diss. Heidelberg 1938.

Sellers, O. R., *The Citadel of Beth-zur*, Philadelphia 1933.

Sellers, O. R., and Albright, W. F., 'The first Campaign of Excavation at Beth Zur', *BASOR* 43, 1931, 2–13.

Sellin, E., *Die Spuren griechischer Philosophie im Alten Testament*, Leipzig 1905.

— *Geschichte des israelitisch-jüdischen Volkes*, Leipzig 1932.

Sevenster, J. N., *Do You Know Greek?*, Leiden 1968.

Seyrig, H., 'La Triade Heliopolitaine et les Temples de Baalbek', *Syria* 10, 1929, 314–56.

— 'A propos de culte de Zeus à Séleucie', *Syria* 20, 1939, 296–301.

— 'Aradus et sa pérée sous les rois Séleucides', *Syria* 28, 1951, 206–20.

— 'Note sur les Cultes de Scythopolis à l'époque romaine', *Syria* 39, 1962, 207–11.

— 'Une idole bétylique', *Syria* 40, 1963, 17–19.

— 'Alexandre le Grand, fondateur de Gérasa', *Syria* 42, 1965, 25–8.

Shotwell, W. A., 'The Problem of the Syrian Akra', *BASOR* 176, 1964, 10–19.

Siebeneck, R. T., 'May their Bones return to Life!—Sirach's Praise of the Fathers', *CBQ* 21, 1959, 411–28.

Simon, M., 'Le judaïsme berbère dans l'Afrique ancienne', *RHPR* 26, 1946, 1–31; 105–45.

— *Verus Israel*, Bibliothèque des Écoles françaises d'Athènes et de Rome 166, Paris 1948, and 'Post-Scriptum', Paris 1964.

Sinclair, L. A., 'An Archaeological Study of Gibeah (Tell el-fûl)', *AASOR* 34/35, 1954–56, New Haven 1960, 1–52.

Sint, J. A., *Pseudonymität im Altertum*, Commentationes Aenipontanae XV, Innsbruck 1960.

Sjöberg, E., *Der Menschensohn im Äthiopischen Henochbuch*, Skrifter . . . Lund 41, 1946.

Sisti, A., 'Riflessi dell'epoca premaccabaica nell'Ecclesiastico', *RivBibl* 12, 1964, 215–56.

Skeat, T. C., 'Notes on Ptolemaic Chronology', *JEA* 46, 1960, 91–4, and *JEA* 47, 1961, 107–12.

Skehan, P. W., 'The Biblical Scrolls from Qumran and the Text of the Old Testament', *BA* 28, 1965, 87–100.

Slotki, J. J., 'The Origin of the Book of Job', *ExpT* 39, 1927/28, 131–4.

Smend, R., *Die Weisheit des Jesus Sirach*, Berlin 1907.

— *Griechisch–Syrisch–Hebräischer Index z. W. d.J.S.*, Berlin 1907.

Smith, Morton, 'The Image of God, Notes on the Hellenization of Judaism with Especial Reference to Goodenough's Work on Jewish Symbols', *BJRL* 40, 1957/58, 473–512.

— 'The Dead Sea Sect in Relation to Ancient Judaism', *NTS* 7, 1960/61, 347–60.

— in: *Fischer Weltgeschichte*, Vol. V, *Griechen und Perser*, ed. H. Bengtson,

356–70, and Vol. VI, *Der Hellenismus*, ed. P. Grimal, 254–70, Frankfurt 1965.

Sokolowski, F., 'Encore sur le decret dionysiaque de Ptolémée Philopator', *JJurPap* 3, 1949, 137–52.

Sourdel, D., *Les Cultes du Hauran à l'époque Romaine*, Bibliotheque Archéologique et historique 53, Paris 1952.

Spengler, O., *The Decline of the West*, London 1932.

Sperber, D., 'A Note on a Coin of Antigonus Mattathias', *JQR* 54, 1963/64, 250–7.

Speyer, W., *Die literarische Fälschung im heidnischen und christlichen Altertum*, HAW I, 2, München 1971.

— *Bücherfunde in der Glaubenswerbung der Antike*, Hypomnemata 24, Göttingen 1970.

Spiro, A., 'Samaritans, Tobiads and Judahites . . .', *PAAJR* 20, 1951, 279–355.

Squarciapino, F. M., 'The Synagogue at Ostia', *Archaeology* 16, 1963, 194–203.

Stamm, J. J., 'Ein Vierteljahrhundert Psalmenforschung', *TR* 23, 1955/56, 1–68.

Starcky, J., 'The Nabateans, A Historical Sketch', *BA* 18, 1955, 84–106.

— 'Les quatre étapes du messianisme à Qumrân', *RB* 70, 1963, 481–505.

Stegemann, H., *Die Enstehung der Qumrangemeinde*, Theol. Diss. Bonn 1971.

Stein, E., *Die allegorische Exegese des Philo aus Alexandreia*, BZAW 51, Giessen 1929.

Stern, M., 'The Death of Onias III', *Zion* 25, 1960, 1–16.

— 'Notes on the Story of Joseph the Tobiad', *Tarbiz* 32, 1962, 35–47 (in Hebrew).

— Review of M. Hengel, *Judentum und Hellenismus* 1969, *Kirjath Sepher* 46, 1970/71, 94–9.

Sticker, B., 'Weltzeitalter und astronomische Perioden', *Saeculum* 4, 1953, 241–9.

Stiehl, R., 'Das Buch Esther', *WZKM* 53, 1957, 4–22.

Stier, H. E., *Roms Aufstieg zur Weltmacht und die griechische Welt*, Arbeitsgem. f. Forschung d. Landes Nordrhein-Westfalen, Köln – Opladen 1957.

Story, C. I. K., 'The Book of Proverbs and Northwest Semitic Literature', *JBL* 64, 1945, 319–37.

Strobel, A., 'Der Termin des Todes Jesu', *ZNW* 51, 1960, 69–101.

— 'Zur kalendarisch-chronologischen Einordnung der Qumrān-Essener', *TLZ* 86, 1961, 179–84.

— 'Zur Funktionsfähigkeit des essenischen Kalenders', *RQ* 3, 1961/62, 395–412.

— 'Der 22. Tag des XI. Monats im essenischen Jahr', *RQ* 3, 1961/62, 539–43.

Strohm, H., 'Studien zur Schrift von der Welt', *MusHelv* 9, 1952, 137–75.

Strugnell, J., 'Notes en marge du volume V des *Discoveries in the Judaean Desert of Jordan*', *RQ* 7, 1969–71, 163–276.

Stuhlmacher, P., *Gerechtigkeit Gottes bei Paulus*, FRLANT 87, Göttingen 1965.

Sukenik, E. L., *Ancient Synagogues in Palestine and Greece*, Schweich Lectures 1930, London 1934.

— 'Paralipomena Palaestinensia', *JPOS* 14, 1934, 178–84.

— 'More about the Oldest Coins of Judaea', *JPOS* 15, 1935, 341–3.

Susemihl, F., *Geschichte der Griechischen Literatur in der Alexandrinerzeit*, Vols. I and II, Leipzig 1891/92.

Swain, J. W., 'The Theory of the Four Monarchies', *ClassPhil* 35, 1940, 1–21.

Swart, W., *De invloed van den griekschen Geest op de boeken Sprewken, Prediker, Job*, Diss. Groningen 1908.

Świderek, A., 'La société grecque en Égypte en III siècle av. n. è. d'après les Archives de Zenon', *JJurPap* 9/10, 1955/56, 355–400.

Taeger, F., *Charisma, Studien zur Geschichte des antiken Herrscherkultes*, Vols. I and II, Stuttgart 1957 and 1960.

Täubler, E., 'Staat und Umwelt, Palästina in der hellenistisch-römischen Zeit', *Tyche, Historische Studien*, Leipzig-Berlin 1926, 116–36.

— 'Jerusalem 201 to 199 B.C.E. On the History of a Messianic Movement', *JQR* 37, 1946/47, 1–30; 125–37; 249–63.

Tarn, W. W., 'Ptolemy II and Arabia', *JEA* 15, 1929, 9–25.

— *The Greeks in Bactria and India*, Cambridge [2]1951.

— *Alexander the Great*, Vols. I–II, Cambridge 1948.

— *Hellenistic Civilization*, rev. by the author and G. T. Griffith, London [3]1959.

Tcherikover, V. (Tscherikower), 'Die hellenistischen Städtegründungen von Alexander dem Gr. bis auf die Römerzeit', *PhilSuppl* 19, 1, 1927, 1–216.

— 'Palestine under the Ptolemies', *Mizraim* 4–5, 1937, 7–90 (*Miz*).

— 'Jewish Apologetic Literature Reconsidered', *Eos* 48, 1956, 169–93 = *Symbolae R. Taubenschlag dedicatae III*, 1957.

— 'The Ideology of the Letter of Aristeas', *HTR* 51, 1958, 59–85.

— 'The Third Book of Maccabees as a Historical Source of Augustus' Time', *ScrHieros* 7, 1961, 1–26.

— *Hellenistic Civilization and the Jews*, Philadephia-Jerusalem [2]1961 (*HC*).

— 'Was Jerusalem a Polis ?', *IEJ* 14, 1964, 61–78.

Teixidor, J., 'Bulletin d'épigraphie sémitique', *Syria* 45, 1968, 353–89.

Testuz, M., *Les idées religieuses du livre des Jubilés*, Genève-Paris 1960.

Théocharis, A., *La sagesse dans le Judaïsme palestinien de l'insurrection Maccabéenne à la fin du Ier siècle*, typescript diss. Strasbourg 1963.

Thesleff, H., *An Introduction to the Pythagorean Writings of the Hellenistic Period*, Acta Academiae Aboensis, Humaniora XXIV.3, Åbo 1961.

Thiersch, H., 'Ein hellenistischer Kolossalkopf aus Beisan', NGG ph.-hist. Kl. 1932, 52–76.

Thissen, H. J., *Studien zum Raphiadekret*, Beiträge zur klassischen Philologie 23, Meisenheim am Glan 1966.

Thompson, H. A., 'Syrian Wheat in Hellenistic Egypt', *APF* 9, 1930, 207–13.

Thorndike, L., *A History of Magic and Experimental Science*, Vol. I, London 1932.

Tondriau, J., 'Tatouage, Lierre et Syncrétismes', *Aeg* 30, 1950, 57–66.

— 'Le décret dionysiaque de Philopator', *Aeg* 26/27, 1946/47, 84–95.

Toombs, L. E., and Wright, G. E., 'The Third Campaign at Balâṭah (Shechem)', *BASOR* 161, 1961, 11–54.

Torrey, C. C., 'Die Briefe 2. Makk. 1, 1–2, 18', *ZAW* 20, 1900, 225–42.

— 'The Letters prefixed to Second Maccabees', *JAOS* 60, 1940, 119–50.

Tournay, R., Review of O. Plöger, *Theokratie und Eschatologie* 1959, *RB* 68, 1961, 444–5.

Trachtenberg, J., *Jewish Magic and Superstition*, Philadelphia 1961.

Treu, M., 'Die neue "orphische" Unterweltsbeschreibung und Vergil', *Hermes* 82, 1954, 24–51.

Tufnell, O., *Lachish III, The Iron Age*, Oxford 1953.

Uebel, F., *Die Kleruchen Ägyptens . . .*, AAB 1968, 3.

Ueberweg, F., – Praechter, K., *Grundriss der Geschichte der Philosophie I, Die Philosophie des Altertums*, Tübingen ¹³1953.

Ullendorff, E., 'The Greek Letters of the Copper Scroll', *VT* 11, 1961, 227–8.

Usener, H., *Götternamen*, Frankfurt ³1948.

Vaux, R. de, 'Les Sacrifices de porcs en Palestine et dans l'Ancien Orient', *Von Ugarit nach Qumran . . . O. Eissfeldt . . . dargebracht*, ed. J. Hempel and L. Rost, BZAW 77, Berlin 1958, 250–5.

— 'Une hachette Essénienne', *VT* 9, 1959, 399–407.

— 'Fouilles de Feshkha', *RB* 66, 1959, 225–55.

— *L'archéologie et les manuscrits de la Mer Morte*, Schweich Lectures 1959, London 1961.

— *Ancient Israel*, London 1965.

Vermes, G., 'The Etymology of "Essenes"', *RQ* 2, 1959–60, 427–43.

Vidman, L., *Sylloge inscriptionum religionis Isiacae et Sarapiacae*, RGVV 28, Berlin 1969.

Viereck, P., *Philadelphia, Die Gründung einer hellenistischen Militärkolonie in Ägypten*, Morgenland (BhAO) 16, 1928.

Vincent, A., *La Religion des Judéo-Araméens d'Elephantine*, Paris 1937.

Vincent, L. H., 'La Palestine dans les papyrus Ptolémaiques de Gerza', *RB* 29, 1920, 161–202.

— 'La Date des Épigraphes d''Araq el Emir', *JPOS* 3, 1923, 55–68.

— 'Acra', *RB* 43, 1934, 205–36.

— *Jérusalem de l'Ancien Testament*, Recherches d'Archéologie et d'Histoire, Vols. I–III, Paris 1954–56.

Visser, E., *Götter und Kulte im ptolemäischen Alexandrien*, Archeologisch-historische Bijdragen 5, Amsterdam 1938.

Vogelstein, H., *History of Jews in Rome*, Philadelphia 1940.

Vogt, E., ' "Mysteria" in textibus Qumrān', *Bibl* 37, 1956, 247–57.

— 'Kalenderfragmente aus Qumran', *Bibl* 39, 1958, 72–7.

Vogt, J., *Sklaverei und Humanität*, Historia Einzelschriften 8, 1965.

— 'Kleomenes von Naukratis – Herr von Ägypten', *Chiron* 1, 1971, 153–7.

Volkmann, H., 'Der Herrscherkult der Ptolemäer in phönikischen Inschriften und sein Beitrag zur Hellenisierung von Kypros', *Historia* 5, 1956, 448–55.

Volz, P., *Die Eschatologie der jüdischen Gemeinde in neutestamentlichen Zeitalter*, Tübingen ²1934.

Vosté, J. M., 'L'oeuvre exégétique de Théodore de Mopsueste au IIᵉ Concile de Constantinople', *RB* 38, 1929, 382–95; 542–54.

Wacholder, B., *Nicolaus of Damascus*, Berkeley and Los Angeles 1962.
— 'Pseudo-Eupolemus' Two Greek Fragments on the Life of Abraham', *HUCA* 34, 1963, 83–113.
— 'Biblical Chronology in the Hellenistic World Chronicles', *HTR* 61, 1968, 451–81.
Wächter, L., 'Der Einfluss platonischen Denkens auf rabbinische Schöpfungsspekulationen', *ZRGG* 14, 1962, 36–56.
Waerden, B. L. v., 'Das grosse Jahr und die ewige Wiederkehr', *Hermes* 80, 1952, 129–55.
— 'History of the Zodiac', *AfO* 16, 1952–53, 216–30.
Wagner, M., *Die lexikalischen und grammatikalischen Aramaismen* . . ., BZAW 96, Berlin 1966.
Wagner, S., *Die Essener in der wissenschaftlichen Diskussion vom Ausgang des 18. bis zum Beginn des 20. Jahrhunderts*, BZAW 79, Berlin 1960.
Walbank, F. W., *A Historical Commentary on Polybius*, Vol. I. Oxford 1957.
Walcot, P., 'Hesiod and the Didactic Literature of the Near East', *REG* 75, 1962, 13–36.
Walter, N., *Der Thoraausleger Aristobulos*, TU 86, 1964.
— 'Zu Pseudo-Eupolemus', *Klio* 43/45, 1965, 282–90.
Walzer, R., *Galen on Jews and Christians*, London 1949.
Watzinger, C., *Denkmäler Palästinas*, Vols. I and II (*DP*), Leipzig 1933/35.
Weber, M., *Gesammelte Aufsätze zur Religionssoziologie*, Vol. II: *Das antike Judentum*, Tübingen 1921.
Weinberg, S. S., 'Tel Anafa', *IEJ* 19, 1969, 250–2.
— 'Tel Anafa: The Hellenistic Town', *IEJ* 21, 1971, 86–109.
Weippert, M., 'Archäologischer Jahresbericht', *ZDPV* 79, 1963, 164–179; 80, 1964, 150–93.
Weiser, A., *Das Buch der zwölf Kleinen Propheten*, I, ATD 24, 1963.
Weiss, H.-F., 'Zur Frage der historischen Voraussetzungen der Begegnung von Antike und Christentum', *Klio* 43–45, 1965, 307–28.
— *Untersuchungen zur Kosmologie des hellenistischen und palästinischen Judentums*, TU 97, 1966.
Weizsäcker, C. F. v., *The Relevance of Science*, London 1964.
Welles, C. B. *Royal Correspondence in the Hellenistic Period*, New Haven 1934.
— 'Ptolemaic Administration in Egypt', *JJurPap* 3, 1949, 21–47.
— 'The Hellenism of Dura-Europos', *Aeg* 39, 1959, 23–8.
— 'The Role of the Egyptians under the First Ptolemies', *Proceedings of the Twelfth International Congress of Papyrology*, American Studies in Papyrology 7, Toronto 1970, 505–10.
Wellhausen, J., 'Über den geschichtlichen Wert des 2. Makkabäerbuches', NGG 1905, 117–63.
— *Israelitische und jüdische Geschichte*, Leipzig [8]1921.
Wellmann, M., *Die ΦΥΣΙΚΑ des Bolos Demokritos und der Magier Anaxilaos aus Larissa*, AAB No. 7, 1928.
— *Marcellus von Side als Arzt und die Koiraniden des Hermes Trismegistos*, PhilSuppl 27, 1934, H.2.

Wendland, P., *Die hellenistisch-römische Kultur . . .; Die urchristlichen Litera-turformen*, HNT I, 2, 3, Tübingen 1912.

Wenschkewitz, H., 'Die Spiritualisierung der Kultusbegriffe', *Angelos* 4, 1932, 70–230.

Wernberg-Møller, P., *The Manual of Discipline*, Studies on the Texts of the Desert of Judah, Vol. I, Leiden 1957.

— 'A Reconsideration of the two Spirits in the Rule of the Community', *RQ* 3, 1961/62, 413–41.

West, M. L., *Early Greek Philosophy and the Orient*, Oxford 1971.

Westermann, W. L., 'The Ptolemies and the Welfare of their Subjects', *AHR* 4, 1937/38, 270–87.

— 'Enslaved persons who are free, Rainer-Papyrus (PER), Inv 24552', *AJP* 59, 1938, 1–30.

— *The Slave Systems of Greek and Roman Antiquity*, Philadelphia 1955.

Whybray, R. N., *Wisdom in Proverbs*, SBT I, 45, London 1965.

Widengren, G., *Literary and Psychological Aspects of the Hebrew Prophets*, UUÅ 1948, No. 10.

— 'Quelques rapports entre Juifs et Iraniens à l'époque des Parthes', *Congress Volume 1956*, SVT 4, 1957, 197–240.

— *Iranisch-semitische Kulturbegegnung in Parthischer Zeit*, Arbeitsgemeinschaft f. Forschung des Landes Nordrhein-Westfalen, Vol. 70, Köln-Opladen 1960.

— *Die Religionen Irans*, in: Die Religionen der Menschheit, Vol. XIV, Stuttgart 1965.

Wilamowitz-Moellendorff, U. v., *Griechische Verskunst*, Berlin 1921.

— *Der Glaube der Hellenen*, Vols. I and II, Darmstadt 1959.

— *Platon*, Berlin ⁵1959.

Wilcken, U., Reports: *APF* 6, 1920, 369; *APF* 7, 1924, on P. Edg., 292–5; *APF* 8, 1927, on PCZ I and II, 275–85; *APF* 10, 1932, on PCZ IV, 238–41; *APF* 12, 1937, 221–3; *APF* 14, 1941, 151–80.

Wilckens, U., *Weisheit und Torheit*, BHT 26, Tübingen 1959.

Wilhelm, A., *Neue Beiträge zur griechischen Inschriftenkunde*, 5. Teil, SAW 214, 4, 1932.

— 'Zu den Judenerlassen des Ptolemaios Philadelphos', *APF* 14, 1941, 30–5.

Will, E., 'Les premières Années du règne d'Antiochos III', *REG* 75, 1962, 71–129.

— *Histoire politique du Monde hellénistique*, Vols. I and II, Nancy 1966f.

Willrich, H., *Juden und Griechen vor der Makkabäischen Erhebung*, Göttingen 1895.

— *Judaica*, Göttingen 1900.

— 'Zur Geschichte der Tobiaden', *APF* 7, 1924, 61–4.

— *Urkundenfälschung in der hellenistisch-jüdischen Literatur*, FRLANT NF 21, Göttingen 1924.

Wilson, R. McL., 'Simon, Dositheos and the Dead Sea Scrolls', *ZRGG* 9, 1957, 21–30.

— *The Gnostic Problem*, London ²1964.

Windisch, H., *Die Orakel des Hystaspes*, Verhandelingen der kon. Akad. v. Wetenschappen te Amsterdam, Afd. Letterkunde NR XXVIII No. 3, 1929.

Winter, P., Review of L. Finkelstein, *The Pharisees*, ³1962, *RQ* 4, 1963/64, 592–4.

Wlosok, A., *Laktanz und die philosophische Gnosis*, AAH ph.-hist. Kl. 1960, Vol. 2.

Wolf, M. J., 'Sibyllen und Sibyllinen', *Arch. f. Kulturgeschichte* 24, 1934, 312–25.

Wolff, H. W., 'Psalm 1', *EvTh* 9, 1949–50, 385–94.

Wolfson, H. A., *Philo*, Vols. I and II, Cambridge, Mass. ²1948.

Wright, G. E., 'The First Campaign at Tell Balâṭah (Shechem)', *BASOR* 144, 1956, 9–20.

— 'The Second Campaign at Tell Balâṭah (Shechem)', *BASOR* 148, 1957, 11–28.

— 'The Samaritans at Shechem', *HTR* 55, 1962, 357–66.

— *Shechem, The Biography of a Biblical City*, London and New York 1964.

Wünsche, A., *Aus Israels Lehrhallen*, Leipzig 1907–9, reprinted in two vols., Hildesheim 1967.

Yadin, Y., *The Scroll of the War of the Sons of Light against the Sons of Darkness*, London 1962.

— 'The Excavation of Masada – 1963/64, Preliminary Report', *IEJ* 15, 1965, 1–120.

Zaehner, R. C., *Zurvan*, Oxford 1955.

Zambelli, M., 'L'ascesa al trono di Antioco IV Epifane di Siria', *Rivista di Filologia e di Istruzione Classica* 38, 1960, 363–89.

Zeitlin, S., 'The Tobias Family and the Hasmonaeans', *PAAJR* 4, 1932/33, 169–223.

— Review of E. Bickermann, *Der Gott der Makkabäer*, *JQR* 31, 1940/41, 199–204.

— *The First Book of Maccabees*, New York 1950.

— *The Second Book of Maccabees*, New York 1954.

— *The Rise and Fall of the Judaean State*, Vol. I, 332–37 B.C.E., Philadelphia 1964.

Zeller, E., 'Die Entwicklung des Monotheismus bei den Griechen', *Vorträge und Abhandlungen*, Vol. I, Berlin ²1875, 1–29.

— 'Über den Ursprung der Schrift von der Welt', *Kleine Schriften*, Vol. I, Berlin 1910, 328–47.

— *Die Philosophie der Griechen*, Parts II and III, Leipzig 1879–1923 (*PhGr*).

Ziebarth, E., *Das griechische Vereinswesen*, Preisschriften der Fürstlich Jablonowski'schen Gesellschaft 34, 1896.

Zimmerli, W., *Die Weisheit des Predigers Salomo*, Aus der Welt der Religion, Vol. II, Berlin 1936.

— *Das Buch des Predigers Salomo*, ATD 16, 1962.

Zimmermann, F., 'The Story of the Three Guardsmen', *JQR* 54, 1963/64, 179–200.

Zobel, M., *Gottes Gesalbter*, Berlin 1938.

Zucker, F., 'Γυμνασίαρχος κώμης', *Aeg* 11, 1931, 485–96.

— *Doppelinschrift spätptolemäischer Zeit aus der Garnison von Hermopolis Magna*, AAB 1937, No. 6, 1938.

Zucker, H., *Studien zur jüdischen Selbstverwaltung im Altertum*, Berlin 1936.

Zuntz, G., 'Greek Words in the Talmud', *JSS* 1, 1956, 129–40.

SELECT INDEX OF PASSAGES FROM ANCIENT WRITERS

All passages discussed in detail are included, but
only the New Testament references are complete

I Old Testament

Genesis

1.1	I, 157
1.1–2.4	I, 156, 196
1.2	II, 105
1.31	II, 105
2.1–4a	I, 167f.
5.24	I, 204
6.1–4	I, 231
6.4	
(LXX)	I, 89
10.9	
(LXX)	I, 89
10.15	II, 195
14.19	II, 200
17.5	
(LXX)	I, 91
25.1–4	I, 72
34.2	I, 89
47.20ff.	I, 29

Exodus

3.14	II, 105
19.17–20	I, 165
20.11	I, 168
33.11	I, 72

Deuteronomy

4.6	I, 161
16.21f.	I, 295
26.5	
(LXX)	II, 8

Judges

1.27	
(LXX)	II, 10

I Samuel

6.9	II, 81
16.14	I, 233
20.26	II, 81

I Kings

5.11	I, 129
5.11ff.	I, 129
5.12	
(LXX)	I, 129
5.14	II, 88
5.15–23	I, 110
5.18	II, 81
10.1	I, 129; II, 88
22.19ff.	II, 100

II Kings

2.11	I, 121
5.15–19	I, 112
20.1–11	I, 112
21.1–18	I, 296

Isaiah

6.3	II, 127
9.10f.	
(LXX)	I, 32

Isaiah

19.19	I, 16
23.11	II, 28
24–27	I, 180f.
26.19	I, 196
38	I, 112
45.9	I, 146
58.6	
(LXX)	I, 51f.
60.19f.	II, 109
63.7	II, 175
65.17	I, 189
66.11	I, 127
66.22	I, 189

Jeremiah

10.16	II, 94
18.4–6	I, 146
23.24	I, 147
27.16	
(LXX)	I, 17
29	I, 110
33.25	I, 172
44.15ff.	II, 11
44.30	I, 93

Ezekiel

16.29	I, 34; II, 28
17.4	I, 34; II, 28
27.11–25a	I, 32

II Old Testament Apocrypha

III Pseudepigrapha

IV Qumran Writings

V New Testament

VI Rabbinic Writings

1. Mishnah

2. Babylonian Talmud

VII Jewish Hellenistic Writings

For fragments not mentioned here (Demetrius the Chronographer, Ezekiel the Tragedian, Cleodemus Malchus, the historian Aristeas and Philo the Elder), see Index of Names and Subjects

Ps.-Philo (Kisch)
60.2   II, 88

Theodotus
FGrHist 732 F 1 (= Eusebius,
  Prep. Ev. 9.22)
            I, 89; II, 61f.

VIII Graeco-Roman Secular Writing

Aeschylus, *Prometheus*
454–505   I, 190; II, 127

Ammianus Marcellinus
19.1.2   II, 124
22.13.1   II, 190

Appian, *Punica*
132   I, 182; II, 122

Apollonius Molon
FGrHist 728 F 1   II, 173
F3 = c. *Ap.* 2. 148   II, 172, 177

Apuleius, *Metamorphoses*
11.23.8   I, 215

Aristophanes, *Peace*
832ff.   I, 197

Aristotle, *Nicomachean Ethics* (By-
water)
1125b ll.33–35   II, 109

Arrian, *Anabasis Alex.*
3.6.1.   II, 51

Athenaeus, *Deipnosophistae*
4.157b   I, 85; II, 57
5.201a   II, 29
12.527e/f   I, 55; II, 41
12.536e   I, 130; II, 88
15.692c   II, 41

Berossus
FGrHist 680 F 4.14f.
            I, 242; II, 164

Censorinus, *De die natali*
18.11   I, 191; II, 128

Cercidas (Knox, LCL)
194.8ff.   I, 122f.; II, 83
237.100ff.   II, 84

Chairemon
FGrHist 618 F 6   I, 213; II,
            140

Chrysippus (SVF)
2.265 Fr. 918   II, 154
2.277 Fr. 954.15–20 II, 161
2.293 Fr. 1000   II, 154
2.305 Fr. 1021   II, 94, 176
2.335 Fr. 1169   II, 95

Cicero
De divinatione
1.30, 63f.   II, 142

De finibus
4.56   I, 87; II, 58

De natura deorum
2.28.71   I, 236
2.56   II, 174

In Pisonem
70   II, 57

De re publica
3.33   II, 103
6.13   II, 132

Claudius Iolaus
FGrHist 788 F 4   II, 50

Cleanthes (SVF)
1.111 Fr. 495   II, 104f.
1.112 Fr. 499   I, 236; II,
            159
1.114 Fr. 510   II, 159
1.121ff. Fr. 537   I, 148; II,
            94, 154
1.125 Fr. 549   II, 60

(Quintus) Curtius Rufus, *Hist. Alex.*
4.6.31   II, 11

Damascius, *Vita Isidori* (Photius,
  Bibl.; Bekker)
345b   II, 202

Democritus (Diels-Kranz)
Fr. 30   II, 170

IX Collections of Manuscripts, Papyri, Inscriptions, etc.

X Early Christian Writings

INDEX OF NAMES AND SUBJECTS

Administrative units
  eparchy, II, 15
  hyparchy, I, 21
  nome, I, 19f., 29
  satrapy, II, 15
  toparchy, I, 19
Adonai, I, 262
Adonis, II, 175
Adora, I, 40; II, 172
Adullam, I, 46
Aegean, I, 32, 60; II, 30, 88, 200
  clay jars from, I, 44
  cultural centres of, I, 88
  economic and cultural exchange
    with Phoenicia and Palestine,
    I, 43, 56; II, 72
  mercenaries from, I, 12
  wine from, I, 39, 44
Aelia Capitolina, I, 307
Aemilius Sura, Roman annalist, I,
  182
Aeneas of Gaza (fifth century AD),
  II, 130
Aeon, I, 121, 125, 190
Aeschylus, I, 69, 109, 190; II, 83,
  91, 95, 127
Africa, I, 74; II, 63
Agabus, prophet, I, 240
Agamemnon (of Aeschylus), II, 91
Agatharcides of Cnidus (second
  century BC), I, 29; II, 173, 203
Agathocles, tyrant of Syracuse
  (361–289 BC), II, 67
Agathos Daimon (Knephis), I, 185
Agenor I, king of Sidon, father of
  Cadmus, I, 72
Agriculture, *see* Domains, Grain,
  Wine, I, 19, 36, 51
Agrippa I, I, 29, 276; II, 40, 162
Agrippa II, I, 77; II, 68
Ahab, I, 295
Aḥer (Elisha b. Abuya), I, 207; II,
  25
Ahriman Hades, I, 193
Ahura Mazda, I, 298, cf. 193
R. Akiba, I, 171, 207, 276; II, 113,
  144

Alcaeus, Lesbian poet (seventh/
  sixth century BC), I, 13
Alchemy, I, 241, 243
Alcimus, high priest (died 159 BC),
  I, 64, 80, 105, 289f.; II, 69,
  149, 186
Alexander the Great (356–323 BC),
  I, 2, 3, 13f., 15, 36, 38, 107,
  185; II, 190
  conquest of Tyre, II, 67
  defence of by Erastosthenes, I, 65
  festivals in Tyre, I, 73
  Jewish mercenaries, I, 15
  ktistēs of the Macedonian colony
    of Gerasa, II, 9
  ktistēs of the Macedonian colony
    of Samaria, I, 13, 282
  total income of, II, 23
Alexander, son of Andronicus,
  Jewish soldier in Egypt (*c.* 200
  BC), I, 63; II, 11
Alexander, son of Dorotheus,
  Jewish ambassador, I, 64
Alexander Balas (died 145 BC), I,
  225, 290, 291
Alexander Jannaeus (103–76 BC), I,
  60, 64, 76, 85, 105, 253, 276,
  306
Alexander Polyhistor (beginning of
  first century BC), I, 70, 88, 89,
  92, 93; II, 49, 52, 76, 178
Alexandria, I, 11, 22, 36, 42f., 49,
  52f., 59, 66, 68ff., 83, 185, 244
  A. Relations with Judaism, I, 17,
    52, 68f., 70, 76, 91, 95f., 101,
    114, 136, 162, 165ff., 171, 241,
    244, 250, 252, 269f., 301, 304
  B. Education and culture, I, 38,
    42, 66, 69, 88, 173, 181, 215,
    230, 241, 246, 273; II, 113
  C. Philosophy and religion, I, 99,
    103, 164, 169, 236, 310
Allat, I, 296
Allegory, *see* Exegesis, I, 164f., 246
Al-Mina, II, 26
Alms, II, 38
Altar, I, 294f., 298, 303, 305

296

Asia Minor, I, 9, 15f., 21, 32, 77,
183, 263, 298, 308; II, 16, 96,
188, 200
Diaspora in, I, 16, 298; II, 177
Asphalt (from Dead Sea), I, 45f.
Assembly
military, I, 13
popular, I, 49
Assimilation (to Hellenistic en-
vironment), *see* Apostasy, I, 66,
74, 77, 114, 176
Associations, nature of, I, 66, 244,
311
Assumption, I, 204
of Moses, I, 99; II, 120
Assyria, I, 13, 182, 187; II, 63
= Syria, I, 85, 93
Astarte, I, 158; II, 99, 100
of Ashkelon, II, 172
-Isis, I, 158
Asteria-Ashtoreth, I, 43, 89
Astibares of Media, king, I, 93
Astral religion, *see* Astrology, Sun,
I, 86, 207, 232f.; II, 134
Astrology (astronomy), I, 86, 89ff.,
182, 184, 189, 191, 193, 196,
201, 207, 214, 215f., 236f.,
242f.; II, 140
Atabyrion-Tabor, I, 8; II, 172, 197
Atargatis = Isis, I, 158; II, 173
Atheism, I, 144
Athene, I, 187, 296; II, 98
Athens, Athenian, I, 32f., 40, 54,
65, 71, 87, 88, 258, 289; II, 30,
34, 42, 47, 67, 84, 183
'Assyrian' = Gadara, I, 34f.
Athenians in Dor in Palestine, I,
32; II, 73
exports of pottery, I, 32, 35
temple of Zeus, I, 285
Atlas, brother of Prometheus,
Titan, I, 89
'Aṭliṭ, I, 13, 34; II, 26, 35
Atomic theories, I, 86
Attalus III (138–133 BC), II, 175
Attica, I, 187; II, 85
Attic alliance, I, 32

Augustine, I, 260, 262
Augustus, emperor, I, 185; II, 20,
48, 190
Autonomy, I, 10
Avesta, II, 130
(Pseudo-Platonic) Axiochus, I, 211,
216
Azariah, Prayer of, II, 120

Baal
of Carmel, II, 172, 198
of Kasion, I, 286
of Tabor, II, 172
of Tyre, I, 295, 302
Baalbek, I, 7; II, 191
Ba'al Šāmēm, I, 259, 297, 299, 303;
II, 181, 197
Ahura Mazda and, I, 298
connection with Dusares, II, 201
god of Zion, I, 298–305
and Helios, I, 297
and *Jupiter summus exsuperantissimus*, II, 199
and Zeus Olympius, I, 94, 128,
286, 297f.; II, 198
Babas and Babatas, sons of Kosnatanus, name in Marisa, I, 62
Babylon, I, 71, 89, 96, 179, 182,
212, 277
Babylonia, *see* Chaldeans, I, 47,
115, 181, 201, 242
astral religion, astrology, I, 191,
193, 201, 207, 212, 235–7,
242; II, 59, 72, 160
doctrine of world cycles, I, 191f.,
232
exile in, II, 127
and Greek mythology, I, 88, 198
influence on apocalyptic, I, 181,
201; II, 156
influence on Essenism, I, 236f.,
246
influence on wisdom, II, 97
and Jewish Diaspora, I, 16, 263;
II, 192
Bacchanalia, I, 299

Religious edicts, *see* Antiochus III, Antiochus IV

Remnant, holy, I, 223, 226f.

Renegades, Jewish, *see* Assimilation, I, 291, 305, 314; II, 196

Repentance, I, 179f., 195, 203, 217, 223, 226f., 251

Reseph Apollo, Phoenician god, II, 10, 172

Reseph Mikal, Cyprus, II, 126

Resurrection, I, 196, 209, 250
  Apocalypse of Isaiah, II, 121
  Ben Sira, I, 153
  Hasidim, I, 196–202
  II Maccabees, I, 97
  Paul, I, 200
  post-Maccabean Judaism, I, 312

Retribution, idea of, *see* Apocalyptic, Theodicy, I, 202
  Ben Sira, I, 128, 138, 142f., 147f.
  I Enoch, I, 200
  Essenes, I, 221
  Greek thought, I, 121f.; II, 67
  Hasidim, I, 198, 250
  Jason of Cyrene, I, 97, 100, 143
  Koheleth, I, 119, 126; II, 84
  repudiation of, I, 119, 122, 142, 303
  Stoics, I, 147, 249

Revelation, I, 154f., 202–18, 222f., 261, 311f.

Reward, idea of, *see* Retribution, Righteousness of God, I, 128, 172

Rheneia, near Delos, II, 34, 201

Rhetoric, I, 69f., 95, 98, 105, 130; II, 68, 142

Rhetoricus (c. AD 500), II, 128

Rhinocolura, I, 158

Rhodes, I, 32, 43, 44, 83; II, 21, 42, 123
  constitution, II, 21
  cultural centre, I, 88
  Jewish colony, II, 202
  trade, I, 32, 43
  Zeus Atabyrios, II, 172, 198

Riches, I, 50ff., 56, 123, 136ff.

Righteousness of God, *see* Theodicy
  demonstrability of, I, 146f.
  'fundamental ordinance of world', I, 221
  questioning of, I, 119, 121f., 126, 143f.

Rigorism, legal, see Law, Zeal, I, 101, 194, 226f.; II, 119

Romances, I, 30, 69, 111

Rome, I, 10ff., 32, 35, 54, 60, 64, 77, 86, 88, 153, 182, 261, 272, 279, 288, 295, 309; II, 41, 123, 125
  annihilation, I, 186, 214
  astrology, I, 236; II, 160
  Bacchanalia, I, 299
  Chaldeans in, I, 236
  Jewish delegations to, I, 54, 60, 98, 183, 263, 291; II, 150
  Jews in, I, 263, 307; II, 114, 201
  law schools, I, 81
  satirists, I, 256
  Theudas affair, II, 182

Royal land, I, 19, 22, 25, 35f., 44f., 46

Rudens (Plautus), I, 201

Ruler cult, I, 19, 30, 67, 153, 285ff., 296, 303

Ruth, I, 111, 113

Sabaeans, I, 42, 129

Sabaoth, Iao, I, 262f.

Sabazius, I, 263, 298, 304
  Jupiter, I, 263

Sabbath, *see* Seven, number, I, 41, 96, 166ff., 178, 189, 235, 281, 289, 292, 294; II, 119, 176, 202

Sabbatistes, I, 308

Sabo, name in Marisa, I, 62

Sacrifice, I, 271, 278f., 283, 291ff.; II, 179

Sadducees, I, 75, 78, 81, 94, 114, 128, 143, 153, 301; II, 115, 150, 167

Safa, I, 297

Šamaʿbaʿal-Diopeithes, Phoenician name, I, 61

Simonides, poet (sixth/fifth century BC), I, 116

Sinai, I, 72, 160, 165, 170, 189; II, 114

Sinope on Black Sea, I, 42, 84

Sirach, *see* Ben Sira

Ps. Skylax, II, 50, 172

Slaves, slave trade, *see* Liberation, Rebellions, I, 14, 16, 21, 23, 41f., 48, 56, 63, 84, 185f., 268, 270, 281; II, 11, 149

Smyrna, II, 132

Social conditions, *see* Poor, Poverty, I, 38f., 48f., 54, 56, 117, 123, 126f., 136ff., 290

Social criticism, I, 136ff.

Social utopia, I, 186

Socrates, philosopher, I, 81, 165, 169, 211, 233, 258, 267; II, 64, 68, 92

Solinus, I, 247

Soloi, in Cilicia, I, 87; II, 49

Solomon, king, I, 73, 79, 166, 167, 241, 297, 302; II, 52f.

  Koheleth and, I, 129f.

  letters in Eupolemus, I, 93, 110

  magician, I, 130

Solstice festival, *see* Hanukkah, I, 298f., 303

Somata laika eleuthera, semi-free population of Palestine, I, 24, 42, 48; II, 17

Sophacians, Cyrenaica, I, 92

Sophocles, II, 95

Sosibius, minister of Ptolemy IV, I, 8

Sosipater, Maccabean cavalry officer, I, 64, 276

Sosus of Ashkelon, Stoic, pupil of Panaitios, I, 86

Soteriology, *see* Redemption

Sotion, Greek biographer, II, 90

Soul, *see* Anthropology, Journey to heaven, I, 124, 149, 192, 198ff., 204, 211f., 216, 233f., 246; II, 131, 142

Sources

  of Jason of Cyrene, I, 98

  of Josephus, see Nicolaus of Damascus, I, 289ff.; II, 179, 182, 193, 202

  of Tacitus, I, 301

  of Tobiad romance, I, 269

Spartans (and Jews), I, 26, 60, 64, 72, 92, 98, 256, 276, 302; II, 52, 123, 150

Sphragis, slave of Zeno, I, 268; II, 33

Star symbol, II, 20

State capitalism, I, 20

Stephen, I, 296, 309

Stoa

  A. Views

    allegory, I, 165, 246

    determinism, I, 191, 230f., 239

    etymology, I, 265; II, 202

    freedom of will, I, 141, 231

    idea of God, I, 147ff., 260, 262f., 266

    physiognomy, II, 160

    soul, I, 198

    sun, I, 236

    world law, I, 160f., 173f., 231

    world soul, I, 163

  B. Relationships

    Ben Sira, I, 141, 147–50, 160, 310

    Koheleth, I, 115

    Late Judaism, I, 248

    Palestine, Phoenicia, I, 86f.

    Rabbis, I, 173f.

    Semitic thought, I, 87, 149

    Wisdom, I, 167, 310

Stones, sacred, *see* Betyl, I, 295

Strabo, I, 44f., 83, 87, 258f.; II, 170, 177

Strato, agent of Zeno, I, 21

Strato, king of Sidon (died 400 BC), I, 32, 61

Strato, king of Tyre (died 340 BC), II, 44

Strato, prince of Arados (died 340 BC), II, 44